*Contemporary Authors*®

# NEW REVISION SERIES

ISSN 0275-7176

# Contemporary Authors®

**A Bio-Bibliographical Guide to Current Writers in Fiction, General Nonfiction, Poetry, Journalism, Drama, Motion Pictures, Television, and Other Fields**

## NEW REVISION SERIES
### volume 227

GALE
CENGAGE Learning®

Detroit • New York • San Francisco • New Haven, Conn • Waterville, Maine • London

**Contemporary Authors, New Revision Series, Vol. 227**

Project Editor: Mary Ruby

Composition and Electronic Capture: Gary Oudersluys

Manufacturing: Rhonda Dover

For product information and technology assistance, contact us at
**Gale Customer Support, 1-800-877-4253.**
For permission to use material from this text or product,
submit all requests online at **www.cengage.com/permissions.**
Further permissions questions can be emailed to
**permissionrequest@cengage.com**

Gale
27500 Drake Rd.
Farmington Hills, MI, 48331-3535

LIBRARY OF CONGRESS CATALOG CARD NUMBER 81-640179

ISBN-13: 978-1-4144-6844-0
ISBN-10: 1-4144-6844-X

ISSN 0275-7176

This title is also available as an e-book.
ISBN-13: 978-1-4144-7261-4
ISBN-10: 1-4144-7261-7
Contact your Gale sales representative for ordering information.

Printed in Mexico
1 2 3 4 5 6 7 15 14 13 12 11

# Contents

# Preface

*Contemporary Authors* (*CA*) provides information on approximately 146,000 writers in a wide range of media, including:

- Current writers of fiction, nonfiction, poetry, and drama whose works have been issued by commercial publishers, risk publishers, or university presses. Authors whose books have been published only by known vanity or author-subsidized firms are ordinarily not included.

- Prominent print and broadcast journalists, editors, photojournalists, syndicated cartoonists, graphic novelists, screenwriters, television scriptwriters, and other media people.

- Notable international authors.

- Literary greats of the early twentieth century whose works are popular in today's high school and college curriculums and continue to elicit critical attention.

A *CA* listing entails no charge or obligation. Authors are included on the basis of the above criteria and their interest to *CA* users. Sources of potential listees include trade periodicals, publishers' catalogs, librarians, and other users.

## How to Get the Most out of *CA*: Use the Index

The key to locating an author's most recent entry is the *CA* cumulative index, which is published separately and distributed twice a year. It provides access to *all* entries in *CA* and *Contemporary Authors New Revision Series* (*CANR*). Always consult the latest index to find an author's most recent entry.

For the convenience of users, the *CA* cumulative index also includes references to all entries in these Gale Group literary series: *African-American Writers, African Writers, American Nature Writers, American Writers, American Writers: The Classics, American Writers Retrospective Supplement, American Writers Supplement, Ancient Writers, Asian American Literature, Authors and Artists for Young Adults, Authors in the News, Beacham's Encyclopedia of Popular Fiction: Analyses, Beacham's Encyclopedia of Popular Fiction: Biography and Resources, Beacham's Guide to Literature for Young Adults, Beat Generation: A Gale Critical Companion, Bestsellers, Black Literature Criticism, Black Literature Criticism Supplement, Black Writers, British Writers, British Writers: The Classics, British Writers Retrospective Supplement, British Writers Supplement, Children's Literature Review, Classical and Medieval Literature Criticism, Concise Dictionary of American Literary Biography, Concise Dictionary of American Literary Biography Supplement, Concise Dictionary of British Literary Biography, Concise Dictionary of World Literary Biography, Contemporary American Dramatists, Contemporary Authors Autobiography Series, Contemporary Authors Bibliographical Series, Contemporary British Dramatists, Contemporary Canadian Authors, Contemporary Dramatists, Contemporary Literary Criticism, Contemporary Novelists, Contemporary Poets, Contemporary Popular Writers, Contemporary Southern Writers, Contemporary Women Dramatists, Contemporary Women Poets, Contemporary World Writers, Dictionary of Literary Biography, Dictionary of Literary Biography Documentary Series, Dictionary of Literary Biography Yearbook, DISCovering Authors, DISCovering Authors 3.0, DISCovering Authors: British Edition, DISCovering Authors: Canadian Edition, DISCovering Authors Modules, Drama Criticism, Drama for Students, Encyclopedia of World Literature in the 20th Century, Epics for Students, European Writers, Exploring Novels, Exploring Poetry, Exploring Short Stories, Feminism in Literature, Feminist Writers, Gay & Lesbian Literature, Guide to French Literature, Harlem Renaissance: A Gale Critical Companion, Hispanic Literature Criticism, Hispanic Literature Criticism Supplement, Hispanic Writers, International Dictionary of Films and Filmmakers: Writers and Production Artists, International Dictionary of Theatre: Playwrights, Junior DISCovering Authors, Latin American Writers, Latin American Writers Supplement, Latino and Latina Writers, Literature and Its Times, Literature and Its Times Supplement, Literature Criticism from 1400-1820, Literature of Developing Nations for Students, Major Authors and Illustrators for Children and Young Adults, Major Authors and Illustrators for Children and Young Adults Supplement, Major 21st Century Writers (eBook version), Major 20th-Century Writers, Modern American Women Writers, Modern Arts Criticism, Modern Japanese Writers, Mystery and Suspense Writers, Native North American Literature, Nineteenth-Century Literature Criticism, Nonfiction Classics for Students, Novels for Students, Poetry Criticism, Poetry for Students, Poets: American and British, Reference Guide to American Literature, Reference Guide to English Literature, Reference Guide to Short Fiction, Reference Guide to World Literature, Science Fiction Writers, Shakespearean Criticism, Shakespeare for Students, Shakespeare's Characters for Students, Short Stories for Students, Short Story Criticism, Something About the Author, Something About the Author Autobiography Series, St. James Guide to Children's Writers, St. James Guide to Crime & Mystery Writers, St. James Guide to Fantasy Writers, St. James Guide to Horror, Ghost & Gothic Writers, St. James Guide to Science Fiction Writers, St. James Guide to Young Adult Writers, Supernatural Fiction*

Writers, *Twayne Companion to Contemporary Literature in English, Twayne's English Authors, Twayne's United States Authors, Twayne's World Authors, Twentieth-Century Literary Criticism, Twentieth-Century Romance and Historical Writers, Twentieth-Century Western Writers, William Shakespeare, World Literature and Its Times, World Literature Criticism, World Literature Criticism Supplement, World Poets, World Writing in English, Writers for Children, Writers for Young Adults,* and *Yesterday's Authors of Books for Children.*

## A Sample Index Entry:

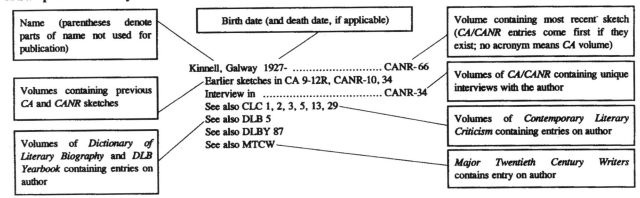

# How Are Entries Compiled?

The editors make every effort to secure new information directly from the authors; listees' responses to our query letters and emails provide most of the information featured in *CA*. For deceased writers, or those who fail to reply to requests for data, we consult other reliable biographical sources, such as those indexed in Gale's *Biography and Genealogy Master Index,* and bibliographical sources, including *National Union Catalog, LC MARC,* and *British National Bibliography.* Further details come from published interviews, feature stories, and book reviews, as well as information supplied by the authors' publishers and agents.

*An asterisk (\*) at the end of a sketch indicates that the listing has been compiled from secondary sources believed to be reliable but has not been personally verified for this edition by the author.*

# What Kinds of Information Does An Entry Provide?

Sketches in *CA* contain the following biographical and bibliographical information:

- **Entry heading:** the most complete form of author's name, plus any pseudonyms or name variations used for writing.

- **Personal information:** author's date and place of birth, family data, ethnicity, educational background, political and religious affiliations, and hobbies and leisure interests.

- **Addresses:** author's home, office, or agent's addresses, plus e-mail and fax numbers, as available.

- **Career summary:** name of employer, position, and dates held for each career post; résumé of other vocational achievements; military service.

- **Membership information:** professional, civic, and other association memberships and any official posts held.

- **Awards and honors:** military and civic citations, major prizes and nominations, fellowships, grants, and honorary degrees.

- **Writings:** a comprehensive, chronological list of titles, publishers, dates of original publication, and production information for plays, television scripts, and screenplays.

- **Adaptations:** a list of films, plays, and other media which that been adapted from the author's work.

- **Sidelights:** a biographical portrait of the author's development; information about the critical reception of the author's works; revealing comments, often by the author, on personal interests, aspirations, motivations, and thoughts on writing.

- **Interview:** a one-on-one discussion with authors conducted especially for *CA*, offering insight into authors' thoughts about their craft.

- **Autobiographical essay:** an original essay written by noted authors for *CA*, a forum in which writers may present themselves, on their own terms, to their audience. These essays are generally accompanied by personal photographs.

- **Biographical and critical sources:** a list of books, periodicals, and Websites in which additional information on an author's life and/or writings appears.

# Related Titles in the *CA* Series

*Contemporary Authors Autobiography Series* complements *CA* original and revised volumes with specially commissioned autobiographical essays by important current authors, illustrated with personal photographs they provide. Common topics include their motivations for writing, the people and experiences that shaped their careers, the rewards they derive from their work, and their impressions of the current literary scene.

*Contemporary Authors Bibliographical Series* surveys writings by and about important American authors since World War II. Each volume concentrates on a specific genre and features approximately ten writers; entries list works written by and about the author and contain a bibliographical essay discussing the merits and deficiencies of major critical and scholarly studies in detail.

## Available in Electronic Formats

**Lit Omni.** *CA* is available on a subscription basis through Lit Omni, an online information resource that features an easy-to-use end-user interface, powerful search capabilities, and ease of access through the World-Wide Web. For more information, call 1-800-877-GALE.

**Licensing.** *CA* is available for licensing. The complete database is provided in a fielded format and is deliverable on such media as disk, CD-ROM, or tape. For more information, contact Gale's Business Development Group at 1-800-877-GALE, or visit us on our website at www.gale.com/bizdev.

## Suggestions Are Welcome

The editors welcome comments and suggestions from users on any aspect of the *CA* series. If readers would like to recommend authors for inclusion in future volumes of the series, they are cordially invited to write the Editors at *Contemporary Authors*, Gale Cengage Learning, 27500 Drake Rd., Farmington Hills, MI 48331-3535; or call at 1-248-699-4253; or fax at 1-248-699-8054.

---

**Indexing note:** All *Contemporary Authors* entries are indexed in the *Contemporary Authors* cumulative index, which is published separately and distributed twice a year.

**As always, the most recent Contemporary Authors cumulative index continues to be the user's guide to the location of an individual author's listing.**

---

# *CA* Numbering System and Volume Update Chart

Occasionally questions arise about the *CA* numbering system and which volumes, if any, can be discarded. Despite numbers like "29-32R," "97-100" and "315" the entire *CA* print series consists of 469 physical volumes with the publication of *CA* Volume 315. The following charts note changes in the numbering system and cover design, and indicate which volumes are essential for the most complete, up-to-date coverage.

**CA First Revision**

- 1-4R through 41-44R (11 books)
  *Cover:* Brown with black and gold trim.
  There will be no further First Revision volumes because revised entries are now being handled exclusively through the more efficient *New Revision Series* mentioned below.

**CA Original Volumes**

- 45-48 through 97-100 (14 books)
  *Cover:* Brown with black and gold trim.
  101 through 315 (215 books)
  *Cover:* Blue and black with orange bands.
  The same as previous *CA* original volumes but with a new, simplified numbering system and new cover design.

**CA Permanent Series**

- *CAP*-1 and *CAP*-2 (2 books)
  *Cover:* Brown with red and gold trim.
  There will be no further Permanent Series volumes because revised entries are now being handled exclusively through the more efficient *New Revision Series* mentioned below.

**CA New Revision Series**

- CANR-1 through CANR-227 (227 books)
  *Cover:* Blue and black with green bands.
  Includes only sketches requiring significant changes; **sketches are taken from any previously published CA, CAP, or CANR volume.**

| If You Have: | You May Discard: |
|---|---|
| *CA* First Revision Volumes 1-4R through 41-44R and *CA Permanent Series* Volumes 1 and 2 | *CA* Original Volumes 1, 2, 3, 4 and Volumes 5-6 through 41-44 |
| *CA* Original Volumes 45-48 through 97-100 and 101 through 315 | **NONE:** These volumes will not be superseded by corresponding revised volumes. Individual entries from these and all other volumes appearing in the left column of this chart may be revised and included in the various volumes of the *New Revision Series*. |
| *CA New Revision Series* Volumes *CANR*-1 through *CANR*-226 | **NONE:** The *New Revision Series* does not replace any single volume of *CA*. Instead, volumes of *CANR* include entries from many previous *CA* series volumes. All *New Revision Series* volumes must be retained for full coverage. |

# A Sampling of Authors and Media People Featured in This Volume

**George W. Bush**

Bush was the forty-third president of the United States. In Bush's 2010 memoir, *Decision Points,* he explains the difficult choices he had to make during his presidency and his life. The book is not a chronological memoir but an arrangement of the topics Bush felt were important to address. He candidly admits where he believes he did not make the right choice but also defends the decisions he believes were correct. As a whole, the book evokes the pressure of the challenging and sometimes ambivalent task of being the president of the United States. Bush was named the *Time* person of the year in 2004.

**Judi Dench**

Equally at home playing historic queens, Shakespearean ladies, and suburban housewives, Dench is one of the most acclaimed English-speaking actresses of her generation. The two-time Academy Award winner draws critical hosannas and audience affection in virtually any role she undertakes. In her native England, Dench is one of the few West End performers whose name guarantees box-office success. She has starred in many theatrical productions and won numerous awards for her work in theater. Dench's memoir, *And Furthermore,* is meant to be the actor's own follow-up to John Miller's *Judi Dench: With a Crack in Her Voice. And Furthermore* is written by Miller, as told by Dench.

**Åke Edwardson**

Swedish novelist Edwardson is a popular and successful crime writer in his native country and in Scandinavia. He is a three-time winner of the Swedish Academy of Crime Writers' Award for best novel. Edwardson has been a journalist, a press officer at the United Nations, and a professor at Sweden's Gothenburg University. Less well known in the United States, Edwardson's detective novels have been appearing in America in English translation since 2005. They feature recurring series character Erik Winter, the chief inspector of police in the Swedish coastal city of Gothenburg.

**Steve Martin**

A famed comedian and actor, Martin has also become an accomplished writer. Playing the part of a "wild and crazy guy," he became one of the most notable stand-up comics of the 1970s. His first two comedy albums won Grammy Awards and sold millions of copies; he scored a hit single with the absurd song "King Tut"; and the book *Cruel Shoes,* his collection of humorous sketches, was a national best-seller. The bizarre incongruity of a junior-

executive type wearing balloons on his head, latex nose and glasses, and a white, custom-tailored, three-piece suit struck the perfect chord with American audiences. Martin's subsequent career is as expansive as it is extraordinary. He has won awards; starred in movies; written screenplays, short stories, novellas, and children's books; and has hosted the Academy Awards, among many other accolades. In 2010 Martin released his first novel, *An Object of Beauty.*

**Helena McEwen**

McEwen was born and raised in Scotland. She studied painting in the late 1980s at the Chelsea School of Art and subsequently taught painting and drawing classes and workshops for adults and children at art galleries in Sheffield, England. McEwen also taught painting at London's Kensington and Chelsea College and University College Falmouth. McEwen's debut novel, *The Big House,* has been compared with the work of such writers as Katherine Mansfield and D.H. Lawrence. In 2006, McEwen won the J.B. Priestley Award for a writer of outstanding promise. Her novel *Invisible* was released in 2011.

**Danielle Steel**

Having produced a score of best-selling novels, Steel has been nothing less than a publishing phenomenon. Since the publication of her first hardcover in 1980, Steel has consistently hit both hardback and paperback best-seller lists; there are reportedly over 580 million of her books in print in twenty-eight languages in forty-seven countries. Her popularity has also spilled over into television, where several film versions of her books have been produced and garnered good ratings. Steel's fiction is peopled by women in powerful or glamorous positions; often they are forced to choose the priorities in their lives. In 2009, Steel was inducted into the California Hall of Fame.

**Di Wang**

Wang is an academic and historian. Born in 1956 in Chengdu, China, he studied history at Sichuan University before earning a Ph.D. from Johns Hopkins University in 1999. Wang lectured at Sichuan University in the 1980s and early 1990s and became an assistant professor of history at Texas A&M University in 1998, becoming a full professor by 2009. Wang has contributed articles and reviews to a number of academic journals on his research interests, which cover the social and cultural history of China. He has also served as a manuscript reviewer for journals and publishing houses. Wang's 2003 book *Street Culture in Chengdu: Public Space, Urban Commoners, and Local Politics, 1870-1930* won the best non-North American book award from the Urban History Association.

**Fay Weldon**
Weldon grew up in New Zealand. As a single mother in her twenties, Weldon supported herself and her son with a variety of odd jobs until she settled into a successful career as a copywriter. After marrying in the early sixties, Weldon had three more sons, underwent psycho-analysis as a result of depression, and subsequently abandoned her work in advertising for freelance creative writing. Her first novel, *The Fat Woman's Joke,* appeared in 1967. Since then she has published many novels, short stories, and plays for the theater, television, and radio. Products of a keen mind concerned with women's issues, Weldon's novels have been labeled "feminist" by many reviewers. Yet, Weldon's views are not easily classified. She has won numerous awards, including a Society of Film and Television Arts award for best series, a Writer's Guild award for best radio play, and a PEN/Macmillan Silver Pen Award.

# Peter Abrahams

## 1947-

### ■ Also Known As

Peter Brian Abrahams
Spencer Quinn

### ■ Personal

Born June 28, 1947; married Diana Gray (a teacher), 1978; children: Seth, Ben, Lily, Rosie. *Education:* Williams College, B.A., 1968.

### ■ Addresses

*Home*—Cape Cod, MA. *E-mail*—pa@cape.com.

### ■ Career

Writer. Worked as a spear fisher in the Bahamas, 1968-70; Canadian Broadcasting Co. (CBC), Toronto, Ontario, Canada, producer.

### ■ Awards, Honors

Edgar Allan Poe Award nominations, Mystery Writers of America, best novel of 1994, for *Lights Out,* and 2007, for *Down the Rabbit Hole;* Agatha Award for best children/young adult fiction, 2006, for *Down the Rabbit Hole;* Edgar Allan Poe Award for best young adult fiction, Mystery Writers of America, 2010, for *Reality Check.*

### ■ Writings

*NOVELS*

*The Fury of Rachel Monette,* Macmillan (New York, NY), 1980.

*Tongues of Fire,* M. Evans (New York, NY), 1982.

*Red Message,* Avon Books (New York, NY), 1986.

*Hard Rain,* Dutton (New York, NY), 1988.

*Pressure Drop,* Dutton (New York, NY), 1989.

*Revolution #9,* Mysterious Press (New York, NY), 1992.

*Lights Out,* Mysterious Press (New York, NY), 1994.

*The Fan,* Warner Books (New York, NY), 1995.

*A Perfect Crime,* Ballantine Books (New York, NY), 1998.

*Crying Wolf,* Ballantine Books (New York, NY), 2000.

*Last of the Dixie Heroes,* Ballantine Books (New York, NY), 2001.

*The Tutor,* Ballantine Books (New York, NY), 2002.

*Their Wildest Dreams,* Ballantine Books (New York, NY), 2003.

*Oblivion,* William Morrow (New York, NY), 2005.

*End of Story,* William Morrow (New York, NY), 2006.

*Nerve Damage,* William Morrow (New York, NY), 2007.

*Delusion,* William Morrow (New York, NY), 2008.

*Reality Check* (young adult), HarperTeen (New York, NY), 2009.

*Bullet Point* (young adult), HarperTeen (New York, NY), 2010.

*"ECHO FALLS MYSTERY" SERIES; YOUNG ADULT FICTION*

*Down the Rabbit Hole,* Laura Geringer Books (New York, NY), 2005.

*Behind the Curtain,* Laura Geringer Books (New York, NY), 2006.

*Into the Dark,* Laura Geringer Books (New York, NY), 2008.

*"CHET AND BERNIE MYSTERY" SERIES; WRITING AS SPENCER QUINN*

*Dog on It*, Atria Books (New York, NY), 2009.
*Thereby Hangs a Tail,* Atria Books (New York, NY), 2010.
*To Fetch a Thief*, Atria Books (New York, NY), 2010.
*The Dog Who Knew Too Much*, Atria Books (New York, NY), 2011.

*OTHER*

(With Sidney D. Kirkpatrick) *Turning the Tide: One Man against the Medellin Cartel* (nonfiction), Dutton (New York, NY), 1991.
(With others) *Up All Night: A Short Story Collection*, introduction by Laura Geringer, Laura Geringer Books/HarperTeen (New York, NY), 2008.
*Quacky Baseball* (picture book), illustrated by Frank Morrison, HarperCollins Children's Books (New York, NY), 2011.
*Robbie Forester and the Outlaws of Sherwood Street* (middle-grade novel), Philomel Books (New York, NY), 2012.

■ **Adaptations**

*The Fan* was adapted for film by Frank Darabont and Phoef Sutton and released by TriStar in 1996.

■ **Sidelights**

Peter Abrahams is the author of many suspenseful novels that have become favorites with readers and critics alike. In an interview with Kay Longcope in the *Boston Globe*, Abrahams explained: "They're all sorts of thrillers, but defining them isn't easy. . . . I think of them as novels but the suspense element plays a strong role. I like to lead my main character to something the reader will dread, then say, 'Given characteristics of that particular character, that had to happen.' I like a bit of humor, too. Generally, thrillers provide a humorless terrain." Further commenting on his books to Longcope, Abrahams stated: "I'm interested in putting ordinary people into extraordinary situations, as Alfred Hitchcock did, rather than making James Bond-type superheroes and putting them in life and death situations. You can generate a lot more dread. I want to directly attack the imagination, to ensnare it. That's the way a good book works for me." Abrahams penned almost twenty popular thrillers for adult readers before turning to novels for young adults as well as an adult detective series narrated by a canine private investigator, the "Chet and Bernie Mysteries" series, written under the pseudonym Spencer Quinn.

### *The Fury of Rachel Monette* and *Tongues of Fire*

Abrahams's early books often feature ordinary heroes and heroines, complicated plot twists, and political intrigue. His first, *The Fury of Rachel Monette*, follows the title character to Morocco, France, and Israel, as she attempts to solve her husband's murder, discover the secret of a 1942 German letter he left behind, and recover her young son, who has been kidnapped by a man posing as a rabbi. *The Fury of Rachel Monette* garnered praise from critics; a *Publishers Weekly* reviewer commented that its "steadily sustained suspense and smooth writing keep the reader hooked," and *Spectator* contributor Harriet Waugh called the book "well written, fast moving, constantly surprising and jolly exciting."

An Israel connection also figures prominently in *Tongues of Fire,* Abrahams's second novel. In it, Isaac Rehv, a former Israeli soldier, flees to the United States after his country is destroyed by Arab invaders. There, Rehv conspires to assassinate an Arab leader and attracts the attention of a zealous CIA agent who tails Rehv around the world, from Canada to Sudan and Mecca. Although some reviewers considered *Tongues of Fire* to be a bit implausible, many praised Abrahams's skill nonetheless. *Publishers Weekly* reviewer Barbara A. Bannon termed the book "fast-paced and exciting," while *Los Angeles Times Book Review* contributor Raymond Mungo called it "a wickedly clever and intricate mystery." According to a writer in the *West Coast Review of Books*, Abrahams's "gripping prose can best be described as throat-grabbing."

### *Hard Rain* and *Pressure Drop*

Abrahams's third thriller to catch the attention of critics was *Hard Rain,* which conjures up the atmosphere of the late 1960s and takes its title from a Bob Dylan tune. In it, Jessie Shapiro is caught up in political intrigue as she searches for her ex-husband and young daughter, who have failed to return from a weekend trip. Defining events of the past, such as Woodstock and the Vietnam War, haunt the present as Jessie treks from Los Angeles to Vermont in search of clues. Writing in the *Los Angeles Times Book Review,* Charles Champlin praised *Hard Rain* as a "top-rank adventure." *Publishers Weekly* reviewer Sybil Steinberg called the book "an intricate, convincing thriller." *New York Times Book Review* contributor William J. Harding was also enthusiastic, commenting that *Hard Rain* has the elements of "a good thriller": "style, atmosphere and a surprising plot."

*Pressure Drop*, Abrahams's follow-up to *Hard Rain,* also generated approval from critics. According to *Quill and Quire* contributor Paul Stuewe: "*The Fury* of *Rachel Monette* and *Hard Rain* were competent thrillers, but Peter Abrahams's latest novel breaks to the front ranks of this extremely crowded field." In *Pressure Drop*, Abrahams sets up two seemingly unrelated plot lines that eventually collide. In one, suspicious and dangerous circumstances develop around Nina Kitchener, whose baby boy, conceived through artificial insemination, is kidnapped from the hospital shortly after birth. In the other, N.H. "Matt" Matthias investigates nagging questions surrounding a scuba-diving accident that took place at his resort in the Bahamas, uncovering a connection between the accident and Nina's tragedy. Reviewing *Pressure Drop* in the *Armchair Detective*, William J. Schafer praised Abrahams's writing as "highly literate, brisk, and graphic," and his characterizations as "fresh and unclichéd."

### *Revolution #9* and *Lights Out*

Flashbacks to 1960s Vietnam War protests provide a backdrop for Abrahams's next novel, *Revolution #9.* The main character is Charlie Ochs, a Cape Cod lobster fisher who has been lying low since a campus protest bombing he was involved in accidentally killed a young boy. Ochs, who has spent nearly twenty years living underground, is finally tracked down by federal agents the night before his wedding. He is given an ultimatum: help the government find the bombing's mastermind, Rebecca Klein, or serve time for his own role in the attack. According to Chicago *Tribune Books* contributor Richard Martins: "Charlie's hunt through the past is an often painful but always gripping story. Abrahams weaves in and out of time and temperament with considerable skill." Although finding *Revolution #9* somewhat "uneven," a *Publishers Weekly* reviewer nonetheless noted that "expert pacing and an intriguing plot hold the reader's interest."

Abrahams followed *Revolution #9* with *Lights Out*, which received an Edgar Allan Poe Award nomination for best novel of 1994. The book's main character is Eddie Nye, who, despite his innocence, has spent fifteen years in prison on drug charges. He is not free long before he is again plunged into dangerous intrigue while investigating his frame-up. According to *Publishers Weekly* writer Sybil Steinberg, Abrahams "creates a fascinating and memorable character in Eddie Nye." Steinberg further noted: "Consistently interesting and suspenseful, his thriller's shocking outcome is revealed only on the very last page." According to the author, *Lights Out* marked the beginning of a new phase in Abrahams's work, where he began to expand beyond the limits of the genre.

### *The Fan* and *A Perfect Crime*

In *The Fan,* Abrahams focuses on Gil Renard, a down-and-out traveling salesman, and Bobby Rayburn, an arrogant and successful baseball player who is riding out a batting slump. Renard, a baseball fanatic, has lost his job and wife and has slid into committing petty crimes. He becomes obsessed with Rayburn, managing to become the caretaker on the ballplayer's estate while he plans to murder the star on the field. *The Fan* was a hit with critics; *Booklist* contributor Wes Lukowsky called it a "first-rate thriller," and *Library Journal* reviewer Marylaine Block termed it an "excellent novel." *The Fan* was filmed in 1996 by Tony Scott, starring Robert DeNiro and Wesley Snipes.

The thriller *A Perfect Crime* tells of Roger Cullingwood's murderous plot against his wife. Though he is in a marriage that lacks depth and has been on unemployment for months, Roger's idyllic perception of his life is not shattered until he learns that his wife, Francie, is romantically involved with a well-known local psychologist. Roger, an extremely intelligent person desperate to restore his enormous ego, engineers a "perfect" plan to kill his wife. He loses control of his plot after he enlists the help of a previously convicted murderer. Although a *Publishers Weekly* critic felt that Roger and his cohort were unrealistic characters who "lack dimension," the critic noted that the other major characters were "well-drawn." In contrast, *Booklist* contributor Thomas Gaughan uniformly praised Abrahams's characterizations as well as complimenting the author's "complex and compelling [plotting]" and "sharp and almost flawless [dialogue]." Gaughan noted, however, that the "satisfying" novel has "a subtle sense of the mathematical certainty to the denouement." "*A Perfect Crime* is fast-paced, tense, even witty as it careens to its bloody conclusion," noted Karen Anderson in her *Library Journal* review.

### *Crying Wolf* and *The Tutor*

The ethics of four young adults from various social classes are exposed and tested in actions and reactions associated with acquiring money and material goods. What will a middle-class kid from a small Colorado town do to pay for a prestigious university education in New England? Abrahams presents one scenario in *Crying Wolf*, "a suspense novel built around kidnapping, extortion and youthful stupidity," related a *Publishers Weekly* reviewer. Nat, a high school valedictorian, uses his two thousand dollar essay contest winnings to help his mother cover the tuition for his freshman year at Inverness. When his mother loses her job, Nat must find another way to subsidize his education. He sets up a kidnapping plot with the help of Grace and Izzie, the wealthy twins Nat becomes involved with at Inverness. As Vanessa Bush indicated in *Booklist,* the trio's plan is devised to be "a 'victimless' crime with one of [the twins] as the kidnapping subject, to get the money from an indifferent father." The father prevents the kidnapping, however, and Freedy, a thief and suspected rapist from the "wrong side" of the college town, takes the trio's kidnapping idea and adapts it, making a more dangerous plan. When Nat tries to expose Freedy's plans, people think that he is just "crying wolf."

The title character in *The Tutor* was likened by a *Publishers Weekly* contributor to the Alfred Hitchcock character Norman Bates of *Psycho* fame: an apparently ordinary and pleasant fellow who gradually emerges as a sinister threat to an entire family. Hired by the suburban Gardner family to prepare son Brandon for his Scholastic Aptitude Test, tutor Julian Sawyer manages to penetrate the weaknesses of the family members, guiding each toward a personalized, destructive objective. It is up to Brandon's teenaged sister Ruby to unravel the emerging clues and save her family from danger. The *Publishers Weekly* reviewer observed: "Once again this author finds menace in dailiness." A contributor to *Kirkus Reviews* called *The Tutor* a reflection of "the familiar laced with lingering irony."

### Their Wildest Dreams **and** Oblivion

The novel *Their Wildest Dreams* features not one but several potential troublemakers and multiple storylines. Single mom Helen Larkin, who works as an exotic dancer, feels eerily uncomfortable about her employer's "intentions." Strip club patron and aspiring crime writer Nicholas Loeb is lured by an Internet literary critic across the line from imagination into the realm of true crime. Larkin's teenage daughter develops a crush on a ranch hand and would-be bank robber at her father's dude ranch. The unlikely cast of characters converges at a small Arizona border town, where all the plot lines come together. A reviewer of *Their Wildest Dreams* commented in *Kirkus Reviews* that Abrahams's attention to minute detail and the flaws of his characters make them not only believable, but "engaging." A *Publishers Weekly* contributor recommended the novel as a "wildly inventive, captivating caper" and a "bravura thrillfest."

In the novel *Oblivion* the threat comes not only from Abrahams's solid and believable characters, but from the foe within. Private detective Nick Petrov

must try to locate a missing teenaged girl while in the throes of memory loss and mental confusion caused by a cerebral hemorrhage that puts a temporary halt to his investigation. Both challenges entwine Nick's career and his personal life in what *New Yorker* writer Joyce Carol Oates referred to as "a Dali landscape of baffling clues, memory lapses, and visual hallucinations." The tension of the investigation is increased by the psychological fear associated with Nick's amnesia. He believes that following the course of his interrupted investigation backward to its roots may help him recover his memory. Instead, the fragmented clues available to him cause Nick to question his own integrity. Could he himself be a criminal—even a murderer? Oates found *Oblivion* to be, like Abrahams's earlier novels, "gratifyingly attentive to psychological detail, richly atmospheric, layered in ambiguity." She concluded that "Peter Abrahams's strongest novels seem to suggest, despite their allegiance to [the thriller] genre, a fascination with something beyond mere form."

### Nerve Damage **and** Delusion

*Nerve Damage* portrays terminally ill sculptor Paul Valois. As he is dying, Paul reminisces about his late wife, Delia. However, Paul continues to struggle to survive, taking an experimental drug for his cancer. He also discovers that Delia's death occurred under suspicious circumstances. Paul sets out to find the truth behind his wife's death, even as he is dying himself. "From the reliably marvelous Abrahams comes another top-drawer psychological thriller," declared *Entertainment Weekly* reviewer Jennifer Reese. Indeed, Reese was not alone in her positive assessment of the novel, as *Booklist* writer Gaughan observed that "there's more than enough substance here to keep readers of literary thrillers engrossed." Calling the book a "gripping political suspense novel," a *Publishers Weekly* contributor remarked that both the "action and suspense are first-rate." According to a reviewer for the *New Yorker,* the author's in-depth characterization "sets him apart from most thriller writers working today." Although *Library Journal* contributor Nicole A. Cooke felt that "the reader must suspend disbelief a bit," she nevertheless commented that "the bulk of his tale is gripping, captivating, and so well written."

Abraham's next thriller, *Delusion,* features Nell Jarreau. Twenty years ago the pregnant Nell was witness to her boyfriend's murder. Her testimony sent Alvin Dupree to jail for two decades. After the trial, Nell married the detective who handled the case, and they raised her daughter together. However, new video evidence emerges that exonerates Dupree of the murder, and Nell is devastated by the news. She can't understand how the video contradicts her own memories. Complicating matters, Nell's husband refuses to investigate. *Library Journal* contributor Cooke applauded the novel, noting that the "characters are extremely well rendered and quite fascinating." Cooke went on to call *Delusion* "a captivating and swiftly moving story." A *Publishers Weekly* reviewer, however, was nonplussed, commenting that "fans of Abrahams's complex earlier novels will hope for a return to form next time." Nevertheless, a *Kirkus Reviews* critic stated that "Abrahams succeeds in making this deeply wronged man [Dupree] dangerous, pitiable and scary."

## "Echo Falls Mystery" Series

Breaking away from thrillers, Abraham began writing a series of mysteries for young adults. The first book in the "Echo Falls Mystery" series is *Down the Rabbit Hole.* Published in 2005, the book was such a great success that the second series installment, *Behind the Curtain,* was published only a year later. The first novel introduces young Ingrid, who lives in Echo Falls, Connecticut. The second novel finds Ingrid attending middle school. Her older brother, Ty, struggles to hold his spot on the high school football team. Ingrid suspects her brother may be using steroids, and she investigates by searching out local drug dealers. Meanwhile, developers are pressuring Ingrid's grandfather to sell the family farm. Thus, when Ingrid is kidnapped, it could be drug dealers or greedy developers. Ingrid escapes her captor and no one believes her tale, so she is forced to discover the identity of the kidnapper alone. "The mystery is entertaining and well constructed," noted Claire Rosser in *Kliatt. School Library Journal* contributor Denise Moore also lauded the book, noting that despite being part of a larger series, "this enjoyable story stands on its own."

*Into the Dark* opens with a murder that occurs on the farm belonging to Ingrid's grandfather. Unfortunately, he is arrested as the prime suspect, and he refuses to give police an alibi. Ingrid begins to investigate, uncovering her grandfather's distinguished service during World War II. Indeed, his days as a soldier may be connected to the murder. Rosser, again writing in *Kliatt,* remarked that "Abrahams is an experienced writer and he knows his craft." *School Library Journal* contributor Sheila Fiscus was also impressed by the novel, noting that "the story is accessible, and Ingrid's ability to not only think through the crime but also solve it is impressive."

### *Reality Check*

Abrahams continues writing for young adults with his 2009 novel, *Reality Check.* Cody Laredo's perfect life is falling apart. From a working class background, he is the standout athlete of his high school football team in Colorado and in love with beautiful Clea Watson. But when her rich father, who does not care to have his daughter matched up with Cody, sends Clea away to a fancy private school in Vermont, Cody's life begins to fall apart. Pining for his lost love, he injures his knee, and this sidelines the sixteen-year-old during the recruiting season for college. Dispirited that he will not be awarded a football scholarship, Cody is unable concentrate on school work, and soon he drops out of school altogether. News that Clea has gone missing in Vermont finally awakens him, and he decides to travel to Vermont to help hunt for his beloved. The search is anything by straightforward, as Cody feels like an outsider among the wealthy kids at Clea's school, but Cody vows to carry on to the end. In the process, he learns some hard truths about himself.

*Booklist* reviewer Lynn Rutan had praise for this offering, terming it a "compulsively readable mystery for older teens—[whose] intriguing puzzle will have readers racing through the pages." *School Library Journal* contributor Amy S. Pattee also applauded the novel, dubbing it "a solid mystery" Higher praise came from a *Kirkus Reviews* writer who thought that by the end of the book readers would be "frantically turning pages and fully invested in Abrahams's message of true love conquering all obstacles." Similarly, a *Publishers Weekly* reviewer found this an "engrossing crime novel," and an "exciting, fastpaced story" with "complex characters with believable motivations and faults."

### *Bullet Point*

A further stand-alone young adult suspense novel is the 2010 *Bullet Point,* focusing on another sixteen-year-old male athlete protagonist. Wyatt is advised by his baseball coach to change high schools when his own school cuts baseball for budgetary reasons. He and a buddy enroll in the upper class Silver City high, but it turns out that his friend is the one who gets the vacant spot on the team. Soon, this disappointment moves to the background, however, when Wyatt begins an affair with sexy if somewhat unstable Greer, a few years his senior. Greer's father happens to be in the local prison and now he tells his daughter that Wyatt's biological dad is there, too. Wyatt, who has never gotten along with his stepfather, is curious to meet this man who is doing a life sentence for armed robbery. Soon he is investigating the robbery that sent his father to prison, for both he and Greer believe the man was wrongly convicted. But there are also those who do not want the cold case being investigated again.

"Questions about innocence, guilt, and justice contribute to a complex story that is a thriller with a dramatic denouement," wrote *Voice of Youth Advocates* contributor Hillary Crew, who additionally termed the work a "very well-written, riveting read for older teens." *Booklist* reviewer Daniel Kraus also had a high assessment of *Bullet Point,* noting that it "wrenches guts" with its "engulfing plot, multifaceted characters, and a plausibility rare to the genre." In a similar vein, *School Library Journal* contributor Shawna Sherman thought this novel is "as gritty and raw as today's headlines."

### Dog on It

Writing as Spencer Quinn, Abrahams initiates a series featuring a dog as the trustworthy and constant assistant to a human private investigator with *Dog on It.* Humor plays a large part in the novels in this series, yet mystery and suspense are still at the heart of things. Abrahams noted in an interview with a contributor to *Newsvine.com,* that his goal with the series "is to entertain readers, and more than that, it's to write a story that, once started, is hard to put down." *Dog on It* is told in the first person from the point of view of Chet the Jet, a canine who failed his K-9 school, and who is now partner of Bernie Little, proprietor of the Little Detective Agency. The investigating duo look into the disappearance of teenage girl in the first installment, and the girl's father, a developer with less than impeccable credentials, may have something to do with the situation. It takes a dog's nose and instincts to solve the case.

*Booklist* reviewer Jessica Moyer felt that "Chet may well be one of the most appealing new detectives on the block." Further praise for this series debut came from a *Kirkus Reviews* contributor who noted: "Stalwart, often mischievous narrator Chet's amusing, perceptive canine take on the human characters should appeal to hard-boiled fans and canine fanciers alike." Likewise, a *Publishers Weekly* reviewer termed *Dog on It* a "winning debut . . . [that] fans of classic mysteries are sure to appreciate."

### Thereby Hangs a Tail and To Fetch a Thief

The series moves forward with *Thereby Hangs a Tail,* in which the dynamic canine and human duo are employed as bodyguards for a famous show dog.

The fee of two thousand dollars per diem seems too good to be true, and indeed it is, when both dog and its mistress are kidnapped. Now Chet and Bernie must really earn their money in this "fast-moving and fun series entry," as *Booklist* reviewer Moyer described the book.

In the third series addition, *To Fetch a Thief,* Chet and Bernie investigate a case of a missing circus pachyderm, Peanut the elephant. "Tender-hearted Chet and literal-minded Bernie are the coolest human/pooch duo this side of Wallace and Gromit," wrote a *Kirkus Reviews* contributor of this series installment. Similarly, a *Publishers Weekly* reviewer felt that Abrahams "radiates pure comedic genius via Chet's doggy bright narrative."

### ■ Biographical And Critical Sources

*PERIODICALS*

*Armchair Detective,* spring, 1990, William J. Schafer, review of *Pressure Drop,* p. 238.

*Booklist,* August, 1992, Peter Robertson, review of *Revolution #9,* p. 1998; February 1, 1994, Wes Lukowsky, review of *Lights Out,* p. 996; January 15, 1995, Wes Lukowsky, review of *The Fan,* p. 868; July, 1998, Thomas Gaughan, review of *A Perfect Crime,* p. 1827; August, 1999, Karen Harris, review of *A Perfect Crime,* p. 2075; January 1, 2000, Vanessa Bush, review of *Crying Wolf,* p. 833; May 1, 2001, Connie Fletcher, review of *Last of the Dixie Heroes,* p. 1618; March 1, 2006, Keir Graff, review of *End of Story,* p. 43; May 1, 2006, Connie Fletcher, review of *Behind the Curtain,* p. 47; February 15, 2007, Thomas Gaughan, review of *Nerve Damage,* p. 37; February 1, 2008, Stephanie Zvirin, review of *Delusion,* p. 5; April 1, 2008, Shauna Yusko, review of *Up All Night: A Short Story Collection,* p. 41; May 1, 2008, Connie Fletcher, review of *Into the Dark,* p. 50; December 1, 2008, Jessica Moyer, review of *Dog on It,* p. 29; July 1, 2009, Lynn Rutan, review of *Reality Check,* p. 56; December 1, 2009, Jessica Moyer, review of *Thereby Hangs a Tail,* p. 30; May 1, 2010, Daniel Kraus, review of *Bullet Point,* p. 49; March 1, 2011, Patricia Austin, review of *Quacky Baseball,* p. 66.

*Boston Globe,* February 22, 1988, interview by Kay Longcope.

*Christianity Today,* May 1, 2010, review of *Thereby Hangs a Tail,* p. 58.

*Entertainment Weekly,* April 21, 1995, Gene Lyons, review of *The Fan,* p. 49; March 16, 2007, Jennifer Reese, review of *Nerve Damage,* p. 72.

*Kirkus Reviews,* May 1, 2002, review of *The Tutor,* p. 588; June 15, 2003, review of *Their Wildest Dreams,* p. 817; December 15, 2004, review of *Oblivion,* p.

1151; February 15, 2006, review of *End of Story*, p. 143; April 1, 2006, review of *Behind the Curtain*, p. 341; February 15, 2008, review of *Delusion*; March 1, 2008, review of *Into the Dark*; April 15, 2008, review of *Up All Night*; November 1, 2008, review of *Dog on It*; April 1, 2009, review of *Reality Check*; August 15, 2010, review of *To Fetch a Thief*.

*Kliatt*, May 1, 2006, Claire Rosser, review of *Behind the Curtain*, p. 4; July 1, 2007, Claire Rosser, review of *Behind the Curtain*, p. 21; March 1, 2008, Claire Rosser, review of *Into the Dark*, p. 6.

*Library Journal*, August, 1980, Samuel Simons, review of *The Fury of Rachel Monette*, p. 1655; April 15, 1982, review of *Tongues of Fire*, p. 823; December, 1987, A.M.B. Amantia, review of *Hard Rain*, p. 126; May 1, 1991, review of *Turning the Tide: One Man against the Medellin Cartel*, p. 89; July, 1992, Michele Leber, review of *Revolution #9*, p. 119; February 1, 1994, Dan Bogey, review of *Lights Out*, p. 109; February 1, 1995, Marylaine Block, review of *The Fan*, p. 97; August, 1998, Karen Anderson, review of *A Perfect Crime*, p. 128; December, 1998, Danna Bell-Russel, review of *A Perfect Crime*, p. 173; June 15, 2003, Marianne Fitzgerald, review of *Their Wildest Dreams*, p. 98; March 15, 2006, Ken Bolton, review of *End of Story*, p. 61; March 1, 2007, Nicole A. Cooke, review of *Nerve Damage*, p. 66; April 15, 2008, Nicole A. Cooke, review of *Delusion*, p. 70.

*Los Angeles Times Book Review*, June 27, 1982, Raymond Mungo, review of *Tongues of Fire*, p. 10; January 17, 1988, Charles Champlin, review of *Hard Rain*, p. 10.

*New Republic*, September 9, 1996, Stanley Kauffmann, review of *The Fan*, p. 37.

*New York*, July 5, 1982, Rhoda Koenig, review of *The Fury of Rachel Monette*, p. 103.

*New Yorker*, April 4, 2005, Joyce Carol Oates, review of *Oblivion*, p. 94; April 2, 2007, review of *Nerve Damage*, p. 79.

*New York Times Book Review*, February 21, 1988, William J. Harding, review of *Hard Rain*, p. 20; October 11, 1998, Marilyn Stasio, review of *A Perfect Crime*, p. 28.

*Penthouse*, February, 1981, Marilyn Stasio, review of *The Fury of Rachel Monette*, p. 48.

*Playboy*, June, 1991, Digby Diehl, review of *Turning the Tide*, p. 38.

*Publishers Weekly*, June 27, 1980, review of *The Fury of Rachel Monette*, p. 79; April 9, 1982, Barbara A. Bannon, review of *Tongues of Fire*, p. 43; November 6, 1987, Sybil Steinberg, review of *Hard Rain*, p. 58; September 29, 1989, review of *Pressure Drop*, p. 60; April 19, 1991, review of *Turning the Tide*, p. 54; June 1, 1992, review of *Revolution #9*, p. 50; January 10, 1994, Sybil Steinberg, review of *Lights Out*, pp. 43-44; January 23, 1995, review of *The Fan*, pp. 58-59; July 3, 1995, p. 26; July 20, 1998, review of *A Perfect Crime*, p. 206; January 10, 2000, review of *Crying Wolf*, p. 42; July 1, 2002, review of *The Tutor*, p. 55; August 4, 2003, review of *Their Wildest Dreams*, p. 56; April 4, 2005, review of *Down the Rabbit Hole*, p. 60; June 25, 2001, review of *Last of the Dixie Heroes*, p. 52; February 27, 2006, review of *End of Story*, p. 34; January 15, 2007, review of *Nerve Damage*, p. 32; February 18, 2008, review of *Delusion*, p. 136; December 22, 2008, review of *Dog on It*, p. 35; May 25, 2009, review of *Reality Check*, p. 58; July 26, 2010, review of *To Fetch a Thief*, p. 55.

*Quill and Quire*, February, 1990, Paul Stuewe, review of *Pressure Drop*, p. 27.

*Reviewer's Bookwatch*, November 1, 2009, Christy Tillery French, review of *Dog on It*.

*School Library Journal*, May, 2005, Susan W. Hunter, review of *Down the Rabbit Hole*, p. 120; April 1, 2006, Denise Moore, review of *Behind the Curtain*, p. 133; March 1, 2008, Sheila Fiscus, review of *Into the Dark*, p. 193; April 1, 2008, Tasha Saecker, review of *Up All Night*, p. 139; October 1, 2008, review of *Up All Night*, p. 71; May 1, 2009, Amy S. Pattee, review of *Reality Check*, p. 100; June 1, 2010, Shawna Sherman, review of *Bullet Point*, p. 93; February 1, 2011, Blair Christolon, review of *Quacky Baseball*, p. 74.

*Spectator*, January 30, 1982, Harriet Waugh, review of *The Fury of Rachel Monette*, pp. 22-23.

*Tribune Books* (Chicago, IL), August 2, 1992, Richard Martins, review of *Revolution #9*, p. 5.

*Voice of Youth Advocates*, August 1, 2010, Hillary Crew, review of *Bullet Point*, p. 240.

*West Coast Review of Books*, July, 1982, review of *Tongues of Fire*, p. 33.

ONLINE

*Chet: A Dog's Life Web site*, http://www.chetthedog.com (July 10, 2011).

*Internet Movie Database*, http://www.imdb.com/ (July 10, 2011), "Peter Abrahams."

*NationalPost.com*, http://network.nationalpost.com/ (March 11, 2009), Mark Medley, "Peter Abrahams' Secret Life as Spencer Quinn."

*Neff Review*, http://neffreview.blogspot.com/ (January 14, 2011), LaVonne Neff, review of *To Fetch a Thief*.

*Newsvine.com*, http://sbutki.newsvine.com/ (February 9, 2009), "An Interview With Spencer Quinn, Author of *Dog On It*."

*Peter Abrahams Home Page*, http://www.peterabrahams.com (July 10, 2011).

# John A. Adams

## 1951-

### ■ Also Known As

John Alfred Adams, Jr.

### ■ Personal

Born April 24, 1951. *Education:* American-Nicaragua School, Managua, Nicaragua, graduate; Texas A&M University, B.A., 1973, M.A., Ph.D.; attended Southern Methodist University Southwestern Graduate School of Banking, Dallas, TX; holds certified economic developer credentials.

### ■ Addresses

*Office*—Enterprise Florida, Inc., Ste. 1300, 390 N. Orange Ave., Orlando, FL 32801.

### ■ Career

Writer, historian, entrepreneur. National Bank of Texas, Laredo, former vice president and manager; Enterprise Florida, Inc., Orlando, president and CEO; Texas A&M International University, Laredo, TX, adjunct professor. GATT negotiations, delegate; World Trade Organization, advisor; U.S. Department of Commerce, chair of Industry Sector Advisory Council for trade policy review. *Military service:* Captain in United States Air Force.

### ■ Writings

*We Are the Aggies: The Texas A&M University Association of Former Students,* foreword by Richard ("Buck") Weirus, Texas A&M University Press (College Station, TX), 1979.

*Damming the Colorado: The Rise of the Lower Colorado River Authority, 1933-1939,* Texas A&M University Press (College Station, TX), 1990.

*Softly Call the Muster: The Evolution of a Texas Aggie Tradition,* foreword by Richard "Buck" Weirus, Texas A&M University (College Station, TX), 1994.

*Mexican Banking and Investment in Transition,* Quorum (Westport, CT), 1997.

*Keepers of the Spirit: The Corps of Cadets at Texas A&M University, 1876-2001,* foreword by Ray M. Bowen, Texas A&M University Press (College Station, TX), 2001.

*Bordering the Future: The Impact of Mexico on the United States,* Praeger (Westport, CT), 2006.

(With Henry C. Dethloff) *Texas Aggies Go to War: In Service of Their Country,* foreword by George H.W. Bush, Texas A&M University Press (College Station, TX), 2006, expanded edition with foreword by George H.W. Bush, Texas A&M University Press (College Station, TX), 2008.

*If Mahan Ran the Great Pacific War: An Analysis of World War II Naval Strategy,* Indiana University Press (Bloomington, IN), 2008.

*Conflict and Commerce on the Rio Grande: Laredo, 1755-1955,* Texas A&M University Press (College Station, TX), 2008.

### ■ Sidelights

John A. Adams is an entrepreneur who has been active for several decades in international trade, focusing on Latin America with a special emphasis on emerging industrial and financial markets in Mexico. A consultant to both the U.S. Department of Commerce and the World Trade Organization, Adams has used this expertise in several of his books, including *Mexican Banking and Investment in Transition* and *Bordering the Future: The Impact of*

*Mexico on the United States.* He also looks at the domestic impact of a major civil engineering project in his 1990 work *Damming the Colorado: The Rise of the Lower Colorado River Authority, 1933-1939.* A graduate of Texas A&M University, Adams has penned a number of books dealing the development of the "Aggie" tradition, as well as the military contributions of A&M University alumni.

### Damming the Colorado

In his *Damming the Colorado,* Adams traces the origins and early construction phase of the Lower Colorado River Authority (LCRA), known locally as "Texas's little TVA," whose initial task was flood control of the Red River. Adams intended to show in his study the positive effects of such reclamation, conservation, and hydroelectric projects of the New Deal. During this time, Adams argued, such resource management migrated from local control to federal management.

Thomas D. Isern, writing in the *Historian,* observed that Adams "notes that the LCRA was an effective force for economic development because it went beyond simple work relief and stimulated industrial growth through provision of cheap power." Isern went on to note that Adams's book was "well crafted and laudable," but at the same time the reviewer found that it was hampered by "its limited intellectual range," failing, as Isern thought, to provide enough background analysis. Gregory Field, writing in the *Business History Review,* offered a similar mixed assessment: "*Damming the Colorado* will prove useful as a brief account of one episode in the history of the New Deal in the West and of the politics of water control. Scholars looking for more than a factual chronicle, however, most likely will be disappointed."

### Mexican Banking and Investment in Transition

Adams turns to economics and Latin America in other works. His 1998 *Mexican Banking and Investment in Transition* "is one of the first works to examine the evolution of Mexican banking and finance up to and including the peso crash and deep recession of 1994-95," according to Miguel Ramirez, writing in the *Journal of Interamerican Studies and World Affairs.* At the time of writing the book, Adams was himself a banker in Texas and had a thorough understanding of practices south of the border. Ramirez found, however, that Adams's own banking background "constrained the book's pre-

sentation to a status quo reporting of the economic events leading up to the peso crisis, as well as their future economic and political implications."

Adams does not, in Ramirez's opinion, offer true analysis; he simply reports and lists. As an example of this, Ramirez noted: "When the author discusses the period known as Stabilizing Development (1954-70), he does not delve into the political economy reasons for the abandonment of the previous strategy." In short, Ramirez observed, *Mexican Banking and Investment in Transition* is "a book that is best read as a set of nine self-contained essays that provide useful factual information and a fairly standard explanation of the economic and political events leading up to the 1994-95 peso crash and recession." Ramirez added: "The nonspecialist or businessperson looking for a clear, nontechnical explanation of the overall structure of, and challenges facing, the Mexican banking system in the post-NAFTA era will not be disappointed."

### Bordering the Future and Keepers of the Spirit

Adams's 2006 title *Bordering the Future* focuses on Mexico's economic influence on the United States in the near future, examining areas such as "agriculture; migration; energy; the Mexican-Chinese relationship; . . . technology transfer, and trade corridors," explained a contributor to *Reference & Research Book News.* Adams employs government, industry, and academic sources for his predictions. According to Kevin J. Middlebrook, writing in the *Journal of Latin American Studies,* "the book's principal contribution is to provide the general reader with an overview of recent economic developments and policy dilemmas in Mexico." Middlebrook observed: "Adams is an enthusiastic advocate of open markets and free trade. This perspective encourages him to highlight some issues that other writers might overlook, such as the pressing transportation infrastructure needs along the Mexico-US border." Tony Payan, writing in the *Political Science Quarterly,* thought that "the value of the book consists in its descriptive nature." Specifically, Payan noted: "Number by number, acronym by acronym, year by year, statistic by statistic, the book weaves a scenario that sheds light on the major problems facing Mexico today."

Typical of Adams's works about Texas A&M University is his *Keepers of the Spirit: The Corps of Cadets at Texas A&M University, 1876-2001.* He "provides a detailed and positive examination of his alma mater," as Jennifer R. Green commented in the *Journal of Southern History.* Adams notes that the university has had a cadet corps since its founding in 1876. The author crafted his narrative history from media coverage, oral histories, archival sources, and interviews. Green felt that Adams "successfully details the history of the corps at the largest civilian military college" and termed the work "well-researched and attractive."

### If Mahan Ran the Great Pacific War

In *If Mahan Ran the Great Pacific War: An Analysis of World War II Naval Strategy*, Adams uses the ideas set forth by the great turn of the century U.S. admiral Alfred Thayer Mahan in his book *The Influence of Sea Power upon History* to examine and evaluate the Pacific naval sea battles of World War II in light of Mahan's powerful naval doctrine. Adams partakes in an examination of the two major strategies used: MacArthur's return to the Philippines and the amphibious campaign of island-hopping.

In *Air Power History*, John F. McConnell deemed the book "truly outstanding" and contended that "the lessons he presents apply to more than purely naval warfare. He discusses the main strategy to be pursued in war and the allocation of resources to that end, along with a refusal to expend resources on relatively minor strategic objectives, no matter how tempting they may seem." Although David J. Fitzpatrick was critical of *If Mahan Ran the Great Pacific War* in *Michigan War Studies Review*, he concluded his review by noting: "*If Mahan Ran the Great Pacific War* has its strengths. For those who wish to understand Mahanian ideas without trudging through *The Influence of Sea Power upon History*, Adams offers a nice summary. The book also has wonderful maps that will help readers better grasp both operational and strategic issues. And, too, there is an interesting, if poorly written, comparison and assessment of the American and Japanese navies at war's start." In *Naval War College Review*, Michael Pearlman reported that Adams's exercise in evaluation using Mahan's theories results in "a lively, interesting exercise in counterfactual history, one that deals both with what occurred and what might have occurred had the high commands of both navies been more true to what one might call 'the revealed Word.'"

## ■ Biographical And Critical Sources

### PERIODICALS

*Air Power History*, March 22, 2010, John F. O'Connell, review of *If Mahan Ran the Great Pacific War: An Analysis of World War II Naval Strategy*, p. 48.

*Business History Review*, winter, 1991, Gregory Field, review of *Damming the Colorado: The Rise of the Lower Colorado River Authority, 1933-1939*.

*Choice*, July 1, 2006, E.L. Whalen, review of *Bordering the Future: The Impact of Mexico on the United States*, p. 2041.

*Ground Water*, January 1, 1992, Kobina Atobrah, review of *Damming the Colorado*, p. 149.

*Historian*, fall, 1992, Thomas D. Isern, review of *Damming the Colorado*, p. 152.

*History: The Journal of the Historical Association*, October 1, 2009, Jeremy Black, review of *If Mahan Ran the Great Pacific War*, p. 515.

*Houston Chronicle*, May 21, 2006, Glenn Dromgoole, "New in Texas," p. 19.

*Journal of American History*, March, 1992, Andrew Gulliford, review of *Damming the Colorado*, p. 1501.

*Journal of Economic History*, June, 1992, Richard Lowitt, review of *Damming the Colorado*, p. 508.

*Journal of Interamerican Studies and World Affairs*, summer, 1998, Miguel Ramirez, review of *Mexican Banking and Investment in Transition*.

*Journal of Latin American Studies*, November, 2006, Kevin J. Middlebrook, review of *Bordering the Future*, p. 883.

*Journal of Military History*, July, 1994, review of *Softly Call the Muster: The Evolution of a Texas Aggie Tradition*, p. 562; October 1, 2009, Jon Sumida, review of *If Mahan Ran the Great Pacific War*, p. 1295.

*Journal of Southern History*, February, 2003, Jennifer R. Green, review of *Keepers of the Spirit: The Corps of Cadets at Texas A&M University, 1876-2001*, p. 202.

*Journal of the West*, April, 1994, G. Richard Marzolf, review of *Damming the Colorado*, p. 100.

*Library Journal*, November 15, 1990, Gwen Gregory, review of *Damming the Colorado*, p. 78.

*Military Review*, March 1, 2010, Prisco R. Hernandez, review of *If Mahan Ran the Great Pacific War*.

*Naval War College Review*, September 22, 2009, Michael Pearlman, review of *If Mahan Ran the Great Pacific War*, p. 170.

*Pacific Historical Review*, November, 1991, James E. Sherow, review of *Damming the Colorado*, p. 560.

*Political Science Quarterly*, winter, 2006, Tony Payan, review of *Bordering the Future*.

*Public Historian*, winter, 1993, review of *Damming the Colorado*.

*Reference & Research Book News*, August, 1997, review of *Mexican Banking and Investment in Transition*, p. 59; May, 2006, review of *Bordering the Future*.

*Roundup,* February 1, 2010, review of *Conflict and Commerce on the Rio Grande: Laredo, 1755-1955,* p. 27.

*Southwestern Historical Quarterly,* January, 1992, L. Patrick Hughes, review of *Damming the Colorado,* p. 423; July, 2002, Ethan S. Rafuse, review of *Keepers of the Spirit,* p. 134.

*Technology and Culture,* July, 1992, Karen L. Smith, review of *Damming the Colorado,* p. 620.

*Transnational Lawyer,* fall, 1997, Michael P. Malloy, review of *Mexican Banking and Investment in Transition.*

*Western Historical Quarterly,* February, 1992, James R. Kimmel, review of *Damming the Colorado,* p. 84.

ONLINE

*Area Development Online,* http://www.areadevelopment.com/ (February 26, 2008), "A Conversation with John Adams, President and CEO of Enterprise Florida."

*Greenwood Publishing Group Web site,* http://www.greenwood.com/ (February 26, 2008), "John A. Adams, Jr."

*Michigan War Studies Review,* http://www.michiganwarstudiesreview/ (July 1, 2009), David J. Fitzpatrick, review of *If Mahan Ran the Great Pacific War.*

*Texas A&M University, Corps of Cadets Web site,* http://corps.tamu.edu/ (August 23, 2011), author profile.*

# George Akita

## 1926-

### ■ Personal

Born April 26, 1926, in Honolulu, HI; son of Jukichi and Takino Akita; married Akiko Teshirogi, December 2, 1950; children: Naomi M., Makoto A., Izumi J. *Education:* University of Hawaii, B.A., 1951; Harvard University, M.A., 1953, Ph.D., 1960.

### ■ Addresses

*Office*—Department of History, University of Hawaii, Honolulu, HI 96822.

### ■ Career

U.S. Department of the Army, researcher and analyst, Tokyo, Japan, 1957-61; University of Hawaii, Honolulu, assistant professor, 1961-63, associate professor, 1963-67, professor of history, beginning 1967; then professor emeritus of history. *Military service:* U.S. Army, 1945-47.

### ■ Member

Association for Asian Studies.

### ■ Writings

*Foundations of Constitutional Government in Modern Japan, 1868-1900,* Harvard University Press (Cambridge, MA), 1967.

(Contributor) Albert Craig and Donald Shively, editors, *Personality in Japanese History,* Center for Japanese and Korean Studies, University of California, Berkeley (Berkeley, CA), 1970.

*Evaluating Evidence: A Positivist Approach to Reading Sources on Modern Japan,* University of Hawaii Press (Honolulu, HI), 2008.

Contributor to professional journals.

### ■ Sidelights

George Akita was born and raised in the Hawaiian Islands in the years before World War II. He joined the U.S. Army in 1945 and served for two years. After earning a bachelor's degree at the University of Hawaii and a master's degree at Harvard University, he went to work for the Department of the Army as a researcher and analyst based in Tokyo, Japan. In 1961, after completing his Ph.D. at Harvard, he began his long career as a professor of history at the University of Hawaii. His published works focus on modern Japan.

In 2008, *Evaluating Evidence: A Positivist Approach to Reading Sources on Modern Japan* was published. The book is the result of thirty years of painstaking research through mostly handwritten records, in collaboration with Japanese historians. Akita argues that it is necessary to use an inductive, rather than deductive, methodology in using primary sources. He believes that historians should not come to the research with a presumption and try to prove it; instead the historian should collect the data, find the patterns, and then draw conclusions from that work. That is what he calls a positivist approach. Akita critiques the difficulties involved with the use of primary sources as documentation and the problems associated with the intervention of the editors and compilers of many of these documents. Akita verifies his observations with illustrations of problems in published texts. He also examines the problem of non-Japanese scholars working to write Japanese history from a non-Japanese perspective.

A contributor to *Reference & Research Book News* commented that Akita is "committed to doing history the old-fashioned way." Hiroaki Sato, on the *Japan Times* Web site, noted that Akita calls the historical approach described in *Evaluating Evidence* "nitty-gritticism." In *Pacific Affairs*, Frederick R. Dickinson pointed out that the book is "an invaluable addition . . . for specialists of modern Japanese political history, Akita offers a wide-ranging, strikingly candid and furtively titillating personal glimpse at many of the leading personalities in our field. For experts and aspiring aficionados alike, he conveniently highlights some of the most important published documentary collections and provides a fascinating glimpse at the actual compilation process. . . . For graduate students, the advice in chapter three on using personal letters, memoranda, diaries and memoirs is a must read."

## ■ Biographical And Critical Sources

*PERIODICALS*

*Pacific Affairs*, March 1, 2010, Frederick R. Dickinson, review of *Evaluating Evidence: A Positivist Approach to Reading Sources on Modern Japan*, p. 178.

*Reference & Research Book News*, August 1, 2008, review of *Evaluating Evidence*.

*ONLINE*

*Japan Times*, http://search.japantimes.co.jp/ (April 5, 2009), Hiroaki Sato, "Looking at History: The Argument for Facts over Theory."

*University of Hawaii at Manoa, Center for Japanese Studies Web site*, http://www.hawaii.edu/ (July 30, 2011), faculty profile.*

# Mark Alpert

## 1961-

---

### ■ Personal

Born April 19, 1961; married; children: two. *Education:* Princeton University, B.A., 1982; Columbia University, M.F.A., 1984.

### ■ Addresses

*Home*—New York, NY. *E-mail*—info@markalpert. com.

### ■ Career

Writer and journalist. *Claremont Eagle Times,* Claremont, NH, reporter, 1984-85; *Montgomery Advertiser,* Montgomery, AL, reporter, 1985-87; *Fortune,* New York, NY, writer, 1987-92; *Popular Mechanics,* New York, NY, freelance writer, c. 1992-97; *Moneyline,* Cable News Network, New York, NY, freelance writer, 1996-97; *Scientific American,* New York, NY, editor, 1998—.

### ■ Writings

*Final Theory: A Novel,* Simon & Schuster (New York, NY), 2008.
*The Omega Theory: A Novel,* Simon & Schuster (New York, NY), 2011.

Contributed articles to newspapers and magazines, including *Claremont Eagle Times, Montgomery Advertiser, Fortune, Popular Mechanics, Scientific American,* and *Playboy.* Contributed to the television program *Moneyline* on the Cable News Network.

### ■ Sidelights

Mark Alpert was born on April 19, 1961, and grew up in New York City. He majored in astrophysics at Princeton University, where he wrote his under-graduate thesis on the application of the theory of relativity to Edwin Abbott's science-fantasy book *Flatland.* Alpert graduated in 1982 and then received an M.F.A. in poetry from Columbia University in 1984. He worked as a reporter on the *Claremont Eagle Times* in New Hampshire and the *Montgomery Advertiser* in Alabama before returning to New York to write about the computer industry and emerging technologies for *Fortune* magazine. In the early 1990s he began working as a freelance writer, contributing pieces to *Popular Mechanics* and the Cable News Network program *Moneyline.* He also published a single short story in *Playboy.* In 1998 he joined the board of editors of *Scientific American.* His job there is to explain complicated scientific concepts like string theory to the magazine's popular audience. Alpert lives in New York, New York, with his wife and two children.

### *Final Theory*

In 2008 Alpert published his first book, *Final Theory: A Novel.* The plot centers on David Swift, a professor at Columbia University who is called to the bedside of his mentor, physicist Walter Kleinman. Moments before his death, Walter passes on a series of numbers that turn out to be a clue to Albert Einstein's Theory of Everything. No sooner does David leave the hospital than he finds himself pursued by both the U.S. Federal Bureau of Investigation and a mysterious assassin. David enlists the aid of his ex-girlfriend, physicist Monique Reynolds, and the two race to solve Einstein's mystery before one or another of their pursuers can put an end to their theorizing once and for all.

Joe Hartlaub, writing for *Bookreporter.com,* said that *Final Theory* was "in equal measures a smart and entertaining thriller." Hartlaub also noted that Alpert "keeps the excitement engine racing at fever pitch" in the book. . . . One who is unfamiliar with the field will be intrigued by the explanations rather than frightened away." A reviewer for *Mysterious Reviews* was somewhat less enthusiastic than Hartlaub, noting that *Final Theory* "is a fine choice for anyone looking for light, escapist entertainment that doesn't tax (in a supremely ironic way) the intellect too greatly. Otherwise, it's rather disappointing." However, Donna Seaman, writing in *Booklist*, found that "video-game players with a head for science and a love of clever, fast-moving mysteries will enjoy this technology-strewn adventure."

### The Omega Theory

Alpert published his second book, *The Omega Theory: A Novel*, in 2011. In this novel, the sequel to *Final Theory*, a radical cult kidnaps the autistic son of science historian David Swift, believing that he knows the formula for Einstein's universal theory. The cult's leader intends to use the theory to create a weapon that will bring about Armageddon and the salvation of his followers by, in effect, reproducing the big bang. David races to save his son and the world while foiling the plans of the cult.

*The Omega Theory* was not as well received as the earlier novel. Although *Seattle Pi* reviewer Scott Butki called the characters "interesting" and characterized the book as "a good thriller," a reviewer in *Kirkus Reviews* found the book "slow going," conceding that "students of quantum physics may be diverted." Jeff Ayers, writing in *Booklist*, believed the book will appeal to "mainstream thriller fans," but a reviewer for *Publishers Weekly* objects to "characters who are little more than plot devices or mouthpieces for exposition."

## ■ Biographical And Critical Sources

### PERIODICALS

*Booklist*, May 1, 2008, Donna Seaman, review of *Final Theory: A Novel*, p. 28; January 1, 2011, Jeff Ayers, review of *The Omega Theory: A Novel*, p. 50.

*Kirkus Reviews*, April 1, 2008, review of *Final Theory*; December 15, 2010, review of *The Omega Theory*.

*New Scientist*, February 5, 2011, Amanda Gefter, review of *The Omega Theory*, p. 45.

*Publishers Weekly*, March 24, 2008, review of *Final Theory*, p. 51; December 13, 2010, review of *The Omega Theory*, p. 36.

### ONLINE

*Big Thrill*, http://www.thebigthrill.org/ (August 26, 2011), Lori Andrews, review of *The Omega Theory*.

*Bookreporter.com*, http://www.bookreporter.com/ (December 12, 2008), Joe Hartlaub, review of *Final Theory*.

*Mark Alpert Home Page*, http://www.markalpert.com (December 12, 2008), author profile.

*My Book, the Movie*, http://mybookthemovie.blogspot.com/ (March 10, 2011), Marshal Zeringue, author interview.

*Mysterious Reviews*, http://www.mysteriousreviews.com/ (December 12, 2008), review of *Final Theory*.

*New Scientist Online*, http://www.newscientist.com/ (July 16, 2008), Dan Falk, review of *Final Theory*.

*New York Times Online*, http://www.nytimes.com/ (May 26, 2008), Janet Maslin, "In Murderous Pursuit of Einstein's Secret," review of *Final Theory*.

*Seattle Pi*, http://www.seattlepi.com/ (April 26, 2011), Scott Butki, brief author interview and review of *The Omega Theory*.

*Simon & Schuster Web site*, http://authors.simonandschuster.com/ (August 15, 2011), brief author profile.

*SimonSays.com*, http://www.simonsays.com/ (December 12, 2008), brief author profile.

*Times Online* (London, England), http://entertainment.timesonline.co.uk/ (June 27, 2008), Peter Millar, review of *Final Theory*.*

# Asoka Bandarage

## 1950-

### ■ Personal

Born May 27, 1950. *Education:* Bryn Mawr College, B.A., 1973; Yale University, M.A., 1975, Ph.D., 1980.

### ■ Addresses

*Office*—Georgetown University, Department of Government, Box 571034, Intercultural Center 681, Washington, DC 20057-1034. *E-mail*—ab479@ georgetown.edu.

### ■ Career

Writer and professor. Brandeis University, instructor, 1979-85; Macalester College, Hubert H. Humphrey Professor, 1988; Mount Holyoke, professor, 1989-2006; *Bulletin of Concerned Asian Scholars*, editorial board; Georgetown University's Public Policy Institute, affiliated associate professor, 2005—.

### ■ Member

Committee on Women, Population, and Environment (member of steering committee), National Women's Dance Troupe of Sri Lanka (founding member), Critical Asian Studies, National Advisory Council on South Asian Affairs.

### ■ Writings

*Colonialism in Sri Lanka: The Political Economy of the Kandyan Highlands, 1833-86* (presented as Ph.D. dissertation), Mouton (Berlin, Germany), 1983.

*Women, Population, and Global Crisis: A Political Economic Analysis,* Zed Books (London, England), 1996.

*The Separatist Conflict in Sri Lanka: Terrorism, Ethnicity, Political Economy,* Routledge (New York, NY), 2008.

### ■ Sidelights

Asoka Bandarage wrote *Colonialism in Sri Lanka: The Political Economy of the Kandyan Highlands, 1833-86* as a dissertation topic for her Ph.D. Meant primarily "for university collections," according to a *Choice* reviewer. The book is a thorough analysis of the development of the Sri Lankan central highlands in the nineteenth century into a plantation economy under European influence. Bandarage describes the precolonial economic and social conditions, the transformation of the economy, and the subsequent effects of colonialism.

According to Ronald J. Herring in *Contemporary Sociology:* "[Bandarage] seeks to mediate between the world views of imperial apologists and nationalists, concluding in the nationalist camp." L. Ananda Wickremeratne in the *Journal of Asian Studies* wrote: "As books on Sri Lanka multiply, it is stimulating to encounter one concerned with wide perspectives. . . . This volume is a valuable addition to our understanding of the economic processes that transformed Sri Lanka in the nineteenth century."

#### *Women, Population, and Global Crisis*

Bandarage's next book, *Women, Population, and Global Crisis: A Political Economic Analysis,* she explains the challenges that women, and women of color in particular, face in today's political and economic climate.

Reviewing the work in *WIN News,* contributor Fran P. Hosken opined: "This book presents an overwhelming amount of research and information, international data and documentation to support the urgent plea, indeed, the demand for fundamental social and economic changes." Martha E. Gimenez, a contributor to the *Monthly Review,* described the work as "a well-written, thoughtful, well-researched and timely book which brings together a wealth of information documenting the connections between economic globalization, increasing economic and reproductive oppression of women, ecological deterioration, worldwide decline in the standard of living of working people, and the uses of Malthusian and neo-Malthusian ideologies to mask the capitalist roots of the crisis." Gimenez also noted: "It is, however, a contradictory book, one which trendy middle-class activists in the United States and elsewhere are likely to welcome, for it captures their cherished main concerns with self-transformation and spirituality based on a synthesis among intellectual and religious, indigenous and non-Western sources."

### The Separatist Conflict in Sri Lanka

Bandarage also wrote *The Separatist Conflict in Sri Lanka: Terrorism, Ethnicity, Political Economy,* a detailed work concerning the path that led to Sri Lanka's civil war.

Reviewing the work in *Pacific Affairs,* contributor Bruce Matthews remarked: "This is a gripping and valuable account of Sri Lanka's descent into civil war, the consequences of which are still being played out. The book is a meticulous record of the country's chaotic last half-century. But it is much more than a description of the crucial events that lie behind one of the world's longest separatist conflicts."

### ■ Biographical And Critical Sources

*PERIODICALS*

*Choice,* July-August, 1984, review of *Colonialism in Sri Lanka: The Political Economy of the Kandyan Highlands, 1833-86,* pp. 1642-1643.
*Contemporary Sociology,* September, 1985, Ronald J. Herring, review of *Colonialism in Sri Lanka,* p. 637.
*Journal of Asian Studies,* February, 1985, L. Ananda Wickremeratne, review of *Colonialism in Sri Lanka,* p. 417.
*Monthly Review,* March 1, 1999, Martha E. Gimenez, review of *Women, Population, and Global Crisis: A Political Economic Analysis,* p. 46.
*Pacific Affairs,* March 1, 2010, Bruce Matthews, review of *The Separatist Conflict in Sri Lanka: Terrorism, Ethnicity, Political Economy,* p. 193.
*WIN News,* September 22, 1998, Fran P. Hosken, review of *Women, Population, and Global Crisis,* p. 15.

*ONLINE*

*Asoka Bandarage Home Page,* http://www.bandarage.com (August 14, 2011).
*Georgetown University, Department of Government Web site,* http://explore.georgetown.edu/ (August 14, 2011), author profile.*

# Alan Bennett

## 1934-

### ■ Personal

Born May 9, 1934, in Leeds, England; son of Walter (a butcher) and Lilian Mary Bennett; partner's name, Rupert Thomas. *Education:* Exeter College, Oxford, B.A. (with honors), 1957. *Religion:* Church of England.

### ■ Addresses

*Home*—London, England. *Agent*—Charles Walker, PFD, Drury House, 34-43 Russell St., London WC2B 5HA, England.

### ■ Career

Playwright, screenwriter, and actor on stage and television, 1959—. Oxford University, Magdalen College, Oxford, England, temporary junior lecturer in history, 1960-62. President, North Craven Heritage Trust, 1968-93. *Military service:* Intelligence Corps, 1952-54.

### ■ Member

British Actors' Equity Association, Actors' Equity Association, American Federation of Television and Radio Artists.

### ■ Awards, Honors

London *Evening Standard* Drama Award, 1961, for *Beyond the Fringe,* 1968, for *Forty Years on,* and 1971, for *Getting On;* Antoinette Perry (Tony) Award, and New York Drama Critics Circle Award, both 1963, both for *Beyond the Fringe;* Guild of Television Producers Award, 1967, for *On the Margin; Plays & Players* Award for best new play, 1977, for *The Old Country,* and 1986, for *Kafka's Dick;* Broadcasters Press Guild TV Award, 1983, British Academy of Film and Television ArtsWriters Award, 1983, and Royal Television Society Award, 1984, all for *An Englishman Abroad;* honorary fellow, Exeter College, 1987; Hawthornden Prize, 1989, for *Talking Heads;* Olivier Award for best comedy, 1989, for *Single Spies,* and for best new play, 2005, for *The History Boys;* D.Litt., Leeds University, 1990; British Book Award, 2001, for best audiobook of the year for *The Laying On of Hands,* 2003, for lifetime achievement, and 2006, for author of the year; New York Drama Critics' Circle Award for best play, *Evening Standard* award for best play, and Tony Award for best play, all 2006, all for *The History Boys;* honorary membership, the Coterie, 2007.

### ■ Writings

*PLAYS*

(With Peter Cook, Jonathan Miller, and Dudley Moore) *Beyond the Fringe* (comedy revue; first produced in Edinburgh, Scotland, 1960; produced in the West End, 1961; produced in New York, NY, 1962), Random House (New York, NY), 1963.
(Coauthor) *Fortune,* produced in London, England, 1961.
(Coauthor) *Golden,* produced in New York, NY, 1962.
*Forty Years On* (two-act; first produced in Manchester, England, 1968; produced in the West End, 1968; also see below), Faber (London, England), 1969.
(With Caryl Brahms and Ned Sherrin) *Sing a Rude Song* (two-act), first produced in London, England, 1969.

*Getting On* (two-act; first produced in Brighton, England, 1971; produced in the West End, 1971; also see below), Faber (London, England), 1972.

*Habeas Corpus* (two-act; first produced in Oxford, England, 1973; produced in the West End, 1973; produced on Broadway, 1975; also see below), Faber (London, England), 1973, Samuel French (New York, NY), 1976.

*The Old Country* (first produced in Oxford, 1977; produced in the West End, 1977), Faber (London, England), 1978.

*Enjoy* (first produced at Richmond Theatre, 1980; produced in the West End, 1980), Faber (London, England), 1980.

*Office Suite* (adaptations of television plays *A Visit from Miss Prothero* and *Doris and Doreen,* produced in London, 1987; also see below), Faber (London, England), 1981.

*Forty Years On, Getting On, Habeas Corpus,* Faber (London, England), 1985.

*Kafka's Dick* (also see below), first produced at Royal Court Theatre, London, England, 1986.

*Two Kafka Plays: Kafka's Dick* [and] *The Insurance Man,* Faber (London, England), 1987.

(And director) *Single Spies* (two one-act plays; contains *A Question of Attribution* and *An Englishman Abroad;* also see below), first produced in London, England, 1988.

*The Wind in the Willows* (based on the novel by Kenneth Grahame; first produced in London, England, 1990), Faber (London, England), 1991.

*The Madness of George III* (also see below; first produced in London, England, 1991; produced in New York, NY, 1993), Faber (London, England), 1992.

*Talking Heads* (also see below; adapted from the teleplay by Bennett; first produced in London, 1992; adaptation produced in New York at the Minetta Lane Theater and directed by Michael Engler, 2003), Parkwest Publications (New York, NY), 1992.

*Bed among the Lentils: A Monologue from "Talking Heads,"* Samuel French (New York, NY), 1998.

*A Cream Cracker under the Settee: A Monologue from "Talking Heads,"* Samuel French (New York, NY), 1998.

*Her Big Chance: A Monologue from "Talking Heads,"* Samuel French (New York, NY), 1998.

*The Complete Talking Heads,* Picador (New York, NY), 2003.

*The History Boys* (first produced on Broadway, 2006), Faber & Faber (New York, NY), 2006.

*The Habit of Art* (first produced at the National Theater, London, England, 2009), Faber and Faber (New York, NY), 2010.

*TELEPLAYS*

*On the Margin* (television series), British Broadcasting Corp. (BBC-TV), 1966.

*A Day Out* (also see below), BBC-TV, 1972.

*Sunset across the Bay,* BBC-TV, 1975.

*A Little Outing,* BBC-TV, 1978.

*A Visit from Miss Prothero,* BBC-TV, 1978.

*Me! I'm Afraid of Virginia Woolf* (also see below), London Weekend Television, 1978.

*Doris and Doreen,* London Weekend Television, 1978.

*The Old Crowd* (also see below), London Weekend Television, 1979.

*One Fine Day* (also see below), London Weekend Television, 1979.

*Afternoon Off* (also see below), London Weekend Television, 1979.

*All Day on the Sands* (also see below), London Weekend Television, 1979.

*Objects of Affection* (contains *Our Winnie, A Woman of No Importance, Rolling Home, Marks,* and *Say Something Happened;* also see below), BBC-TV, 1982.

*Intensive Care* (also see below), BBC-TV, 1982.

*An Englishman Abroad* (also see below), BBC-TV, 1982.

*Objects of Affection and Other Plays* (includes *Intensive Care, A Day Out,* and *An Englishman Abroad*), BBC Publications (London, England), 1982.

*The Writer in Disguise* (includes *Me! I'm Afraid of Virginia Woolf, The Old Crowd, One Fine Day, Afternoon Off,* and *All Day on the Sands*), Faber (London, England), 1985.

*The Insurance Man* (also see below), BBC-TV, 1986.

*Talking Heads* (series), BBC-TV, 1987, BBC Publications (London, England), 1988.

*Dinner at Noon* (documentary), BBC-TV, 1988.

(And director) *Bed among the Lentils,* Public Broadcasting Service, 1989.

*Poetry in Motion,* Channel 4, 1990.

*102 Boulevard Haussmann,* BBC-TV, 1991.

*A Question of Attribution,* BBC-TV, 1991.

*Poetry in Motion 2,* Channel 4, 1992.

*Portrait or Bust* (documentary), BBC-TV, 1993.

*The Abbey* (documentary), BBC-TV, 1995.

*Talking Heads 2,* BBC-TV, 1998.

*Telling Tales* (autobiography), BBC-TV, 2000.

Also author of *An Evening with Alan Bennett, Famous Gossips, Ashenden, In My Defense,* and *A Chip in the Sugar.*

*OTHER*

*A Private Function* (screenplay), Handmade Films, 1984, Faber (London, England), 1985.

*Uncle Clarence* (radio talk), 1986.

*Prick Up Your Ears* (screenplay; adapted from the biography by John Lahr; produced by Samuel Goldwyn, 1987), Faber (London, England), 1988.

*The Lady in the Van* (produced, 1990), Faber (London, England), 2001.

*The Madness of King George* (screenplay; based on his play *The Madness of George III*, produced by Samuel Goldwyn, 1994), Random House (New York, NY), 1995.

*Writing Home* (memoir and essays), Faber (London, England), 1994, Random House (New York, NY), 1995.

*The Laying On of Hands* (short stories), Profile (London, England), 2000.

*The Clothes They Stood Up In* (novella), Random House (New York, NY), 2001.

*Three Stories* (contains "Father! Father! Burning Bright," "The Clothes They Stood Up In," and "Laying On of Hands"), Profile (London, England), 2003.

*Me, I'm Afraid of Virginia Woolf*, Faber (London, England), 2003.

*Alan and Thora*, BBC Consumer Publishing (London, England), 2004.

*Untold Stories* (memoir and essays), Farrar, Straus & Giroux (New York, NY), 2006.

*The History Boys* (screenplay, based on his play *The History Boys*), Fox Searchlight Pictures, 2006.

(With Nicholas Hytner) *The History Boys: The Film*, Faber and Faber (New York, NY), 2006.

*The Uncommon Reader* (novella), Farrar (New York, NY), 2007.

*A Life like Other People's* (memoir), Farrar (New York, NY), 2010.

*Smut: Two Unseemly Stories*, Faber and Faber: Profile Books (London, England), 2011.

Contributor to periodicals, including *Listener* and the *London Review of Books*.

## ■ Sidelights

Alan Bennett is a playwright, screenwriter, and entertainer best known for his work on stage and on television in Great Britain. His contributions to *Beyond the Fringe* and *Talking Heads* have established him as one of the premiere satirists in the United Kingdom. "Whatever their ostensible subjects, Alan Bennett's plays consistently dramatize man's desire to define himself and his world through teasingly inadequate language, whether conventional adages, women's magazine prose, government jargon, or quotations from the 'Greats,'" noted an essayist for *Contemporary Dramatists*. "The resulting parodies simultaneously mock and honor this impulse to erect linguistic safeguards in a frightening world."

Bennett began his career as an actor. He was studying medieval history at Oxford University when he and fellow student Dudley Moore were asked, along with Cambridge University students Peter Cook and Jonathan Miller, to come up with a comedy review for the Edinburgh Festival. Using minimal props, they created a series of routines that included a Shakespearean parody, a skit about working as a coal miner, and a farce about a train robbery and the overly literal police officer who investigates it. In these and many other segments of the review, they featured anarchic, irreverent humor that was a forerunner of many other significant comedy ensembles to come, including *Laugh-In, Monty Python's Flying Circus*, and *Saturday Night Live*.

### Forty Years On

Bennett's first solo creation, *Forty Years On*, first produced in 1968, consists of a play within a play. It follows the changing of the guard at a boys' boarding school, as the headmaster's retirement inspires the performance of a comic revue. It was a "fragmented, ambiguous, oddly interesting assortment of a play," according to *Village Voice* writer Molly Haskell, and it marked the author's transition from someone who could write clever skits to legitimate playwright.

Highlighting the satire in *Forty Years On* is the author's flair for language; "as we know from [his previous work], Bennett has a mean ear for cliché and the verbal ingenuity to twist it into appealingly absurd shapes," Benedict Nightingale remarked in the *New Statesman*. In contrast, *New York Times* critic Clive Barnes felt that the satire is "fundamentally . . . cheap and nasty," and he faulted the play for "pretentiousness and ineptness." Jeremy Kingston, however, praised *Forty Years On* for hitting its satirical targets, writing in *Punch* that Bennett "scores bull's-eyes and winners all down the line."

### Kafka's Dick

In the 1970s and early 1980s, Bennett wrote more than fifteen television scripts, garnering many awards. Despite critical acclaim for his work for television, however, Bennett wanted to return to writing for the stage, and in 1986 he did so with the work *Kafka's Dick*. *Kafka's Dick* is a "kind of leisurely vaudeville about the tormented Kafka of litcrit and biographical legend," wrote *Observer* contributor Michael Ratcliffe. Examining the relationships between biographers and their subjects, *Kafka's Dick* follows the investigations and trials of an insurance salesman who is obsessed with the famous Czech author, and the play includes characters such as Max Brod, Kafka's friend and literary executor, Kafka's father, and the author himself.

In the London *Times*, Irving Wardle called the play a "head-on challenge to literary myth," and he added: "There is a great deal more than that, too much in fact, to the play." Other reviewers likewise criticized the work as perhaps too ambitious; Ratcliffe observed that the work is "a mordant attack on twentieth-century trivialisation and barbarity by a playwright who cannot resist blunting the force and intensity of his attack by a constant stream of gags." "On the one hand, [Bennett] tilts at what Englishness stifles," Jim Hiley wrote in the *Listener*, and yet the playwright himself "refuses to get 'too' serious. He perches fretfully on the fence." Nevertheless, the critic believed that *Kafka's Dick* "provides a rewardingly inventive, provoking, often hilarious night out—a nutritious confection with pins in the cream." Wardle likewise maintained that while Bennett "has taken more on board than he can deal with . . . there remains, of course, the Bennett dialogue, which is as rich as ever in exquisitely turned domestic banalities and literary give-aways."

### The Madness of George III

Bennett's 1991 play, *The Madness of George III,* is "part court spectacle, part history lesson, part medical thriller," in the words of William A. Henry III of *Time.* The play is based on the life of the English king who reigned from 1760 to 1820. It focuses on two years during which the king lost the American colonies and, later, his mind. "The uniqueness of [this] play," according to Robert Brustein in the *New Republic*, "lies in the way it manages to evoke an entire historical epoch. . . . Before long we are deep in the intrigues of Georgian politics." As the king descends into madness, those about him—members of parliament, the Prince of Wales—scheme and vie for power. According to some critics this portrayal of England's political intrigue is the play's chief weakness.

Donald Lyons commented in the *New Criterion:* "Bennett writes these pols and docs on one note; once put on stage, they wrangle all too predictably. He has no Shavian knack for dramatizing ideas, or,

better to describe what Shaw does, to play and toy articulately with ideas." Jonathan Yardley offered a similar view in the *Washington Post.* He suggested that "the [grand] production of the play cannot quite disguise the flimsiness of its superstructure." Yardley conceded that *The Madness of George III* "may possess in any single scene more wit and energy than most American playwrights or screenwriters can summon up in an entire evening, but in other respects it bears a striking similarity to the intermittent attempts that are made over here— mostly on television—to reinterpret history through dramatization." Bennett adapted his play about King George into a screenplay for the 1994 film, *The Madness of King George,* directed by Nicholas Hytner and produced by the Samuel Goldwyn Company. The film brought Bennett's talents to a much wider audience in the United States.

### Prick Up Your Ears

It was not his first screenplay, however. He had previously written *A Private Function,* a film that skewers the class system in Great Britain. The film follows a middle-class couple in postwar England as they attempt to ascend the social ladder by serving pork—forbidden by rationing laws—at a society banquet. In 1986, Bennett took a more serious turn with *Prick Up Your Ears,* a film biography of English playwright Joe Orton. At the age of thirty-four, Orton was murdered by his longtime male lover, who then committed suicide.

*Los Angeles Times* film critic Sheila Benson termed Bennett's screenplay "a bracingly outrageous portrait of the playwright, his free-ranging life and remarkably constricted times." *Prick Up Your Ears* follows Orton's life through a series of flashbacks framed by the investigations of the playwright's biographer, John Lahr. Some critics thought that the film focuses too much on the details of Orton's life and not enough on his work. Vincent Canby, for example, commented in the *New York Times* that it "goes on to record little more than the facts of the Orton life, [and] the mere existence of the plays." Benson expressed a similar criticism, but commended the film for having "the rhythm and even the insolence of an Orton play, without its dialogue."

### Writing Home

The man behind the plays and movies, or at least his public persona, emerges in *Writing Home,* a collection of Bennett's diaries, essays, character sketches, and play prefaces. "Bennett has said," according to Peter Parker in the *Times Literary Supplement,* "that all writers play (rather than are) themselves in public, and *Writing Home . . .* a fragmentary but illuminating and engaging autobiography, is a classic performance." Evident in these occasional pieces are the characteristics that provide the basis for Bennett's work and account for his reception in the world of letters. Events from his unremarkable childhood in the north of England lie behind much of the writing in his television plays. Many of his insights into the supporting characters seem to be drawn from his own awkward experiences. "Mr. Bennett talks a fair amount about himself," observed Ben Brantley in the *New York Times Book Review,* "but it is self as defined almost exclusively by self-consciousness, a free-floating, pained awareness of everything he isn't and of life as a minefield of potential embarrassments."

Also evident is the humor that permeates Bennett's work. At times, this humor comes from his command of language and timing. Philip Hensher wrote in the *Spectator:* "What makes Bennett remarkable . . . is a linguistic spark, an unerring sense for the surprising, right word; the word which is going to slide like a banana skin, at the point where the reader expects to place his foot." Humor also comes, noted Hensher, from Bennett's keen powers of observation. "Bennett's comedy never seems to try; it is addicted to the bathetic shrug after the laugh; it modestly tells us that its best lines are not invented but overheard; the pinpoint accuracy of its vocabulary is passed off as that of an *object trouvé.*"

In the opinion of Richard Eder in the *Los Angeles Times Book Review,* not all of the pieces in *Writing Home* are of equal value. He maintained that the book "calls for prospecting, not straight reading; a vein of iron and more dazzling stuff are to be found under the topsoil." *New York Times* critic Michiko Kakutani admitted that "there are a few noticeable gaps in Mr. Bennett's book. . . . The reader notices these gaps, however, only because Mr. Bennett is such a delightful raconteur: this is a book you don't want to end." Fiona MacCarthy offered this evaluation in the *Observer:* "You finish this book liking Alan Bennett less than you imagined, but admiring him much more." For Peter Parker, what Bennett displays in *Writing Home* "is part of the reason why he is one of our most considerable, as well as one of our most popular, playwrights."

### The Clothes They Stood Up In and The Laying On of Hands

In 2001 Bennett turned to fiction, publishing the slender novel *The Clothes They Stood Up In.* The darkly comic work examines the marriage of a middle-class British couple through the lens of a burglary and its aftermath. When Mr. and Mrs. Ransome return from a night at the opera to find their flat completely cleaned out by burglars, they each learn lessons about the power of possessions to shape and define their lives. In his *Washington Post* review of the work, Jonathan Yardley wrote: "To call it a novella borders on exaggeration. Yet there is more to it—more wit, more complexity and ambiguity, more depth, more sheer pleasure and satisfaction—than there is to just about any new novel of whatever length that I have read since Saul Bellow's *Ravelstein* or Michael Chabon's *The Amazing Adventures of Kavalier & Clay.*" Yardley called the book "absolutely delicious, near-perfect," and concluded: "You will read it in a couple of hours at most, but you will think about it for a long, long time."

Bennett showed his skill with the short story form in the collection *The Laying On of Hands.* The title piece, a novella, is set at the memorial service for a young masseur whose promiscuous lifestyle was well known by those in attendance. It is widely assumed that he died of AIDS, so there is great anxiety among many of the mourners that perhaps they, too, have contracted the deadly disease. Even the clergyman presiding over the service has been an intimate of the dead man, and when he opens the floor for people wishing to share their personal memories, the results are somewhat shocking. According to Michele Leber, a *Booklist* reviewer, the story comments "provocatively on broader issues of morality with wry wit." In another story, "Miss Fozzard Finds Her Feet," a woman finds release for her sexual predilections through regular appointments with her podiatrist. The final offering in the collection is another novella, "Father! Father! Burning Bright," which depicts a middle-aged man who, while faithfully visiting his ailing father in the hospital, enters into a strange sexual relationship with his father's nurse. A *Kirkus Reviews* writer recommended the collection as "deft, light, observant, and very funny indeed."

### Untold Stories

Bennett drew more praise for his prose collection *Untold Stories,* which contains diary excerpts, political commentary, personal memories, and bits of conversation overheard by Bennett. He writes about art, about writing, and about his own sexual history. He takes an overview of his family's history and describes his fight with cancer. Diagnosed with the disease in 1997, he was told he had only a fifty percent chance for survival. He told almost nobody, in part because he did not want to deal with the additional correspondence he knew his news would engender.

In telling his story, he is "honest, urbane, humane," commented Stephen Smith in the Toronto *Globe & Mail,* as well as "funny, mordantly funny," even though his book is "shot through with pain, shadowed by death." Although the author believed that the pieces in this book might be published posthumously, he in fact survived his cancer and was able to see the book in print.

### The History Boys

Bennett returned to playwriting with the comedy *The History Boys,* which was produced on Broadway in 2006. The play, which won many prestigious awards, concerns a group of bright students at an English boys' school during the 1980s. The drama turns on the very different methods used by two of the instructors there. One, Hector, is a free thinker who believes in giving the students a truly well-rounded education. The other, Irwin, is focused on getting good exam results from the boys. Noting that the situation could have lent itself to much use of cliché, *Hollywood Reporter* reviewer Frank Scheck praised Bennett for avoiding that trap, and he called the play as a whole "messy and digressive but ultimately very entertaining." Scheck added that although the play "takes a long time getting to where it wants to go . . . it provides plenty of theatrical riches along the way." Scheck also praised *The History Boys* as "a sharp-edged and complex portrait of its milieu, leavened with frequent doses of uproarious humor." *Advocate* reviewer Don Shewey described *The History Boys* as "dense and epigrammatic." John Lahr, commenting on the play in the *New Yorker,* stated that it shows Bennett "in the fullness of his talent. . . . He is not only one of Britain's most popular storytellers onstage and on-screen; he is the iconic voice of its comic disenchantment, charting the spiritual attrition of the country's concessions to the marketplace and to modernism."

Bennett's successful play was adapted for a feature film with its original director, Nicholas Hytner, leading the direction of Bennett's screenplay. Gilbey Ryan in the *New Statesman* found the movie and concept wanting. Ryan noted: "In cinematic form [*The History Boys*] is no more than a gay *Dead Poets Society,* or *The Breakfast Club* with A-levels," and complained of "the script's graceless stabs at Profundity." Michael Koresky, reviewing the film for *Interview,* found it "straightforward and dramatically inert." Similarly, *Hollywood Reporter* reviewer Kirk Honeycutt observed that "precious little has been done to accommodate the change in medium" from stage to film. For Honeycutt, "performances border on the theatrical." Despite these criticisms, Honeycutt still believed "the movie makes for an intellectually invigorating couple of hours," further commenting that "while Bennett's satire no doubt aims at Thatcherite values, American viewers can certainly substitute the Reaganite push for a results-oriented society and heavy reliance on spin and glibness." Other reviewers also found much to like in the movie. *U.S. Catholic* contributor Patrick McCormick called it a "sparkling coming-of-age comedy." Likewise, *New York* contributor David Edelstein wrote: "The movie is brilliant and infectious, much like Bennett's voice."

### The Uncommon Reader

With his 2007 work, *The Uncommon Reader,* Bennett returned to fiction with a novella about the joys and dangers of reading. His protagonist is none other than the queen of England, who has never been much of a reader. One day a mobile library van pays a weekly visit outside the gates of Buckingham Palace and draws her attention. She borrows a book, and then the next week another, and yet another. Guided in her reading by a former kitchen boy with a penchant for homosexual authors, the queen is soon consumed with the delights of reading, querying the French president on the works of Jean Genet and forming a most unpleasant distaste for the longueurs of Henry James. Literary figures such as the Canadian short story writer Alice Munro become respected visitors at the palace, and soon the queen's entourage is concerned about her new obsession. When she decides to turn to writing rather than ruling, a constitutional crisis arises in "this crafty work of satire [that] should find an appreciative American audience," according to *Booklist* contributor Brad Hooper.

Other reviewers also commended Bennett's novella. A *Kirkus Reviews* critic noted of *The Uncommon Reader:* "Those who love reading will recognize the process of the Queen's enrapturing, how one book inevitably leads to another, and so many others, and that the richness of the reading life will always be offset by the recognition that time grows shorter as the list of books grows longer." A *Publishers Weekly* contributor called *The Uncommon Reader* "briskly original and subversively funny," as did an *Atlantic Monthly* contributor who found it a "witty novella. . . . Delectable, yes, but also nutritionally sound." Bob Minzesheimer, writing for *USA Today,* similarly found the work a "hilarious and pointed novella," as well as a "lovely lesson in the redemptive and subversive power of reading." *New York Times Book Review* writer Jeremy McCarter added to the chorus of praise, dubbing *The Uncommon Reader* a "kind of palace fairy tale for grown-ups." *Financial Times* critic Christopher Bray found the novella to be a "delight," while *Boston Globe* reviewer Katherine A. Powers felt it was "filled with sly jokes against the spirit of the age and beautifully spare in style." Jane Shilling, writing for the London *Times,* concluded that *The Uncommon Reader* was "an exquisitely produced jewel of a book."

### The Habit of Art

Bennett turned to theater once again with his 2009 play, *The Habit of Art,* dealing with a meeting between poet W.H. Auden and British composer Benjamin Britten in 1972. Britten was at work on his opera *Death in Venice* at the time and had hit a creative block. Auden and Britten had successfully collaborated in the 1930s, but had little contact with one another after that time. Bennett presents this meeting in a framed play within a play that takes the audience backstage during rehearsals for a theater piece that deals with the reunion. "Bennett continues his concern with the relationship between homosexuality and creativity," wrote Henry Hitchings in the London *Evening Standard Online.* "Sexual misunderstandings provide moments of ripe humour."

Hitchings found *The Habit of Art* "funny, and sometimes brilliantly so, but strangely uninvolving. . . . Fundamentally, though, this is a cerebral and self-referential play." Paul Taylor, writing in the London *Independent Online,* found more to like in this piece, dubbing it "hilariously provocative," while London *Guardian Online* reviewer Charlotte Higgins noted: "Bennett's work is utterly attentive to the joy, hardship, loneliness, comradeship, bitterness and solid, habitual drive to make work, whether that's music, poetry, or drama: the habit of art." Michael Billington, also reviewing the play in the *Guardian Online,* similarly felt that "Bennett's play is at its strongest when it deals with the theme implicit in its title: the idea that, for the artist, creativity is a constant, if troubling imperative." Billington termed *The Habit of Art* a "deeply moving play . . . [about] the ennobling power, in art, of sheer diurnal persistence."

### A Life like Other People's

Bennett returned to memoir for his 2010 work, *A Life like Other People's,* in which he details his parents' marriage and his mother's attempts to fight her depression. The mother's depression in fact defined the family, though for much of Bennett's life it was hidden from him. Then, later in his mother's life when she underwent a bout of depres-

sion, he learned the truth about earlier episodes from his father, and about the truth of his grandfather's suicide. Bennett's maternal aunts, Kathleen and Myra, also become a focus of this tale, much of which was already told in Bennett's earlier work, *Untold Stories.*

London *Independent Online* reviewer Lesley McDowell felt that Bennett's memoir is "clear-eyed, touching, occasionally waspish, not always charitable, and ever honest." Similarly, a *Bookbag* Web site contributor noted of the memoir: "The book is, of course, a delight. Alan Bennett never produces anything less. The writing is superb—appearing effortless and with never a wasted word. The observations are acute but always kindly and whilst we might laugh it will never be done in malice. And just occasionally we will chuckle with our author at himself."

### Smut

With *Smut: Two Unseemly Stories,* Bennett offers two novellas that have "fun with notions of respectability and gentility," according to an *Irish Independent Online* contributor. In the first tale, "The Greening of Mrs. Donaldson," a fifty-five-year-old widow ekes out a precarious living at a hospital faking illnesses so that medical students can find the correct diagnosis. She also takes in lodgers; her current boarders, Laura and Andy, cannot pay the rent and instead offer the frustrated woman a sex show in payment. Another lady, Mrs. Forbes, is at the center of the second novella, "The Shielding of Mrs. Forbes." She is upset that her son is marrying a girl with little to recommend her. In fact, the son, Graham, is marrying out of convenience, as he is gay and has been leading a double life, one that is about to be shattered by a blackmailing former lover. Meanwhile, henpecked Mr. Forbes forms an online liaison.

The reviewer for the *Irish Independent Online* felt this is "minor Bennett, never less than entertaining but nowhere as shrewd, perceptive, funny or poignant than the wonderful pieces to be found in his two essay collections, *Writing Home* and *Untold Stories.*" London *Guardian Online* reviewer Sarah Churchwell similarly noted: "If *Smut* is undeniably slight . . . it also offers plenty of Bennett's trademark pleasures." Churchwell added: "It would be too much to say that [Bennett is] challenging himself, but the book is by no means lazily written and it's consistently amusing, full of witty turns of phrase." London *Independent Online* contributor Arifa Akbar likewise termed this a "light, readable book." Akbar went on to note: "The characters are endearingly conventional who are merely owning up to their carnality. It is good, old-fashioned British humour with the lightest of subversive twists." Australia's *Age Online* reviewer Michael Shmith added praise for the work, writing: "Smut, the perfect title for this elegant little volume, is exactly what the stories are about. On a wider scale, however, they expose the hidden foibles of human nature in a way that is witty and wise but always acutely observed." *Financial Times Online* contributing editor Simon Schama similarly noted: "The stories have a dark, knowing, shrewdness about erotic mischief, young and old, but then we always knew, didn't we, that behind Bennett's tousled owlishness there was a Bit of Lad. The trick of these tales is to sprinkle middle-class, middle-aged life with a dash of dirty—a spot of nookie amid the nasturtiums."

With each new play and fictional work, Bennett has furthered his standing in the eyes of many critics. *New York Times* theater critic Ben Brantley called Bennett the "slyest and—along with Tom Stoppard—most elegant of contemporary British dramatists." David Nokes asserted in the *Times Literary Supplement:* "Alan Bennett's beguiling modesty has all but deflected recognition that he is probably our greatest living dramatist. His characteristic style is unpretentious, small-scale and domestic. His genius lies in an unerring ear for the idioms of lower-middle-class life, the verbal doilies of self-respect and self-repression."

## ■ Biographical And Critical Sources

### BOOKS

Bennett, Alan, *Writing Home,* Faber (London, England), 1994, Random House (New York, NY), 1995.

Bennett, Alan, *Untold Stories* (memoir), Farrar, Straus & Giroux (New York, NY), 2006.

*Contemporary Dramatists,* 6th edition, St. James Press (Detroit, MI), 1999.

Wolfe, Peter, *Understanding Alan Bennett,* University of South Carolina Press (Columbia, SC), 1998.

### PERIODICALS

*Advocate,* June 6, 2006, Don Shewey, review of *The History Boys,* p. 56.

*America,* September 9, 1989, Gary Seibert, review of *Single Spies,* p. 145.

*America's Intelligence Wire,* November 24, 2006, "Alan Bennett's Sensational Play 'The History Boys' Comes to the Big Screen with Original Cast."

*Antioch Review,* January 1, 2007, Ianthe Brautigan, review of *Untold Stories,* p. 196.

*Atlantic Monthly,* October 1, 2007, review of *The Uncommon Reader,* p. 138.

*Back Stage East,* June 15, 2006, "'Boys' Night Out at the Tonys: 'Jersey Boys'; 'History Boys' Named Broadway's Best," p. 2; March 6, 2008, review of *The Wind in the Willows,* p. 24.

*Baltimore Sun,* December 22, 2006, "Fresh Writing Earns 'History Boys' High Marks."

*Biography,* winter, 2006, Stephen Smith, review of *Untold Stories,* p. 200.

*Book,* March, 2001, Paul Evans, review of *The Clothes They Stood Up In,* p. 82.

*Booklist,* June 1, 2002, Michele Leber, review of *The Laying On of Hands,* p. 167; August 1, 2007, Brad Hooper, review of *The Uncommon Reader,* p. 40.

*Bookseller,* June 17, 2005, review of *Untold Stories,* p. 36; June 16, 2006, "Another Call for Bennett," p. 8.

*Boston Globe,* September 23, 3007, Katherine A. Powers, review of *The Uncommon Reader.*

*Buffalo News* (Buffalo, NY), December 22, 2006, review of *The History Boys.*

*Chicago Tribune,* December 8, 2006, "'History' Feels Stagey, but Is Still Moving."

*Christian Science Monitor,* November 24, 2006, review of *The History Boys,* p. 14.

*Columbus Dispatch* (Columbus, OH), December 22, 2006, "Yanks Need Translator for British Tale."

*Commonweal,* May 23, 2008, "Tenderized," p. 20.

*Economist,* February 23, 1991, review of *The Wind in the Willows,* p. 98; October 29, 1994, review of *Writing Home,* p. 105.

*Europe Intelligence Wire,* June 12, 2006, "History Boys Celebrates Comprehensive Tony Triumph"; September 8, 2006, "Making History"; October 12, 2006, "Bennett's Play Is Making History"; November 24, 2006, "New York Laps Up Bennett's Slice of History."

*Film Journal International,* December 1, 2006, David Noh, review of *The History Boys,* p. 62; December 1, 2006, "Yorkshire Lads: Original Cast of History Boys Graduates to Big Screen," p. 16.

*Financial Times,* January 8, 2007, Alastair Macaulay, review of *The History Boys,* p. 13; September 22, 2007, Christopher Bray, "Crown Prints the Queen Discovers Literature, with a Little Help from Alan Bennett," p. 37.

*Gay & Lesbian Review Worldwide,* March 1, 2007, "The History Teacher."

*Globe & Mail* (Toronto, Ontario, Canada), October 7, 2005, Kamal Al-Solaylee, review of *Habeas Corpus,* p. R27; October 15, 2005, Kamal Al-Solaylee, review of *Habeas Corpus,* p. R7; October 28, 2005, Warren Clements, review of *Beyond the Fringe,* p.

R34; December 10, 2005, Stephen Smith, review of *Untold Stories*, p. D18; May 3, 2006, Kamal Al-Solaylee, review of *The History Boys*, p. R4.

*GP*, March 3, 2006, Fiona Gilroy, review of *Untold Stories*, p. 62.

*Guardian*, February 17, 1989, p. 26; May 14, 2004, Aida Edemariam, "Guardian Profile: Alan Bennett"; May 19, 2004, Charles Spencer, review of *The History Boys*, and Michael Billington, review of *The History Boys*; October 1, 2005, Nicholas Wroe, "Sketchy Beginnings."

*Harper's Bazaar*, September, 1989, Christa Worthington, "Bringing Down the House," p. 46.

*Hollywood Reporter*, April 26, 2006, Frank Scheck, review of *The History Boys*, p. 12; June 13, 2006, "'Boys' Night Out at Tony Awards: Bennett Earns Eight Nods; Valli Story Named Top Musical," p. 53; November 2, 2006, Kirk Honeycutt, review of *The History Boys*, p. 25.

*Hudson Review*, winter, 1990, reviews of *An Englishman Abroad* and *A Question of Attribution*, p. 636.

*Interview*, December 1, 2006, Michael Koresky, review of *The History Boys*, p. 98.

*Kirkus Reviews*, May 1, 2002, review of *The Laying On of Hands*, p. 590; January 15, 2006, review of *Untold Stories*, p. 68; July 15, 2007, review of *The Uncommon Reader*.

*Law Society Journal*, July 1, 2006, Richard Krever, review of *Untold Stories*, p. 79.

*Library Journal*, January 1, 2001, Judith Kicinski, review of *The Clothes They Stood Up In*, p. 151; January 1, 2006, Pam Kingsbury, review of *Untold Stories*, p. 114; August 1, 2007, Christina Bauer, review of *The Uncommon Reader*, p. 63.

*Listener*, October 2, 1986, Jim Hiley, review of *Kafka's Dick*.

*Los Angeles Times*, May 1, 1987, Sheila Benson, review of *Prick Up Your Ears*.

*Los Angeles Times Book Review*, September 24, 1995, Richard Eder, review of *Writing Home*.

*New Republic*, April 20, 1987, Stanley Kauffman, review of *Prick Up Your Ears*, p. 28; February 17, 1992, Robert Brustein, review of *The Madness of George III*, p. 28; December 18, 2006, "Histories, Fresh and Final," p. 22.

*Newsday*, November 21, 2006, "Teachers' Wit Makes 'History.'"

*New Statesman*, November 8, 1968, Benedict Nightingale, review of *Forty Years On*; November 7, 1986, Victoria Radin, review of *Kafka's Dick*, p. 25; May 22, 1987, Judith Williamson, review of *Prick Up Your Ears*, p. 23; May 31, 2004, Rosie Millard, review of *The History Boys*, p. 43; October 16, 2006,

Gilbey Ryan, "Please, Sir, Can I Be Excused? Alan Bennett's Saccharine Tale Does Not Work Well on the Big Screen," p. 45.

*New Statesman and Society*, December 6, 1991, Andy Lavender, review of *The Madness of George III*, p. 37.

*Newsweek*, April 20, 1987, David Ansen, review of *Prick Up Your Ears*, p. 89; January 9, 1989, Jack Kroll, review of *Single Spies*, p. 53; January 21, 1991, Jack Kroll, review of *The Wind in the Willows*, p. 60; September 27, 1993, Jack Kroll, review of *The Madness of George III*, p. 74.

*Newsweek International*, August 2, 2004, Tara Pepper, review of *The History Boys*, p. 53.

*New York*, April 20, 1987, David Denby, review of *Prick Up Your Ears*, p. 76; February 13, 1989, John Leonard, review of *Bed among the Lentils: A Monologue from 'Talking Heads,'* p. 71; September 27, 1993, John Simon, review of *The Madness of George III*, p. 72; November 27, 2006, David Edelstein, "Top of Its Class: The History Boys Shows Why Dead Poets Society Was Such a Sham," p. 120.

*New Yorker*, May 4, 1987, Pauline Kael, review of *Prick Up Your Ears*, p. 128; September 6, 1993, Clive Barnes, review of *Forty Years On*, p. 92; October 11, 1993, John Lahr, review of *The Madness of George III*, p. 124; April 14, 2003, John Lahr, review of *Talking Heads*, p. 88; May 1, 2006, John Lahr, review of *The History Boys*, p. 92.

*New York Review of Books*, September 24, 1987, Gabriele Annan, review of *Prick Up Your Ears*, p. 3A; April 13, 1989, Noel Annan, review of *Single Spies*, p. 24; February 16, 1995, Ian Buruma, review of *The Madness of George III*, p. 15.

*New York Sun*, September 28, 2007, Michael Schulman, review of *The Uncommon Reader*.

*New York Times*, November 5, 1968, Clive Barnes, review of *Forty Years On*; March 1, 1985, Vincent Canby, review of *A Private Function*; May 17, 1987, John Gross, review of *Prick Up Your Ears*; March 3, 1992, Frank Rich, review of *The Madness of George III*, p. C13; September 17, 1993, Frank Rich, review of *The Madness of George III*, p. C1; September 26, 1995, Michiko Kakutani, review of *Writing Home*, p. B2; November 21, 2006, "From the Stage to the Screen, History Worth Repeating," p. 1.

*New York Times Book Review*, October 15, 1995, Ben Brantley, review of *Writing Home*, p. 13; September 30, 2007, Jeremy McCarter, "Ruined by a Book," p. 11.

*New York Times Magazine*, September 30, 1990, J.B. Miller, "Far beyond the Fringe," p. 13.

*Observer*, September 28, 1986 Michael Ratcliffe, review of *Kafka's Dick*; October 9, 1994, Fiona Mc-Carthy, review of *Writing Home*, p. 20.

*Orlando Sentinel* (Orlando, FL), December 22, 2006, "History Repeats Itself in Lackluster 'Boys.'"

*O, the Oprah Magazine*, April, 2006, David Gates, review of *Untold Stories*, p. 218; September 1, 2007, "What She's Reading," p. 248.

*Philadelphia Inquirer*, December 11, 2006, Carrie Rickey, review of *The History Boys*.

*Publishers Weekly*, December 4, 2000, review of *The Clothes They Stood Up In*, p. 51; May 27, 2002, review of *The Laying On of Hands*, p. 35; July 16, 2007, review of *The Uncommon Reader*, p. 142.

*Punch*, November 6, 1968, Jeremy Kingston, review of *Forty Years On*.

*Quadrant*, July 1, 2007, "The Drama of Teaching and the Recent Past"; December 1, 2007, Anne Warburton, "The Morality of *The History Boys*," p. 5.

*Seattle Times* (Seattle, WA), December 15, 2006, "*The History Boys*: The Joy and Heartbreak of Learning, Teaching."

*Spectator*, October 8, 1994, Philip Hensher, review of *Writing Home*, p. 39; December 18, 1999, Sheridan Morley, review of *The Lady in the Van*, pp. 90-91; December 16, 2000, Paul Routledge, review of *Telling Tales*, pp. 78-79; October 6, 2001, Hilary Mantel, review of *The Laying On of Hands*, p. 63; May 29, 2004, Rachel Halliburton, review of *The History Boys*, p. 44; October 22, 2005, Ferdinand Mount, review of *Untold Stories*, p. 49; April 1, 2006, review of *The Old Country*, p. 69; October 7, 2006, Andrew Roberts, "The History Boys Film Gets Me All Wrong"; October 14, 2006, "Too Faithful"; September 1, 2007, Sam Leith, "Waking Up Late at the Palace," p. 29.

*Star Tribune* (Minneapolis, MN), December 14, 2006, Colin Covert, "Class Act; Alan Bennett's 'History Boys' Graduates from Stage to Screen with Honors," p. 25.

*Sunday Times* (London, England), September 2, 2007, Lindsay Duguid, review of *The Uncommon Reader*.

*Tampa Tribune* (Tampa, FL), December 22, 2006, "Thought Intelligent Cinema Was 'History'? Think Again," p. 4.

*Time*, September 13, 1993, William A. Henry III, review of *The Madness of George III*, p. 75.

*Time International*, June 7, 2004, Richard Corliss, review of *The History Boys*, p. 69.

*Times* (London, England), September 6, 1986, Irving Wardle, review of *Kafka's Dick*, p. 10; August 25, 2007, Jane Shilling, review of *The Uncommon Reader*.

*Times Literary Supplement*, December 16, 1991, David Nokes, review of *The Madness of George III*, p. 18; October 7, 1994, Peter Parker, review of *Writing Home*, p. 38; December 24, 1999, Robert Shore, review of *The Lady in the Van*, p. 17; September 14, 2007, "A Book of One's Own," p. 21.

*USA Today*, October 2, 2007, Bob Minzesheimer, review of *The Uncommon Reader*, p. 6.

*U.S. Catholic*, February 1, 2007, Patrick McCormick, review of *The History Boys*, p. 44.

*Variety*, February 3, 1992, John Goff, reviews of *In My Defense* and *A Chip in the Sugar*, p. 87; November 9, 1992, p. 66; April 7, 2003, review of *Talking Heads*, p. 4; April 14, 2003, Charles Isherwood, review of *Talking Heads*, p. 28; May 31, 2004, Matt Wolf, review of *The History Boys*, p. 32; April 3, 2006, David Benedict, review of *The Old Country*, p. 77.

*Video Business*, March 19, 2007, Irv Slifkin, review of *The History Boys*, p. 9.

*Village Voice*, January 30, 1969, Molly Haskell, review of *Forty Years On*.

*Vogue*, September, 1993, Georgina Howell, interview with Alan Bennett, p. 324.

*Wall Street Journal*, December 29, 1994, Amy Gamerman, review of *The Madness of King George*, p. A8.

*Washington Post*, April 29, 1985, Paul Attanasio, review of *A Private Function*, p. C2; February 19, 1992, Jonathan Yardley, review of *The Madness of George III*, p. C1; January 25, 2001, Jonathan Yardley, review of *The Clothes They Stood Up In*, p. C2.

*Washington Post Book World*, October 7, 2007, "What Would Happen If Her Royal Highness Got Hooked on Books?," p. 10.

*World Entertainment News Network*, September 1, 2006, "Bennett: 'I Thought I'd Die before Biography Published'"; October 8, 2006, "Bennett: 'The Queen Is Hilarious'"; October 9, 2006, "Bennett Disrespected on Set."

ONLINE

*Age Online*, http://www.theage.com.au/ (June 11, 2011), Michael Shmith, "It's Dirty Work, Coughing Up Our Foibles," review of *Smut: Two Unseemly Stories*.

*Asylum*, http://theasylum.wordpress.com/ (September 2, 2007), John Self, review of *The Uncommon Reader*.

*Bookbag*, http://www.thebookbag.co.uk/ (August 9, 2011), review of *A Life like Other People's*.

*Complete Review*, http://www.complete-review.com/ (September 1, 2006), review of *The History Boys*.

*Contemporary Writers,* http://www.contemporary writers.com/ (October 14, 2011), Guy Woodward, biography of Alan Bennett.

*Curled Up with a Good Book,* http://www.curledup. com/ (June 16, 2008), review of *The Uncommon Reader.*

*Evening Standard Online,* http://www.thisislondon. co.uk/ (November 18, 2009), Henry Hitchings, "Alan Bennett Is Back in the Habit with Brilliant but Flawed Play."

*Financial Times Online,* http://www.ft.com/ (April 22 2011), Simon Schama, review of *Smut.*

*Grumpy Old Bookman,* http://grumpyoldbookman. blogspot.com/ (February 5, 2007), review of *Untold Stories.*

*Guardian Online,* http://www.guardian.co.uk/ (September 30, 2007), Edward Marriott, review of *The Uncommon Reader;* (November 18, 2009), Michael Billington, review of *The Habit of Art;* (November 18, 2009), Charlotte Higgins, review of *The Habit of Art;* (April 23, 2011), Sarah Churchwell, review of *Smut.*

*Independent Online,* http://www.independent.co. uk/ (November 18, 2009), Paul Taylor, review of *The Habit of Art;* (April 22, 2011), Arifa Akbar, review of *Smut;* (May 2, 2010), Lesley McDowell, review of *A Life like Other People's.*

*Internet Movie Database,* http://www.imdb.com/ (August 9, 2011). "Alan Bennett."

*Irish Independent Online,* http://www.independent. ie/ (July 2, 2011), review of *Smut.*

*Lambda Literary Review Online,* http://www. lambdaliterary.org/ (April 26, 2011), Frank Pizzoli, review of *A Life like Other People's.*

*List,* http://www.list.co.uk/ (August 23, 2007), review of *The Uncommon Reader.*

*London Review of Books Online,* http://www.lrb.co. uk/ (November5, 2009), "Alan Bennett Writes about His New Play."

*Mostly Fiction Book Reviews,* http://www.mostly fiction.com/ (September 14, 2007), Mary Whipple, review of *The Uncommon Reader.*

*Museum of Broadcast Communications Web site,* http://www.museum.tv/ (September 1, 2006), Brendan Kenny, "Alan Bennett."

*Telegraph Online,* http://www.telegraph.co.uk/ (May 9, 2009), William Langley, "Alan Bennett: A Writer Who Endures an Embarrassment of Talents."

*University of Leeds Reporter,* http://reporter.leeds.ac. uk/ (June 16, 2008), "Telling Tales on Alan Bennett."

*West End Whingers,* http://westendwhingers. wordpress.com/ (November 12, 2009), review of *The Habit of Art.**

# Suzanne Berne

## 1961-

■ **Personal**

Born January 17, 1961, in Washington, DC; daughter of Henry (a psychotherapist) and Patricia (a psychologist) Berne; married Kenneth Kimmell (an attorney), September 24, 1989; children: Avery Patricia, Louisa Berne. *Education:* Wesleyan University, B.A., 1982; University of Iowa Writers Workshop, M.F.A., 1985. *Politics:* Democrat.

■ **Addresses**

*Agent*—Colleen Mohyde, Doe Coover Agency, P.O. Box 668, Winchester, MA 01890. *E-mail*—cmohyde@aol.com.

■ **Career**

Harvard University, Cambridge, MA, expository writing preceptor, 1988-92, member of extension school faculty, 1989-95; Radcliffe College Seminars faculty member, 1990-93, instructor in fiction, 1995-99, Department of English Briggs-Copeland fellow, 1999-2000, visiting lecturer in English, 2000-01; Boston College, Chestnut Hill, MA, adjunct lecturer in English, 2007—.

■ **Member**

PEN New England Center.

■ **Awards, Honors**

College Fiction Award, *Ms.* magazine, 1981; Bay Area Fiction Award, 1987; National Endowment for the Arts fellowship, 1994; PEN/Discovery honoree for fiction, 1995; Massachusetts Cultural Council artist grant, 1996; Art Seidenbaum Award finalist, *Los Angeles Times,* 1997, Edgar Allan Poe Award finalist, Mystery Writers of America, 1997, and Orange Prize winner (Great Britain), 1999, all for *A Crime in the Neighborhood;* notable book designation, *New York Times,* 1997, for *A Crime in the Neighborhood,* and 2001, for *A Perfect Arrangement.*

■ **Writings**

*A Crime in the Neighborhood,* Algonquin Books (Chapel Hill, NC), 1997.

*A Perfect Arrangement,* Algonquin Books (Chapel Hill, NC), 2001.

*The Ghost at the Table: A Novel,* Algonquin Books (Chapel Hill, NC), 2006.

*Missing Lucile: Memories of a Grandmother I Never Knew,* Algonquin Books of Chapel Hill (Chapel Hill, NC), 2010.

Contributor of essays to anthologies, including *The Place Within: Essays on Landscape by Twenty Contemporary American Writers,* W.W. Norton (New York, NY); and *The Quiet Center: Women Writers Reflecting on Life's Passages,* Hearst Books. Contributor of short fiction to periodicals, including *Epoch, Threepenny Review, Cimarron Review, Playgirl, Mademoiselle, Conjunctions,* and *Ms.* Contributor of essays and reviews to periodicals, including *New York Times Magazine, New York Times Book Review, New York Times, Ploughshares, Harvard Review, Boston Globe Magazine, Bloomsbury Review, Boston Review, Belles Lettres, Commonweal, Victoria, House Beautiful, San Francisco Chronicle, Guardian,* and *Independent.*

Berne's novels have been translated into several languages.

## ■ Sidelights

Suzanne Berne is a family-oriented writer who focuses her novels on the average suburban neighborhood. The genuine feeling behind her writing and her ability to communicate the fragility of her characters' emotions and circumstances have earned the author considerable praise.

### A Crime in the Neighborhood

Berne's multi-award-winning debut novel, 1997's *A Crime in the Neighborhood*, takes place in the early 1970s and focuses on the Eberhardt family as they are rocked by the adultery of father Larry, the brutal murder of a young neighborhood boy, and the unfolding Watergate scandal. Berne's narrator, the daughter of Larry Eberhardt, tells the story as a grown woman, recounting her experiences and emotions as an impressionable ten-year-old.

Dubbing the novel an "impressive literary debut," *Booklist* contributor Michele Leber pointed to the author's ability to express "the potentially devastating effects of one person's actions on others." Praising the novel's "seamless narrative structure" and "extraordinary sense of lightness and suspense," a *Publishers Weekly* contributor called *A Crime in the Neighborhood* "a resonant portrait of a girl's, a community's and a country's loss of innocence."

### A Perfect Arrangement

In her second novel, *A Perfect Arrangement*, Berne once again focuses on a family overcoming the difficulties of modern life. Here a married couple struggles to reconnect after having been emotionally distant due to busy schedules and the demands of job and family. Meanwhile, the seemingly perfect caregiver they hired for their children appears to be unusually possessive.

Imbued with "chilling inevitability, this carefully observed, beautifully written book proceeds to a horrifying finale," remarked Judith Kicinski in a review for *Library Journal*. While a *Publishers Weekly* contributor criticized Berne's characters as "studiously drawn archetypes," the reviewer gave the novel high marks overall. "Berne is an assured writer and is at her best with careful, observant descriptions of family life," the contributor concluded.

### The Ghost at the Table

Five years separated the publication of Berne's second novel and her third, 2006's *The Ghost at the Table: A Novel*, another piece of fiction focusing on the family. It is, according to Ron Charles writing in the *Washington Post Book World*, "very much a novel about the way we shape and sanctify our memories and then allow those memories to control us." Berne's novel turns out to be a feat of historical exhumation as two estranged sisters gather for Thanksgiving at their family home in Concord, Massachusetts; one is eager to put the past behind her, the other is controlled by family history. Frances hopes to bring the family back together again with this holiday visit, but the younger Cynthia is not overly eager to return to her childhood home from her new life as a writer in San Francisco. The reader views the proceedings largely through the voice of Cynthia, a narrator who cannot always be relied upon for objective observation. Meanwhile, Frances's recollections of the same incidents take on a more positive hue, and the reader is left to sort out the truth.

Writing in the *Guardian Online*, Carrie O'Grady observed that Berne opts for a risky technique in this third novel: instead of finally unraveling the past for the reader, "she skillfully knots the threads still further, revealing fresh complexities in every chapter." Central to the book are the death of Mrs. Fiske, the sisters' mother, when they were teenagers, and their philandering father's subsequent remarriage to the young woman who was their tutor at the time. Both have viewed this incident in vastly different ways. This establishes the twin points of view of the main characters: Frances, who views the family history through the rosy lens of her childhood optimism, and Cynthia, whose cynicism charges all of her recollections.

Critics on both sides of the Atlantic had high praise for *The Ghost at the Table*. Writing in the *Boston Globe*, Carol Iaciofano commented: "Berne masterfully explores the parallel realities that can endure after a great sadness." A *Kirkus Reviews* critic called *The Ghost at the Table* a "substantial tale of a dysfunctional family reunion [that] promises a holiday, and a read, to remember." A reviewer for *O, the Oprah Magazine* termed the novel a "crash course in sibling rivalry, with its cutthroat dueling for dominance and parental love," while Jennifer Reese, writing in *Entertainment Weekly*, observed: "Berne turns a witty tale of holiday dysfunction into a transfixing borderline gothic." Likewise, a *Publishers Weekly* reviewer praised Berne's "astute observation and narrative cunning" in this "taut psychological drama." Reviewers in the United Kingdom were also won over by the novel. Zoe Paxton, writing in the London *Times*, described it as "an immaculately executed character study [that] becomes an altogether more intelligent and unnerving critique of the pitfalls of memory." Reviewing the novel in the *London Independent Online*, Charlie Lee-Potter considered *The Ghost at the Table* "a satisfying and complex story that adds up to more than its parts." And O'Grady concluded that the novel is not only "gripping and hugely satisfying, filled with Berne's characteristic appreciation of small, sensual details, but it reminds you that other families may be in even worse shape than your own."

### Missing Lucile

After a gap of several years, Berne turned to the memoir with the 2010 publication of *Missing Lucile: Memories of a Grandmother I Never Knew.* The memoir is about her paternal grandmother, Lucile Kroger, a member of the Kroger grocery chain family who died when Berne's father was a child and whose death led to his lifelong sadness and sense of loss. Sifting through scraps of information, Berne created a portrait based partly on fact and partly on speculation. In an interview on the *Algonquin Books Blog,* Berne describes her grandmother: "Lucile was an intellectual, an early feminist, a business executive, a relief worker, a wife and mother."

The critical reaction to *Missing Lucile* was somewhat mixed. Many reviewers offered a favorable judgment. Writing in *The Wall Street Journal,* reviewer Stephen Birmingham said that "as a work of history or biography *Missing Lucile* is of little interest, but as a piece of writing it is a surprisingly lively read," one that "artfully weaves actual events of the early twentieth century with what Lucile might or might not have been doing or thinking at the time." In the *Citizen Times,* Linda Elisabeth Beattie wrote that Berne's "venture into the genre of memoir" is a "delightful gamble." Karna Converse, in *Internet Review of Books,* concluded that the book's "narrative skillfully ties Lucile's childhood to major events that are occurring at the turn of the century" and called the book's writing "beautiful." On *Elder Statesman Blog,* Bill Duncan called the book a "good read," and Pam Kelley, writing in the *Charlotte Observer,* described *Missing Lucile* as a "beautifully written story." A reviewer in *Kirkus Reviews* concurred, praising the book as "a lyrical character sketch, vivid even through the smoky glass of time."

### Berne told *CA:*

"In trying to think of something interesting to say about my writing process, I find that not much comes to mind that hasn't already been said, with varying degrees of eloquence and frustration, by many other writers before me. Not that many other writers have had the same writing process as mine,

but there is a good deal of commonality: You sit down, you put something on paper, and you rewrite it. Eventually, if you have worked hard enough, and are lucky enough, whatever you wrote gets published. And then you start all over again. People never believe that's all there is to it, and they're right—so much else goes into writing a story than sitting down in front of a piece of paper (or a computer screen nowadays)—but they're also wrong: sitting down and putting something on paper is the writing process.

"The only aspect of my writing process that might be a little unusual is that I like to begin with a technical problem. It makes starting something new seem less intimidating if you start by thinking you're simply experimenting with narrative perspective or shifting tenses or writing about a murder when you've done anything like that before. That's how I began my first novel—as a simple exercise: write about a murder. My second novel began when I decided to try to create three different points of view that all were experiencing the same set of events, but quite differently.

"Doesn't that sound easy? But it takes years and years, after you get started, to make any sense out of those first ideas, however they arrive. At least it takes me years and years. I spent seven years writing a novel that will never be published (because it's not very good). The next one took five. . . . Flannery O'Connor once said that being a fiction writer requires 'a grain of stupidity,' the need to stare and stare before you understand something. I would agree with that analysis."

## ■ Biographical And Critical Sources

### PERIODICALS

*Booklist,* April 15, 1997, Michele Leber, review of *A Crime in the Neighborhood,* p. 1385; August 1, 2006, Joanne Wilkinson, review of *The Ghost at the Table: A Novel,* p. 36; September 1, 2010, Allison Block, review of *Missing Lucile: Memories of a Grandmother I Never Knew,* p. 31.

*Boston Globe,* October 18, 2006, Carol Iaciofano, review of *The Ghost at the Table.*

*Entertainment Weekly,* October 20, 2006, Jennifer Reese, review of *The Ghost at the Table,* p. 84.

*Kirkus Reviews,* August 1, 2006, review of *The Ghost at the Table,* p. 737; August 15, 2010, review of *Missing Lucile.*

*Library Journal,* May 1, 2001, Judith Kicinski, review of *A Perfect Arrangement,* p. 125; July 1, 2006, Leigh Anne Vrabel, review of *The Ghost at the Table,* p. 61.

*New Statesman,* November 6, 2006, Elinor Cook, review of *The Ghost at the Table,* p. 60.

*New York Times Book Review,* November 21, 2010, "The Missing Piece," p. 8.

*O, the Oprah Magazine,* November, 2006, review of *The Ghost at the Table,* p. 240.

*Publishers Weekly,* March 31, 1997, review of *A Crime in the Neighborhood,* p. 59; April 16, 2001, review of *A Perfect Arrangement,* p. 45; June 12, 2006, review of *The Ghost at the Table,* p. 26.

*School Library Journal,* January, 2007, Jenny Gasset, review of *The Ghost at the Table,* p. 164.

*Times* (London, England), October 21, 2006, Zoe Paxton, review of *The Ghost at the Table.*

*Wall Street Journal Eastern Edition,* October 21, 2010, Stephen Birmingham, "The Cincinnati Grocer's Kid; an Heiress of the Kroger Fortune Proves to Be an Elusive Subject," p. 15.

*Washington Post Book World,* October 15, 2006, Ron Charles, review of *The Ghost at the Table,* p. 6.

ONLINE

*Algonquin Books Blog,* http://www.algonquinbooks blog.com/ (October 13, 2010), interview with Suzanne Berne.

*Charlotte Observer,* http://www.charlotteobserver. com/ (October 10, 2010), Pam Kelley, review of *Missing Lucile.*

*Citizen Times* (Asheville, NC), http://www.citizen-times.com/ (November 22, 2006), Linda Elisabeth Beattie, review of *Missing Lucile.*

*Elder Statesman Blog site,* http://www.theduncans online.com/ (August 26, 2011), Bill Duncan, review of *Missing Lucile.*

*Guardian Online,* http://books.guardian.co.uk/ (October 28, 2006), Carrie O'Grady, review of *The Ghost at the Table.*

*Independent Weekly Online* (Raleigh-Durham-Chapel Hill, NC), http://www.indyweek.com/ (November 22, 2006), Adam Sobsey, review of *The Ghost at the Table.*

*Internet Review of Books,* http://www.indyweek. com/ (November 20, 2010), Karna Converse, review of *Missing Lucile.*

*London Independent Online,* http://enjoyment. independent.co.uk/ (November 19, 2006), Charlie Lee-Potter, review of *The Ghost at the Table.*

*Suzanne Berne Home Page,* http://www.suzanne berne.net/ (August 17, 2011), author profile.

*Washington Post Book World,* http://www. washingtonpost.com/ (October 14, 2010), Carolyn See, review of *Missing Lucile.**

# Donald Bogle

## 1944-

■ **Personal**

Born July 13, 1944, in Philadelphia, PA. *Education:* Lincoln University (with honors); attended Indiana University, Harvard University, and Columbia University.

■ **Addresses**

*Home*—New York, NY.

■ **Career**

Historian, editor, and writer. Worked as a staff writer and assistant editor at *Ebony* magazine. Lectured at Lincoln University, University of Pennsylvania, and New York University's Tisch School of the Arts.

■ **Awards, Honors**

Theatre Library Association Award, best film book of the year, for *Toms, Coons, Mulattoes, Mammies, and Bucks: An Interpretive History of Blacks in American Films*; Hurston/Wright Literary Award, 2006.

■ **Writings**

*Toms, Coons, Mulattoes, Mammies, and Bucks: An Interpretive History of Blacks in American Films*, Viking Press (New York, NY), 1973, 4th edition, Continuum (New York, NY), 2001.
*Brown Sugar*, Harmony Books (New York, NY), 1980, revised edition published as *Brown Sugar*, Continuum (New York, NY), 2007.

*Blacks in American Films and Television: An Encyclopedia*, Garland (New York, NY), 1988.
(Editor) *Black Arts Annual 1987/88*, Garland (New York, NY), 1989.
*Dorothy Dandridge: A Biography*, Amistad (New York, NY), 1997.
*Primetime Blues: African Americans on Network Television*, Farrar, Straus & Giroux (New York, NY), 2001.
*Bright Boulevards, Bold Dreams: The Story of Black Hollywood*, One World Ballantine Books (New York, NY), 2005.
*Heat Wave: The Life and Career of Ethel Waters*, HarperCollins (New York, NY), 2011.

Contributor to books, including *Louis Armstrong: A Cultural Legacy* (essays), edited by Marc Miller, Queens Museum of Art (New York, NY), 1994.

■ **Adaptations**

*Brown Sugar: Eighty Years of America's Black Female Superstars* was made into a series by Public Broadcasting Service (PBS). Whitney Houston Products purchased the film rights to *Dorothy Dandridge: A Biography*.

■ **Sidelights**

Donald Bogle grew up in Philadelphia, Pennsylvania, and like many American children of the 1960s, he spent much of his leisure time going to the movies or, as he says in the introduction to his book *Primetime Blues: African Americans on Network Television*, "plopped in front of the TV set." As a black American, Bogle was especially drawn to performances by black actors and began pondering the types of characters they played, sensing that a fundamental racism was at work in their stereotypical roles. "Even as a kid," he points out in his introduction, "I often found myself asking all sorts of questions about what I was seeing *and* enjoying."

### *Toms, Coons, Mulattoes, Mammies, and Bucks*

Bogle's interest in movies and television led him to a career as a writer and a film historian. His first book, *Toms, Coons, Mulattoes, Mammies, and Bucks: An Interpretive History of Blacks in American Films,* takes a comprehensive look at blacks in American films from the silent-movie era on. Bogle places his commentary within the appropriate cultural and social context of the times that the films were made. In addition to discussing the films, Bogle also provides information on the performers' lives. Throughout the book, he discusses the stereotypes that black actors have been forced to play, noting that, even given these stereotypes, these films provided black actors with the opportunity for work.

Although reviewer Edward Mapp, writing in the *Library Journal,* felt that "Bogle fails to convince me of the validity of his interpretations," most reviewers found the book to be insightful and important. *Commentary* reviewer Richard Schickel remarked that Bogle "has responded to a complex subject with a complex, non-ideological, aesthetically aware work, infused throughout with a patient humanity and written in a carefully tempered tone." A reviewer in the *New York Times Book Review* commented that Bogle's book "is a model of 'interpretative history,' temperate but shrewd in its judgments . . . well organized, well-written, solidly grounded in historical and biographical fact." The reviewer also called the book "non-ideological, esthetically aware, graceful in tone and humane in its point of view."

### *Brown Sugar* and *Blacks in American Films and Television*

Bogle's next book, 1980's *Brown Sugar: Eighty Years of America's Black Female Superstars,* chronicles the lives and works of numerous legendary black female entertainers, from Bessie Smith, Josephine Baker, and Ethel Waters to Diana Ross, Cicely Tyson, and disco queen Donna Summer. Bogle also mentions many lesser-known performers.

Writing in *Booklist,* reviewer William Bradley Hooper noted that Bogle writes "with great spirit and earnestness."

In *Blacks in American Films and Television: An Encyclopedia,* Bogle provides critical interpretations of more than 260 films and more than one hundred television shows, including commentary on how black characters have evolved since the advent of television. Bogle also presents numerous biographical profiles of black actors and actresses and other blacks involved in movies and television, such as black film directors. As a reference book, *Blacks in American Films and Television* includes a substantial index and bibliography. However, as a reviewer pointed out in *American Libraries,* "this is no dull merely descriptive encyclopedia." Rather, the reviewer noted, Bogle's "lively and candid style . . . offers insightful interpretations," while Joseph W. Palmer, writing in *American Reference Books Annual,* called it "a meaty volume crammed with facts and strong opinions."

### *Dorothy Dandridge*

For his book *Dorothy Dandridge: A Biography* Bogle spent several years interviewing family, friends, and associates of the actress, whose success in Hollywood was short-lived and ultimately led to tragedy. The book includes many reminiscences of black entertainers such as Diahann Carroll, Sammy Davis, Jr., and Bobby Short. Bogle recounts how Dandridge rose through the ranks of the entertainment industry, starting out as a child performer and singer in church, vaudeville, and on the "chitlin' circuit," small black nightclubs and "honky tonks" located primarily in the South. Eventually, she began making cameos in mainstream Hollywood movies, like the Marx Brothers film *A Day at the Races,* and then starred in two low-budget "race movies," films produced by black-owned independent film companies. She was then cast in *Carmen Jones* by director Otto Preminger and was nominated for an Oscar for her role. Still, good roles for black actors remained rare. After her role as Bess in the 1959 film *Porgy and Bess,* Dandridge quickly fell from the spotlight. As the press cast aspersions on her for her marriage and affairs with white men and her reputation grew as being "difficult," both her acting and nightclub careers faded. Dandridge died in 1965 from a drug overdose with two dollars and fourteen cents in the bank.

While Bogle focuses on Dandridge in his work, Ed Guerrero, writing in *Cineaste,* pointed out that the author also "vividly charts the professional and evolutionary stages of black entertainment in America" as he tells Dandridge's story. Guerrero also noted that while Bogle clearly delineates "the socially charged performance of race in America," he never "hectors or editorializes." Rather, said

Guerrero, Bogle "lets the events and evidence speak for the frank systemic racism of the day that all blacks, from kitchen maids to movie stars, endured." Writing on the *BookPage* Web site, Robert Fleming noted: "He gives the finest view yet of the gutsy, beautiful black actress fighting to survive in Jim Crow Hollywood despite a flood of slights and tragedies."

### Primetime Blues

Bogle returned to his childhood love of television in his book *Primetime Blues*. This comprehensive history of blacks working on network television series begins with the early days of television following World War II through the 1990s. Bogle traces the early stereotypes that blacks were forced to play on such shows as *Beulah*, in which the famed black entertainer Ethel Waters played a loyal and not-too-bright maid to a white family, and the infamous *Amos 'n' Andy*, which perhaps epitomized what Bogle calls "parts that were shameless, dishonest travesties of African American life and culture." Nevertheless, says Bogle, many of the performers were able to present portrayals in ways that that allowed the black community to identify with them. Although blacks gained more prominence on network television in the seventies, Bogle points out that ethnic urban comedies like *Sanford and Son* and *Good Times* also presented blacks in a less-than-stellar light. Bogle also analyzes such popular shows in the 1980s as *The Cosby Show* and explores the black-white buddy relationship in programs like *Miami Vice*.

*New Republic* reviewer John McWhorter found Bogle's fixation on stereotypes to be an "ideological straightjacket." Although John Anderson, writing in the *Nation*, called the history presented in *Primetime Blues* "fascinating," he disagreed with Bogle's seeming emphasis that a "positive image or political message" should be inherent in black acting roles on television. "In this," wrote Anderson, "Bogle skirts the two basic aspects of television's nature. First, that it is craven, soulless and bottom-line fixated. And second that it is aimed at morons." Nevertheless, Anderson and other viewers generally praised Bogle's work as the first comprehensive view of black actors on television. McWhorter called Bogle's chapters focusing on the 1950s and 1960s "masterful." In a review in *Entertainment Weekly*, Ken Tucker called the history "thorough" and "engagingly opinionated." Vanessa Bush, writing in *Booklist*, called *Primetime Blues* "an extensive and even-handed look at how television has mirrored and distorted race images and issues in the premier multiracial society."

### Bright Boulevards, Bold Dreams

In *Bright Boulevards, Bold Dreams: The Story of Black Hollywood*, Bogle takes a look at the black film community that coexisted almost in a "parallel universe," according to *Booklist* reviewer Vanessa Bush, to the mainstream white Hollywood up until the 1950s. This parallel universe had its own stars—such as Dorothy Dandridge, Lena Horne, Mantan Moreland, Hattie McDaniel, and Stepin Fetchit—and its own nightspots and fans. Employing archival research as well as numerous interviews with black artists, Bogle devotes a chapter to each decade between 1910 and 1950, tracing the social and political story of black Hollywood.

Bush felt that Bogle "celebrates the black movie colony" in *Bright Boulevards, Bold Dreams*. Writing in *Gay & Lesbian Review Worldwide*, Charles Michael Smith noted that "in addition to a factual history, Bogle has captured a sense of what life was like to be an African-American in the early days of Hollywood" in this work. Likewise, *Cineaste* reviewer Patrick McGilligan called Bogle's book a "sweeping social history bursting with characters." In a similar vein, a *Variety* contributor felt that Bogle's book is "filled with amusing and telling details," and *Black Issues Book Review* writer Antoinette Dykes found it a "bright and bold work that all Americans should read."

### Heat Wave

As he did in his biography of Dorothy Dandridge, Bogle documents the life of the singer Ethel Waters in *Heat Wave: The Life and Career of Ethel Waters*. Bogle traces the life of Waters from her birth into poverty in Pennsylvania in 1896, to her first marriage at age thirteen, through her early musical career (beginning at age twenty-one) on the "chitlin' circuit" singing racy songs, and on to singing in nightclubs in New York's Harlem. She attracted audiences across the color line in the 1920s and 1930s with her renditions of such popular songs as *Am I Blue?*, and *Stormy Weather*. Waters's style influenced later artists, including Supremes star Diana Ross, and helped usher in the craze for buying records. From Harlem clubs Waters went on to Broadway and film careers, as well as television, where she performed into the 1970s. Waters was, as Bogle shows, a woman of firsts. She was one of the first black women to sing on radio, she was among the first black women to take the lead role in a Broadway drama, and she went on to be the first black woman to have her own television sitcom, *Beulah*, which went on the air in 1950. Later, in declining health, she turned to religion. Waters died in 1977. Bogle is forthcoming about Waters's private life, as David Hajdu noted in the *New York Times Book Review*: "Waters was sexually venturesome, apparently, and she probably had same-sex partners on and off throughout her life, Bogle suggests. He handles this dimension of Waters's life matter-of-factly, much to his credit. Bogle makes no misguided effort to reposition Waters as an unsung hero of transgressive sexual identity. After all, sexual fluidity was so common among the early blues queens that it was scarcely transgressive in their sphere; it was practically the norm."

Reviewers responded warmly to Bogle's biography. *Washington Post Online* contributor Wil Haygood wrote: "Donald Bogle has wrapped the life of Ethel Waters in empathy, and that is no small achievement." A *Publishers Weekly* reviewer termed this a "powerful" as well as "thorough and unflinchingly honest" biography presented in "vivid though often exhausting detail." Similarly, *Booklist* contributor Bush called *Heat Wave* a "penetrating look at a woman of massive talent and determination." A *Kirkus Reviews* contributor also praised Bogle's biography, terming it a "lush and often lyrical valentine to an extraordinarily talented and complicated artist." Likewise, *Library Journal* reviewer John Frank thought: "This work is everything a biography should be."

## ■ Biographical And Critical Sources

*PERIODICALS*

*American Libraries*, May, 1989, review of *Blacks in American Films and Television: An Encyclopedia*, p. 410.

*American Reference Books Annual*, Volume 20, 1989, Joseph W. Palmer, review of *Blacks in American Films and Television*, p. 509.

*Black American Literature Forum*, winter, 1991, Edward Mapp, review of *Blacks in American Films and Television*, p. 793.

*Black Issues Book Review*, May, 2005, Antoinette Dykes, "Dreams, Promises and Disappointments: Hollywood's Racial Past, Virginia's Forgotten Free Enclave, Jamaica Kincaid's Search for Flowers and Other Offerings," review of *Bright Boulevards, Bold Dreams: The Story of Black Hollywood.*

*Booklist*, June 15, 1980, William Bradley Hooper, review of *Brown Sugar: Eighty Years of America's Black Female Superstars*, p. 1479; July, 1994, review of *Blacks in American Films and Television*, pp. 1966-1967; February 15, 1998, Ray Olson, review of *Dorothy Dandridge: A Biography*, p. 978; January 1, 2001, Vanessa Bush, review of *Primetime Blues: African Americans on Network Television*, p. 896.

*Bookwatch*, August, 1990, review of *Brown Sugar*, p. 6; February 1, 2005, Vanessa Bush, review of *Bright Boulevards, Bold Dreams*, p. 933; February 1, 2011, Vanessa Bush, review of *Heat Wave: The Life and Career of Ethel Waters*, p. 25.

*Choice*, November, 1973, review of *Toms, Coons, Mulattoes, Mammies, and Bucks: An Interpretive History of Blacks in American Films*, p. 1395; September, 1988, C.A. Larson, *Blacks in American Films and Television: An Encyclopedia*, p. 74.

*Cineaste*, fall, 1998, Ed Guerrero, review of *Dorothy Dandridge*, p. 60; fall, 2005, Patrick McGilligan, review of *Bright Boulevards, Bold Dreams*, p. 73.

*Commentary*, November, 1973, Richard Schickel, review of *Toms, Coons, Mulattoes, Mammies, and Bucks*, pp. 90, 92-94.

*Encore*, August, 1980, "A Talk with Critic Donald Bogle," p. 38.

*Entertainment Weekly*, March 2, 2001, Ken Tucker, "Color Blind: Donald Bogle Takes an Incisive Look at Small-Screen Depictions of African Americans in *Primetime Blues*," p. 62; January 28, 2005, Tom Sinclair, review of *Bright Boulevards, Bold Dreams*, p. 87.

*Essence*, April, 2005, "Black Hollywood's Heyday: On the Big Screen, Hattie McDaniel and Stepin Fetchit Played Stereotypical Servants to Icons like Katherine Hepburn and Clark Gable. Film Historian Donald Bogle's Latest Book Documents Their Glamorous Lives Off-screen," review of *Bright Boulevards, Bold Dreams*, p. 102.

*Film Comment*, January, 2005, Wesley Morris, "Blind Spot: Donald Bogle Takes a Look at Hollywood's Black Film Community in the First Half of the 20th Century," review of *Bright Boulevards, Bold Dreams.*

*Film Quarterly*, summer, 2008, Arthur Knight, review of *Bright Boulevards, Bold Dreams*, p. 89.

*Gay & Lesbian Review Worldwide*, May 1, 2005, Charles Michael Smith, "Race on the Set," review of *Bright Boulevards, Bold Dreams.*

*Journalism & Mass Communication Quarterly*, spring, 1998, S. Craig Watkins, review of *Toms, Coons, Mulattoes, Mammies, and Bucks*, p. 226.

*Kirkus Reviews*, December 15, 2010, review of *Heat Wave.*

*Library Bookwatch*, June 1, 2005, review of *Bright Boulevards, Bold Dreams.*

*Library Journal*, July, 1973, Edward Mapp, review of *Toms, Coons, Mulattoes, Mammies, and Bucks*, p. 2141; June 15, 1980, review of *Brown Sugar: Eighty Years of America's Black Female Superstars*, p. 1405; November 1, 1997, Corinne Nelson, review of *Dorothy Dandridge*, p. 75; November 1, 2000, Ann

Burns and Emily Joy Jones, review of *Primetime Blues,* p. 104; January 1, 2001, David M. Lisa, review of *Primetime Blues,* p. 109; January 1, 2011, John Frank, review of *Heat Wave,* p. 98.

*Los Angeles Times,* February 26, 2001, Lynell George, "Tuned in to TV's Racial Divide," interview, p. E1.

*Nation,* April 16, 2001, John Anderson, review of *Primetime Blues,* p. 28.

*New Republic,* March 5, 2001, "Gimme a Break! Blacks, Television, and the Decline of Racism in America," p. 30.

*New Yorker,* August 18, 1997, Hilton Als, review of *Dorothy Dandridge,* p. 68.

*New York Times Book Review,* August 26, 1973, review of *Toms, Coons, Mulattoes, Mammies, and Bucks,* p. 8; February 27, 2011, David Hajdu, "Stormy Weather," review of *Heat Wave,* p. 13.

*Publishers Weekly,* November 13, 2000, review of *Primetime Blues,* p. 91; November 20, 2006, "Hurston/Wright Literary Awards," p. 6; December 20, 2010, review of *Heat Wave,* p. 45.

*St. Petersburg Times* (St. Petersburg, FL), February 27, 2005, Roger K. Miller, "Inside Black Hollywood," review of *Bright Boulevards, Bold Dreams,* p. 4.

*Santa Fe New Mexican* (Santa Fe, NM), March 6, 2005, Robert Nott, "Book Tells of the Unsung Heroes in the Old Black Hollywood," review of *Bright Boulevards, Bold Dreams,* p. 7.

*Variety,* March 7, 2005, review of *Bright Boulevards, Bold Dreams,* p. 53.

ONLINE

*BookPage,* http://www.bookpage.com/ (March 30, 2002), Robert Fleming, review of *Dorothy Dandridge.*

*Museum of Television & Radio Web site,* http://www.mtr.org/ (September 12, 2002), excerpt from Donald Bogle's introduction in *Primetime Blues.*

*New York Journal of Books,* http://www.nyjournalofbooks.com/ (February 8, 2011), Vinton Rafe McCabe, review of *Heat Wave.*

*Washington Post Online,* http://www.washingtonpost.com/ (January 28, 2011), Wil Haygood, review of *Heat Wave.*

OTHER

*Hollywood and the Black Actor* (sound recording), interview with Donald Bogle and others about the portrayal and stereotyping of blacks in American movies, J. Norton Publishers.*

# Brian Boyd

## 1952-

■ **Also Known As**

Brian David Boyd

■ **Personal**

Born July 30, 1952, in Belfast, Northern Ireland; immigrated to New Zealand, 1957; son of David Boyd and Jean Abernethy; married Janet Eden, 1974 (divorced, 1980); married Bronwen Nicholson (an editor), 1994; stepchildren: Cassandra, Thomasin, Alexandra. *Education:* University of Canterbury, B.A., 1972, M.A. (with honors), 1974; University of Toronto, Ph.D., 1979.

■ **Addresses**

*Home*—Auckland, New Zealand. *Office*—Department of English, University of Auckland, Private Bag 92019, Auckland 1142, New Zealand. *Agent*—Georges Borchardt, 136 E. 57th St., New York, NY 10022. *E-mail*—b.boyd@auckland.ac.nz.

■ **Career**

Writer, educator. Victoria University, Wellington, New Zealand, junior lecturer, 1974; University of Auckland, Auckland, New Zealand, postdoctoral fellow, 1979-80, lecturer, 1980-85, senior lecturer, 1986-91, associate professor, 1992-99, professor of English, 1999-2001, university distinguished professor, 2001—. Visiting professor at University of Nice at Sophia Antipolis, 1994-95, and V.V. Nabokov Museum, St. Petersburg, Russia, 2002.

■ **Member**

International Vladimir Nabokov Society, Human Behavior and Evolution Society, New Zealand Society of Authors.

■ **Awards, Honors**

Thomas Carter Essay Prize, *Shenandoah*, 1989, for a chapter of *Vladimir Nabokov: The Russian Years*; Robert and Suzanne Weiss fellow, Amherst College, 1992; James Cook fellow, Royal Society of New Zealand, 1997-99; Einhard Prize (Germany), 2001; New Zealand Academy of the Humanities fellowship, 2009—.

■ **Writings**

*Nabokov's Ada: The Place of Consciousness*, Ardis (Ann Arbor, MI), 1985, 2nd edition, Cybereditions (Christchurch, New Zealand), 2001.

*Vladimir Nabokov* (biography), Princeton University Press (Princeton, NJ), Volume 1: *The Russian Years*, 1990, Volume 2: *The American Years*, 1991.

(Editor) *Nabokov: Novels and Memoirs, 1941-1951*, Library of America (New York, NY), 1996.

(Editor) *Nabokov: Novels, 1955-1962*, Library of America (New York, NY), 1996.

(Editor) *Nabokov: Novels, 1969-1974*, Library of America (New York, NY), 1996.

*Nabokov's Pale Fire: The Magic of Artistic Discovery*, Princeton University Press (Princeton, NJ), 1999.

(Editor) Vladimir Nabokov, *Speak Memory: An Autobiography Revisited*, Knopf (New York, NY), 1999.

(Editor, with Robert Martin Pyle, and coauthor of annotations and introductions) *Nabokov's Butterflies: Unpublished and Uncorrected Writings by Vladimir Nabokov*, translated by Dmitri Nabokov, Beacon Press (Boston, MA), 2000.

(Editor) *Words That Count: Essays on Early Modern Authorship in Honor of MacDonald P. Jackson*, University of Delaware Press (Newark, NJ), 2004.

(Editor, with Stanislav Shvabrin, and author of introduction) Vladimir Nabokov, *Verses and Versions: Three Centuries of Russian Poetry* (Nabokov's translations of verse by other poets), Harcourt (Orlando, FL), 2008.

*On the Origin of Stories: Evolution, Cognition, and Fiction,* Belknap Press of Harvard University Press (Cambridge, MA), 2009.

(Editor, with Joseph Carroll and Jonathan Gottschall) *Evolution, Literature, and Film: A Reader,* Columbia University Press (New York, NY), 2010.

(Editor) Vladimir Nabokov, *Pale Fire: A Poem in Four Cantos by John Shade,* Gingko Press (Berkeley, CA), 2011.

*Stalking Nabokov: Selected Essays,* Columbia University Press (New York, NY), 2011.

Contributor to books, including introduction to *Speak, Memory: An Autobiography Revisited,* by Vladimir Nabokov, Knopf (New York, NY), 1999; and foreword, *Alphabet in Color,* by Nabokov, Gingko Press (Corte Madera, CA), 2005. Contributor to periodicals, including *Shenandoah, Scripsi, Southern Review, Islands, Landfall, Times Literary Supplement, Natural History, Shakespeare Quarterly, Philosophy and Literature, American Scholar, Washington Post,* and *New York Times.*

Boyd's work has been translated into Chinese, Czech, Dutch, French, German, Greek, Italian, Japanese, Korean, Polish, Portuguese, Russian, Slovenian, Spanish, Swedish, and Turkish.

## ■ Sidelights

Brian Boyd, University Distinguished Professor at the University of Auckland, New Zealand, is an acknowledged expert on the life and literary works of the writer Vladimir Nabokov. Boyd has written or edited twelve books on or by the Russian author; he has edited volumes by Nabokov published by Library of America and has produced studies of classic works by the writer, including *Ada* and *Pale Fire.* He is also the author of a two-volume biography of Nabokov, published by Princeton University Press, which has, since its publication in 1991, become the standard reference for the author's life and works in Russia and the United States.

### *Vladimir Nabokov*

Boyd's *Vladimir Nabokov* is a two-volume biography of the celebrated writer whose works include the novels *Lolita* and *Pale Fire.* The first volume, *The Russian Years,* traces the first half of Nabokov's life, ending as Nabokov leaves Paris for America in 1940, while the second volume, *The American Years,* is concerned with the remaining years of Nabokov's life, which he split between the United States and Switzerland. *New York Times Book Review* contributor Sergei Davydov called the first volume "superb" and credited Boyd with bringing "back to life a most remarkable man, who valued literature above all else," adding: "We will not need another biography of Nabokov for the foreseeable future." Walter Kendrick, also writing in the *New York Times Book Review,* called the second volume "a truly monumental achievement" and observed that "Nabokov has found, at last, a biographer worthy of him." Jay Parini wrote in the *Los Angeles Times Book Review:* "Prof. Boyd . . . has done his homework with almost superhuman diligence, tracking his subject to the far ends of the Earth, and it shows." Parini concluded: "*The Russian Years* is an exquisitely written book that will not be superseded for a very long time." "In every respect then," Michael Dirda noted in the *Washington Post Book World,* "this is yet another of those masterly literary biographies of recent years, eligible to sit at the right hand of Richard Ellmann's *James Joyce,*" which won a National Book Award in 1960.

In *The American Years,* Boyd describes Nabokov's life in America, where he taught literature at Stanford University, Wellesley College, and Cornell University. Butterfly collecting, a passion Nabokov had developed in his youth, occupied much of his time throughout his life, and he spent many summers pursuing that interest in the American West. In the twenty-one years Nabokov lived in America, he never owned a house. Instead, he and his family lived in "sublets" and motels until 1961, when they took up residence in a hotel in Montreux, Switzerland, where they remained until Nabokov's death in 1977. In 1960, Nabokov had become independently wealthy due to the huge success of his novel *Lolita,* enabling him to give up his teaching career and focus on his writing in relative seclusion. In the last eighteen years of his life he published a book virtually every year; his last completed novel, *Look at the Harlequins!,* came out in 1974.

### *Speak Memory* **and** *Nabokov's Pale Fire*

Nabokov also published an autobiography, *Speak, Memory,* which, years later, was reprinted with an introduction by Boyd. *Speak, Memory: An Autobiography Revisited* was released five decades after Nabokov wrote his account of his life and marked the 100th anniversary of Nabokov's birth. The publisher Random House posted some of Boyd's comments about the acclaimed author's autobiography on its

Web site: "*Speak, Memory* is the one Nabokov work outside his finest novels—*The Gift, Lolita, Pale Fire, Ada*—that is a masterpiece on their level. . . . [It is] the most artistic of autobiographies. . . . [It] fuses truth to detail with perfection of form, the exact with the evocative, and acute awareness of time with intimations of timelessness."

Boyd's interest in Nabokov started at an early age; he read *Pale Fire* three times when he was sixteen. Around the age of forty-seven, Boyd published a study of that work, *Nabokov's Pale Fire: The Magic of Artistic Discovery*, in which he "skillfully peels away the layers of [that] novel in a feast of literary detective work," observed *Library Journal* contributor Ronald Ratliff. In *Nabokov's Pale Fire*, Boyd refutes some people's contentions that *Pale Fire* is merely a satire of the literary life.

### Nabokov's Butterflies

Boyd collaborated with butterfly expert Robert Martin Pyle to edit, annotate, and introduce *Nabokov's Butterflies: Unpublished and Uncorrected Writings by Vladimir Nabokov*, a publication that contains some text translated from Russian by Nabokov's son, Dmitri. *Nabokov's Butterflies* is "a fascinating volume" that brings to light "Nabokov's obsession with butterflies," noted Jay Parini in the *Guardian*. *Nabokov's Butterflies* contains segments of Nabokov's diaries, correspondence, interviews, poems, stories, novels, drawings, and autobiography, as well as scientific writing.

Reviewers such as *New York Times Book Review* contributor Laurie Adlerstein noted that *Nabokov's Butterflies*, particularly the portions of heavily scientific writings by Nabokov, would be tiring if read through completely. Parini, however, found relief in the editorial decision to truncate some of Nabokov's more scientific text and appreciated Boyd and Pyle's inclusion of multiple forms of Nabokov's writing.

"In his shrewd introduction [to *Nabokov's Butterflies*] Boyd teases out the connections between the writer and the lepidopterist," observed Parini, explaining: "One comes to understand Vladimir Nabokov as novelist more completely and precisely by understanding that science gave this canny author 'a sense of reality that should not be confused with modern (or "postmodern") epistemological nihilism.'" "I had not realized the extent to which Nabokov's fiction depended on his attention to the natural world," revealed Parini, who concluded: "Nabokov offered, in his magnificent fiction, a complete taxonomy of the human spirit. He might not have been so meticulous and thorough were it not for the parallel interest in lepidoptery." In contrast, Adlerstein said that "*Nabokov's Butterflies* juxtaposes science and art, but cannot integrate them."

Discussing the importance of *Nabokov's Butterflies* in the *Spectator*, John Fowles commented: "We can't begin to enter Nabokov's world, or worlds, unless we realize that, like every great writer of fiction, he had a vital sense of humour. This scholarly book (an outstanding triumph for Anglo-American publishing) constantly hints at or suggests this. It is expertly edited and annotated. . . . It gives an unbelievably rich portrait of a genius. . . . Nobody who has not read this book can call himself a true natural historian."

### On the Origin of Stories

Boyd turns from Nabokov to the larger issue of the meaning and importance of stories in human evolution with the 2009 *On the Origin of Stories: Evolution, Cognition, and Fiction*. Boyd examines why people tell stories through an examination of the evolution of language itself and the means by which literature helps people better understand themselves. *American Scientist* contributor Michael Berube succinctly described Boyd's central thesis, noting that the author "attempts an evolutionary explanation of the appearance of art—and, more specifically, of the utility of fiction." For Boyd, art is a specifically human adaptation; literary art has developed from play and has distinct survival advantages by increasing social cognition, encouraging cooperation, and inspiring creativity. The need to hold an audience's attention while storytelling leads to innovative solutions for distinctly universal human problems, Boyd explains. This in turn aids people's universal perceptions. Using this evolutionary foundation, Boyd then examines examples of literature from Homer to Dr. Seuss to demonstrate how fiction initiates emotion and why certain stories hold an audience's attention more than others. "It is impossible here to summarize adequately the details of the arguments in such a large, ambitious, and scholarly volume; it would be easy to misrepresent it by simplification," noted George Levine on the Web site for the British Society for Literature and Science. "Roughly, however, this is Boyd's approach. For each book, he uses an evolutionary perspective that attends to familiar elements of narrative, like 'character, plot, structure, dramatic irony, and theme,' and he does so by returning to what he calls 'first principles,' treating fiction 'as a human activity arising naturally out of other human and animal behavior.'"

Levine found Boyd's study "brilliant and ambitious." *Library Journal* reviewer Pam Kingsbury similarly dubbed this work a "fascinating blend of the humanities and the sciences." Berube also praised the work, calling it a "fascinating book, even a necessary book." However, Berube also felt that Boyd's literary examples are too limited for the sweeping nature of his arguments. An even more critical assessment was offered by *Marvels & Tales* contributor Jack Zipes, who observed: "Boyd's study, based on Darwinist theory, provides few historical clues to explain how types of tales originated and developed. Instead, he is more interested in writing a bible for the propagation of evolutionary psychological principles to grasp our natural inclination for narrative." Much higher praise, though, came from *Choice* reviewer K. Wein, who found *On the Origin of Stories* a "compelling, erudite, and thoroughly original work," as well as "beautifully written and wide-ranging."

### Evolution, Literature, and Film

Acting as editor, with Joseph Carroll and Jonathan Gottschall, Boyd offers a similar analysis in the 2010 collection, *Evolution, Literature, and Film: A Reader.* The collected essays attempt to provide a new framework for the study of film and literature by engaging the science of evolutionary biology into the critical mix. Various sections of the book deal with aspects such as evolution and human nature, why humans are artistic, the divide between cultural constructivists and evolutionists in such studies, and interpretations of literature and film. Writing in *Choice*, E.T. Klaver found this a "first-rate contribution to the field."

### Boyd once told CA:

"Biography offers a writer a rare combination: to undertake exhaustive scholarly research on a figure of major intellectual importance and yet to excite an audience far beyond academia. Although Nabokov was highly regarded—in the 1960s he was often considered the best writer alive—many have thought of him as primarily an astonishing stylist, a verbal magician. I wanted to suggest that there was much more to him than that: that he had a coherent and highly individual philosophy that shaped his style, his structures, his strategies, and that there was meaning in his magic."

Boyd later added: "Over the last few years I have tried to develop a new approach to literary study. I had felt strongly for some time that academic literary studies had taken a wrong turn, that the humanities absurdly overplayed the importance of language, culture, and cultural difference, and underplayed the physical, biological, and neurological worlds, and human similarities. Along with others I think we need to find an approach to literature that reflects the fact that humans have evolved, that we are shaped in part by our deep past. What can fields like evolutionary anthropology, evolutionary psychology, evolutionary economics, and cognitive neuroscience offer literary study? Why as a species do we spend so much time in telling or attending to stories that both sides know are untrue? How do we make up and understand stories so effortlessly? How can evolutionary lenses deepen our vision of the human nature depicted and appealed to in literature?

"Before I had found an evolutionary way out of my dissatisfaction with the literary-critical fads of the 1980s and 1990s, I had thought of another way out: biography. I looked for a literary writer, a twentieth-century figure, who would inspire me enough for years of intense work and hadn't already been the subject of a first-rate biography, but there wasn't one who satisfied my personal criteria. But I found myself being drawn irresistibly to a *non*-literary writer who, like Nabokov, had received world recognition, and had at one time been considered at the top of his field, but was now not appreciated as I think he deserves. That is the philosopher of science Karl Popper, who has been rated as one of the most important philosophers, even *the* most important, of the twentieth century. He certainly has had more impact on science, politics, and economics than any other twentieth-century philosopher. And the common critiques of his supposed ideas leave his *actual* ideas intact."

## ■ Biographical And Critical Sources

*BOOKS*

Boyd, Brian, *Vladimir Nabokov,* Volume 1: *The Russian Years,* Princeton University Press (Princeton, NJ), 1990.

*PERIODICALS*

*American Scientist,* January, 2010, Michael Berube, "The Play's the Thing," review of *On the Origin of Stories: Evolution, Cognition, and Fiction.*

*Choice,* January, 2010, K. Wein, review of *On the Origin of Stories,* p. 886; December, 2010, E.T. Klaver, review of *Evolution, Literature, and Film: A Reader,* p. 665.

*Guardian* (London, England), March 25, 2000, Jay Parini, "The Wings of Desire."

*Library Journal*, October 15, 1999, Ronald Ratliff, review of *Nabokov's Pale Fire: The Magic of Artistic Discovery*, p. 70; May 1, 2009, Pam Kingsbury, review of *On the Origin of Stories*, p. 78.

*Los Angeles Times Book Review*, November 11, 1990, Jay Parini, review of *Vladimir Nabokov*, Volume 1: *The Russian Years*, pp. 1, 8.

*Marvels & Tales*, April, 2010, Jack Zipes, review of *On the Origin of Stories*, p. 152.

*New York Times Book Review*, October 14, 1990, Sergei Davydov, review of *Vladimir Nabokov*, Volume 1: *The Russian Years*, pp. 3, 26-27; September 22, 1991, Walter Kendrick, review of *Vladimir Nabokov*, Volume 2: *The American Years*, pp. 1, 22-23; May 7, 2000, Laurie Adlerstein, review of *Nabokov's Butterflies: Unpublished and Uncorrected Writings by Vladimir Nabokov*.

*Publishers Weekly*, March 13, 2000, review of *Nabokov's Butterflies*, p. 74.

*Quadrant*, April, 1991, Jill Kitson, "Nabokov and Fate," pp. 71-74.

*Spectator*, April 15, 2000, John Fowles, "The High Ridges of Knowledge," pp. 36-37.

*Times Literary Supplement* (London, England), August 21, 2009, Laura Dietz, "Book Doctors," p. 17.

*Washington Post Book World*, October 21, 1990, Michael Dirda, review of *Vladimir Nabokov*, Volume 1: *The Russian Years*, pp. 1, 11.

*World Literature Today*, July 1, 2009, David Shook, review of *Verses and Versions: Three Centuries of Russian Poetry*.

ONLINE

*Bomb*, http://www.bombsite.com/ (June 1, 2000), Thomas Bolt, author interview.

*British Society for Literature and Science*, http://www.bsls.ac.uk/ (July 3, 2011), George Levine, review of *On the Origin of Stories*.

*Rorotoko*, http://rorotoko.com/ (September 20, 2011), author interviews.

*University of Auckland, Faculty of Arts Web site*, http://artsfaculty.auckland.ac.nz/ (July 3, 2011), "Brian Boyd."

# Sally Ryder Brady

## 1939-

### ■ Also Known As

Ryder Brady

### ■ Personal

Born May 26, 1939, in Boston, MA; daughter of Francis C. (an administrator) and Dorothy Ryder; married Upton R. Brady (director of Atlantic Monthly Press), November 17, 1962; children: Sarah, Andrew, Nathaniel, Alexander. *Education:* Attended Barnard College, 1956-57, 1960-61. *Politics:* Independent. *Religion:* Roman Catholic.

### ■ Addresses

*Home*—Bedford, MA.

### ■ Career

Writer, teacher, freelance editor.

### ■ Writings

(Under pseudonym Ryder Brady) *Instar* (novel), Doubleday (Garden City, NY), 1976.

*A Yankee Christmas: Feasts, Treats, Crafts, and Traditions of Wintertime New England: Featuring Nantucket Noel,* Yankee Press (Emmaus, PA), 1992.

*Featuring Vermont Celebrations: Feasts, Treats, Crafts, and Traditions of Wintertime New England,* Yankee Press (Emmaus, PA), 1993.

(With others) *Sweet Memories: A Gingerbread Family Scrapbook,* Bloomsbury (New York, NY), 2006.

*A Box of Darkness: The Story of a Marriage* (memoir), St. Martin's (New York, NY), 2011.

Contributor to *House Beautiful, Boston Globe, Good Housekeeping, Yankee, Woman's Day, Boston Review of the Arts,* and newspapers.

### ■ Sidelights

Sally Ryder Brady is a writer, teacher, and freelance editor who has written in a variety of genres in her thirty-five-year career as an author. She has written *Sweet Memories: A Gingerbread Family Scrapbook,* a humorous picture book about a gingerbread couple; two nonfiction books featuring New England traditions; a novel, *Instar;* and a memoir, *A Box of Darkness: The Story of a Marriage.*

Brady once wrote: "Following a brief theatrical career, I had four children in five years, thereby limiting extra activities. While writing my first novel, I recognized the similarity between acting and writing, both arts demanding the same energetic and economical projection into other characters. This likeness intrigues me and makes me eager to attempt a screenplay at some point. I am also interested in psychic and electromagnetic energy and their effects on people. Thus far, my novels have been about fear and power. For lack of a better label, I call them psychological thrillers."

Brady had what, by all appearances, was a perfect life. She was married to Upton Brady, executive editor of Atlantic Monthly Press, and had a successful writing career and a lovely family of four children. That all changed upon his death in 2008, when Brady discovered his secret life laid out in his personal papers. In her memoir, *A Box of Darkness,* Brady retraces the signs and evidence that she should have seen, as they struggled to stay married for nearly fifty years, to recognize that he was a homosexual, including his admission ten years into their marriage that he had had a homosexual encounter. Brady discussed the memoir in *Harper's Bazaar,* considered: "When he died suddenly in 2008, my world was drained of light, yet I had no idea of the utter darkness that awaited me." She also noted: "Someone recently asked me why I didn't leave Upton. The answer is simple: I loved him. His pain was so huge, its roots so deep, I could not possibly abandon him. His toxic secret was the shadow beneath his light, the pain he drank to relieve, the prompt for my prayer, and the missing piece in a story of enduring love." In *Library Journal,* Kathryn Stewart described the book as Brady's "attempt to understand her tumultuous marriage," which also included his controlling behaviors, debt, and alcoholism.

A contributor to *Kirkus Reviews* considered *A Box of Darkness* to be a "bittersweet memoir of a highly stressed marriage that somehow endured for nearly half a century." In *Publishers Weekly,* a reviewer contended that "her memoir is as searing and tender as the life she describes." In *Booklist,* Donna Seaman lauds the memoir as an "engrossing chronicle" that "offers generous and enlightening testimony to the true meaning of love." Anne Kingston, in a review for *Maclean's,* found *A Box of Darkness* to be "jarringly discordant" and determined that the story "depicts a complex man who adored and resented his children and his wife, a woman who remains remarkably steadfast in her love—and complicity—even now." The *New York Times Book Review'*s Donna Rifkind concluded that "though we as readers may be troubled by the certainty that Upton would have been horrified by his wife's public version of their story, it's to her credit that we feel as much compassion for his suffering as we do for hers."

## ■ Biographical And Critical Sources

### BOOKS

Brady, Sally Ryder, *A Box of Darkness: The Story of a Marriage,* St. Martin's (New York, NY), 2011.

### PERIODICALS

*Booklist,* January 1, 2011, Donna Seaman, review of *A Box of Darkness: The Story of a Marriage,* p. 36.

*Harper's Bazaar,* February 1, 2011, "I Discovered My Husband's Secret Gay Life: Author Sally Ryder Brady Long Suspected That Her Husband of 45 Years Was Leading a Double Life, but It Wasn't until His Death That the Truth Came Out," p. 119.

*Kirkus Reviews,* December 15, 2010, review of *A Box of Darkness.*

*Library Journal,* December 1, 2010, Kathryn Stewart, review of *A Box of Darkness,* p. 122.

*Maclean's,* March 7, 2011, Anne Kingston, review of *A Box of Darkness,* p. 75.

*New York Times Book Review,* February 6, 2011, "My Husband, the Stranger," p. 23.

*Publishers Weekly,* November 8, 2010, review of *A Box of Darkness,* p. 51.

*Washington Post,* February 6, 2011, Marie Arana, review of *A Box of Darkness.*

### ONLINE

*Boston.com,* http://articles.boston.com/ (January 30, 2011), Jan Gardner, "Inside Stories."

*Sally Ryder Brady Home Page,* http://www.sallyryderbrady.com (August 23, 2011).

# Mark D. Brewer

## 1971-

### ■ Personal

Born May 6, 1971. *Education:* Syracuse University, Ph.D.

### ■ Addresses

*Office*—Department of Political Science, 229 N. Stevens Hall, University of Maine, Orono, ME 04469. *E-mail*—mark.brewer@umit.maine.edu.

### ■ Career

University of Maine, Orono, associate professor. Former visiting assistant professor, Colby College, Waterville, ME.

### ■ Writings

(With Jeffrey M. Stonecash and Mack D. Mariani) *Diverging Parties: Social Change, Realignment, and Party Polarization,* Westview Press (Boulder, CO), 2003.

*Relevant No More? The Catholic/Protestant Divide in American Electoral Politics,* Lexington Books (Lanham, MD), 2003.

(With Jeffrey M. Stonecash) *Split: Class and Cultural Divides in American Politics,* CQ Press (Washington, DC), 2007.

(With L. Sandy Maisel) *Parties and Elections in America: The Electoral Process,* 5th edition (Brewer not associated with earlier editions), Rowman & Littlefield (Lanham, MD), 2008, 6th edition, Rowman & Littlefield (Lanham, MD), 2011.

*Party Images in the American Electorate,* Routledge (New York, NY), 2009.

*Dynamics of American Political Parties,* Cambridge University Press (New York, NY), 2009.

Contributor of articles to journals, including *Political Research Quarterly, Political Behavior, Legislative Studies Quarterly,* and *Journal for the Scientific Study of Religion.*

### ■ Sidelights

A professor of political science, Mark D. Brewer focuses his research on topics including religion in politics, the connection between public opinion and public policy, and the effects on partisanship in the electoral process.

#### *Relevant No More?*

In his 2003 book *Relevant No More? The Catholic/Protestant Divide in American Electoral Politics,* he investigates the first of these research interests. Written in the run-up to the 2004 presidential elections in which Senator John Kerry's Catholicism became a minor campaign issue, Brewer's book looks at "how Catholics have responded at the polls in the latter half of the twentieth century," according to Elizabeth Pollard-Grayson for *Humanities and Social Sciences Online.* Brewer's major thesis in the study is that Catholics remain much more heavily connected to the Democratic Party than do Protestants, despite the party's stand on social issues such as abortion rights. In the course of this study, Brewer provides a historical perspective on the turbulent relations between Catholics and Protestants in the United States, a discussion of the relationship of Catholics with the Democratic Party, and an investigation of the voting trends by Catholics during the twentieth century by employing statistical analysis and research numbers from sources such as the American National Election Studies Cumulative Data File.

"The most monumental task in *Relevant No More?* is Brewer's attempt to find the reasons that Catholics remain so much more likely to be Democrats than Protestants," wrote Pollard-Grayson. Brewer concludes in this context that the Catholic worldview of sharing and a tradition of doing good works is more compatible with Democratic beliefs than with Republican beliefs. Pollard-Grayson went on to note: "Overall, Brewer's book accomplishes its task of demonstrating that Catholics are more Democratic than Protestants as a whole. His explanation of the Catholic worldview offers a plausible explanation for this continuing pattern despite conundrums such as the Democratic party's support of abortion rights in opposition to the Catholic Church's condemnation."

### Split

Collaborating with Jeffrey M. Stonecash, Brewer wrote *Split: Class and Cultural Divides in American Politics*, a book that examines the relative importance of class and cultural conflicts in the political process. Writing in *Political Science Quarterly*, Jeremy C. Pope felt that *Split* "makes an important contribution" to the study of these cleavages in American politics.

The authors assert that although cultural differences are generally considered more critical than class differences in current assessments of the split in the body politic, in fact both remain significantly divisive. By examining such factors as political party platforms, acceptance speeches by presidents, and a selection of votes in Congress, the authors detect both cultural and class divides at work in the U.S. political system.

### Party Images in the American Electorate

In just 117 pages of *Party Images in the American Electorate*, Brewer describes the typical mental pictures Americans have about each political party and how that perception affects voting behavior. His examination spans more than fifty years and delves into the image question for important political subgroups, including by race and ethnicity, gender, class, and religion. Brewer also analyzes the effects of party image on the political polarization that has beset the nation in the early twenty-first century.

In *Politics* magazine, Elizabeth Abraham felt that the contribution of *Party Images in the American Electorate* is "an ever-increasing understanding of how parties are actually evaluated." Joel David Bloom found that the book "is long on potential but short on execution. It remains an interesting read that will illuminate the nature of partisan beliefs for most readers. The book's high price and thin findings make it difficult to justify using as a supplemental text for a political parties course, presumably its primary audience." Bloom continued: "Nonetheless, Brewer's methodology and comprehensive approach show promise and I would consider using subsequent editions if they address some of the shortcomings discussed here."

### ■ Biographical And Critical Sources

*PERIODICALS*

*Choice*, May, 2003, H.L. Reiter, review of *Diverging Parties: Social Change, Realignment, and Party Polarization*, p. 1626; March, 2004, E.J. Eisenach, review of *Relevant No More? The Catholic/Protestant Divide in American Electoral Politics*, p. 1371; July, 2007, J.F. Kraus, review of *Split: Class and Cultural Divides in American Politics*, p. 1985.

*Political Science Quarterly*, spring, 2008, Jeremy C. Pope, review of *Split*, p. 188; March 22, 2010, Joel David Bloom, review of *Party Images in the American Electorate*, p. 160.

*Politics*, May 1, 2009, Elizabeth Abraham, review of *Party Images in the American Electorate*, p. 52.

*Reference & Research Book News*, November, 2003, review of *Relevant No More?*, p. 165; November 1, 2006, review of *Split*; February 1, 2008, review of *Parties and Elections in America: The Electoral Process*.

*ONLINE*

*CQ Press Web site*, http://www.cqpress.com/ (April 20, 2009), "Mark D. Brewer."

*H-Net: Humanities and Social Sciences Online*, http://www.h-net.org/ (June 1, 2004), Elizabeth Pollard-Grayson, review of *Relevant No More?*

*Politico's Bookshop*, http://www.politicos.co.uk/ (April 20, 2009), "Mark D. Brewer."

*University of Maine, Political Science Department Web site*, http://umaine.edu/ (August 23, 2011), "Mark Brewer."*

# Ken Bruen

## 1951-

■ **Personal**

Born January 3, 1951, in Galway, Connacht, Ireland; married; wife's name Phil; children: Grace. *Education:* Trinity College, Ph.D. *Hobbies and other interests:* Sailing, travel, soccer.

■ **Addresses**

*Home*—Galway, Ireland. *Agent*—Marianne Gunn O'Connor Literary Agency, Morrison Chambers, Ste. 17, 32 Nassau St., Dublin 2, Republic of Ireland. *E-mail*—ken@kenbruen.com.

■ **Career**

Writer. Worked as an English teacher in Africa, Japan, Southeast Asia, and South America, and for a brief period as a security guard at the World Trade Center; actor in a horror film directed by Roger Corman.

■ **Member**

PEN, Irish Writers Union.

■ **Awards, Honors**

Shamus Award, Private Eye Writers of America, 2003, for *The Guards,* and 2007, for *The Dramatist;* Macavity Awards Best Novel winner, 2005, for *The Killing of the Tinkers;* Barry Award for Best British Crime Novel, 2007, for *Priest;* David Loeb Goodis Award, 2008.

■ **Writings**

*Shades of Grace* (crime novel), Images Booksellers, 1993.

*Martyrs* (crime novel), Minerva Press (London, England), 1994.

*Rilke on Black* (crime novel), Serpent's Tail (New York, NY), 1996.

*The Hackman Blues* (crime novel), Bloodlines (London, England), 1997.

*Her Last Call to Louis MacNeice,* Serpent's Tail (New York, NY), 1998.

*London Boulevard* (crime novel), Do-Not Press (London, England), 2001, Minotaur Books (New York, NY), 2009.

*Dispatching Baudelaire,* Sitric Books (Dublin, Ireland), 2004.

(Editor) *Dublin Noir: The Celtic Tiger vs. the Ugly American,* Akashic Books (New York, NY), 2006.

*American Skin* (crime novel), Justin, Charles & Co. (Boston, MA), 2006.

*Once Were Cops,* St. Martin's Minotaur (New York, NY), 2008.

(With Reed Farrel Coleman) *Tower,* edited by Allan Guthrie, Busted Flush Press (Houston, TX), 2009.

*"JACK TAYLOR" SERIES; CRIME NOVELS*

*The Guards,* Brandon (Dingle, Ireland), 2001, St. Martin's Minotaur (New York, NY), 2003.

*The Killing of the Tinkers,* Brandon (Dingle, Ireland), 2002, St. Martin's Minotaur (New York, NY), 2004.

*The Magdalen Martyrs,* Brandon (Dingle, Ireland), 2003, St. Martin's Minotaur (New York, NY), 2005.

*The Dramatist,* Brandon (Dingle, Ireland), 2003, St. Martin's Minotaur (New York, NY), 2006.

*Priest,* Bantam (London, England), 2006, St. Martin's Minotaur (New York, NY), 2007.

*Cross,* Bantam (London, England), 2007, St. Martin's Minotaur (New York, NY), 2008.

*Sanctuary,* Transworld Ireland (Dublin, Ireland), 2008, St. Martin's Minotaur (New York, NY), 2009.

*The Devil,* Minotaur Books (New York, NY), 2010.

*Headstone,* Mysterious Press (New York, NY), 2011.

### "BRANT" SERIES; CRIME NOVELS

*A White Arrest* (also see below), Bloodlines (London, England), 1998.

*Taming the Alien* (also see below), Bloodlines (London, England), 1999.

*The McDead* (also see below), Bloodlines (London, England), 2000.

*The White Trilogy* (contains *A White Arrest, Taming the Alien,* and *The McDead*), Kate's Mystery Books (Boston, MA), 2003.

*Blitz,* Do-Not Press (London, England), 2003, St. Martin's Minotaur (New York, NY), 2004.

*Vixen,* Do-Not Press (London, England), 2003, St. Martin's Minotaur (New York, NY), 2005.

*Calibre,* St. Martin's Minotaur (New York, NY), 2006.

*Ammunition,* St. Martin's Minotaur (New York, NY), 2007.

### "MAX AND ANGELA" SERIES; WITH JASON STARR

*Bust,* Hard Case Crime (London, England), 2006.

*Slide,* Hard Case Crime (London, England), 2007.

*The Max,* Hard Case Crime (London, England), 2008.

### COLLECTIONS

*Funeral: Tales of Irish Morbidities,* Dorrance Publishing (Pittsburgh, PA), 1991.

*Sherry: And Other Stories,* Adelphi Press (London, England), 1994.

*The Time of Serena-May: And Other Stories,* Adelphi Press (London, England), 1995.

*Murder by the Book,* Busted Flush Press (Houston, TX), 2005.

*A Fifth of Bruen: Early Fiction of Ken Bruen,* Busted Flush Press (Houston, TX), 2006.

(Contributor) *Requiems for the Departed* (e-book), CreateSpace, 2010.

## ■ Adaptations

*The Guards, Blitz, Her Last Call to Louis MacNeice,* and *London Boulevard* were adapted for film or television series; rights to *The White Trilogy* were purchased for television by Deep Indigo Productions.

## ■ Sidelights

Ken Bruen has worked as an English teacher in Africa, Japan, Southeast Asia, and South America. In 1979 Bruen took a teaching position in Rio de Janeiro, Brazil. Soon after he arrived there he was arrested for his involvement in a fight that occurred in a bar. His captors tortured and sexually assaulted him. When he was released and returned to London, Bruen was so traumatized by his experience that he contemplated suicide. Instead, he said in his author autobiography at the Justin, Charles, & Company Web site, "I decided to write books, just to prove to myself that I was still alive if nothing else." Thus, his writing career was launched.

### *The Hackman Blues* and *London Boulevard*

One of Bruen's first books, *Rilke on Black,* elicited praise for its rendering of the dregs of contemporary popular culture. This was followed by *The Hackman Blues,* in which Tony Brady is hired by Jack Dunphy, who happens to resemble the actor Gene Hackman, to find his daughter, Roz. Tony easily finds Roz, who is being held by club owner Leon in a rough London neighborhood. Jack instructs Tony to pay off Leon in order to get his daughter back, but Tony has a plan of his own. He decides to kidnap Roz himself, keep Jack's money, and then get more cash from Leon. Tony's plan backfires, however, and he soon finds his life in danger. "Readers of hard-boiled British mysteries such as those by Quintin Jardine and Ian Rankin should enjoy this gritty page-turner," predicted *Library Journal* contributor Bob Lunn. *Booklist* contributor David Pitt added: "Bruen's sojourn among London's underclass is a cutting-edge British thriller."

In *London Boulevard,* a man named Mitchell is freed from jail, where he was serving time for a crime he committed while in a drunken stupor. Determined to make a change in his life, Mitchell finds an honest job as a handyman and also starts dating a nice woman. Something happens, however, that throws Mitchell back into a shady past he cannot escape. *Booklist* contributor Emily Melton observed: "This one packs one hell of a powerful punch."

### *The Guards*

In *The Guards* Bruen's series character Jack Taylor makes his debut when he is kicked out of the Guards, Ireland's police force. Now he spends most of his time at a Galway bar getting drunk and making a meager living as a private investigator. When

Ann Henderson's daughter Sarah is found dead in Galway, the Guards claim she is one of several recent suicide cases involving young girls. Ann strongly feels that her daughter would not commit suicide and that she was murdered. She hires Jack to find out who murdered her daughter and why. Jack takes the job, and along the way he falls in love with Ann.

*Bookview Ireland* Web site contributor Pauline Ferrie commented: "Though not without humor *The Guards* is essentially a dark tale of perversion, evil and violence." *Booklist* contributor Keir Graff noted that "Bruen has a sly, dark humor that is appealing."

### The Killing of the Tinkers and The Magdalen Martyrs

Bruen continued the adventures of Taylor in several other installments. The author explained the origin of the character to *Publishers Weekly* contributor Patrick Millikin: "Jack Taylor is a tribute to the American private eye, but like myself, his greatest gift was a library ticket as a child. To go to the library in the old days, you had to go to the courthouse and pass all these huge [police] Guards and it lodged in my mind: Guards and books." Speaking with Milton C. Toby on the *Big Thrill* Web site, Bruen described the difficulties in having an unlikeable series protagonist: "I try to keep Jack interesting in that even though he is an arsehole, he is loyal to his few friends and will risk all if he believes he is right. . . . I think he appeals because he is so desperately flawed and speaks to the human condition as we are, not as the TV, movie heroes would have us believe. And too, he knows his own act, whatever else he does, he is honest with his own self, to his terrible cost."

In *The Killing of the Tinkers,* Taylor, still struggling with his addictions, returns to Galway only to be caught up in an investigation of the deaths of several young tinkers. Taylor continues his unorthodox investigation methods in this "strong piece of crime writing," as *Booklist* contributor Graff described the novel. Graff went on to observe that Taylor "may be a drunken shambles, but his wry humor, regret, and sense of impending mortality . . . keep readers coming along." High praise came from a *Publishers Weekly* reviewer who concluded that *The Killing of the Tinkers* is "a remarkable book from a singular talent."

Taylor next appears in *The Magdalen Martyrs,* which is, according to *Booklist* contributor David Wright, a "stiff shot of evil chased with heartbreaking irony."

Here Taylor, battling with alcohol and cocaine, is summoned by a Galway criminal to find a missing woman. Taylor's search leads him to several other mistreated women, as well, who are all connected to a Catholic laundry where unwed mothers have been sent. Wright noted that it was not the procedural bits that were the book's strength, but rather the "the eclectic, lyrical screeds pouring forth from the narrator's ruined heart." A reviewer for *Publishers Weekly* found that Buren's "noir mystery-thriller crackles with his trademark tough-guy bravado."

### The Dramatist and Priest

In *The Dramatist* Taylor is off alcohol and drugs and is trying to put his life back in order. His next commission comes from his former drug dealer who is now in prison and anxious to have his sister's killer brought to justice. This young woman was the first of several dead women found with a copy of the works of Irish playwright J.M. Synge near their bodies. A *Publishers Weekly* contributor called the book "a riveting mystery and a deftly rendered protagonist."

*Priest,* the fifth book in the series, finds Taylor just being released from a rehabilitation asylum, where he was incarcerated after his drinking led to the death of a young child. Taylor's lingering guilt is put on hold when he is hired by a priest to find the murderer of a fellow man of the cloth, a pedophile, who has been beheaded. A reviewer for *Publishers Weekly* described this tale as "a kind of savage poetry, at once exhausting and exhilarating."

### Cross and Sanctuary

*Cross* finds Taylor in his favorite pubs but exercising restraint. He learns from Ridge, a lesbian and an old friend from the Guard, that a young boy has been found crucified. Then the boy's sister is burned to death in her car. In order to discover why dogs have been disappearing, Taylor hires alcoholic Eoin Heaton, a former Guard, to investigate, but he is then found dead, floating in a canal with a dog tied to him.

Ali Karim reviewed *Cross* for *Rap Sheet* online, concluding that "Bruen's writing in *Cross* has a beguiling quality. The story is told in very intimate first-person, allowing us to crawl right into the tightest corners of Taylor's mind and poke around in his thoughts. We acquire a good view of Jack Taylor's existential thoughts about life, death, and whatever is meant by the word 'humanity.'"

As *Sanctuary,* begins, Taylor is about to depart for New York when he receives a list of "victims" that includes two Guards, one judge, and a nun. The list is signed Benedictus. He can't get involved because he has his tickets in hand, but when a child is added to the list of victims, it becomes impossible not to.

### The Devil

The eighth installment in the Jack Taylor series, *The Devil,* appeared in 2010. Here Jack appears to be doing battle with the devil himself. He turns back to drugs, alcohol, and cigarettes after he is refused access to a flight to the United States at the airport in Ireland. Taking comfort in shots of Jameson, he meets a man name Kurt who imparts a mysterious message to him about evil and redemption. Not much later, Jack becomes involved in cases of suicide and murder that seem to be connected to a certain Mr. K. Later still Jack meets the mysterious Kurt again in the guise of Carl Franz, and each meeting leads to violence for others. Finally Jack is forced to go back into his own case histories to solve this one, revisiting crimes from the first seven books in the series.

"What happens, though, matters far less in Bruen's books than the boozy, doped-up ride along Jack's Joycean consciousness," wrote P.G. Koch in a *Houston Chronicle* review, "the narrative delivered in chopped up sentences stacked like lines in a poem." A *Publishers Weekly* reviewer termed this an "atmospheric, metaphysically tinged" novel that supplies "lots of . . . delicious moments" for fans of the series. *Library Journal* reviewer Eric Norton was less enthused with this installment, however, noting that Jack Taylor "spends most of his time going from one bar to the next" instead of actually investigating the identity of Kurt. Norton thought this one was for readers who like protagonists who are "Irish and well soaked in alcohol." A contributor to *Kirkus Reviews* offered a higher assessment, concluding: "Between all the Xanax-popping and Jameson-swilling, Bruen keeps Jack and his adventures as mordantly funny as ever." *Booklist* reviewer Thomas Gaughan also had praise for *The Devil,* observing that it "will go down nicely with a large Jameson."

### The White Trilogy

In addition to the works featuring Taylor, Bruen has written a series featuring Detective Sergeant Tom Brant. The first two titles in the series are *A White Arrest* and *Taming the Alien.* On the *Things I'd Rather Be Doing* blog, Bruen explained: "I write Brant to chill me out and Taylor to torment myself. . . . Brant is pure fun, Taylor is me disgusted with our new rich Ireland."

In *The McDead,* Chief Inspector James Roberts's brother is found beaten to death. Even though he has not seen or talked to his brother in ten years, Roberts vows to get revenge. The killer is Tommy Logan, and soon Inspector Roberts and Detective Tom Brant are on his trail. At the same time, other detectives are trying to capture a rapist who preys on black women. *Booklist* contributor Wes Lukowsky believed that "fans of British procedurals and noir novels will savor every speck of grit in this unrelenting crime novel."

The first three volumes of the series are collected in *The White Trilogy.* This is a book filled with violence and clipped dialogue that inspired *Booklist* writer Graff to conclude: "This stuff smokes like cordite, but it blows a hole in your stomach instead of filling your belly." The series featuring Brant has often been likened to American author Ed McBain's "87th Precinct" series, and Bruen has said in interviews that he much admires McBain's work.

### Blitz and Vixen

Bruen carries the series forward with *Blitz,* which finds the team of Southeast London police chasing a cop killer who dubs himself The Blitz. Meanwhile, each of the main characters struggles with his or her own personal difficulties. Graff, writing again in *Booklist,* observed: "This one is more satisfyingly plotted than its predecessors, ending with a bang instead of just skidding to a stop." A *Publishers Weekly* critic had a more positive assessment of *Blitz,* terming it an "intelligent, uncompromising hard-boiled crime novel."

Writing in *Booklist,* Wright described Bruen's fifth installment in the series, *Vixen,* as a "vicious, black-sheep cousin of McBain's 87th precinct series." In this novel, the police have to deal with a gang of bombers bent on extortion.

### Calibre and Ammunition

A serial murder is at work in *Calibre,* a "superb . . . pulp-inspired novel," according to a *Publishers Weekly* contributor. The same contributor concluded that "Bruen's furious hard-boiled prose, chopped down to its trademark essence, never fails to astonish."

In *Ammunition,* Brant is sitting in one of his favorite bars having a whiskey when hit man Terry Banks shoots him in the back. He was paid by wealthy Rodney Lewis, but the neophyte killer bungles the job. When it is thought that Brant will die, cops and criminal alike celebrate, but Brant pulls through to avenge himself. Sergeant Elizabeth Falls is the target of a woman who wants to settle the score, and a senior citizen who is part of a group of elderly vigilantes is killed. A *Publishers Weekly* contributor concluded: "Bruen keeps this train wreck on proper course to a wholly satisfying, and very noir, conclusion."

### *American Skin* and *Once Were Cops*

Bruen is equally at home with stand-alone titles. Taking to the road, he delivers a "dark tribute to the Irish fascination with the American dream" with his *American Skin,* according to a *Publishers Weekly* reviewer. Here an Irish bank robber and his girlfriend are trying to lose themselves in the American Southwest, only to be pursued by an IRA (Irish Republican Army) hit man who wants part of their takings. A *Kirkus Reviews* critic felt that "this is Bruen beyond noir into full-out stygian." The same writer called Bruen the "poster boy for Irish noir."

Taylor is losing his battle with the bottle in *Once Were Cops,* a spinoff from the series, and he is replaced by Matthew Patrick O'Shea, who inflicts "biblical damage" on his victims and sees rosary beads as a weapon to be used in the strangulation of beautiful women. O'Shea wants to experience violence on a higher level and wangles a spot in an exchange program that takes him to New York. There he becomes friendly with brutish New York copy Kurt "Kebar" Browski, but Browski has a beautiful handicapped sister who could become a target of the Irish thug.

A *Kirkus Reviews* contributor concluded: "Readers asked at year's end to list the nastiest, most violent cop novels of 2008 will certainly remember this one." Gaughan wrote in *Booklist* that this is "a chilling and deeply creepy read."

### *Tower*

Bruen teams up with fellow noir mystery writer Reed Farrel Coleman for the 2009 stand-alone title, *Tower.* The collaborators tell two tales here of friends Nick and Todd and their journey through life and crime. The two come of age on the mean streets of Brooklyn, both on the outs with their families. They go into crime together, running errands for Boyle, a vicious criminal who happily quotes from the Bible, and rise through his organization, seeming destined for either jail or a coffin. Bruen writes incidents from the point of view of Nick, while Coleman takes the perspective of Todd, rendering the same events from a different angle.

A reviewer for *Publishers Weekly* felt that "Bruen and Coleman shine" in this "short, brutally poetic tour of the underside of Brooklyn, Boston and Philadelphia." Gaughan, writing again in *Booklist,* felt that "Bruen's prose is some of the leanest, meanest writing crime fans will find." *Pulp Serenade* Web site contributor Cullen Gallagher also commended this collaborative effort, writing: "What's most remarkable about *Tower* is that not only do Bruen and Coleman perfectly complement each other while retaining their own voices, but that their juxtaposition creates a literary polyphony that enriches the narrative all the more. It's like a jam session between your favorite musicians, riffing off each other while still working together. They each get their solo, but one without the other wouldn't be a song—together, it's a tour de force."

### *Bust, Slide,* and *The Max*

Bruen and Jason Starr cowrote *Bust,* in which New York businessman Max Fisher hires a hit man to kill his wife so that he can pursue a romance with Angela Petrakos, his secretary. Ken Tucker in *Entertainment Weekly* described it as being a "terse, sometimes brutal, often funny caper." In *Slide,* Max has become a crack dealer and Angela is in Ireland, home to Slide, an Irish psychopath who wants to follow in the footsteps of infamous American serial killers, Dahmer, Bundy, and Berkowitz. *Booklist* reviewer Thomas Gaughan felt that the two writers "had as much fun writing *Slide* as crime fans will have reading it."

Both Max and Angela wind up in prison in *The Max.* Max is in Attica, and Angela is incarcerated on the Greek island of Lesbos. Wright noted in *Booklist* that "Bruen and Starr's dirty rotten scoundrels and natural born killers do some very bad things in this sleazy grind house."

Bruen continues to teach English while writing in the early morning hours of each day and churning out sometimes several novels per year. Writing in *Booklist,* Graff quipped that "Bruen is so prolific that there is mounting evidence he could supply his own book-of-the-month club." The critic continued: "It doesn't seem to affect his quality, though."

## ■ Biographical And Critical Sources

*PERIODICALS*

*Booklist,* March 15, 1998, David Pitt, review of *The Hackman Blues,* p. 1204; April 1, 2000, Thomas Gaughan, review of *Taming the Alien,* p. 1438; May 1, 2001, Wes Lukowsky, review of *The McDead,* p. 1624; December 15, 2002, Keir Graff, review of *The Guards,* p. 736; January 21, 2003, Emily Melton, review of *London Boulevard;* February 1, 2003, Keir Graff, review of *The White Trilogy,* p. 975; March 1, 2003, Keir Graff, review of *Blitz,* p. 1148; November 15, 2003, Keir Graff, review of *The Killing of the Tinkers,* p. 583; January 1, 2005, David Wright, review of *The Magdalen Martyrs,* p. 826; August, 2005, David Wright, review of *Vixen,* p. 1997; January 1, 2006, Keir Graff, review of *The Dramatist,* p. 63; April 1, 2006, Keir Graff, review of *Bust,* p. 22; May 1, 2006, Keir Graff, review of *Calibre,* p. 18; July 1, 2007, Thomas Gaughan, review of *Slide,* p. 36; January 1, 2008, Thomas Gaughan, review of *Cross,* p. 47; May 15, 2008, David Wright, review of *The Max,* p. 25; August 1, 2008, Thomas Gaughan, review of *Once Were Cops,* p. 46; August 1, 2009, Thomas Gaughan, review of *Tower,* p. 41; August 1, 2010, Thomas Gaughan, review of *The Devil,* p. 31.

*Entertainment Weekly,* March 10, 2006, Tina Jordan, review of *The Dramatist,* p. 71; April 28, 2006, Ken Tucker, review of *Bust,* p. 139; November 21, 2008, Tina Jordan, review of *Once Were Cops,* p. 123.

*Europe Intelligence Wire,* January 7, 2006, review of *Priest.*

*Hollywood Reporter,* December 8, 2010, Ray Bennett, review of *London Boulevard,* p. 63.

*Houston Chronicle,* September 26, 2010, P.G. Koch, "Devil Makes Life a Living Hell: Satan Determined to Wreak Havoc in Ken Bruen's Latest Novel," review of *The Devil,* p. 14.

*Kirkus Reviews,* May 1, 1997, review of *Rilke on Black,* p. 680; February 1, 1998, review of *The Hackman Blues,* p. 154; March 15, 2000, review of *Taming the Alien,* p. 337; March 1, 2001, review of *The McDead,* p. 293; October 15, 2002, review of *The Guards,* p. 1505; February 15, 2003, review of *Blitz,* p. 271; November 1, 2003, review of *The Killing of the Tinkers,* p. 1295; February 15, 2005, review of *The Magdalen Martyrs,* p. 198; January 15, 2006, review of *The Dramatist,* p. 62; June 1, 2006, review of *Calibre,* p. 547; August 15, 2006, review of *American Skin,* p. 810; July 1, 2007, review of *Ammunition;* January 15, 2008, review of *Cross;* September 1, 2008, review of *Once Were Cops.* November 1, 2009, review of *London Boulevard;* August 1, 2010, review of *The Devil.*

*Library Journal,* June 1, 1998, Bob Lunn, review of *The Hackman Blues,* p. 167; June 1, 2004, Rex E. Klett, review of *Blitz,* p. 107; January 1, 2005, Craig Shufelt, review of *The Magdalen Martyrs,* p. 85; August 1, 2005, Craig Shufelt, review of *Vixen,* p. 59; February 1, 2006, Jo Ann Vicarel, review of *The Dramatist,* p. 56; August 1, 2008, Bob Lunn, review of *Once Were Cops,* p. 64; July 23, 2010, Eric Norton, review of *The Devil.*

*New York Times Book Review,* January 11, 2004, Marilyn Stasio, review of *The Killing of the Tinkers,* p. 19.

*Publishers Weekly,* February 9, 1998, review of *The Hackman Blues,* p. 77; May 24, 1999, review of *A White Arrest,* p. 71; March 19, 2001, review of *The McDead,* p. 80; November 25, 2002, review of *The Guards,* p. 46; February 3, 2003, review of *The White Trilogy,* p. 58; December 22, 2003, review of *The Killing of the Tinkers,* p. 35, Patrick Millikin, "Hibernian Noir," interview with Ken Bruen, p. 36; May 31, 2004, review of *Blitz,* p. 55; February 14, 2005, review of *The Magdalen Martyrs,* p. 57; January 16, 2006, review of *The Dramatist,* p. 39; March 13, 2006, review of *Bust,* p. 47; June 5, 2006, review of *Calibre,* p. 40; August 21, 2006, review of *American Skin,* p. 53; January 22, 2007, review of *Priest,* p. 165; June 25, 2007, review of *Ammunition,* p. 38; January 21, 2008, review of *Cross,* p. 157; August 18, 2008, review of *Once Were Cops,* p. 38; July 6, 2009, review of *Tower,* p. 39; October 12, 2009, review of *London Boulevard,* p. 31; July 26, 2010, review of *The Devil,* p. 55.

*Reviewer's Bookwatch,* April, 2008, Theodore Feit, review of *Cross.*

*ONLINE*

*Agony Column,* http://trashotron.com/agony/ (June 14, 2004), Terry D'Auray, review of *The Killing of the Tinkers.*

*Big Thrill,* http://www.thrillerwriters.org/ (December 31, 2009), Milton C. Toby, "Between the Lines with Ken Bruen."

*Bookview Ireland,* http://www.bookviewireland.ie/ (January 21, 2003), Pauline Ferrie, reviews of *The Killing of the Tinkers* and *The Guards.*

*Busted Flush Press,* http://bustedflushpress.blogspot.com/ (June 27, 2009), Craig McDonald, "Tower Interview #1: Ken Bruen."

*Charlotte Austin Review,* http://collection.nlc-bnc.ca/ (January 21, 2003), Lisa Eagleson-Roever, review of *Taming the Alien.*

*Crime Scenes NI,* http://crimescenesni.blogspot.com/ (November 20, 2008), interview.

*Crime Scenes Scotland Reviews,* http://www.crimescenesscotlandreviews.blogspot.com/ (August 1, 2006), Russel D. Mclean, review of *A Fifth of Bruen: Early Fiction of Ken Bruen.*

*Culture Northern Ireland,* http://www.culturenorthernireland.org/ (August 10, 2010), "Interview: Ken Bruen."

*Detective Fiction*, http://detective-fiction.suite101.com/ (December 7, 2008), Sandra Webster, review of *Cross*.

*Drowning Machine*, http://drowningmachine.blogspot.com/ (July 22, 2010), review of *The Devil*.

*Euro Crime*, http://www.eurocrime.co.uk/ (February 16, 2009), Norman Price, review of *Cross*.

*Galway Advertiser Online*, http://www.galwayadvertiser.ie/ (May 10, 2006), Kernan Andrews, review of *A Fifth of Bruen*.

*Internet Movie Database*, http://www.imdb.com/ (July 3, 2011), "Ken Bruen."

*Irish Echo Online*, http://www.irischecho.com/ (March 7, 2007), Pól Ó Conghaile, "To Hell and Back."

*Justin, Charles & Company Web site*, http://www.justincharles.com/ (January 21, 2003), "Ken Bruen."

*Ken Bruen Home Page*, http://www.kenbruen.com (July 3, 2011).

*Murder by the Book*, http://www.murderbooks.com/ (March 19, 2007), "Mystery Author Interviews: Ken Bruen."

*Mystery Reader*, http://www.themysteryreader.com/ (March 19, 2007), Martin Kich, review of *The Killing of the Tinkers*.

*Pulp Serenade*, http://www.pulpserenade.com/ (July 23, 2009), Cullen Gallagher, review of *Tower*.

*Rap Sheet*, http://therapsheet.blogspot.com/ (January 8, 2007), Ali Karim, review of *Cross*.

*Shots Online*, http://www.shotsmag.co.uk/ (January 21, 2003), Liz Hatherall, review of *London Boulevard*; Calum Macleod, reviews of *The Guards* and *The Killing of the Tinkers*; (March 19, 2007), Ali Karim, "Callin Galway: A Conversation with Ken Bruen."

*Spinetingler*, http://www.spinetinglermag.com/ (February 23, 2011), Theodore Feit, review of *The Devil*.

*Things I'd Rather Be Doing*, http://www.tirbd.com/ (January 28, 2007), interview with Bruen.*

# Bill Bryson

## 1951-

■ **Also Known As**

William Bryson

■ **Personal**

Born December 8, 1951, in Des Moines, IA; son of William (a sports columnist) and Mary Bryson; married; wife's name Cynthia (a nurse); children: David, Felicity, Catherine, Samuel. *Education:* Attended Drake University.

■ **Addresses**

*Home*—Norfolk, England.

■ **Career**

Journalist and author. Worked at a newspaper in Bournemouth, England, beginning 1977, and for business sections of the *Times* and the *Independent*, London, England. Guest on television programs, including *Good Morning America* and *Sunday Morning*. Appointed an English Heritage Commissioner, 2003; chancellor of Durham University in northern England, 2005-11; president of the Campaign to Protect Rural England, 2007—.

■ **Awards, Honors**

Aventis Prize for best general science book, 2004, and Descartes Prize for science communication, 2005, both for *A Short History of Nearly Everything*; President's Award, Royal Society of Chemistry, 2005; honorary Order of the British Empire (OBE), from the British government, 2006; James Joyce Award of the Literary and Historical Society of University College Dublin, 2007. Awarded numerous honorary degrees, including from Bournemouth University and the Open University.

■ **Writings**

*The Facts on File Dictionary of Troublesome Words*, Facts on File (New York, NY), 1984, revised edition, 1988, published as *The Penguin Dictionary of Troublesome Words*, Penguin (New York, NY), 1984, revised edition, Viking (New York, NY), 1988, published as *Bryson's Dictionary of Troublesome Words*, Broadway Books (New York, NY), 2002.

(As William Bryson) *The Palace under the Alps, and Over Two Hundred Other Unusual, Unspoiled, and Infrequently Visited Spots in Sixteen European Countries*, Congdon & Weed (New York, NY), 1985.

*The Lost Continent: Travels in Small-town America*, Harper (New York, NY), 1989.

*The Mother Tongue: English and How It Got That Way*, Morrow (New York, NY), 1990.

*Neither Here nor There: Travels in Europe*, Secker & Warburg (London, England), 1991, Morrow (New York, NY), 1992.

*The Penguin Dictionary for Writers and Editors*, Viking (New York, NY), 1992, published as *Bryson's Dictionary for Writers and Editors*, Broadway Books (New York, NY), 2008.

*Made in America: An Informal History of the English Language in the United States*, Morrow (New York, NY), 1994.

*Notes from a Small Island: An Affectionate Portrait of Britain*, Morrow (New York, NY), 1995.

*A Walk in the Woods: Rediscovering America on the Appalachian Trail*, Broadway Books (New York, NY), 1998.

*I'm a Stranger Here Myself: Notes on Returning to America after Twenty Years Away,* Broadway Books (New York, NY), 1999.

(Editor, with Jason Wilson) *The Best American Travel Writing, 2000,* Houghton Mifflin (Boston, MA), 2000.

*In a Sunburned Country,* Broadway Books (New York, NY), 2000, published as *Down Under,* Doubleday (London, England), 2000.

*Bill Bryson's African Diary,* Broadway Books (New York, NY), 2002.

*A Short History of Nearly Everything,* Broadway Books (New York, NY), 2004.

*A Short History of Nearly Everything: Special Illustrated Edition,* Broadway Books (New York, NY), 2005.

*The Life and Times of the Thunderbolt Kid,* Broadway Books (New York, NY), 2006.

*Shakespeare: The World as Stage,* Atlas Books/ HarperCollins (New York, NY), 2007.

(Author of foreword) Andy Singleton and David Joy, *Barns of the Yorkshire Dales,* photography by Christopher Walker, Great Northern (Ilkley, West Yorkshire, England), 2008.

*A Really Short History of Nearly Everything* (for younger readers), Delacorte Press (New York, NY), 2009.

(Editor and author of introduction) *Seeing Further: The Story of Science, Discovery, and the Genius of the Royal Society,* William Morrow (New York, NY), 2010.

*At Home: A Short History of Private Life,* Doubleday (New York, NY), 2010.

Author of "Notes from a Big Country," a weekly column in *Mail on Sunday.* Contributor to periodicals, including *Travel and Leisure, National Geographic,* and the *New York Times.*

## ■ Adaptations

*Neither Here nor There* was adapted for audio recording by Random House (New York, NY), 1999; *In a Sunburned Country* was adapted for audio recording by BDD Audio (New York, NY), 2000.

## ■ Sidelights

Bill Bryson's works can be divided into two categories, according to some reviewers. "In his adoptive Britain," Norman Oder explained in *Publishers Weekly*, "Bryson reached best-seller status with wiseacre travelogues. . . . In the United States, he's best known for excursions into the lore of the English language." Bryson has since broadened his literary scope, tackling topics as dauntingly large as his popular science book, *A Short History of Nearly Everything,* or as seemingly mundane—yet fascinating—as the 2010 title *At Home: A Short History of Private Life.*

### The Lost Continent

For the first of the travelogues, the American-born journalist returned from his home in North Yorkshire, England, to his native Iowa and set out on a journey by car across the North American continent to write *The Lost Continent: Travels in Small-town America.* The work is an account of a thirty-eight-state tour Bryson began in 1987, having decided to embark on the kind of motor trip his family once took in their blue Rambler station wagon. Bryson's quest was to find the perfect small town in which, as he explains in *The Lost Continent,* "Bing Crosby would be the priest, Jimmy Stewart mayor, Fred MacMurray the high school principal, Henry Fonda a Quaker farmer. Walter Brennan would run the gas station, a boyish Mickey Rooney would deliver groceries, and somewhere, at an open window, Deanna Durbin would sing."

Throughout his travels, however, Bryson offers descriptions of what he finds as "parking lots and tallish buildings surrounded by a sprawl of shopping centers, gas stations and fast-food joints." His observations about small-town America are laced with a sharp-edged humor; at one point he notes that "talking about a scenic route in southeast Iowa is like talking about a good Barry Manilow album," which alienated some reviewers. *Los Angeles Times Book Review* contributor Wanda Urbanska termed *The Lost Continent* "merely a forum for the put-down humor so popular these days." *Newsweek* contributor Jim Miller, however, noted that the book "is paradoxically touching—a melancholy memoir in the form of a snide travelogue." *The Lost Continent* proved more popular with readers, becoming a Book-of-the-Month Club alternate selection. "You have to be able to laugh at yourself to understand this book, and I know that is asking a lot of some people," Bryson explained in the *Chicago Tribune.* "It really is a fond portrait."

### Neither Here Nor There
### and Notes from a Small Island

Bryson again took to the road with his next book, although this time journeying the European continent. *Neither Here nor There: Travels in Europe* describes his adventures in places such as France, Italy, Norway, and Turkey. As with *The Lost Conti-*

*nent,* some reviewers expressed reservations about *Neither Here nor There,* complaining that the book's humor sometimes wears thin. Dervla Murphy in the *Times Literary Supplement* found that "sometimes Bill Bryson's humour recalls [P.G.] Wodehouse, sometimes Flann O'Brien. More often it is distinctive, depending on his cunning use of flamboyant exaggerations, grotesque but always successful metaphors and the deft juxtapositions of incongruous images—the whole presented in a style that boldly veers from laid-back colloquial American to formal clean-cut English."

In the mid-1990s, Bryson moved back to the United States, where he settled with his family in Hanover, New Hampshire. Before leaving England, where he had lived for more than twenty years, the author toured the island one last time, confining himself to public transportation and foot travel. *Notes from a Small Island: An Affectionate Portrait of Britain* represents what some reviewers have likened to a fond farewell. "This affectionate valediction lauds British eccentricity, endurance, and genius for adversity," Oder wrote. British critic Boyd Tonkin reported in *New Statesman and Society* that, beneath the humor of Bryson's "all-smiles, easy reading jaunt," there flows an undercurrent of lament for days gone by. "The Britain he loves is quaint, quiet and deeply welfare-statist," Tonkin wrote, and Bryson's criticisms of "the damage wrought by market-minded dogmas," however witty, left the critic "unpersuaded. . . . He seldom reads our mustn't-grumble tolerance as a sign of surrender, not just of civility." In the United States, on the other hand, some reviewers were delighted with Bryson's "trenchant, witty and detailed observations," as a *Publishers Weekly* critic noted. *Publishers Weekly* recommended *Notes from a Small Island* as an "immensely entertaining" account, and *Booklist* reviewer Alice Joyce hailed Bryson's writing as "delightfully irreverent."

### A Walk in the Woods

Bryson marked his return to the land of his birth with an exploration of one of America's longest and oldest footpaths—the Appalachian Trail. His goal was to walk the entire trail, more than two thousand miles long, from Georgia to Maine. He set out optimistically from a Georgia state park with a companion of his boyhood and completed the first hundred miles with relative ease. "Initially, it didn't seem an impossible task," Bryson told Oder in an interview. "But your expectations cannot match reality." Citing difficulties ranging from "drudgery" to the whimsical reliability of maps and map makers to the defection of his partner, Stephen Katz, Bryson

abridged his plan. According to *New Statesman* critic Albert Scardino: "He decides he doesn't have to walk the whole trail to absorb its spirit." In various segments over a period of time, Bryson eventually completed more than eight hundred miles of hiking and observation. *A Walk in the Woods: Rediscovering America on the Appalachian Trail* is the memoir of his journey.

A *Forbes* reviewer remarked that the author's "humor is winning and succinct" and displays a talent "for boiling down his observations to their absurd essences." *Library Journal* critic Nancy J. Moeckel wrote: "Bryson shares some truly laugh-out-loud moments" in his "amiable" account of the journey and the people he meets along the way. A British reviewer for the *Economist* compared Bryson's talents to the "droll American mix of folksy intelligence and aw-shucks wit" of Garrison Keillor, and Ron Antonucci recommended the memoir to *Booklist* readers as "a marvelous description and history of the trail."

### Bryson's Dictionary of Troublesome Words

Oder suggested that *A Walk in the Woods* represents a combination of both sides of Bryson's career: "picaresque traveler and lore-gatherer." The lore-gatherer emerges in several books about words and language, beginning with *The Penguin Dictionary of Troublesome Words.* A third edition of the book was released in 2002 as *Bryson's Dictionary of Troublesome Words* and contains "some sixty percent" new or updated material, according to the author. Created initially by Bryson as an editorial tool for personal use, it remains a concise guide to common English language problems. Features include lists of words and phrases often misused, clarification of differences between British and American English, redundant wording, examples of blatant errors found in prominent publications, and a glossary of punctuation and grammatical terms.

A *Booklist* reviewer described this book as "admittedly narrow in range" but a "pithy guide [that] will work fine in conjunction with a full-blown style manual." Lilli McCowan of the *European Business Journal* concluded that "Bryson can help us to get stylish and even better, understood."

### The Mother Tongue and Made in America

*The Mother Tongue: English and How It Got That Way* is an anecdotal, historical survey of what Bryson calls "the most important and successful language in the world." *The Mother Tongue* was warmly received by critics, who considered the book lively and engaging. *New York Times Book Review* contributor Burt Hochberg found reading Bryson's presentation of such topics as etymology, pronunciation, spelling, dialects, grammar, origins of names, and wordplay "an enthralling excursion."

In *Made in America: An Informal History of the English Language in the United States,* Bryson, according to Oder, "uses the evolution of American English to slalom through American History and culture." The *Economist* reviewer described Bryson as "an easy, intelligent and good-humoured writer" but warned: "Towards its end the book threatens to become little more than a history of consumption and consumer goods: how the automobile, shopping mall, aeroplane, hamburger, came to America." That reviewer also warned of errors—a caution echoed by other critics as well. In *People,* Elaine Kahn identified some of the mistakes that could lead an unwary reader astray. Others reviewers were less critical, however. Albert Kim of *Entertainment Weekly* was engaged by Bryson's "unabashed curiosity" about the English language and the "sheer delight" he derives from transmitting the information to his readers. George W. Hunt summarized the work in *America* as, overall, "a leisurely history . . . of a nation's growth as dramatized by its changing vocabulary," and a *Publishers Weekly* reviewer called the book "a treasure trove of trivia about American culture past and present."

### The Best American Travel Writing, 2000 and *I'm a Stranger Here Myself*

Bryson revisited his favored genre of travel writing and his editorial past for *The Best American Travel Writing, 2000.* As guest editor, Bryson shared duties with series editor Jason Wilson to publish this volume of Houghton Mifflin's "Best American" series. This collection of travel anthologies was described by Nicholas Howe in the *New Republic* as "'testosterone travel' or 'exploraporn' . . . today's versions of the adventure stories that ran thirty or fifty years ago in barbershop or cigar-store magazines." Bryson chose travel pieces he liked for this collection, penned by writers who, according to a *Publishers Weekly* contributor, "share a love of a place, a moment, a people," and who have written tales to "remind us of how amazing the world truly is."

Bryson recorded his return to the world of his roots in a collection of essays originally written for the British magazine *Night and Day.* The book *I'm a Stranger Here Myself: Notes on Returning to America after Twenty Years Away* is filled with funny anecdotes describing contemporary American life from the absurd, witty, and unique vantage of Bryson, who chose to make his birth land home after twenty years as an expatriate. "This is humor writing at its sharpest," noted Brad Hooper in *Booklist,* who went on to say that "his saving grace is that he does more laughing with us than at us." Wilda Williams of *Library Journal* reported that the book is filled with Bryson's "trademark humor," but also "a bit slight and choppy," a small criticism that she does not expect to have any impact on the book's popularity.

### In a Sunburned Country

*In a Sunburned Country* is Bryson's appropriately eccentric and humorous depiction of Australia, the continent he claims "has more things that will kill you than anywhere else," an opinion he expands, saying: "If you are not stung or pronged to death in some unexpected manner, you may be fatally chomped by sharks or crocodiles, or helplessly carried out to sea by irresistible currents, or left to stagger to an unhappy death in the baking outback." Harry Levins, writing in the *St. Louis Dispatch,* warned that "*In a Sunburned Country* is not a travel guide or tour book," yet he recommended Bryson's "witty, curious, and fiendishly observant" book as good traveling company. Robert Zeller in *Antipodes* reported that "Bryson is at his best in portraying the various characters he encounters . . . and in conveying his sense of wonder at his discoveries."

Not all reviewers found *In a Sunburned Country* to be Bryson's most sterling book. David Gates in *Newsweek* found Bryson's "leaden whimsy and faux-conversational tone" to be annoying and "the wealth of gee-whiz factoids [to be] almost . . . worth the trip."

Perhaps the most accurate description of the book, its author, and the subject was from a reviewer in *Publishers Weekly* who commented that "a land as vast as Australia needs a primer to make it accessible, and Bryson has accomplished that with humor and relentless curiosity."

### A Short History of Nearly Everything

In 2004, Bryson published his hefty work, *A Short History of Nearly Everything.* The book, while neither short nor covering anywhere near "everything," is an entertaining overview that provides a grounding in the history of a number of the sciences. The result is that humankind appears to be rather small and insignificant in the face of some of the miraculous and all-encompassing pieces of knowledge that Bryson chooses to share. He begins with an overview of the theories that explain the beginning of the universe, with a focus on Big Bang theory. Other subjects covered include the distances between points in space and how long space travel might take, the theory of relativity and other work by Albert Einstein, the structure of DNA and a history of what we know about it, and the studies and thought of such diverse scientific personalities as Charles Darwin and Edwin Hubble. Over the course of the book, he discusses various theories of physics, biology, astronomy, chemistry, geology, and evolution.

Christopher Martyn, in a review for the *British Medical Journal,* took issue with the lack of hard scientific explanation accompanying Bryson's less serious narrative, dubbing his effort "a bumper book of jaw-dropping facts transformed into a jaunty narrative by a professional writer." However, a reviewer for *Astronomy* found the book "entertaining and accessible," and concluded that "readers fond of Bryson's keen eye for atmospheric detail won't be disappointed." Orla Smith, in a review for *Science,* commented that "although the tome is generally a delight to read, it begins to sag under the weight of the author's daunting task somewhere between quarks and the troposphere. Some parts succeed better than others."

### The Life and Times of the Thunderbolt Kid and Shakespeare

*The Life and Times of the Thunderbolt Kid,* loosely framed as Bryson's memoir, takes a look back at the city of Des Moines, Iowa, during the time that Bryson lived there as a child. The Thunderbolt Kid of the title is the self-appointed persona that Bryson would adopt when he felt the need of some bravado going up against the town bullies, or the town morons, depending on the circumstances. The book includes commentary on both politics and pop culture of the day, giving readers a look at the world of yesteryear through Bryson's witty and sarcastic lens. Allison M. Lewis, writing for *Library Journal,* observed that "the larger world of 1950s America emerges through the lens of 'Billy's' world."

At a time when new books on the life and works of William Shakespeare appear faster than readers can work their way through them, Bryson has thrown his hat into the ring with *Shakespeare: The World as Stage.* Part of the "Penguin Lives" series, the book takes a concise and amusing look at the life of the

Bard. Bryson is up front regarding the difficulties about chronicling Shakespeare's days, pointing out that despite the large number of biographies that have been written on the subject, very few facts are actually known with regards to who Shakespeare was and what he accomplished over the course of his life. Bryson does not claim to have made any earth-shattering discoveries, nor to offer up any original ideas regarding who might have written the works of Shakespeare if Shakespeare himself was not responsible. Instead, he provides a clear and lucid look at the life of the playwright and seeks to set the record straight regarding what is fact and what is simply speculation. Desmond Ryan, in a review for the *Philadelphia Inquirer,* concluded that "Bryson's unassuming and enjoyable survey is a useful introduction that students and playgoers will find handy. It is the work of a man who clearly loves Shakespeare and is bold enough to hold the conviction, heretical as it may be in some quarters, that he actually wrote the immortal texts that bear his name." *Booklist* contributor Ray Olson wrote that "Bryson doesn't seem the obvious choice for a Shakespeare biography, but he does the job quite wonderfully." A reviewer for *Publishers Weekly* wrote: "Bryson is a pleasant and funny guide to a subject at once overexposed and elusive."

### A Really Short History of Nearly Everything

Bryson offers an illustrated abridgement of his classic *A Short History of Nearly Everything* with his 2009 title, *A Really Short History of Nearly Everything.* Geared for middle-grade and junior high readers, this book "addresses the same set of sprawling questions as the original," according to *School Library Journal* reviewer Jeffrey Hastings. Thus, the book goes into the origin and size of the universe, the age of Earth, and the means by which human life emerged from the microbe. It presents such hefty concepts in language adapted for younger readers and in Bryson's "breezy Brit voice," as Hastings further noted.

Ian Chipman, writing in *Booklist,* termed this a "kid-friendly version" of the original, praising Bryson's "accessible, even exciting, writing" in this "irreverent and illuminating edutainment, good for the science-phobic and -centric alike." Hastings also felt that this book "succeeds largely because . . . there's clearly still a curious kid living in Bryson's head." In a similar vein, a *Kirkus Reviews* contributor thought that Bryson "makes a genial guide" in this "tour of time, space and science."

### Seeing Further

Bryson serves as editor for *Seeing Further: The Story of Science and the Royal Society,* a volume celebrating the 350th anniversary of the Royal Society. The book's twenty-two contributors include Richard Dawkins, Margaret Atwood, Richard Holmes, and Neal Stephenson, among others, each of whom write on various aspects of this society formed in 1660 following a presentation on astronomy by the young Christopher Wren. The gathered scholars that night thought that it might be good to form a society for the advancement of science, and thus was born the Royal Society, which has counted among its fellows such scientific luminaries as Isaac Newton, Charles Darwin, Albert Einstein, Robert Hooke, Robert Boyle, Joseph Banks, Humphry Davy, and Alexander Fleming, as well as sixty-nine Nobel laureates. Essays are both generalist and scientific. Atwood, for example, offers one on the origins of the mad scientist motif by Atwood, while geneticist Steven Jones writes on the theory of biodiversity; the social critic Dawkins opines on how Darwin arrived at his theories, and Richard Holmes, a historian, delves into the rage of ballooning in the eighteenth century and what it meant for science.

This work "has something for everyone," thought *Booklist* contributor Gilbert Taylor. Similar praise came from *Maclean's* reviewer Brian Bethune, who felt that "the society richly deserves the stellar array of commentators in this thought-provoking tribute volume." Likewise, a *Kirkus Reviews* contributor dubbed the offerings in this tribute "premium vest-pocket histories of science," while for *Library Journal* writer Gregg Sapp, it is a "semischolarly and at times quaint anthology."

### *At Home*

Bryson provides an informal history of private life with his *At Home,* which is, on one level, a tour of his own home, an old parsonage in England. Each room, and each piece of furniture or domestic bric-a-brac tells a story, and Bryson takes the reader into ten thousand years of domestic life via such objects. For example, in the kitchen Bryson diverges into a discussion of gluttony; the bedroom leads to a discussion of surgery before the modern age; and the scullery takes him into a disquisition on the trying lives servants had. He also goes into the price of various household goods over time, and compares these to the average income, giving readers an index to the relative cost of such items through history and thus the corresponding standard of living.

"Bryson follows his inquisitiveness wherever it goes, from Darwinian evolution to the invention of the lawnmower, while savoring eccentric characters and untoward events," wrote a reviewer for *Publishers Weekly* of *At Home. Policy Review* contributor David R. Henderson also had praise for this work, noting: "Bryson has pulled off a marvelous feat." Henderson went on to explain that via the tour of his Victorian home and what is in it now and what was at one time in such rooms, Bryson "produces an important economic history, only some of which will be familiar to economic historians and almost all of which will be unfamiliar to pretty much everyone else." *Christian Science Monitor* contributor Sean Hughes also had a positive assessment of *At Home,* terming it a "delightful history of household life." Similarly, a *Kirkus Reviews* writer called it "informative, readable and great fun," and *Booklist* reviewer Vanessa Bush found it a "beautifully written ode to the ordinary and overlooked things of everyday life in the home."

### ■ Biographical And Critical Sources

*BOOKS*

Bryson, Bill, *The Lost Continent: Travels in Small-town America,* Harper (New York, NY), 1989.
Bryson, Bill, *The Mother Tongue: English and How It Got That Way,* Morrow (New York, NY), 1990.
Bryson, Bill, *The Life and Times of the Thunderbolt Kid,* Broadway Books (New York, NY), 2006.

*PERIODICALS*

*America,* November 25, 1995, George W. Hunt, review of *Made in America: An Informal History of the English Language in the United States,* p. 2.
*Antipodes,* December, 2000, Robert Zeller, review of *In a Sunburned Country,* p. 175.
*Astronomy,* January 1, 2004, "One Book Fits All," p. 96.
*Booklist,* May 1, 1996, Alice Joyce, review of *Notes from a Small Island: An Affectionate Portrait of Britain,* p. 1486; April, 1998, Ron Antonucci, review of *A Walk in the Woods: Rediscovering America on the Appalachian Trail,* pp. 1297-1299; April 1, 1999, Brad Hooper, review of *I'm a Stranger Here Myself: Notes on Returning to America after Twenty Years Away,* p. 363; August, 1999, Karen Harris, review of *Neither Here nor There: Travels in Europe,* p. 2075; September 15, 1999, Whitney Scott, review of *A Walk in the Woods,* p. 276; September 15, 2000, Brad Hooper, review of *The Best American Travel Writing, 2000,* p. 97; July, 2002, Joanne Wilkinson, review of *Bryson's Dictionary of Troublesome Words,* p. 1805; October 15, 2007, Ray Olson, review of *Shakespeare: The World as Stage,* p. 21; November

15, 2009, Ian Chipman, review of *A Really Short History of Nearly Everything*, p. 39; October 15, 2010, Gilbert Taylor, review of *Seeing Further: The Story of Science, Discovery, and the Genius of the Royal Society*, p. 9; October 15, 2010, Vanessa Bush, review of *At Home: A Short History of Private Life*, p. 9.

*Boston Herald*, June 6, 1999, Erica Noonan, review of *I'm a Stranger Here Myself*, p. 64; June 29, 2000, review of *In a Sunburned Country*, p. 62.

*British Medical Journal*, October 25, 2003, Christopher Martyn, review of *A Short History of Nearly Everything*, p. 994.

*Chicago Tribune*, September 20, 1989, interview with Bill Bryson, pp. 1, 10.

*Christian Science Monitor*, October 15, 2010, Sean Hughes, review of *At Home*.

*Economist*, August 20, 1994, review of *Made in America*, p. 69; November 15, 1997, review of *A Walk in the Woods*, pp. S5-S7.

*Entertainment Weekly*, May 5, 1995, Albert Kim, review of *Made in America*, p. 63; June 7, 1996, Curt Feldman, review of *Notes from a Small Island*, p. 54.

*European Business Journal*, spring, 2002, Lilli Mc-Cowan, review of *Bryson's Dictionary of Troublesome Words*, p. 53.

*Forbes*, May 4, 1998, review of *A Walk in the Woods*, p. S140.

*Fortune*, July 10, 2000, "The Books of Summer," review of *In a Sunburned Country*, p. 314.

*Guardian*, October 16, 1999, review of *I'm a Stranger Here Myself*, p. 11; December 21, 2002, review of *In a Sunburned Country*, p. 14.

*History Today*, June 1, 2010, Andrew Robinson, review of *Seeing Further*, p. 64.

*Houston Chronicle*, July 30, 2000, review of *In a Sunburned Country*, p. 14.

*Insight on the News*, October 16, 2000, Rex Roberts, review of *In a Sunburned Country*, p. 33.

*Kirkus Reviews*, September 1, 2009, review of *A Really Short History of Nearly Everything*; August 15, 2010, review of *At Home*; September 1, 2010, review of *Seeing Further*.

*Library Journal*, April 1, 1998, Nancy J. Moeckel, review of *A Walk in the Woods*, pp. 114-116; May 15, 1999, Wilda Williams, review of *I'm a Stranger Here Myself*, p. 114; September 1, 1999, Carolyn Alexander, review of *Neither Here nor There*, p. 255; March 1, 2000, review of *In a Sunburned Country*, p. S1; June 1, 2000, Joseph L. Carlson, review of *In a Sunburned Country*, p. 174; December, 2000, Robert Zeller, review of *In a Sunburned Country*, p. 175; September 15, 2001, Nancy Pearl, review of *A Walk in the Woods*, p. 61; August, 2002, review of *Bryson's Dictionary of Troublesome Words*; September 1, 2006, Alison M. Lewis, review of

*The Life and Times of the Thunderbolt Kid*, p. 155; September 1, 2010, Frederick J. Augustyn, review of *At Home*, p. 118; October 15, 2010, Gregg Sapp, review of *Seeing Further*, p. 100.

*Los Angeles Times*, August 23, 1990, Wand Urbanska, review of *The Lost Continent*, pp. E1, E13.

*Maclean's*, January 31, 2011, Brian Bethune, review of *Seeing Further*, p. 61.

*New Republic*, August 6, 2001, Nicholas Howe, review of *The Best American Travel Writing, 2000*, p. 34.

*New Statesman*, December 12, 1997, Albert Scardino, review of *A Walk in the Woods*, pp. 43-45.

*New Statesman & Society*, October 4, 1991, Marek Kohn, review of *Neither Here nor There*, pp. 35-36; September 15, 1995, Boyd Tonkin, review of *Notes from a Small Island*, p. 34.

*Newsweek*, August 14, 1989, Jim Miller, review of *The Lost Continent: Travels in Small-town America*, p. 51; June 5, 2000, David Gates, review of *In a Sunburned Country*, p. 73.

*New York*, September 18, 1989, Chris Smith, review of *The Lost Continent*, p. 26.

*New York Times*, June 5, 2000, Janet Maslin, review of *In a Sunburned Country*, p. B6.

*New York Times Book Review*, September 17, 1989, Michele Slung, review of *The Lost Continent*, p. 26; August 5, 1990, Burt Hochberg, review of *The Mother Tongue*, p. 8; May 30, 1999, Elizabeth Gleick, review of *I'm a Stranger Here Myself*, p. 10; August 20, 2000, Annette Kobak, review of *In a Sunburned Country*, p. 105; December 3, 2000, "Travel Review," p. 58.

*People*, April 17, 1995, Elaine Kahn, review of *Made in America*, p. 32.

*Philadelphia Inquirer*, November 28, 2007, Desmond Ryan, review of *Shakespeare*.

*Policy Review*, February, 2011, David R. Henderson, "Home Economics," review of *At Home*, P. 108.

*Publishers Weekly*, February 13, 1995, review of *Made in America*, p. 71; March 4, 1996, review of *Notes from a Small Island*, p. 40; February 23, 1998, review of *A Walk in the Woods*, p. 57; May 4, 1998, Norman Oder, "Bill Bryson: An Ex-expat Traveling Light," author interview, pp. 191-193; March 22, 1999, review of *I'm a Stranger Here Myself*, p. 76; May 15, 2000, review of *In a Sunburned Country*, p. 95; September 18, 2000, review of *The Best American Travel Writing, 2000*, p. 96; June 3, 2002, review of *Bryson's Dictionary of Troublesome Words*, p. 75; September 3, 2007, review of *Shakespeare*, p. 47; August 9, 2010, review of *At Home*, p. 41.

*St. Louis Post-Dispatch*, June 18, 2000, review of *In a Sunburned Country*, p. F8; May 30, 2001, Harry Levins, review of *In a Sunburned Country*, p. E1.

*School Library Journal*, February 1, 2010, Jeffrey Hastings, review of *A Really Short History of Nearly Everything*, p. 128.

*Science*, February 13, 2004, Orla Smith, "Moving Mountains," p. 960.

*Spectator*, July 22, 2000, Michael Davie, review of *Down Under*, p. 35; December 15, 2001, Christopher Howse, review of *Bryson's Dictionary of Troublesome Words*, p. 61.

*Times* (London, England), July 5, 2000, James Bone, "Our Rumpled Tour-guide to the Familiar," p. B12.

*Times Literary Supplement*, October 18, 1991, Dervla Murphy, review of *Neither Here nor There*, p. 28; July 28, 2000, Robert Drewe, review of *Down Under*, p. 8.

*U.S. News and World Report*, June 12, 2000, Holly J. Morris, review of *In a Sunburned Country*, p. 69.

*Wall Street Journal*, May 14, 1999, Kate Flatley, review of *I'm a Stranger Here Myself*, p. W9.

*Washington Post*, October 18, 2000, Elizabeth Ward, review of *In a Sunburned Country*, p. C8.

ONLINE

*Bill Bryson Home Page*, http://www.billbryson.co.uk (July 11, 2011).

*Random House Web site*, http://www.randomhouse.com/ (November 9, 2003), "Bill Bryson."*

# Michael Burlingame

## 1941-

■ **Personal**

Born September 13, 1941, in Washington, DC; son of Harry (a civil servant) and Estelle (a homemaker) Burlingame; married Sara Lee Silberman (divorced, 1980); married Lois Erickson McDonald; children: Rebecca, Jessica. *Ethnicity:* "White Anglo-Saxon Protestant." *Education:* Princeton University, B.A., 1964; Johns Hopkins University, Ph.D., 1971. *Hobbies and other interests:* Opera, concerts, hockey, lacrosse, tennis.

■ **Addresses**

*Home*—Springfield, IL. *Office*—History Department, University Hall, Bldg. 3050, University of Illinois at Springfield, One University Plaza, Springfield, Illinois 62703-5407. *E-mail*—mburl2@uis.edu.

■ **Career**

Writer, educator, historian. Connecticut College, New London, professor of history, 1968-2001, Buckley Sadowski Professor of History Emeritus, 2001—; University of Illinois at Springfield, Chancellor Naomi B. Lynn Distinguished Chair in Lincoln Studies, 2009—. Abraham Lincoln Institute of the Mid-Atlantic, member of board of directors; Abraham Lincoln Studies Center, member of board of advisers.

■ **Member**

National Association of Scholars, Historical Society (member of board of governors), Abraham Lincoln Association (member of board of directors).

■ **Awards, Honors**

Abraham Lincoln Association Prize, 1995, for *An Oral History of Lincoln;* Lincoln Diploma of Honor, Lincoln Memorial University, 1998; inductee, Lincoln Academy of Illinois, 2009; cowinner, Abraham Lincoln Institute book prize, Russell P. Strange Book Award, Illinois State Historical Society, and Lincoln Prize, Gilder-Lehrman Institute for American History and Gettysburg College, 2010, all for *Abraham Lincoln: A Life.*

■ **Writings**

*The Inner World of Abraham Lincoln,* University of Illinois Press (Champaign, IL), 1994.

(Editor) *An Oral History of Lincoln: John G. Nicolay's Interviews and Essays,* Southern Illinois University Press (Carbondale, IL), 1996.

(Editor, with John R. Turner Ettlinger) *Inside Lincoln's White House: The Complete Civil War Diary of John Hay,* Southern Illinois University Press (Carbondale, IL), 1997.

(Editor) *Lincoln Observed: Civil War Dispatches of Noah Brooks,* Johns Hopkins University Press (Baltimore, MD), 1998.

(Editor) *Lincoln's Journalist: John Hay's Anonymous Writings for the Press, 1860-1864,* Southern Illinois University Press (Carbondale, IL), 1998.

(Editor) Walter B. Stevens, *A Reporter's Lincoln,* University of Nebraska Press (Lincoln, NE), 1998.

(Editor) *With Lincoln in the White House: Letters, Memoranda, and Other Writings of John G. Nicolay, 1860-1865,* Southern Illinois University Press (Carbondale, IL), 2000.

(Editor) William O. Stoddard, *Inside the White House in War Times: Memoirs and Reports of Lincoln's Secretary,* University of Nebraska Press (Lincoln, NE), 2000.

(Editor) *At Lincoln's Side: John Hay's Civil War Correspondence and Selected Writings,* Southern Illinois University Press (Carbondale, IL), 2000.

(Editor) Benjamin P. Thomas, *"Lincoln's Humor" and Other Essays,* University of Illinois Press (Urbana, IL), 2002.

(Editor) Jesse W. Weik, *The Real Lincoln: A Portrait,* University of Nebraska Press (Lincoln, NE), 2002.

(Editor) William O. Stoddard, *Dispatches from Lincoln's White House: The Anonymous Civil War Journalism of Presidential Secretary William O. Stoddard,* University of Nebraska Press (Lincoln, NE), 2002.

(Editor) *Abraham Lincoln: The Observations of John G. Nicolay and John Hay,* Southern Illinois University Press (Carbondale, IL), 2007.

*Abraham Lincoln: A Life,* Johns Hopkins University Press (Baltimore, MD), 2008.

*Lincoln and the Civil War,* Southern Illinois University Press (Carbondale, IL), 2011.

Contributor of articles to professional journals.

## ■ Sidelights

Michael Burlingame is a historian whose professional career has been devoted to researching about the life and times of President Abraham Lincoln. The May Buckley Sadowski Professor of History Emeritus at Connecticut College, where he taught from 1968 to 2001, he became in 2009 the Chancellor Naomi B. Lynn Distinguished Chair in Lincoln Studies at the University of Illinois at Springfield. Burlingame has written several works on Lincoln, including the 1994 title, *The Inner World of Abraham Lincoln,* the award-wining 2008 biography, *Abraham Lincoln: A Life,* and his 2011 study, *Lincoln and the Civil War.* He has also edited numerous volumes on aspects of Lincoln, including his years in the White House, remembrances by close associates, and the president's sense of humor. Burlingame's interest in the sixteenth president of the United States was spurred as a college freshman at Princeton University where he took a class on the Civil War taught by the Lincoln scholar David Herbert Donald, who later made Burlingame a research assistant. After earning his doctorate at Johns Hopkins University, Burlingame joined the faculty of Connecticut College. Burlingame once told *CA:* "I write about Abraham Lincoln because I like and admire him and because, improbable as it may sound, his life story has never been told adequately before. My principal contribution to the field is my willingness to dig up new information by visiting archives and libraries that others have neglected."

### *The Inner World of Abraham Lincoln*

In his first Lincoln publication, *The Inner World of Abraham Lincoln,* Burlingame turns to psychobiography, as he notes in his introduction, to explain attitudes and emotions of the president, from his hatred of slavery to his attitude toward women and difficult relations with his wife, his bouts of anger and cruelty, his role as a father to his children, and his strongly felt ambitions. Burlingame synthesizes the work of other historians who have taken a psychological look at Lincoln, including Charles B. Strozier, who wrote *Lincoln's Quest for Union.* The author also employs contemporary papers, including those of Lincoln's law partner, William H. Herndon, and newspaper accounts of the time. Thus, rather than viewing Lincoln's life from the vantage point of the president himself, Burlingame examines it from that of what his contemporaries experienced and later recalled. As *Journal of American History* writer William Hanchett noted, Burlingame subscribes to Herndon's oft-contested description of Lincoln's marriage to Mary Todd as a domestic nightmare. Hanchett found this extensive and final chapter of the book the "most controversial."

*Library Journal* contributor Boyd Childress felt that Burlingame's "analysis is an important new look at the man who shaped the course of a nation in peril." *American Heritage* reviewer Geoffrey C. Ward, however, was less impressed with this biography, describing it as a "grab bag of evidence, some of it fresh and fascinating . . . but adding up to a good deal less than its compiler repeatedly promises." For example, Ward points to Burlingame's chapter on Lincoln's aversion to or dislike of women, stating that the author "demonstrates only that he was sometimes shy and awkward in their presence." Similarly, a chapter on Lincoln's supposed anger and cruelty "actually shows precious little 'cruelty'," according to Ward. Hanchett, on the other hand, had a much higher assessment of *The Inner World of Abraham Lincoln,* noting that it is "original and important." Hanchett added: "The Lincoln who walks out of its pages is a real person, a fallible but admirable human being. That is a measure of what Burlingame has accomplished."

### *An Oral History of Lincoln* and *Lincoln Observed*

Burlingame has edited numerous volumes on Lincoln, most of them remembrances by his private secretaries or journalists. In *An Oral History of Lincoln: John G. Nicolay's Interviews and Essays,* Burlingame gathers interviews conducted by Lincoln's private secretary from 1860 to 1865, John G. Nicolay, done for an official biography of Lincoln that Nicolay wrote with fellow secretary John Hay. "Burlingame's editorial work is solid," noted *Civil War History* contributor Judith A. Rice. "The introduction presents a brief biographical sketch of Nicolay and discusses his approach toward oral history. . . . Lincoln scholars should find this volume useful because of the information it brings together in one place and stimulating because of the larger questions it raises concerning the use of historical evidence."

Burlingame also serves as editor for *Lincoln Observed: Civil War Dispatches of Noah Brooks.* Brooks was an American journalist and author who first met and befriended Lincoln during the 1856 presidential campaign. Representing a California newspaper, Brooks served as a correspondent in Washington during the Civil war and wrote 258 articles based on personal weekly visits to the Lincoln White House. A *Publishers Weekly* reviewer observed that Burlingame "salvages these important dispatches for posterity, providing a riveting day-to-day insider's view of Lincoln's dealing with important personalities and issues." Similarly, *Booklist* contributor Jay Freeman felt these "candid vignettes . . . provide a revealing portrait of Lincoln." Freeman called *Lincoln Observed* a "compact, readable, and highly informative work."

### Inside the White House in War Times and Dispatches from Lincoln's White House

Burlingame also edited *Inside the White House in War Times: Memoirs and Reports of Lincoln's Secretary.* The private secretary in question is William O. Stoddard, who served as assistant to Lincoln's two secretaries during the Civil War. Here Burlingame gathers together in one volume the memoir that Stoddard published in 1890, along with thirteen sketches he published a newspaper in 1866 regarding his years in the White House working for Lincoln. *Journal of Southern History* reviewer Lucas E. Morel noted of this work that it is "yet another product of what has become a cottage industry for Michael Burlingame: keenly edited and footnoted reprints of the writings of President Lincoln's earliest commentators."

In *Dispatches from Lincoln's White House: The Anonymous Civil War Journalism of Presidential Secretary William O. Stoddard,* Burlingame collects 120 of the anonymous newspaper reports that Stoddard wrote during the Civil War. Writing in *Presidential Studies Quarterly,* Michael E. Long observed that "Burlingame's latest work is thoroughly researched and well documented." Long added: "Twenty-five pages of endnotes guide the reader to a variety of primary and secondary sources. . . . [Burlingame's] interpretation of the Stoddard dispatches helps us understand Abraham Lincoln and the complex historical and political environment in which he lived." Further praise came from *Journal of Southern History* writer Silvana R. Siddali, who felt that this book "continues Michael Burlingame's valuable work of editing primary sources related to the Lincoln administration."

### Abraham Lincoln

Burlingame retired in 2001 from Connecticut College in order to devote himself fully to his long-planned multivolume biography of Lincoln, *Abraham Lincoln,* which appeared in time for the bicentennial year of Abraham Lincoln's birth. Burlingame's effort is large in scale, running to two thousand pages, including extensive notes and index. The biography draws on Burlingame's several decades of Lincoln research, including contemporary accounts and reminiscences, newspaper accounts of the time, Lincoln's previously lost early journalism, notes from earlier Lincoln biographers, and manuscript archives. "What sets Burlingame's magnum opus apart is its extensive reliance upon 'reminiscence material': namely, the recollections of contemporaries of Lincoln whose encounters and conversations with him were documented years after—in many cases, decades after—their interaction occurred," noted *Books & Culture* reviewer Lucas E. Morel. Burlingame's years of editing the memoirs and reminiscences of private secretaries to Lincoln or of journalists who covered him for the newspapers, such as John G. Nicolay, John Hay, William O. Stoddard, and Noah Brooks, aided greatly in the depth of research included in this work. In the first volume of the biography, Burlingame deals with Lincoln's childhood and his harsh, bleak years as a farm boy in Indiana and Illinois, followed by his legal training, and then the drive for political office that eventually led to a term in Congress in the 1840s; the second volume carries the story forward to Lincoln's life during his presidency and the Civil War, providing new insights into Lincoln's relationships with his associates as well as political rivals and detractors, and a portrait of his domestic life, including the tragic deaths of two sons from illness and his stormy marriage to Mary Todd.

*Atlantic* contributor Christopher Hitchens noted: "No review could do complete justice to the magnificent two-volume biography that has been so well-wrought by Michael Burlingame." Similarly, Morel felt that "Lincoln and his world come to life in Burlingame's biography with all the virtue and vice, reason and emotion, that wrestled for supremacy in the burgeoning American republic." *Journal of Southern History* Nicole Etcheson found Burlingame's biography "monumental," further noting that it "must certainly be considered the definitive one." A contributor to the *New York Times Book Review* also had praise for this biography, terming it a "magisterial enterprise . . . [that] is not likely to be soon overtaken in scope or timeliness." Similarly, *Publishers Weekly* reviewer James L. Swanson called Burlingame's study "the most meticulously researched Lincoln biography ever written." Swanson added: "This book supplants Sandburg and supersedes all other biographies. Future Lincoln books cannot be written without it, and from no other book can a general reader learn so much about Abraham Lincoln."

## ■ Biographical And Critical Sources

*PERIODICALS*

*American Heritage,* February, 1995, Geoffrey C. Ward, review of *The Inner World of Abraham Lincoln,* p. 14.

*Atlantic,* May 22, 2009, Christopher Hitchens, review of *Abraham Lincoln: A Life.*

*Booklist,* May 1, 1998, Jay Freeman, review of *Lincoln Observed: Civil War Dispatches of Noah Brooks,* p. 1496.

*Books & Culture,* November, 2009, "Bicentennial Abe," review of *Abraham Lincoln,* p. 16.

*Civil War History,* June, 1997, Judith A. Rice, review of *An Oral History of Lincoln: John G. Nicolay's Interviews and Essays,* p. 176; September, 1998, Thomas R. Turner, review of *Inside Lincoln's White House: The Complete Civil War Diary of John Hay,* p. 226.

*Historian,* January, 2002, DeAnne Blanton, review of *Inside the White House in War Times: Memoirs and Reports of Lincoln's Secretary,* p. 427.

*Journal of Southern History,* November, 2001, Lucas E. Morel, review of *Inside the White House in War Times,* p. 876; November, 2003, Silvana R. Siddali, review of *Dispatches from Lincoln's White House: The Anonymous Civil War Journalism of Presidential Secretary William O. Stoddard,* p. 937; May, 2010, Nicole Etcheson, "Abraham Lincoln and the Nation's Greatest Quarrel: A Review Essay," review of *Abraham Lincoln,* p. 401.

*Library Journal,* October 1, 1994, Boyd Childress, review of *The Inner World of Abraham Lincoln,* p. 88; January 1, 1999, Brooks D. Simpson, review of *A Reporter's Lincoln,* p. 124; February 1, 1999, Grant A. Fredericksen, review of *Lincoln's Journalist: John Hay's Anonymous Writings for the Press, 1860-1864,* p. 106.

*New York Times Book Review,* February 8, 2009, "Lincoln Monuments," review of *Abraham Lincoln,* p. 1.

*Presidential Studies Quarterly,* summer, 1997, Charles B. Strozier, review of *An Oral History of Abraham Lincoln,* p. 601; June, 2004, Michael E. Long, review of *Dispatches from Lincoln's White House,* p. 465.

*Publishers Weekly,* May 4, 1998, review of *Lincoln Observed,* p. 199; November 3, 2008, James L. Swanson, review of *Abraham Lincoln,* p. 50.

*White House Studies,* summer, 2003, William D. Pederson, review of *Lincoln Observed,* p. 371.

*ONLINE*

*Day.com,* http://www.theday.com/ (May 2, 2011), Kenton Robinson, "Five Questions with Lincoln Scholar Michael Burlingame."

*Michael Burlingame Home Page,* http://www.michael burlingame.com (July 22, 2011).

*News at Illinois Springfield,* http://news.uis.edu/ (May 27, 2009), "Renowned Lincoln Scholar Michael Burlingame Accepts Lincoln Chair."

# George W. Bush

## 1946-

■ **Also Known As**

George Walker Bush

■ **Personal**

Born July 6, 1946, in New Haven, CT; son of George Herbert Walker (a businessman, diplomat, government official, and president of the United States) and Barbara (a homemaker) Bush; married Laura Welch (a librarian and teacher); children: Barbara, Jenna. *Education:* Yale University, B.A., 1968; Harvard University, M.B.A., 1975. *Politics:* Republican. *Religion:* Methodist. *Hobbies and other interests:* Golf, baseball, fishing, hunting.

■ **Addresses**

*Home*—Dallas, TX. *Office*—Office of George W. Bush, P.O. Box 259000, Dallas, TX 75225-9000.

■ **Career**

Writer and motivational speaker. Bush Exploration, founder and chief executive officer, 1975-83; Spectrum 7, chief executive officer, 1983-87; Texas Rangers Baseball Organization, managing general partner, 1989-94; governor of Texas, 1995-2000; president of the United States, 2001-09. Republican nominee for U.S. House of Representatives, 1978; George H.W. Bush presidential campaign, senior advisor, 1988; Republican National Convention, cochair, 1996. Also the subject of the documentary *George W. Bush: Faith in the White House. Military service:* Texas Air National Guard, 1968-73, F-102 fighter pilot.

■ **Awards, Honors**

Big D Award, Dallas All Sports Association, 1989; Person of the Year, *TIME,* 2004.

■ **Writings**

(With Karen Hughes) *A Charge to Keep,* William Morrow (New York, NY), 1999.

*Our Mission and Our Moment: Speeches since the Attacks of September 11,* The White House (Washington, DC), 2001.

*United We Stand: A Message for All Americans,* Mundus (Ann Arbor, MI), 2001.

(Edited by Jacob Weisberg, with a foreword by Garry Trudeau) *More George W. Bushisms: More of Slate's Accidental Wit and Wisdom of Our Forty-third President,* Fireside (New York, NY), 2002.

(Edited by Jacob Weisberg, with a foreword by Al Franken) *Still More George W. Bushisms: Neither in French, nor in English, nor in Mexican,* Simon & Schuster (New York, NY), 2003.

*We Will Prevail: President George W. Bush on War, Terrorism, and Freedom,* Continuum (New York, NY), 2003.

*George W. Bush Speaks to America: Speeches,* Merril Press (Bellevue, WA), 2004.

*George W. Bush on God and Country,* Allegiance Press (Fairfax, VA), 2004.

*The Quotable George W. Bush: A Portrait in His Own Words,* Andrews McMeel (Kansas City, MO), 2004.

*The George W. Bush Foreign Policy Reader: Presidential Speeches and Commentary,* M.E. Sharpe (Armonk, NY), 2005.

(Edited by Jacob Weisberg) *George W. Bushisms V: New Ways to Harm Our Country,* Fireside (New York, NY), 2005.

*George W. Bush Out of Office Countdown Handbook: Hand in There! It's Almost Over,* Sourcebooks Hysteria (Naperville, IL), 2006.

*The Selected Quotations of George W. Bush,* Sabre Press (Troy, MI), 2007.

(Edited by Jacob Weisberg) *The Ultimate George W. Bushisms: Bush at War (with the English Language),* Simon & Schuster (New York, NY), 2007.

*Decision Points* (memoir), Crown (New York, NY), 2010.

## ■ Sidelights

President George W. Bush's campaign autobiography, written with his press secretary, Karen Hughes, outlines the president's personal and political development. *A Charge to Keep,* released in the middle of the 2000 presidential campaign, includes many memories of the prominent family into which Bush was born in Connecticut. His real home, however, became the state of Texas, where the family moved in 1948 and where Bush grew up. After attending Yale University and Harvard Business School, Bush returned to Texas, where he built a career in the oil business and later owned the Texas Rangers baseball team. Elected governor of Texas in 1994, Bush focused on education reform and tax cuts in the state. He was reelected in 1998 with nearly seventy percent of the vote, making him the first Texas governor to win consecutive four-year terms. Bush's popular leadership in Texas, along with his family connections, made him a powerful figure in the Republican Party, which nominated him for president in 2000.

In *A Charge to Keep,* Bush deals frankly with his much-publicized youthful indiscretions, discusses his maturation, and attempts to define his policy goals, particularly his hallmark "compassionate conservatism." Bush chronicles the many important events in his life, including his marriage to Laura Welch, a pivotal encounter with the Reverend Billy Graham, and his successful efforts to cut taxes in Texas and make sweeping education reforms.

As is typical with campaign memoirs, reviewers tended to be lukewarm toward *A Charge to Keep* (whose title was taken from a Methodist evangelical hymn). Many felt the book was hastily written, mostly by ghostwriter Hughes. Lars-Erik Nelson in the *New York Review of Books* called it a "slapdash affair" that gives little evidence of the fact that Bush is indeed "an intelligent man, with a formidable memory, enormous charm, and a sense of humor." Zachary Karabell, in a critique in the *Los Angeles Times Book Review,* charged that the book "avoids moral subtlety or human complexity," but he pointed out that "there are glimmers of content, especially . . . when Bush outlines his policy of 'compassionate conservatism.' It's vision lite, but it is not completely visionless."

Although *New York Times Book Review* critic Adam Clyer expressed disappointment with the book's political content, he suggested that Bush is at his best when he reveals his private self, as in the passages that deal with his grief over the death of his young sister Robin or his shock at witnessing racist behavior in the mid-1960s. This "simple, not very deep tone rings true," wrote Clymer. *New York Times* writer Frank Bruni, however, considered Bush's political message less doubtful. *A Charge to Keep,* in his view, "reads . . . like an astute act of political positioning" and reveals its author as "someone willing to chart a politically risky course for something he believes is right."

### Our Mission and Our Moment and *George W. Bush Speaks to America*

Published in 2001, Bush's next book, *Our Mission and Our Moment: Speeches since the Attacks of September 11,* is a compilation of the speeches Bush gave during his first term in office as U.S. president. The book presents the speech Bush gave in front of a joint session of Congress following the September 11, 2001, terrorist attacks. The volume also includes a timeline tracing events beginning with the attacks and ending nine days later. Other books by Bush include *United We Stand: A Message for All Americans,* also published in 2001, and *We Will Prevail: President George W. Bush on War, Terrorism, and Freedom,* which was released in 2003.

A second collection of Bush's speeches as president was released as *George W. Bush Speaks to America: Speeches* in 2004. Also published that year was *George W. Bush on God and Country,* an exploration of Bush's politics and faith. Notably, 2004, the eve of Bush's second term, was a prolific year, as he also released *The Quotable George W. Bush: A Portrait in His Own Words.* Given that 2004 was an election year for Bush, it is likely that these books served the same purpose that *A Charge to Keep* did during his 2000 presidential campaign.

### The George W. Bush Foreign Policy Reader

The following year, after commencing his second term as president, Bush released *The George W. Bush Foreign Policy Reader: Presidential Speeches and Commentary.* Aside from being a collection of speeches pertaining to foreign policy, the volume also includes an introductory essay to each chapter and quotes from American foreign policy experts. Topics addressed include the war on terrorism, global and domestic security issues, and diplomatic relationships between the United States and Asia, Europe, and the Middle East.

However, a contributor to *Reference & Research Book News* felt that the book was missing valuable information, such as administration documents that "might have shed further light on Bush's approach."

### George W. Bush

In addition to these books, Bush was featured as the subject of the documentary *George W. Bush: Faith in the White House,* which explores the role of religion in Bush's presidency. Discussing the documentary online for *Christianity Today,* Mark Moring noted that it offers "a fine and fitting conclusion." However, he also wished the filmmakers "had remained focused on the title—and not tried to set it up as an 'alternative'" to Michael Moore's documentary *Fahrenheit 911.* Despite this, Moring noted that "a movie about our President's strong faith is a valid project, and one that should inspire us all."

### Decision Points

In Bush's 2010 memoir, *Decision Points,* he explains the difficult choices he has had to make during his presidency and his life. The book is not a chronological memoir but an arrangement of the topics Bush felt were important to address. He candidly admits where he believes he did not make the right choice but also defends the decisions he believes were right. As a whole, the book evokes the pressure of the challenging and sometimes ambivalent task of being the president of the United States.

Reviewing the work in the *Weekly Standard* contributor Philip Terzian said of the work: "It successfully conveys what we know of the quality and character of George W. Bush, and the sound of his voice. Bush is neither omnipotent nor especially defensive in tone; he admits to mistakes and misgivings, and acknowledges regret and uncertainty. He is careful to explain the principles that informed his actions, and describe the options and dissenting arguments as he reached those decisions." A *Kirkus Reviews* contributor said that in the work, Bush "accepts blame for a number of mistakes and misjudgments, while also standing up for decisions he felt were right." The contributor described the work as "honest, of course, but also surprisingly approachable and engaging." George C. Edwards III, a contributor to *Presidential Studies Quarterly,* observed: "As the former president hopes, reading this material will be a useful resource for students of the first decade of the twenty-first century. From stem cell research to the interrogation of prisoners, we see a

president weighing options, many of which are unattractive, and doing the best he can in a complex and uncertain environment." Daniel Weiss, a contributor to *Campaigns and Elections,* explained: "Most of *Decision Points . . .* is naturally concerned with the momentous events that dominated his two terms as president—9/11, the Afghanistan and Iraq wars, Hurricane Katrina and the financial crisis. But it also includes clues about how Bush evolved."

### ■ Biographical And Critical Sources

*BOOKS*

Alterman, Eric, and Mark J. Green, *The Book on Bush: How George W. (Mis)leads America,* Viking Penguin (New York, NY), 2004.

Begala, Paul, *Is Our Children Learning? The Case against George W. Bush,* Simon & Schuster (New York, NY), 2000.

Begala, Paul, *It's Still the Economy, Stupid: George W. Bush, America's CEO,* Simon & Schuster (New York, NY), 2002.

Bush, George W., and Karen Hughes, *A Charge to Keep,* William Morrow (New York, NY), 1999.

Corn, David, *The Lies of George W. Bush: Mastering the Politics of Deception,* Crown (New York, NY), 2003.

*Encyclopedia of World Biography, Supplement,* Volume 21, Gale (Detroit, MI), 2001.

Greenstein, Fred, *The George W. Bush Presidency: An Early Assessment,* Johns Hopkins University Press (Baltimore, MD), 2003.

Hatfield, James, *Fortunate Son: George W. Bush and the Making of an American President,* Soft Skull Press (Brooklyn, NY), 2002.

Ivins, Molly, and Lou Dubose, *Shrub: The Short but Happy Political Life of George W. Bush,* Vintage (New York, NY), 2000.

Ivins, Molly, and Lou Dubose, *Bushwhacked: Life in George W. Bush's America,* Random House (New York, NY), 2003.

Lind, Michael, *Made in Texas: George W. Bush and the Southern Takeover of American Politics,* Basic Books (New York, NY), 2003.

Mansfield, Stephen, *Faith of George W. Bush,* Tarcher, 2003.

Mitchell, Elizabeth, *W: Revenge of the Bush Dynasty,* Hyperion Press (New York, NY), 2000.

Phillips, Kevin, *American Dynasty: Aristocracy, Fortune, and the Politics of Deceit in the House of Bush,* Viking Penguin (New York, NY), 2004.

Scheer, Christopher, Robert Scheer, and Lakshmi Chaudhry, *The Five Biggest Lies Bush Told Us about Iraq,* Seven Stories Press (New York, NY), 2003.

Suskind, Ron, *The Price of Loyalty: George W. Bush, the White House, and the Education of Paul O'Neill,* Simon & Schuster (New York, NY), 2004.

Vidal, Gore, *Dreaming War: Blood for Oil and the Cheney-Bush Junta,* Thunder's Mouth Press (New York, NY), 2002.

Woodward, Bob, *Bush at War,* Simon & Schuster (New York, NY), 2003.


*PERIODICALS*

*Campaigns & Elections,* November 1, 2010, Daniel Weiss, review of *Decision Points.*

*Entertainment Weekly,* January 14, 2000, Bruce Fretts, "Meet the Prez?," p. 68.

*Kirkus Reviews,* December 15, 2010, review of *Decision Points.*

*Los Angeles Times Book Review,* January 16, 2000, Zachary Karabell, "Yeah, Yeah, Yeah," pp. 7-8.

*National Review,* December 31, 1999, Ramesh Ponnuru, interview with George W. Bush, p. 33.

*New York Review of Books,* February 24, 2000, Lars-Erik Nelson, "Legacy," pp. 4-6.

*New York Times,* November 15, 1999, Frank Bruni, "Book Lets Bush Explain His Life and His Politics," p. A20.

*New York Times Book Review,* December 5, 1999, Adam Clymer, review of *A Charge to Keep,* p. 52.

*Presidential Studies Quarterly,* June 1, 2011, George C. Edwards, review of *Decision Points,* p. 411.

*Publishers Weekly,* November 3, 2003, review of *Still More George W. Bushisms: Neither in French, nor in English, nor in Mexican,* p. 65.

*Reference & Research Book News,* August 1, 2005, review of *The George W. Bush Foreign Policy Reader: Presidential Speeches and Commentary,* p. 70.

*Texas Monthly,* June, 1999, Pamela Colloff, "The Son Rises," p. 105.

*Time,* June 21, 1999, "How George Got His Groove," p. 4; August 7, 2000, Walter Isaacson, interview with George W. Bush, p. 55.

*United Press International,* September 27, 2001, "Bush Speech on Attacks to Be Instant Book."

*Weekly Standard,* December 6, 1999, Andrew Ferguson, review of *A Charge to Keep;* November 22, 2010, "Only Yesterday; a President Remembers What Some Have Forgotten."


*ONLINE*

*Christianity Today,* http://www.christianitytoday.com/ (January 1, 2004), Mark Moring, review of *George W. Bush: Faith in the White House.*

*White House Web site,* http://www.whitehouse.gov/ (February 3, 2002), biography of George W. Bush; (August 25, 2011), biography of George W. Bush.*

# Victor D. Cha

## 1961-

### ■ Personal

Born 1961, in NY. *Education:* Columbia University, B.A., 1983, M.I.A, 1988, Ph.D., 1994; University of Oxford, M.A., 1986.

### ■ Addresses

*Office*—Department of Government, 681 ICC, Georgetown University, Washington, DC 20057. *E-mail*—chav@georgetown.edu.

### ■ Career

Political scientist, educator, and writer. Georgetown University, Washington, DC, professor of government, 1995—; Center for Strategic & International Studies, senior advisor and Korea Chair.

### ■ Awards, Honors

Recipient of numerous academic awards including the two Fulbright scholarships and MacArthur Foundation fellowships.

### ■ Writings

*Alignment Despite Antagonism: The U.S.-Korea-Japan Security Triangle,* Stanford University Press (Stanford, CA), 1999.

(With David Kang) *Nuclear North Korea: A Debate on Engagement Strategies,* Columbia University Press (New York, NY), 2004.

*Beyond the Final Score: The Politics of Sport in Asia,* Columbia University Press (New York, NY), 2009.

(Contributor, with others) *Asia's Response to Climate Change and Natural Disasters: Implications for an Evolving Regional Architecture,* edited by Robert S. Wang and Jeffrey D. Bean, Center for Strategic & International Studies (Washington, DC), 2010.

### ■ Sidelights

Victor D. Cha authored *Nuclear North Korea: A Debate on Engagement Strategies,* with the scholar David Kang. The book is organized as a debate between Cha and Kang regarding how the United States should approach the problem of North Korea.

Reviewing the work in the *Korean Studies* journal, contributor Leon V. Sigal assessed: "In *Nuclear North Korea,* Victor Cha and David Kang make a commendable effort to get beyond the bumper-sticker sloganeering that passes for public discourse in the United States to conduct a civilized debate on what to do about North Korea. For the most part, the book lives up to their aspirations 'to produce scholarship on Korea that is empirically rich, analytical rigorous, and policy-relevant.'" *Journal of East Asian Studies* contributor Peter Sylvestre remarked: "This book is refreshing in that each author has reached a logical, sound conclusion, both of which fortuitously converge. If George W. Bush is to read one book this year, I recommend *Nuclear North Korea.*" *Pacific Affairs* contributor Ruediger Frank lauded: "The book is good and extraordinary. It is a delight to read, and the authors should not be too disappointed to find it on the book shelves of their colleagues at universities and think tanks or as a textbook in international relations and East Asian politics courses, rather than under the pillows of world leaders."

## ■ Biographical And Critical Sources

*PERIODICALS*

*Economist* (U.S.), January 24, 2004, review of *Nuclear North Korea: A Debate on Engagement Strategies*, p. 74.

*Journal of East Asian Studies,* January 1, 2005, Peter Sylvestre, review of *Nuclear North Korea.*

*Korean Studies,* January 1, 2005, Leon V. Sigal, review of *Nuclear North Korea,* p. 170.

*Nation,* June 7, 2004, Selig S. Harrison, review of *Nuclear North Korea,* p. 23.

*Pacific Affairs,* September 22, 2005, Ruediger Frank, review of *Nuclear North Korea,* p. 504; March 1, 2010, Hyung-Gu Lynn, review of *Beyond the Final Score: The Politics of Sport in Asia.*

*Washington Post,* May 1, 2007, Glenn Kessler, "NSC Post a Real-World Lesson for Cha."

*ONLINE*

*Center for Strategic & International Studies Web site,* http://csis.org/ (August 14, 2011), author profile.

*George Bush White House Web site,* http://georgew bush-whitehouse.archives.gov/ (August 14, 2011), author profile.

*Georgetown University Web site,* http://explore. georgetown.edu/ (August 14, 2011), author profile.*

# C.S. Challinor

## ■ Also Known As

Caroline S. Challinor

## ■ Personal

Born in Bloomington, IN; married. *Education:* Holds degrees from the University of Kent, Canterbury, England, and the Pushkin Institute, Moscow, Russia.

## ■ Addresses

*Home*—FL. *E-mail*—readermail@rexgraves.com.

## ■ Career

Author of mystery novels. Previously worked in real estate.

## ■ Member

Authors Guild, Sisters in Crime.

## ■ Writings

*"REX GRAVES MYSTERY" SERIES*

*Christmas Is Murder,* Midnight Ink (Woodbury, MN), 2008.
*Murder in the Raw,* Midnight Ink (Woodbury, MN), 2009.
*Phi Beta Murder,* Midnight Ink (Woodbury, MN), 2010.

*Murder on the Moor,* Midnight Ink (Woodbury, MN), 2011.

Contributor of fiction to women's magazines in the United States and United Kingdom.

## ■ Sidelights

A former real estate agent, C.S. Challinor is known for her "Rex Graves" series of mysteries. This series follows Scottish barrister Rex Graves as he uses his prosecutorial prowess to untangle mysteries.

### Christmas Is Murder

Reviewers praised Challinor's 2008 debut in the "Rex Graves" series, *Christmas Is Murder.* Graves finds himself snowed in at Swanmere Manor, a country bed-and-breakfast where several guests suffer unfortunate and fatal accidents. As he investigates, Graves uncovers a complex web of half-truths and mixed motivations. "The first installment in this new mystery series is a winner," Judy Coon wrote in *Booklist.* Coon was especially taken with the protagonist, noting that this "charming new sleuth" makes the book "a must for cozy fans."

According to Lori Graham, reviewing *Christmas Is Murder* for the *Once upon a Romance* blog, the novel is "a real who-done-it. . . . This isn't a suspense that keeps you griping the edge of your seat but a true mystery that uses your mind to puzzle things out." A contributor to the *Mysterious Reviews* Web site likewise found the book to be "an engaging whodunit populated with an interesting and imaginative mix of characters. . . . [The novel] effortlessly combines elements of a classic country house mystery with an Agatha Christie-style denouement to great effect. . . . This quick-reading mystery will keep readers guessing."

### Murder in the Raw and Phi Beta Murder

Challinor followed *Christmas Is Murder* with *Murder in the Raw.* The new owners of Swanmere Manor pay for Rex to travel to the Caribbean and help sort out the matter of a missing actress. When he arrives, he discovers not only a new tangle of crossed alliances and murderous motivations, but also that the resort where he is staying is exclusively for nudists. Although fans enjoyed this second installment, some reviewers were less enthusiastic, with a contributor to *Kirkus Reviews* quipping that the novel is "the most untitillating nudist company imaginable."

Series novel number three, *Phi Beta Murder,* finds Rex visiting his son, Campbell, at college in Jacksonville, Florida. While Rex is there, a student is found hanged in his dorm room under suspicious circumstances. Rex, of course, begins his own investigation, between spending time with Campbell and dealing with an ex-girlfriend who has followed him to Florida and is emotionally unstable. In a *Booklist* review, Judy Coon felt that, when compared with the other novels in the series, "although the humor of Challinor's writing is still in evidence, this novel is a bit more subdued." However, a contributor to *Publishers Weekly* noted that "Rex focuses on sleuthing and being a good dad in this lightweight cozy."

### Murder on the Moor

In the fourth book of the series, *Murder on the Moor,* Rex and his girlfriend, Helen d'Arcy, host a housewarming party at his new estate, Gleneagle Lodge, in the highlands of Scotland, which is attended by his colleague, Alistair, who is also staying with Rex. As a barrister, Alistair has just lost a high-profile conviction in the infamous Moor Murders. The murderer is now on the premises, as well his ex-girlfriend, Moira, who winds up dead in the bathtub, obviously murdered. The local police are looking for a child killer and can offer no help, so Rex must solve the murder.

"Challinor's feel for setting is very good, as is her plotting. As spring approaches, it's a pleasure to read about someplace with worse weather than here. The good writing is a delight as well," P.J. Coldren concluded in a review for *ReviewingThe Evidence.com.* A contributor to *Kirkus Reviews* described *Murder on the Moor* as "a slim volume in the style of Agatha Christie, lightweight but fun to read." Similarly, a *Publishers Weekly* contributor concluded that "traditional mystery fans will appreciate the retro Agatha Christie style."

## ■ Biographical And Critical Sources

*PERIODICALS*

*Booklist,* September 15, 2008, Judy Coon, review of *Christmas Is Murder,* p. 27; February 1, 2010, Judy Coon, review of *Phi Beta Murder,* p. 34.

*Kirkus Reviews,* July 15, 2008, review of *Christmas Is Murder;* March 1, 2009, review of *Murder in the Raw;* December 15, 2010, review of *Murder on the Moor.*

*Publishers Weekly,* January 4, 2010, review of *Phi Beta Murder,* p. 33; December 13, 2010, review of *Murder on the Moor,* p. 40.

*ONLINE*

*AuthorsDen,* http://www.authorsden.com/ (April 6, 2009), C.S. Challinor, "Author Spends Three Weeks in the Nude"; (May 8, 2009), profile of author.

*C.S. Challinor Home Page,* http://www.rexgraves. com (May 8, 2009).

*Midnight Ink Press Web site,* http://www.midnight inkbooks.com/ (May 8, 2009), profile of author.

*Mysterious Reviews,* http://www.mysteriousreviews. com/ (May 8, 2009), review of *Christmas Is Murder.*

*Once upon a Romance,* http://www.onceupona romance.net/ (May 8, 2009), Lori Graham, review of *Christmas Is Murder.*

*PRWeb: Press Release Newswire,* http://www.prweb. com/ (July 24, 2008), "Author's Support for the Wounded No Mystery."

*ReviewingTheEvidence.com,* http://www.reviewing theevidence.com/ (March 1, 2011), P.J. Coldren, review of *Murder on the Moor.*

*Rex Graves Series Web Site,* http://www.rexgraves. com/ (August 23, 2011).

*Undiscovered Scotland,* http://www.undiscovered scotland.com/ (August 23, 2011), review of *Murder on the Moor.**

# Laura Childs

## ■ Also Known As

Gerry Schmitt

## ■ Personal

Married, husband a college professor.

## ■ Career

Writer, novelist, and copywriter. Copywriter and producer at national advertising agencies; Mission Critical Marketing (marketing and advertising firm), Minneapolis, MN, former owner, chief executive officer, and creative director.

## ■ Writings

*"TEA SHOP MYSTERIES" SERIES*

*Death by Darjeeling,* Berkley Prime Crime (New York, NY), 2001.

*Gunpowder Green,* Berkley Prime Crime (New York, NY), 2002.

*The English Breakfast Murder,* Berkley Prime Crime (New York, NY), 2003.

*Shades of Earl Grey,* Berkley Prime Crime (New York, NY), 2003.

*The Jasmine Moon Murder,* Berkley Prime Crime (New York, NY), 2004.

*Chamomile Mourning,* Berkley Prime Crime (New York, NY), 2005.

*Blood Orange Brewing,* Berkley Prime Crime (New York, NY), 2006.

*Dragonwell Dead,* Berkley Prime Crime (New York, NY), 2007.

*The Silver Needle Murder,* Berkley Prime Crime (New York, NY), 2008.

*Oolong Dead,* Berkley Prime Crime (New York, NY), 2009.

*The Teaberry Strangler,* Berkley Prime Crime (New York, NY), 2010.

*Scones & Bones,* Berkley Prime Crime (New York, NY), 2011.

*"SCRAPBOOKING MYSTERIES" SERIES*

*Keepsake Crimes,* Berkley Prime Crime (New York, NY), 2003.

*Photo Finished,* Berkley Prime Crime (New York, NY), 2004.

*Bound for Murder,* Berkley Prime Crime (New York, NY), 2004.

*Death by Design* (omnibus), Berkley Prime Crime (New York, NY), 2006.

*Motif for Murder,* Berkley Prime Crime (New York, NY), 2006.

*Frill Kill,* Berkley Prime Crime (New York, NY), 2007.

*Death Swatch,* Berkley Prime Crime (New York, NY), 2008.

*Tragic Magic,* Berkley Prime Crime (New York, NY), 2009.

*Fiber & Brimstone,* Berkley Prime Crime (New York, NY), 2010.

*Skeleton Letters,* Berkley Prime Crime (New York, NY), 2011.

*"CACKLEBERRY CLUB MYSTERIES" SERIES*

*Eggs in Purgatory,* Berkley Prime Crime (New York, NY), 2008.

*Eggs Benedict Arnold,* Berkley Prime Crime (New York, NY), 2009.

*Bedeviled Eggs,* Berkley (New York, NY), 2010.

## ■ Sidelights

Laura Childs is the pseudonym of Gerry Schmitt, a mystery novelist and former marketing director whose "Tea Shop Mysteries," "Scrapbooking Mysteries," and "Cackleberry Club Mysteries" books have as their protagonists women entrepreneurs who also solve crimes. The "Tea Shop Mysteries" series centers on Theodosia Browning, who, like Childs, once worked in advertising, and who is now proprietor of the Indigo Tea Shop in a historic section of Charleston, South Carolina. The "Scrapbooking Mysteries" are set in another richly historic, atmospheric area, the French Quarter of New Orleans, and focus on Carmela Bertrand, who sells scrapbooks and related craft supplies at a store called Memory Mine. The former series includes recipes, the latter tips on making scrapbooks, and several reviewers have described both as falling into the "cozy" category of mysteries, without extensive descriptions of violence. In the "Cackleberry Club Mysteries," Childs features three women of a certain age—Suzanne, Toni, and Petra—who open a cozy breakfast café in the little town of Kindred. They specialize in eggs at the Cackleberry Club in the mornings and delve into amateur sleuthing in the afternoons and evenings.

Childs once told an interviewer for the Web site *In the Library Reviews* that the idea for her first series came from her editor, who "wanted 'a mystery featuring a snoopy woman who owns a tea shop!'" According to the pseudonymous novelist, "the rest of the concept sprang from my imagination." The author explained that, that while working in advertising, she met many women who wanted to do what Theodosia has done—leave the corporate world and operate a small business. The scrapbook series, the author continued, "was completely my idea." The author continued: "I figured that old photos and new clippings—the stuff that goes into scrapbooks—would yield a bounty of clues!" The popularity of her mystery novels enabled the author to sell her advertising firm and write full-time.

### *Death by Darjeeling* and *Gunpowder Green*

*Death by Darjeeling* introduces Theodosia; her valued employees, Drayton and Haley, who help her prepare teas and bakery goods; and her dog, Earl Grey, a dalmatian-labrador mix. The story finds Theo providing refreshments during a tour of landmark Charleston homes; one of the participants, a local real estate developer, dies after drinking poisoned tea. Theo, wishing to keep her business above suspicion, decides to seek out the poisoner, and in the process learns of the conflicts between developers and historic preservationists.

This debut and others in the series have won praise for their portrayals of engaging people and places. *Death by Darjeeling* "offers readers a good setting and a promising cast of characters," commented Jennifer Monahan Winberry in a review for the *Mystery Reader* Web site, the critic adding that it is "a good beginning" to the series. The follow-up, *Gunpowder Green,* takes its title from a special tea Theo and Drayton have created for a party connected with a yacht race; the party turns deadly, however, when the finishing-line gun explodes and kills the man firing it. Theo alone thinks this was no accident, so she begins to investigate. "The story line engages the audience from the start," remarked Harriet Klausner, writing for the *AllReaders.com.* Winberry, again contributing to the *Mystery Reader* Web site, called the novel "a delightful cozy that will warm readers the way a good cup of tea does," while *RT Book Reviews* contributor Toby Bromberg deemed it "a charming mystery of manners."

### *The English Breakfast Murder* and *Shades of Earl Grey*

The third book in the series, *The English Breakfast Murder,* features Theo at the beach one night with others, tending to newly hatched loggerhead turtles, when she comes across a dead body floating in the ocean. Harper Frisk, the dead man, did underwater salvaging as a hobby. Theo begins her investigation by going to a meeting of Harper's friends called the English Breakfast Club. It turns out that Harper's friends were not that friendly after all, and more than one had a strong motive for killing the man. "Readers will be charmed and beguiled by this delicious amateur sleuth mystery and will feel like visiting Charles Street to have a cup at the Indigo Tea Shop," commented Harriet Klausner in a review for the *Best Reviews* Web site. Sharyn McGinty, writing for the *In the Library Reviews* Web site, called *The English Breakfast Murder* "a fantastic read from beginning to end."

*Shades of Earl Grey* features Theo at a high-society wedding party when the roof collapses, killing the groom. In the confusion, the 70,000-dollar wedding ring disappears, leading Theo to suspect a cat burglar was involved. "What can I say about *Shades of Earl Grey*? Other than it's a keeper, I'm at a loss," wrote Sharyn McGinty for the Web site *In the Library Reviews.* Harriet Klausner, writing on the *Best Reviews* Web site, noted: "There is a surplus of suspects with means and opportunity," adding that "readers will want to finish . . . in one sitting to see who the perpetrator is in this delicious cozy."

### *The Jasmine Moon Murder* and *Chamomile Mourning*

In *The Jasmine Moon Murder,* Theo and the staff at the Indigo Tea Shop are working at serving tea and goodies during a tour of the famous Jasmine Cemetery when Dr. Jasper Davis is murdered. Davis is the uncle of Jory, Theo's love interest, which makes her want to investigate despite being warned off doing so by Detective Burt Tidewell. Before long, Theo is investigating a link between the doctor's murder and the company he worked for, Cardiotech, a medical products company. "Fans will enjoy the rich brew of murder, tea lore and mouth-watering descriptions of food (recipes included)," commented a contributor to *Publishers Weekly.* Writing for *In the Library Reviews,* McGinty opined that she has seen improvements in the author's mysteries, noting that the "greatest sign of her maturity is how much more difficult it is to discover the culprit's identity."

The sixth book in the series, *Chamomile Mourning,* revolves around murder at another gala event; the victim, an auction-house owner, is shot and falls from a balcony into a cake Theo's shop has catered for the party. His widow believes the victim's girlfriend is the murderer, as do the police, but Theo has other ideas. A *Publishers Weekly* contributor thought this novel the best so far in the series and termed its author "a master of Southern local color." In a similar vein, a *Kirkus Reviews* contributor described the book as an "homage to the Low Country and all things tea-related," while Klausner, reviewing for *MBR Bookwatch Online,* noted that Charleston itself is one of the story's primary characters, providing "the ambience that makes this series so special." As for human protagonist Theo, she "is one of the most realistic and likeable characters" in mystery fiction, Klausner observed.

### *Blood Orange Brewing* and *Dragonwell Dead*

The seventh book in the "Tea Shop Myteries" series, *Blood Orange Brewing* finds Theo investigating the murder of Duke Wilkes, a local businessman and political big shot, during a fund raiser for the Heritage Society. To find the murderer, Theo must sort through various suspects, including developers who the dead man opposed in his efforts for historic preservation. "Childs has a great eye for local color," wrote a *Publishers Weekly* contributor. A contributor to *Kirkus Reviews* called the mystery "a paean to Charleston, the genteel enjoyment of tea and the tasty treats that accompany it."

*Dragonwell Dead* takes place during the annual Spring Plantation Ramble in Charleston. Theo and staff are serving tea at a local plantation when the owner of a local bread and breakfast establishment collapses and dies. Theo, of course, suspects murder. A *California Bookwatch* contributor called *Dragonwell Dead* an "absorbing, fun mystery." Harriet Klausner, writing for the *Best Reviews* Web site, noted: "The story line is fast-paced."

### *The Silver Needle Murder* and *Oolong Dead*

*The Silver Needle Murder* published in 2008, takes place during the first-ever Charleston Film Festival, with Theo and her staff under pressure to serve tea and food at several parties. However, Theo is soon sidetracked into investigating the murder of director Jordan Cole, who is shot during the opening of the newly renovated Belvedere Theatre. A contributor to *Kirkus Reviews* commented that the author "again [presents] a love letter to Charleston, tea and fine living, with the usual addition of recipes."

Murder strikes close to home for Theo in *Oolong Dead,* in which the sister of a former boyfriend of Theo's is murdered. An investigative reporter, Abby Davis, had her fair share of enemies, and Theo did not get along with her either. But when the former boyfriend and police detective Burt Tidewell ask her to help out in the investigation, she obliges, even though this doesn't please Theo's current boyfriend, Parker Scully. The investigation leads to adventures in the swamps and in an old mansion in this story "filled with uniquely warm characters," according to *Booklist* reviewer Judy Coon. Similarly, a *Publishers Weekly* contributor felt that Theo's "dogged yet always elegant sleuthing" is as "satisfying as sipping a cup of jade oolong." Similar praise came from *BookLoons* Web site contributor Mary Ann Smyth, who thought that "the plot is tightly woven with intrigue, a good mystery, and a glimpse into the life of high society in Charleston."

### *The Teaberry Strangler* and *Scones & Bones*

In the eleventh "Tea Shop Mysteries" installment, *The Teaberry Strangler,* Theo comes upon a murder in the making as she sees a neighboring shopkeeper,

Daria, attacked and killed in an alley. The scent of mint at the crime scene serves as a clue as Theo investigates. A *Publishers Weekly* reviewer found this a "tepid" series addition, noting that the "mystery never quite catches fire as it simmers to a close." However, *Best Reviews* Web site contributor Harriet Klausner had a more positive assessment of the novel, terming it a "spectacular whodunit."

*Scones & Bones* finds Theo investigating the theft of a diamond-studded cup made from the skull of Blackbeard, the pirate. Taken from the Heritage Society, the skull cup is only part of the crime, for the robber also stabbed and killed a young intern and also attacked the office manager. Meanwhile, Theo finds herself divided between her boyfriend, Parker Scully, and a new museum director in town. A *Publishers Weekly* contributor found this a "charming" installment with "tempting recipes." A *Kirkus Reviews* writer offered a more mixed assessment, concluding: "A weak mystery, worth reading for the extensive tea lore, the loving portrayal of Charleston and the appended recipes."

### *Keepsake Crimes, Photo Finished,* and *Bound for Murder*

*Keepsake Crimes* inaugurates the "Scrapbooking Mysteries" series as its heroine, Carmela, sets up in business after her husband leaves her. After a man dies during the Mardi Gras parade, her estranged husband, Shamus, is suspected of murder; he was seen fighting with the deceased. Shamus seeks Carmela's aid, and she finds a customer's scrapbook helpful in her search for the true perpetrator. As with the other series, some reviewers found Childs's protagonist and locale particularly appealing. Writing for *AllReaders.com,* Klausner dubbed Carmela "plucky and likable" and noted that the novel powerfully evokes the atmosphere of New Orleans and Mardi Gras. It is also "well-written" and truly mysterious, with a wide selection of suspects, Klausner related.

The next in the series, *Photo Finished,* concerns the murder of the disreputable owner of the antiques shop located next door to Carmela's shop, Memory Mine, while the third, *Bound for Murder,* finds Carmela investigating the killing of a friend's fiancée. Reviewing the former book, Klausner wrote in *AllReaders.com* that it is fast-paced and full of action, while also offering "a heroine that is impossible to not like" and a "realistic" view of New Orleans. *RT Book Reviews* contributor Shari Melnick noted that the novel "exudes Southern charm and humor" and is "sure to please fans of light-hearted mysteries."

Also in *RT Book Reviews,* contributor Cindy Harrison called *Bound for Murder* "truly suspenseful" and described its characters and setting as "beguiling."

### *Motif for Murder* and *Frill Kill*

The next book in the "Scrapbooking Mysteries" series, *Motif for Murder,* finds Carmela and Shamus once again in marital bliss and living together in a mansion belonging to Shamus's sister, Glory, who does not like Carmela. One morning, Carmela sees Shamus being hauled off in a car's trunk and then finds Uncle Henry shot dead. Glory demands that Carmela leave the mansion, and kidnappers soon contact Carmela asking for a ransom. After Carmela rescues Shamus with the help of her friend, Ava, she soon discovers that she is targeted for murder by the mastermind of the kidnapping plot. A *Publishers Weekly* contributor called *Motif for Murder* an "engaging read from this reliable cozy author."

The mystery in *Frill Kill* involves the murder of a fashion model in New Orleans, where Carmela is living while once again separated from her husband, Shamus. Carmela discovers the woman's body at the shop of her friend, Ava, and then Carmela is knocked unconscious. The prime suspects are Giovanni, a fortune teller that Ava hired to work in her shop, and his brother, Santino, who has a circus act involving wolves. As Carmela investigates, she also finds that her scrapbooking shop is more popular than ever as Halloween approaches. A contributor to *Kirkus Reviews* commented that the mystery "contains bushels of Big Easy ambiance, quirky characters, scrapbooking tips and recipes." Another reviewer, writing for *Publishers Weekly,* referred to *Frill Kill* as "sprightly."

### *Death Swatch* and *Tragic Magic*

Childs continues her scrapbooking series with the 2008 *Death Swatch,* in which Mardi Gras is approaching. Attending a party in honor of the upcoming festivities, Carmela and Ava find a dead body, apparently strangled with a strand of barbed wire. The corpse turns out to be that of someone working with float designer Jekyl Hardy, and soon Carmela is helping Hardy track down the killer. A secret passage leads the amateur investigators on a merry chase after a reputed treasure of Jean Lafitte, the infamous pirate. At the same time, Carmela's romance with a detective is also developing. "So much detail about Mardi Gras and so many recipes and scrapbooking tips, that only mystery fans will notice all the loose ends," noted a *Kirkus Reviews* contributor of this cozy mystery. *Booklist* reviewer Sue O'Brien found more to like, noting that "well-developed main and secondary characters mesh nicely with the vibrant setting." Similarly, a *Publishers Weekly* reviewer called this an "enjoyable" series addition, adding: "Childs paints a picture of New Orleans sure to appeal to cozy fans."

Carmela and friend Ava, proprietor of the Juju Voodoo shop, are once again investigating in *Tragic Magic*. Helping to transform an old mansion, Medusa Manor, into a haunted house for an imminent horror convention, the two are soon involved in real horror when the owner of the mansion dies spectacularly. There are plenty of suspects for Carmela to sift through, and she is also busy with her own scrapbooking business. Reviewing this novel in *Booklist*, Coon felt that it (and the series of which it is a part) is "one of the best in the current wave of crime-and-crafts novels." A *Publishers Weekly* contributor also commended the manner in which the author "conjures up the abiding charm of New Orleans," but at the same time felt that the "rushed resolution disappoints." An online *Two Lips Reviews* writer was more impressed with this work, calling it "a fun, light read that leaves you wondering whodunit until the end."

### Fiber & Brimstone

Carmela and Ava are helping out in another bit of scariness in *Fiber & Brimstone*. Here they are assisting in preparations for the annual Halloween parade in New Orleans, constructing the head of a giant monster. At the same time but in a different part of the workshop, Bret Fowler is found dead, stabbed by the huge horns of a Minotaur puppet. Carmela decides to investigate, once again to the disappointment of her new boyfriend, NOPD detective Edgar Babcock. Fowler has lots of enemies, including those he has taken in by his Ponzi schemes, his business partner, float designer Jekyl Hardy who had an altercation with Fowler not long before the man was killed, and even Fowler's own wife.

A *Kirkus Reviews* contributor found this to be a "too-cute" novel and series. *Fresh Fiction* Web site reviewer Paula Myers however, had no such criticism, terming *Fiber & Brimstone* a "fun and fast-paced read." Likewise, a *Publishers Weekly* reviewer termed this a "colorful, briskly plotted" installment.

### Eggs in Purgatory and Eggs Benedict Arnold

*Eggs in Purgatory* inaugurates Childs's third series, the "Cackleberry Club Mysteries." Fortyish and recently widowed, Suzanne decides to open a cozy

café devoted to eggs dishes of all descriptions (with recipes accompanying each book). Teaming up with her single friends Toni and Petra—who have lost husbands to Alzheimer's and a younger woman—she converts an older establishment on the outskirts of Kindred, Tennessee, into the Cackleberry Club, part café, and part book nook and knitting corner. More than eggs are served up, however, when Suzanne's lawyer, Bobby White, is found dead in his car behind her newly opened establishment. When Sheriff Doogie suspects Suzanne's egg delivery man, she dons a sleuthing cap and starts to investigate the killing for herself. The investigation is made more complicated when Suzanne discovers that her own late husband may have had some shady dealings with Bobby. A nearby cult and a runaway girl add to the complications in this "great start to another terrific series," as online *Mystery Reader* contributor Jennifer Monahan Winberry termed the novel. *Best Reviews* Web site writer Dawn Dowdle also commended this series opener, noting: "The author does a great job of crafting and intertwining the plots. Her characters are very likeable and believable."

The egg action continues in *Eggs Benedict Arnold*, in which the local mortician ends up on his own slab and the ladies of the Cackleberry Club are once again on the trail of a killer who has also murdered the mortician's assistant. Suzanne does not recognize the danger she is in with this investigation, for the killer is prepared to do anything to stop her snooping. Online *Best Reviews* contributor Klausner found this second novel in the series an "extremely entertaining amateur sleuth mystery . . . wrapped inside a sisterhood tale of three women who forge a strong bond." *BookLoons* Web site reviewer Smyth added praise, observing that the "plot is well-thought out and the characters as delicious as the food served in the tea room"

### Bedeviled Eggs

Kindred is rocked by two high-profile murders in the third series installment, *Bedeviled Eggs*. First, the town's candidate for mayor is shot between the eyes with a crossbow while speaking with Suzanne. Then, Suzanne comes across the dead body of the town deputy while walking in the woods. Understandably, she takes these deaths personally and starts investigating. When the killer sends threats for her to stop, this only serves to redouble the efforts of the spunky widow, who is helped in her investigation by the new doctor in town.

"Along with toothsome recipes, Childs dishes up plenty of smalltown charm," wrote a *Publishers Weekly* reviewer of this novel. Similarly, a contributor for the online *Lesa's Book Critiques* dubbed this third book in the series a "combination of well-written mystery, good friends, good food, a little humor, and, now, a little romance."

## ■ Biographical And Critical Sources

*PERIODICALS*

*Booklist*, September 1, 2008, Sue O'Brien, review of *Death Swatch*, p. 53; March 15, 2009, Judy Coon, review of *Oolong Dead*, p. 46; October 1, 2009, Judy Coon, review of *Tragic Magic*, p. 30.

*California Bookwatch*, May, 2007, review of *Dragonwell Dead*.

*Kirkus Reviews*, April 1, 2005, review of *Chamomile Mourning*, p. 386; March 1, 2006, review of *Blood Orange Brewing*, p. 209; August 15, 2007, review of *Frill Kill*; February 1, 2008, review of *The Silver Needle Murder*; July 15, 2008, review of *Death Swatch*; August 15, 2010, review of *Fiber & Brimstone*; January 15, 2011, review of *Scones & Bones*, pp. 91-92.

*Library Journal*, September 1, 2004, Rex E. Klett, review of *The Jasmine Moon Murder*, p. 121; May 1, 2005, Rex E. Klett, review of *Chamomile Mourning*, p. 66.

*Publishers Weekly*, August 23, 2004, review of *The Jasmine Moon Murder*, p. 40; April 18, 2005, review of *Chamomile Mourning*, p. 47; February 20, 2006, review of *Blood Orange Brewing*, p. 139; July 31, 2006, review of *Motif for Murder*, p. 57; January 22, 2007, review of *Dragonwell Dead*, p. 167; August 6, 2007, review of *Frill Kill*, p. 172; January 28, 2008, review of *The Silver Needle Murder*, p. 44; July 21, 2008, review of *Death Swatch*, p. 145; February 2, 2009, review of *Oolong Dead*, p. 35; August 24, 2009, review of *Tragic Magic*, p. 45; January 18, 2010, review of *The Teaberry Strangler*, p. 32; August 2, 2010, review of *Fiber & Brimstone*, p. 32; October 25, 2010, review of *Bedeviled Eggs*, p. 33; January 17, 2011, review of *Scones & Bones*, p. 33.

*ONLINE*

*AllReaders.com*, http://www.allreaders.com/ (September 28, 2005), David Loftus, review of *Death by Darjeeling*; Abby White, review of *The English Breakfast Murder*; Harriet Klausner, reviews of *Gunpowder Green*, *Shades of Earl Grey*, *The English Breakfast Murder*, *The Jasmine Moon Murder*, *Chamomile Mourning*, *Keepsake Crimes*, *Photo Finished*, and *Bound for Murder*.

*Always with a Book*, http://alwayswithabook. blogspot.com/ (January 1, 2011), review of *Fiber & Brimstone*.

*Best Reviews*, http://thebestreviews.com/ (December 4, 2002), Harriet Klausner, review of *Shades of Earl Grey*; (July 13, 2003), Harriet Klausner, review of *The English Breakfast Murder*; (July 19, 2006), Harriet Klausner, review of *Blood Orange Brewing*; (August 29, 2006), Harriet Klausner, review of *Motif for Murder*; (February 27, 2007), Harriet Klausner, review of *Dragonwell Dead*; (March 4, 2009), Dawn Dowdle, review of *Eggs in Purgatory*; (December 4, 2009), Harriet Klausner, review of *Eggs Benedict Arnold*; (October 27, 2010), Harriet Klausner, review of *The Teaberry Strangler*.

*BookLoons*, http://www.bookloons.com/ (July 3, 2011), Mary Ann Smyth, review of *Oolong Dead*; (August 11, 2011), Mary Ann Smyth, review of *Eggs Benedict Arnold*.

*Cajun Book Lady*, http://www.thecajunbooklady. com/ (February 2, 2010), review of *Tragic Magic*; (February 3, 2010), "Q&A with the Author of *Tragic Magic* Laura Childs"; (January 7, 2011), review of *Bedeviled Eggs*.

*Fresh Fiction*, http://freshfiction.com/ (December 12, 2010), Paula Myers, review of *Fiber & Brimstone*; (February 9, 2011), Audrey Lawrence, review of *Scones & Bones*.

*In the Library Reviews*, http://www.inthelibrary reviews.net/ (July 5, 2003), Sharyn McGinty, review of *Shades of Earl Grey*; (November 15, 2003), Sharyn McGinty, review of *The English Breakfast Murder*; (October 13, 2005), interview with "Laura Childs"; (February 4, 2005), Sharyn McGinty, review of *The Jasmine Moon Murder*.

*Laura Childs Home Page*, http://www.laurachilds. com (August 11, 2011).

*Lesa's Book Critiques*, http://lesasbookcritiques. blogspot.com/ (December 10, 2010), review of *Bedeviled Eggs*.

*MBR Bookwatch Online*, http://www.midwestbook review.com/ (October 13, 2005), Harriet Klausner, review of *Chamomile Mourning*.

*Mystery Reader*, http://www.themysteryreader.com/ (June 3, 2001), Jennifer Monahan Winberry, review of *Death by Darjeeling*; (May 23, 2002), Jennifer Monahan Winberry, review of *Gunpowder Green*; (August 11, 2011), Jennifer Monahan Winberry, review of *Eggs in Purgatory*.

*RT Book Reviews*, http://rtbookreviews.com/ (March 1, 2002), Toby Bromberg, review of *Gunpowder Green*; (January 1, 2004), Shari Melnick, review of *Photo Finished*; (November 1, 2004), Cindy Harrison, review of *Bound for Murder*.

*Star Tribune Online*, http://www.startribune.com/ (March 2, 2009), Laurie Hertzel, "Murder amid the Chamomile."

*Two Lips Reviews*, http://www.twolipsreviews.com/ (April 26, 2011), review of *Tragic Magic*.*

# Christopher Coker

## 1953-

■ **Personal**

Born March 28, 1953, in England.

■ **Addresses**

*Office*—London School of Economics and Politics, Houghton St., London WC2A 2AE, England. *E-mail*—c.coker@lse.ac.uk.

■ **Career**

London School of Economics and Political Science, London, professor of international relations; Norwegian Staff College, adjunct professor.

■ **Member**

Washington Strategy Seminar, Institute for Foreign Policy Analysis, Black Sea University Foundation, Moscow School of Politics, IDEAS (advisory board), Czech Diplomatic Academy (academic board).

■ **Awards, Honors**

Honorable mention for Senior Information Book Award, *Times Educational Supplement*, 1986, for *Terrorism*.

■ **Writings**

*NONFICTION*

*U.S. Military Power in the 1980s*, Macmillan (London, England), 1983.

*The Future of the Atlantic Alliance*, Macmillan (London, England), 1984.

*The Soviet Union, Eastern Europe, and the New International Economic Order*, Praeger (New York, NY), 1984.

*NATO, the Warsaw Pact, and Africa*, St. Martin's Press (New York, NY), 1985.

*A Nation in Retreat? Britain's Defence Commitment*, Brassey's (London, England), 1986.

*The United States and South Africa, 1968-1985: Constructive Engagement and Its Critics*, Duke University Press (Durham, NC), 1986.

*British Defence Policy in the 1990s: A Guide to the Defence Debate*, Brassey's, 1987.

*South Africa's Security Dilemmas*, Praeger (New York, NY), 1987.

(Editor) *The United States, Western Europe, and Military Intervention Overseas*, St. Martin's (New York, NY), 1988.

*Reflections on American Foreign Policy since 1945*, St. Martin's (New York, NY), 1989.

(Editor) *Drifting Apart? The Superpowers and Their European Allies*, Brassey's (London, England), 1989.

(Editor) *Shifting into Neutral? Burden Sharing in the Western Alliance in the 1990s*, Brassey's (London, England), 1990.

*War and the Twentieth Century: A Study of War and Modern Consciousness*, Brassey's (London, England), 1994.

*The Western Alliance in Decline*, Danish Commission on Security and Disarmament (Copenhagen, Denmark), 1995.

*Twilight of the West*, Westview (Boulder, CO), 1998.

*War and the Illiberal Conscience*, Westview (Boulder, CO), 1998.

*Humane Warfare*, Routledge (New York, NY), 2001.

*Globalisation and Insecurity in the Twenty-first Century: NATO and the Management of Risk,* Oxford University Press for the International Institute for Strategic Studies (New York, NY), 2002.

*Waging War without Warriors? The Changing Culture of Military Conflict,* Lynne Rienner Publishers (Boulder, CO), 2002.

*Empires in Conflict: The Growing Rift between Europe and the United States,* Royal United Services Institute for Defence and Security Studies (London, England), 2003.

*Future of War: The Re-enchantment of War in the Twenty-first Century,* Blackwell Pub (Oxford, England), 2004.

*The Warrior Ethos: Military Culture and the War on Terror,* Routledge (New York, NY), 2007.

*Ethics and War in the Twenty-first Century,* Routledge (New York, NY), 2008.

*War in an Age of Risk,* Polity (Cambridge, MA), 2009.

*Barbarous Philosophers: Reflections on the Nature of War from Heraclitus to Heisenberg,* Columbia University Press (New York, NY), 2010.

(Editor, with Caroline Holmqvist-Jonsäter) *The Character of War in the 21st Century,* Routledge (New York, NY), 2010.

*JUVENILE NONFICTION*

*Terrorism,* Gloucester Press (New York, NY), 1986.

*Terrorism and Civil Strife,* F. Watts (New York, NY), 1987.

Contributor to periodicals, including the *Economist* and *Society*.

## ■ Sidelights

British scholar Christopher Coker is an authority in international relations. He has written or edited many books on this subject, including *U.S. Military Power in the 1980s, NATO, the Warsaw Pact and Africa,* and *War and the Twentieth Century*. Several of his works have been published in the United States, and he has also written two nonfiction books for young readers on the subject of terrorism.

### U.S. Military Power in the 1980s and NATO, the Warsaw Pact, and Africa

Coker's first book was 1983's *U.S. Military Power in the 1980s*. Anthony Verrier in *British Book News* praised the effort because, in his opinion, it discusses the true factors determining the strength of the United States's armed forces rather than rehashing old themes such as the cold war and the communist threat. Coker "places the requirements for military power firmly within a diplomatic context," Verrier concluded.

One of Coker's most widely reviewed efforts was 1985's *NATO, the Warsaw Pact, and Africa*. In this book, he debunks such beliefs as the idea that NATO (North Atlantic Treaty Organization) was secretly allied with the then-apartheid state of South Africa. He also discusses why most emerging African nations felt less threatened by alliance with the communist nations of the former Warsaw Pact than by alliance with such countries as Great Britain or France that were their former colonial masters.

Crawford Young in the *Political Science Quarterly* called *NATO, the Warsaw Pact, and Africa* a book with "a distinctive niche" that "makes a valuable contribution." Similarly, Ruth B. Russell in *Perspective* found it to be "an unusually interesting study."

### The United States and South Africa, 1968-1985 and Reflections on American Foreign Policy since 1945

Coker focused more explicitly on the relationship between the United States and South Africa in 1986's *The United States and South Africa, 1968-1985: Constructive Engagement and Its Critics.* "Constructive engagement" was the term used to describe the U.S. policy of trying to influence South Africa to abandon racial apartheid without outright sanctions and other punishments. Coker saw hope for this strategy—more so than for U.S. President Jimmy Carter's stricter policy during his administration—but within the span the book covers, the author never saw the method correctly employed. K.W. Grundy in *Choice* applauded the volume's "excellent, thorough, and sober analysis." Coker focused in even more narrowly to write 1987's *South Africa's Security Dilemmas.*

Another well-known part of Coker's bibliography is the 1989 work *Reflections on American Foreign Policy since 1945.* Here the author asserts that the United States has long based its military policy on distorted mythological perceptions of its own greatness. According to Wesley M. Bagby in the *Journal of American History,* Coker divides this mythology into three sections, which he labels "manifest destiny, Kennedy's New Frontier, and Jefferson's Beacon of Light." Bagby further noted that these "have been the means by which an often rootless United States retained its identity plus 'the self-confidence to tackle tasks which would have defeated most other nations.'" R.H. Immerman in *Choice* called *Reflec-*

*tions* "a provocative study that forces the reader to ask uncomfortable questions about the U.S. and its role in the world."

Looking among the works of contemporary philosophers, "Coker lines up for us all the usual suspects, and then some," according to Michael Howard in the *Times Literary Supplement.* Howard felt that Coker had not provided readers with a link between these intellectual sources and more popular culture, but conceded that "this new work shows a considerable and ambitious extension of his range."

*War and the Illiberal Conscience,* like *War and the Twentieth Century,* shows Coker as "a cultural historian of conflict," observed Daniel Johnson in the *Times Literary Supplement.* In this work Coker examines the various belief systems that developed in opposition to liberalism in the twentieth century, with particular attention to the influence of Friedrich Nietzsche—the nineteenth-century German philosopher who posited that society should be run by a group of "supermen"—and how these ideas have been used to justify war. "The main themes of illiberalism, as they emerge here, are familiar: the militarization of life, the sense of historical destiny, the apotheosis of the nation and the will to power," Johnson explained.

Coker also demonstrates that these concepts held some attraction for liberals and "that their disappearance from the late twentieth century has left liberal patriotism enfeebled," added Johnson.

Reviewers saw some flaws in the book; *Foreign Affairs* contributor Francis Fukuyama criticized Coker's text as bouncing from significant thinkers to negligible ones, while Johnson commented that "Coker's scholarship . . . is wide rather than deep" and wished the author had discussed how an understanding of illiberalism might help in dealing with modern totalitarian regimes. Nevertheless, Fukuyama considered *War and the Illiberal Conscience* "a welcome contrast" to other scholarly writings on war, which he found "excessively theoretical," and Johnson pronounced the volume "stimulating and original."

### Twilight of the West

*Twilight of the West* is the most extensively reviewed of Coker's works. In *Perspectives on Political Science* George MacLean wrote: "the aging of western culture is what Coker refers to as his 'three axioms' of a declining society: the contradiction between what the West says and what it intends the state-

ment to mean; the irony created between appearance and reality; and what the West states and actually does. Although these axioms may reflect traditional conclusions about the 'decline' of the West the road that Coker takes us on to get there is invigorating and provocative."

In the *National Interest* John O'Sullivan, commenting on the author's "shrewd and sardonic argument," believed the "case for Coker's predictions make itself." "Coker thinks that the western brothers have quarreled so irrevocably that there is nothing for it but for them to divide the estate and go out to seek profitable alliances with their former retainers." In a review in the British journal *Prospect* diplomat Robert Cooper, praising "this stimulating book" took issue with its "Spenglerian gloom" but added: "It may be possible to feel more optimistic about the 'west' than Coker does but he is still right that the West needs to reinvent itself in a post-cold war and that it can do so only in communication with others."

### War in an Age of Risk

In Coker's book *War in an Age of Risk,* Coker provides his suggestions for amending the manner in which wars are conducted. Much of the work concerns the notion of a "risk society," or a society that is preoccupied with its safety in the future. In *War in an Age of Risk* Coker analyzes how living in a risk society can alter peoples' attitudes towards war. Coker explains how a risk society functions, and how anxiety is frequently the most prominently driving force in a risk society. Providing several case studies, Coker thoroughly explains how risk societies operate, and where their pitfalls lie.

In the journal of *Ethics & International Affairs* contributor Claudia Aradau summarized: "Risk and the 'risk society' thesis have recently entered the vocabulary of international relations scholarship. Moving from deterrence, defense, and imminent dangers, security scholars have paid increasing attention to the language and practices of risk, prevention, preemption, precaution, surveillance, and vulnerability. Christopher Coker's War in an Age of Risk intervenes in these debates with an eye to the changing practices of war. As the preface points out, 'war has become risk management in all but name.'"

### ■ Biographical And Critical Sources

*PERIODICALS*

*Air & Space Power Journal,* December 22, 2009, John Farrell, review of *The Warrior Ethos: Military Culture and the War on Terror,* p. 125.

*British Book News*, May, 1984, Anthony Verrier, review of *U.S. Military Power in the 1980s*, p. 282.

*Choice*, November, 1986, K.W. Grundy, review of *The United States and South Africa, 1968-1985: Constructive Engagement and Its Critics*, p. 546; R.H. Immerman, review of *Reflections on American Foreign Policy since 1945*.

*English Historical Review*, November, 1999, Brian Bond, review of *War and the Illiberal Conscience*, p. 1392.

*Ethics & International Affairs*, March 22, 2010, Claudia Aradau, review of *War in an Age of Risk*, p. 110.

*Foreign Affairs*, September-October, 1998, Francis Fukuyama, review of *War and the Illiberal Conscience*, p. 146.

*History: Review of New Books*, winter, 1999, Troy Paddock, review of *War and the Illiberal Conscience*, p. 92.

*Journal of American History*, March, 1991, Wesley M. Bagby, *Reflections on American Foreign Policy since 1945*, p. 1410.

*Military Review*, May-June, 2004, John R. Sutherland, review of *Waging War without Warriors? The Changing Culture of Military Conflict*, p. 73; March 1, 2006, Tommy J. Tracy, review of *Future of War: The Re-enchantment of War in the Twenty-first Century*, p. 115.

*National Interest*, spring, 1999, John O'Sullivan, review of *Twilight of the West*, pp. 87-98.

*Perspective*, May-June, 1986, Ruth B. Russell, review of *NATO, the Warsaw Pact, and Africa*, pp. 91-92.

*Perspectives on Political Science*, winter, 1999, George MacLean, review of *Twilight of the West*, pp. 57-58.

*Political Science Quarterly*, fall, 1999, David L. Blaney, review of *War and the Illiberal Conscience*, p. 536.

*Prospect*, December, 1998, Robert Cooper, review of *Twilight of the West*, pp. 60-63

*Times Educational Supplement*, November 14, 1986, "Terrorism," p. 28.

*Times Literary Supplement*, January 6, 1995, Michael Howard, review of *War and the Twentieth Century*, p. 5; April 9, 1999, Daniel Johnson, review of *War and the Illiberal Conscience*, p. 30.

ONLINE

*London School of Economics and Political Science Web site*, http://www2.lse.ac.uk/ (August 14, 2011), author profile.*

# Paul K. Conkin

## 1929-

■ **Also Known As**

Paul Keith Conkin

■ **Personal**

Born October 25, 1929, in Chuckey, TN; son of Harry T. and Dorothy Conkin; married Dorothy L. Tharp, August 14, 1954; children: Keith Tharp, Claudia Sue, Lydia Kathleen. *Education:* Milligan College, B.A., 1951; Vanderbilt University, M.A., 1953, Ph.D., 1957.

■ **Addresses**

*Home*—Nashville, TN. *E-mail*—paul.k.conkin@ vanderbilt.edu.

■ **Career**

University of Southwestern Louisiana, Lafayette, assistant professor of philosophy and history, 1957-59; University of Maryland at College Park, College Park, assistant professor, 1959-61, associate professor, 1961-66, professor of history, 1966-67; University of Wisconsin—Madison, Madison, professor of history, 1967-76, Merle Curti Professor of History, beginning 1976; Vanderbilt University, Nashville, TN, distinguished professor of history, 1979-2000, distinguished research professor, 2000-02, professor emeritus, 2002—. *Military service:* U.S. Army, 1953-55.

■ **Member**

Organization of American Historians, Southern Historical Association (president, 1996-97).

■ **Awards, Honors**

Albert J. Beveridge Award in American History, American Historical Association, 1958; Guggenheim fellow, 1966-67; National Endowment for the Humanities, senior fellow, 1972-73, university fellowship, 1990; Thomas Jefferson Award, Vanderbilt University, 1990.

■ **Writings**

*Tomorrow a New World: The New Deal Community Program,* Cornell University Press (Ithaca, NY), 1959.

*Two Paths to Utopia: The Hutterites and the Llano Colony,* University of Nebraska Press (Lincoln, NE), 1964.

*F.D.R. and the Origins of the Welfare State,* Crowell (New York, NY), 1967, also published as *The New Deal,* Crowell, 1967, 2nd edition, H. Davidson (Arlington Heights, IL), 1975.

*Puritans and Pragmatists: Eight Eminent American Thinkers,* Dodd (New York, NY), 1968.

(With Roland N. Stromberg) *The Heritage and Challenge of History,* Dodd (New York, NY), 1971.

*Self-Evident Truths,* Indiana University Press (Bloomington, IN), 1974.

(With David Burner) *A History of Recent America,* Crowell (New York, NY), 1974.

(Editor, with John Higham) *New Directions in American Intellectual History,* Johns Hopkins University Press (Baltimore, MD), 1979.

*Prophets of Prosperity: America's First Political Economists,* Indiana University Press (Bloomington, IN), 1980.

(Editor, with Erwin C. Hargrove) *TVA, Fifty Years of Grass-Roots Bureaucracy,* University of Illinois Press (Urbana, IL), 1983.

*Two Paths to Utopia: The Hutterites and the Llano Colony,* Greenwood Press (Westport, CT), 1983.

(With Henry Lee Swint and Patricia S. Miletich) *Gone with the Ivy: A Biography of Vanderbilt University,* University of Tennessee Press (Knoxville, TN), 1985.

*Big Daddy from the Pedernales: Lyndon Baines Johnson,* Twayne Publishers (Boston, MA), 1986.

*The Southern Agrarians,* University of Tennessee Press (Knoxville, TN), 1988.

(With Roland N. Stromberg) *Heritage and Challenge: The History and Theory of History,* Forum Press (Arlington Heights, IL), 1989.

*Cane Ridge, America's Pentecost,* University of Wisconsin Press (Madison, WI), 1990.

*The Four Foundations of American Government: Consent, Limits, Balance, and Participation,* Harlan Davidson (Arlington Heights, IL), 1994.

*The Uneasy Center: Reformed Christianity in Antebellum America,* University of North Carolina Press (Chapel Hill, NC), 1995.

*American Originals: Homemade Varieties of Christianity,* University of North Carolina Press (Chapel Hill, NC), 1997.

*When All the Gods Trembled: Darwinism, Scopes, and American Intellectuals,* Rowman & Littlefield (Lanham, MD), 1998.

*A Requiem for the American Village,* Rowman & Littlefield (Lanham, MD), 2000.

*Peabody College: From a Frontier Academy to the Frontiers of Teaching and Learning,* Vanderbilt University Press (Nashville, TN), 2002.

*The State of the Earth: Environmental Challenges on the Road to 2100,* University Press of Kentucky (Lexington, KY), 2007.

*A Revolution Down on the Farm: The Transformation of American Agriculture since 1929,* University Press of Kentucky (Lexington, KY), 2008.

Contributor to journals.

## ■ Sidelights

*F.D.R. and the Origins of the Welfare State,* written by historian and educator Paul K. Conkin in 1967, is considered to be one of the best-known titles in a popular series of books about American history. In it, the author paints a rich portrait of Franklin Delano Roosevelt and his associates, while detailing the domestic policies adopted during Roosevelt's term as president of the United States.

Accessible even to readers who are not historians, Conkin's book *Heritage and Challenge: The History and Theory of History,* written with Roland N. Strom-

berg, provides a brief, coherent history of historical writing along with an analysis of the issues (philosophical and theoretical) that challenge historians.

### *The Four Foundations of American Government* and *The Uneasy Center*

*The Four Foundations of American Government: Consent, Limits, Balance, and Participation* is Conkin's concise exploration of the items and concepts named in the title: the consent of a sovereign people, limited government, balanced government, and democratic participation.

Conkin outlines the origins of America's Reformed churches in his next book, *The Uneasy Center: Reformed Christianity in Antebellum America.* In this work he also explains the traditions, disputes, and forms of worship and organization of each of these churches during the years prior to the Civil War. In reviewing *The Uneasy Center,* W. Clark Gilpin observed in *Christian Century* that this book "displays all the virtues of an experienced teacher who has thought regularly and deeply about a subject with changing generations of students. Clear, balanced and richly informative, it not only engages current scholarship but also offers fresh readings of the pivotal primary texts and contexts."

### *American Originals* and *When All the Gods Trembled*

In *American Originals: Homemade Varieties of Christianity,* Conkin provides a history and defined the forms of Christianity in the United States. *American Originals* was labeled "helpful for all readers who need a nonbiased account on these groups" by Leroy Hommerding in *Library Journal.* The chapters in this book were reviewed by scholars of the doctrines and practices about which Conkin wrote.

*When All the Gods Trembled: Darwinism, Scopes, and American Intellectuals* is Conkin's account of the famous Scopes "Monkey Trial" of 1925 and the intellectual and religious debates surrounding it. This work also includes an original analysis of Charles Darwin's *Origin of Species* and illustrates how Americans in the twentieth century attempted to reconcile Darwin's theories with existing religious traditions.

### *A Requiem for the American Village* and *Peabody College*

Conkin's book *A Requiem for the American Village* was portrayed as a wide-ranging collection of seventeen "wise, trenchant, iconoclastic essays" by a reviewer for *Publishers Weekly.* This reviewer also commented that "Conkin celebrates American pluralism and tolerance of diversity as he mourns tight-knit local communities, which, in his estimation, have all but disappeared." This work also includes a look by the author at different forms of "colonies" and his examination of the reasons these collective and communal living arrangements have failed. In this work, Conkin also described how America's earliest towns and villages in reality could be exclusive, repressive, restrictive places, the reviewer pointed out.

*Peabody College: From a Frontier Academy to the Frontiers of Teaching and Learning* is really a genealogy of the George Peabody College for Teachers in Nashville, Tennessee. Now a part of Vanderbilt University, the school has an interesting social and educational history that dates back to before the Civil War. "Peabody alumni will appreciate the book, and historians of the South and of education will no doubt find Conkin's history of this important southern institution useful and revealing," concluded Charles A. Israel in a review of the book for the *Journal of Southern History.*

### A Revolution Down on the Farm

*A Revolution Down on the Farm: The Transformation of American Agriculture since 1929* maps the changes that have occurred in farming since the start of the Great Depression. Conkin uses statistical data to provide both an economic and historical analysis of the technological changes, advancement in farming skills, and creation of state and federal government policies starting with the New Deal that have combined to produce more food with fewer farmers yet complicate farming further. He also examines the growing phenomenon of corporate farming, advances in biological and chemical applications, and provides alternatives for future farming. In *Southeastern Geographer,* Russell Graves opined that Conkin's "affinity for rural community life runs parallel to his telling of the rapid 20th-century transformation of American agriculture in alternating chapters through the first half of the book. While some might find this narrative approach a bit disjointed, I found Conkin to be a master storyteller. Whether reflecting upon his own life growing up in a family and community whose livelihood depended upon the sale of tobacco or describing the potentially mundane details of the history of federal agricultural policy changes since Roosevelt's New Deal, Conkin never loses sight of his audience by diverting into needless historiography or burying his narrative in a sea of statistics."

*A Revolution Down on the Farm* is "a clearly written and organized" book, stated a contributor to *Sci*

*Tech Book News.* In *California History,* Stephanie Pincetl remarked that the book "provides an accessible overview of the evolution of American agriculture in the twentieth century that is personal as well. Having grown up on a small Tennessee farm, he contrasts the daily life of his childhood with farm life today." Pincetl also commented that the book "offers the most readable and comprehensible overview of farm policies that this reviewer knows." Monica R. Gisolfi, in a review for the *Journal of Southern History,* aptly pointed out that "the history of American agribusiness is central to the study of twentieth-century American history, and Conkin contributes to the study of this critical topic."

### ■ Biographical And Critical Sources

*PERIODICALS*

*Agricultural History,* January 1, 2010, Jon Lauck, review of *A Revolution Down on the Farm: The Transformation of American Agriculture since 1929,* p. 136.

*American Historical Review,* December, 1972, review of *The Heritage and Challenge of History,* p. 1402.

*Business History Review,* June 22, 2010, Sarah Phillips, review of *A Revolution Down on the Farm,* p. 425.

*California History,* June 22, 2009, Stephanie Pincetl, review of *A Revolution Down on the Farm,* p. 75.

*Choice,* May 1, 2007, D. Goldblum, review of *The State of the Earth: Environmental Challenges on the Road to 2100,* p. 1552.

*Christian Century,* September 13, 1995, W. Clark Gilpin, review of *The Uneasy Center: Reformed Christianity in Antebellum America,* p. 856.

*Christian Science Monitor,* August 23, 1969, review of *Puritans and Pragmatists: Eight Eminent American Thinkers,* p. 9.

*Journal of American History,* September, 1975, review of *Self-Evident Truths,* p. 379; June 1, 2009, Shane Hamilton, review of *A Revolution Down on the Farm,* p. 263.

*Journal of Economic History,* June 1, 2009, Alan L. Olmstead, review of *A Revolution Down on the Farm,* p. 608.

*Journal of Southern History,* February, 1975, review of *Self-Evident Truths,* p. 97; November 1, 2004, Charles A. Israel, review of *Peabody College: From a Frontier Academy to the Frontiers of Teaching and Learning,* p. 947; February 1, 2010, Monica R. Gisolfi, review of *A Revolution Down on the Farm,* p. 192.

*Library Journal,* August, 1997, Leroy Hommerding, review of *American Originals: Homemade Varieties of Christianity,* p. 93.

*Publishers Weekly*, February 28, 2000, review of *A Requiem for the American Village*, p. 74.

*Reviews in American History*, December 1, 2009, "Field Work by the Sage of East Tennessee," p. 584.

*SciTech Book News*, June 1, 2010, review of *A Revolution Down on the Farm*.

*Southeastern Geographer*, June 22, 2010, Russell Graves, review of *A Revolution Down on the Farm*, p. 283.

*Wall Street Journal*, September 29, 2008, "Where Yields Are Still High; a *Revolution down on the Farm*, by Paul K. Conkin," p. 23.

*William and Mary Quarterly*, April, 1975, review of *Self-Evident Truths*, p. 349.

ONLINE

*Vanderbilt University Division of Public Affairs Web site*, http://www.vanderbilt.edu/ (August 1, 2011), faculty profile.

# Michael Cunningham

## 1952-

### ■ Personal

Born November 6, 1952, in Cincinnati, OH; partner of Ken Corbett, beginning 1988. *Education:* Stanford University, B.A., 1975; University of Iowa, M.F.A., 1980.

### ■ Addresses

*Home*—New York, NY. *Agent*—Barclay Agency, 12 Western Ave., Petaluma, CA 94952.

### ■ Career

Writer. Worked for Carnegie Corp., New York, NY, beginning 1986; Brooklyn College, NY, fiction instructor; Fine Arts Work Center, Provincetown, MA, Yale University, New Haven, CT, professor. Has appeared on television and in the 2009 documentaries, *Ptown Diaries* and *Making the Boys.*

### ■ Member

ACT-UP.

### ■ Awards, Honors

Guggenheim fellowship, 1993; Whiting Writers' Award, 1995; *Lambda* Literary Award for gay men's fiction, 1995 and 1996, for *Flesh and Blood*; National Endowment for the Arts Fellowship, 1998; PEN/ Faulkner Award for fiction, Gay, Lesbian, Bisexual, and Transgendered Book Award, and Pulitzer Prize for fiction, all 1999, all for *The Hours.*

### ■ Writings

*NOVELS*

*Golden States,* Crown (New York, NY), 1984.
*A Home at the End of the World,* Farrar, Straus (New York, NY), 1990.
*Flesh and Blood,* Farrar, Straus (New York, NY), 1995.
*The Hours,* Farrar, Straus (New York, NY), 1998.
*Specimen Days,* Farrar, Straus (New York, NY), 2005.
*By Nightfall,* Farrar (New York, NY), 2010.

*OTHER*

(Author of text) *I Am Not This Body: Photographs,* photographs by Barbara Ess, Aperture (New York, NY), 2001.
*Land's End: A Walk through Provincetown,* Crown (New York, NY), 2002.
(Editor) Walt Whitman, *Laws for Creation,* Picador (New York, NY), 2006.
(With Susan Minot; and producer) *Evening* (screenplay), Focus Features, 2007.
(Author of introduction) *Fall River Boys,* Charles Lane Press (New York, NY), 2009.

Author of screen adaptation for *A Home at the End of the World,* 2004. Contributor of fiction to anthologies, including *The Best American Short Stories,* 1989; and *O. Henry Prize Stories,* 1999. Contributor of fiction and nonfiction to periodicals, including *New Yorker, Atlantic, Los Angeles Times, Mother Jones,* and *Paris Review.*

### ■ Adaptations

*The Hours* was adapted for a film of the same title, directed by Stephen Daldry and starring Nicole Kidman, Julianne Moore, and Meryl Streep, Miramax, 2002; *A Home at the End of the World* was adapted for a film of the same title, Warner Independent, 2004.

■ **Sidelights**

Michael Cunningham has won critical acclaim, commercial success, and major literary awards for his novels. His works frequently feature homosexual characters and themes, but they do not lose sight of the world beyond the gay community. "Homosexuality is a lens through which the world is viewed, not a world unto itself," stated Joseph M. Eagan in *Gay and Lesbian Literature*. In novels that explore themes of family, friendship, identity, and commitment, he "places his gay and bisexual characters in the mainstream of American life, [viewing] their homosexuality as only one aspect of their identity," according to Eagan. The critic further noted that Cunningham has "been widely praised for his prose, sense of place, use of imagery, and psychological insight into his characters."

**Early Novels**

In 1984 Cunningham published his first novel, *Golden States*, which concerns an adolescent boy coming of age in Southern California. The boy, twelve-year-old David Stark, is initially portrayed as a victim of his own preoccupations and manias. Living with his mother, older stepsister, and tirelessly obnoxious younger sister, David seems obsessed with safeguarding his home and family. At one point, he even sojourns, with an unloaded pistol, to San Francisco in a harebrained scheme to "save" his stepsister from her presumably dangerous fiancé. Eventually, David begins to understand and control his fears and anxieties even as his life becomes one of increasing isolation and domestic instability. Though abandoned by his father and rejected by his best friend, David develops a sense of security and self-understanding. Ever the protector, however, he continues to guard his suburban neighborhood home from prowling coyotes.

*Golden States* was generally perceived as a successful first venture into novel writing. Elizabeth Royte, writing in the *Village Voice*, deemed Cunningham's debut "a sweetly appealing book," while Alice F. Wittels declared in the *Los Angeles Times Book Review* that the work was "exceedingly well-written." Wittels objected only to the end, which she claimed "left a bad taste," but conceded that the book's "first seven-eighths was terrific." Ruth Doan MacDougall was more enthusiastic in her *Christian Science Monitor* appraisal. "However much one might object to the theme of the protection of women, one cannot help savoring every moment of this novel," she wrote. "Funny, tender, [*Golden States*] is a joy to read."

Despite the favorable reviews, *Golden States* only "sold seven or eight copies," the author joked to *Publishers Weekly* interviewer Michael Coffey. His real breakthrough came with his second novel, *A Home at the End of the World*, a story about sexual liberation in the age of acquired immune deficiency syndrome (AIDS). The novel provides perspectives on four characters—Jonathan, Bobby, Clare, and Alice—in detailing the complexities of a childhood friendship that develops into romantic love. Jonathan and Bobby meet as young boys in Cleveland, and in the ensuing years they become close friends. When Jonathan leaves for college in New York City, Bobby, whose own family life is empty, becomes a mainstay in his friend's family home. There, Bobby grows particularly close to Jonathan's mother, Alice, whose marriage is collapsing. Eventually, Bobby and Jonathan are reunited in New York City, where they begin living together. They are joined in their quarters by Clare, a young divorced woman who is still rebelling against her wealthy family. Clare hopes to bear Jonathan's child. Instead, she bears Bobby's, a daughter. Jonathan becomes jealous of Bobby and Clare's relationship, but soon all three adults, plus child, begin living together in upstate New York. This idyll is undone, however, when one of Jonathan's former lovers arrives stricken with AIDS.

*A Home at the End of the World* has earned praise as a compelling portrait of modern times. In the *New York Times Book Review* Joyce Reiser Kornblatt likened Cunningham to Charles Dickens and E.M. Forster, and she hailed Cunningham's work as one of power and depth. She found *A Home at the End of the World* "memorable and accomplished." Another enthusiast, Richard Eder, was particularly impressed with Cunningham's craft, affirming in the *Los Angeles Times Book Review* that the novelist "writes with power and delicacy" and adding that the entire book "is beautifully written." And Patrick Gale, in his review in the *Washington Post Book World*, noted both the profundity of Cunningham's work and the subtlety with which he wrote it. Observing that the theme of the novel is nothing less than "the family and its alternatives in the overlapping aftermaths of sexual liberation and AIDS," Gale commended Cunningham for his work's "careful structure." Especially successful to Gale is the use of memory, which enables *A Home at the End of the World* to provide readers with "a pleasing sense . . . of resolution, even if the characters are no less happy at the close than they were before."

*Flesh and Blood*, published in 1995, demonstrates Cunningham's continuing concerns for honoring all kinds of unconventional family units. This long, multigenerational saga centers around a Greek immigrant and his family. On the surface, Constantine and his wife, Mary, seem to have achieved the American dream: a nice house in the suburbs and three children. But Mary cannot curb her compulsion to shoplift, nor can Constantine resist the beauty of his eldest daughter. A cross-dressing son and a drug-using daughter who raises her illegitimate child with a transvestite partner fill out the picture. All the characters and their troubles "ring true, heartbreakingly true. And beautiful in a way no camera could capture," praised Kelli Pryor in *Entertainment Weekly*. A *Publishers Weekly* reviewer affirmed that, as in *A Home at the End of the World*, Cunningham's prose "is again rich, graceful and luminous, and he exhibits a remarkable maturity of vision and understanding of the human condition." The book was also praised by *Booklist* reviewer Donna Seaman, who called it "empathic and searing," and concluded: "Cunningham, in a remarkable performance, inhabits the psyche of each of his striking characters."

## Later Novels

Remarkably, Cunningham received even higher praise for his 1998 publication, *The Hours*. This book, which won a Pulitzer Prize and a prestigious PEN/Faulkner award, and was adapted as a successful feature film, is a complex tribute to author Virginia Woolf and her classic novel *Mrs. Dalloway*. Woolf is a character in the book, which is strongly influenced by her unique style. A day in Woolf's life is skillfully meshed with brief episodes from two other lives: a lonely homemaker who escapes her family for a day to read *Mrs. Dalloway*, and a Greenwich Village lesbian who is called "Mrs. Dalloway" by her dying lover. *Advocate* contributor Robert Plunket confided: "I have a very low tolerance for arty writers who publish stories in the *New Yorker* and then write novels that turn out to be homages to Virginia Woolf, which makes my reaction to Michael Cunningham's new novel . . . all the more remarkable. . . . Reading this book, I was overwhelmed by the possibilities of art." A *Publishers Weekly* reviewer declared that Cunningham's book "makes a reader believe in the possibility and depth of a communality based on great literature, literature that has shown people how to live and what to ask of life." Similarly, *Booklist* contributor Seaman called *The Hours* "a graceful and passionate homage to Virginia Woolf."

After this success, Cunningham turned to screenwriting, adapting *A Home at the End of the World* and coauthoring and producing *Evening*. He also wrote the nonfiction work *Land's End: A Walk through Provincetown*. In 2005, he returned to the novel with *Specimen Days*, a book with a similar structure and

theme to *The Hours*. Again, Cunningham weaves three separate stories around a literary figure; this time the writer is American poet Walt Whitman. Specifically, Whitman's long poem *Leaves of Grass* links the three novellas. While Susan H. Greenberg, writing in *Newsweek*, felt that "Cunningham's writing is as lyrically evocative as ever," she also complained that *Specimen Days* is a "strained and familiar novel that doesn't quite work." Similarly, Joseph O'Neill, writing in the *Atlantic Monthly*, called Cunningham "one of the most humane and moving writers we have," while at the same time despairing that the plots of the three novellas are ultimately "reduced to melodrama." Theo Tait, writing in the *New Statesman*, was also unimpressed by *Specimen Days*, finding it "as muddled, and as silly, as it sounds." However, other critics had a more positive assessment of Cunningham's novel. *Booklist* contributor Seaman, for example, thought it was "galvanizing," as well as a "genuine literary event." Similarly, a *Publishers Weekly* critic called it "daring, memorable fiction," while *Library Journal* contributor Henry L. Carrigan, Jr., noted that the author's "vivid prose captures the intricate weave of love and expectation that propels the hopes of one generation as it fades into another."

In *By Nightfall*, New York City arts dealer Peter Harris experiences a midlife crisis in the form of a sexual reawakening. Peter's marriage to Rebecca, an art magazine editor, has grown stale, but it is enlivened by a visit from Rebecca's far younger brother, Ethan. A reformed drug addict, Ethan is determined to begin a career in the arts. Peter finds himself strangely drawn to his brother-in-law, and he is unsure whether this is because he envy's Ethan's lack of responsibilities, or because Ethan resembles Rebecca as a young woman. "From the complex triptychs of his previous two books, Cunningham has moved to a svelte story with just a touch of actual plot about an art dealer feeling cramped by his own smallness," Ron Charles remarked in *Washington Post Book World*. He concluded: "If the novel's final revelation seems a bit bland, it's more than compensated for by the insight and humor that come before. Admittedly, *By Nightfall* doesn't have the emotional breadth of *The Hours*, but it's a cerebral, quirky reflection on the allure of phantom ideals and even, ultimately, on what a traditional marriage needs to survive." According to Hermione Lee in the London *Guardian*, "one of Cunningham's gifts is to be able to shift gears when he wants, out of banal everydayness into an intense rhapsodic meditation on the meaning and purpose of life. This is always risky, and at times lands up in preciousness. . . . When the transitions work, though, there really is a sense of people's lives deepening and changing—even if these are not people we mind about very much."

# ■ Biographical And Critical Sources

## BOOKS

*Contemporary Literary Criticism*, Volume 34, Gale (Detroit, MI), 1985, pp. 40-42.

*Gay and Lesbian Literature*, Volume 2, St. James Press (Detroit, MI), 1998.

## PERIODICALS

*Advocate*, June 13, 1995, review of *Flesh and Blood*, p. 62; December 8, 1998, Robert Plunket, "Imagining Woolf," p. 87; May 25, 1999, Robert L. Pela, "Pulitzer Surprise," p. 83.

*Atlantic Monthly*, June, 2005, Joseph O'Neill, review of *Specimen Days*, p. 113.

*Best Sellers*, June, 1984, review of *Golden States*, p. 87.

*Booklist*, March 15, 1984, review of *Golden States*, p. 1027; January 15, 1995, Donna Seaman, review of *Flesh and Blood*, p. 868; September 15, 1998, Donna Seaman, review of *The Hours*, 173; May 1, 2005, Donna Seaman, review of *Specimen Days*, p. 1501.

*Bookseller*, August 12, 2005, review of *Specimen Days*, p. 38.

*Chicago*, July, 1984, review of *Golden States*, p. 156.

*Christian Science Monitor*, May 4, 1984, Ruth Doan MacDougall, review of *Golden States*, p. 20.

*Christopher Street*, Volume 13, number 9, 1990, review of *A Home at the End of the World*, pp. 4-5.

*Criterion*, June, 1999, Brooke Allen, review of *The Hours*, p. 81.

*Entertainment Weekly*, May 8, 1992, review of *A Home at the End of the World*, p. 52; April 14, 1995, Kelli Pryor, review of *Flesh and Blood*, p. 59.

*Glamour*, November, 1990, review of *A Home at the End of the World*, p. 174; April, 1995, review of *Flesh and Blood*, p. 198.

*Guardian* (London, England), January 15, 2011, Hermione Lee, review of *By Nightfall*.

*Harper's*, June, 1999, Jonathan Dee, review of *The Hours*, p. 76.

*Interview*, August, 2004, John Beatty, review of *A Home at the End of the World*, p. 78.

*Kirkus Reviews*, September 1, 1998, review of *The Hours*; May 1, 2002, review of *Land's End: A Walk through Provincetown*, p. 632.

*Lambda Book Report*, May-June, 1995, review of *Flesh and Blood*, p. 14; January, 1999, Sarah Van Arsdale, review of *The Hours*, p. 14.

*Library Journal*, April 1, 1984, review of *Golden States*, p. 732; October 15, 1990, review of *A Home at the End of the World*, p. 102; April 15, 1995, review of *Flesh and Blood*, p. 112; October 1, 1998, Marc A.

Kloszewski, review of *The Hours*, p. 131; May 15, 2005, Henry L. Carrigan, Jr., review of *Specimen Days*, p. 104.

*London Review of Books*, February 22, 1996, review of *Flesh and Blood*, pp. 27-31.

*Los Angeles Times Book Review*, April 22, 1984, Alice F. Wittels, review of *Golden States*, p. 6; November 18, 1990, Richard Eder, review of *A Home at the End of the World*, pp. 3, 12; April 9, 1995, review of *Flesh and Blood*, pp. 3, 7.

*Nation*, July 1, 1991, David Kaufman, review of *A Home at the End of the World*, pp. 21-25.

*New Leader*, May-June, 2005, Angeline Goreau, review of *Specimen Days*, p. 39.

*New Republic*, August 8, 2005, Deborah Friedell, review of *Specimen Days*, p. 35.

*New Statesman*, August 29, 2005, Theo Tait, review of *Specimen Days*, p. 38.

*Newsweek*, June 13, 2005, Susan H. Greenberg, review of *Specimen Days*, p. 75.

*New York*, November 12, 1990, review of *A Home at the End of the World*, p. 30; April 10, 1995, review of *Flesh and Blood*, pp. 72-73.

*New Yorker*, April 30, 1984, review of *Golden States*, p. 118; October 5, 1998, review of *The Hours*, p. 107.

*New York Times Book Review*, November 11, 1990, Joyce Reiser Kornblatt, review of *A Home at the End of the World*, pp. 12-13; April 16, 1995, review of *Flesh and Blood*, p. 13; November 22, 1998, review of *The Hours*, p. 6.

*People*, May 7, 1984, review of *Golden States*, p. 19; February 19, 2003, Allison Adato, "Man of the Hours," p. 105; June 20, 2005, Jonathan Durbin, review of *Specimen Days*, p. 49.

*Publishers Weekly*, February 3, 1984, review of *Golden States*, p. 393; August 17, 1990, Sybil Steinberg, review of *A Home at the End of the World*, p. 52; January 23, 1995, review of *Flesh and Blood*, p. 60; August 31, 1998, review of *The Hours*, p. 46; November 2, 1998, interview with Michael Coffey, "Michael Cunningham: New Family Outings," p. 53; May 20, 2002, review of *Land's End*, p. 55; May 9, 2005, review of *Specimen Days*, p. 44.

*School Library Journal*, October, 2005, Matthew L. Moffett, review of *Specimen Days*, p. 200.

*Times Literary Supplement*, August 11, 1995, review of *Flesh and Blood*, p. 20.

*Tribune Books* (Chicago, IL), November 4, 1990, review of *A Home at the End of the World*, p. 6.

*Vanity Fair*, May, 1995, review of *Flesh and Blood*, p. 96.

*Village Voice*, September 4, 1984, Elizabeth Royte, review of *Golden States*, p. 52.

*Vogue*, January, 1989, review of *A Home at the End of the World*, p. 62; November, 1998, review of *The Hours*, p. 247.

*Voice of Youth Advocates,* October, 1984, review of *Golden States,* p. 196.

*Washington Post Book World,* December 9, 1990, Patrick Gale, review of *A Home at the End of the World,* p. 7; April 2, 1995, review of *Flesh and Blood,* pp. 72-73; October 6, 2010, Ron Charles, review of *By Nightfall,* p. C1.


ONLINE

*Barclay Agency Web site,* http://www.barclayagency. com/ (October 16, 2006), "Michael Cunningham."

*Internet Movie Database,* http://www.imdb.com/ (October 16, 2006), "Michael Cunningham."

*Literati.net,* http://www.literati.net/ (October 16, 2006), "Michael Cunningham."

*Michael Cunningham Home Page,* http://www. michaelcunninghamwriter.com (August 8, 2011).

*Powell's Books,* http://www.powells.com/ (October 16, 2006), Dave Weich, "The Same Old, Brand New Michael Cunningham."

*Salon.com,* http://www.salon.com/ (November 10, 1998), Georgia Jones-Davis, review of *The Hours.**

# Charles E. Curran

## 1934-

■ **Personal**

Born March 30, 1934, in Rochester, NY. *Education:* St. Bernard's Seminary and College, B.A., 1955; Pontifical Gregorian University, Rome, Italy, S.T.D., 1957, S.T.L., 1959, S.T.D., 1961; Academia Alfonsiana, Rome, S.T.D., 1961.

■ **Addresses**

*Office*—317 Dallas Hall, Southern Methodist University, P.O. Box 750317, Dallas, TX 75275-0317. *E-mail*—ccurran@smu.edu.

■ **Career**

Writer, theologian. Ordained Roman Catholic priest, 1958. St. Bernard's Seminary, Rochester, NY, professor of moral theology, 1961-65; Catholic University of America, Washington, DC, assistant professor, 1965-67, associate professor, 1967-71, professor of moral theology, 1971-89; Southern Methodist University, Dallas, TX, Elizabeth Scurlock University Professor of Human Values, 1991—. Senior research scholar, Kennedy Center for Bioethics, Georgetown University, 1972; external examiner in Christian ethics, University of the West Indies, 1982-86; visiting Kaneb Professor of Catholic Studies, Cornell University, 1987-88; University of Southern California, visiting Brooks Professor of Religion, 1988-89, visiting Firestone Professor of Religion, 1989-90; visiting Goodwin-Philpott Eminent Scholar in Religion, Auburn University, 1990-91.

■ **Member**

American Society of Christian Ethics (president, 1971-72), American Theological Society (vice president, 1988-89; president, 1989-90), Catholic Theological Society of America (vice president, 1968-69; president, 1969-70), College Theology Society.

■ **Awards, Honors**

"Man in the News" citation, *New York Times*, 1967; faculty fellowship, American Association of Theological Schools, 1971; John Courtney Murray Award, Catholic Society of America, 1972, for distinguished achievement in theology; "Person of the Week," American Broadcasting Company (ABC), August, 1986; honorary doctorate, University of Charleston, 1987, and Concordia College, 1992; Presidential Award, College Theology Society, for a lifetime of scholarly achievements in moral theology, 2003; Call to Action leadership award, 2005.

■ **Writings**

*NONFICTION; THEOLOGY*

*Christian Morality Today: The Renewal of Moral Theology,* Fides (Notre Dame, IN), 1966.

*A New Look at Christian Morality,* Fides (Notre Dame, IN), 1968.

(Editor) *Absolutes in Moral Theology?*, Corpus Books (Washington, DC), 1968.

(With Robert E. Hunt and others) *Dissent in and for the Church: Theologians and Humanae Vitae,* Sheed & Ward (New York, NY), 1969.

(With others) *The Responsibility of Dissent: The Church and Academic Freedom,* Sheed & Ward (New York, NY), 1969.

(Editor) *Contraception: Authority and Dissent,* Herder & Herder (New York, NY), 1969.

*Contemporary Problems in Moral Theology,* Fides (Notre Dame, IN), 1970.

(Editor, with George J. Dyer) *Shared Responsibility in the Local Church,* Catholic Theological Society of America, 1970.

*Catholic Moral Theology in Dialogue,* Fides (Notre Dame, IN), 1972.

*The Crisis in Priestly Ministry,* Fides (Notre Dame, IN), 1972.

*Politics, Medicine, and Christian Ethics: A Dialogue with Paul Ramsey,* Fortress (Philadelphia, PA), 1973.

*New Perspectives in Moral Theology,* Fides (Notre Dame, IN), 1974.

*Ongoing Revision: Studies in Moral Theology,* Fides (Notre Dame, IN), 1975.

*Themes in Fundamental Moral Theology,* University of Notre Dame Press (Notre Dame, IN), 1977.

*Issues in Sexual and Medical Ethics,* University of Notre Dame Press (Notre Dame, IN), 1978.

*Transition and Tradition in Moral Theology,* University of Notre Dame Press (Notre Dame, IN), 1979.

*Moral Theology: A Continuing Journey,* University of Notre Dame Press (Notre Dame, IN), 1982.

*American Catholic Social Ethics: Twentieth-Century Approaches,* University of Notre Dame Press (Notre Dame, IN), 1982.

*Critical Concerns in Moral Theology,* University of Notre Dame Press (Notre Dame, IN), 1984.

*Directions in Catholic Social Ethics,* University of Notre Dame Press (Notre Dame, IN), 1985.

*Directions in Fundamental Moral Theology,* University of Notre Dame Press (Notre Dame, IN), 1985.

*Faithful Dissent,* Sheed & Ward (Kansas City, MO), 1986.

*Toward an American Catholic Moral Theology,* University of Notre Dame Press (Notre Dame, IN), 1988.

*Sexualitaet und Ethik,* Athenaum (Frankfurt, Germany), 1988.

*Tensions in Moral Theology,* University of Notre Dame Press (Notre Dame, IN), 1988.

*Catholic Higher Education, Theology, and Academic Freedom,* University of Notre Dame Press (Notre Dame, IN), 1990.

(Editor) *Moral Theology: Challenges for the Future; Essays in Honor of Richard A. McCormick,* Paulist Press (New York, NY), 1990.

*The Living Tradition of Catholic Moral Theology,* University of Notre Dame Press (Notre Dame, IN), 1992.

*The Church and Morality: An Ecumenical and Catholic Approach,* Fortress (Minneapolis, MN), 1993.

*History and Contemporary Issues: Studies in Moral Theology,* Continuum (New York, NY), 1996.

*The Origins of Moral Theology in the United States: Three Different Approaches,* Georgetown University Press (Washington, DC), 1997.

*The Catholic Moral Tradition Today: A Synthesis,* Georgetown University Press (Washington, DC), 1999.

*Moral Theology at the End of the Century,* Marquette University Press (Milwaukee, WI), 1999.

*Catholic Social Teaching, 1891-Present: A Historical, Theological, and Ethical Analysis,* Georgetown University Press (Washington, DC), 2002.

*The Moral Theology of Pope John Paul II,* Georgetown University Press (Washington, DC), 2005.

*Loyal Dissent: Memoir of a Catholic Theologian,* Georgetown University Press (Washington, DC), 2006.

*Catholic Moral Theology in the United States: A History,* Georgetown University Press (Washington, DC), 2008.

*The Social Mission of the U.S. Catholic Church: A Theological Perspective,* Georgetown University Press (Washington, DC), 2011.

EDITOR; "READINGS IN MORAL THEOLOGY" SERIES

(With Richard A. McCormick) *Readings in Moral Theology Number 1: Moral Norms and Catholic Tradition,* Paulist Press (New York, NY), 1979.

(With Richard A. McCormick) *Readings in Moral Theology Number 2: The Distinctiveness of Christian Ethics,* Paulist Press (New York, NY), 1980.

(With Richard A. McCormick) *Readings in Moral Theology Number 3: The Magisterium and Morality,* Paulist Press (New York, NY), 1982.

(With Richard A. McCormick) *Readings in Moral Theology Number 4: The Use of Scripture in Moral Theology,* Paulist Press (New York, NY), 1984.

(With Richard A. McCormick) *Readings in Moral Theology Number 5: Official Catholic Social Teaching,* Paulist Press (New York, NY), 1986.

(With Richard A. McCormick) *Readings in Moral Theology Number 6: Dissent in the Church,* Paulist Press (New York, NY), 1988.

(With Richard A. McCormick) *Readings in Moral Theology Number 7: Natural Law and Theology,* Paulist Press (New York, NY), 1991.

(With Richard A. McCormick) *Readings in Moral Theology Number 8: Dialogue about Catholic Sexual Teaching,* Paulist Press (New York, NY), 1993.

(With Margaret A. Farley) *Readings in Moral Theology Number 9: Feminist Ethics and the Catholic Moral Tradition,* Paulist Press (New York, NY), 1996.

(With Richard A. McCormick) *Readings in Moral Theology Number 10: John Paul II and Moral Theology,* Paulist Press (New York, NY), 1998.

(With Richard A. McCormick) *Readings in Moral Theology Number 11: The Historical Development of Fundamental Moral Theology in the United States,* Paulist Press (New York, NY), 1999.

(With Leslie Griffin) *Readings in Moral Theology Number 12: The Catholic Church, Morality and Politics,* Paulist Press (New York, NY), 2001.

*Readings in Moral Theology Number 13: Change in Official Catholic Moral Teachings,* Paulist Press (New York, NY), 2002.

*Readings in Moral Theology Number 14: Conscience,* Paulist Press (New York, NY), 2004.

(With Julie Hanlon Rubio) *Readings in Moral Theology Number 15: Marriage,* Paulist Press (New York, NY), 2009.

(With Lisa A. Fullam) *Readings in Moral Theology Number 16: Virtue,* Paulist Press (Mahwah, NJ), 2011.

*OTHER*

Contributor to books, including *Ecumenical Dialogue at Harvard,* edited by S.H. Miller and G.E. Wright, Harvard University Press (Cambridge, MA), 1964; *Law for Liberty,* edited by James E. Biechler, Helicon (La Jolla, CA), 1967; and *The Situation Ethics Debate,* edited by Harvey Cox, Westminster (Philadelphia, PA), 1968. Contributor to periodicals, including *Jurist, Commonweal,* and *Homiletic.* Member of editorial board, *International Christian Digest, Eglise et Theologie,* and *Horizons.*

■ **Sidelights**

In April 1967, Charles E. Curran became a *cause célèbre* for priestly academic freedom when he was fired by Catholic University of America, supposedly (although the university gave no reasons for the dismissal) for his liberal views on birth control. The popular teacher chose to fight the ouster, and the Catholic University faculty voted 400 to eighteen not to hold classes until he was reinstated. The boycott closed the university for three days before Curran was rehired with the announcement that he would be promoted from assistant to associate professor the following semester.

In the summer of 1968, Curran was, he once told *CA,* "the organizer and chief spokesman of a group of American Catholic theologians, ultimately totaling about six hundred, who dissented from the papal encyclical *Humanae Vitae,*" which reaffirmed the church's traditional stand against artificial birth control. "The day after the encyclical was issued in Rome, I spoke for eighty-nine Roman Catholic theologians . . . indicating that one could be a loyal Roman Catholic and still disagree with this particular teaching. This dissent was widely carried in the newspaper and television accounts of those days. . . . These events are recorded in . . . *Dissent in and for the Church: Theologians and Humanae Vitae.*"

In 1989 Curran explained further to *CA* about his difficulties with the Catholic University of America and the Vatican: "The Vatican's Congregation for the Doctrine of the Faith [declared] that I was no longer suitable nor eligible to teach Catholic theology at Catholic University of America. Subsequent to that, the university said that I could not teach Catholic theology there and had to sign a statement saying I would agree with the Vatican declaration. I refused to do so, on the grounds that it was a violation of my academic freedom. I took the case to court in the Superior Court of the District of Columbia, but the judge ruled that Catholic University did not always have to come down on the side of academic freedom and that I had no case against them. However, a committee of the American Association of University Professors has concluded that Catholic University has violated my academic freedom and my tenure rights."

Banned by the Vatican from teaching moral theology at the university, Curran left the Catholic University of America in 1989. He has been the Elizabeth Scurlock Professor of Human Values at Southern Methodist University in Dallas, Texas, since 1991. A prolific writer and editor, Curran focuses his work on the moral theology of the church, including the "Readings in Moral Theology" series he coedits with Richard A. McCormick and others.

*The Origins of Moral Theology in the United States and Catholic Social Teaching, 1891-Present*

Curran is generally lauded by critics for his scholarly analyses and balanced reasoning on issues of moral theology, despite the church's position that he is unfit to teach moral issues. Lawrence Cunningham wrote in *Commonweal* of Curran's *The Origins of Moral Theology in the United States: Three Different Approaches:* "Curran analyzes in some depth the writing of all three men [Aloysius Sabetti, Thomas Boquillon, and John Hogan] as well as offers a concise and illuminating history of the development of moral theology. . . . Though scholarly, this study should be of interest to anyone concerned with theology."

Curran's *Catholic Social Teaching, 1891-Present: A Historical, Theological, and Ethical Analysis* was also hailed as a major achievement. Curran emphasizes the historical development of the church's social teachings, which traditionally focus on social, economic, and political matters and not subjects relating to women's rights, family, or environmental responsibility. He examines the influence of major documents, including the papal encyclicals *Dignitatis humanae* from the second Vatican Council, and *The Challenge of Peace* and *Economic Justice for All* from the U.S. Catholic bishops. In the view of *National Catholic Reporter* contributor Andrew Skotnicki, Curran's analysis of the disagreements and compromises that shaped the creation of these documents is one of the particular strengths of the book. According to *Church History* contributor Debra Campbell, *Catholic Social Teaching, 1891-Present* is a "major milestone in Catholic intellectual history." David Hollenbach, writing in *Theological Studies*, called it "the single best analysis of the modern tradition of Catholic social teaching to be found in one place."

### The Moral Theology of Pope John Paul II and *Loyal Dissent*

In *The Moral Theology of Pope John Paul II*, Curran analyzes the foundations of John Paul's ethical teachings. The book "rightly notes that the key concern and unifying theme of John Paul's ethics is the truth about the human person, disclosed in and by Jesus Christ," wrote Darlene Fozard Weaver in *Commonweal*. In Curran's view, however, John Paul's focus on duty, obedience, and the common good "cannot deal adequately with the concrete realities of each individual called in a unique way to respond to the gift of God and the needs of others in our complex world." According to *Theological Studies* critic Mark J. Allman, the book "reconfirms [Curran's] well-earned reputation as one of the most intelligent and consistently progressive voices in Catholic moral theology."

Curran's exploration of his own development as a moral thinker, *Loyal Dissent: Memoir of a Catholic Theologian,* received significant attention. Curran describes his call to the priesthood, his moral studies in seminary, and his early clash with church authorities on teachings about sexual morality; he also discusses how the consequences of his choices to confront the church hierarchy have affected him. Writing in *America*, Maura Anne Ryan observed that "the virtue of *Loyal Dissent . . .* is its ability to place [Curran's] public choices, and ultimately their costs, in the context not only of deeply held theological convictions, but also of his vocation as a priest-theologian." As a result, Ryan added, the book "is more than a reflection on Charles Curran's life. It is also a reflection on the American Catholic Church in the aftermath of Vatican II." *Library Journal* reviewer John-Leonard Berg admired the book's bluntness and honesty, writing that Curran challenges established teachings "with the brilliance of a scholar and the sensitivity of a seasoned pastor."

### Catholic Moral Theology in the United States

In *Catholic Moral Theology in the United States: A History,* Curran provides a historical overview of Catholic moral theology from the nineteenth century

to present-day America. Of the book's ten chapters, the first three deal with pre-Vatican II during the nineteenth and twentieth centuries. In the section on the nineteenth century, Curran focuses on manuals of moral theology intended to prepare seminarians as confessors. "The manuals are not ancient history," noted Russell B. Connors, Jr., in *America*. "The moral methodology of these textbooks continues to serve as the foundation of current Catholic teachings on many medical and sexual issues." Three further chapters deal with the effect on moral theology of Vatican II and the 1968 encyclical of Pope Paul VI, Humanae Vitae, a reaffirmation of, among other things, the church's opposition to any form of birth control. The final four chapters examine specific topics: "Fundamental Moral Theology," "Sexuality and Marriage," "Bioethics," and "Social Ethics." Connors noted that while these chapters "are well connected to the chapters that precede them, they could stand alone for readers looking for an overview of these areas of Catholic moral theology subsequent to Vatican II."

*Conscience* reviewer Thomas A. Shannon called this work an "outstanding volume," as well as a "tour de force on the development of moral theology in the US from the 19th century forward." Shannon further noted: "One of the important elements of the book is the way in which Curran situates the history of moral theology in both secular and ecclesiological history and culture. He recognizes that there is a strong relationship between theology and its various settings which he spells out clearly. . . . In this book—as in all of Curran's writings, presentations and teaching is his sense of impeccable fairness to the authors he discusses." Connors similarly felt that in this work, Curran "has chronicled history fairly and clearly." Further praise for *Catholic Moral Theology in the United States* came from *National Catholic Reporter* contributor David O'Brien, who felt that Curran's "chapters on the period of his own work before, during and after Vatican II are an invaluable summary of the intellectual issues that have divided and damaged the church." O'Brien added: "Curran is scrupulously fair to his critics, so that the reader gets an evenhanded presentation. . . . This book and Curran's work generally deserve the attention of all those Catholics who believe that history matters." Likewise, *Church History* reviewer Aline H. Kalbian observed that "fans of Curran, of which there are many, will welcome this latest offering for its ambitious sweep and comprehensive treatment of the subject." *Theological Studies* writer Julia Fleming also commended this volume, concluding: "When done well, the study of history reminds us that something has not always been, nor need always be, as we know it today. [Curran's] text provides a much-needed framework for analyzing the past and tracing the trajectories of U.S. Catholic ethical reflection. This account of the discipline's development will serve as a standard resource for both theological education and historical research."

### The Social Mission of the U.S. Catholic Church

With *The Social Mission of the U.S. Catholic Church: A Theological Perspective,* Curran provides a similar overview, as *National Catholic Reporter* contributor Michael Baxter noted: "The plot line, the church's social mission from colonial Maryland up to the 2008 national election, highlights Catholics' movement out of their own subculture into the U.S. mainstream." Curran's work focuses on the twentieth century, and Curran shows that during the early decades of the century, the church focused its social mission on hospitals, schools, and charities. After Vatican II, however, the emphasis switched to social, political, and civic issues in the United States and elsewhere. Curran pays special attention to several issues that are representative of the church's sense of social mission since Vatican II: abortion, war and peace, and labor.

Writing for the *Catholic Books Review,* Richard Shields noted that Curran's book "is an undertaking that shows deep respect both for the tradition and the development of contemporary moral consciousness." Shields added: "By examining various examples of social mission as faithful responses of the Catholic community, Curran paints a picture of the Church as a living body interpreting the 'signs of the time' and discerning the Gospel calling in the world today."

## ■ Biographical And Critical Sources

### BOOKS

Curran, Charles E., *The Moral Theology of Pope John Paul II,* Georgetown University Press (Washington, DC), 2005.
Curran, Charles E., *Loyal Dissent: Memoir of a Catholic Theologian,* Georgetown University Press (Washington, DC), 2006.

### PERIODICALS

*America,* July 31, 2006, Maura Anne Ryan, "Search and Witness," p. 34; September 8, 2008, Russell B. Connors, Jr., "'Participant Observer'," review of *Catholic Moral Theology in the United States: A History,* p. 35.
*Church History,* March, 2005, Debra Campbell, review of *Catholic Social Teaching, 1891-Present: A Historical, Theological, and Ethical Analysis,* p. 210; September, 2009, Aline H. Kalbian, review of *Catholic Moral Theology in the United States,* p. 720.

*Commonweal,* November 21, 1997, Lawrence S. Cunningham, review of *The Origins of Moral Theology in the United States: Three Different Approaches,* p. 27; December 16, 2005, Darlene Fozard Weaver, "How to Be Good," p. 27; September 8, 2006, J. Peter Nixon, review of *Loyal Dissent: Memoir of a Catholic Theologian,* p. 30.
*Conscience,* summer, 2007, Rosemary Radford Ruether, "For the Good of the Church"; winter, 2008, Thomas A. Shannon, "The Inside Man: History from a Participant's Expert Perspective," review of *Catholic Moral Theology in the United States,* p. 45.
*Ecumenical Review,* July, 2004, Thomas J. Massaro, review of *Catholic Social Teaching, 1891-Present,* p. 378.
*First Things: A Monthly Journal of Religion and Public Life,* April, 2003, review of *Catholic Social Teaching, 1891-Present,* p. 69.
*Library Journal,* May 15, 2006, John-Leonard Berg, review of *Loyal Dissent,* p. 106.
*National Catholic Reporter,* February 1, 2002, Andrew Skotnicki, review of *Catholic Social Teaching, 1891-Present,* p. 27; February 20, 2009, David O'Brien, "Catholic Moral Theology Based on Real Life," review of *Catholic Moral Theology in the United States,* p. 15; April 15, 2011, Michael Baxter, "Curran Charts Catholic Move to the Mainstream," review of *The Social Mission of the U.S. Catholic Church: A Theological Perspective,* p. 17.
*New York Times Book Review,* March 19, 1989, John Garvey, review of *Tensions in Moral Theology,* p. 11. October 24, 1999, John T. Noonan, Jr., review of *The Catholic Moral Tradition Today: A Synthesis.*
*Science & Sprit,* May-June, 2006, review of *Loyal Dissent.*
*Theological Studies,* June, 2003, David Hollenbach, review of *Catholic Social Teaching, 1891-Present,* p. 437; September, 2006, Mark J. Allman, review of *The Moral Theology of Pope John Paul II,* p. 695; June, 2007, Joseph A. Selling, review of *Loyal Dissent,* p. 468; June, 2009, Julia Fleming, review of *Catholic Moral Theology in the United States,* p. 493; June, 2010, Mary M. Doyle Roche, review of *Readings in Moral Theology Number 15: Marriage,* p. 484.

### ONLINE

*Catholic Books Review,* http://catholicbooksreview.org/ (July 3, 2011), review of *Readings in Moral Theology Number 15: Marriage*; Richard Shields, review of *The Social Mission of the U.S. Catholic Church.*
*Southern Methodist University, Perkins School of Theology Web site* http://www.smu.edu/ (July 3, 2011), "Charles E. Curran."*

# Mary Daheim

## 1937-

■ **Also Known As**

Mary Richardson Daheim

■ **Personal**

Surname is pronounced "*day*-hime"; born November 7, 1937, in Seattle, WA; daughter of Hugh E. (a marine engineer) and Monica (a legal secretary) Richardson; married David C. Daheim (a professor of humanities), December 18, 1965; children: Barbara, Katherine, Magdalen. *Education:* University of Washington, Seattle, B.A., 1960. *Politics:* Democrat. *Religion:* Roman Catholic.

■ **Addresses**

*Home*—Seattle, WA. *E-mail*—mary@authormary daheim.com.

■ **Career**

Author and communications consultant. Pacific Northwest Bell, Seattle, WA, public relations manager and communications consultant, 1960—. Consultant to banks and telecommunications companies.

■ **Member**

Romance Writers of America, Mystery Writers of America, Authors Guild.

■ **Awards, Honors**

Pacific Northwest Writers Association Achievement Award, 2000.

■ **Writings**

*HISTORICAL ROMANCE NOVELS*

*Love's Pirate,* Avon (New York, NY), 1983.
*Destiny's Pawn,* Avon (New York, NY), 1984.
*Pride's Captive,* Avon (New York, NY), 1986.
*Passion's Triumph,* Avon (New York, NY), 1988.
*King's Ransom,* Harlequin (London, England), 1990.
*Improbable Eden,* Harlequin (London, England), 1991.
*Gypsy Baron,* Harlequin (London, England), 1992.

*"BED AND BREAKFAST" MYSTERY SERIES*

*Just Desserts,* Avon (New York, NY), 1991.
*Fowl Prey,* Avon (New York, NY), 1991.
*Holy Terrors,* Avon (New York, NY), 1992.
*Dune to Death,* Avon (New York, NY), 1993.
*Bantam of the Opera,* Avon (New York, NY), 1993.
*A Fit of Tempera,* Avon (New York, NY), 1994.
*Major Vices,* Avon (New York, NY), 1995.
*Murder, My Suite,* Avon (New York, NY), 1995.
*Auntie Mayhem,* Avon (New York, NY), 1996.
*Nutty as a Fruitcake,* Avon (New York, NY), 1996.
*September Mourn,* Avon (New York, NY), 1997.
*Wed and Buried,* Avon (New York, NY), 1998.
*Snow Place to Die,* Avon (New York, NY), 1998.
*Legs Benedict,* Avon (New York, NY), 1999.
*Creeps Suzette,* Avon (New York, NY), 2000.
*A Streetcar Named Expire,* Avon (New York, NY), 2001.
*Suture Self,* William Morrow (New York, NY), 2001.
*Silver Scream,* William Morrow (New York, NY), 2002.
*Hocus Croakus,* William Morrow (New York, NY), 2003.

*This Old Souse,* William Morrow (New York, NY), 2004.

*Dead Man Docking,* William Morrow (New York, NY), 2005.

*Saks & Violins,* William Morrow (New York, NY), 2006.

*Scots on the Rocks,* William Morrow (New York, NY), 2007.

*Vi Agra Falls,* William Morrow (New York, NY), 2008.

*Loco Motive,* William Morrow (New York, NY), 2010.

*All the Pretty Hearses,* William Morrow (New York, NY), 2011.

*"ALPINE" SERIES*

*The Alpine Advocate,* Ballantine (New York, NY), 1992.

*The Alpine Betrayal,* Ballantine (New York, NY), 1993.

*The Alpine Christmas,* Ballantine (New York, NY), 1993.

*The Alpine Decoy,* Ballantine (New York, NY), 1994.

*The Alpine Escape,* Ballantine (New York, NY), 1995.

*The Alpine Fury,* Ballantine (New York, NY), 1996.

*The Alpine Gamble,* Ballantine (New York, NY), 1996.

*The Alpine Hero,* Ballantine (New York, NY), 1996.

*The Alpine Icon,* Ballantine (New York, NY), 1998.

*The Alpine Journey,* Ballantine (New York, NY), 1998.

*The Alpine Kindred,* Ballantine (New York, NY), 1998.

*The Alpine Legacy,* Ballantine (New York, NY), 1999.

*The Alpine Menace,* Ballantine (New York, NY), 2000.

*The Alpine Nemesis,* Ballantine (New York, NY), 2001.

*The Alpine Obituary,* Ballantine (New York, NY), 2002.

*The Alpine Pursuit,* Ballantine (New York, NY), 2004.

*The Alpine Quilt,* Ballantine Books (New York, NY), 2005.

*The Alpine Recluse,* Ballantine (New York, NY), 2006.

*The Alpine Mysteries Omnibus,* Wings Books (New York, NY), 2006.

*The Alpine Scandal,* Ballantine (New York, NY), 2007.

*The Alpine Traitor,* Ballantine Books (New York, NY), 2008.

*The Alpine Uproar,* Ballantine Books (New York, NY), 2009.

*The Alpine Vengeance,* Ballantine Books (New York, NY), 2010.

*The Alpine Winter,* Ballantine Books (New York, NY), 2011.

*OTHER*

(With others) *Jessica Fletcher Presents "Murder, They Wrote,"* Boulevard Books (New York, NY), 1997.

(With Carolyn Hart, Jane Isenberg, and Shirley Rousseau Murphy) *Motherhood Is Murder* (mystery collection), Avon (New York, NY), 2003.

*Sugarplums and Scandal* (novel), HarperCollins (New York, NY), 2006.

Also author of *Sound of Surrender,* Avon (New York, NY), and other historical romance novels. Managing editor of *Anacortes American Bulletin,* 1960; reporter and columnist for *Port Angeles Daily News,* 1966-69; former staff member of *Pacific Search* (now *Northwest* magazine). Contributor to magazines and newspapers.

■ **Sidelights**

As a child in the Pacific Northwest, Mary Daheim aspired to a career as a sports reporter. Friends and relatives told her that women do not become sports reporters. When she asked her grandmother why, she was told: "Because those boys don't want you to see them with their clothes off." Daheim turned to writing novels instead and became the author of the popular "Bed and Breakfast" and "Alpine" mystery series.

After penning a number of historical romances, Daheim realized she was working in a field that did not reflect her interests as a reader. She was actually a fan of mystery novels, and she proceeded to launch two successful mystery series. Both series are set in the Pacific Northwest and feature casts of characters drawn from her own experiences. The "Bed and Breakfast" series takes place on the coastal island of Chavez where its protagonist, Judith McMonigle Flynn, runs the only B&B when she is not too busy solving crimes. The "Alpine" series is based in Alpine, Washington, which a reviewer from *Publishers Weekly* characterized as a "soap-opera small town." It features amateur sleuth Emma Lord, editor of the *Alpine Advocate.* In addition to writing solo, Daheim has also contributed to several mystery collections.

**Daheim once told *CA*:**

"I've always written, never wanted to do anything else. I use the historical romance to inform, entertain, and amuse. I like research and do a lot of it. I consider myself a storyteller, not a novelist. While the genre isn't exactly suited to one-liners, I try to inject at least a hint of humor. I have as much fun writing the books as I hope readers will have reading them.

"I try to create characters that fit the romantic novel genre without being clichés. I also use historical personages as much as possible to give authenticity while presenting their characters with what I term interpretive accuracy. Stories with a strong historical background suit my style best, using the actual events as a springboard for my characters, real and imagined.

"The personal views I present tend to deal with my own interpretation of historical events, though I know that the historian must, by definition, deal in hindsight. To compensate I try to show how characters reacted to events within the context of their time and personal experiences. For me, history is not a grand, faceless panorama, but the meshing of individual personalities, needs, ambitions, and every other human emotion that eventually becomes what we later call 'history.'"

### The Alpine Fury, The Alpine Gamble, and The Alpine Pursuit

Daheim's mysteries have received a mixed critical response. In the sixth novel of the "Alpine" series, *The Alpine Fury,* the town is suffering the economic effects of a failed logging industry when rumors begin to circulate that its only bank is headed for a merger. Emma Lord begins to investigate in her capacity as a journalist. However, when the bank's bookkeeper turns up murdered, her role soon switches to that of detective. A reviewer for *Publishers Weekly* stated: "The book's small town ambience makes a good contrast to this high-finance, very 1980s mystery. The town's quirky characters . . . add a nice, honest feel to the tale." However, another *Publishers Weekly* reviewer found nothing to praise in the seventh novel in the series, *The Alpine Gamble,* describing it as a "predictable, mundane book."

Despite such occasional criticism, Daheim has had considerable success with the "Alpine" series. The author made her hardcover debut with the sixteenth novel in the series, *The Alpine Pursuit,* in which Emma investigates the shooting death of an actor killed onstage during the performance of a play. *Library Journal* reviewer Rex Klett remarked that the novel contains "solid prose, remarkable characters, and [an] entertaining plot."

### The Alpine Quilt and The Alpine Recluse

In *The Alpine Quilt,* Emma finds herself once again juggling a million tasks, including a good dose of sleuthing. In her role as publisher of the weekly paper, she has to deal with the local photography studio regarding some changes in policy and discuss the home section with the appropriate editor. On a personal level, she must fit in a visit with her brother Ben, a missionary, who has just returned to town. When Emma learns that the photographer's mother Genevieve is soon to visit after decades away, she decides to interview her on top of all of her other duties, in an effort to get a feel for what the town was like during a bygone era. But when Genevieve and another woman are poisoned while having a reunion dinner, Emma's plans take a sharp turn, particularly when Genevieve does not survive the incident. Instead of an interview, Emma sets out on an investigation, determined to learn who is responsible for the woman's death. A contributor to *Kirkus Reviews* opined that the book "amiably captures the rhythms and crosscurrents of small-town life."

*The Alpine Recluse* is the next volume in the series, and finds Emma and her friends suffering through a sweltering heat wave. Temperatures rise even higher one evening when Tim and Tiffany Rafferty's house burns to the ground. The next day, Tim is discovered dead inside the house, and a preliminary investigation suggests that he was already dead prior to the rampaging fire. A number of questions swiftly come up in the wake of this discovery, with the town wondering if Tiffany, who is quite pregnant, was in any way abused by her husband, making her and her protective parents potential suspects in what is now a murder investigation. A stranger was also seen lurking around the house prior to the fire. While the sheriff makes very little headway with his investigation, Emma manages to see things a little more clearly and get to the bottom of the situation. A *Kirkus Reviews* contributor remarked that "the ending is a bit of a cheat, but if you prefer your mysteries small, insular and chatty, Daheim . . . is your gal."

### The Alpine Traitor

Emma Lord is jarred into past memories when a former fiancé's children try to buy out her paper. Memories of this man, Tom Cavanaugh, who left her pregnant and is now long dead, are further stirred when one of those involved in the deal is found murdered and Emma herself becomes a suspect. Now she must investigate to protect herself and the newspaper as further violence strikes closer to home. Meanwhile, she is also trying to help a new reporter learn how to write journalism.

*Booklist* reviewer Sue O'Brien praised Daheim's protagonist as an "engaging narrator" and remarked that the daily task of operating the local newspaper serves as a "fascinating frame" for the story. A *Publishers Weekly* contributor also commended this twentieth series installment, noting that an "intriguing plot and the usual cast of lovable characters make this another winner."

### The Alpine Uproar

An apparent barroom brawl leaves Alvin De Muth dead in *The Alpine Uproar.* For once Emma can run the story fresh in her weekly paper as it happens just before her deadline. But Sheriff Milo Dodge is not sure about the cause of death, and when a highway accident leaves two dead and another on life support, Emma and the sheriff begin wondering if the two incidents are related.

A *Kirkus Reviews* contributor found this novel very "chatty" but added that if "small-town minutiae and insularity appeal to you, this is top of the line." O'Brien, writing again in *Booklist,* commended the "well-delineated main and recurring characters," but she also noted there are so many that even loyal fans of the series "may have some trouble keeping [them] straight." A *Publishers Weekly* reviewer had higher praise for this series addition, noting: "Daheim's premise—that random occurrences are connected—keeps the reader turning the pages."

### The Alpine Vengeance

*The Alpine Vengeance* finds Emma investigating a ten-year-old murder to shed light on recent crimes, including the shooting of a reclusive artist. The original crime, part of an earlier episode in the "Alpine" series, involved the supposed murder of a sibling over control of a bank. When the convicted killer dies in prison, mysterious letters start arriving demanding the wrongly convicted man be exonerated.

A *Kirkus Reviews* contributor had praise for this installment, writing: "Daheim's series—like Alpine, the kind of town that considers you a newcomer if you've only lived there 10 years—bustles with small-town charm and convoluted family relationships." A *Publishers Weekly* reviewer offered a more mixed assessment, noting: "While the investigation drags in places, the unexpected conclusion is sure to please series fans."

### Holy Terrors, Wed and Buried, and September Mourn

Daheim's "Bed & Breakfast" series has also established itself as a popular mystery series. In *Holy Terrors,* the third book in the series, investigator Judith McMonigle falls in love with homicide detective (and future husband) Joe Flynn as the two search for the murderer of a local woman. A *Publishers Weekly* reviewer observed that "Daheim creates a credible and sympathetic character in McMonigle."

In *Wed and Buried,* the twelfth installment in the "Bed and Breakfast" series, Judith believes she has seen a murder outside of her hotel's reception area. To the consternation of her husband, Judith investigates. Observed a *Publishers Weekly* reviewer: "Luckily clues contrive to drop into Judith's lap because, generally speaking, she doesn't seem competent enough to find them herself. . . . All in all, neither the characters nor the construction of the plot seems believable or coherent."

In contrast, another *Publishers Weekly* reviewer credited *September Mourn,* the eleventh book in the series, with "inventive plot twists" and praised Daheim's portrayal of the book's "picturesque backdrop."

### Creeps Suzette, Silver Cream, and Hocus Croakus

Daheim added installations to her "Bed & Breakfast" series, including *Creeps Suzette, Silver Scream,* and *Hocus Croakus.* In *Creeps Suzette,* Judith and her cousin look after an elderly woman who is convinced that someone is trying to kill her. A *Publishers Weekly* critic felt that Daheim's "acerbic wit and sarcasm propel the dialogue" in this mystery.

*Silver Scream* finds Judith's B&B overrun by Hollywood as actors, directors, and producers descend upon Hillside Manor on Halloween weekend. When a famous producer turns up dead, Judith begins a murder investigation. A contributor to *Publishers Weekly* wrote: "The fog, mist, and rain of a Pacific Northwest October add to the Halloween atmosphere" as Judith searches for clues among the strange cast of characters. The critic concluded: "Fans will be enthralled." While *Silver Scream* contains many Halloween tricks and treats, *Hocus Croakus* offers only tricks. Judith, on vacation from her beloved B&B, investigates the murder of a magician's assistant who turns up dead at a casino. A *Publishers Weekly* reviewer deemed *Hocus Croakus* a "winning addition."

### Dead Man Docking and Scots on the Rocks

*Dead Man Docking* finds cousins Judith and Renie taking off for a girls' trip to San Francisco as their husbands remain behind. Renie has gotten them a free cruise through one of her clients, and the two are ready to set sail. However, the owner of the ship is killed onboard during a cocktail party before the boat can even leave the dock, promptly mooring the cruise. As police investigate, a second person is killed, and the situation is just too intriguing for Judith and Renie to ignore. The two pair up for their own investigation, one that takes them wandering all over the city of San Francisco and teams them up with Rick and Rhoda St. George, Daheim's answer to Nick and Nora Charles. Jenny McLarin, writing for *Booklist*, praised the novel, labeling it "more madcap fun from the always-reliable Daheim."

In *Scots on the Rocks*, Judith and Renie once again go traveling, only this time they take their husbands along for the adventure. The two couples head for Scotland for their vacation, checking into a small bed and breakfast in a tiny town off the beaten path. Their intention is to relax and to alleviate some of the stress of running their own inn. However, when Harry Gibb, whom they have just met, is killed, the peace and quiet of their vacation fly out the window as Judith immediately feels the need to investigate the crime. Even on short acquaintance, she had pegged Harry Gibb as a good man, and can't imagine why anyone would want him dead. She looks into his marriage, as his wife is now a widow for the second time, as well as all of his business dealings, hoping to find a clue, and putting a firm end to her vacation. A reviewer for *Publishers Weekly* wrote that "the local color—fine wool, romantic castles, freely flowing whiskey and tea—is charming."

### Vi Agra Falls

In the twenty-fourth series installment, *Vi Agra Falls*, Judith has recently remarried her former husband, Joe Flynn. Complications arise, however, when Joe's former wife, Vivian, arrives in town and indicates she has plans to build a large condominium complex nearby. Judith vows to fight the project, but when a man's body is found hanging from a tree on Vivian's property, the innkeeper dons her sleuth's hat instead.

"Endearingly eccentric characters are a plus" in this "entertaining" series addition, according to a *Publishers Weekly* contributor. *BestSellersWorld.com* reviewer Nancy Eaton similarly observed that "zany characters really make this novel stand out."

### Loco Motive and All the Pretty Hearses

In *Loco Motive*, Judith and Renie are again on a trip. Here they are on Amtrak, headed for the East Coast to meet up with their husbands, who are on a business jaunt to Boston. Murder and mayhem take place en route, and the cousins match wits against the perpetrator.

A *Kirkus Reviews* contributor termed this series addition "fast-paced, droll and lively fun." However, a *Publishers Weekly* reviewer found it "plodding," with "convoluted plotting and irksome characters [that] may leave new readers cold." A contributor to *Mystery Librarian* Web site found more to like in this work, calling it an "excellent addition" and concluding: "An entertaining read, *Loco Motive* will be of particular interest to those who love train travel."

Daheim's 2011 series addition, *All the Pretty Hearses*, finds Judith's private investigator husband, Joe, the suspect in a murder case when a crook he's been following is shot. Judith goes to work to try and clear him, but her investigations are slowed somewhat by a flotilla of quarrelsome guests at her bed and breakfast. "Series fans will cheer as Judith sorts everything out with her usual combination of humor and exasperation," noted a *Publishers Weekly* reviewer.

### ■ Biographical And Critical Sources

*BOOKS*

*Detecting Women*, Purple Moon Press (Dearborn, MI), 1994.

*PERIODICALS*

*Booklist*, January 1, 2001, Jenny McLarin, review of *Suture Self*, p. 924; August 1, 2005, Jenny McLarin, review of *Dead Man Docking*, p. 1998; March 1, 2008, Sue O'Brien, review of *The Alpine Traitor*, p. 54; May 1, 2009, Sue O'Brien, review of *The Alpine Uproar*, p. 13.

*Kirkus Reviews*, July 15, 2003, review of *Hocus Croakus*, p. 938; March 1, 2005, review of *The Alpine Quilt*, p. 261; February 1, 2006, review of *The Alpine Recluse*, p. 112; May 15, 2009, review of *The Alpine Uproar*; August 15, 2010, review of *Loco Motive*; January 15, 2011, review of *The Alpine Vengeance*.

*Library Journal*, February 1, 2004, Rex Klett, review of *The Alpine Pursuit*, p. 128.

*Publishers Weekly*, February 24, 1992, review of *Holy Terrors*, p. 50; November 2, 1992, review of *The Alpine Advocate*, p. 67; November 13, 1995, review of *The Alpine Fury*, p. 58; June 17, 1996, review of *The Alpine Gamble*, p. 62; September 30, 1996, review of *Nutty as a Fruitcake*, p. 80; July 7, 1997, review of *September Mourn*, p. 66; January 12, 1998, review of *Wed and Buried*, p. 57; December

14, 1998, review of *The Alpine Kindred,* p. 72; December 13, 1999, review of *Creeps Suzette,* p. 69; April 29, 2002, review of *Silver Scream,* p. 46; January 1, 2001, review of *Suture Self,* p. 71; April 29, 2002, review of *Silver Scream,* p. 46; August 26, 2002, review of *The Alpine Obituary,* p. 50; June 16, 2003, review of *Hocus Croakus,* p. 54; June 11, 2007, review of *Scots on the Rocks,* p. 41; January 7, 2008, review of *The Alpine Traitor,* p. 39; June 30, 2008, review of *Vi Agra Falls,* p. 166; April 27, 2009, review of *The Alpine Uproar,* p. 115; August 2, 2010, review of *Loco Motive,* p. 33; February 7, 2011, review of *The Alpine Vengeance,* p. 39; June 20, 2011, review of *All the Pretty Hearses,* p. 37.

*ONLINE*

*BestSellersWorld.com,* http://www.bestsellersworld.com/ (July 3, 2011), Nancy Eaton, review of *Vi Agra Falls;* (July 3, 2011), Caryn St. Clair, review of *Loco Motive.*

*Fresh Fiction,* http://freshfiction.com/ (November 2, 2010), Paula Myers, review of *Loco Motive.*

*Mary Daheim Home Page,* http://authormarydaheim.com (July 3, 2011).

*Mystery Librarian,* http://mysterylibrarian.com/ (May 9, 2011), review of *Loco Motive.**

# MaryJanice Davidson

## 1969-

---

### ■ Also Known As

Janice Pohl

### ■ Personal

Born 1969; married Anthony Alongi (a writer); children: two.

### ■ Addresses

*Home*—MN. *E-mail*—maryjanice@maryjanice davidson.net.

### ■ Career

Writer. Worked as a manager of operations for a brokerage firm.

### ■ Awards, Honors

Sapphire Award for Excellence in Science Fiction Romance, 2000, for story "Love's Prisoner."

### ■ Writings

*NOVELS; UNLESS OTHERWISE NOTED*

*By Any Other Name*, Hard Shell Word Factory (Amherst Junction, WI), 2001.
*Canis Royal: Bridefight* (e-book; novel), Ellora's Cave (Stow, OH), 2002.
*Under Cover* (stories), Brava (New York, NY), 2003.

*Beggarman, Thief* (e-book; novel), Loose-ID Publications (Carson City, NV), 2004.
*The Royal Treatment*, Brava (New York, NY), 2004.
*Derik's Bane*, Berkley Sensation (New York, NY), 2005.
*Hello, Gorgeous!*, Brava (New York, NY), 2005.
*The Royal Pain*, Brava (New York, NY), 2005.
*Really Unusual Bad Boys*, Brava (New York, NY), 2005.
*Drop Dead, Gorgeous!*, Kensington (New York, NY), 2006.
*Dead and Loving It*, Berkley Sensation (New York, NY), 2006.
*Royal Mess*, Brava (New York, NY), 2007.
*Doing It Right*, Brava (New York, NY), 2007.
(With others) *Over the Moon*, Berkley Sensation (New York, NY), 2007.
*No Rest for the Witches*, St. Martin's (New York, NY), 2007.
*Dead over Heels*, Berkley Sensation (New York, NY), 2008.
*Outta the Bag* (Kindle edition), St. Martin's Press (New York, NY), 2010.
*Me, Myself, and Why?*, St. Martin's Press (New York, NY), 2010.
*Wolf at the Door*, Berkley Trade (New York, NY), 2010.

*"UNDEAD" SERIES*

*Undead and Unwed*, Berkley Sensation (New York, NY), 2004.
*Undead and Unemployed*, Berkley Sensation (New York, NY), 2004.
*Undead and Unappreciated*, Berkley Sensation (New York, NY), 2005.
*Undead and Unreturnable*, Berkley Sensation (New York, NY), 2005.

*Undead and Unpopular,* Berkley Sensation (New York, NY), 2006.

*Undead and Uneasy,* Berkley Sensation (New York, NY), 2007.

*Undead and Unworthy,* Berkley Sensation (New York, NY), 2008.

*Undead and Unwelcome,* Random House (New York, NY), 2009.

*Undead and Unfinished,* Berkley Sensation (New York, NY), 2010.

*Undead and Undermined,* Berkley Sensation (New York, NY), 2011.

*Undead and Unstable,* Berkley Sensation (New York, NY), 2011.


*"FRED THE MERMAID" SERIES*

*Sleeping with the Fishes,* Jove (New York, NY), 2006.
*Swimming without a Net,* Jove (New York, NY), 2007.
*Fish out of Water,* Jove Books (New York, NY), 2008.


*YOUNG ADULT NOVELS*

*Adventures of the Teen Furies,* Hard Shell Word Factory (Amherst Junction, WI), 2001.

(With husband, Anthony Alongi) *Jennifer Scales and the Ancient Furnace,* Berkley Jam Books (New York, NY), 2005.

(With Anthony Alongi) *Jennifer Scales and the Messenger of Light,* Berkley Jam Books (New York, NY), 2006.

(With Anthony Alongi) *The Silver Moon Elm: A Jennifer Scales Novel,* Berkley Jam Books (New York, NY), 2007.

(With Anthony Alongi) *Seraph of Sorrow: A Jennifer Scales Novel,* Ace Books (New York, NY), 2009.

(With Anthony Alongi) *Rise of the Poison Moon,* Ace (New York, NY), 2010.

(With Anthony Alongi) *Evangelina,* Ace (New York, NY), 2011.


*OTHER*

Also author of e-books, including the novels *Thief of Hearts* and *Love Lies,* Ellora's Cave (Stow, OH), and *Dying for Ice Cream* Fiction Works and the nonfiction work *Escape the Slush Pile,* Fiction Works. Contributor of short fiction to anthologies, including *Men at Work* Berkley Sensation (New York, NY), 2004; *Bite,* Jove (New York, NY), 2004; *Bad Boys with Expensive Toys,* 2004; *Cravings,* Jove (New York, NY), 2004; *How to Be a "Wicked" Woman,* Brava (New York, NY), 2004; *"Wicked" Women Whodunit,* Brava (New York, NY), 2005; *Charming the Snake: Savage Scavenge,* Loose-ID (Carson City, NV), 2005; *Romance at the Edge,* Loose ID (Carson City, NV), 2005; *Valentine's Day Is Killing Me,* Brava (New York, NY), 2006; *Surf's Up,* Berkley Sensation (New York, NY), 2006; *Demon's Delight,* Berkley Sensation (New York, NY), and *Secrets,* Volumes 6 and 8, Red Sage. Contributor, under pseudonym Janice Pohl, to *Reunions: Four Inspiring Romance Stories of Friends Reunited.*


■ **Adaptations**

A number of Davidson's books have been adapted for audio.


■ **Sidelights**

MaryJanice Davidson is a writer of romance novels and short stories who works within a variety of subgenres, including paranormal, science fiction, young adult, mystery, erotica, and combinations thereof. Her work often features copious helpings of humor and frank sexuality. Davidson has written extensively for publication in both print and e-book form, and the success of her e-books has helped build her print career.

*Writer Unboxed* Web site interviewer Kathleen Bolton wrote that "Davidson has made a career out of taking the most feared creatures of mythology and the underworld, and putting them smack in the middle of a hilarious yarn that has the reader laughing out loud."

Bolton asked Davidson: "What draws you to the strange and fantastical?" Davidson replied: "My teeny, tiny brain. I can't write straight, guy-meets-girl romance. Just can't do it. The one time I tried, the heroine turned out to be bionic, and the hero was a cyborg. *Doing It Right* was as close as I came and even then, the heroine was a black belt who could break a forearm with one hand while sipping a milkshake with the other."


### *Undead and Unwed* **and** *Undead and Unemployed*

*Undead and Unwed,* a novel about a young, single, fashion-conscious female vampire, was originally published as an e-book, and it caught the attention of an editor at Berkley. After the company published the novel in print form, it released several other books by Davidson. *Undead and Unwed* inaugurates the "Undead" series and introduces readers to Betsy Taylor, a woman who joins the undead after dying in a traffic accident. Unlike most vampires, Betsy can go out in the daytime and is not bothered by religious symbols, and these qualities make her a candidate for queen of the vampires. But she also must do battle with another candidate, an evil, 500-year-old vampire named Nostro. Assisting her in this effort is Eric Sinclair, a vampire who is handsome and sexy but nevertheless does not appeal to Betsy. Describing the novel as a "chick-lit foray into the paranormal," *Booklist* critic Diana Tixier Herald dubbed the story "sexy," "funny," and "delightful."

In *Undead and Unemployed,* Betsy has become vampire queen, but she still needs a job in the mortal world, so she goes to work in a department store selling designer shoes. Meanwhile, she has to fight off a gang of vampire slayers and come to the aid of an enigmatic young girl. *Booklist* critic Herald called the story "wickedly clever and amusing." The series has continued with a number of titles, including *Undead and Unreturnable,* in which Betsy is writing a column for a vampire newsletter and preparing for her wedding.

### Undead and Uneasy **and** Undead and Unwelcome

In the 2007 series installment, Betsy, Queen of the Vampires, is down to the wire in preparations for her wedding to Sinclair and still has not picked out a dress. Things get even worse when friends and family suddenly disappear and she must rely totally on her own skills for the first time since awaking an Undead. *Booklist* contributor Herald found this series addition "filled with breezy dialogue, kick-ass action, and endearing characters."

In the eighth book in the series, *Undead and Unwelcome,* Betsy and Sinclair head to New England in hopes of averting a vampire-werewolf war over the death of werewolf Antonia. *RT Book Reviews* Web site contributor Jill M. Smith felt that the "tone is decidedly more somber yet still outrageously wacky" in this installment.

### Undead and Unfinished **and** Undead and Undermined

*Undead and Unfinished* sees Betsy traveling with her half-sister Laura to hell in hopes of learning more about *The Book of the Dead* and her adopted son, Eric. While in hell, Betsy follows a door into the Salem witch trials and attempts to intervene. She also catches a glimpse of a telling incident out of Eric's past in this "potential horror story" that is softened by "fun and wackiness," as Smith noted in the online *RT Book Reviews. Best Reviews* Web site

writer Harriet Klausner also commended this novel, noting that fans of the series will "enjoy . . . the acerbic comedic commentary."

Betsy continues her exploits in hell in the second part of this trilogy within the "Undead" series, *Undead and Undermined.* "Betsy is as wacky, selfish and hilariously self-absorbed as always," wrote Smith for *RT Book Reviews.*

### Derik's Bane **and** Hello, Gorgeous!

Vampires are not the only supernatural creatures to appear in Davidson's writings. The hero of *Derik's Bane* is attractive young werewolf Derik Gardner. His wolf pack sends him on a mission to kill Morgan le Fay, the wicked enchantress of the King Arthur legends, in order to stop what the werewolves believe is Morgan's plot to destroy the world. Morgan has been reincarnated in modern-day Northern California as Dr. Sara Gunn, with whom Derik falls in love after failing to kill her. Sara, at first skeptical, eventually comes to believe she is indeed Morgan, but she claims Morgan has been falsely accused of evil intentions, and she and Derik join in fighting an Arthur-worshipping cult that is truly threatening the planet. Harriet Klausner, writing in *MBR Bookwatch,* found *Derik's Bane* to be "a unique well-written romantic fantasy with a Camelot twist," adding that Derik and Sara are humorous and appealing. Herald, again reviewing for *Booklist,* also noted the book's comic aspects, writing that it "will elicit delighted howls of laughter."

*Hello, Gorgeous!* is a venture into science fiction involving a young woman who is brought back to life after a fatal car crash through the implantation of mechanical parts. The procedure gives this "bionic woman," Caitlyn James, superpowers, so the U.S. government enlists her as a secret agent with a mission to track and thwart a computer hacker. Herald predicted that readers would enjoy the novel's "over-the-top humor and raunchily funny sex scenes"

### The Royal Treatment

In *The Royal Treatment* Davidson envisions an alternate reality in which the state of Alaska is an independent country ruled by a monarchy. The royals like to mingle with the common people, and one day the king brings home a rootless young woman as a bride for his eldest son, the crown prince. The woman and the prince do fall in love, but they are not wholly compatible, and they must overcome their personal differences while dealing with troubles facing the kingdom. *Booklist* contributor Maria Hatton deemed the book "quirky" and "fun."

### Sleeping with the Fishes and Swimming without a Net

The protagonist in *Sleeping with the Fishes* is a grumpy mermaid named Fred who can't swim and is allergic to shellfish. Fred, the sometime marine biologist and part-time mermaid, returns in *Swimming without a Net*. Here she is participating in a "merpeople" conference in the Caymans in which it is being decided whether or not to let humans know of their existence. Romantic interests for Fred abound, in the form of two who are vying for her affections: Prince Artur, the prospective leader of the merpeople, and Thomas, another marine biologist with a very healthy bank account. *Booklist* reviewer Herald dubbed this a "wickedly funny romp" and called Davidson the "queen of paranormal comedy." Similarly, Smith, writing on *RT Book Reviews*, felt that this novel offers "lots of laughs as well as biting social commentary."

### Fish out of Water

Fred is back in *Fish out of Water*, and she is as confused as ever about her place in the world. Now that Thomas has left her behind for a full-blooded mermaid, Fred is the girlfriend of Prince Artur, who wants her to join him in the seas. But Fred is unsure, wanting only to hide away somewhere. The impending marriage of her human friend Jonas brings her out of herself to work on his wedding plans. Then comes an unexpected visitor: her merman father shows up. Fred has never met him, but he definitely has plans for her.

*Booklist* reviewer Shelley Mosley felt this novel is a "swimmingly good finale" to the novels dealing with Fred the mermaid. Likewise, *RT Book Reviews* Web site contributor Smith dubbed this "vintage Davidson wackiness."

### The Silver Moon Elm and Rise of the Poison Moon

Davidson also writes a young adult paranormal series with her husband, Anthony Alongi. The first of these is *Jennifer Scales and the Ancient Furnace*. Jennifer is a teen who can change into a dragon twice a month. The third in the series, *The Silver Moon Elm: A Jennifer Scales Novel*, finds Jennifer awaking to an alternate universe where "wereachnids" rule and weredragons are all but extinct. Writing in *Kliatt*, Cara Chancellor felt this "exceptional tale" has a plot "as complex and far-reaching as any adult-level fantasy novel." Writing for *RT Book Reviews*, Smith similarly thought that this YA series is "much darker and filled with teenage angst" than Davidson's other paranormal romances.

*Rise of the Poison Moon* has Jennifer and her family cut off from the outside world by a magic barrier. Meanwhile long-lasting feuds keep the dragons, wereachnids, and dragons, at each other's throats. Smith, again writing for *RT Book Reviews*, gave "kudos to this terrific storytelling duo."

### Me, Myself, and Why?

Davidson creates what a *Publishers Weekly* reviewer called an "odd chick lit thriller cozy" with her 2010 novel *Me, Myself, and Why?* The novel features federal agent Cadence Jones, who belongs to a secret FBI group based in Minneapolis, Minnesota, known as the BOFFO group—an acronym for Bureau of False Flags Ops. Jones, along with her cohorts, is part of an assemblage of agents who all have psychological problems. In Jones's case, she has multiple personality disorder; her partner, George Pinkham, is a sociopath. Others are kleptomaniacs, pyromaniacs, and even a paranoid psychotic individual. Jones and the team are after a serial killer dubbed the "ThreeFer" in this novel that is the first in a proposed trilogy.

The *Publishers Weekly* contributor thought that this book would "either delight or horrify," leaving Davidson's romance fans "scratching their heads." Herald, writing in *Booklist*, was more impressed, praising Davidson's "over-the-top humor and outrageous situations that have made her a best-seller." Similar praise came from online *RT Book Reviews* contributor Annette Elton, who told readers: "Prepare yourself for a wild and entertaining ride."

## ■ Biographical And Critical Sources

*PERIODICALS*

*Booklist*, March 15, 2004, Diana Tixier Herald, review of *Undead and Unwed*, p. 1274; May 1, 2004, Maria Hatton, review of *The Royal Treatment*, p. 1550; August, 2004, Diana Tixier Herald, review of *Undead and Unemployed*, p. 1908; December 1, 2004, Diana Tixier Herald, review of *Derik's Bane*, p.

641; February 1, 2005, Diana Tixier Herald, review of *Hello, Gorgeous!*, p. 948; June 1, 2005, Diana Tixier Herald, review of *Undead and Unappreciated*, p. 1763; October 1, 2005, Diana Tixier Herald, reviews of *The Royal Pain* and *Undead and Unreturnable*, p. 40; May 15, 2007, Diana Tixier Herald, review of *Undead and Uneasy*, p. 27; December 15, 2007, Diana Tixier Herald, review of *Swimming without a Net*, p. 31; November 15, 2008, Shelley Mosley, review of *Fish out of Water*, p. 22; September 15, 2010, Diana Tixier Herald, review of *Me, Myself, and Why?*, p. 48.

*Kirkus Reviews*, May 1, 2005, review of *Undead and Unappreciated*, p. 492.

*Kliatt*, November, 2007, Jodi Israel, review of *Undead and Uneasy*, p. 44; January, 2008, Cara Chancellor, review of *The Silver Moon Elm: A Jennifer Scales Novel*, p. 18.

*MBR Bookwatch*, January, 2005, Harriet Klausner, reviews of *Derik's Bane* and *Men at Work*; February, 2005, Harriet Klausner, review of *Bad Boys with Expensive Toys*.

*Publishers Weekly*, June 7, 2004, review of *Cravings*, p. 37; June 7, 2004, review of *Cravings*, p. 37; January 3, 2005, review of *Bite*, p. 42; August 9, 2010, review of *Me, Myself, and Why?*, p. 30.

*ONLINE*

*All about Romance*, http://www.likesbooks.com/ (March 25, 2005), Megan Frampton, review of *Under Cover*; (August 19, 2007), Laurie, "Writer's Corner for March, 2005," interview with author.

*AllReaders.com*, http://www.allreaders.com/ (March 25, 2005), L. Watson, review of *Hello, Gorgeous!*

*Allscifi.com*, http://www.allscifi.com/ (March 25, 2005), review of *Canis Royal: Bridefight*.

*Best Reviews*, http://thebestreviews.com/ (November 24, 2008), Harriet Klausner, review of *Fish out of Water*; (August 9, 2010), Harriet Klausner, review of *Undead and Unfinished*.

*Fresh Fiction*, http://freshfiction.com/ (September 9, 2010), Paula Myers, review of *Me, Myself, and Why?*

*Jennifer Scales Web site*, http://www.jenniferscales.com (August 19, 2007).

*Mama Kitty Reviews*, http://mamakittyreviews.com/ (August 6, 2010), review of *Undead and Unfinished*.

*MaryJanice Davidson Home Page*, http://www.maryjanicedavidson.net (July 3, 2011).

*Medieval Bookworm*, http://medievalbookworm.com/ (July 3, 2011), review of *Undead and Unwelcome*.

*MJ's Musings*, http://maryjanicedavidson.blogspot.com/ (July 3, 2011), author blog.

*Reading with Monie*, http://www.readingwithmonie.com/ (August 1, 2010), review of *Undead and Unfinished*.

*RT Book Reviews*, http://www.rtbookreviews.com/ (June 1, 2007) Jill M. Smith, review of *The Silver Moon Elm*; (December 1, 2007), Jill M. Smith, review of *Swimming without a Net*; (December 1, 2008), Jill M. Smith, review of *Fish out of Water*; (July 1, 2009), Jill M. Smith, review of *Undead and Unwelcome*; (July 1, 2010), Jill M. Smith, review of *Undead and Unfinished*; (August 1, 2010), Jill M. Smith, review of *Rise of the Poison Moon*; (October 1, 2010), Annette Elton, review of *Me, Myself, and Why?*; (July 1, 2011), Jill M. Smith, review of *Undead and Undermined*.

*Writer Unboxed*, http://writerunboxed.com/ (February 16, 2007), Kathleen Bolton, interview with Davidson.*

# David DeKok

## 1953-

■ **Also Known As**

David Paul DeKok

■ **Personal**

Surname is pronounced "De-*Cook*"; born July 17, 1953, in Holland, MI; son of Paul W. (a chemist) and Olga K. (a homemaker) DeKok. *Education:* Hope College, B.A., 1975; attended George Washington University. *Religion:* Lutheran.

■ **Addresses**

*Home*—Harrisburg, PA. *Office*—Patriot, 812 King Blvd., Harrisburg, PA 17101. *Agent*—Michael Steinberg, P.O. Box 274, Glencoe, IL 60022.

■ **Career**

Writer. *News-Item*, Shamokin, PA, reporter, 1975-87; *Patriot*, Harrisburg, PA, reporter, 1987-2008. Film consultant.

■ **Member**

Society of Professional Journals/Sigma Delta Chi (Central Pennsylvania chapter).

■ **Awards, Honors**

Keystone Press Awards, Pennsylvania Newspaper Publishers Association, first place award in news series category, 1979, for stories about the mine fire in Centralia, PA, first place award in feature story category, 1986, for story "Family's Dilemma: Illness, Loss of Jobs, Insensitive Bureaucracy," first place award in news story category, 1987, for story "Man Dead, Wife Hurt in Shooting"; first place award in public service category, Associated Press Managing Editors of Pennsylvania, 1981, for stories on the mine fire in Centralia.

■ **Writings**

*Unseen Danger: A Tragedy of People, Government, and the Centralia Mine Fire,* University of Pennsylvania Press, 1986, iUniverse, 2000.
*Fire Underground: The Ongoing Tragedy of the Centralia Mine Fire,* GPP (Guilford, CT), 2010.
*The Epidemic: A Collision of Power, Privilege, and Public Health,* Lyons Press (Guilford, CT), 2011.

■ **Sidelights**

David DeKok's book, *Fire Underground: The Ongoing Tragedy of the Centralia Mine Fire,* DeKok tells the story of the mine fire that destroyed Centralia, Pennsylvania. DeKok explains that after the fire began, government officials failed to take the appropriate measures to contain it. He also carefully details the toll the fire took on Centralia and its inhabitants.

Reviewing the work on the *History on Air* Web site, a contributor claimed that in the work DeKok "does a good job of capturing the ineptitude of the government officials and the anguish of the residents suffering through the decades it took to finally come to the conclusion of evacuation."

### The Epidemic

In DeKok's next book, *The Epidemic: A Collision of Power, Privilege, and Public Health,* DeKok explains how a wealthy businessman, William T. Morris, was responsible for the typhoid epidemic that ravaged Ithica, New York in 1903. Eighty-two people died, including twenty-nine Cornell University students. William T. Morris, who owned the local water plant, decided not to add a filtration system to the plant that could have sanitized the water. Typhoid bacteria entered the water supply and infected over one thousand people at a time when there was no cure.

Reviewing the work in the *Patriot-News*, contributor Lewis E. Silverman lauded: "In David DeKok's gripping new book, *The Epidemic* greed, ignorance and denial merge to form a perfect storm of chaos and death." A *Kirkus Reviews* contributor opined: "This tale of 'criminal stupidity' would have had far more impact as a long-form magazine article."

### DeKok Once Told *CA*:

"My book *Unseen Danger* grew out of the reporting I did for the *News-Item*, a small newspaper in Shamokin, Pennsylvania. The mine fire under Centralia, Pennsylvania, which is the topic of my book, was endlessly fascinating to me as a reporter. Writing factual, fair, but hard-hitting stories about Centralia's plight was the best way that I, as a concerned fellow human, could help the people there. I also hoped that my writing would make it more difficult for such a tragedy to occur again.

"I think that writing about environmental disasters like Centralia, particularly if done repeatedly, can be the catalyst that stirs an unconcerned bureau-cracy to action. Even if it does not move the bureaucratic mountain, it may move elected officials to action, as it did in the case of Centralia."

## ■ Biographical And Critical Sources

### PERIODICALS

*Kirkus Reviews*, December 15, 2010, review of *The Epidemic: A Collision of Power, Privilege, and Public Health.*

*News-Item*, September 20, 2009, "Centralia Book Updated: Pa.'s New Open Records Law Helps Author Uncover More on Mine Fire."

*New York Times Book Review*, January 4, 1987, review of *Unseen Danger: A Tragedy of People, Government, and the Centralia Mine Fire*, p. 16.

*Patriot-News* (Harrisburg, PA), February 20, 2011, Lewis E. Silverman, review of *The Epidemic.*

*Reference & Research Book News*, May 1, 2010, review of *Fire Underground: The Ongoing Tragedy of the Centralia Mine Fire.*

### ONLINE

*David DeKok Home Page*, http://daviddekok.com/ (August 20, 2011).

*History on Air*, http://historyonair.com/ (January 30, 2011), review of *Fire Underground.**

# Judi Dench

## 1934-

■ **Also Known As**

Judith Olivia Dench

■ **Personal**

Born December 9, 1934, in York, England; daughter of Reginald Arthur and Eleanora Olave (Jones) Dench; married Michael Williams (an actor), February 5, 1971 (died January, 2001); children: Tara Cressida Frances ("Finty") Williams. *Education:* Studied at Mount School, York, England; trained for the stage at the Central School of Speech Training and Dramatic Art. *Religion:* Society of Friends (Quaker). *Hobbies and other interests:* Painting, drawing, sewing, swimming, catching up with letters.

■ **Addresses**

*Agent*—Tor Belfrage, Julian Belfrage Associates, 46 Albemarle St., London W1X 4PP, England; William Morris Agency, 151 El Camino Dr., Beverly Hills, CA 90212.

■ **Career**

Actress. Old Vic Company, London, England, member of the company, 1957-61. Film appearances include: (uncredited) *The Third Secret,* Twentieth Century-Fox, 1964; *Four in the Morning,* West One Film Producers, 1965; *A Study in Terror* (also known as *Fog*), Columbia, 1966; *A Midsummer Night's Dream,* Eagle, 1969; *Luther,* American Film Theatre, 1974; *Dead Cert,* United Artists, 1974; *Nela,* 1980; *Wetherby,* Metro-Goldwyn-Mayer/United Artists, 1985; *The Angelic Conversation,* British Film Institute, 1985; *A*

*Room with a View,* Cinecom, 1986; *84 Charing Cross Road,* Columbia, 1987; *A Handful of Dust,* New Line Cinema, 1988; *Henry V,* Samuel Goldwyn Company, 1989; *Jack and Sarah,* Gramercy Pictures, 1994; *A Little Night Music,* 1995; *Golden Eye,* Metro-Goldwyn-Mayer/United Artists, 1995; *Hamlet* (also known as *William Shakespeare's Hamlet*), Columbia/Sony Pictures Entertainment, 1996; *Mrs. Brown* (also known as *Her Majesty, Mrs. Brown*), Miramax, 1996; *After Murder Park,* [Great Britain], 1997; *Tomorrow Never Dies,* Metro-Goldwyn-Mayer/United Artists, 1997; *Tea with Mussolini,* Universal, 1998; *The World Is Not Enough* (also known as *Bond 19, Bond 2000, Death Waits for No Man, Fire and Ice, Pressure Point,* and *T.W.I.N.E.*), Metro-Goldwyn-Mayer/United Artists, 1998; *Shakespeare in Love,* Miramax, 1998; *Chocolat,* Miramax, 2000; (narrator) *Into the Arms of Strangers* (documentary), Warner Bros., 2000; *Therese Raquin,* October Films, 2001; *Iris,* 2001; and *The Importance of Being Earnest,* Miramax, 2002.

Television series appearances include: *A Fine Romance,* London Weekend Television, 1981-84; and *As Time Goes By,* British Broadcasting Corporation (BBC), 1993-2000. Television miniseries appearances include: *Talking to a Stranger,* BBC-2, 1966; *Love in a Cold Climate,* Thames Television, 1980, later broadcast on *Masterpiece Theatre,* Public Broadcasting System (PBS), 1982; *Playing Shakespeare,* London Weekend Television, 1984; *Mr. and Mrs. Edgehill* (also known as *Star Quality: Mr. and Mrs. Edgehill*), 1985, later broadcast on *Masterpiece Theatre,* Public Broadcasting System, 1988; and (voiceover) *Angelina Ballerina,* 2002. Television movie appearances include: *Saigon—Year of the Cat,* Thames Television, 1983; *The Browning Version,* BBC, 1985; *Behaving Badly,* Channel Four, 1988; *Can You Hear Me Thinking?,* BBC America, 1990; *Absolute Hell,* 1991; and *Last of the Blonde Bombshells,* BBC/Home Box Office, 2000. Other television appearances include: *Play of the Month,* BBC; *Playhouse,* BBC-2; *Hey Mr. Producer* (also known as *Hey Mr. Producer! The Musical World of Cameron Mackintosh*), PBS, 1998; *Broadway '99: Launching the Tony Awards*, PBS, 1999; and *The Cherry Orchard*, BBC America, 1999. Director, *Look Back in Anger*, Thames Television, 1999. Radio appearances include: *Whom Do I Have the Honour of Addressing?* (solo play), BBC Radio Four, 1989. Guest on talk shows, including *Late Night with Conan O'Brien, Charlie Rose Show, Today Show,* and *60 Minutes.*

Stage appearances include: *A Midsummer Night's Dream*, Old Vic Company, London, England, 1957; *Hamlet*, Old Vic Company, Liverpool, England, then London, England, 1957; *Twelfth Night*, Old Vic Company, London, 1957-58; *Henry V*, Old Vic Company, Broadway production, 1958; *The Merry Wives of Windsor*, Old Vic Company, London, 1959; *Romeo and Juliet*, Old Vic Company, London, 1959-61; *A Midsummer Night's Dream*, Old Vic Company, London, 1960; *Romeo and Juliet*, Paladino d'Argentino, Venice, Italy, Festival, 1961; *The Cherry Orchard*, Aldwych Theatre, London, England, 1961; *A Penny for a Song*, Aldwych Theatre, 1962; *Measure for Measure*, Royal Shakespeare Company, Stratford-upon-Avon, England, 1962; *A Midsummer Night's Dream*, Royal Shakespeare Company, 1962; *A Shot in the Dark*, Lyric Theatre, London, England, 1963; *Macbeth*, Nottingham Playhouse, Nottingham, England, 1963; *The Twelfth Hour*, Oxford Playhouse Company, Great Britain, 1964; *The Three Sisters*, Oxford Playhouse Company, 1964; *Private Lives*, Nottingham Playhouse, 1965; *The Alchemist*, Oxford Playhouse Company, 1965; *Measure for Measure*, Nottingham Playhouse, 1965; *The Firescreen*, Oxford Playhouse Company, 1965; *Romeo and Jeanette*, Oxford Playhouse Company, 1965; *The Astrakhan Coat*, Nottingham Playhouse, 1966; *St. Joan*, Nottingham Playhouse, 1966; *The Rules of the Game*, Oxford Playhouse, 1966; *The Promise*, Oxford Playhouse, 1966, then Fortune Theatre, London, England, 1967; *Cabaret*, Palace Theatre, London, England, 1968; *Women Beware Women*, Royal Shakespeare Company, England, 1969; *The Winter's Tale*, Royal Shakespeare Company, England, 1969; *Twelfth Night*, Royal Shakespeare Company, England, 1969; *Major Barbara*, Royal Shakespeare Company, 1970-71; *London Assurance*, Royal Shakespeare Company, 1970-71; *The Winter's Tale*, Aldwych Theatre, 1970-71; *Twelfth Night*, Aldwych Theatre, 1970-71; *The Duchess of Malfi*, Royal Shakespeare Company, England, 1971; *Toad of Toad Hall*, Royal Shakespeare Company, England, 1971; *The Merchant of Venice*, Royal Shakespeare Company, England, 1971; *Twelfth Night*, Royal Shakespeare Company, England, 1971; *London Assurance*, New Theatre, London, England, 1972; *Content to Whisper*, Theatre Royal, York, England, 1973; *The Wolf*, London, England, 1973; *The Good Companions*, Her Majesty's Theatre, London, England, 1974; *Too True to Be Good*, Royal Shakespeare

Company, 1975; *The Gay Lord Quex*, Albery Theatre, London, England, 1975; *Much Ado about Nothing*, Royal Shakespeare Company, 1976; *Macbeth*, Royal Shakespeare Company, 1976; *King Lear*, Royal Shakespeare Company, 1976; *The Comedy of Errors*, Royal Shakespeare Company, 1976-77; *The Comedy of Errors*, Aldwych Theatre, 1977-78; *Much Ado about Nothing*, Aldwych Theatre, 1977-78; *Macbeth*, Aldwych Theatre, 1977-78; *Pillars of the Community*, Aldwych Theatre, 1977-78; *The Way of the World*, Aldwych Theatre, 1977-78; *Cymbeline*, Royal Shakespeare Company, 1979; *Juno and the Paycock; The Importance of Being Earnest*, Royal National Theatre Company, Lyttleton Theatre, London, England, 1982; *Pack of Lies*, Lyric Theatre, 1983; *Mother Courage*, Royal Shakespeare Company, 1984-85; *Waste*, Royal Shakespeare Company, 1985; *Mr. and Mrs. Nobody*, Garrick Theatre, London, England, 1987; *Antony and Cleopatra*, Royal National Theatre Company, 1987-88; *Entertaining Strangers*, Royal National Theatre Company, 1987-88; *Hamlet*, Royal National Theatre Company, 1989; *Star Quality*, Richmond Theatre, London, England, 1989; *The Cherry Orchard*, Aldwych Theatre, 1989-90; *The Plough and the Stars*, Young Vic Theatre, London, England, 1991-92; *The Sea*, Lyttleton Theatre, 1991-92; *Coriolanus*, Chichester Theatre Festival, Chichester, England, 1992; *The Gift of the Gorgon*, 1992-93; *The Seagull*, 1994; *A Little Night Music*, Royal National Theatre Company, 1995; *Absolute Hell*, London, England, c. 1996; *Amy's View*, Royal National Theatre Company, 1997, then Ethel Barrymore Theatre, New York, NY, 1999; *Filumena*, Peter Hall Company, Piccadilly Theatre, London, England, 1998; and *Into the Woods* (voiceover), 2002. Director of plays, including: *Look Back in Anger*, Renaissance Theatre Company, Coliseum Theatre, London, Theatre, 1989; and *The Boys from Syracuse*, Open Air Theatre, London, England, 1991. Also directed *Romeo and Juliet*, Open Air Theatre; *As You Like It* and *Much Ado about Nothing*, both Renaissance Theatre Company, London, England; and *Macbeth*, Central School of Speech Training and Dramatic Art, London, England. Major tours include *Twelfth Night*, across West Africa and Japan, 1963, 1972.

Albums and taped readings include *Kids' Stuff*, His Master's Voice/EMI, 1986; *A Midsummer Night's Dream*, Deutsche Grammophon, 1994; *Silas Marner*, 1988; *The Importance of Being Earnest*, Trafalgar Square, 1995; *The Ultimate Fairy Tale Collection*, Trafalgar Square, 1995; *Penguin English Verse: The Sixteenth Century, the Seventeenth Century, the Eighteenth Century, the Romantics, the Victorians, the Early Twentieth Century*, Volume 12, Penguin Highbridge Audio, 1996; *Lark Rise to Candleford*, Penguin Highbridge Audio, 1996; *Hans Christian Andersen's Fairy Tales*, Trafalgar Square, 1997; *Pooh Goes Visiting: And Other Stories*, Trafalgar Square, 1998; *The*

*Winnie-the-Pooh Gift Pack,* Trafalgar Square, 1998; *Lady Chatterley's Lover,* Media Books, 1999; and *Shakespeare: His Life and Work,* Audio Partners Publishing Corporation, 2000.

## ■ Awards, Honors

British Academy of Film and Television Arts (BAFTA) Film Award for most outstanding newcomer to leading film roles, 1965, for *Four in the Morning;* BAFTA Film Award for best television actress, and Guild of Directors Award for best actress, both 1967, both for *Talking to a Stranger;* London Critics Award for best actress, Variety Club of Great Britain, 1967, for *The Promise;* Laurence Olivier Award for actress of the year, Society of West End Theatre, 1977, for *Macbeth;* Laurence Olivier Award for best actress, c. 1978, for *The Comedy of Errors; Evening Standard* Award for best actress and *Plays and Players* Award for best actress, Laurence Olivier Award for best actress of the year, Society of West End Theatre for best actress of the year, and Variety Club of Great Britain Award for best actress of the year, all 1980, all for *Juno and the Paycock;* BAFTA Television Awards for best television actress, 1981, for *Going Gently* and for *The Cherry Orchard;* BAFTA Television Awards for best television actress, 1981, and for best light entertainment performance, 1984, both for *A Fine Romance; Plays and Players* Award for best actress and *Evening Standard* Award for best actress, both 1983, both for *The Importance of Being Earnest;* Laurence Olivier Award for best actress, and *Plays and Players* Award for best actress, both 1983, both for *Pack of Lies; Evening Standard* Award for best actress, 1983, for *A Kind of Alaska;* American Cinema Editors Award for best actress, c. 1985, for *Mr. and Mrs. Edgehill;* BAFTA Film Award for best actress in a supporting role, 1986, for *A Room with a View;* BAFTA Film Award nomination for best actress in a supporting role, 1986, for *Wetherby;* Laurence Olivier Award for actress of the year, *Evening Standard* Award for best actress, and *Drama* Award, all 1987, all for *Antony and Cleopatra;* BAFTA Film Award nomination for best actress in a supporting role, 1988, for *84 Charing Cross Road;* American Cinema Editors Award, 1988, for *Ghosts;* named Dame Commander of the British Empire, 1988; BAFTA Film Award nomination for best actress in a supporting role, 1989, for *A Handful of Dust;* BAFTA Television Award nomination for best actress, 1990, for *Behaving Badly;* Laurence Olivier Awards for best actress and best actress in a musical, both 1996, both for *A Little Night Music;* Laurence Olivier Award for best actress, 1996, for *Absolute Hell;* Rothermore Award for lifetime achievement, 1997; Online Film Critics Society Award for best actress, and Critics Circle Award, both 1997, Golden Globe Award for best performance by an actress in a supporting role in a motion picture, BAFTA Film Award and BAFTA Scotland Award, both for best performance by an actress in a leading role, Chicago Film Critics Association Award for best actress, Golden Satellite Award for best performance by an actress in a motion picture—drama, Academy Award nomination for best actress, and Screen Actors Guild Award nomination for outstanding performance by a female actor in a leading role, all 1998, all for *Mrs. Brown;* Critics Circle Drama Award, 1997, and Antoinette Perry Award for best actress in a play, 1999, both for *Amy's View;* Academy Award and National Society of Film Critics Award, both for best supporting actress, BAFTA Film Award for best performance by an actress in a supporting role, Screen Actors Guild Award (with others) for outstanding performance by a cast, Golden Globe Award nomination for best performance by an actress in a supporting role in a motion picture, and Screen Actors Guild Award nomination for outstanding performance by an actress in a supporting role, all 1999, all for *Shakespeare in Love;* Laurence Olivier Award nomination, c. 1999, for *Filumena;* United Kingdom Entertainment Personality of the Year Award, Variety Club of Great Britain, 1999; *Evening Standard* Award, *Plays and Players* Awards, and Drama Award, all for *Other Places;* Academy Award, outstanding performance by an actress in a supporting role, 2000, for *Chocolat;* Golden Globe Award, 2000, for *Last of the Blonde Bombshells;* London Film Critics Circle Award for best lead actress and Academy Award nomination for outstanding lead actress, both 2002, both for *Iris;* Critics Circle Award, for "outstanding service to the arts"; Gold Medal, Elsie Fogarty Prize, and William Poel Memorial Prize, all from the Central School of Speech Training and Dramatic Art. Honorary doctor of letters, Warwick University, 1978, and York University, 1983; named to the Order of the British Empire, 1980.

## ■ Writings

(With Nigel Rideout) *First Steps toward an Acting Career,* A & C Black (London, England), 1996.

(With Patsy Rodenburg) *The Actor Speaks: Voice and the Performer,* St. Martin's Press New York, NY), 2000.

(With John Miller) *And Furthermore,* St. Martin's Press (New York, NY), 2011.

Also author of *Judi Dench: A Great Deal of Laughter.*

*OTHER*

(Author of foreword) Robin May, *Who's Who in Shakespeare,* Taplinger (New York, NY), 1972.

(Author of foreword) Judith Cook, *Directors' Theatre,* Harrap (London, England), 1974.

(Author of foreword) John Doyle and Ray Lischner, *Shakespeare for Dummies,* IDG Books Worldwide (Foster City, CA), 1999.

■ **Sidelights**

Equally at home playing historic queens, Shakespearean ladies, and suburban housewives, Judi Dench is one of the most acclaimed English-speaking actresses of her generation. The two-time Academy Award winner draws critical hosannas and audience affection in virtually any role she undertakes. In her native England, Dench is one of the few West End performers whose name guarantees box-office success.

A product of York, England, Dench as a youth chose to follow the Quaker religion, even though her parents were not of that faith. The much-loved youngest child of a doctor, Dench grew up in a sprawling Victorian house, where she had an attic bedroom and was allowed to draw on the walls. As a child she harbored dreams of becoming a ballerina or a designer, but she soon discovered acting. After high school, Dench was accepted at the Central School of Speech Training and Dramatic Art in London. From there she was plucked out of the crowd as an unknown ingenue and cast as Ophelia in an Old Vic production of *Hamlet.* Over the next several years, Dench became a favorite of the Royal Shakespeare Company, featured not just in Shakespeare's plays but also in dramas like Anton Chekhov's *The Cherry Orchard.*

The actress "came of age just as the definitions of femininity were being rewritten," according to John Lahr in a *New Yorker* profile of Dench, "and she was an incarnation of the free-wheeling, bumptious independence of the eternally young New Woman. With a cap of close-cropped hair, a strong chin, high cheekbones, alert eyes, and a wide smile, the five-foot-two Dench cut a gamine figure onstage." Dench's unmistakable husky voice placed her in good stead when in 1968 she created the role of Sally Bowles for the first London production of the musical *Cabaret.* This rare singing appearance provided her the opportunity to interpret the free-spirited Sally as a character complex in her childishness and corruption. Hal Prince, the director of *Cabaret,* considered Dench "the most effective of all the people who played the part," as he was quoted in the *New Yorker* piece. In 1971 Dench married actor Michael Williams, who would be her husband and occasional costar (in the British series *A Fine Romance*) until his death in 2001. Their daughter,

Finty Williams, has followed in her parents' footsteps by becoming an actress; in 2002 mother and daughter teamed up to provide voiceovers for the animated series *Angelina Ballerina.*

Film soon beckoned Dench. In the 1980s she appeared in English period pieces, including *84 Charing Cross Road* and *A Room with a View.* Dench's breakthrough film role came in 1995 when she played Queen Victoria in the sleeper hit *Mrs. Brown.* Based on true events, the movie tells of how the queen dealt with her grief over the death of her husband, Albert, the Prince Consort, by developing a discrete but deep affection for her horse trainer, John Brown. So scandalized was her court over this friendship—they nicknamed the queen "Mrs. Brown"—that the very state of the monarchy was threatened. In this role, Dench, "her face clamped in anguish, radiates the stern ecstasy of grief," said *Time* critic Richard Corliss. A *Film Comment* reviewer was also taken by the actress's visage: "Judi Dench's face is tremulous with self-control, as bulbously round and polished, for all the scratchmark-wrinkes of age, as a bossed mirror. She looks as if she could implode with her own genteel self-containment." To a *Maclean's* writer, Dench "does more with a pursed mouth, a raised eyebrow or a sudden inflection in her voice than most actors do with a bagful of Method-acting tricks."

Dench earned her first Academy Award nomination for *Mrs. Brown;* though she did not win, the accompanying acclaim helped establish her in Hollywood. She went on to commercial success playing "M," Agent 007's no-nonsense superior in three James Bond films. But she would find an even more enthusiastic audience with her second "royal" role. In 1999's blockbuster *Shakespeare in Love,* Dench plays Elizabeth I as a woman with a deadpan wit who is not afraid to put snobs in their place. She parlayed that small role into another Academy Award nomination, and this time Dench took the podium as winner of an Oscar for best supporting actress.

With the Oscar nod, Dench found herself at age sixty-five a hot commodity. A star turn in the West End and Broadway productions of *Amy's View* reestablished the actress's stage career; at the same time, Dench was costarring in a hit British sitcom, *As Time Goes By,* where she played a lively wife to actor Geoffrey Palmer's bemused husband. The film *Chocolat* brought Dench back to the big screen, this time as a tart-tongued landlady who bonds with her grandson despite her estrangement from her daughter. Critics and audiences showed their appreciation again; as *Entertainment Weekly* reporter Clarissa Cruz noted, "never underestimate a woman who can nab an Oscar with less than nine minutes of screen time." But the 2001 Academy Award (and a Golden Globe nod for a television movie, *Last of the Blonde Bombshells*) was a bittersweet honor for Dench, who had lost her husband to cancer just months before.

After her husband's death, Dench threw herself into her work. She finished three films—*The Importance of Being Earnest, The Shipping News,* and *Iris*—and premiered onstage in *The Royal Family,* all in just ten months. *Iris,* in particular, proved to be a challenging project. In her portrayal of author Iris Murdoch, who battled Alzheimer's disease before succumbing to the illness in 1999, Dench was required to portray the ravages of a debilitating condition. Again, she made a strong impression, even during the filming: "There were members of the [*Iris*] crew who were so affected by Dench's animal outburst of grief at the burial of Murdoch's best friend Janet Stone— almost clawing at the coffin to get her back—that they came away from the shooting feeling as if they had spent the day at a real and unusually traumatic funeral," noted London *Times* reporter Alan Franks. That Dench was filming this and other death- oriented scenes so soon after the passing of her husband was not lost on the actress. Her sense of loss over Williams's death, she told Franks, "will go on for ages, I expect. I do feel he would have wanted me to do all this work." Grief, she told the reporter, "is something that comes over you and you can barely breathe." Dench's work in *Iris* earned her a fourth Academy Award nomination.

### The Actor Speaks

Though far better known as a performer than as a writer, Dench has contributed to several books on the technique involved in her craft. One of them, *The Actor Speaks: Voice and the Performer,* offers voice training for the "seven stages" of an actor's life. The actress who made her name in so many Shake- spearean roles also contributed the foreword to the volume *Shakespeare for Dummies.*

The acclaim and celebrity aside, Dench remains a private person. "I have to have quietness inside me somewhere, otherwise I'd burn myself up," she is quoted as saying in Lahr's article. Acting, she said, is part of the service industry: "It's a very unselfish job. It's about being true to an author, a director, a group of people, and stimulating a different audi- ence every night. If you're out for self-glorification, then you're in the wrong profession."

### And Furthermore

Dench's memoir, *And Furthermore,* is meant to be the actor's own follow-up to John Miller's 1998 biography of her, *Judi Dench: With a Crack in Her Voice. And Furthermore* is written by Miller, as told by Dench. Dench's aim was to fill in the pieces that the prior biography left out.

Reviewing the work in the *Los Angeles Times* con- tributor Jessica Gelt assessed: "There are glimpses of what the book could have been if Dench had chosen to focus on fewer details and instead looked intently at the really important events and anecdotes. . . . The reader's frustration of not being let into the great actress's life exists only because Dench—even hastily sketched—is such a charming, vivid and compelling person. We want more. In the end, however, we are given an actor's mask." *New York Times Book Review* contributor Brooks Barnes noted: "*And Furthermore* will disappoint fans who want a peek at Ms. Dench's personal life. It's strictly off-limits. ('I think you're entitled to keep those things to yourself if that's what you wish,' she said.) But readers will walk away with a keen sense of her philosophy on life: take your art seriously but never yourself." London *Observer* contributor Kate Kellaway remarked: "Dench is superstitiously unrevealing. My guess is she has an understandable fear that were she to attempt to explain the mystery of her acting, her miraculous gift might take offence or flight." London *Daily Mail* contributor Jan Moir opined: "It is obvious that *And Furthermore* has not been written by Dench herself, but dictated with celerity to her biographer John Miller. Yes, much of her crisp intelligence is there on the page, alongside her puckish sense of humour and her evident good- ness—yet it is somehow remote; a memoir once removed. Quite often it is a memoir characterised by what she does not say, rather than what she does."

■ **Biographical And Critical Sources**

*BOOKS*

Miller, John, *Judi Dench: With a Crack in Her Voice,* Orion (London, England), 1999, revised edition, 2002.
*Newsmakers 1999,* Issue 4, Gale (Detroit, MI), 1999.

*PERIODICALS*

*Advocate,* February 5, 2002, Lawrence Ferber, "Cock- tails with Dame Judi."
*Biography,* March, 2002, Bart Mills, "Great Dame!"
*Entertainment Weekly,* March 1, 1999, p. 49; January 11, 2001, Owen Gleiberman, "Grim Lasse-tude," p. 48; February 23, 2001, "Judi Dench: *Chocolat,*" p. 60.

*Film Comment,* July-August, 1997, Harlan Kennedy, review of *Mrs. Brown,* p. 6.

*Hello,* April 4, 1989, Madeline Kingsley, "Judi Dench: The Classy Dame of the British Empire!"

*Los Angeles Times,* March 22, 2011, Jessica Gelt, review of *And Furthermore.*

*Maclean's,* August, 11, 1997, Diane Turbide, review of *Mrs. Brown,* p. 54.

*New Republic,* August 4, 1997, Stanley Kauffmann, review of *Mrs. Brown,* p. 26; February 11, 2002, Stanley Kauffmann, "Toward the Shadows," p. 26.

*New Statesman,* January 29, 1999, David Jays, review of *Shakespeare in Love,* p. 39; February 11, 2002, Anne Chisholm, "The Severed Head," p. 38.

*Newsweek,* November 27, 1995, Jack Kroll, review of *Golden Eye,* p. 86; July 28, 1997, David Ansen, review of *Mrs. Brown,* p. 69; April 26, 1999, Jack Kroll, "Nothing like the Dame," p. 68.

*New Yorker,* January 21, 2002, John Lahr, "The Player Queen."

*New York Times Book Review,* February 14, 2011, Brooks Barnes, review of *And Furthermore.*

*Observer* London, England, October 17, 2010, Kate Kellaway, review of *And Furthermore.*

*Publishers Weekly,* August 28, 2000, review of *The Actor Speaks: Voice and the Performer,* p. 72.

*Radio Times,* August, 2000, "As Time Goes Bye-bye?"

*Skipton Life,* spring, 2002, "Judi Still Packs a Punch."

*Time,* July 21, 1997, Richard Corliss, review of *Mrs. Brown,* p. 70.

*USA Today,* January 26, 2011, Craig Wilson, author interview.

ONLINE

*A.V. Club,* http://www.avclub.com/ (March 24, 2011), Tasha Robinson, review of *And Furthermore.*

*Daily Mail Online,* http://www.dailymail.co.uk/ (October 27, 2010), Jan Moir, review of *And Furthermore.*

*Dame Judi Dench Web site,* http://www.djd chronology.com (April 25, 2002).

*Internet Movie Database,* http://www.imdb.com/ (August 25, 2011), author profile.*

# Alan M. Dershowitz

## 1938-

■ **Also Known As**

Alan Dershowitz
Alan Morton Dershowitz

■ **Personal**

Born September 1, 1938, in Brooklyn, NY; son of Harry (a store owner) and Claire Dershowitz; divorced; remarried Carolyn Cohen (a psychologist); children: three, including Elon Marc, Jamin Seth. *Education:* Brooklyn College (now Brooklyn College of the City University of New York), B.A., 1959; Yale University, LL.B., 1962. *Religion:* Jewish.

■ **Addresses**

*Office*—Harvard Law School, 1563 Massachusetts Ave., Cambridge, MA 02138. *E-mail*—dersh@law. harvard.edu.

■ **Career**

Lawyer, educator, writer, editor, and lecturer. Admitted to the Bar, 1962; practicing civil liberties lawyer, 1962—; Harvard University, Law School, Cambridge, MA, assistant professor, 1964-67, professor of law, 1967-93, Felix Frankfurter Professor of Law, 1993—. Also visiting professor of law at the Hebrew University, Jerusalem, Israel, 1988. Radio talk-show host, 1995-96. Consultant, National Institute of Mental Health.

■ **Member**

American Civil Liberties Union, Phi Beta Kappa, Order of Coif, Anti-Defamation League of B'nai B'rith.

■ **Awards, Honors**

Guggenheim fellowship; William O. Douglas First Amendment Award, Anti-Defamation League of B'nai B'rith, 1983, for "compassionate eloquent leadership and persistent advocacy in the struggle for civil and human rights"; Golden Plate Award, c. 1991; Freedom of Speech Award, National Association of Radio Talk Show Hosts, 1996, for hosting radio talk-show about the law. Also honorary degrees and medals from Yeshiva University, Syracuse University, Hebrew Union College, the University of Haifa, Bar Ilan University, Monmouth College, Fitchburg College, and Brooklyn College.

■ **Writings**

(With Jay Katz and Joseph Goldstein) *Psychoanalysis, Psychiatry and the Law,* Free Press (New York, NY), 1967.

(With Joseph Goldstein and Richard Schwartz) *Criminal Law: Theory and Process,* Free Press (New York, NY), 1974.

*The Best Defense,* Random House (New York, NY), 1982.

*Reversal of Fortune: Inside the von Bulow Case,* Random House (New York, NY), 1986.

*Taking Liberties: A Decade of Hard Cases, Bad Laws, and Bum Raps,* Contemporary Books (Chicago, IL), 1988.

*Chutzpah,* Little, Brown (Boston, MA), 1991.

*Contrary to Popular Opinion,* Pharos Books (New York, NY), 1992.

*The Advocate's Devil* (novel), Warner Books (New York, NY), 1994.

*The Abuse Excuse and Other Cop-Outs, Sob Stories, and Evasions of Responsibility* (essays), Little, Brown (Boston, MA), 1994.

*Reasonable Doubts: The O.J. Simpson Case and the Criminal Justice System,* Simon & Schuster (New York, NY), 1996.

*The Vanishing American Jew: In Search of Jewish Identity for the Next Century,* Little, Brown (Boston, MA), 1997.

*Sexual McCarthyism: Clinton, Starr, and the Emerging Constitutional Crisis,* Basic Books (New York, NY), 1998.

*Just Revenge* (novel), Warner Books (New York, NY), 1999.

*The Genesis of Justice: Ten Stories of Biblical Injustice That Led to the Ten Commandments and Modern Law,* Warner Books (New York, NY), 2000.

*Supreme Injustice: How the High Court Hijacked Election 2000,* Oxford University Press (New York, NY), 2001.

*Letters to a Young Lawyer,* Basic Books (New York, NY), 2001.

*Shouting Fire: Civil Liberties in a Turbulent Age,* Little, Brown (Boston, MA), 2002.

*Why Terrorism Works: Understanding the Threat, Responding to the Challenge,* Yale University Press (New Haven, CT), 2002.

*The Case for Israel,* John Wiley (Hoboken, NJ), 2003.

*America Declares Independence,* John Wiley (Hoboken, NJ), 2003.

*America on Trial: Inside the Legal Battles That Transformed Our Nation,* Warner Books (New York, NY), 2004.

*Rights from Wrongs,* Basic Books (New York, NY), 2005.

*The Case for Peace: How the Arab-Israeli Conflict Can Be Resolved,* John Wiley (Hoboken, NJ), 2005.

(Editor) *What Israel Means to Me,* John Wiley (Hoboken, NJ), 2006.

*Preemption: A Knife That Cuts Both Ways,* W.W. Norton (New York, NY), 2006.

*Blasphemy: How the Religious Right Is Hijacking Our Declaration of Independence,* John Wiley & Sons (Hoboken, NJ), 2007.

*The Case against Israel's Enemies: Exposing Jimmy Carter and Others Who Stand in the Way of Peace,* John Wiley & Sons (Hoboken, NJ), 2008.

*Is There a Right to Remain Silent? Coercive Interrogation and the Fifth Amendment after 9/11,* Oxford University Press (New York, NJ), 2008.

*Finding Jefferson: A Lost Letter, a Remarkable Discovery, and the First Amendment in an Age of Terrorism,* John Wiley & Sons (Hoboken, NJ), 2008.

*The Trials of Zion* (novel), Grand Central Pub. (New York, NY), 2010.

(Author of foreword) Salo Aizenberg, *Postcards from the Holy Land: A Pictorial History of the Ottoman Era, 1880-1918,* Society of Israel Philatelists (Shaker Heights, OH), 2010.

Also contributor of background papers to *Fair and Certain Punishment: Report of the Twentieth Century Fund Task Force on Criminal Sentencing,* McGraw-Hill (New York, NY), 1976; contributor to the sound recording *Freedom and the Criminal Code,* Center for the Study of Democratic Institutions (Santa Barbara, CA), 1982; author of introductions to *Say It Ain't So, Joe! The True Story of Shoeless Joe Jackson,* by Donald Gropman, Carol Publishing, 1992, and *The Story of My Life,* by Clarence Darrow, Da Capo (New York, NY), 1996. Contributor to periodicals, including the *New York Times Magazine,* and *New York Times Book Review.* He has also published hundreds of articles in magazines and journals such as the *New York Review, Saturday Review, Harvard Law Review, Yale Law Journal, Stanford Law Review, American Bar Association Journal, Israel Law Review, Commentary, New Republic, Chronicle of Higher Education, Journal of Legal Education, Nation, Der Spiegel, George, Psychology Today, New Women, Harper's, Atlantic, TV Guide, Sports Illustrated, JD Jungle, Punch, American Film, Good Housekeeping, Partisan Review, Jerusalem Post, International Herald Tribune, Yahoo! Internet Life, Slate, Washington Post, Moment, Life,* and *Penthouse.* Author of the *Alan Dershowitz Web log.* Writings have been translated into foreign languages, including French, German, Hebrew, Japanese, Thai, Chinese, Korean, Italian, Spanish, Portuguese, Swedish, Danish, Dutch, and Russian.

■ **Adaptations**

Author's books have been made into sound recordings, including *Chutzpah!,* 1991, *Contrary to Popular Opinion,* 1992, and *The Advocate's Devil,* 1994, all Dove Audio (Beverly Hills, CA); *Reasonable Doubts,* Simon & Schuster (New York, NY), 1996; *Just Revenge,* Audio Renaissance (Los Angeles, CA), 1999; *The Genesis of Justice,* Time Warner AudioBooks (New York, NY), 2001; *The Case for Peace,* Recorded Books (Prince Frederick, MD), 2005.

■ **Sidelights**

Alan M. Dershowitz, the youngest tenured professor in the history of Harvard Law School, is "the attorney of last resort for the desperate and despised, counselor for lost causes and forlorn hopes," according to Elaine Kendall in the *Los Angeles Times. The Best Defense* is Dershowitz's account of many of the cases he has undertaken as an appellate defense attorney, cases that were lost at the trial stage but that he agreed to appeal because no one else would take them or because they involved interesting points in law.

Dershowitz has built his reputation on the defense of a number of notorious clients, most notably former football star O.J. Simpson. Dershowitz's other clients of note have included Jewish Defense League terrorist Sheldon Seigel, who set a bomb that killed an innocent young woman; nursing home owner Rabbi Bernard Bergman, called "the meanest man in New York" by the press; Manhattan hotel magnate Leona Helmsley; adult film star Harry Reems; the Tison brothers, who helped their father escape from prison and were with him when he later murdered an entire family; Stanford professor H. Bruce Franklin, faced with dismissal because his communist politics led him to incite students to wage a "people's war" against the university; and corrupt defense lawyer Edmund Rosner, the U.S. Attorney's Office's "public enemy number one" whose trial formed the basis for the film *The Prince of the City*. Other clients have included Anatoly Shcharansky and other Soviet dissidents; nude bathers on a Cape Cod beach; trial lawyer F. Lee Bailey; and former CIA agent Frank Snepp, who refused to submit his book manuscript to the agency for approval.

### The Best Defense

"[*The Best Defense*] is more than a book by a lawyer about his cases," wrote David S. Tatel in *Washington Post Book World*. "It is an articulate defense of many fundamental principles that are under attack in our country today." Tatel added: "Dershowitz's book is a compelling answer to those who . . . seek to dilute the Bill of Rights. It is particularly persuasive because his arguments emanate from courtrooms where constitutional principles are transformed from inspiring words to life and death realities." Indeed, in *The Best Defense* Dershowitz demonstrates that he is deeply committed to protecting the civil liberties of all citizens; many of his cases challenge the constitutionality of certain laws or procedures, or question police and prosecution methods in obtaining the original conviction. "*The Best Defense* is a labor of love for the law by a man who has lost some of his illusions but kept his faith intact," noted Kendall. "He believes that the adversary process, allowing a defendant to challenge the government, is the foundation of American liberty; he is prepared to fight for that cause whenever and however it seems jeopardized. If some of our cherished preconceptions about the legal system are casualties of that battle, the system itself will not only survive but be strengthened by his efforts."

"The basic dilemma presented by *The Best Defense* is the propriety of a lawyer's using every legal device he can think of to get off a man who he knows to be guilty," declared Joseph W. Bishop, Jr., in *Commentary*. Dershowitz was horrified that Sheldon Seigel was freed because of government misconduct in gathering evidence against the Jewish Defense

League, but he says, quoting former Chief Justice Oliver Wendell Holmes: "It is a lesser evil that some criminals should escape than that the government should play an ignoble role." In the case of the Tison brothers, Dershowitz questioned the legality of sentencing someone to death for a murder he did not actually commit. The defense of Harry Reems, H. Bruce Franklin, Frank Snepp, and the nude bathers was, for Dershowitz, a defense of the Bill of Rights. It is clear that Dershowitz believes, noted Bishop, that "the first person a good advocate convinces is himself, and what he convinces himself of is that his client may be a criminal but that he is not guilty of the crime with which he is charged, or at least he is being treated unfairly."

While questioning the actual magnitude of the accusations Dershowitz levels against the government, the courts, and the prosecution, *New Leader* contributing critic Barry Gewen conceded that the case histories Dershowitz presents are "immensely readable, thought-provoking, often troubling," and acknowledged that "perhaps there are no satisfactory answers . . . in many of the . . . cases included in *The Best Defense* where public safety is set against civil liberties. Bringing such ethical conundrums to the general attention could be the book's greatest virtue." John Greenya observed in the *Detroit News* that Dershowitz "writes well enough so his passion for his clients and their legal predicaments comes through loud and clear. One can feel the 'last resort' desperation that must always be at one's back, and not just in capital cases. Dershowitz is successful in doing something much more difficult than portraying the human drama: he makes the *law* exciting, the intellectual wrestling that embodies the best advocacy confrontation, especially on the appellate level."

Dershowitz's basic contention is that there are serious problems with the American judicial system, stemming from, among other things, prosecutorial and magisterial disregard for the constitutional rights and civil liberties of the defendant and from the frequent collusion between prosecution and the judges. The justice system, Dershowitz contends, is corrupt. *Commentary* contributor Joseph W. Bishop, Jr., supported Dershowitz's attempts to uphold constitutional principles even if it sometimes means freeing a guilty man. "Dershowitz has seen too much . . . to think that the unjust acquittal of some criminals is too high a price to pay to avoid Communist justice," Bishop concluded.

### The Advocate's Devil and Just Revenge

With *The Advocate's Devil*, a novel, Dershowitz departed from his long string of nonfiction writings. The story features the attorney Abe Ringel, who, according to Cheryl Lavin in the *Chicago Tribune,* "faces an ethical crisis when he believes his client—a famous basketball player charged with rape—is guilty." Given Dershowitz's role in the defense of former football star O.J. Simpson, then on trial for the murder of his estranged wife Nicole and her friend Ron Goldman, Lavin asked Dershowitz, at the outset of a lengthy interview, just how autobiographical the book was. Dershowitz, while pointing out that "Ringel is my mother's family name and Abe is my Hebrew name," insisted that "it's not autobiographical. I'm more skeptical than Abe."

The novel, observed Kinky Friedman in the *New York Times Book Review,* "may not disrupt John Grisham's sleep patterns, but it earns a thumbs-up verdict in the pleasant-surprise department. Not only does this novel accomplish what was considered unthinkable by some—that is, a fun romp with Alan Dershowitz—it also acquits itself rather nicely on several semiliterary levels" in view of the legal insight it offers. "With his inside view of practically every sensational trial of the last decade," pointed out Cosima von Bulow in the *Spectator,* "it must have been a challenge indeed to create a work of fiction as bizarre and fascinating as his life." The reviewer added: "Bursting at the seams with topical details, *The Advocate's Devil* keeps its finger on the pulse of the American legal system today." A reviewer writing in *Books* commented: "In this debut novel Dershowitz has crafted with spellbinding precision a drama which opens the Pandora's Box of our most measured legal belief: innocent until proven guilty."

Ringel appears for a second time in the 1999 novel *Just Revenge,* in which he is defending a Holocaust survivor who takes revenge on the man who killed his pregnant wife, son, and extended family in Lithuania in 1942. A *Publishers Weekly* contributor praised the "dramatic and tragic events that frame the plot, and the intensity of [the author's] moral argument" in this novel. *Booklist* reviewer Stephanie Zvirin, on the other hand, was less enthusiastic about this second outing for Abe Ringel. Zvirin found the courtroom drama "realistic enough" and the plot premise "intriguing," but she complained of "stiff and sometimes trite" dialogue and called parts of the novel "undramatic." A higher assessment was offered by *New York Times Book Review* wrier Adam Liptak, who felt "there is much that is instructive and entertaining" in this courtroom drama.

### Reasonable Doubts **and** The Abuse Excuse

The issue of reasonable doubt would particularly attract the notice of reviewers when Dershowitz published *Reasonable Doubts: The O.J. Simpson Case and the Criminal Justice System,* his account of the Simpson trial; but in the meantime he offered up *The Abuse Excuse and Other Cop-Outs, Sob Stories, and Evasions of Responsibility.* In the book he examines such prominent 1990s legal cases as those of Lyle and Erik Menendez, who killed their parents and blamed the act on sexual abuse suffered as children; Colin Ferguson, who opened fire on a Long Island subway, killing six people and wounding nineteen, because of "black rage"; and Lorena Bobbitt, who blamed her abusive husband for driving her to slice off his penis while he was sleeping.

"Although the title may suggest that you've read or heard all this before," wrote Clarence Petersen of *The Abuse Excuse and Other Cop-Outs, Sob Stories, and Evasions of Responsibility* in the Chicago *Tribune Books,* "chances are you have not encountered it in terms of how the law is being violated in many high-profile cases." Referring to a point that would come to prominence during the Clinton impeachment inquiries three years later, Petersen noted: "Dershowitz takes up the 'everyone does it' excuse for official corruption, in which liberal Democrats and right-wing Republicans alike are scored."

"For all the fun that is made of him—and he is good grist for fun-makers—Alan Dershowitz is a deeply thoughtful man." So began William F. Buckley's *National Review* commentary on *Reasonable Doubts.* Regarding Dershowitz's stated opinion that the Simpson jury was right to maintain "reasonable doubts" regarding the guilt of Simpson, who was exonerated but widely believed to be guilty nonetheless, Buckley asked: "Does [Dershowitz] himself believe this? Therein hangs a tale." Nicholas Lemann in the *New York Times Book Review* observed that Dershowitz "is first out of the gate with a book on the O.J. Simpson trial—which is a good strategic move, because he doesn't have very much juicy inside stuff and might have been overwhelmed in a direct competition with some of the other entrants." But Dershowitz does offer some extremely strong criticisms of prosecutor Marcia Clark, noted A.W.B. Simpson in the *Times Literary Supplement.* "His discussion and analysis of the [disagreement] between white perceptions and the outcome of the trial is valuable and moderately expressed," wrote Simpson.

### The Vanishing Jew **and** The Genesis of Justice

With *The Vanishing American Jew: In Search of Jewish Identity for the Next Century* Dershowitz departs from his usual focus on the legal system and "inventories the Jewish elements of his and his generation's identity, then works his way toward a prescription for securing Jewish existence into the future," according to Yehudah Mirsky in *New Leader*. In addition to analyzing the future of Judaism in the United States, Dershowitz touches on related issues such as Jewish intermarriage, Jewish relations with African Americans, and anti-Semitism in the militia movement. *Booklist* contributor Ilene Cooper asserted that while *The Vanishing American Jew* is of primary interest to Jews, "Dershowitz's notoriety and lively writing style broaden its appeal." Jonathan Rosen, in the *New York Times Book Review*, also found Dershowitz's voice engaging, asserting that "Mr. Dershowitz writes with characteristic optimism and audacity." Rosen added that "only time will tell whether he is indeed leading [future generations] back to Judaism or merely following them into the wilderness."

In *The Genesis of Justice: Ten Stories of Biblical Injustice That Led to the Ten Commandments and Modern Law*, Dershowitz delves into the Old Testament stories of Adam and Eve, the murder of Cain, Noah's Ark, and others to show how injustices as described in the Bible led to a just system of law. In a review in *Midstream*, Milton Birnbaum noted: "Dershowitz approaches the book of Genesis in a lawyer's robes, with reason and logic as his guidelines."

### *Supreme Injustice* and *Letters to a Young Lawyer*

The author tackles the 2000 U.S. presidential election controversy in *Supreme Injustice: How the High Court Hijacked Election 2000*. The book revolves around the Supreme Court's ultimate decision on who won the disputed 2000 presidential race between George W. Bush and Al Gore, and Dershowitz presents his viewpoint that the court practiced partisan politics in making its decision that Bush won the election. A *Publishers Weekly* contributor called the book "an excellent analysis of a troubling case." Steven Puro, writing in the *Library Journal*, commented: "This well-reasoned and controversial book asks central questions about American democracy."

*Letters to a Young Lawyer* is a commentary written as thirty-six letters by Dershowitz on the law field with an emphasis on advice to fledgling lawyers. "His reflections touch on many of his long-standing obsessions, particularly the unethical practices he contends compromise our criminal justice system," wrote a *Kirkus Reviews* contributor. Mary Carroll, writing in *Booklist*, noted that "much of Dershowitz's advice can be applied in other workplaces as well." In a review in *Trial*, Carolyn Magnuson wrote: "Dershowitz's overall message is a good one. He advises young lawyers to vow, from the start of their careers, to keep their idealism and maintain their ethical footing despite rough terrain."

### *Why Terrorism Works, The Case for Israel,* and *The Case for Peace*

*Why Terrorism Works: Understanding the Threat, Responding to the Challenge* presents Dershowitz's belief that much of the modern terrorism movement has resulted from factors such as Western misdeeds conducted around the world, as well as the lack of success in battling it effectively. The author also presents his take on how the war on terror should be conducted. "Sensible overall, with little of the grandstanding or self-aggrandizement," wrote a *Kirkus Reviews* contributor. James R. Holmes, writing in the *Library Journal*, referred to the book as "bracing" and noted that the author "is always worth reading."

Dershowitz writes in the form of a legal brief in *The Case for Israel*, in which the author avoids discussing specific Israeli government polices but instead looks at overall prejudice and discrimination behind some of the criticisms aimed at the government. Jay Freeman, writing in *Booklist*, noted that the author "is a passionate but generally fair and honest advocate for his position." In *The Case for Peace: How the Arab-Israeli Conflict Can Be Resolved*, Dershowitz presents a plan for peace in the Middle East and argues against extremists who try to thwart such efforts. Elizabeth R. Hayford, writing in the *Library Journal*, noted that the author's "analysis of the prospects for peace has some merit."

### *America Declares Independence* and *America on Trial*

*America Declares Independence* is a look at the prominent rise of the Christian religious right in American politics and Dershowitz's argument that the idea of a "Christian nation" goes against the intentions of the America's founding fathers. *Loyalist Gazette* contributor William Manning commented: "Many of the author's insights may surprise the reader."

Dershowitz writes about some of the most notorious and famous cases in American legal history in *America on Trial: Inside the Legal Battles That Transformed Our Nation*. Among the cases he discusses are the Salem witch trials, the Dred Scott decision, and the O.J. Simpson trial. A *Publishers Weekly* contributor commented that the author "displays a keen sense of history to go along with his knowledge of the law."

### *Rights from Wrongs* and *Preemption*

*Rights from Wrongs*, focuses on the issue of "inalienable" human rights, which are mentioned in the U.S. Declaration of Independence. The author traces how the notion of "rights" evolved and states his case that these "natural" laws do not, however, stem from formal law or religion. Writing in *Publishers Weekly* a reviewer noted "the insightful thoughts that mark . . . [the author's] latest work."

In *Preemption: A Knife That Cuts Both Ways*, the author discusses his views on how a government should respond to a perceived but as yet unrealized threat. In the process he discusses such issues as preemptive war and restrictions on freedom of speech. In a review in *Booklist*, Brendan Driscoll commented that the author "admits that constructing a jurisprudence for a democracy is a daunting task not well served by narrow political stances." *Commentary* contributor Andrew C. McCarthy noted that Dershowitz "has asked the right questions, pointed to the right data, and demonstrated the urgent necessity of confronting the most serious threats right now—while they are still at bay, though rising ominously on the horizon."

### *Blasphemy* and *Finding Jefferson*

With *Blasphemy: How the Religious Right Is Hijacking Our Declaration of Independence*, the author contends that the religious right in the United States is intent on creating a Christian theocracy with ruling principles governed by the Bible. As evidence, he points to the insistence by these Christian conservatives that the Founding Fathers intended to create a nation based on Christian beliefs, using language from the Declaration of Independence such as "Creator" and "Divine Providence" to bolster their arguments. Countering this, Dershowitz points to the Constitution itself and its assertion of separation of church and state as stipulated in First Amendment. *Booklist* reviewer Brad Hooper felt that "this book will prompt intense dialogue—surely the author's intention."

In *Finding Jefferson: A Lost Letter, a Remarkable Discovery, and the First Amendment in an Age of Terrorism*, Dershowitz describes and analyzes a letter from Thomas Jefferson that he unexpectedly came across in a New York antiquarian bookstore and purchased. In it, this founding father describes his opinion on the constitutional limitations of freedom of speech, and in so doing also sheds new light, according to Dershowitz, on the intent of other framers of the Constitution. In Dershowitz's interpretation, Jefferson held that political and religious speech should not be censored, even if it advocates violence, as such censorship only harms democracy and will not deter violence. The author also details his love of collecting rarities such as this letter. Writing in *Library Journal*, Gilles Renaud felt this book is of "vital importance in illuminating current debate on the subject of terrorism and the right to express unpopular opinions and politics." For a *Publishers Weekly* reviewer, "the main contribution here is the publication of Jefferson's letter."

### *Is There a Right to Remain Silent?*

Dershowitz examines the Fifth Amendment's right to remain silent in *Is There a Right to Remain Silent? Coercive Interrogation and the Fifth Amendment after 9/11*. The book is a "serious examination," according to a *Publishers Weekly* reviewer, of a 2003 Supreme Court decision allowing coercion of testimony from subjects under certain circumstances. In Dershowitz's view, such a decision creates a slippery slope in the war on terror. In the book he urges that there be some legal restraints put on the possible interpretations of this 2003 decision.

Writing in the *New York Times Book Review*, Jonathan Mahler felt that Dershowitz's book "serves as a kind of primer in analyzing and interpreting constitutional law, the murky business of divining the framers' intentions and of reconciling seemingly contradictory Supreme Court opinions." *Trial* contributor Lee Hunt felt that "reading this book is reminiscent of sitting in a law school class and debating the different models of constitutional interpretation and judicial decision-making." Hunt added: "Dershowitz is at his best when forcing the reader to think critically about the limits of, and the need for, the right to remain silent." *Library Journal* reviewer Becky Kennedy also had praise for this study, terming it an "excellent book."

### *The Trials of Zion*

Dershowitz turns again to fictional defense attorney Abe Ringel in the 2010 novel *The Trials of Zion*. Here, Abe's daughter Emma, a recent Yale graduate in law, plans to help defend a young Palestinian accused of setting off an explosion that has killed several of the world's leaders in Israel. Eventually Abe is drawn into the proceedings; he must win the Palestinian's case or risk losing his daughter forever.

A contributor to *Kirkus Reviews* thought that *The Trials of Zion* offers a "solid display of Dershowitz's legal chops, if not always his narrative ones." Similarly, *Library Journal* writer Stacy Alesi complained of "one-dimensional characters and awkward dialog," but she also noted that "legal fans will enjoy learning about the differences between American and Israeli law." A *Publishers Weekly* reviewer had a similar mixed assessment, commending the book's "interesting legal issues and clever courtroom action," but also citing the "clunky dialogue and perfunctory thriller plotting." Higher praise came from *Booklist* reviewer Barbara Bibel, who called it a "thought-provoking page-turner."

## ■ Biographical And Critical Sources

PERIODICALS

*Book*, November-December, 2001, James Schiff, review of *Letters to a Young Lawyer*, p. 59.

*Booklist*, January 1, 1997, Ilene Cooper, review of *The Vanishing American Jew: In Search of Jewish Identity for the Next Century*, p. 777; August, 1999, Stephanie Zvirin, review of *Just Revenge*, p. 1985; July, 2001, Brad Hooper, review of *Supreme Injustice: How the High Court Hijacked Election 2000*, p. 1948; October 1, 2001, Mary Carroll, review of *Letters to a Young Lawyer*, p. 267; September 1, 2003, Jay Freeman, review of *The Case for Israel*, p. 2; November 1, 2004, Vernon Ford, review of *Rights from Wrongs*, p. 442; January 1, 2006, Brendan Driscoll, review of *Preemption: A Knife That Cuts Both Ways*, p. 21; May 1, 2007, Brad Hooper, review of *Blasphemy: How the Religious Right Is Hijacking Our Declaration of Independence*, p. 4; September 1, 2010, Barbara Bibel, review of *The Trials of Zion*, p. 52.

*Books*, January/February, 1995, review of *The Advocate's Devil*, p. 25.

*California Bookwatch*, May, 2006, review of *Preemption*.

*Chicago Tribune*, February 1, 1995, Cheryl Lavin, interview with author, p. T1.

*Commentary*, October, 1982, Joseph W. Bishop, Jr., review of *The Best Defense*; July-August, 2006, Andrew C. McCarthy, review of *Preemption*, p. 88; July, 2006, Andrew C. McCarthy, "Early Action," review of *Preemption*.

*Contemporary Review*, June, 2002, review of *Supreme Injustice*, p. 382.

*Detroit News*, August 29, 1982, John Greenya, review of *The Best Defense*.

*Harvard Law Review*, June, 2005, review of *Rights from Wrongs*, p. 2932.

*Humanist*, May-June, 2005, David A. Niose, review of *Rights from Wrongs*, p. 41.

*Journal of Church and State*, autumn, 2005, Nathan R. Lynn, review of *The Case for Israel*, p. 896.

*Kirkus Reviews*, September 1, 2001, review of *Letters to a Young Lawyer*, p. 1260; December 1, 2001, review of *Shouting Fire: Civil Liberties in a Turbulent Age*, p. 1659; July 1, 2002, review of *Why Terrorism Works: Understanding the Threat, Responding to the Challenge*, p. 929; January 1, 2006, review of *Preemption*, p. 26; August 15, 2010, review of *The Trials of Zion*.

*Library Journal*, August, 2001, Steven Puro, review of *Supreme Injustice*, p. 136; February 15, 2002, Steven Puro, review of *Shouting Fire*, p. 164; September 1, 2002, James R. Holmes, review of *Why Terrorism Works*, p. 196; May 1, 2004, Harry Charles, review of *America on Trial: Inside the Legal Battles That Transformed Our Nation*, p. 128; June 1, 2004, I. Pour-El, review of *The Case for Israel*, p. 197; September 1, 2005, Elizabeth R. Hayford, review of *The Case for Peace: How the Arab-Israeli Conflict Can Be Resolved*, p. 162; October 15, 2007, Gilles Renaud, review of *Finding Jefferson: A Lost Letter, a Remarkable Discovery, and the First Amendment in an Age of Terrorism*, p. 80; March 1, 2008, Becky Kennedy, review of *Is There a Right to Remain Silent? Coercive Interrogation and the Fifth Amendment after 9/11*, p. 95; September 15, 2010, Stacy Alesi, review of *The Trials of Zion*, p. 58.

*Los Angeles Times*, June 15, 1982, Elaine Kendall, profile of author.

*Loyalist Gazette*, spring, 2004, William Manning, review of *America Declares Independence*, p. 53.

*Middle East Quarterly*, winter, 2004, Max Abrahms, review of *The Case for Israel*, p. 79.

*Midstream*, January, 2001, Milton Birnbaum, review of *The Genesis of Justice: Ten Stories of Biblical Injustice That Led to the Ten Commandments and Modern Law*, p. 43.

*Nation*, August 7-14, 1982, David Bruck, review of *The Best Defense*.

*National Journal*, September 8, 2001, David G. Savage, review of *Supreme Injustice*, p. 2764.

*National Review*, July 1, 1996, William F. Buckley, review of *Reasonable Doubts: The O.J. Simpson Case and the Criminal Justice System*, p. 63.

*New Leader*, July 12-26, 1982, Barry Gewen, review of *The Best Defense*; May 19, 1997, Yehudah Mirsky, review of *The Vanishing American Jew*, pp. 22-23.

*New York Times Book Review*, June 13, 1982, Tom Goldstein, review of *The Best Defense*; January 1, 1995, Kindy Friedman, review of *The Advocate's Devil*, p. 12; March 3, 1996, Nicholas Lemann, review of *Reasonable Doubts*, p. 7; March 30, 1997, Jonathan Rosen, review of *The Vanishing American Jew*, p. 7; August 29, 1999, Adam Liptak, review of *Just Revenge*; September 14, 2008, Jonathan Mahler, "Torture and Taking the Fifth," review of *Is There a Right to Remain Silent?*, p. 24.

*Publishers Weekly*, August 2, 1999, review of *Just Revenge*, p. 71; June 18, 2001, Sarah F. Gold, "PW Talks with Alan Dershowitz," p. 74, and review of *Supreme Injustice*, p. 75; January 7, 2002, review of *Shouting Fire*, p. 59; July 8, 2002, review of *Why Terrorism Works*, p. 39; March 3, 2003, review of *America Declares Independence*, p. 64; August 4, 2003, review of *The Case for Israel*, p. 67; April 12, 2004, review of *America on Trial*, p. 56; May 17, 2004, review of *America on Trial*, p. 48; November 1, 2004, review of *Rights from Wrongs*, p. 56; May 8, 2006, review of *What Israel Means to Me*, p. 58; September 3, 2007, review of *Finding Jefferson*, p. 50; February 18, 2008, review of *Is There a Right to Remain Silent?*, p. 143; August 25, 2008, review of *The Case against Israel's Enemies: Exposing Jimmy Carter and Others Who Stand in the Way of Peace*, p. 64; August 2, 2010, review of *The Trials of Zion*, p. 28.

*Reference & Research Book News*, May, 2006, review of *Preemption*.

*Shofar*, spring, 2004, review of *The Case for Israel*, p. 194.

*Skeptic*, fall, 2005, Kenneth W. Krause, review of *Rights from Wrongs*, p. 75.

*Spectator*, March 4, 1995, Cosima von Bulow, review of *The Advocate's Devil*, p. 36; April 29, 2006, Jonathan Sumption, review of *Preemption*.

*Theological Studies*, March, 2006, Michael J. Kerlin, review of *Rights from Wrongs*, p. 222.

*Times Literary Supplement*, July 19, 1996, A.W.B. Simpson, review of *Reasonable Doubts*, p. 28.

*Trial*, April, 2002, Carolyn Magnuson, review of *Letters to a Young Lawyer*, p. 66; May, 2005, Emily Sack, review of *Rights from Wrongs*, p. 78; August, 2006, Emily J. Sack, review of *Preemption*, p. 64; November, 2008, Lee Hunt, review of *Is There a Right to Remain Silent?*, p. 70.

*Tribune Books* (Chicago, IL), September 10, 1995, Clarence Petersen, review of *The Abuse Excuse and Other Cop-Outs, Sob Stories, and Evasions of Responsibility*, p. 8.

*Washington Post Book World*, June 6, 1982, David S. Tatel, review of *The Best Defense*.

ONLINE

*Alan Dershowitz Home Page*, http://www.alan dershowitz.com (July 3, 2011).

*Harvard Law School Web site*, http://www.law. harvard.edu/ (July 3, 2011), faculty profile of author.

*Internet Movie Database*, http://www.imdb.com/ (July 3, 2011), "Alan Dershowitz."*

# Jonathan Dimbleby

## 1944-

### ■ Personal

Born July 31, 1944, in Aylesbury, Buckinghamshire, England; son of Richard (a journalist and broadcaster) and Dilys (a journalist) Dimbleby; married Beryl Ann Mooney (a broadcaster, author, and journalist), February 23, 1968 (divorced 2004); married Jessica Ray, 2007; children: Daniel Richard, Katharine Rose (from first marriage), Daisy, Gwendolyn (from second marriage). *Education:* University College, London, B.A., 1969.

### ■ Addresses

*Agent*—David Higham Associates Ltd., 5-8 Lower John St., Golden Sq., London W1R 4HA, England.

### ■ Career

Freelance broadcaster, journalist, and writer. Member of National Commission for UNESCO, 1978-79; sponsor of Amnesty International and Centre for Peace Building Studies; trustee of the Butler Trust and Richard Dimbleby Cancer Fund; director of TV-am News Ltd.

### ■ Member

International Broadcasting Trust (board member), United Nations Association of Great Britain (president, 1977-78), Voluntary Service Overseas Council.

### ■ Awards, Honors

Richard Dimbleby Award from Society of Film and Television Arts, 1974.

### ■ Writings

*Richard Dimbleby* (biography), Hodder & Stoughton (London, England), 1975.

*The Palestinians,* photographs by Donald McCullin, Quartet Books (London, England), 1979.

*The Prince of Wales* (biography), William Morrow (New York, NY), 1994.

(Also presenter) *Prince Charles—The Private Man, the Public Role,* Central Independent Television Plc, 1995.

(Author of foreword) *Derbyshire: Detail and Character: A Celebration of Its Towns and Villages,* A. Sutton (London, England), 1996.

*The Last Governor: Chris Patten and the Handover of Hong Kong,* Little, Brown (New York, NY), 1997.

*Russia: A Journey to the Heart of a Land and Its People,* BBC Books (London, England), 2008.

### ■ Sidelights

The biography *Richard Dimbleby* is Jonathan Dimbleby's account of his late father's personal and professional life. Considered one of Britain's premier news broadcasters, Richard Dimbleby broke new ground as a British Broadcasting Corporation (BBC) radio correspondent during World War II with his on-site reporting; he later worked in television as a broadcast commentator and central figure of the BBC's "Panorama."

"His became the voice of our generation, the most telling voice on BBC radio or television so far," commented Paul Fox, reviewing the book for the *Spectator.* "Jonathan Dimbleby's biography of his father is an engrossing book that depicts in a clear and unhurried way the story of the greatest broadcaster of our time." "Written with affection and pride, [this book] is filled with details of Richard Dimbleby's daily existence at home and abroad," Grace Wyndham Goldie reported in the *New Statesman.* "What, perhaps inevitably, seems to have escaped from this devoted account is the quality of his professional excellence which many of us who worked with him found so remarkable and so impressively his own."

### The Palestinians

In another work, *The Palestinians,* Jonathan Dimbleby humanizes the Arab-Israeli conflict by interviewing members of the Palestinian diaspora, hoping to capture how they think and feel. From all walks of life and many countries, these displaced Arabs are "always passionate, always enterprising, always proud and always extremely keen to talk about themselves," described Christopher Hitchens in the *New Statesman.* "Since [Dimbleby] has done the book with Donald McCullin, who is the best photographer we have on this kind of story, there is rarely a description or an anecdote which does not have a vivid illustration to lend it some depth. It would be impossible to turn these pages and retain the conviction that the word 'Palestinian' is just another synonym for terrorist or desperado."

Reviewing *The Palestinians* for the *Spectator,* Edward Mortimer noted that—while undeniably pro-Arab—"the main thrust of the book is descriptive rather than prescriptive. It proposes no solution to the problem, beyond warning that no solution that ignores the Palestinians will work." *Listener* critic Peter Mansfield shared a similar observation, writing: "Dimbleby does not argue so much as describe." He continued: "The truth is that there are still very few books which describe who the Palestinians are or how they feel and exist. *The Palestinians* is therefore a major contribution to the knowledge of humanity." And Hitchens remarked that while Dimbleby plays "journalistic advocate for the Palestinians," he "writes well, managing to remain *engage* without slipping into the pitfalls of sentimentality which sometimes yawn in his path. . . . He has caught the flavour of the Palestinians themselves."

### Russia

Dimbleby spent eighteen-weeks traveling across Russia in preparation for his next book, *Russia: A Journey to the Heart of a Land and Its People.* The book provides an outsider's perspective on contemporary Russian culture. During his eighteen-week journey, Dimbleby conducted formal interviews, interacted with many Russian people, and generally spent his time observing his surroundings. *Russia* constitutes his most interesting findings. Dimbleby sought to

provide a well-rounded portrait of the variety of cultures that can be found in Russia. He spoke to a wide array of people, including successful business owners in Moscow and the Altai mountain people. Though Dimbleby provides some musings about the future of Russian politics and economics, the majority of the work is focused strictly on Russian culture. From his interviews, Dimbleby attempts to glean an understanding of Russian attitudes towards democracy, and other issues. Dimbleby also divulges a bit of personal information, addressing the issues he was facing in his own life during the trip.

Reviewing the work in the *Journal of International Affairs,* James Wesley Jeffers remarked: "From being homesick to hating travel, to a new marriage Dimbleby never stops reflecting on his own life. This often feels superfluous."

## ■ Biographical And Critical Sources

*PERIODICALS*

*Bookseller,* April 25, 2008, review of *Russia: A Journey to the Heart of a Land and Its People,* p. 12.
*Cancer Nursing Practice,* October 1, 2005, "Dimblebys' Fund Palliative Care Research," p. 5.
*Journal of International Affairs,* March 22, 2010, James Wesley Jeffers, review of *Russia.*
*Listener,* September 6, 1979, Peter Mansfield, review of *The Palestinians,* p. 314.
*New Statesman,* October 10, 1975, Grace Wyndham Goldie, review of *Richard Dimbleby;* September 14, 1979, Christopher Hitchens, review of *The Palestinians,*
*Spectator,* October 18, 1975, Edward Mortimer, review of *Richard Dimbleby,* p. 509.
*Telegraph* (London, England), March 30, 2008, Laura Donnelly, "BBC's Jonathan Dimbleby Was 'a Wreck'"; April 21, 2008, Niall Firth, "Jonathan Dimbleby: Why I Left My Wife of 35 Years to Be with My Dying Lover."
*Times* (London, England), April 20, 2008, Margarette Driscoll, "Jonathan Dimbleby Reveals How an Unstoppable Force Called Susan Changed His Life."

*ONLINE*

*BBC Radio 4,* http://www.bbc.co.uk/radio4/ (August 14, 2011), author profile.
*Internet Movie Database,* http://www.imdb.com/ (August 14, 2011), author profile.
*Russia Web site,* http://www.dimblebys-russia.co.uk/ (August 14, 2011).*

# Åke Edwardson

## 1953-

### ■ Personal

Born 1953.

### ■ Career

Writer, journalist, educator, and novelist. Gothenburg University, professor. Worked as a journalist and as a press officer for the United Nations.

### ■ Awards, Honors

Swedish Academy of Crime Writers' Award (three-time recipient).

### ■ Writings

*Genomresa* (title means "En Route"), Norstedt (Stockholm, Sweden), 1999.

*Jukebox,* Norstedt (Stockholm, Sweden), 2003.

*Till allt som varit dott* (title means "Everything That Has Been Dead"), ManPocket (Stockholm, Sweden), 2003.

*Samurajsommar* (title means "Samurai Summer"; young adult novel), ManPocket (Stockholm, Sweden), 2005.

*Drakmanod,* (title means "Dragon Mouth"; young adult novel), ManPocket (Stockholm, Sweden), 2006.

*Svalorna flyger så högt att ingen längre kan se dem,* Leopard foerlag (Stockholm, Sweden), 2010.

*Moet mig i Estepona,* Leopard foerlag (Stockholm, Sweden), 2011.

*"INSPECTOR WINTER" SERIES*

*Dans med en angel,* ManPocket (Stockholm, Sweden), 1998, translation by Ken Schubert published as *Death Angels: An Inspector Erik Winter Novel,* Penguin Books (New York, NY), 2009.

*Rop fran langt avstand,* Norstedt (Stockholm, Sweden), 1998, translation by Per Carlsson published as *The Shadow Woman: An Inspector Erik Winter Novel,* Penguin Books (New York, NY), 2010.

*Sol och skugga,* Norstedt (Stockholm, Sweden), 1999, translation by Laurie Thompson published as *Sun and Shadow: An Inspector Erik Winter Novel,* Viking (New York, NY), 2005.

*Lat det aldrig ta slut,* ManPocket (Stockholm, Sweden), 2000, translation by Laurie Thompson published as *Never End: An Inspector Erik Winter Novel,* Viking (New York, NY), 2006.

*Himlen ar en plats pa Jorden,* Norstedt (Stockholm, Sweden), 2001, translation by Laurie Thompson published as *Frozen Tracks: An Inspector Erik Winter Novel,* Viking (New York, NY), 2007.

*Segel av sten* (title means "Sail of Stone"), Norstedt (Stockholm, Sweden), 2002.

*Rum nummer 10* (title means "Room Number 10"), Norstedt (Stockholm, Sweden), 2005.

*Vanaste land* (title means "Fairest Land"), Norstedt (Stockholm, Sweden), 2006.

*Nastan dod man* (title means "Nearly Dead Man"), Norstedt (Stockholm, Sweden), 2007.

*Den sista vintern* (title means "The Last Winter"), Norstedt (Stockholm, Sweden), 2008.

Also author of books on journalism and creative writing.

### ■ Sidelights

Swedish novelist Åke Edwardson is a popular and successful crime writer in his native country and in Scandinavia. He is a three-time winner of the Swedish Academy of Crime Writers' Award for best novel. Edwardson has been a journalist, a press officer at the United Nations, and a professor at Sweden's Gothenburg University.

## Sun and Shadow

Less well known in the United States, Edwardson's detective novels have been appearing in America in English translation since 2005. They feature recurring series character Erik Winter, the chief inspector of police in the Swedish coastal city of Gothenburg. Experienced and in his forties, Winter is still the youngest chief inspector in Sweden. When not unraveling complicated crimes, he is a jazz enthusiast and a gourmet cook. In *Sun and Shadow: An Inspector Erik Winter Novel,* the character's inaugural book in the United States, Winter is facing serious life changes. His girlfriend, Angela, a doctor, is pregnant, and the two are preparing to marry. Elsewhere, his aging father, retired in Spain, has a serious heart attack. He travels to Spain to do what he can for his father and take care of his mother, encountering a sun-drenched world so different from his day-to-day life in dreary Gothenburg as to be surreal.

Back in Sweden, Winter's next case begins to unfold as Christian and Louise Valker, a sexually adventurous young couple, are savagely murdered in their apartment, then discovered weeks after the brutal crime. The case is no simple homicide, however, as the pair were found strangely mutilated, their heads severed and transposed and their bodies carefully posed and arranged, with loud death metal music playing in a continuous loop in the background. A cryptic message, scrawled in blood on the apartment wall, adds an even more sinister element to the crime. To find answers, Winter must learn about death metal fans, sexual swingers, and other subcultures far removed from his generally staid lifestyle. Soon, a similar second crime occurs, and one of the survivors gives testimony that suggests a police officer might be the perpetrator. Worse, the sense of doom moves closer to Winter's homestead as Angela receives odd phone calls and feels that she is being watched.

Critical reaction to Edwardson's American debut was generally positive. *Library Journal* reviewer Michele Leber commented that this "dark police procedural is a topnotch work, suspenseful to the very end, with appealing characters." Within the space of "its first few chapters, *Sun and Shadow* provides an evocative description of life in downtown Gothenburg: not the Sweden of Christmas cards, but the seedier side of drunks and petty crime," observed reviewer Maxine Clark on *Eurocrime.* "It's a relatively lengthy book, but passes quite swiftly," commented Fiona Walker in a *Mystery Ink* review. "The writing is excellent and the plot moves very well. There are several very pleasing side-strands to the book—the teenagers Maria and Patrik, who wander the Gothenburg streets at all hours to get away from home, are superb and touch-ing characters—and the impression is of a well-rounded crime-novel, not just a successful puzzle," Walker continued. A *Kirkus Reviews* critic called the novel a "solid procedural neatly balancing the professional and personal lives of Winter" and his colleagues. Writing in *Booklist,* Bill Ott also had praise for this novel, noting that by its standards, it appears to be the first of "what promises to be a superior procedural series."

## Never End

*Never End: An Inspector Erik Winter Novel* reverses impressions of Sweden as a cold Scandinavian country and places Winter's next case in the atmosphere of a sweltering summer heat wave. Winter is called in to investigate when a recently graduated nineteen-year-old woman is raped after taking a nighttime shortcut through the local park. Sometime later, a second rape ends with the victim dead, and Winter begins to notice similarities between these crimes and a nearly identical unsolved rape from five years prior. With worries about his wife, Angela, and the couple's newborn baby daughter firmly in the back of his mind, Winter sets out in search of answers among uncooperative witnesses, former victims, and long-cold clues. Edwardson pays particular attention to the interactions between Winter and his police colleagues as they undertake their methodical investigation.

This novel and the others in Edwardson's Erik Winter series are "as much about character interaction as it is about story, but he is no slouch at building suspense," commented Bill Ott in *Booklist.* Walker, in another *Mystery Ink* review, remarked that the novel is "plotted really well, and the plot itself, which could have been nothing particularly original, is given a nice little twist from the potential five-year gap in a killer/rapists activity, and the intriguing possible links between the cases."

## Frozen Tracks

Two seemingly unconnected crimes veer toward an unexpected connection in *Frozen Tracks: An Inspector Erik Winter Novel,* the third Winter novel to appear in America. Christmas is fast approaching, and the days are growing shorter as Winter and his team investigate the beatings of several male university students in areas around the city. The vicious attacks are linked by distinctive marks left on each victim by the unusual weapon used by the attacker. Elsewhere in Gothenburg, nursery school children are being lured away and abducted by a strange man in a car who promises them candy and treats. Winter's investigation takes him into the dismal landscape of rural Sweden, and ultimately into a tense race against time to save a kidnapped young boy from impending peril.

Edwardson "creates endlessly interesting characters," particularly series protagonist Erik Winter, who "tackles crime after crime with a shrewd mind and a heavy heart," observed Allison Block, writing in *Booklist.* A *Publishers Weekly* reviewer was, however, less impressed with this series addition, noting that "the reader stays perpetually ahead of the irritatingly slow detectives." Julie Elliott had a far more favorable assessment of *Frozen Tracks,* noting that the quotidian lives of Edwardson's Swedish characters "make the narrative compelling," while various elements of the mysteries also make for a "page-turner."

### Death Angels

The fourth Winter procedural to be made available in English, *Death Angels: An Inspector Erik Winter Novel,* is actually a translation of his 1998 series opener, *Dans med en angel.* Here Winter teams up with Scotland Yard in the hunt for the perpetrator or perpetrators of a series of grisly murders that have taken place both in Winter's turf, Gothenburg, and in London. Hitchcock is the name the police are using for this murderer, who has evidently filmed the murders, and soon Winter and his colleagues are following clues into the snuff film industry.

A *Publishers Weekly* reviewer termed this only a "middling . . . police procedural." *Reviewing the Evidence* Web site contributor Barbara Fister also offered a mixed assessment of this series debut, noting that "the lurid story is clothed in an elegant narrative style, but Edwardson holds the reader at arm's length." Fister went on to note: "There's something aloof and unengaging in the series and its hero. In the final analysis, Erik Winter is likely to leave many readers cold." Glen Harper, however, writing in the online *International Noir Fiction,* found much more to like: "Though it seems to take a while getting started, *Death Angels* is a good foundation for a series that has since then gotten better and better." Likewise, a *Scandinavian Books* Web site contributor found this novel a "well constructed police procedural . . . with some very neat twists in the tale."

### The Shadow Woman

*The Shadow Woman: An Inspector Erik Winter Novel,* from 2010, the fifth English translation, continues the out-of-sequence translation of the Winter novels. In this second installment of the original Swedish series, Winter investigates a cold-case murder to discover new dimensions to a contemporary homicide. The death of a woman at the weeklong festival, Gothenburg Party, leads Winter into the past and takes him to Denmark in search of the killer in historical biker wars.

Block, reviewing the novel in *Booklist,* thought that the "compelling characters and vivid renderings of a landscape [are] by turns beautiful and bleak." A *Kirkus Reviews* contributor called the book "an expert melding of sociological observation and psychological acuity. The criminals, introduced late in the story, are especially gripping." A *Publishers Weekly* reviewer also commended this offering, calling it a "thoroughly satisfying police procedural." Jean King, writing in *Library Journal,* noted that Edwardson "reveals more insights into Inspector Winter's character, making him more human and more sympathetic to readers."

## ■ Biographical And Critical Sources

*PERIODICALS*

*Booklist,* June 1, 2005, Bill Ott, review of *Sun and Shadow: An Inspector Erik Winter Novel,* p. 1760; August 1, 2006, Bill Ott, review of *Never End: An Inspector Erik Winter Novel,* p. 49; May 1, 2007, Bill Ott, "A Hard-Boiled Gazetteer to Scandinavia," p. 8; August, 2007, Allison Block, review of *Frozen Tracks: An Inspector Erik Winter Novel,* p. 43; September 15, 2010, Allison Block, review of *The Shadow Woman: An Inspector Erik Winter Novel,* p. 35.

*Kirkus Reviews,* May 1, 2005, review of *Sun and Shadow,* p. 511; August 15, 2010, review of *The Shadow Woman.*

*Library Journal,* May 15, 2005, Michele Leber, review of *Sun and Shadow,* p. 110; June 1, 2006 Susan O. Moritz, review of *Never End,* p. 94; Julie Elliott, review of *Frozen Tracks,* p. 57; September 1, 2010, Jean King, review of *The Shadow Woman,* p. 94.

*New York Times Book Review,* June 25, 2006, Marilyn Stasio, "Offbeat Cops," review of *Never End.*

*Publishers Weekly,* May 2, 2005, review of *Sun and Shadow,* p. 176; June 25, 2007, review of *Frozen Tracks,* p. 33; August 10, 2009, review of *Death Angels: An Inspector Erik Winter Novel,* p. 39; August 23, 2010, review of *The Shadow Woman,* p. 32.

*ONLINE*

*Åke Edwardson Fansite,* http://akeedwardson.com/ (December 3, 2009), "Åke Edwardson: Biography."

*BlogCritics,* http://blogcritics.org/ (August 25, 2010), Jack Goodstein, review of *The Shadow Woman.*

*Complete Review,* http://www.complete-review.com/ (May 22, 2008), review of *Sun and Shadow.*

*Euro Crime,* http://www.eurocrime.co.uk/ (May 22, 2008), Maxine Clarke, review of *Sun and Shadow;* Maxine Clarke, review of *Never End.*

*International Noir Fiction,* http://internationalnoir.blogspot.com/ (October 7, 2009), Glenn Harper, review of *Death Angels.*

*Mostly Fiction Book Reviews,* http://bookreview.mostlyfiction.com/ (November 27, 2010), Lynn Harnett, review of *The Shadow Woman.*

*Mystery Ink,* http://www.mysteryinkonline.com/ (May 22, 2008), Fiona Walker, review of *Sun and Shadow;* Fiona Walker, review of *Never End.*

*Penguin Group Web site,* http://us.penguingroup.com/ (May 22, 2008), biography of Åke Edwardson.

*Pop Goes Fiction,* http://popgoesfiction.blogspot.com/ (October 29, 2009), review of *Death Angels.*

*Random House Web site,* http://www.randomhouse.co.uk/ (May 22, 2008), biography of Åke Edwardson.

*Reviewing the Evidence,* http://www.reviewingtheevidence.com/ (October, 2009), Barbara Fister, review of *Death Angels;* (October, 2010), Larissa Kyzer, review of *The Shadow Woman.*

*Scandinavian Books,* http://www.scandinavianbooks.com/ (August 6, 2011), "Åke Edwardson," (August 6, 2011), review of *Death Angels.*

*Spinetingler,* http://www.spinetinglermag.com/ (May 18, 2011), Theodore Feit, review of *The Shadow Woman.*

*What's Sarah Reading?,* http://www.tcpl.org/sarah/ (March 6, 2007), review of *Never End.**

# Katherine Ellison

## 1957-

### ■ Also Known As

Katherine Esther Ellison

### ■ Personal

Born August 19, 1957, in Minneapolis, MN; daughter of Ellis (a physician) and Bernice Ellison; married Jack Epstein (a newspaper editor); children: two sons. *Education:* Stanford University, B.A., 1979.

### ■ Addresses

*Home*—San Anselmo, CA. *Agent*—Michelle Tessler/ Tessler Literary Agency, 27 W. 20th St., Ste. 1003, New York, NY, 10011. *E-mail*—kathyellison@ comcast.net.

### ■ Career

Writer, journalist. Intern at *Foreign Policy,* Center for Investigative Reporting, and *Los Angeles Times; Washington Post,* Washington, DC, intern, 1979; *Newsweek,* London, England, intern, 1979-80; *Mercury News,* San Jose, CA, staff member, beginning 1980, reporter from San Jose, beginning 1983, bureau chief in Mexico City, Mexico, 1987-92; *Miami Herald,* Latin American correspondent from Rio de Janeiro, Brazil, 1992-99. Media Alliance, San Francisco, CA, member of board of directors, beginning 1986. Writing or speech consultant for Google.org, Packard Foundation, the Ford Foundation, the Native Conservancy, Stanford University, and Kleiner, Perkins, Caulfield & Byers.

### ■ Awards, Honors

Award for outstanding print reporting, Media Alliance of San Francisco, 1985; (with others) Pulitzer Prize for international reporting, 1986, George Polk Memorial Award, Long Island University, and Investigative Reporters and Editors Award, all 1986, for "Hidden Billions," a series of articles on Ferdinand Marcos; award from Inter American Press Association, 1994-95; Media Award, Latin American Studies Association, 1994; award, National Association of Hispanic Journalists, 1997.

### ■ Writings

*Imelda: Steel Butterfly of the Philippines,* McGraw-Hill (New York, NY), 1988.

(With Gretchen C. Daily) *The New Economy of Nature: The Quest to Make Conservation Profitable,* Island Press (Washington, DC), 2002.

*The Mommy Brain: How Motherhood Makes Us Smarter,* Basic Books (New York, NY), 2005.

*Buzz: A Year of Paying Attention,* Voice (New York, NY), 2010.

Contributor to periodicals, including the *Smithsonian, Working Mother, Atlantic Monthly, Fortune,* and *Conservation in Practice.* Monthly columnist, *Frontiers in Ecology and the Environment.* Contributor, *The Atlas of Global Conservation,* University of California Press (Berkeley, CA), 2010.

### ■ Sidelights

Katherine Ellison is an award-winning journalist and author of four nonfiction books. During her twenty-two years in journalism (over a dozen of them spent as bureau chief in Mexico City and in Rio de Janeiro for the Knight Ridder Newspapers), she won a collective Pulitzer Prize for work about the financial dealings of Philippines leader Ferdinand Marcos and his wife Imelda. This international reporting ultimately led to Ellison's first book, the 1988 *Imelda: Steel Butterfly of the Philippines.* During her reporting career she experienced adventures from traveling in Ethiopia with Eritrean guerrillas to covering the U.S.-sponsored wars in Central America. As noted on her author home page, Ellison has also "hunted for Nazis in Paraguay and Argentina and spent a week traveling with a band of Huichol Indians during their annual ceremonial peyote hunt in central Mexico." Additionally, "she has been taken hostage by Mexican peasants, arrested by Cuban police, tear-gassed in Panama, [and] chased by killer bees." Since leaving journalism, she has worked as a speech and writing consultant, and has penned books dealing with the environment and neuroscience, including *The New Economy of Nature: The Quest to Make Conservation Profitable, The Mommy Brain: How Motherhood Makes Us Smarter,* and *Buzz: A Year of Paying Attention.*

### Imedla

With her 1988 biography of the wife of Philippines president Ferdinand Marcos, *Imelda,* Ellison is, according to *New York Times Book Review* contributor Caroline Rand Herron, "on the track of bigger game" than she was in her Pulitzer Prize-winning series on the Marcoses' financial dealings. As Herron noted, Ellison is attempting in this book to portray "the soul of the country as well as of her subject." The author details Imelda's rise from poverty to becoming the wife and co-equal of the most powerful man in the Philippines. Imelda's family led a middle-class life in Manila until hard economic times drove them out of the country and to family property on the island of Leyte. Imelda became a beauty queen there before returning to Manila after World War II. There she met Marcos, a wealthy lawyer and up-and-coming politician. The couple was married, and after Marcos ascended to the presidency in 1965, Imelda held numerous positions in the government until 1986, when fabled excesses of the pair led to Marcos's ouster. Such financial reaches included the nearly three thousand pairs of shoes in Imelda's wardrobe.

Writing in *Library Journal,* Donald Clay Johnson termed *Imelda* "an absorbing biography." Similarly, *Publishers Weekly* reviewer Genevieve Stuttaford found the book "well-researched" and observed that Ellison's goal in the work is to demonstrate how Imelda "made comic opera out of a historic opportunity for greatness."

### The New Economy of Nature

Working with Stanford University research scientist and leading ecologist Gretchen C. Daily, Ellison published *The New Economy of Nature* in 2002, a work that explores how new, ecologically friendly technologies can transform the economic paradigm. The authors provide ecological and economic case studies to show the way to a greener future. For example, instead of spending more than eight billion dollars for a water purification system, New York City workers figured out that it would be more economical by far to protect the city's watershed in the Catskills. The authors also provide examples of schemes to trade emissions and plans in Australia and Costa Rica to turn wasteland and waste into useful products. Thus, the authors demonstrate that old-fashioned enlightened self-interest can lead to endeavors that are not only profitable but also sustainable. *European Business Forum* reviewer Eric Lambin amplified on the book's thesis: "The main argument proposed in the prologue by ecologist Gretchen Daily and journalist Katherine Ellison is that conservation cannot succeed by charity or philanthropy alone. The challenge is to change the rules of the game so as to produce new incentives for environmental protection, geared to both society's long-term well-being and individual self-interest."

According to an *E* reviewer, the authors "provide eminently readable examples where this is already happening." Similarly, writing in *Women's Review of Books,* Paula DiPerna noted: "Each chapter presents an innovative scheme that recognizes the economic values inherent in nature, including environmentally sound forestry practices, carbon dioxide emissions trading, ecotourism, floodplain management and botanical prospecting." *American Forests* contributor Deborah Gangloff likewise observed: "This book proves the claim that 'conservation doesn't cost, it pays.'" *Science* reviewer David Pearce thought that this "highly readable and openly journalistic book maximizes the chances politicians, entrepreneurs, and venture capitalists will pick up the theme that paying for the environment works." Pearce also noted that "Daily and Ellison's account is full of fascinating mini-biographies of some of today's leading players."

### The Mommy Brain

In *The Mommy Brain,* Ellison, the mother of two boys, calls into question the pejorative phrase "mommy brain," meaning a forgetfulness and distractedness brought on by the tensions of motherhood. Instead, she argues that motherhood improves a woman's intelligence. Researchers may have shown reduced scores on standardized neuropsychological tests for new mothers, but Ellison demonstrates that these women later show greatly improved performance in many areas. The author also shows that fathers who participate heavily in child-rearing also achieve such mental improvement. Ellison recommends societal improvements to help new mothers (including good daycare and more flex time), as well as helpful individual practices (including sufficient rest, socializing, and exercise), and she provides anecdotes from her own parenting life as well as scientific studies. "Ellison has done her homework," noted *Library Journal* reviewer Mary Ann Hughes, "citing legitimate social and neurological research to back up her conclusions."

A *Publishers Weekly* contributor had praise for Ellison's study, writing: "Ellison's often humorous and always thorough approach reveals plenty of other illustrations of these skills that will amuse and intrigue smart mothers everywhere." Similarly, a *Kirkus Reviews* writer noted: "Moms may say they have no time to read—but they'll make time for this discussion of brainy motherhood. . . . Sure to be controversial, as well as encouraging to many, many women." *Herizons* reviewer Wendy Robbins also had praise for *The Mommy Brain*, writing: "Ellison's provocative book adds new fuel to the nature/culture debate and challenges patriarchy's long tradition of ridicule of the learned or 'brainy' woman."

### *Buzz*

Ellison delves more deeply into memoir as well as neuroscience with her 2010 work, *Buzz*. The title for the book comes from her nickname for one of her sons, who suffers from attention deficit hyperactivity disorder (ADHD). When Ellison learned that she, too, has ADHD, she determined to do all the research she could to find out how two such people could live in the same house together. She takes the readers through a year in her and her family's life, supplying anecdotes of what did and did not work as treatment. In her family's case, meditation and neurofeedback were the most helpful. She also provides historical information about the treatment of impulsive behavior and also introduces readers to standard treatment options.

*Booklist* contributor Karen Springen called *Buzz* a "funny, well-written memoir" and added that "parents of kids with ADHD should find comfort in this book." A *Kirkus Reviews* writer also had a high assessment of the book, terming it an "absorbing, sharply observed memoir." Writing on the *Parent-Dish* Web site, Christopher Healy noted of *Buzz*: "In it, [Ellison] is boldly honest about the frustrating and unpredictable struggles she faced in her unfor-

tunately not-so-unique situation. . . . But Ellison never plays victim or martyr; she is just as frank about her own distractions and overreactions. The resulting story is as informative as it is entertaining. It's inspirational without being maudlin, and often quite funny."

### ■ Biographical And Critical Sources

*PERIODICALS*

*American Forests,* January, 2003, Deborah Gangloff, review of *The New Economy of Nature: The Quest to Make Conservation Profitable,* p. 17.
*BioScience,* February, 2003, Brian Czech, "Roll Over, Adam Smith: *The New Economy of Nature,* Overlooks the Origins of Money," review of *The New Economy of Nature,* p. 180.
*Booklist,* September 15, 2010, Karen Springen, review of *Buzz: A Year of Paying Attention,* p. 11.
*Business Week,* December 12, 1988, Maria Shao, review of *Imelda: Steel Butterfly of the Philippines,* p. 18.
*Chemical & Engineering News,* October 31, 2005, Bette Hileman, review of *The Mommy Brain: How Motherhood Makes Us Smarter,* p. 40.
*Choice,* December, 2005, V.L. Bullough, review of *The Mommy Brain,* p. 742.
*Christian Century,* November 20, 2002, Katherine Ellison, "Stopping Traffic," p. 8.
*E,* September, 2002, "Money Makes the World Go Round," review of *The New Economy of Nature,*
*Endangered Species Update,* March, 2003, Gloria E. Helfand, review of *The New Economy of Nature.*
*European Business Forum,* June 22, 2003, Eric Lambin, "Profits and the Planet," review of *The New Economy of Nature,* p. 93.
*Far Eastern Economic Review,* September 14, 1989, Steven Knipp, review of *Imelda,* p. 59.
*Herizons,* March 22, 2007, Wendy Robbins, review of *The Mommy Brain,* p. 45.
*Houston Chronicle* (Houston, TX), August 14, 2005, Erica Noonan, "Mom's IQ Gets Boost from Baby; Research Based Primarily on Studies of Mice," review of *The Mommy Brain,* p. 24.
*Issues in Science and Technology,* summer, 2002, David Simpson, review of *The New Economy of Nature,* p. 84.
*Journal of Economic Literature,* December, 2002, review of *The New Economy of Nature,* p. 1423.
*Journal of the West,* summer, 2004, Paul H. Carlson, review of *The New Economy of Nature,* p. 89.
*Kirkus Reviews,* January 1, 2005, review of *The Mommy Brain,* p. 32; July 15, 2010, review of *Buzz.*

*Library Journal,* October 15, 1988, Donald Clay Johnson, review of *Imelda,* p. 93; March 1, 2005, Mary Ann Hughes, review of *The Mommy Brain,* p. 99.

*National Post,* July 23, 2005, Erica Noonan, "Motherhood Can Make You Smarter," review of *The Mommy Brain,* p. 13.

*National Review,* September 12, 2005, Susan Konig, "Mother Wit," review of *The Mommy Brain,* p. 49.

*Natural Resources & Environment,* fall, 2002, JoAnne L. Dunec, review of *The New Economy of Nature,* p. 107.

*Natural Resources Journal,* January, 2004, Patrick Wilson, review of *The New Economy of Nature,* p. 336.

*Nature,* April 25, 2002, Norman Myers, review of *The New Economy of Nature,* p. 788.

*New York Times Book Review,* January 8, 1989, review of *Imelda,* p. 23.

*People,* October 25, 2010, "Books," p. 47.

*Psychology Today,* May 1, 2005, Jennifer Drapkin, "New Mom, Ph.D.," review of *The Mommy Brain.*

*Publishers Weekly,* September 2, 1988, Genevieve Stuttaford, review of *Imelda,* p. 92; February 21, 2005, review of *The Mommy Brain,* p. 167.

*San Francisco Chronicle,* May 12, 2002, Alex Barnum, review of *The New Economy of Nature,* p. 3.

*Science,* August 9, 2002, David Pearce, "Gold from Green Paths," review of *The New Economy of Nature,* p. 941.

*Self,* May, 2005, Katherine Ellison, "The Myth of Mommy Brain," p. 135.

*Sierra,* July, 2002, Bob Schildgen, "Green Revolution in Economics," review of *The New Economy of Nature,* p. 69.

*Times Literary Supplement,* July 23, 2004, Zoe Young, "Market Gardeners," review of *The New Economy of Nature,* p. 30.

*Washington Post Book World,* April 10, 2005, Anne Glusker, "The Mother Load," review of *The Mommy Brain,* p. 10.

*Women's Review of Books,* June, 2002, Paula DiPerna, "The End of the Free Ride," review of *The New Economy of Nature,* p. 15.

ONLINE

*AMHC Web site,* http://www.amhc.org/ (August 6, 2011), David Van Nuys, "An Interview with Katherine Ellison on ADHD."

*Center for Conservative Biology Web site,* http://www.stanford.edu/ (June 23, 2011), "Katherine Ellison."

*Examiner.com,* http://www.examiner.com/ (October 11, 2010), Gabriella West, "Diagnosed ADHD Herself, Katherine Ellison Writes about Parenting an ADHD Kid."

*Huffington Post,* http://www.huffingtonpost.com/ "Katherine Ellison."

*Katherine Ellison Home Page,* http://www.katherineellison.com (June 23, 2011).

*Mommy Brain Home Page,* http://themommybrain.com/ (June 23, 2011), "Katherine Ellison."

*ParentDish,* http://www.parentdish.com/ (October 29, 2011), Christopher Healy, "Katherine Ellison, Author of *Buzz: A Year of Paying Attention,* Understands Distraction."

*SFGate.com,* http://articles.sfgate.com/ (October 11, 2010), Jessica Werner Zack, "Son's ADD Leads to Mom's Own Diagnosis and a Critical Book on Parenting."

*Time Online,* http://www.time.com/ (April 24, 2005), Amanda Bower, review of *The Mommy Brain.*

OTHER

*Morning Edition,* November 1, 2010, Jon Hamilton, "Train the Brain: Using Neurofeedback to Treat ADHD," transcript of a National Public Radio (NPR) interview with Katherine Ellison.

# Kathleen Ernst

## 1959-

### ■ Also Known As

Kathleen A. Ernst

### ■ Personal

Born May 7, 1959, in Scranton, PA; daughter of Henry (a Methodist minister) and Priscilla Johnston Angotti (a librarian) Ernst; married Scott C. Meeker; children: Meghan McGill Meeker. *Education:* West Virginia University, B.S., 1981; Antioch University, M.A., 1993. *Politics:* "Independent liberal." *Religion:* Unitarian Universalist. *Hobbies and other interests:* Travel, hiking, kayaking, baking, sewing, quilting.

### ■ Addresses

*Home*—Middleton, WI. *Agent*—Andrea Cascardi, Transatlantic Literary Agency, Inc., 72 Glengowan Rd., Toronto, Ontario M4N IG4, Canada. *E-mail*—k. ernst@kathleenernst.com.

### ■ Career

Writer and writing instructor. Old World Wisconsin Historic Site, Eagle, WI, interpreter and curator of education and collections, 1982-93; Wisconsin Educational Communications Board, Madison, instructional programs developer and project director, 1994-2003. Instructor at Mount Mary College and University of Wisconsin-Madison, Carroll College, and Edgewood College. Civil War interpreter at living-history presentations.

### ■ Member

Society of Children's Book Writers and Illustrators, Mystery Writers of America, Women Writing the West.

### ■ Awards, Honors

Award of Excellence, Central Education Network, 1996, for *Exploring Wisconsin Our Home*; Books for the Teen Age listing, New York Public Library, 1998, for *The Night Riders of Harpers Ferry*; Crystal Award, Association for Educational Communications and Technology, 2000, for *Investigating Wisconsin History*; Edgar Allan Poe Award nomination, Mystery Writers of America, 2001, for *Trouble at Fort La Pointe*; Arthur Tofte Juvenile Fiction Book Award, Council for Wisconsin Writers, 2001, for *Retreat from Gettysburg*, 2004, for *Ghosts of Vicksburg*, and 2005, for *Betrayal at Cross Creek*; Emmy for Outstanding Children's Programming—Children's Series, National Academy of Television Arts & Sciences, Midwest Chapter, 2002, for *Cultural Horizons of Wisconsin*; Aurora Award Gold Medal, Aurora Independent Film and Video Competition, for *Cultural Horizons of Wisconsin*; Wilbur Schramm Award for Excellence, National Educational Telecommunications Association, 2003, for *Cultural Horizons*; Judge's Award for Instructional Innovation, National Educational Telecommunications Association, and Aurora Award Platinum Medal for Best of Show, Aurora International Independent Film and Video Corporation, both 2004, both for *Cultural Horizons*; Arthur Tofte Juvenile Fiction Book Award, Council for Wisconsin Writers, 2004, for *Ghosts of Vicksburg*, and 2005, for *Betrayal at Cross Creek*; Flora MacDonald Award, 2006; Scottish Heritage Service Award, 2006, for *Betrayal at Cross Creek*; Children's Literature Award, Society of Midland Authors, Arthur Tofte/Betty Ren Wright Children's Literature Award, Council for Wisconsin Writers, Editors' Choice Selection, Books for the Teen Age listing, all 2007, all for *Hearts of Stone*.

## ■ Writings

*Too Afraid to Cry: Maryland Civilians in the Antietam Campaign* (nonfiction), Stackpole (Mechanicsburg, PA), 1999.

*HISTORICAL NOVELS; YOUNG ADULT*

*The Night Riders of Harpers Ferry*, White Mane (Shippensburg, PA), 1996.
*The Bravest Girl in Sharpsburg*, White Mane Kids (Shippensburg, PA), 1997.
*Retreat from Gettysburg*, White Mane Kids (Shippensburg, PA), 2000.
*Ghosts of Vicksburg*, White Mane Kids (Shippensburg, PA), 2003.
*Hearts of Stone*, Dutton Children's Books (New York, NY), 2006.
*Highland Fling*, Cricket Books (Chicago, IL), 2006.

Contributor to periodicals, including *America's Civil War, Civil War Times Illustrated, Columbiad, Wilderness, Boundary Waters Journal, Wisconsin Trails,* and *Quilters' Newsletter Magazine.*

*"AMERICAN GIRL HISTORY MYSTERIES" SERIES; FOR YOUNG ADULTS*

*Trouble at Fort La Pointe*, Pleasant Company (Middleton, WI), 2000.
*Whistler in the Dark*, Pleasant Company (Middleton, WI), 2002.
*Betrayal at Cross Creek*, Pleasant Company (Middleton, WI), 2004.
*Danger at the Zoo: A Kit Mystery*, American Girl (Middleton, WI), 2005.
*Secrets in the Hills: A Josefina Mystery*, Pleasant Company (Middleton, WI), 2006.
*Midnight in Lonesome Hollow: A Kit Mystery*, American Girl (Middleton, WI), 2007.
*The Runaway Friend: A Kirsten Mystery*, American Girl (Middleton, WI), 2008.
*Clues in the Shadows: A Molly Mystery*, American Girl (Middleton, WI), 2009.

*"CHLOE ELLEFSON MYSTERY" SERIES; FOR ADULTS*

*Old World Murder*, Midnight Ink (Woodbury, MN), 2010.
*The Heirloom Murders*, Midnight Ink (Woodbury, MN), 2011.

*FOR TELEVISION*

(With others) *Exploring Wisconsin, Our Home*, Wisconsin Educational Communications Board/ Wisconsin Public Television, 1995.

*New Dawn of Tradition: A Wisconsin Powwow*, Wisconsin Educational Communications Board, 1998.
*Investigating Wisconsin History*, Wisconsin Educational Communications Board/Wisconsin Public Television, 1998.
(And project director) *Cultural Horizons of Wisconsin* (series), Wisconsin Educational Communications Board/Wisconsin Public Television, 2002–03.

## ■ Sidelights

Kathleen Ernst's professional writing career began with work as a magazine freelancer and as a screenwriter for the Wisconsin Educational Communications Board. Ernst's fiction writing started much earlier, however. "I started writing seriously when I was in my teens," Ernst once commented. "Twenty years passed before I got my first book contract. Obviously I enjoy the processing of writing, although getting published is pretty darn nice too." Ernst is the author of over twenty novels for young readers, most of them historicals. She is also the author of a series of cozy mysteries for adult readers featuring Wisconsin museum curator Chloe Ellefson.

Ernst once commented: "I love research. It's like a treasure hunt! Researching books has taken me from university libraries to the Cincinnati Zoo; from tiny museums in rural Scotland to the Smithsonian Institution; from Ojibwe reservations to hiking trails in Colorado; from Highland Games in North Carolina to ghost tours in New Mexico. What could be more fun than that?"

Ernst also offered the following advice to aspiring writers: "One: Take the time to learn your craft. Two: Get connected—join a professional writer's group, and hook up with other writers who can help critique your work. Three: Read a lot. Keep up with work being published in your genre. Read like a writer—take time to analyze what you like, and why."

### *The Night Riders of Harpers Ferry* and *The Bravest Girl in Sharpsburg*

Ernst's first book contract was for *The Night Riders of Harpers Ferry*, a novel of the U.S. Civil War. Based on a true story, the novel centers around Solomon Hargreave, a Union soldier in the New York Cavalry Regiment stationed at Harpers Ferry. Solomon saves the life of a young woman, only to find out that her brother is a member of the Confederate army. When Solomon is asked to spy on her family, he must decide who is worthy of his trust. Carolyn Phelan, writing for *Booklist*, remarked that *The Night Riders* of *Harpers Ferry* "conveys the strain of divided families, misguided loyalties," and the difficulties of life during the Civil War.

*The Bravest Girl in Sharpsburg*, Ernst's second novel, also takes place during the U.S. Civil War. Teresa Kretzer and Savilla Miller, best friends who once shared the reputation for being the bravest girls in Sharpsburg, find themselves at political odds as civil war looms over Maryland. Their difficulties come to a head as both girls must face the Battle of Antietam. Ernst once commented about why she chose to write on historical topics: "Most of my work is historical fiction because that's what I grew up reading, and I still love to disappear into a good historical novel. Novelists know that history is about stories, not strings of dates and facts. When I'm settling in on a new project, I try to find themes and stories that haven't been covered already in fiction—stories that might otherwise be lost."

## Too Afraid to Cry

Having grown up in Maryland, Ernst spent many years visiting the Antietam Battlefield and the small towns nearby. As she once explained: "At that time there was little interest in social history, but I always looked at the old houses near the battlefield and wondered what happened to the people living there when the armies came. That interest led to my lone adult nonfiction book, *Too Afraid to Cry: Maryland Civilians in the Antietam Campaign*, which took over a decade to research and write. The first three Civil War novels I had published stemmed from research I did for that project, too."

*Too Afraid to Cry* focuses on the changes civilians were forced to make when the Civil War landed on their doorsteps. The Battle of Antietam was the single bloodiest day in the history of the United States, and while there are numerous military studies of the event, very few books discuss the effect the battle had on the people living in the area, according to Theresa McDevitt of *Library Journal*, who considered it a "fascinating topic." Sharon Seager, writing in *Civil War History*, praised Ernst's book, noting that "the writing is vivid, skillfully blending military and social history."

## Retreat from Gettysburg and Ghosts of Vicksburg

Ernst followed her adult nonfiction book with a third young-adult novel focusing on the same era in history. In *Retreat from Gettysburg* young Chigger O'Malley's father and three brothers were killed while serving in the Union Army, and Chigger hopes that the Confederates will suffer a sound defeat. However, when he and his mother are forced

to take in a wounded Confederate soldier, he begins to question his own faith in what is right and what is wrong. "Meticulous attention to history is the strong point" of the novel, according to Carolyn Phelan in *Booklist*. Toniann Scime, writing in *School Library Journal*, praised the novel as "an excellent example of how to teach history through fiction."

Jamie Carswell and his cousin Althea find themselves on opposite sides of the Civil War in *Ghosts of Vicksburg*. Although Jamie currently serves in the Fourteenth Wisconsin Infantry Regiment, he grew up summering in Mississippi with his cousins. As Jamie watches while he and the other soldiers cause civilians to suffer, he begins to wonder if the army is doing the right thing. Nancy P. Reeder wrote in her *School Library Journal* review that Ernst "does a commendable job of remaining neutral."

## Trouble at Fort La Pointe and Betrayal at Cross Creek

As well as penning historical fiction, Ernst has written several titles for Pleasant Company's American Girl imprint. She once explained: "I came to mystery writing unexpectedly when an editor from American Girl invited me to submit a story for the new series being planned, 'History Mysteries.'" Ernst's first novel in the series is *Trouble at Fort La Pointe*, which takes place in the 1730s. Suzette Choudoir's mother is Ojibwe and her father is a French fur trapper who spends most of the year away from his family. If he wins a fur competition, he will be able to spend the winter with Suzette and her mother, but just as it seems he is about to win, Mr. Choudoir is framed for a crime of theft. Suzette knows her father is not guilty, and she sets out to prove his innocence. Ernst "does a commendable job of integrating setting and cultural details into the story," according to Kay Weisman in a *Booklist* article, while Maureen Griffin of *Kliatt* called it "a delight."

Another of Ernst's "History Mysteries" is *Betrayal at Cross Creek*, which takes place during the American Revolution. Elspeth and her family are Scottish immigrants to the North Carolina territory; her grandfather fought in the war for Scottish independence years earlier and now wants nothing to do with a new war. When the patriots come to convince Elspeth's family to fight, the family is mysteriously put in danger, and Elspeth takes it upon herself to discover the identity of the person who would cause them harm. A *Kirkus Reviews* contributor considered *Betrayal at Cross Creek* "a grand read and an important addition" to the historical novels for young adults about the Revolutionary Era. Hazel Rochman, writing in *Booklist*, noted that Ernst's "characters are drawn with extraordinary depth," while

Kristen Oravec of *School Library Journal* commented, "This well told story has an intriguing plot. . . . The element of mystery keeps readers guessing."

### Secrets in the Hills and Midnight in Lonesome Hollow

In *Secrets in the Hills: A Josefina Mystery,* another historical mystery for the "American Girl" series, a mysterious stranger shows up at the home of Josefina, a young girl who lives on a ranch in New Mexico during the 1820s. He is injured, and the family cares for him. While washing the man's clothes, Josefina finds a treasure map. A subplot includes a mystery about a ghost, and readers also see Josefina trying to develop her skills as a *curandera,* or healer. Gillian Engberg, a reviewer for *Booklist,* felt that "readers will be easily drawn in" by the story, and will "see themselves" in Josefina's place.

In *Midnight in Lonesome Hollow: A Kit Mystery,* Ernst spins a tale of Depression-era mystery. Kit Kittredge was first introduced in Ernst's 2005 *Danger at the Zoo: A Kit Mystery,* in which the sixth grader gets some work writing for the local paper and subsequently helps solve a mystery at a nearby zoo. In *Midnight in Lonesome Hollow,* Kit travels to Appalachia to visit an aunt and ends up helping a visiting researcher who is studying regional basket weaving. Soon, however, it becomes apparent that someone does not want Kit or the researcher investigating anything around Lonesome Hollow. *Booklist* reviewer Ilene Cooper felt that Ernst "does a fine job of showing . . . the poverty of Appalachia during the Depression." Similarly, *School Library Journal* contributor Krista Tokarz termed this mystery "nicely paced" and noted that the author manages to blend historical information into the narrative.

### The Runaway Friend and Clues in the Shadows

A young Swedish girl, Kirsten, slowly adapts to her new life in Minnesota in the nineteenth century in *The Runaway Friend: A Kirsten Mystery.* When a neighbor, Erik, disappears, Kirsten investigates, despite her parents' objections. They think that he has just run away from debt, but Kirsten thinks otherwise. "Throughout the story, the author weaves in information about the dangers of frontier life," noted *School Library Journal* reviewer Donna Atmur of this novel.

*Clues in the Shadows: A Molly Mystery* features a young girl named Molly during World War II. Here the war is drawing to a close and Molly's dad has returned uninjured but sadly changed by all he has seen and experienced. Molly is still volunteering at

the Junior Red Cross, but when a leader there mysteriously quits, Molly finds herself in the midst of another mystery that needs solving. *School Library Journal* reviewer Natasha Forrester noted that "red herrings interspersed throughout the story keep readers guessing."

### Hearts of Stone and Highland Fling

Ernst turns to stand-alone titles with *Hearts of Stone* and *Highland Fling.* With the former, the author created Hannah Cameron, a girl whose father must leave home to join the Union army during the Civil War. After her father and mother are both killed, Hannah looks for refuge in Nashville, a city crowded with starving refugees. According to a *Kirkus Reviews* writer, the "memorable tale demonstrates in vivid detail how wars affect women and children." Although the historical foundation of the book is sound, its greatest value lies in its depiction of the human emotions and conflicts stirred up by war, according to Nancy P. Reeder in *School Library Journal.* She suggested that the book provides good material for "discussions about authority, family bonds, and selflessness."

*Highland Fling* features Tanya, a fifteen-year-old who has to move from Wisconsin to North Carolina after her parents' divorce. Tanya's mother and sister are enthusiastic about their Scottish heritage and enjoy taking part in cultural events, such as Highland Games and dances, but Tanya feels alienated. The book contains information about Scots culture and documentary filmmaking, as well as exploring deeper themes of the effects of divorce and the nature of history and culture. "There are a lot of strands here and Ernst balances them nicely for the most part," remarked a *Kirkus Reviews* writer.

### Old World Murder and Heirloom Murders

Ernst produced her first fiction for adult readers with the 2010 mystery, *Old World Murder,* which introduces her series protagonist, Chloe Ellefson, a curator of living history at Old World Wisconsin. The series debut finds Chloe still reeling from a bad romance. She has left Switzerland to return to her hometown, and she takes the job of curator at the local museum, which focuses on the history of local immigrant communities. Her first day at work turns out to be difficult, for a local woman has a request. Berget Lundquist, an old widowed woman, once donated a family memento, a Norwegian ale bowl, to the museum, and now she inexplicably wants it back. Chloe has no idea where the bowl might be, for the museum has been left in a mess by her predecessor. She promises the woman that she will try to find the bowl, which does not seem to please

Mrs. Lundquist. After leaving the museum to dive home, the elderly woman apparently has a heart attack and crashes her car, dying at the scene. Chloe thereafter attempts to find the bowl, but she discovers that it is missing. Then, when Mrs. Lundquist's only friend is found dead, Chloe begins to wonder if this is mere coincidence. The local policeman, Roelke McKenna, also seems interested in the bowl—or attracted to Chloe—but now they must work together to solve the crime.

A *Kirkus Reviews* contributor did not have a high opinion of this series debut, calling it "a gentle puzzler best appreciated by amateur genealogists and folk artists. The slow pace will bore most others." *Library Journal* reviewer Jo Ann Vicarel found more to like in this work, dubbing it a "charming cozy . . . with a dab of antique lore." Similar praise came from *Booklist* writer Sue O'Brien, who found it an "engaging story of a woman devastated by a failed romantic relationship whose sleuthing helps her heal." Likewise, a *Publishers Weekly* reviewer thought that "clever plot twists and credible characters make this a far from humdrum cozy."

In the second series installment, *The Heirloom Murders,* Chloe's romance with good-looking policeman Roelke McKenna is put on hold when her ex-boyfriend from Switzerland suddenly gets second thoughts and shows up on her doorstep. Roelke, meanwhile, is looking into the suicide of Bonnie Sabatola, but something tells him this might not be a suicide after all. Chloe is also drawn into this case when she helps out her friend Dellyn, who is Bonnie's sister. The two have been left a huge assortment of artifacts by their parents and plan to donate these to a local historical society. Chloe helps to go through these things, and Dellyn jokes about a famous diamond that might be among the clutter. When Chloe is later attacked, the joke about the diamond no longer seems humorous; perhaps there is a connection between Bonnie's death and the collection of artifacts. "Complex characterization and a stronger mystery make Ernst's second more likely to appeal to a broader audience than her debut," wrote a contributor to *Kirkus Reviews.*

■ **Biographical And Critical Sources**

*PERIODICALS*

*Booklist*, January 1, 1997, Carolyn Phelan, review of *The Night Riders of Harpers Ferry*, p. 842; September 15, 2000, Carolyn Phelan, review of *Retreat from Gettysburg*, p. 239; October 1, 2000, Kay Weisman, review of *Trouble at Fort La Pointe*, p. 339; September 15, 2003, Traci Todd, review of *Trouble at Fort La Pointe*, p. 254; March 1, 2004, Hazel Rochman, review of *Betrayal at Cross Creek*, p. 1203; April 15, 2006, Chris Sherman, review of *Highland Fling*, p. 40; May 15, 2006, Gillian Engberg, review of *Secrets in the Hills: A Josefina Mystery*, p. 45; November 1, 2006, Anne O'Malley, review of *Hearts of Stone*, p. 53; May 15, 2007, Ilene Cooper, review of *Midnight in Lonesome Hollow: A Kit Mystery*, p. 47; October 1, 2010, Sue O'Brien, review of *Old World Murder*, p. 35.

*Civil War History*, June, 2000, Sharon Seager, review of *Too Afraid to Cry: Maryland Civilians in the Antietam Campaign*, p. 171.

*Kirkus Reviews*, February 15, 2004, review of *Betrayal at Cross Creek*, p. 77; February 15, 2006, review of *Highland Fling*, p. 182; October 1, 2006, review of *Hearts of Stone*, p. 1013; August 15, 2010, review of *Old World Murder*; June 15, 2011, review of *The Heirloom Murders*.

*Kliatt*, January, 2004, Maureen Griffin, review of *Trouble at Fort La Pointe*, p. 51; November 1, 2006, Claire Rosser, review of *Hearts of Stone*, p. 10.

*Library Journal*, June 15, 1999, Theresa McDevitt, review of *Too Afraid to Cry*, p. 89; September 1, 2010, Jo Ann Vicarel, "Mystery," review of *Old World Murder*, p. 94.

*Publishers Weekly*, August 9, 2010, review of *Old World Murder*, p. 34.

*School Library Journal*, December, 2000, Carrie Schadle, review of *Trouble at Fort La Pointe*, p. 144, and Toniann Scime, review of *Retreat from Gettysburg*, p. 144; July, 2003, Katherine Devine, review of *Trouble at Fort La Pointe*, p. 71; December, 2003, Nancy P. Reeder, review of *Ghosts of Vicksburg*, p. 150; May, 2004, Kristen Oravec, review of *Betrayal at Cross Creek*, p. 146; April, 2006, review of *Secrets in the Hills*, p. 138; June, 2006, Catherine Ensley, review of *Highland Fling*, p. 154; December, 2006, Nancy P. Reeder, review of *Hearts of Stone*, p. 138; May, 2007, Krista Tokarz, review of *Midnight in Lonesome Hollow*, p. 86; November 1, 2008, Donna Atmur, review of *The Runaway Friend: A Kirsten Mystery*, p. 88; July 1, 2009, Natasha Forrester, review of *Clues in the Shadows: A Molly Mystery*, p. 62.

*Voice of Youth Advocates*, February, 2007, Stacey Hayman, review of *Hearts of Stone*, p. 524.

*ONLINE*

*American Girl Publishing Web site*, http://www.americangirlpublishing.com/ (June 23, 2011), "Kathleen Ernst."

*Fantastic Fiction*, http://www.fantasticfiction.co.uk/ (June 23, 2011), "Kathleen Ernst."

*Kathleen Ernst Home Page*, http://www.distaff.net/ (June 23, 2011).

*Mystery Writers of America*, http://www.mysterywriters.org/ (June 23, 2011), "Kathleen Ernst."*

# Janet Evanovich

## 1943-

■ **Also Known As**

Steffie Hall

■ **Personal**

Born April 22, 1943, in South River, NJ; married; husband's name Pete (a manager); children: Peter, Alex (daughter). *Education:* Attended Douglass College.

■ **Addresses**

*Home and office*—Naples, FL. *E-mail*—janet@ evanovich.com.

■ **Career**

Writer.

■ **Member**

Romance Writers of America, Sisters in Crime.

■ **Awards, Honors**

John Creasey Memorial, Last Laugh, and Silver Dagger award, all from Crime Writers Association; Lefty award, Left Coast Crime; Dilys award, Independent Booksellers Association; Quill Award, Mystery/ Suspense/Thriller category, 2006, for *Twelve Sharp;* Golden Leaf Award, New Jersey Romance Writers.

■ **Writings**

*"STEPHANIE PLUM" SERIES*

*One for the Money,* Scribner (New York, NY), 1994.
*Two for the Dough,* Scribner (New York, NY), 1996.
*Three to Get Deadly,* Scribner (New York, NY), 1997.
*Four to Score,* St. Martin's Press (New York, NY), 1998.
*High Five,* St. Martin's Press (New York, NY), 1999.
*Hot Six,* St. Martin's Press (New York, NY), 2000.
*Seven Up,* St. Martin's Press (New York, NY), 2001.
*Three Plums in One* (contains *One for the Money, Two for the Dough,* and *Three to Get Deadly*), Scribner (New York, NY), 2001.
*Hard Eight,* St. Martin's Press (New York, NY), 2002.
*To the Nines,* St. Martin's Press (New York, NY), 2003.
*Ten Big Ones,* St. Martin's Press (New York, NY), 2004.
*Eleven on Top,* St. Martin's Press (New York, NY), 2005.
*Twelve Sharp,* St. Martin's Press (New York, NY), 2006.
*Lean Mean Thirteen,* St. Martin's Press (New York, NY), 2007.
*More Plums in One* (includes *Four to Score, High Five,* and *Hot Six*), St. Martin's Press (New York, NY), 2007.
*Fearless Fourteen,* St. Martin's Press (New York, NY), 2008.
*Finger Lickin' Fifteen,* St. Martin's Press (New York, NY), 2009.
*Sizzling Sixteen,* St. Martin's Press (New York, NY), 2010.
*Smokin' Seventeen,* Bantam Books (New York, NY), 2011.
*Explosive Eighteen,* Bantam (New York, NY), 2011.

Other omnibus collections from the series include *The Stephanie Plum Novels*, 2002; *Three to Get Deadly/Four to Score/High Five/Hot Six*, 2002; *Hot Six, Seven Up, Hard Eight*, 2006; *Seven Up/Hard Eight/To the Nines*, 2007; and *Ten Big Ones/Eleven on Top/Twelve Sharp*, 2007.

*"STEPHANIE PLUM BETWEEN THE NUMBERS" SERIES*

*Visions of Sugar Plums*, St. Martin's Press (New York, NY), 2002.

*Plum Lovin'*, St. Martin's Press (New York, NY), 2007.

*Plum Lucky*, St. Martin's Press (New York, NY), 2008.

*Plum Spooky*, St. Martin's Press (New York, NY), 2009.

Also author of omnibus *Between the Plums*, 2009.

*"MAX HOLT" SERIES*

(As Steffie Hall) *Full House*, Second Chance at Love, 1989, reprinted, St. Martin's Press (New York, NY), 2002.

(With Charlotte Hughes) *Full Tilt*, St. Martin's Press (New York, NY), 2003.

(With Charlotte Hughes) *Full Speed*, St. Martin's Press (New York, NY), 2003.

(With Charlotte Hughes) *Full Blast*, St. Martin's Press (New York, NY), 2004.

(With Charlotte Hughes) *Full Bloom*, St. Martin's Press (New York, NY), 2005.

(With Charlotte Hughes) *Full Scoop*, St. Martin's Press (New York, NY), 2006.

Also author of omnibus *The Full Box*, 2006.

*ROMANCE NOVELS*

(As Steffie Hall) *Hero at Large*, Second Chance at Love, 1987.

*The Grand Finale*, Bantam (New York, NY), 1988.

*Thanksgiving*, Bantam (New York, NY), 1988.

*Manhunt*, Bantam (New York, NY), 1988, reprinted, HarperTorch (New York, NY), 2005.

(As Steffie Hall) *Foul Play*, Second Chance at Love, 1989.

*Ivan Takes a Wife*, Bantam (New York, NY), 1989, published as *Love Overboard*, HarperTorch (New York, NY), 2005.

*Back to the Bedroom*, Bantam (New York, NY), 1989, reprinted, HarperTorch (New York, NY), 2005.

*Wife for Hire*, Bantam (New York, NY), 1990.

*Smitten*, Bantam (New York, NY), 1990, reprinted, HarperCollins (New York, NY), 2006.

*The Rocky Road to Romance*, Bantam (New York, NY), 1991.

*Naughty Neighbor*, Bantam (New York, NY), 1992, HarperCollins (New York, NY), 2008.

*"ALEXANDRA BARNABY" SERIES*

*Metro Girl*, HarperCollins (New York, NY), 2004.

*Motor Mouth*, HarperCollins (New York, NY), 2006.

(With Alex Evanvovich) *Troublemaker, Book One* (graphic novel; see also below), illustrated by Joelle Jones, Dark Horse Comics (Milwaukie, OR), 2010.

(With Alex Evanvovich) *Troublemaker, Book Two*, (graphic novel; see also below), illustrated by Joelle Jones, Dark Horse Comics (Milwaukie, OR), 2010.

(With Alex Evanvovich) *Troublemaker* (graphic novel; paperback reprint containing both *Troublemaker, Book One* and *Troublemaker, Book Two*), illustrated by Joelle Jones, Dark Horse Comics (Milwaukie, OR), 2011.

*OTHER*

(With Ina Yaloff and Alex Evanvovich) *How I Write: Secrets of a Bestselling Author* (nonfiction), St. Martin's Griffin (New York, NY), 2006.

(With Leanne Banks) *Hot Stuff*, St. Martin's Paperbacks (New York, NY), 2007.

*Wicked Appetite*, St. Martin's Press (New York, NY), 2010.

■ **Adaptations**

*One for the Money* was adapted for film by TriStar, 2011.

■ **Sidelights**

Janet Evanovich is the author of a successful series of humorous detective novels set in Trenton, New Jersey. The works feature protagonist Stephanie Plum, a feisty Jersey girl who turns to bounty hunting when she loses her job as a lingerie buyer. Characterized by a flamboyant wardrobe, big hair, and an impertinent manner, Plum tracks bail jumpers for her cousin Vinnie, a bail bondsman. In addition to the score of novels written featuring wisecracking Stephanie Plum, Evanovich has also written several novels in a series featuring Alexandra Barnaby, as well as a number of stand-alone novels. Evanovich's novels have combined sales of more than seventy-five million copies worldwide as of 2011.

### One for the Money

In 1994's *One for the Money*, the novel in which she is introduced, Plum tackles her first assignment, the capture of Joe Morelli, a police officer and accused murderer who also happens to be the man to whom she lost her virginity when she was sixteen. Reviewing *One for the Money*, Marilyn Stasio in the *New York Times Book Review* delighted in a bounty-hunting protagonist "with Bette Midler's mouth and Cher's fashion sense." Stasio wrote: "With [Plum's] brazen style and dazzling wardrobe, who could resist this doll?"

Calling the novel "funny and ceaselessly inventive," Charles Champlin in the *Los Angeles Book Review* applauded Evanovich's use of first-person narration. According to Champlin, "Stephanie's voice, breezy and undauntable, is all her own. . . . [Her] moral seems to be that when the going gets tough, the tough get funny." However, Marvin Lachman, writing in *Armchair Detective*, complained that "Plum's . . . voice becomes irritating, largely due to its consistently unsophisticated speech." In addition, calling the plot "minimal," Lachman indicated that the story "cannot sustain a book of two hundred and ninety pages," specifically noting that "reader suspension of disbelief is . . . threatened" by Plum's prior relationship with Morelli. Kate Wilson, in a mixed review in *Entertainment Weekly*, suggested that Evanovich's inexperience as a novelist is evident in occasionally contrived dialogue, but nevertheless described heroine Plum as "intelligent, cheery, and genuine." Dwight Garner in the *Washington Post Book World* characterized *One for the Money* as "a lightweight but very funny crime novel" and a "bright, bracing book [that] comes roaring in like a blast of very fresh air."

### Two for the Dough

Evanovich's follow-up novel, *Two for the Dough*, depicts Plum's pursuit of fugitive Kenny Mancuso. The case is complicated by a secondary mystery involving two dozen coffins missing from a local mortuary and intensified by the protagonist's ongoing relationship with Morelli, who also has an interest in the case. Ultimately, Plum's grandmother gets involved, and, in the words of *Times Literary Supple-*

*ment* contributor Natasha Cooper, "does her hamfisted best to assist Stephanie, falling into coffins, firing off bullets, and upsetting the entire neighborhood."

In the *Christian Science Monitor*, Michelle Ross praised *Two for the Dough*, noting: "Evanovich has created not just an immediately likeable heroine, but an entire real, vibrant, and . . . colorful world. We call it wild and sassy, we call it wonderful." In the *New York Times Book Review*, Stasio again lauded heroine Plum, whom she described as "the motor-mouthed Jersey girl from Trenton . . . with her pepper spray, stun gun, up-to-here hair and out-to-there attitude." An *Entertainment Weekly* contributor, however, called the "local color . . . a bit too forcibly hued" and complained that the "dialogue has a mechanical, insular feel." A critic writing in *Belles Lettres* found that although "there are some great lines" in *Two for the Dough*, it "isn't as funny" as the first Plum mystery. In the *Times Literary Supplement*, however, Cooper called the work "an entertaining parody of the hard-boiled American crime novel."

### Three to Get Deadly and Four to Score

The third volume in the series, *Three to Get Deadly*, details Plum's search for "Uncle Mo," a candy store owner and local hero who skipped out on a concealed weapons charge. A reviewer in *Library Journal* noted that *Three to Get Deadly* brings "more fast and funny action from a winning writer." Stasio, in an assessment in the *New York Times Book Review*, called the novel "another rollicking chapter in the madcap career of . . . Evanovich's sassy bounty hunter." A *Publishers Weekly* reviewer appreciated the way the heroine "muddles through another case full of one-liners as well as corpses," and wrote that "the redoubtable Stephanie is a character crying out for a screen debut."

In the fourth "Stephanie Plum" mystery, *Four to Score*, Stephanie is called on to find a waitress who has jumped bail after a car-theft charge. *Four to Score* includes some familiar characters as well as a supporting cast of eccentrics. *New York Times Book Review* contributor Stasio again praised Evanovich's work, calling this novel a "brashly funny adventure."

### High Five and Hot Six

*High Five*, the next volume in the series, became Evanovich's first hardcover best seller. Its plot involves a missing uncle, a stalker, some photos of body parts in garbage bags, and Stephanie's adventures—or misadventures—working odd jobs when her bounty-hunting business slows down. The novel "deftly combines eccentric, colorful characters, wacky humor, and nonstop . . . action," observed Wilda Williams in *Library Journal.* "The action never stops," noted a *Publishers Weekly* reviewer, who praised the book's "snappy" dialogue and sharply drawn characters.

No less popular was *Hot Six,* in which Stephanie agrees to help her mentor, Ranger, clear himself after being accused of killing Homer Ramos, a drug and gun dealer. Admiring the book as a "lunatic tapestry of nonstop action" and bizarre yet funny characters, a writer for *Publishers Weekly* commented that "Evanovich just keeps getting better."

### Seven Up and Hard Eight

In *Seven Up,* which *New York Times Book Review* contributor Stasio described as "pure, classic farce—Jersey girl style," Stephanie goes after Eddie DeChooch, an aging mobster who happens to be dating her grandmother. Though a reviewer for *Publishers Weekly* found this effort less successful than its predecessor, *Booklist* contributor GraceAnne A. DeCandido hailed it as both hilarious and sensitive to all of its characters, even the unattractive Eddie. "No character, no matter how broadly draw[n], stays a caricature for long," wrote DeCandido, who added that "it's difficult to read Evanovich in public places, so frequently do chuckles turn into belly laughs."

*Hard Eight* finds the wisecracking bounty hunter on the trail of Evelyn Soder and her young daughter, who have left behind an angry ex-husband and a child custody bond. Soon, however, the business gets personal for Stephanie as someone is trailing her as well. Her car is blown up and then a dead boy appears on her sofa. Morelli, the cop and Stephanie's occasional boyfriend, joins this investigation, which becomes far more than Stephanie envisioned.

### To the Nines

Evanovich's 2003 offering, *To the Nines,* finds Stephanie on the silly, sexy, and sometimes terrifying case of missing Indian contract worker, Samuel Singh. Her cousin and employer, Vinnie, has teamed her up with the always intriguing Ranger, who continues to provide romantic competition for Stephanie's temporary roommate, Joe Morelli. There

is a serial killer on the loose and Stephanie, the recipient of sinister floral deliveries, appears to be on his list. This least likely of bounty hunters finds herself in Las Vegas as the plot thickens around Evanovich's trademark host of lively characters. Her sidekicks, office manager Connie and ex-prostitute turned bounty hunter Lulu, provide entertainment to rival that of the Elvis and Tom Jones impersonators Stephanie inevitably encounters. The Plum family is reliably eccentric with appearances from Grandma Mazur and Stephanie's mom, who has reached her limit while housing Stephanie's pregnant, unwed sister, Valerie.

A *Publishers Weekly* contributor called *To the Nines* "nonstop, zany adventure." Although Marianne Fitzgerald in *Library Journal* maintained that the trip to Las Vegas is an unsatisfactory deviation from the usual New Jersey stomping grounds, she recommended this installment to those "clamoring for their Stephanie fix." A *Kirkus Reviews* contributor stated that "the plot is—as usual—a shambles" but went on to acknowledge that "the people and their dialogue are as sharp and funny as ever," which may have contributed to the book's nine-week stint as a best-selling hardcover.

### Ten Big Ones

In the tenth episode of the series, *Ten Big Ones,* Stephanie hunts down more elusive, idiosyncratic bail jumpers, including a woman who held up a Frito-Lay truck for corn chips, bringing a quick end to her "no-carb" diet, and a man arrested for urinating on his neighbor's rose bushes. Early in the novel, Stephanie finds herself in hot water when she witnesses a convenience store robbery and, because she can identify the culprits, becomes a target for a local street gang. She seeks cover at Ranger's apartment, intensifying the Morelli-Ranger romantic drama.

While *Entertainment Weekly* contributor Karen Karbo felt that the book "clearly suffers from book-a-year syndrome," a *Publishers Weekly* contributor related that "Evanovich is at her best in her tenth Stephanie Plum adventure," which, according to the reviewer, "reads like the screenplay for a 1930s screwball comedy: fast, funny, and furious." In a *People* review, contributor Samantha Miller expressed "one quibble" with the book: "*Ten Big Ones* wraps up so abruptly that readers might feel payoff-deprived." Overall, however, Miller praised Evanovich, commenting that the author's series "is as addictive as Fritos—and ten books in, not losing any of its salty crunch." *Booklist* contributor Stephanie Zvirin found that "the strain of keeping her formula fresh and funny shows." However, Zvirin also noted: "Fortunately, a dynamite finish—unexpected and very funny—saves the day." Even reviewers who were not impressed by the book's plot were often compelled to praise the author for her usual cast of amusing and eccentric characters.

### Eleven on Top

Next in the series is *Eleven on Top,* which finds Stephanie tiring of the rough treatment she receives from her criminal clients. In a bold career move, Stephanie leaves her cousin's bounty-hunting business and gets a job at a button factory, then a dry cleaning business. When neither enterprise works out, and after her car is blown to bits, Stephanie gets a job at a fast-food restaurant, which ends when the store is blown up as well. On top of the constant explosions around her, Stephanie keeps receiving creepy, threatening notes from a stalker, who is obviously keeping tabs on her whereabouts. When Stephanie's stalker runs over Joe with a car, Stephanie joins Lula, who has taken over her duties, in hunting criminals and trying to solve the mystery that has come too close to her personal life for comfort.

"Each Stephanie Plum book is better than the one before," wrote Harriet Klausner in a review of *Eleven on Top* on her *Harriet Klausner's Review Archive* Web site. "Janet Evanovich is a creative writer who brilliantly spins slapstick into life-threatening events," Klausner noted. While a *Publishers Weekly* contributor wrote that the lead character of the series "stumbles out of the gate due to some forced humor," the reviewer added that she "eventually hits her usually entertaining stride." Other reviewers found the book humorous from start to finish. DeCandido commented in *Booklist* that the eleventh book in the series is "brimming with lines that will have readers howling with laughter," adding that "it's wonderful to watch both a beloved character and a cherished author grow." In a review for the *ABC Wide Bay Qld* Web site, Sue Gammon expressed disappointment with the tenth book, commenting that *Ten Big Ones,* "while enjoyable, was also fairly predictable." After reading *Eleven on Top,* however, Gammon acknowledged that "Evanovich is back on top form with this light-hearted and funny episode in the perils of Plum."

### Twelve Sharp

In *Twelve Sharp,* "Evanovich uses all of her considerable arsenal" of plot and storytelling techniques to create a tale focused on Stephanie Plum's bounty hunting partner and sometime lover, Ranger Manoso, noted DeCandido in *Booklist.* Unable to make a romantic decision between the quietly powerful Ranger and police officer Joe Morelli, Stephanie is astonished when a woman who claims to be Ranger's wife suddenly storms into her life. The alleged Carmen Manoso warns Stephanie away from Ranger, but shortly afterward she is found shot to death in an SUV outside Plum's bond agency. Worse, reports are surfacing that Ranger has kidnapped his ten-year-old daughter, Julie, from the girl's mother and stepfather in Florida. Stephanie discovers that it is not Ranger who committed the act, but a deranged impersonator and identity thief intent on acquiring all aspects of Ranger's life, including Stephanie herself. Evanovich "finds exactly the tight tone of danger-laden farce for Stephanie's duel with the false Ranger," noted a *Kirkus Reviews* contributor. The author is "one of the very few writers whose skill can turn what should be serious moments into boisterously funny scenes. And her technique shines in *Twelve Sharp,*" commented Oline H. Cogdill in the *South Florida Sun-Sentinel.* "The boundaries of good taste are deliciously stretched; low-brow comedy becomes an art in Evanovich's hands," Cogdill remarked.

### Lean Mean Thirteen

The author furthers her "Stephanie Plum" series with *Lean Mean Thirteen.* Called "eminently satisfying" by *Booklist* contributor DeCandido, the novel features Stephanie, who, despite her better judgment, is doing a favor for her bounty hunter friend, Carlos Manoso, aka Ranger. Ranger wants Stephanie to meet with her ex-husband, Dickie Orr, so she can plant a listening device on the womanizing ex-lawyer. When Dickie goes missing, leaving behind only a smattering of blood at his brokerage firm offices, Stephanie is soon the number-one suspect, resulting in her setting out to learn whether Dickie is alive or dead. In addition, Stephanie has to deal with Joyce Barnhardt, the woman she caught Dickie having an affair with many years ago and the reason she divorced Dickie in the first place. Joyce also thinks Stephanie might have killed Dickie and begins to stalk her. Paul Katz, writing in *Entertainment Weekly,* noted that the author "boosts this . . . series with amusing side characters."

### Fearless Fourteen and Finger Lickin' Fifteen

In *Fearless Fourteen,* Stephanie is helping Morelli on the case of his own home burglaries. Morelli has been the victim of repeated break-ins, though this may be because Morelli's cousin Dom has buried the loot from a bank robbery there. While on the case, Stephanie and Ranger take a side job working security for Brenda, a singer who bears a striking resemblance to Dolly Parton.

"This Plum adventure won't disappoint those looking for the perfect summer beach read," commended a *Publishers Weekly* reviewer. DeCandido was also impressed, finding that "fans will be delighted." However, she remarked that those "who stumble into the series at this advanced point," may need to read the series from the beginning. On the *Blogcritics* Web site, Katie Trattner noted that the series has indeed changed over time, observing that "*Fearless Fourteen* is entertaining and fun, even if it is the same old thing dressed up in something new. The series isn't as serious as it used to be back in the days of *One for the Money* and *Two for the Dough;* it's lighter and funnier but this doesn't make it bad." *Finger Lickin' Fifteen,* the next installment in the series, was also praised by critics, with a Publishers Weekly reviewer finding that "Evanovich dishes up her usual mixture of shoot-'em-up action . . . and quirky characters."

### Sizzling Sixteen

Plum is back in action in the 2010 series installment, *Sizzling Sixteen,* and this time she has to come to the rescue of her cousin Vinnie, who has been kidnapped and is being held for a hefty ransom. Vinnie's gambling has gotten him into serious debt to the right kind of folks, and now Stephanie feels the tug of family duty to save the man, as he did he give her the first job tracking bail jumpers. So, with office manager Connie and buddy Lula in tow, the three women set off once again to save the day.

A *Publishers Weekly* reviewer was not enthused by this sixteenth in the series, calling it a "tepid Stephanie Plum adventure," and noting that the "larger story simply recycles elements from previous installments." DeCandido, reviewing the title in *Booklist,* had a much more favorable impression, calling it "funny, scary, silly, and sweet." A *Kirkus reviews* contributor felt that this novel is less about plot than humor and concluded: "Worth celebrating, not for the tangled story, but for gems like Lula's four ways of managing stress: 'There's drugs, there's alcohol, there's sex, and there's doughnuts.'"

### Visions of Sugar Plums and Plum Lovin'

Evanovich has also featured Stephanie in a separate series called the "Stephanie Plum Between the Numbers." Each novel takes place in a holiday setting. *Visions of Sugar Plums* occurs during the Christmas holidays and introduces the character of Diesel, who not only helps Stephanie track down a bail skipper but also might be an angel, as evidenced by some strange powers he seems to possess. Although helpful, it turns out that Diesel is really after someone else and is using Stephanie's case to pursue his own goals. "Throw in some elves, a mad hunt for a Christmas tree and a few fires and you have a Plum-crazy Christmas classic," wrote a *Publishers Weekly* contributor.

*Plum Lovin',* published in 2006, is a Valentine's Day tale featuring Stephanie and the return of Diesel, who is helping a matchmaker named Annie Hart hide out. However, Stephanie has been looking for Annie, as she is wanted on a charge of assault. DeCandido wrote in *Booklist* that the author "keeps the language light and sweet and the action nonstop."

### Plum Lucky and Plum Spooky

The 2008 novel *Plum Lucky* has a St. Patrick's Day theme and features a criminal who believes he is a leprechaun. A *Kirkus Reviews* contributor commented that "the frantic, anything-for-a-laugh jokes are brand new and nonstop." Populated with most of the characters from the detective novels, *Plum Lucky* finds everyone congregating in Atlantic City trying to save Grandma Mazur, who has been kidnapped by the mobster whom the supposed leprechaun double-crossed to get the loot. Also on hand is the enigmatic Diesel. DeCandido, writing in *Booklist,* called the novel "silly, hilarious, delightful." A *Publishers Weekly* contributor referred to it as "a delightful miniadventure sure to whet [readers'] appetites for the next full-length Plum escapade."

*Plum Spooky* finds Diesel reentering Stephanie's life. Explaining the plot in the *Tampa Tribune,* Mary Beth Thompson remarked that Diesel comes "back into Stephanie's complicated, barely-making-it-as-a-bounty-hunter life. Diesel is on the hunt for his bad cousin, Wulf, who is involved with the latest bail jumper Stephanie is trying to apprehend." This elusive culprit is Martin Munch, a man who looks like a twelve-year-old boy. Much of the search occurs in the isolated Pine Barrens in New Jersey. The eerie surroundings make "this is the perfect book to be read at Halloween, with some very strange goings on in the Pine Barrens," noted a *Reviewer's Bookwatch* contributor. DeCandido, again writing in *Booklist,* praised the book for its signature humor, stating that "the repartee sparkles and shimmies from razor wit to toilet humor (and back again)." A *Kirkus Reviews* writer, however, found that "this time even the humor, which depends on such staples as pet monkeys and fart jokes, is a mite synthetic as well." Nevertheless, the writer still felt that "this weirdly plotted adventure [is] very funny."

### Wicked Appetite

Diesel takes center stage in Wicked Appetite, the first in a Evanovich's "Unmentionable" series. Stephanie Plum does not make an appearance in this series; instead, the series is narrated by a new character altogether, Elizabeth "Lizzy" Tucker, a baker who lives in Salem, Massachusetts. She, like Diesel, is an Unmentionable, someone with supernatural powers. All the books in the series will deal with the Seven Deadly Sins; Wicked Appetite focuses on gluttony. Other characters from the Stephanie Plum books, including Wulf and Carl the Monkey, also make appearances. In the series opener, Diesel is trying to stop the devilish Wulf from getting his hands on the Stones of SALIGIA, which have somehow found their way to Massachusetts. Each of the seven stones represents one of the Seven Deadly Sins, and whoever owns them has incredible powers in his or her hands. In order to keep the stones from coming into Wulf's possession, Diesel must convince Lizzy that she is the only person in the world who can stop this from happening.

A Kirkus Reviews contributor offered a mixed assessment of Wicked Appetite, writing: "Instead of the slapdash mysteries Stephanie solves, there's a frantic pursuit of the paranormal. Fans attracted by the comic-book plotting and pacing will doubtless re-enlist for the pursuit of the other six Stones." Higher praise came from Booklist reviewer DeCandido, who felt that "classic Evanovich tropes . . . are in evidence" in this new series for fans "to revel in." Similarly, Library Journal contributor Stacey Hayman found this the first in an "entertaining new paranormal series." Hayman further remarked: "It's hard to find a reliably humorous author, but Evanovich always delivers."

### Metro Girl and Motor Mouth

With Metro Girl, Evanovich steps away from the "Stephanie Plum" series to concentrate on a new series hero, Alexandra "Barney" Barnaby. The first novel tells of Alexandra's search for her missing brother, who has run afoul of an exiled Cuban warlord.

In the second book in the series, Motor Mouth, Alexandra, an engineer and racing enthusiast, works as a spotter for NASCAR driver Sam Hooker, helping him to avoid trouble on the track during races. She and Sam are also estranged lovers, whose relationship suffered a rift when he was caught in a one-night stand with a sales clerk. Alexandra retains her professionalism and continues to work as Sam's spotter, but otherwise she has little contact with him. When Sam loses a close race, Alexandra believes that the opposing team cheated, and the search begins for an electronic device that gives the other side an illegal upper hand. The stakes get even higher when a murder is discovered and the villains take an interest in stopping Alexandra and Sam from ferreting out their secret. Evanovich plumbs NASCAR trivia and lore to fill in the background of a story based firmly in the big-money, high-RPM world of professional racing. The protagonists "find themselves in one outrageously hilarious situation after another," commented De-Candido in another Booklist review, noting that Evanovich "appears to have another winner on her hands."

### Troublemaker

Evanovich, collaborating with her daughter, Alex Evanovich, and illustrator Joelle Jones, takes the books featuring Alexandra Barnaby in a new direction with the third series installment, a graphic novel, Troublemaker. "I have always loved comics," Evanovich noted in an interview with Publishers Weekly contributor Sasha Watson. "We always thought the Barnaby series would make a great graphic novel. . . . It's got Miami, flashy cars, and a Saint Bernard—what more could you want?" In this series addition Barney's friend Rosa is kidnapped, and her disappearance is linked to a dangerous voodoo priest. Barney and Hooker's subsequent attempts to rescue her involved the pair in a chase in the swamps, breaking and entering, and a quarrelsome cougar, among other adventures.

Reviewing the graphic novel in Library Journal, Martha Cornog felt that "comics aficionados may be entertained, but prose-inclined fans won't get much of a fix." A Publishers Weekly reviewer had a somewhat higher assessment of this graphic novel, noting: "For those not already Evanovich fans, it's rather like a grown-up Scooby Doo." Voice of Youth Advocates contributor Jennifer Rummel had higher praise for this work, writing: "As with Evanovich's novels, action and danger fuel the story, with humor and a touch of romance thrown in for good measure."

### How I Write

After a solid and successful career as a novelist, Evanovich has acquired considerable insight on the process of writing and publishing. She shares this information in *How I Write: Secrets of a Bestselling Author,* written with Ina Yaloff and daughter Alex Evanovich. While coauthor Yaloff covers some of the nuts-and-bolts basics of writing, Evanovich offers expert commentary and answers to questions readers and hopeful writers have posed to her on her Web site. She explains in detail her techniques for writing dialogue, accurate crime scenes, story lines, and plots. Her real-world examples also amount to a great deal of background and inside information on the creation and writing of the "Stephanie Plum" novels.

Reviewer Ilene Cooper, writing in *Booklist,* commented that although much of Evanovich's advice can be found in other forms in other resources, "what you can't find in most writers' guides is her inimitable voice and a wealth of examples" drawn from her own successful novels. "Learning how best-selling author Janet Evanovich writes might not guarantee success to all those aspiring writers out there, but she does offer much constructive advice beyond the usual 'show, don't tell' offerings in the plethora of how-to-write books on the market," noted *Bookreporter.com* contributor Roz Shea.

## ■ Biographical And Critical Sources

*PERIODICALS*

*America's Intelligence Wire,* June 21, 2011, Mary Ann Grossmann, "Author Janet Evanovich Meant to Work on Another Series, but Had to Keep Going with Adventures of Bounty Hunter Stephanie Plum."

*Armchair Detective,* summer, 1995, Marvin Lachman, review of *One for the Money,* p. 287.

*Belles Lettres,* January, 1996, review of *Two for the Dough,* p. 15.

*Booklist,* May 1, 2000, GraceAnne A. DeCandido, review of *Hot Six,* p. 1622; May 1, 2001, Bill Ott, review of *Hot Six,* p. 1598, GraceAnne A. DeCandido, review of *Seven Up,* p. 1628, and "Story behind the Story: Stephanie Plum as Indiana Jones," p. 1629; May 1, 2004, Stephanie Zvirin, review of *Ten Big Ones,* p. 1506; March 15, 2005, Shelley Mosley, review of *Full Bloom,* p. 1272; May 15, 2005, GraceAnne A. DeCandido, review of *Eleven on Top,* p. 1612; July 1, 2006, GraceAnne A. DeCandido, review of *Twelve Sharp,* p. 7; September 1, 2006, Ilene Cooper, review of *How I Write: Secrets of a Bestselling Author,* p. 36; September 15, 2006, GraceAnne A. DeCandido, review of *Motor Mouth,* p. 5; December 15, 2006, GraceAnne A. DeCandido, review of *Plum Lovin',* p. 5; June 1,
2007, GraceAnne A. DeCandido, review of *Lean Mean Thirteen,* p. 5; January 1, 2008, GraceAnne A. DeCandido, review of *Plum Lucky,* p. 22; May 15, 2008, GraceAnne A. DeCandido, review of *Fearless Fourteen,* p. 4; December 15, 2008, GraceAnne A. DeCandido, review of *Plum Spooky,* p. 4; June 1, 2010, GraceAnne A. DeCandido, review of *Sizzling Sixteen,* p. 5; August 1, 2010, GraceAnne A. DeCandido, review of *Wicked Appetite,* p. 8.

*Christian Science Monitor,* July 25, 1996, Michelle Ross, review of *Two for the Dough,* p. 21.

*Detroit Free Press,* June 21, 2006, Marta Salij, "Evanovich Is as Sharp as Ever in Latest Plum Adventure," review of *Twelve Sharp.*

*Entertainment Weekly,* November 11, 1994, Kate Wilson, review of *One for the Money,* p. 68; February 23, 1996, review of *Two for the Dough,* p. 119; June 15, 2004, Karen Karbo, review of *Ten Big Ones,* p. 172; June 23, 2006, J.P. Mangalindan, review of *Twelve Sharp,* p. 73; June 22, 2007, Paul Katz, review of *Lean Mean Thirteen,* p. 73; June 20, 2008, Mandi Bierly, review of *Fearless Fourteen,* p. 71.

*Kirkus Reviews,* June 1, 2003, review of *To the Nines,* p. 781; May 15, 2005, review of *Eleven on Top,* p. 565; June 1, 2006, review of *Twelve Sharp,* p. 548; September 15, 2006, review of *Motor Mouth,* p. 922; June 15, 2007, review of *Lean Mean Thirteen;* January 1, 2008, review of *Plum Lucky;* June 15, 2010, review of *Sizzling Sixteen;* August 1, 2010, review of *Wicked Appetite.*

*Kliatt,* July, 2005, Mary Purucker, review of *Full Bloom,* p. 53; January 1, 2009, review of *Plum Spooky;* June 15, 2009, review of *Finger Lickin' Fifteen.*

*Library Journal,* December, 1996, review of *Three to Get Deadly,* p. 151; June 1, 1999, Wilda Williams, review of *High Five,* p. 186; May 1, 2000, Wilda Williams, review of *Hot Six,* p. 158; June 1, 2001, Wilda Williams, review of *Seven Up,* p. 224; July, 2003, Marianne Fitzgerald, review of *To the Nines,* p. 130; June 1, 2004, Rex E. Klett, review of *Ten Big Ones,* p. 107; August 13, 2010, Stacey Hayman, review of *Wicked Appetite;* September 15, 2010, Martha Cornog, review of *Troublemaker,* p. 50.

*Los Angeles Times Book Review,* November 20, 1994, Charles Champlin, review of *One for the Money,* p. 8.

*New York Times,* June 24, 2011, Julie Bosman, "Sales Are Smokin' for Evanovich Book," p. 3.

*New York Times Book Review,* September 4, 1994, Marilyn Stasio, review of *One for the Money,* p. 17; January 21, 1996, Marilyn Stasio, review of *Two for the Dough,* p. 31; February 16, 1997, Marilyn Stasio, review of *Three to Get Deadly,* p. 28; July 19, 1998, Marilyn Stasio, review of *Four to Score,*

p. 20; June 27, 1999, Marilyn Stasio, review of *High Five*, p. 26; July 22, 2001, Marilyn Stasio, review of *Seven Up*, p. 22; June 22, 2005, Edward Wyatt, "For This Author, Writing Is Only the Beginning," profile of Janet Evanovich, p. E1.

*People*, June 21, 2004, Samantha Miller, review of *Ten Big Ones*, p. 49.

*Publishers Weekly*, November 25, 1996, review of *Three to Get Deadly*, p. 59; June 21, 1999, review of *High Five*, p. 60; July 5, 1999, "A High Five Family," p. 23; November 8, 1999, "Good Seven for *High Five*," p. 14; May 1, 2000, review of *Hot Six*, p. 52; May 7, 2001, review of *Seven Up*, p. 227; October 21, 2002, review of *Visions of Sugar Plums*, p. 58; June 23, 2003, review of *To the Nines*, p. 50; June 7, 2004, review of *Ten Big Ones*, pp. 35-36; July 5, 2004, Daisy Maryles, "It's 10 for the Money," review of *Ten Big Ones*, p. 13; March 14, 2005, review of *Full Bloom*, p. 51; May 30, 2005, review of *Eleven on Top*, p. 43; May 22, 2006, review of *Twelve Sharp*, p. 33; December 18, 2006, review of *Plum Lovin'*, p. 43; December 24, 2007, review of *Plum Lucky*, p. 31; May 19, 2008, review of *Fearless Fourteen*, p. 35; May 25, 2009, review of *Finger Lickin' Fifteen*, p. 39.

*Reviewer's Bookwatch*, November 1, 2009, Christy Tillery French, review of *Plum Spooky*; May 17, 2010, Sasha Watson, "Janet Evanovich Mixes It Up," p. 25; May 31, 2010, review of *Sizzling Sixteen*, p. 29; August 16, 2010, review of *Troublemaker, Book One*, p. 41.

*South Florida Sun-Sentinel*, June 21, 2006, Oline H. Cogdill, "*Twelve Sharp*: Plum Tale Darker, but Still Juicy," review of *Twelve Sharp*.

*Swiss News*, September, 2007, review of *Lean Mean Thirteen*, p. 52.

*Tampa Tribune*, January 4, 2009, Mary Beth Thompson, review of *Plum Spooky*, p. 8.

*Times Literary Supplement*, March 15, 1996, Natasha Cooper, review of *Two for the Dough*, p. 24.

*Voice of Youth Advocates*, February 1, 2011, Jennifer Rummel, review of *Troublemaker, Book One*, p. 552.

*Washington Post Book World*, August 28, 1994, Dwight Garner, review of *One for the Money*, p. 6.

ONLINE

*A&C Book Junkies*, http://acbookjunkies.blogspot.com/ (January 30, 2011), review of *Wicked Appetite*.

*ABC Wide Bay Qld Web site*, http://www.abc.net.au/ (February 6, 2007), Sue Gammon, review of *Eleven on Top*.

*All about Romance*, http://www.likesbooks.com/ (September 18, 1998), Lorna Jean, "Quickie with Janet Evanovich on Her Stephanie Plum Series," interview with Janet Evanovich.

*Blogcritics*, http://blogcritics.org (February 11, 2010), Katie Trattner, review of *Fearless Fourteen*.

*BookPage.com*, http://www.bookpage.com/ (February 6, 2007), Bruce Tierney, "Janet Evanovich: Mystery Maven Keeps Readers Coming Back for More," interview with Janet Evanovich; "Meet the Author: Janet Evanovich," biography of Janet Evanovich.

*Bookreporter.com*, http://www.bookreporter.com/ (February 6, 2007), Roz Shea, reviews of *Two for the Dough*, *Three to Get Deadly*, *Four to Score*, *High Five*, *Hot Six*, *Seven Up*, *Hard Eight*, *Visions of Sugar Plums*, *Ten Big Ones*, *Metro Girl*, *Eleven on Top*, *Twelve Sharp*, *How I Write*, *Motor Mouth*, and *Plum Lovin'*; Maggie Harding, review of *To the Nines*.

*Brazen Bookworm*, http://www.brazenbookworm.com/ (June 24, 2011), review of *Smokin' Seventeen*.

*Fantastic Fiction*, http://www.fantasticfiction.co.uk/ (February 6, 2007), bibliography of Janet Evanovich.

*Harriet Klausner's Review Archive*, http://harrietklausner.wwwi.com/ (February 6, 2007), Harriet Klausner, review of *Eleven on Top*.

*Janet Evanovich Home Page*, http://www.evanovich.com (July 4, 2011).

*Look at OKC*, http://newsok.com/ (September 12, 2010), Betty Lytle, review of *Wicked Appetite*.

*Writers Write*, http://www.writerswrite.com/ (February 6, 2007), Claire E. White, "A Conversation with Janet Evanovich."

# Scott Eyman

## 1951-

■ **Personal**

Born March 2, 1951, in Cleveland, OH; married.

■ **Addresses**

*Office*—Palm Beach Post, P.O. Box 24700, West Palm Beach, FL 33405. *Agent*—Fran Collin, Don Congdon Associates, Inc., 156 5th Ave., Ste. 625, New York, NY 10010. *E-mail*—scott_eyman@pbpost.com.

■ **Career**

Journalist and writer. *Fort Lauderdale Sun-Sentinel*, Fort Lauderdale, FL, journalist and critic; *Miami News*, Miami, FL, journalist and entertainment editor; *Palm Beach Post*, West Palm Beach, FL, affiliate, beginning 1989, books editor, beginning 1991.

■ **Writings**

(With Louis D. Giannetti) *Flashback: A Brief History of Film*, Prentice Hall (Englewood Cliffs, NJ), 1986, 6th edition, Pearson Education (Boston, MA), 2009.

*Five American Cinematographers: Interviews with Karl Struss, Joseph Ruttenberg, James Wong Howe, Linwood Dunn, and William H. Clothier*, Scarecrow Press (Metuchen, NJ), 1987.

*Mary Pickford, America's Sweetheart*, Donald I. Fine (New York, NY), 1990.

*Ernst Lubitsch: Laughter in Paradise*, Simon & Schuster (New York, NY), 1993.

*The Speed of Sound: Hollywood and the Talkie Revolution, 1926-1930*, Simon & Schuster (New York, NY), 1997.

*Print the Legend: The Life and Times of John Ford*, Simon & Schuster (New York, NY), 1999.

*Lion of Hollywood: The Life and Legend of Louis B. Mayer*, Simon & Schuster (New York, NY), 2005.

(With Robert Wagner) *Pieces of My Heart: A Life*, HarperEntertainment (New York, NY), 2008.

*Empire of Dreams: The Epic Life of Cecil B. DeMille*, Simon & Schuster (New York, NY), 2010.

Contributor to newspapers and periodicals, including *New York Observer, New York Times, Washington Post*, and *Chicago Tribune*.

■ **Sidelights**

Journalist and film critic Scott Eyman has written biographies of the actress Mary Pickford and the directors Ernst Lubitsch and John Ford, in addition to books about the history of cinema.

### *Five American Cinematographers* and *Mary Pickford, America's Sweetheart*

*Five American Cinematographers: Interviews with Karl Struss, Joseph Ruttenberg, James Wong Howe, Linwood Dunn, and William H. Clothier* provides an honest look into the film industry over the twentieth century and is enriched by anecdotes about famous directors and the actors with whom they worked. John Nangle, in *Films in Review*, said about the five: "Their styles may have had nothing in common, but the vigor of their work is apparent on each page."

Genevieve Stuttaford in *Publishers Weekly* called Eyman's biography of the silent film star Mary Pickford "far superior to many movie star biographies." Pickford, born Gladys Smith in Toronto, Canada, in 1892, became the family breadwinner at age six, when she first performed on stage. New York movie producer David Belasco gave her the name Mary Pickford, and she began her career as the sweet, curly-haired star of such silent films as *Poor Little Rich Girl, Little Annie Rooney*, and *My Best Girl.* Behind her wholesome demeanor was the mind of a shrewd businesswoman, and she soon became the most famous, and most highly paid, woman in film. Her second husband was the screen idol Douglas Fairbanks, with whom Pickford, Charlie Chaplin, and D.W. Griffiths founded United Artists. By age forty Pickford had left the movies, as they turned from silent to talking pictures. Although she remained wealthy, she turned to alcohol abuse and lived her last years as a recluse. In her mid-eighties she was awarded an honorary Oscar.

Leah Rozen, in a review of *Mary Pickford, America's Sweetheart* for *People,* wrote that Eyman presented Pickford's story "with detail, perspective and a measured affection." *Saturday Night* reviewer George Galt found the book "prodigious in its research" but containing "flat-footed and disjointed prose," while *Spectator* reviewer Lindsay Anderson called it "authoritative as well as gripping" and a "remarkable" and "valuable" book.

### *Ernst Lubitsch* and *The Speed of Sound*

Eyman's fourth book, *Ernst Lubitsch: Laughter in Paradise,* is a biography of the German-born Jewish film director, who came to the United States in 1922 and spent a decade at Paramount, where he was made head of production in the 1930s. Lubitsch made a smooth transition to sound pictures from silent movies. He directed such actors as Jeanette McDonald, Jack Benny, Greta Garbo, and Miriam Hopkins in some of their finest performances. His movies included *Trouble in Paradise, Heaven Can Wait,* and *To Be or Not to Be.* The director was known for his intriguing sets and his sexual innuendos in a time when the content of adult comedies was far more restricted than it is today. His was the "Lubitsch touch," which became known to moviemakers and moviegoers alike.

Critics offered praise for Eyman's research and writing, although several expressed disappointment with the manner in which Eyman integrates the

discussion of Lubitsch's personal life and his career. Dave Kehr, writing in the *Los Angeles Times Book Review,* thought that Eyman did "a superlative job of arranging the facts . . . though he misses the connection between the life and the work." *Washington Post Book World* reviewer Joel E. Siegel found the book well researched but noted the author's "inability to interpret and articulate the fruits of his scholarship." *Atlantic Monthly* reviewer Dennis Drabelle called it "solid but awkwardly written." Henry Zorich, writing in *Rapport,* stated that Eyman "devotes a great deal to allow us to know the man himself, and based on what we learn, that wasn't an easy feat."

Eyman's book *The Speed of Sound: Hollywood and the Talkie Revolution, 1926-1930* covers the transition, in the late 1920s, from silent pictures to sound film and the impact of this transition on actors, directors, producers, and the public. Mick LaSalle, in a review for the *San Francisco Chronicle,* pointed out that Eyman's book is "the first to deal extensively with all three aspects of the transition—business, art and technology." *Cineaste* reviewer Thomas Doherty concluded that the book "appreciates both the glory of the silent cinema working at the peak of its powers . . . and the excitement of a new technology being born and obliterating the old art, with no regrets." *New York Times Book Review* contributor Richard Barrios questioned Eyman's "relentless procession of vignettes" and said the book "does not really convey" the breadth of "grandeur and greed and folly" of the age, but Gavin Lambert, writing in the *Los Angeles Times Book Review,* described the book as a "colorful and richly researched history."

### *Print the Legend*

*Print the Legend: The Life and Times of John Ford* is a biography of the Hollywood director, whose career spanned the first half of the twentieth century, from 1914 to 1962. Ford made movies that fed his perception of the American dream, about the valor of the West, World War II, and the working man. His films included *The Iron Horse, Stagecoach, Drums along the Mohawk, The Grapes of Wrath, Fort Apache,* and *The Man Who Shot Liberty Valance.* Ford worked with such stars as Harry Carey, Will Rogers, Shirley Temple, John Wayne, John Carradine, and Henry Fonda. One of the industry's most successful directors and a multiple Academy Award winner, Ford was an elusive man who cared more about his art than his family and his health, as evidenced by his alcoholism.

Tom Huntington, reviewing the book in *American History,* commented that Eyman "manages to portray Ford's monstrous side without alienating the reader, and he also finds evidence of the man's better nature." Similarly, *National Review* contributor Randy Roberts called Eyman's detailing of Ford's professional life "brilliantly successful." *New Republic* reviewer David Thomson noted that "Eyman sometimes seems more fixed on the riddle of Ford's psyche than on the depth of his movies." But Malcolm Jones, writing in *Newsweek,* concluded that "everything about this model biography is a pleasure." And *St. Louis Post-Dispatch* contributor Allen Barra dubbed *Print the Legend* "one of the most important books ever written on the subject of movies." Actor-director-writer Peter Bogdanovich, in a review for the *Wall Street Journal,* commented: "The book captures extremely well the twofold emotions of worship and terror that Ford generally provoked," and he called Eyman's biography "the best . . . yet published about the creator of work that constitutes America's single most representative and complicated national cinematic treasure."

### Lion of Hollywood

Louis B. Mayer was another filmmaker whose dynamism evoked both respect and criticism. In *Lion of Hollywood: The Life and Legend of Louis B. Mayer* Eyman portrays a tyrant and genius, according to reviewers. He credits Mayer's formative years as an immigrant scrap machinery dealer in Canada for the determination and ruthlessness that enabled him to propel Metro-Goldwyn-Mayer to the very apex of the Hollywood studio system. But he also suggests that Mayer's humble origins may have been responsible for the confrontational attitude that repelled many of his colleagues and actors. Eyman describes Mayer's dedication to high-quality films and old-fashioned American values without whitewashing the filmmaker's propensity for philandering or his talent for manipulating others into obeying his will. *Lion of Hollywood* is based on more than one hundred interviews and access to documents that had been unavailable until recent years.

Stephen Rees described *Lion of Hollywood* in his *Library Journal* review as "more factual and less sensational than competing titles." A *Publishers Weekly* reviewer commented that Eyman's "scrupulous research . . . make this biography an often revelatory delight."

### Pieces of My Heart

Eyman collaborated with Robert Wagner to write *Pieces of My Heart: A Life* in 2008. The book tells Wagner's life story from the day as a child when he saw four movie stars playing golf to his own rise to stardom. He also talks about the loves of his life, including the tragic drowning death of Natalie Wood in 1981. Full of stories, gossip, analysis, and photographs, it reveals the personality of fifty years in the life of a true Hollywood legend.

Christopher Hart noted in the London *Sunday Times:* "He's also a tremendous gossip, a perceptive analyst of other people, and quite a ladies' man. His memoirs cannot help but be entertaining." In *Hollywood Reporter,* Robert Osborne commented that *Pieces of My Heart* is "a terrific read: classy like Wagner and full of interesting showbiz stories and insights."

### Empire of Dreams

Eyman's other 2008 publication was *Empire of Dreams: The Epic Life of Cecil B. DeMille.* The pioneering Hollywood director Cecil B. DeMille (1881-1959) got his start in 1913. He became the driving force for Paramount Pictures and is best known for his epic biblical films, including *The Ten Commandments* and *King of Kings.* Eyman was provided first-time access to the DeMille family papers to put together a biography that examines DeMille's career, personal life, and friendships. "Eyman reminds us in this beautifully written, deeply researched and appropriately 'epic' biography how DeMille's rise in early Hollywood not only paralleled the industry's ascent to global prominence, but was inextricably intertwined with it," concluded John Patterson on the Directors Guild of American Web site.

In the *Washington Post,* Adam Bernstein suggested that in *Empire of Dreams,* Eyman succeeds in honoring DeMille, and stated that "even if his films kept a devoted audience, after his death DeMille's reputation fell precipitously among film critics and scholars, who considered his rousing adventures and Bible-based epics anachronistic. Readers are left with Eyman's helpful insights into the films themselves. Not only does he believe they hold up and are worthy of reevaluation, but he also emphasizes the exceptional skill it takes to finance and produce an epic." In *Booklist,* Mike Tribby thought that "Eyman's sprawling biography fully gives the master his due." A *Kirkus Reviews* contributor felt that not only is the book a biography presenting DeMille "in grand style, befitting the great man," but it is also "engrossing and comprehensive—an essential text for readers interested in the history of movies."

## ■ Biographical And Critical Sources

*PERIODICALS*

*American Enterprise,* April-May, 2000, Brock Yates, "Model 'A' Ford," p. 58.

*American History,* June, 2000, Tom Huntington, review of *Print the Legend: The Life and Times of John Ford,* pp. 66-67, and "Talking with Scott Eyman," p. 66.

*Atlantic Monthly,* March, 1994, Dennis Drabelle, "A Touch of Sophistication," p. 124.

*AudioFile,* February 1, 2009, S.J. Henschel, review of *Pieces of My Heart: A Life.*

*Booklist,* October 15, 1993, Gordon Flagg, review of *Ernst Lubitsch: Laughter in Paradise,* p. 406; February 15, 1997, Gordon Flagg, review of *The Speed of Sound: Hollywood and the Talkie Revolution, 1926-1930,* p. 991; October 1, 1999, Gordon Flagg, review of *Print the Legend,* p. 333; September 15, 2010, Mike Tribby, review of *Empire of Dreams: The Epic Life of Cecil B. DeMille,* p. 14.

*Book World,* October 5, 2008, "Star Light, Star Bright," p. 9.

*Chicago Sun-Times,* December 29, 1999, Robert Sklar, review of *Print the Legend,* p. 44.

*Choice,* November, 2005, C. McCutcheon, review of *Lion of Hollywood: The Life and Legend of Louis B. Mayer,* p. 492.

*Cineaste,* summer, 1998, Thomas Doherty, review of *The Speed of Sound,* pp. 51-52; March 22, 2011, Patrick McGilligan, review of *Empire of Dreams,* p. 69.

*Entertainment Weekly,* April 22, 2005, Gregory Kirschling, review of *Lion of Hollywood,* p. 68.

*Film Comment,* September 1, 2010, "The Blockbuster Godfather DeMille Gets His Close-up."

*Film Quarterly,* winter, 1998, Matt Severson, review of *The Speed of Sound,* p. 61; spring, 2007, Bernard F. Dick, review of *Lion of Hollywood,* p. 96.

*Films in Review,* May, 1988, John Nangle, review of *Five American Cinematographers: Interviews with Karl Struss, Joseph Ruttenberg, James Wong Howe, Linwood Dunn, and William H. Clothier,* p. 311.

*Hollywood Reporter,* September 22, 2008, "These True Hollywood Stories Prove It: The Movies Can Make a Great Book," p. 22.

*Investor's Business Daily,* December 2, 2010, "Cecil B. DeMille's Epic Vision Go Big: The Iconic Director Gave Film Fans More, and More, of What They Wanted," p. 3.

*Kirkus Reviews,* August 1, 2010, review of *Empire of Dreams.*

*Library Journal,* February 15, 1997, Thomas Wiener, review of *The Speed of Sound,* p. 137; February 1, 1998, Barbara Mann, review of *The Speed of Sound,* pp. 130-131; October 1, 1999, Stephen Rees, review of *Print the Legend,* p. 96; March 15, 2005, Stephen Rees, review of *Lion of Hollywood,* p. 87.

*Los Angeles Times Book Review,* November 28, 1993, Dave Kehr, "When a Gesture Told All," pp. 2, 11; March 30, 1997, Gavin Lambert, review of *The Speed of Sound,* p. 9.

*National Review,* December 31, 1999, Randy Roberts, "The Mythmaker," p. 46.

*New Republic,* January 31, 2000, David Thomson, "How False Was My Valley," pp. 40-45.

*Newsweek,* November 15, 1999, Malcolm Jones, "Cut! And That's a Wrap!," p. 90; September 20, 2010, "Run of DeMille," p. 66.

*New York Review of Books,* September 30, 2010, "The Greatest Show in Town," p. 61.

*New York Times Book Review,* March 9, 1997, Richard Barrios, "All Talking!," p. 20; January 9, 2000, Richard Schickel, "The Man Who Shot the West," p. 9.

*People,* May 21, 1990, review of *Mary Pickford, America's Sweetheart,* p. 40.

*Publishers Weekly,* February 2, 1990, Genevieve Stuttaford, review of *Mary Pickford, America's Sweetheart,* p. 70; October 11, 1993, review of *Ernst Lubitsch,* p. 74; January 20, 1997, review of *The Speed of Sound,* p. 385; October 11, 1999, review of *Print the Legend,* p. 66; March 21, 2005, review of *Lion of Hollywood,* p. 45; August 11, 2008, review of *Pieces of My Heart,* p. 35; August 11, 2008, review of *Pieces of My Heart,* p. 35; July 19, 2010, review of *Empire of Dreams,* p. 124.

*Rapport,* June-July, 1994, Henry Zorich, "The 1994 Movie Book Roundup," pp. 14-17.

*St. Louis Post-Dispatch,* January 2, 2000, Allen Barra, "Contradictory John Ford Is the Stuff of Legend," p. F10.

*San Francisco Chronicle,* March 11, 1997, Mick LaSalle, "The Film Innovation Everybody Was Talking About," p. E5.

*Saturday Night,* March, 1990, George Galt, review of *Mary Pickford, America's Sweetheart,* p. 56.

*Spectator* (London, England), April 25, 1992, Lindsay Anderson, "The Guiding Star of a Whole Brave Nation," p. 32.

*Tribune Books* (Chicago, IL), January 2, 1994, Bruce Cook, "The Lubitsch Touch," p. 7.

*Vanity Fair,* September 1, 2010, "In Short, but All Fondness," p. 184.

*Wall Street Journal,* November 26, 1999, Peter Bogdanovich, "The Man Who Shot the Movies," p. W81.

*Washington Post,* October 22, 2010, Adam Bernstein, review of *Empire of Dreams.*

*Washington Post Book World,* May 13, 1990, Dennis Drabelle, review of *Mary Pickford, America's Sweetheart,* p. 10; January 2, 1994, Joel E. Siegel, "Importance of Being Ernst," p. 3; October 5, 2008, John DiLeo, review of *Pieces of My Heart,* p. 9.

*Xpress Reviews,* August 20, 2010, Teri Shiel, review of *Empire of Dreams.*

ONLINE

*American Association of Sunday and Feature Editors,* http://www.aasfe.org/ (November 5, 2003), "AASFE's 2002 Writing Competition Winners."

*Cleveland.com,* http://www.cleveland.com/ (September 1, 2010), David Walton, "Scott Eyman's Biography Gives Us Cecil B. DeMille, Forming Hollywood in His Own Image."

*Directors Guild of America,* http://www.dga.org/ (September 1, 2010), John Patterson, review of *Empire of Dreams.*

*Palm Beach Post Online,* http://www.palmbeachpost.com/ (November 5, 2003), author profile.

*Scott Eyman Home Page,* http://www.scotteyman.com (August 2, 2011).

*Sunday Times* (London, England), http://entertainment.timesonline.co.uk/ (March 8, 2009), Christopher Hart, review of *Pieces of My Heart.**

# Noah Feldman

## 1970-

---

## ■ Also Known As

Noah R. Feldman

## ■ Personal

Born May 22, 1970, in Boston, MA; married Jeannie Suk (an author). *Education:* Harvard University, A.B., 1992; Oxford University, D.Phil., 1994; Yale Law School, J.D., 1997.

## ■ Addresses

*Office*—Harvard Law School, Hauser 210, Cambridge, MA 02138. *E-mail*—nfeldman@law.harvard. edu.

## ■ Career

Legal scholar and author. Yale University, New Haven, CT, visiting lecturer, 1996; New York University School of Law, assistant professor, 2001-04, associate professor of law, 2004-06, Cecelia Goetz Professor of Law, 2006-07; Harvard Law School, Cambridge, MA, Bemis Professor of law, 2007—. Visiting associate professor of law at Yale Law School, 2004, and Harvard Law School, 2005. Has also served as a law clerk to Chief Judge Harry T. Edwards, U.S. Court of Appeals for the DC Circuit, 1997-98, and to Associate Justice David H. Souter, U.S. Supreme Court, 1998-99; New America Foundation, Washington, DC, former adjunct fellow; Council on Foreign Relations, former adjunct senior fellow; chief U.S advisor for the writing of Iraq's new constitution, 2003.

## ■ Awards, Honors

Rhodes Scholar, Oxford University; Junior Fellow, Harvard University Society of Fellows, 1999-2001; Carnegie Scholar, 2005; named "Most Beautiful Brainiac," *New York Magazine;* among listees of "most influential people of the 21st century," *Esquire,* 2008.

## ■ Writings

*After Jihad: America and the Struggle for Islamic Democracy,* Farrar, Straus & Giroux (New York, NY), 2003.

*What We Owe Iraq: War and the Ethics of Nation Building,* Princeton University Press (Princeton, NJ), 2004.

*Divided by God: America's Church-State Problem and What We Should Do about It,* Farrar, Straus & Giroux (New York, NY), 2005.

*The Fall and Rise of the Islamic State,* Princeton University Press (Princeton, NJ), 2008.

*Scorpions: The Battles and Triumphs of FDR's Great Supreme Court Justices,* Twelve (New York, NY), 2010.

Also author of scholarly articles on topics such as constitutional law, law and religion, and legal theory.

## ■ Adaptations

*Scorpions* was adapted for audiobook, Hachette Audio, 2011, read by Feldman.

## ■ Sidelights

At the age of only thirty-two, Noah Feldman, a New York University School of Law professor, was tapped by the Bush administration to head its attempt to bring constitutional government to Iraq. Feldman's book, *After Jihad: America and the Struggle for Islamic Democracy,* argues that Iraq and other Middle Eastern nations are capable of forming their own versions of democratic government compatible with Islamic teachings. Feldman has written further about Iraq and the Islamic world in *What We Owe*

Iraq: War and the Ethics of Nation Building and The Fall and Rise of the Islamic State, and he has addressed domestic issues in Divided by God: America's Church-State Problem and What We Should Do about It and Scorpions: The Battles and Triumphs of FDR's Great Supreme Court Justices.

Feldman completed his undergraduate work at Harvard in Near Eastern languages and civilizations and, as a Rhodes scholar, earned a doctorate from Oxford University in Islamic thought. Feldman also received a law degree from Yale University Law School and served as law clerk to Supreme Court Justice David H. Souter. In an interview with the Journal News, Feldman stated that the aftermath of the regime change in Iraq would test the mettle of the United States and its allies: "We're on the verge of one of the most important processes of our political history of the last twenty-five years."

### After Jihad

In After Jihad, Feldman suggests that the world needs to prepare for life after a period of Islamist extremism, and that the world can be fairly optimistic about that prospect. Feldman argues that both Islam and democracy are "mobile" ideas that can be defined in both a "modern" and an Islamic way. After Jihad examines the compatibility of Islam and democracy, discusses the problems and prospects of democratization, and tries to influence the policy debate on the Middle East in the United States.

Some reviewers of the book did not share Feldman's optimism. Nader Hashemi, in an otherwise positive review in the Toronto Globe & Mail, said that Feldman's assertion that Jordan is making progress toward democracy is flawed: "Attempts at democratization have really been about regime survival in the face of a hostile population." A Kirkus Reviews critic noted that in Feldman's text "the words 'perhaps' and 'maybe' appear so often that they begin to sound like wishful thinking." In the Middle East Quarterly, Jonathan Schanzer also argued that Feldman fails to take the dangers of militant Islamist movements seriously enough.

Other reviewers were more sanguine. Margaret Flanagan in Booklist wrote that "this thought-provoking discourse couldn't be published at a more appropriate time." Washington Post writer Emran Qureshi pointed out that Feldman's picture of the possibilities for democracy in the Middle East is not entirely optimistic, because the author fears for democracy in states like Saudi Arabia, whose oil wealth effectively prevents the need to follow democratic movements. Qureshi, however, concluded that Feldman "has written a substantial and

important defense of why America should support democratic reform and not the authoritarian status quo in much of the Muslim world."

### What We Owe Iraq

Feldman furthers his analysis of Iraq following the U.S. invasion with his 2004 book, What We Owe Iraq, in which he supports the merchandising analogy of "we broke it, we bought it." Robert Kagan noted in the New York Times Book Review: "When the United States invaded Iraq, Feldman argues, it did more than topple a tyrant. It undertook a 'trusteeship' on behalf of the Iraqi people." Thus, as Political Science Quarterly writer Robert I. Rotberg stated, "Feldman puts the Iraqi imbroglio into a framework of ethical responsibility." The author contends that the United States has a moral and ethical, as well as a practical obligation to Iraq and the Iraqi people to construct a new functioning and stable government. He arrives at this conclusion following a "crisp and provocative examination of international law and historical experiences with colonialism, trusteeships, and mandates," wrote Foreign Affairs contributor L. Carl Brown. Regarding Feldman's central thesis, New Statesman contributor Rodric Braithwaite asserted: "Feldman is right, of course. But he offers no confidence at all that this is achievable." Similarly, Middle East Quarterly contributor Patrick Clawson observed: "Feldman's optimism about Washington's ability to transform Iraqi politics would be more convincing if he demonstrated a better understanding of the obstacles ahead." Feldman further argues in his book that it is to the advantage not just of Iraq and the United States that the country be stabilized; it also benefits Iraq's neighbors in the region and Europe.

Kagan noted that What We Owe Iraq is, "like its author, . . . an unusual blend: part theoretical treatise, part political analysis, part memoir." Kagan went on to note: "Above all, it is a plea to the American conscience to take seriously the responsibility the United States has assumed to help the Iraqi people build the democracy Feldman believes they need and deserve." Kagan termed this thesis both "powerful and important." A Publishers Weekly reviewer felt that "Feldman's book nicely bridges theory and practice, even as some events outpace it." Parameters contributor Raymond A. Millen had praise for Feldman's study, calling it a "thought-provoking and enlightening study of modern nation-building." Millen added: "Feldman's book is a valuable tool for political-military specialists as well as strategists. He has successfully distilled the essential principles required for nation-building, the likely political and ethical dilemmas, and the milestones needed to achieve Iraqi sovereignty. The author's logic is well-grounded, addressing America's national security concerns without compromising its ethical obligations. In short, Feldman has succeeded in providing a useful primer for nation-building, regardless of the context or state."

### Divided by God

With *Divided by God*, Feldman turns his attention to the concept of separation of church and state, written into the U.S. Constitution and hotly debated ever since. Here he attempts to find a middle ground between those wishing for more religion in public life and those seeking to keep public life secular. Feldman examines the thoughts of the Founding Fathers on this subject, and follows the arguments and counter-arguments over the past two centuries to conclude that the debate can be partially resolved simply following the First Amendment: namely, that public money not be spent on any church institution or its auxiliary, and that religious expression not be interfered with or inhibited in public places or speech. *New York Times Book Review* writer Franklin Foer put this suggestion into concrete terms: "[Feldman] proposes a simple solution for this mess: a compromise that gives evangelicals and secularists what they want most. Liberals would be granted an unambiguous ban on the financing of religion, ending school vouchers to religious institutions and President Bush's faith-based initiative. In return, they would stop challenging religion's prominence in public symbols like the Pledge of Allegiance, and objecting to politicians who offer theological justifications for policy positions."

*Booklist* reviewer Ray Olson found this book "intelligently respectful of both secularist and religious camps." Similarly, *Library Journal* contributor Thomas J. Baldino thought Feldman's book "offers a balanced overview of the subject" as well as a "reasonable approach for reconciling the differences." Baldino went on to term *Divided by God* an "excellent, very readable work." Likewise, a *Kirkus Reviews* writer called it "a reasoned, reasonable and consensus-seeking argument that is, of course, in danger of going unheard amid all the shouting." Further praise for the work came from a *Publishers Weekly* reviewer who thought it a "lucid and careful study . . . [that] will leave readers on all sides far more informed." In a similar vein, an *Economist* contributor dubbed the book "an elegant and fair primer on a contentious issue."

### The Fall and Rise of the Islamic State

Feldman describes various forms that Islamic rule has taken over the centuries in *The Fall and Rise of the Islamic State*. He also focuses on the differences between contemporary Islamic states and those of the past, from Ottoman times on. Putting Islamic administration in a historical context, he attempts to show how Islamic or shari'a law was in many cases the only restraint put on the power of despotic rulers. Thus, for many Muslims, this legal tradition is the only one they have a connection to, never having experienced democratic alternatives. A contributor for the *Economist* noted regarding this perception: "That perceived dilemma—either Muslim law and scholarship, or unfettered dictatorship—is not just a hangover from history; it also reflects the fact that many secular regimes which replaced traditional Muslim empires were dictatorships, with no separation of powers." In this context, shari'a law should look less alarming to the West, according to Feldman, for it was simply an attempt at putting in codified order a system of laws that would apply equally to all. *Commentary* reviewer Paul Marshall noted of Feldman's thesis: "This book makes the provocative and counterintuitive argument that the West and the world may have nothing to fear, and even something to gain, if Muslim nations were to become 'Islamic states'—by which Feldman means states governed not by Islamist dictators but by Islamic law, or shari'a."

The contributor for the *Economist* found this a "short, incisive and elegant book," but also voiced a criticism: "One huge question, unanswered by this book, is how minorities—practitioners of other religions or none—can expect to fare in countries where a form of political Islam is practised by the will of the majority." Similarly, Marshall commented: "Feldman's thesis depends on a heavily scrubbed and buffed depiction of shari'a. He conspicuously does not address its dual hierarchical structure, specifying separate and highly unequal rights for men and women, Muslims and non-Muslims, the Islamic realm and the rest of the world." Likewise, a contributor for the *New Yorker* found *The Fall and Rise of the Islamic State* "compelling as a theoretical exercise," yet lacking in real usefulness because of the author's "failure to confront practical considerations such as the rights of women."

### Scorpions

Feldman leaves Islamic law behind to examine an aspect of the American legal system in *Scorpions*, a study of the lasting achievements of four of the nine Supreme Court justices Franklin Delano Roosevelt appointed during his long tenure as U.S. president. The four memorable justices—Felix Frankfurter, Robert Jackson, Hugo Black, and William O. Douglas—all served together on the court from 1941 through 1954 (ending with the landmark Brown v.

Board of Education decision on school segregation), and were part of an attempt by Roosevelt to get rid of the conservative Supreme Court that blocked so much of his progressive legislative agenda during the New Deal. Feldman sets out to show whether or not Roosevelt's liberal agenda was actually served by these justices, and he concludes with a "complicated" answer, according to online *Slate* contributor Dahlia Lithwick. These four justices, Lithwick noted, "so fundamentally reshaped 20th-century constitutional thought that their influences still dominate modern doctrine today." Yet, as Lithwick further observed, these four "scorpions" were so "consistently egotistical and inflexible, so fractious and combative, that they worked at cross purposes for most of their lives." Feldman's book takes readers behind the scenes, showing the workings of conferences between the justices as decisions were worked out. In the end, though they might have been appointed with supposed liberal credentials, once these four justices put on their robes they each found their own personal way to interpret law.

Lithwick termed *Scorpions* a "terrific new book." *Booklist* reviewer Gilbert Taylor also had praise for the book, noting: "The interpersonal factor in court politics is knowledgeably displayed in Feldman's intriguing account." Similarly, a *Kirkus Reviews* writer called the book an "immensely readable history that goes behind the facade of our most august institution to reveal the flesh-and-blood characters who make our laws." *Publishers Weekly* reviewer Jeffrey Rosen also had a high assessment of *Scorpions*, commenting: "The pleasure of this book comes from Feldman's skill as a narrator of intellectual history." Rosen went on to call the book a "first-rate work of narrative history that succeeds in bringing the intellectual and political battles of the post-Roosevelt Court vividly to life." Likewise, *Foreign Affairs* contributor Walter Russell Mean commended "Feldman's admirable ability to weave a compelling narrative out of a complicated and abstract plot."

# ■ Biographical And Critical Sources

*PERIODICALS*

*America*, November 28, 2005, Gene Roman, "Split in Two," review of *Divided by God: America's Church-State Problem and What We Should Do about It*, p. 26.

*American Lawyer*, February, 2004, Carolyn Kolker, "Founding Facilitator," interview with Feldman.

*Asian Affairs*, November, 2008, Ivor Lucas, review of *The Fall and Rise of the Islamic State*, p. 419.

*AudioFile*, February, 2011, Joseph A. Harris, review of *Scorpions: The Battles and Triumphs of FDR's Great Supreme Court Justices*.

*Booklist*, April 15, 2003, Margaret Flanagan, review of *After Jihad: America and the Struggle for Islamic Democracy*, pp. 1430-1431; August 1, 2005, Ray Olson, review of *Divided by God*, p. 1973; October 15, 2010, Gilbert Taylor, review of *Scorpions*, p. 6.

*California Law Review*, December, 2005, Jedediah Purdy, review of *What We Owe Iraq: War and the Ethics of Nation Building*, p. 1773.

*Choice*, October, 2008, S. Zuhur, review of *The Fall and Rise of the Islamic State*, p. 384.

*Christian Century*, November 29, 2005, Robert Westbrook, "Mission Impossible: The Iraq Mistake," review of *What We Owe Iraq*, p. 29.

*Commentary*, November, 2005, Adam Wolfson, "Over the Wall," review of *Divided by God*, p. 92; June, 2008, Paul Marshall, "Islamophilia," review of *The Fall and Rise of the Islamic State*, p. 60.

*Commonweal*, November 18, 2005, Richard W. Garnett, "Permanent Conflict," review of *Divided by God*, p. 24.

*Constitutional Commentary*, spring, 2010, Asifa Quraishi, review of *The Fall and Rise of the Islamic State*, p. 297.

*Economist*, July 2, 2005, "But Whose Law Should Prevail? Church, State and the Courts in America," review of *Divided by God*, p. 73; May 3, 2008, "Power Points; Religion and Secularism," review of *The Fall and Rise of the Islamic State*, p. 90; November 20, 2010, "The Scorpions' Stratagems; Franklin Roosevelt's Supreme Court," review of *Scorpions*, p. 96.

*Education Next*, spring, 2006, review of *Divided by God*, p. 86.

*Ethics*, October, 2007, Chad Flanders, review of *Divided by God*, p. 147.

*Federal Lawyer*, February, 2006, David M. Ackerman, review of *Divided by God*, p. 59.

*First Things: A Monthly Journal of Religion and Public Life*, January, 2006, "There Is a Great Deal to Like about Noah Feldman's *Divided by God: America's Church-State Problem and What We Should Do about It*," p. 70.

*Foreign Affairs*, March, 2005, L. Carl Brown, review of *What We Owe Iraq*; January, 2006, Walter Russell Mead, review of *Divided by God*; September, 2008, L. Carl Brown, review of *The Fall and Rise of the Islamic State*; March, 2011, Walter Russell Mead, review of *Scorpions*.

*Globe & Mail* (Toronto, Ontario, Canada), May 17, 2003, Nader Hashemi, "The Fundamentals of Democracy," p. D5.

*Harvard Law Review*, December, 2005, review of *Divided by God*, p. 701.

*Historian*, summer, 2010, Leor Halevi, review of *The Fall and Rise of the Islamic State*, p. 404.

*International Affairs*, January, 2005, Andrew Rathmell, review of *What We Owe Iraq*, p. 249.

*International History Review,* June, 2009, John O. Voll, review of *The Fall and Rise of the Islamic State,* p. 373.

*International Journal,* summer, 2006, Arzoo Osanloo, review of *What We Owe Iraq,* p. 766.

*Journal News,* April 13, 2003, interview with Feldman.

*Journal of Law and Religion,* fall, 2006, Perry Dane, review of *Divided by God,* p. 545; spring, 2010, Abdullahi A. Gallab, review of *The Fall and Rise of the Islamic State,* p. 381.

*Kirkus Reviews,* February 15, 2003, review of *After Jihad,* p. 284; May 15, 2005, review of *Divided by God,* p. 574; August 1, 2010, review of *Scorpions.*

*Law and Social Inquiry,* January, 2010, Molly Greene, "Goodbye to the Despot: Feldman on Islamic Law in the Ottoman Empire," p. 219.

*Library Journal,* July 1, 2005, Thomas J. Baldino, review of *Divided by God,* p. 100.

*London Review of Books,* March 31, 2005, Rory Stewart, "Degrees of Not Knowing," review of *What We Owe Iraq,* p. 9.

*Los Angeles Lawyer,* April, 2011, Jeffrey Andrew Hartwick, review of *Scorpions,* p. 64.

*Middle East Quarterly,* winter, 2004, Jonathan Schanzer, review of *After Jihad,* pp. 74-75; spring, 2005, Patrick Clawson, review of *What We Owe Iraq,* p. 94.

*National Review,* March 7, 2011, Joseph Tartakovsky, "Begaveled Neuroses," review of *Scorpions,* p. 49.

*New Leader,* July, 2005, Eugen Weber, "Divided We Stand," review of *Divided by God,* p. 18.

*New Statesman,* June 26, 2006, Rodric Braithwaite, "The War That Will Never Be Won; There Is No Such Thing as a Humanitarian Intervention: If You Invade a Country You Will Always Kill People. Rodric Braithwaite on the Folly of Our Campaign in Iraq," review of *What We Owe Iraq,* p. 60.

*New Yorker,* May 26, 2008, review of *The Fall and Rise of the Islamic State,* p. 77.

*New York Law Journal,* January 4, 2011, Walter Barthold, review of *Scorpions.*

*New York Times,* May 11, 2003, Jennifer Lee, "Aftereffects: The Law; American Will Advise Iraqis on Writing New Constitution," section 1, p. 14.

*New York Times Book Review,* July 6, 2003, Jonathan D. Tepperman, "A Delicate Balance," p. 16; July 24, 2005, Franklin Foer, "One Nation, under Whomever," review of *Divided by God,* p. 14; August 20, 2006, "Paperback Row," p. 20; November 14, 2004, Robert Kagan, review of *What We Owe Iraq;* November 7, 2010, Adam Cohen, "Jousting Justices," review of *Scorpions,* p. 12.

*Parameters,* winter, 2005, Raymond A. Millen, review of *What We Owe Iraq,* p. 133.

*Political Science Quarterly,* spring, 2005, Robert I. Rotberg, review of *What We Owe Iraq,* p. 133.

*Publishers Weekly,* March 3, 2003, review of *After Jihad,* pp. 63-64; August 9, 2004, review of *What We Owe Iraq,* p. 237; June 6, 2005, review of *Divided by God,* p. 54; August 9, 2010, Jeffrey Rosen, review of *Scorpions,* p. 38.

*Shofar,* spring, 2004, review of *After Jihad,* p. 202.

*Survival,* winter, 2006, Toby Doge, "What We Owe Iraq: War and the Ethics of Nation Building," p. 157.

*Tulane Law Review,* December, 2005, Don Willenburg, review of *Divided by God,* p. 713.

*Washington Lawyer,* October, 2010, Ronald Goldfarb, review of *Scorpions,* p. 42.

*Washington Post,* May 4, 2003, Emran Qureshi, "Building Bridges," section T, p. 8.

*Washington Post Book World,* November 21, 2004, Richard A. Clarke, "War of Ideas," review of *What We Owe Iraq,* p. 3; July 10, 2005, E.J. Dionne, Jr., "American Spirit," review of *Divided by God,* p. 7; July 27, 2008, Geneive Abdo, "Islamic Democracy," review of *The Fall and Rise of the Islamic State,* p. 11.

*World Politics,* January 1, 2007, Jason Brownlee, "Can America Nation-build?," p. 314.

*Yale Journal of International Law,* summer, 2005, Adil Ahmad Haque, review of *What We Owe Iraq,* p. 605; winter, 2009, Maryam Khan, review of *The Fall and Rise of the Islamic State,* p. 260.

## ONLINE

*Council on Foreign Relations Web site,* http://www.cfr.org/ (June 23, 2011), "Noah Feldman."

*Front Page,* http://www.frontpagemag.com/ (June 16, 2003), Martin Kramer, "Jihad Is Over (If Noah Feldman Wants It)."

*Harper's Online,* http://www.harpers.org/ (April 3, 2008), Scott Horton, "Six Questions for Noah Feldman, Author of *The Fall and Rise of the Islamic State.*"

*Harvard Law School Web site,* http://www.law.harvard.edu/ (June 23, 2011), "Noah Feldman."

*Slate,* http://www.slate.com/ (November 17, 2010), Dahlia Lithwick, review of *Scorpions.*

## OTHER

*International Wire,* October 15, 2003, "Security Council Considers U.S. Resolution on Iraq: Interview with *After Jihad* Author Noah Feldman," transcript of television interview by John Gibson on Fox News; December 15, 2003, "Interview with Noah Feldman," transcript of television interview by John Gibson on Fox News.*

# Martin Fletcher

## 1947-

### ■ Personal

Born August 16, 1947, in London, England. *Education:* Graduated from University of Bradford, 1970.

### ■ Career

National Broadcasting Company (NBC News), Tel Aviv, Israel, correspondent, 1982—, bureau chief, 1990—. Visnews, television news programming writer, 1970-71, cameraman/writer and field producer, beginning 1973; British Broadcasting Corp. (BBC-TV), writer for "9 O'Clock News," 1971-73; Also worked as a French and German interpreter for Common Market in Brussels, Belgium, and has been based as a reporter in Johannesburg, Paris, and Frankfurt.

### ■ Awards, Honors

Emmy Award, 1988, for reporting on the Palestinian intifada, 1994, for coverage of Rwanda, 1999, for Kosovo coverage, 2002, for coverage of the Palestinian uprising, and 2006, for coverage of Israel's war with Hezbollah; Citation for Excellence, Overseas Press Club of America, 1988, for coverage of the first Palestinian uprising, 1994, for coverage in Bosnia, and 2001, for coverage of the second Palestinian uprising; Overseas Press Club award, 1999, for Kosovo coverage, and 2002, for coverage of the Palestinian uprising; DuPont award, 2002, for coverage of the Palestinian uprising; Cameraman of the Year, British Royal Society of Television; Jewish National Book Award, 2011, for *Walking Israel.*

### ■ Writings

*Breaking News: A Stunning and Memorable Account of Reporting from Some of the Most Dangerous Places in the World,* Thomas Dunne Books/St. Martin's Press (New York, NY), 2008.

*Walking Israel: A Personal Search for the Soul of a Nation,* St. Martin's Press (New York, NY), 2010.

*The List,* Thomas Dunne Books (New York, NY), 2011.

### ■ Sidelights

NBC News bureau chief and correspondent Martin Fletcher is known to millions of people as the network's primary contact in Tel Aviv, Israel. "From his base in Tel Aviv, Fletcher has covered a full spectrum of breaking news developments throughout the Middle East and around the world," wrote a contributor to *MSNBC.com.* Fletcher was also the first television reporter to enter the American embassy in Teheran in 1979, when the hostage situation was developing. "When NATO and American troops were hunting for General Aidid, the Somali warlord responsible for killing eighteen American soldiers in Somalia," the *MSNBC.com.* writer reported, "Fletcher was the only person to find and interview him for NBC Nightly News." Fletcher also worked in Cambodia, finding and interviewing major figures in the Khmer Rouge movement who were responsible for the murder of millions of Cambodian citizens during the late 1970s.

#### *Breaking News*

Fletcher's *Breaking News: A Stunning and Memorable Account of Reporting from Some of the Most Dangerous Places in the World* is a memoir that recounts his decades of adventures while on assignment all around the globe. For the NBC correspondent, however, the creation of the book was as much an interior odyssey as it was a chronicle of his world trips.

"One day everyone takes stock of their life. When I did that, I realised that the days, which I had taken one by one, added up to an extraordinary record," Fletcher stated in an article he wrote for the *Gather* Web site. "Slowly I realized—by confronting the suffering of the world, I was coming to understand the suffering closer to home." Fletcher's family, including his parents and two sisters, had survived the Holocaust, which had claimed the lives of all but five of his closest relatives. In a way, he stated in his *Gather* Web site article, *Breaking News* became a way for him to deal with the pain of his own loss. "Through it all," stated a *Kirkus Reviews* contributor in an assessment of *Breaking News*, "Fletcher tries but cannot fully explain his love for a job that has brought him face-to-face with human suffering and mass carnage." Nonetheless, *Breaking News* is "a historical overview, an example of a successful journalist's career," Joel W. Tscherne wrote in *Library Journal*, "and a journalistic tour de force."

*Breaking News* also became a way for Fletcher to clarify his own moral compass. In his travels he encountered situations where his duty as a reporter conflicted with his own wishes. He lists a story he did on a Somali girl who died of starvation while he was filming her and his relationship with the Al-Aksa Martyr's Brigade, which sent suicide bombers to kill Israeli citizens as examples of times when his professional duty as a reporter conflicted with his personal morality. "How polite should I be when interviewing someone responsible for killing up to two million Cambodians?" he was quoted by *Wisconsin State Journal* reporter William R. Wineke as saying. "Is it wrong to stay in the home of a brutal Somali warlord, eating lavish food prepared by his Italian-trained chef, in order to report on, among other things, his theft of the same food from international aid organizations?" At other times, his work as a reporter led him into conflict with governments as well as individuals and non-government bodies. In 1988, reported Richard Zoglin in *Time*, the Israeli government withdrew Fletcher's credentials after the NBC correspondent filed a story stating that Israeli agents had planned and carried out the assassination of a major PLO figure. "Fletcher," declared a *Publishers Weekly* reviewer, "has a clear understanding of the ambiguities of his position as a purveyor of misery and death."

### Walking Israel

For Fletcher's Next book, *Walking Israel: A Personal Search for the Soul of a Nation*, he literally walked Israel from the Lebanese border to Gaza. This book is the result of what he learned on his pedestrian journey. In the work, he chronicles all of the differ-

ent people and cultures he encountered along the way, and debunks stereotypes about Arabs and Jews, Muslims and Zionists, Palestinians and Israelis. Thus, *Walking Israel* is a complex portrait of a much disputed nation.

Reviewing the work on the *Middle East Mirror* Web site, contributor Valerie Saturen lauded: "Fletcher's excellent storytelling makes him an engaging guide on this tour of the most fascinating 170 miles on the planet. With a veteran journalist's nose for a good story, he investigates the lives of ordinary Israelis." *Booklist* contributor Bryce Christensen called the work: "A much-needed corrective to media stereotypes." *Library Journal* contributor Paul Kaplan remarked that the book is "recommended for those seeking to stay informed about Israel and its diverse peoples." A *Kirkus Reviews* contributor explained the work as "a dogged reporter reveals essential truths, from his home and his heart, never broadcast on the evening news-a welcome bit of sanity."

## ■ Biographical And Critical Sources

*PERIODICALS*

*Booklist*, September 15, 2010, Bryce Christensen, review of *Walking Israel: A Personal Search for the Soul of a Nation*, p. 26.

*Kirkus Reviews*, February 1, 2008, review of *Breaking News: A Stunning and Memorable Account of Reporting from Some of the Most Dangerous Places in the World*; August 1, 2010, review of *Walking Israel*.

*Library Journal*, February 1, 2008, Joel W. Tscherne, review of *Breaking News*, p. 82; November 1, 2010, Paul Kaplan, review of *Walking Israel*, p. 80.

*Los Angeles Times*, April 27, 1988, "Israel Curbs 2 U.S. Journalists for Assassination Reports," p. 6.

*New York Times*, April 27, 1988, "Israel Withdraws Credentials of Two Western Journalists," p. 10.

*Publishers Weekly*, January 14, 2008, review of *Breaking News*, p. 52.

*Time*, May 9, 1988, "Dialogue in a Demilitarized Zone; ABC's Nightline Plays Diplomat and Journalist in Israel," p. 74.

*TV Guide*, January 3, 1981, "The War TV Can't Cover: The Iran-Iraq Conflict Has Been an Exercise in Frustration for Reporters and Film Crews," p. 4.

*Washington Post*, April 27, 1988, "Israel Lifts Accreditation of Post, NBC Reporters," p. 26.

*Wisconsin State Journal*, March 29, 2008, William R. Wineke, "War Correspondent Martin Fletcher Writes Memoir."

*ONLINE*

*Forward*, http://blogs.forward.com/ (September 29, 2010), review of *Walking Israel*.
*Gather*, http://www.gather.com/ (October 22, 2008), Martin Fletcher, "Why I Wrote *Breaking News*."

*Middle East Mirror*, http://www.middleeastmirror.com/ (December 18, 2010), Valerie Saturen, review of *Walking Israel*.
*MSNBC.com*, http://www.msnbc.msn.com/ (October 22, 2008), "Martin Fletcher;" (August 14, 2011), author profile.

# Ian Frazier

## 1951-

■ **Personal**

Born 1951, in Cleveland, OH; son of David (a chemist) and Peggy (a teacher, actress, and director) Frazier; married Jacqueline Carey (a writer); children: Cora, Thomas. *Education:* Attended Western Reserve Academy; Harvard University, B.A., 1973.

■ **Addresses**

*Home*—Montclair, NJ.

■ **Career**

Writer, essayist, and journalist. *Oui* magazine, Chicago, IL, staff writer; *New Yorker,* New York, NY, staff writer, twenty-one years. Former staff member, *Harvard Lampoon.*

■ **Writings**

*NONFICTION*

*Dating Your Mom* (essays), Farrar, Straus & Giroux (New York, NY), 1986, Picador (New York, NY), 2003.

*Nobody Better, Better than Nobody* (essays), Farrar, Straus & Giroux (New York, NY), 1987.

*Great Plains,* Farrar, Straus & Giroux (New York, NY), 1989.

*Family,* Farrar, Straus & Giroux (New York, NY), 1994.

*Coyote v. Acme* (essays), Farrar, Straus & Giroux (New York, NY), 1996.

(Editor, with Robert Atwan) *The Best American Essays: 1997,* Houghton Mifflin (Boston, MA), 1997.

*On the Rez,* Farrar, Straus & Giroux (New York, NY), 2000.

*Lamentations of the Father,* illustrated by Bruce Zick, Westminster John Knox Press (Louisville, KY), 2000.

*Great Plains,* Picador (New York, NY), 2001.

(Contributor of essays, with Douglas R. Nickel) Joel Sternfeld, *Stranger Passing,* Bulfinch (Boston, MA), 2001.

*The Fish's Eye: Essays about Angling and the Outdoors,* Farrar, Straus & Giroux (New York, NY), 2002.

*Gone to New York: Adventures in the City* (essays), Farrar, Straus & Giroux (New York, NY), 2005.

(Author of introduction) Joel Smith, *Steinberg at the New Yorker,* Harry N. Abrams (New York, NY), 2005.

*Lamentations of the Father: Essays* (different collection from earlier book of the same name), Farrar, Straus & Giroux (New York, NY), 2008.

*Travels in Siberia,* Farrar, Straus & Giroux (New York, NY), 2010.

(Editor) *Humor Me: An Anthology of Funny Contemporary Writing (Plus Some Great Old Stuff Too),* Ecco (New York, NY), 2010.

*OTHER*

(Translator) Daniil Kharms, *It Happened Like This: Stories and Poems,* pictures by Katya Arnold, Farrar, Straus & Giroux (New York, NY), 1998.

Contributor to books, including *They Went: The Art and Craft of Travel Writing,* edited by William Zinsser, Houghton Mifflin, 1991.

■ **Sidelights**

Journalist and essayist Ian Frazier is known for his comic, ironic essays and for his affectionate explorations of rural America. A native of Ohio who splits his time between New York City and Montana, Frazier has kept alive his ties to the Midwest by writing about it in the pages of the *New Yorker* magazine and in books. His humorous reflections on home and country, city life, and modern society are collected in a series of nonfiction books, including *Dating Your Mom, Great Plains,* and *Family.* He explores the contemporary lives of Native Americans in his book *On the Rez. New York Times* contributor Christopher Lehmann-Haupt cited Frazier for his "original point of view" and the "antic sense of fun he brings to whatever he writes."

## Early Essay Collections

Collections of essays Frazier originally wrote for the *New Yorker* formed the basis of his first two books, *Dating Your Mom* and *Nobody Better, Better than Nobody.* The twenty-five pieces that make up *Dating Your Mom* showcase Frazier's deadpan humor and wit. In the title story, for instance, Frazier counsels single men to give up the arduous process of dating strangers and instead date their mothers, since these men are already familiar with and loved by their moms. In "LGA-ORD," another piece from the book, Frazier offers a witty parody of the playwright Samuel Beckett as a commercial pilot making his way from New York to Chicago, Illinois. Critics praised Frazier's bizarre fantasies and his ability to see humor in small details. As Mordecai Richler noted in the *New York Times Book Review,* "Frazier is an elegant miniaturist, a much needed mockingbird with a fine eye for the absurd." *Los Angeles Times Book Review* contributor Shelly Lowenkopf commented that the essays in the book "sing with Frazier's understated irreverence, reminding us that there is nothing so sacred it cannot or should not be laughed at."

In his second collection of humorous essays, *Nobody Better, Better than Nobody,* Frazier again turns to a wide range of seemingly average people and events. He writes of a fishing store owner in New York, of the woman who produces the *Hints from Heloise* newspaper column, and of bears in Montana. As in his first collection, Frazier's humor is often couched in the guise of serious storytelling, such as his description of an angry dog he encountered while fishing, as quoted by Paul Gray in *Time:* "The woman told me to hold still and the dog wouldn't bite me. I held still, and the dog bit me in the right shoulder. I told the woman that the dog was biting me." Reviewers have noted that in *Nobody Better, Better than Nobody,* Frazier tempers the wicked sarcasm of his first collection with sympathy for his subjects, while maintaining his astute eye for ironic

detail. *New York Times* contributor Lehmann-Haupt commented: "It's the rare combination of humor and empathy that gives these casual pieces their special appeal." Other reviewers lauded Frazier's ability to heighten his comedic effects with stylistic devices, particularly with his tendency toward extremely long sentences and equally long series of oddly juxtaposed images. Gray praised the "loopy laziness" of Frazier's prose and noted that "the reader winds up laughing and knowing a great deal about subjects . . . that most people can live without." Another collection of essays, *Coyote v. Acme,* features a parody of Bob Hope's memoirs; a legal brief of a case filed by the Warner Bros., Inc., cartoon character, the Coyote, against the explosives manufacturer, Acme, addressing his many mishaps while trying to catch the Roadrunner; and "Boswell's Life of Don Johnson." A *Publishers Weekly* contributor noted that *Coyote v. Acme* proves "Frazier's great comic range, however trite the subject."

## Later Essays

*The Fish's Eye: Essays about Angling and the Outdoors* features the author's ruminations about his love of fishing and fish. The essays in the collection are from the author's previous writings for magazines such as *Outside* and *Sports Afield.* In them, the author reveals that he can find connections to his love of fishing in almost any environment, from a fishing shop near New York's Grand Central Station to writing about catching a bass fish at the New York City Beach to a story about a family fishing trip. In the process, the author provides keen observations about the outdoors.

"His paeans to the angling experience set the standard in this subgenre," wrote a contributor to *Publishers Weekly.* In a review of *The Fish's Eye* in *Booklist,* Dennis Dodge noted that the author "unfailingly communicates an infectious fascination—a passion, really—for woods and water and fish."

For his next book, *Gone to New York: Adventures in the City,* Frazier switches his focus to his beloved New York. Combining new and previously published essays, the author writes about everything from New York traffic to various profile pieces, such as the story of a typewriter repairman in the age of the computer. In another article, he profiles a man who tried to climb the World Trade Center in 1977. Although Frazier is known primarily for his humor, the book also contains more serious perspectives of the city, such as "Street Scene," which tells of a woman who collapses on the city's streets and the effort to revive her. The author also writes about the psyche of a post-9/11 New York.

"A vivid collection of essays expertly blending reporting, history, humor and one man's abiding affection for a city's quirks," wrote a *Kirkus Reviews* contributor of *Gone to New York.* A reviewer in *Publishers Weekly* commented that the author's "evocation of the city over three decades is thoughtful, entertaining and occasionally moving."

Although it has almost the same title as an earlier book, *Lamentations of the Father: Essays,* published in 2008, does not focus on parenting and family life but features thirty-three wide-ranging essays by the author written over the prior thirteen years. The title essay is, however, connected to the earlier book of the same title. Other essays include a satire about the U.S. founding fathers and the cartoon character Elmer Fudd, a tale of the author's imagined marriage to the actress Elizabeth Taylor, and some advice about how to use a shower curtain, written in the form of an instructional manual for hotel guests.

Writing in *Library Journal,* Anthony Pucci noted that the essays in *Lamentations of the Father: Essays* represent "more reasons to consider *New Yorker* contributor Frazier one of America's premier humorists." A *Kirkus Reviews* contributor observed: "His sense of humor is so uncanny and surprising it's nearly impossible not to be charmed."

### Other Nonfiction

For his third book, *Great Plains,* Frazier spent several years exploring the interior of the United States. Among many other sites, he visited gigantic ranches in Wyoming, American Indian monuments in South Dakota, and obscure museums in Kansas. His observations of the area, while often funny and ironic, express a sadness that the rural lifestyle that characterizes the vast plains of inner America will inevitably disappear as people abandon farms for cities. Frazier describes the uniqueness of the plains landscape—flat and barren under an enormous sky—and the diversity of figures, both past and present, who inhabit that landscape. As quoted by Sue Hubbell in the *New York Times Book Review,* the author writes that "the Great Plains have plenty of room for the past. Often, as I drove around, I felt as if I were in an enormous time park." Critics praised the mix of humor, wit, nostalgia, and sadness with which Frazier infuses his observations.

Frazier continues his exploration of the American heartland in his well-received 1994 book *Family.* The work is a profile of Frazier's white, Anglo-Saxon, Protestant, Midwestern, middle-class fore-

bears and their quite ordinary—if illuminating—lives. "*Family* . . . is more than an extended family photo album minus the photos," wrote David Klinghoffer in the *National Review.* "There is an unmistakable tide in the history of these families, which Frazier notices early on and conveys in a powerful, because personal, way. It's the slow evaporation of noble sentiment, reflected in a wider way in American culture." In the *New York Times Book Review,* David Willis McCullough characterized *Family* as "a book of a lifetime, . . . that rarest of events, a family reunion worth inviting strangers to attend."

*Great Plains* introduces readers to Le War Lance, an Oglala Sioux Frazier met in his travels. Lance was notable for the wild tales of his real and imagined life in New York, as a world traveler, and on the Pine Ridge Indian Reservation in South Dakota. In *On the Rez,* Frazier recounts how he moved his family from New York to Montana and began regular trips to the reservation. "What motivates the book is Frazier's own search for something he believes can be found in Indian society but which white society seems to him unable to produce: the capacity to be personally free," explained Christine Gray in *Washington Monthly.* The author examines the quality of Native American life, through history, observation, and stories of Native American heroes of the past and present.

Acknowledging his status as an "Indian wannabe," Frazier nevertheless defends his privilege to write about any subject he chooses. Even so, Gray questioned his authority to write *On the Rez,* claiming: "Frazier's friendship with Lance, one senses, is compromised by Frazier's agenda and, in the end, the portrait of Indianness that Frazier offers is just the creation of another set of stereotypes drawn by a white man. Seeking to enlarge his own truncated vision, and ours, too, one feels that Frazier has stuffed a whole people into the shape and size of his own dream of freedom." Sharply differing with that judgment, *Booklist* reviewer Donna Seaman declared that "by weaving the past with the present and illuminating so many aspects of Indian life, Frazier's frank and adroitly improvised narrative will stand as one of literature's most complex yet most clarifying testaments to the essence of American Indian culture." An *Entertainment Weekly* contributor affirmed the value of *On the Rez,* crediting Frazier with "fusing warm essayism and cold reportage." Gray wrote in another *Time* review: "As Frazier serendipitously shuttles his narrative between Pine Ridge visits and snippets of Indian history, a fascinating picture emerges of a people struggling with the consequence of old wrongs and human orneriness."

In his 2000 book, *Lamentations of the Father,* illustrated by Bruce Zick, the author provides his own humorous perspective on parenting based on an earlier essay. Borrowing from the language of Deuteronomy in the Bible, Frazier provides a code of conduct for children composed of a series of statues and ordinances pertaining to topics such as life at the dinner table, screaming, sippy cups, and numerous other aspects of a young family's life. Mary-Jane Donnellan, writing on the *AD2000* Web site, commented that the book "offers a delightful yet insightful perspective on parenting."

A travelogue of sorts, *Travels in Siberia* portrays Frazier's explorations of Siberia. The author visited the barren region of Russia five times over a twelve-year period, and the book reflects his varying impressions and experiences. The volume even includes Frazier's sketches of the region. Several critics compared *Travels in Siberia* favorably to *Great Plains*, and online *Bookslut* reviewer Janet Potter found that it "does a great service to its subject." She added: "The region is usually shrugged off for its unapproachable climate, depressing historical connotations, and mind-boggling scope, and of course those factors are enormous in the Siberian experience. But the reality of Siberia, while not a hidden utopia, is a place of charm. Frazier, an enormously gifted observer and writer who is both in love with the smell of Siberian air and not afraid to complain about its plumbing problems, is the perfect man to tell us about it." Carmela Ciuraru pointed out in the *San Francisco Chronicle*: "There are many reasons to love it, including the fantastic ending, possibly the best of any book in recent memory. *Travels in Siberia* is a masterpiece of nonfiction writing—tragic, bizarre and funny. Once again, the inimitable Frazier has managed to create a genre of his very own."

## ■ Biographical And Critical Sources

*PERIODICALS*

*American Heritage*, July-August, 1995, Geoffrey C. Ward, review of *Family*, p. 16.
*American Scholar*, autumn, 2002, Franklin Burroughs, review of *The Fish's Eye: Essays about Angling and the Outdoors*, p. 144.
*American Spectator*, December, 1989, Wayne Michael Sarf, review of *Great Plains*, p. 50; February 18, 2006, Alexander Chancellor, review of *Gone to New York: Adventures in the City*, p. 48.
*Booklist*, October 1, 1994, Brad Hooper, review of *Family*, p. 233; November 15, 1999, Donna Seaman, review of *On the Rez*, p. 578; March 1, 2002, Dennis Dodge, review of *The Fish's Eye*, p. 1077; September 15, 2005, Brad Hooper, review of *Gone to New York*, p. 24; March 15, 2008, Donna Seaman, review of *Lamentations of the Father: Essays*, p. 16.

*Business Week*, February 14, 2000, review of *On the Rez*, p. 18; May 6, 2002, review of *The Fish's Eye*, p. 14.
*Commonweal*, December 7, 1990, Jean Bethke Elshtain, review of *Great Plains*, p. 726; December 2, 1994, review of *Family*, p. 24.
*Economist*, March 24, 1990, review of *Great Plains*, p. 96.
*English Journal*, January, 1999, Lewis Cobbs, review of *Great Plains*, p. 118.
*Entertainment Weekly*, November 11, 1994, Tom de Haven, review of *Family*, p. 67; January 27, 1995, "Ian Frazier: What I'm Reading," p. 43; February 4, 2000, review of *On the Rez*, p. 66; May 9, 2008, Gary Susman, review of *Lamentations of the Father: Essays*, p. 69.
*Interview*, May, 1996, John Howell, "What Is Ian Frazier?," author interview, p. 70.
*Kirkus Reviews*, February 1, 2002, review of *The Fish's Eye*, p. 157; October 1, 2005, review of *Gone to New York*, p. 1062; April 1, 2008, review of *Lamentations of the Father: Essays*.
*Library Journal*, January, 1986, Edward B. St. John, review of *Dating Your Mom*, p. 101; June 15, 1987, Jo Cates, review of *Nobody Better, Better than Nobody*, p. 70; October 15, 1994, Barbara Conaty, review of *Family*, p. 69; June 15, 1996, William Gargan, review of *Coyote v. Acme*, p. 65; November 15, 1999, Nathan Ward, review of *On the Rez*, p. 87; November 15, 2005, Anthony Pucci, review of *Gone to New York*, p. 67; March 15, 2008, Anthony Pucci, review of *Lamentations of the Father: Essays*, p. 72.
*Los Angeles Times Book Review*, August 31, 1986, Shelly Lowenkopf, review of *Dating Your Mom*, p. 5; November 27, 1994, review of *Family*, pp. 3, 12; June 1, 2008, Tim Rutten, review of *Lamentations of the Father: Essays*.
*Manhattan, Inc.*, April, 1989, Amy Virshup, review of *Great Plains*, p. 128.
*Mother Jones*, January, 2000, review of *On the Rez*, p. 88.
*National Review*, December 19, 1994, David Klinghoffer, review of *Family*, pp. 57-59.
*New Republic*, August 7, 1989, Sara Mosle, review of *Great Plains*, p. 39.
*New Statesman*, February 27, 1987, Nick Kimberley, review of *Dating Your Mom*, p. 30.
*Newsweek*, February 3, 1986, review of *Dating Your Mom*, p. 70; June 12, 1989, Laura Shapiro, review of *Great Plains*, p. 64; November 7, 1994, Malcolm Jones, Jr., review of *Family*, p. 73.
*New York*, January 13, 1986, Rhoda Koenig, review of *Dating Your Mom*, p. 52; November 21, 1994, Bob Ickes, review of *Family*, p. 50; January 3, 2000, Walter Kirn, review of *On the Rez*, p. 86.

*New Yorker,* December 18, 1989, review of *Great Plains,* p. 114; January 31, 2000, Scott L. Malcoms, review of *On the Rez,* p. 92.

*New York Review of Books,* February 10, 2000, Larry McMurtry, review of *On the Rez,* p. 26.

*New York Times,* December 23, 1985, review of *Dating Your Mom,* p. 15; April 16, 1987, Christopher Lehmann-Haupt, review of *Nobody Better, Better than Nobody,* p. 19; June 5, 1989, review of *Great Plains,* p. B2; November 21, 1994, review of *Family,* p. B2; June 20, 1996, Christopher Lehmann-Haupt, review of *Coyote v. Acme;* January 4, 2000, Michiko Kakutani, review of *On the Rez.*

*New York Times Book Review,* January 5, 1986, Mordecai Richler, review of *Dating Your Mom,* p. 5; January 25, 1987, Patricia T. O'Conner, review of *Dating Your Mom,* p. 32; May 3, 1987, Robert R. Harris, review of *Nobody Better, Better than Nobody,* p. 9; June 18, 1989, Sue Hubbell, review of *Great Plains,* p. 9; November 6, 1994, David Willis McCullough, review of *Family,* p. 9; June 23, 1996, James Gorman, review of *Coyote v. Acme,* p. 16; December 6, 1998, Bill Bryson, review of *Great Plains,* p. 10; January 16, 2000, Tracy Kidder, review of *On the Rez,* p. 6; April 7, 2002, Tyler D. Johnson, review of *The Fish's Eye,* p. 24.

*People,* February 3, 1986, Campbell Geelin, review of *Dating Your Mom,* p. 18; August 7, 1989, Michael Neill, "What's So Great about the Great Plains? Ian Frazier Took the Time to Find Out," p. 104; August 19, 1996, Peter Carlin, review of *Coyote v. Acme,* p. 34; January 31, 2000, review of *On the Rez,* p. 39.

*Publishers Weekly,* November 15, 1985, Genevieve Stuttaford, review of *Dating Your Mom,* p. 51; March 20, 1987, Genevieve Stuttaford, review of *Nobody Better, Better than Nobody,* p. 58; January 27, 1989, Genevieve Stuttaford, review of *Great Plains,* p. 462; August 29, 1994, review of *Family,* p. 58; November 14, 1994, "Ian Frazier: 'I Do Believe in Predestination,'" author interview, p. 49; March 25, 1996, review of *Coyote v. Acme,* p. 68; September 29, 1997, review of *The Best American Essays: 1997,* p. 72; December 20, 1999, review of *On the Rez,* p. 67; March 11, 2002, review of *The Fish's Eye,* p. 61; September 5, 2005, review of *Gone to New York,* p. 48; March 3, 2008, review of *Lamentations of the Father: Essays,* p. 41.

*San Francisco Chronicle,* October 24, 2010, Carmela Ciuraru, review of *Travels in Siberia.*

*School Library Journal,* February, 1999, review of *It Happened Like This: Stories and Poems,* p. 108.

*Seattle Times,* April 19, 2002, Eric Sorensen, "Ian Frazier's *The Fish's Eye:* Hooking into a Dream," p. 20.

*Texas Monthly,* July, 1989, Suzanne Winckler, review of *Great Plains,* p. 109.

*Time,* March 3, 1986, Paul Gray, review of *Dating Your Mom,* p. 75; May 25, 1987, Paul Gray, review of *Nobody Better, Better than Nobody,* p. 67; June 5, 1989, John Skow, review of *Great Plains,* p. 64; October 31, 1994, review of *Family,* p. 86; January 24, 2000, Paul Gray, review of *On the Rez,* p. 74; "*PW* Talks with Ian Frazier," p. 67.

*Tribune Books* (Chicago, IL), July 5, 1987, review of *Nobody Better, Better than Nobody,* p. 3; May 28, 1989, review of *Great Plains,* p. 4; November 13, 1994, review of *Family,* p. 5.

*U.S. News & World Report,* September 25, 1989, Miriam Horn, "Our Imaginary Plains: A New Breed of Writers Advances a Darker Vision West," p. 51.

*Village Voice Literary Supplement,* October, 1994, review of *Family,* p. 23.

*Vogue,* January, 1986, Tracy Young, review of *Dating Your Mom,* p. 120.

*Washington Monthly,* January, 2000, Christine Gray, review of *On the Rez,* p. 52.


ONLINE

*AD2000,* http://www.ad2000.com.au/ (January 15, 2008), Mary-Jane Donnellan, review of *Lamentations of the Father: Essays.*

*Bookslut,* http://www.bookslut.com/ (August 8, 2011), Janet Potter, review of *Travels in Siberia.*

*Salon.com,* http://www.salon.com/ (February 1, 2000), Craig Seligman, "From the *New Yorker* to the Rez."*

# Robert Eric Frykenberg

## 1930-

■ **Also Known As**

Robert E. Frykenberg

■ **Personal**

Born June 8, 1930, in Ootacamund, India; son of American missionaries, C. Eric and Doris Frykenberg; married Carol Addington, July 1, 1952; children: Ann, Brian, Craig. *Education:* Bethel College and Seminary, St. Paul, MN, B.A., 1951, B.D., 1954; University of Minnesota, M.A., 1953; University of California, Berkeley, graduate study, 1954-58; School of Oriental and African Studies, London, Ph.D., 1961.

■ **Addresses**

*Home*—Madison, WI. *Office*—University of Wisconsin—Madison, Department of History, 3211 Mosse Humanities Bldg., 455 N. Park St., Madison, WI 53706-1483. *E-mail*—refryken@wisc.edu.

■ **Career**

Writer, educator, historian. Oakland City College, Oakland, CA, instructor in political science and history, 1957-58; University of Chicago, Chicago, IL, visiting assistant professor of Indian history, 1961-62; University of Wisconsin—Madison, assistant professor, 1962-67, associate professor, 1967-70, professor of history and South Asian studies, 1971-98; professor emeritus of history and South Asian studies, 1998—; chair of department of South Asian studies, and director of Centre for South Asian Studies, 1970-73; University of Edinburgh, *History of*

*Christian Missions,* cogeneral editor, 1997—. Lecturer for National Council of Churches (ten lectures) at Drexel University and University of Hawaii, both summer, 1968; teacher, Peace Corps, 1964. South Asian Microform Project, founder and director, 1962-66, and in conferences and seminars in Poona and New Delhi, Hong Kong, Tokyo, Kuala Lumpur, Hyderabad, Madras, London, and Paris.

■ **Member**

American Historical Association, Association for Asian Studies, Royal Asiatic Society (fellow), Royal Historical Society (fellow), Institute for Asian Studies (India), Institute of Historical Studies (fellow; India), International Association of Tamil Research, South India Society, India International Centre.

■ **Awards, Honors**

Rockefeller Foundation fellow, 1958-61; Carnegie and Ford Foundation fellowships, 1962-63; American Council of Learned Societies-Social Science Research Council fellow, 1963, 1967, 1973; Fulbright fellow, 1965-66; Guggenheim fellow, 1968-69; National Endowment for the Humanities fellow, 1975; AIIS Senior Research Fellow in India, 1987-88; Rockefeller Scholar in Residence, Rockefeller Foundation's Bellagio Study Center, 1988; fellow, Woodrow Wilson International Center for Scholars, 1992; presenter, Radhakrishnan Memorial Lectures, Oxford University, 1998; presenter, Becker Memorial Lecture, University of Northern Iowa, 1998; presenter, Harshbarger Lecture, Penn State University, 2008; Murdoch University International Scholar for 2009.

# ■ Writings

*Guntur District, 1788-1848: A History of Local Influence and Central Authority in South India*, Clarendon Press (London, England), 1965.

*Today's World in Focus: India* (textbook), Ginn (Boston, MA), 1968.

(Editor and contributor) *Land Control and Social Structure in Indian History*, University of Wisconsin Press (Madison, WI), 1969.

(Contributor) *European History in World Perspective*, Heath (London, England), 1975.

(Editor and contributor) *Land Tenure and Peasant in South Asia*, Wisconsin Land Tenure Center (Madison, WI), 1976.

(Editor and contributor) *India's Imperial Tradition*, Indo-British Historical Society (Madras), 1976.

(Editor, with Pauline Kolenda) *Studies of South India: An Anthology of Recent Research and Scholarship*, New Era Publications (Madrid, Spain), 1985.

(Editor) *Delhi Through the Ages: Essays in Urban History, Culture, and Society*, Oxford University Press (New York, NY), 1986.

*History and Belief: The Foundations of Historical Understanding*, Eerdmans (Grand Rapids, MI), 1996.

(Editor, with Judith M. Brown) *Christians, Cultural Interactions, and India's Religious Traditions*, W.B. Eerdmans (Grand Rapids, MI), 2002.

(Editor, and author of biographical introduction) Pandita Ramabai Sarasvati, *Pandita Ramabai's America: Conditions of Life in the United States*, translated by Kshitija Gomes, William B. Eerdmans Pub. (Grand Rapids, MI), 2003.

(Editor, with Alaine Low) *Christians and Missionaries in India: Cross-Cultural Communication since 1500, with Special Reference to Caste, Conversion, and Colonialism*, W.B. Eerdmans Pub. (Grand Rapids, MI), 2003.

*Christianity in India: From Beginnings to the Present*, Oxford University Press (New York, NY), 2008.

Author of study guides; contributor of over sixty articles and reviews to professional journals and chapters to scholarly books.

# ■ Sidelights

Robert Eric Frykenberg is, according to *International Bulletin of Missionary Research* contributor Atul Y. Aghamkar, "a historian of high caliber who has contributed significantly toward a better understanding and interpretation of Christianity in India." An emeritus professor at the University of Wisconsin, Frykenberg devoted his professional career to the elucidation of the history of India in its agricultural, social, and religious aspects. The son of American missionaries, Frykenberg was born in India in 1930, earned his doctorate at the School of Oriental and African Studies in London, England, and spent almost all of his academic career at the University of Wisconsin—Madison, where he was a professor of history and South Asian studies. Frykenberg is the writer or editor of thirteen books, including *Christians, Cultural Interactions, and India's Religious Traditions, Pandita Ramabai's America: Conditions of Life in the United States, Christians and Missionaries in India: Cross-Cultural Communication since 1500, with Special Reference to Caste, Conversion, and Colonialism*, and the 2008 title, *Christianity in India: From Beginnings to the Present.*

### *Christians, Cultural Interactions, and India's Religious Traditions*

Frykenberg served as editor, along with Judith M. Brown, a history professor at Oxford University, on the 2002 work, *Christians, Cultural Interactions, and India's Religious Traditions*, a collection of essays that looks at the relationship in nineteenth-century India between Christians and adherents of other religions and sects. Writing in the *International Bulletin of Missionary Research* Roger E. Hedlund noted that the gathered writings examine "interactions of Christianity in India's modern history and indicate a considerable give-and-take between Christian faith and local cultures." The essays chosen by Frykenberg and Brown thus show the important role that Christianity has had throughout India's history, but especially in the nineteenth and twentieth centuries, when, under British rule, India was visited by a large number of Protestant missionaries. The growth of modern communication which occurred at the same time amplified the effect of these missionaries with all levels of society, from rich to poor. Some essays deal with the reaction of Muslim and Hindu leaders to the message of Christian missionaries, revamping their own religious rhetoric to show that their religions were the superior ones. Such revised thinking among both Muslim and Hindu thinkers had to do with the concept of the rise and fall of civilizations and with the idea of progress. Another essay deals with the Tamil poet Vedanayaka Sastri, who wrote verse celebrating the Tamil Evangelical tradition. Still other essays deal with Christian conversion and the Indian caste system and the challenges faced in translating the Bible into Indian languages, among other topics.

*Church History* contributor Chandra Mallampalli felt that this "volume's well-crafted and highly provocative essays cross the terrain of many disciplines," and that the "editors should be credited for producing a volume that highlights indigenous actors and agents in the story of Indian Christianity." Mallam-palli went on to observe: "[The essays] will be of great interest to those examining the history of religious apologetics, pluralism, conversion, and popular movements in South Asia. The volume also brings an important India component to the emerging scholarship on world Christianity." Similarly, Hedlund thought that *Christians, Cultural Interactions, and India's Religious Traditions* is "essential reading for anyone serious about knowing the place of Christianity in the history and development of India."

### Pandita Ramabai's America and Christians and Missionaries in India

Frykenberg again serves as editor, as well as the author of a biographical introduction, for *Pandita Ramabai's America.* Also known as Pandita Ramabai Sarasvati, she was a Christian convert from a well-placed Brahmin family. She was a late-nineteenth-century social reformer who campaigned widely for the emancipation of Indian women. In her writings Pandita Ramabai championed education for females and also shed light on darker aspects of the condition of women in India, from child brides to the practice of *sati,* or the immolation of a widow on the funeral pyre of her deceased spouse. She also traveled widely, both in England and the United States; *Pandita Ramabai's America* is the first English translation of her observations during the latter journey. She held up the relatively emancipated role of women in the United States at the time as a model for India, but she also had critical words for race relations in the United States. Writing in the *International Bulletin of Missionary Research,* Richard Fox Young felt that "Frykenberg's introduction rides his favorite historiographical hobbyhorses a bit hard," but also found that this translation is "lively."

Frykenberg also edited the 2003 collection of sixteen essays, *Christians and Missionaries in India,* a work that examines the "beginning, progress, and challenges of Christian cross-cultural communication in India," according to *International Bulletin of Missionary Research* reviewer Daniel Jeyaraj. Fourteen of the essays were written by Western academics and two by Indian. "With convincing examples these authors illustrate how Indian Christians have been interacting with Indian cultures, religions, languages, and people groups," observed Jeyaraj, who further termed the book a "remarkable volume."

### Christianity in India

Working on his own, Frykenberg produced a major study of the development of the Christian religion in India with his *Christianity in India.* The author begins his survey with the supposed arrival of the Apostle Thomas in India in 52 AD and the development of Thomas Christianity in South India. Frykenberg looks at further developments over the ages, including the introduction of Catholicism in the sixteenth and seventeenth centuries, as well as the rise of Protestantism during the British Raj. Much of the work focuses on developments in South India, a particular research specialty of the author. Frykenberg additionally demonstrates in this history how India reshaped Christianity, and how, Christianity, in turn, shaped India and Hinduism.

Arun W. Jones, writing in *Church History,* felt there was not a better person to assay such an overview, noting: "Prof. Frykenberg has been studying the religious and political history of India for approximately fifty years, and he would be one of a small group of scholars who could make a serious attempt at this possibly impossible endeavor." "Christian Century" contributor Philip Jenkins similarly noted: "Robert Frykenberg is a brave man. He attempts to trace the whole story of the Christian experience in India over a period of 1,900 years and through a vast territory that comprises many cultures and languages." In the event, Jenkins felt that the author "succeeds wonderfully, with a book that is richly informative on countless aspects of Indian history quite apart from its contributions to the study of Christianity." Further praise for *Christianity in India* came from *International Bulletin of Missionary Research* reviewer John C.B. Webster, who concluded: "This is the best single-volume history of Christianity in India written so far. It is both genuinely Indo-centric and genuinely ecumenical. Within its chapters are extensive illustrations of ways that Frykenberg's distinctive way of being Indo-centric . . . might be applied to regions and topics he did not cover. While written primarily for Westerners, it does provide Indian Christians with further evidence, in their current struggle with Hindutva propaganda, that Christianity is not a foreign religion."

### ■ Biographical And Critical Sources

*PERIODICALS*

*Christian Century,* May 5, 2009, Philip Jenkins, review of *Christianity in India: From Beginnings to the Present,* p. 43.

*Church History,* December, 2004, Chandra Mallampalli, review of *Christians, Cultural Interactions, and India's Religious Traditions,* p. 903; December, 2009, Arun W. Jones, review of *Christianity in India,* p. 947.

*International Bulletin of Missionary Research,* January, 2003, Roger E. Hedlund, review of *Christians, Cultural Interactions, and India's Religious Traditions,* p. 45; January, 2005, Daniel Jeyaraj, review of *Christians and Missionaries in India: Cross-Cultural Communication since 1500, with Special Reference to Caste, Conversion, and Colonialism,* p. 45; July, 2005, Richard Fox Young, review of *Pandita Ramabai's America: Conditions of Life in the United States,* p. 155; July, 2009, John C.B. Webster, review of *Christianity in India,* p. 155; July, 2010,

Atul Y. Aghamkar, "India and the Indianness of Christianity: Essays on Understanding—Historical, Theological, and Bibliographical—in Honor of Robert Eric Frykenberg," p. 184.

*ONLINE*

*University of Wisconsin—Madison, Department of History Web site,* http://history.wisc.edu/ (July 12, 2011), "Robert Eric Frykenberg."

# Gary W. Gallagher

## 1950-

### ■ Also Known As

Gary William Gallagher

### ■ Personal

Born October 8, 1950, in Glendale, CA; son of William (a farmer) and Shirley (a homemaker) Gallagher; children: William Paul. *Education:* Adams State College, B.A., 1972; University of Texas at Austin, M.A., 1977, Ph.D., 1982.

### ■ Addresses

*Office*—University of Virginia, Corcoran Department of History, 227 Randall Hall, Charlottesville, VA 22903-3284. *E-mail*—gallagher@virginia.edu.

### ■ Career

National Archives and Records Administration, Washington, DC, archivist at Lyndon Baines Johnson Library, 1977-86; Pennsylvania State University, University Park, assistant professor, 1986-89, associate professor, 1989-91, professor of history, 1991-98, head of department, 1991-95; University of Virginia, Charlottesville, professor of history, 1998-99, John L. Nau III Professor of the History of the American Civil War, 1999—.

University of Texas at Austin, visiting lecturer, 1986, George W. Littlefield lecturer, 1995-96; Organization of American Historians Lecturer, 2002—, Pennsylvania State University, Steven and Janice Brose Distinguished Lecturer in the Civil War Era, 2004; Gettysburg College, Robert Fortenbaugh Memorial

Lecturer, 2005; Huntington Library, scholar in residence, 2008. American Battlefield Protection Foundation, member of board of trustees, 1991—.

### ■ Member

Organization of American Historians, Society of Civil War Historians, Association for the Preservation of Civil War Sites (president, 1987-94, trustee, 1994-96), Southern Historical Association.

### ■ Awards, Honors

Grant, National Endowment for the Humanities, 1985; Mellon fellow, Virginia Historical Society, 1988 and 1989; grant, American Council of Learned Societies, 1989-90; Daniel Harvey Hill Award, 1990; Douglas Southall Freeman Prize, 1990, and Founder's Award, 1991, both for *Fighting for the Confederacy;* Nevins-Freeman Award, 1991; Society of American Historians citation, 1996; Fletcher Pratt Award, 1998; distinguished fellow at Huntington Library, Times-Mirror Foundation, 2001-02; Cavaliers' Distinguished Teaching Professorship, University of Virginia, 2010.

### ■ Writings

*Stephen Dodson Ramseur: Lee's Gallant General,* University of North Carolina Press (Chapel Hill, NC), 1985.

*Jubal A. Early, the Lost Cause, and Civil War History: A Persistent Legacy,* Marquette University Press (Milwaukee, WI), 1995.

*The Confederate War: How Popular Will, Nationalism, and Military Strategy Could Not Stave Off Defeat,* Harvard University Press (Cambridge, MA), 1997.

*Lee and His Generals in War and Memory,* Louisiana State University Press (Baton Rouge, LA), 1998.

*Lee and His Army in Confederate History,* University of North Carolina Press (Chapel Hill, NC), 2001.

*The American Civil War: The War in the East, 1861-May 1863,* Fitzroy Dearborn Publishers (Chicago, IL), 2001.

*Causes Won, Lost, and Forgotten: How Hollywood and Popular Art Shape What We Know about the Civil War,* University of North Carolina Press (Chapel Hill, NC), 2008.

(Author of foreword) *The Civil War: A History,* New American Library (New York, NY), 2010.

*The Union War,* Harvard University Press (Cambridge, MA), 2011.

### EDITOR

*Fighting for the Confederacy: The Personal Recollections of General Edward Porter Alexander,* University of North Carolina Press (Chapel Hill, NC), 1989.

(With Margaret E. Wagner and Paul Finkelman) *The Library of Congress Civil War Desk Reference,* Simon & Schuster (New York, NY), 2002.

(With Joseph T. Glatthaar) *Leaders of the Lost Cause: New Perspectives on the Confederate High Command,* Stackpole Books (Mechanicsburg, PA), 2004.

*Two Witnesses at Gettysburg: The Personal Accounts of Whitelaw Reid and A.J.L. Fremantle,* Wiley-Blackwell (Malden, MA), 2009.

(With Alan T. Nolan) *The Myth of the Lost Cause and Civil War History,* Indiana University Press (Bloomington, IN), 2010.

(With Robert O'Neill) *The Civil War: Bull Run and Other Eastern Battles, 1861-May 1863,* Rosen (New York, NY), 2011.

### EDITOR AND CONTRIBUTOR

*Essays on Southern History: Written in Honor of Barnes F. Lathrop,* General Libraries, University of Texas at Austin (Austin, TX), 1980.

*Antietam: Essays on the 1862 Maryland Campaign,* Kent State University Press (Kent, OH), 1989.

*Struggle for the Shenandoah: Essays on the 1864 Valley Campaign,* Kent State University Press (Kent, OH), 1991.

*The First Day at Gettysburg: Essays on Confederate and Union Leadership,* Kent State University Press (Kent, OH), 1992.

*The Second Day at Gettysburg: Essays on Confederate and Union Leadership,* Kent State University Press (Kent, OH), 1993.

*The Third Day at Gettysburg and Beyond,* University of North Carolina Press (Chapel Hill, NC), 1994.

*The Fredericksburg Campaign: Decision on the Rappahannock,* University of North Carolina Press (Chapel Hill, NC), 1995.

*Lee the Soldier,* University of Nebraska Press (Lincoln, NE), 1996.

*Chancellorsville: The Battle and Its Aftermath,* University of North Carolina Press (Chapel Hill, NC), 1996.

*The Wilderness Campaign,* University of North Carolina Press (Chapel Hill, NC), 1997.

*The Spotsylvania Campaign,* University of North Carolina Press (Chapel Hill, NC), 1998.

*The Antietam Campaign,* University of North Carolina Press (Chapel Hill, NC), 1999.

*Three Days at Gettysburg: Essays on Confederate and Union Leadership,* Kent State University Press (Kent, OH), 1999.

(With Alan T. Nolan) *The Myth of the Lost Cause and Civil War History,* Indiana University Press (Bloomington, IN), 2001.

*The Richmond Campaign of 1862: The Peninsula and the Seven Days,* University of North Carolina Press (Chapel Hill, NC), 2002.

*The Shenandoah Valley Campaign of 1862,* University of North Carolina Press (Chapel Hill, NC), 2003.

*The Shenandoah Valley Campaign of 1864,* University of North Carolina Press (Chapel Hill, NC), 2006.

(With Edward L. Ayers and Andrew J. Torget) *Crucible of the Civil War: Virginia from Secession to Commemoration,* University of Virginia Press (Charlottesville, VA), 2006.

(With Joan Waugh) *Wars within a War: Controversy and Conflict over the American Civil War,* University of North Carolina Press (Chapel Hill, NC), 2009.

Editor, *"Civil War America,"* series, University of North Carolina Press, 1993—; editor, *"Military Campaigns of the Civil War"* series, University of North Carolina Press, 1994—; coeditor, *"American Civil War Classics"* series, University of South Carolina Press, 2001-05; coeditor, *"The Littlefield History of the Civil War Era,"* series, University of North Carolina Press, 2008—. Work represented in anthologies, including *The Civil War Battlefield Guide,* edited by Frances H. Kennedy, Houghton Mifflin, 1990; *The Confederate General,* edited by William C. Davis, six volumes, National Historical Society, beginning 1991; *Why the Confederacy Lost,* edited by Gabor S. Boritt, Oxford University Press, 1991; *Ken Burns's "The Civil War": Historians Respond,* edited by Robert Brent Toplin, Oxford University Press, 1996; *New Perspectives on the Civil War: Myths and Realities of the National Conflict,* edited by John Y. Simon and Michael E. Stevens, Madison House, 1998; and *Writing the Civil War: The Quest to Understand,* edited by James M. McPherson and William J. Cooper, Jr.,

University of South Carolina Press, 1998. Contributor of articles and reviews to history and military journals.

## ■ Sidelights

Gary W. Gallagher is a prolific and prominent historian of the U.S. Civil War, dealing with both the actual events of the war and the mythology that has developed around them. *Chicago Tribune* contributor James A. Ramage has described Gallagher as "one of today's foremost Civil War historians," and *Washington Times* commentator Mackubin Thomas Owens has called him "one of the best of a new generation of Civil War scholars." His work, as both writer and editor, has emphasized the importance of military history at a time when it had fallen out of favor among some academics. He has chronicled many of the major campaigns of the war's eastern theater, dissected both romantic and revisionist views of the Confederacy, and scrutinized the generalship and postwar reputation of Southern commander Robert E. Lee.

### Early Nonfiction

In *The Confederate War: How Popular Will, Nationalism, and Military Strategy Could Not Stave Off Defeat,* Gallagher disputes the idea held by many late-twentieth-century historians that the Southern war effort was fatally undermined by dissension within the Confederacy, including resentment of economic inequities, distrust of centralized government, and perhaps an unconscious distaste for defending the institution of slavery. On the contrary, he asserts, there was deep and wide support for the war; more than three-quarters of Southern white men of military age served in the army, as opposed to half of the North's available fighters, and civilians had great loyalty to their young country and reverence for Lee. It was only the North's greater military might, not any lack of Southern resolve, that brought the Union victory, he contends. He draws on hundreds of Civil War letters and diary entries to provide examples of this resolve.

Gallagher "argues that the current emphasis on class, race and gender on the home front exaggerates tensions in Southern society and distorts the picture," related Ramage in the *Chicago Tribune*. His case, Ramage added, is "well-organized and well-presented." Jonathan Yardley, writing in the *Washington Post Book World,* deemed Gallagher's evidence "impressive if limited," but thought the author failed to address "a central and well-founded tenet

of the conventional wisdom: that the South was doomed from the outset by an agrarian economy" with little heavy industry. Yardley allowed, however, that the South "prolonged the conflict to an almost unimaginable extent precisely for the reasons Gallagher cites: its puissant nationalism, its devotion to its 'cause,' the genius of its chief military leaders and the dogged bravery of its soldiers." *Civil War History* reviewer Christopher Phillips described *The Confederate War* as "an extremely satisfying book" that demonstrates the importance of studying military history, and Ramage concluded that Gallagher's "bold revisions make this one of the most significant works in this generation of Civil War literature."

Gallagher returns to this theme in *Lee and His Army in Confederate History,* a collection of essays on the Southern military leader and key battles. "Gallagher revives the overwhelming numbers and resources explanation for Confederate defeat, shorn of its false aura of inevitability," commented James M. McPherson in the *New York Review of Books.* McPherson continued that Gallagher argues "forcefully and convincingly" that the South's "white unity and strength of purpose," even with its army outnumbered and outgunned, made it a tenacious foe for the Union throughout the conflict.

### Later Nonfiction

In *Lee and His Generals in War and Memory,* Gallagher makes a "persuasive" case that Lee himself was "a significant factor in prolonging the life of the Confederacy," observed Joseph L. Harsh in *Civil War History.* This book, according to *Washington Times* contributor Owens, "provides a balanced assessment of Lee the soldier—avoiding the dual pitfalls of Lost Cause hagiography and the Lee bashing that too often characterizes the work of revisionists." Gallagher's work, Owens continued, offers a picture of "Lee's great qualities, including most of all his ability to compensate for weak subordinates," as well as discussion of instances where his strategies went wrong, such as at Gettysburg.

Gallagher devotes space to several of Lee's subordinate commanders, both the weak and the strong, and shows how one of them, Jubal A. Early, helped develop and popularize the romanticized "lost cause" view of the Confederacy. Early crafted "for future generations a written record that celebrated the Confederacy's hopeless but heroic military resistance against the overwhelming power of the Union," Owens remarked. This view also idealized Lee, downplayed slavery, and portrayed the South as fighting primarily for independence. It gained many adherents in the late nineteenth century and far into the twentieth, even though modern academic historians have put forth some decidedly different views. "Gallagher illustrates how even today, the Lost Cause interpretation dominates both historiography and popular images of the war," commented Owens. Willard Carl Klunder, reviewing the book in the *Historian,* noted that Gallagher "cogently argues that the romantic image of the 'Lost Cause' is based as much on perception as fact." *Lee and His Generals in War and Memory,* Klunder added, "augments Gallagher's reputation as a thoughtful interpreter of Civil War military history."

Gallagher revisits Lee in his next volume, *Lee and His Army in Confederate History,* and he continues to address the Civil war in such books as *The American Civil War: The War in the East, 1861-May 1863, Causes Won, Lost, and Forgotten: How Hollywood and Popular Art Shape What We Know about the Civil War,* and *The Union War.* In the latter, a companion volume to *The Confederate War,* Gallagher argues that the Civil War was not fought over slavery but to keep the Southern states from seceding. The author draws on pertinent letters and documents to support his claims. He notes that Americans in the North and West were devoted to the Union and felt that slavery undermined the United States and democracy. In fact, Gallagher finds that slavery was largely abolished to chastise the Southern states for attempting to secede. "Gallagher offers not so much a history of wartime patriotism as a series of meditations on the meaning of the Union to Northerners, the role of slavery in the conflict and how historians have interpreted (and in his view misinterpreted) these matters," Eric Foner observed in the *New York Times Book Review.* However, the critic complained that "Gallagher devotes many pages—too many in a book of modest length—to critiques of recent Civil War scholars, whom he accuses of exaggerating the importance of slavery in the conflict and the contribution of black soldiers to Union victory. Often, his complaint seems to be that another historian did not write the book he would have written."

A more evenhanded assessment of *The Union War* was given by an online *Soldier Voices* critic, who commented: "My hope is that Gallagher's book expands the discussion to once again include those patriotic and 'exceptionalism' aspects of motivation for Northern soldiers. Certainly we must continue to discuss the role of race and slavery, but it is not the be all or end all." Yardley, writing again in *Washington Post Book World,* called *The Union War* an "exceptionally fine book." Explaining this assertion, Yardley pointed out: "Gallagher . . . is far more interested in pursuing historical truth than in mas-

saging whatever praiseworthy sentiments he may harbor on race, gender, class or anything else. He knows that for the historian the central obligation is to understand and interpret the past, not to judge it. This is what he has done, to exemplary effect." The reviewer concluded: "I suspect that one of his motives in writing it may have been to remind us of what a precious thing our Union is, a Union that we have come to take for granted. Fighting for its preservation was a noble thing, in and of itself."

## Edited Works

*The Myth of the Lost Cause and Civil War History,* which Gallagher edited with Alan T. Nolan, further addresses the growth and persistence of the "lost cause" viewpoint, with Gallagher contributing an essay on Early's role. Gallagher's work as an editor and contributor to volumes of essays also includes anthologies on Lee and on major battles including Gettysburg, Antietam, Fredericksburg, Chancellorsville, Spotsylvania, and the Virginia Peninsula campaign. Critiquing *The Richmond Campaign of 1862: The Peninsula and the Seven Days* in *Civil War History,* Richard J. Sommers praised Gallagher's "graceful and learned editorship." *The Spotsylvania Campaign,* George C. Rable wrote in *History: Review of New Books,* is "a fine piece of work," gathering varied perspectives and challenging conventional viewpoints. In *Chancellorsville: The Battle and Its Aftermath,* with historians emphasizing new interpretations and including firsthand observations from, among others, children and military doctors, Gallagher "has again shown why he is a master editor-historian," in the opinion of *Civil War History* contributor Ervin L. Jordan, Jr. With both his writing and editing work, Phillips reported in that same journal, Gallagher "has become one of the most well-regarded of our Civil War scholars."

In *The Shenandoah Valley Campaign of 1862* and *The Shenandoah Valley Campaign of 1864* Gallagher has edited and contributed to two volumes on key Civil War campaigns. The former book focuses on the Union Army of the Potomac, led by General George B. McClellan, and its attempts to take the Shenandoah Valley. It then details General Thomas Jonathan Jackson's attempts to hold the valley with only 4,000 soldiers. According to *Journal of Southern History* reviewer Archie P. McDonald, *The Shenandoah Valley Campaign of 1862* is "one of the most interesting volumes for readers whose Civil War focus is on General Thomas Jonathan Jackson." Charles M. Dobbs, writing in *Canadian Journal of History,* was also impressed, stating that the book "will interest both the knowledgeable and casual reader, the dedicated military scholar and more general reader alike." Dobbs went on to note: "Each of the articles is well researched and interestingly written. Because the articles cover a range of topics, different articles will appeal to different readers. While military historians might not approve the mix of articles, these articles help provide a more complete view of a campaign that really needs its own detailed monographic study."

# ■ Biographical And Critical Sources

## PERIODICALS

*America's Civil War*, March 1, 2010, Gordon Berg, review of *Wars within a War: Controversy and Conflict over the American Civil War*, p. 68.

*Armor*, May 1, 2007, Philip L. Bolte, review of *Leaders of the Lost Cause: New Perspectives on the Confederate High Command*.

*Booklist*, October 15, 2000, Jay Freeman, review of *The Myth of the Lost Cause and Civil War History*, p. 415.

*Canadian Journal of History*, August 1, 2004, Charles M. Dobbs, review of *The Shenandoah Valley Campaign of 1862*, p. 394; December 22, 2008, Theodore W. Eversole, review of *Causes Won, Lost, and Forgotten: How Hollywood and Popular Art Shape What We Know about the Civil War*, p. 573.

*Chicago Tribune*, October 1, 1997, James A. Ramage, "A Well-Reasoned View of What Kept the South Going," Tempo section, p. 3.

*Civil War History*, September, 1997, Ervin L. Jordan, Jr., review of *Chancellorsville: The Battle and Its Aftermath*, pp. 250-251; March, 1998, Arthur W. Bergeron, Jr., review of *The Wilderness Campaign*, p. 62; September, 1998, Christopher Phillips, review of *The Confederate War: How Popular Will, Nationalism, and Military Strategy Could Not Stave Off Defeat*, p. 221; June, 1999, Joseph M. Priest, review of *The Spotsylvania Campaign*, p. 163; September 1, 1999, Joseph L. Harsh, review of *Lee and His Generals in War and Memory*, p. 271; December 1, 1999, Arthur W. Bergeron, Jr., review of *The Antietam Campaign*, p. 357, Jeffry D. Wert, review of *Three Days at Gettysburg: Essays on Confederate and Union Leadership*, p. 363; December 1, 2001, James Tice Moore, review of *The Myth of the Lost Cause and Civil War History*, p. 354; June, 2002, Richard J. Sommers, review of *The Richmond Campaign of 1862: The Peninsula and the Seven Days*, p. 172.

*Historian*, spring, 2000, Willard Carl Klunder, review of *Lee and His Generals in War and Memory*, p. 655; fall, 2000, Daniel E. Sutherland, review of *The Antietam Campaign*, p. 148; September 22, 2007, Charles D. Grear, review of *The Shenandoah Valley Campaign of 1864*, p. 538.

*History: Review of New Books*, spring, 1999, George C. Rable, review of *The Spotsylvania Campaign*, p. 105; June 22, 2007, Daniel E. Sutherland, review of *Crucible of the Civil War: Virginia from Secession to Commemoration*, p. 135.

*Journal of Southern History*, May, 2002, James M. Morris, review of *The Richmond Campaign of 1862*, p. 575; August 1, 2004, Archie P. McDonald, review of *The Shenandoah Valley Campaign of 1862*, p. 685; November 1, 2007, W. Eric Emerson, review of *The Shenandoah Valley Campaign of 1864*, p. 923; February 1, 2008, Martin Crawford, review of *Crucible of the Civil War*, p. 190; February 1, 2011, Robert Cook, review of *Wars within a War*, p. 183.

*Library Journal*, June 15, 1998, Brooks D. Simpson, review of *Lee and His Generals in War and Memory*, p. 91; October 15, 2000, Jim Doyle, review of *The Myth of the Lost Cause and Civil War History*, p. 84.

*New York Review of Books*, June 13, 2001, James M. McPherson, "Could the South Have Won?," pp. 23-25.

*New York Times Book Review*, April 29, 2011, Eric Foner, review of *The Union War*.

*Washington Post Book World*, September 24, 1997, Jonathan Yardley, "A New Perspective on a Lost Cause," p. D2; April 16, 2011 Jonathan Yardley, review of *The Union War*.

*Washington Times*, September 27, 1997, Kevin Levin, "'Lack of Will' Theory Takes a Beating," p. B3; December 16, 2000, Kevin Levin, "Finding the Truth about 'Lost Cause,'" p. B3; September 25, 1999, Mackubin Thomas Owens, "Lee, Flaws and Genius Intact," p. B3.

## ONLINE

*Soldier Voices*, http://www.soldierstudies.org/ (May 22, 2011), review of *The Union War*.

University of Virginia Web site, http://www.virginia.edu/ (August 12, 2011), author profile.*

# Steven M. Gelber

## 1943-

### ■ Also Known As

Steven Michael Gelber

### ■ Personal

Born February 21, 1943, in New York, NY; son of Leonard (a high school principal) and Edith Gelber; married Hester Goodenough, June 18, 1965 (marriage ended); married Catherine Bell (a professor of religious studies; died, 2007); children: (first marriage) Gideon. *Education:* Cornell University, B.S., 1965; University of Wisconsin—Madison, M.S., 1967, Ph.D., 1972.

### ■ Addresses

*Home*—San Jose, CA 95117.

### ■ Career

Writer, historian, educator. University of Santa Clara, Santa Clara, CA, assistant professor of history and professor of history, 1969-2009. Member of Santa Clara Bicentennial Committee, 1973-74.

### ■ Member

American Historical Association, Organization of American Historians.

### ■ Awards, Honors

National Endowment for the Humanities grant, 1973-74.

### ■ Writings

*Business Ideology and Black Employment: A Case Study in Cultural Adaptation,* Addison-Wesley (Reading, MA), 1973.

*Black Men and Businessmen: The Growing Awareness of a Social Responsibility,* Kennikat (Foster, RI), 1974.

(With Martin L. Cook) *Saving the Earth: The History of a Middle-Class Millenarian Movement,* University of California (Berkeley, CA), 1990.

*Hobbies: Leisure and the Culture of Work in America,* Columbia University Press (New York, NY), 1999.

*Horse Trading in the Age of Cars: Men in the Marketplace,* Johns Hopkins University Press (Baltimore, MD), 2008.

### ■ Sidelights

Steven M. Gelber was a professor of history at California's University of Santa Clara from 1969 to his retirement in 2009. His research and writing has dealt with aspects of business and leisure in American life, from African Americans in the business world to automobile sales and hobbies.

#### *Hobbies*

Gelber's 1999 title, *Hobbies: Leisure and the Culture of Work in America,* utilizes a wide array of research, from popular magazines to newspaper articles and how-to books, to examine the rise of hobbies in nineteenth-century America, a "middle ground between work and leisure," as Daniel J. Walkowitz noted in the *Journal of Social History.* Focusing on collecting and crafts, Gelber traces the rise of hobbies, noting that after the 1880s these activities appeared to be less a matter of obsession and more a constructive use of leisure time. Thus hobbies became a sort of hidden or disguised leisure, an acceptable activity in the America of growth capitalism and the work ethic where idleness was distrusted. For advocates of such beliefs, hobbies became an acceptable use of one's spare time. As Gelber notes, hobbies were both an extension of the work ethic after hours and a venue for relief and release from the tedium of the workplace. Gelber also looks at the gendered nature of hobbies, noting that while men generally preferred the use of tools in crafts, women generally became involved in needlework. In collecting, though women did participate in certain aspects, it was by and large men who collected stamps and coins, hobbies with a potential lucrative value. During the Depression, the author also notes, crafts gave unemployed men a means to feel useful and productive, which ultimately led, as Gelber notes in the book, to an area of "domestic masculinity," with workshops in basements. The rise of hobbies in the nineteenth century led directly, as Gelber shows, to the do-it-yourself culture of the twentieth and twenty-first centuries.

Walkowitz termed Gelber's book a "very serious and sophisticated history of crafts and hobbies in America," noting that it is not only a "a trip down a memory lane, first of collecting—stamps, coins, picture cards, dolls, and so forth—and, then, of hobbies such as embroidery for girls or modeling for boys," but it also "illuminates the reorganization of social space in which they took place and the changing gendered character of hobbies and crafts." Walkowitz concluded: "*Hobbies* will not be the last word on this subject; it will, however, be the starting point for future work. Provocative, entertaining, even personally disquieting, it deserves a wide readership." Similar praise came from *American Historical Review* contributor Cindy S. Aron, who felt that this is a "closely analyzed and well-researched book [that] explains that hobbies served-important functions for an industrializing, capitalist economy." Aron further noted of *Hobbies:* "Gelber takes an unusual and little studied topic—the history of hobbies—and shows us its depth, its breadth, and its importance. This is a fine book, one that reminds us that the study of leisure is also the study of work, gender, and culture."

### Horse Trading in the Age of Cars

With his 2008 work, *Horse Trading in the Age of Cars: Men in the Marketplace,* Gelber examines the continuity between horse trading and the buying and selling of cars. Haggling between men was the preferred method of negotiating the sale of a horse, and with the advent of a new form of transportation, the automobile, the same business model ap-

plied to its sales. This happened, Gelber shows in his study, despite the fact that at the same time, fixed prices were being instituted with other mass-produced goods sold in department stores. As Clay McShane noted in the *Journal of Social History,* Gelber argues that this happened because the car "filled the role of the horse." McShane added: "As Gelber points out, bargaining over such animals was asymmetric. Invariably sellers knew more than buyers. . . . In modern car-buying the same asymmetry remains, especially over the crucial issue of price, often played out over the issue of trade-in value." Aspects such as male rivalry and truth-stretching, common practice in horse trading, thus also became enshrined in the sales of cars, and they have endured to contemporary times.

McShane had praise for Gelber's book, noting that it is "praiseworthy because it avoids the kind of temporal parochialism that characterizes so many contemporary monographs, covering the entire automobile age." Further praise came from *Historian* reviewer Eric J. Morser, who called the study "an original work that accomplishes something admirable." Morser added: "It sheds important light on how gender shaped a familiar aspect of American life while offering modern-day readers a cautionary manual on how to survive an often unnerving national rite of passage: their first tentative journey to the automobile sales lot." Similarly, *Business History Review* contributor Thomas A. Kinney termed *Horse Trading in the Age of Cars* an "intriguing account," and a reviewer for *SciTech Book News* found it an "occasionally humorous but serious look" at the business of buying and selling cars.

### ■ Biographical And Critical Sources

*PERIODICALS*

*American Historical Review,* June, 2001, Cindy S. Aron, review of *Hobbies: Leisure and the Culture of Work in America,* p. 1002.

*Business History Review,* spring, 2010, Thomas A. Kinney, review of *Horse Trading in the Age of Cars: Men in the Marketplace,* pp. 179-181.

*Historian,* winter, 2010, Eric J. Morser, review of *Horse Trading in the Age of Cars,* p. 921.

*Journal of Social History,* fall, 2001, Daniel J. Walkowitz, review of *Hobbies,* p. 205; spring, 2010, Clay McShane, review of *Horse Trading in the Age of Cars,* p. 757.

*SciTech Book News,* June 1, 2009, review of *Horse Trading in the Age of Cars.*

*ONLINE*

*Santa Clara University, Department of History Web site,* http://www.scu.edu/ (March 7, 2011), "Steven Gelber."*

# Todd Gitlin

## 1943-

### ■ Personal

Born January 6, 1943, in New York, NY; son of Max (a teacher) and Dorothy (a teacher) Gitlin; married Laurel Cook, November 3, 1995; stepchildren: Shoshana, Justin, Fletcher. *Education:* Harvard University, B.A., 1963; University of Michigan, M.A., 1966; University of California, Berkeley, Ph.D., 1977.

### ■ Addresses

*Home*—New York, NY. *Office*—Columbia University Graduate School of Journalism, 2950 Broadway, New York, NY 10027. *Agent*—Ellen Levine, Trident Media Group, 41 Madison Ave., 36th Fl., New York, NY 10010. *E-mail*—toddgitlin@toddgitlin.net.

### ■ Career

Writer, educator, journalist, sociologist. *San Francisco Express Times*, San Francisco, CA, writer, 1968-69; San Jose State College (now University), San Jose, CA, lecturer, 1970-76; University of California, Santa Cruz, lecturer, 1974-77; University of California, Berkeley, assistant professor, 1978-83, associate professor, 1983-87, professor of sociology and director of mass communications program, 1987-95; New York University, New York, NY, professor of culture and communication, journalism, and sociology, 1995-2002; Columbia University, New York, NY, professor of journalism and sociology, chair of the Ph.D. program in Communications, 2002—. Holder of Chair in American Civilization, Ecole des Hautes Etudes en Sciences Sociales, French-American Foundation, Paris, 1994-95; visiting professor of political science, Yale University, 2000. Also visiting professor at University of Oslo, the University of Toronto, East China Normal University in Shanghai, the Institut Superieur des Langues de Tunis in Tunisia, and the American University of Cairo.

### ■ Member

PEN American Center (cochair of San Francisco branch, 1987-88).

### ■ Awards, Honors

Anne Parsons Educational Trust grant, 1962; Laras Fund grant, 1976; National Endowment for the Humanities grant, 1981; Rockefeller Foundation fellowship, 1981; nonfiction award, Bay Area Book Reviewers Association, 1984, for *Inside Prime Time*; finalist, Robert F. Kennedy Book Award and Bay Area Book Reviewers Association, 1988, for *The Sixties*; grant for research and writing in international peace and security, MacArthur Foundation, 1988-89; fellowship, Media Studies Center, 1998-99; Harold U. Ribalow Prize, 2000, for *Sacrifice*; Bosch Fellow in Public Policy, American Academy in Berlin; fellow, Media Studies Center, New York, NY.

### ■ Writings

(With Nanci Hollander) *Uptown: Poor Whites in Chicago,* Harper (New York, NY), 1970.

(Editor) *Campfires of the Resistance: Poetry from the Movement,* Bobbs-Merrill (New York, NY), 1971.

*Busy Being Born* (poems), Straight Arrow Books (New York, NY), 1974.

*The Whole World Is Watching: Mass Media in the Making and Unmaking of the New Left*, University of California Press (Berkeley, CA), 1980.

*Inside Prime Time*, Pantheon (New York, NY), 1983, revised edition, 1994, republished with new introduction, University of California Press (Berkeley, CA), 2000.

(Editor and contributor) *Watching Television*, Pantheon (New York, NY), 1987.

*The Sixties: Years of Hope, Days of Rage*, Bantam (New York, NY), 1987.

*The Murder of Albert Einstein* (novel), Farrar, Straus (New York, NY), 1992.

*The Twilight of Common Dreams: Why America Is Wracked by Culture Wars*, Metropolitan/Henry Holt (New York, NY), 1995.

*Sacrifice* (novel), Metropolitan Books (New York, NY), 1999.

*Media Unlimited: How the Torrent of Images and Sounds Overwhelms Our Lives*, Metropolitan (New York, NY), 2001.

*Letters to a Young Activist*, Basic Books (New York, NY), 2003.

*The Intellectuals and the Flag*, Columbia University Press (New York, NY), 2006.

*The Bulldozer and the Big Tent: Blind Republicans, Lame Democrats, and the Recovery of American Ideals*, John Wiley & Sons (Hoboken, NJ), 2007.

(With Liel Leibovitz) *The Chosen Peoples: America, Israel, and the Ordeals of Divine Election*, Simon & Schuster (New York, NY), 2010.

*Undying* (novel), Counterpoint Press (Berkeley, CA), 2011.

Contributor to numerous books. Columnist, *New York Observer*, 1992-99. Contributor to periodicals, including *Harper's, New York Times, Washington Post, Theory and Society, American Journalism Review, World Policy Journal, New Republic, Boston Globe, Dissent, San Francisco Examiner, American Journalism Review, Columbia Journalism Review,* and *Yale Review*. Member of editorial board, *Dissent*.

## ■ Sidelights

Todd Gitlin's writing explores myriad interconnected facets of contemporary life, including the way mass media affects society and vice versa, historical analysis of the recent past, and the changing state of American politics. He is the author or editor of three notable books of the 1980s on mass media: *The Whole World Is Watching: Mass Media in the Making and Unmaking of the New Left, Inside Prime Time,* and *Watching Television*. All three works reflect

Gitlin's political viewpoint; the author, a New Left liberal, was for a time president of Students for a Democratic Society (SDS), well known in the 1960s as a breeding ground for countercultural activism. Gitlin focuses on those counterculture days in *The Sixties: Years of Hope, Days of Rage*. In *The Twilight of Common Dreams: Why America Is Wracked by Culture Wars*, he examines the disintegration of the American left since his days in the SDS. Other books from Gitlin that have a political message include *The Intellectuals and the Flag, The Bulldozer and the Big Tent: Blind Republicans, Lame Democrats, and the Recovery of American Ideals*, and *The Chosen Peoples: America, Israel, and the Ordeals of Divine Election*, the last in collaboration with Liel Leibovitz. Gitlin is also the author of three novels: *The Murder of Albert Einstein, Sacrifice,* and the 2011 work, *Undying*.

### The Whole World Is Watching

In *The Whole World Is Watching*, Gitlin uses his experiences with the Students for a Democratic Society to make the point that in 1965 the relationship between the SDS and media was minimal, but it grew into "something like an active partnership just a few years later," as Frank Viviano reported in a *Washington Post* review. According to the author, continued Viviano, the expectations of the media—especially television—resulted in increasing coverage of SDS activities, which brought in new members to the organization and also fulfilled the cameras' need for "good copy and photogenic media events" by the youthful activists.

*New York Times Book Review* critic Walter Goodman praised Gitlin's thesis but also expressed some reservations. The most interesting and enjoyable parts of *The Whole World Is Watching*, Goodman stated, are when Gitlin "reports on the effects that the heady attentions of reporters and cameramen had on SDS leaders."

### Inside Prime Time and Watching Television

*Inside Prime Time* is the "best book ever written" about the mindset of the television executives of Hollywood, wrote David Crook in the *Los Angeles Times Book Review*. Gitlin infiltrated media ranks there—the major network television production centers in California—to produce his study of television's power structures, tacit agreements, and dependence on advertisers' standards. The book has "many trenchant observations," commented

*Washington Post* critic Jonathan Yardley. Yardley concluded that *Inside Prime Time* is a "thorough and sensitive exploration."

*Watching Television*, a book Gitlin edited and to which he contributed an essay, is composed of seven essays that express "serious complaints about the role television plays in our lives," commented Neil Postman in the *Los Angeles Times Book Review.* Together the essays form a sort of "treatise in social psychology." As for Gitlin's contribution, Postman pointed out that the editor gives the book a "coherent spirit." Brent Staples concluded in a *New York Times Book Review* article that *Watching Television* should be seen as a "prolegomenon to any further television criticism."

### The Sixties

Departing from mass-media themes, Gitlin produced *The Sixties* in 1987, a year that itself saw much interest sparked in sixties recollection. The book "fuses research, personal witness and a willingness to discuss shortfalls and successes alike," according to Abe Peck in a Chicago *Tribune Books* review. The most valuable parts of *The Sixties* "are autobiographical," remarked *New York Times Book Review* writer Jim Miller. The critic reported that Gitlin's reminiscences center mainly on his college days, where in the early years of the decade he "began to learn about left-wing politics."

From there *The Sixties* covers events in Berkeley and Chicago, where Gitlin joined such activists as Abbie Hoffman and Thomas Hayden in movements like SDS. Sometimes Gitlin "seems overwhelmed by his material," found Miller, who nonetheless added that in many places, through careful reconstruction of key events, "he succeeds admirably in bringing this 'gone time' back to life."

### The Twilight of Common Dreams

Gitlin takes a look at where the American left has gone since the 1960s in *The Twilight of Common Dreams*. Gitlin observes that the growth of "identity politics" catering to specialized groups such as women, Latinos, gays, and so forth has led to the near-death of anything that can really be identified as an American left. The idea of a common "American dream" has died as each group has chosen to pursue its own ends.

The author's "survey of the left's demise is cogent and useful," wrote Jonathan Alter in *Washington Monthly.* *Tikkun* reviewer Frank Browning remarked that the author "brings a moving sense of anguish" to the book.

### Sacrifice

Gitlin tried his hand at fiction in 1992 with *The Murder of Albert Einstein* and again in 1999 with the novel *Sacrifice.* The latter concerns the suicide of a well-known social activist and psychiatrist, and the repercussions of his death on his adult son, Paul. After inheriting his father's journals, Paul embarks on a journey of discovery about his estranged father's emotional life, the reasons his marriage disintegrated, and what led him to the final self-destructive act. Woven within the story is the text of a book written by the character of Paul's father, which Paul reads for the first time along with the journals. The book-within-a-book is an analysis of the biblical stories of Abraham, Isaac, and Esau. With that device, according to *Booklist* reviewer Frank Caso, the author "provides an interesting explication of the Bible tales."

*New York Times Book Review* contributor Judith Dunford described *Sacrifice* as an "ambitious work." However, Dunford complained that what she considered disjointed aspects of the book do not "necessarily add up to a successful novel." She faulted *Sacrifice* as emotionally unconvincing and marred by the author's overly earnest writing. A *Kirkus Reviews* writer allowed that "Chester's journals and the world they evoke provide a fine portrait of a tortured soul."

### The Intellectuals and the Flag and The Bulldozer and the Big Tent

In 2006, Gitlin returned to nonfiction with the book *The Intellectuals and the Flag.* This collection of seven essays divided into three parts addresses the author's liberal-minded audience, like many of his previous works. The first section of essays focuses on David Riesman, C. Wright Mills, and Irving Howe, notable intellectuals from recent history. In the second section, Gitlin writes essays criticizing two popular intellectual trends as well as values the mass media represents. The final section and essay, bearing the book's title, encourages left-leaning citizens to engage in a patriotism that is fitting for their ideals. Gitlin relates his own experiences as a

New Yorker after the attacks of September 11, 2001, and how he found his own sense of patriotism as a result. Critics responded positively to *The Intellectuals and the Flag* overall, citing the book's thoughtful reflections and demonstrative arguments. Gitlin has an "excellent grasp of the adversarial mindset," wrote Paul Hollander in a review for *New Criterion*. Others appreciated the author's use of his own personal experiences. The "best parts of Gitlin's book . . . are his reflections on patriotism," noted *Commonweal* contributor Alan Wolfe.

The following year, Gitlin published his next book, *The Bulldozer and the Big Tent*. The book primarily examines the reign of the Republican Party at the beginning of the twenty-first century, with Gitlin describing the party's approach to politics as similar to that of a bulldozer. He argues that the actions of Republican leaders like President George W. Bush have damaged the image of the country both at home and abroad, and these actions have created an atmosphere of secrecy and corruption. The author reviews the history of the Bush administration and tries to determine why and how the country followed this path. He also offers lessons the country and people can learn from the errors of the administration and how to avoid similar mistakes in the future. While many critics praised *The Bulldozer and the Big Tent*, some found the author's writing style to be a bit over the top. Gitlin's "taste for grandiloquence sometimes leads to cartoonish overstatement," observed Michael Crowley in a review for the *New York Times*. Others found much wisdom and insight in the book. *The Bulldozer and the Big Tent* "offers lessons to be learned," wrote *Booklist* contributor Vanessa Bush.

### The Chosen Peoples

Gitlin teams up with Leibovitz, a graduate student at Columbia and a blogger, for *The Chosen Peoples*, "a critique of Israeli and American religious-based exceptionalism," according to *Commentary Online* contributor Sam Siegel. The book follows a similar theme throughout Jewish and American history— namely, that their people are chosen by God. The study is, as a *Publishers Weekly* reviewer noted, an "ambitious religio-political meditation on American and Israeli history." The authors examine the concept of "chosenness," finding that the concept leads to assumptions of superiority. In the case of Israel and the "Promised Land," it has led to fierce and dogged wars, with the Canaanites and later the Palestinians. In the case of the United States, the

concept of manifest destiny and exceptionalism led to the wars with and virtual eradication of American Indians. The authors also deplore the concept of chosenness as an duty to work toward certain ideals, such as social justice. They find this theme elucidated in the Torah and the writings of Abraham Lincoln. However, as the authors point out, such goals lead to a feeling of divine sanction on the part of the governments of Israel and the United States, serving as mere cover for territorial expansion and imperial intentions. The authors also argue that this shared sense of chosenness in part explains the strong bond between the two countries.

The *Publishers Weekly* reviewer felt that Gitlin and Leibovitz "load too great an explanatory burden onto a forced comparison between the two nations" in this study. *Christian Science Monitor* contributor Chuck Leddy had a higher assessment of the work, noting that the authors "shed light on the strong messianic impulses in the history of both 'chosen' nations, especially Israel." Higher praise still came from a *Kirkus Reviews* writer who thought the book provides "lively, approachable scholarship for the lay reader and student of history alike," and that it is a "nuanced, carefully considered comparison of the deep-seated beliefs that pervade both groups." Likewise, *Forward Online* reviewer Gordon Haber found the work a "valuable addition to the public discussion of religion and politics (or religion in politics)." Haber went on to note: "And I don't mean to be dismissive when I say that the book is brisk and entertaining." Online *Huffington Post* contributor Andrei Markovits also had praise for *The Chosen Peoples*, terming it a "thought-provoking book that deserves much attention and debate."

### Undying

Gitlin returns to the novel with *Undying*, a fictionalized memoir of his own experience with cancer. In the book, professor of philosophy Alan Meister, suffering from cancer, reflects on his life. Initially, he wonders if there is some synchronicity between his cancer diagnosis and the reelection in 2004 of President George W. Bush. Journal entries follow the course of treatment and also document his life with wife, Melanie, a former graduate student of his, and with his daughter, Natasha, who returns to the family fold for a time because of her father's illness. Meister also ruminates on the philosophy and life of Nietzsche, who becomes a beacon leading him through his cancer treatment.

A *Publishers Weekly* reviewer felt that, despite "some lovely moments" in descriptions of life in New York, Gitlin presents a "a jumbled and heavy-handed reflection on life and illness" in this "unpolished" novel. A similar mixed assessment was offered by *Booklist* writer Michael Aurrey, who termed it "loosely autobiographical and loosely novelistic." *Library Journal* contributor Henry Bankhead, however, offered a much different evaluation of the novel, calling it "an engaging journal documenting a different take on the experience of cancer and recovery." For Bankhead, even the parts of the book dealing with chemotherapy are "captivating and even humorous."

**Gitlin once told *CA*:**

"Since my college days, my profession—my calling, to use the old-fashioned word—has been that of the writer, the writer before anything else. Why I took a Ph.D. in sociology and spent many years in a sociology department is a long story, the details of which are idiosyncratic, but the key element, I think, is that I wanted a certificate and a location which would permit me to write as much about whatever interested me, in the ways that interested me, as possible. In a specialized world, writing about media and popular culture gave me a way of slicing into a whole tangle of political, social, cultural, and intellectual questions. Since publishing *The Sixties,* I continue to write regularly on the mass media as a way of slicing into all kinds of social and cultural questions.

"I have been more 'writerly' than before. I published a novel, *The Murder of Albert Einstein,* a thriller set in the worlds of television, politics, and physics. In the conventions of American writing, a thriller is a low form, not taken very seriously, not regarded as 'about anything' especially, but this book, in my estimation, was also an exploration of moral questions. My second novel, *Sacrifice,* was quite different in form and style, more inward, formally more complex, more intense. I plan a third novel, musing and scribbling as I pursue other projects.

"Another major project of recent years was a nonfiction book, *The Twilight of Common Dreams.* This was an attempt to transcend the stale debates about American identity, multiculturalism, and so forth, and to explain why American politics has developed its distracted quality, its paralysis. The book was an extended essay in American history, philosophy, social theory, and sociology. I am now writing about the contemporary experience of all-encompassing media.

"In fiction, I need not respect the truth of details, only the truth of the intricacy of the truth. Here I go with Picasso: 'Art is the lies by which the truth is known.' Nonfiction has other obligations. I need both."

## ■ Biographical And Critical Sources

### BOOKS

Gitlin, Todd, *The Sixties: Years of Hope, Days of Rage,* Bantam (New York, NY), 1987.

### PERIODICALS

*Booklist,* March 1, 1999, Frank Caso, review of *Sacrifice,* p. 1150; September 1, 2007, Vanessa Bush, review of *The Bulldozer and the Big Tent: Blind Republicans, Lame Democrats, and the Recovery of American Ideals,* p. 24; February 15, 2011, Michael Aurrey, review of *Undying,* p. 52.

*Canadian Journal of Sociology,* July-August, 2007, Neil McLaughlin, review of *The Intellectuals and the Flag.*

*Chicago Tribune,* February 24, 1987, Steve Daley, review of *Watching Television,* p. 3.

*Christianity Today,* April, 2006, Allen C. Guelzo, review of *The Intellectuals and the Flag.*

*Christian Science Monitor,* September 15, 2010, Chuck Leddy, review of *The Chosen Peoples: America, Israel, and the Ordeals of Divine Election.*

*Commonweal,* March 24, 2006, Alan Wolfe, review of *The Intellectuals and the Flag,* p. 26.

*Kirkus Reviews,* February 1, 1999, review of *Sacrifice;* October 1, 2005, review of *The Intellectuals and the Flag,* p. 1062; August 1, 2010, review of *The Chosen Peoples.*

*Library Journal,* March 1, 1999, Francisca Goldsmith, review of *Sacrifice,* p. 109; February 1, 2011, Henry Bankhead, review of *Undying,* p. 53.

*Los Angeles Times Book Review,* October 23, 1983, David Crook, review of *Inside Prime Time,* p. 1; March 22, 1987, Neil Postman, review of *Watching Television,* p. 1; December 27, 1987, Sam Hurst, review of *The Sixties: Years of Hope, Days of Rage,* p. 5.

*Nation,* May 3, 1980, Tom Smucker, review of *The Whole World Is Watching: Mass Media in the Making and Unmaking of the New Left,* p. 526.

*New Criterion,* May, 2006, Paul Hollander, review of *The Intellectuals and the Flag,* p. 75.

*New Republic,* April 4, 1981, Michael Schudson, review of *The Whole World Is Watching,* p. 36.

*New York Times,* October 14, 2007, Michael Crowley, review of *The Bulldozer and the Big Tent.*

*New York Times Book Review,* August 31, 1980, Walter Goodman, review of *The Whole World Is Watching,* p. 11; October 2, 1983, Robert Sklar, review of *Inside Prime Time,* p. 12; February 8, 1987, Brent Staples, review of *Watching Television,* p. 7; November 8, 1987, Jim Miller, review of *The Sixties,* p. 13; July 18, 1999, Judith Dunford, review of *Sacrifice,* p. 23.

*Perspectives on Political Science,* winter, 2006, Howard L. Reiter, review of *The Intellectuals and the Flag,* p. 51.

*Publishers Weekly,* June 28, 2010, review of *The Chosen Peoples,* p. 117; December 20, 2010, review of *Undying,* p. 30.

*Tikkun,* September-October, 1996, Frank Browning, review of *The Twilight of Common Dreams: Why America Is Wracked by Culture Wars,* p. 86.

*Tribune Books* (Chicago, IL), October 25, 1987, review of *Sacrifice,* p. 6; February 12, 1989, Abe Peck, review of *The Sixties,* p. 9.

*Washington Monthly,* January, 1996, Jonathan Alter, review of *The Twilight of Common Dreams,* p. 55.

*Washington Post,* September 19, 1980, Frank Viviano, review of *The Whole World Is Watching,* p. 4; October 5, 1983, Jonathan Yardley, review of *Inside Prime Time,* p. 1; February 4, 1987, Jonathan Yardley, review of *Watching Television,* p. 2.

*ONLINE*

*Commentary Online,* http://www.commentary magazine.com/ (September, 2010), Sam Siegel, review of *The Chosen Peoples.*

*Forward Online,* http://www.forward.com/ (September 1, 2010), Gordon Haber, review of *The Chosen Peoples.*

*Huffington Post,* http://www.huffingtonpost.com/ (September 23, 2010), Andrei Markovits, review of *The Chosen Peoples.*

*Todd Gitlin Home Page,* http://toddgitlin.net (July 4, 2011).*

# Jim Gorant

## 1967-

## ■ Personal

Born February 23, 1967. *Education:* Villanova University, B.A.; New York University, M.A.

## ■ Addresses

*Agent*—Matthew Carnicelli, Trident Media Group, 41 Madison Ave., Fl. 36, New York, NY 10010.

## ■ Career

*Sports Illustrated*, New York, NY, editor, beginning 2004, currently senior editor. Also worked for *Sports Illustrated Golf Plus, Men's Health, GQ, Outside, Sports Afield Travel & Leisure Golf*, and others.

## ■ Writings

(With Boris Kuzmic) *Fit for Golf: A Personalized Conditioning Routine to Help You Improve Your Score, Hit the Ball Farther, and Enjoy the Game More,* McGraw-Hill (New York, NY), 2004.

*Fanatic: Ten Things All Sports Fans Should Do before They Die,* Houghton Mifflin Company (Boston, MA), 2007.

*The Lost Dogs: Michael Vick's Dogs and Their Tale of Rescue and Redemption,* Gotham Books (New York, NY), 2010.

Contributor to periodicals, including *Men's Journal, Travel & Leisure, GQ,* and *Men's Health.* Also author of the blog *Fanatic: 10 Things All Sports Fans Should Do B4 They Die.*

## ■ Sidelights

Sportswriter Jim Gorant has been part of the *Sports Illustrated* editorial team since 2004. His specialty is golf; in addition to writing for *Sports Illustrated Golf*

*Plus* and *Travel & Leisure Golf,* he has composed (with golf pro Boris Kuzmic) the guide *Fit for Golf: A Personalized Conditioning Routine to Help You Improve Your Score, Hit the Ball Farther, and Enjoy the Game More.* He believes, he stated on his author blog, that this path to a sports writing career allowed him to reach an important stage in his professional development with his basic sports-fan instincts intact. "In 2004," he wrote in his blog, "I realized there were a lot of big-time, elemental sports events I'd never been to. So I spent one year traveling to the ten greatest sports events, or at least the ten that topped my list and wrote a book about the experience." The result was *Fanatic: Ten Things All Sports Fans Should Do before They Die.*

### *Fanatic*

*Fanatic* is an examination of the experience of attending sporting events. Gorant, wrote a contributor on the *Cynical Bastard* Web site, "starts [the book] with the Super Bowl in January of 2005 in Jacksonville, Florida and ends it with opening day for the Boston Red Sox at Fenway Park in Boston in April of 2006. In between he attends some of the biggest sporting events anywhere including the NCAA Men's Final Four, Wimbledon and the Kentucky Derby among others."

What *Fanatic* is examining just as much as the events themselves, however, is the culture of the attendees at the events—the fans. These included rabid NASCAR fans (including one whose devotion to auto racing caused a delay in the launching of the space shuttle), and "Ignatius 'Kelly' Giglio," wrote Vince Darcangelo in the *Rocky Mountain News,* "the longest-tenured Boston Red Sox season ticketholder who held his seats from 1935 until his death in 2005, but stuck around long enough to see his hard-luck team finally win the big one." At the same time, noted a reviewer on the *Joy of Sox* Web site, *Fanatic* "is also part-memoir, as Gorant looks back, exploring how his own relationship to sports has changed as he has gotten older, from an obsessive who sulked all night after a loss to someone who still watches and cheers, but at an emotional distance." In *Fanatic,* wrote a contributor to the *BookPage* Web site, Gorant has "combined an engaging travelogue with a study of human nature and a tale of internal exploration."

### The Lost Dogs

In Gorant's book *The Lost Dogs: Michael Vick's Dogs and Their Tale of Rescue and Redemption,* he chronicles the paths of the dogs that were rescued from National Football League (NFL) player Michael Vick's horrifying dog fighting circle. He details the mistreatment of Vick's dogs, but also explains how their lives have been improved since they were rescued, and Vick was convicted of illegal dog fighting.

Reviewing the work on the *Badrap Blog,* contributor Tim Racer explained: "This is a book for those who want to know more details about the case, for those who want to know about the present status of the dogs, and for those who want to learn more about Vick's true role in Bad Newz Kennels as some still believe he merely bankrolled the operation." Ross Currie, a contributor to the *Phillyist* Web site, stated: "The power of Gorant's book lies in that it doesn't have an agenda. Not every dog from a fight situation can be rehabilitated into an adoptable pet. Some are so traumatized by their upbringing that they'll never be 'normal' dogs. . . . Gorant's narrative shares the bad with the good, and it's both heartbreaking and uplifting." *Washington Post Book World* contributor Mark Caro criticized: "*The Lost Dogs* feeling more like pit bull advocacy than dynamic storytelling. By the end of the twenty-one-page 'Where Are They Now?' epilogue covering each of the dogs, it's the reader who's in danger of being put to sleep."

## ■ Biographical And Critical Sources

*PERIODICALS*

*Publishers Weekly,* March 19, 2007, review of *Fanatic: Ten Things All Sports Fans Should Do before They Die,* p. 53.
*Rocky Mountain News,* June 22, 2007, Vince Darcangelo, review of *Fanatic.*
*Washington Post Book World* October 10, 2010, Mark Caro, review of *The Lost Dogs: Michael Vick's Dogs and Their Tale of Rescue and Redemption.*

*ONLINE*

*Badrap Blog,* http://badrap-blog.blogspot.com/ (August 14, 2010), Tim Racer, review of *The Lost Dogs.*
*BookPage,* http://www.bookpage.com/ (November 24, 2007), "Hello, Sports Fans."
*Cynical Bastard,* http://cynicalbstd.blogspot.com/ (November 24, 2007), review of *Fanatic.*
*Examiner.com,* http://www.examiner.com/ (September 7, 2010), Pamela Kramer, review of *The Lost Dogs.*
*Golf.com,* http://www.golf.com/ (November 24, 2007), "Jim Gorant, Senior Editor, Sports Illustrated."
*Houghton Mifflin Web site,* http://www.houghton mifflinbooks.com/ (November 24, 2007), author biography.
*Huffington Post,* http://www.huffingtonpost.com/ (August 14, 2011), author profile.
*I Heart Paws,* http://www.iheartpaws.com/ (September 14, 2010), Christina Harvey-Dusenberry, review of *The Lost Dogs.*
*Joy of Sox,* http://joyofsox.blogspot.com/ (November 24, 2007), review of *Fanatic.*
*Lost Dogs Web site,* http://www.thelostdogsbook.com/ (August 14, 2011).
*Phillyist,* http://phillyist.com/ (September 21, 2010), Ross Currie, review of *The Lost Dogs.**

# Posie Graeme-Evans

## 1952-

■ **Personal**

Born 1952, in Nottingham, England; daughter of Frank (a Royal Air Force pilot) and Eleanor (novelist) Graeme-Evans; married Tim Jacobs (divorced); married Andrew Blaxland (a television producer); children: two daughters, one son.

■ **Addresses**

*Home*—Sydney, New South Wales, Australia. *E-mail*—writeback@millennium.au.com.

■ **Career**

Author, 2004—. Australian Broadcasting Commission, director and field producer for news and current affairs, sports, and drama; producer, *Sons and Daughters, Rafferty's Rules, Elly and Jools, The Miraculous Mellops, Mirror Mirror,* and *Doomrunners,* 1997. Creator, with Helena Harris, of preschool series *Hi-5,* 1998, and *Cushion Kids.* Producer, with husband and business partner Andrew Blaxland, of *McLeod's Daughters,* Millennium Television, 2001. Coauthor of eleven of the twelve songs on *McLeod's Daughters* CD.

■ **Awards, Honors**

Named Australian Independent Producer of the Year, Screen Producers of Australia, 2001; "Twenty Significant Women in Film and Television" citation, *Variety,* 2002.

■ **Writings**

*Freya Dane,* Hodder & Stoughton (London, England), 2008.

*The Dressmaker: A Novel,* Atria Paperback (New York, NY), 2010.

*"WAR OF THE ROSES" SERIES*

*The Innocent: A Novel,* Atria Books (New York, NY), 2004.
*The Exiled: A Novel,* Atria Books (New York, NY), 2005.
*The Uncrowned Queen: A Novel,* Atria Books (New York, NY), 2006; also published as *The Beloved,* Simon & Schuster Australia (Pymble, New South Wales, Austrailia), 2006.

■ **Sidelights**

Posie Graeme-Evans, an Australian television producer, is also the author of several novels set in the mid-fifteenth century during the English War of the Roses, detailing the love between the fictitious Anne de Bohun and the historical King Edward IV. In the first book, *The Innocent: A Novel,* Anne begins her relationship with the already married king. Born a member of the royal Plantagenet house, Anne has been raised a peasant and, through her foster mother, has developed a reputation for healing. She comes to the king's attention when the queen develops complications during pregnancy. But Anne is a member of a lineage whose claim to the throne is better than Edward's own—she is the unacknowledged daughter of Henry VI, the man whom Edward displaced as king of England—and, as such, she has a truly momentous decision to make: whether to seize her destiny or to cleave to the man she loves.

For Edward's part, said Kristen LeBlanc in her *Kliatt* review of the novel, his decision is equally heart-rending: "He truly cares for this intelligent young woman who helps to save his wife and daughter during a difficult birth."

### The Exiled

Anne's and Edward's story continues in *The Exiled: A Novel* and *The Uncrowned Queen: A Novel.* By the time of the final volume, in 1470, Anne and Edward have a love-child and she is living in genteel exile in Brugge. Then Edward, forced from the throne by a twist of fate, flees to the Low Countries. From there he hopes to win assistance from his brother-in-law Charles, Duke of Burgundy. Anne is the person who can best provide the needed link between Charles and Edward. However, if she does so, she condemns her father to an uncertain fate.

"Set amidst a turbulent period in European history," Janelle Martin wrote in the *Eclectic Closet*, "Graeme-Evans has created a compelling love story which manages to hold up amidst the political drama which drives the plot."

### The Dressmaker

In *The Dressmaker: A Novel,* set in Victorian England, protagonist Ellen Gowan is a well-loved but poor girl. After being left by her first husband, Ellen becomes a dressmaker to support herself and her daughter. Soon her work is widely celebrated, and she creates clothes for all of England's elite.

Reviewing the work on the *Story Girl* Web site, a contributor stated: "Overall, this book was fun and frivolous—a soap opera of a novel, but an entertaining one. If you are a fan of historical fiction and light romance, this book will probably appeal to you. However, if you are looking for something serious with deeper themes, you'll find yourself wanting more." A *Here There and Everywhere* contributor explained: "While I found the characters, descriptions, plotlines and dialogues pretty awful, I loved reading about the fashions, and I found reading about the social status of women—not all that long ago—where women in England had few choices and fewer opportunities—fascinating." A contributor to the *Single Minded Woman* Web page stated:

"In *The Dressmaker,* the romance of Jane Austen, the social commentary of Charles Dickens and the very contemporary voice of Posie Graeme-Evans combine."

## ■ Biographical And Critical Sources

*PERIODICALS*

*Daily Variety,* December 18, 2002, Michaela Boland, "Nine Knights Drama Chief," p. 16.

*Hollywood Reporter,* December 17, 2002, Jacqueline Lee Lewes, "Staff Changes Continue at Nine: Drama Director Noble Latest to Exit under New Management," p. 66.

*Kliatt,* July, 2004, Kristen LeBlanc, review of *The Innocent: A Novel,* p. 18.

*Publishers Weekly,* April 17, 2006, review of *The Uncrowned Queen: A Novel,* p. 166.

*Variety,* March 22, 2004, Don Groves, "Taking Dramatic Turn: Auds Tune out Reality to Turn on Oz, U.S. Skeins," p. 27.

*ONLINE*

*Eclectic Closet,* http://antheras.blogspot.com/ (June 20, 2007), Janelle Martin, review of *The Uncrowned Queen.*

*Here There and Everywhere,* http://intlxpatr.wordpress.com/ (March 9, 2011), review of *The Dressmaker: A Novel.*

*Life is Short, Read Fast,* http://lifeisshort-readfast.blogspot.com/ (May, 2011), review of *The Dressmaker.*

*Posie Graeme-Evans Home Page,* http://www.posiegraemeevans.com (June 20, 2007); (August 14, 2011).

*Read in a Single Sitting,* October 7, 2010, review of *The Dressmaker.*

*Single Minded Woman,* http://singlemindedwomen.com/ (August 14, 2011), review of *The Dressmaker.*

*Story Girl,* http://thestorygirlbookreviews.blogspot.com/ (March 29, 2011), review of *The Dressmaker.**

# Colin S. Gray

## 1943-

### ■ Personal

Born December 29, 1943. *Education:* University of Manchester, B.A. (with honors), 1965; Lincoln College, Oxford, D.Phil., 1970.

### ■ Addresses

*Office*—Department of Politics and International Relations, University of Reading, Whiteknights, P.O. Box 218, Reading, Berkshire RG6 6AA, England. *E-mail*—c.s.gray@reading.ac.uk.

### ■ Career

Writer, educator. University of Reading, Reading, England, professor of international politics and strategic studies; has also taught at Lancaster University, Bailrigg, Lancaster, England; University of York, Toronto, Ontario, Canada; University of Hull, Hull, England; and University of British Columbia, Vancouver, British Columbia, Canada. Canadian Institute of International Affairs, Toronto, former executive secretary of the strategic studies commission; International Institute for Strategic Studies, London, England, former assistant director; Hudson Institute, Croton-on-Hudson, NY, former director of national security studies, beginning 1976; National Institute for Public Policy, Fairfax, VA, founding president and chair, 1981—; National Institute for Public Policy, Fairfax, senior fellow. Member of President's General Advisory Committee on Arms Control and Disarmament, 1982-87; member of Panel of Experts, United Kingdom Strategic Defense Review, 1997-98; Force Development and Integration Center, U.S. Army Space and Missile Defense Command, Arlington, VA, director, c. 2000. Former advisory panel member for the U.S.

Army and Air Force, for the Congressional Office of Technology Assessment, and for the U.S. Space Command; has also served as an advisor to the British Royal Navy.

### ■ Awards, Honors

Superior Public Service Award, U.S. Department of the Navy, 1987.

### ■ Writings

*Canadian Defence Priorities: A Question of Relevance,* foreword by John W. Holmes, Clarke, Irwin (Toronto, Ontario, Canada), 1972.

*Canada's Maritime Forces,* Canadian Institute of International Affairs (Toronto, Ontario, Canada), 1973.

(Editor, with R.B. Byers) *Canadian Military Professionalism: The Search for Identity,* Canadian Institute of International Affairs (Toronto, Ontario, Canada), 1973.

*The Soviet-American Arms Race,* Lexington Books (Lexington, MA), 1976.

*The Geopolitics of the Nuclear Era: Heartland, Rimlands, and the Technological Revolution,* Crane (New York, NY), 1977.

(With Leon Gouré and William G. Hyland) *The Emerging Strategic Environment: Implications for Ballistic Missile Defense,* Institute for Foreign Policy Analysis (Cambridge, MA), 1979.

*SALT: Deep Force Level Reductions,* Hudson Institute (Croton-on-Hudson, NY), 1981.

*The MX ICBM and National Security,* Praeger (New York, NY), 1981.

*Strategic Studies and Public Policy: The American Experience,* University Press of Kentucky (Lexington, KY), 1982.

*Strategic Studies: A Critical Assessment,* Greenwood Press (Westport, CT), 1982.

*American Military Space Policy: Information Systems, Weapon Systems, and Arms Control,* Abt Books (Cambridge, MA), 1982.

*Nuclear Strategy and Strategic Planning,* Foreign Policy Research Institute (Philadelphia, PA), 1984.

(Editor, with Keith B. Payne) *The Nuclear Freeze Controversy,* foreword by Sam Nunn, University Press of America (Lanham, MD), 1984.

(Editor, with Barry R. Schneider and Keith B. Payne) *Missiles for the Nineties: ICBMs and Strategic Policy,* Westview Press (Boulder, CO), 1984.

*Missiles against War: The ICBM Debate Today,* National Institute for Public Policy (Fairfax, VA), 1985.

*Maritime Strategy, Geopolitics, and the Defense of the West,* Ramapo Press (New York, NY), 1986.

*Nuclear Strategy and National Style,* Madison Books, 1986.

*The Geopolitics of Super Power,* University Press of Kentucky (Lexington, KY), 1988.

(Editor, with Roger W. Barnett) *Seapower and Strategy,* Naval Institute Press (Annapolis, MD), 1989.

*War, Peace, and Victory: Strategy and Statecraft for the Next Century,* Simon & Schuster (New York, NY), 1990.

*The Leverage of Sea Power: The Strategic Advantage of Navies in War,* Free Press (New York, NY), 1992.

*House of Cards: Why Arms Control Must Fail,* Cornell University Press (Ithaca, NY), 1992.

*Weapons Don't Make War: Policy, Strategy, and Military Technology,* University Press of Kansas (Lawrence, KS), 1993.

*The Navy in the Post-Cold War World: The Uses and Value of Strategic Sea Power,* Pennsylvania State University Press (University Park, PA), 1994.

(Author of notes and introduction) C.E. Callwell, *Military Operations and Maritime Preponderance: Their Relations and Interdependence,* Naval Institute Press (Annapolis, MD), 1996.

*Explorations in Strategy,* Greenwood Press (Westport, CT), 1996.

(Editor, with Geoffrey Sloan) *Geopolitics, Geography, and Strategy,* Frank Cass (Portland, OR), 1999.

*The Second Nuclear Age,* Lynne Rienner Publishers (Boulder, CO), 1999.

*Modern Strategy,* Oxford University Press (New York, NY), 1999.

*Defining and Achieving Decisive Victory,* Strategic Studies Institute (Carlisle Barracks, PA), 2002.

*Strategy for Chaos: Revolutions in Military Affairs and the Evidence of History,* foreword by Murray Williamson, Portland (London, England), 2002.

(Editor, with John Baylis and James J. Wirtz) *Strategy in the Contemporary World: An Introduction to Strategic Studies,* Oxford University Press (New York, NY), 2002, 3rd edition, 2010.

*Maintaining Effective Deterrence,* Strategic Studies Institute (Carlisle Barracks, PA), 2003.

*The Sheriff: America's Defense of the New World Order,* University Press of Kentucky (Lexington, KY), 2004.

*Another Bloody Century: Future Warfare,* Weidenfeld & Nicolson (London, England), 2005.

*Irregular Enemies and the Essence of Strategy: Can the American Way of War Adapt?,* Strategic Studies Institute (Carlisle Barracks, PA), 2006.

*Strategy and History: Essays on Theory and Practice,* Routledge (New York, NY), 2006.

*The Implications of Preemptive and Preventive War Doctrines: A Reconsideration,* Strategic Studies Institute (Carlisle Barracks, PA), 2007.

*War, Peace and International Relations: An Introduction to Strategic History,* Routledge (New York, NY), 2007, 2nd edition, 2011.

*Fighting Talk: Forty Maxims on War, Peace, and Strategy,* Praeger Security International (Westport, CT), 2007.

*After Iraq: The Search for a Sustainable National Security Strategy,* U.S. Army War College (Carlisle, PA), 2009.

*National Security Dilemmas: Challenges and Opportunities,* foreword by Paul K. Van Riper, Potomac Books (Washington, DC), 2009.

*Schools for Strategy: Teaching Strategy for 21st Century Conflict,* Strategic Studies Institute (Carlisle, PA), 2009.

*Understanding Airpower: Bonfire of the Fallacies,* Airpower Research Institute (Maxwell Air Force Base, AL), 2009.

*The Strategy Bridge: Theory for Practice,* Oxford University Press (New York, NY), 2010.

Contributor to *SALT II, Rest in Peace: A Roundtable Discussion: The Louis Lehrman Auditorium, the Heritage Foundation, March 28, 1985,* Heritage Foundation (Washington, DC), 1985. Contributor to periodicals, including *Wilson Quarterly, Foreign Affairs, Washington Quarterly, International Security, Foreign Policy, Survival,* and the *National Interest.* Member of editorial board, *Comparative Strategy, Naval War College Review, Journal of Strategic Studies,* and the *Journal of Terrorism and Organized Crime.*

## ■ Sidelights

A respected scholar of military history and strategy who, as a dual citizen of the United Kingdom and the United States, has served as an advisor to both countries' militaries, as well as the North Atlantic Treaty Organization, Colin S. Gray is also a university professor and founding chair of the National Institute for Public Policy in Fairfax, Virginia.

Mackubin Thomas Owens asserted in a 2006 *National Review* article that "no one is more qualified to address the issue of future war than Gray, who has been the most consistently brilliant and prolific strategic thinker in the English-speaking world for the past three decades." Regarded as a classical realist in his writings and lectures, Gray is among those military thinkers who "take their lead from the writings of Thucydides, Sun Tzu, and [Carl von] Clausewitz and calculate strategy in terms of power and geography, or geostrategy," explained Mark T. Clark in a *Naval War College Review* of *The Sheriff: America's Defense of the New World Order*. In many of his books, Gray emphasizes that many students of the military and even political leaders fail to take lessons from history; they also tend to sacrifice solid military strategy for a faith in new technologies and outdated tactics against such threats as Muslim terrorism. Gray uses both the past and present to advise his readers on strategies for today and the future of the military.

## War, Peace, and Victory

American leaders should not be overly impressed by their own military firepower, Gray warns in his 1990 book, *War, Peace, and Victory: Strategy and Statecraft for the Next Century*. The work examines military strategies going back to ancient Greece and Rome, then explores the theories of Clausewitz and Alfred Mahan, two theorists upon whom Gray frequently relies in his writings, before continuing on to discuss the American mindset on tactics. Gray emphasizes, in a book published before the end of the Cold War, the need of military leaders to understand more completely the advantages and disadvantages of land versus sea power. It is Gray's assertion that, of the two, America's strength lies in its navy, as well as its air force, and so he protests Congress's efforts at the time to cut these branches while boosting land forces for combat in the Middle East. (This is a point he also makes in his books *The Leverage of Sea Power: The Strategic Advantage of Navies in War* and *The Navy in the Post-Cold War World: The Uses and Value of Strategic Sea Power*.)

While Ralph De Toledano observed in the *National Review* that many of Gray's arguments center on the U.S.-Soviet situation and that, therefore, "his theorems will involve different variables" if considered under different circumstances, the critic attested that his "postulates remain valid." Genevieve Stuttaford, writing for *Publishers Weekly*, called *War, Peace, and Victory* "impressively broad" and "authoritative."

Some critics of Gray's work have found his positions controversial. For example, he has argued that a nuclear conflict can be winnable and not necessar-

ily equate to a total annihilation of civilization. In a review of *War, Peace, and Victory*, *Washington Monthly* contributor Adam Yarmolinsky wondered why, "if Gray sees so little military utility in nuclear weapons, he is not more interested in reducing their numbers." Indeed, although Gray has maintained that nuclear weapons caches are useful for deterrence, in most cases he argues that traditional military conflicts between warring states will continue to be a fact of life.

## Explorations in Strategy and Modern Strategy

Gray's *Explorations in Strategy* discusses the importance of America's air force. While also acknowledging the usefulness of special forces, Gray continues to emphasize strategy over technology in terms of winning conflicts. As James A. Huston put it in his *Perspectives on Political Science* review: "Gray recognizes that the 'information war' is a revolution in warfare, but the microchip is not the final stage any more than was the crossbow, gun powder, or the atomic bomb. Strategy must remain, as Clausewitz put it, the use of engagements for the object of the war."

*Modern Strategy, Strategy for Chaos: Revolutions in Military Affairs and the Evidence of History*, and *Strategy and History: Essays on Theory and Practice* are more examples of Gray's continuing plea for an emphasis on strategy over mere military might and reliance on technology. The first title lays the groundwork of what Gray would contend in other books, as well: that while technology and politics might change, the basic art of warfare does not. Lamenting again the lack of strategic thinkers among America's politicians and even academics, Gray "describes the problem but offers no help in finding the solution," criticized Glen C. Collins in a *Parameters* review.

## Strategy for Chaos and Strategy and History

*Strategy for Chaos* reiterates Gray's warning against supplanting genuine strategy with impressive-seeming high-tech military devices. "Gray is right to condemn incautious assertions—even by American Secretaries of Defense—that precision munitions or cyberspace weapons are altering the nature of war or strategy," commented Barry Watts in the *Joint Force Quarterly*. Other advances, such as nuclear weapons and guided missiles, are also discussed. Although the critic described the book as "an uneven work with good intentions," that "is not entirely successful in laying out either theory or evidence," he concluded that it "will be of interest to those who follow the RMA [revolutions in military affairs] debate. The book is an invaluable goad for thoughtful readers to think beyond the RMA bumper stickers and slogans Gray rightly condemns and to determine their own positions on the subject." *Strategy and History* makes Gray's case that strategists must learn military history, which is still relevant to today's conflicts. *Parameters* critic Stephen J. Blank praised this title as a reflection of "Gray's independence of mind, intellectual rigor, and willingness to challenge the political correctness or conventional wisdom of the time." Gray reiterated this position in his more recent *War, Peace and International Relations: An Introduction to Strategic History.*

Much of the debate occurring at the national and international level in the early twenty-first century has involved the United States' role as the world's leading military power.

### The Sheriff

Two books by Gray that address this issue are *The Sheriff* and *Another Bloody Century: Future Warfare.* In the former, the author asserts, as many others have, that the United States should be involved in international conflicts in order to help insure political stability in the world. "Gray explains that 'sheriff is of course a metaphor. By its use I mean to argue that the United States will act on behalf of others, as well as itself, undertaking some of the tough jobs of international security that no other agent or agency is competent to perform,'" reported Clark. Clark went on to note that this has been the aim of U.S. policy for some time, but that the country lost its focus, "particularly during the years of the Clinton administration."

Asserting that *The Sheriff* "does not acknowledge that there are compelling arguments against a global sheriff," *Air Power History* critic John L. Cirafici wrote: "It is not that Gray is incorrect when he argues that America has a leading role to play in maintaining global stability. He may have missed the point, however, by not recognizing that stability arises from collective wisdom and global commitment to the ideal." Despite disagreeing with Gray's position, Cirafici recommended the book "for no other reason than [to understand] its perspective." Damon Coletta, writing in *Parameters,* felt that Gray's classical realism approach "can take us only so far" in understanding the current role of America's military, but concluded: "Taken as a whole, *The Sheriff* effectively demonstrates why traditional realism, geopolitics, and the cyclical view of history, after 2,500 years, retain their relevance."

### Another Bloody Century

*Another Bloody Century* offers Gray's look into the future of warfare, and he concludes that classic notions of war will remain applicable. "This is not to say that there is nothing new out there waiting for us. Quite on the contrary, *strategic surprise* is more than likely to occur. Strategic history is cyclical, but it does not repeat itself with high fidelity," explained a contributor to the Center for Security and International Studies Web site.

The critic continued: "One of the central theses of Colin Gray's book is that *irregular warfare,* in the sense it is understood today, as the Global War on Terrorism for instance, or largely against low-intensity conflicts that spur *within* states *is not the future of warfare.* In fact, Gray argues that irregular warfare has a healthy future, but not as we imagine it today. His predictions indicate that terrorism is a faint threat that will run its course in the next two decades at the most, and then will see its decline." While disagreeing with "Gray's claim that war can only be controlled indirectly," such as through international law, the reviewer recommended *Another Bloody Century* as "definitely a 'must read' for any serious student or scholar of strategic and security studies, but it should also be remembered that no theory is without fallacy and that Gray's has some, too."

### War, Peace, and International Relations and *Fighting Talk*

Gray's book, *War, Peace, and International Relations: An Introduction to Strategic History,* is one of two published in 2007, and is an examination of the last two centuries of strategic history, covering all the major wars during that time. Arguing that these wars have been transformative events in world history, Gray explores three major themes: the factors in strategy that have changed over the years and those that have not; the connection between war and politics; and finally the difference between tactical and strategic conduct of war. Once again, Gray "takes an unabashedly Clauzewitzian or slightly amended Clauzewitzian point of view with regard to strategy; the use or threat of force for achieving the ends of policy, as one of its main theses," as *Parameters* contributor Stephen J. Blank noted. Some of the conflicts Gray examines are the Napoleonic wars, World War I and World War II, as well as the U.S. involvement in Iraq and Afghanistan. "This book bears all the hallmarks of his labors in the field: immense erudition, an appealing and no-nonsense style which pulls no punches and does not equivocate, and a strong authorial voice," noted Blank.

Gray's second book from 2007, *Fighting Talk: Forty Maxims on War, Peace, and Strategy,* was inspired and once again informed by the thoughts of military strategist Carl von Clausewitz. Here Gray provides forty rules or maxims that cover most of the basics of strategy, along with accompanying explanatory essays for each maxim. These rules are laid out in parts dealing with topics from war and peace to warfare and military policy, security and insecurity, strategy, and history and the future. For example, the first ten maxims fall into the "war and peace" category, and discuss the various perspectives that different players bring to this relationship. On the one hand there are those concerned in a practical manner in such questions, including politicians and the military, and those involved at a more theoretical level, such as strategists. In the section on strategy, the ten maxims deal with the transformation of political will into military action. A major focus of this lengthy section is a discussion of three writers on war who Gray considers the essential thinkers on strategy: Clausewitz and his *On War,* Sun-tzu and *Art of War,* and Thucydides, and *Peloponnesian War.* Gray's fourteenth maxim is, in fact: "If Thucydides, Sun-tzu, and Clausewitz did not say it, it probably is not worth saying." Todd Manyx, writing in *Joint Force Quarterly,* felt that "Gray's attempt to shed light on the nature of war, peace, and strategy is a great success." According to Manyx, *Fighting Talk* "serves as a primer on topics relating to strategic policy that will help interested parties at all levels understand that behind political jargon and rhetoric, more than an invisible hand is guiding a strategist's counsel."

### National Security Dilemmas

In his 2009 work, *National Security Dilemmas: Challenges and Opportunities,* Gray presents a primer for the most pressing contemporary issues facing the U.S. in regards to national security. Here he "provides a sound argument for the need for a coherent and inclusive national strategy that orchestrates power and political aims," according to *Military Review* contributor Matthew Eberhart. Gray examines, among other topics, the policy of deterrence; the need to transform the military to changing needs and enemies, especially those who wage an irregular war; the use of new technologies in warfare; and the difficulties posed for U.S. policy in waging defensive versus preemptive wars.

For Douglas Peifer, writing in *Joint Force Quarterly, National Security Dilemmas* "brings together eight thought-provoking essays by one of today's leading scholar-strategists." Peifer further noted: "This eclectic collection offers a Clausewitzean, realist examination of security dilemmas from deterrence to irregular warfare, combining broad macro-analysis with specific recommendations and critiques. This collection should prove most useful for those unfamiliar with Gray's work or in search of a convenient, single-volume collection of his contributions to the Strategic Studies Institute over the past seven years." Similarly, Eberhart felt that the study "provides a complete view of the road-blocks to crafting an effective, coherent strategy in light of current challenges and discusses how the challenges may be met." Further praise for the work came from *Parameters* contributor Robert Bateman, who felt that Gray's "writing is clear, strong, and admirably lacking in the high-sounding mucky buzzwords-of-the-day that often grip so many writers working at the strategic level." Bateman added: "Each chapter is a standalone feast for the mind."

### ■ Biographical And Critical Sources

*BOOKS*

Gray, Colin S., *National Security Dilemmas: Challenges and Opportunities,* foreword by Paul K. Van Riper, Potomac Books (Washington, DC), 2009.

*PERIODICALS*

*Air Power History,* fall, 2006, John L. Cirafici, review of *The Sheriff: America's Defense of the New World Order.*
*Air & Space Power Journal,* winter, 2003, Gilles Van Nederveen, review of *Strategy for Chaos: Revolutions in Military Affairs and the Evidence of History.*
*American Political Science Review,* September, 1991, John P. Lovell, review of *War, Peace, and Victory: Strategy and Statecraft for the Next Century,* p. 1084; March, 2000, Gregory Paul Domin, review of *The Second Nuclear Age,* p. 239.
*Annals of the American Academy of Political and Social Science,* May, 1984, "Strategic Studies and Public Policy," p. 193.
*Bulletin of the Atomic Scientists,* December, 1983, "Strategic Studies and Public Policy: The American Experience," p. 42.
*California Bookwatch,* June, 2006, review of *Another Bloody Century: Future Warfare.*
*Choice,* March, 1993, R.A. Strong, review of *House of Cards: Why Arms Control Must Fail,* p. 1238; June, 1993, A.N. Sabrosky, review of *Weapons Don't Make War: Policy, Strategy, and Military Technology,* p. 1705; December, 1996, review of *Explorations in Strategy,* p. 688; January, 2000, D. McIntosh, review of *The Second Nuclear Age,* p. 1010; Febru-

ary, 2003, M.A. Morris, review of *Strategy for Chaos*, p. 1055; February, 2005, A.C. Tuttle, review of *The Sheriff*, p. 1094.

*Comparative Strategy*, January 1, 2005, C. Dale Walton, review of *The Sheriff*, p. 99; December, 2005, Stephen J. Cimbala, review of *Another Bloody Century*, p. 439.

*Current History*, May, 1983, "Strategic Studies and Public Policy," p. 220.

*Emory International Law Review*, spring, 1993, Bernard L. McNamee, review of *House of Cards*.

*Encounter*, June, 1988, review of *The Geopolitics of Super Power*, p. 57.

*Ethics*, October, 1983, "Strategic Studies: A Critical Assessment," p. 185.

*Foreign Affairs*, spring, 1984, "American Military Space Policy"; fall, 1988, Gregory F. Treverton, review of *The Geopolitics of Super Power*; summer, 1990, Lucy Edwards Despard, review of *War, Peace, and Victory*; summer, 1993, Eliot A. Cohen, review of *Weapons Don't Make War*; January, 2003, review of *Strategy for Chaos*, p. 163.

*Historian*, fall, 2005, Lorraine M. Lees, review of *The Sheriff*.

*International Affairs*, spring, 1989, "The Geo-Politics of Superpower"; January, 1994, Theo Farrell, review of *Weapons Don't Make War*, p. 134; July, 1995, Eric Grove, review of *The Navy in the Post-Cold War World: The Uses and Value of Strategic Sea Power*, p. 601; May, 2003, Paul Hirst, review of *Strategy for Chaos*, p. 652.

*International History Review*, May, 1996, Richard D. Challener, review of *The Navy in the Post-Cold War World*, p. 491; December, 2003, Geoffrey Blainey, review of *Strategy for Chaos*, p. 995.

*International Journal*, summer, 1993, review of *The Leverage of Sea Power: The Strategic Advantage of Navies in War*.

*Joint Force Quarterly*, July, 2005, Barry Watts, review of *Strategy for Chaos*, p. 109; July, 2008, Todd Manyx, review of *Fighting Talk: Forty Maxims on War, Peace, and Strategy*, p. 141; October, 2009, Douglas Peifer, review of *National Security Dilemmas: Challenges and Opportunities*, p. 169.

*Journal of American History*, June, 1989, review of *The Geopolitics of Super Power*, p. 313.

*Journal of American Studies*, August, 1989, review of *The Geopolitics of Super Power*, pp. 329-330; December, 2005, Patrick Fagan, review of *The Sheriff*, p. 556.

*Journal of Military History*, October, 1990, Dean C. Allard, review of *Seapower and Strategy*, p. 491; January, 1992, William H. McNeill, review of *War, Peace, and Victory*, p. 123; October, 1993, Kenneth

P. Werrell, review of *Weapons Don't Make War*, p. 749; October, 1995, Malcolm Muir, review of *The Navy in the Post-Cold War World*, p. 745.

*Journal of Politics*, May, 1989, review of *The Geopolitics of Super Power*, p. 456.

*Library Journal*, June 15, 1990, Richard Weitz, review of *War, Peace, and Victory*, p. 124; November 1, 1992, Harold N. Boyer, review of *The Leverage of Sea Power*, p. 102.

*Military Law Review*, spring, 1987, "Maritime Strategy, Geopolitics, and the Defense of the West."

*Military Review*, January, 2010, Matthew Eberhart, review of *National Security Dilemmas*.

*National Interest*, winter, 1992, Gideon Rose, review of *House of Cards*.

*National Review*, January 28, 1991, Ralph De Toledano, review of *War, Peace, and Victory*, p. 55; April 10, 2006, "A Brutal Constant," p. 48.

*New Republic*, September 29, 1986, Paul Kennedy, review of *Nuclear Strategy and National Style*, p. 38.

*New York University Journal of International Law and Politics*, fall, 1989, review of *The Geopolitics of Super Power*; spring, 1992, David Soskin, review of *War, Peace, and Victory*.

*Orbis*, spring, 1993, Bruce D. Berkowitz, review of *House of Cards*; spring, 1997, Michael P. Noonan, review of *Explorations in Strategy*.

*Parameters*, winter, 2000, Glen C. Collins, review of *Modern Strategy*; summer, 2005, Damon Coletta, review of *The Sheriff*; summer, 2007, Stephen J. Blank, review of *Strategy and History: Essays on Theory and Practice*; spring, 2009, Stephen J. Blank, review of *War, Peace, and International Relations: An Introduction to Strategic History*, p. 111; winter, 2009, Robert Bateman, review of *National Security Dilemmas*, p. 146.

*Perspectives on Political Science*, summer, 1997, James A. Huston, review of *Explorations in Strategy*.

*Policy Review*, winter, 1989, review of *Nuclear Strategy and National Style*.

*Political Science Quarterly*, fall, 1993, James J. Wirtz, review of *Weapons Don't Make War*; winter, 1995, Edward Rhodes, review of *The Navy in the Post-Cold War World*.

*Political Studies*, June, 2000, Tarak Barkawi, review of *Modern Strategy*, p. 668.

*Prairie Schooner*, fall, 1993, review of *Weapons Don't Make War*; winter, 1995, review of *The Navy in the Post-Cold War World*.

*Publishers Weekly*, May 18, 1990, Genevieve Stuttaford, review of *War, Peace, and Victory*, p. 72; May 24, 1991, review of *War, Peace, and Victory*, p. 56; October 12, 1992, review of *The Leverage of Sea Power*, p. 60.

*Reference & Research Book News*, February, 1990, review of *Seapower and Strategy*, p. 41; August, 1993, review of *House of Cards*, p. 26; November, 1999, review of *The Second Nuclear Age*, p. 206; February, 2000, review of *Geopolitics, Geography, and Strategy*, p. 111; February, 2003, review of *Strategy for Chaos*, p. 240; August, 2007, review of *Fighting Talk*; August, 2007, review of *War, Peace and International Relations*.

*Science Books & Films*, September, 1984, review of *American Military Space Policy: Information Systems, Weapon Systems, and Arms Control*, p. 11; July, 2000, review of *The Second Nuclear Age*, p. 156.

*Survival*, spring, 1994, Ivo H. Daalder, review of *House of Cards*.

*Times Literary Supplement*, March 9, 2001, Adam Roberts, review of *Modern Strategy*, p. 26; September 23, 2005, "After the Peace," p. 10.

*Virginia Quarterly Review*, winter, 1989, review of *The Geopolitics of Super Power*; summer, 2000, review of *Modern Strategy*.

*Washington Monthly*, July 1, 1990, Adam Yarmolinsky, review of *War, Peace, and Victory*, p. 58.

ONLINE

*Center for Security and International Studies Web site*, http://www.csis.ro/ (February 2, 2008), review of *Another Bloody Century*.

*Johns Hopkins University Applied Physics Laboratory Web site*, http://www.jhuapl.edu/ (February 2, 2008), faculty profile of Colin S. Gray.

*Strategic Studies Institute of the U.S. Army War College Web site*, http://www.strategicstudiesinstitute.army.mil/ (February 2, 2008), brief biography of Colin S. Gray.

*United States Army War College, Strategic Studies Institute Web site*, http://www.strategicstudiesinstitute.army.mil/ (July 12, 2011), "Colin S. Gray."

*University of Reading Department of Politics and International Relations Web site*, http://www.spirs.reading.ac.uk/ (February 2, 2008), faculty profile of Colin S. Gray.

*University of Reading, School of Politics and International Relations Web site*, http://www.reading.ac.uk/ (July 12, 2011), "Colin S. Gray."*

# Sara Gruen

## 1969(?)-

### ■ Personal

Born c. 1969, in Vancouver, British, Columbia, Canada; married; children: three. *Education:* Carleton University, B.A.

### ■ Addresses

*Home*—P.O. Box 6135, Chicago, IL 60606-6135. *Agent*—Emma Sweeney Agency, LLC, 245 E. 80th St., New York, NY 10021. *E-mail*—sara@saragruen. com.

### ■ Career

Writer.

### ■ Writings

*Riding Lessons* (novel), HarperTorch (New York, NY), 2004.
*Flying Changes* (novel), HarperTorch (New York, NY), 2005.
*Water for Elephants* (novel), Algonquin Books (Chapel Hill, NC), 2006.
*Ape House,* Spiegel & Grau (New York, NY), 2010.

### ■ Adaptations

*Water for Elephants* was adapted for film and released by Twentieth Century-Fox, 2011.

### ■ Sidelights

Sara Gruen's debut novel, *Riding Lessons,* concerns an Olympic-level rider named Annemarie Zimmer, who loses her prized horse and her promising career in a terrible accident. The incident proves to be the first link in a chain of events that culminates two decades later. At that point, Annemarie has lost her job, is in the midst of a divorce from her husband, and has discovered that her father is terminally ill. Taking her highly rebellious, teenage daughter with her, she returns to her parents' riding school in New Hampshire to regroup. There, she encounters a former love interest, Dan Garibaldi. She also finds a neglected horse with rare, brindled coloring; it is the same coat pattern as Highland Harry, her mount who died in the accident twenty years before. The coloration is so unusual that Annemarie feels there must be a connection between the two animals, and she becomes determined to discover what it is. Eventually, she learns that the horse is Harry's brother.

"*Riding Lessons* is an exciting character study that uses the equestrian world as a backdrop to a family drama," wrote Harriet Klausner in a review for *AllReaders.com.* Klausner praised the "vivid story line" and the author's "insight into the heroine who remains the center of a powerful tale of redemption." Jill M. Smith, a contributor to *RT Book Reviews,* advised that "painful estranged relationships form the core of this emotionally complex and dark novel." A contributor to *Publishers Weekly* wrote that *Riding Lessons* is "beautifully nuanced" and added: "The book's appealing horse scenes depicted with unsentimental affection help build a moving story of loss, survival and renewal." A *Booklist* writer praised Gruen's writing skill, calling *Riding Lessons* "so exquisitely written it's hard to believe that it's also a debut."

#### *Flying Changes*

*Flying Changes* continues the story of Annemarie, who is now engaged to be married and struggling to come to terms with her new life. When her headstrong daughter displays a natural talent for riding, Annemarie is forced to choose between protecting her daughter from possible harm and encouraging her to reach for her dreams.

Leslie Poston commented in a review for *Suite101* that *Flying Changes* is "one of those books that balances delicately on the telling of a good, meandering story."

### Water for Elephants

Gruen was inspired to write *Water for Elephants* after reading about the traveling circuses of the 1920s and 1930s. The story is told from the perspective of Jacob, a lonely elderly man finishing out his days in a nursing home. An upcoming field trip to a local circus sends him back seventy years when, as a recently orphaned twenty-three-year-old, he dropped out of veterinary school and joined the Benzini Brothers' Most Spectacular Show on Earth. Charged with taking care of the circus animals, Jacob is witness to untold cruelties to animals and workers alike, and he is drawn into conflict when he falls in love with the head trainer's wife.

*Bookreporter.com* critic Jennifer Krieger remarked that Gruen "has a finely-tuned radar for the magic and mysteries of the human heart." Krieger continued: "With lines of startling beauty, haunting and evocative scenes and finely-drawn characters who dance off the page, readers can dip in and out of the novel, immersing themselves in Jacob's memories. The story and its characters will haunt readers long after they have resurfaced." In a review for the *Library Journal,* Jim Coan commented: "Old-fashioned and endearing, this is an enjoyable, fast-paced story." "With a showman's expert timing," wrote *New York Times Book Review* contributor Elizabeth Judd, Gruen "transform[s] a glimpse of Americana into an enchanting escapist fairy tale."

### Ape House

Gruen's next novel, *Ape House,* though not quite as well received as *Water for Elephants,* still received many positive reviews. The novel follows Isabel Duncan and the clan of bonobo monkeys that she studies.

Reviewing the work in the *New York Times Book Review,* contributor Leah Hager Cohen assessed: "The novel includes scenes illuminating the horrors

of some scientific research, and indirectly raises the question of what bonobos might teach us about our own capacity for empathy. At such moments, *Ape House* seems to want to be a different kind of book, one that would seek unabashedly to move us, to leave us changed." London *Independent* contributor James Urquhart lauded: "*Ape House* is gripping, emotionally exhilarating and, by a large margin, the best novel I've read in the past 12 months. Or perhaps 24." Diane Baker Mason, a contributor to the Toronto *Globe and Mail,* explained: "Despite the premise, this is not a story told by the bonobos or from the bonobos' point of view: It is not *Watership Down.* It is very much about the humans and their relationships, with each other and with animals." London *Guardian* contributor Jane Smiley mused: "*Ape House* is an ambitious novel in several ways, for which it is to be admired, and it is certainly an easy read, but because Gruen is not quite prepared for the philosophical implications of her subject, it is not as deeply involving emotionally or as interesting thematically as it could be."

## ■ Biographical And Critical Sources

*PERIODICALS*

*Booklist,* April 1, 2004, Shelley Mosley, review of *Riding Lessons,* p. 1355.

*Globe and Mail* (Toronto, Ontario, Canada), September 10, 2010, Diane Baker Mason, review of *Ape House.*

*Guardian* (London, England), March 26, 2011, Jane Smiley, review of *Ape House.*

*Independent* (London, England), February 13, 2011, James Urquhart, review of *Ape House.*

*Library Journal,* March 15, 2006, Jim Coan, review of *Water for Elephants,* p. 62.

*New York Times Book Review,* June 4, 2006, Elizabeth Judd, review of *Water for Elephants,* p. 35; September 3, 2010, Leah Hager Cohen, review of *Ape House.*

*Publishers Weekly,* March 1, 2004, review of *Riding Lessons,* p. 55.

*Washington Post Book World,* September 8, 2010, Ron Charles, review of *Ape House.*

*ONLINE*

*AllReaders.com,* http://www.allreaders.com/ (December 14, 2004), Harriet Klausner, review of *Riding Lessons.*

*Bookreporter.com,* http://www.bookreporter.com/ (May, 2006), Jennifer Krieger, review of *Water for Elephants.*

*Internet Movie Database,* http://www.imdb.com/ (August 14, 2011), author profile.

*ReadersRead.com,* http://www.readersread.com/ (December 14, 2004), Sarah Reaves White, review of *Riding Lessons.*

*RT Book Reviews,* http://www.rtbookreviews.com/ (December 14, 2004), Jill M. Smith, review of *Riding Lessons.*

*Sara Gruen Home Page,* http://www.gruenzoo.com (August 14, 2011).

*Suite101,* http://www.suite101.com/ (June 6, 2006), Leslie Poston, review of *Water for Elephants.*\*

# Kevin Guilfoile

## 1968-

■ **Personal**

Born July 16, 1968, in Teaneck, NJ; married; wife's name Mo; children: Max. *Education:* Graduated from University of Notre Dame.

■ **Addresses**

*Home*—Chicago, IL. *E-mail*—kevin@guilfoile.net.

■ **Career**

Writer. Commentator for National Public Radio; worked variously for Houston Astros (professional baseball team) and in advertising in Chicago, IL.

■ **Writings**

(And illustrator, with John Warner) *Modern Humorist Presents My First Presidentiary: A Scrapbook by George W. Bush*, edited by Michael Colton, Three Rivers Press (New York, NY), 2001.
*Cast of Shadows* (novel), Knopf (New York, NY), 2005.
*The Thousand*, Alfred A. Knopf (New York, NY), 2010.

Guilfoile's writings have been anthologized in *Created in Darkness by Troubled Americans: The Best of McSweeney's Humor, May Contain Nuts: A Very Loose Canon of American Humor, 101 Damnations,* and *The Humorists' Tour of Personal Hells.* Contributor of short humor to periodicals, including *McSweeney's, New Republic, Modern Humorist, Chicago Reader,* and *Morning News* online.

■ **Adaptations**

*Cast of Shadows* was adapted as an audiobook by Random House Audio, 2005.

■ **Sidelights**

Although Kevin Guilfoile established his writing credentials as a humorist, his first novel, *Cast of Shadows,* is a combination science-fiction, mystery, and legal thriller. In an interview with *Publishers Weekly* contributor Michael Archer, Guilfoile explained that he has always been interested in thrillers and noted that "writing humor and writing suspense are the same in that with both you're trying to get an involuntary response out of people, whether it's to make them laugh or to scare them."

### Cast of Shadows

The plot of *Cast of Shadows* takes place in the future and revolves around Dr. David Moore, whose seventeen-year-old daughter has been raped and murdered. The police cannot find the killer, and when they return Moore's daughter's belongings to him, they inadvertently include a vial of sperm from the evidence files. An expert in the future world of advanced cloning and a fertility doctor, Moore uses his own contested technology to clone the DNA and artificially impregnate a woman with the goal of creating a copy of his daughter's murderer. He then becomes involved in the child's life, seeking clues to who the killer is through the child's face and actions, which are observed through a private investigator. The child, Justin Finn, grows up, and he confronts Moore when he is fifteen years old and announces that he knows he is a clone and that he may have clues to the killer's identity. Complicating the plot is the suspicion that Finn may possess some of the evil characteristics of the murderer. The answer to Moore's search for the killer may also involve a real-time video game called Shadow World, which reflects the real city of Chicago, where Moore lives and where the murder took place. Moore suspects that the murderer may play the game, not only to kill women virtually but also as a precursor to doing so in real life.

In a review of *Cast of Shadows* for *MBR Bookwatch*, Harriet Klausner commented that the author "cooks up an extremely exciting tale with several intriguing moral questions." Christopher J. Korenowsky, writing in *Library Journal*, noted that the novel's plot unfolds in a "logical yet compelling fashion" as it centers on issues surrounding "good and evil, past lives, and scientific cloning." A *Publishers Weekly* contributor called *Cast of Shadows* an "engrossing debut novel" and felt that the work "as a whole is rich and involving." Michiko Kakutani wrote in the *New York Times* that the "story occasionally stumbles into the clichés thrillers are prone to" but added that "Guilfoile's tricky, high-concept plot continually subverts and plays with the reader's expectations." Calling the novel "gripping," Kakutani went on comment that the author "knows how to create suspense that not only relies on police-blotter developments but also stems from his characters' personalities, their sense of right and wrong, [and] their intuitions about fate and choice and will."

### The Thousand

Guilfoile's next novel, a thriller titled *The Thousand*, was published in 2010. The novel centers on a bizarre secret society called The Thousand, who study and admire the work of the ancient Greek mathematician Pythagoras.

Reviewing the work in the *New York Times Book Review*, contributor Michiko Kakutani lauded: "The real pleasures of reading *The Thousand* have less to do with the story's portentously withheld secrets than with Mr. Guilfoile's keenly observed characters, his gritty feel for the city of Chicago and his ability to weave artfully all sorts of philosophical questions—like the relationship of music and math, and the morality of using scientific knowledge—into his hectic, bloodstained plot." Chicago *Tribune Books* critic Rick Kogan described the book as "filled with vivid characters, chills and thrills and a Chicago

and some of its personalities brought to inventive, creative life." *Los Angeles Times* contributor Marion Winik criticized: "If you like Scott Turow, Stan Lee, Dan Brown or Michael Crichton, then you are in the target audience for Kevin Guilfoile's novel *The Thousand*. Unfortunately, like smoked duck ravioli with wasabi-tomatillo sauce, Guilfoile has fallen under the sway of one influence too many." *Bookreporter.com* contributor Joe Hartlaud lauded: "*The Thousand* could easily have been one of those 500-page books that collapses under the weight of its own gravitas. Guilfoile doesn't let that happen. He demonstrates, for example, his understanding of the teachings of Pythagoras without turning the novel into a treatise. He also doesn't skimp on plot, characterization, or action, particularly in the last half of the book."

### ■ Biographical And Critical Sources

*PERIODICALS*

*Kirkus Reviews*, January 15, 2005, review of *Cast of Shadows*, p. 73.

*Library Journal*, March 1, 2005, Christopher J. Korenowsky, review of *Cast of Shadows*, p. 78.

*MBR Bookwatch*, May, 2005, Harriet Klausner, review of *Cast of Shadows*.

*New York Times*, April 19, 2005, Michiko Kakutani, review of *Cast of Shadows*.

*New York Times Book Review*, August 27, 2010, Michiko Kakutani, review of *The Thousand*.

*People*, April 11, 2005, Sue Corbett, review of *Cast of Shadows*, p. 52.

*Publishers Weekly*, January 24, 2005, Michael Archer, "Kevin Guilfoile: *Cast of Shadows*," interview, p. 119; January 31, 2005, review of *Cast of Shadows*, p. 48.

*Tribune Books* (Chicago, IL), August 20, 2010, Rick Kogan, review of *The Thousand*.

*ONLINE*

*BellaOnline.com*, http://www.bellaonline.com/ (June 29, 2005), Laura Lehman, review of *Cast of Shadows*.

*Best Reviews Online*, http://www.thebestreviews.com/ (May 2, 2005), Harriet Klausner, review of *Cast of Shadows*.

*Big Thrill*, http://www.thrillerwriters.org/ (July 28, 2010), John Darrin, review of *The Thousand*.

*Bookreporter.com,* http://www.bookreporter.com/ (August 14, 2011), Joe Hartlaub, review of *The Thousand.*

*Kevin Guilfoile Home Page,* http://www.guilfoile.net (August 14, 2011).

*Los Angeles Times,* http://articles.latimes.com/ (August 30, 2010), Marion Winik, review of *The Thousand.*

*Morning News Online,* http://www.themorning news.org/ (May 24, 2005), Robert Birnbaum, "Birnbaum v. Kevin Guilfoile," interview with author.

*RoundTableReviews.com,* http://www.roundtable reviews.com/ (June 29, 2005), review of *Cast of Shadows.*

*Salon.com,* http://www.salon.com/ (June 6, 2005), Laura Miller, review of *Cast of Shadows.*

# Gerald Hammond

## 1926-

### ■ Also Known As

Arthur Douglas
Gerald Arthur Douglas Hammond
Dalby Holden

### ■ Personal

Born March 7, 1926, in Bournemouth, Hampshire, England; son of Frederick Arthur Lucas (a physician) and Maria Birnie (a nursing sister) Hammond; married Gilda Isobel Watt (a nurse), August 20, 1952; children: Peter, David, Steven. *Education:* Aberdeen School of Architecture, diploma, 1952. *Politics:* Conservative. *Hobbies and other interests:* Shooting, fishing.

### ■ Addresses

*Home*—Aboyne, Aberdeenshire, Scotland.

### ■ Career

Writer, architect. Navy, Army, and Air Force Institutes, Claygate, Surrey, England, assistant architect, 1952-53; Aberdeen County Council, Aberdeen, Scotland, assistant architect, 1953-60; University of Dundee, Dundee, Argus, Scotland, assistant to resident architect, 1960-69; Livingston Development Corp., Livingston, Scotland, deputy chief architect and planning officer for Livingston New Town, 1969-82. Member, Royal Institute of British Architects; fellow and former chair of Scottish branch of Chartered Institute of Arbitrators. *Military service:* British Army, 1944-45.

### ■ Member

Crime Writers Association, Society of Authors, Muzzle Loaders Association, Shooting Club (founder; president).

### ■ Writings

*CRIME NOVELS; EXCEPT AS NOTED*

(Under pseudonym Dalby Holden) *Doldrum,* R. Hale (London, England), 1987.

*Cash and Carry,* Macmillan (London, England), 1992.

*A Running Jump,* Severn House (London, England), 1998.

*Flamescape,* Severn House (London, England), 1998.

*Fine Tune,* Severn House (London, England), 1998.

*Into the Blue,* Severn House (London, England), 2000.

*The Language of Horse Racing* (nonfiction), Routledge (London, England), 2000.

*Grail for Sale,* Severn House (London, England), 2002.

*Down the Garden Path,* Severn House (London, England), 2003.

*The Snatch,* Severn House (London, England), 2003.

*The Hitch,* Severn House (London, England), 2004.

*The Outpost,* Severn House (London, England), 2004.

*Saving Grace,* Allison & Busby (London, England), 2004.

*Dead Letters,* Allison & Busby (London, England), 2005.

*Heirs and Graces,* Magna (London, England), 2005.

*Cold in the Heads,* Severn House (London, England), 2006.

*Cold Relations,* Allison & Busby (London, England), 2006.

*On the Warpath,* Severn House (London, England), 2006.

*Keeper Turned Poacher,* Severn House (London, England), 2006.

*A Dead Question,* Allison & Busby (London, England), 2007.

*Waking Partners,* Severn House (London, England), 2007.

*Loving Memory,* Severn House (London, England), 2007.

*His or Her Grace,* Allison & Busby (London, England), 2007.

*Hit and Run,* Severn House (London, England), 2008.

*Crash,* Severn House (London, England), 2008.

*Well and Good,* Severn House (London, England), 2009.

*The Fingers of One Foot,* Severn House (London, England), 2009.

*Silent Intruder,* Severn House (London, England), 2009.

*A Dog's Life,* Severn House (London, England), 2010.

*Snitch* Severn House (London, England), 2011.

*With My Little Eye,* Severn House (London, England), 2011.

"BEAU PEPYS" SERIES

*Fred in Situ,* Hodder & Stoughton (London, England), 1965.

*The Loose Screw,* Hodder & Stoughton (London, England), 1966.

*Mud in His Eye,* Hodder & Stoughton (London, England), 1967.

"KEITH CALDER" SERIES

*Dead Game,* Macmillan (London, England), 1979.

*The Reward Game,* St. Martin's Press (New York, NY), 1980.

*The Revenge Game,* Macmillan (London, England), 1981.

*Fair Game,* St. Martin's Press (New York, NY), 1982.

*The Game,* Macmillan (London, England), 1982.

*Cousin Once Removed,* St. Martin's Press (New York, NY), 1984.

*Sauce for the Pigeon,* St. Martin's Press (New York, NY), 1984.

*Pursuit of Arms,* St. Martin's Press (New York, NY), 1985.

*Silver City Scandal,* St. Martin's Press (New York, NY), 1986.

*The Executor,* St. Martin's Press (New York, NY), 1986.

*The Worried Widow,* Macmillan (London, England), 1987, St. Martin's Press (New York, NY), 1988.

*Adverse Report,* Macmillan (London, England), 1987.

*Stray Shot,* Macmillan (London, England), 1988.

*A Brace of Skeet,* Macmillan (London, England), 1989.

*Let Us Prey,* Macmillan (London, England), 1990.

*Home to Roost,* Macmillan (London, England), 1990.

*In Camera,* Macmillan (London, England), 1991.

*Snatch Crop,* Macmillan (London, England), 1991.

*Thin Air,* Macmillan (London, England), 1993.

*Hook or Crook,* Macmillan (London, England), 1994.

*Carriage of Justice,* Macmillan (London, England), 1995.

*Sink or Swim,* Macmillan (London, England), 1996.

*Follow That Gun,* Macmillan (London, England), 1996.

"CAPTAIN JOHN CUNNINGHAM" SERIES

*Dog in the Dark,* Macmillan (London, England), 1989.

*Doghouse,* Macmillan (London, England), 1989.

*Whose Dog Are You?,* Macmillan (London, England), 1990.

*Give a Dog a Name,* Macmillan (London, England), 1992.

*The Curse of the Cockers,* Macmillan (London, England), 1993.

*Sting in the Tail,* Macmillan (London, England), 1994.

*Mad Dogs and Scotsmen,* Macmillan (London, England), 1995.

*Bloodlines,* Macmillan (London, England), 1996, St. Martin's Press (New York, NY), 1998.

*Twice Bitten,* Macmillan (London, England), 1998, St. Martin's Press (New York, NY), 1999.

*A Shocking Affair,* Macmillan (London, England), 1999.

*Dead Weight,* Macmillan (London, England), 2000.

*Illegal Tender,* Macmillan (London, England), 2001.

NOVELS; UNDER PSEUDONYM ARTHUR DOUGLAS

*The Goods,* Macmillan (London, England), 1985.

*Last Rights,* Macmillan (London, England), 1986, St. Martin's Press (New York, NY), 1987.

*A Very Wrong Number,* Macmillan (London, England), 1987.

*A Worm Turns,* Macmillan (London, England), 1988, St. Martin's Press (New York, NY), 1989.

Contributor to magazines and periodicals. Author of monthly column, "The Abominable Dog," for *Sporting Gun.*

■ **Adaptations**

The novel *Give a Dog a Name* was adapted for audio, narrated by Donald Douglas, Isis Publishing, 2000.

■ **Sidelights**

Gerald Hammond has used his profound knowledge of firearms and hunting dogs to create two unique mystery series, one featuring a Scottish gunsmith, Keith Calder, and the other focusing on

John Cunningham, a retired soldier turned dog breeder. Hammond has also written a number of stand-alone mysteries; indeed, since 2001 the veteran crime novelist has focused on nonseries novels.

### "Beau Pepys" and "Keith Calder" Series

The author originally set out to write humor, but he found that publishers had little interest in humorous novels. Still, his first three books—*Fred in Situ, The Loose Screw,* and *Mud in His Eye*—have a somewhat humorous bent. Their protagonist is Beau Pepys, an architect and amateur race driver who becomes involved in mysteries. *St. James Guide to Crime and Mystery Writers* contributor Judith Rhodes described them as "light-hearted" and "fairly implausible" but "nevertheless pleasant."

Hammond relates in the *St. James Guide to Crime and Mystery Writers* that after writing these first novels he began trying to come up with a new set of characters and a background he would not have to research much: "I was (and am) deeply involved with gundogs and shooting, generally, and was irritated by the stereotypes of the shooting fraternity which seemed to be universal. I set out to depict the shooting scene (particularly in Scotland) as I knew it, most of [it] centered around the character of Keith Calder, a gunsmith of unreliable habits and an enquiring mind" and "a randy but loveable rogue."

Numerous critics found the Calder series to be unique in the mystery genre because of its heavily detailed lore about dogs and hunting. Rhodes explains: "Keith Calder burst upon the scene in *Dead Game,* bombarding the reader, and any character in the book who will pay him any attention, with intricate details of firearms and firearm history. Calder, in his capacity as gunsmith, shooting instructor, and poacher, is in his younger days none too choosey about which side of the law he operates on. As the series progresses . . . he marries, sets up a gunshop, and as the years pass becomes a relatively respectable figure, upon whom his former adversary Chief Inspector Munro comes unwillingly to rely." Reviewing one title in the series, *Pursuit of Arms,* a *Booklist* contributor approved of its "interesting gun lore, subtle characterization, smashing action, and . . . taut suspense." As the series unfolded, Calder frequently relinquished his role as narrator to other characters. Three of the later novels are written in the voice of Simon Parbitter, a London-born writer who moves next to Calder; others are narrated by Calder's daughter Deborah, his partner Wallace James, or Ian Fellowes, a detective who eventually marries Deborah. The series of twenty-six books ended in 1996 with *Follow That Gun.*

### "Captain John Cunningham" Series

Hammond's special knowledge of the hunting world figures prominently in another mystery series, this one featuring John Cunningham, a soldier who was discharged from the army after contracting a debilitating tropical disease. He takes up a career as a professional breeder and trainer of Springer spaniels, working with kennel maid Beth Cattrell and hard-drinking veterinarian Isobel Kitts.

This trio finds itself repeatedly drawn into mysteries, and as Rhodes pointed out: "The joint expertise of the three partners (Cunningham's in guns, Isobel's in dog-breeding, and Beth's in sheer commonsense) helps in solving murders and associated canine and ballistic puzzles." Rhodes noted that the Cunningham books are more formulaic than the Calder efforts, but conceded that each one "provides an interesting and entertaining read." The series of eleven books came to a conclusion in 2001 with *Illegal Tender.*

### Nonseries Novels

Hammond's nonseries crime novels include his lighthearted *Grail for Sale,* which brings together Scottish historian Jeremy Carpenter and Hazel Tripp, an American who has lost her job in an antiques store. Upon comparing notes, the two discover that both of their predicaments arise from the same source: wealthy blackguard Gordon McKennerty. They concoct an antiques scam through which they plan to exact revenge. A *Publishers Weekly* contributor felt that "Hammond fans should enjoy his new tack and new readers might easily become fans. . . . Everyone should be grateful that the author has yet to retire."

*The Snatch* finds twenty-something Alice Dunwoodie storming out of the house after a dispute with her father and meeting her friend, Sarah McLeod, at a local bar. As the two young women walk home, they are kidnapped by Foxy Brett and Tod Bracken, who intend to hold them for ransom. But the women convince them that there is no money to be made, and that, instead, they should all work together and divide the spoils of a supermarket robbery. They succeed, but with consequences that provide an entirely new challenge. *Library Journal* reviewer Rex Klett wrote that Hammond's "lively plot and light prose" are "energized by frequent humor."

Alice and Sarah return in *The Hitch* with a burglary plot that also involves Alice's father, Robin. Unfortunately, even Alice's carefully laid plans can go awry, and Robin is caught and jailed. The three decide to go straight, but a fax received by accident just before Robin's release from prison reignites the trio's larcenous fires. The errant fax is from wealthy pop music star Mona Lisa, who is trying to reserve the Scottish retreat of Angus Castle for her upcoming wedding. They decide to correspond with the star as if they were representatives of the castle, constantly requesting more and more payments for reservations, materials, and other expenses for the lavish wedding. If they can keep up the subterfuge long enough, they can bilk the singer out of plenty of cash—but more people know about their chicanery than they realize. Their plot involves a complex balancing act, keeping not only the famous pop star in the dark, but representatives of the real Angus Castle, and some dangerous criminals, as well. *Booklist* reviewer Emily Melton appreciated the novel for its "appealing characters, an imaginative plot, and cracking good action."

*The Outpost* has a plot that is "wildly implausible, but the book is such good fun it doesn't matter," remarked Melton in another *Booklist* review. Hallelujah Brown, the daughter of a British army officer, is wooed into military service less for her skills than for the fact that she is a black woman whose recruitment is good public relations. At Sandhurst, a military training school, Hallelujah proves she is much more than a prime recruiting statistic; she is also an outstanding soldier with a brilliant military mind. Assigned to a post in Maveria, her language skills prove useful when her superior officer is captured by neighboring Liboonese rebels. After the perils of war transform her into the senior officer, she finds herself in a leadership role hatching battle plans, devising strategy, and developing a ferocious reputation among the Liboonese.

Lady P, the protagonist of *Cold in the Heads,* is an engineer, detective, and grandmother. What she thought was going to be a typical day of caring for her grandson while her daughter and son-in-law take some time off turns into an unexpectedly dark experience. When her daughter and son-in-law return after a day of sailing, they announce a startling discovery: a dead body in the boat's cabin. Lady P enthusiastically takes up the investigation and discovers that the dead woman is Molly Gallagher, a secretary from the county architect's office who disappeared eight months earlier. However, the pathologist determines that the woman died much more recently, raising the question of what happened to her from the time she disappeared to the time she died. Lady P is determined to find out, though she is stymied by an uncooperative local police detective, thugs intent on doing her physical harm, and corrupt local officials who are obviously involved in the murder. A *Kirkus Reviews* critic called Lady P an "appealingly free-spirited detective." In a *Booklist* review, Melton concluded that "for those who enjoy understated but uproarious humor and delightfully weird characters . . ., this is just the ticket."

The protagonist in *On the Warpath* is octogenarian Helen Mercer, who served with the French Resistance and then became a journalist who covered wars and disasters globally. Now retired, she lives in England, where her grandson has become the victim of a con artist who has stolen the Jaguar he has been restoring. Helen comes to his aid in hunting down the criminal, drawing on her experience from her days in the Resistance.

In *Keeper Turned Poacher,* Joan Lightfoot is the keeper who has also been living with her employer, Tasker O'Neill, but when she is implicated in a crime, she escapes on his stolen motorcycle and hides in his country cottage. After taking in a badly treated dog, she begins to steal to buy dog food. Joan meets gamekeeper Ken Whetsone, who left his research to work for an MP. His wife has abandoned him, and when her body turns up, he and Joan search for the murderer, fearing that Ken will be arrested.

In *Waking Partners,* Aubrey Merryhill, owner of an import business, is in involved in an accident while driving his beloved MG and falls into a coma. His wife asks his assistant to take over the business, and he does such a good job of it that the company makes a profit for the first time in its history. The money is needed as Aubrey requires brain surgery. The police investigate and suspect that Aubrey's crash wasn't an accident, and his wife and employees become suspects. Melton concluded in her *Booklist* review that *Waking Partners* is "a pleasantly entertaining, cleverly plotted, and witty mystery from a reliable genre veteran."

The title of *Loving Memory* refers to a memory card that contains explicit photographs of Kate, friend of Detective Inspector Honey Laird. Honey, who is on maternity leave, searches for the card and, when she finds it, discovers that it now also contains a photograph of a dead woman who, it turns out, knew that her MP boss was embezzling from his company.

Octogenarian Luke Grant, who has lived an exciting life as a photographer, now finds himself the guardian of two spirited great-grandchildren in *Hit and Run.* His grandson died years earlier in an aircraft accident, and now his sharp-tongued wife is in the hospital after being injured by a hit-and-run driver. The case is being investigated as sixteen-year-old Violet and nine-year-old Jane adjust to life with Luke and Pepper, his retriever. Luke worries about Violet's attention to a classmate and calls on Helen Harper, a love interest, to help with the girls.

Julian Custer isn't the victim in *Crash,* but he could become one after offering help to Delia Barrow, whom he saves from a burning vehicle and whose brother has died in the accident. Delia has recently arrived in Scotland from New Zealand, and her identification is lost in the blaze. Julian offers to help the injured woman, but they soon discover that the crash may have been planned, and that both their lives are in danger. Melton praised the story in *Booklist,* adding that the author "also injects warmhearted, feel-good romance and an authentic portrait of life in rural Scotland."

Luke Grant, the octogenarian photographer from *Hit and Run,* returns in the 2009 novel *Well and Good.* Having adopted his granddaughters, Violet and Jane, Luke sees boy trouble ahead for the teenagers. Violet has a crush on Roddy McWilliams and talks Luke into having him over for dinner. When he fails to show up, Violet starts worrying that something has happened to him. In fact, someone has pushed him down a well, and sister Jane helps to save him. Now Luke investigates the matter along with a local police inspector, Ian Fellowes, in this "pleasantly entertaining, cleverly plotted, and nicely written" cozy mystery, as *Booklist* reviewer Melton described it.

Luke Grant's granddaughter Jane Highsmith is the focus of *The Fingers of One Foot.* Here she has recently been certified as a veterinarian, and she has also lost her beloved grandfather. Though he was ninety at the time of his death, he was in good shape, and Jane cannot believe that he somehow stumbled and fell to his death from the bridge that he had used daily for years. Jane, however, is alone in her belief; even DI Ian Fellowes does a pass on this investigation. Jane, however, finds an ally in village newcomer Roland Fox, an impoverished writer whose dog she treats. Fox barters for Jane's services, taking on the investigation into Luke's death. In the event he quickly ascertains that the elderly gentleman was killed, but then both Fox and Jane are stricken with mysterious illnesses, and the reading of Luke's will further complicates matters, as it could cause a deterioration of relations between Jane and sister Violet. "The low-stress detection leads to two separate perpetrators, neither of whom Hammond . . . makes as memorable as the local canines," noted a *Kirkus Reviews* contributor, who added: "The hero and heroine, though, are charming." Similarly, Melton, writing again in *Booklist,* dubbed this an "appealing read" and praised Hammond's "solid writing, engaging characters, and . . . vivid picture of life in a rural Scottish village."

A canine again is at the center of *A Dog's Life.* Scottish novelist Tim Russell is out walking his dog when he comes across a young woman, Ann, who seems homeless. He does not immediately recognize her, but soon discovers that she is the daughter of a friend of his who died in an accident. Ann turns out to be very good company, and Tim invites her home with him. Tim is lonely and ultimately invites Ann to stay with him; slowly their relationship grows closer and closer. Then Tim is attacked for no apparent reason. But there are reasons and motives, for Tim, unbeknownst to himself, has been making enemies because of his relationship with Ann. First among these is Ann's stepfather, who stole her house from her, and there is also a dealer who cheated her in the purchase of her household items. A further motive for many comes when it is discovered that Ann's uncle has died and left her a wealthy heiress. When Tim and Ann make plans for a marriage, murder ensues, and Tim's dog helps solve the crime. A *Kirkus Reviews* contributor noted of this novel: "More village romance than mystery, and none the worse for it." Barbara Bibel, writing in *Booklist,* also felt that "animal lovers and cozy fans will enjoy this quirky mystery." Similarly, a *Publishers Weekly* reviewer noted that "Hammond avoids the maudlin as Tim and Ann grow closer while trying to solve the crime."

In *Silent Intruder,* Scottish couple Michael McGinnis and Hilda Gilmour return from a vacation in Switzerland to discover the police are at their cottage investigating a charge of child pornography. They find nothing on Michael's computer, but now the couple fear that someone was living in their home while they were gone. A neighbor also appears to be missing, and Michael is assaulted when a thug comes looking for this person. Soon the pair is helping the police in their search for the neighbor, and they are also caught up in a "world of illegal gambling, computer fraud, violence, and deceit," as a *Publishers Weekly* reviewer noted. The same contributor termed this a "pedestrian effort." *Booklist* reviewer Sue O'Brien, however, had a higher assessment of *Silent Intruder,* calling it an "engaging story" with "suspense, plot twists, [and] well-developed characters."

## Hammond once told *CA:*

"I try very hard to be technically accurate, and this may be why my novels bring me correspondence from all over the world. Americans, in particular, send me supporting material which I wish I had while writing that particular book. A fictional incident in one of my novels suggested to a detective in San Francisco the solution to a real crime, and convictions followed.

"I never set out to become a propagandist for the shooting man but this, again, happened without my conscious volition. In Britain, perhaps more than the States, an attitude is growing that shooting must *ipso facto* be cruel and that wildlife would achieve a delightful balance, patterned on Walt Disney, if left severely alone. My series of novels has proved ideal (and, I hope, useful) in putting across, one piece at a time, the facts that the balance of nature (in Britain) is entirely man-made or man-influenced, that it owes a major debt to shooting interests, and that the withdrawal of hunting pressures would spell disaster to wildlife as we know it here.

"My primary motivation for writing is escape from boredom into a rich fantasy world. My writing process is to look for a starting idea and start writing. Characters will usually develop themselves. I enjoy the final development more than the plotting.

"I used to write against backgrounds of my enthusiasms. A change was partly triggered by a desire to try my hand at noncrime fiction. This introduced a change in style. I leave it to others to interpret."

## ■ Biographical And Critical Sources

### BOOKS

*St. James Guide to Crime and Mystery Writers,* St. James Press (Detroit, MI), 1996.

### PERIODICALS

*Booklist,* December 15, 1985, review of *Pursuit of Arms,* p. 608; February 15, 1992, Peter Robertson, review of *In Camera,* p. 1091; March 15, 2004, Emily Melton, review of *The Hitch,* p. 1271; September 15, 2004, Emily Melton, review of *The Outpost,* p. 212; November 1, 2005, Emily Melton, review of *Cold in the Heads,* p. 28; March 15, 2006, Emily Melton, review of *On the Warpath,* p. 31; March 1, 2007, Emily Melton, review of *Waking Partners,* p. 67; September 1, 2007, Emily Melton, review of *Loving Memory,* p. 62; October 1, 2008, Emily Melton, review of *Crash,* p. 26; June 1, 2008, Emily Melton, review of *Hit and Run,* p. 50; April 1, 2009, Emily Melton, review of *Well and Good,* p. 25; September 1, 2009, Emily Melton, review of *The Fingers of One Foot,* p. 44; March 15, 2010, Sue O'Brien, review of *Silent Intruder,* p. 26; December 15, 2010, Barbara Bibel, review of *A Dog's Life,* p. 25.

*Kirkus Reviews,* April 1, 2002, review of *Grail for Sale,* p. 457; May 1, 2003, review of *The Snatch,* p. 645; March 15, 2004, review of *The Hitch,* p. 251; December 15, 2005, review of *Cold in the Heads,* p. 1302; November 15, 2006, review of *Keeper Turned Poacher,* p. 1155; April 15, 2008, review of *Hit and Run;* October 15, 2008, review of *Crash;* September 15, 2009, review of *The Fingers of One Foot;* December 15, 2010, review of *A Dog's Life.*

*Library Journal,* April 15, 2000, Barbara E. Kemp, review of *Into the Blue,* p. 122; June 1, 2003, Rex Klett, review of *The Snatch,* p. 171.

*Publishers Weekly,* April 23, 2001, review of *Illegal Tender,* p. 52; April 22, 2002, review of *Grail for Sale,* p. 53; August 27, 2007, review of *Loving Memory,* p. 65; March 22, 2010, review of *Silent Intruder,* p. 56; December 13, 2010, review of *A Dog's Life,* p. 41.

### ONLINE

*Fantastic Fiction,* http://www.fantasticfiction.co.uk/ (January 30, 2009), profile.*

# Steve Hendricks

## ◼ Also Known As

Stephen Bicknell

## ◼ Personal

Born Stephen Bicknell, in AR; married Jennifer Hendricks (a professor and lawyer); children: one son. *Education:* Yale University, B.A.

## ◼ Addresses

*Home*—Boulder, CO. *Agent*—Andrew Wylie, The Wylie Agency, 250 W. 57th St., Ste. 2114, New York, NY 10107. *E-mail*—steve@stevehendricks.org.

## ◼ Career

Freelance writer.

## ◼ Writings

*The Unquiet Grave: The FBI and the Struggle for the Soul of Indian Country*, Thunder's Mouth Press (New York, NY), 2006.
*A Kidnapping in Milan: The CIA on Trial*, W.W. Norton (New York, NY), 2010.

Contributor to periodicals and other venues, including *Washington Post Book World, Boston Globe, San Francisco Chronicle, DoubleTake, Orion, Sierra, AlterNet.org,* Progressive Media Project, and Montana Public Radio.

## ◼ Sidelights

Steve Hendricks is a freelance writer and journalist with a particular interest in politics. He considered a career in public service, running for office twice in

Helena, Montana, but lost both times, a result that convinced him to turn to writing full-time. His work has appeared in a number of periodicals, including *DoubleTake, Sierra, Orion, Boston Globe, San Francisco Chronicle,* and the *Nation,* and he has also written for the Progressive Media Project and Montana Public Radio. Hendricks's first book, *The Unquiet Grave: The FBI and the Struggle for the Soul of Indian Country,* stemmed from his interest in the treatment of the Native Americans by the FBI. He first read about the conflict in Peter Matthiessen's book *In the Spirit of Crazy Horse,* after which he began doing his own research on the topic.

On an interview on his home page, Hendricks stated: "I wanted to know what had been found out in the years since—what more had been learned about the conflict over Indian rights, particularly in the main battleground state of South Dakota. It turned out just about nothing had been written since." At first, Hendricks found himself blocked at every turn, as the FBI refused to provide him with documentation that should have been made available under the Freedom of Information Act. He sued the FBI and won the release of thousands of documents, which enabled him to write the book. He wrote *The Unquiet Grave* in an attempt to shed light on the immensity of the cover-up regarding this area in recent U.S. history. Steve Weinberg, writing for *Booklist,* called the book "a citizen indictment based on extensive and impressive research," and a contributor to *Kirkus Reviews* found it to be "a blistering, important work."

### *A Kidnapping in Milan*

Hendricks's second book, *A Kidnapping in Milan: The CIA on Trial,* is an exposé on United States sanctioned counterterrorism efforts in Italy. In an interview regarding the work on the *Biblioklept* Web site, Hendricks stated: "I came to the story somewhat sideways—less because of Abu Omar's rendition itself than because I was frustrated that no one had written a compelling account of the horror of America's torture-by-proxy; that is, the horror of the torture that our client states were inflicting on our captives in what amounted to our offshore dungeons."

Reviewing the work in the *New York Times Book Review*, contributor Mark Mazzetti noted: "Hendricks is particularly strong in tracing Abu Omar's roots in the jihadist world of the Middle East and his travels to Pakistan, Albania and eventually the rundown fringes of Milan. When Abu Omar arrived in Italy, he was just one among a flood of immigrants who had come to work in factories churning out Armani suits and Prada shoes." Steve Fiffer, a contributor to Chicago *Tribune Books,* opined: "[The] absurd near-kidnapping in Egypt provides one of the few light moments in this skillfully crafted, highly disturbing account of the officially sanctioned actions of U.S. operatives in Europe and elsewhere after September 11, 2001."

## ■  Biographical And Critical Sources

### PERIODICALS

*Bellingham Herald* (Bellingham, WA), October 5, 2006, "Author Talks on Badlands Death."
*Booklist,* August 1, 2006, Steve Weinberg, review of *The Unquiet Grave: The FBI and the Struggle for the Soul of Indian Country,* p. 32.

*Kirkus Reviews,* July 1, 2006, review of *The Unquiet Grave,* p. 662.
*New York Times Book Review,* November 12, 2010 (November 12, 2010), Mark Mazzetti, review of *A Kidnapping in Milan: The CIA on Trial.*
*Publishers Weekly,* June 26, 2006, review of *The Unquiet Grave,* p. 44.
*Tribune Books* (Chicago, IL), September 22, 2010, Steve Fiffer, review of *A Kidnapping in Milan.*

### ONLINE

*Biblioklept,* http://biblioklept.org/ (January 31, 2011), author interview.
*Devourer of Books,* http://www.devourerofbooks.com/ (February 21, 2011), review of *A Kidnapping in Milan.*
*Great Salt Lake Book Festival Web page,* http://www.utahhumanities.org/BookFestival/ (February 26, 2007), author biography.
*Harper's,* http://harpers.org/ (October 13, 2010), Scott Horton, author interview.
*Progressive on the Prairie,* http://prairieprogressive.com/ (November 29, 2010), review of *A Kidnapping in Milan.*
*Steve Hendricks Home Page,* http://www.stevehendricks.org (February 26, 2007); (August 14, 2011).
*Torture Report,* http://www.thetorturereport.org/ (December 13, 2010), Larry Siems, review of *A Kidnapping in Milan.*

# David C. Hendrickson

## 1953-

### ■ Personal

Born March 22, 1953, in Oklahoma City, OK; son of Calvin W. (a lawyer) and Frances Hendrickson; married Clelia deMoraes (an editor), June 30, 1979; children: Wesley, Whitney, and Marina. *Education:* Colorado College, B.A., 1976; Johns Hopkins University, Ph.D., 1982.

### ■ Addresses

*Office*—Department of Political Science, Colorado College, Colorado Springs, Colo. 80903.

### ■ Career

Writer. Colorado College, Colorado Springs, assistant professor of political science, 1983-96, professor, 1996-2004, chair of political science department, 2000-03, Robert J. Fox Distinguished Service Professor, 2004—.

### ■ Member

Council on Foreign Relations.

### ■ Writings

(With Robert W. Tucker) *The Fall of the First British Empire: The Origins of the War of American Independence,* Johns Hopkins University Press (Baltimore, MD), 1982.

*The Future of American Strategy,* Holmes & Meier (Teaneck, NJ), 1987.

*Reforming Defense: The State of American Civil Military Relations,* Johns Hopkins University Press (Baltimore, MD), 1988.

(With Robert W. Tucker) *Empire of Liberty: The Statecraft of Thomas Jefferson,* Oxford University Press (New York, NY), 1990.

(With Robert W. Tucker) *The Imperial Temptation: The New World Order and America's Purpose,* Council on Foreign Relations Press (New York, NY), 1992.

*Peace Pact: The Lost World of the American Founding,* University Press of Kansas (Lawrence, KS), 2003.

(With Robert W. Tucker) *Revisions in Need of Revising: What Went Wrong in the Iraq War,* Strategic Studies Institute, U.S. Army War College (Carlisle Barracks, PA), 2005.

*Union, Nation, or Empire: The American Debate over International Relations, 1789-1941,* University Press of Kansas (Lawrence, KS), 2009.

### ■ Sidelights

The prevailing view among twentieth-century social historians is that the American Revolution was precipitated by misrule of British ministers following the Seven Years War. David C. Hendrickson and his coauthor Robert W. Tucker dismiss this explanation, insisting in *The Fall of the British Empire: The Origins of the War of American Independence* that the Americans themselves assisted in creating the problems that led to the revolution.

Paul Langford, writing for the *English Historical Review,* praised the authors for displaying "a marked readiness to accept the intractability of the American problem from the British standpoint," and for placing "emphasis . . . on the imperial dilemma, rather than the colonial predicament." Ian R. Christie in the *Times Higher Education Supplement* called *The Fall of the British Empire* "an intellectually enjoyable work, lively and provoking in its critical judgments, and an admirable example of the stiffening which can be given to historical discussion by the skills of the political scientist."

### The Future of American Strategy and Reforming Defense

*The Future of American Strategy,* Hendrickson's 1987 work, discusses American economic policies concerning Western Europe, the Middle East, and "the maintenance of strategic nuclear stability," according to Michael Howard in the *Times Literary Supplement.* The critic praised the author, judging that "on all of these [strategies] he has wise things to say, and he says them in a language which is not only intelligible to the layman, but a pleasure to read." Hendrickson's third book, *Reforming Defense: The State of American Military Relations,* defines and analyzes the three major military reform movements that have arisen in the 1980s. The "organizational reformers," he writes, hope for change in the military as an institution; the "administrative reformers" look for change in the vast military bureaucracy; and the "military reformers" claim basic military theories must be overhauled in order to suit the government's changing military strategies.

### Union, Nation, or Empire

Henrickson's work, *Union, Nation, or Empire: The American Debate over International Relations, 1789-1941,* is an examination of American foreign policy up until World War II. Hendrickson examines how historical attitudes towards international relations are relevant today.

Reviewing the work on *H-Net: Humanities and Social Sciences Online,* contributor John Kane observed: "This is an excellent book, rich in incident and analysis, that pursues its theme steadfastly, evenhandedly, and for the most part convincingly. By exploring the centrality of union to Americans' understanding of their political experience, it reveals why that experience had such resonance in and for the wider world even at times when the United States seemed most eager to be disconnected from it. The book presumes some knowledge of the

sweep of American history but rewards reading by anyone with an interest in that history." *Political Science Quarterly* contributor Robert J. McMahon explained: "Hendrickson seeks to establish his big themes through a methodical description and analysis. . . . *Union, Nation, or Empire* helps recapture the passion, high stakes, and contingency of some of the country's most contentious foreign policy debates. It provides a welcome and original addition to the literature on early American foreign relations." A contributor to *Foreign Affairs* described the work as "a book that no serious student of the United States' political tradition can afford to ignore."

## ■ Biographical And Critical Sources

### PERIODICALS

*Choice,* February 1, 2010, R. Vitalis, review of *Union, Nation, or Empire: The American Debate over International Relations, 1789-1941,* p. 1165.

*English Historical Review,* fall, 1985, Paul Langford, review of *The Fall of the First British Empire: The Origins of the War of American Independence.*

*Foreign Affairs,* November 1, 2009, Walter Russell Mead, review of *Union, Nation, or Empire.*

*Political Science Quarterly,* March 22, 2010, Robert J. McMahon, review of *Union, Nation, or Empire,* p. 168.

*Times Higher Education Supplement,* June 3, 1983, Ian R. Christie, review of *The Fall of the First British Empire.*

*Times Literary Supplement,* October 14, 1983, September 18-24, 1987, Michael Howard, review of *The Future of American Strategy.*

### ONLINE

*Colorado College Web site,* http://personalwebs.coloradocollege.edu/ (August 23, 2011), author profile.

*H-Net: Humanities and Social Sciences Online,* http://www.h-net.org/ (September 12, 2011), John Kane, review of *Union, Nation, or Empire.*

*United States Army War College, Strategic Studies Institute Web site,* http://www.strategicstudiesinstitute.army.mil/ (August 23, 2011), author profile.*

# Nigel Hey

## 1936-

### ■ Also Known As

Nigel Stewart Hey

### ■ Personal

Born June 23, 1936, in Morecambe, Lancashire, England; son of Aaron and Margery Hey; married Miriam Lamb, October 13, 1960 (divorced, 1977); children: Brian, Jocelyn. *Education:* University of Utah, B.A., 1958.

### ■ Addresses

*Home*—Albuquerque, NM. *Office*—IMS World Publications, York House, 37 Queen Sq., London WCIN 3BH, England.

### ■ Career

Writer. United Press International, newsman in Salt Lake City, UT, 1958; *Kentish Express* (weekly newspaper), Ashford, Kent, England, copy editor, 1959-60; *Bermuda Mid-Ocean News* (daily newspaper), Hamilton, Bermuda, associate editor, 1958-59, 1960-61; Weltech College, Salt Lake City, director, 1962-64; Newspaper Printing Corp., Albuquerque, NM, editor, 1964-66; Sandia Laboratories (research and development firm), Albuquerque, science writer, 1966-72, senior administrator, until 2001; IMS World Publications, London, England, editorial director, beginning 1972. Member of board of directors, New Mexico Conference on Social Welfare, 1966-70.

### ■ Member

American Institute of Aeronautics and Astronautics, National Association of Science Writers, International Association of Science Writers, Association of British Science Writers.

### ■ Awards, Honors

New Mexico State Press Association awards for editorial and feature writing in weekly newspapers.

### ■ Writings

*The Mysterious Sun*, Putnam (New York, NY), 1971.
(With Science Book Associates editors) *How Will We Feed the Hungry Billions?*, Messner (New York, NY), 1971.
*How We Will Explore the Outer Planets*, Putnam (New York, NY), 1973.
*Solar System*, Weidenfeld & Nicolson (London, England), 2002.
*The Star Wars Enigma: Behind the Scenes of the Cold War Race for Missile Defense*, Potomac Books (Washington, DC), 2006.

Writer of film, *The Space Age and You*, and short television film clips on science; cowriter of other full-length science films.

### ■ Sidelights

Nigel Hey, who has speared barracuda off Bermuda and driven a tunnel into a Greek mountain, looks on research for books as another, semi-vicarious, type of adventure. He writes: "We must . . . learn to think of technology as the farmer thinks of his plow—as a means of husbanding the finite fields of earth. Most vital subject? Easy—it's the race between population, the restoration of natural ecological balances, and the management of world food, water and energy resources."

#### *Solar System*

Hey's book *Solar System* was published in 2002. In the work Hey offers an explanation of the nine planets, the sun, and other space matter in our solar system. He brings the reader up to date on modern space technology, and astronomer's current theories about the solar system.

A *Science News* contributor called the book "a solid introduction to space studies." Allison Boyle and Ken Grimes, contributors to *Astronomy,* assessed: "In its current format it's too dense for the novice tourist and too messily arranged to be a useful reference for seasoned travelers. It's a fun tour destination, but the package needs improving."

### The Star Wars Enigma

Hey's book *The Star Wars Enigma: Behind the Scenes of the Cold War Race for Missile Defense,* is a detailed study of the Strategic Defense Initiative enacted by President Reagan during the cold war.

Reviewing the work on the *Space Review* Web site, contributor Taylor Dinerman stated: "This book will not satisfy those who are looking for a solid set of conclusions, but for those who want to have some idea as to what the SDI debate in the 1980s was all about, they could do worse." *Air & Space Power*

*Journal* contributor Eric J. Kolb recommended: "*The Star Wars Enigma* is a worthwhile read for anyone in the Air Force or NMD community who seeks a concise, entertaining, and accessible account of the SDI saga and its contributions to our current effort."

## ■ Biographical And Critical Sources

### PERIODICALS

*Air & Space Power Journal,* June 22, 2010, Eric J. Kolb, review of *The Star Wars Enigma: Behind the Scenes of the Cold War Race for Missile Defense,* p. 108.
*Astronomy,* March 1, 2003, Alison Boyle, review of *Solar System,* p. 102.
*Mechanical Engineering-CIME,* November 1, 2006, review of *The Star Wars Enigma,* p. 49.
*Science News,* December 21, 2002, review of *Solar System,* p. 401.

### ONLINE

*Space Review,* http://www.thespacereview.com/ (October 15, 2007), Taylor Dineran, review of *The Star Wars Enigma.**

# James Holland

## 1970-

## ■ Personal

Born June 27, 1970, in Salisbury, Wiltshire, England; married; children: one son and one daughter. *Education:* Graduated from Durham University, 1992.

## ■ Addresses

*Home*—England. *E-mail*—info@secondworldwar forum.com.

## ■ Career

Writer and historian. Random House UK, London, England, worked in public relations and marketing, 1992-96; Reed Publishers, London, worked in public relations, 1996-97; Penguin Books UK, Ltd., London, worked in public relations, 1997-2002; freelance writer.

## ■ Member

British Commission for Military History, Guild of Battlefield Guides.

## ■ Writings

*"SERGEANT JOHN TANNER" SERIES*

*The Odin Mission*, Bantam Press (London, England), 2008.
*Darkest Hour*, Bantam Press (London, England), 2009.

*Blood of Honour*, Bantam Press (London, England), 2010.
*Hellfire*, Bantam Press (London, England), 2011.

*NOVELS*

*The Burning Blue*, William Heinemann (London, England), 2004.
*A Pair of Silver Wings*, William Heinemann (London, England), 2006.
*Duty Calls: Dunkirk*, Puffin (London, England), 2011.

*NONFICTION*

*Fortress Malta: An Island under Siege, 1940-1943*, Orion (London, England), 2003.
*Together We Stand: Turning Tide in the West: North Africa, 1942-1943*, HarperCollins (London, England), 2005.
*Twenty-one: Coming of Age in the Second World War*, HarperCollins (London, England), 2006.
*Heroes: The Greatest Generation and the Second World War*, HarperPerennial (London, England), 2007.
*Italy's Sorrow: A Year of War, 1944-1945*, St. Martin's Press (New York, NY), 2008.
*The Battle of Britain: Five Months That Changed History May-October 1940*, Bantam Press (London, England), 2010, St. Martin's Press (New York, NY), 2011.

Contributor to periodicals, including the *Daily Telegraph, Times, Sunday Times, BBC History Magazine, Mail on Sunday, Sunday Express,* and *New Statesman.*

## ■ Sidelights

James Holland was born and raised in Salisbury, Wiltshire, England, near Stonehenge and Salisbury Cathedral, an area steeped in history. He attended

Durham University, where he studied history, and went on to work in the publicity department of several major publishers in London, promoting the work of such notable clients as celebrity chef Jamie Oliver. His writing has appeared in a variety of national newspapers and magazines, and he has written both fiction and nonfiction books that draw on his interest and education in history.

### Fortress Malta

*Fortress Malta: An Island under Siege, 1940-1943,* for instance, takes a look at the conditions on the island during World War II, a small parcel of land that has nevertheless become the most bombed place in the world. A British colony since 1814, Malta bore the brunt of numerous flyover attacks from both the Germans and the Italians during the war, resulting in King George VI of England awarding the island the George Cross for Gallantry. Holland concerns himself more with the personal stories of the war, delving into the histories of the people who lived on Malta through the attacks, and how they survived the devastation.

Carlton Sherwood, in a review for the *Washington Times,* observed that Holland "fashions a remarkably seamless history that introduces his readers to dozens of unlikely characters." *Library Journal* contributor Brian K. DeLuca remarked: "The Maltese people's stories of personal courage and suffering . . . shine through in Holland's superb documentation." Nicholas Roe, writing for the *Guardian,* stated: "The broad perspective is done well, albeit without challenging or revising received accounts." Roe also noted: "Ranging through the military and civilian communities, Holland shows the war's destruction of everyday life as food, water, fuel, electricity, transport and buildings gradually disappeared."

### Together We Stand

*Together We Stand: Turning Tide in the West: North Africa, 1942-1943* addresses the end of the British campaigns in North Africa during World War II, a dramatic period due to the scale of the endeavor as well as the wartime military personalities involved. Holland compares the later attempts to the earlier years of the campaigns, examining the organization of the different forces and analyzing the level of preparedness and training of each nation. He also looks at the way the arrival of the Americans, timed with the reorganization of the British troops, turned the tide in Africa. Holland interviewed veterans and incorporated their individual stories with the more commonly described history of the military operations.

"Holland's narrative is leisurely and anecdotal," according to a *Kirkus Reviews* critic, "drawing on the memories of dozens of players, including the photographer Cecil Beaton and the journalist and author Alan Moorehead." A *Publishers Weekly* reviewer called Holland's book "a compelling and detailed account," and an "exhaustively researched narrative." Gilbert Taylor predicted in *Booklist* that the volume, "flavored with his tendency to kibitz about strategy and tactics, will keep readers engaged."

### Italy's Sorrow

In 2008 Holland published *Italy's Sorrow: A Year of War, 1944-1945.* The account covers the Italian campaign of Allied soldiers reaching across Italy at the end of World War II. Holland faults the lack of enough amphibious assault vehicles and a poor supply chain for slowing the Allied progress of invading the Italian peninsula. Holland also notes that many Allied forces were permanently relocated to West Europe for the invasion at Normandy.

Raleigh Trevelyan, writing on the *Literary Review* Web site, summarized that "Holland's research is quite staggering. His aim has been to illuminate the story with personal reminiscences and details of the backgrounds of his main characters, high and low, from army commanders to contadini. Recorded interviews with German soldiers make this book stand out among the many histories of the war in Italy, especially the interview with Hans Golda of the seventy-one Werfer Regiment, who is evidently rather a jolly person but gives vivid accounts of times in extremis, such as the horror of seeing comrades drowning as they tried to escape across the Po." A contributor to the *Blogging the Second World War* Web site pointed out that the various "elements of the civilian experience of war are often under explored in history and military history books, yet they are at the forefront of Holland's history. For this, he deserves much credit for these eye opening accounts of *Italy's Sorrow.*" Dominic Sandbrook, reviewing the book in the London *Telegraph,* remarked that "above all, it is for the human interest, the emotional texture, the vicarious experience of men under the most terrible pressure, that we read military history, and in this book James Holland cements his reputation as the rising star of the genre." A contributor to *Military.com* commented that "Holland has written a first-rate story of an underappreciated campaign. . . . Holland's *Italy's Sorrow* [offers] a definitive account of a controversial campaign and 'a truly terrible' fight." A critic writing in *Kirkus Reviews* found the book to be "less engaging than Rick Atkinson's *The Day of Battle: The War in Sicily and Italy, 1943-1944* (2007), but still of much value to WWII buffs and generalists." *Booklist* contributor Margaret Flanagan remarked: "Those more familiar with martial history will welcome this inclusive chronicle." Caroline Moorehead, reviewing the book in *Spectator*, felt that "as a picture of a country slowly consumed and destroyed by war, *Italy's Sorrow* is a memorable book."

### The Battle of Britain

Holland's book *The Battle of Britain: Five Months That Changed History May-October 1940*, he details the battle that marked the beginning of the fall of Nazi Germany, particularly focusing on the faceoff between the Royal Air Force and the German Luftwaffe.

Reviewing the work in *Library Journal*, contributor Daniel K. Blewett said the work "is recommended for all history buffs and World War II students." A *Kirkus Reviews* contributor described the book as "A painstakingly detailed history of the battle that exposed the myth of Nazi invincibility." A contributor to the *Economist* criticized: "Published to mark the 70th anniversary of the battle of Britain, this book should sell well. But it will leave many readers unsatisfied. One problem is its glibness. . . . A bigger problem is that the author's enthusiasm for his subject is not matched by his grip of history. He peddles the Anglocentric myth that Britain was 'alone' in the summer of 1940 (insultingly forgetting Greece, Poland and the entire British empire). Too many characters appear, with annoyingly similar potted biographies." A *Publishers Weekly* contributor remarked: "This work enhances Holland's . . . developing reputation as a writer of popular military history." A *Military Review* contributor called the work a "groundbreaking new book."

## ■ Biographical And Critical Sources

*PERIODICALS*

*Booklist*, February 1, 2006, Gilbert Taylor, review of *Together We Stand: Turning Tide in the West: North Africa, 1942-1943*, p. 18; February 15, 2008, Margaret Flanagan, review of *Italy's Sorrow: A Year of War, 1944-1945*, p. 24.

*Bookseller*, February 4, 2005, review of *Together We Stand*, p. 35.
*Contemporary Review*, August, 2003, review of *Fortress Malta: An Island under Siege, 1940-1943*, p. 123.
*Economist*, May 15, 2010, "Boys in Blue; Britain and the Second World War," p. 93.
*Guardian* (London, England), May 1, 2004, Nicholas Roe, "Against All Odds."
*Historian*, summer, 2007, Charles Cogan, review of *Together We Stand*, p. 380.
*Kirkus Reviews*, January 1, 2006, review of *Together We Stand*, p. 28; January 1, 2008, review of *Italy's Sorrow*; December 15, 2010, review of *The Battle of Britain: Five Months That Changed History May-October 1940*.
*Library Journal*, October 1, 2003, Brian K. DeLuca, review of *Fortress Malta*, p. 94; March 1, 2011, Daniel K. Blewett, review of *The Battle of Britain*, p. 84.
*Military Review*, May 1, 2011, review of *The Battle of Britain*.
*Observer* (London, England), August 19, 2007, review of *Italy's Sorrow*, p. 28.
*Publishers Weekly*, December 5, 2005, review of *Together We Stand*, p. 44; December 6, 2010, review of *The Battle of Britain*, p. 39.
*Spectator*, March 15, 2008, Caroline Moorehead, review of *Italy's Sorrow*, p. 58.
*Telegraph* (London, England), January 4, 2008, Dominic Sandbrook, review of *Italy's Sorrow*, p. 94.
*Times Literary Supplement*, June 30, 2006, Andrew Taylor, review of *Twenty-one: Coming of Age in the Second World War*, p. 33; June 27, 2008, Michael Howard, review of *Italy's Sorrow*, p. 12.
*Washington Post Book World*, December 7, 2003, review of *Fortress Malta*, p. 12.
*Washington Times*, November 7, 2006, Carlton Sherwood, "Revealing Horrors of Most Bombed Place on Earth," review of *Fortress Malta*.

*ONLINE*

*Blogging the Second World War*, http://secondworldwar.wordpress.com/ (May 15, 2008), review of *Italy's Sorrow*.
*Fantastic Fiction*, http://www.fantasticfiction.co.uk/ (November 7, 2006), author profile.
*James Holland Home Page*, http://www.secondworldwarforum.com (October 4, 2008), author biography; (August 23, 2011).
*Literary Review*, http://www.literaryreview.co.uk/ (October 4, 2008), Raleigh Trevelyan, review of *Italy's Sorrow*.
*Military.com*, http://www.military.com/ (October 4, 2008), review of *Italy's Sorrow*.*

# Hannah Holmes

## 1963-

### ■ Personal

Born December 22, 1963; married. *Education:* University of Southern Maine, B.A. (magna cum laude), 1988.

### ■ Addresses

*Home*—South Portland, ME.

### ■ Career

Writer. Discovery Channel Online, science and natural-history writer; "Science Live," show cohost.

### ■ Writings

*The Secret Life of Dust: From the Cosmos to the Kitchen Counter, the Big Consequences of Little Things,* Wiley (New York, NY), 2001.
*Suburban Safari: A Year on the Lawn* (nonfiction), Bloomsbury (New York, NY), 2005.
*The Well-Dressed Ape: A Natural History of Myself,* Random House (New York, NY), 2009.
*Quirk: Brain Science Makes Sense of Your Peculiar Personality,* Random House (New York, NY), 2011.

Contributor to *Outside, Islands, Escape, Sierra, New York Times Magazine,* and *Los Angeles Times Magazine;Casco Bay Weekly,* news editor, 1988; editor of *Garbage* magazine, 1989-2001; scriptwriter with Matthew A. Borten of the documentary *Operation in Orbit: Hubble Telescope's Space Doctors,* Big Shot Productions, 1998.

### ■ Sidelights

Science and natural-history writer Hannah Holmes explores the minute realm of dust in her first book, *The Secret Life of Dust: From the Cosmos to the Kitchen Counter, the Big Consequences of Little Things.* The author's extensively researched book takes the reader from comet dust to the Sahara sand and discusses dust's impact on a wide range of issues, including the environment, allergies, and even the evolution of planets.

Writing in *Library Journal,* Michael D. Cramer noted that the author discusses "technical points in language that is clear and comprehensible even for those lacking a science background." A *Publishers Weekly* contributor noted that Holmes "teases many tantalizing facts from this particulate microscopic substance." A reviewer writing in *Science News* commented that "from various vantage points, Holmes provides a compelling and enjoyable look at the world of these tiny flecks." *Saturday Evening Post* contributor Ted Kreiter noted: "The research in her book makes it clear that dust is far from the dry subject we might think it to be," adding that "Holmes demonstrates that dust, be it ever so humble, plays an amazing role in our lives."

#### *Suburban Safari*

In *Suburban Safari: A Year on the Lawn,* Holmes follows the four seasons and local wildlife on the lawn of her Portland, Maine, suburban home. The author's musings include not only insights into birds, insects, and other animals, but also a discussion of lawns and their sociological history. The author dedicated the book to a chipmunk named Cheeky that she tamed during her backyard sojourn.

A *Kirkus Reviews* contributor called the book "a cracking good reminder that an appreciation of the wonders of nature need not be reserved for special occasions." "For readers who believe lawns are simply something needing mowing," George Cohen commented in *Booklist*, "science writer Holmes has news for them." A *Publishers Weekly* contributor noted that "Holmes gives names and personalities . . . [to the animals] but she keeps her naturalist credibility intact by inviting scientists and other experts to join her in her lawn chair vigil."

### The Well-Dressed Ape

Holmes published *The Well-Dressed Ape: A Natural History of Myself* in 2009. The account is a biological fact sheet for humans. The author compares statistics and rankings of animals with humans, which she describes in the terms of being yet another species of animal. Holmes also covers the evolutionary reasons why humans are the ways they are, and not more like their animal relatives in certain areas.

A contributor writing on the *Public Square* Web site noted that "Holmes offers an admirable number throughout the book" of evolutionary theories. Kristin Thiel, writing in Portland's *Oregonian*, opined that "Holmes' style is enjoyable: smart and easygoing, yet well-written and well-organized—reading her brief discussions on human territoriality, diet and our impact on the ecosystem, among our other descriptors, is like attending a lecture that leaves you feeling warmer and wiser than when you entered." Reviewing the book in the *St. Petersburg Times*, Diane Roberts called it "a hoot," appending that "Holmes cheerfully declares, 'Hello! I'm not a scientist,' nevertheless, she knows her stuff. She can explain how human brain chemistry evolved to maximize our chances for breeding and surviving a famine, and she does it in a way that doesn't make your head explode. Indeed, she offers the best excuse you've ever heard for falling off the diet wagon."

Yoni Goldstein, writing in Canada's *National Post*, claimed that the book's major flaw is "that Holmes is too deep in the evolutionary camp—for every wonder of human existence she offers a cold Origin of Species-style answer." Goldstein added that the book is "plagued by a jarring mix of tones: quasi-scientific jargon and cutesy personal revelations don't blend well." Kimberley Jones, writing in the *Austin Chronicle*, commented that "the book is indeed quite dense—but throughout she makes the material hugely engaging, peppered with wry asides . . . and the occasional startlingly lyrical moment." Naomi Barr, writing in *O, the Oprah Magazine*, called the book "wry," adding that the author does not "pull any punches when tackling the big issues of our time." Rick Kleffel, writing on the *Agony Column* Web site, called *The Well-Dressed Ape* "a fine work of science writing, a book in which the prose craftsmanship plays as important a part as the facts

that underlie the work. This is humanity as we might seem if viewed by benevolent aliens, surveying all the life on earth."

A *Kirkus Reviews* contributor stated that, in the novel, "Careful science meets good writing." The same contributor remarked: "The careful reader will learn scads of facts to attend to all kinds of questions they may not have known they had." Abe Streep, writing in *Mother Jones*, summarized: "Using the framework of a mock science textbook on the species Homo sapiens, Holmes tackles a variety of questions about our basest instincts." *Time* contributor Lev Grossman noticed that "Holmes describes us quite wonderfully, and she's a tireless compiler of biological trivia. She scours the extremes of the earth for anomalous and specially adapted humans." A contributor reviewing the book in *Publishers Weekly* noted: "Holmes makes the scientific personal in prose that is juicy and humorous, if occasionally a bit too cute."

*Booklist* contributor Vanessa Bush wrote: "Holmes brings fresh eyes to her look at our old species." Don Oldenburg, reviewing the book in *USA Today*, commented: "Trying to understand ourselves is an attribute exclusive to Homo sapiens. To that end, her book succeeds affably." Oldenburg criticized, however, that "where it falters, the result of excessive wordplay and obsessive science, well, that's only human, too." Michael D. Cramer, reviewing the book in *Library Journal*, lauded that "Holmes comfortably uses herself as the example for the topic, and the personalization works well."

### Quirk

In Holmes's fourth book *Quirk: Brain Science Makes Sense of Your Peculiar Personality*, she explores the science behind what composes each person's unique personality. Each of the eighteen chapters in this study focus on a different part of the brain, and how it contributes to personality.

*Oregonian* contributor B.T. Shaw said in a review of the work: "Conversational, good-humored and clear, the chapters in *Quirk* hum along, fueled by Holmes' considerable curiosity. And although the quizzes initially struck me as broad and somewhat leading, I eventually found myself cornering housemates and friends, coaxing them to weigh in on themselves." A *Kirkus Reviews* contributor described the book as "an intriguing but hardly groundbreaking consideration of the qualities that distinguish us." *Wilson Quarterly* contributor Emily Anthes observed: "Holmes has a gift for making complex science clear and accessible, but Quirk has one flaw: It exhibits more than a whiff of biological determinism. . . . Even if Holmes wanted to maintain her rigid focus on genes and neurotransmitters, it would have been worthwhile to remind readers that brains and genes are just part of the puzzle. With personality, as with most human traits, it's nature and nurture. Holmes's book, interesting as it is, addresses only half of the equation." A *Publishers Weekly* contributor pointed out: "The author's take is relentlessly mechanistic: personality, in her view, is largely the product of genes."

## ■ Biographical And Critical Sources

### BOOKS

Holmes, Hannah, *Suburban Safari: A Year on the Lawn*, Bloomsbury (New York, NY), 2005.

### PERIODICALS

*American Scientist*, May 15, 2001, review of *The Secret Life of Dust: From the Cosmos to the Kitchen Counter, the Big Consequences of Little Things*, p. 458.

*Austin Chronicle*, February 6, 2009, Kimberley Jones, review of *The Well-Dressed Ape: A Natural History of Myself.*

*Book*, July, 2001, review of *The Secret Life of Dust*, p. 13.

*Booklist*, June 1, 2001, Bryce Christensen, review of *The Secret Life of Dust*, p. 1809; January 1, 2005, George Cohen, review of *Suburban Safari*, p. 794; December 1, 2008, Vanessa Bush, review of *The Well-Dressed Ape*, p. 10.

*Choice*, January, 2002, C.G. Wood, review of *The Secret Life of Dust*, p. 899.

*Discover*, February, 2009, review of *The Well-Dressed Ape*, p. 22.

*Entertainment Weekly*, February 5, 2005, Tina Jordan, review of *Suburban Safari*, p. 106.

*Guardian* (London, England), January 30, 2009, review of *The Well-Dressed Ape*, p. 39.

*Kirkus Reviews*, May 15, 2001, review of *The Secret Life of Dust*, p. 723; December 15, 2004, review of *Suburban Safari*, p. 1182; November 1, 2008, review of *The Well-Dressed Ape*; December 15, 2010, review of *Quirk: Brain Science Makes Sense of Your Peculiar Personality.*

*Library Journal*, July, 2001, Michael D. Cramer, review of *The Secret Life of Dust*, p. 117; November 1, 2008, Michael D. Cramer, review of *The Well-Dressed Ape*, p. 98.

*Mother Jones*, January-February, 2009, Abe Streep, review of *The Well-Dressed Ape*, p. 70.

*National Post* (Don Mills, Ontario, Canada), March 21, 2009, Yoni Goldstein, review of *The Well-Dressed Ape*, p. 13.

*Nature*, autumn, 2001, review of *The Secret Life of Dust*, p. 51.

*New Scientist*, September 15, 2001, Elizabeth Sourbut, review of *The Secret Life of Dust*, p. 46.

*Oregonian* (Portland, OR), January, 2009, Kristin Thiel, review of *The Well-Dressed Ape*; February 19, 2011, B.T. Shaw, review of *Quirk.*

*O, the Oprah Magazine*, February, 2009, Naomi Barr, review of *The Well-Dressed Ape.*

*Portland Press Herald*, March 6, 2011, "Author Q&A: It's All about Me."

*Publishers Weekly*, July 30, 2001, review of *The Secret Life of Dust*, p. 76; January 3, 2005, review of *Suburban Safari*, p. 43; November 10, 2008, review of *The Well-Dressed Ape*, p. 41; December 20, 2010, review of *Quirk*, p. 47.

*Ruminator Review*, spring, 2002, review of *The Secret Life of Dust*, p. 37.

*St. Petersburg Times*, February 5, 2009, Diane Roberts, review of *The Well-Dressed Ape.*

*Saturday Evening Post*, September-October, 2003, Ted Kreiter, review of *The Secret Life of Dust*, p. 27.

*Science Books & Films*, March, 2002, review of *The Secret Life of Dust*, p. 360.

*Science News*, May 3, 2003, review of *The Secret Life of Dust*, p. 287.

*Scientific American*, February, 2002, review of *The Secret Life of Dust*, p. 97.

*Scitech Book News*, December, 2005, review of *Suburban Safari.*

*Time*, January 26, 2009, Lev Grossman, review of *The Well-Dressed Ape*, p. 60.

*Times Educational Supplement*, June 21, 2002, review of *The Secret Life of Dust*, p. 29.

*USA Today*, March 3, 2009, Don Oldenburg, review of *The Well-Dressed Ape*, p. 5D.

*Whole Earth*, fall, 2002, review of *The Secret Life of Dust*, p. 89.

*Wilson Quarterly*, March 22, 2011, "Who Are You?," p. 102.

### ONLINE

*Agony Column*, http://trashotron.com/agony/ (April 4, 2009), Rick Kleffel, review of *The Well-Dressed Ape.*

*Hannah Holmes Home Page*, http://www.hannahholmes.net (July 1, 2009), author biography and interview.

*My Daily*, http://www.mydaily.com/ (March 7, 2011), Amanda Chatel, author interview.

*Powells.com*, http://www.powells.com/ (July 1, 2009), author interview.

*Public Square*, http://www.zocalopublicsquare.org/ (July 1, 2009), review of *The Well-Dressed Ape.**

# Sonya Huber

## 1971-

---

### ■ Personal

Born January 30, 1971, in Evergreen Park, IL; children: Ivan. *Education:* Carleton College, B.A., 1993; Ohio State University, M.A., 2000, M.F.A., 2004.

### ■ Addresses

*Office*—Department of Writing and Linguistics, Georgia Southern University, P.O. Box 8026, Statesboro, GA 30460. *E-mail*—shuber@georgiasouthern. edu.

### ■ Career

Writer, educator. Georgia Southern University, Statesboro, assistant professor; Ashland University, Ashland, OH, instructor. Has had numerous other part-time jobs.

### ■ Awards, Honors

PEO research scholar, 2003; Robert McCloy fellowship, American Council on Germany, 2003; StorySouth's Million Writers Award for notable story, 2004; Excellence in Education Award, Coastal Business, Technology, and Education Alliance, 2007.

### ■ Writings

*Opa Nobody* (novel), University of Nebraska Press (Lincoln, NE), 2008.
*The Backwards Research Guide for Writers: Using Your Life for Reflection, Connection and Inspiration* (textbook), Equinox Books (London, England), 2009.

*Cover Me: A Health Insurance Memoir,* University of Nebraska Press (Lincoln, NE), 2010.

Author of blog. Contributor to anthologies. Contributor of short fiction, poetry, and essays to periodicals and online journals, including *Fourth Genre, Sub-Lit, Topic, Passages North, McSweeney's Internet Tendency, Pudding House, Main Street Rag, Literary Mama, Kaleidoscope, Washington Post Magazine, Chronicle of Higher Education, Psychology Today, In These Times, Sojourner, Earth Island Journal,* and *Hotel Amerika.*

### ■ Sidelights

Writing on her home page, Sonya Huber explained the significance of the title of her debut novel, *Opa Nobody:* "'Opa' is grandfather in German, and 'Nobody' refers to the fact that my grandfather's political life was invisible, at least to me, when I was growing up." Writing on her MySpace page, Huber described the work as a "book of fiction and creative nonfiction" and remarked: "The main story is about my grandfather, who was an anti-Nazi activist in Germany in World War II. I talk to him, imagine his life, and try to make sense of mine (unsuccessfully, of course)." The work was begun as a project for her graduate degree in writing and blends factual, historical writing with techniques of fiction writing, such as a sense of scene, description, and narrative. To complete the book, Huber took a college course about German history, read widely about the history and culture of the Ruhr area of Germany where her family originated, and traveled to Germany to interview surviving family members and research local archives.

Huber's inspiration for the book came from her own commitment to political activism, from fighting against the American war in Iraq to preserving old-growth forests. Hearing from her immigrant mother stories of her grandfather Heina Buschman's commitment to fighting for the proletariat in the face of the new Nazi dictatorship and the toll it took on his family, she decided to try to recreate his life to uncover the links between activism and family life. A mother herself, Huber wanted to discover whether she could actually combine activism with being a parent. Writing in the *Christian Century*, Valerie Weaver-Zercher observed: "Through her admirably candid writing, Huber makes visible the inability of political activism to manage failure and despair." Weaver-Zercher further noted: "Huber's research had led her to no satisfactory answer, and her own experience of trying to merge activism with motherhood only complicated the question."

Reviewing the work in Florida's *Orlando Sentinel*, Karrie Higgins noted that "Huber is always careful to explain where research ends and imagination begins." Higgins also commented: "By connecting with history on such a personal level, [Huber] reveals how ordinary citizens can get swept up into movements of all kinds; allegiance is never as simple as a membership card." A *Kirkus Reviews* critic offered a mixed assessment of *Opa Nobody*, describing it as "bumpy, but a unique, imaginative take on the family memoir." Higher praise came from *Booklist* contributor Deborah Donovan, who found the book a "thoughtful discourse on political activism and the toll exacted from those dedicated to unpopular causes."

### Cover Me

In Huber's next book, *Cover Me: A Health Insurance Memoir*, she chronicles her struggles with the Health Care System in the United States. In an interview concerning the work with Shannon Drury on the *Literary Mama* Web site, Hubar explained why she chose to writer about health insurance: "I have written journalistic and policy documents about health insurance, but I wanted to see what all that mess looked like in a normal person's life. So I started from the beginning, trying to pick up any threads of insurance I could find in my life story, from childhood through college through career and childbirth and beyond. The book tries to show how my health insurance options—and lack of options—limited and curtailed my sense of what was possible in my life."

Reviewing the work on the *Sophisticated Dorkiness* Web site, a contributor opined: "I like my memoirs on the informative side, and this one just didn't do that for me. If you're less neurotic than I am about the information side of narrative nonfiction, there are stories to enjoy in this memoir. But if you want a book that can give you some background to current health-care issues, I'd suggest looking elsewhere." However, reviewing the work on the *Brevity Book Reviews* Web site, contributor Sarah Werthan Buttenwieser expressed: "What I found so compelling about Huber's story is her ability to make the personal resonate so much more loudly than the political ideas or theories, while capably insuring that her own story underscores her political stance on health care." A *Kirkus Reviews* contributor described the work as "a harrowing though not uncommon story."

### ■ Biographical And Critical Sources

*PERIODICALS*

*Booklist*, March 1, 2008, Deborah Donovan, review of *Opa Nobody*, p. 46.

*Christian Century*, May 6, 2008, Valerie Weaver-Zercher, review of *Opa Nobody*, p. 55.

*Kirkus Reviews*, January 1, 2008, review of *Opa Nobody*; July 15, 2010, review of *Cover Me: A Health Insurance Memoir*.

*Orlando Sentinel* (Orlando, FL), March 23, 2008, Karrie Higgins, review of *Opa Nobody*.

*ONLINE*

*Ashland MFA News*, http://ashlandmfa.blogspot.com/ (August 30, 2010), Joan Hanna, author interview.

*Ashland University Web site*, http://www.ashland.edu/ (August 22, 2008), "MFA at Ashland: Sonya Huber."

*Brevity Book Reviews*, http://www.creativenonfiction.org/ (August 14, 2011), Sarah Werthan Buttenwieser, review of *Cover Me*.

*Georgia College Web site*, http://infox.gcsu.edu/ (January 18, 2011), author profile.

*Georgia Southern University Web site*, http://personal.georgiasouthern.edu/ (August 14, 2011), author profile.

*Literary Mama*, http://www.literarymama.com/ (March 5, 2011), Shannon Drury, author interview.

*Red Room*, http://www.redroom.com/ (August 22, 2008), "Sonya Huber."

*Sonya Huber Home Page*, http://www.sonyahuber.com (August 22, 2008); (August 14, 2011).

*Sonya Huber MySpace Page*, http://www.myspace.com/sonyahuber (August 22, 2008).

*Sophisticated Dorkiness*, http://www.sophisticateddorkiness.com/ (March 2, 2011), review of *Cover Me*.

# Stephen Hunter

## 1946-

### ■ Personal

Born March 25, 1946, in Kansas City, MO; son of Charles Francis (an academic) and Virginia (an executive) Hunter; married Lucy Hageman (a teacher and journalist), September 13, 1969; children: James H., Amy E. *Education:* Northwestern University, B.S.J., 1968.

### ■ Addresses

*Home*—Baltimore, MD.

### ■ Career

Journalist. *Baltimore Sun*, Baltimore, MD, copy reader, 1971-73, book review editor, 1973-82, film critic, 1982-97; *Washington Post*, Washington, DC, film critic, 1997—. *Military service:* U.S. Army, Infantry, 1968-70.

### ■ Awards, Honors

Pulitzer Prize finalist, 1995, 1996; American Society of Newspaper Editors award, 1998, for distinguished writing in criticism; Pulitzer Prize, 2003, for criticism.

### ■ Writings

#### NOVELS

*The Master Sniper*, Morrow (New York, NY), 1980.
*The Second Saladin*, Morrow (New York, NY), 1982.

*The Spanish Gambit*, Crown (New York, NY), 1985, published as *Tapestry of Spies*, Dell (New York, NY), 1997.
*Target*, Warner Books (New York, NY), 1985.
*The Day before Midnight*, Bantam (New York, NY), 1989.
*Dirty White Boys*, Random House (New York, NY), 1994.
*Soft Target: A Thriller*, Simon & Schuster (New York, NY), 2011.

#### "BOB LEE SWAGGER" SERIES

*Point of Impact*, Bantam (New York, NY), 1993.
*Black Light*, Doubleday (New York, NY), 1996.
*Time to Hunt*, Doubleday (New York, NY), 1998.
*The 47th Samurai*, Simon & Schuster (New York, NY), 2007.
*Night of Thunder*, Simon & Schuster (New York, NY), 2008.
*I, Sniper*, Simon & Schuster (New York, NY), 2009.
*Dead Zero*, Simon & Schuster (New York, NY), 2010.

#### "EARL SWAGGER" SERIES

*Hot Springs*, Simon & Schuster (New York, NY), 2000.
*Pale Horse Coming*, Simon & Schuster (New York, NY), 2001.
*Havana*, Simon & Schuster (New York, NY), 2003.

#### NONFICTION

*Violent Screen: A Critic's 13 Years on the Front Lines of Movie Mayhem*, Bancroft Press (Baltimore, MD), 1995.

*Now Playing at the Valencia: Pulitzer Prize-Winning Essays on the Movies,* Simon & Schuster (New York, NY), 2005.

(With John Bainbridge, Jr.) *American Gunfight: The Plot to Kill Harry Truman, and the Shoot-Out That Stopped It,* Simon & Schuster (New York, NY), 2005.

Contributor to periodicals, including *Crawdaddy.*

## ■ Adaptations

*Point of Impact,* was adapted as the film *Shooter,* released by Paramount, 2007.

## ■ Sidelights

Stephen Hunter is a veteran journalist and film critic who has also won a large readership with his action-packed suspense novels. Though marked by fast-paced plotting and graphic violence, his fiction has won praise from reviewers for its multifaceted characters, particularly Bob Lee Swagger, a retired Marine sniper, and his father, Earl Swagger, a World War II veteran.

### Novels

One of the author's early novels, *The Spanish Gambit* (later reissued under the title *Tapestry of Spies*), is based on the true story of Kim Philby, one of the most infamous double agents of the twentieth century. Philby was a Cambridge-educated British intelligence operative who spied for the Soviet Union and defected to that country in the early 1960s. Hunter explored Philby's stint as a correspondent for the London *Times* during the Spanish Civil War, and speculates on the manner in which he was recruited as a Soviet agent. *Armchair Detective* contributor Jeanne F. Bedell described *The Spanish Gambit* as "more complex psychologically and richer in historical background than most espionage fiction."

In *The Day before Midnight,* a military-political thriller, a shadowy cadre of military men seizes control of an American missile base and threatens to launch an attack on the Soviet Union. *New York Times Book Review* critic Newgate Callendar acknowledged the novel's strength as entertainment, pointing out its "nonstop action and mounting tension," although he wondered if the book would age well, asking: "What will authors do if, in a few years, the Russians are our friends?"

*Dirty White Boys* presents an elaborate cat-and-mouse game between a homicidal prison escapee and the Oklahoma highway patrolman who pursues him. In the novel's opening scenes, convicted killer Lamar Pye escapes from Oklahoma's maximum security McAlester State Penitentiary accompanied by his cousin Odell, a mentally retarded giant with a cleft palate, and Richard Peed, a scholarly, rather effeminate man whose sketches have captivated Lamar. Led by Lamar, this awkward trio cuts a swath of murder and mayhem across Oklahoma and Texas, eventually taking refuge in the farmhouse of a psychotic young woman who becomes their partner in crime and Lamar's lover. Their chief antagonist is Oklahoma Highway Patrol Sergeant Bud Pewtie, a veteran cop and family man whose normal stolidity is disrupted by two obsessions: his adulterous affair with his partner's wife, and capturing Lamar Pye. *New York Times Book Review* contributor Marilyn Stasio hailed *Dirty White Boys* as "an exhilarating crime novel" with a "big, mythic theme," and she observed: "Of all the killings in *Dirty White Boys* . . . the death of the American family is the most monstrous." According to Daniel Woodrell in the *Washington Post Book World,* "Hunter is extremely knowledgeable about small arms, criminal behavior, and law enforcement techniques. He writes very well, in direct and savory prose, poetically evocative and rough-and-tumble by turns."

### "Bob Lee Swagger" Series

Hunter has achieved his greatest popular success, as well as his most enthusiastic critical reception, with his books about Bob Lee Swagger, including *Point of Impact* and *Hot Springs,* and about Swagger's father, Earl, featured in *Hot Springs* and *Pale Horse Coming.*

Bob Swagger killed eighty-seven people in Vietnam, his accuracy as a sniper earning him the nickname "The Nailer." Twenty years after the war, Bob lives in the Arkansas mountains, where he hunts and takes care of his gun collection. This quiet way of life is interrupted when he is contacted by Ram-Dyne, a mysterious company linked to military intelligence. He is hired as a consultant to help protect the president from assassination, but Swagger soon realizes that his job is merely a setup. Before long he is the most wanted man in America, pursued by the police, the FBI, and hired killers from RamDyne who need to silence him. Fleeing through the underworld, Swagger finds an ally in another expert marksman in the twilight of his career at the FBI. The two embark on a bloody quest for justice and retribution, and the story concludes with a dramatic court case. In a *New York Times Book*

*Review* article, Callendar wrote: "More than a mere action novel, *Point of Impact* is superbly written. Mr. Hunter has made a fine effort to get into the mind of his protagonist." Writing in *Armchair Detective,* Christine E. Thompson called *Point of Impact* an "excellent novel" that delivered "top-notch emotional experience."

In *Black Light,* Bob Lee Swagger returns, this time teaming up with Russell Pewtie, the son of Oklahoma Highway Patrolman Bud Pewtie. In *Dirty White Boys,* Russell Pewtie is a studious, Princeton-bound teenager; in *Black Light,* he is a young newspaperman helping Bob Lee Swagger investigate the four-decades-old murder of the latter's father, a crime found to have connections to, among other things, the CIA and corrupt Arkansas politicians. According to *Los Angeles Times* reviewer Dick Lochte, "the result is a big, bristly bear of a book, edgy and violent." In the opinion of a *Publishers Weekly* critic, *Black Light* confirms Hunter's "status as one of the most skilled hands in the thriller business."

Swagger appears again in *Time to Hunt,* which finds him married to the widow of one of his closest comrades in Vietnam, Danny Fenn. The two of them are horseback riding with another companion in Arizona when a sniper's shot kills their friend. Somehow, the murder is linked to events in the early 1970s, when Danny was ordered to spy on peace-movement activists. Now Swagger and his wife both seem to be targets, and their deaths to be the intended conclusion of events set into motion years before. *Time to Hunt* is "both a gripping war novel and a complex thriller," noted Charles Michaud in *Library Journal. Booklist* reviewer Wes Lukowsky mused: "Swagger is a near-mythic character without peer in mystery fiction."

Hunter published the fourth book in the "Bob Lee Swagger" series, *The 47th Samurai,* in 2007. Swagger's father, Earl, took the samurai sword of a Japanese officer after winning the battle of Iwo Jima. Earl decided to return it to the officer's son in Japan. After he does so, however, the family is slain and the sword stolen as it a significant piece of craftsmanship with a history. Bob Lee decides to retrieve the sword and avenge the family.

Jules Brenner, writing on the *Jules Brenner's Critical Mystery Tour* Web site, declared that "Hunter has gone to extremes in his study of swords and samurai so as to enrich his mystery with the most intimate and detailed course on human dissection methodology imaginable. The cold, impersonal tone of its formalized cross-body slicing maneuvers is as objectively described as one might hear discussed in a surgical ward. Incorporating it into the narra-

tive invests it with considerable authenticity." Mike Riley, reviewing the book on the *Shots* Web site, observed that "no one writes better scenes of violent action and Hunter knows every familiar trick from the movies, both Japanese and traditional Westerns, and he utilises them splendidly here." A critic writing in *Kirkus Reviews* remarked that the novel "gets a bit operatic toward the end, but Swagger—never to be taken seriously—is always fun." *Booklist* contributor Bill Ott observed that "Hunter celebrates the samurai soldier while showing the appalling underside of the samurai way of life and the ideals that drive it." A contributor to *Publishers Weekly* recorded that "while the action builds to the inevitable climax, the joy of the journey will keep readers" interested.

Hunter continues to detail Swagger's adventures in *Night of Thunder, I, Sniper,* and *Dead Zero, In I, Sniper,* 1970s antiwar extremists are being murdered one by one. The killer is an expert sniper, and Swagger is enlisted by the FBI to find the culprit. Vast information about the killer and his craft ensue as Swagger gives chase. "The level of detail did become a little repetitive after a few shots were taken," an online *Bookbag* contributor noted. "This apart, though, I did enjoy *I, Sniper* as it neatly wove together several different plot strands and aspects of life in Washington into a very readable story. It may not be the most welcoming of crime thrillers, but it certainly offers something a little different and it is one of the more entertaining ones." Theodore Feit, writing on the *Spinetingler* Web site, observed: "Despite its length, the novel moves swiftly, except for all kinds of minutiae on the life of a sniper." He went on to call the novel "recommended." In his *Library Journal* assessment, Robert Conroy remarked: "Hunter's thrillers are always taut, exciting, and well written, and his latest is no exception." According to a *Kirkus Reviews* critic, "even the somewhat squeamish . . . and even certifiable gun-dummies, may once again find chivalric, heroic Bob Lee just about irresistible."

Swagger must hunt down a rogue sergeant in *Dead Zero.* Sergeant Roy Cruz is ordered to assassinate an Afghan warlord, but his mission fails and Cruz goes missing. The warlord soon befriends American troops, and the assassination order is cancelled. When Cruz resurfaces, he refuses to believe that the warlord has been reformed. Swagger must then stop Cruz from killing against direct orders. Ott, writing in *Booklist,* called the novel "a topnotch thriller . . . showing that Bob the Nailer is just as (well, almost as) compelling a hero without his guns." On the *Oregonian* Web site, Steve Duin was less impressed, dubbing *Dead Zero* "a disappointment, not a total loss. I can only hope it's the novel that finally convinces Hunter to flesh out the history of a new sniper and allow Bob the Nailer the retirement he so richly deserves." However, *TruthaboutGuns.com* contributor William C. Montgomery observed: "The tempo of the book is brisk and the action sequences are well done. Hunter proves his craft in a climatic shootout in downtown Washington D.C. . . . Despite yet another movie-reference literary crutch . . . the scene is an epic shootout that almost makes the rest of the book worth reading."

### "Earl Swagger" Series

Hunter created a prequel to his Bob Swagger books so that he could write about Bob Swagger's father, Earl. The novel, titled *Hot Springs,* is set in an Arkansas town that teems with corruption and is known as a playground for criminal types and their hangers-on. Earl is weary from the terrible things he has seen and done in World War II but is set to work cleaning up Hot Springs, a job as dangerous as fighting in the Pacific. Comparing *Hot Springs* to the work of Dashiell Hammett, *Booklist* writer Ott described it as "a violent book about the allure of violence." Jan Tarasovic in *School Library Journal* stated that "readers who find violence exciting will get their fill, but they will also see that the scars it leaves may never heal, and that winning the war may be just the start of the battle." A *Publishers Weekly* writer praised Hunter's character development and his prose, which includes "some wonderful stretches of backwoods dialect and gritty scenes of physical and emotional turmoil" and "has that rare visual quality that takes the action off the page and into the mind."

In *Pale Horse Coming,* Earl Swagger's story continues as he attempts to liberate a horrific Mississippi prison for black men, run by a gang of vicious, racist guards. In addition to the overt abuse they face, it seems the prisoners may be the subjects of secret medical experiments. Less nuanced than the previous book, it nevertheless makes for compelling reading, according to *Booklist* reviewer Ott, who remarked: "The character of Earl Swagger, equal parts gristle and determination, remains compelling, both as archetype and as complex human being." *Pale Horse Coming* is a "virtually un-put-downable gothic chiller about unspeakable evil," commented a *Publishers Weekly* critic, with "unforgettable characters in vivid settings. . . . Once again, Hunter proves he is a master of cinematic prose."

### Nonfiction

In 2005 Hunter coauthored *American Gunfight: The Plot to Kill Harry Truman, and the Shoot-Out That Stopped It* with John Bainbridge, Jr. The account revives the scenario when a group of Puerto Rican nationalists attempted to assassinate U.S. president Harry Truman in 1950.

Lawrence Henry, writing in *American Spectator,* commented that "fans of his fiction would find it difficult to urge his former work on a wider audience than adventure and action readers. With *American Gunfight,* Hunter makes it clear what he's been up to all along, and under what stylistic rubric: He works in New Journalism, that splendid rich vein of American literature largely untapped since Tom Wolfe's *The Right Stuff* in 1979." Henry added: "Until now, Hunter has confined this style to what appears to be fiction. . . . Now it is clear that Hunter has been a historian all along." A contributor to *Publishers Weekly* explained: "Interpretations are presented as such, and their handling of the recorded events is not only convincing but compelling." A critic writing in *Kirkus Reviews* found that "those with patience for run-on sentences may enjoy this long footnote to history." The critic admitted that the account is "an intrinsically interesting story" but felt that the authors layer on "incidental details" too widely and employ "breathless Dragnet-speak" in doing so.

In an article in the *Weekly Standard,* Tom Kelly stated: "This book is without substantial new facts, but loaded with suppositions, deductions, and opinions. The main players are long dead, but Hunter and Bainbridge seem able to move back in time and into the heads and hearts of the assassins, as well as bystanders, innocent or not, at home and abroad, and hear with their ears, see with their eyes, and read the thoughts that ran around in their brains." *Booklist* contributor Taylor concluded: "Skillfully dramatized, it will captivate readers interested in the crime and the killers' motivations."

Hunter also published *Now Playing at the Valencia: Pulitzer Prize-Winning Essays on the Movies* in 2005. The book outlines hundreds of films through the collection of essays and critiques the author published in the decade prior to releasing this book.

*Booklist* contributor Gordon Flagg proposed that Hunter's "love of plebeian pleasures seems to blind him to the rewards of more elevated fare." A critic writing in *Kirkus Reviews* described the book as "a smart and riotous glorification of everything that is fantastic about the cinema." A contributor to *Publishers Weekly* summarized: "Written in a vigorous, demotic style, these essays are more fun than the films they discuss."

## ■ Biographical And Critical Sources

### PERIODICALS

*American Handgunner,* March-April, 2003, Michael Bane, author interview.

*American Libraries*, February, 2001, Bill Ott, review of *Hot Springs*, p. 60.

*American Spectator*, March 10, 2006, Lawrence Henry, review of *American Gunfight: The Plot to Kill Harry Truman, and the Shoot-Out That Stopped It.*

*Armchair Detective*, summer, 1993, Christine E. Thompson, review of *Point of Impact*, p. 118; fall, 1993, Jeanne F. Bedell "The Spanish Gambit," p. 22.

*Baltimore City Paper*, January 2, 1995, David Louis Edelman, author interview.

*Baltimore Sun*, March 8, 2007, Dan Rodricks, author interview.

*Booklist*, April 15, 1980, review of *The Master Sniper*, p. 1180; July, 1985, review of *The Spanish Gambit*, p. 1518; November 15, 1988, review of *The Day before Midnight*, p. 514; May 1, 1996, Wes Lukowsky, review of *Black Light*, p. 1468; April 15, 1998, Wes Lukowsky, review of *Time to Hunt*, p. 1384; May 1, 2000, Bill Ott, review of *Hot Springs*, p. 1623; January 1, 2001, review of *Dirty White Boys*, p. 1016; May 1, 2001, Bill Ott, review of *Hot Springs*, p. 1598; October 15, 2001, Bill Ott, review of *Pale Horse Coming*, p. 385; February 15, 2002, Nancy Spillman, review of *Hot Springs*, p. 1039; August, 2003, Bill Ott, review of *Havana*, p. 1925; October 15, 2005, Gilbert Taylor, review of *American Gunfight*, p. 9; November 1, 2005, Gordon Flagg, review of *Now Playing at the Valencia: Pulitzer Prize-Winning Essays on the Movies*, p. 19; July 1, 2007, Bill Ott, review of *The 47th Samurai*, p. 7; September 1, 2008, Bill Ott, review of *Night of Thunder*, p. 6; October 1, 2009, Bill Ott, review of *I, Sniper*, p. 5; December 1, 2010, Bill Ott, review of *Dead Zero*, p. 30.

*Christian Science Monitor*, June 7, 1993, Burke Wilkinson, review of *Point of Impact*, p. 13.

*Denver Post* (Denver, CO), October 14, 2001, review of *Pale Horse Coming*, p. K5; July 2, 2002, review of *Hot Springs*, p. F1.

*Detroit Free Press*, July 28, 2002, review of *Pale Horse Coming*, p. 5E.

*Entertainment Weekly*, December 23, 1994, Gene Lyons, "Dirty White Boys," p. 61; October 10, 2003, Adam B. Vary, review of *Havana*, p. 128.

*Esquire*, June, 1998, review of *Time to Hunt*, p. 44.

*Globe and Mail* (Toronto, Ontario, Canada), July 15, 2000, review of *Hot Springs*, p. D13; November 24, 2001, review of *Pale Horse Coming*, p. D44; October 11, 2003, review of *Havana*, p. D26.

*Japan Times* (Tokyo, Japan), August 26, 2007, Mark Schreiber, author interview.

*Kirkus Reviews*, January 1, 1980, review of *The Master Sniper*, p. 26; May 15, 1982, review of *The Second Saladin*, p. 616; June 1, 1985, review of *The Spanish Gambit*, p. 491; December 15, 1992, review of *Point of Impact*, p. 1527; September 1, 1994, review of *Dirty White Boys*, pp. 1152-1153; April 1, 1996, review of *Black Light*, p. 470; May 1, 1998, review of *Time to Hunt*, p. 604; April 1, 2000, review of *Hot Springs*, p. 407; September 1, 2001, review of *Pale Horse Coming*, p. 1235; July 15, 2003, review of *Havana*, p. 928; September 1, 2005, review of *American Gunfight*, p. 957; September 15, 2005, review of *Now Playing at the Valencia*, p. 1013; September 15, 2007, review of *The 47th Samurai*; November 15, 2009, review of *I, Sniper*; December 15, 2010, review of *Dead Zero.*

*Library Journal*, March 15, 1980, Nadia Taran, review of *The Master Sniper*, p. 972; June 15, 1982, review of *The Second Saladin*, p. 1241; August, 1985, review of *The Spanish Gambit*, p. 116; February 1, 1993, V. Louise Saylor, review of *Point of Impact*, p. 112; October 15, 1994, David Keymer, review of *Dirty White Boys*, p. 87; November 15, 1995, Carol J. Binkowski, review of *Violent Screen: A Critic's 13 Years on the Front Lines of Movie Mayhem*, pp. 76-77; April 1, 1996, Adam Mazmanian, review of *Black Light*, p. 117; September 15, 1996, Kristen L. Smith, review of *Black Light*, p. 112; May 1, 1998, Charles Michaud, review of *Time to Hunt*, p. 138; May 15, 2000, Thomas L. Kilpatrick, review of *Hot Springs*, p. 124; December, 2000, Beth Farrell, review of *Hot Springs*, p. 212; October 1, 2003, Thomas Kilpatrick, review of *Havana*, p. 116; August 1, 2007, Robert Conroy, review of *The 47th Samurai*, p. 69; October 15, 2009, Robert Conroy, review of *I, Sniper*, p. 70.

*Los Angeles Times*, June 23, 1996, review of *Black Light*, p. 10; August 20, 2000, review of *Hot Springs*, p. 9.

*News & Record* (Piedmont Triad, NC), November 25, 2001, review of *Hot Springs*, p. R3.

*New Statesman*, June 27, 1980, Martin Walker, review of *The Master Sniper*, p. 972.

*New York*, August 8, 2007, "Pulitzer Prize Winner Stephen Hunter: Our Nation's Shame."

*New York Times Book Review*, July 6, 1980, Martin Levin, review of *The Master Sniper*, p. 9; April 23, 1989, Newgate Callendar, review of *The Day before Midnight*, p. 33; February 28, 1993, Newgate Callendar, review of *Point of Impact*, p. 24; November 20, 1994, Marilyn Stasio, review of *Dirty White Boys*, p. 44; June 9, 1996, review of *Black Light*, p. 29; December 8, 1996, review of *Black Light*, p. 94; August 27, 2000, John D. Thomas, review of *Hot Springs*, p. 18.

*Observer* (London, England), June 26, 1983, review of *The Second Saladin*, p. 31; August 20, 2000, review of *Hot Springs*, p. 12; April 28, 2002, Peter Guttridge, review of *Pale Horse Coming*, p. 19.

*People*, August 26, 1985, Campbell Geeslin, review of *The Spanish Gambit*, p. 21; January 23, 1995, Louisa Ermelino, review of *Dirty White Boys*, p. 28; June 17, 1996, J.D. Reed, review of *Black Light*, p. 32.

*Publishers Weekly*, January 11, 1980, review of *The Master Sniper*, p. 217; May 14, 1982, review of *The*

*Second Saladin*, p. 207; March 31, 1985, review of *The Spanish Gambit*, p. 45; November 11, 1988, review of *The Day before Midnight*, p. 41; January 4, 1993, review of *Point of Impact*, p. 57; September 19, 1994, review of *Dirty White Boys*, p. 49; April 29, 1996, review of *Black Light*, p. 51; May 27, 1996, review of *The Master Sniper*, p. 75; March 30, 1998, review of *Time to Hunt*, p. 67; June 5, 2000, review of *Hot Springs*, p. 72; September 24, 2001, review of *Pale Horse Coming*, p. 67; July 21, 2003, review of *Havana*, p. 171; August 15, 2005, review of *Now Playing at the Valencia*, p. 45; October 3, 2005, review of *American Gunfight*, p. 66; July 23, 2007, review of *The 47th Samurai*, p. 45; July 28, 2008, review of *Night of Thunder*, p. 53.

*Rocky Mountain News*, July 16, 2000, Peter Mergendahl, review of *Hot Springs*, p. 2E.

*San Francisco Examiner*, July 11, 2000, review of *Hot Springs*, p. B3.

*School Library Journal*, March, 2001, Jan Tarasovic, review of *Hot Springs*, p. 281.

*Seattle Times*, August 26, 2000, Bill Norton, review of *Hot Springs*, p. D8.

*Tribune Books* (Chicago, IL), March 5, 1989, review of *The Day before Midnight*, p. 6; February 21, 1993, review of *Point of Impact*, p. 7; November 20, 1994, review of *Dirty White Boys*, p. 6; November 18, 2001, review of *Pale Horse Coming*, p. 7.

*USA Today*, November 11, 2003, review of *Havana*, p. 5D.

*Wall Street Journal*, July 3, 2000, Tom Nolan, review of *Hot Springs*, p. A10.

*Washington Business Journal*, September 28, 2001, Greg A. Lohr, "A Difficult Man."

*Washingtonian*, May 1, 2008, Tim Wendel, "Gunslinger Stephen Hunter."

*Washington Post*, December 7, 1999, author interview.

*Washington Post Book World*, August 4, 1985, Dennis Drabelle, review of *The Spanish Gambit*, p. 6; January 8, 1995, Daniel Woodrell, review of *Dirty White Boys*, p. 4; June 14, 1998, review of *Time to Hunt*, p. 9; February 20, 2000, review of *Hot Springs*, p. 4; August 6, 2000, "Soaking Up Trouble," p. 4; December 3, 2000, review of *Hot Springs*, p. 15; October 31, 2001, David L. Ulin, "The Swamp of the Human Heart," p. 10; December 1, 2002, review of *Dirty White Boys*, p. 3; September 7, 2003, review of *Havana*, p. 3; November 13, 2005, Ted Widmer, review of *American Gunfight*, p. 3; October 7, 2007, Daniel Woodrell, review of *The 47th Samurai*, p. 6.

*Weekly Standard*, March 27, 2006, Tom Kelly, review of *American Gunfight*.

*Western American Literature*, fall, 1995, review of *Dirty White Boys*, p. 312.

*Xpress Reviews*, December 10, 2010, Robert Conroy, review of *Dead Zero*.

ONLINE

*Bookbag*, http://www.thebookbag.co.uk/ (August 22, 2011), review of *I, Sniper*.

*Book Browse*, http://www.bookbrowse.com/ (August 22, 2008), author profile.

*Jules Brenner's Critical Mystery Tour*, http://variagate.com/b-47samr.htm?bookrevs/ (August 22, 2008), review of *The 47th Samurai*.

*Oregonian*, http://www.oregonlive.com/ (January 14, 2011), Steve Duin, review of *Dead Zero*.

*Shots*, http://www.shotsmag.co.uk/ (August 22, 2008), Mike Riley, review of *The 47th Samurai*.

*Spinetingler*, http://www.spinetinglermag.com/ (March 26, 2010), Theodore Feit, review of *I, Sniper*.

*TruthaboutGuns.com*, http://thetruthaboutguns.com/ (February 1, 2011), William C. Montgomery, review of *Dead Zero*.

*Unofficial Stephen Hunter Web site*, http://www.stephenhunter.net/ (August 22, 2011), author profile.*

# J.A. Jance

## 1944-

■ **Also Known As**

Judith Ann Jance

■ **Personal**

Born October 27, 1944, in Watertown, SD; daughter of Norman (in insurance sales) and Evelyn Busk; married Jerry Joseph Teale Jance, January 29, 1967 (divorced, 1980); married William Alan Schilb, 1985; children: (first marriage) Jeanne Teale, Josh Mikki; (second marriage) two stepsons, one stepdaughter. *Education:* University of Arizona, B.A., 1966, M.Ed., 1970; American College, C.L.U., 1980.

■ **Addresses**

*Home*—Bellevue, WA; Tucson, AZ. *Agent*—Alice Volpe, Northwest Literary Agency, 4500 108th NE, Kirkland, WA 98033. *E-mail*—jajance@jajance.com.

■ **Career**

Pueblo High School, Tucson, AZ, teacher, 1966-68; Indian Oasis Schools, Sells, AZ, librarian, 1968-73; Equitable Life Assurance Society, New York, NY, life insurance salesperson and district manager, 1974-84. Writer, 1985—.

■ **Member**

Sisters in Crime, Mystery Writers of America, Denny Regrade Business Association (president, 1983-84), Seattle Free Lances (president, 1989-90).

■ **Awards, Honors**

D.H.L., University of Arizona, 2000.

■ **Writings**

*"J.P. BEAUMONT" SERIES; MYSTERY NOVELS*

*Until Proven Guilty* (also see below), Avon (New York, NY), 1985.
*Injustice for All* (also see below), Avon (New York, NY), 1986.
*Trial by Fury* (also see below), Avon (New York, NY), 1987.
*Improbable Cause,* Avon (New York, NY), 1987.
*A More Perfect Union,* Avon (New York, NY), 1988.
*Dismissed with Prejudice,* Avon (New York, NY), 1989.
*Minor in Possession,* Avon (New York, NY), 1990.
*Payment in Kind,* Avon (New York, NY), 1991.
*Without Due Process,* Morrow (New York, NY), 1992.
*Failure to Appear,* Morrow (New York, NY), 1993.
*Lying in Wait,* Morrow (New York, NY), 1994.
*Name Withheld,* Morrow (New York, NY), 1995.
*Breach of Duty,* Avon (New York, NY), 1999.
*Birds of Prey,* Morrow (New York, NY), 2001.
*Sentenced to Die* (omnibus; includes *Until Proven Guilty, Injustice for All,* and *Trial by Fury*), William Morrow (New York, NY), 2005.
*Long Time Gone,* William Morrow (New York, NY), 2005.
*Justice Denied,* William Morrow (New York, NY), 2007.
*Fire and Ice,* William Morrow (New York, NY), 2009.
*Betrayal of Trust,* William Morrow (New York, NY), 2011.

*"JOANNA BRADY" SERIES; MYSTERY NOVELS*

*Desert Heat*, Avon (New York, NY), 1993.
*Tombstone Courage*, Morrow (New York, NY), 1994.
*Shoot/Don't Shoot*, Avon (New York, NY), 1995.
*Dead to Rights*, Avon (New York, NY), 1997.
*Skeleton Canyon*, Avon (New York, NY), 1997.
*Rattlesnake Crossing*, Avon (New York, NY), 1998.
*Outlaw Mountain*, Avon (New York, NY), 1999.
*Devil's Claw*, Morrow (New York, NY), 2000.
*Paradise Lost*, Morrow (New York, NY), 2001.
*Dead Wrong*, Morrow (New York, NY), 2001.
*Partner in Crime*, Morrow (New York, NY), 2002.
*Exit Wounds*, Morrow (New York, NY), 2003.
*Damage Control*, William Morrow (New York, NY), 2008.

*"SHERIFF BRANDON WALKER" SERIES; MYSTERY NOVELS*

*Hour of the Hunter*, Morrow (New York, NY), 1991.
*Kiss of the Bees*, Avon (New York, NY), 2000.
*The Day of the Dead*, William Morrow (New York, NY), 2004.
*Queen of the Night*, William Morrow (New York, NY), 2010.

*"ALI REYNOLDS" SERIES; MYSTERY NOVELS*

*Edge of Evil*, Avon Books (New York, NY), 2006.
*Web of Evil*, Touchstone (New York, NY), 2007.
*Hand of Evil*, Touchstone (New York, NY), 2007.
*Cruel Intent*, Thorndike Press (Waterville, ME), 2008.
*Trial by Fire*, Simon & Schuster (New York, NY), 2009.
*Fatal Error*, Simon & Schuster (New York, NY), 2011.

*FOR CHILDREN*

*It's Not Your Fault*, Charles Franklin (Edmonds, WA), 1985.
*Dial Zero for Help: A Story of Parental Kidnapping*, Charles Franklin (Edmonds, WA), 1985.
*Welcome Home, Stranger: A Child's View of Family Alcoholism*, Charles Franklin (Edmonds, WA), 1986.

*OTHER*

*After the Fire* (poetry), Lance Publications, 1984.
(With others) *Naked Came the Phoenix* (serial novel), St. Martin's (New York, NY), 2001.
(With others) *Bark M for Murder* (anthology), Avon Books (New York, NY), 2006.

*Left for Dead: A Mystery*, Touchstone (New York, NY), 2012.

## ■ Sidelights

J.A. Jance is best known for her mystery novels, especially the books that depict the adventures of Seattle police detective J.P. Beaumont and those featuring Arizona sheriff Joanna Brady. Jance has been producing titles in these two mystery series for two decades and is quite comfortable with her two very different protagonists. Beaumont is a hard-boiled but decent recovering alcoholic working out of Seattle, Washington, and Brady is a tender-hearted working mother in a small desert town; both of them manage to solve dangerous and life-threatening crimes while contending with issues in their personal lives. A *Publishers Weekly* reviewer declared that Jance's mysteries are "distinguished by authentic dialogue, honest emotions and characters readers will care about."

### "J.P. Beaumont" Series

The first Beaumont tale, *Until Proven Guilty*, was published in 1985 in paperback. It establishes the protagonist's wealth, which is the outcome of a relationship with a woman named Anne Corley. This and later titles reveal Beaumont as a resentful, morose man who is battling alcoholism and an unstable love life. Critics found him a compelling character. *Booklist* contributor Bill Ott noted that the "J.P. Beaumont" series "has a lot going for it," principally because Jance "is an excellent plotter . . . offering genuine surprises throughout."

Jance became interested in police work following an incident in which her husband was driven home from work by a person who turned out to be a serial killer and later began stalking them. The police investigation that followed inspired Jance to depict police procedures in her work. The "J.P. Beaumont" series has been praised by critics for its accurate descriptions of Seattle and for its well-drawn characterizations. In a review of *Dismissed with Prejudice*, a *Publishers Weekly* contributor praised "the dexterous characterizations that have become the hallmarks of [Jance's] mysteries."

*Long Time Gone* finds J.P. Beaumont dealing with a murder investigation that involves two of his friends. An old school friend, Bonnie Jean Dunleavy, is now Sister Mary Katherine and serves as the Mother Superior at a local convent. She goes to visit another school friend who works as a hypnotherapist when her nightmares become so painful that she can barely sleep. When the therapist uncovers suppressed memories that indicate the Sister was the witness to a murder four decades earlier, the pair take the information to Beaumont. Meanwhile, in another case, a paraplegic friend of Beau's is accused of murdering his ex-wife, with whom he was fighting for custody of their daughter. Beau must determine if his friend is truly guilty or covering for someone else. A contributor to *Kirkus Reviews* found the book to be "the literary equivalent of a paint-by-numbers kit, with no real surprises but no major flaws."

*Justice Denied* is the eighteenth installment in Jance's "J.P. Beaumont" series. When ex-con LaShawn Tompkins is murdered, Beau feels the case belongs more to the mainstream police department in Seattle, rather than his highly focused Special Homicide Investigation Team. However, his boss, Attorney General Ross Alan Connors, feels the investigation requires an extra close look of the type for which Beau is famous. So Beau takes the case, intrigued by Connors's request for added discretion that includes putting nothing in writing and reporting to him in person. The deeper he gets into his investigation, the more Beau realizes that there are major political considerations linked to Connors, and that racism may have a hand in the circumstances. A contributor to *Kirkus Reviews* dubbed the book "a solid, satisfying procedural," adding that there is "no fancy stepping here, but those who've danced with Jance . . . have come to prefer the waltz to the bossa nova."

Beau is joined by Joanna Brady in *Fire and Ice*. He is investigating a likely serial killer; six unidentified women have been killed and their bodies burned. Back in Arizona, Joanna is also working a murder case; her victim worked as a caretaker at an ATV recreation park. They come together when Beau discovers that one of his victims is likely the missing sister of one of Joanna's detectives, Jaime Carbajal. Jaime travels to Seattle to join Beau while Joanna stays behind to look into a nursing home that is mistreating its residents. Applauding the novel in *Publishers Weekly*, a critic called it "a gripping tale that's easily one of . . . [Jance's] best." Teresa L. Jacobsen, writing in *Xpress Reviews*, lauded the story as well, commending the "complex themes of immigration, drug running, and alternative lifestyles." As Stephanie Zvirin observed in her *Booklist* review, "the clever story unfolds smoothly, with characters kept nicely distinct throughout." Zvirin went on to declare that "fans of both characters will be pleased."

## "Sheriff Brandon Walker" Series

In 1991 Jance, a former librarian on a Native American reservation, switched gears from the "J.P. Beaumont" series to produce *Hour of the Hunter*, a novel set on a reservation in Arizona and the first in the "Sheriff Brandon Walker" series. The novel features a recently released killer who seeks revenge against a woman who was instrumental in putting him behind bars. Bill Farley, writing in *St. James Guide to Crime & Mystery Writers*, lauded this novel as "Jance's most complex and compelling work to date."

A sequel to *Hour of the Hunter* titled *Kiss of the Bees* was published in 1999. In this novel Jance reintroduces the heroine from the former work, but it is now the heroine's adopted teenage daughter who faces the wrath of a killer bent upon revenge. The story blends graphic action with Native American folklore, especially the tales of the Tohono O'othham tribe. A *Publishers Weekly* correspondent praised Jance's "sure hand" in creating "a coherent and engrossing novel," and Emily Melton in *Booklist* concluded that the "riveting tale . . . is certain to generate widespread demand."

The next book in the "Sheriff Brandon Walker" series is *The Day of the Dead*. The book is loosely connected to Jance's own experiences in 1970, when she and her family found themselves being targeted by a serial killer. The action begins in that year, when highway workers in Arizona come across the body of Roseanne Orozco, a teenager who has been murdered. Over the next thirty years, the case languishes unsolved, until Walker becomes involved through the request of Roseanne's mother. A member of the Last Chance, an organization specifically organized to look into cold cases such as this one, Walker sets out to get justice for Roseanne and to find closure for her family. Joe Hartlaub, reviewing the novel in *Bookreporter.com*, praised the book, declaring that "Brandon Walker, in the short space of three novels, may well be on his way to becoming Jance's most memorable character."

The fourth Walker Family book, *Queen of the Night*, brings a second generation forward, Brandon and Diana Ladd, Walker's adopted daughter, and a new character, an Apache border patrol officer working on the reservation. Together they work to save a child targeted by a serial killer.

## "Joanna Brady" Series

Jance has attracted a wide readership for her works featuring Cochise County sheriff Joanna Brady. *Desert Heat*, the first book in the "Joanna Brady" series, concludes with the murder of Joanna's husband during his campaign for sheriff. Following her husband's death, Joanna decides to run for sheriff herself. *Tombstone Courage* begins with Joanna winning the election. This book depicts Joanna's experiences as the first female sheriff in Arizona. In subsequent outings, Joanna has had to contend with serial killers, drug rings, suspicious suicides, and her own crowded personal life, often simultaneously. In other words, as Susan A. Zappia observed in *Library Journal*, Joanna "wears a tough gal's badge yet remains a sensitive, caring . . . mom and friend." In *Booklist*, George Needham declared that in the "remarkable" "Joanna Brady" series, Jance "has created a fully realized universe."

*Exit Wounds*, the tenth installment in the "Joanna Brady" series, finds Joanna and her husband expecting a baby. Determined not to let pregnancy slow her down, Joanna is also in the middle of running for reelection as sheriff. However, when Carol Mossman is discovered dead in her trailer, having been shot, along with her seventeen dogs who all died from the heat, Joanna must set aside her campaigning and her preparations for motherhood and immerse herself in the investigation. Two reporters were killed in the vicinity, and Joanna must discover if there is a connection and whether a local cult also plays a role. Nanci Milone Hill, writing in *Library Journal*, declared that "Jance expertly weaves plot and family saga to produce another first-rate page-turner."

### "Ali Reynolds" Series

In 2006, Jance began the new "Ali Reynolds" series with *Edge of Evil*. This first installment introduces Allison Reynolds during a very bad week of her life. A television anchorwoman, she has just been replaced at work by a younger woman, and her husband, who works at the network and was aware of the change, did not see fit to warn her about her impending firing. Then her best friend Renee goes missing and is later found dead in her wreck of a car, a supposed suicide. But when Ali visits Renee's family, she learns the suicide note was unsigned and written on a computer, and soon discovers other suspicious details that make her question the police's conclusions. Harriet Klausner, writing on the *Books 'n' Bytes* Web site, remarked of the book that "the mystery itself is well thought out with the usual amount of red herrings and unexpected twists to keep the reader off guard," and predicted that readers "will finish it in one sitting."

Jance continues her "Ali Reynolds" series with *Web of Evil*. Now the successful proprietor of the *Cut Loose* blog, Ali finds herself reaching out to the cy-

ber community for support as she goes through the trials and tribulations of divorcing her unfaithful husband. When her soon-to-be ex is murdered, Ali becomes the primary suspect in the investigation. In an effort to prove her innocence, Ali sets out to figure out who really killed her husband, a journey that brings her into contact with April, his eight-months-pregnant mistress. A contributor to *Kirkus Reviews* commented that this was not one of Jance's more accomplished offerings, calling it a "slapdash effort."

*Web of Evil* was followed in quick succession by *Hand of Evil* and *Cruel Intent*. In *Trial by Fire*, the fifth series installment, Ali has moved to Sedona, Arizona, where she takes a temporary job as the county-sheriff's media-relations official. In her new job, Ali comes across a woman nearly burned to death in a fire that was later determined to be arson. The woman has complete amnesia, and although the case is handed over to federal investigators, Ali is asked to stay involved by patient advocate sister Anselm. Not long afterward, sister Anselm is kidnapped. "Though evil does land some heavyweight punches, it's overmatched in the end," a *Kirkus Reviews* contributor observed. However, the contributor called *Trial by Fire* "meticulously formulaic" and "mostly for the base." A *Publishers Weekly* critic felt the plot was somewhat tame but acknowledged that "a desert shoot-out tacked on toward the end adds some excitement." Sue O'Brien, writing in *Booklist*, was more impressed, commending the "fast pacing, surprising plot twists, and a strong, principled heroine."

Ali appears again in *Fatal Error*, which begins with the series protagonist's plans to catch up with her old coworker, Brenda Riley. During their friendly outing, Brenda tells Ali that she is engaged to Richard Lattimer, a man who she only knows through their online conversations. Richard has disappeared, and Brenda does not even have a picture to help her find him. Ali then discovers that Brenda's mysterious fiance is actually Richard Lowensdale, an Internet lothario known for getting woman to fall for him before blocking their e-mails. Once Brenda knows the truth, she vows to keep Richard from hurting other women, and she reveals his real identity and intentions to potential victims. Five months pass; Richard is found murdered, and Brenda is the prime suspect. "In her inimitable, take-no-prisoners style, Ali sorts it all out, of course," a *Kirkus Reviews* contributor wrote. The contributor called the story "formulaic," but added that "main character Ali manages to disarm."

According to an online *I'm Booking It* reviewer, "One of the things I was looking forward to in this book was the technological aspect, and I was a little disappointed. Once I suspended disbelief, it was fine, but I knew enough to know some of it doesn't completely hold together." Michele Leber, writing in *Booklist*, proffered more straightforward praise, remarking: "This sixth outing in the series . . . offers an entertaining mix of sleuthing and human relationships." Noting that the story takes place "over several months," a *Publishers Weekly* critic asserted: "The plot never stalls and leads to a logical and exciting finale."

### Jance Told *CA*:

"Writing has provided a means of rewriting my own history, both in terms of the children's books and the murder thrillers. The children's books confront difficult issues—sexual molestation, parental kidnapping, and a child's view of family alcoholism. The murder thrillers are escapist fare with no redeeming social value."

"I've always wanted to be a writer from the time I read the *Wizard of Oz* books in second grade.

"The ancient sacred charge of the storyteller is to beguile the time. I regard myself as a storyteller and hope my books can take people away from their own concerns during times of stress and carry them away to some other place and time."

## ■ Biographical And Critical Sources

### BOOKS

Pederson, Jay P., editor, *St. James Guide to Crime & Mystery Writers*, 4th edition, St. James Press (Detroit, MI), 1996.

### PERIODICALS

*Booklist*, April 15, 1998, Emily Melton, review of *Rattlesnake Crossing*, p. 1386; February 15, 1999, Bill Ott, review of *Breach of Duty*, p. 1045; April 15, 1999, Emily Melton, review of *Outlaw Mountain*, p. 1480; November 15, 1999, Emily Melton, review of *Kiss of the Bees*, p. 580; May 1, 2000, George Needham, review of *Devil's Claw*, p. 1619; February 1, 2001, Bill Ott, review of *Birds of Prey*, p. 1020; June 1, 2009, Stephanie Zvirin, review of *Fire and Ice*, p. 42; November 15, 2009, Sue O'Brien, review of *Trial by Fire*, p. 24; June 1, 2010, Michele Leber, review of *Queen of the Night*, p. 41; December 15, 2010, Michele Leber, review of *Fatal Error*, p. 22.

*Kirkus Reviews*, January 15, 2001, review of *Birds of Prey*, p. 83; June 15, 2005, review of *Long Time Gone*, p. 666; November 15, 2006, review of *Web of Evil*, p. 1155; June 1, 2007, review of *Justice Denied*; October 15, 2009, review of *Trial by Fire*; July 1, 2010, review of *Queen of the Night*; December 15, 2010, review of *Fatal Error*; June 1, 2011, review of *Betrayal of Trust*.

*Library Journal*, July, 1999, Susan Zappia, review of *Outlaw Mountain*, p. 142; May 15, 2003, Nanci Milone Hill, review of *Exit Wounds*, p. 132.

*Publishers Weekly*, January 25, 1999, review of *Breach of Duty*, p. 75; December 20, 1999, review of *Kiss of the Bees*, p. 58; June 26, 2000, review of *Devil's Claw*, p. 53; September 29, 2008, review of *Cruel Intent*, p. 59; June 15, 2009, review of *Fire and Ice*, p. 33; September 21, 2009, review of *Trial by Fire*, p. 35; May 24, 2010, review of *Queen of the Night*, p. 35; November 29, 2010, review of *Fatal Error*, p. 27; May 23, 2011, review of *Betrayal of Trust*, p. 26.

*Xpress Reviews*, June 26, 2009, Teresa L. Jacobsen, review of *Fire and Ice*.

### ONLINE

*Bookreporter.com*, http://www.bookreporter.com/ (May 4, 2008), Joe Hartlaub, review of *The Day of the Dead*.

*Books 'n' Bytes*, http://www.booksnbytes.com/ (May 4, 2008), Harriet Klausner, review of *Edge of Evil*.

*I'm Booking It*, http://blog.imbookingit.com/ (March 17, 2011), review of *Fatal Error*.

*J.A. Jance Home Page*, http://www.jajance.com (August 29, 2011).

# Steven Johnson

## 1968-

### ■ Also Known As

Steve Berlin Johnson

### ■ Personal

Born June 6, 1968; married; children: three sons. *Education:* Brown University, B.A.; Columbia University, M.A.

### ■ Addresses

*Home*—Brooklyn, NY. *E-mail*—sbj6668@earthlink. net.

### ■ Career

Writer, editor, educator, cultural critic, and computer expert. *Feed* (online magazine), founder and editor-in-chief; New York University, New York, NY, Distinguished Writer-in-Residence; lecturer to corporate and educational institutions; Columbia University Journalism school, Hearst New Media Professional-in-Residence, 2009.

### ■ Awards, Honors

Ranked in ten best nonfiction books of 2006, *Entertainment Weekly,* for *The Ghost Map; Where Good Ideas Come From* was ranked one of the year's best books by the *Economist.*

### ■ Writings

#### NONFICTION

*Interface Culture: How New Technology Transforms the Way We Create and Communicate,* HarperEdge (San Francisco, CA), 1997.

*Emergence: The Connected Lives of Ants, Brains, Cities, and Software,* Scribner (New York, NY), 2001.

*Mind Wide Open: Your Brain and the Neuroscience of Everyday Life,* Scribner (New York, NY), 2004.

*Everything Bad Is Good for You: How Today's Popular Culture Is Actually Making Us Smarter,* Riverhead Books (New York, NY), 2005, with a new afterword by the author, Riverhead Books (New York, NY), 2006.

*The Ghost Map: The Story of London's Most Terrifying Epidemic—and How It Changed Science, Cities, and the Modern World,* Riverhead Hardcover (New York, NY), 2006.

*The Invention of Air: A Story of Science, Faith, Revolution, and the Birth of America,* Riverhead Books (New York, NY), 2009.

(Editor) *The Best of Technology Writing, 2009,* Yale University Press (New Haven, CT), 2009.

*Where Good Ideas Come From: The Natural History of Innovation,* Riverhead Books (New York, NY), 2010.

Contributor to periodicals, including the *Guardian* (London, England), *Lingua Franca, Harper's, Brill's Content,* the *New Yorker,* the *Wall Street Journal,* and the *New York Times.* Contributing editor, *Wired;* monthly columnist, *Discover* magazine.

### ■ Sidelights

Steven Johnson is a writer, media expert, and science maven whose books confront the complexities of the zones where science and culture meet. In 1995, Johnson founded the now-defunct online journal *Feed,* which examined the front lines of Web life and the development of computers and interconnectivity as a normal part of everyday existence.

## Interface Culture

In *Interface Culture: How New Technology Transforms the Way We Create and Communicate,* Johnson explores in-depth how digital information technology, particularly the Internet, interacts with and changes the commonplace acts of communication. As much as prior innovations such as the printing press and television, Johnson says, computer-based means of interacting with the world are creating fundamental changes in the most basic cultural interactions. "*Interface Culture* is one of the first books to analytically critique and explore the forces unleashed by this new media and their broad cultural consequences," wrote Deborah A. Salazar in a review for the *Journal of Cultural Geography.*

The "information space" where general users spend time "creating and exploring environments that reflect cultural values and aesthetics"—particularly the online world—is influenced not only by cultural preferences but by the tools and interfaces used to explore that world, Salazar wrote. Johnson's theory is that Web browsers, computer desktops, online chat rooms, hyperlinks, Windows, Web sites, search engines—all of these interfaces between humans and technology serve to help users understand and utilize the technical advances going on around them, much the same way that novels helped readers in Victorian times make sense of their own society and surroundings. The design of the interface itself affects what type of information is available, how that information is retrieved, and what kind of material cannot be retrieved through that particular interface. "The interface serves as a kind of translator, mediating between the two parties, making one sensible to the other," Johnson maintains.

A *Publishers Weekly* contributor remarked that readers familiar with *Feed* might be "disappointed" by Johnson's "engaging but superficial analysis of the way personal computers are changing our lives." However, Salazar found *Interface Culture* to be "an excellent introduction to a culturally based critique of what is happening in information space both from a design perspective, but more fundamentally, from a human cultural orientation as well." Harvey Blume, writing in the *American Prospect,* called the book "probably the single most memorable volume to come out of the Internet explosion of the 1990s. It was an intellectually bold, often exhilarating read, full of unexpected perspectives on culture and digital media."

## Emergence

Johnson's 2001 book, *Emergence: The Connected Lives of Ants, Brains, Cities, and Software,* expands on arguments in *Interface Culture* and ties them into the concept of emergence. Johnson defines emergence as "the movement from low-level rules to high-level sophistication." Emergent systems do not derive their organization and structure from a king, manager, dictator, or any type of centralized authority. Instead, the emergent system organizes itself, independent of any overall knowledge of the whole, into a fully functioning unit made up of the individual actions of its components. These individual actions naturally contribute to the function and well-being of the entire system without being directed by any sort of centralized manager or system of laws. The complex behavior of an entire emergent system is brought about by the simple, seemingly insignificant actions of the individuals in the system. "This delightful book introduces readers to the subject of complex adaptive systems (such as ant colonies), and discusses how large-scale order emerges from a series of small-scale interactions," wrote Peter Merholz in *New Architect.*

The prime example of an emergent system in Johnson's book is that of an ant colony. Individually, a single ant may forage for food, build tunnels, or defend the colony. These actions are driven by instinct and can be altered by chemical signals from other members of the colony; a forager can stop looking for food and take up another activity if the communication it receives from other individuals indicates that food is plentiful and other work is necessary. This type of message, however, does not come down as orders from the colony's queen; instead, the message to adapt behavior comes from other individual components of the system. The emergent system of the ant colony regulates itself, changing almost immediately to adapt to different conditions. No command from a monarch is necessary; the system polices itself, and the individual components alter their behavior to best benefit the society as a whole.

Johnson also provides other examples of emergent systems. Under conditions of abundant food, slime mold cells swarm and move about, consuming vegetation; but when conditions worsen, the cells disband into individual units. *Slashdot*, a popular online community, is not governed by an editor or moderator, but is instead controlled by the participants who constantly review content, assign it ratings, and encourage the proliferation of content that meets overall approval while discouraging objectionable material. Programmer Danny Hillis created a "genetic algorithm" that evolved thousands of individual data-sorting programs into a single functional and efficient sorting program—one that Hillis himself could not understand.

Even cities can display emergent behavior in development of business districts, suburbs, slums, and population centers. "Cities seem to have emergent lives of their own, governed by the usually unwitting actions of their inhabitants over many generations," wrote a contributor to the *Guardian*. "We are the ants, in other words, and cities are our colonies."

A *Publishers Weekly* contributor remarked that the "wide scope of the book may leave some readers wanting greater detail, but it does an excellent job of putting the Web into historical and biological context, with no dotcom diminishment." A *Guardian* contributor called *Emergence* "a fascinating book, full of surprises and insights, and written in an easy, engaging style." In *Emergence,* Blume observed in *American Prospect,* "Johnson has put some powerful ideas through a literary feedback loop that will, in all likelihood, accelerate and magnify their effect on our culture."

### Mind Wide Open

For Johnson's third book, *Mind Wide Open: Your Brain and the Neuroscience of Everyday Life,* he turns his attentions to matters of the mind. Johnson subjected himself to a series of tests ranging from brain imaging techniques to neurochemical analysis to get at the heart of the mind-brain connection.

"Johnson is an engaging and intelligent guide," remarked *Discover* contributor Robert Wilson. "One follows him eagerly when he explores the neurophysiology of laughter or allows himself to be inserted into a magnetic resonance imaging machine," Wilson continued. Through his various self-experiments, Johnson formed conclusions on how the brain influences how we think, feel, and act. "Johnson weaves disparate strands of brain research and theory smoothly into the narrative," observed a contributor to *Publishers Weekly.* "Only a concluding section on Freud's modern legacy feels like a tangent," added the reviewer. *Top Producer* reviewer John Phipps pointed out that "while the working of the mind is not simple or easily described, Johnson's accounts of current research do offer realistic ideas that may well be confirmed by later, more rigorous studies." "Johnson very capably reduces the hard science of mind research into readable and even usable tools for all of us," noted Phipps.

### Everything Bad is Good for You

Johnson's fourth book, *Everything Bad Is Good for You: How Today's Popular Culture Is Actually Making Us Smarter,* delivers his controversial contrarian standpoint that video games, television, and the Internet are actually making people smarter.

David Eaves pointed out in his review of the book on *Eaves.ca* that "Johnson is not applauding or even condoning the content of pop culture, what he is celebrating is how the increasing complexity of TV shows, video games and internet content is forcing us to work harder to explore, understand, engage and even guide, the content." Johnson uses the collective rise in IQ points (at three points per decade) over the past thirty years as proof that Americans are getting smarter, and he connects it to the advent of more sophisticated television shows and video games. "But how direct is this link, if it exists at all? And how would someone whose cultural diet has not changed at all over the same period measure up? Without a control group to make such comparisons, Johnson wisely turns his focus to various cultural genres and the specific skills they inspire," maintained *San Francisco Chronicle* contributor Peter Hyman. "When he compares contemporary hit crime dramas like *The Sopranos* and *24*—with their elaborate, multilevel plotlines, teeming casts of characters and open-ended narrative structures—with popular numbskull clunkers of yore like *Starsky and Hutch . . .* it's almost impossible not to agree with him that television drama has grown up and perhaps even achieved a kind of brilliance that probably rubs off on its viewers," observed *New York Times* contributor Walter Kirn. Johnson, however, does "see risks, for example, if children watch too much television or play too many video games. And some cultural works 'are more rewarding than others,' he writes, acknowledging that good literature ought to command people's attention, too," stated *Boston Globe* contributor Joseph Rosenbloom.

### The Ghost Map

Johnson's 2006 study, *The Ghost Map: The Story of London's Most Terrifying Epidemic—and How It Changed Science, Cities, and the Modern World,* deals with the cholera epidemic in London's Soho district in 1854 that killed nearly 700 people in two weeks and was one of the worst cholera outbreaks in London's history.

In this book, "Johnson adds a new and welcome element—old-fashioned storytelling flair, another form of street knowledge—to his fractal, multifaceted method of unraveling the scientific mysteries of everyday life," commended *Los Angeles Times* contributor Mark Coleman. Conventional wisdom of the period regarded miasma (smelly air in dirty spaces) as the culprit for the outbreak. However, physician John Snow believed that cholera was spread through water, a result of London's horrifically unsanitary methods of dealing with waste. Along with clergyman Henry Whitehead (who initially set out to prove Snow wrong), Snow was able to successfully back up his theory. His map (referred to as a "ghost map") depicting where people died in relation to their water source finally convinced city leaders to take action. Kevin Crowley, reviewing for *Inthenews.co.uk,* believed that Johnson's "narration of the intertwining tales of Snow and Whitehead is undermined by explaining their findings within the first fifty pages thus quashing any sense of tension." The book does more than tell their story, though: "Johnson shows the reader a vast, interconnected picture about urban and bacterial life: how information and illness spreads, how ideas and sewage flow; in short, the whole ecosystem of what a city 'means,'" noted Stuart Kelly, reviewer for *Scotland on Sunday.* "*The Ghost Map* is not just a remarkable story, but a remarkable study in what we might learn from that story," added Kelley.

### The Invention of Air

In his next book, *The Invention of Air: A Story of Science, Faith, Revolution, and the Birth of America,* Johnson presents a portrait of Joseph Priestly, an eighteenth-century scientist and theologian. The author evaluates Preistly's friendship with the founding fathers of the United States, including Thomas Jefferson, John Adams, and Benjamin Franklin, and examines Priestly's role in the nation's development intellectually. As Johnson points out, Priestly was held in high regard by the founding fathers. As evidence, the author notes that the historical correspondence between John Adams and Thomas Jefferson later in their lives included fifty-two references to Priestly, who was British but spent the last ten years of his life in the United States, while only mentioning Benjamin Franklin five times and George Washington three times.

In an interview with Blake Wilson for the *New York Times,* Johnson noted that he was supposed to write another book "about how important ideas emerge and spread through society." However, Johnson commented: "I came across the story of Joseph Priestley when I was researching the ideas book, and got so enthralled that I decided to write about Priestley first."

The author examines numerous ideas that changed the world as he provides a narrative of Priestly's life and accomplishments, which include seminal contributions to the discovery of oxygen and the founding of the Unitarian Church. However, as noted by Johnson, Priestly was also a radical thinker who, even though he was British, was a strong supporter of the American Revolution. While Johnson pays due attention to Priestly's role in the discovery of oxygen and his contributions to the Unitarian faith and the United States, the author is much more interested in another contribution by Priestly that has important implications in the modern world.

"Johnson's book throws a certain amount of cold water on the oxygen claim, but more important, Johnson sees all of that as secondary to Priestley's greatest accomplishment, a paradigm-changing discovery that neither he nor anyone else in the 18th century was entirely equipped to understand," wrote Andrew O'Hehir in a review for *Salon.com.* As Johnson points out in his book, among the group of scientists from various places who played a role in discovering the existence of oxygen, Priestly probably understood the discovery and its implications less than the others involved. He never understood that oxygen was important for combustion and continued to proffer a notion that rose up around medieval times that burning objects let out something called phlogiston into the air, making it poisonous.

According to Johnson, however, Priestly should be highly revered for making another discovery. Priestly was conducting an experiment that included having mint and mice together in a jar. He observed that the mint sprigs could keep mice alive, which was the beginning of science's ability to isolate a gaseous element. However, according to Johnson, Priestly's discovery was even more important in that it was leading to "a whole new way of thinking about the planet itself, and its capacity for sustaining life." Essentially, according to Johnson, Priestly's experiment represented "a microcosm of a vast system that had been evolving on Earth for two billion years."

Priestly wrote to Franklin about his experiment, leading Franklin to ponder it; according to *Salon.com* contributor O'Hehir: "Franklin came eerily close, in his 18th-century language, to nailing the entire concept of ecosystem science in one shot." O'Hehir went on to note that Franklin's description of the earth's "ecosystem" does not accurately represent in detail what scientists today know about the ecosystem. Nevertheless, O'Hehir observed that "it's a remarkable insight" for Priestly and Franklin to have made at the time, adding: "At least momentarily, Franklin and Priestley seemed to glimpse a branch of scientific inquiry that would not reach the mainstream until the mid-20th century: the study of all planetary life as a single interlocking system, a complex web of energy flows and chemical interactions that extended from the smallest microorganism to giant redwoods and blue whales."

Several reviewers commented that *The Invention of Air* defies easy classification. Noting that the book is not a "straightforward biography" or a simple recounting of Priestly's achievements in science or in other areas, a *PhiloBiblos* Web site contributor added: "Nor is it a history of the Enlightenment processes which contributed to Priestley's world-view, or an exploration of how that worldview shaped and was shaped by the times, or a treatise on the interstices of science, government and religion." Nevertheless, the reviewer commented: "Each of those elements plays a role in Johnson's story."

Throughout the book, Johnson also takes readers on various intellectual sidetracks. For example, at one point, according to *New York Times Book Review* contributor Russell Shorto, the author "offers a brilliant 'Intermezzo' set in 300 million B.C., which roots Priestley's work on oxygen, and the whole advent of life on earth as we know it, in the Carboniferous era, when supersize plant-life—130-foot-high mosses, trees with three-foot leaves—led to a rise in the oxygen content of the atmosphere." Shorto noted that another aside examines how the discovery and early widespread use of coffee might have impacted the Enlightenment.

A *Kirkus Reviews* contributor called *The Invention of Air* "another rich, readable examination of the intersections where culture and science meet from a scrupulous historian who never offers easy answers to troubling, perhaps intractable questions." In a review for the *Seattle Times*, Bruce Ramsey compared *The Invention of Air* to Johnson's earlier book *The Ghost Map*, noting: "Both are about a moment in science that illuminates how science comes about and what it means for human society."

### Where Good Ideas Come From

In Johnson's next book, *Where Good Ideas Come From: The Natural History of Innovation*, he argues that good ideas are too often viewed as the momentary epiphanies of geniuses. According to Johnson, innovative ideas are highly dependent on the environment from which they spring, and they are usually the result of a collaboration between many individuals.

Reviewing the work in the London *Independent*, contributor Peter Forbes lauded: "What do coral reefs, Italian Renaissance city states and Twitter have in common? Steven Johnson's achievement in *Where Good Ideas Come From* is to establish such connections entirely convincingly. The book is subtitled 'a natural history of innovation', and delivers precisely this, shedding equal light on evolution in the natural world and in human culture and technology." London *Telegraph* contributor Leo Hollis commented: "This book is bigger than the sum of its parts. Like *The Tipping Point* and *Freakonomics* it goes beyond the traditional 'big think' guides that promise to teach us how to get ahead or why things went so wrong; instead, it explores what makes us tick." Jason B. Jones, a contributor to the *Chronicle of Higher Education* Web site, explained: "*Where Good Ideas Come From* attempts to describe the features of an idea-rich ecology, the sort of environment where innovation comes almost naturally. It also looks to demystify creativity, shifting focus away from the solitary genius toward the interactions among people, networks, and other forces that allow innovation to happen."

## ■ Biographical And Critical Sources

### BOOKS

Johnson, Steven, *Interface Culture: How New Technology Transforms the Way We Create and Communicate*, HarperEdge (San Francisco, CA), 1997.

Johnson, Steven, *The Invention of Air: A Story of Science, Faith, Revolution, and the Birth of America*, Riverhead Books (New York, NY), 2009.

### PERIODICALS

*American Prospect*, November 19, 2001, Harvey Blume, review of *Emergence: The Connected Lives of Ants, Brains, Cities, and Software*, pp. 42-45.

*American Scholar*, autumn, 2001, Alex Soojung-Kim Pang, review of *Emergence*, pp. 138-142.

*Booklist*, July, 2001, review of *Emergence*, p. 1953; December 1, 2008, Ray Olson, review of *The Invention of Air: A Story of Science, Faith, Revolution, and the Birth of America*, p. 20.

*Boston Globe*, May 1, 2005, Joseph Rosenbloom, review of *Everything Bad Is Good for You: How Today's Popular Culture Is Actually Making Us Smarter*.

*Discover*, July 1, 2004, Robert Wilson, review of *Mind Wide Open: Your Brain and the Neuroscience of Everyday Life*, p. 82.

*Economist*, October 27, 2001, review of *Emergence*.

*Guardian* (London, England), November 24, 2001, review of *Emergence*, p. 10; August 24, 2002, review of *Emergence*, p. 25.

*Humanities*, November/December, 2006, Bruce Cole, "A Conversation with Steven Johnson," interview.

*Independent* (London, England), October 9, 2001, Roz Kaveny, review of *Emergence*, p. 5; October 8, 2010, Peter Forbes, review of *Where Good Ideas Come From: The Natural History of Innovation*.

*Journal of Cultural Geography*, fall-winter, 2001, Deborah A. Salazar, review of *Interface Culture: How New Technology Transforms the Way We Create and Communicate*, pp. 140-142.

*Kirkus Reviews*, December 1, 2003, review of *Mind Wide Open*, p. 1393; October 15, 2008, review of *The Invention of Air*.

*Library Journal*, December 1, 2008, Eric D. Albright, review of *The Invention of Air*, p. 155.

*Los Angeles Times*, October 15, 2006, Mark Coleman, review of *The Ghost Map: The Story of London's Most Terrifying Epidemic—and How It Changed Science, Cities, and the Modern World*.

*New Architect*, March, 2002, Peter Merholz, review of *Emergence*, p. 56.

*New Statesman*, April 26, 2004, Bryan Appleyard, review of *Mind Wide Open*, p. 53.

*New Yorker*, February 2, 2009, review of *The Invention of Air*, p. 67.

*New York Times*, December 9, 2001, Steven Johnson, "Populist Editing," p. 90; April 6, 2002, Steven Johnson, "Games People Play on Computers," p. A15; May 22, 2005, Walter Kirn, review of *Everything Bad Is Good for You*; May 26, 2005, Janet Maslin, review of *Everything Bad Is Good for You*; February 6, 2009, Blake Wilson, "Stray Questions for: Steven Johnson."

*New York Times Book Review*, January 25, 2009, Russell Shorto, "Breath of Thought," review of *The Invention of Air*.

*Pittsburgh Post-Gazette*, January 18, 2009, Glenn C. Altschuler, "When Science and Politics Worked Hand in Hand," review of *The Invention of Air*.

*Plain Dealer* (Cleveland, OH), November 4, 2001, Dan Tranberg, "Straightforward Writing Makes the Complex Simple; An Easy Look at the Concept of Emergence," p. 112.

*Publishers Weekly*, October 27, 1997, review of *Interface Culture*, p. 60; July 23, 2001, review of *Emergence*, p. 61; December 1, 2003, review of *Mind Wide Open*, p. 50; November 10, 2008, Simon Winchester, review of *The Invention of Air*, p. 40.

*St. Petersburg Times* (St. Petersburg, FL), February 19, 2009, David L. Beck, "Science, Politics and a Young U.S.," review of *The Invention of Air*.

*San Francisco Chronicle*, May 22, 2005, Peter Hyman, review of *Everything Bad Is Good for You*, p. F3; January 9, 2009, Troy Jollimore, review of *The Invention of Air*.

*School Library Journal*, October 1, 2005, Catherine Gilbride, review of *Everything Bad Is Good for You*, p. 201.

*Scotland on Sunday*, November 19, 2006, Stuart Kelly, review of *The Ghost Map*.

*Seattle Times*, January 11, 2009, Bruce Ramsey, "*The Invention of Air* Captures a Moment in Scientific Time; Books and Authors," p. 4.

*Spectator*, December 29, 2001, Hugh Lawson-Tancred, review of *Emergence*, p. 38.

*Telegraph* (London, England), November 21, 2010, Leo Hollis, review of *Where Good Ideas Come From*.

*Time*, May 9, 2005, James Poniewozik, review of *Everything Bad Is Good for You*, p. 67.

*Time International*, December 18, 2006, Michael Brunton, review of *The Ghost Map*, p. 6.

*Top Producer*, December 4, 2005, John Phipps, review of *Mind Wide Open*.

*WorldLink*, January-February, 2002, Lance Knobel, review of *Emergence*, pp. 186-187.

ONLINE

*800ceoRead*, http://blog.800ceoread.com/ (December 28, 2010), Kate Mytty, author interview.

*Ape Culture*, http://www.apeculture.com/ (February 6, 2006), Mary E. Ladd, review of *Everything Bad Is Good for You*.

*Arrow through the Sun*, http://arrowthroughthesun.blogspot.com/ (May 27, 2009), review of *The Invention of Air*.

*Atlantic Unbound*, http://www.theatlantic.com/ (September 17, 2002), Harvey Blume, interview with Johnson.

*Best Reviews*, http://thebestreviews.com/ (June 25, 2009), Viviane Crystal, "The Building Innovation," review of *The Invention of Air*.

*Bookslut*, http://www.bookslut.com/ (June, 2005), Liz Miller, review of *Everything Bad Is Good for You*.

*Chronicle of Higher Education*, http://chronicle.com/ (October 15, 2010), Jason B. Jones, review of *Where Good Ideas Come From*.

*Daily Beast*, http://www.thedailybeast.com/ (October 9, 2010), review of *Where Good Ideas Come From*.

*Dallas News Online*, http://www.dallasnews.com/ (January 4, 2009), Alexandra Witze, review of *The Invention of Air*.

*Eaves.ca*, http://eaves.ca/ (February 27, 2007), David Eaves, review of *Everything Bad Is Good for You*.

*Fiddle and Burn*, http://www.fiddleandburn.com/ (January 23, 2009), Jason Pomerantz, review of *The Invention of Air*.

*Freakonomics*, http://www.freakonomics.com/ (October 1, 2010), Stephen J. Dubner, author interview.

*Frontline Web site,* http://www.pbs.org/wgbh/pages/frontline/ (January 24, 2002), Wen Stephenson, "Beyond the Bubble," interview with Johnson.

*Inthenews.co.uk,* http://www.inthenews.co.uk/ (December 12, 2006), review of *The Ghost Map.*

*Oregonian,* http://blog.oregonlive.com/ (January 9, 2009), Paul Collins, review of *The Invention of Air.*

*O'Reilly Network Web site,* http://www.oreillynet.com/ (September 17, 2002), David Sims and Rael Dornfest, interview with Johnson.

*Peterme.com,* http://www.peterme.com/ (December 30, 2008), review of *The Invention of Air.*

*PhiloBiblos,* http://philobiblos.blogspot.com/ (January 28, 2009), review of *The Invention of Air.*

*PopMatters,* http://www.popmatters.com/ (April 6, 2007), Jason B. Jones, "Long Zoom: Interview with Steven Johnson"; (January 19, 2009) Michael Patrick Brady, review of *The Invention of Air.*

*Salon.com,* http://www.salon.com/ (September 17, 2002), Scott Rosenberg, review of *Interface Culture;* (January 9, 2009) Andrew O'Hehir, "Father of the Ecosystem," review of *The Invention of Air.*

*Seattle Times,* http://seattletimes.nwsource.com/ (October 2, 2010), review of *Where Good Ideas Come From.*

*Stating the Obvious,* http://www.theobvious.com/ (January 21, 1998), Michael Sippey, "Just One Question for Steven Johnson," interview.

*Steven Johnson Home Page,* http://www.stevenberlinjohnson.com (August 14, 2011).*

# Jan Karon

## 1937-

- **Also Known As**

Janice Meredith Wilson

- **Personal**

Born Janice Meredith Wilson, March 14, 1937, in Lenoir, NC; children: Candace Freeland.

- **Addresses**

*Home*—Blowing Rock, NC.

- **Career**

Novelist; worked for various advertising agencies as copywriter.

- **Awards, Honors**

Abby Honor Book award, 1996, and Logos award, 1997, for best fiction for *At Home in Mitford*; ECPA Gold Medallion and Christy awards for best fiction, 2000, for *A New Song*; Parent's Choice award for *Jeremy: The Tale of an Honest Bunny*.

- **Writings**

*"MITFORD" SERIES*

*At Home in Mitford* (also see below), Lion (Elgin, IL), 1994.

*A Light in the Window* (also see below), Penguin (New York, NY), 1996, 2nd edition, RiverOak (Colorado Springs, CO), 2005.
*These High, Green Hills* (also see below), Lion (Colorado Springs, CO), 1996.
*Out to Canaan* (also see below), Viking (New York, NY), 1997.
*A New Song* (also see below), Viking (New York, NY), 1999.
*A Common Life: The Wedding Story*, Viking (New York, NY), 2001.
*The Mitford Years* (five-volume set; contains *At Home in Mitford, A Light in the Window, These High, Green Hills, Out to Canaan,* and *A New Song*), Viking (New York, NY), 2001.
*Father Timothy A. Kavanaugh*, Viking (New York, NY), 2001.
*The Mitford Snowmen: A Christmas Story*, Viking (New York, NY), 2001.
*In This Mountain*, Viking (New York, NY), 2002.
*Esther's Gift: A Mitford Christmas Story*, Viking (New York, NY), 2002.
*Shepherds Abiding: Christmas in Mitford*, Knopf (New York, NY), 2003.
*Light from Heaven*, Viking (New York, NY), 2005.
*The Mitford Bedside Companion*, Viking (New York, NY), 2006.

*"FATHER TIM" SERIES*

*Home to Holly Springs*, Viking (New York, NY), 2007.
*In the Company of Others*, Viking (New York, NY), 2010.

*NONFICTION*

*The Trellis and the Seed: A Book of Encouragement for All Ages*, Viking (New York, NY), 2003.

*Jan Karon's Mitford Cookbook & Kitchen Reader,* Viking (New York, NY), 2004.

*A Continual Feast: Words of Comfort and Celebration Collected by Father Tim,* Viking (New York, NY), 2005.

FOR CHILDREN

*Miss Fannie's Hat,* illustrations by Toni Goffe, Augsburg (Minneapolis, MN), 1998.

*Jeremy: The Tale of an Honest Bunny,* illustrations by Terry Weidner, Viking (New York, NY), 2000.

*Jan Karon Presents Cynthia Coppersmith's Violet Comes to Stay* (story by Melanie Cecka), Viking Children's Books (New York, NY), 2006.

*Jan Karon Presents Cynthia Coppersmith's Violet Goes to the Country* (story by Melanie Cecka), Viking Children's Books (New York, NY), 2007.

Also author of foreword, *Never Let It End: Poems of a Lifelong Love,* by Ruth Bell Graham, Baker Books, 2001. Contributor to *A Southern Style Christmas,* compiled by Lucinda Secrest McDowell, Shaw (Colorado Springs, CO), 2000.

## ■ Adaptations

Many of Karon's books have been adapted for audio cassette, read by the author or John McDonough. Karon's "Mitford" series has been adapted to a play called *Welcome to Mitford* by Robert Inman, published by Dramatic Publishing, 2010.

## ■ Sidelights

Jan Karon is the author of a very popular series of novels set in Mitford, a fictional village in the Blue Ridge Mountains. The stories feature an Episcopal priest, Father Tim, and an engaging cast of townspeople, all of them with plenty of human foibles. The books carry Christian themes, expressed through the stories of Father Tim and his fellow residents. After completing numerous books in the "Mitford" series, Karon moved Father Tim to his hometown, Holly Springs, to start a somewhat different series with him at the center. She has also published several books that are peripheral to the main series, including collections of wisdom attributed to Father Tim, special stories for Christmastime, and even a cookbook related to the "Mitford" series.

Karon and her younger sister were reared by their grandparents on a farm in North Carolina. There, the author reported on her home page, Karon's creativity flourished: "On the farm there is time to muse and dream. . . . As a young girl I couldn't wait to get off that farm, to go to Hollywood or New York. But living in those confined, bucolic circumstances was one of the best things that ever happened to me." She noted in an interview with Betty Smartt Carter for *Christianity Today* that it was as a child that she developed "an ear for dialect."

Karon knew from an early age that she wanted to be a writer, and she penned her first novel at age ten. With just eight years of formal schooling, she got her start as a copywriter for an ad agency, where she worked first as a receptionist. After a forty-year career in advertising—during which time she won numerous awards and climbed the corporate ladder to a vice president position with a national agency—she decided to leave advertising to write books. Throughout her advertising years, she told Carter, "I was fighting my calling. I didn't know how to be an author." Upon her retirement from the advertising world, Karon moved to the small town of Blowing Rock, North Carolina, in the Blue Ridge mountains. Her brother had a summer home there and, she told Renee Crist in *Publishers Weekly,* she "wanted to be back in the mountains." While Karon still has a home and family in Blowing Rock, she spends most of her time now in Virginia "for creative privacy" reasons, as Phyllis Ten Elshof explained in the *Christian Reader.*

Blowing Rock is the model for Mitford, North Carolina, the fictional town where Karon's popular novels take place. "Mitford is the literary equivalent of Bedford Falls, the small town of *It's a Wonderful Life,*" wrote Emily Mitchell in *People.* "None of the people in Mitford are actually based upon anyone in Blowing Rock," Karon noted on her Web site. "Yet, the spirit of my characters is found throughout this real-life village." Asked by Carter in *Christianity Today* if someone can "find small-town life just by moving to the country," Karon responded, "No. . . . If you will read a Mitford book carefully, you will see that everybody is helping Mitford happen. Mitford isn't free. You've got to reach out if you want Mitford."

### "Mitford" Series

Karon's "Mitford" novels are a "best-selling, prize-winning series of life in a small town," wrote Elshof in the *Christian Reader.* Malcolm Jones in *Newsweek* commented: "The goings-on in Mitford revolve around church life because the church is the community's social as well as spiritual center. There's no violence, no sex and no cussing." The main character of these novels is Father Tim Kavanaugh, an Episcopal priest. Karon describes Father Tim as "an ordinary human being, sweet and tender, and a man of God, who lives out his convictions in the midst of a town filled with other ordinary people." Karon's characters "win respect, not with extraordinary feats over uncommon odds," said Elshof, "but by moving through life's struggles, surprises, and interactions with an innate devotion to things that really matter."

Elshof believes that the relationship of these ordinary people to God is what most attracts readers to Karon's books. Karon stated: "I'm going out there, and I'm talking about Jesus. I'm talking about people's relationships with him." Karon committed herself to Christianity at age forty-two, following a divorce that ended a three-and-a-half-year marriage and left her with a baby to raise on her own. "In my books," she is quoted as saying by Lauren F. Winner in *Christianity Today*, "I try to depict not a glorious faith with celestial fireworks, but a daily faith, a routine faith, a seven-days-a-week faith. . . . I try to depict how our faith may be woven into our daily life." Winner stated: "The Mitford books may not have inspired mass conversions, but they have shaped the faith of many readers."

As Karon explained to Crist in *Publishers Weekly*, her first novel started as a serial in the local paper, the *Blowing Rocket*, with her compensation consisting of free copies of each issue. The serial ran in the paper every week for two years, at which time Karon decided to try to get it published. Lion, an evangelical Christian publisher, agreed to do so. Eventually Lion and publishing house Penguin "struck a co-publishing deal," noted Crist, whereby "Lion would distribute the books to Christian bookstores, and Penguin would handle the mainstream market." Many of Karon's later books have been published exclusively by Viking.

Jones referred to Karon in *Newsweek* as a "marketing wizard," but he found her "every bit as sincere as she is slick and never smarter than when defining what her readers find in her books: 'They find themselves.'" Karon and her books have been written about in many publications. Zachary Karabell referred to Karon in the *Los Angeles Times Book Review* as "a writer who reflects contemporary culture more fully than almost any other living novelist. Karon spins a fantasy of a town full of lovable yet decent people who struggle with love and marriage, with domestic disputes and unpredictable weather, with ghosts of their past and, most of all, with faith and God." Mary Ellen Quinn in *Booklist* observed: "Karon's great skill is writing novels that are cozy, comfortable, and folksy but never pious or

sentimental." Carter wrote in *Christianity Today*: "Though the Mitford books never gloss over or trivialize the sorrows of life, it's hard to carry sorrow away from them; the reader feels . . . consoled."

"Karon's series has been growing in popularity since her first novel, *At Home in Mitford*, was released by Lion in 1994," reported Crist in *Publishers Weekly*. Crist also said: "Karon's books differ from most Christian fiction, much of which is genre fiction and agenda-driven rather than character-and plot-driven. . . . It's rare for a writer to cross over from the Christian market to the mainstream, but Karon has done so with aplomb." "Distinguished by their rare tone of kindness," observed Keddy Ann Outlaw in *Library Journal*, "Karon's Mitford novels create instant warmth and coziness." Quinn in *Booklist* noted Karon's "gentle humor" and stated: "Although Mitford and its close-knit community seem quaint and idyllic, Karon's portrayal is never sentimentalized."

Reviewing *In This Mountain*, the seventh volume in the "Mitford" series, *Bookreporter* writer Kate Ayers called it "the ultimate feel good book," noting that the same could be said for all of the other books in the series as well. She added: "If everyone periodically read one of Jan Karon's 'Mitford Years' novels, the world would be a happier place." In the novel *In This Mountain* Father Tim continues to minister to his flock, while his wife Cynthia finds that her children's books about Violet the Cat have become unexpectedly popular, leading to a book tour, awards, and a trip to New York City. Dooley Barlowe, a young man whom Father Tim has unofficially adopted, leaves for college but returns periodically, in part because he hopes for a romance with his childhood friend Lace Turner. Though retired, Father Tim has plenty to fill his days: serving as a guest preacher, visiting patients at the hospital, and helping the townspeople to deal with large and small mishaps. Familiar elements such as the relationship between Father Tim and his secretary, Emma, and the threat of trouble from his adversary, Edith Mallory, are present in the series. Father Tim is also challenged by his diabetes and his weakness for sweets and other inappropriate foods, a failing that eventually puts him in the hospital. Quinn, a contributor to *Booklist*, found *In This Mountain* to be "a deeper book" than previous titles in the series, one that would appeal both to die-hard fans and to those who may have been growing a little tired of Mitford and its inhabitants.

The Mitford series concluded in 2005 with *Light from Heaven*, which features Karon's "trademark talents in full view," according to Cindy Crosby in

*Christianity Today.* The story revolves around Holy Trinity church, a small mountain parish that has been mostly abandoned but still waits patiently for a new pastor. Father Tim is sent to do the job, while at the same time attempting to salvage the life of Sammy, Dooley's wayward younger brother, and to find Kenny, Sammy and Dooley's long-lost brother. The narrative contains humor, sermons, hymns, and even recipes for mountain food, including soup made from squirrel meat. According to Debra Bendis in *Christian Century,* visiting the gentle world of the Mitford series is "refreshing." In Karon's world, said Bendis, "relationships are nourished in slow time. Father Tim slows down to honor the sacredness of each encounter, believing that he and another are only a subset of a larger and more glorious gathering of friends and neighbors."

### "Father Tim" Series

Many readers were saddened by the announced end of the "Mitford" series, but the end of the series did not mean the end of Father Tim. Karon continued his story in a new set of books, the "Father Tim" novels, beginning with *Home to Holly Springs.* In this novel, the priest returns to his home town after receiving some mysterious notes. He is both delighted and saddened by what he finds there. Family secrets come to light, including the fact that Father Tim has a half-brother he never knew existed. In an interview for *Bookreporter,* Karon commented: "The new series embodies, I feel, the spirit of the old. That is to say, redemption continues to be the overarching theme in this, and all, my work. It's different in that we're given a far deeper look into the soul of a man we've come to know well—but until now, not as completely." Lauren Winner reviewed the book for *Christianity Today* and praised Karon's writing, her treatment of faith issues, and most of all, her examination of racism in the modern South, a "still-persistent social sin" that must be scrutinized. "It is to that scrutiny and reckoning that Jan Karon's new novel, perhaps willy-nilly, bids us," commented Winner. Cindy Crosby, reviewing for *Bookreporter,* called *Home to Holly Springs* "an auspicious beginning" to the "Father Tim" series and predicted that fans of the first series "will be happy to discover the same wonderful brand of fiction they've grown to love."

Karon continued the "Father Tim" series with her 2010 work *In the Company of Others.* In this installment the now-retired Father Tim and his wife Cynthia head to vacation in Ireland. Tim and Cynthia bond with the other guests at the inn where they are staying after a string of burglaries in the building draws them together. When Tim and Cynthia walk in on the thief ransacking their hotel room, they are forced into a scuffle, and Cynthia obtains a leg injury from the fight. This keeps them hotel bound for the remainder of the trip.

Reviewing the work, *Booklist* contributor Carol Haggas claimed that the "latest installment will be equally attractive to new readers, especially those whose who enjoy Irish fiction." However, a *Kirkus Reviews* contributor noted: "Readers who are not devoted followers of Karon may be impatient with the glacial pace of this installment." Jocelyn McClurg, a contributor to *USA Today,* stated: "*Company* does have moments when it's, well, good company. There's the inn's shoe-chomping Jack Russell terrier, who finds a pal in Tim." A *Publishers Weekly* contributor commented: "Though it's not the ideal entry point to the expansive world of Father Tim, fans will relish this." Jan Blodgett, a contributor to *Xpress Reviews,* opined: "The novel is at its best when the Irish characters are on stage."

### Other Books

The popularity of Father Tim and Mitford gave rise to several related books, including some short Christmas stories, such as *Esther's Gift: A Mitford Christmas Story* and *Shepherds Abiding: Christmas in Mitford,* some collections of wise words and sermons, including *The Trellis and the Seed: A Book of Encouragement for All Ages* and *A Continual Feast: Words of Comfort and Celebration Collected by Father Tim,* and even a cookbook, *Jan Karon's Mitford Cookbook & Kitchen Reader,* recommended by Crosby as an entertaining "carb-fest of comforting, sweet-tooth ticklin' recipes." Even the children's books featuring Violet the Cat, which, in the "Mitford" series, are written by Father Tim's wife, are brought to life in picture books based on the character and written by Melanie Cecka.

Karon also publishes a biannual *Mitford Newsletter,* which is offered free to anyone who is interested. Karon says she enjoys meeting readers of her books and answers every fan letter she receives.

### Children's Books

Karon' first children's book, *Miss Fannie's Hat,* is the story of a ninety-nine-year-old woman who sells her favorite hat to help raise money for her church. *Publishers Weekly* called it "a cheerful story that offers a worthy message while avoiding a didactic tone." Angela J. Reynolds said in *School Library Journal* that it is "a sweet, gentle story." The book includes reusable stickers and a storyboard.

Karon's second children's book, *Jeremy: The Tale of an Honest Bunny*, has sometimes been compared to Margery Williams's *The Velveteen Rabbit*. A reviewer for *Kirkus Reviews* described it as "a sweet, sketchy novella about a handmade rabbit who decides to walk to his new owner's house rather than be mailed." Marta Segal in *Booklist* called it an "old-fashioned story that's part Kenneth Grahame and part C.S. Lewis." "Karon's characters are as consciously quaint as her settings," observed a contributor to *Publishers Weekly*.

## ■ Biographical And Critical Sources

### PERIODICALS

*Book*, July 1, 2002, Beth Kephart, review of *In This Mountain*.

*Booklist*, July, 1996, Mary Ellen Quinn, review of *These High, Green Hills*, p. 1802; April 1, 1997, Mary Ellen Quinn, review of *Out to Canaan*, p. 1268; March 1, 1999, Mary Ellen Quinn, review of *A New Song*, p. 1103; April 15, 2000, Marta Segal, review of *Jeremy: The Tale of an Honest Bunny*, p. 1542; February 15, 2001, Mary Ellen Quinn, review of *A Common Life: The Wedding Story*, p. 1084; May 15, 2002, Mary Ellen Quinn, review of *In This Mountain*, p. 1554; November 15, 2006, Carolyn Phelan, review of *Jan Karon Presents Cynthia Coppersmith's Violet Comes to Stay*, p. 52; September 1, 2007, Carolyn Phelan, review of *Jan Karon Presents Cynthia Coppersmith's Violet Goes to the Country*, p. 130; September 15, 2010, Carol Haggas, review of *In the Company of Others*, p. 28.

*Christian Century*, December 12, 2006, Debra Bendis, review of *Light from Heaven*, p. 40.

*Christianity Today*, September 1, 1997, Betty Smartt Carter, "Postmarked Mitford: Readers Are Finding a Home in Jan Karon's Novels," p. 18; July 12, 1999, Lauren F. Winner, "Karon's Agenda" and "New Song, Familiar Tune," p. 64; February 1, 2006, Cindy Crosby, review of *Light from Heaven*, p. 98.

*Christian Reader*, May, 2001, Phyllis Ten Elshof, "Why Jan Karon Left Mitford," p. 60.

*Fort Worth Star-Telegram*, Kathy Harris, July 16, 2002, review of *In This Mountain*.

*Kirkus Reviews*, March 15, 1997, review of *Out to Canaan*, pp. 406-407; March 1, 1999, review of *A New Song*, p. 330; December 1, 1999, review of *Jeremy*, p. 1886; September 15, 2006, Melanie Cecka, review of *Jan Karon Presents Cynthia Coppersmith's Violet Comes to Stay*, p. 957; August 1, 2007, Melanie Cecka, review of *Jan Karon Presents Cynthia Coppersmith's Violet Goes to the Country*; September 1, 2007, review of *Home to Holly Springs*; August 15, 2010, review of *In the Company of Others*.

*Kliatt Young Adult Paperback Book Guide*, March, 1997, Nancy Crowder Chaplin, review of audio versions of *At Home in Mitford* and *A Light in the Window*, p. 39.

*Library Journal*, November 1, 1994, Henry Carrigan, Jr., review of *At Home in Mitford*, p. 65; May 1, 1997, Keddy Ann Outlaw, review of *Out to Canaan*, p. 140; April 1, 1999, Jan Blodgett, review of *A New Song*, p. 129, and Leah Sparks, review of audio version of *The Mitford Years*, p. 146; October 15, 1999, Joanna Burkhardt, review of *A New Song*, p. 122; February 1, 2001, Melanie C. Duncan, review of *A Common Life*, p. 77.

*Los Angeles Times Book Review*, August 22, 1999, Zachary Karabell, "Look Homeward Angel: Why the Literati Snub the Christian Fiction of Jan Karon," pp. 3-4.

*Mississippi*, Jennifer Barnes Moffett, January 1, 2008, "A Sense of Place: Jan Karon Takes a Mitford Character into New Territory for Her Novel Home to Holly Springs."

*Newsweek*, May 3, 1999, Malcolm Jones, "Touched by the Angels," p. 71.

*People*, December 15, 1997, Emily Mitchell, "The Mitford Years," pp. 31-32.

*Publishers Weekly*, June 6, 1994, review of *At Home in Mitford*, p. 60; June 10, 1996, review of *These High, Green Hills*, p. 87; April 14, 1997, review of *Out to Canaan*, p. 52; May 26, 1997, Renee Crist, "Jan Karon: The Good Life in Mitford," p. 60; February 23, 1998, review of *Miss Fannie's Hat*, p. 66; March 8, 1999, review of *A New Song*, p. 47; January 31, 2000, review of *Jeremy*, p. 103; March 19, 2001, review of *A Common Life*, p. 77; May 20, 2002, review of *In This Mountain*, p. 48; June 9, 2003, "All the Buzz," p. 24; November 3, 2003, review of *Shepherds Abiding: Christmas in Mitford*, p. 55; August 30, 2004, review of *Jan Karon's Mitford Cookbook & Kitchen Reader*, p. 49; January 17, 2005, review of *A Continual Feast: Words of Comfort and Celebration Collected by Father Tim*, p. 50; September 17, 2007, review of *Home to Holly Springs*, p. 37; August 30, 2010, review of *In the Company of Others*, p. 27.

*School Library Journal*, June, 1998, Angela J. Reynolds, review of *Miss Fannie's Hat*, p. 111; September, 2000, Karen K. Radtke, review of *Jeremy*, p. 200; July 1, 2003, Susan Hepler, review of *The Trellis and the Seed: A Book of Encouragement for All Ages*, p. 99; November 1, 2006, Judith Constantinides, review of *Jan Karon Presents Cynthia Coppersmith's Violet Comes to Stay*, p. 98.

*USA Today*, November 23, 2010, "Karon Remains Pleasant 'Company'," p. 7.

*Washington Post Book World*, November 10, 1996, Louise Titchener, review of *These High, Green Hills*, p. 10.

*Xpress Reviews*, October 8, 2010, Jan Blodgett, review of *In the Company of Others*.

*ONLINE*

*Beliefnet,* http://www.beliefnet.com/ (July 31, 2008), Lauren Winner, "A God-given Story," interview with Jan Karon.

*BookPage,* http://www.bookpage.com/ (July 31, 2008), Jay MacDonald, "Jan Karon's Cookbook Is a Sumptuous Southern Treat."

*Bookreporter.com,* http://www.bookreporter.com/ (December 14, 2007), interview with Jan Karon; (July 31, 2008) Cindy Crosby, reviews of *Home from Holly Springs, Light from Heaven, Shepherds Abiding: Christmas in Mitford,* and *Jan Karon's Mitford Cookbook & Kitchen Reader;* Carol Fitzgerald, review of *Esther's Gift: A Mitford Christmas Story;* Kate Ayers, review of *In This Mountain.*

*Christianity Today,* http://www.christianitytoday.com/ (December 27, 2007), Lauren Winner, review of *Home to Holly Springs.*

*Jan Karon's Home Page,* http://www.mitfordbooks.com (July 31, 2008).

*Mitford Books,* http://www.mitfordbooks.com/ (August 14, 2011).*

# Ben Katchor

## 1951-

■ **Personal**

Born November 19, 1951, in New York, NY. *Education:* Attended School of Visual Arts, New York, NY; Brooklyn College of the City University of New York, B.A.

■ **Addresses**

*Agent*—Wylie Agency, 250 W. 57th St., Ste. 2114, New York, NY 10107. *E-mail*—ben@katchor.com.

■ **Career**

Writer and cartoonist. Worked as a partner in a graphic design firm; School of Visual Arts, New York, NY, teacher, 1996—. National Public Radio, creator of a radio drama series based on his comic strip "Julius Knipl, Real Estate Photographer," 1994, and of more than a dozen Julius Knipl episodes, broadcast in the television series *Weekend Edition Saturday.* Visiting lecturer or artist at educational institutions, including Bard College and California College of Arts and Crafts, 1996, Syracuse University, 1999, Yale University, Swarthmore College, and Brown University.

■ **Awards, Honors**

Award for Excellence in Cartoon, Caricature, and Comic-Strip Art, Swann Foundation, 1990; named "best cartoonist" by *New York* magazine, 1994; Guggenheim fellow, 1995-96; Obie Award for theater, *Village Voice,* 2000; MacArthur fellowship, 2000; fellow at American Academy in Berlin, 2002; award from Pew Charitable Trust, 2002; multi-arts production grant from Rockefeller Foundation, 2003.

■ **Writings**

*Cheap Novelties: The Pleasures of Urban Decay* (collected comic strips), Penguin (New York, NY), 1991.

*Julius Knipl, Real Estate Photographer: Stories* (collected comic strips), Little, Brown (New York, NY), 1996.

*The Jew of New York* (graphic novel), Pantheon (New York, NY), 1999.

(And designer and director) *The Carbon Copy Building* (opera libretto), music by David Lang, Julia Wolfe, and Michael Gordon, produced in Turin, Italy, at Settembre Festival, 1999.

*Julius Knipl, Real Estate Photographer: The Beauty Supply District* (collected comic strips), Pantheon (New York, NY), 2000.

*The Cardboard Valise* (graphic novel), Pantheon Books (New York, NY), 2011.

Also designer, director, and librettist for the musical theater productions *The Slug Bearers of Kayrol Island,* music by Mark Mulcahy, 2003; and *The Rosenbach Company,* music by Mark Mulcahy, 2004. Weekly comic strips include *"Julius Knipl, Real Estate Photographer,"* beginning 1988; "The Jew of New York," in *Forward,* beginning 1993; "The Cardboard Valise," 1998; "Hotel & Farm," 2000; and "Shoehorn Technique," 2005; creator of a monthly strip in *Metropolis,* beginning 1998. Contributor to magazines and newspapers, including *Village Voice* and *New Yorker.* Also maintains a blog at http://benkatchor.wordpress.com.

■ **Sidelights**

Ben Katchor is an American writer and cartoonist whose work has been published in outlets such as the *New Yorker.* His graphic novel *The Cardboard Valise* explores motifs of consumerism, tourism, language, and many others. In a complicated and winding plot, Emile Delilah, the main character, travels from country to country, having no homeland of his own.

Reviewing the book in the Toronto *Globe and Mail,* contributor Seth said of Katchor's work: "He performs that often promised yet rarely accomplished feat of transforming the mundane into the sublime. He conjures up otherworldly alternative realities for the banal objects of our everyday world—figuratively tossing them up into the air, then magically recombining them into new and amusing forms." *Fiction Writers Review* Web site contributor Sara Henkin reported: "'Katchor's' illustrations change continuously across the eight frames on each page, capturing buildings, streetscapes, and other curious settings both at close range and from afar. Meanwhile, the narrative—which is inserted across the top of each rectangular frame—and the dialogue are both hand-printed by Katchor in capital letters, making the experience feel both personal and informal." *Publishers Weekly* contributor Sasha Watson explained: "[Katchor's] themes move between recognizable critiques of consumer culture and mainstream entertainment, and moody riffs whose meanings are harder to grasp."

Katchor once told *CA:* "My career in the field of comic-strip art began when I contributed to various small-press magazines during my teenage years. In college I tried to integrate my study of literature and art in the form of narrative paintings and prints. After college I renewed my interest in commercial, high-speed, offset lithography as an alternative to the traditional forms of art printmaking. I acquired an extensive background in book and print production, working for ten years as a partner in a graphic design company.

"In 1986 I edited and published my own *Picture Story* magazine and began working as a freelance illustrator and cartoonist. In 1988 I began the weekly comic strip, 'Julius Knipl, Real Estate Photographer.' In 1993 I began a weekly strip titled 'The Jew of New York' for the English-language edition of the *Forward*. In 1994 I began to work, in collaboration with producer David Isay, on a series of radio dramas based on my Julius Knipl strip. Eight of these were aired. As a result of listener response to this show, a new series of fifteen episodes were produced and broadcast monthly."

### ■ Biographical And Critical Sources

*PERIODICALS*

*American Book Review,* July, 1997, review of *Julius Knipl, Real Estate Photographer: Stories,* p. 19.
*American Heritage,* December, 1993, review of *Cheap Novelties: The Pleasures of Urban Decay,* p.
*Bomb,* summer, 2004, interview by Alexander Theroux.
*Booklist,* December 1, 1998, Ray Olson, review of *The Jew of New York,* p. 643.

*Entertainment Weekly,* February 5, 1999, review of *The Jew of New York,* p. 64.
*Globe & Mail* (Toronto, Ontario, Canada), February 15, 1997, review of *Julius Knipl, Real Estate Photographer: Stories,* p. D10; March 11, 2011, Seth, review of *The Cardboard Valise.*
*Kirkus Reviews,* December 15, 2010, review of *The Cardboard Valise.*
*New Republic,* February 1, 1999, Hillel Halkin, review of *The Jew of New York,* p. 36.
*New York,* January 11, 1999, review of *The Jew of New York,* p. 89.
*New Yorker,* November 25, 1996, review of *Julius Knipl, Real Estate Photographer: Stories,* p. 117; January 11, 1999, review of *The Jew of New York,* p. 89.
*New York Review of Books,* November 15, 2001, Anthony Grafton, review of *Julius Knipl, Real Estate Photographer: The Beauty Supply District,* p. 26.
*New York Times,* October 1, 1996, Michiko Kakutani, review of *Julius Knipl, Real Estate Photographer: Stories,* p. C15.
*New York Times Book Review,* December 22, 1996, Edward Sorel, review of *Julius Knipl, Real Estate Photographer: Stories,* p. 4; January 10, 1999, J. Hoberman, review of *The Jew of New York,* p. 6; June 6, 1999, review of *The Jew of New York,* p. 36; December 5, 1999, review of *The Jew of New York,* p. 74.
*Observer* (London, England), December 5, 1999, review of *The Jew of New York,* p. 13.
*Publishers Weekly,* October 11, 1993, review of *Cheap Novelties,* p. 55; December 21, 1998, Daisy Maryles, "Xmas in South Park," p. 18, and review of *The Jew of New York,* p. 56; November 30, 2010, Sasha Watson, review of *The Cardboard Valise.*
*School Library Journal,* May, 1999, Francisca Goldsmith, review of *The Jew of New York,* p. 162.
*Yale Review,* July, 1999, John Crowley, review of *The Jew of New York,* p. 159.

*ONLINE*

*A.V. Club,* http://www.avclub.com/ (April 22, 2011), Sam Adams, author interview.
*Ben Katchor Home Page,* http://www.katchor.com (August 25, 2011).
*Daily Beast,* http://www.thedailybeast.com/ (March 4, 2011), Malcolm Jones, "Cartoonist Ben Katchor captures the city in his book, *The Cardboard Valise.*"
*Fiction Writers Review,* http://fictionwritersreview.com/ (June 30, 2011), Sara Henkin, review of *The Cardboard Valise.*
*Name of This Cartoon Is Brunswick,* http://brunswick.wordpress.com/ (May 3, 2011), review of *The Cardboard Valise.*
*Straight.com,* http://www.straight.com/ (April 26, 2011), John Lucas, review of *The Cardboard Valise.*

# Stephen King

## 1947-

### ■ Also Known As

Richard Bachman
Eleanor Druse
Stephen Edwin King
Steve King
John Swithen

### ■ Personal

Born September 21, 1947, in Portland, ME; son of Donald (a merchant sailor) and Nellie Ruth King; married Tabitha Jane Spruce (a novelist), January 2, 1971; children: Naomi Rachel, Joseph Hill, Owen Phillip. *Education:* University of Maine, Orono, B.Sc., 1970. *Politics:* Democrat. *Hobbies and other interests:* Reading (mostly fiction), jigsaw puzzles, playing the guitar ("I'm terrible and so try to bore no one but myself"), movies, bowling.

### ■ Addresses

*Home*—Bangor, ME. *Agent*—Rand Holston, Creative Artists Agency, 9830 Wilshire Blvd., Beverly Hills, CA 90212.

### ■ Career

Writer. Hampden Academy (high school), Hampden, ME, English teacher, 1971-73; University of Maine, Orono, writer-in-residence, 1978-79. Owner, Philtrum Press (publishing house), and WZON-AM (rock 'n' roll radio station), Bangor, ME. Has worked as a janitor, as a laborer in an industrial laundry, and in a knitting mill. Has made cameo appearances in films, including *Knightriders*, 1981, *Creepshow*, 1982, *Maximum Overdrive*, 1986, *Pet Sematary*, 1989, and *The Stand*, 1994; has also appeared in American Express credit card television commercial; narrator for *Black Ribbons* album, 2010. Served as judge for 1977 World Fantasy Awards in 1978. Participated in radio honor panel with George A. Romero, Peter Straub, and Ira Levin, moderated by Dick Cavett, WNET, 1980.

### ■ Member

Authors Guild, Screen Artists Guild, Writers Guild, Screen Writers of America, Authors League of America.

### ■ Awards, Honors

Balrog Awards, second place in best novel category, for *The Stand*, and second place in best collection category for *Night Shift*, both 1979; named to the American Library Association's list of best books for young adults, 1979, for *The Long Walk*, and 1981, for *Firestarter;* World Fantasy Award, 1980, for contributions to the field, and 1982, for story "Do the Dead Sing?"; Career Alumni Award, University of Maine at Orono, 1981; special British Fantasy Award for outstanding contribution to the genre, British Fantasy Society, 1982, for *Cujo;* Hugo Award, World Science Fiction Convention, 1982, for *Stephen King's Danse Macabre;* named Best Fiction Writer of the Year, *Us* magazine, 1982; Locus Award for best collection, Locus Publications, 1986, for *Stephen King's Skeleton Crew;* Bram Stoker Award for Best Novel, Horror Writers Association, 1988, for *Misery;* Bram Stoker Award for Best Collection, 1991, for *Four Past Midnight;* World Fantasy award for short story, 1995, and O. Henry Award, 1996, both for "The Man in the Black Suit"; Bram Stoker Award for Best Novelette, Horror Writers Association, 1996, for *Lunch at the Gotham Cafe;* Bram Stoker Award for Best Novel, 1997, for *The Green Mile*, and 1999, for

*Bag of Bones;* Medal for Distinguished Contribution to American Letters, National Book Award, 2003; *The Stand* was voted one of the nation's 100 best-loved novels by the British public as part of the BBC's The Big Read, 2003; Lifetime Achievement Award, World Fantasy Awards, 2004; Quill Book Award, sports category, 2005, for *Faithful: Two Die-Hard Boston Red Sox Fans Chronicle the Historic 2004 Season;* named "Grand Master," Mystery Writers of America, 2006; Bram Stoker Award, 2008, for novel *The Duma Key* and for short-story collection *Just after Sunset;* Alex Award, 2009, for *Just after Sunset;* Black Quill Award, 2009, for *Duma Key;* British Fantasy Award for best collection, 2011, for *Full Dark, No Stars.*

## ■ Writings

*NOVELS*

*Carrie: A Novel of a Girl with a Frightening Power* (also see below), Doubleday (New York, NY), 1974, movie edition published as *Carrie,* New American Library/Times Mirror (New York, NY), 1975, published in a limited edition with introduction by Tabitha King, Plume (New York, NY), 1991.

*Salem's Lot* (also see below), Doubleday (New York, NY), 1975, television edition, New American Library (New York, NY), 1979, published in a limited edition with introduction by Clive Barker, Plume (New York, NY), 1991, new edition, photographs by Jerry N. Uelsmann, Doubleday (New York, NY), 2005.

*The Shining* (also see below), Doubleday (New York, NY), 1977, movie edition, New American Library (New York, NY), 1980, published in a limited edition with introduction by Ken Follett, Plume (New York, NY), 1991.

*The Stand* (also see below), Doubleday (New York, NY), 1978, enlarged and expanded edition published as *The Stand: The Complete and Uncut Edition,* Doubleday (New York, NY), 1990.

*The Dead Zone* (also see below), Viking (New York, NY), 1979, movie edition published as *The Dead Zone: Movie Tie-In,* New American Library (New York, NY), 1980.

*Firestarter* (also see below), Viking (New York, NY), 1980, with afterword by King, 1981, published in a limited, aluminum-coated, asbestos-cloth edition, Phantasia Press (Huntington Woods, MI), 1980.

*Cujo* (also see below), Viking (New York, NY), 1981, published in limited edition, Mysterious Press (New York, NY), 1981.

*Pet Sematary* (also see below), Doubleday (New York, NY), 1983, reprinted, Pocket Books (New York, NY), 2001.

*Christine* (also see below), Viking (New York, NY), 1983, published in a limited edition, illustrated by Stephen Gervais, Donald M. Grant (Hampton Falls, NH), 1983.

(With Peter Straub) *The Talisman,* Viking Press/Putnam (New York, NY), 1984, published in a limited two-volume edition, Donald M. Grant (Hampton Falls, NH), 1984, reprinted, Random House (New York, NY), 2001.

*The Eyes of the Dragon* (young adult), limited edition, illustrated by Kenneth R. Linkhauser, Philtrum Press, 1984, new edition, illustrated by David Palladini, Viking (New York, NY), 1987.

*It* (also see below), Viking (New York, NY), 1986.

*Misery* (also see below), Viking (New York, NY), 1987.

*The Tommyknockers* (also see below), Putnam (New York, NY), 1987.

*The Dark Half* (also see below), Viking (New York, NY), 1989.

*Needful Things* (also see below), Viking (New York, NY), 1991.

*Gerald's Game,* Viking (New York, NY), 1992.

*Dolores Claiborne* (also see below), Viking (New York, NY), 1993.

*Insomnia,* Viking (New York, NY), 1994.

*Rose Madder,* Viking (New York, NY), 1995.

*The Green Mile* (serialized novel), Signet (New York, NY), March-August, 1996, published as *The Green Mile: A Novel in Six Parts,* Plume (New York, NY), 1997.

*Desperation,* Viking (New York, NY), 1996.

(And author of foreword) *The Two Dead Girls,* Signet (New York, NY), 1996.

*Bag of Bones,* Viking (New York, NY), 1998.

*Hearts in Atlantis,* G.K. Hall (Thorndike, ME), 1999.

*The Girl Who Loved Tom Gordon,* Scribner (New York, NY), 1999.

*Dreamcatcher,* Simon & Schuster (New York, NY), 2001.

(With Peter Straub) *Black House* (sequel to *The Talisman*), Random House (New York, NY), 2001.

(Editor) Ridley Pearson, *The Diary of Ellen Rimbauer: My Life as Rose Red,* Hyperion (New York, NY), 2001.

*From a Buick 8,* Scribner (New York, NY), 2002.

(Under name Eleanor Druse) *The Journals of Eleanor Druse: My Investigation of the Kingdom Hospital Incident,* Hyperion (New York, NY), 2004.

*Cell,* Scribner (New York, NY), 2006.

*Lisey's Story,* Scribner (New York, NY), 2006.

*Blaze,* Scribner (New York, NY), 2007.

*Duma Key,* Scribner (New York, NY), 2008.

*Under the Dome,* Scribner (New York, NY), 2009.

*11/22/63,* Scribner (New York, NY), 2011.

## "DARK TOWER" SERIES

*The Dark Tower: The Gunslinger* (also see below), Amereon (New York, NY), 1976, published as *The Gunslinger*, New American Library (New York, NY), 1988, published in limited edition, illustrated by Michael Whelan, Donald M. Grant (Hampton Falls, NH), 1982, 2nd limited edition, 1984, revised and expanded edition, Viking (New York, NY), 2003.

*The Dark Tower II: The Drawing of the Three* (also see below), illustrated by Phil Hale, New American Library (New York, NY), 1989, reprinted, Plume Book (New York, NY), 2003.

*The Dark Tower III: The Waste Lands* (also see below), illustrated by Ned Dameron, Donald M. Grant (Hampton Falls, NH), 1991.

*The Dark Tower Trilogy: The Gunslinger; The Drawing of the Three; The Waste Lands* (box set), New American Library (New York, NY), 1993, reprinted, Penguin Group (New York, NY), 2003.

*The Dark Tower IV: Wizard and Glass*, Plume (New York, NY), 1997.

*The Dark Tower V: Wolves of the Calla*, Plume (New York, NY), 2003, premium edition, illustrated by Bernie Wrightson, Pocket Books (New York, NY), 2006.

*The Dark Tower VI: The Songs of Susannah*, Donald M. Grant (Hampton Falls, NH), 2004.

*The Dark Tower VII: The Dark Tower*, Scribner (New York, NY), 2004.

*The Gunslinger Born* ("Dark Tower" graphic novels), Marvel Books (New York, NY), 2007.

(With Peter David, Robin Furth, and Richard Isanove) *The Long Road Home* ("Dark Tower" graphic novels), illustrated by Jae Lee, Marvel Books (New York, NY), 2008.

## NOVELS; UNDER PSEUDONYM RICHARD BACHMAN

*Rage* (also see below), New American Library/Signet (New York, NY), 1977.

*The Long Walk* (also see below), New American Library/Signet (New York, NY), 1979.

*Roadwork: A Novel of the First Energy Crisis* (also see below) New American Library/Signet (New York, NY), 1981.

*The Running Man* (also see below), New American Library/Signet (New York, NY), 1982.

*Thinner*, New American Library (New York, NY), 1984.

*The Regulators*, Dutton (New York, NY), 1996.

## SHORT FICTION

(Under name Steve King) *The Star Invaders* (privately printed stories), Triad/Gaslight Books (Durham, ME), 1964.

*Night Shift* (story collection; also see below), introduction by John D. MacDonald, Doubleday (New York, NY), 1978, published as *Night Shift: Excursions into Horror*, New American Library/Signet (New York, NY), 1979.

*Different Seasons* (novellas; contains *Rita Hayworth and the Shawshank Redemption: Hope Springs Eternal* [also see below]; *Apt Pupil: Summer of Corruption*; *The Body: Fall from Innocence*; and *The Breathing Method: A Winter's Tale*), Viking (New York, NY), 1982.

*Cycle of the Werewolf* (novella; also see below), illustrated by Berni Wrightson, limited portfolio edition published with "Berni Wrightson: An Appreciation," Land of Enchantment (Westland, MI), 1983, enlarged edition including King's screenplay adaptation published as *Stephen King's Silver Bullet*, New American Library/Signet (New York, NY), 1985.

*Stephen King's Skeleton Crew* (story collection), illustrated by J.K. Potter, Viking (New York, NY), 1985, limited edition, Scream Press (Los Angeles, CA), 1985.

*My Pretty Pony*, illustrated by Barbara Kruger, Knopf (New York, NY), 1989, limited edition, Library Fellows of New York's Whitney Museum of American Art (New York, NY), 1989.

*Four Past Midnight* (contains "The Langoliers," "Secret Window, Secret Garden," "The Library Policeman," and "The Sun Dog"; also see below), Viking (New York, NY), 1990.

*Nightmares and Dreamscapes* (story collection), Viking (New York, NY), 1993.

*Lunch at the Gotham Cafe*, published in *Dark Love: Twenty-two All Original Tales of Lust and Obsession*, edited by Nancy Collins, Edward E. Kramer, and Martin Harry Greenberg, ROC (New York, NY), 1995.

*Everything's Eventual: 14 Dark Tales*, Scribner (New York, NY), 2002.

*Just after Sunset* (story collection), Scribner (New York, NY), 2008.

*Full Dark, No Stars* (novella collection), Scribner (New York, NY), 2010.

*UR* (novella), Hodder Headline Limited (London, England), 2010.

*Blockade Billy* (novella), Cemetery Dance Publications (Baltimore), 2010.

## SCREENPLAYS

*Stephen King's Creep Show: A George A. Romero Film* (based on King's stories "Father's Day," "The Lonesome Death of Jordy Verrill" [previously published as "Weeds"], "The Crate," and "They're Creeping Up on You"; released by Warner Bros. as *Creepshow*, 1982), illustrated by Berni Wrightson and Michele Wrightson, New American Library (New York, NY), 1982.

*Cat's Eye* (based on King's stories *"Quitters, Inc.,"* *"The Ledge,"* and *"The General"*), Metro-Goldwyn-Mayer/United Artists, 1984.

*Stephen King's Silver Bullet* (based on and published with King's novella *Cycle of the Werewolf;* released by Paramount Pictures/Dino de Laurentiis's North Carolina Film Corp., 1985), illustrated by Berni Wrightson, New American Library/Signet (New York, NY), 1985.

(And director) *Maximum Overdrive* (based on King's stories *"The Mangler,"* *"Trucks,"* and *"The Lawnmower Man"*; released by Dino de Laurentiis's North Carolina Film Corp., 1986), New American Library (New York, NY), 1986.

*Pet Sematary* (based on King's novel of the same title), Laurel Production, 1989.

*Stephen King's Sleepwalkers,* Columbia, 1992.

(Author of introduction) Frank Darabont, *The Shawshank Redemption: The Shooting Script,* Newmarket Press (New York, NY), 1996.

*Storm of the Century* (also see below), Pocket Books (New York, NY), 1999.

(Author of introductions, with William Goldman and Lawrence Kasdan) William Goldman and Lawrence Kasdan, *Dreamcatcher: The Shooting Script,* Newmarket Press (New York, NY), 2003.

*Riding the Bullet,* Innovation Film Group, 2004.

*Secret Window,* Columbia, 2004.


*TELEPLAYS*

*Stephen King's Golden Years,* CBS-TV, 1991.

(And executive producer) *Stephen King's The Stand* (based on King's novel *The Stand*), ABC-TV, 1994.

(With Chris Carter) *"Chinga," The X-Files,* Fox-TV, 1998.

*Storm of the Century,* ABC-TV, 1999.

*Rose Red* (also see below), ABC-TV, 2001.

*Stephen King's Kingdom Hospital,* ABC-TV, 2004.

*Desperation,* USA, 2004.


*OMNIBUS EDITIONS*

*Another Quarter Mile: Poetry,* Dorrance (Philadelphia, PA), 1979.

*Stephen King's Danse Macabre* (nonfiction), Berkley Books (New York, NY), 1981.

*Stephen King* (contains *The Shining, Salem's Lot, Night Shift,* and *Carrie*), W.S. Heinemann/Octopus Books (London, England), 1981.

*The Plant* (privately published episodes of a comic horror novel in progress), Philtrum Press (Bangor, ME), Part 1, 1982, Part 2, 1983, Part 3, 1985.

*Black Magic and Music: A Novelist's Perspective on Bangor* (pamphlet), Bangor Historical Society (Bangor, ME), 1983.

(And author of introduction) *The Bachman Books: Four Early Novels* (contains *Rage, The Long Walk, Roadwork,* and *The Running Man*), New American Library (New York, NY), 1985.

*Dolan's Cadillac,* Lord John Press (Northridge, CA), 1989.

*Stephen King* (contains *Desperation* and *The Regulators*), Signet (New York, NY), 1997.

*Stephen King's Latest* (contains *Dolores Claiborne, Insomnia,* and *Rose Madder*), Signet (New York, NY), 1997.


*OTHER*

*Nightmares in the Sky: Gargoyles and Grotesques* (nonfiction), photographs by F. Stop FitzGerald, Viking (New York, NY), 1988.

*Midnight Graffiti,* Warner Books (New York, NY), 1992.

*On Writing: A Memoir of the Craft,* Scribner (New York, NY), 2000.

(With Stewart O'Nan) *Faithful: Two Die-Hard Boston Red Sox Fans Chronicle the Historic 2004 Season,* Scribner (New York, NY), 2004.

*The Colorado Kid,* Hard Case Crime (New York, NY), 2004.

Also author of teleplay *Battleground* (based on short story of same title; optioned by Martin Poll Productions for NBC-TV), and *"Sorry, Right Number,"* for television series *Tales from the Dark Side,* 1987.

Author of short stories under his name and under pseudonym John Swithen. Contributor of short stories to *The Last Dangerous Visions,* and *Robert Bloch's Psychos,* edited by Robert Bloch. Also contributor to anthologies and collections, including *The Year's Finest Fantasy,* edited by Terry Carr, Putnam (New York, NY), 1978; *Shadows,* edited by Charles L. Grant, Doubleday (New York, NY), Volume 1, 1978, Volume 4, 1981; *New Terrors,* edited by Ramsey Campbell, Pocket Books (New York, NY), 1982; *World Fantasy Convention 1983,* edited by Robert Weinberg, Weird Tales, 1983; *The Writer's Handbook,* edited by Sylvia K. Burack, Writer (Boston, MA), 1984; *The Dark Descent,* edited by David G. Hartwell, Doherty Associates, 1987; *Prime Evil: New Stories by the Masters of Modern Horror,* by Douglas E. Winter, New American Library (New York, NY), 1988; and *Dark Visions,* Gollancz (London, England), 1989.

Author of e-book *The Plant,* self-published first two chapters on his Web site (www.stephenking.com), August, 2000. Author of weekly column "King's Garbage Truck" for *Maine Campus,* 1969-70, and of monthly book review column for *Adelina,* 1980. Contributor of short fiction and poetry to numerous magazines, including *Art, Castle Rock: The Stephen King Newsletter, Cavalier, Comics Review, Cosmopolitan, Ellery Queen's Mystery Magazine, Fantasy and Science Fiction, Gallery, Great Stories from Twilight Zone, Heavy Metal, Ladies' Home Journal, Magazine of Fantasy and Science Fiction, Maine, Maine Review, Marshroots,* Marvel comics, *Moth, Omni, Onan, Playboy, Redbook, Reflections, Rolling Stone, Science-Fiction Digest, Startling Mystery Stories, Terrors, Twilight Zone, Ubris, Whisper,* and *Yankee.* Contributor of book reviews to *New York Times Book Review.*

Most of King's papers are housed in the special collection of the Folger Library at the University of Maine at Orono.

## ■ Adaptations

Many of King's novels have been adapted for the screen. *Carrie* was produced as a motion picture in 1976 by Paul Monash for United Artists, screenplay by Lawrence D. Cohen, directed by Brian De Palma, featuring Sissy Spacek and Piper Laurie, and was also produced as a Broadway musical in 1988 by Cohen and Michael Gore, developed in England by the Royal Shakespeare Company, featuring Betty Buckley; *Salem's Lot* was produced as a television miniseries in 1979 by Warner Brothers, teleplay by Paul Monash, featuring David Soul and James Mason, and was adapted for the cable channel TNT in 2004, with a teleplay by Peter Filardi and direction by Mikael Salomon; *The Shining* was filmed in 1980 by Warner Brothers/Hawks Films, screenplay by director Stanley Kubrick and Diane Johnson, starring Jack Nicholson and Shelley Duvall, and it was filmed for television in 1997 by Warner Brothers, directed by Mick Garris, starring Rebecca De Mornay, Steven Weber, Courtland Mead, and Melvin Van Peebles; *Cujo* was filmed in 1983 by Warner Communications/Taft Entertainment, screenplay by Don Carlos Dunaway and Lauren Currier, featuring Dee Wallace and Danny Pintauro; *The Dead Zone* was filmed in 1983 by Paramount Pictures, screenplay by Jeffrey Boam, starring Christopher Walken; was adapted as a cable television series starring Anthony Michael Hall by USA Network, 2002; *Christine* was filmed in 1983 by Columbia Pictures, screenplay by Bill Phillips; *Firestarter* was produced in 1984 by Frank Capra, Jr., for Universal Pictures in association with Dino de Laurentiis, screenplay by Stanley Mann, featuring David Keith and Drew Barrymore; *Stand by Me* (based on King's novella *The Body*) was filmed in 1986 by Columbia Pictures, screenplay by Raynold Gideon and Bruce A. Evans, directed by Rob Reiner; *The Running Man* was filmed in 1987 by Taft Entertainment/Barish Productions, screenplay by Steven E. de Souza, starring Arnold Schwarzenegger; *Misery* was produced in

1990 by Columbia, directed by Reiner, screenplay by William Goldman, starring James Caan and Kathy Bates; *Graveyard Shift* was filmed in 1990 by Paramount, directed by Ralph S. Singleton, adapted by John Esposito; *Stephen King's It* (based on King's novel *It*) was filmed as a television miniseries by ABC-TV in 1990; *The Dark Half* was filmed in 1993 by Orion, written and directed by George A. Romero, featuring Timothy Hutton and Amy Madigan; *Needful Things* was filmed in 1993 by Columbia/Castle Rock, adapted by W.D. Richter and Lawrence Cohen, directed by Fraser C. Heston, starring Max Von Sydow, Ed Harris, Bonnie Bedelia, and Amanda Plummer; *The Tommyknockers* was filmed as a television miniseries by ABC-TV in 1993; *The Shawshank Redemption,* based on King's novella *Rita Hayworth and Shawshank Redemption: Hope Springs Eternal,* was filmed in 1994 by Columbia, written and directed by Frank Darabont, featuring Tim Robbins and Morgan Freeman; *Dolores Claiborne* was filmed in 1995 by Columbia; *Thinner* was filmed by Paramount in 1996, directed by Dom Holland, starring Robert John Burke, Joe Mantegna, Lucinda Jenney, and Michael Constantine; *Night Flier* was filmed by New Amsterdam Entertainment/Stardust International/Medusa Film in 1997, directed by Mark Pavia, starring Miguel Ferrer, Julie Entwisle, Dan Monahan, and Michael H. Moss; *Apt Pupil* was filmed in 1998 by TriStar Pictures, directed by Bryan Singer, starring David Schwimmer, Ian McKellen, and Brad Renfro; *The Green Mile* was filmed in 1999 by Castle Rock, directed by Frank Darabont, who also wrote the screenplay, starring Tom Hanks; *Hearts in Atlantis* was filmed in 2001 by Castle Rock, directed by Scott Hicks, screenplay written by William Goldman, starring Anthony Hopkins; *Dreamcatcher* was released in 2003 by Warner Brothers and Castle Rock Entertainment and was directed by Lawrence Kasdan, written by William Goldman, starring Morgan Freeman. Several of King's short stories have also been adapted for the screen, including *The Boogeyman,* filmed by Tantalus in 1982 and 1984 in association with the New York University School of Undergraduate Film, screenplay by producer-director Jeffrey C. Schiro; *The Woman in the Room,* filmed in 1983 by Darkwoods, screenplay by director Frank Darabont, broadcast on public television in Los Angeles, 1985 (released with *The Boogeyman* on videocassette as *Two Mini-Features from Stephen King's Nightshift Collection* by Granite Entertainment Group, 1985); *Children of the Corn,* produced in 1984 by Donald P. Borchers and Terrence Kirby for New World Pictures, screenplay by George Goldsmith; *The Word Processor* (based on King's "The Word Processor of the Gods"), produced by Romero and Richard Rubenstein for Laurel Productions, 1984, teleplay by Michael Dowell, broadcast November 19, 1985, on *Tales from the Darkside* series and released on videocassette by Laurel Entertainment, 1985; *Gramma,* filmed by

CBS-TV in 1985, teleplay by Harlan Ellison, broadcast February 14, 1986, on *The Twilight Zone* series; *Creepshow 2* (based on "The Raft" and two unpublished stories by King, "Old Chief Wood'nhead" and "The Hitchhiker"), was filmed in 1987 by New World Pictures, screenplay by Romero; *Sometimes They Come Back*, filmed by CBS-TV in 1987; "The Cat from Hell" is included in a three-segment anthology film titled *Tales from the Darkside—The Movie*, produced by Laurel Productions, 1990; *The Lawnmower Man*, written by director Brett Leonard and Gimel Everett for New Line Cinema, 1992; *The Mangler*, filmed by New Line Cinema, 1995; and *The Langoliers*, filmed as a television mini-series by ABC-TV in 1995; the short fiction "Secret Window, Secret Garden" was adapted into the film *Secret Window*, distributed by Columbia Pictures, written and directed by David Koepp; 2004; the short story "All That You Love Will Be Carried Away" from the collection *Everything's Eventual* has been adapted and made into a short film by James Renner; film rights to the short story "1408" from the collection *Everything's Eventual* has been optioned by Dimension Films; *From a Buick 8* has been optioned by Chesapeake Films; *Gunslinger* has been optioned for adaptation as a comics miniseries by Marvel Comics, 2005; "The Dark Tower" series has been optioned for film by Universal Pictures and NBC; the television series *Haven*, 2010, is based on *The Colorado Kid*; *Bag of Bones* was adapted as a television series, 2011. Most of King's books have also been adapted for audio, including *The Dark Tower: The Gunslinger*, New American Library, 1988; *The Dark Tower II: The Drawing of the Three*, New American Library, 1989; *The Dark Tower III: The Waste Lands*, Penguin-HighBridge Audio, 1991; *Needful Things*, Penguin-HighBridge Audio, 1991; *The Girl Who Loved Tom Gordon*, Simon & Schuster Audio, 1999; *Blood and Smoke*, Simon & Schuster Audio, 2000; *Dreamcatcher*, Simon & Schuster Audio, 2001; *On Writing: A Memoir of the Craft*, Recorded Books, 2001; *The Talisman*, Simon & Schuster Audio, 2001; *From a Buick 8*, Simon & Schuster Audio, 2002; *Riding the Bullet*, Simon & Schuster Audio, 2002; *Black House*, Books on Tape, 2003; *Wolves of the Calla*, Simon & Schuster Audio, 2003.

## ■ Sidelights

"With Stephen King," mused a contributor to *Fear Itself: The Horror Fiction of Stephen King*, "you never have to ask 'Who's afraid of the big bad wolf?'—You are. And he knows it." Throughout a prolific array of novels, short stories, and screen work in which elements of horror, fantasy, science fiction, and humor meld, King deftly arouses fear from dormancy. The breadth and durability of his popularity alone evince his mastery as a compelling storyteller. Although the critical reception of his work has not necessarily matched its sweeping success with readers, colleagues and several critics alike discern within it a substantial and enduring literary legitimacy.

While striking a deep and responsive chord within its readers, the genre of horror is frequently trivialized by critics who tend to regard it, when at all, less seriously than mainstream fiction. In an interview with Charles Platt in *Dream Makers: The Uncommon Men and Women Who Write Science Fiction*, King said he suspects that "most of the critics who review popular fiction have no understanding of it as a whole." Regarding the "propensity of a small but influential element of the literary establishment to ghettoize horror and fantasy and instantly relegate them beyond the pale of so-called serious literature," King told Eric Norden in a *Playboy* interview: "I'm sure those critics' nineteenth-century precursors would have contemptuously dismissed [Edgar Allan] Poe as the great American hack." In a panel discussion at the 1984 World Fantasy Convention in Ottawa, reprinted in *Bare Bones: Conversations on Terror with Stephen King*, he predicted that horror writers "might actually have a serious place in American literature in a hundred years or so."

King's ability to comprehend "the attraction of fantastic horror to the denizen of the late twentieth century," according to a contributor to *Fear Itself*, partially accounts for his unrivaled popularity in the genre. However, what distinguishes him is the way in which he transforms the ordinary into the horrific. A contributor to *Discovering Stephen King* wrote that King is "a uniquely sensitive author" within the Gothic literary tradition, which he described as "essentially a literature of nightmare, a conflict between waking life and the darkness within the human mind." Perpetuating the legacy of Edgar Allan Poe, Nathaniel Hawthorne, Herman Melville, Henry James, and H.P. Lovecraft, "King is heir to the American Gothic tradition in that he has placed his horrors in contemporary settings and has depicted the struggle of an American culture to face the horrors within it," explained Crawford, and because "he has shown the nightmare of our idealistic civilization." Observing that children suspend their disbelief easily, King argued in his *Stephen King's Danse Macabre* that, ironically, they are actually "better able to deal with fantasy and terror *on its own terms* than their elders are." Adults are capable of distinguishing between fantasy and reality, but in the process of growing up, laments King in *Stephen King's Danse Macabre*, they develop "a good case of mental tunnel vision and a gradual ossification of the imaginative faculty"; thus, he perceives the task of the fantasy or horror writer as enabling one to become, "for a little while, a child again."

Not surprisingly, throughout most of King's adolescence, the written word afforded a powerful diversion. "Writing has always been it for me," King indicated in a panel discussion at the 1984 World Fantasy Convention in Ottawa, reprinted in *Bare Bones.* Science fiction and adventure stories comprised his first literary efforts. Having written his first story at the age of seven, King began submitting short fiction to magazines at twelve, and published his first story at eighteen. In high school, he authored a small, satiric newspaper titled "The Village Vomit"; and in college he penned a popular and eclectic series of columns called "King's Garbage Truck." He also started writing the novels he eventually published under the pseudonymous ruse of Richard Bachman—novels that focus more on elements of human alienation and brutality than supernatural horror. After graduation, King supplemented his teaching salary through various odd jobs and by submitting stories to men's magazines. Searching for a form of his own, King responded to a friend's challenge to break out of the machismo mold of his short fiction. Because King completed the first draft of *Carrie: A Novel of a Girl with a Frightening Power* at the time William Peter Blatty's *The Exorcist* and Thomas Tryon's *The Other* were being published, the novel was marketed as horror fiction, and the genre had found its juggernaut. Or, as a contributor to *Fear Itself* noted: "Like a mountain, King is there."

"King has made a dent in the national consciousness in a way no other horror writer has, at least during his own lifetime," noted a contributor to *Discovering Stephen King.* "He is a genuine phenomenon." A newsletter—"Castle Rock"—has been published since 1985 to keep his ever-increasing number of fans well informed, and Book-of-the-Month Club has been reissuing all of his best sellers as the Stephen King Library collection. Resorting to a pseudonym to get even more work into print accelerated the process for King; but according to a contributor to *Kingdom of Fear,* although the ploy was not entirely "a vehicle for King to move his earliest work out of the trunk," it certainly triggered myriad speculations about, as well as hunts for, other possible pseudonyms he may also have used. In his essay "Why I Was Bachman" in *The Bachman Books: Four Early Novels,* King recalled that he simply considered it a good idea at the time, especially since he wanted to try to publish something without the attendant commotion that a Stephen King title would have unavoidably generated. Also, his publisher believed that he had already saturated the market. King's prodigious literary output and multimillion-dollar contracts, though, have generated critical challenges to the inherent worth of his fiction. Deducing that he has been somehow compromised by commercial success, some critics imply that he writes simply to

fulfill contractual obligations. But as King told *Playboy* contributor Norden, "Money really has nothing to do with it one way or the other. I love writing the things I write, and I wouldn't and 'couldn't' do anything else."

King writes daily, exempting only Christmas, the Fourth of July, and his birthday. He likes to work on two things simultaneously, beginning his day early with a two-or three-mile walk: "What I'm working on in the morning is what I'm *working* on," he said in a panel discussion at the 1980 World Fantasy Convention in Baltimore, reprinted in *Bare Bones.* He devotes his afternoon hours to rewriting. And according to his *Playboy* interviewer, while he is not particular about working conditions, he is about his output. Despite chronic headaches, occasional insomnia, and even a fear of writer's block, he produces six pages daily.

Regarding what he finds to be an essential reassurance that underlies and impels the genre itself, King remarked in *Stephen King's Danse Macabre* that "beneath its fangs and fright wig" horror fiction is really quite conservative. Comparing horror fiction with the morality plays of the late Middle Ages, for instance, he believes that its primary function is "to reaffirm the virtues of the norm by showing us what awful things happen to people who venture into taboo lands." Also, there is the solace in knowing "when the lights go down in the theater or when we open the book that the evildoers will almost certainly be punished, and measure will be returned for measure." However, King admitted to Norden that despite all the discussion by writers generally about "horror's providing a socially and psychologically useful catharsis for people's fears and aggressions, the brutal fact of the matter is that we're still in the business of public executions."

"Death is a significant element in nearly all horror fiction," wrote Michael A. Morrison in *Fantasy Review,* "and it permeates King's novels and short stories." Remarking that "evil is basically stupid and unimaginative and doesn't need creative inspiration from me or anybody else," King told Norden, for instance, that "despite knowing all that rationally, I have to admit that it is unsettling to feel that I could be linked in any way, however tenuous, to somebody else's murder."

### Early Novels

The empowerment of estranged young people is a theme that recurs throughout King's fiction. His first novel, *Carrie,* is about a persecuted teenage girl. "The novel examines female power," stated a *Dictionary of Literary Biography* contributor, "for Carrie gains her telekinetic abilities with her first menstruation." "It is," the contributor noted, "a compelling character study of a persecuted teenager who finally uses her powers to turn the table on her persecutors. The result is a violent explosion that destroys the mother who had taught her self-hatred and the high-school peers who had made her a scapegoat." An alienated teenage boy is the main character in King's *Christine,* and *Rage* features Charlie Decker, a young man who tells the story of his descent into madness and murder. In *The Shining* and *Firestarter,* Danny Torrance and Charlie McGee are alienated not from their families—they have loving, if sometimes weak, parents—but through the powers they possess and by those who want to manipulate them: evil supernatural forces in *The Shining,* the U.S. Government in *Firestarter.* Children also figure prominently, although not always as victims, in *Salem's Lot, The Tommyknockers, Pet Sematary, The Eyes of the Dragon,* and *The Talisman.*

King's most explicit examination of alienation in childhood, however, comes in the novel *It.* The eponymous IT is a creature that feeds on children—on their bodies and on their emotions, especially fear. IT lives in the sewers of Derry, Maine, having arrived there ages ago from outer space, and emerges about every twenty-seven years in search of victims. King organizes the tale as two parallel stories, one tracing the activities of seven unprepossessing fifth-graders—the 'Losers' Club'—who discovered and fought the horror in 1958, the other describing their return to Derry in 1985 when the cycle resumes." The surviving members of the Losers' Club return to Derry to confront IT and defeat IT once and for all. The only things that appears to hurt IT are faith, humor, and childlike courage. "*It* involves the guilts and innocences of childhood and the difficulty for adults of recapturing them," Christopher Lehmann-Haupt stated in the *New York Times.* "*It* questions the difference between necessity and free will. *It* also concerns the evil that has haunted America from time to time in the forms of crime, racial and religious bigotry, economic hardship, labor strife and industrial pollution." The evil takes shape among Derry's adults and older children, especially the bullies who terrorize the members of the Losers' Club.

An example of King's ability to "pour new wine from old bottles" is his experimentation with narrative structure. In *It, Carrie,* and *The Stand,* declared Tony Magistrale in the study *Landscape of Fear: Stephen King's American Gothic,* King explores story forms—"stream of consciousness, interior monologues, multiple narrators, and a juggling of time sequences—in order to draw the reader into a direct and thorough involvement with the characters and events of the tale." In *Gerald's Game,* Jessie Burlingame has lost her husband to heart failure. He "has

died after handcuffing her to the bed at their summer home," explained a contributor to the *Dictionary of Literary Biography,* "and Jessie must face her life, including the memory that her father had sexually abused her, and her fears alone." *Dolores Claiborne* is the story of a woman suspected of murdering her employer, a crusty old miser named Vera Donovan. Dolores maintains her innocence, but she freely confesses that she murdered her husband thirty years previously after she caught him molesting their daughter.

"There are a series of dovetailing, but unobtrusive, connections," stated a *Locus* contributor, "linking the two novels and both Jessie and Dolores." Like *It,* both *Gerald's Game* and *Dolores Claiborne* are set in the town of Derry, Maine. They are also both psychological portraits of older women who have been subjected to sexual abuse. *Dolores Claiborne* differs from *Gerald's Game,* however, because it uses fewer of the traditional trappings of horror fiction, and it is related entirely from the viewpoint of the title character. *Dolores Claiborne* "is, essentially, a dramatic monologue," stated Kit Reed in the *Washington Post Book World,* "in which the speaker addresses other people in the room, answers questions and completes a narrative in actual time." "King has taken horror literature out of the closet and has injected new life into familiar genres," a contributor to the *Dictionary of Literary Biography* wrote. "He is not afraid to mix those genres in fresh ways to produce novels that examine contemporary American culture."

*Insomnia,* King's 1994 novel, continues the example set by *Gerald's Game* and *Dolores Claiborne.* It is also set in Derry, and its protagonist is an elderly man named Ralph Roberts, a retired salesman, newly widowed and suffering severely from insomnia. Ralph begins to see people in a new way: their auras become visible to him. "Ralph finds himself a man in a classic situation, a mortal in conflict with the fates—literally," declared a *Locus* contributor. "How much self-determination does he really possess? And how much is he acted upon?" Ralph also finds himself in conflict with his neighbor Ed Deepeneau, a conservative Christian and antiabortion activist who beats his wife and has taken up a crusade against a visiting feminist speaker. "There are some truly haunting scenes in the book about wife abuse and fanaticism, as well as touching observations about growing old, but they're quickly consumed by more predictable sensationalism," remarked Chris Bohjalian in the *New York Times Book Review.*

King delighted his readers and astounded his critics by issuing three new major novels in 1996: *Desperation, The Regulators*—under the pseudonym Richard Bachman—and *The Green Mile,* the last a Depression-era prison novel serialized in six installments. A

*Publishers Weekly* contributor wrote that "if the publishing industry named a Person of the Year, this year's winner would be Stephen King." The critic noted that, with *Desperation*, "King again proves himself the premier literary barometer of our cultural clime." Released on the same day from two different publishers, *Desperation* and *The Regulators* have interlocking characters and plots; each works as a kind of distorted mirror image of the other. In *Desperation*, which many critics agree is the better book, a group of strangers drive into Desperation, Nevada, where they encounter a malign spirit (Tak) in the body of police officer Collie Entragian. The survivors of this apocalyptic novel are few, but include David Carver, an eleven-year-old boy who talks to God, and John Edward Marinville, an alcoholic novelist. Mark Harris, writing in *Entertainment Weekly*, remarked that King "hasn't been this intent on scaring readers—or been this successful at it—since *The Stand*," noting that "King has always been pop fiction's most compassionate sadist."

While *The Regulators* received little critical praise, King's experiment in serialization with *The Green Mile* captured the imagination of both readers and critics. An *Entertainment Weekly* reviewer called it a novel "that's as hauntingly touching as it is just plain haunted," and a *New York Times* contributor claimed that in spite of "the striking circumstances of its serial publication," the novel "manages to sustain the notes of visceral wonder and indelible horror that keep eluding the Tak books." Set in the Deep South in 1932, *The Green Mile*—a prison expression for death row—begins with the death of twin girls and the conviction of John Coffey for their murder. Block superintendent Paul Edgecombe, who narrates the story years later from his nursing home in Georgia, slowly unfolds the story of the mysterious Coffey, a man with no past and with a gift for healing.

King's next major novel, *Bag of Bones*, appeared in 1998. This tale of a writer struggling with grief for his dead wife and with writer's block while living in a haunted cabin met with a great deal of acclaim from critics. Also acclaimed was the following year's *Hearts in Atlantis*, which Tom De Haven described in *Entertainment Weekly* as "a novel in five stories, with players sometimes migrating from one story to the next." De Haven went on to note that "there's more heartbreak than horror in these pages, and a doomy aura that's more generational than occult." He also reported that the "last two stories are drenched in sadness, mortality, regret, and finally absolution," concluding that *Hearts in Atlantis* "is wonderful fiction." Similarly, Ray Olson praised the volume in *Booklist* as "a rich, engaging, deeply moving generational epic." *The Girl Who Loved Tom Gordon* also saw print in 1999. This novel, short by King's standards, centers on a nine-year-old girl

from a broken home who gets lost in a forest for two weeks. She has her radio with her and survives her ordeal by listening to Boston Red Sox games and imagining conversations with her hero, Red Sox relief pitcher Tom Gordon.

While these books were making their way to readers, however, King suffered a serious health challenge. On June 19, 1999, he was struck by a van while walking alongside a road near his home, sustaining injuries to his spine, hip, ribs, and right leg. One of his broken ribs punctured a lung, and he nearly died. He began a slow progress toward recovery, cheered by countless cards and letters from his fans. During his recovery, he began experimenting with publishing his fiction electronically. In August 2000, King self-published the first two installments of his e-book *The Plant* on his Web site. Pricing the installments at one dollar each, King promised to publish additional chapters if at least seventy-five percent of those who downloaded the first two installments paid for them. King also published a short story, "Riding the Bullet," in March, only distributed as an e-book publication in a number of formats. This tale was later reprinted in the 2002 collection *Everything's Eventual: 14 Dark Tales*.

### Later Novels

Some of the novels King has published since the beginning of the twenty-first century, including *Dreamcatcher* and *From a Buick 8*, have brought strong comparisons from critics with his earlier novels; in these specific cases, *It* and *Christine*, respectively. These books, however, were followed by an announcement King made in 2002 that he was planning to retire from publishing. In an interview with Chris Nashawaty in *Entertainment Weekly*, King clarified: "First of all, I'd never stop writing because I don't know what I'd do between nine and one every day. But I'd stop publishing. I don't need the money." Yet *Dreamcatcher* and *From a Buick 8* have garnered praise from reviewers as well. Rene Rodriguez, writing in the *Miami Herald*, maintained that "*Dreamcatcher* marks [King's] bracing return to all-out horror, complete with trademark grisly gross-outs, a panoramic cast of deftly drawn characters and a climactic race against time, with the fate of the planet hanging in the balance." Salem Macknee in the Charlotte *Observer*, noting surface similarities between *From a Buick 8* and *Christine*, assured readers that "this strange counterfeit of a Buick Roadmaster is no rerun. Stephen King has once again created an original, a monster never seen before, with its own frightful fingerprint."

With *Cell*, a 2006 novel that *Booklist* contributor Olson considered "the most suspenseful, fastest-paced book King has ever written," the author uses cell phone signals as a source for inducing zombie-like violence in the majority of the population. A *Publishers Weekly* contributor found "King's imagining . . . rich," and the dialogue "jaunty and witty" in this novel that borrows technique from Richard Matheson and George A. Romero, the horror legends to whom the book is dedicated. Olson noted that with the publication of *Cell*, "King blasts any notion that he's exhausted or dissipated his enormous talent."

King presents a good old-fashioned yarn in his book *The Colorado Kid*. As told by two veteran newspaper reporters to a cub reporter named Stephanie Mc-Cann, the story revolves around the discovery of a body by two high school sweethearts twenty years earlier on Moosie's beach in Moose-Lookit Island, Maine. The story reveals how the two reports eventually discovered that the man was from Colorado. "King is especially good at describing the monumental sadness of sifting through the remnants of a dead loved one's life, and depicting the secret and sometimes even nauseatingly cute code-talk of long relationships," wrote Mark Rahner in the *Seattle Times*. Several reviewers noted that *The Colorado Kid* is difficult to classify, especially in terms of King's other novels in that it contains elements of horror, mystery, and pulp fiction. Keir Graff, writing in *Booklist*, commented that the author "appears to be fumbling in his tackle box when, in fact, he's already slipped the hook into our cheeks." In a review in the *Library Journal*, Nancy McNicol commented that "this slim (by King standards) volume will speak to those who appreciate good storytelling."

In *Lisey's Story*, King tells the tale of Lisey Landon beginning two years after her famous novelist husband, Scott Landon, has died. Besieged by researchers and others wanting Scott's papers, Lisey decides to prepare his work for donation when she begins to receive threatening phone calls and notes, as well as a dead cat in her mailbox. In the meantime, Lisey has been hearing Scott's voice and it leads her to a netherworld called Boo'Ya Moon where Scott and his brother used to go to escape their brutal father. Although Lisey escapes to this world to learn about Scott's past and her own strength, she does not elude the psychopath who has threatened her. "The book is also, perhaps, a parable about love and imagination that affirms love as the more salvific of the two," wrote Olson in *Booklist*.

Once again, reviewers welcomed King's novel. Noting that the author "is surprisingly introspective and mature here," a *Kirkus Reviews* contributor went on to call *Lisey's Story* "one of King's finest works." Charles De Lint, writing in the *Magazine of Fantasy and Science Fiction*, commented that "sometimes even established writers can surprise us by stretch-

ing in a new direction, or telling a new kind of story while still using the favorite tools in their toolbox. That's the case here, and it's worth talking about." Some reviewers addressed specific aspects of the author's writing. For example, Jim Windolf wrote in the *New York Times Book Review* that the novel "has an abundance of solid descriptions . . . and indelible images." Windolf also commented on the magical world that King creates, noting that "it's as real as J.M. Barrie's Never-Never Land, L. Frank Baum's Oz or the Grimms' forest."

In the aftermath of his horrific 1999 accident, King made a decision to relocate—on at least a part-time basis—from his Maine home to Florida. "A few years [after the accident], after developing a severe case of pneumonia, the king of chills decided to embrace warmth," explained *Time* contributor Gilbert Cruz. "'It's the law,' he jokes from his part-time home on the Gulf Coast. 'You get a little bit older, and you have to move to Florida.' So, in one of the rare cliché moments of his life, King . . . and his wife Tabitha flew south for the winter."

While his previous novels had all been set in his native Maine, *Duma Key* draws for the first time on King's new Florida surroundings. It tells the story of Edgar Freemantle, a construction chief and self-made millionaire who undergoes a catastrophic, life-changing accident. A construction crane collapses on the truck he is in, crushing his hip, shattering his skull, and damaging his right arm so badly that it has to be amputated. "Anyone who has ever screamed in post-traumatic pain or cursed his physical therapist during an agonizing session of stretching limbs in directions they don't want to go," wrote Mark Graham in the *Rocky Mountain News*, "will find it hard to read the first 50 pages of *Duma Key*, as Edgar describes the feeling of 'ground glass' in his leg and hip during his rehabilitation." Many reviewers speculated that King drew on his own long and painful recuperation for inspiration. "When King writes in Freemantle's voice that 'everything hurt all the time. I had a constant ringing headache; behind my forehead it was always midnight in the world's biggest clock-shop,'" Minzesheimer stated, "he's not just imagining it."

Moreover, the accident's effects go well beyond the purely physical: the combination of pain, medication, and brain damage changes Edgar's personality. "He becomes prone to fits of rage. His wife leaves him," explained *USA Today* reviewer Bob Minzesheimer. "A psychiatrist advises him to find a new life elsewhere, so he moves to an isolated island in Florida." He sets up shop on the small, privately owned island of Duma Key. "There," reported Emily Lambert in *Media Wales*, "he discovers a talent for painting and becomes obsessed with the horizon. And an imaginary boat called Perse."

Freemantle "wrestles with a talent he doesn't comprehend and familiarizes himself with his new neighbors, elderly heiress Elizabeth Eastlake and her caretaker, Jerome Wireman," stated *San Francisco Chronicle* contributor Michael Bery. "All three harbor secrets, and as they size each other up, they all sense that occult forces have been set in motion around them. Edgar's freaky paintings seem to contain portents of future tragedies, while Eastlake's descent into Alzheimer's masks the origin of the evil that lurks on the key's deserted shore." "You could say that *Duma Key* is about how Edgar gets his life back," wrote Charles Taylor in a review posted on *Bloomberg.com.* "The skeleton-grin irony is that what he gets back is not quite his life."

Slowly the realization dawns on Freemantle that his presence on the island is not accidental, and that his paintings reveal truths that some, including East-lake, have chosen not to reveal. "As King expertly peels back layers of suspense and back story, Edgar realizes he has been drawn to Duma Key, which seems to want desperately wounded people for its own occult purposes," declared *Houston Chronicle* reviewer Chauncey Mabe. "The island, no surprise, is haunted—by ghosts, memories, and an elemental evil of immense power and malice. "The paintings hold significance, though Edgar does not initially understand them," Ali Karim wrote on the *January* magazine Web site. "This changes when his youngest daughter comes to visit." Ilse (most often called Illy) cheers her father up, but at the same time sensitizes him to the fact that Duma Key is not the peaceful, idyllic spot it appears outwardly to be. "When Illy gets sick after they explore the Island," Karim continued, "Edgar starts to realize that there are things within Duma Key that might hold danger to him and his daughter and when Illy recovers, he sends her away." "*Duma Key* is a terrifying book about friendship and the random events that make life what it is," Karim concluded. "It chases down the idea that even though we might sometimes hear the balls in the lottery machine ahead of time, the ability to do so comes with consequences and is perhaps linked to a greater evil and to things we don't—can't?—understand.

"'Trying to re-invent the ordinary, make it new by turning it into a dream,' is how Edgar comes to define his art, and this is King's quest also," explained *Chicago Tribune* contributor Richard Rayner. "He writes as always with energy and drive and a wit and grace for which critics often fail to give him credit." In addition, Rayner continued, "there's the thrilling sense of a master determined not only to flex his muscles but develop them too." "King may be meditating on the diverse powers of the creative soul," wrote *Washington Post Book World* contributor Brigitte Weeks, "but he has in no way lost his unmatched gift for ensnaring and chilling his readers with 'terrible fishbelly fingers.'" "When it comes to spine-tingling stories capable of melding the mundane with monstrous fears, both real and imagined," concluded Erik Spanberg, writing in the *Christian Science Monitor,* "nobody does it better."

### Nonfiction

King had also begun work on a writer's manual before his accident, and the result, 2000's *On Writing: A Memoir of the Craft,* sold more copies in its first printing than any previous book about writing. In addition to King's advice on crafting fiction, however, the book includes a great deal of autobiographical material. The author chronicles his childhood, his rise to fame, his struggles with addiction, and the horrific accident that almost ended his life. "King's writing about his own alcoholism and cocaine abuse," noted John Mark Eberhart in the Kansas City *Star,* "is among the best and most honest prose of his career." Similarly, Jack Harville reported in the Charlotte *Observer* that "the closing piece describes King's accident and rehabilitation. The description is harrowing, and the rehab involves both physical and emotional recovery. It is beautifully told in a narrative style that would have gained Strunk and White's approval."

In 2004, King varied a bit from his usual formula to write, in conjunction with Stewart O'Nan, a nonfiction book about one of his great loves, the Boston Red Sox. When the two authors began keeping diaries of every team-related moment in the year, *Faithful: Two Die-Hard Boston Red Sox Fans Chronicle the Historic 2004 Season* was originally expected to be the story of yet another disappointing season for fans of the seemingly cursed team. Instead the Red Sox won the World Series that season for the first time in eighty-six years.

### Short Fiction

King received a great deal of praise for his short story collection *Everything's Eventual.* Among other selections, the volume includes a few that he published previously in the *New Yorker.* Notable among these is "The Man in the Black Suit," which won the 1996 O. Henry Award for best short story and brought King comparisons with great nineteenth-century American fiction writer Nathaniel Hawthorne. "As a whole," concluded Rodriguez in another *Miami Herald* review, "*Everything's Eventual* makes a perfect showcase for all of King's strengths: His uncanny talent for creating vivid, fully realized characters in a few strokes, his ability to mine horror out of the mundane, . . . and his knack for leavening even the most preposterous contraptions with genuine, universal emotions."

In 2010, King focused his writing efforts on the novella, releasing four in the collection *Full Dark, No Stars.* Each selection focuses on the darker side of human nature in tales of horror and suspense. "1922" is narrated by Wilf James, a man who killed his wife in 1922 to prevent her from selling part of their farm. Wilf disposed of the body in the well, but her spirit stayed behind. In "Big Driver," a mystery writer who was sexually assaulted exacts her revenge, while "A Good Marriage" features a married couple who has been together for nearly thirty years. Of course, the wife discovers her husband's awful secret. The final novella in the collection, "Fair Extension," features a man named Mr. Elvid (i.e., the devil), who revels in others' dark sides. King explores "greed, revenge, and self-deception," Daniel Kraus remarked in *Booklist.* "Rarely has King gone this dark, but to say there are no stars here is crazy." According to a *Kirkus Reviews* critic, "each [novella] deals in some way with the darkest recesses of the human soul." The result is "a collection of page-turning narratives for those who prefer the prolific tale spinner at his pulpiest."

London *Telegraph* reviewer Tim Martin observed: "*Full Dark, No Stars* isn't King's best work, but of course, many or most of his readers will read it whether he's on form or not. Like Woody Allen films for some and Bob Dylan albums for others, one buys them because there's usually a flicker of genius somewhere and, if not, it's worth supporting him until it comes back." He added: "What keeps us reading? One answer is habit; another is that this writer rarely disappoints in matters of structure. Almost all his novels are lessons in scenic form." Proffering further praise, Martin wrote: "King's most striking effects have traditionally come when he rebels against the traditions of genre, but sometimes he just likes to have fun. In this collection, never less than entertaining, he does both." Neil Gaiman in the London *Guardian* was highly impressed, asserting that "these are stories of retribution and complicity: of crimes that seem inevitable, of ways that we justify the world to ourselves and ourselves to the world. Powerful, and each in its own way profoundly nasty." Gaiman reported: "In his afterword, King states that he wanted the stories to linger in the imagination. And they do. They linger, and perhaps sometimes they even fester. But they are never less than satisfying and are fine stories to take with us into the night."

Two stand-alone novellas, *UR* and *Blockade Billy,* also followed in 2010. The latter is narrated by a retired third-base coach. Set during the late 1950s,

the novella presents the coach's recollections of William "Billy" Blakely, a fresh recruit from the minor leagues. Billy is a great catcher and power hitter, but a dark aura surrounds him. "A good writer . . . can make any subject interesting, and that's certainly the case" in *Blockade Billy* De Lint remarked in the *Magazine of Fantasy and Science Fiction.* He stated that the story is "excellent so long as you like King in character-development mode, as opposed to sturm und drang." In the online *Bright Hub,* Dylan Lambert felt that the novella "shows a changing style in his writing. Instead of being a supernatural horror novel, *Blockade Billy* is more about real horror, as it is based on real events. It shows the horror that people are capable of inflicting on each other."

## "Dark Tower" Series

While King has played with the idea of giving up publishing his writings, his legion of fans continues to be delighted that the idea has not yet become a reality. In 2004, under the pseudonym of Eleanor Druse, King published *The Journals of Eleanor Druse: My Investigation of the Kingdom Hospital Incident.* He has also continued with his "Dark Tower" series (the illustrated novels featuring Roland the gunslinger) with the publication of *The Dark Tower V: Wolves of the Calla* in 2003. The book was published more than five years after the publication of the previous installment in the series, *The Dark Tower IV: Wizard and Glass.* King completed the final two installments of the series in 2004, *The Dark Tower VI: The Songs of Susannah* and *The Dark Tower VII: The Dark Tower.* In a surprise for fans, King introduced himself as a character in the sixth installment, which a *Publishers Weekly* reviewer called a "gutsy move" and commented: "There's no denying the ingenuity with which King paints a candid picture of himself."

Although he does not necessarily feel that he has been treated unfairly by critics, King has described what it is like to witness the written word turned into filmed images that are less than generously received by reviewers. In his essay "Why I Was Bachman," he readily admits that he has little to complain about: "I'm still married to the same woman, my kids are healthy and bright, and I'm being well paid for doing something I love." And despite the financial security and recognition, or perhaps because of its intrinsic responsibility, King strives to improve at his craft. "It's getting later and I want to get better, because you only get so many chances to do good work," he stated in a panel discussion at the 1984 World Fantasy Convention in Ottawa. "There's no justification not to at least try to do good work when you make the money."

According to a contributor to *Discovering Stephen King,* there is absolutely nothing to suggest that success has been detrimental to King: "As a novelist, King has been remarkably consistent." Noting, for instance, that "for generations it was given that brevity was the soul of horror, that the ideal format for the tale of terror was the short story," Warren pointed out that "King was among the first to challenge that concept, writing not just successful novels of horror, but long novels." Moreover, wrote Warren, "his novels have gotten longer."

Influenced by the naturalistic novels of writers such as Theodore Dreiser and Frank Norris, King once confessed that his personal outlook for the world's future is somewhat bleak. On the other hand, one of the things he finds most comforting in his own work is an element of optimism. "In almost all cases, I've begun with a premise that was really black," he said in a panel discussion at the 1980 World Fantasy Convention in Baltimore, reprinted in *Bare Bones.* "And a more pleasant resolution has forced itself upon that structure." However, as a contributor to *Kingdom of Fear* maintained: "Unlike some other horror writers who lack his talents and sensitivity, Stephen King never ends his stories with any cheap or easy hope. People are badly hurt, they suffer and some of them die, but others survive the struggle and manage to grow. The powers of evil have not yet done them in." According to a contributor to *Fear Itself,* though, the reassurance King brings to his own readers derives from a basic esteem for humanity itself: "For whether he is writing about vampires, about the death of ninety-nine percent of the population, or about innocent little girls with the power to break the earth in half, King never stops emphasizing his essential liking for people."

Douglas E. Winter assessed King's contribution to the horror genre in his study *Stephen King: The Art of Darkness* this way: "Death, destruction, and destiny await us all at the end of the journey—in life as in horror fiction. And the writer of horror stories serves as the boatman who ferries people across that Reach known as the River Styx. . . . In the horror fiction of Stephen King, we can embark upon the night journey, make the descent down the dark hole, cross that narrowing Reach, and return again in safety to the surface—to the near shore of the river of death. For our boatman has a master's hand."

■ **Biographical And Critical Sources**

*BOOKS*

Beahm, George W., editor, *The Stephen King Companion,* Andrews & McMeel (Kansas City, MO), 1989.

Beahm, George W., *The Stephen King Story,* revised and updated edition, Andrews & McMeel (Kansas City, MO), 1992.

Blue, Tyson, *Observations from the Terminator: Thoughts on Stephen King and Other Modern Masters of Horror Fiction,* Borgo Press (San Bernardino, CA), 1995.

Collings, Michael R., *Stephen King As Richard Bachman,* Starmont House (Mercer Island, WA), 1985.

Collings, Michael R., *The Works of Stephen King: An Annotated Bibliography and Guide,* edited by Boden Clarke, Borgo Press (San Bernardino, CA), 1993.

Collings, Michael R., *Scaring Us to Death: The Impact of Stephen King on Popular Culture,* 2nd edition, Borgo Press (San Bernardino, CA), 1995.

*Contemporary Literary Criticism,* Gale (Detroit, MI), Volume 12, 1980, Volume 26, 1983, Volume 37, 1985, Volume 61, 1990.

*Contemporary Theatre, Film, and Television,* Volume 63, Gale (Detroit, MI), 2005.

Davis, Jonathan P., *Stephen King's America,* Bowling Green State University Popular Press (Bowling Green, OH), 1994.

*Dictionary of Literary Biography,* Volume 143: *American Novelists since World War II, Third Series,* Gale (Detroit, MI), 1994.

*Dictionary of Literary Biography Yearbook: 1980,* Gale (Detroit, MI), 1981.

Docherty, Brian, editor, *American Horror Fiction: From Brockden Brown to Stephen King,* St. Martin's Press (New York, NY), 1990.

Hoppenstand, Gary, and Ray B. Browne, editors, *The Gothic World of Stephen King: Landscape of Nightmares,* Bowling Green State University Popular Press (Bowling Green, OH), 1987.

Keyishian, Amy, and Marjorie Keyishian, *Stephen King,* Chelsea House (Philadelphia, PA), 1995.

King, Stephen, *Stephen King's Danse Macabre,* Everest House (New York, NY), 1981.

King, Stephen, *The Bachman Books: Four Early Novels,* New American Library (New York, NY), 1985.

King, Stephen, *On Writing: A Memoir of the Craft,* Scribner (New York, NY), 2000.

Magistrale, Tony, editor, *Landscape of Fear: Stephen King's American Gothic,* Bowling Green State University Popular Press (Bowling Green, OH), 1988.

Magistrale, Tony, editor, *A Casebook on "The Stand,"* Starmont House (Mercer Island, WA), 1992.

Magistrale, Tony, *Stephen King: The Second Decade—"Danse Macabre" to "The Dark Half,"* Twayne (New York, NY), 1992.

Platt, Charles, *Dream Makers: The Uncommon Men and Women Who Write Science Fiction,* Berkley (New York, NY), 1983.

Saidman, Anne, *Stephen King, Master of Horror,* Lerner Publications (Minneapolis, MN), 1992.

Schweitzer, Darrell, editor, *Discovering Stephen King,* Starmont House (Mercer Island, WA), 1985.

*Short Story Criticism,* Volume 17, Gale (Detroit, MI), 1995.

Underwood, Tim, and Chuck Miller, editors, *Fear Itself: The Horror Fiction of Stephen King*, New American Library (New York, NY), 1982.

Underwood, Tim, and Chuck Miller, editors, *Kingdom of Fear: The World of Stephen King*, New American Library (New York, NY), 1986.

Underwood, Tim, and Chuck Miller, editors, *Bare Bones: Conversations on Terror with Stephen King*, McGraw-Hill (New York, NY), 1988.

Underwood, Tim, and Chuck Miller, editors, *Feast of Fear: Conversations with Stephen King*, Carroll & Graf (New York, NY), 1992.

Underwood, Tim, and Chuck Miller, editors, *Fear Itself: The Early Works of Stephen King*, foreword by King, introduction by Peter Straub, afterword by George A. Romero, Underwood Miller (San Francisco, CA), 1993.

Winter, Douglas E., *Stephen King: The Art of Darkness*, New American Library (New York, NY), 1984.

PERIODICALS

*Associated Content*, October 1, 2008, Lori Titus, review of *Duma Key*.

*Atlantic Monthly*, September, 1986, review of *It*, p. 102; November 1, 2006, review of *Lisey's Story*, p. 125.

*Book*, November-December, Chris Barsanti, review of *The Dark Tower V: Wolves of the Calla*, p. 75; September 1, 2001, Stephanie Foote, review of *Black House*, p. 80.

*Booklist*, January 1, 1976, review of *Salem's Lot*, p. 613; December 1, 1978, review of *The Stand*, p. 601; September 1, 1979, review of *The Dead Zone*, p. 24; September 1, 1998, Ray Olson, review of *Bag of Bones*, p. 6; February 15, 1999, Bonnie Smothers, review of *Storm of the Century*, p. 1003; July, 1999, Ray Olson, review of *Hearts in Atlantis*, p. 1893; May 1, 2004, Ray Olson, review of *The Dark Tower VI: The Songs of Susannah*, p. 1483; September 1, 2004, Ray Olson, review of *The Dark Tower VII: The Dark Tower*, p. 6; September 1, 2001, Ray Olson, review of *Black House*, p. 4; September 1, 2005, Keir Graff, review of *The Colorado Kid*, p. 6; January 1, 2006, Ray Olson, review of *Cell*, p. 24; June 1, 2006, Ray Olson, review of *Lisey's Story*, p. 6; May 15, 2007, Ray Olson, review of *Blaze*, p. 5; December 1, 2007, Ray Olson, review of *Duma Key*, p. 4; September 15, 2008, Ray Olson, review of *Just after Sunset*, p. 5; May 1, 2010, Bill Ott, review of *Blockade Billy*, p. 6; September 15, 2010, Daniel Kraus, review of *Full Dark, No Stars*, p. 38.

*Books*, November 19, 2006, "Stephen King Fuses Serious Writing and Horror: A Widow's Tale of Loss, Mourning and Terror," p. 8.

*Boston Globe*, January 19, 2008, Erica Noonan, "In Long or Short Form, He's King of Horror"; November 15, 2008, Erica Noonan, review of *Duma Key*.

*California Bookwatch*, January 1, 2009, review of *Just after Sunset*.

*Chicago Tribune*, August 26, 1990, review of *Four Past Midnight*, p. 3; November 7, 1993, review of *Nightmares and Dreamscapes*, p. 9; February 9, 2008, Richard Rayner, review of *Duma Key*.

*Christian Science Monitor*, January 22, 1990, Thomas D'Evelyn, review of *The Dark Half*, p. 13; January 25, 2008, review of *Duma Key*.

*Columbus Dispatch* (Columbus, OH), November 11, 2009, Nick Chordas, review of *Just after Sunset*.

*Deseret News* (Salt Lake City, UT), November 16, 2008, Valerie Parsons, review of *Just after Sunset*.

*English Journal*, January, 1979, review of *The Shining*, p. 58; January, 1983, review of *Cujo*, p. 79; December, 1983, review of *Different Seasons*, p. 69; December, 1984, review of *Pet Sematary*, p. 66.

*Entertainment Weekly*, October 14, 1994, review of *Insomnia*, p. 52; June 16, 1995, review of *Rose Madder*, p. 54; March 22, 1996, review of *The Two Dead Girls*, p. 63; April 26, 1996, "The Mouse on the Mile," p. 49; May 31, 1996, review of "Coffey's Hands," p. 53; June 28, 1996, review of "The Bad Death of Eduard Delacroix," p. 98; August 2, 1996, "Night Journey," p. 53; September 6, 1996, "Coffey on the Mile," p. 67; October 4, 1996, Mark Harris, review of *Desperation*, p. 54; December 27, 1996, review of *The Green Mile*, p. 142; September 25, 1998, "King of the Weird," p. 95; September 17, 1999, Tom De Haven, "King of 'Hearts': He May Be the Master of Horror, but Stephen King Is Also Adept at Capturing Everyday America. In *Hearts in Atlantis*, His Take on the 60s, including the Effects of Vietnam, Is Scarily Accurate," p. 72; September 21, 2001, Bruce Fretts, "Back in 'Black': Stephen King and Peter Straub Return to the Shadows with the Delightfully Creepy Black House," p. 76; September 27, 2002, Chris Nashawaty, "Stephen King Quits," p. 20; June 25, 2004, Gregory Kirschling, review of *The Dark Tower VI*, p. 172; October 7, 2005, Gilbert Cruz, "The New King of Pulp," p. 83; June 15, 2007, Tanner Stransky, review of *Blaze*, p. 83.

*Esquire*, November, 1984, review of *The Talisman*, p. 231; February 21, 2008, Benjamin Percy, review of *Duma Key*.

*Fantasy Review*, January, 1984, Michael A. Morrison, review of *Pet Sematary*, p. 49

*Guardian* (London, England), November 5, 2010, Neil Gaiman, review of *Full Dark, No Stars*.

*Houston Chronicle*, September 20, 1998, Bruce Westbrook, "Stephen King Finds Love among 'Bones'," p. 17; February 8, 2008, Chauncey Mabe, "Return of the King."

*Independent* (London, England), August 15, 1998, Kim Newman, review of *Bag of Bones*; November 10, 1999, David Usborne, review of *Misery*; October 12, 2001, Charles Shar Murray, review of

*Black House;* January 20, 2008, Matt Thorne, review of *Duma Key;* November 9, 2008, Matt Thorne, review of *Just after Sunset.*

*Kirkus Reviews,* March 1, 1974, review of *Carrie: A Novel of a Girl with a Frightening Power,* p. 257; December 1, 1977, review of *Night Shift,* p. 1285; June 15, 2006, review of *Lisey's Story,* p. 594; December 15, 2007, review of *Duma Key;* September 1, 2008, review of *Just after Sunset;* September 15, 2010, review of *Full Dark, No Stars.*

*Library Journal,* March 1, 2004, Kristen L. Smith, review of *The Dark Tower V,* p. 126; May 15, 2004, Nancy McNicol, review of *The Dark Tower VI,* p. 115; September 15, 2004, Nancy McNicol, review of *The Dark Tower VII,* p. 49; September 15, 2005, Nancy McNicol, review of *The Colorado Kid,* p. 60; July 1, 2006, Nancy McNicol, review of *Lisey's Story,* p. 66; July 1, 1998, Mark Annichiarico, review of *Bag of Bones,* p. 137; November 1, 2003, Michael Rogers, review of *The Gunslinger,* p. 129; January 1, 2008, Carolann Curry, review of *Duma Key,* p. 84; September 15, 2008, Nancy McNicol, review of *Just after Sunset,* p. 51; October 1, 2010, Carolann Curry, review of *Full Dark, No Stars,* p. 71.

*Locus,* September, 1992, review of *Gerald's Game,* p. 21; November, 1992, review of *Dolores Claiborne,* p. 19; February, 1994, review of *Dolores Claiborne,* p. 58; October, 1994, review of *Nightmares and Dreamscapes,* p. 54.

*Los Angeles Times,* May 8, 1983, review of *Christine,* p. 3; November 20, 1983, review of *Pet Sematary,* p. 17; November 18, 1984, review of *The Talisman,* p. 13; August 25, 1985, review of *Stephen King's Skeleton Crew,* p. 4.

*Magazine of Fantasy and Science Fiction,* January 1, 2007, Charles De Lint, review of *Lisey's Story,* p. 38; May 1, 1999, Elizabeth Hand, review of *Bag of Bones,* p. 41; December 1, 2007, review of *Blaze,* p. 28; July 1, 2008, Charles De Lint, review of *Duma Key,* p. 26; September 1, 2010, Charles De Lint, review of *Blockade Billy.*

*Metro,* January 24, 2009, Robert Murphy, review of *Duma Key.*

*Miami Herald,* March 21, 2001, Rene Rodriguez, review of *Dreamcatcher;* March 27, 2002, Rene Rodriguez, review of *Everything's Eventual: 14 Dark Tales.*

*Midwest Quarterly,* spring, 2004, Tom Hansen, "Diabolical Dreaming in Stephen King's 'The Man in the Black Suit,'" p. 290.

*National Review,* September 1, 1998, James Bowman, review of *Bag of Bones,* p. 46.

*New Republic,* February 21, 1981, Michele Slung, review of *Firestarter,* p. 38.

*New Statesman,* September 15, 1995, Kevin Harley, review of *Rose Madder,* p. 33.

*Newsweek,* August 31, 1981, Jean Strouse, review of *Cujo,* p. 64; May 2, 1983, review of *Christine,* p. 76.

*New York Daily News,* February 2, 2008, David Hinckley, review of *Duma Key.*

*New Yorker,* January 15, 1979, review of *The Stand,* p. 109; September 30, 1996, review of *Desperation,* p. 78

*New York Review of Books,* October 19, 1995, review of *Dolores Claiborne,* p. 54.

*New York Times,* March 1, 1977, review of *The Shining,* p. 35; November 28, 1977, review of *Night Shift,* p. 46; March 26, 1978, review of *The Stand,* p. 13; August 17, 1979, Christopher Lehmann-Haupt, review of *The Dead Zone,* p. C23; August 14, 1981, review of *Cujo,* p. 19; August 11, 1982, review of *Different Seasons,* p. 25; April 12, 1983, review of *Christine,* p. 27; October 21, 1983, review of *Pet Sematary,* p. 21; November 8, 1984, review of *The Talisman,* p. 25; August 21, 1986, Christopher Lehmann-Haupt, review of *It,* p. 17; June 29, 1992, review of *Gerald's Game,* p. B2; November 16, 1992, review of *Dolores Claiborne,* p. B1; June 26, 1995, review of *Rose Madder,* p. B2; October 26, 1996, "Coffey on the Mile," p. 16.

*New York Times Book Review,* May 26, 1974, review of *Carrie,* p. 17; February 20, 1977, Jack Sullivan, review of *The Shining,* p. 8; September 11, 1977, review of *Carrie,* p. 3; March 26, 1978, review of *Night Shift,* p. 13; February 4, 1979, review of *The Stand,* p. 15; May 10, 1981, review of *Stephen King's Danse Macabre,* p. 15; August 29, 1982, review of *Different Seasons,* p. 10; April 3, 1983, review of *Christine,* p. 12; November 6, 1983, review of *Pet Sematary,* p. 15; November 4, 1984, review of *The Talisman,* p. 24; June 9, 1985, review of *Stephen King's Skeleton Crew,* p. 11; February 22, 1987, review of *The Eyes of the Dragon,* p. 12; May 13, 1990, review of *The Stand: The Complete and Uncut Edition,* p. 3; September 2, 1990, review of *Four Past Midnight,* p. 21; September 29, 1991, review of *The Waste Lands,* p. 14; August 16, 1992, review of *Gerald's Game,* p. 3; December 27, 1992, review of *Dolores Claiborne,* p. 15; October 24, 1993, review of *Nightmares and Dreamscapes,* p. 22; October 30, 1994, review of *Insomnia,* p. 24; July 2, 1995, review of *Rose Madder* p. 11; October 20, 1996, review of *The Green Mile,* p. 16; September 21, 1998, Christopher Lehmann-Haupt, review of *Bag of Bones;* March 20, 2000, Christopher Lehmann-Haupt, "Click If You Dare: It's the Cybercrypt," p. 7; January 25, 2002, Ron Wertheimer, "'Rose Red,' Victims Blue in a Stephen King Thriller," p. 36; November 12, 2006, Jim Windolf, "Scare Tactician," review of *Lisey's Story,* p. 1; January 21, 2008, Janet Maslin, review of *Duma Key;* March 2, 2008, James Campbell, "Dark Art," p. 9; November 4, 2008, Janet Maslin, review of *Just after Sunset.*

*Observer* (Charlotte, NC), October 4, 2000, Jack Harville, review of *On Writing: A Memoir of the Craft;* Salem Macknee, review of *From a Buick 8.*

*Oregonian* (Portland, OR), February 29, 2008, Vernon Peterson, review of *Duma Key.*

*Penthouse,* April, 1982, Bob Spitz, interview with author.

*People Weekly,* April 16, 1984, Mark Donovan, review of *Cycle of the Werewolf,* p. 16; August 24, 1987, Mark Donovan, review of *Misery,* p. 13; November 7, 1988, Mark Donovan, review of *The Dark Tower: The Gunslinger,* p. 38; September 28, 1998, Alex Tresniowski, review of *Bag of Bones,* p. 51.

*Playboy,* June, 1983, Eric Norden review of *Christine* and interview with King, p. 38.

*Publishers Weekly,* February 25, 1974, review of *Carrie,* p. 102; June 7, 1976, review of *Salem's Lot,* p. 73; November 14, 1977, review of *The Shining,* p. 64; September 25, 1978, review of *The Stand,* p. 127; November 12, 1979, review of *The Stand,* p. 56; April 1, 1996, review of *The Two Dead Girls,* p. 38; June 24, 1996, review of *Desperation,* p. 43; July 14, 1997, review of *The Dark Tower IV: Wizard and Glass,* p. 65; June 22, 1998, review of *Bag of Bones,* p. 81; January 25, 1999, review of *Storm of the Century,* p. 75; April 19, 2004, review of *The Dark Tower VI,* p. 37; August 15, 2005, Orson Scott Card, review of *The Colorado Kid,* p. 40; January 2, 2006, review of *Cell,* p. 37; August 28, 2006, review of *Lisey's Story,* p. 27; May 21, 2007, review of *Blaze,* p. 34; November 19, 2007, Paul Pope, review of *Dark Tower: The Gunslinger,* p. 45; October 2, 2007, Laura Hudson, "Marvel's Dark Tower Team Talks to Stephen King"; December 10, 2007, review of *Duma Key,* p. 37; September 27, 2010, review of *Full Dark, No Stars,* p. 34.

*Rapport,* annual, 1992, reviews of *The Waste Lands,* p. 21, and *Gerald's Game,* p. 26.

*Rocky Mountain News* (Denver, CO), January 18, 2008, Mark Graham, review of *Duma Key.*

*St. Petersburg Times* (St. Petersburg, FL), December 14, 2008, Colette Bancroft, review of *Just after Sunset.*

*San Francisco Chronicle,* February 3, 2008, Michael Berry, review of *Duma Key.*

*Saturday Review,* September, 1981, Michelle Green, review of *Cujo,* p. 59; November, 1984, review of *The Talisman* p. 85.

*Scotland on Sunday* (Edinburgh, Scotland), November 9, 2008, Janet Maslin, review of *Just after Sunset.*

*Seattle Times,* October 27, 2006, Mark Rahner, review of *Lisey's Story.*

*South Florida Sun-Sentinel* (Fort Lauderdale, FL), November 23, 2008, Carole Goldberg, review of *Just after Sunset.*

*Spectator,* October 13, 2001, Sam Phipps, review of *Black House,* p. 58.

*Star* (Kansas City, MO), October 4, 2000, John Mark Eberhart, review of *On Writing.*

*Star* (Toronto, Ontario, Canada), February 10, 2008, review of *Duma Key.*

*Star Tribune* (Minneapolis, MN), September 13, 1998, James Lileks, "In Stephen King's Latest, Things . . . Happen; but *Bag of Bones* Is Not a Gorefest; This Novel Has Depth," p. 19.

*Sydney Morning Herald,* June 21, 2005, "Woman Sues Stephen King over *Misery* Character."

*Telegraph* (London, England), February 8, 2008, Justin Williams, "The Horror of Stephen King's Decline"; February 8, 2008, Tim Martin, "Let the Bones Keep Rattling"; November 5, 2010, Tim Martin, review of *Full Dark, No Stars.*

*Time,* August 30, 1982, Paul Gray, review of *Different Seasons,* p. 87; July 1, 1985, review of *Stephen King's Skeleton Crew,* p. 59; October 6, 1986, review of *It,* p. 74; June 8, 1987, review of *Misery,* p. 82; December 7, 1992, review of *Dolores Claiborne,* p. 81; September 2, 1996, review of *The Green Mile,* p. 60; October 12, 1998, Nadya Labi, review of *Bag of Bones,* p. 116; January 17, 2008, Gilbert Cruz, "King's New Realm."

*Times* (London, England), January 20, 2008, John Dugdale, review of *Duma Key;* January 24, 2008, Peter Millar, review of *Duma Key.*

*USA Today,* January 22, 2008, Carol Mommott, review of *Duma Key;* January 23, 2008, Bob Minzesheimer, review of *Duma Key.*

*Valdosta Daily Times* (Valdosta, GA), March 28, 2008, review of *Duma Key.*

*Village Voice,* April 29, 1981, review of *Stephen King's Danse Macabre,* p. 45; October 23, 1984, review of *The Talisman,* p. 53; March 3, 1987, review of *It,* p. 46.

*Voice Literary Supplement,* September, 1982, review of *Creepshow,* p. 6; November, 1985, review of *Salem's Lot,* p. 27.

*Washington Post Book World,* May 26, 1974, review of *Carrie,* p. 17; April 12, 1981, review of *Stephen King's Danse Macabre,* p. 4; August 22, 1982, review of *Different Seasons,* p. 1; November 13, 1983, review of *Pet Sematary,* p. 1; June 16, 1985, review of *Stephen King's Skeleton Crew,* p. 1; August 26, 1990, review of *Four Past Midnight,* p. 9; September 29, 1991, review of *Needful Things,* p. 9; July 19, 1992, review of *Gerald's Game,* p. 7; December 13, 1992, Kit Reed, review of *Dolores Claiborne,* p. 5; October 10, 1993, review of *Nightmares and Dreamscapes,* p. 4; October 9, 1994, review of *Insomnia,* p. 4; October 29, 2006, "Admit It: You've Been a Horrible Snob about Stephen King," p. 1; January 16, 2008, Brigitte Weeks, "Stephen King Wields an Artist's Dark Palette."

*Xpress Reviews,* April 30, 2010, Charli Osborne, review of *Blockade Billy.*


ONLINE

*2 Walls Webzine,* http://www.2walls.com/ (June 3, 2009), Chris Orcutt, review of *The Gunslinger.*

*Agony Column,* http://www.trashotron.com/ (June 3, 2009), Rick Kleffel, reviews of *Bag of Bones* and *Black House.*

*American Chronicle,* http://www.americanchronicle.com/ (June 3, 2009), Jamieson Villeneuve, review of *Bag of Bones.*

*Blog Critics,* http://blogcritics.org/ (June 3, 2009), Ronald C. McKito, review of *The Gunslinger;* (June 3, 2009), Mel Odom and Amanda Banker, reviews of *Duma Key.*

*Bloomberg.com,* http://www.bloomberg.com/ (June 3, 2009), Charles Taylor, "Stephen King Goes to Florida, Finds Twitching Limb."

*BookPage,* http://www.bookpage.com/ (June 3, 2009), James Neal Webb, review of *Bag of Bones.*

*Bookreporter.com,* http://www.bookreporter.com/ (June 3, 2009), Marlene Taylor, review of *Bag of Bones.*

*BookStove,* http://www.bookstove.com/ (June 3, 2009), N.R. Richards, "Stephen King's Misery."

*Boston Phoenix,* http://weeklywire.com/ (June 3, 2009), Charles Taylor, "Unlocking Stephen King's Bag of Bones."

*Bright Hub,* http://www.brighthub.com/ (July 8, 2010), Dylan Lambert, review of *Blockade Billy.*

*Comic Book Resources Reviews,* http://www.comicbookresources.com/ (June 3, 2009), Timothy Callahan, review of *The Long Road Home.*

*ComicCritique.com,* http://www.comiccritique.com/ (June 3, 2009), review of *The Long Road Home.*

*Entertainment Weekly Online,* http://www.ew.com/ (June 3, 2009), Tom De Haven, review of *Bag of Bones;* (June 3, 2009), Maitland McDonagh, "'Misery' Gets Company"; (June 3, 2009), Kate Ward, review of *Duma Key;* Gregory Kirschling, review of *Just after Sunset;* (June 3, 2009), Jeff Jensen, "When Stephen King Met the 'Lost' Boys."

*Examiner.com,* http://www.examiner.com/ (June 3, 2009), reviews of *Duma Key* and *Just after Sunset;* "Stephen King's Bag of Bones Heads for the Silver Screen."

*Fairfield Weekly,* http://www.fairfieldweekly.com/ (June 3, 2009), "'Stephen King Goes to the Movies' Is Pretty Lousy."

*Fandomania,* http://fandomania.com/ (June 3, 2009), Kelly Melcher, review of *The Gunslinger.*

*First Post* http://www.thefirstpost.co.uk/ (June 3, 2009), review of *The Gunslinger Born.*

*GMA News,* http://www.gmanews.tv/ (June 3, 2009), "Latest King Stories about Twilight, not Darkness."

*Horror Fiction,* http://horror-fiction.suite101.com/ (June 3, 2009), Lisa Rufle, review of *Duma Key.*

*January,* http://januarymagazine.com/ (June 3, 2009), Ali Karim, review of *Duma Key.*

*List,* http://www.list.co.uk/ (June 3, 2009), Mark Edmundson, review of *Duma Key.*

*Maine Campus* (University of Maine), http://media.www.mainecampus.com/ (June 3, 2009), Zach Dionne, review of *Just after Sunset.*

*Media Wales,* http://www.walesonline.co.uk/ (June 3, 2009), Emily Lambert, review of *Duma Key.*

*Onyx Reviews,* http://www.bevvincent.com/ (June 3, 2009), review of *Just after Sunset.*

*OpenZine,* http://www.openzine.com/ (June 3, 2009), reviews of *Bag of Bones* and *Just after Sunset.*

*Portland Mercury Online* (Portland, OR), http://www.portlandmercury.com/ (June 3, 2009), Erik Henriksen, review of *Duma Key.*

*Salon.com,* http://www.salon.com/ (June 3, 2009), Andrew O'Hehir, review of *Bag of Bones.*

*Science Fact & Science Fiction Concatenation,* http://www.concatenation.org/ (June 3, 2009), Tony Chester, review of *Duma Key.*

*Sci-Fi/Fantasy Fiction,* http://scififantasyfiction.suite101.com/ (June 3, 2009), Derek Clendening, review of *Just after Sunset.*

*SFFWorld.com,* http://www.sffworld.com/ (June 3, 2009), Victor J. Smith, review of *Misery;* Darren Burn and Harriet Klausner, reviews of *The Drawing of the Three;* reviews of *Black House* and *Bag of Bones.*

*SF Site,* http://www.sfsite.com/ (June 3, 2009), Pat Caven, review of *Bag of Bones;* Matthew Peckham, reviews of *The Dark Tower II: The Drawing of the Three* and *The Dark Tower: The Gunslinger.*

*Slate.com,* http://www.slate.com/ (June 3, 2009), Michael Wood, review of *Bag of Bones.*

*Speaking Volumes,* http://www.speakingvolumesonline.org.uk/ (June 3, 2009), review of *Bag of Bones.*

*Stephen King Book Reviews,* http://www.king-stephen.com/ (June 3, 2009), reviews of *Misery, Bag of Bones, Black House, The Gunslinger, The Drawing of Three, Roadwork, The Running Man, Thinner,* and *Cycle of the Werewolf.*

*Stephen King Home Page,* http://www.stephenking.com (August 29, 2011).

*Strange Horizons,* http://www.strangehorizons.com/ (June 3, 2009), Colin Harvey, review of *Just after Sunset;* Adam Roberts, review of *Duma Key.*

*Tech* (Massachusetts Institute of Technology), http://tech.mit.edu/ (June 3, 2009), Freddy Funes, review of *Black House.*

*Time Out Sydney,* http://www.timeoutsydney.com.au/ (June 3, 2009), Will Gore, review of *Duma Key.*

*Vue Weekly,* http://www.vueweekly.com/ (June 3, 2009), Josef Braun, "Still King."*

# P.F. Kluge

## 1942-

### ■ Also Known As

Paul Frederick Kluge

### ■ Personal

Born January 24, 1942, in Berkeley Heights, NJ; son of Walter (a machinist) and Maria Kluge; married Pamela Hollie (a journalist), February 14, 1977. *Education:* Kenyon College, B.A., 1964; University of Chicago, M.A., 1965, Ph.D., 1967.

### ■ Addresses

*Home*—Gambier, OH. *Office*—Department of English, Kenyon College, Gambier, OH 43022-9623. *E-mail*—pfk@xoxopress.com; klugef@kenyon.edu.

### ■ Career

Writer, 1969—. U.S. Peace Corps, Washington, DC, volunteer in Saipan, Northern Mariana Islands (of Micronesia); worked as a speech writer and political aide in Micronesia, 1960s; *Wall Street Journal*, New York, NY, staff reporter, 1969, 1970; *Life*, assistant editor, 1970, 1971, *National Geographic Traveler*, Washington, DC, contributing editor. Kenyon College, Gambier, OH, visiting professor, 1987-97, writer in residence, beginning 1997.

### ■ Writings

*NOVELS*

*The Day That I Die,* Bobbs-Merrill (Indianapolis, IN), 1976.

*Eddie and the Cruisers,* Viking (New York, NY), 1980.
*Season for War,* Freundlich Books (New York, NY), 1984.
*MacArthur's Ghost,* Arbor House (New York, NY), 1987.
*Biggest Elvis,* Viking (New York, NY), 1996.
*Final Exam,* XOXOX Press (Gambier, OH), 2005.
*Gone Tomorrow,* Overlook Press (New York, NY), 2008.
*A Call from Jersey,* Overlook Press (New York, NY), 2010.

*OTHER*

*The Edge of Paradise: America in Micronesia,* Random House (New York, NY), 1991.
*Alma Mater: A College Homecoming,* Addison-Wesley (Reading, MA), 1993.

Contributor to periodicals, including *Playboy, Rolling Stone, Smithsonian,* and *Islands.* Contributing editor, *National Geographic Traveler.*

### ■ Adaptations

*Eddie and the Cruisers* was filmed by Embassy Pictures, 1983; the film *Dog Day Afternoon* was based on "The Boys in the Bank," a nonfiction article about a bank robbery and hostage crisis that Kluge coauthored and published in *Life* magazine.

### ■ Sidelights

P.F. Kluge's book *Alma Mater: A College Homecoming* chronicles a year at Kenyon College in Ohio, where he began teaching in 1987, and compares life at the modern-day college to the way it was when he was a student there in the early 1960s. The small, private liberal arts college was once all-male and is still largely white, with only a dozen black students, less than one percent of the total. Kluge depicts Kenyon as a college trying to diversify the student body beyond the white and wealthy. The school's effort suffers from many of the pressures common in academia in the late twentieth century: a never-ending need to raise funds, devalued grades, unmotivated students, and faculty members polarized by issues of race and gender. Professors are reluctant to issue bad grades because they have to justify themselves to angry students; meanwhile, debates among the faculty, according to Kluge, descend to the level of "you suck."

"He suggests that faculty today assume no sense of collective responsibility for institutional quality—only for their own classes," observed Richard H. Hersh in *Change*. "That's not enough, he implies, for the whole college must indeed be greater than the sum of its parts." Hersch continued that "Kluge, for all his worry, retains a romantic optimism for the soul-survival of his liberal arts alma mater." Kluge writes: "Whenever I'm here, I can't stop imagining how much better we could be if we asked more of ourselves. . . . I picture a college more diverse and more intense, a college where students of all races and backgrounds can flunk out, a more daunting college, a place that graduates remember not only with affection but with awe. . . . I picture a faculty that engages openly in disagreement but feels a larger commitment to this place and realizes that being here, every day, is a gorgeous blessing. I may be wrong." A *Kirkus Reviews* contributor dubbed Kluge's book "rueful, tender, eloquent: an evenhanded view of the allure and penalties of academic life that should be required reading for everyone connected with a liberal-arts college," while a *Publishers Weekly* critic called it "a chatty, informative portrait that lightly probes the current challenges in higher education."

### Biggest Elvis

Kluge has published more novels than nonfiction works, including the novel *Biggest Elvis*. In this story, the protagonists are three entertainers who portray Elvis Presley at different stages in his life: eager young rock-and-roller, known as "Baby Elvis"; sophisticated movie star, "Dude Elvis"; and bloated, rhinestone-clad Las Vegas showman, "Biggest Elvis." The three perform their act for U.S. Navy personnel and local prostitutes in a club called Graceland (after Presley's home in Memphis, Tennessee) in the town of Olongapao in the Philippines. Chester and Albert Lane, the two young brothers who play Baby Elvis and Dude Elvis, do not take

their work particularly seriously, but Wade Wiggins, a former college professor who plays Biggest Elvis, sees the effort as a mission; for him, Presley is a Christ-like figure. For a time, the success of the three Elvises provides an economic and spiritual lift to Olongapao, but when they go on tour, the situation changes rapidly.

Richard Eder commented in the *Los Angeles Times Book Review* that *Biggest Elvis* is "a serious book as well as a very entertaining one." He explained: "*Biggest Elvis* charts an illusion and its passing: America's confidence that its message suits the rest of the world, both in its own right and in the allure it gains from our national preeminence." *Cleveland Plain Dealer* reviewer Brooke Horvath noted: "Elvis and his avatars come to embody whatever America is and has been at its best and worst. Similarly, American colonialism stands exposed as the wreck of possibly good intentions clumsily pursued." In much the same vein, Sarah Ferguson, writing in the *New York Times Book Review,* called the novel "a dreamy, melancholy tale of economic and pop-cultural imperialism." *Boston Globe* contributor Suzanne Freeman made special mention of Kluge's depiction of the Philippines, where he has spent much time: "His understanding of the place, the people and their complicated relationship with Americans gives wonderful emotional weight to this novel." *Booklist* reviewer Joanne Wilkinson observed that Kluge's enthusiasm for rock music (an earlier novel, *Eddie and the Cruisers*, is about a rock band) "invest[s] his musical scenes with surging emotion and an almost mythic resonance." Freeman concluded: "Like Biggest Elvis himself, this novel could stand some paring down in spots. But, also like its title character, it wins us over anyway with its intelligence, compassion and strength."

### Final Exam

Another novel, *Final Exam*, is a murder mystery set in a small college town in Ohio. The story begins when the corpse of a controversial feminist studies professor is found near a fraternity lodge, and the body count grows quickly as the story proceeds. Before long, college administrators begin to fear that a serial killer is aiming to destroy the school itself.

Writing in *Booklist*, Leon Wagner wrote about Kluge's skewering of campus life, concluding that despite some plot contrivances, the novel offers "a clever twist on the academic thriller."

### Gone Tomorrow

The novel *Gone Tomorrow* also has an academic setting. The novel focuses on the recently deceased George Canaris, identified in the first line of the novel as "the first faculty member of this college in half a century whose death merited an obituary in the *New York Times."* Canaris, who had written two celebrated novels in his youth, had spent the ensuing decades at Canaris while ostensibly working on his magnum opus, nicknamed *The Beast.* But as the writer became less and less relevant to younger generations of students, the college finally forced him to retire, replacing him with a trendier young literary superstar. After Canaris dies in a hit-and-run accident, his literary executor, Mark May, searches for the manuscript of *The Beast* but instead finds a memoir titled *Gone Tomorrow.* This describes the writer's early life in Prague, where he was born; his move to California and his famous novel about Hollywood; his subsequent life in Ohio and in Manhattan; and his return, in late middle age, to Prague. Canaris comments witheringly on the frustrations of dealing with college administrators, clueless students, and the discouraging aspects of teaching; he also writes about his complicated amorous life and his inspiration for beginning work on *The Beast.* As May reads through this account, he confronts perplexing questions about the deceased writer and about the larger themes of inspiration, the creative process, and the vagaries of literary celebrity.

*Gone Tomorrow,* said a writer for *Publishers Weekly,* "combines elements of *Citizen Kane* and *Goodbye Mr. Chips."* Reviewers seemed to enjoy the author's witty observations of academic life, as well as his character's more rueful ruminations on fame, reputation, and mortality. Janet Maslin, writing in the *New York Times,* called *Gone Tomorrow* "a sharply observed yet tender novel," and *Entertainment Weekly* contributor Jennifer Reese described it as "witty and astute." *Library Journal* reviewer M. Neville also expressed admiration for the novel for its lack of pedantry and the "lively gems of wisdom about the writing process" that Kluge scatters throughout the book. Observing that Kluge "vibrates like a turning fork to the foibles of academe," *Cleveland Plain Dealer* contributor Karen R. Long said the ending of *Gone Tomorrow* is "just right."

### *A Call from Jersey*

Kluge's next novel, *A Call from Jersey,* follows a German immigrant named Hans Greifinge and his son as they travel through New York and New Jersey in the 1920s.

Reviewing the work on the *Cleveland Plain Dealer* Web site, contributor Bill Eichenberger commented: "Much of *A Call from Jersey* concerns either leaving or staying: The characters who stay mostly regret it and are in some way broken; the characters who go regret that choice, too, and are broken in different ways." A *Kirkus Reviews* contributor lauded: "Kluge shifts perspective between George and Hans, lending each character a distinct, equally compelling voice. He sketches a difficult but ultimately loving father/son relationship with a rare sincerity and welcome humor." John Coyne, a contributor to the *Peace Corps Worldwide* Web site, opined: *"A Call from Jersey* doesn't disappoint. Kluge captures his beloved New Jersey, showing us how this melting pot came to be and how it has changed. Kluge has said that his subject matter here isn't sexy or chic, but that he hopes the work has a certain 'magic.' Here is another way of putting it: what the novel lacks in action and suspense, it makes up for in charm and wisdom."

### Kluge once told *CA:*

"I tell my students that being a writer is a fate, perhaps a doom. It is not a career choice. It's something you have to do, difficult to live with, impossible to live without. In newspapers and magazines, in and out of the college that employs me—Kenyon College—I have always written: novels, works of nonfiction, numerous magazine articles. I have many subjects, perhaps too many: rock and roll, college life, immigrant experience in America, American experience overseas, especially in the Philippines and Micronesia. I write the kind of books that I would like to read. They get harder to find, it seems. I write first in pencil, then on one of an increasingly hard-to-maintain collection of manual typewriters. I enjoy my non-dependence on technology, I like my work, I like working. Every day isn't heel-clickingly happy, but I love the feeling of handwritten, hand-typed pages adding up. I have all the standard complaints about editors and publishing, the reading public, the bookselling business. Yet I haven't lost my conviction—which I attempt to pass on—that a writer is a good thing to be."

## ■ Biographical And Critical Sources

### BOOKS

Kluge, P.F., *Alma Mater: A College Homecoming,* Addison-Wesley (Reading, MA), 1993.
Kluge, P.F., *Gone Tomorrow,* Overlook Press (New York, NY), 2008.

### PERIODICALS

*American Scholar,* autumn, 1996, Felicia Ackerman, review of *Alma Mater: A College Homecoming,* p. 621.

*Best Sellers*, January, 1985, review of *Season for War*, p. 368.

*Booklist*, February 15, 1976, review of *The Day That I Die*, p. 839; September 15, 1980, review of *Eddie and the Cruisers*, p. 99; October 15, 1984, review of *Season for War*, p. 282; September 1, 1987, review of *MacArthur's Ghost*, p. 27; March 15, 1991, review of *The Edge of Paradise: America in Micronesia*, p. 1450; October 1, 1993, Roland Wulbert, review of *Alma Mater*, p. 225; July, 1996, Joanne Wilkinson, review of *Biggest Elvis*, p. 1803; April 1, 1998, review of *Biggest Elvis*, p 1305; April 15, 2005, Leon Wagner, review of *Final Exam*, p. 1435; October 1, 2008, Heather Paulson, review of *Gone Tomorrow*, p. 22.

*Boston Globe*, August 4, 1996, Suzanne Freeman, review of *Biggest Elvis*.

*Change*, November-December, 1994, Richard H. Hersh, review of *Alma Mater*, p. 53.

*Cleveland Plain Dealer*, August 11, 1996, Brook Harvath, "Fine-tuned Pop Profundity in Philippines"; December 27, 2008, Karen R. Long, review of *Gone Tomorrow*; September 9, 2010, Bill Eichenberger, review of *A Call from Jersey*.

*Contemporary Pacific*, spring, 1993, review of *The Edge of Paradise*, p. 208.

*Economist*, September 7, 1991, review of *The Edge of Paradise*, p. 96.

*Entertainment Weekly*, October 4, 1996, Megan Harlan, review of *Biggest Elvis*, p. 57; October 31, 2008, Jennifer Reese, review of *Gone Tomorrow*, p. 67.

*ForeWord*, November-December, 2008, Christine Canfield, review of *Gone Tomorrow*.

*Kaselehlie Press*, January 9, 2008, Bill Jaynes, author interview.

*Kirkus Reviews*, August 1, 1980, review of *Eddie and the Cruisers*, p. 1009; April 15, 1984, review of *Season for War*, p. 772; August 1, 1987, review of *MacArthur's Ghost*, p. 1101; October 1, 1993, review of *Alma Mater*, p. 1248; June 1, 1996, review of *Biggest Elvis*, p. 771; October 1, 2008, review of *Gone Tomorrow*; August 15, 2010, review of *A Call from Jersey*.

*Library Journal*, February 1, 1976, review of *The Day That I Die*, p. 548; October 1, 1980, Henri C. Veit, review of *Eddie and the Cruisers*, p. 2110; October 15, 1984, Edwin B. Burgess, review of *Season for War*, p. 1960; April 15, 1991, Glenn Peterson, review of *The Edge of Paradise*, p. 110; November 1, 1993, Samuel T. Huang, review of *Alma Mater*, p. 108; July, 1996, Nancy Pearl, review of *Biggest Elvis*, p. 161; August 1, 2008, M. Neville, review of *Gone Tomorrow*, p. 68.

*Los Angeles Times*, December 13, 1987, review of *MacArthur's Ghost*, p. 12; October 15, 1995, review of *Alma Mater*, p. 10.

*Los Angeles Times Book Review*, August 4, 1996, Richard Eder, review of *Biggest Elvis*, p. 2.

*New Yorker*, July 22, 1991, review of *The Edge of Paradise*, p. 83.

*New York Times Book Review*, December 30, 1984, Mona Simpson, review of *Season for War*, p. 16; May 4, 1991, Kenneth Brower, review of *The Edge of Paradise*, p. 16; February 6, 1994, Douglas A. Sylva, review of *Alma Mater*, p. 22; September 1, 1996, Sarah Ferguson, review of *Biggest Elvis*, p. 16; November 17, 2008, Janet Maslin, review of *Gone Tomorrow*.

*Publishers Weekly*, December 1, 1975, review of *The Day That I Die*, p. 61; August 15, 1980, review of *Eddie and the Cruisers*, p. 44; August 24, 1984, review of *Season for War*, p. 75; August 7, 1987, review of *MacArthur's Ghost*, p. 436; October 4, 1993, review of *Alma Mater*, p. 58; June 10, 1996, review of *Biggest Elvis*, p. 85; June 30, 2008, review of *Gone Tomorrow*, p. 158.

*Rapport: Modern Guide to Books, Music & More*, annual, 1996, review of *Biggest Elvis*, p. 36.

*Reference & Research Book News*, May, 1994, review of *Alma Mater*, p. 39.

*School Library Journal*, November, 1980, Cyrisse Jaffee, review of *Eddie and the Cruisers*, p. 93.

*Smithsonian*, December, 1991, David Nevin, review of *The Edge of Paradise*, p. 128.

*Southern Review*, autumn, 1995, review of *Alma Mater*, p. 948.

*Star-Ledger* (Newark, NJ), http://blog.nj.com/ (September 9, 2010), Mark Di Ionno, "Worldly Author P.F. Kluge Rediscovers His N.J. Past with Latest Book, *A Call from Jersey*.

*Voice of Youth Advocates*, April, 1981, review of *Eddie and the Cruisers*, p. 34.

*Washington Post Book World*, May 12, 1991, review of *The Edge of Paradise*, p. 4; November 14, 1993, review of *Alma Mater*, p. 3.

*Weekly Standard*, January 19, 2009, David Skinner, review of *Gone Tomorrow*.

ONLINE

*Dan's Journal*, http://grumpydan.blogspot.com/ (October 5, 2010), review of *A Call from Jersey*.

*Internet Movie Database*, http://www.imdb.com/ (August 14, 2011), author profile.

*Kenyon College Web site*, http://www.kenyon.edu/ (August 14, 2011), author profile.

*Peace Corps Worldwide*, http://peacecorpsworldwide.org/ (July 8, 2010), review of *A Call from Jersey*.

*P.F. Kluge Home Page*, http://www.pfkluge.com (August 14, 2011).

*Teabrarian*, http://www.teabrarian.com/ (December 9, 2010), Laura Rancani, review of *A Call from Jersey*.

*XOXOX Press Web site*, http://xoxoxpress.com/ (June 25, 2009), author profile.*

# Steven Kotler

## 1967-

### ■ Personal

Born May 25, 1967, in Chicago, IL; son of Harvey (in business) and Norma (a teacher) Kotler; married Joy Nicholson. *Ethnicity:* "White." *Education:* University of Wisconsin, B.A., 1989; Johns Hopkins University, M.A., 1993. *Politics:* "Not at present, but open to new ideas." *Religion:* "See politics."

### ■ Addresses

*Home*—Chimayo, NM. *Agent*—May Evans, May Evans, Inc., 242 E. 5th Ave., New York, NY 10003. *E-mail*—steven@stevenkotler.com.

### ■ Career

Freelance journalist. *GQ*, writer-at-large; Rancho de Chihuahua Dog Sanctuary, cofounder (with wife).

### ■ Awards, Honors

William L. Crawford IAFA Fantasy Award, 2000, for *The Angle Quickest for Flight*; Top Ten Dog Books, *Bark* magazine, 2010, for *A Small Furry Prayer*; PEN West finalist, for *West of Jesus.*

### ■ Writings

*The Angle Quickest for Flight* (novel), Four Walls Eight Windows (New York, NY), 1999.

*West of Jesus: Surfing, Science, and the Origins of Belief,* Bloomsbury/Holtzbrinck Publishers (New York, NY), 2006.

*A Small Furry Prayer: Dog Rescue and the Meaning of Life,* Bloomsbury (New York, NY), 2010.

Also author of foreword for *Instant Karma: The Heart and Soul of a Ski Bum,* by Wayne K. Sheldrake, Ghost Road Press (Denver, CO), 2007. *PsychologyToday.com,* "The Playing Field" blogger. Contributor to more than sixty publications, including *New York Times Magazine, LA Times, Wired, GQ, Discover, Popular Science, Outside, Details,* and *National Geographic.*

### ■ Sidelights

Freelance journalist Steven Kotler published his first novel, *The Angle Quickest for Flight,* in 1999. He then switched to nonfiction with *West of Jesus: Surfing, Science, and the Origins of Belief* in 2006. The following year, Kotler wrote the foreword to *Instant Karma: The Heart and Soul of a Ski Bum,* by Wayne K. Sheldrake. Kotler's next book, *A Small Furry Prayer: Dog Rescue and the Meaning of Life,* relates Kotler's attempts to woo his girlfriend by caring for rescued canines. The gesture clearly worked, and after Kotler and his girlfriend married, the couple moved to Chimayo, New Mexico, and founded the Rancho de Chihuahua Dog Sanctuary out of their home. Kotler recounts adopting unwanted shelter dogs and rehabilitating them for permanent homes. From nursing sick canines to training those with behavioral issues, Kotler remarks on the unique bonds he forged with each dog that came into his care. The author speaks of the rescue dogs that died in his arms and mourns those who were successfully places in adoptive homes. He also explores the history and culture of pet ownership.

*Booklist* contributor Rick Roche remarked that *A Small Furry Prayer* contains "rough language and frank descriptions," but he also noted that it is "full of well-told stories." Furthermore, Roche found that "Kotler's book will please many animal advocates." A *Kirkus Reviews* critic acknowledged: "Kotler offers a touching account of Chihuahua adventures alongside interesting blurbs on the history of pet ownership." The critic added that *A Small Furry Prayer* is "a heartfelt example of humanitarianism at work." Barbara Hoffert, writing in *Library Journal*, lauded the book, commenting that it is "highly recommended not only for dog lovers but for readers of memoir, biology, and anthropology and seekers generally." According to *Christian Science Monitor* reviewer Randy Dotinga, "at first glance, *A Small Furry Prayer* looks like yet another entry in the endless series of books about adorable canine scamps"; however, "this gritty journey into 'a world made of dog' is unlike any dog story you've ever read." Explaining this statement, Dotinga observed: "It's the original tale of one couple's star-crossed love affair with dangerous, dying, and dumb dogs. It also chronicles the author's quest through science and the sacred to understand the complex emotional ties between man and beast." A *Publishers Weekly* critic pointed out: "Brimming with humor, gratitude, and grace, this is a remarkable story."

## ■ Biographical And Critical Sources

### BOOKS

Kotler, Steven, *A Small Furry Prayer: Dog Rescue and the Meaning of Life*, Bloomsbury (New York, NY), 2010.

### PERIODICALS

*Booklist*, May 15, 1999, Michelle Kaske, review of *The Angle Quickest for Flight*, p. 1669; September 1, 2010, Rick Roche, review of *A Small Furry Prayer: Dog Rescue and the Meaning of Life*, p. 24.

*Christian Science Monitor*, November 1, 2010, Randy Dotinga, review of *A Small Furry Prayer*.

*Kirkus Reviews*, July 15, 2010, review of *A Small Furry Prayer*.

*Library Journal*, June 15, 1999, Jim Dwyer, review of *The Angle Quickest for Flight*, p. 108; August 1, 2010, Barbara Hoffert, review of *A Small Furry Prayer*, p. 104.

*Los Angeles*, June 1, 2006, "Surf & Turf," p. 144.

*MBR Bookwatch*, September 1, 2006, John Taylor, review of *West of Jesus: Surfing, Science, and the Origins of Belief*.

*Publishers Weekly*, April 19, 1999, review of *The Angle Quickest for Flight*, p. 62; April 3, 2006, review of *West of Jesus*, p. 49; June 28, 2010, review of *A Small Furry Prayer*, p. 117.

*Review of Contemporary Fiction*, March 22, 2002, Alan Tinkler, review of *The Angle Quickest for Flight*, p. 147.

### ONLINE

*Steven Kotler Home Page*, http://www.stevenkotler.com (August 9, 2011).

# Alice Kuipers

## 1979-

■ **Personal**

Born 1979, in London, England. *Education:* Manchester Metropolitan University, graduated.

■ **Addresses**

*Home*—Saskatoon, Saskatchewan, Canada.

■ **Career**

Author.

■ **Writings**

*Life on the Refrigerator Door: Notes between a Mother and Daughter* (novel), Harper (New York, NY), 2007.
*Lost for Words* (novel), HarperTeen (New York, NY), 2010.

■ **Sidelights**

Born in London, England, Alice Kuipers settled in Saskatoon, Saskatchewan, Canada, where she has been slowly building a writing career. Her first efforts included the unpublished novels *Repeat, Aquaplane,* and *Always Present,* the last one being about incest. "I think lots of first time writers have a book about incest in them," she observed wryly in a *Thin Air* Web site interview with Daria Salamon. In addition to these unsuccessful first attempts—the author called *Repeat* a "really awful" initial effort—she also completed two short-story collections, "both of which I like for different reasons," although neither of these has been published. Kuipers at last hit the mark with *Life on the Refrigerator Door: Notes between a Mother and Daughter,* which was released in 2007.

### Life on the Refrigerator Door

*Life on the Refrigerator Door* is about a mother-daughter relationship. Claire is a fifteen-year-old whose mother is a very busy, divorced obstetrician. Because of their hectic schedules—especially Mom's—the two main characters rarely see each other, and so they communicate largely by leaving notes on the refrigerator door. Kuipers uses the device of telling her story entirely from the text that is written in these notes. Although the notes are cursory, the reader is easily able to follow events over the course of a year. Kuipers describes how Claire often has to shop and cook for herself while her mother is away at work; mother and daughter argue about Claire's on again, off again boyfriend, Michael, and their fighting about him leads Claire to move in with her father temporarily. Later notes reveal that Claire's mother has found a lump in her breast, and this later is found to be cancerous. She undergoes chemotherapy, and a range of emotions engulfs mother and daughter as they deal with anger and fear. In the end, Mom dies from her disease, and the last notes on the refrigerator are from Claire, expressing her love for her mother.

While some reviewers of the novel found the narrative technique intriguing, others pointed out flaws. The question arose, for example, as to why a doctor would not have a cell phone or pager with her in order to communicate not only with her office but with her daughter. Instead, she resorts to low-tech Post-it notes. Janice Harayda, writing on the *One-Minute Book Reviews* Web site, noted that *Life on the Refrigerator Door* is more like a children's book than an adult book, and remarked that she ran the text through a Microsoft readability program to find out that the reading level was measured to be at the second grade. Harayda declared the novel to be "dumber than Mitch Albom's *For One More Day*," though she called the note technique "modestly clever." A *Kirkus Reviews* contributor considered the character Claire to be "too good to be true." Although the young teen sometimes complains about wanting money, for the most part she is "independent yet loving and responsible." The reviewer commented that the debut "makes for an easy read for those looking for sad-lite."

Other reviewers received *Life on the Refrigerator Door* more positively. A *Publishers Weekly* writer called it a "haunting debut." "Bittersweet, funny and achingly real," the novel was praised by this reviewer for its important message that time can run out quickly and that we should value the loved ones in our lives. Caitlyn Pilkington, writing on *ButYouDontLookSick.com*, praised the characterizations in the novel, adding: "Kuipers takes petty teenage issues, along side intense grown-up situations, and places the two together, creating a memorable novel about coming of age and family ties."

### *Lost for Words*

Kuipers's next novel, *Lost for Words*, involves a girl named Sophie who is struggling to deal with the loss of her sister. The story is told in the first person via Sophie's journal, which her therapist has instructed her to use to record her feelings.

In an interview on the *Book Butterfly* Web site, the author described her biggest challenge in writing the novel: "The same scene was both hardest and easiest to write. It is the scene where you as a reader find out what happened to Sophie and her sister. It involved a lot of research. I read and listened to upsetting stories. I wondered how to get the tone right."

Reviewing the work on the *Girl in the Stacks* Web site, a contributor lauded: "I think this is a great story about grief and the power of hope and perseverance. This is a must read for everyone." In a review of the work on the *Falling off the Shelf* Web site a contributor expressed: "Towards the end of this book I was bawling my eyes out, and practically hiccuping because I was so gripped by the story. It made me appreciate the family that I have." A contributor to the *Reading Angel* Web site re-

marked: "My main complaint with this book is that the author didn't tell us what actually happened to Sophie's sister until almost the very end of the book."

## ■ Biographical And Critical Sources

*PERIODICALS*

*Bookseller,* January 19, 2007, "Yann Martel's Partner Alice Kuipers Signs with Pan Mac," p. 7.

*Chatelaine,* October, 2007, Rebecca Caldwell, "Yann Martel and Alice Kuipers: The Booker Prize—Winning Author of Life of Pi and His Novelist Partner Share the Story of Their Love—Post-it Notes and Car Accidents Included," p. 67.

*Kirkus Reviews,* July 15, 2007, review of *Life on the Refrigerator Door: Notes between a Mother and Daughter.*

*Publishers Weekly,* July 16, 2007, review of *Life on the Refrigerator Door,* p. 143.

*ONLINE*

*Alice Kuipers Home Page,* http://www.alicekuipers.com (August 14, 2011).

*Book Butterfly,* http://thebookbutterfly.com/ (July 12, 2010), author interview.

*BookLoons,* http://www.bookloons.com/ (March 26, 2008), review of *Life on the Refrigerator Door.*

*ButYouDontLookSick.com,* http://www.butyoudontlooksick.com/ (December 1, 2007), Caitlyn Pilkington, review of *Life on the Refrigerator Door.*

*Falling off the Shelf,* http://fallingofftheshelf.blogspot.com/(May 9, 2010), review of *Lost for Words.*

*Girl in the Stacks,* http://girlsinthestacks.com/ (August 14, 2011), review of *Lost for Words.*

*Life on the Refrigerator Door Web site,* http://www.refrigeratordoor.ca (March 26, 2008).

*One-Minute Book Reviews,* http://oneminutebookreviews.wordpress.com/ (February 5, 2008), Janice Harayda, review of *Life on the Refrigerator Door.*

*Reading Angel,* http://www.readingangel.com/ (July 21, 2010), review of *Lost for Words.*

*Read It Again, Mom!,* http://readitagainmom.blogspot.com/ (April 16, 2011), review of *Lost for Words.*

*Thin Air,* http://thinair2007.blogspot.com/ (September 25, 2007), Daria Salamon, "Interview: Alice Kuipers."

*Trashionista,* http://www.trashionista.com/ (August 1, 2007), interview with Alice Kuipers.

*Vancouver International Writers & Readers Festival Web site,* http://www.writersfest.bc.ca/ (August 14, 2011), author profile.*

# Barbara Leaming

## ■ Personal

Born in Philadelphia, PA; daughter of James F. and Muriel Leaming; married David Packman (a professor), February 21, 1975. *Education:* Smith College, B.A.; New York University, Ph.D.

## ■ Addresses

*Home*—CT. *Agent*—Wallace & Sheil Agency, Inc., 177 E. 70th St., New York, NY 10021.

## ■ Career

Former professor of theater and film at Hunter College of the City University of New York, New York, NY; writer.

## ■ Writings

### BIOGRAPHIES

*Grigori Kozintsev,* Twayne (Boston, MA), 1980.

*Polanski: The Filmmaker as Voyeur,* Simon & Schuster (New York, NY), 1981, published as *Polanski: His Life and Films,* Hamish Hamilton (London, England), 1982.

*Orson Welles: A Biography,* Viking Penguin (New York, NY), 1985.

*If This Was Happiness: A Biography of Rita Hayworth,* Viking (New York, NY), 1989.

*Bette Davis: A Biography,* Simon & Schuster (New York, NY), 1992.

*Katherine Hepburn,* Crown (New York, NY), 1995.

*Marilyn Monroe,* Crown (New York, NY), 1998.

*Mrs. Kennedy: The Missing History of the Kennedy Years,* Free Press (New York, NY), 2001.

*Jack Kennedy: The Education of a Statesman,* W.W. Norton (New York, NY), 2006.

*Churchill Defiant: Fighting On, 1945-1955,* Harper (New York, NY), 2010.

Contributor of articles to periodicals, including *Vanity Fair* and the *New York Times Magazine.*

## ■ Sidelights

Biographer Barbara Leaming's *Polanski: The Filmmaker as Voyeur* details the life and work of the controversial filmmaker who fled the United States while being tried for statutory rape in 1977. Leaming traces Roman Polanski's years as an abandoned child in World War II Europe. She also analyzes the possible influence his tragic experiences—such as the murder of his wife, actress Sharon Tate, by Charles Manson's clan—may have had on his work, including the gruesome *Macbeth* and the pessimistic *Chinatown.*

*Los Angeles Times* critic Irwin R. Blacker viewed the biography as "an insightful and useful study of both the artist and his work." A reviewer for the *Fort Worth Star-Telegram* reached a similar conclusion, calling *Polanski* "an appreciative but hardly gentle study."

### *Orson Welles*

Leaming explored such a relationship in her next biography, turning her attention to the legendary cinematic giant Orson Welles. The appearance of *Orson Welles: A Biography* was timely, for it was published within weeks of his death in 1985. Reviewer Louis Parks saw it as a triumph in the *Houston Chronicle:* "The book is not only timely, it is also unusual and fascinating, an exceptionally intimate, personal look at a remarkable public figure. Leaming achieves what all biographers want but few manage—she gets at her subject from the inside."

Initially, when Leaming approached Welles to write his authorized biography, he refused. She pursued him for a number of years, all the while accumulating information on him from a multitude of sources. Leaming was on the verge of composing an unauthorized biography when Welles decided to speak. The meetings to follow were not mere interviews, for it is said by various reviewers that Welles slowly opened his soul to Leaming. According to Leaming, it is the achievement of such closeness which has made her work a success. Parks quoted Leaming: "If Orson Welles had died without talking, the private man just never would have appeared. There were hints (of him) in things people told me, but he just wasn't there. . . . That legend of his is so entrenched—a larger-than-life figure, arrogant and terrifying, unreachable and cold. But when you know him, he's shy and vulnerable. He's the most approachable, warm, amusing person you can imagine. It's something I would never have known if Orson hadn't decided to take the chance."

The fact that Leaming was able to get so close to Welles is viewed favorably by some critics and skeptically by others. Whereas *Financial Times* critic Nigel Andrews professed that Leaming "obtained near limitless access to the Master, and has repaid the privilege with a biography that is as revealing, confiding and sumptuously wide-ranging as any autobiography," Jay Scott noted in the Toronto *Globe and Mail:* "Leaming wooed and won the recalcitrant Welles and, at the same time, one suspects, fell in love with him. . . . We are told in [others' biographies of Welles] that Welles could charm birds out of trees; he certainly charmed Leaming out of her critical faculties and with a few exceptions she accepts his memories as Holy Writ and his rationalizations as fact." Other reviewers express opinions similar to Scott's, asserting that Leaming was so taken in by Welles that he moved her to plead for all of his life's mistakes. *Detroit News* commentator Bruce Cook called it a "singular lack of objectivity" and believed Welles found the ideal biographer, "so protective of him that very often she seems more an amanuensis than a biographer." Nevertheless, Cook felt the biography is a "good and wonderfully readable book." Others have also been pleased with Leaming's work. According to David Elliott in the *Chicago Sun Times*, "Welles is alive in [Leaming's] book as he has never been before in print. . . . Here

is Welles as a talking, eating, sexing, stirringly emotive man. . . . Leaming should have spent more time on the films and plays, a little less with 'look what I found' stuff (courtesy of Welles, mostly) on his prodigious sex life. But for the first time his wives, and not just Rita Hayworth, are more than mere appendages. . . . Leaming has written the best of the Welles books, full of body heat, and a generosity that rarely blunts insight." Sarah Bradford, writing in *Spectator,* believed Welles's life was told in a "fascinating, skillfully assembled biography."

### If This Was Happiness

In her next two books, Leaming looked at two other film legends: Welles's former wife and World War II pin-up girl Rita Hayworth, and the combative Bette Davis, flamboyant star of the Warner Brothers studio during the 1940s. Both women, according to Leaming, were products of abusive childhoods, and both of them reflected this damage in their later histories. Both Davis and Hayworth were unable to keep their public images—Hayworth as a "sex kitten," Davis as a feisty, strong-willed feminist—from influencing their off-screen lives.

Rita Hayworth, according to *If This Was Happiness: A Biography of Rita Hayworth,* was sexually abused by her sometime dance partner and father, Eduardo Cansino, who recruited his teenage daughter to work with him in his nightclub act. "According to Ms. Leaming," wrote Susan Braudy in the *New York Times Book Review,* "her father's abusive treatment was the key to her emotional development and led to a lifetime of disastrous relationships." Hayworth married five times: the first, at age eighteen, to a much older man who exploited her, stated Braudy, by "threaten[ing] her with physical abuse and disfigurement," and "offer[ing] her to any man he thought would advance her career." Her second husband was Orson Welles, who married her in 1943. However, Welles was unable to meet Hayworth's emotional needs and soon sought solace outside the marriage. Three other marriages—to Prince Aly Khan, heir to the throne of the Aga Khan, to the singer Dick Haymes, and to the director James Hill—also ended in divorce. Hayworth became an alcoholic and in 1980 was diagnosed with Alzheimer's disease. Her daughter, Princess Yasmin Khan, cared for her until her death in 1987.

Many critics celebrated Leaming's convincing portrayal of Hayworth. "The meticulous research," stated Braudy, "makes the painful story of Hayworth's personal problems vivid, which may diminish some envy of her public successes. The book teaches a harder lesson: Rita Hayworth's tortured childhood . . . shaped her. . . . Hollywood did not destroy her." "Leaming's prose can gush," declared Paul Gray in *Time*, ". . . and regularly descends to write-by-the-numbers cliche. But the material is poignant, another reminder of the chasm that can exist between public images and private pain." Hayworth "claimed to have been happy with Welles," Gray concluded, "at least before his infidelities became too blatant. 'If this was happiness,' Welles told Leaming years later, 'imagine what the rest of her life had been.'"

### Bette Davis

Leaming also presents Bette Davis as a person haunted by her childhood in *Bette Davis: A Biography*. Davis's father, a Boston lawyer, deserted his family when Bette was ten years old. Bette's mother, Ruthie, compensated by pushing her older daughter into an acting career and making personal sacrifices to maintain Bette's schooling. "When Bette ultimately achieved success," wrote James Kotsilibas-Davis in the *Washington Post Book World*, "Ruthie would exact her toll, living like a queen on her daughter's earnings." In part because of these troubles, Davis evolved into a woman and an actress who practiced what *Los Angeles Times Book Review* contributor David Elliott called "empress tactics." Elliott continued: "A friend said later, 'She began to imitate herself as an actress and to refuse to know that she was doing that.'" Davis's self-destructive practices helped to end all four of her marriages—including those to abusive husbands such as William Grant Sherry and Gary Merrill—and to alienate her daughter.

"Leaming's biography," declared Richard Christiansen in the *Chicago Tribune*, "walks delicately between pity and scorn for its subject. The author records the traumas Davis inflicted on her daughter B.D., yet she carefully notes the deep pain that B.D., a born-again Christian, inflicted on her mother with the publication of *My Mother's Keeper*," her tell-all, vituperative autobiography.

### Katherine Hepburn

After the Davis biography, Leaming turned her attention to one of Davis's contemporaries, Katherine Hepburn, the most celebrated actress of her generation. Although Hepburn granted Leaming an interview, *Katherine Hepburn* is an unauthorized biography, its contents not approved by its subject.

Describing her single meeting with Hepburn, Leaming stated: "She was so smart and so perceptive, irresistible. She would go so far in the interview and then be deliberately contrary if she thought she wasn't controlling it." Some critics suggested that in *Katherine Hepburn* Leaming reveals significant aspects of the star's character that have not been previously portrayed. Both in her own biographical writings and in her film personas, Hepburn emerges as a self-determined and spirited woman, a feminist model of her day.

According to Ellis Nassour, writing in *Back Stage*: "Leaming uncovers a Katherine Hepburn in stark contrast with the independent, opinionated, fearless Kate." Delving back two generations, Leaming shows how Hepburn's tragic family background shaped her life. It was a family plagued by suicides, five in all; Hepburn discovered her own brother's body after he hanged himself. It is Leaming's contention that these suicides were instrumental in shaping Hepburn's character, particularly her choice of men. Wary of committing to and losing a man, Hepburn had numerous affairs with married men, such as director John Ford and Spencer Tracy, who were not really available. Leaming depicts Tracy as an abusive and domineering alcoholic who often manipulated Hepburn, and Hepburn herself as a woman far less self-assured than her public image would have us believe. Yet despite its often critical frankness, Leaming's biography is more an insightful and sympathetic portrait than a sordid expose. "As feisty and fascinating as Hepburn herself," stated Ilene Cooper in *Booklist*, "Leaming's book catches all the angles of light reflected through the prism of a fascinating life." Lisa Schwarzbaum, writing in *Entertainment Weekly*, felt that "Leaming's great accomplishment in *Katherine Hepburn* is to make the Great Kate come alive as a regular woman and to tell that story with an empathy and acuity desperately rare in the biographies of stars."

### Marilyn Monroe

For her sixth film biography, Leaming chose a subject about whom countless biographies, memoirs, and other books had already appeared: Marilyn Monroe. Could Leaming find anything new or worthwhile to say about the blonde bombshell that had not already been said? The answer to this question, as well as critical response to Leaming's *Marilyn Monroe*, varies greatly.

According to *Booklist* critic Brad Hooper, "Leaming . . . has lots to say, and she's worth listening to. . . . We come away from Leaming's detailed, explicit, sympathetic picture with more understanding of Monroe's demons and more comprehension of her talents." A *People* reviewer commented: "Leaming does not dwell on rumor and gossip about Monroe's life and death. Instead, basing her account on dozens of interviews and thousands of primary documents, she brings new insight—and a woman's perspective—to Monroe's professional and psychological struggles." Yet other reviewers felt that Leaming's book offered little information of value about Monroe. "This survey of the tragically brief life and career of the 1950s sex symbol," observed Stephen Rees in a *Library Journal* review, "devotes so much space to the men in Monroe's life (Joe DiMaggio, Arthur Miller, Laurence Olivier, Elia Kazan, and many others) that she almost becomes a background player in her own drama. . . . Leaming shows little interest in Monroe's actual film work and provides little information on her involvement with the Kennedys." Similarly, a *Publishers Weekly* reviewer noted: "Leaming relays the precise dates when Monroe signed contracts, called in sick, filmed for half a day, etc. It's an approach that does little to explain Monroe's dynamic screen presence, her warmth and charm."

### Mrs. Kennedy

Leaming turned from biographies of film stars to celebrities of another sort, the Kennedys, in a pair of books profiling John F. Kennedy and his wife, Jacqueline Kennedy. The 2001 *Mrs. Kennedy: The Missing History of the Kennedy Years* takes on the question of the role Jackie played in the Kennedy White House, "arguing that Jackie played a key part in her husband's presidency," according to *Time* critic Laura Miller. As with many of the female film stars she has profiled, Leaming once again goes to Jackie Kennedy's childhood and youth to explain her later actions. Leaming portrays a troubled childhood with a mother that largely rejected her; this later made Jackie keep an emotional distance between herself and others. As First Lady, Leaming asserts, Jackie used her social skills to make the president—youthful and politically naive—seem more mature and august than he in fact was. Miller did not think that Leaming made her case for a Jackie Kennedy who was intimately involved in decision-making.

Miller concluded: "However gracefully [Jackie] intervened in shaping the public face of [JFK's] Administration, her efforts, even by Leaming's highly sympathetic account, were intermittent at best." Likewise, Sally Bedell Smith, writing in the *New York Times Book Review*, felt Leaming "repeatedly misses the mark." However, Ilene Cooper, writing in *Booklist*, observed that whether the reader accepts Leaming's thesis or not, the author "has clearly done her research, and she tells a darn good story." Similarly, a *Publishers Weekly* reviewer thought Leaming "provides a fascinating glimpse into the psychodynamics of one of the 20th century's most famous marriages." A critic for *Kirkus Reviews* had much higher praise, describing *Mrs. Kennedy* as "admirably detailed, stunningly successful, and likely to become the definitive biography of the Kennedy marriage."

### Jack Kennedy

With *Jack Kennedy: The Education of a Statesman,* Leaming focuses on the president and his ties to England. Jeff Broadwater, writing in *History,* thought this was a "serious book with a provocative thesis: John F. Kennedy brought to the White House a distinctive approach to foreign policy derived from his deep ties to Great Britain." While still a youth, Kennedy witnessed firsthand—as the son of the then U.S. ambassador to Great Britain—the failed attempts at appeasing Hitler prior to World War II. He also made lasting friendships with men who would later hold important office in England. Leaming also demonstrates how Kennedy learned much about foreign policy from Prime Minister Harold Macmillan. Broadwater felt that Leaming gave "an intriguing human face on the fabled 'special relationship' between the United States and the United Kingdom" in this work.

For Geoffrey Wheatcroft, writing in the *New York Times,* Leaming "has written what is in part an absorbing and enjoyable book; whether her thesis really stands up is another matter." Less positive was the review of a *Publishers Weekly* contributor who felt that Leaming "overreaches and overstates in her first attempt at political biography." On the other hand, *Library Journal* reviewer William D. Pederson felt the book was "engagingly written . . . [and] provides new insights into JFK's behavior." Further praise came from a *Kirkus Reviews* critic who found the same work "thoroughly well written and constructed, with fresh views on the Kennedy presidency and the difficult path that led to Camelot."

### Churchill Defiant

Leaming's next biography, *Churchill Defiant: Fighting On, 1945-1955,* provides a portrait of the period of Churchill's political career that is less frequently addressed by biographers.

Reviewing the work on the *Daily History Blog*, a contributor lamented: "I wanted to like this book. But, sadly, the manner in which it is based on what are loosely described as 'conversations' with conservative party figures makes it hard for me to think of it as a work of History. The paucity of references is disappointing." A contributor to *Open Letters Monthly* opined: "Leaming has done the refreshing favor of focusing on these later years passed over by numerous biographies. The popularly known Churchill endures, with a tenacious fix on the inseparable goals of peace and getting back on top. We see little else from Leaming's sympathetic writing, and she reveals how the triumphs and defeats of Churchill's second term mimic the undying character seen in the first." Reviewing the work in *Kirkus Reviews*, a contributor stated: "Using a variety of material, Leaming executes a smooth, succinct narrative. Tight, polished and effectively focused on the lesser-known end of Churchill's career." *Publishers Weekly* contributor Jon Meacham remarked: "Taken all in all . . . the book is a well-told political drama about the greatest figure of an epic century. Not a bad achievement, that."

### Leaming once told *CA*:

"I am a professor of film history and aesthetics. Both the [Grigori] Kozintsev and Polanski books were written out of my long-term study of Soviet and East European cinema and culture. I also have a special interest in the relationship between American film and its cultural context."

## ■ Biographical And Critical Sources

### BOOKS

Leaming, Barbara, *Orson Welles: A Biography*, Viking Penguin (New York, NY), 1985.

### PERIODICALS

*Back Stage*, December 1, 1995, Ellis Nassour, review of *Katherine Hepburn*, p. 30.
*Biography*, summer, 2006, Geoffrey Wheatcroft, review of *Jack Kennedy: The Education of a Statesman*, p. 526.
*Book*, November-December, 2001, Penelope Mesic, review of *Mrs. Kennedy: The Missing History of the Kennedy Years*, p. 57.
*Booklist*, March 1, 1995, Ilene Cooper, review of *Katherine Hepburn*, p. 1139; September 1, 1998, Brad Hooper, review of *Marilyn Monroe*, p. 4;

September 1, 2001, Ilene Cooper, review of *Mrs. Kennedy*, p. 2; September 1, 2010, Gilbert Taylor, review of *Churchill Defiant: Fighting On, 1945-1955*, p. 30.
*Canberra Times* (Canberra, Australia), August 5, 2006, "Limits in JFK's Getting of Winston."
*Chattanooga Times*, February 13, 1982, review of *Polanski: The Filmmaker as Voyeur*.
*Chicago Sun Times*, September 8, 1985, David Elliott, review of *Orson Welles: A Biography*.
*Chicago Tribune*, May 17, 1992, Richard Christiansen, review of *Bette Davis: A Biography*, p. 3.
*Contemporary Review*, March, 1986, review of *Orson Welles*.
*Detroit Free Press*, October 13, 1985, review of *Orson Welles*; November 9, 2001, John Smyntek, review of *Mrs. Kennedy*.
*Detroit News*, October 13, 1985, Bruce Cook, review of *Orson Welles*.
*Entertainment Weekly*, May 12, 1995, Lisa Schwarzbaum, review of *Katherine Hepburn*, p. 56.
*Financial Times*, October 19, 1985, Nigel Andrews, review of *Orson Welles*.
*Fort Worth Star-Telegram*, February 14, 1982, review of *Polanski*.
*Globe and Mail* (Toronto, Ontario, Canada), October 5, 1985, Jay Scott, review of *Orson Welles*; November 2, 1985, review of *Orson Welles*.
*History*, summer, 2005, Jeff Broadwater, review of *Jack Kennedy*, p. 113.
*Houston Chronicle*, October 20, 1985, Louis Parks, review of *Orson Welles*.
*Kirkus Reviews*, September 15, 1998, review of *Marilyn Monroe*; September 1, 2001, review of *Mrs. Kennedy*, p. 1268; April 15, 2006, review of *Jack Kennedy*, p. 393; July 15, 2010, review of *Churchill Defiant*.
*Library Journal*, October 15, 1998, Stephen Rees, review of *Marilyn Monroe*, p. 73; September 1, 2001, Cynthia Harrison, review of *Mrs. Kennedy*, p. 196; April 1, 2006, William D. Pederson, review of *Jack Kennedy*, p. 104.
*Los Angeles Times*, April 11, 1982, Irwin R. Blacker, review of *Polanski*; September 9, 1985, review of *Orson Welles*.
*Los Angeles Times Book Review*, May 17, 1992, David Elliott, review of *Bette Davis*, pp. 2, 8.
*New Republic*, March 17, 1986, review of *Orson Welles*.
*New York Review of Books*, June 10, 1982, review of *Polanski*.
*New York Times*, September 6, 1985, review of *Orson Welles*; April 16, 1995, review of *Katherine Hepburn*; June 25, 2006, Geoffrey Wheatcroft, "A Special Relationship," review of *Jack Kennedy*.

*New York Times Book Review,* September 15, 1985, review of *Orson Welles;* November 19, 1989, Susan Braudy, review of *If This Was Happiness: A Biography of Rita Hayworth,* pp. 7, 9; November 5, 2001, Sally Bedell Smith, review of *Mrs. Kennedy,* p. 14.

*Observer* (London, England), November 18, 2001, Andrew Rawnsley, "I'm Not All Right, Jack," review of *Mrs. Kennedy.*

*Orlando Sentinel* (Orlando, FL), November 23, 2001, Loraine O'Connell, review of *Mrs. Kennedy.*

*People,* May 1, 1995, review of *Katherine Hepburn,* p. 28; November 23, 1998, review of *Marilyn Monroe,* p. 47; December 3, 2001, David Cobb Craig, review of *Mrs. Kennedy,* p. 45.

*Philadelphia Inquirer,* December 12, 2001, Donald Newlove, review of *Mrs. Kennedy.*

*Publishers Weekly,* March 13, 1995, review of *Katherine Hepburn,* p. 53; October 26, 1998, review of *Marilyn Monroe,* p. 53; September 3, 2001, review of *Mrs. Kennedy,* p. 71; August 3, 2006, review of *Jack Kennedy,* p. 59; July 26, 2010, Jon Meacham, review of *Churchill Defiant,* p. 61.

*Reference & Research Book News,* August, 2006, review of *Jack Kennedy.*

*Seattle Times* (Seattle, WA), April 11, 1982, review of *Polanski.*

*Spectator,* April 3, 1982, review of *Polanski;* November 9, 1985, Sarah Bradford, review of *Orson Welles;* November 17, 2001, Sarah Bradford, review of *Mrs. Kennedy,* p. 49.

*Time,* October 7, 1985, review of *Orson Welles;* December 4, 1989, Paul Gray, review of *If This Was Happiness,* pp. B8, 97; October 22, 2001, Laura Miller, review of *Mrs. Kennedy,* p. 78.

*Times Literary Supplement,* November 28, 1986, review of *Orson Welles.*

*Village Voice,* October 15, 1985, review of *Orson Welles.*

*Village Voice Literary Supplement,* March, 1982, review of *Polanski.*

*Washington Post Book World,* September 17, James Kotsilibas-Davis, review of *Bette Davis,* 1992, p. 8.

*ONLINE*

*Daily History Blog,* http://dalyhistory.wordpress.com/ (November 6, 2010), review of *Churchill Defiant.*

*Open Letters Monthly,* http://www.openlettersmonthly.com/ (August 14, 2011), review of *Churchill Defiant.**

# Buddy Levy

## 1960-

---

### ■ Also Known As

Lynn Levy

### ■ Personal

Born February 2, 1960, in New Orleans, LA; married, 1987; wife's name Camie Ann; children: Logan, Hunter. *Education:* University of Idaho, B.A., 1986, M.A., 1988.

### ■ Addresses

*Home*—P.O. Box 9575, 105 E. Second ST., Ste. 6, Moscow, ID 83843. *Home and office*—Moscow, ID. *Agent*—Scott Waxman, Waxman Literary Agency, 80 5th Ave., Ste. 1101, New York, NY 10011. *E-mail*—buddy@buddylevy.com.

### ■ Career

Writer and academic. University of Idaho, Moscow, instructor, 1988-93; Washington State University, Pullman, clinical assistant professor, then clinical associate professor, 1988-2009. Served as a host for the History Channel.

### ■ Writings

*Echoes on Rimrock: In Pursuit of the Chukar Partridge,* foreword by Jack Hemingway, illustrated by David Fleming, Pruett (Boulder, CO), 1998.

*American Legend: The Real-life Adventures of David Crockett,* Putnam (New York, NY), 2005.

*Conquistador: Hernán Cortés, King Montezuma, and the Last Stand of the Aztecs,* Bantam Books (New York, NY), 2008.

*River of Darkness: Francisco Orellana's Legendary Voyage of Death and Discovery down the Amazon,* Bantam Books (New York, NY), 2011.

Contributor to anthologies, including *The Gift of Birds: True Encounters with Avian Spirits,* Traveler's Tales, 1999; and *Chicken Soup for the Chiropractic Soul,* HCI, 2003. Columnist for *Hooked on the Outdoors* and *MountainZone.com;* contributor to periodicals and Web sites, including *Big Sky Journal, Canoe & Kayak, Trail Runner, Adventure Sports, Backpacker, Out-Post, Discover, Poets & Writers, TV Guide, VIA, High Desert Journal, River Teeth, Utne Reader,* and *Field & Stream.*

### ■ Sidelights

Buddy Levy is an American writer and academic. Born in New Orleans, in 1960, he earned bachelor's and master's degrees from the University of Idaho. Levy has covered many sports events for various magazines and Web sites. He also served as a clinical professor at Washington State University from 1988 until 2009.

#### *American Legend* and *Conquistador*

In *American Legend: The Real-life Adventures of David Crockett,* Levy chronicles the life of the Tennessean who was born in 1786 and died defending the Alamo in 1836. He notes that the folk hero was a three-time congressman, a potential presidential candidate, and a soldier in the War of 1812. Crockett came from humble beginnings and spent much of his life on a small farm, where his wife died during childbirth. Levy comments that Crockett's popular 1834 autobiography "prefigures by some fifty years the literary genre of 'realism,' with nothing remotely like it" until Mark Twain published his *Adventures of Huckleberry Finn.* A *Publishers Weekly* contributor reported that Levy covers the familiar aspects of Crockett's life, but he also includes more "in the way of background and complexity, and is willing to expose some of Crockett's deficiencies without making judgements."

In 2008 Levy published *Conquistador: Hernán Cortés, King Montezuma, and the Last Stand of the Aztecs.* Levy sets the popular record straight on how the Spanish conquistadors were able to conquer the mighty Aztec Empire. Contrary to the belief that Hernán Cortés, aided by a small group of soldiers and superior European technology, destroyed the Aztec population, Levy shows how it was the Spanish who were almost defeated. This drawn-out campaign, Levy argues, turned in favor of the Spanish after they were able to make amphibious attacks against the Aztec and gained the support of rival tribes who had been oppressed by the Aztec. Levy compiles his information from both Aztec and Spanish records, showing the range of diplomatic and militaristic campaigns employed. Levy pays particular attention to the personal characteristics of the leaders of each camp.

Arthur Herman, writing in the *Wall Street Journal,* observed that "Levy offers a fascinating account of the first and most decisive" encounter between Montezuma and Cortés. Herman also noted that "Levy has an eye for vivid detail and manages to build a compelling narrative out of this almost unbelievable story of missionary zeal, greed, cruelty and courage. By avoiding the kind of ideological posturing that usually distorts re-tellings of the conquest of the New World, Mr. Levy rightly focuses his reader's attention on the story's antagonists." A contributor writing on *Cadre Comments* stated: "I appreciate the author's readable style and modest length, but some key points suffer from his relative brevity. A related issue is the relative lack of discussion of dissenting views or scholarly disputes." The contributor also commented that "the author's focus on Cortés's hypocrisy (thus personalizing responsibility for the Spanish Inquisition and Reconquest) is especially interesting given the author's more nuanced understanding of ritual human sacrifice on what is likely the largest scale in human history."

*Booklist* contributor Jay Freeman observed that "this is a superb work of popular history, ideal for general readers." A contributor to *Kirkus Reviews* commented that the book "conveys with ghastly power the relentlessness of [the conquistadors], the tragedy of [the Aztec leader], the brutality of battle and the utter bewilderment of one culture in the face of the other." Stephen H. Peters, reviewing the book in *Library Journal,* remarked that "this well-written book is a good starting point for those seeking to understand the conquest of Mexico."

## River of Darkness

Levy published *River of Darkness: Francisco Orellana's Legendary Voyage of Death and Discovery down the Amazon,* in 2011. The account covers the sixteenth-century expedition of Spanish conquistador Francisco Orellana along the Amazon River in search of El Dorado. In his race against conquistador Gonzalo Pizarro, Orellana and his men became the first Europeans to navigate the entire length of the large river and to encounter the numerous tribes of the Amazon Basin.

Writing in the *A.V. Club,* Rowan Kaiser observed that "Levy is clearly fascinated by Orellana, and does his best to humanize the conquistador." Kaiser also pointed out that "Levy successfully conveys the Amazon's power and majesty, while shedding light on the futility of humanity's attempt to tame it." In a review in the *Wall Street Journal,* Gerard Helferich stated: "Focused on adventure more than reflection, Mr. Levy rushes along almost as resolutely as Orellana himself without lingering over the moral ambiguities of his hero's predicament." Writing in the Portland *Oregonian,* Katie Schneider exclaimed: "The dramatic title says it all." Calling *River of Darkness* "a treasure hunt of history," in *BookPage,* John T. Slania called the account "a worthwhile read because of such swashbuckling adventure," adding that "Levy is a gifted writer who makes it all the more enjoyable; his narrative flows as smoothly and rapidly as the Amazon River." Writing in the *Washington Times,* Stephen Goode lauded that "Levy tells Orellana's riveting story with the ease of someone who has mastered the material and loves the story he's telling."

## ■ Biographical And Critical Sources

### PERIODICALS

*Booklist,* December 15, 2005, George Cohen, review of *American Legend: The Real-life Adventures of David Crockett,* p. 15; June 1, 2008, Jay Freeman, review of *Conquistador: Hernán Cortés, King Montezuma, and the Last Stand of the Aztecs,* p. 25.

*Kirkus Reviews,* April 15, 2008, review of *Conquistador;* December 15, 2010, review of *River of Darkness: Francisco Orellana's Legendary Voyage of Death and Discovery down the Amazon.*

*Library Journal,* May 15, 2008, Stephen H. Peters, review of *Conquistador,* p. 113.

*Oregonian* (Portland, OR), July 9, 2011, Katie Schneider, review of *River of Darkness.*

*Publishers Weekly,* November 28, 2005, review of *American Legend,* p. 35; January 10, 2011, review of *River of Darkness,* p. 41.

*Roundup,* October, 2007, review of *American Legend,* p. 24.

*Wall Street Journal,* July 10, 2008, Arthur Herman, review of *Conquistador,* p. A13; February 22, 2011, Gerard Helferich, review of *River of Darkness.*

*Washington Post Book World,* December 17, 2006, Rachel Hartigan Shea, review of *American Legend,* p. 11.

*Washington Times,* May 16, 2011, Stephen Goode, review of *River of Darkness.*

ONLINE

*A.V. Club,* http://www.avclub.com/ (March 17, 2011), Rowan Kaiser, review of *River of Darkness.*

*BookPage,* http://www.bookpage.com/ (August 13, 2011), John T. Slania, review of *River of Darkness.*

*Buddy Levy Home Page,* http://www.buddylevy.com (August 13, 2011).

*Cadre Comments,* http://christiancadre.blogspot.com/ (January 6, 2009), review of *Conquistador.*

*Current Intelligence,* http://www.currentintelligence.com/ (December 9, 2010), John Matthew Barlow, author interview.

*GoodReads,* http://www.goodreads.com/ (August 13, 2011), author profile.

*Red Room,* http://www.redroom.com/ (February 11, 2009), author profile.

*Washington State University, English Department Web site,* http://libarts.wsu.edu/english/ (August 13, 2011), author profile.

# Pauline Maier

## 1938-

### ■ Also Known As

Pauline Rubbelke Maier

### ■ Personal

Born April 27, 1938, in St. Paul, MN; daughter of Irvin Louis (a fireman) and Charlotte Rubbelke; married Charles Steven Maier (an academic), June 17, 1961; children: Andrea Nicole, Nicholas Winterer, Jessica Elizabeth Heine. *Education:* Radcliffe College, A.B., 1960; Harvard University, Ph.D., 1968; studied at the University of London. *Religion:* Roman Catholic.

### ■ Addresses

*Home*—Cambridge, MA. *Office*—History Faculty, Massachusetts Institute of Technology, 77 Massachusetts Ave., Bldg. E51-279, Cambridge, MA 02139. *E-mail*—pmaier@mit.edu.

### ■ Career

Academic and historian. University of Massachusetts—Boston, assistant professor, 1968-72, associate professor of history, 1972-77; University of Wisconsin—Madison, Robinson Edwards Professor of History, 1977-78; Massachusetts Institute of Technology, Cambridge, professor of history, beginning 1978, became William R. Kenan, Jr., Professor of American History. American Academy of Arts and Sciences history fellow. Has appeared on national television interviews and programs, including C-SPAN2, *Charlie Rose.*

### ■ Member

Society of American Historians (president, 2011), American Antiquarian Society, American Historical Association, Colonial Massachusetts Society.

### ■ Awards, Honors

Fulbright scholar, London School of Economics and Political Science, University of London, 1960-61; National Book Critics Circle Award nominee, 1997, for *American Scripture;* Killian Award, Massachusetts Institute of Technology, 1998; Douglass Adair Award for article in *William and Mary Quarterly;* George Washington Book Prize, 2011; Fraunces Tavern Museum Book Prize (shared with Ron Chernaw); Paolucci/Walter Bagehot Prize.

### ■ Writings

(Editor, with Bruce Bank and Brayton Polka) *A Select Bibliography of History,* revised edition, [Cambridge], 1963.

*From Resistance of Revolution: Colonial Radicals and the Development of American Opposition to Britain, 1765-1776,* Knopf (New York, NY), 1973.

(With Jack P. Greene) *Interdisciplinary Studies of the American Revolution,* Sage (Beverly Hills, CA), 1976.

(With Alfred Kazin and Michael G. Kammen) *Perspectives on the American Revolution: Lectures Presented at the York Campus, the Pennsylvania State University, April-May 1976,* Pennsylvania State University (York, PA), 1976.

*The Old Revolutionaries: Political Lives in the Age of Samuel Adams,* Knopf (New York, NY), 1980.

*Boston and New York in the Eighteenth Century,* American Antiquarian Society (Worcester, MA), 1981.

*The American People: A History,* D.C. Heath (Lexington, MA), 1986.

*American Scripture: Making the Declaration of Independence,* Knopf (New York, NY), 1997.

*The Declaration of Independence and the Constitution of the United States,* Bantam Books (New York, NY), 1998.

(With Merritt Roe Smith, Alexander Keyssar, and Daniel J. Kevles) *Inventing America: A History of the United States,* Norton (New York, NY), 2002.

*Declaring Independence: The Origin and Influence of America's Founding Document: Featuring the Albert H. Small Declaration of Independence Collection,* edited by Christian Y. Dupont and Peter S. Onuf, University of Virginia Library (Charlottesville, VA), 2008.

*Ratification: The People Debate the Constitution, 1787-1788,* Simon & Schuster (New York, NY), 2010.

Contributor to the *William and Mary Quarterly, Washington Post,* and *New York Times.*

## ■ Sidelights

Pauline Maier is the author of a number of books on American history, particularly the colonial period. Her *American Scripture: Making the Declaration of Independence* takes a look at the circumstances behind the writing of the Declaration of Independence. In *Inventing America: A History of the United States,* Maier and her coauthors present a history of the United States that highlights the role played by science and technology.

### American Scripture

Maier's *American Scripture* tells the story of how Thomas Jefferson and a committee including John Adams, Benjamin Franklin and others, was charged by the Continental Congress with writing a document declaring America's sovereignty. While Jefferson wrote most of the document, the committee edited and cut Jefferson's original text. Maier examines existing early drafts to explain what had been changed or deleted and why. She notes that the committee was under a severe time limit to produce the document and that Jefferson drew on earlier texts to complete his work on time.

Michael J. Ybarra in the *San Francisco Chronicle* found that Maier offers "a sharp and engaging textual analysis of the evolving document" and "has created an impressive piece of work herself: a meticulous examination of American history that is full of fascinating details and scintillating insights." Besides a careful analysis of the Declaration of Independence itself, Maier also presents "the context of the times in which it was written, as well as the English tradition of ideas, petitions and

declarations from whence it flowed," according to Steve Forbes in *Forbes* magazine. Some critics believed that Maier's book made Jefferson's role in writing the Declaration of Independence seem less important than it was. Milton R. Konvitz, in *New Leader,* pointed out that previous scholars already had acknowledged the role of others in writing and revising the Declaration. He noted that the section where the committee made the most changes, the list of grievances against King George III, was the least important section. "It is the first section that is transcendently and permanently valuable," Konvitz stated, "not only for Americans but for mankind. And that part is 99 per cent pure Jefferson." But Maier explained her feelings about Jefferson to Bonnie Blodgett in *MPLS-St. Paul* magazine: "I have no desire to debunk the man, only to cut him back to size." "In the end," R.S. Hill admitted in his review of the book for the *National Review,* "we know nothing that would deny Jefferson the principal credit" for writing the Declaration.

### Inventing America

Maier teamed with Merritt Roe Smith, Alexander Keyssar, and Daniel J. Kevles to write *Inventing America.* Taking the approach that America has always been a nation of innovation and creativity, the authors present the history of the United States as a series of creative ventures ranging from the invention of the electric light bulb to the idea of constitutional government. Among the new details provided by this focus on innovation is the reason why the American Civil War was so deadly—firearms had been built to be more accurate at a longer distance than ever before, but military strategy still called for soldiers to march in close ranks.

"Reading *Inventing America,* looking at the nation's history through the powerful lens of ceaseless innovation, you see events falling into place in ways they never have before," according to Malcolm Jones in *Newsweek.* Alan Earls, in the *Christian Science Monitor,* suggested that "the additional focus on invention and inventiveness as an important element in the nation's history adds interest and vitality to a familiar story. Indeed, this is probably a new dimension that most readers have not considered much before."

### Ratification

Maier published *Ratification: The People Debate the Constitution, 1787-1788,* in 2010. Meier traces the development of the Constitution's ratification by popularly elected state conventions between September 17, 1987, when the Federal Convention adjourned, and September 13, 1788, when the Confederation Congress officially declared the Constitution ratified. The book also includes a prologue that gives necessary background information by looking at George Washington's agonized decision to attend the Federal Convention, an epilogue that takes the story of amendments through the first Federal Congress, and a postscript that tells what happened to some prominent participants in the ratification debates. In this process, she elaborates on a fuller picture of the tug and pull that went on at the convention as different interests and individuals asserted their influence on the document.

Writing in *Library Journal*, Brian Odom claimed that "Maier's monumental study, filled with penetrating conclusions, stands presently as the authoritative account of the ratification of the Constitution." A *Kirkus Reviews* critic noted that Maier "brilliantly" works through the topic of her book, and described it as "a scrupulously even-handed presentation based on impressive scholarship." A contributor to *American Heritage* found the account to be "sweeping." Reviewing *Ratification* in *American Spectator*, John R. Coyne called *Ratification* a "solid and splendidly organized and written block of a book." Coyne observed that "Maier is scrupulously fair to the Anti-Federalists, and refuses to call them that." Coyne noted that the author "writes with a narrative flair and the conviction that history must be written to be read beyond the classroom. She succeeds admirably," pointing out that "if there's a flaw here, it's that Maier's portrait of Washington at this moment in his life is so compelling that he very nearly hijacks her work." *Booklist* reviewer Gilbert Taylor concluded that with this book, "Maier eruditely yet accessibly revives a neglected but critical passage in American history."

■ **Biographical And Critical Sources**

*PERIODICALS*

*American Archivist*, March 22, 2001, review of *American Scripture: Making the Declaration of Independence*, p. 159.

*American Heritage*, January 1, 2011, review of *Ratification: The People Debate the Constitution, 1787-1788*, p. 62.

*American Historical Review*, October 1, 1981, review of *The Old Revolutionaries: Political Lives in the Age of Samuel Adams*, p. 916; April 1, 1999, review of *American Scripture*, p. 560.

*American Spectator*, March 1, 2011, John R. Coyne, Jr., review of *Ratification*, p. 74.

*Booklist*, March 15, 1998, review of *American Scripture*, p. 1210; October 1, 2010, Gilbert Taylor, review of *Ratification*, p. 8.

*Books and Culture*, July 1, 1998, review of *American Scripture*, p. 18.

*Books of the Times*, December 1, 1980, review of *The Old Revolutionaries*, p. 585.

*Boston Globe*, October 27, 2002, Diana Muir, review of *Inventing America: A History of the United States*.

*Chicago Tribune Books*, August 10, 1997, review of *American Scripture*, p. 4.

*Choice*, March 1, 1981, review of *The Old Revolutionaries*, p. 1013; November 1, 1997, review of *American Scripture*, p. 549.

*Christian Science Monitor*, January 2, 2003, Alan Earls, review of *Inventing America*.

*Contemporary Review*, August 1, 1999, review of *American Scripture*, p. 107.

*Curriculum Review*, September 1, 1987, review of *The American People: A History*, p. 50.

*Economist*, December 6, 1997, review of *American Scripture*, p. 95.

*Entertainment Close-Up*, May 31, 2011, "Pauline Maier Wins the George Washington Book Prize for Ratification."

*Forbes*, August 24, 1998, Steve Forbes, review of *American Scripture*, p. 32.

*Historian*, November 1, 1981, review of *The Old Revolutionaries*, p. 116.

*Journal of American History*, June 1, 1981, review of *The Old Revolutionaries*, p. 115.

*Journal of Popular Culture*, November 1, 2003, Amos St. Germain, review of *Inventing America*, p. 367.

*Journal of Southern History*, February 1, 1999, review of *American Scripture*, p. 151.

*Kirkus Reviews*, July 15, 1980, review of *The Old Revolutionaries*, p. 962; May 1, 1997, review of *American Scripture*, p. 700; August 15, 2010, review of *Ratification*.

*Kliatt*, November 1, 1998, review of *American Scripture*, p. 32.

*LC Information Bulletin*, August 1, 1997, John Martin, "American Scripture: Author Pauline Maier and the Declaration of Independence."

*Library Journal*, August 1, 1980, review of *The Old Revolutionaries*, p. 1630; June 1, 1997, review of *American Scripture*, p. 114; September 15, 2010, Brian Odom, review of *Ratification*, p. 85.

*Los Angeles Times Book Review*, August 10, 1997, review of *American Scripture*, p. 8.

*MIT News*, May 28, 1998, "MIT Historian Pauline Maier, Author of *American Scripture*, Wins Coveted Faculty Award."

*MPLS-St. Paul,* November 1, 1997, Bonnie Blodgett, "Declarations under Glass," p. 62.

*National Review,* September 15, 1997, R.S. Hill, review of *American Scripture,* p. 76.

*New England Quarterly,* March 1, 1998, review of *American Scripture,* p. 136.

*New Leader,* September 22, 1997, Milton R. Konvitz, review of *American Scripture,* p. 18.

*New Republic,* June 30, 1997, review of *American Scripture,* p. 34.

*Newsweek,* January 20, 2003, Malcolm Jones, review of *Inventing America.*

*New Yorker,* January 12, 1981, review of *The Old Revolutionaries,* p. 101; September 15, 1997, review of *American Scripture,* p. 87.

*New York Review of Books,* August 14, 1997, review of *American Scripture,* p. 37.

*New York Times Book Review,* October 12, 1980, review of *The Old Revolutionaries,* p. 12; July 6, 1997, review of *American Scripture,* p. 9; December 7, 1997, review of *American Scripture,* p. 12; July 5, 1998, review of *American Scripture,* p. 20; December 6, 1998, review of *American Scripture,* p. 96; September 15, 2002, Sylvia Nasar, review of *Inventing America,* p. 17.

*Political Science Quarterly,* June 22, 1981, review of *The Old Revolutionaries,* p. 353.

*PR Newswire,* May 25, 2011, "George Washington Book Prize Goes to Pauline Maier for Ratification."

*Publishers Weekly,* August 15, 1980, review of *The Old Revolutionaries,* p. 46; June 2, 1997, review of *American Scripture,* p. 59.

*Reference and User Services Quarterly,* March 22, 1998, review of *American Scripture,* p. 274.

*Review of Politics,* March 22, 1998, Michael Zuckert, review of *American Scripture,* p. 355.

*Reviews in American History,* September 1, 1981, review of *The Old Revolutionaries,* p. 330.

*San Francisco Chronicle,* June 29, 1997, Michael J. Ybarra, review of *American Scripture,* p. 5.

*Sewanee Review,* July 1, 1998, review of *American Scripture,* p. 505.

*Times Literary Supplement* (London, England), February 27, 1998, review of *American Scripture,* p. 28.

*Voice of Youth Advocates,* October 1, 1998, review of *American Scripture,* p. 255.

*Washington Post Book World,* July 6, 1997, review of *American Scripture,* p. 1; August 2, 1998, review of *American Scripture,* p. 12.

*William and Mary Quarterly,* July 1, 1982, review of *The Old Revolutionaries,* p. 557; July 1, 1998, review of *American Scripture,* p. 463.

*World and I,* November 1, 1997, review of *American Scripture,* p. 268.

ONLINE

*BookPage,* http://www.bookpage.com/ (July 1, 1997), Roger Bishop, review of *American Scripture.*

*Massachusetts Institute of Technology Web site,* http://web.mit.edu/ (August 14, 2011), author profile.

# Steve Martin

## 1945-

## ■ Personal

Born August 14, 1945, Waco, TX; son of Glenn (a realtor) and Mary Martin; married Victoria Tennant (an actress), 1986 (divorced, 1994); married Anne Stringfield (a writer), July 28, 2007. *Education:* Attended California State University, Long Beach and the University of California, Los Angeles. *Hobbies and other interests:* Reading old magic books, art books, museum catalogs, and the *New Yorker*, playing horseshoes, skiing.

## ■ Addresses

*Home*—Beverly Hills, CA. *Office*—P.O. Box 929, Beverly Hills, CA 90213. *Agent*—Ed Limato, International Creative Management, 8942 Wilshire Blvd., Beverly Hills, CA 90211.

## ■ Career

Comedian, actor, and writer. Partner in the Aspen Film Society and 40 Share Productions. Performer in coffeehouses, c. 1963; comedy writer for television programs, including *The Smothers Brothers Comedy Hour*, 1968, *The John Denver Rocky Mountain Christmas Show*, 1975, and *Van Dyke and Company*, 1975, and for performers, including Glen Campbell, Ray Stevens, Pat Paulsen, John Denver, and Sonny and Cher. Guest appearances on television programs, including *Saturday Night Live, The Tonight Show Starring Johnny Carson, Dinah!, The Merv Griffin Show, The Dick Cavett Show*; executive producer, *Domestic Life* (television series), Columbia Broadcasting System (CBS), 1984; actor in motion pictures, including *The Absent-Minded Waiter*, 1977, *The Jerk*, 1979, *Pennies from Heaven*, 1981, *Dead Men Don't Wear Plaid*, 1982, *The Man with Two Brains*, 1983, *The Lonely*

*Guy*, 1984, *All of Me*, 1984, *Little Shop of Horrors*, 1986, *Three Amigos!*, 1986, *Roxanne*, 1987, *Planes, Trains, and Automobiles*, 1987, *Dirty Rotten Scoundrels*, 1988, *Parenthood*, 1989, *My Blue Heaven*, 1990, *Father of the Bride*, 1991, *Grand Canyon*, 1991, *L.A. Story*, 1991, *Housesitter*, 1992, *Leap of Faith*, 1993, *Mixed Nuts*, 1994, *A Simple Twist of Fate*, 1994, *Father of the Bride Part II*, 1995, *Sgt. Bilko*, 1996, *Bowfinger*, 1999, *The Out of Towners*, 1999, *Joe Gould's Secret*, 2000, *Novocaine*, 2001, *Bringing Down the House*, 2003, *Cheaper by the Dozen*, 2003, *Shopgirl*, 2005, *Baby Mama*, 2008, *The Pink Panther 2*, 2009, and *It's Complicated*, 2009; also actor in (theater) *Waiting for Godot*, 1988, and (television) *And the Band Played On*, 1993.

Banjo musician for "Foggy Mountain Breakdown" and performer with In the Minds of the Living. Also worked at Disneyland and Knott's Berry Farm, early 1960s.

## ■ Member

Screen Actors Guild, American Guild of Variety Artists, American Federation of Television and Radio Artists.

## ■ Awards, Honors

Emmy Award, National Academy of Television Arts and Sciences, 1969, for best achievement in comedy, variety, or music for *The Smothers Brothers Comedy Hour*; Emmy Award nomination, 1975, for best writing in a comedy, variety, or music special for *Van Dyke and Company*; Georgie Award, American Guild of Variety Artists, 1977; Academy Award nomination, Academy of Motion Picture Arts and Sciences, 1977, for *The Absent-Minded Waiter*; Jack Benny Award, University of California at Los Angeles,

1978, for entertainment excellence; Grammy Award, National Academy of Recording Arts and Sciences, 1978, for *Let's Get Small*, and 1979, for *A Wild and Crazy Guy*; National Society of Film Critics Award and New York Film Critics Circle Award, both 1984, both for role in *All of Me*; best actor award, Los Angeles Film Critics Association, and best screenplay award, Writers Guild of America, both 1987, both for *Roxanne*; two New York Critics Outer Circle Awards, best play and best playwright, 1996, for *Picasso at the Lapin Agile*; Boston Film Excellence Award, 2001. Grammy Award for best country instrumental performance, 2002, for "Foggy Mountain Breakdown"; Mark Twain Prize for American Humor, 2002; Disney Legend Award, 2005; 30th Annual Kennedy Center Honors, 2007; Grammy Award for best bluegrass album, 2009, for *The Crow: New Songs for the 5-String Banjo*. Honorary Doctor of Humane Letters, California State University Long Beach, 1989.

■ **Writings**

*PLAYS*

*Picasso at the Lapin Agile* (also see below), first produced in Chicago by Steppenwolf Theater, 1993.
*WASP* (also see below), first produced in New York City at the Public Theater, 1995.
*Picasso at the Lapin Agile and Other Plays*, Grove Press (New York, NY), 1996.
*Meteor Shower*, first produced in Los Angeles, 1997.
*WASP and Other Plays*, Samuel French (New York, NY), 1998.

*SCREENPLAYS*

*The Absent-Minded Waiter*, Paramount (Los Angeles, CA), 1977.
(With Carl Reiner) *The Jerk*, Universal (Los Angeles, CA), 1979.
(With Carl Reiner and George Gipe) *Dead Men Don't Wear Plaid*, Universal (Los Angeles, CA), 1982.
(Coauthor) *The Man with Two Brains*, Warner Bros. (Los Angeles, CA), 1983.
(With Lorne Michaels and Randy Newman; and executive producer) *Three Amigos!*, Orion (Los Angeles, CA), 1986.
(And executive producer) *Roxanne* (based on *Cyrano de Bergerac* by Edmond Rostand), Columbia (Los Angeles, CA), 1987.
*L.A. Story*, Tri-Star (Los Angeles, CA), 1991.
*A Simple Twist of Fate* Buena Vista Pictures (Los Angeles, CA), 1994.

*L.A. Story* [and] *Roxanne: Two Screenplays*, Grove Press (New York, NY), 1997.
*Bowfinger*, Universal (Los Angeles, CA), 1999.
*Shopgirl* (based on Martin's novella, see below), Touchstone Pictures (Burbank, CA), 2005.

*RECORDINGS*

*Let's Get Small*, Warner Bros. (Los Angeles, CA), 1977.
*A Wild and Crazy Guy*, Warner Bros. (Los Angeles, CA), 1978.
*King Tut*, Warner Bros. (Los Angeles, CA), 1978.
*Comedy Is Not Pretty* (also see below), Warner Bros. (Los Angeles, CA), 1979.
*The Steve Martin Brothers*, Warner Bros. (Los Angeles, CA), 1982.
*The Crow: New Songs for the 5-String Banjo*, 40 Share Productions, 2009.

*TELEPLAYS*

*Steve Martin: A Wild and Crazy Guy*, National Broadcasting Corporation (NBC), 1978.
*Comedy Is Not Pretty*, NBC, 1980.
*Steve Martin's Best Show Ever*, NBC, 1981.

*FICTION*

*Pure Drivel* (stories), Hyperion (New York, NY), 1998.
*Shopgirl* (novella), Hyperion (New York, NY), 2000.
*The Pleasure of My Company* (novella), Hyperion (New York, NY), 2003.
*An Object of Beauty* (novel), Grand Central (New York, NY), 2010.

*OTHER*

*Cruel Shoes* (humorous sketches), Press of the Pegacycle Lady (Los Angeles, CA), 1977, revised and enlarged edition, Putnam (New York, NY), 1979.
*Born Standing Up: A Comic's Life* (memoir), Scribner (New York, NY), 2007.
(With Roz Chast) *The Alphabet from A to Y with Bonus Letter Z!* (children's book), Flying Dolphin Press (New York, NY), 2007.
(With Arthur C. Danto and Robert Enright) *Eric Fischl, 1970-2007*, Monacelli Press (New York, NY), 2008.
*Late for School* (children's book), Grand Central (New York, NY), 2010.

Also adapted Carl Sternheim's play *The Underpants* for a production by the Classic Stage Company, 2002. Author of the concept for the film *Traitor*, screenplay by Jeffrey Nachmanoff, Overture Films, 2008. Contributor of essays to *New Yorker, Rolling Stone,* and *New York Times.*

## ■ Adaptations

*Picasso at the Lapin Agile*, adapted and directed by Fred Schepisi, was produced in 2003.

## ■ Sidelights

"Well, EXCUUUUSE MEEEE!!!" Steve Martin would roar during his stand-up comedy routine, his entire body shaking with indignation, and the audience, many sporting giant bunny ears or a fake arrow through the head, would erupt with howls, cheers, and an ovation comparable to those heard at rock concerts. The bizarre incongruity of a junior-executive type wearing balloons on his head, latex nose and glasses, and a white, custom-tailored, three-piece suit struck the perfect chord with American audiences in the 1970s. Martin's sudden attacks of "happy feet" took him lurching across the stage; he twisted balloons into absurd shapes, then named them "Puppy dog! Venereal disease! The Sistine Chapel!" He performed magic tricks that did not quite work. But most of all, Martin parodied the whole idea of a comedian standing on stage telling jokes. Playing the part of a "wild and crazy guy," Martin became one of the most notable stand-up comics of the decade. His first two comedy albums won Grammy Awards and sold millions of copies; he scored a hit single with the absurd song "King Tut"; and the book *Cruel Shoes*, his collection of humorous sketches, was a national best seller. By 1979 Martin had graduated to films, making the box-office smash *The Jerk* and following with a string of other films throughout the 1980s. His performance in 1984's *All of Me* earned popular acclaim as well as awards from the National Society of Film Critics and the New York Film Critics Circle. *Roxanne* showed him capable of touching character portrayals, while *Planes, Trains, and Automobiles* gave Martin the chance to play the straight man.

In the 1990s Martin's evolution continued, this time in unexpected directions. He began to write pieces for the *New Yorker*, and these reflected not only his comedic talents but a literary bent as well. He also began to write plays, including the popular *Picasso at the Lapin Agile*. The dawn of the twenty-first century found Martin to be less engaged in television and film comedy and more engaged in serious creative endeavors, including his well-received novellas, *Shopgirl* and *The Pleasure of My Company.*

Martin's fascination with the entertainment world stems back to his childhood. He was stage-struck at the age of three and grew up idolizing such comedians as Laurel and Hardy, Jerry Lewis, and Red Skelton. By the age of five, he was memorizing Red Skelton's television skits and performing them at school show-and-tells. When his family moved to California, he hiked over to the new Disneyland amusement park and got a part-time job selling guidebooks, magic tricks, and Frontierland rodeo ropes.

During working hours he would sneak away to watch an old vaudevillian comic, Wally Boag, at Disneyland's Golden Horseshoe Revue. The comedian performed a routine of songs, jokes, and balloon tricks that Martin committed to memory. Soon Martin was performing the tricks he sold, twirling a lasso, playing the banjo, and appearing in a Boag production called "It's Vaudeville Again." After eight years at the Magic Kingdom, Martin left for nearby Knott's Berry Farm to act in melodrama at the Birdcage Theatre and perform his own fifteen-minute routines of comedy, magic, and banjo music.

Martin's budding career was cut short by his discovery of education. He fell in love with Stormy, an actress in the Birdcage company, who persuaded him to read Somerset Maugham's *The Razor's Edge*. Afterward, Martin enrolled at Long Beach State College where he studied philosophy for the next three years. But when he came across the arguments of Ludwig Wittgenstein concerning semantics and the philosopher's contention that nothing was absolutely true, his interest in philosophy waned. He transferred to the University of California and changed his major to theater.

### Comedy

Martin's first big break in show business came when he submitted some of his written material to Mason Williams, the head writer for CBS-TV's *The Smothers Brothers Comedy Hour*. At the time, Martin was broke, living in a maid's quarters in Bel Air, struggling as a performer at small clubs and coffeehouses, and studying television writing at UCLA. Williams invited him to join the writing staff of the show, one of the highest-rated on television at the time. CBS cancelled the show in 1968, but Martin and the show's ten other writers won an Emmy for their work. The award tripled Martin's value as a writer, and he was soon making 1,500 dollars a week writing for entertainers like Glen Campbell, Ray Stevens, Pat Paulsen, John Denver, and Sonny and Cher. Still, his ambition was to work onstage: "I decided to stop writing for other people and perform full-time again," he told Kathy Lowry in the *New Times*. "I was bored with writing all that formula stuff. I wanted to deal directly with the audience."

The early 1970s proved to be a dismal period in Martin's career. He took his stand-up act on the road, playing every small club he could find and opening for rock groups whose drugged, impatient audiences shouted him off the stage. "Back then they didn't know what a comedian was," Martin told Janet Coleman in *New York*. He later satirized the period in one of his routines: a marijuana-smoking hippie is watching Martin perform, nods slowly, then drawls, "These guys are *good*." Coleman noted that Martin is "still annoyed by the ritual sloppiness and inattention of the 'love generation' audience."

Success as a stand-up comedian came when Martin developed a distinctive stage persona. He was a pioneer of postmodernist comedy, or comedy poking fun at the entertainment industry itself. When doing his act, Martin became a parody of a comedian. His character was shallow and slick, desperate for acceptance, full of insincere show-business asides to the audience, and unaware of his own stupidity. Balloon gags, juggling, banjo playing, and rabbit ears were all used in a deliberately hokey attempt to get laughs.

His usual performance would begin with Martin walking out in his six-hundred-dollar white suit, an expensive banjo slung over his shoulder, and announcing: "Hi, I'm Steve Martin, and I'll be out in *just* a minute!" For a few moments, he would goof in the spotlight, hum to himself, look around aimlessly. He was "waiting for the drugs to take effect," he would explain. Then: "Okay, you paid the money, you're expecting to see a professional show, so let's not waste any more time, here we go with Professional Show Business, let's go, hey!" He would step back, start tuning the banjo, plucking one string then another, turning a peg or two, then move up and smash his nose into the microphone. "Okay, we're moving now, eh folks? Yes, these are the good times and we're having them, ah ha ha ha."

"And that's the whole point." Lowry explained: "Steve Martin just wants to get a laugh; he doesn't much care about being profound or pricking society's conscience." Speaking to a *U.S. News & World Report* interviewer, Martin revealed: "The '60s was a time of humorlessness in America. Everybody was so dead earnest. . . . During this time, the cheapest way to get a laugh was to make a political joke. . . . When I made my breakthrough in comedy in the early 1970s, politics was very much on everybody's mind. I saw it as my job to take it off their minds and so left politics out of my comedy. I think that was a big part of my success. There was no moralizing, no left, no right; it was just about a human being."

### Film

Martin transferred his stage persona to the screen in 1979's *The Jerk,* a film that grossed over seventy million dollars at the box office. Playing the white son in a poor black family (obviously an adopted son, but Martin doesn't realize it), he goes on to win and lose a fortune with a crazy invention. Audiences loved the movie, but critics found it wanting, expecting it to be somehow more "relevant" or provocative. Martin's next few efforts were also met with critical coolness. Audience appeal was also limited. *Pennies from Heaven*, a lush musical set in the 1930s, lost money; *Dead Men Don't Wear Plaid*, a spoof of the hard-boiled detective genre that incorporated scenes from vintage movies, was a box-office disappointment.

It was only with *All of Me*, in which Martin costarred with Lily Tomlin, that he discovered a comfortable screen character. Ironically for the comic who had made his reputation as a "wild man," Martin's new character was a normal fellow who is beset with unusual problems. In the film, Martin plays a lawyer who becomes possessed by the spirit of a dead woman. One side of his body is controlled by the woman, the other side by him. Martin's amazing ability to portray this absurd physical condition—half male and half female—drew widespread critical praise and won him two major film awards as well. In addition to the film's physical humor, Jack Barth maintained in *Film Comment*: "*All of Me* is Martin's first comedy to subjugate gags to story and characterization. . . . [It] is also the first Martin film to deliver a satisfying ending." The result pleased the film-going public as well as the critics.

Martin further developed his new screen character in subsequent films, particularly in *Roxanne*, a gentle, updated version of the classic *Cyrano de Bergerac*. Martin plays a small-town fireman with an absurdly long nose. Called upon to help a friend woo the new woman in town, Martin falls in love with her himself.

By the late 1980s Martin had left his stand-up "wild and crazy" image behind him. He had become, in the words of Richard Corliss in *Time*, "this decade's most charming and resourceful comic actor." A wide variety of film comedy roles were suddenly available to him. In *Planes, Trains, and Automobiles* Martin played the straight man to John Candy, in *Dirty Rotten Scoundrels* he played a con man with Michael Caine, and in *Parenthood* he was a middle-class father. And all three films, in pleasant contrast to several earlier Martin efforts, were solid box-office hits.

## Writing

Martin's fame as a film star has overshadowed the considerable efforts he has put into writing over the years. He created his own stand-up comedy routines and has screenplay credits in many of his films, including *Dead Men Don't Wear Plaid, L.A. Story, Roxanne*, and *Bowfinger*. It was therefore a natural progression for him to move into other genres as a creative writer, and he has enjoyed some significant successes with plays, essays, and fiction. In 1993 his play *Picasso at the Lapin Agile* had its premiere in Chicago at the Steppenwolf Theater Company, and the show has since been performed on national tour and in London. The play provides a whimsical look at what might have happened if Albert Einstein, Pablo Picasso, and Elvis Presley all met at a celebrated Parisian bar circa 1910. *WASP,* another Martin theater piece, made its debut at New York City's Public Theater.

Another breakthrough for Martin occurred when the *New Yorker* began to publish his humorous essays. These pieces, collected in the book *Pure Drivel*, demonstrate his facility with wordplay as well as his talent as a satirist. "Twenty years ago you wouldn't have thought of Steve in the tradition of James Thurber and S.J. Perelman, but now he's really established himself as a prose writer," noted publisher David Ebershoff in the online *Yahoo! News.* Ebershoff added: "Steve is a rare figure in American humor because these days, rightly or wrongly, humor is thought of in terms of performance and not writing." In her *New York Times Book Review* critique of *Pure Drivel*, Susan Shapiro praised the work for its "chameleon quality," noting that the tone "ranges from parody to irony to just plain silliness." *Booklist* correspondent Donna Seaman commended *Pure Drivel* for its "intelligent, innovative, and self-conscious humor." Seaman also observed that Martin crafts prose "as notable for its meticulousness as for its drollery." A *Kirkus Reviews* critic deemed the pieces "lighter-than-air mockery. Often ingenious."

*Shopgirl,* Martin's first novella, shows the artist working a different vein of material. While not completely lacking in humor, the tale of a young store clerk and her affair with a noncommittal middle-aged businessman is an earnest exploration of mismanaged relationships and thwarted ambitions. "The funny thing about Steve Martin's first work of extended fiction, *Shopgirl,* is that it's not funny," wrote Richard Corliss in *Time.* "*Shopgirl* . . . offers quieter pleasures: a delicate portrait of people inflicting subtle pain on others and themselves, and an appeal to the intelligent heart." In the *New York Times Book Review,* John Lanchester described the novella as "elegant, bleak, desolatingly sad," adding that the work "has an edge to it, and a deep unassuageable loneliness. Steve Martin's most achieved work to date may well have the strange effect of making people glad not to be Steve Martin." A *Publishers Weekly* reviewer was impressed by Martin's ability to write serious fiction, concluding that *Shopgirl* is "yet another of this intelligent performer's attempts to expand his range." Bonnie Smothers made a similar observation in *Booklist* when she suggested that the novella "may mark a new direction in a noteworthy writer's career."

Martin's second novella, *The Pleasure of My Company,* is about a somewhat neurotic, obsessive-compulsive man, Daniel Pecan Cambridge, who lives alone in a rundown Santa Monica, California, apartment. Cambridge cannot hold a job and passes his dull, lonely days imagining romances and awaiting visits from his social worker. He is also driven to keep exactly 1,125 watts of lightbulbs burning at all times in his apartment, and he relies on driveways when walking around his neighborhood since he cannot bring himself to step over curbs. A *Publishers Weekly* reviewer found the book to be "funnier than *Shopgirl* but put together just as smartly," adding: "What's most remarkable about it, though, is its tenderness, a complex mix of wit, poignancy and Martin's clear, great affection for his characters." A critic in *Kirkus Reviews* agreed that *The Pleasure of My Company* is "a joy. . . . Although Martin succumbs to a banal plot choice later on, when his neurotic goes on a road trip, this is a genuinely funny and surprisingly touching tale."

Continuing his authorial efforts, Martin wrote two children's books, a memoir about his comedic career, and the novel *An Object of Beauty.* His heroine, Lacey Yeager is an arts world dealer in New York City during the late 1990s. She sleeps with her clients and deals easily with the dark underbelly of the art world. Through her ruthless actions, Lacey is finally able to open her own gallery. Lacey's art world life progresses toward the inevitable; although the 9/11 attacks shake Manhattan, Lacey remains unfazed, driven only by her unchecked ambition. The story is narrated by Lacey's friend, reporter Daniel Franks, and critics have noted that the narrator may be a stand-in for Martin himself.

Martin "offers an enlightening explication" of the art world Joanne Wilkinson commented in *Booklist.* "This thoroughly engaging primer on the art world is unusual on a number of levels." Craig Seligman, writing in *Hollywood Reporter,* proffered praise as well, asserting: "The book is a treat, and with the unsentimental Lacey as its heroine, it's harder-edged than Martin's previous novels." Seligman then observed: "You might think somebody who makes it as a comic, an actor, a playwright, a novelist, a collector and even a musician would inspire envy instead of affection. Some people you just can't dislike." *An Object of Beauty* is "an ambitious and heartfelt analysis of both the complexity and absurdity of the Manhattan art market," a *Kirkus Reviews* critic declared. It is also "an artfully told tale of trade, caste and the obsessive mindset of collectors." According to Ian Dunlop in the *Spectator,* "Martin has . . . avoided the obvious storylines of most art novels. So although a stolen work of art is mentioned, it is a minor diversion from the main plot. Nor is it a simple romantic comedy, where the girl eventually finds the right man. The book is subtler than that because it has something intelligent to say about how taste and collecting have changed over the past ten years." Offering additional applause in her *New York Times Book Review* article, Alexandra Jacobs remarked: "The expertise of Martin, himself a longtime collector . . . is dazzlingly in evidence here. The text is as useful an idiosyncratic art-history primer as it is a piece of fiction." She added that the novel "is thoroughly delightful, evoking a vanished gilded age with impertinence but never contempt (and with a feather-light touch; the terrorist attacks of Sept. 11, for example, appear literally as a minor impediment to Lacey's bicycle ride down the primrose path)."

Martin has noted that he does not intend to retire from films, but that he is encouraged by the new direction his career has taken and by what serious writing has taught him. He told the *Detroit Free Press:* "It was time to focus on a more narrow range of interest. I talk to my friend Marty Short about this conscious withdrawal from competing in the Hollywood world. It would be embarrassing if we didn't. I know a little bit more about myself now, enough to write. I know now that other people exist." Asked by the *Knight-Ridder/Tribune News Service* about his methods, he said: "I'm lazy. I do most of my writing when I'm on my bicycle in the park, and I come home and type it up. So when I get a line, I always remember where I was when I wrote it. It's sort of nice actually—like remembering where you were when you first met someone."

## ■ Biographical And Critical Sources

### BOOKS

*Contemporary Literary Criticism,* Volume 30, Gale (Detroit, MI), 1984.

Lenburg, Greg, Randy Skretvedt, and Jeff Lenburg, *Steve Martin: The Unauthorized Biography,* St. Martin's Press (New York, NY), 1980.

Martin, Steve, *Born Standing Up: A Comic's Life,* Scribner (New York, NY), 2007.

### PERIODICALS

*Booklist,* September 1, 1998, Donna Seaman, review of *Pure Drivel;* July, 2000, Bonnie Smothers, review of *Shopgirl,* p. 1974; September 1, 2010, Joanne Wilkinson, review of *An Object of Beauty,* p. 45.

*Detroit Free Press,* November 1, 2000, Bruce Weber, "Actor Branches Out to Book Writing," p. D9.

*Film Comment,* January, 1979, Jack Barth, review of *All of Me.*

*Hollywood Reporter,* December 8, 2010, Craig Seligman, review of *An Object of Beauty,* p. 64.

*Kirkus Reviews,* September 1, 1998, review of *Pure Drivel;* August 1, 2003, review of *The Pleasure of My Company,* p. 982; April 1, 2008, review of *The Alphabet from A to Y with Bonus Letter Z!;* August 1, 2010, review of *Late for School;* August 1, 2010, Ilene Cooper, review of *An Object of Beauty.*

*Knight-Ridder/Tribune News Service,* December 6, 1995, Chris Hewitt, "Steve Martin Downplays His Contribution to *Father of the Bride* Sequel," p. K2855; April 11, 1997, Lynn Carey, "Probing the Agile Comic Mind behind *Picasso at the Lapin Agile,*" p. K6300; October 18, 2000, John Mark Eberhart, "More Writers Find Solace in the Novella," p. K4898.

*Library Journal,* November 15, 2007, Richard A. Dickey, review of *Born Standing Up,* p. 61; September 1, 2010, Christine Perkins, review of *An Object of Beauty,* p. 103.

*New Republic,* March 11, 1991, Stanley Kauffmann, review of *L.A. Story,* p. 28.

*New Statesman,* January 7, 2008, "Star Quality," p. 53.

*New Times,* September 2, 1977, Kathy Lowry, interview with Steve Martin.

*New York,* August 22, 1977, Janet Coleman, interview with Steve Martin.

*New York Times Book Review,* September 13, 1998, Susan Shapiro, review of *Pure Drivel;* October 29, 2000, John Lanchester, "The Counter Life"; November 28, 2010, Alexandra Jacobs, "Only Collect," p. 9.

*People,* February 25, 1991, Ralph Novak, review of *L.A. Story,* p. 11; October 16, 2000, Kyle Smith, review of *Shopgirl,* p. 55.

*Publishers Weekly,* August 7, 2000, review of *Shopgirl,* p. 72; September 15, 2003, review of *The Pleasure of My Company,* p. 44; October 1, 2007, review of *The Alphabet from A to Y with Bonus Letter Z!,* p. 55; December 31, 2007, review of *Born Standing Up,* p. 39; August 9, 2010, review of *Late for School,* p. 49; September 27, 2010, review of *An Object of Beauty,* p. 34.

*Saturday Evening Post,* March 1, 2008, "A Comedian's Memoir: Steve Martin Looks Back at a Person He Used to Know."

*School Library Journal,* January 1, 2008, Donna Cardon, review of *The Alphabet from A to Y with Bonus Letter Z!,* p. 144.

*Spectator,* November 27, 2010, Ian Dunlop, "Ring of Truth," p. 40.

*Texas Monthly,* December 1, 2007, Mike Shea, review of *Born Standing Up,* p. 74.

*Time,* October 16, 2000, Richard Corliss, "But Seriously, Folks: Steve Martin Talks about His First Novella, a Delicate, Poignant Modern Romance about a Shy Shopgirl," p. 113.

*U.S. News & World Report,* June 17, 1985, interview with Steve Martin.

ONLINE

*ABC News.com,* http://abcnews.go.com/ (October 19, 2000), Buck Wolf, "Steve Martin, Renaissance Clown."

*Steve Martin Home Page,* http://www.stevemartin.com (October 19, 2000).

*Yahoo! News,* http://dailynews.yahoo.com/ (October 4, 2000), Hillel Italie, "Steve Martin Gets Literary."*

# Helena McEwen

## 1961-

### ■ Personal

Born March, 1961, in Marchmont, Scotland. *Education:* Chelsea School of Art, B.A. (with honors), 1989; Kensington and Chelsea College, city and guilds teacher's training certificate, 1995.

### ■ Addresses

*Home*—Scotland. *Agent*—A.M. Heath, 6 Warwick Ct., London WC1R 5DJ, England.

### ■ Career

Painter, writer, and educator. Teacher of painting and drawing classes and workshops for adults and children at art galleries in Sheffield, England, 1995-98; Kensington and Chelsea College, London, England, painting teacher, 1998-2000, 2003. Teacher of creative expression workshops, 1997; Chelsea Estates Youth Group, leader of arts activities, 1999-2000; Trinity Hospice, facilitator, 2001; Hypatia Trust, creative writing teacher, 2004-05; University College Falmouth, part-time lecturer, 2005-06; gives readings from her works.

### ■ Awards, Honors

J.B. Priestley Award for writer of outstanding promise, 2006.

### ■ Writings

NOVELS

*The Big House*, Bloomsbury (London, England), 1999.
*Ghost Girl*, Bloomsbury (London, England), 2004.

*Invisible River*, Bloomsbury USA (New York, NY), 2011.

### ■ Sidelights

Helena McEwen was born and raised in Scotland. She studied painting in the late 1980s at the Chelsea School of Art and subsequently taught painting and drawing classes and workshops for adults and children at art galleries in Sheffield, England. McEwen also taught painting at London's Kensington and Chelsea College and University College Falmouth.

### *The Big House* and *Ghost Girl*

McEwen's debut novel, *The Big House,* has been compared with the work of such writers as Katherine Mansfield and D.H. Lawrence. The story opens with the suicide of the narrator's brother, James, and the drowning death of her sister, Kitty. To cope with the loss of her siblings, the narrator, Elizabeth, returns to her childhood home and relives childhood memories. Christina Patterson wrote in the London *Observer:* "Elizabeth returns to her memories of childhood in a large Scottish mansion. She describes, with breathtaking clarity and simplicity, a world of nursery teas, roaring fires, fierce nannies, hunts and a mother who sweeps in and out of the children's orbit." "McEwen writes with such fierce charm and conviction, and the world she creates is so hermetically complete, that there is barely a chink for doubt to creep in," observed reviewer Candice Rodd in the London *Times Literary Supplement.* "McEwen succeeds brilliantly in capturing those universal themes of childhood: fear, confusion and wonder," commented Frances Atkinson in the Melbourne *Age.*

*Ghost Girl,* while not a sequel, explores the next stage in the growth of a young girl. Cath is about thirteen when her parents, posted to faraway lands, enroll her in a convent boarding school. They entrust her holiday supervision to her older sister Verity, a would-be artist who lives and looks for adventure in the bohemian neighborhoods of 1970s London. The contrast between school and city—forbidding religious atmosphere versus liberating decadence of the outside world—enables McEwen to depict the soul of a girl who belongs to neither world, a girl who spends much of her time inside her own head while her body drifts in ghostly fashion from one venue to the other. As Jennie Renton described it in the *Glasgow Sunday Herald:* "With a clairvoyant acuity that refuses to be staunched, Cath discovers a sense of belonging in her own cosmic vision." *Ghost Girl* earned its author the serious attention of several critics. Kate Salter observed in the London *Times Literary Supplement* that "*Ghost Girl* succeeds in rising above more conventional treatments of [coming of age in the 1970s] chiefly thanks to the authenticity of its central voice." *Time Out* contributor Anna Scott wrote: "McEwen captures the impressionability of youth, as well as the visceral nature of emotions which have yet to be dulled by experience."

### Invisible River

In 2011, McEwen published the novel *Invisible River.* Eve finds freedom studying painting in London after growing up with her alcoholic father in Cornwall. Happy for the first time in her life, she is forced to deal with her turbulent past when her father arrives in London in worse shape than ever before.

Writing in the London *Guardian,* Shena Mackay observed that the novel "is about looking, seeing and understanding, about passing through the invisible curtain that separates one reality from another, and it is an evocative reminder of how it feels to be young." London *Telegraph* contributor Amanda Craig opined, however, that "what is genuinely captivating about *Invisible River* is, however, not its story of young love, but its glowing portrait of London, and 'the feeling of hope, of possibilities that London exudes.'" Reviewing the novel in the London *Independent,* Lesley McDowell remarked that "McEwen's very spare and precise prose makes private moments of intensity vibrate with emotion." A *Kirkus Reviews* critic stated: "Banality and radiance combine oddly in a novel

that achieves immediacy but risks claustrophobia." Writing in the Edinburgh *Scotsman,* Allan Massie noted that "it would seem that she writes only when she has something to say, and perhaps mostly out of her own experience, or her experience as she imagines it might have been. That may make her sound the literary equivalent of a Sunday painter, but there is nothing amateurish about her writing."

## ■ Biographical And Critical Sources

*PERIODICALS*

*Age* (Melbourne, Victoria, Australia), March 20, 2000, Frances Atkinson, review of *The Big House.*

*Booklist,* December 15, 2010, Michele Leber, review of *Invisible River,* p. 19.

*Books,* March 22, 2001, review of *The Big House,* p. 20.

*Glasgow Sunday Herald* (Glasgow, Scotland), June 27, 2004, Jennie Renton, review of *Ghost Girl.*

*Guardian* (London, England), March 19, 2011, Shena Mackay, review of *Invisible River.*

*Independent* (London, England), January 16, 2000, Maggie O'Farrell, review of *The Big House;* February 6, 2011, Lesley McDowell, review of *Invisible River.*

*Kirkus Reviews,* December 15, 2010, review of *Invisible River.*

*Library Journal,* January 1, 2010, Mara Dabrishus, review of *Invisible River,* p. 85.

*Observer* (London, England), January 16, 2000, Christina Patterson, review of *The Big House,* p. 13.

*Publishers Weekly,* November 15, 2010, review of *Invisible River,* p. 36.

*Scotsman* (Edinburgh, Scotland), February 13, 2011, Allan Massie, review of *Invisible River.*

*Spectator,* January 29, 2000, Olivia Glazebrook, review of *The Big House,* p. 52.

*Telegraph* (London, England), February 22, 2011, Amanda Craig, review of *Invisible River.*

*Time Out,* July 30, 2004, Anna Scott, review of *Ghost Girl.*

*Times Literary Supplement* (London, England) January 14, 2000, Candice Rodd, review of *The Big House,* p. 27; June 11, 2004, Kate Salter, review of *Ghost Girl,* p. 20.

*ONLINE*

*Week,* http://www.theweek.co.uk/ (April 4, 2002), review of *The Big House.**

# Jonathan Miles

## 1952-

■ **Personal**

Born 1952; married; children: a daughter. *Education:* Graduated from University College (magna cum laude) and Jesus College, Ph.D.

■ **Addresses**

*Home*—Paris, France. *Agent*—Julian Alexander, LAW Writers' and Artists' Agency, 14 Vernon St., London W14 0RJ, England; George Lucase, Inkwell Management, 521 5th Ave., 25th Fl., New York, NY 10175.

■ **Career**

Art historian and writer. Has also worked as a lecturer.

■ **Writings**

*Backgrounds to David Jones: A Study in Sources and Drafts,* University of Wales Press (Cardiff, Wales), 1990.

*Eric Gill & David Jones at Capel-y-ffin,* Seren Books (Bridgend, Mid Glamorgan, Wales), 1992.

(With Derek Shiel) *David Jones: The Maker Unmade,* Seren (Bridgend, Mid Glamorgan, Wales), 1995.

*The Wreck of the Medusa,* Atlantic Monthly Press (New York, NY), 2007, published as *Medusa: The Shipwreck, the Scandal, the Masterpiece,* Jonathan Cape (London, England), 2007.

*The Dangerous Otto Katz: The Many Lives of a Soviet Spy,* Bloomsbury USA (New York, NY), 2010.

*The Dangerous Otto Katz* has been translated into French, Russian, and Czech.

■ **Sidelights**

Jonathan Miles is a writer whose works include books on the English poet and artist David Jones and a recounting of a famous sea disaster and the masterpiece it inspired. Born in 1952, he worked as an art historian and writer after earning degrees from University College and Jesus College. He was raised in the United States and Canada and has additionally worked as a lecturer.

*David Jones*

Miles and Derek Shiel wrote *David Jones: The Maker Unmade.* This illustrated book is a major critical study as well as a biography of Jones that introduces readers to both Jones's famous artwork and previously unpublished materials, including sketches, watercolors, carvings, engravings, and inscriptions. The authors place Jones within the context of twentieth-century British art and in relation to continental art movements as they discuss his many styles. Although he painted at a time when abstract art was gaining popularity, Jones was basically a religious artist who also painted dreamy landscapes and illustrated the tale of Lancelot and Guinevere.

In their study of Jones and his work, Miles and Shiel relate Jones's work to events in his life, including his experience as a soldier in World War I, his conversion to Catholicism, and his strong interest in neo-romantic symbolism and Celtic mysticism. They also detail the author's personal trials and tribulations, including poverty, mental breakdowns, and his ordeal with agoraphobia, a condition in which panic attacks become so severe that people often do not leave their homes. A *Publishers Weekly* contributor noted that the authors "have unearthed a trove of Jones's . . . [works], which will surprise even those familiar with Jones's writing and art."

## The Wreck of the Medusa

In *The Wreck of the Medusa*, published in England as *Medusa: The Shipwreck, the Scandal, the Masterpiece,* Miles interweaves the stories of a controversial shipwreck, the resulting political scandal, and the famous and initially highly controversial painting of the wreck by Théodore Géricault, titled *The Raft of the Medusa,* or *Le Radeau de la Méduse.*

The wreck occurred on July 2, 1816, when the French frigate *Medusa* struck a reef on its way to Senegal. The incompetent cowardly captain and his cronies took the lifeboats for themselves, setting 148 passengers and crew adrift on a rickety, makeshift raft. Of those on the raft, only fifteen survived, primarily by resorting to murder and cannibalism. An exposé written by a survivor named Alexandre Corréard accused the corrupt French Restoration government as being responsible for the tragedy because the captain was inexperienced but a friend of the government due to his anti-Bonapartist views. Writing in *Booklist,* Gilbert Taylor noted that the author "is wary about Corréard's factual fidelity, lending historical depth to the narrative." Nevertheless, Corréard's report inspired Géricault to make his masterpiece, a political statement that depicts the desperate survivors of the raft as it strikes the Bank of Arguin off the coast of Mauritania and they are apparently rescued.

Commenting on *The Wreck of the Medusa,* Miles told Anna Mundow in an interview for the *Boston Globe* that it was the painting that first inspired him to write the book. Miles noted: "I was looking at it in the Louvre—this was post 9/11 and before the Iraq invasion—and it struck me that the Medusa story had echoes for our time, with the West being steered towards disaster by leaders who don't understand what they are doing and, in the case of [President George W.] Bush, for very mixed motives. Then I read about Corréard, a marvelous, combative figure . . . who kept battering at the doors of the establishment. All of that hooked me into the story."

In his book, the author delves into the intense friendship that developed between survivor Corréard and artist Géricault, who went so far as to bring parts of cadavers back to his studio to inspire his painting and make it realistic. He also explores how the artist used the painting to make several statements about the French government. For example, as noted by Kelly Grovier in her London *Observer* review of the book, only one black man was on the raft but Géricault made the decision to include three. According to Grovier, these three "comprise a micro-drama within the larger tragedy," adding: "At the time of the shipwreck and the exhibition of the painting, France had resisted calls to extricate itself from the slave trade, generating the fog of moral failure from which the work summons much of its power. By depicting one of the three black men as dead, another frozen in anguish, and a third transfixed on a distant salvation, Géricault was advocating a social trajectory 'from despair and victimization to an enlightened future.'"

*The Wreck of the Medusa* received widespread critical acclaim from many reviewers. Noting that Miles, "the author of this excellent account, tells the story quickly and well," *American Scholar* contributor Anthony Brandt wrote in the same review: "Miles has taken a shipwreck and placed it into its political and historical and artistic context. We can only hope he writes more books as fine and compelling as *The Wreck of the Medusa.*" A *Kirkus Reviews* contributor referred to the book as a "diligent deconstruction of a shipwreck and a scandal."

## The Dangerous Otto Katz

In 2010, Miles published *The Dangerous Otto Katz: The Many Lives of a Soviet Spy.* Miles begins with Katz's Bohemian childhood and builds the story of how he eventually became one of the most infamous European spies of the mid-twentieth century. A loyal communist, Miles shows how Katz was an advocate against Nazism but eventually became uncomfortable with Stalin's harsh tactics.

Writing in Glasgow's *Herald,* Tim Sharp summarized that "Miles has unearthed some fascinating information from the files of security services across the globe. But spies, whatever their nationality, are not noted for their frankness. By the very nature of the subject, this isn't a conventional biography. By the end we still don't really know who Katz is, exactly what role he played, what motivated him. But what we do have is a fascinating introduction to the forces operating under the surface when Europe was at a crucial turning point." Reviewing the book in the *Cleveland Plain Dealer,* Tricia Springstubb commented that "the narrative's dense thicket of names and places sometimes brings a heart-pounding account of courage or treachery to a thudding halt." A *Kirkus Reviews* critic described *The Dangerous Otto Katz* as "an intriguing spy biography that ably demonstrates how fierce adherence to an ideology can lead to human suffering on terms both intimate and global." In a review in the *Chicago Sun-Times,* Carlo Wolff opined that the "portrait of Katz is masterful and ultimately sad." Writing in the *Los Angeles Times,* Richard Schickel concluded that "in a certain sense, Katz's end was more typical than his life—as at least 20 million similar deaths testify. That life, however, was unique in the annals of the secret world. And Miles' book is unique among accounts of that world—always clear-eyed about the tyranny Katz served, yet as sympathetic as it is possible to be to a man who eventually, predictably fell in this most dubious of battles."

## ■ Biographical And Critical Sources

*PERIODICALS*

*American Scholar,* September 22, 2007, Anthony Brandt, "Swept Away: When Gericault Painted The Raft of the Medusa, He Immersed Himself in His Subject's Horrors," p. 131.

*Atlantic,* March 1, 2008, review of *The Wreck of the Medusa,* p. 105.

*Booklist,* May 15, 2007, Gilbert Taylor, review of *The Wreck of the Medusa,* p. 15; October 15, 2010, Gilbert Taylor, review of *The Dangerous Otto Katz: The Many Lives of a Soviet Spy,* p. 4.

*Bookwatch,* January 1, 2011, review of *The Dangerous Otto Katz.*

*Boston Globe,* November 4, 2007, Anna Mundow, "From Disaster, a Modern Vision Is Born," interview with author.

*Burlington,* April 1, 1996, review of *David Jones: The Maker Unmade,* p. 261.

*Chicago Sun-Times,* accessed August 13, 2011, Carlo Wolff, review of *The Dangerous Otto Katz.*

*Cleveland Plain Dealer,* December 15, 2010, Tricia Springstubb, review of *The Dangerous Otto Katz.*

*Contemporary Review,* December 22, 2007, review of *Medusa,* p. 535.

*Herald* (Glasgow, Scotland), July 26, 2010, Tim Sharp, "The Nine Lives of Otto Katz."

*Kirkus Reviews,* August 1, 1996, review of *David Jones,* p. 1142; May 15, 2007, review of *The Wreck of the Medusa;* August 15, 2010, review of *The Dangerous Otto Katz.*

*Library Journal,* April 15, 2007, Marie Marmo Mullaney, review of *The Wreck of the Medusa,* p. 103; November 1, 2010, Maria Bagshaw, review of *The Dangerous Otto Katz,* p. 67.

*London Review of Books,* July 5, 2007, Graham Robb, review of *Medusa,* p. 17.

*Los Angeles Times,* November 21, 2010, Richard Schickel, review of *The Dangerous Otto Katz.*

*Modern Language Review,* July 1, 1992, M.J. Alexander, review of *Backgrounds to David Jones: A Study in Sources and Drafts,* p. 724.

*National Post* (Toronto, Ontario, Canada), April 21, 2007, Michael Prodger, review of *Medusa,* p. 16.

*New York Times Book Review,* December 2, 2007, Florence Williams, review of *The Wreck of the Medusa,* p. 44.

*Observer* (London, England), October 29, 1995, review of *David Jones,* p. 16; April 22, 2007, Kelly Grovier, review of *Medusa.*

*Publishers Weekly,* August 12, 1996, review of *David Jones,* p. 76; March 12, 2007, review of *The Wreck of the Medusa,* p. 44.

*Quadrant,* December 1, 1996, review of *David Jones,* p. 85.

*Spectator,* April 21, 2007, William Boyd, "All at Sea."

*Times Literary Supplement* (London, England), April 5, 1996, Julian Bell, review of *David Jones,* p. 9; April 13, 2007, Alex Danchev, "Horror into Art," p. 4.

*University of Toronto Quarterly,* March 22, 1997, William Blissett, review of *Backgrounds to David Jones,* p. 479.

*Yale Review,* January 1, 1998, Ben Downing, review of *David Jones,* p. 154.


*ONLINE*

*Jonathan Miles Home Page,* http://jonathanmiles.net (August 14, 2011).

# Roger Moorhouse

## 1968-

### ■ Personal

Born October 14, 1968, in Stockport, Cheshire, England; married; children: two. *Education:* University of London, M.A., 1994; postgraduate research at Heinrich Heine University Dusseldorf, and University of Strathclyde.

### ■ Addresses

*Home*—Buckinghamshire, England. *E-mail*—roger@rogermoorhouse.com.

### ■ Career

Historian, writer, editor, and translator. Senior researcher and editorial assistant to Professor Norman Davies, 1995—. Also works as a public speaker and guest lecturer; has appeared on various television and radio programs.

### ■ Member

British-German Association, Royal Society of Arts.

### ■ Awards, Honors

Honorary diploma, City of Wroclaw, 2002.

### ■ Writings

(With Norman Davies) *Microcosm: Portrait of a Central European City,* Jonathan Cape (London, England), 2002.
*Killing Hitler: The Plots, the Assassins, and the Dictator Who Cheated Death,* Bantam Books (New York, NY), 2006.
*Berlin at War,* Basic Books (New York, NY), 2010.

Contributor to periodicals, including *History Today, Independent on Sunday Financial Times,* and *BBC History* magazine; author of the *Historian at Large* blog.

### ■ Sidelights

Roger Moorhouse is a British historian who writes, edits, and translates. He earned a master's degree from the University of London in 1994 and undertook additional studies at Heinrich Heine University Dusseldorf, and the University of Strathclyde. Moorhouse served as the senior researcher and editorial assistant to Professor Norman Davies since 1995. He has served as a public speaker and guest lecturer.

#### *Microcosm* and *Killing Hitler*

Moorhouse published his first book, *Microcosm: Portrait of a Central European City,* with Davies. In their book, the authors tell the story of Wroclaw, a city in modern-day Poland, close to the borders with the Czech Republic and Germany. The city has had many names over its long existence, most notably the German name Breslau, which it carried until the end of World War Two. It has also undergone numerous changes in government and national and ethnic influence over the years. Moorhouse and Davies explore such issues as national identity and examine the city's many instances of social turmoil. "Davies and Moorhouse set out to present the history of the city, a microcosm of Central Europe, as evenhandedly as possible, freeing it from the straitjackets of German and Polish nationalisms, and giving due weight to its Jewish and Czech components," wrote Richard Butterwick in the *English Historical Review.* Butterwick added that "*Microcosm* must be acclaimed as exemplary." Writing in the *Spectator,* Antony Beevor noted the book's "scholarship and objectivity," adding that it "also makes a fascinating story."

In *Killing Hitler: The Plots, the Assassins, and the Dictator Who Cheated Death,* Moorhouse presents case studies of eight attempts to assassinate German dictator Adolf Hitler. The author examines the people and reasons behind the attempts and also explores how each of the failures, along with the other many failed attempts to assassinate the dictator, helped to lead Hitler and his coterie to the belief that they were unstoppable. "Moorhouse's documentation and analysis of this comprehensive history will keep readers interested to the end," wrote George Cohen in *Booklist.* A *Publishers Weekly* contributor wrote: "Accessible prose, suspenseful narration and ample historical context make this a page-turner."

### *Berlin at War*

*Berlin at War* looks at the lives of Berliners from 1939 until 1945. Using diaries, memoirs, and interviews, Moorhouse recreates the challenges of the residents of the city and also how many were willing to be stripped of their humanity in the anti-Jew campaigns promoted by the government.

Writing in the London *Telegraph,* Ian Thomson claimed that "in this vitally important work, Moorhouse shows how a great German city was disrupted in different ways by the war, depending on whether its citizens were Jewish, pro-Hitler, or simply willing to be degraded into collaboration. As a leading historian of modern Germany, Moorhouse has chronicled a largely unknown story with scholarship, narrative verve and, at times, an awful, harrowing immediacy." *Washington Post Book World* contributor Jonathan Yardley noted that "there is more than enough pain in *Berlin at War* to satisfy all but the most masochistic readers." Yardley pointed out that as the twenty-first century begins, "Berlin has regained its standing as one of the world's great cities. That it started at zero is made all too clear by this excellent book." In a review in the London *Independent,* C.J. Schüler commented that "Moorhouse's meticulous and painstaking research is matched by his narrative verve, wide-ranging sympathy and eye for telling detail." A contributor to *A Common Reader* stated: "I enjoyed this book greatly, not least because it is so very readable. This is far from being an academic book, but it is full of information which fills out a picture already well-known with personal stories and anecdotes." "This book, it is fair to say, is not one that restores one's faith in human nature. It is, however, as readable as a first-rate novel, and choc-full of gripping stories of suffering, endurance, cowardice, and courage," concluded Nigel Jones in a review for the *Military Times.*

### ■ Biographical And Critical Sources

*PERIODICALS*

*Booklist,* March 1, 2006, George Cohen, review of *Killing Hitler: The Plots, the Assassins, and the Dictator Who Cheated Death,* p. 57.

*Christian Century,* December 14, 2010, Richard Kauffman and David Heim, review of *Berlin at War,* p. 24.

*Christian Science Monitor,* November 5, 2010, Terry Hartle, review of *Berlin at War.*

*Economist,* April 27, 2002, review of *Microcosm: Portrait of a Central European City.*

*English Historical Review,* June 1, 2004, Richard Butterwick, review of *Microcosm,* p. 743.

*Independent* (London, England), August 20, 2010, C.J. Schüler, review of *Berlin at War.*

*Kirkus Reviews,* July 15, 2010, review of *Berlin at War.*

*Library Journal,* March 1, 2006, Frederic Krome, review of *Killing Hitler,* p. 103.

*Maclean's,* November 29, 2010, Brian Bethune, review of *Berlin at War,* p. 100.

*Publishers Weekly,* February 27, 2006, review of *Killing Hitler,* p. 52; August 30, 2010, review of *Berlin at War,* p. 42.

*Slavonic and East European Review,* April 1, 2002, W.H. Zawadzki and Juergen Kurz, review of *Microcosm,* pp. 348-350.

*Spectator,* March 30, 2002, Antony Beevor, review of *Microcosm,* p. 42.

*Telegraph* (London, England), August 8, 2010, Ian Thomson, review of *Berlin at War.*

*Washington Post Book World,* October 3, 2010, Jonathan Yardley, review of *Berlin at War,* p. B8.

*ONLINE*

*A Common Reader,* http://acommonreader.org/ (July 30, 2011), review of *Berlin at War.*

*Historian at Large,* http://historian-at-large.blogspot.com (August 24, 2011), author blog.

*History in an Hour,* http://www.historyinanhour.com/ (September 7, 2010), Rupert Colley, author interview.

*Military Times,* http://www.military-times.co.uk/ (July 30, 2011), Nigel Jones, review of *Berlin at War.*

*Random House Web site,* http://www.randomhouse.com/ (November 28, 2006), brief profile of author.

*Roger Moorhouse Home Page,* http://www.rogermoorhouse.com (July 30, 2011).

# Tamar Myers

## 1948-

■ **Personal**

Given name is accented on the second syllable; born September 21, 1948, in the Belgian Congo (now Zaire); became U.S. citizen; daughter of Russell F. (a minister and missionary) and Helen (a missionary) Schnell; married Jeffrey Myers (an engineer), November 28, 1970; children: Sarah, David, Dafna. *Ethnicity:* "Swiss/Danish/German." *Education:* American College in Jerusalem, B.A., 1970; Eastern Kentucky University, M.A., 1973. *Politics:* Independent. *Religion:* Jewish. *Hobbies and other interests:* Gardening, oil painting, teaching piano, and cooking.

■ **Addresses**

*Home*—Charlotte, NC. *Agent*—Nancy Yost, Lowenstein Associates, Inc., 121 W. 27th St., Ste. 601, New York, NY 10001. *E-mail*—tamar@tamarmyers.com.

■ **Career**

Writer.

■ **Member**

Mystery Writers of America, Novelists, Inc., Sisters in Crime, Politeia, Southeastern Palm and Exotic Plant Society, Blue Stockings Literary Club.

■ **Writings**

*Angels, Angels Everywhere* (stories), Avon (New York, NY), 1995.

*The Dark Side of Heaven* (novel), Bella Rosa Books (Rock Hill, SC), 2006.

*The Witch Doctor's Wife* ("Amanda Brown" series), Avon (New York, NY), 2009.

*The Headhunter's Daughter* ("Amanda Brown" series), William Morrow (New York, NY), 2011.

*"PENNSYLVANIA DUTCH" MYSTERY SERIES*

*Too Many Crooks Spoil the Broth,* Doubleday (New York, NY), 1994.

*Parsley, Sage, Rosemary, and Crime,* Doubleday (New York, NY), 1995.

*No Use Dying over Spilled Milk,* Dutton (Bergenfield, NJ), 1996.

*Just Plain Pickled to Death,* Dutton (New York, NY), 1997.

*Between a Wok and a Hard Place,* Signet (New York, NY), 1998.

*Play It Again, Spam,* Signet (New York, NY), 1999.

*The Hand That Rocks the Ladle,* Signet (New York, NY), 2000.

*The Crepes of Wrath,* New American Library (New York, NY), 2001.

*Eat, Drink, and Be Wary,* Thorndike Press (Thorndike, ME), 2001.

*Gruel and Unusual Punishment,* New American Library (New York, NY), 2002.

*Custard's Last Stand,* New American Library (New York, NY), 2003.

*Thou Shalt Not Grill,* New American Library (New York, NY), 2004.

*Assault and Pepper,* New American Library (New York, NY), 2005.

*Grape Expectations,* New American Library (New York, NY), 2006.

*Hell Hath No Curry,* New American Library (New York, NY), 2007.

*As the World Churns,* Obsidian (New York, NY), 2008.

*Batter off Dead,* Obsidian (New York, NY), 2009.

*Butter Safe than Sorry,* New American Library (New York, NY), 2010.

*"DEN OF ANTIQUITY" MYSTERY SERIES*

*Larceny and Old Lace,* Avon (New York, NY), 1996.

*Gilt by Association,* Avon (New York, NY), 1996.

*The Ming and I,* Avon (New York, NY), 1997.

*So Faux, So Good,* Avon (New York, NY), 1997.

*Baroque and Desperate,* Avon (New York, NY), 1999.

*Estate of Mind,* Avon (New York, NY), 1999.

*A Penny Urned,* Avon (New York, NY), 2000.

*Nightmare in Shining Armor,* Avon (New York, NY), 2001.

*Splendor in the Glass,* Avon (New York, NY), 2002.

*Tiles and Tribulations,* Avon (New York, NY), 2003.

*Statue of Limitations,* Avon (New York, NY), 2004.

*Monet Talks,* Avon (New York, NY), 2005.

*The Cane Mutiny,* Avon (New York, NY), 2006.

*Death of a Rug Lord,* Avon (New York, NY), 2008.

*Poison Ivory,* Avon Books (New York, NY), 2009.

*The Glass Is Always Greener,* Avon (New York, NY), 2011.

## ■ Sidelights

Tamar Myers is the author of mystery novels in several different series. Most of her works are divided between two ongoing series featuring amateur sleuths: the "Pennsylvania Dutch" mystery series, starring irascible Mennonite innkeeper Magdalena Yoder, and the "Den of Antiquity" series, with Abigail Timberlake, a diminutive antiques dealer from Charleston. Both series rely heavily on humor—Magdalena is particularly fond of crisp one-liners; Abigail often finds herself in funny situations with oddball characters; and the books' titles are puns with direct relevance to the stories. In both series, Myers, who comes from a Mennonite background, offers realistic details on Pennsylvania Amish and Mennonite life and the world of antiques collectors. In addition, the Magdalena Yoder books include recipes for several of the dishes highlighted within each individual story.

### "Pennsylvania Dutch" Series

Sometimes cantankerous, sometimes wryly observant, Magdalena holds her own in such books as *Just Plain Pickled to Death,* in which a dead body turns up in a barrel of sauerkraut given to her as a wedding present, and *Gruel and Unusual Punishment,* in which Magdalena must work to clear her name after an inmate in a local prison dies from arsenic poisoning in a meal she provided. In *Custard's Last Stand,* she opposes plans by developer Colonel Custard to build a luxury hotel in her hometown of Hernia, Pennsylvania. When the colonel is discovered shot to death in Magdalena's inn, the authorities believe they have their culprit in the man's chauffeur, Ivan. Magdalena, however, thinks the murderer is someone else, and she sets out to prove it. "Scrawny, pesky, irresistibly funny Magdalena will have you overlooking plot glitches and reading on for her next amusing one-liner," commented a *Kirkus Reviews* contributor.

In *Assault and Pepper,* Magdalena gears up for her church's annual chili cook-off. When Reverend Schrock keels over and dies after eating some chili, it is found that the reverend had a deadly peanut allergy and someone has spiked his food with peanut butter. As Magdalena investigates, she discovers that the reverend was not as good as everyone thought. In fact, he enjoyed drinking, gambling, and regular massage parlor visits. As more harm comes to members of Reverend Schrock's family, Magdalena investigates why a man of the cloth would have so many determined enemies.

Myers returns to the adventures of Magdalena Yoder with *Grape Expectations.* This time, Magdalena faces competition to her inn from the newly arrived Felicia Bacchustelli, a beauty who is opening a spa. When Felicia is found murdered, Magdalena is the prime suspect and must track down the murderer herself to clear her name. "Magdalena's fans will . . . enjoy another of her tongue-in-cheek adventures," wrote a *Kirkus Reviews* contributor.

Magdalena appears again in *Hell Hath No Curry.* She is investigating the murder of playboy Cornelius Wever, who dies in the bed of the local police chief, Olivia Hornsby-Anderson, just before he is to be married to Priscilla Livingood. However, the coroner finds that Cornelius's supposed heart attack was brought on by a dose of Elavil put in his dish of curry. As Magdalena investigates, she encounters the numerous women that Cornelius bedded, all of them suspects. In the meantime, her Mennonite background leads to the dissolution of Magdalena's engagement. A *Kirkus Reviews* contributor referred to *Hell Hath No Curry* as "a masterful Mennonite mystery." Kathy Perschmann, writing on the *Armchair Interviews* Web site, called this series entry "every bit as tasty as the previous books!" Perschmann added: "The curry recipes in this book are authentic."

Additional "Pennsylvania Dutch" installments include *As the World Churns, Batter off Dead,* and *Butter Safe than Sorry.* In the former, Magdalena is newlywed and honeymooning when she learns that her brother-in-law, a convicted murderer, has escaped. Magdalena is unable to track him down, and her inn is fully booked thanks to the local bovine festival and contest. The veterinarian responsible for judging entrants is attacked as mystery and hilarity ensue in equal measure. Ice-cream recipes ranging from the traditional to the experimental are also included. Myers presents readers with "plenty of humorous by-play," Mark Knoblauch observed in his *Booklist* assessment. A *Kirkus Reviews* critic pointed out: "Fans of the clever, sarcastic, engaging Magdalena will doubtless find this adventure just as rollicking as all her others." Nancy L. Cox, writing in *MBR Bookwatch,* was equally impressed, noting: "Magdalena is a memorable sleuth who slings puns, jokes, and words as easily as Pennsylvania Dutch potato pancakes." She went on to call *As the World Churns* "a rollicking romp through the pastures of all imagination with many a laugh for free." Proffering praise in the online *Best Reviews,* Harriet Klausner commented: "*As the World Churns* is as tasty as shoofly pie. This is a delightful mystery due to the characters, especially the secondary and recurring ones."

### "Den of Antiquity" Series

Abigail Timberlake struggles to balance her personal and professional lives throughout the "Den of Antiquity" series. In *Nightmare in Shining Armor* she throws a costume party to celebrate the purchase of her new home. The party starts disastrously, with the appearance of Tweetie, her ex-husband's much-younger wife, and ends badly, with burned drapes and spilled punch, but the worst is yet to come when Abigail discovers Tweetie's body stuffed into a suit of armor and crammed under her bed.

Sympathetic to the perils of new homeownership, Abigail helps a friend clean some ghosts out of her newly acquired mansion in *Tiles and Tribulations.* The psychic hired to do the job, Madam Woo-Woo, concludes that the ghosts appear because there is a body still hidden behind a set of priceless seventeenth-century tiles in the house. When Madam Woo-Woo later dies of an apparent poisoning, Abigail investigates the decidedly nonsupernatural elements of the case. "Fans of laugh-out-loud mystery fare are sure to find this an exceptional delight," commented a *Publishers Weekly* critic.

### "Amanda Brown" Series

Myers begins the fledgling "Amanda Brown" series with *The Witch Doctor's Wife.* The novel is based on Myers's own experiences as a child of missionaries in the Congo. Set in the 1950s, the story follows Amanda Brown, a missionary from South Carolina. Amanda manages a guesthouse in the isolated small town of Belle Vue. The witch doctor's wife hides her power behind her pronounced limp. Amanda's housekeeper, named Protruding Navel, is cantankerous. Belle Vue is filled with many similarly colorful characters, all of whom clash over a large diamond discovered in the town's confines. Critics applauded the story as a wonderful new direction in Myers's writing, and they also praised the author's expert fictionalization of her childhood memories. For instance, *Booklist* reviewer Allison Block noted that Myers "was born and raised in the Congo, and she writes vividly about her childhood home." Seconding this opinion in *Kirkus Reviews,* a contributor felt that the author's "personal experience as a child brought up by missionaries in the Congo lends authenticity to every word." The contributor also called *The Witch Doctor's Wife* "a radical but welcome departure" from Myers's previous mysteries. According to a *Publishers Weekly* writer, *The Witch Doctor's Wife* is "a major breakthrough for Myers as she displays storytelling skills not recently seen in" her other series novels.

Amanda brown returns in *The Headhunter's Daughter.* It is 1958, and Amanda learns that there is a white girl being raised by a clan of headhunters. Amanda suspects the girl may be a baby that was kidnapped from the area thirteen years ago. Amanda and her maid, along with Captain Pierre, hope to find out. The plot hinges on the taut racial tensions of the Congo during the mid-twentieth-century. Thus, a *Kirkus Reviews* critic commended "the evocative descriptions of life in the Congo . . . and the skillful portrayal of the vast disconnect between the white and black inhabitants." Jessica Moyer, writing in *Booklist,* lauded the novel as well, remarking that it is filled "with atmosphere" and announcing: "The novel is a gentle read." Moyer also called *The Headhunter's Daughter* "an excellent choice for book groups." According to a *Coffee Time Romance* Web site reviewer, "I found myself becoming entranced, almost against my will, in the unfolding drama of this ultimately uniquely mesmerizing narrative."

### Myers Told *CA:*

"I was born and raised in the Belgian Congo, where my parents were Mennonite missionaries to a tribe of headhunters. We lived in a very remote region, hundreds of miles away from the nearest English-language bookstore. We had no radio or television. I wrote my first book-length manuscript at age ten to amuse myself and my three sisters.

"I began writing fiction in earnest in college, but it took twenty-three years to make my first sale. During that time I accumulated a stack of unsold manuscripts. Then, fortunately, I attempted a mystery with a humorous bent, using my background as a Mennonite of Amish descent. The novel sold immediately. In three years I signed contracts for ten humorous mystery novels: six centering on my Amish-Mennonite sleuth, Magdalena Yoder, and four featuring Abigail Timberlake, the owner of an antique shop called the Den of Antiquity. Because I now write four books a year, writing is a full-time job."

■ **Biographical And Critical Sources**

*PERIODICALS*

*Booklist*, September 1, 1997, GraceAnne A. DeCandido, review of *Just Plain Pickled to Death*, p. 66; March 1, 2008, Mark Knoblauch, review of *As the World Churns*, p. 51; December 1, 2008, Judy Coon, review of *Batter off Dead*, p. 27; November 15, 2009, Allison Block, review of *The Witch Doctor's Wife*, p. 24; February 15, 2011, Jessica Moyer, review of *The Headhunter's Daughter*, p. 55.

*Charlotte Observer*, May 12, 2007, Jeri Krentz, "Mystery Writer Is Accustomed to Adventure."

*Drood Review of Mystery*, July, 2000, review of *A Penny Urned*.

*Kirkus Reviews*, December 1, 2002, review of *Custard's Last Stand*, p. 1737; December 15, 2004, review of *Assault and Pepper*, p. 1168; December 15, 2005, review of *Grape Expectations*, p. 1303; November 15, 2006, review of *Hell Hath No Curry*, p. 1156; December 1, 2007, review of *As the World Churns*; April 15, 2010, review of *The Witch Doctor's Wife*; December 15, 2010, review of *The Headhunter's Daughter*.

*Library Journal*, February 1, 2003, Rex E. Klett, review of *Custard's Last Stand*, p. 121; January 1, 2005, Rex E. Klett, review of *Assault and Pepper*, p. 84.

*MBR Bookwatch*, February, 2005, Harriet Klausner, review of *Assault and Pepper*; February 1, 2008, Nancy L. Cox, review of *As the World Churns*.

*Publishers Weekly*, November 11, 1996, review of *Gilt by Association*, p. 72; November 27, 2000, review of *The Crepes of Wrath*, p. 57; July 2, 2001, review of *Nightmare in Shining Armor*, p. 57; January 28, 2002, review of *Gruel and Unusual Punishment*, p. 274; February 3, 2003, review of *Tiles and Tribulations*, p. 60; December 19, 2005, review of *Grape Expectations*, p. 44; November 27, 2006, review of *Hell Hath No Curry*, p. 35; November 24, 2008, review of *Batter off Dead*, p. 41; September 28, 2009, review of *The Witch Doctor's Wife*, p. 44.

*ONLINE*

*Armchair Interviews*, http://reviews.armchair interviews.com/ (July 13, 2007), Kathy Perschmann, review of *Hell Hath No Curry*.

*Best Reviews*, http://www.thebestreviews.com/ (December 10, 2005), Harriet Klausner, review of *Custard's Last Stand*; (January 31, 2008), Harriet Klausner, review of *As the World Churns*.

*Book Loons*, http://www.bookloons.com/ (December 10, 2005), Mary Ann Smyth, review of *Gruel and Unusual Punishment*.

*Books 'n' Bytes*, http://www.booksnbytes.com/ (December 10, 2005), Harriet Klausner, reviews of *The Crepes of Wrath*, *Gruel and Unusual Punishment*, and *Nightmare in Shining Armor*.

*Coffee Time Romance*, http://www.coffeetime romance.com/ (August 30, 2011), review of *The Headhunter's Daughter*.

*Mystery Reader*, http://www.themysteryreader.com/ (December 10, 2005), Monica Pope, review of *The Hand That Rocks the Ladle*.

*Romance Readers Connections*, http://www.the romancereadersconnection.com/ (July 13, 2007), "February Mystery Author Spotlight."

*Tamar Myers Home Page*, http://www.tamarmyers. com (August 30, 2011).

# James Peck

## 1944-

## ■ Personal

Born 1944.

## ■ Addresses

*Home*—New York, NY. *E-mail*—jlpeck1098@aol.com.

## ■ Career

Writer, editor, and educator. U.S.-China Book Publication Project, director; New York University, New York, NY, adjunct professor in East Asian studies; Yale University Press Culture and Civilization of China Project, founder; China International Publishing Group, Beijing, China, founder.

## ■ Writings

(Editor, with Victor Nee) *China's Uninterrupted Revolution: From 1840 to the Present*, Pantheon Books (New York, NY), 1975.

(Editor) Noam Chomsky, *The Chomsky Reader*, Pantheon Books (New York, NY), 1987.

(With Sirin Phathanothai) *The Dragon's Pearl*, Simon & Schuster (New York, NY), 1994.

*Washington's China: The National Security World, the Cold War, and the Origins of Globalism*, University of Massachusetts Press (Amherst, MA), 2006.

*Ideal Illusions: How the U.S. Government Co-opted Human Rights*, Metropolitan Books (New York, NY), 2010.

Contributor to *New York Times* and *San Francisco Chronicle*.

## ■ Sidelights

James Peck is a writer and editor specializing in East Asia. As editor of *The Chomsky Reader*, Peck also presents the writings of Noam Chomsky, a philosopher, political activist, and writer who first gained notoriety for his outspoken opposition to the Vietnam War and has also written about the Middle East and numerous other political and socioeconomic issues.

### *The Dragon's Pearl* and *Washington's China*

Peck collaborated with Sirin Phathanothai to write *The Dragon's Pearl*. Peck helps Phathanothai tell her tale of being sent at the age of eight from her home in Thailand to China, along with her brother, as a token of goodwill between the two enemy countries. As a result, Phathanothai spent her youth living with China's leaders, include Mao Tse-tung. The book recounts how Phathanothai witnessed the Cultural Revolution and the many changes that China underwent as a result. Mary Ellen Sullivan, writing in *Booklist*, commented that the "account of these times is fascinating."

Peck is also author of the 2006 book, *Washington's China: The National Security World, the Cold War, and the Origins of Globalism*. The book is a reassessment of American policy toward China at the beginning of the Cold War. *California Bookwatch* contributor Diane C. Donovan noted that the issues in this book "are especially meaningful today" because of China's growing importance in the world as a global power.

### *Ideal Illusions*

In 2010, Peck published *Ideal Illusions: How the U.S. Government Co-opted Human Rights*. The account outlines the history of the human rights movement on the global stage and also shows how the United States government has appropriated it for its own benefit, even using the movement as a political weapon. With the passage of the 1948 UN Declaration of Human Rights, the United States warily dodged taking the movement as its centerpiece for foreign relations, opting instead for freedom, modernization, and anticommunism. By the late 1970s, however, human rights became a part of the American foreign policy platform, using it to criticize ideological opponents on the world stage and as justification for intervention. Peck covers the streams of civil and political rights, as well as cultural, educational, and economic rights, and how the American government has favored the former over the latter domestically and internationally.

Reviewing the book in *Library Journal*, April Younglove called the book "an engaging and original look at America's foreign policy, accessible and well researched." A *Kirkus Reviews* critic described *Ideal Illusions* as being "a prodigiously researched, provocative critique." A contributor to *Publishers Weekly* found the book to be "a useful, thought-provoking challenge to the Western human rights consensus."

## ■ Biographical And Critical Sources

*PERIODICALS*

*American Historical Review*, April 1, 2008, Michael Schaller, review of *Washington's China: The National Security World, the Cold War, and the Origins of Globalism*, pp. 531-532.

*Booklist*, July 1, 1994, Mary Ellen Sullivan, review of *The Dragon's Pearl*, p. 1920.

*California Bookwatch*, March 1, 2007, Diane C. Donovan, review of *Washington's China*.

*Far Eastern Economic Review*, November 24, 1994, Alison Hardie, review of *The Dragon's Pearl*, p. 118.

*International History Review*, September 1, 2008, Gordon H. Chang, review of *Washington's China*, pp. 690-692.

*Journal of American History*, December 1, 2007, Marc Gallicchio, review of *Washington's China*, p. 984.

*Kirkus Reviews*, December 15, 2010, review of *Ideal Illusions: How the U.S. Government Co-opted Human Rights*.

*Library Journal*, June 15, 1994, Mark Meng, review of *The Dragon's Pearl*, p. 84; January 1, 2011, April Younglove, review of *Ideal Illusions*, p. 113.

*Nation*, May 7, 1988, Brian Morton, review of *The Chomsky Reader*, p. 646.

*Progressive*, August 1, 1988, review of *The Chomsky Reader*, p. 30.

*Publishers Weekly*, June 6, 1994, review of *The Dragon's Pearl*, p. 52; December 6, 2010, review of *Ideal Illusions*, p. 38.

*ONLINE*

*Command Posts*, http://www.commandposts.com/ (August 14, 2011), author profile.*

# Peter John Perry

## 1937-

## Personal

Born December 22, 1937, in Sherborne, Dorsetshire, England; son of Leslie John (a headmaster) and Marjorie F. Perry; married Rachel-Mary Stewart Armitage (a nurse and midwife), December 1, 1973. *Education:* Clare College, Cambridge University, B.A., 1959, M.A., 1963, Ph.D., 1963. *Politics:* Independent. *Religion:* Church of England.

## Addresses

*Home*—Christchurch, New Zealand. *Office*—Dept. of Geography, University of Canterbury, Christchurch 1 N2, New Zealand.

## Career

Academic and geographer. University of Canterbury, Christchurch, New Zealand, beginning 1966, began as lecturer, became senior lecturer in geography, reader in geography, and professor of geography.

## Member

Institute of British Geographers, New Zealand Geographical Society, British Agricultural History Society, Economic History Society.

## Writings

(Editor) *British Agriculture, 1875-1914*, Methuen (London, England), 1973.

*British Farming in the Great Depression, 1870-1914: An Historical Geography*, David & Charles (Newton Abbot, Devon, England), 1974.
*Political Corruption and Political Geography*, Ashgate (Brookfield, VT), 1997.
*Political Corruption in Australia: A Very Wicked Place?*, Ashgate (Burlington, VT), 2001.
*Myanmar (Burma) since 1962: The Failure of Development*, Ashgate (Burlington, VT), 2007.

## Sidelights

Peter John Perry is a British academic and geographer. Born in England in 1937, he earned a Ph.D. from Cambridge University in 1963. In 1966, Perry began working as a lecturer at New Zealand's University of Canterbury, eventually becoming a professor in geography. He writes in the areas of political and economic geography.

### Myanmar (Burma) since 1962

Perry published *Myanmar (Burma) since 1962: The Failure of Development* in 2007. The account looks at how the resource-rich country of Myanmar, formerly known as Burma, had become one of the least-developed countries in the world by the end of the twentieth century. Perry uses economic data and models to show where things went wrong and how, primarily through better resource management, the country can turn their economic prospects around.

Writing in *Pacific Affairs*, Anne Booth claimed that *Myanmar (Burma) since 1962* is "welcomed, even if it is mainly a survey of work done by other scholars," adding that it "gives a useful background to anyone wishing to understand how contemporary Burma reached its present parlous state." Writing in the

*Journal of Southeast Asian Studies,* David I. Steinberg commented that "there is less on politics in the volume than might have been desired, given, as the author notes, that politics has often driven economic positions, but one cannot ask the author to write a different book." Nevertheless, Steinberg concluded that "this volume is recommended to those with serious interests in that country, and taken together with a variety of other contemporary commentaries, it has helpful perspectives on the sorry state of affairs in Myanmar." Reviewing the book in *Sojourn: Journal of Social Issues in Southeast Asia,* Ardeth Maung Thawngmung mentioned that "although the book does not offer any new insights for Burma specialists, its comprehensive coverage gives a good overview and understanding of Burma's development policies and their consequential impacts on the population, society, and environment."

## ■ Biographical And Critical Sources

*PERIODICALS*

*Asian Affairs,* November 1, 2008, Robert H. Taylor, review of *Myanmar (Burma) since 1962: The Failure of Development,* pp. 458-459.

*Choice: Current Reviews for Academic Libraries,* December 1, 1997, review of *Political Corruption and Political Geography,* p. 704; May 1, 2008, E. Pang, review of *Myanmar (Burma) since 1962,* p. 1589.

*Far Eastern Economic Review,* May 1, 2007, Michael Grosberg, review of *Myanmar (Burma) since 1962,* p. 72.

*Journal of Contemporary Asia,* May 1, 1999, Herb Thompson, review of *Political Corruption and Political Geography,* p. 277.

*Journal of Southeast Asian Studies,* February 1, 2009, David I. Steinberg, review of *Myanmar (Burma) since 1962,* p. 215.

*Pacific Affairs,* March 1, 2010, Anne Booth, review of *Myanmar (Burma) since 1962.*

*Reference & Research Book News,* November 1, 1997, review of *Political Corruption and Political Geography,* p. 106; May 1, 2002, review of *Political Corruption in Australia: A Very Wicked Place?,* p. 42.

*Sojourn: Journal of Social Issues in Southeast Asia,* April 1, 2008, Ardeth Maung Thawngmung, review of *Myanmar (Burma) since 1962,* p. 137.*

# Robert Michael Pyle

## 1947-

■ **Personal**

Born July 19, 1947, in Denver, CO; son of Robert Harold (a sales representative) and Helen Lee (a secretary) Pyle; married JoAnne R. Clark (divorced, 1973); married Sarah Anne Hughes (divorced, 1983); married Thea Linnaea Peterson (a botanist and silk-screen artist), October 19, 1985; stepchildren: Thomas Michael Hellyer, Dorothea Alix Hellyer. *Ethnicity:* "Anglo." *Education:* University of Washington, Seattle, B.S., 1969, M.S., 1973; Yale University, M.Phil., 1975, Ph.D., 1976. *Politics:* Democrat. *Hobbies and other interests:* Natural history, walking, reading, butterfly watching, birding.

■ **Addresses**

*Home*—Gray's River, WA. *Office*—Central Washington University, Dept. of Geography, 400 E. University Way, Ellensburg, WA 98926. *Agent*—Laura Blake Peterson, Curtis Brown Ltd., 10 Astor Pl., New York, NY 10003.

■ **Career**

Academic and lepidopterist. Resource person and writer for U.S. Forest Service, Washington State Parks, and Sierra Club, between 1967 and 1973; University of Washington, Seattle, teacher of creative writing, 1972; Yale University, New Haven, CT, curatorial assistant at Peabody Museum of Natural History, 1973-74; Vale of Catmose College, Oakham, England, teacher of creative writing, 1976-77; nature conservation consultant in Papua New Guinea, 1977; Nature Conservancy, Portland, OR, Northwest land steward, 1977-79; International Union for the Conservation of Nature and Natural Resources/ World Wildlife Fund, Cambridge, England, editor and manager, 1979-81; freelance writer, lecturer, and

educator, 1982—. Green and Pleasant Tours, proprietor and tour guide, with excursions in the Rocky Mountains, the Pacific Northwest, and England. Utah State University, visiting professor, 2002; University of Montana, Kittredge Distinguished Writer, 2004; teacher or lecturer at numerous other institutions, including Olympic Park College and Evergreen State College, 1988-89, Olympic Park Institute, North Cascades Institute, and National Wildlife Federation, 1988-93, and Lewis and Clark College, 1991-93; workshop presenter and public speaker; guest on media programs, including *All Things Considered,* National Public Radio, and *Good Morning America;* gives readings from his works. Sequoia National Park, ranger-naturalist, 1969; Washington State Department of Natural Resources, member of Natural Heritage Advisory Council; Rocky Mountain Biological Laboratory, member; consultant to World Conservation Centre, U.S. Fish and Wildlife Service, and National Park Service.

■ **Member**

John Burroughs Association, Authors Guild, Authors League of America, Poets and Writers, Xerces Society (founder), Evergreen Aurelians (cofounder), Lepidopterists Society (member of executive committee, 1981-83, 2005-07), National Association of Railroad Passengers, Association for the Study of Literature and Environment, Nature Conservancy, Orion Society, Patrons of Husbandry (Grange), Willapa Hills Audubon Society.

■ **Awards, Honors**

Fulbright fellow at Monks Wood Experimental Station in England, 1971-72; fellow of National Wildlife Federation, 1974-75; Governor's Writers Awards, 1985, for *The Audubon Society Handbook for Butterfly Watchers,* 1987, for *Wintergreen,* and 2000, for *Chas-*

ing *Monarchs: A Migration with the Butterflies of Passage;* John Burroughs Medal and award from Pacific Northwest Booksellers Association, both 1987, for *Wintergreen;* Guggenheim fellow, 1989; distinguished service award, Society for Conservation Biology, 1997; Harry B. Nehls Award in Nature Writing, Portland Audubon Society, 2002; John Adams Comstock Award, Lepidopterists Society, 2004; grants from Sigma Xi, National Science Foundation, Colorado-Wyoming Academy of Sciences, and International Union for the Conservation of Nature and Natural Resources.

## ■ Writings

*Watching Washington Butterflies,* Seattle Audubon Society (Seattle, WA), 1974.

*The Audubon Society Field Guide to North American Butterflies,* Knopf (New York, NY), 1981, revised edition, 1985.

(With S.M. Wells and N.M. Collins) *The IUCN Invertebrate Red Data Book,* World Wildlife Fund (Gland, Switzerland), 1983.

*The Audubon Society Handbook for Butterfly Watchers,* Scribner (New York, NY), 1984, published as *Handbook for Butterfly Watchers,* Houghton Mifflin (Boston, MA), 1992.

*Wintergreen: Rambles in a Ravaged Land* (essays), Scribner (New York, NY), 1986, published as *Wintergreen: Listening to the Land's Heart,* Houghton Mifflin (Boston, MA), 1986.

*The Thunder Tree: Lessons from an Urban Wildland,* Houghton Mifflin (Boston, MA), 1993.

(With Kristin Kest) *Peterson Field Guide to Insects Coloring Book,* Houghton Mifflin (Boston, MA), 1993.

(With Roger Tory Peterson and Sarah Anne Hughes) *A Field Guide to Butterflies Coloring Book,* Houghton Mifflin (Boston, MA), 1993.

*Where Bigfoot Walks: Crossing the Dark Divide,* Houghton Mifflin (Boston, MA), 1995.

*Chasing Monarchs: A Migration with the Butterflies of Passage,* Houghton Mifflin (Boston, MA), 1999.

(Editor, with Brian Boyd, and coauthor of annotations) *Nabokov's Butterflies: Unpublished and Uncollected Writings,* translations by Dmitri Nabokov, Beacon Press (Boston, MA), 2000.

*Walking the High Ridge: Life as a Field Trip,* Milkweed Editions (Minneapolis, MN), 2000.

*The Butterflies of Cascadia: A Field Guide to All the Species of Washington, Oregon, and Surrounding Territories,* Seattle Audubon Society (Seattle, WA), 2002.

*Sky Time in Gray's River: Living for Keeps in a Forgotten Place,* Houghton Mifflin (Boston, MA), 2007.

*Mariposa Road: The First Butterfly Big Year,* Houghton Mifflin Harcourt (Boston, MA), 2010.

(Author of foreword) David G. James and David Nunnallee, *Life Histories of Cascadia Butterflies,* Oregon State University Press (Corvallis, OR), 2011.

Work represented in anthologies, including *Butterfly Gardening: Creating Summer Magic in Your Garden,* Sierra Books, 1990; *The Norton Book of Nature Writing,* W.W. Norton (New York, NY), 1990; *Getting Over the Color Green: Contemporary Environmental Literature of the Southwest,* edited by Scott Slovic, University of Arizona Press (Tucson, AZ), 2001; *Blessed "Pests" of the Beloved West: An Affectionate Collection on Insects and Their Kin,* edited by Yvette A. Schnoeker-Shorb and Terril L. Shorb, Native West Press (Prescott, AZ), 2004; and *Holding Common Ground: The Individual and Public Lands in the American West,* edited by Paul Lindholdt and Derrick Knowles, Eastern Washington University Press (Spokane, WA), 2005.

Author of "The Tangled Bank," a bimonthly column in *Orion Afield,* 1997-2002, and *Orion,* 2003—.

Contributor of more than 300 articles, short stories, and poems to periodicals, including *Audubon, Natural History, High Country News, Horticulture, Biological Conservation, International Wildlife, Rain, Petroglyph, North American Review,* and *Pacific Northwest.* Founding editor, *Atala, Rutland Review,* and *Willapa Review.*

## ■ Sidelights

Robert Michael Pyle is a highly regarded author whose works combine scholarly knowledge of the natural world with a writer's eye for description, anecdote, and adventure. He is best known for his work on butterflies, especially *The Audubon Society Field Guide to North American Butterflies.* Living in the American West, it is perhaps not surprising that Pyle should also be an expert on the monarch butterfly and its epic annual migration from Canada and the northern United States to Southern California and Mexico.

### *Chasing Monarchs* and *Nabokov's Butterflies*

Pyle's *Chasing Monarchs: A Migration with the Butterflies of Passage* approaches the monarch migration from a different perspective: the author set out to follow individual butterflies as far as he could, to more precisely map their torturous journeys. Considering the fact that butterflies do not always follow roadways, Pyle's fifty-seven day, 9,462-mile journey proved quite a challenge indeed. In the process of the trip, however, he was able to prove that monarchs west of the Rockies do not all migrate to California, as was commonly believed. In a *Publishers' Weekly* review of *Chasing Monarchs,* a contributor wrote that Pyle's "memoir serves both as tribute to this majestic insect and as a thoughtful tour of the contemporary American West." And in her *New York Times* review of the book, Michiko Kakutani observed: "The author's evident passion for and understanding of butterflies invest his narrative with energy and interest. By far the most absorbing portions of this book deal with Mr. Pyle's interaction with the monarchs (tagging and tracking them and watching them feed and navigate) and his musings on their history and their habits."

Pyle combined his love of butterflies and enjoyment of literature when he set out, with biographer Brian Boyd, to capture and collect every specimen he could find of writings that demonstrate author Vladimir Nabokov's passion for butterflies. The result of this quest is the massive collection titled *Nabokov's Butterflies: Unpublished and Uncollected Writings.* It may surprise readers to learn that the literary giant was also a respected collector of butterflies who conducted his own expeditions and contributed substantially to the scientific knowledge of the butterflies known colloquially as "blues." Nabokov's published works are liberally sprinkled with references to the delicate creatures, but here, in nearly 800 pages, Pyle and Boyd present letters, scientific papers, unpublished poems, and fragments of other writings that also contain references to butterflies. A *Publishers Weekly* contributor made special note of a long essay translated from Russian by Nabokov's son Dmitri, as well as the short story "The Admirable Anglewing," written near the end of Nabokov's career and never published in his lifetime.

### Where Bigfoot Walks

In the late 1980s Pyle received a Guggenheim fellowship to track and study a truly elusive creature: the legendary Bigfoot, which resulted in the publication of *Where Bigfoot Walks: Crossing the Dark Divide.* While not a staunch believer in Bigfoot himself, Pyle interviewed dozens of people who claimed to have seen the animal, including Native Americans of the Northwest whose stories abound in sightings of the beast.

As Robert Sullivan stated in the *New York Times Book Review,* the author's aim was "to examine the myth surrounding the controversial creature and the human characters who have concerned themselves with its fate." This is not to say that Pyle conducted his research from the safety of home and hearth; instead, he donned a backpack and hiked through a

wilderness area in southwestern Washington that is known for its Bigfoot sightings. Sullivan wrote: "For those unfamiliar with the Bigfoot legend, *Where Bigfoot Walks* is a good primer. For those up to speed, the story Mr. Pyle has recorded of a Sasquatch-like encounter as told around the campfire by a former Haisla Nation chief from coastal British Columbia may be worth all the rehashing; it is one of the best I've ever read." An *American Heritage* contributor characterized *Where Bigfoot Walks* as "a natural history of the Northwest as well as an education in forestry." The critic added: "Even if the creature is only a metaphor for our diminishing wilderness, by the end of this book it remains a far more powerful symbol than the spotted owl or marbled murrelet. To Pyle it is a myth worth rescuing 'from the gutter' and the tabloids."

### Wintergreen and Sky Time in Gray's River

In 1986 Pyle introduced readers to his home in the Willapa Hills of the Pacific Northwest in the essay collection *Wintergreen: Rambles in a Ravaged Land.* Some twenty years later, in *Sky Time in Gray's River: Living for Keeps in a Forgotten Place,* he approaches the remote location from a different direction. Pyle told *CA:* "*Sky Time in Gray's River* is a close examination of life in one rural place three decades, a love song to staying put, and a personal phenomenology of place."

*Wintergreen* "painted a broad picture" of Gray's River, according to Ilse Heidmann in *Library Journal,* appropriate for readers visiting the place for the first time. In *Sky Time in Gray's River* he writes about the small details of daily living, accumulated over thirty years of observation and musing. The essays are arranged in the form of a monthly record that proceeds from one season of the year to the next, in a place where the years themselves appear to have changed very little over time. "Pyle has the ability to find wonder in the mundane and beauty in the unpretentious," observed Heidmann.

### Mariposa Road

Pyle published *Mariposa Road: The First Butterfly Big Year* in 2010. The account serves as Pyle's travelogue when he set off on the road to document as many species of butterflies that he could in a single year. Pyle followed the migration routes and managed to document 477 different species. In addition to highlighting each one, he also shares the personal story of his journey.

Writing in the *Seattle Times,* Irene Wanner commented that "this account is not rocket science (luckily). There are some scientific names to negotiate, but armchair travelers who love a good yarn will find Pyle's exuberance catching." Reviewing the book in the Minneapolis *Star Tribune,* James P. Lenfestey found that "it's a joy to ride along on Pyle's 'Butterfly Big Year.' At 588 pages, the book appears a heavy load, but turning the pages is as breezy as, well, stopping the car, getting out and chasing something miraculous." A contributor to *Kirkus Reviews* suggested that the book is more than "a sweet, unhurried travelogue; it can easily be used as a guidebook, as Pyle is scrupulous in detailing where and when he found each of the butterflies." Finding the book "delightful," *Booklist* contributor Nancy Bent concluded that "this one is great fun."

### Pyle once told *CA:*

"Unlike several authors working from the landscape today, I was trained in natural history, science, and conservation much more than in literature. This was undertaken by design, and with difficulty, in an era when nature study was considered passé. I was stimulated by the early nature writers and by personal contact with Edwin Way Teale, and I always wrote during my career in conservation biology. My minimal writing instruction from good teachers (Jack Cady and Linda Daniel) and my own random reading provided one side of whatever literary background I acquired along the way. The rest has come from writing, particularly in close collaboration with excellent editors, especially Harry Foster at Houghton Mifflin.

"My early books were about a great love, butterflies. Recent books have been inspired by landscapes I have been close to, and the love of damaged lands, a particular concern of mine. For many years I have been independent, with the writing having assumed the primary position in my work-world as conservation and biology have receded; they remain important to me, but on a voluntary, avocational level.

"I consider conservation of natural diversity and limitation of human population effects to be the most important work in the world, and my own response to those imperatives has shifted from scientific to artistic, with a good dose of activism remaining. The greatest challenge is to write, remain active, communicate (teach, correspond), and live, while remaining a 'real' naturalist who goes frequently afield."

"As of 2006, I have had the platform of my column in *Orion* in which to address many of my current concerns and responses to the world around me. As a result of this outlet, I have devoted relatively little effort to other magazine work, concentrating instead on book projects and, more and more, on poetry.

My novel in progress, *Magdalena Mountain,* is entering its thirty-second year and eighth draft; I consider it a long-term apprenticeship in fiction, but I do intend to conclude and publish it soon. My greatest challenge as a freelance writer remains what Jackson Brown elegantly described as 'being caught between the longing for love and the struggle for the legal tender,' and the difficult balance that poses between travel for supportive work engagements and unbroken periods of writing at home. The advent of e-mail has facilitated certain aspects of the work, while dramatically hobbling one's concentration. I no longer find it possible to be online at home and still maintain devotion to page and place. By using a community computer center now and then, I keep my study free from the infinite distraction of e-mail and the ever-so-well-named sticky web of electrons. As always I write by attending closely to the physical details of the world and responding to them. I do not believe that nature writing exists apart from writing in general, as I know nothing outside of nature that can be written about. However, that which goes beyond the strictly human, and extends to the out-of-doors, remains most compelling to me.

## ■ Biographical And Critical Sources

*BOOKS*

*Dictionary of Literary Biography,* Volume 275: *American Nature Writers,* Gale (Detroit, MI), 2003.

Pyle, Robert Michael, *Mariposa Road: The First Butterfly Big Year,* Houghton Mifflin Harcourt (Boston, MA), 2010.

Satterfield, Terre, and Scott Slovic, *What's Nature Worth? Narrative Expressions of Environmental Values,* University of Utah Press (Salt Lake City, UT), 2004.

*PERIODICALS*

*American Heritage,* September 1, 1995, review of *Where Bigfoot Walks: Crossing the Dark Divide,* p. 91.

*American West,* November 1, 1984, review of *The Audubon Society Handbook for Butterfly Watchers,* p. 68.

*Amicus Journal,* December 22, 2000, Fred Baumgarten, review of *Chasing Monarchs: A Migration with the Butterflies of Passage,* p. 44.

*Atlantic,* August 1, 1995, review of *Where Bigfoot Walks,* p. 106.

*Audubon,* March 1, 2000, Christopher Camuto, review of *Chasing Monarchs,* p. 157.

*Birder's World,* April 1, 2011, review of *Mariposa Road,* p. 17.

*Bloomsbury Review,* July 1, 1994, review of *The Thunder Tree: Lessons from an Urban Wildland,* p. 5; July 1, 1994, review of *Wintergreen: Rambles in a Ravaged Land,* p. 5; March 1, 1996, review of *Where Bigfoot Walks,* p. 17.

*Booklist,* May 1, 1993, Angus Trimnell, review of *The Thunder Tree,* p. 1555; July 1, 1999, Donna Seaman, review of *Chasing Monarchs,* p. 1912; October 15, 2010, Nancy Bent, review of *Mariposa Road,* p. 8.

*Bookwatch,* July 1, 1993, review of *The Thunder Tree,* p. 8.

*Choice: Current Reviews for Academic Libraries,* October 1, 1993, review of *The Thunder Tree,* p. 293; October 1, 2000, M. Gochfeld, review of *Nabokov's Butterflies: Unpublished and Uncollected Writings,* p. 354.

*Conservationist,* February 1, 1993, Arthur Woldt, review of *The Audubon Society Handbook for Butterfly Watchers,* p. 43.

*E,* January 1, 2002, review of *Wintergreen,* p. 60.

*English Journal,* November 1, 1994, James LeMonds, review of *The Thunder Tree,* p. 106; October 1, 1996, James LeMonds, review of *Where Bigfoot Walks,* p. 122.

*Environment,* March 1, 1999, review of *Wintergreen,* p. 9.

*Globe & Mail* (Toronto, Ontario, Canada), September 18, 1999, review of *Chasing Monarchs,* p. D17.

*Hungry Mind Review,* December 22, 1995, review of *Where Bigfoot Walks,* p. 7.

*Kirkus Reviews,* March 15, 1993, review of *The Thunder Tree,* p. 357; May 15, 1995, review of *Where Bigfoot Walks,* p. 692; June 15, 1999, review of *Chasing Monarchs,* p. 945; July 15, 2010, review of *Mariposa Road.*

*Kliatt,* November 1, 1992, review of *The Audubon Society Handbook for Butterfly Watchers,* p. 43; January 1, 2002, Katherine E. Gillen, review of *Nabokov's Butterflies,* p. 33.

*Library Journal,* June 15, 1984, review of *The Audubon Society Handbook for Butterfly Watchers,* p. 1233; February 1, 1987, Carol J. Lichtenberg, review of *Wintergreen,* p. 85; April 15, 1993, William H. Wiese, review of *The Thunder Tree,* p. 123; July 1, 1995, Valerie Vaughan, review of *Where Bigfoot Walks,* p. 116; June 1, 1996, Michael Rogers, review of *Wintergreen,* p. 158; July 1, 1999, Gregg Sapp, review of *Chasing Monarchs,* p. 127; November 1, 2006, Ilse Heidmann, review of *Sky Time in Gray's River: Living for Keeps in a Forgotten Place,* p. 106.

*Los Angeles Times,* June 2, 1996, review of *Wintergreen,* p. 15.

*Natural History,* July 1, 1995, review of *Where Bigfoot Walks,* p. 69.

*New Criterion,* September 1, 2000, Guy Davenport, review of *Nabokov's Butterflies,* p. 74.

*New Scientist,* August 5, 1995, Toby Howard, review of *Where Bigfoot Walks,* p. 45; December 25, 1999, review of *Chasing Monarchs,* p. 81.

*New York Review of Books,* June 21, 2001, Michael Wood, review of *Nabokov's Butterflies,* p. 39.

*New York Times Book Review,* July 30, 1995, Robert Sullivan, review of *Where Bigfoot Walks,* p. 21; August 13, 1999, Michiko Kakutani, review of *Chasing Monarchs,* p. B42; August 15, 1999, Stewart Kellerman, review of *Chasing Monarchs,* p. 15; May 7, 2000, Laurie Adlerstein, review of *Nabokov's Butterflies,* p. 22.

*Peninsula,* September 22, 1992, Jane Elder Wulff, "Dr. Robert Michael Pyle: A Meticulous Observer of Life," pp. 18-21.

*Poets and Writers,* March 1, 1996, Ray Kelleher, "An Interview with Robert Michael Pyle," pp. 45-61.

*Publishers Weekly,* November 21, 1986, Genevieve Stuttaford, review of *Wintergreen,* p. 42; March 15, 1993, review of *The Thunder Tree,* p. 75; June 12, 1995, review of *Where Bigfoot Walks,* p. 55; June 7, 1999, review of *Chasing Monarchs,* p. 62; March 13, 2000, review of *Nabokov's Butterflies,* p. 74; October 16, 2006, review of *Sky Time in Gray's River,* p. 43.

*Review of Contemporary Fiction,* September 22, 2000, Irving Malin, review of *Nabokov's Butterflies,* p. 154.

*Science,* October 6, 2000, May Berenbaum, review of *Nabokov's Butterflies,* p. 57.

*Science Books & Films,* March 1, 2007, Albert Edward Feldman, review of *Sky Time in Gray's River,* p. 65.

*SciTech Book News,* September 1, 1992, review of *The Audubon Society Handbook for Butterfly Watchers,* p. 24.

*Seattle Times,* October 11, 2010, Irene Wanner, review of *Mariposa Road.*

*Sierra,* May 1, 1987, Christopher Camuto, review of *Wintergreen,* p. 83.

*Star Tribune* (Minneapolis, MN), December 4, 2010, James P. Lenfestey, review of *Mariposa Road.*

*Times Higher Education Supplement,* July 7, 2000, Rod Mengham, review of *Nabokov's Butterflies,* p. 23.

*Virginia Quarterly Review,* June 22, 2007, Hugh Gildea, review of *Sky Time in Gray's River,* p. 268.

*Washington Post Book World,* July 16, 1995, review of *Where Bigfoot Walks,* p. 8.

*Western American Literature,* September 22, 1995, review of *Wintergreen* and *The Thunder Tree,* p. 296; September 22, 1995, review of *Where Bigfoot Walks,* p. 298.

*Whole Earth,* September 22, 2000, review of *Nabokov's Butterflies,* p. 37.

*Wilderness,* June 22, 1988, Charles E. Little, review of *Wintergreen,* p. 60.

ONLINE

*Central Washington University, Department of Geography Web site,* http://www.cwu.edu/ (July 29, 2011), author profile.*

# Charles Rappleye

## ■ Personal

Married Tulsa Kinney; children: two.

## ■ Addresses

*Home*—Los Angeles, CA. *E-mail*—chasrap@sbc global.net.

## ■ Career

Journalist, editor, and writer. *Artillery* magazine, cofounder; previously worked as an editor at *LA Weekly*.

## ■ Awards, Honors

Best book of 2006, American Revolution Round Table, 2006, for *Sons of Providence*; George Washington Book Prize, 2007, for best book on the colonial era.

## ■ Writings

(With Ed Becker) *All American Mafioso: The Johnny Rosselli Story*, Doubleday (New York, NY), 1991.

*Sons of Providence: The Brown Brothers, the Slave Trade, and the American Revolution*, Simon & Schuster (New York, NY), 2006.

*Robert Morris: Financier of the American Revolution*, Simon & Schuster (New York, NY), 2010.

Contributor to periodicals and journals, including *Virginia Quarterly Review, American Journalism Review, Columbia Journalism Review, LA Weekly, Los Angeles City Beat*, and *OC Weekly*.

## ■ Sidelights

Charles Rappleye is a longtime journalist who has written largely about media, law enforcement, and organized crime. He and his wife, Tulsa Kinney, founded the magazine *Artillery*. Prior to that, Rappleye served as an editor for *LA Weekly*.

### *All American Mafioso* and *Sons of Providence*

Rappleye collaborated with private detective Ed Becker on his first book, *All American Mafioso: The Johnny Rosselli Story*. The book follows Rosselli's life as a young immigrant from Italy who began working for the notorious Al Capone and became a leader in organized crime well into the 1970s, when he was murdered. The authors trace the Mafioso's career to Hollywood and the film industry, Las Vegas, and even to the political powers in Washington. "The biography will be much discussed," wrote a *Publishers Weekly* contributor.

In his next book, a solo effort titled *Sons of Providence: The Brown Brothers, the Slave Trade, and the American Revolution,* Rappleye tells the story of John and Moses Brown, brothers from a wealthy family who were diametrically opposite in their viewpoints and activities associated with slavery. While John worked in and defended the slave trade, Moses was an early abolitionist and wrote the first Federal law in America banning slave trading. Ironically, the first person convicted under the law was his brother John. Comparing *Sons of Providence* to Brown's first book, *All American Mafioso, Washington Post Book World* contributor Jonathan Yardley noted: "The leap from the Mafia to colonial New England is a long one, but Rappleye makes it with style. He is a diligent researcher . . . and a fair-minded, unjudgmental chronicler of the Browns' complicated story."

Other reviewers also commended Rappleye for his history of the Brown brothers and their conflict. "Rappleye . . . skillfully details the complex relationship between these brothers," wrote David S. Reynolds in the *New York Times Book Review.* Referring to the book as "incisive," a *Publishers Weekly* contributor went on to write that *Sons of Providence* "provides unique insight into the festering wound of slavery." Several reviewers noted how the Browns's saga not only reflects much of the internal struggle of America's attitudes concerning slavery but also a broader struggle that has persisted throughout American history. For example, Vernon Ford, writing for *Booklist,* commented that the story "reflects on many issues that remain American dilemmas: the balance between commercial and religious and political ideals."

### Robert Morris

In 2010, Rappleye published *Robert Morris: Financier of the American Revolution.* Liverpool native Robert Morris was one of the most successful businessmen of his era and He served as superintendent of finance in the early 1780s and was a desired Cabinet choice by both Washington and Jefferson. Morris's funding of the American revolutionary armies played a crucial role in their campaigns against the British. However, his post-revolution business failures, bankruptcy, and eventual imprisonment tempered the significance of his national contributions.

Reviewing the book in *Public Contract Law Journal,* James F. Nagle observed that "Rappleye's book is thorough with an astonishing number of references to contemporaneous letters and diaries. . . . It provides fascinating insights into the American Revolution and shows it was not as clear in terms of the British and Tories versus Patriots as you might have been led to believe." Nagle concluded that *Robert Morris* "helps restore Morris to his rightful place among the Founding Fathers." A contributor to *Kirkus Reviews* also believed that the book "provides thorough coverage of a deserving subject." A *New Yorker* reviewer found the account to be an "illuminating account of the Revolution's improvised and even dodgy finances." In a review in *Library Journal,* Bryan Craig claimed that "Rappl-

eye has written a definitive biography of Morris that neither scholars nor history buffs should ignore."

## ■ Biographical And Critical Sources

*PERIODICALS*

*Booklist,* September 15, 1991, review of *All American Mafioso: The Johnny Rosselli Story,* p. 103; June 1, 2006, Vernon Ford, review of *Sons of Providence: The Brown Brothers, the Slave Trade, and the American Revolution,* p. 29.
*Choice: Current Reviews for Academic Libraries,* April 1, 2007, R.T. Brown, review of *Sons of Providence,* p. 1402.
*Historian,* December 22, 2007, Barbara Ryan, review of *Sons of Providence,* p. 791.
*Journal of the Early Republic,* March 22, 2008, Lesley Doig, review of *Sons of Providence,* p. 140.
*Kirkus Reviews,* July 15, 1991, review of *All American Mafioso,* p. 915; August 1, 2010, review of *Robert Morris: Financier of the American Revolution.*
*Library Journal,* September 1, 1991, Gregor A. Preston, review of *All American Mafioso,* p. 213; May 15, 2006, Robert Flatley, review of *Sons of Providence,* p. 112; September 15, 2010, Bryan Craig, review of *Robert Morris,* p. 82.
*New Yorker,* November 22, 2010, review of *Robert Morris,* p. 135.
*New York Times Book Review,* May 14, 2006, David S. Reynolds, review of *Sons of Providence.*
*Public Contract Law Journal,* March 22, 2011, James F. Nagle, review of *Robert Morris,* p. 891.
*Publishers Weekly,* June 28, 1991, review of *All American Mafioso,* p. 95; March 27, 2006, review of *Sons of Providence,* p. 70; September 6, 2010, review of *Robert Morris,* p. 32.
*Virginia Quarterly Review,* accessed May 23, 2007, author profile.
*Washington Post Book World,* June 11, 2006, Jonathan Yardley, review of *Sons of Providence,* p. BW2.

*ONLINE*

*Anchor Rising Blog,* http://www.anchorrising.com/ (May 24, 2006), Carroll Andrew Morse, "History: Charles Rappleye, author interview.
*Charles Rappleye Home Page,* http://www.rapwest.com (May 23, 2007).
*Simon & Schuster Web site,* http://www.simonsays.com/ (May 23, 2007), author profile.*

# Ruth Rendell

## 1930-

### ■ Also Known As

Ruth Barbara Grasemann
Ruth Rendell, Baroness of Babergh
Barbara Vine

### ■ Personal

Born February 17, 1930, in London, England; daughter of Arthur (a teacher) and Ebba (a teacher) Grasemann; married Donald Rendell, 1950 (divorced, 1975; remarried, 1977; deceased, c. 1999); children: Simon. *Hobbies and other interests:* Reading, walking, opera.

### ■ Addresses

*Home*—London, England. *Agent*—PFD, Drury House, 34-43 Russell St., London WC2B 5HA, England.

### ■ Career

Writer, novelist, short-story writer, and journalist. Express and Independent Newspapers, West Essex, England, reporter and subeditor for the Chigwell *Times*, 1948-52. Member of British House of Lords.

### ■ Awards, Honors

Edgar Allan Poe Award, Mystery Writers of America, 1975, for story "The Fallen Curtain," 1976, for collection *The Fallen Curtain and Other Stories,* 1984, for story "The New Girlfriend," and 1986, for novel *A Dark-Adapted Eye;* Gold Dagger Award, Crime Writers Association, 1977, for *A Demon in My View,* 1986, for *Live Flesh,* and 1987, for *A Fatal Inversion;* British Arts Council bursary, 1981; British Arts Council National Book Award, 1981, for *The Lake of Darkness;* Popular Culture Association Award, 1983; Silver Dagger Award, Crime Writers Association, 1984, for *The Tree of Hands;* Angel Award for fiction, 1988, for *The House of Stars; Sunday Times* award for Literary Excellence, 1990; Gold Dagger Award, Crime Writers Association, 1991, for *King Solomon's Carpet;* Cartier Diamond Dagger Award for a lifetime's achievement in the field, Crime Writers Association, 1991; named Commander of the British Empire, 1996; Grand Master Award, Mystery Writers of America, 1997; named Baroness Rendell of Babergh, 1997; *Mystery Ink* Gumshoe Award for Lifetime Achievement, 2004; Crime Writers Association; *Sunday Times* Literary Award.

### ■ Writings

*MYSTERY NOVELS*

*To Fear a Painted Devil,* Doubleday (New York, NY), 1965.

*Vanity Dies Hard,* John Long (London, England), 1966, published as *In Sickness and in Health,* Doubleday (New York, NY), 1966.

*The Secret House of Death,* John Long (London, England), 1968, Doubleday (New York, NY), 1969.

*One Across, Two Down,* Doubleday (New York, NY), 1971.

*The Face of Trespass,* Doubleday (New York, NY), 1974.

*A Demon in My View,* Doubleday (New York, NY), 1977.

*A Judgment in Stone,* Hutchinson (London, England), 1977, Doubleday (New York, NY), 1978.

*Make Death Love Me,* Doubleday (New York, NY), 1979.

*The Lake of Darkness,* Doubleday (New York, NY), 1980.

*Master of the Moor,* Pantheon (New York, NY), 1982.

*The Killing Doll,* Pantheon (New York, NY), 1984.

*The Tree of Hands,* Pantheon (New York, NY), 1984.

*Live Flesh,* Pantheon (New York, NY), 1986.

*Heartstones,* Harper (New York, NY), 1987.

*Talking to Strangers,* Hutchinson (London, England), 1987, published as *Talking to Strange Men,* Pantheon (New York, NY), 1987.

*The Bridesmaid,* Mysterious Press (New York, NY), 1989.

*Going Wrong,* Mysterious Press (New York, NY), 1990.

*The Crocodile Bird,* Crown (New York, NY), 1993.

*Ginger and the Kingsmarkham Chalk Circle,* Phoenix (London, England), 1996.

*The Keys to the Street,* Random House (New York, NY), 1996.

*Bloodlines: Long and Short Stories,* Wheeler (Rockland, MA), 1997.

*Whydunit (Perfectly Criminal 2),* Severn House (London, England), 1997.

*Thornapple,* Travelman (London, England), 1998.

*A Sight for Sore Eyes: A Novel,* Crown (New York, NY), 1999.

*Adam and Eve and Pinch Me,* Crown (New York, NY), 2001.

*The Rottweiler,* Crown (New York, NY), 2004.

*Thirteen Steps Down,* Crown Publishers (New York, NY), 2004.

*The Water's Lovely,* Crown Publishers (New York, NY), 2007.

*Portobello,* Doubleday Canada (Toronto, Ontario, Canada), 2008.

*Tigerlily's Orchids,* Doubleday Canada (Toronto, Ontario, Canada), 2010.

## "INSPECTOR WEXFORD" SERIES; MYSTERY NOVELS

*From Doon with Death* (also see below), John Long (London, England), 1964, Doubleday (New York, NY), 1965, reprinted Ballantine Books (New York, NY), 2007.

*Wolf to the Slaughter,* John Long (London, England), 1967, Doubleday (New York, NY), 1968, reprinted, Ballantine Books (New York, NY), 2008.

*A New Lease of Death* (also see below), Doubleday (New York, NY), 1967, published as *Sins of the Fathers,* Ballantine (New York, NY), 1970.

*The Best Man to Die,* John Long (London, England), 1969, Doubleday (New York, NY), 1970.

*A Guilty Thing Surprised,* Doubleday (New York, NY), 1970.

*No More Dying Then,* Hutchinson (London, England), 1971, Doubleday (New York, NY), 1972.

*Murder Being Once Done,* Doubleday (New York, NY), 1972.

*Some Lie and Some Die,* Doubleday (New York, NY), 1973.

*Shake Hands Forever,* Doubleday (New York, NY), 1975.

*A Sleeping Life,* Doubleday (New York, NY), 1978.

*Put on by Cunning,* Hutchinson (London, England), 1981, published as *Death Notes,* Pantheon (New York, NY), 1981.

*The Speaker of Mandarin,* Pantheon (New York, NY), 1983.

*An Unkindness of Ravens,* Pantheon (New York, NY), 1985.

*The Veiled One,* Pantheon (New York, NY), 1988.

*Kissing the Gunner's Daughter,* Mysterious Press (New York, NY), 1992.

*Simisola,* Random House (New York, NY), 1995.

*Road Rage,* Crown (New York, NY), 1997.

*Harm Done,* Crown (New York, NY), 1999.

*The Babes in the Wood,* Crown (New York, NY), 2002.

*End in Tears,* Crown (New York, NY), 2006.

*Not in the Flesh,* Crown (New York, NY), 2007.

*The Monster in the Box,* Doubleday Canada (Toronto, Ontario, Canada), 2009.

*The Vault,* Scribner (New York, NY), 2011.

## STORY COLLECTIONS

*The Fallen Curtain and Other Stories,* Hutchinson (London, England), 1976, published as *The Fallen Curtain: Eleven Mystery Stories by an Edgar Award-Winning Writer,* Doubleday (New York, NY), 1976.

*Means of Evil and Other Stories,* Hutchinson (London, England), 1979, published as *Five Mystery Stories by an Edgar Award-Winning Writer,* Doubleday (Garden City, NY), 1980.

*The Fever Tree and Other Stories,* Hutchinson (London, England), 1982, Pantheon (New York, NY), 1983, published as *The Fever Tree and Other Stories of Suspense,* Ballantine (New York, NY), 1984.

*The New Girlfriend and Other Stories,* Hutchinson (London, England), 1985, published as *The New Girlfriend and Other Stories of Suspense,* Pantheon (New York, NY), 1986.

(Editor) *A Warning to the Curious: The Ghost Stories of M.R. James,* Hutchinson (London, England), 1986.

*Collected Short Stories,* Hutchinson (London, England), 1987, published as *Collected Stories,* Pantheon (New York, NY), 1988.

*The Copper Peacock and Other Stories*, Mysterious Press (New York, NY), 1991.

*Blood Lines: Long and Short Stories*, Crown (New York, NY), 1996.

*Piranha to Scurfy and Other Stories*, Vintage (New York, NY), 2002.

*Collected Stories II*, Hutchinson (London, England), 2008.

*NOVELS; UNDER PSEUDONYM BARBARA VINE*

*A Dark-Adapted Eye*, Viking (New York, NY), 1985.

*A Fatal Inversion*, Bantam (New York, NY), 1987.

(With others) *Yes, Prime Minister: The Diaries of the Right Honorable James Hacker*, Salem House Publishers, 1988.

*The House of Stairs*, Harmony Books (New York, NY), 1989.

*Gallowglass*, Harmony Books (New York, NY), 1990.

*King Solomon's Carpet*, Harmony Books (New York, NY), 1992.

*Anna's Book*, Harmony Books (New York, NY), 1993.

*No Night Is Too Long*, Harmony Books (New York, NY), 1994.

*The Brimstone Wedding*, Harmony Books (New York, NY), 1996.

*The Chimney Sweeper's Boy*, Harmony Books (New York, NY), 1998.

*Grasshopper*, Harmony Books (New York, NY), 2000.

*The Blood Doctor*, Shaye Areheart Books (New York, NY), 2002.

*The Minotaur*, Shaye Areheart Books (New York, NY), 2005.

*The Birthday Present*, Crown (New York, NY), 2009.

*OTHER*

*"People Don't Do Such Things"* (episode of *Tales of the Unexpected*), Independent Television (ITV), 1985.

(With Colin Ward) *Undermining the Central Line*, Chatto & Windus (London, England), 1989.

(With photographs by Paul Bowden) *Ruth Rendell's Suffolk* (nonfiction), Hutchinson (London, England), 1992.

(Editor) *The Reason Why: An Anthology of the Murderous Mind*, Crown (New York, NY), 1996.

Contributor to anthologies, including *Haunted Houses: The Greatest Stories*, edited by Martin H. Greenberg, 1983; *Haunting Women*, edited by Alan Ryan, Avon Books (New York, NY), 1988; *Scare Care*, edited by Graham Masterson, St. Martin's Press (New York, NY), 1989; *The New Gothic: A Collection of Contemporary Gothic Fiction*, edited by Patrick McGrath and Bradford Morrow, Random House

(New York, NY), 1991; *I Shudder at Your Touch*, edited by Michelle Slung, ROC (New York, NY), 1992; *Little Deaths*, edited by Ellen Datlow, Dell (New York, NY), 1995; *Mistresses of the Dark: 25 Macabre Tales by Master Storytellers*, edited by Stefan R. Dziemianowicz, Denise Little, and Robert E. Weinberg, Barnes & Noble Books, 1998; and *The Mammoth Book of Haunted House Stories*, edited by Peter Haining, Carroll & Graf (New York, NY), 2000. Also contributor of short stories to *Ellery Queen's Mystery Magazine*.

Author's works have been translated into fourteen languages.

# ■ Adaptations

*A Judgment in Stone* was filmed as *The Housekeeper*, Rawfilm/Schulz Productions, 1987; several of Rendell's Wexford mysteries have been adapted for British television and subsequently aired on the Arts and Entertainment network's "Masters of Mystery" series; numerous Ruth Rendell and Barbara Vine short stories and novels have been adapted to film and television as stand-alone programs and as part of the "Ruth Rendell Mysteries" series, including *An Affair in Mind*, 1988, *A Guilty Thing Surprised*, 1988, *Shake Hands Forever*, 1988, *Tree of Hands*, 1989, *No More Dying Then*, 1989, *The Veiled One*, 1989, *The Best Man to Die*, 1990, *Put on by Cunning*, 1990, *A New Lease of Death*, 1991, *Murder Being Once Done*, 1991, *From Doon with Death*, 1991, *Talking to Strange Men*, 1992, *A Fatal Inversion*, 1992, *The Speaker of Mandarin*, 1992, *Kissing the Gunner's Daughter*, 1992, *Gallowglass*, 1993, *Vanity Dies Hard*, 1995, *The Secret House of Death*, 1996, *Simisola*, 1996, *Road Rage*, 1998, *Lake of Darkness*, 1999, *The Fallen Curtain*, 1999, *Harm Done*, 2000, and *No Night Is Too Long*, 2002; *The Tree of Hands* was adapted as the film *Betty Fisher et autres histoires* (also known as *Alias Betty*), 2001.

# ■ Sidelights

Ruth Rendell is a prolific author who, writing under her own name and the pseudonym Barbara Vine, has enthralled both the general public and literary critics with her skillfully written mysteries and suspenseful stories. She has the ability, according to *Dictionary of Literary Biography* contributor Patricia A. Gabilondo, to render tales that could be considered formulaic into something "always suspenseful and viscerally compelling." In her first novel, *From Doon with Death*, the author introduces Chief Inspector Reginald Wexford, a proper Englishman whose town of Kingsmarkham, Sussex, is plagued by many murders. Wexford has been the subject of numerous sequels and has won much praise for his creator for the deft characterizations, clever plots, and surprising endings that mark these books. While the Wexford books are straightforward police procedural novels, the books Rendell publishes under the Vine pseudonym are more gothic, often involving twisted psychology to produce edgy thrillers. David Lehman in *Newsweek* commented that "few detective writers are as good at pulling such last-second rabbits out of their top hats—the last page making us see everything before it in a strange, new glare."

## "Inspector Wexford" Series

Rendell's Wexford character is middle-aged, happily married, and the father of two grown daughters. His extensive reading allows him to quote from a wide range of literature during his murder investigations, but despite his erudition, Wexford is not cynical, eccentric, or misanthropic as are many literary detectives. His well-adjusted manner serves as contrast to the many strange mysteries he investigates. Social differences are frequently illuminated in these mysteries, and Rendell has been singled out as particularly skillful at portraying England's social stratification, even in the details of her descriptions of architectural features. Gabilondo mused: "Her meticulous description of setting serves to create atmosphere and, more important, to communicate the intimate relation between the physical and the psychological, especially in terms of the way that landscapes, whether urban or rural, take on the imprints of sociological change and personal conflict."

Wexford is also notable for his philosophical turn of mind and his keen empathy for his fellow man regardless of circumstance. His sensitivity makes him quite desirable to the women he encounters, yet Wexford remains determinedly devoted to his wife. Wexford's greatest disdain is for the "inanities of modernity," wrote Gabilondo. "Through Wexford's often ironic eye, Rendell paints a remarkably specific portrait of the changes that have occurred in English life—the encroachment of suburban sprawl, the banal homogenization of consumer culture, the dispossessed youth, the problems with unemployment, and the growing complexities of civil bureaucracies. Able to see both sides of any issue, as well as to grasp the essential poignancy of the human condition, Wexford finds himself often at odds with his official role, for his reliance on intuition and the imagination usually runs counter to the official line, offering a rich resource of dramatic tension," concluded Gabilondo. Wexford's open-mindedness is contrasted with the more narrow vision and rigid morality of his partner, Inspec-

tor Michael Burden. Unlike many series characters, Wexford and Burden age and go through many significant changes as the series progresses.

Rendell's early Wexford mysteries deal with desire and taboo, while in her later books she takes on social issues in a more direct manner. Feminism, ecoterrorism, and other modern concerns are examined, not always in a flattering light. In *A Sleeping Life*, gender-identity conflicts figure prominently in the murder case, while Wexford's daughter becomes involved in a radical feminist group. Rendell actually drew the ire of real-life feminist groups after the publication of *An Unkindness of Ravens*, which features a man-hating group called Action for the Radical Reform of Intersexual Attitudes (ARRIA). Members of the group vow to carry weapons and refrain from marriage; it even seems that some members advocate the murder of a man as an initiation rite. The author also ruffled feathers with *Kissing the Gunner's Daughter*, which challenges the popular notion that class stratification is much less meaningful in Britain than it has been in the past. Racism is addressed in *Simisola*, another Wexford novel; the problems of urban and suburban sprawl are considered in *Road Rage*; and the subject of wife-beating is approached in *Harm Done*.

*The Babes in the Wood* finds Inspector Wexford on the trail of teenage brother and sister Giles and Sophie Dade, who have gone missing, along with their babysitter, Joanna Troy, after heavy storms and torrential rains flood the Sussex countryside. Fears arise that the trio died in the floodwaters, but when the babysitter's body is discovered alone in her car, there is reason to hope that the children are still alive. As time passes, the likelihood of finding them alive grows dimmer, until the sudden and unexpected reappearance of the girl. Her return prompts as many questions as it answers, particularly where she has been and what has happened to her brother. Wexford's investigation reveals dreadful family secrets, shocking revelations about Giles and Sophie, and answers that are not revealed until the book's final pages. Throughout, "Rendell's gift for intelligent, coolheaded storytelling remains undiminished," commented Mark Harris in *Entertainment Weekly*.

*End in Tears* explores the sometimes criminal lengths that hopeful parents will go to in order to conceive, find, or acquire a child. Rendell also delineates the predatory element that will manipulate and exploit this primal desire for offspring. Teenage mother Amber Marshalson is found dead outside her home, her head bashed in with a brick. Sometime later, her pregnant friend Megan Bartlow is killed in a dingy row house. Inspector Wexford, dismayed by the moral decay he sees represented by the burgeoning numbers of teen pregnancies, steps in to investigate the murders of the young women. Suspicion focuses on several potential murderers, including a pair of sinister twins, a heavily tattooed and pierced ex-boyfriend, and a tall, thin man in a hooded jacket. Even Amber's grieving father, her hostile step-mother, and the wealthy parents of her baby's father are not above suspicion. Complicating Wexford's at-titude in the case is his daughter Sylvia's willing-ness to serve as surrogate mother for her ex-husband Neil and his new wife Naomi. In this book, Rendell still "proves a master at rendering the joys and sorrows of human relationships," stated *Booklist* reviewer Allison Block. A *Kirkus Reviews* critic called the story "average for Rendell's distinguished list of whodunits, which makes it just a whisker below state of the art."

*Not in the Flesh,* which was published in 2007, finds Wexford attempting to determine how the remains of two bodies wound up on the Grimble property. At first, a truffle dog finds a human hand, and the nearby body, from whence the hand came, is thought to have been buried for about a decade. Soon after this discovery, another body is found on the property, this time under a woodpile. Wexford begins gathering evidence, visiting potential wit-nesses, and the landowners, whom he suspects of the murders. The book features a cast of characters that includes Owen Tredown, who lives with his two ex-wives, Claudia and Maeve. The local Somali immigrant enclave and seasonal fruit-pickers also figure into the plot. Connie Fletcher, writing in *Booklist,* noted that "for devoted fans of the series, of whom there are many, this [book] will be much anticipated and, as always, satisfying." Comment-ing on the story's suspenseful plot, a *Publishers Weekly* reviewer stated that "the last pieces of the puzzle click elegantly yet unexpectedly into place." Another laudatory review came from a *Kirkus Re-views* writer, who called the book "rich, tangled and as sharply observed as ever."

### Stand-alone Novels

Various types of psychological torment are central in Rendell's other books. *A Judgment in Stone* portrays an illiterate woman whose inability to read has led to a life of shame, isolation, and regression. *The Killing Doll* features Dolly Yearman, a schizo-phrenic whose delusions eventually lead her to murder. *Live Flesh* is told from the point of view of a convicted murderer and rapist, who lives in a strange symbiotic relationship with the police of-ficer he crippled with a gunshot wound. In *The Bridesmaid,* the Pygmalion myth is turned inside out

as a beautiful girl is shown to be marred by her mental instability. Despite her flaws, she becomes the object of sexual obsession for Philip; eventually, she brings him to the brink of murder. One of the author's most ambitious novels is *The Keys to the Street,* which uses the concentric circles and paths of London's Regent Park to follow the interconnected threads of human lives, particularly those of a well-to-do man who lives on the streets in the wake of a family tragedy and a young woman struggling to assert her independence. Although it may be the author's "most compassionate and most complex treatment of the human condition," according to Gabilondo, it left "most reviewers disappointed in her failure to bring all the strands together. The ef-fectiveness of the structure, however, lies in this intentional failure to make everything connect. In Rendell's psychological thrillers, those avenues of emotional connection, like the misaligned arcs of Regent's Park, often do not meet, frustrating the hopes and dreams of her characters' lives." A very positive assessment of the book was offered by Emily Melton in *Booklist,* however; she wrote that it is "at once tragic, shocking, satisfying, and hope-ful," and added: "Without a doubt, Rendell ranks with today's finest writers, and this book is one of her best. . . . Superbly written and beautifully constructed, the story is unique, powerful, and provocative."

*Adam and Eve and Pinch Me* is a "gem from the Brit-ish master," wrote a *Publishers Weekly* reviewer, filled with characters "so vivid they live beyond the frame of the novel." At the center of the plot is Minty Knox, a woman in her thirties who works in a dry-cleaning business and is obsessed with germs and cleanliness. Her hygiene phobias, as well as the ghosts she imagines she sees, figure prominently in a plot that is "intricate but brisk," according to the writer, "a literary page-turner, both elegant and ac-cessible." *Booklist* reviewer Fletcher called the book "madly absorbing," and declared: "Rendell's charac-ters are fully drawn, and we become completely caught up in their struggles." Discussing her writ-ing with a *Publishers Weekly* interviewer, Rendell commented: "I do write about obsession, but I don't think I have an obsession for writing. I'm not a compulsive writer. I like to watch obsession in other people, watch the way it makes them behave."

*The Rottweiler* focuses on a bestial serial killer stalk-ing the streets of London, garroting his victims and stealing small keepsake items from their bodies. The killer earned his sobriquet from bite marks on the neck of his first victim, which he is chagrined to note were not inflicted by him. When items taken from the killer's victims begin to surface in Inez Ferry's antique shop, the police believe that the killer is one of the several boarders living in rooms above the shop. However, their investigation fails to uncover which of the eccentric residents shares his or her skin with the brutal Rottweiler. "The various characters involved including Inez herself are . . . brilliantly drawn," remarked Antonia Fraser in *Spectator*. When Rendell reveals the Rottweiler's identity a third of the way through the book, the reader's relationship with the story changes to one of knowledge tinged with dread, waiting for the killer to strike again while hoping the authorities will make an arrest before more victims die. *Entertainment Weekly* reviewer Tina Jordan called the novel "classic Rendell, macabre and fast-paced." The novel is "unusually three-dimensional for a mystery novel, with a set of characters who engage interest on their own merits," remarked Janet Maslin in the *New York Times Book Review*. "Whether they turn out to be linked to the Rottweiler's evil streak is almost a secondary matter," Maslin observed. *Orlando Sentinel* reviewer Ann Hellmuth concluded: "Ruth Rendell is the perfect storyteller, never resorting to cliches and tired formats but transfixing and enthralling with intelligent writing, clever plotting, and character development."

Obsession fuels the pathological behaviors of the characters in *Thirteen Steps Down*. Mix Cellini is an exercise-machine repairman who nurses twin obsessions: one for local supermodel Nerissa Nash, who he believes will eventually marry him, and one for another local hero, serial killer Harold Christie. Mix rents an attic room from bitter, snobbish widow Gwendolen Chawcer, who has seen her better days along with St. Blaise House, her crumbling London mansion. Gwendolen nurses a longtime obsession of her own, a romantic attachment to Dr. Stephen Reeves, who treated her dying mother 1953 and who courted her for a bit. She has not seen Reeves in almost a half century, but when she learns that his wife has died, she foresees a reunion that Reeves does not expect. Mix and Gwendolen thoroughly despise each other, but their animosity adds a frisson to their embattled relationship that mutual respect or affection would not provide. Within this volatile psychological atmosphere, madness will arise, control will be lost, and murders will occur. *New York Times Book Review* contributor Marilyn Stasio called the book a "profoundly unnerving psychological suspense novel about a young man gripped by obsessions that can lead only to madness and murder." Rendell's novel offers "vivid characters, a plot addictive as crack, and a sense of place unequaled in crime fiction," remarked a *Publishers Weekly* critic.

*The Water's Lovely*, which was published in 2007, introduces a London family torn apart by a long-buried murder. Told mostly in flashbacks, the story portrays Guy Rolland, stepfather to sisters Heather and Ismay. Twelve years ago, at age fifteen, Ismay accepted Guy's flirtations, but thirteen-year-old Heather did not. Heather ultimately kills her perverted stepfather by drowning him in the bathtub. The death is officially ruled an accident, and the family boards up the bathroom where Guy drowned, continuing to live in the house as if nothing ever happened. Now that Heather and Ismay are both adults with their own love interests, the long-ago murder begins to haunt them. As Heather prepares to wed her fiancé, Edmund Litton, Ismay feels compelled to tell her future brother-in-law of the murder. Ismay's relationship with her boyfriend, a lawyer named Andrew Campbell-Sedge, also begins to suffer. Meanwhile, a retired detective keeps an eye on the sisters, suspicious of Guy's "accidental" death. Critics applauded the book, especially the story's highly suspenseful plot. Fletcher, again writing in *Booklist*, noted: "Combining potent imagery and exquisite plotting, Rendell twists the knife of suspense in a wonderfully excruciating way." Echoing this opinion, a *Kirkus Reviews* critic observed that "the sense of impending calamity is palpable." The critic added that *The Water's Lovely* is "one of the most deeply pleasurable thrillers from the genre's leading practitioner." Yet another laudatory review came from Jennifer Resse, writing in *Entertainment Weekly*. Reese noted that "while she never explicitly judges her characters, Rendell has crafted for each a cruelly perfect fate, one that reflects, sometimes humorously and sometimes tragically, the kinds of lives they have lived."

Rendell followed *The Water's Lovely* with the novels *Portobello* and *Tigerlily's Orchids*. In the latter, Rendell explores the lives of the residents of Lichfield House, a condominium building in North London. The characters include aging alcoholic Olwen Curtis, lothario Stuart Font, and a janitor who is also a pedophile. Additional characters include three college students and two neighbors (Marius Potter and Rose Preston-Jones) who are falling for one another. The members of Lichfield House are fascinated by the building on the opposite side of the street, where immigrants from Hong Kong are rumored to be harvesting hothouse orchids. The story is "a tragicomedy that follows very much the same formula as *Portobello*," a *Kirkus Reviews* contributor remarked. "No new ground is broken, but fans will be pleased." However, Amy Nolan, writing in *Library Journal*, felt that "the penetrating prose communicates moments of tragedy and humor." *Booklist* reviewer Joanne Wilkinson was equally impressed, stating that the author "ever so lightly relays the effects of global warming and human trafficking." The tale is "subtle and ever so skillful." A *Publishers Weekly* critic announced that "Rendell spices the action with just the right gothic ingredients."

## Short Stories

In addition to her many novels, Rendell is also the author of numerous well-received short stories that have appeared in anthologies and collections over the years. *The Copper Peacock and Other Stories* "delights with its fine-tuned psychological effects," commented a *Publishers Weekly* reviewer. In the book's title story, Bernard is a writer who borrows a friend's apartment to find the solitude needed to work on a book. He takes an interest in the lovely Judy, the maid who cleans the apartment and fixes his lunch. Curiously, she exhibits increasingly severe bruises and injuries as time goes on, and Bernard is stunned when she gives him an ugly but expensive peacock-shaped bookmark. The story's "denouement is a master stroke," the *Publishers Weekly* critic stated. "The Fish Sitter" posits human prey for the dwellers in an aquarium. A cat-based mystery finds a regal feline ascending to her proper place in the royal hierarchy after the death of another cat. In "Mother's Help," a handsome and charming father enlists his children's help in disposing of unwanted wives. Chief Inspector Wexford appears in "An Unwanted Woman," wherein he tries to help a moody and unnerving teenage runaway.

"Rendell is one of the finest writers of our time," stated *Booklist* reviewer Melton, and her story collection *Blood Lines: Long and Short Stories,* is "a must-have collection by one of the world's most talented authors," Melton concluded. Rendell explores a wide field of psychological aberration in the stories, including the shame that results from obsession in "Clothes," the search for love and companionship in "The Strawberry Tree," and anger resulting from damaged egos in "The Man Who Was the God of Love." She uncovers the humanity inherent in her characters but does not shy away from the inhumanity that sometimes dwells deep within as well. "For all the stories' differences, however, Rendell's hand remains rock-steady throughout," observed Pam Lambert in a *People* review. A *Publishers Weekly* critic noted that in these stories, "Rendell's deft touch and keen insight (and sometimes wry wit) can wring abject horror from even the smallest vignette."

## Novels Written under the Pseudonym Barbara Vine

With the books written under her pen name of Barbara Vine, Rendell manages to "escape the strictures of the detective novel and concentrate on the darker peculiarities of human nature," observed Katie Owen in *New Statesman*. In *The Blood Doctor,* for example, Martin Nanther, a biographer and once the fourth Lord Nanther, undertakes a biography of his great-grandfather Henry, the first Lord Nanther, who was awarded a hereditary peerage by Queen Victoria in recognition for his research into hemophilia and his services as royal physician. Martin's life is complicated by the recent loss of the privileges and benefits of his title when the House of Lords opts to eliminate hereditary peerages. As the novel progresses, Martin learns that he and his wife's failure to conceive a child is the result of faulty genes, and that if they want to have a child, they will have to turn to modern science and genetic manipulation to create a baby designed to their specifications. Meanwhile, his research uncovers numerous unpleasant things about his great-grandfather Henry, the "architect of a crime that has outlived him for generations," and parallels with his own life and marital troubles, according to a *Kirkus Reviews* writer, who named the book a "dense, dazzling exploration of the biographer as detective, and of the truism that blood will tell."

In *The Minotaur,* also written under the Vine pseudonym, young Swedish nurse Kerstin Kvist is hired to care for John Cosway, a once-brilliant mathematical genius who has seemingly succumbed to schizophrenia. Living with John at Lydstep Old Hall is his harridan mother and four odious middle-aged sisters. As Kerstin interacts with John, she begins to realize that his troubles are not caused by mental illness but by heavy doses of brain-addling drugs. John, she finds, is the owner of Lydstep Old Hall, and it behooves the mother and sisters to keep him incapacitated so that they can continue to live there as long as they wish. A considerable sum of money is also tied up in John's name. A plot is under way, she realizes, to strip John Cosway of his rightful home and fortune, and soon this plot brings murder down to Lydstep. *Booklist* reviewer Fletcher called the novel "very satisfying reading." A *Kirkus Reviews* critic stated: "Using the conventions of a Victorian pastiche, Vine presents as satisfying a family of monsters as you're likely to find. It's like watching a house of cards collapse in exquisite slow-motion." Vine, concluded *Detroit Free Press* critic Ron Bernas, "is one of the best, a writer of literate thrillers that never fail to draw in readers, even though they know where she's going."

Another examination of human foibles is *The Birthday Present,* a novel told by two unrelated narrators. The story follows Ivor Tesham, a politician whose promising career is ruined when his mistress is killed in a car accident. The tragic accident occurred during a tawdry role-playing adventure, and Ivor decides to disavow any knowledge of the incident. This fateful decision eats away at Ivor as well as his family and friends. Slowly, the consequences destroy everyone connected to the accident.

"It's never quite clear whether *The Birthday Present* is a thriller which happens to have a Westminster setting or a book which aims to say something about the nature of Tory politics—or, indeed, which version of the Tory party she has in mind," Joan Smith mused in the London *Independent*. However, Carrie O'Grady in the London *Guardian*, found that "Vine is so good at sweeping us into the minds of ordinary people that she can make us react with horror to acts that, out of context, might not seem all that bad." Despite these statements, O'Grady was somewhat disheartened: "There are plenty of dark hints and false leads, but the twist in the tale leaves most of the loose ends hanging. . . . the suspense worked up so potently in earlier Vine novels is not in evidence." Explaining these reactions on the *Euro Crime* Web site, Fiona Walker observed that the novel "may be a disappointment, but it is still certainly worth a read for its social insights and psychological portraits. It's a good novel, and I enjoyed reading it." She added: "Non-Vine fans, or readers who prefer satires or political novels, may well—unclouded by expectation—find much indeed to like here. So, for almost any reader it is certainly one to have a crack at. It is, after all, brilliantly written. And that is a worthwhile pleasure for anyone."

Carolyn See, writing in the *Washington Post Book World*, proffered additional praise, announcing: "Within the first five pages of *The Birthday Present*, you know you're in the hands of a mystery/thriller writer who's in perfect control of her material. In addition to that fabulous control, Rendell/Vine maintains a matronly, almost magisterial tone that lends unexpected dignity to the goriest, creepiest material. It is her trademark." See also pointed out that Vine's "tone in every line is maternal, soothing, proper. You really do feel cradled. You can keep on reading this with tranquillity even as your plane lurches down out of the sky."

Gabilondo concluded of the author's work: "Rendell's greatest contribution, in addition to her gifts as a storyteller, has been to track the social and the psychological circulation of that vast system—political, familial, cultural, and genetic—in which people are forced to play out their lives, through a body of work that takes readers not into the cozy drawing rooms of traditional English mystery but into the lives and psyches of men and women in a vividly contemporary Britain."

## ■ Biographical And Critical Sources

*BOOKS*

*Contemporary Literary Criticism,* Gale (Detroit, MI), Volume 28, 1984, Volume 48, 1988, Volume 50, 1988.

*Dictionary of Literary Biography,* Gale (Detroit, MI), Volume 87: *British Mystery and Thriller Writers since 1940,* 1989, Volume 276: *British Mystery and Thriller Writers since 1960,* 2003.

*Mystery and Suspense Writers: The Literature of Crime, Detection, and Espionage,* Scribner (New York, NY), 1998.

*PERIODICALS*

*Advertiser* (Adelaide, Australia), July 27, 2002, Katharine England, review of *The Blood Doctor,* p. W13.

*America's Intelligence Wire,* December 9, 2005, Jill Lawless, "Queen of Suspense Ruth Rendell Tackles Celebrity and Murder in *Thirteen Steps Down,*" profile of Ruth Rendell.

*Antioch Review,* winter, 1997, review of *The Keys to the Street,* p. 122.

*Belles Lettres: A Review of Books by Women,* spring, 1994, Lorraine E. McCormack, review of *The Crocodile Bird,* p. 13.

*Booklist,* December 1, 1994, Emily Melton, review of *No Night Is Too Long,* p. 635; October 1, 1995, Emily Melton, review of *The Brimstone Wedding,* p. 213; March 1, 1996, Emily Melton, review of *Blood Lines: Long and Short Stories,* p. 1077; August, 1996, Emily Melton, review of *The Keys to the Street,* p. 1856; August, 1997, Emily Melton, review of *Road Rage,* p. 1848; December 1, 1998, Emily Melton, review of *A Sight for Sore Eyes: A Novel,* p. 620; April 15, 1999, review of *Kissing the Gunner's Daughter,* p. 1458; August, 1999, review of *A Judgment in Stone,* p. 2025; September 1, 1999, Stephanie Zvirin, review of *Harm Done,* p. 8; November 1, 1999, Karen Harris, review of *A Sight for Sore Eyes,* p. 551; June 1, 2000, Mary McCay, review of *Harm Done,* p. 1922; August, 2000, Bill Ott, review of *Grasshopper,* p. 2077; November 1, 2000, Connie Fletcher, review of *Piranha to Scurfy and Other Stories,* p. 493; November 15, 2001, Connie Fletcher, review of *Adam and Eve and Pinch Me,* p. 524; May 15, 2002, Stephanie Zvirin, review of *The Blood Doctor,* p. 1556; September 1, 2003, Stephanie Zvirin, review of *The Babes in the Wood,* p. 7; July, 2005, Connie Fletcher, review of *Thirteen Steps Down,* p. 1877; December 1, 2005, Connie Fletcher, review of *The Minotaur,* p. 7; May 1, 2006, Allison Block, review of *End in Tears,* p. 39; May 1, 2007, Connie Fletcher, review of *The Water's*

*Lovely,* p. 37; March 15, 2008, Connie Fletcher, review of *Not in the Flesh,* p. 5; August 1, 2009, Connie Fletcher, review of *The Monster in the Box,* p. 9; May 1, 2010, Connie Fletcher, review of *Portobello,* p. 40; March 15, 2011, Joanne Wilkinson, review of *Tigerlily's Orchids,* p. 26.

*Bookseller,* June 10, 2005, review of *Thirteen Steps Down,* p. 13; December 2, 2005, Frances Harvey, review of *End in Tears,* p. 15.

*British Medical Journal,* July 29, 2000, Judy Jones, "Concern Mounts over Female Genital Mutilation," p. 262; November 30, 2002, Jeff Aronson, review of *The Blood Doctor,* p. 1307.

*Christian Science Monitor,* July 20, 2007, review of *The Water's Lovely,* p. 12.

*Detroit Free Press,* March 15, 2006, Ron Bernas, review of *The Minotaur.*

*Entertainment Weekly,* February 14, 1992, review of *Gallowglass,* p. 50; July 17, 1998, Darcy Lockman, review of *The Chimney Sweeper's Boy,* p. 78; April 23, 1999, "The Week," review of *A Sight for Sore Eyes,* p. 58; March 15, 2002, review of *Adam and Eve and Pinch Me,* p. 72; October 31, 2003, Mark Harris, review of *The Babes in the Wood,* p. 77; November 19, 2004, Tina Jordan, review of *The Rottweiler,* p. 88; September 30, 2005, Jennifer Reese, "Mistress of the Dark: In *Thirteen Steps Down,* Ruth Rendell Pulls Off the Almost-perfect Crime Novel," review of *Thirteen Steps Down,* p. 96; December 30, 2005, Jennifer Reese, "Literature of the Year," review of *Thirteen Steps Down,* p. 148; July 21, 2006, Jennifer Reese, "Deep 'End,'" review of *End in Tears,* p. 74; July 20, 2007, Jennifer Reese, "Sisters in Crime," review of *The Water's Lovely,* p. 77.

*Europe Intelligence Wire,* October 20, 2002, Katie Owen, review of *The Babes in the Wood;* November 2, 2002, Rachel Simhon, review of *The Babes in the Wood;* July 29, 2005, Graham Chalmers, "In Conversation: Ruth Rendell, Cedar Court Hotel, Harrogate," interview with Ruth Rendell.

*Financial Times,* August 25, 2007, Melissa McClements, review of *Not in the Flesh,* p. 40.

*Guardian* (London, England), October 4, 2008, Carrie O'Grady, review of *The Birthday Present.*

*Independent* (London, England), August 18, 2001, Jane Jakeman, review of *Adam and Eve and Pinch Me,* p. 9; June 15, 2002, Jane Jakeman, "Where Does Ruth Rendell End and 'Barbara Vine' Begin?," p. 30; September 12, 2008, Joan Smith, review of *The Birthday Present.*

*Kirkus Reviews,* May 15, 2002, review of *The Blood Doctor,* p. 698; July 15, 2003, review of *The Babes in the Wood,* p. 942; July 1, 2005, review of *Thirteen Steps Down,* p. 706; January 15, 2006, review of *The Minotaur,* p. 61; May 15, 2006, review of *End in Tears,* p. 500; June 1, 2007, review of *The Water's Lovely;* April 15, 2008, review of *Not in the Flesh;*

August 15, 2009, review of *The Monster in the Box;* August 1, 2010, review of *Portobello;* March 1, 2011, review of *Tigerlily's Orchids;* July 1, 2011, review of *The Vault.*

*Library Journal,* March 15, 1998, Francine Fialkoff, review of *The Chimney Sweeper's Boy,* p. 97; February 1, 1999, Caroline Mann, review of *A Sight for Sore Eyes,* p. 122; August, 1999, Michael Rogers, review of *Some Lie and Some Die,* p. 149; September 1, 1999, Francine Fialkoff, review of *Harm Done,* p. 237, and Michael Rogers, review of *Murder Being Once Done,* p. 238; October 1, 1999, Sandy Glover, review of *A Sight for Sore Eyes,* p. 150; May 15, 2000, Danna Bell-Russel, review of *Harm Done,* p. 142; June 15, 2000, Michael Rogers, review of *A Judgment in Stone,* p. 122; October 15, 2000, Zaheera Jiwaji, review of *Grasshopper,* p. 105; December, 2000, Jane la Plante, review of *Piranha to Scurfy and Other Stories,* p. 194; February 15, 2001, Michael Rogers, review of *The Fallen Curtain and Other Stories,* p. 206; December, 2001, Caroline Mann, review of *Adam and Eve and Pinch Me,* p. 175; June 15, 2002, Caroline Mann, review of *The Blood Doctor,* p. 98; October 1, 2003, Caroline Mann, review of *The Babes in the Wood,* p. 122; August 1, 2005, Jane la Plante, review of *Thirteen Steps Down,* p. 71; January 1, 2006, Rebecca Vnuk, review of *The Minotaur,* p. 106; June 15, 2006, Caroline Mann, review of *End in Tears,* p. 64; June 15, 2007, Linda Oliver, review of *The Water's Lovely,* p. 63; April 15, 2008, Caroline Mann, review of *Not in the Flesh,* p. 79; July 1, 2010, Linda Oliver, review of *Portobello,* p. 78; April 15, 2011, Amy Nolan, review of *Tigerlily's Orchids,* p. 88.

*New Statesman,* September 6, 1996, Carol Birch, review of *The Keys to the Street,* p. 47; October 30, 1998, Francis Gilbert, review of *A Sight for Sore Eyes;* July 3, 2000, Nicola Upson, "Crime Waves," review of *Grasshopper,* p. 58; June 10, 2002, Katie Owen, "Novel of the Week," review of *The Blood Doctor,* p. 53; October 4, 2004, Rebecca Gowers, "Murky Depths," review of *Thirteen Steps Down,* p. 54.

*New Statesman & Society,* March 12, 1993, Bill Greenwell, review of *Anna's Book,* p. 38; August 20, 1993, Julie Wheelwright, review of *The Crocodile Bird,* p. 40; May 20, 1994, Wendy Brandmark, review of *No Night Is Too Long,* p. 39; April 5, 1996, Patricia Craig, review of *The Brimstone Wedding,* p. 39.

*Newsweek,* September 21, 1987, David Lehman, review of *Talking to Strange Men,* p. 77.

*New Yorker,* November 7, 2005, review of *Thirteen Steps Down,* p. 139.

*New York Times Book Review,* October 13, 1996, Marilyn Stasio, review of *The Keys to the Street,* p. 29; September 7, 1997, Marilyn Stasio, review of *Road Rage,* p. 34; April 4, 1999, Marilyn Stasio, review of *A Sight for Sore Eyes,* p. 20; November 21, 1999, Marilyn Stasio, review of *Harm Done,* p. 80; March 3, 2002, Marilyn Stasio, review of *Adam and Eve and Pinch Me,* p. 21; August 4, 2002, Marilyn Stasio, review of *The Blood Doctor,* p. 19; November 18, 2004, Janet Maslin, "A Killer Is on the Loose, but Life's Demands Continue," review of *The Rottweiler;* November 27, 2005, Marilyn Stasio, "Killer in the Attic," review of *Thirteen Steps Down;* March 26, 2006, Marilyn Stasio, "The Madman in the Attic," review of *The Minotaur,* p. 15; July 23, 2006, Marilyn Stasio, "Unhappy Families," review of *End in Tears,* p. 22.

*Orlando Sentinel,* December 29, 2004, Ann Hellmuth, review of *The Rottweiler.*

*People,* February 6, 1984, review of *The Fever Tree and Other Stories,* p. 12; April 7, 1986, Campbell Geeslin, review of *The New Girlfriend and Other Stories,* p. 16; July 20, 1987, Campbell Geeslin, review of *Heartstones,* p. 12; October 18, 1992, William A. Henry III, review of *Anna's Book,* p. 40; July 15, 2006, Pam Lambert, review of *Blood Lines,* p. 41.

*Publishers Weekly,* March 9, 1990, review of *Gallowglass,* p. 53; August 17, 1990, review of *Going Wrong,* p. 50; August 16, 1991, review of *The Copper Peacock and Other Stories,* p. 49; March 2, 1992, review of *King Solomon's Carpet,* p. 51; June 21, 1993, review of *Anna's Book,* p. 87; December 19, 1994, review of *No Night Is Too Long,* p. 47; April 22, 1996, review of *Blood Lines,* p. 61; July 29, 1996, review of *The Keys to the Street,* p. 73; July 7, 1997, review of *Road Rage,* p. 53; March 23, 1998, review of *The Chimney Sweeper's Boy,* p. 80; February 8, 1999, review of *A Sight for Sore Eyes,* p. 197; October 18, 1999, review of *Harm Done,* p. 73; August 28, 2000, review of *Grasshopper,* p. 50; November 13, 2000, review of *Piranha to Scurfy and Other Stories,* p. 89; January 28, 2002, review of *Adam and Eve and Pinch Me,* p. 274, and interview with Ruth Rendell, p. 275; June 24, 2002, review of *The Blood Doctor,* p. 43; September 29, 2003, review of *The Babes in the Wood,* p. 46; August 15, 2005, review of *Thirteen Steps Down,* p. 37; January 16, 2006, review of *The Minotaur,* p. 39; May 29, 2006, review of *End in Tears,* p. 40; May 14, 2007, review of *The Water's Lovely,* p. 34; April 21, 2008, review of *Not in the Flesh,* p. 39; August 17, 2009, review of *The Monster in the Box,* p. 48; July 26, 2010, review of *Portobello,* p. 45; April 25, 2011, review of *Tigerlily's Orchids,* p. 109.

*Richmond Times-Dispatch,* August 5, 2007, "A Twisted Family and Death in the Bathtub."

*San Jose Mercury News,* December 19, 2003, John Orr, review of *The Babes in the Wood.*

*School Library Journal,* March, 1997, Judy McAloon, review of *The Keys to the Street,* p. 16.

*Seattle Times,* February 10, 2002, Adam Woog, review of *Adam and Eve and Pinch Me,* p. J11.

*Spectator,* June 1, 2002, Charlotte Joll, "Trying to Climb the Family Tree," review of *The Blood Doctor,* p. 37; October 4, 2003, Antonia Fraser, "And Now for My Next Trick . . .," review of *The Rottweiler,* p. 55; April 9, 2005, Anita Brookner, "A Nest of Ungentle Essex Folk," review of *The Minotaur,* p. 36; November 26, 2005, Harriet Waugh, "Recent Crime Novels," review of *End in Tears,* p. 49; November 4, 2006, Andrew Taylor, "Looking on the Dark Side," review of *The Water's Lovely.*

*Telegraph* (London, England), November 4, 2005, "Her Dark Materials," interview with Ruth Rendell.

*Time,* May 5, 1986, William A. Henry III, review of *The New Girlfriend and Other Stories,* p. 74; August 18, 1986, William A. Henry III, review of *A Dark-Adapted Eye,* p. 72; August 17, 1987, William A. Henry III, review of *A Dark-Adapted Eye,* p. 64; February 1, 1988, William A. Henry III, review of *Talking to Strange Men,* p. 65; August 8, 1988, William A. Henry III, review of *The Veiled One,* p. 74; June 19, 1989, review of *The House of Stairs,* p. 65; July 2, 1990, Stefan Kanfer, review of *Gallowglass,* p. 67.

*Washington Post Book World,* March 13, 2009, Carolyn See, review of *The Birthday Present.*

*Xpress Reviews,* September 18, 2009, Linda Oliver, review of *The Monster in the Box.*

ONLINE

*Euro Crime,* http://www.eurocrime.co.uk/ (August 15, 2011), Fiona Walker, review of *The Birthday Present.*

*Internet Movie Database,* http://www.imdb.com/ (February 10, 2007), author profile.*

# David A.J. Richards

## 1944-

### ■ Personal

Born in 1944. *Education:* Harvard University, B.A., 1966, J.D., 1971; Oxford University, Ph.D., 1971.

### ■ Addresses

*Office*—New York University School of Law, Vanderbilt Hall, 40 Washington Sq. S, Ste. 421, New York, NY 10012-1066. *E-mail*—david.richards@nyu.edu.

### ■ Career

Legal scholar, author, and educator. Admitted to the bar of New York State, 1972. Cleary, Gottlieb, Steen & Hamilton, New York, NY, associate, 1971-74; Fordham University, New York, associate professor, 1974-77; Barnard College, New York, visiting professor of philosophy, 1974-77; New York University, New York, associate professor, 1977-79, professor of law, 1979—, Edwin D. Webb Professor of Law.

### ■ Member

Society for Philosophy and Public Affairs, Austinian Society.

### ■ Awards, Honors

Best book in criminal justice ethics, Institute of Criminal Justice Ethics, 1982, for *Sex, Drugs, Death, and the Law: An Essay on Human Rights and Overcriminalization*; Rockefeller grantee, Austinian Society and Center for Study of Law and Society; Mellon fellow, Aspen Institute for Humanistic Studies.

### ■ Writings

*A Theory of Reasons for Action*, Oxford University Press (New York, NY), 1971.

*The Moral Criticism of Law,* Dickenson-Wadsonth (Encino, CA), 1977.

*Sex, Drugs, Death, and the Law: An Essay on Human Rights and Overcriminalization*, Rowman & Littlefield (Totowa, NJ), 1982.

*Toleration and the Constitution*, Oxford University Press (New York, NY), 1986.

*Foundations of American Constitutionalism*, Oxford University Press (New York, NY), 1989.

*Conscience and the Constitution: History, Theory, and Law of the Reconstruction Amendments*, Princeton University Press (Princeton, NJ), 1993.

*Women, Gays, and the Constitution: The Grounds for Feminism and Gay Rights in Culture and Law*, University of Chicago Press (Chicago, IL), 1998.

*Identity and the Case for Gay Rights: Race, Gender, Religion as Analogies*, University of Chicago Press (Chicago, IL), 1999.

*Italian American: The Racializing of an Ethnic Identity*, New York University Press (New York, NY), 1999.

*Free Speech and the Politics of Identity*, Oxford University Press (New York, NY), 2000.

*Tragic Manhood and Democracy: Verdi's Voice and the Power of Musical Art*, Sussex Academic Press (East Sussex, England), 2004.

*Disarming Manhood: Roots of Ethical Resistance*, Swallow Press (Athens, OH), 2005.

*The Case for Gay Rights: From Bowers to Lawrence and Beyond*, University Press of Kansas (Lawrence, KS), 2005.

(With Nicholas C. Bamforth) *Patriarchal Religion, Sexuality, and Gender: A Critique of New Natural Law*, Cambridge University Press (New York, NY), 2007.

*The Sodomy Cases: Bowers v. Hardwick and Lawrence v. Texas,* University Press of Kansas (Lawrence, KS), 2009.

(With Carol Gilligan) *The Deepening Darkness: Patriarchy, Resistance, and Democracy's Future,* Cambridge University Press (New York, NY), 2009.

*Fundamentalism in American Religion and Law: Obama's Challenge to Patriarchy's Threat to Democracy,* Cambridge University Press (New York, NY), 2010.

## ■ Sidelights

New York University law professor David A.J. Richards has made important contributions to the theory of rights-based constitutional interpretation. In his 1982 book, *Sex, Drugs, Death, and the Law: An Essay on Human Rights and Overcriminalization,* he examines the issue of "victimless" crimes such as drug use and consensual sex acts. *Annals of the American Academy of Political and Social Science* reviewer Joseph E. Jacoby pointed out that discussions of this issue had traditionally come from two vantage points: Authors favoring criminalization tended to use moral arguments, while those favoring decriminalization tended to use utilitarian arguments that claimed that criminalization did not work. Richards took a different path, favoring decriminalization for moral reasons and admitting that utilitarian arguments for decriminalization had not been successful either politically or philosophically. In other words, Richards finds that decriminalization would depend on showing that the moral arguments of the criminalizers were mistaken or obsolete. For Richards, personal autonomy is a primary social goal that should be limited only when competing rights of at least equal importance are seriously threatened.

Jacoby, impressed by Richards's broad range of sources and sophisticated critical argument, called the book "an important contribution to the debate about the proper role of the state." Jacoby stated that the author assembled arguments that "thoroughly and convincingly supports his position," and claimed that Richards had posited "a serious challenge to existing law."

### Foundations of American Constitutionalism

In *Foundations of American Constitutionalism,* Richards offers a somewhat interdisciplinary approach to constitutional analysis, the two disciplines being history and political philosophy. For Richards, constitutional interpretation ought to be based on the intent of the Constitution's founders. Understanding the founders' intent demands an appreciation of their Lockean philosophical roots and their humanist worldview. As interpreters of history and philosophy in their own right, the founders established the process of ongoing constitutional interpretation as one of the most enduring forces in American democracy and as an underpinning of the national government's political legitimacy.

For *Annals of the American Academy of Political and Social Science* contributor John S. Robey, Richards's treatment of this subject was "scholarly and well written," offering "new and compelling methodologies in legal analysis. . . . It is a significant step forward."

### Conscience and the Constitution

In his 1993 *Conscience and the Constitution: History, Theory, and Law of the Reconstruction Amendments,* Richards examines the thirteenth, fourteenth, and fifteenth amendments to the Constitution, known collectively as the Reconstruction Amendments because they were passed in the aftermath of the Civil War. These amendments made slavery unconstitutional and established equal protection of the law for all. Sometimes viewed as an extension of the Bill of Rights, the Reconstruction Amendments have been crucial sources of justification for twentieth-century developments in civil rights and affirmative action. For Richards, they demonstrate the existence of a national political philosophy based on the principles of inalienable human rights. Courts, Richards believes, must apply these amendments both to rights enumerated by the Constitution, such as free speech and association, and those not enumerated. He argues for a broad definition of the equal protection clause and the privileges and immunities clause of the Fourteenth Amendment, in contrast to what he considers an excessive reliance the courts place on the due process clause of that amendment. Because the Reconstruction Amendments condemn slavery as economically unjust, Richards finds that they offer a justification for such restitutive policies as affirmative action. *American Historical Review* contributor Roberta Sue Alexander stated that "Richards presents an attractive jurisprudence that calls on courts to . . . protect inalienable rights." Alexander believed that Richards's analysis is weakest in its historical aspect. Richards, she commented, has focused on the views of a minority of Reconstruction-era politicians and thinkers, overlooking the piecemeal, ground-level development of varied political philosophies in a palpable context of events and policies. She concluded, however, that "legal theorists and jurists seek clear answers, and Richards's volume provides a compelling one because of his broad, humanistic, interdisciplinary approach."

Judith A. Baer, writing in the *Journal of American History*, was sympathetic to Richards's rights-based theory of the Constitution and his view that the Reconstruction Amendments extended the American Revolution. She regretted that Richards does not extend his arguments even further by questioning the courts' monopoly on constitutional interpretation. That, she claimed, "would have been an impressive contribution to jurisprudence," although it would still have obliged Richards and his fellow rights-based theorists to defend their views against critics with other political philosophies. For Baer, any theory-based approach is inevitably selective and thus open to criticism based on what it excludes. Richards has not made a case for the preferability of rights-based over non-rights-based theories, Baer asserted, but nevertheless, "Richards's juxtaposition of abolitionist and proslavery discussions of rights makes masterly use of history and philosophy." For Christopher E. Smith, writing in the *Annals of the American Academy of Political and Social Science*, Richards's book constitutes "a bold, impressively documented argument that sheds new light on the spirit and substantive meaning" of the Reconstruction Amendments. The author "has developed a comprehensive theory and approach for advancing our contemporary applications of constitutional law," Smith concluded.

### The Sodomy Cases

*Women, Gays, and the Constitution: The Grounds for Feminism and Gay Rights in Culture and Law* was published in 1998. It was followed in 1999 by *Identity and the Case for Gay Rights: Race, Gender, Religion as Analogies* and *Italian American: The Racializing of an Ethnic Identity*. Books that Richards authored in the early 2000s include *Free Speech and the Politics of Identity* and *Tragic Manhood and Democracy: Verdi's Voice and the Power of Musical Art*. The author then revisited gay and gender rights in his ensuing titles, *The Case for Gay Rights: From Bowers to Lawrence and Beyond* (2005), *Patriarchal Religion, Sexuality, and Gender: A Critique of New Natural Law* (2007), and *The Sodomy Cases: Bowers v. Hardwick and Lawrence v. Texas* (2009).

In *The Sodomy Cases*, Richards explores two book-ended Supreme Court Rulings, one that upheld antisodomy laws and another that did not. In doing so, the author touches on changing societal and judicial views of the body, gender, and the right to privacy. In 1986, the Supreme Court upheld Georgia's antisodomy laws in Bowers v. Hardwick, but in 2003, it overturned the same Texas laws in Lawrence v. Texas. In the interim, Richards explained, gender and privacy rulings in the Supreme Court illustrated the belief that both topics fell under the purview of the rights of the individual. Richards goes on to support this argument by exploring both rulings in light of the 1973 conclusion to Roe v. Wade. This approach, Philip Y. Blue observed in *Library Journal*, is "recommended for academic, public, and law libraries." Jonathan F. Parent, writing in the *Political Science Quarterly*, was also impressed, calling *The Sodomy Cases* "a well-organized and accessible piece that would provide a useful introduction to anyone who is interested in the background of the Bowers and Lawrence decisions and who may have little previous experience with constitutional law or legal studies."

## ■ Biographical And Critical Sources

*PERIODICALS*

*American Historical Review*, April, 1995, Roberta Sue Alexander, review of *Conscience and the Constitution: History, Theory, and Law of the Reconstruction Amendments*, pp. 570-571.

*Annals of the American Academy of Political and Social Science*, March, 1983, Joseph E. Jacoby, review of *Sex, Drugs, Death, and the Law: An Essay on Human Rights and Overcriminalization*, pp. 240-241; May, 1991, John S. Robey, review of *Foundations of American Constitutionalism*, pp. 196-197; January, 1995, Christopher E. Smith, review of *Conscience and the Constitution*, pp. 192-193.

*Chronicle of Higher Education*, May 6, 2005, "Pacifists and the Women Who Shaped Them."

*Journal of American History*, December, 1994, Judith A. Baer, review of *Conscience and the Constitution*, pp. 1324-1325.

*Library Journal*, February 15, 2009, Philip Y. Blue, review of *The Sodomy Cases: Bowers v. Hardwick and Lawrence v. Texas*, p. 120.

*Political Science Quarterly*, June 22, 2006, "Courts, Liberalism, and Rights: Gay Law and Politics in the United States and Canada," p. 348; March 22, 2010, Jonathan F. Parent, review of *The Sodomy Cases*, p. 148.

*Women's Review of Books*, November 1, 2009, "The Imperial Presidency."

*ONLINE*

*New York University, School of Law Web site*, https://its.law.nyu.edu/ (August 24, 2011), author profile.

# Eugene Robinson

## 1954-

## ■ Also Known As

Eugene Harold Robinson

## ■ Personal

Born March 12, 1954, in Orangeburg, SC; son of Harold I. and Louisa Robinson; married Avis Collins, September 23, 1978; children: Aaron E., Lowell E. *Education:* University of Michigan, B.A., 1974.

## ■ Addresses

*Home*—Arlington, VA. *Office*—Washington Post, 1150 15th St. NW, Washington, DC 20071.

## ■ Career

Journalist. *San Francisco Chronicle,* San Francisco, CA, reporter, 1975-80; *Washington Post,* city hall reporter, 1980-82, assistant city editor, 1982-84, city editor, 1984-87, South American correspondent, 1988-92, London correspondent, 1992-94, foreign editor, 1994—, assistant managing editor. International Women's Media Foundation board member.

## ■ Member

National Association of Black Journalists, Council on Foreign Relations.

## ■ Awards, Honors

Harvard University, Nieman fellow, 1988; several journalism awards; Pulitzer Prize for Commentary, 2009.

## ■ Writings

*Coal to Cream: A Black Man's Journey beyond Color to an Affirmation of Race* (memoir), Free Press (New York, NY), 1999.
*Last Dance in Havana: The Final Days of Fidel and the Start of the New Cuban Revolution,* Free Press (New York, NY), 2004.
*Disintegration: The Splintering of Black America,* Doubleday (New York, NY), 2010.

Contributor to the *PostPartisan* blog; opinion columnist for *Washington Post,* 2005—.

## ■ Sidelights

Eugene Robinson is an African American journalist who grew up in the segregated South. Robinson, whose career with the *Washington Post* began in 1980, covered South America for the paper for four years, beginning in 1988. He traveled to Brazil, a country with more than sixty million people of African heritage, which has a reputation for a lack of racism. "Initially, Robinson thought of Brazil as a 'Colored People's Promised Land' free of racial tension and anger," wrote Sherri L. Barnes in *Library Journal.* But what Robinson found was a different kind of approach toward race, one based on shades of color rather than labels of black or white.

### *Coal to Cream*

*Coal to Cream: A Black Man's Journey beyond Color* is Robinson's insight into the attitudes about race, both as he knew them to be in the United States and as he observed them in Brazil. *Booklist* reviewer Vernon Ford said the book "provides a compelling look at American views on race and the often false promise of racial color blindness." Although in the United States anyone with even a trace of black heritage is categorized as black, Robinson was told by Brazilians that he could be whatever he wished. In spite of this seemingly indifferent attitude toward race, Robinson saw that the poor and people holding lower-level jobs tended to be dark, while white or paler people filled positions of more importance. "American society sees race but not color," Robinson wrote. "Brazilian society sees color but not race."

Anthony Walton wrote in the *New York Times Book Review* that Robinson concludes that the difference "is deeply pernicious, robbing Brazil's dark multitudes of an organizing principle that would allow them to join together in a mass movement with the more educated and generally lighter middle classes, as American blacks did in the 1950s and 1960s." *Foreign Affairs* reviewer Kenneth Maxwell judged that the book does not indicate that Robinson interacted with activists or that he has read the most recent literature on race and class in Brazil. Maxwell claimed that "despite its personal honesty," the book "offers little insight into the Brazilian racial dilemma." "Robinson wryly hammers home his key points on the destructive nature of racial prejudice in America," wrote a *Publishers Weekly* contributor, who concluded by saying that the book "is full of provocative and worthy insights." Gregory H. Williams averred in *Washington Post Book World* that "the Brazilian experience suggests that we recognize that race—just as much as place—affects how persons of color are perceived, where in society they land, and how the social fabric of this country is drawn. . . . Robinson's conclusion provides a powerful lesson."

### *Disintegration*

In 2010 Robinson published *Disintegration: The Splintering of Black America*. Robinson argues that the segregation-era black community in the United States has since splintered into four groups: the middle-class majority, those living in poverty, the elites, and the new black immigrants and children of mixed parentage. Robinson focuses largely on those still living in poverty, a group he refers to as the Abandoned, noting that they fall further into the abyss as the other groups rise.

Writing in the *New York Times Book Review*, Raymond Arsenault commented that *Disintegration* "is full of facts, figures and telling anecdotes related to the

disintegration of black America, but its real power resides elsewhere. Sometimes writers tell us something familiar . . . but they do it in such a creative and cleareyed way and with such force that we begin to see things differently independent of any new information. This is exactly what Eugene Robinson" achieves. In a review in the *New Republic*, John McWhorter opined that "*Disintegration* is a columnist's book, essentially a string of extended op-eds, so many of them rehashing well-trodden ground that the text would be useful as a young person's introduction to Race in America 101." McWhorter pointed out that Robinson "nicely nails why so many black movers and shakers hesitated to support Obama for so long." *San Francisco Chronicle* contributor Paul Devlin found the book to be "sober, careful, and engaging." In a review in the *Los Angeles Times*, Erin Aubry Kaplan remarked that "Robinson's fleet-footedness and frequent sense of humor while detailing a nearly hopeless situation rescues *Disintegration* from being well meaning but didactic; he knows how to be circumspect and play devil's advocate without blunting his own message or sacrificing the integrity of his own vision of change." Reviewing the book in *Polite Society*, Marc W. Polite noted that "ultimately, Eugene Robinson's book challenges us to see the components of Black America in all our complexity, and urges that we move forward by dealing with our differences," adding that "this book is a step in the right direction."

## ■ Biographical And Critical Sources

*BOOKS*

Robinson, Eugene, *Coal to Cream: A Black Man's Journey beyond Color to an Affirmation of Race*, Free Press (New York, NY), 1999.

*PERIODICALS*

*Booklist*, July 1, 1999, Vernon Ford, review of *Coal to Cream: A Black Man's Journey beyond Color to an Affirmation of Race*, p. 1903; July 1, 2004, Terry Glover, review of *Last Dance in Havana: The Final Days of Fidel and the Start of the New Cuban Revolution*, p. 1812; October 1, 2010, Vernon Ford, review of *Disintegration: The Splintering of Black America*, p. 8.
*California Bookwatch*, December 1, 2010, review of *Disintegration*.
*Civil Rights Journal*, September 22, 1999, review of *Coal to Cream*, p. 58.

*Foreign Affairs,* November 1, 1999, Kenneth Maxwell, review of *Coal to Cream,* p. 139.

*Kirkus Reviews,* June 15, 1999, review of *Coal to Cream,* p. 946; April 15, 2004, review of *Last Dance in Havana,* p. 381; August 15, 2010, review of *Disintegration.*

*Library Journal,* July 1, 1999, Sherri L. Barnes, review of *Coal to Cream,* p. 106; June 15, 2004, Thomas A. Karel, review of *Last Dance in Havana,* p. 86; September 15, 2010, Robert Bruce Slater, review of *Disintegration,* p. 91.

*Los Angeles Times,* November 22, 2010, Erin Aubry Kaplan, review of *Disintegration.*

*New Republic,* October 5, 2010, John McWhorter, review of *Disintegration.*

*New York Times Book Review,* September 1, 1999, Anthony Walton, "Another Country," p. 30; December 29, 2010, Raymond Arsenault, review of *Disintegration.*

*Publishers Weekly,* July 5, 1999, review of *Coal to Cream,* p. 52; May 31, 2004, review of *Last Dance in Havana,* p. 65; August 9, 2010, review of *Disintegration,* p. 37.

*San Francisco Chronicle,* November 7, 2010, Paul Devlin, review of *Disintegration.*

*Washington Post Book World,* August 1, 1999, Gregory H. Williams, review of *Coal to Cream,* p. 9; accessed August 16, 2011, author profile.


ONLINE

*Polite Society,* http://politeonsociety.com/ (January 23, 2011), Marc W. Polite, review of *Disintegration.**

# Peter Robinson

## 1950-

### ■ Personal

Born March 17, 1950, in Castleford, Yorkshire, England; son of Clifford Robinson (a photographer) and Miriam Jarvis (a homemaker); married Sheila Halladay (a lawyer). *Education:* University of Leeds, B.A. (with honors), 1974; University of Windsor, M.A., 1975; York University, Ontario, Canada, Ph.D., 1983. *Politics:* "Liberal humanist." *Religion:* "Under consideration." *Hobbies and other interests:* Music, travel, walking, reading, pubs.

### ■ Addresses

*Home*—Toronto, Ontario, Canada. *Agent*—Dominick Abel, 146 W. 82nd St., Ste. 1B, New York, NY 10024. *E-mail*—peter@inspectorbanks.com.

### ■ Career

University of Toronto, School of Continuing Studies, Toronto, Ontario, Canada, writing instructor; teacher of college writing and literature classes, 1983—; University of Windsor, Windsor, Ontario, writer-in-residence, 1992-93.

### ■ Member

International Association of Crime Writers, Crime Writers of Canada, Mystery Writers of America, Crime Writers' Association.

### ■ Awards, Honors

Arthur Ellis Award for best short story, 1990, for "Innocence," and 2001, for "Murder in Utopia"; Arthur Ellis Award for best novel, 1990, for *The Hanging Valley,* 1991, for *Past Reason Hated,* 1996, for *Innocent Graves,* and 2000, for *Cold Is the Grave;* Torgi award for best talking book, Canadian National Institute for the Blind, 1994, for *Past Reason Hated;* Author's Award, Foundation for the Advancement of Canadian Letters, 1995, for *Final Account;* Macavity Award, 1998, for "The Two Ladies of Rose Cottage"; Anthony Award, 1999, Barry Award, Grand Prix de Littérature Policière, 2001, and Martin Beck Award, 2001, both for *In a Dry Season;* Edgar Award for best short story, Mystery Writers of America, 2001, for "Missing in Action"; Dagger in the Library Award, Crime Writers of America, 2002; Spoken Word Bronze Award, 2003, for *The Hanging Valley;* Palle Rosenkrantz Award, 2006, for *Cold Is the Grave;* Toronto Public Library Celebrates Reading Award, 2008; Harbourfront Festival Prize, 2010.

### ■ Writings

*"INSPECTOR BANKS" SERIES*

*Gallows View,* Viking (Toronto, Ontario, Canada), 1987, reprinted as *Gallows View: The First Inspector Banks Novel,* Harper Paperbacks (New York, NY), 2010.

*A Dedicated Man,* Viking (Toronto, Ontario, Canada), 1988, Scribner (New York, NY), 1991.

*A Necessary End,* Viking (Toronto, Ontario, Canada), 1989, Scribner (New York, NY), 1992.

*The Hanging Valley,* Viking (Toronto, Ontario, Canada), 1989, Scribner (New York, NY), 1992.

*Past Reason Hated,* Viking (Toronto, Ontario, Canada), 1991, Scribner (New York, NY), 1993.

*Wednesday's Child,* Viking (Toronto, Ontario, Canada), 1992, Scribner (New York, NY), 1994.

*Final Account,* Viking (Toronto, Ontario, Canada), 1994, Berkley (New York, NY), 1995, published as *Dry Bones That Dream,* Constable (London, England), 1995.

*Innocent Graves,* Berkley (New York, NY), 1996.

*Blood at the Root,* Avon (New York, NY), 1997.

*In a Dry Season,* Avon Twilight (New York, NY), 1999.

*Cold Is the Grave,* William Morrow (New York, NY), 2000.

*Aftermath,* William Morrow (New York, NY), 2001.

*The Summer That Never Was,* McClelland & Stewart (Toronto, Ontario, Canada), 2003, published as *Close to Home,* William Morrow (New York, NY), 2003.

*Playing with Fire,* William Morrow (New York, NY), 2004.

*Strange Affair,* William Morrow (New York, NY), 2005.

*Piece of My Heart,* William Morrow (New York, NY), 2006.

*Friend of the Devil,* William Morrow (New York, NY), 2007.

*All the Colors of Darkness,* William Morrow (New York, NY), 2009.

*Bad Boy,* William Morrow (New York, NY), 2010.

## NOVELS

*Caedmon's Song,* Viking (Toronto, Ontario, Canada), 1990, published as *The First Cut,* Perennial Dark Alley (New York, NY), 2004.

*No Cure for Love,* Viking (Toronto, Ontario, Canada), 1995.

*Before the Poison,* William Morrow (New York, NY), 2011.

## OTHER

*With Equal Eye* (poems), Gabbro Press (Toronto, Ontario, Canada), 1979.

*Nosferatu* (poems), Gabbro Press (Toronto, Ontario, Canada), 1981.

*Not Safe after Dark and Other Stories,* Crippen & Landru Publishers (Norfolk, VA), 1998.

(Editor, with Roy Fisher) *News for the Ear: A Homage to Roy Fisher,* Stride Publications (Devon, England), 2000.

*The Price of Love and Other Stories,* William Morrow (New York, NY), 2010.

Also contributor to anthologies, including *Cold Blood II,* Mosaic Press, 1989; *Cold Blood III; Cold Blood IV; Cold Blood V;* and *A Merry Band of Murderers,* Poisoned Pen Press (Scottsdale, AZ), 2006. Contributor of short stories to periodicals, such as *Ellery Queen's Mystery* magazine. Robinson's works have been translated into nineteen languages.

## ■ Adaptations

Several Robinson books have been adapted for audio, including *Playing with Fire* and *Strange Affair; Aftermath* was adapted as *DCI Banks* (two-part television special), ITV, 2010.

## ■ Sidelights

Mystery writer Peter Robinson sets most of his books in the English countryside of Yorkshire, where he was born and raised. He has written a series of novels featuring Detective Inspector Alan Banks, who solves murder cases for the Yorkshire police. The "Inspector Banks" series has proven popular in Canada, England, and the United States, with a *Publishers Weekly* contributor calling it "one of the best collections of procedurals extant." The reviewer concluded: "The measured effectiveness of [Robinson's] prose and the increasingly complex life of Inspector Banks make this an ever more compelling series." In the *New York Times Book Review,* Marilyn Stasio wrote of Banks: "He loves the opera and appreciates a lively, intelligent woman, even if she happens not to be his wife. He's no pushover, but he can sympathize with the human frailties that make decent folk go bad. All in all, Chief Inspector Alan Banks shapes up admirably as a civilized detective of the old school of British justice." To quote another *Publishers Weekly* reviewer: "The inhabitants of Robinson's Yorkshire are a far cry from James Herriot's sturdy farmers. . . . Nevertheless, Robinson . . . creates an appealing Yorkshire setting with evocative descriptions of the . . . town, dales, and seaside."

### "Inspector Banks" Series

The first of Robinson's "Inspector Banks" mysteries, *Gallows View,* was published in 1987, while the author was still working on his doctoral dissertation. The book was nominated by the Crime Writers of Canada as the best first novel of the year. Banks, who has recently arrived in Yorkshire after police service in London, learns quickly that the quieter life he sought in the countryside is simply not to be. Faced with a peeping tom, a rash of burglaries, and a possible murder, Banks "adds his own dimension to detecting through his logical, instinctive, and persistent nature," according to *St. James Guide to Crime and Mystery Writers* essayist Bruce Southworth. Southworth likewise commented that this first Banks procedural "sets the stage for this intelligent, insightful, and entertaining series." Banks returns in *A Dedicated Man,* in which he investigates the strange death of Harry Steadman, a university professor who is found covered in rocks and with a fatal head injury. It becomes apparent that foul play is involved; suspects include his wife, the businessman who wants to develop a field that Steadman had proclaimed a historic site, and a possible mistress.

*A Necessary End*, Robinson's next "Inspector Banks" novel, depicts a murder that initially seems to be the act of a violent mob of protesters but later proves to have been premeditated. Deeply involved in the plot is Maggie's Farm, a commune full of New Age types. Stasio, writing in the *New York Times Book Review*, observed that "like the region that breeds them, the people in Mr. Robinson's mysteries flaunt their colors but keep their secrets." In *The Hanging Valley* Inspector Banks is confronted with two different murders and a mysterious disappearance that may be related. *New York Times Book Review* contributor Stasio approved of *The Hanging Valley* as well, calling it an "emotionally rich novel, in which death seems preferable to life in endless exile from the 'green and pleasant land' of one's home."

Banks is back in *Past Reason Hated*, Robinson's 1991 effort. This time the inspector investigates the killing of a beautiful lesbian; possible perpetrators include both past lovers and the scorned ex-partners of these lovers. Also introduced in this novel is a new character, Detective Constable Susan Gay. Gay has accompanied Banks on his more recent forays into crime solving, including *Wednesday's Child*, *Innocent Graves*, and *Blood at the Root*. In all of these novels, matters are not what they seem: a child is abducted by people posing as ardent social workers; a teenager is found strangled in a churchyard with multiple suspects nearby; a neo-Nazi's death in a brawl may have been staged by members of his own group. In a *People* review of *Innocent Graves*, Jeff Brown noted that Robinson's Banks mysteries "may be genre stuff—police procedural, English village—but it's first-class work. Banks and his assistant Susan Gay are good company, the plot twists frequent and surprising." The *Publishers Weekly* contributor wrote: "If Banks has occasionally appeared a shade too decent and placid in past works, this eighth appearance finds him with a new, sharper edge. Banks is still a kindly enough soul, but he knowingly occupies a world that has suddenly become more richly treacherous."

Southworth contended that in all of Robinson's "Inspector Banks" series books, the detective "attempts, in his cases as in life, to strip away the veil of mystery or facade and reveal what lies beneath." The critic noted of Robinson: "The richness of his characters, his ability to successfully examine the events of modern life in the context of a rural setting and yet weave gripping and entertaining novels, sets Robinson apart from the majority of crime novelists. . . . Though his output is comparatively small, he consistently delivers on the promise of each of his earlier novels and can look for a long career at the top of his field."

Robinson's tenth novel featuring Inspector Banks is the Anthony Award-winning *In a Dry Season*. During what appears to be a routine case, Banks discovers a community's secrets from a half a century ago as he investigates the discovery of a murder victim's skeletal remains in a dried-up reservoir. In the book, Robinson's narrative switches back and forth from the present to the time of the murder during World War II. Caroline Mann, writing in *Library Journal*, commented that "Robinson tells a compelling story of wartime England that rings true."

In *Cold Is the Grave*, Robinson presents a tale of a young girl who has run away from home and become involved in Internet porn and, as is later discovered, murder. The investigation is complicated because the girl happens to be the daughter of Inspector Banks's boss, Chief Constable Riddle, with whom he shares a mutual dislike. Further adding to the inspector's dilemma are his own personal demons, including his relationships with his ex-wife and his sometime girlfriend, Annie Cabbot. Wilda Williams, writing in *Library Journal*, called the book a "great read for those dark and stormy nights."

In *Aftermath*, Robinson's twelfth "Inspector Banks" mystery, the author begins the novel with a twist: the actual capture of the murderer during a routine domestic violence call. What follows is a tale focusing on the aftermath of capturing the serial rapist and killer of young girls, including questions about the killer's wife and her involvement in the crimes. Another issue concerns the brutal police beating of the killer after he murders one of the police officers trying to arrest him. Oline H. Cogdill, writing in the *Knight-Ridder/Tribune News Service*, noted that, despite focusing on issues such as child abuse and domestic violence, the book is a psychological thriller and avoids gratuitous violence. Cogdill added: "While Robinson is careful not to make *Aftermath* a sociological study, he explores the cycle of domestic abuse better than novels that are merely soapboxes in disguise." In a *Library Journal* review of *Aftermath*, Francine Fialkoff commented that this series installment "puts Robinson firmly in the upper echelon of British mystery writers."

As for Robinson, he noted on his personal home page that he struggled with several versions of *Aftermath* and did not really succeed until he decided to make it an "Inspector Banks" book. "*Aftermath* isn't a comfortable book; it's a book that involves and challenges the reader," wrote Robinson. "But as anyone who has read the last few Banks books already knows, I don't like to follow a formula."

In *Close to Home* Banks is forced into grim nostalgia when the remains of Graham Marshall, an old childhood friend who disappeared while on his newspaper route in 1965, are uncovered. Cutting short a Greek island vacation, Banks travels back to his Cambridgeshire home town of Peterborough, where he confronts his guilt at an unrevealed clue that might have helped the investigation into Graham's disappearance. As he becomes unofficially involved in the case, he finds himself falling for investigator Michelle Hart while recalling his past. Meanwhile, in the present, Annie Cabbot is investigating the disappearance of fifteen-year-old Luke Armitage, the reserved and intellectual son of a deceased rock star and a teen who has also disappeared under unexplained circumstances. Banks explores his own past and the current culture of teenagers as he works to solve Luke's disappearance and discover a link between the two teenagers' cases. In addition to the mystery, Robinson explores some more abstract concepts associated with youth and aging: "the illusory nature of nostalgia; the dark, secret lives of small towns; middle age; and the oft-lamented challenges of going home again," explained a *Publishers Weekly* contributor. Fans of Banks "will enjoy watching the grizzled veteran get to know his younger self," commented Keir Graff in *Booklist*.

*Playing with Fire* teams Banks and ex-lover Cabbot again as they investigate two suspicious fires that destroyed two canal boats and killed two squatters living on them: teenage drug addict Tina Aspern and impoverished landscape painter Thomas McMahon. High on the list of suspects are Mark Siddons, Tina's philandering boyfriend, and Dr. Patrick Aspern, her pedophilic stepfather. When another fire claims the life of Roland Gardner, a college friend of McMahon's, the stakes become even higher. Meanwhile, as Annie starts a relationship with an art forgery expert, Banks tries to sort out his still-conflicted feelings for her. *People* writer Arion Berger called *Playing with Fire* "the most accomplished of the Detective Chief Inspector Alan Banks series."

At the beginning of *Strange Affair*, Banks is recovering from a fire that nearly killed him in the previous novel. When his wealthy, estranged younger brother, Roy, leaves a message on his answering machine, pleading for help, Banks is perplexed. He

had not heard from Roy in years, but his plea sounds genuine. Unable to contact Roy, Banks heads to London to see what he can do. When he arrives at Roy's house, he finds the place unlocked and empty, with Roy nowhere to be found. What he does find, however, are unsavory clues that suggest the source of Roy's wealth and that hint at the dilemma he appears to be in. As Banks searches for his sibling, Annie Cabbot investigates the death of a young woman along the roadway who has been shot execution style. Oddly, the girl had in her possession a letter addressed to Banks. When the letter is discovered, the "reader knows that Robinson will tie the two investigations together in fiendishly clever ways," observed *Booklist* reviewer Connie Fletcher. Reviewing *Strange Affair* in *Library Journal*, Deborah Shippy called the Banks novels a "police procedural series that just keeps getting better."

*Philadelphia Inquirer* contributor David Hiltbrand reviewed *Piece of My Heart* and reported on a reading by Robinson at McGillin's Olde Ale House in Philadelphia. "With his scant hair and observant eyes, Peter Robinson looks more like a vicar than a rocker. But give the guy his props. He was in the audience when The Who recorded the masterful 'Live at Leeds' in 1970. And he was there recently when the band (minus John Entwistle and Keith Moon) reprised the show. Both performances took place in the refectory at Leeds University, Robinson's alma mater. 'I was invited by the vice chancellor,' Robinson says of The Who's return. 'I guess I'm sort of an old boy made good.'"

This latest novel, the title of which was a Janis Joplin hit, contains two separate investigations. The current one by Banks is of the death of rock journalist Nicholas Barber, whose head was bashed in with a poker during a blackout, and in a parallel case, in 1969, Detective Inspector Stanley Chadwick investigates the death of young hippie Linda Lofthouse who was found stabbed in her sleeping bag at an outdoor rock concert in Yorkshire. Robinson calls up rock groups from the period, including Led Zeppelin, Pink Floyd, Pentangle, Savoy Brown, and others, and the book's Web site features a playlist of the songs mentioned in the novel. Chadwick, who knows nothing of the rock culture of the time, is at odds with his daughter, Yvonne, who is immersed in it, and his worries about her intrude on his concentration in investigating the case. Reviewing the book in the *South Florida Sun-Sentinel*, Cogdill noted that Robinson offers "a perceptive view" of the similarities and differences between generations and between parents and children, "and how music can unite, or drive a wedge between age groups. Robinson succinctly weaves this theme into a thoughtful, intense novel that mixes a gripping plot with intense character studies."

Reviewing *Friend of the Devil*, Joe Hartlaub wrote in *Bookreporter.com* that Robinson "does for London what Raymond Chandler and Ross MacDonald did for southern California, using his stories against the backdrop of an urban locale to function as a documentation of social and psychological mores of a point in time." The novel picks up threads from Robinson's *Aftermath* by incorporating into the story serial killers Terry and Lucy Payne. The story opens with the discovery by a jogger of the body of a homicide victim sitting at the edge of a cliff in a wheelchair while sea gulls encircle her. Banks is now in his fifties and has mellowed a bit. He is no long smoking and limits his alcohol to a glass of wine. He more often enjoys listening to music, reading, and watching films, and he has met a beautiful woman who is very attentive to him, threatening his ongoing off-and-on relationship with Cabbot. Banks is at home when he is notified of another killing, of nineteen-year-old Haley Daniels in The Maze, an area of Eastvale. Haley's body was found in a warehouse in the business district after she had spent a night drinking.

Cabbot, on the other hand, has been drinking more, and she wakes up after a night of hard partying next to a much younger man she obviously picked up in a club. She worries that she is losing control and immerses herself in solving the "wheelchair murder" of the paraplegic girl whose throat was slit.

A *Publishers Weekly* contributor called the novel "stunning," and wrote that readers will be well rewarded as Banks and Cabbot "explore not only the depths of human depravity but also their own murky relationship." Reviewing the mystery in the online *Mostly Fiction Book Reviews,* Eleanor Bukowsky wrote: "*Friend of the Devil* is a deliciously complex, finely textured, and harrowing look at the walking wounded among us who suffer the terrible and long-lasting aftereffects of physical and psychological trauma."

*All the Colors of Darkness,* the eighteenth installment in the "Inspector Banks" series, begins when a man's corpse is found hanging in a tree. Cabbot attempts to notify the dead man's long-term lover, but that man is also found murdered, this time by stabbing. Banks and Cabbot believe the deaths may have been a murder-suicide, but they change their minds upon further investigation. Indeed, the hanged man was a jovial fellow with a great career, working as a costume and set designer. Critics mostly commended this addition to the series, and London *Independent* reviewer Barry Forshaw noted that the novel is told in "deceptively unspectacular language." Forshaw went on to assert: "Robinson

. . . does plotting with unspectacular assurance— the kind of plotting, in fact, that exerts a considerable grip. Just try putting the book down after a chapter or so: you'll have a problem." Fletcher, writing once more in *Booklist,* was equally impressed, stating: "Robinson shows a deft hand at using forensic science, conflict between characters, and recurring series themes."

Banks's daughter, Tracy, takes a central role in *Bad Boy.* She feels as if her life is in stasis; she retains her dead-end job at a bookstore while her brother's music career begins to skyrocket. Unable to decide on a suitable vocation or even discern what she wants out of life, Tracy falls under the influence of Jaff McCready. Charming, good-looking, and completely wrong for her, Jaff only makes Tracy's life worse. Tracy's roommate is arrested when she is found with an illegal gun, but the firearm belongs to Jaff. In order to avoid capture, Jaff convinces Tracy to flee the country with him, and he ends up holding her hostage instead. *Booklist* contributor Fletcher lauded the book, calling it "a change of pace for the series, to be sure, but another outstanding crime novel from Robinson." Forshaw, reviewing Robinson's work again in the *Independent,* observed: "It's neither the setting nor even the characters that makes Robinson's work so satisfying, but the plotting of a Swiss-watch precision." He added: "We are treated to a masterclass in the organisation of narrative." Proffering additional praise, *Xpress Reviews* commentator Linda Oliver announced that the "excellent characterization and skillful plotting make this an engrossing read." A *Publishers Weekly* critic observed that "Robinson deftly integrates Banks's personal life . . . in this strong entry in a superb series."

## Other

The novel *Caedmon's Song,* published in the United States as *The First Cut,* tells the story of a young woman named Kirsten who is the sole survivor of an attack by a brutal serial rapist and killer. She is, however, terribly maimed. *Caedmon's Song* focuses on her slow, struggling recovery as well as the mystery of her attacker, who is coming back for her because he believes she can identify him.

Southworth called the novel "gripping" and observed that with its publication, "Robinson solidifies his place in the realms of both mystery and horror." A *Publishers Weekly* reviewer declared *The First Cut* an "intricately constructed, standalone novel of suspense and revenge," while a *Kirkus Reviews* critic called it a "brutally efficient page-turner that shows a welcome new side to Banks's accomplished creator."

### Robinson Once Told *CA:*

"Though my background is academic and I began my writing career with poetry, it seemed natural to turn to crime fiction because that is a field where a great deal of fine writing is being done these days. Though I have a series character, I try to make each book a little different and constantly work at improving my narrative skills. 'It must tell a story,' said E.M. Forster of the novel in general, and crime novelists are perhaps more aware of this than anyone else. The challenge to me, though, is not so much in the nuts and bolts of plotting—though they are, indeed, a challenge—but in getting the characters right and creating a strong, concrete sense of place. The Inspector Banks novels are set in the Yorkshire Dales, an area I revisit every year, and as I always found the sense of place fascinating in other authors—from Thomas Hardy to Seamus Heaney—I give it perhaps more precedence than many other crime writers.

"I started the first Inspector Banks novel as a break from writing my Ph.D. dissertation and was lucky enough to have it accepted by the first publisher I sent it to. I didn't have an agent . . . and my novel was the only unsolicited manuscript Penguin accepted that year."

## ■ Biographical And Critical Sources

*BOOKS*

*Contemporary Novelists*, 7th edition, Gale (Detroit, MI), 2001.
*St. James Guide to Crime and Mystery Writers*, 4th edition, St. James Press (Detroit, MI), 1996.

*PERIODICALS*

*Booklist*, November 15, 1998, review of *Not Safe after Dark and Other Stories*, p. 573; September 1, 2001, Connie Fletcher, review of *Aftermath*, p. 57; January 1, 2003, Keir Graff, review of *Close to Home*, p. 856; February 1, 2005, Connie Fletcher, review of *Strange Affair*, p. 947.
*Bookseller*, May 19, 2006, Stuart Lemon, review of *Piece of My Heart*, p. 13; December 1, 2008, Connie Fletcher, review of *All the Colors of Darkness*; July 1, 2010, Connie Fletcher, review of *Bad Boy*.
*Entertainment Weekly*, February 29, 2008, Jennifer Reese, review of *Friend of the Devil*, p. 63.

*Gazette* (Cedar Rapids, IA), June 8, 2008, review of *Friend of the Devil*.
*Globe and Mail* (Toronto, Ontario, Canada), May 8, 1999, review of *In a Dry Season*, p. D12.
*Independent* (London, England), August 13, 2008, Barry Forshaw, review of *All the Colors of Darkness*; August 24, 2010, Barry Forshaw, review of *Bad Boy*.
*Kirkus Reviews*, October 1, 1998, review of *Not Safe after Dark and Other Stories*, p. 1419; March 1, 1999, review of *In a Dry Season*, p. 335; November 1, 2002, review of *Close to Home*, p. 1576; July 15, 2004, review of *The First Cut*, p. 663; May 1, 2006, review of *Piece of My Heart*, p. 435; October 15, 2007, review of *Friend of the Devil*.
*Knight-Ridder/Tribune News Service*, November 28, 2001, Oline H. Cogdill, review of *Aftermath*, p. K2588.
*Library Journal*, April 1, 1999, Caroline Mann, review of *In a Dry Season*, p. 131; October 1, 2000, Wilda Williams, review of *Cold Is the Grave*, p. 152; September 1, 2001, Francine Fialkoff, review of *Aftermath*, p. 239; July, 2004, Deborah Shippy, review of *The First Cut*, p. 65; February 1, 2005, Deborah Shippy, review of *Strange Affair*, p. 58; June 15, 2006, Linda Oliver, review of *Piece of My Heart*, p. 64.
*New York Times Book Review*, April 5, 1992, Marilyn Stasio, review of *A Necessary End*, p. 14; January 3, 1993, Marilyn Stasio, review of *The Hanging Valley*, p. 15; April 18, 1999, review of *In a Dry Season*, p. 101; February 20, 2005, Marilyn Stasio, review of *Strange Affair*, p. 21.
*People*, October 14, 1996, Jeff Brown, review of *Innocent Graves*, p. 42; March 8, 2004, Arion Berger, review of *Playing with Fire*, p. 39.
*Philadelphia Inquirer*, July 4, 2006, David Hiltbrand, review of *Piece of My Heart*.
*Publishers Weekly*, June 7, 1993, review of *Past Reason Hated*, p. 54; January 31, 1994, review of *Wednesday's Child*, p. 78; July 3, 1995, review of *Final Account*, p. 51; June 3, 1996, review of *Innocent Graves*, p. 64; October 13, 1997, review of *Blood at the Root*, p. 58; October 19, 1998, review of *Not Safe after Dark and Other Stories*, p. 59; September 4, 2000, review of *Cold Is the Grave*, p. 88; August 27, 2001, review of *Aftermath*, p. 57; December 9, 2002, review of *Close to Home*, p. 60; July 26, 2004, review of *The First Cut*, p. 36; April 24, 2006, review of *Piece of My Heart*, p. 37; November 5, 2007, Carol Schneck, review of *Friend of the Devil*, p. 15; October 8, 2007, review of *Friend of the Devil*, p. 36; November 19, 2007, Jordan Foster, "An Introspective Inspector: Talks with Peter Robinson," interview, p. 32; June 14, 2010, review of *Bad Boy*.

*School Library Journal*, September, 1999, review of *Friend of the Devil*, p. 244.

*South Florida Sun-Sentinel*, June 7, 2006, Oline H. Cogdill, review of *In a Dry Season*.

*Times* (London, England), February 22, 1999, review of *Piece of My Heart*, p. 68; August 27, 2001, review of *In a Dry Season*, p. 57.

*Times Literary Supplement*, April 19, 1991, Patricia Craig, review of *Aftermath*, p. 22.

*Xpress Reviews*, July 16, 2010, Linda Oliver, review of *Bad Boy*.

ONLINE

*Bookreporter.com*, http://www.bookreporter.com/ (August 21, 2008), Joe Hartlaub, review of *Caedmon's Song*; Ray Palen, review of *Piece of My Heart*.

*Mostly Fiction Book Reviews*, http://www.mostlyfiction.com/ (May 7, 2008), Eleanor Bukowsky, review of *Friend of the Devil*.

*Peter Robinson Home Page*, http://www.peterrobinsonbooks.com (August 24, 2011).*

# Alex Ross

## 1968-

### ■ Personal

Born 1968, in Washington, DC; married in Canada to Jonathan Lisecki (an actor and film director), 2005. *Education:* Harvard University, B.A. (summa cum laude), 1990.

### ■ Addresses

*Home*—New York, NY. *Office*—New Yorker, 4 Times Sq., New York, NY, 10036. *Agent*—Tina Bennett, Janklow & Nesbit Associates, 445 Park Ave., New York, NY 10022.

### ■ Career

Writer, journalist, and music critic. *New York Times,* music critic, 1992-96; *New Yorker,* music critic, 1996—. MacArthur Fellow, 2008.

### ■ Awards, Honors

Three-time recipient, ASCAP-Deems Taylor Award, for music criticism; Holtzbrinck fellowship, American Academy of Berlin; Banff Centre fellowship; National Book Critics Circle Award for criticism, 2007, Best Books of 2007 list, *New York Times, Los Angeles Times, Washington Post, New York* magazine, *Time, Newsweek,* and *Economist,* First Book Award, London *Guardian,* Premio Napoli, Grand Prix des Muses, and Pulitzer Prize finalist for general nonfiction, 2008, all for *The Rest Is Noise;* Arts and Letters Award, American Academy of Arts and Letters; MacArthur fellow, 2008; Belmont Prize, Pèlerinages Art Festival, 2011, for contemporary music; honorary doctorate, New England Conservatory of Music; honorary doctorate, Manhattan School of Music.

### ■ Writings

*The Rest Is Noise: Listening to the Twentieth Century,* Farrar, Straus, and Giroux (New York, NY), 2007.
*Listen to This,* Farrar, Straus, and Giroux (New York, NY), 2010.

Contributor to periodicals, including the *New Republic, Lingua Franca, Slate, London Review of Books, Fanfare,* and *Feed;* author of *The Rest Is Noise* blog.

### ■ Sidelights

Alex Ross, music critic for the *New Yorker,* wrote Jan Swafford in a review for *Wilson Quarterly,* is "one of our most talented practitioners of the art of the feuilleton, the popular journal piece." Born and raised in Washington, DC, Ross bought his first album, a recording of Anton Bruckner's Ninth Symphony, at age ten. From an early age, he had a fondness for classical music; he did not discover the music of Bob Dylan, for example, until he was in his twenties. Ross attended Harvard University in Cambridge, Massachusetts, studying music under the composer Peter Lieberson, and was also the classical music disc jockey for the campus radio station. Also majoring in English, Ross graduated summa cum laude in 1990 and began writing freelance music reviews for *Fanfare* magazine, earning a meager two dollars per review. He did not think of himself as a music critic at this stage, but when he placed a review with the *New Republic,* editor Leon Wieseltier convinced Ross that he should consider music criticism as a profession. Through the intercession of Wieseltier, Ross was employed by the *New York Times* as "a stringer writing about classical music for the culture desk," stated Doree Shafrir in a review in the *New York Observer.* Soon, he also began placing articles with the *New Yorker,* and by 1996 he was the magazine's full-time classical music critic. In 2004, Ross wrote an article for the *New Yorker* that stirred controversy among music critics and musicians alike. He contended that classical music had been in a way "held captive" to an elite group for over a century, and he was determined to demonstrate that classical music could be appreciated by a much wider audience than it had been in the past. Meanwhile, Ross was also gathering notes for a musical tour of the twentieth century.

### The Rest Is Noise

His first book, *The Rest Is Noise: Listening to the Twentieth Century,* was published in the United States in 2007 and in England in 2008. As Swafford noted in *Wilson Quarterly,* "Ross has turned his feuilletonist's sensibility to a longer form, the book, and he's made a terrific debut on the big stage." Ross's book opens with *Salome,* by Richard Strauss, and ends with *Nixon in China,* by John Adams, "emblematic operas from the beginning and the end of a challenging musical epoch," as described by *New York Sun* contributor Adam Kirsch. In between an analysis of these works, Ross studies composers, from Gustav Mahler and Jean Sibelius to Arnold Schoenberg, Dmitri Shostakovich, Aaron Copland, and George Gershwin; from post-romanticism to atonality and avant-garde modernism. "Wherever music has flourished or struggled valiantly for survival, over the last hundred years, Mr. Ross is there," observed Kirsch, who also commented: "The result is a massively erudite book that takes care to wear its learning lightly."

Ross divides the twentieth century into three epochs: 1900-33, 1933-45, and 1945-2000. In the first era covered in the book, he includes not only Strauss, Sibelius, and Mahler, but also Claude Debussy, Schoenberg, Igor Stravinsky, Béla Bartók, Maurice Ravel, Kurt Weill, Hanns Eisler, and Carl Orff. In the second era, Ross discusses composers such as Shostakovich, Sergei Prokofiev, Paul Hindemith, and Hans Pfitzner. He also includes American composers such as Copland and Gershwin. In the third section, Ross writes about composers including Olivier Messiaen, Pierre Boulez, Karlheinz Stockhausen, Benjamin Britten, and John Cage. As Shafrir noted, Ross's book offers "a rereading of the conventional wisdom about 20th-century classical music: that avant-garde, atonal music was the important music of the century and that in some ways all modern classical music is derived from it." Instead, Ross attempts to provide, Shafrir added, "a complete reorientation of how classical music is appreciated: as part of culture as a whole, not a hermetically sealed world unto itself."

Thus, Ross focuses on music criticism for about a fifth of the book's 640 pages. The rest of the book includes biographical profiles and cultural criticism, making it as much a history of the twentieth century as it is a survey of twentieth-century music. Neither does Ross confine himself to the major composers of the twentieth century, but he also introduces readers to the work of Duke Ellington, the Velvet Underground, and Lou Reed, among numerous others. *The Rest Is Noise* earned critical acclaim both in the United States and England, won the National Book Critics Circle Award for criticism in 2007, and was a finalist for the Pulitzer Prize for general nonfiction in 2008. *Library Journal* contributor Larry Lipkis found the book to be a "rich and engrossing history," while Susan Miron, a reviewer for *Christian Science Monitor,* called it "a brilliant, hugely enjoyable, cultural history." In a review for the *Denver Post,* Kyle MacMillan commented that Ross's book was a "towering accomplishment," a "genuine page-turner," and "a fresh, eloquent and superbly researched book." Bryan Appleyard, in a review for the London *Times,* termed it a "marvellous book." Beryl Bainbridge, a contributor to the London *Observer,* stated that Ross, as a writer, "will fascinate, challenge and delight you, but above all he will never, ever patronise you." His book, Bainbridge added, "is littered with great tales—of scandal, revolution, intrigue, lust, greed, shattered dreams and vaunting ambition and they all give this book its extraordinary zest and fluency." A *New Criterion* critic also praised for *The Rest Is Noise,* and termed it "elegant, witty, often even poetic." The same critic, however, identified numerous editing and spelling errors in the text. Other critics voiced disappointment in the seeming exclusion of some important composers, especially British composers, such as Ralph Vaughan Williams, William Elgar, and Michael Tippett, while others did not agree with the eminence Ross ascribes to some of his favorites, such as Shostakovich and Britten.

On the whole, however, most critics concurred with Swafford, who concluded that Ross "consistently connects classical music to the life of creators and of cultures, and so conveys as few writers do the human reality of the music." Most reviewers agreed with *Opera News* writer Jonathan Rabb, who observed: "Ross's achievement is all the more astounding because it makes music essential to the understanding of history beyond the history of the music itself."

### Listen to This

Ross published his second book, *Listen to This,* in 2010. The collection of essays compiles a number of Ross's writings on popular and classical music artists. From Renaissance to rock and Brahms to Björk, the essays cover a wide range of topics while highlighting to the reader the ability of all types of music to express the human condition.

Reviewing the book in the London *Observer,* Peter Conrad said that the book "really needs an exclamation mark. The tone is hortatory; Ross is an enthusiast, as irrepressible and enlivening as a circus barker." Conrad mentioned of Ross that "as a writer he is of course frustrated, like Griffiths, by the way that sounds slip through his verbal net," but allowed that his "gestures of gratified defeat do not mean that Ross fails at his task of describing the indescribable. Relying on metaphor, he deftly catches the way music uses technical inventions to unlock emotion." London *Guardian* contributor Charles Hazlewood lauded that in this book, "Ross liberates music from yet another of its straitjackets— the habit of limiting itself to a single genre." Hazlewood also noted that "the magical mystery tour of a read is also full of piquant phrases." Reviewing the book in the London *Telegraph,* Ivan Hewett observed: "It's easy to see where Ross's heart really lies, in the sense that the essays on Schubert, Mozart, and Brahms are so much more deeply felt and insightful than the others. Nevertheless, running through the book is the same Utopian dream that surfaced in *The Rest Is Noise:* that one day the old categories of classical and pop will melt away, and we will all live together in music's universal republic." Writing in the *Washington Post Book World,* Michael Dirda remarked that "there's a huge amount to admire in this collection of essays about music." In the *Seattle Times,* Alan Moores contended that "running through every piece is a spirit of adventure, common sense, joy and, ultimately, engagement."

## ■ Biographical And Critical Sources

*PERIODICALS*

*Booklist,* October 15, 2007, Alan Hirsch, review of *The Rest Is Noise: Listening to the Twentieth Century,* p. 18; September 1, 2010, Alan Moores, review of *Listen to This,* p. 27.

*Bookmarks,* January 1, 2008, review of *The Rest Is Noise,* p. 66; March 1, 2011, review of *Listen to This,* p. 47.

*Bookseller,* May 21, 2010, review of *Listen to This,* p. 37.

*Choice: Current Reviews for Academic Libraries,* April 1, 2008, J.P. Ambrose, review of *The Rest Is Noise,* p. 1348.

*Christian Science Monitor,* October 23, 2007, Susan Miron, review of *The Rest Is Noise,* p. 15; September 21, 2010, F. Cord Volkmer, review of *Listen to This.*

*Commentary,* October 1, 2007, Terry Teachout, review of *The Rest Is Noise.*

*Denver Post,* February 9, 2008, Kyle MacMillan, review of *The Rest Is Noise.*

*Economist,* October 27, 2007, review of *The Rest Is Noise,* p. 98.

*Guardian* (London, England), December 11, 2010, Charles Hazlewood, review of *Listen to This.*

*Kirkus Reviews,* September 1, 2007, review of *The Rest Is Noise;* August 1, 2010, review of *Listen to This.*

*Library Journal,* October 1, 2007, Larry Lipkis, review of *The Rest Is Noise,* p. 74; July 1, 2010, Barry Zaslow, review of *Listen to This,* p. 91.

*Nation,* October 29, 2007, David Schiff, review of *The Rest Is Noise,* p. 25.

*National Post* (Toronto, Ontario, Canada), December 8, 2007, Craig Seligman, review of *The Rest Is Noise,* p. 13.

*New Criterion,* January 1, 2008, review of *The Rest Is Noise,* p. 72.

*New Republic,* December 31, 2007, Joseph Kerman, review of *The Rest Is Noise,* p. 39.

*New Statesman,* March 24, 2008, Anna Picard, review of *The Rest Is Noise,* p. 54.

*New York Observer,* October 9, 2007, Doree Shafrir, "The Best Listener in America," author interview.

*New York Sun,* September 26, 2007, Adam Kirsch, review of *The Rest Is Noise.*

*New York Times Book Review,* October 28, 2007, Geoff Dyer, review of *The Rest Is Noise,* p. 1.

*Notes,* September 1, 2008, Richard D. Burbank, review of *The Rest Is Noise,* p. 75.

*Observer* (London, England), February 17, 2008, Beryl Bainbridge, review of *The Rest Is Noise;* November 28, 2010, Peter Conrad, review of *Listen to This.*

*Opera News,* November 1, 2007, Jonathan Rabb, review of *The Rest Is Noise,* p. 76; March 1, 2011, Fred Cohn, review of *Listen to This,* p. 71.

*Publishers Weekly,* July 23, 2007, review of *The Rest Is Noise,* p. 55; August 30, 2010, review of *Listen to This,* p. 38.

*Reference & Research Book News,* February 1, 2008, review of *The Rest Is Noise.*

*Scotsman* (Edinburgh, Scotland), March 16, 2008, John Burnside, review of *The Rest Is Noise.*

*Seattle Times,* October 9, 2010, Alan Moores, review of *Listen to This.*

*Seattle Weekly,* October 17, 2007, Gavin Borchert, review of *The Rest Is Noise.*

*Southern Humanities Review,* September 22, 2008, Stanley Hauer, review of *The Rest Is Noise,* p. 403.

*Spectator,* March 1, 2008, Rupert Christiansen, review of *The Rest Is Noise,* p. 31.

*Teaching Music,* January 1, 2009, review of *The Rest Is Noise,* p. 64; January 1, 2011, review of *Listen to This,* p. 63.

*Telegraph* (London, England), May 23, 2008, Ivan Hewett, review of *The Rest Is Noise;* November 16, 2010, Ivan Hewett, review of *Listen to This.*

*Time Out New York,* October 11, 2007, Hank Shteamer, review of *The Rest Is Noise.*

*Times* (London, England), February 24, 2008, Bryan Appleyard, review of *The Rest Is Noise.*

*Tribune Books* (Chicago, IL), December 29, 2007, James Marcus, "Not So Harmonious: Alex Ross Takes a Look at Contemporary Classical Music and Artists," review of *The Rest Is Noise,* p. 10.

*Washington Post Book World,* October 7, 2010, Michael Dirda, review of *Listen to This,* p. C3.

*Wichita Eagle* (Wichita, KS), December 16, 2007, "'Noise' Brings Harmony to Modern Music," review of *The Rest Is Noise.*

*Wilson Quarterly,* September 22, 2007, Jan Swafford, review of *The Rest Is Noise,* p. 95.


ONLINE

*Bookreporter.com,* http://www.bookreporter.com/ (June 30, 2008), "2007 National Book Critics Circle Award Finalists," author information.

*High Hat,* http://www.thehighhat.com/ (June 30, 2008), Steve Hicken, review of *The Rest Is Noise.*

*H-Net: Humanities and Social Sciences Online,* http://www.h-net.org/ (April 1, 2010), Daniel Morat, review of *The Rest Is Noise.*

*Rest Is Noise Blog,* http://www.therestisnoise.com/ (August 25, 2011), author profile.

*Salon.com,* http://www.salon.com/ (November 2, 2007), Kevin Berger, review of *The Rest Is Noise.**

# Hazel Rowley

## 1951-2011

### ■ Personal

Born November 16, 1951, in London, England; immigrated to Australia, in 1959; died of a MRSA-related cerebral hemorrhage, March 1, 2011, in New York, NY; daughter of Derrick (a scientist) and Betty (a homemaker) Rowley. *Education:* Adelaide University, B.A., 1974, Ph.D., 1982. *Politics:* "Left of center."

### ■ Career

Deakin University, Melbourne, Victoria, Australia, lecturer, 1989-94, senior lecturer, beginning 1995; University of Texas-Austin, resident scholar, 1994-95; affiliated with the W.E.B. Du Bois Institute at Harvard University.

### ■ Awards, Honors

National Book Award for Nonfiction, 1993, National Book Council Banjo Award for Nonfiction (Australia), Walter McRae Russell Award from the Association for the Study of Australian Literature, and *New York Times* Notable Book distinction, all 1994, all for *Christina Stead.*

### ■ Writings

*Christina Stead: A Biography,* Heinemann (Port Melbourne, Australia), 1993, Holt (New York, NY), 1994.

*The Art of Self-Invention,* Heinemann (Port Melbourne, Australia), 1996.

(Editor, with Wenche Ommundsen) *From a Distance: Australian Writers and Cultural Displacement,* Deakin University Press (Geelong, Victoria, Australia), 1996.

*Richard Wright: The Life and Times,* Holt (New York, NY), 2001.

*Tête-à-Tête: Simone de Beauvoir and Jean-Paul Sartre,* HarperCollins (New York, NY), 2005.

(Translator, with Kevin Michel Capé) Tahar Ben Jelloun, *The Last Friend* (novel), New Press (New York, NY), 2006.

*Franklin and Eleanor: An Extraordinary Marriage,* Farrar, Straus, and Giroux (New York, NY), 2010.

Contributor to anthologies, including *The Best Australian Essays.* Contributor to periodicals, including *Partisan Review, Antioch Review, Mississippi Quarterly, Prose Studies, Contemporary Literature, Texas Studies in Literature and Language, Southerly and Westerly, Times Higher Education Supplement, Los Angeles Times, Washington Post, Boston Globe,* and *Nation.* Rowley's books have been translated into more than twelve languages.

### ■ Sidelights

Hazel Rowley was born in England, but she spent much of her adult life in Australia and other foreign countries. She wrote two well-received biographies of authors from her adopted countries (one of Australian writer Christina Stead and one of American author Richard Wright) as well as other nonfiction works. Rowley died from a cerebral hemorrhage at the age of fifty-nine, shortly after completing her final biography.

#### *Christina Stead*

Rowley's award-winning first book, *Christina Stead: A Biography,* is a comprehensive study of the life and work of Stead, the novelist best remembered for her book *The Man Who Loved Children,* which was first published in 1940. Before her death, Stead destroyed virtually all of her personal papers and diaries, making a biography such as Rowley's all the more valuable to those who desire a deeper insight into Stead's life and art. Several critics praised *Christina Stead,* among them *New York Newsday* reviewer Diane Cole, who revealed that she had once considered writing Stead's biography. "Fortunately, I did not," Cole remarked. "Because in *Christina Stead,* . . . Hazel Rowley has written the book that I longed to read when I first discovered Stead—a perceptive and comprehensive examination of an extraordinary writer's life and her uncompromising artistic vision. . . . Rowley's account of Stead's life provides as intensely detailed, absorbing, and complex a portrait as any of her subject's fictional characters. Her reconstruction of Stead's early years allows us rare insight into the way the artistic imagination can spin parallel worlds in fiction out of the most hurtful realities."

*Los Angeles Times* critic Merle Rubin offered similar comments about *Christina Stead,* finding that "Rowley's is not the first biography of Christina Stead, but it is the most complete and detailed account of her life to date. . . . Rowley has undertaken her task with zeal and understanding. Her sprawling biography presents a great deal of material culled from letters, articles, and personal interviews in a lively, cogent fashion. She examines multiple aspects of Stead's life and work without losing the thread of the story. Whether evaluating Stead's Communist sympathies or trying to assess the extent of her various infatuations, Rowley shows sound judgment and honesty."

Further praise came from Michael Upchurch, who reviewed *Christina Stead* in the *New York Times Book Review.* "The challenge for any would-be biographer," Upchurch observed, "is to establish the book's importance and relation to one another; to give a sense of the historical backgrounds and personalities from which Stead drew her inspiration; and to portray the woman herself, a task complicated by the fact that Stead burned many of her personal papers late in her life. Hazel Rowley . . . meets the challenge splendidly on all three counts. Juggling a vast amount of detail, her biography of Christina Stead is a model of clarity. Ms. Rowley's shrewd selectivity and handling of anecdote make the book compellingly readable. . . . *Christina Stead* is everything a literary biography should be." Rowley's profile of Stead was also applauded by critic Lorna Sage. Writing in the London *Times Literary Supplement,* Sage observed that Stead's "rediscovery and canonization, which began in the mid-1960s, have been in many quarters more a matter of lip-service than conviction. She remains too

hard to 'place,' even for a world that professes to admire slipperiness and fragmented selves. So it's a godsend to have a full account of her long wandering life. . . . Hazel Rowley, in this splendidly detailed account, much the fullest life to date, supplies the narrative that makes sense of the novel's angry, many-voiced, impatient, digressive brilliance."

### Richard Wright

For her biography of author Richard Wright, Rowley sifted through 136 boxes of his papers, which are archived at Yale University, as well as his correspondence with friends. Although the outlines of Wright's life story, from his birth to poor sharecroppers in Mississippi to his eventual self-imposed exile in France, were already well known, Rowley did manage to flesh out some new aspects of Wright's past. His relationship with fellow African American writer Ralph Ellison and his early days as a writer living in Chicago, for example, are areas noted by reviewers where Rowley had made important contributions.

"This ranks as one of the more revealing biographies" of Wright, wrote *Black Issues Book Review* contributor Robert Fleming. In a review for *Booklist,* Donna Seaman also praised Rowley, calling her "a precise, straight-ahead biographer who eschews facile analysis." Seaman concluded: "For the first time, Wright's complicated life and work and fully and justly illuminated."

### Tête-à-Tête

In *Tête-à-Tête: Simone de Beauvoir and Jean-Paul Sartre* Rowley tells the intricate story of the many relationships forged by existentialist icons and intellectuals Jean-Paul Sartre and Simone de Beauvoir. For almost fifty years, from 1929 until Sartre's death in 1980, de Beauvoir and Sartre were involved in a complex intellectual and romantic relationship that found the two inseparably committed to each other, but far from monogamous. "Without undue prurience, Rowley . . . romps through the major entanglements, loves, triangles, friendships and affairs" of Sartre and de Beauvoir, remarked a *Publishers Weekly* reviewer. "Drawing from a trove of unpublished letters and interviews, Rowley brings fresh psychological insight to both her subjects," noted Megan O'Grady in *Vogue.* Rowley covers aspects of each personality, within and outside their mutual relationship. The physically unattractive Sartre, for example, delighted in seduction and conquest, particularly of beautiful women with whom he could foster a feeling of neediness and dependence on him. De Beauvoir had relationships with many men, though her attentions and affections kept returning to Sartre. Both claimed to be completely open with each other about other lovers they had, though de Beauvoir may have successfully hidden her bisexual affairs from Sartre, and Sartre himself admits that he was never completely truthful with de Beauvoir. "Sartre financially supports the lovers he betrays, while Beauvoir is stunningly two-faced," observed Seaman, again writing in *Booklist*.

Marni Jackson, reviewing *Tête-à-Tête* in the Toronto *Globe & Mail*, commented: "While Rowley's book is fair, straightforwardly written, and deserves a spot on the creaking shelf of Sartre-de Beauvoir literature, the focus on the romantic shenanigans wears thin. It sometimes goes beyond juicy to creepy." However, Jackson also noted that Rowley "presents a surprisingly sympathetic portrait of Sartre—generous, playful and charming—a hambone who loved playing hooky with women from the realm of ideas." A *Kirkus Reviews* contributor called Rowley's biography a "neatly assembled record of people behaving badly in the name of literature, philosophy, and amour." Rowley's "lively and fulfilling portrait" is "thoroughly researched and well written," concluded Jason Moore in *Library Journal*.

### Franklin and Eleanor

Just a year before her untimely death, Rowley published the joint biography *Franklin and Eleanor: An Extraordinary Marriage*. The account looks into the inner workings of the marriage between U.S. President Franklin D. Roosevelt and his distant cousin, Eleanor. Rowley shows that these two strong personalities lived fairly separate lives and each had several other lovers. However, they were a unique complement to each other, offering support and pressure to push forward with their causes.

Reviewing the book in the *Los Angeles Times*, Wendy Smith pointed out that "earlier appraisals of their marriage may have overly emphasized its negatives, but Rowley's unduly minimizes infidelities, jealousy and exasperation on both sides. Franklin and Eleanor's marriage was in many ways dysfunctional. It was also a triumph of shared purpose and dedication." In a review on the *Readings* Web site, Sybil Nolan suggested that the book's "greatest achievement is to show us the Roosevelts eye-to-eye and heart-to-heart in the early and middle phases of their marriage, loving each other but accommodat-

ing each other as well." A contributor to *Book Review Plus* opined: "As a political history, this book does a great job of documenting the various causes these two championed. They were ahead of their time (especially Eleanor) in their views on human rights, civil rights, women's rights and labor rights." Writing in the *Christian Science Monitor*, Terry Hartle concluded that "Rowley has clearly read and analyzed the extensive literature about the Roosevelts and undertook an extensive review of the documentary evidence at the Roosevelt Library in Hyde Park. Despite an occasional tendency toward overstatement, her analysis is sound, and the conclusions seem fair and on-target. The result is compelling history with first-rate character portraits of the Roosevelts and their closest friends."

### Rowley once told *CA*:

"I am interested in the cultural, historical, emotional and intellectual forces that form the individual writer. And I am absorbed by the subject of self-presentation in writing. How do particular writers present themselves, 'invent' themselves?

"I speak French and German and have lived several years in Europe and the United States, which has left me with a strong interest in cultural difference, its manifestations and implications."

## ■ Biographical And Critical Sources

### PERIODICALS

*American History*, June 1, 2011, review of *Franklin and Eleanor: An Extraordinary Marriage*, p. 75.

*American Scholar*, September 22, 2001, John Freeman, review of *Richard Wright: The Life and Times*, p. 145.

*Australian Book Review*, July 1, 1993, review of *Christina Stead: A Biography*, p. 8.

*Australian Journal of Language and Literacy*, August 1, 1997, Alan Meyer, review of *From a Distance: Australian Writers and Cultural Displacement*, p. 246.

*Biography*, December 22, 2006, Marni Jackson and Christina Nehring, review of *Tête-à-Tête: Simone de Beauvoir and Jean-Paul Sartre*, p. 198.

*Black Issues Book Review*, January 1, 2002, Robert Fleming, review of *Richard Wright*, p. 65.

*Book*, July 1, 2001, Paul Evans, "American Exile," p. 22.

*Booklist,* September 1, 1994, Brad Hooper, review of *Christina Stead,* p. 19; July, 2001, Donna Seaman, review of *Richard Wright,* p. 1969; February 15, 2002, Brad Hooper, review of *Richard Wright,* p. 1002; October 1, 2005, Donna Seaman, review of *Tête-à-Tête,* p. 17; February 1, 2006, Ray Olson, review of *The Last Friend,* p. 26; October 15, 2010, Margaret Flanagan, review of *Franklin and Eleanor,* p. 16.

*Business Week,* September 24, 2001, "Furious Writer," p. 20E6.

*Canadian Literature,* September 22, 1994, review of *Christina Stead,* p. 249.

*Chicago Tribune Books,* December 25, 1994, review of *Christina Stead,* p. 4; July 28, 2002, review of *Richard Wright,* p. 6.

*Choice: Current Reviews for Academic Libraries,* March 1, 1995, review of *Christina Stead,* p. 1120.

*Christian Science Monitor,* November 15, 2001, review of *Richard Wright,* p. 14; March 13, 2011, Terry Hartle, review of *Franklin and Eleanor.*

*Cleveland Plain Dealer,* November 16, 2010, Susan Ager, review of *Franklin and Eleanor.*

*Detroit Free Press,* September 2, 2001, review of *Richard Wright,* p. 4E.

*Entertainment Weekly,* August 3, 2001, review of *Richard Wright,* p. 63; September 7, 2001, "The Week," p. 158; October 14, 2005, Michelle Kung, review of *Tête-à-Tête,* p. 161.

*Essence,* September, 2001, "Bookmark," p. 84.

*Globe & Mail* (Toronto, Ontario, Canada), November 12, 2005, Marni Jackson, "The Goblin, the Beaver—and Their Lovers," review of *Tête-à-Tête,* p. D11.

*Guardian* (London, England), February 12, 1995, review of *Christina Stead,* p. 29.

*Hypatia,* January 1, 2008, Julien S. Murphy, review of *Tête-à-Tête,* p. 208.

*Independent* (London, England), January 20, 2006, Joan Smith, review of *Tête-à-Tête.*

*Kirkus Reviews,* July 1, 1994, review of *Christina Stead,* p. 917; June 1, 2001, review of *Richard Wright,* p. 790; August 1, 2005, review of *Tête-à-Tête,* p. 835; July 15, 2010, review of *Franklin and Eleanor.*

*Law Institute Journal,* August 1, 1993, Simon Caterson, review of *Christina Stead,* p. 757.

*Law Society Journal,* March 1, 2011, Philip Burgess, review of *Franklin and Eleanor,* p. 84.

*Library Journal,* August 1, 1994, Denise Johnson, review of *Christina Stead,* p. 87; July 1, 2001, Henry L. Carrigan, Jr., review of *Richard Wright,* p. 68; September 15, 2005, Jason Moore, review of *Tête-à-Tête,* p. 68; May 15, 2006, Debbie Bogenschutz, review of *The Last Friend,* p. 89; September 1, 2010, William D. Pederson, review of *Franklin and Eleanor,* p. 116.

*London Review of Books,* June 8, 1995, review of *Christina Stead,* p. 36.

*Los Angeles Times,* November 20, 1994, Merle Rubin, review of *Christina Stead,* p. 2; November 23, 2010, Wendy Smith, review of *Franklin and Eleanor.*

*Meanjin,* June 22, 1993, review of *Christina Stead,* p. 783.

*Ms.,* September 1, 1994, review of *Christina Stead,* p. 76.

*Nation,* November 21, 1994, Louise Yelin, review of *Christina Stead,* p. 620.

*New Crisis,* November 1, 2001, William Jelani Cobb, review of *Richard Wright,* pp. 62-63.

*New Statesman & Society,* February 10, 1995, Guy Mannes-Abbott, review of *Christina Stead,* p. 47.

*New Yorker,* February 6, 1995, Claudia Roth Piermont, review of *Christina Stead,* p. 85; October 22, 2001, review of *Richard Wright,* p. 77.

*New York Newsday,* October 2, 1994, Diane Cole, review of *Christina Stead.*

*New York Review of Books,* December 4, 1994, review of *Christina Stead,* p. 66; November 1, 2001, Darryl Pinckney, review of *Richard Wright,* p. 68.

*New York Times,* August 26, 2001, Michael Anderson, "A Native Son in Exile."

*New York Times Book Review,* October 2, 1994, Michael Upchurch, review of *Christina Stead,* p. 3.

*Observer* (London, England), November 28, 1993, review of *Christina Stead,* p. 4.

*Publishers Weekly,* August 1, 1994, review of *Christina Stead,* p. 66; June 18, 2001, review of *Richard Wright,* p. 68; August 1, 2005, review of *Tête-à-Tête,* p. 58; December 19, 2005, review of *The Last Friend,* p. 38; September 20, 2010, review of *Franklin and Eleanor,* p. 59.

*Reference & Research Book News,* February 1, 2006, review of *Tête-à-Tête.*

*Times Educational Supplement,* March 24, 1995, review of *Christina Stead,* p. 13.

*Times Literary Supplement,* August 20, 1993, Lorna Sage, review of *Christina Stead,* p. 3.

*Village Voice Literary Supplement,* October 1, 1994, review of *Christina Stead,* p. 18.

*Vogue,* October 1, 2005, Megan O'Grady, review of *Tête-à-Tête,* p. 266.

*Wall Street Journal,* September 4, 2001, Michael J. Ybarra, "A Literary Sensation, a Precarious Existence," p. A20; September 5, 2001, review of *Richard Wright,* p. A20.

*Washington Post Book World,* October 2, 1994, review of *Christina Stead,* p. 4; August 12, 2001, Jake Lamar, review of *Richard Wright,* p. 1.

*Women's Review of Books,* February, 1995, Helen Yglesias, review of *Christina Stead,* p. 7.

*Women's Studies Quarterly,* September 22, 2006, Sarah Glazer, review of *Tête-à-Tête,* p. 234.

*World Literature Today,* June 22, 1994, David Coad, review of *Christina Stead,* p. 633; April 1, 2003, Daniel Garrett, review of *Richard Wright,* p. 109; September 1, 2006, Willis G. Regier, review of *Tête-à-Tête,* p. 77.

*ONLINE*

*BookPage,* http://www.bookpage.com/ (September 30, 2001), Robert Fleming, review of *Richard Wright.*

*Book Review Plus,* http://www.bookreviewplus.com/ (February 25, 2011), review of *Franklin and Eleanor.*

*Hazel Rowley Web site,* http://www.hazelrowley.com/ (August 1, 2011), author profile.

*NPR's Fresh Air,* http://www.npr.org/ (November 18, 2010), review of *Franklin and Eleanor.*

*Readings Web site,* http://www.readings.com.au/ (February 1, 2011), Sybil Nolan, review of *Franklin and Eleanor.*

# ■ Obituaries

*PERIODICALS*

*Age* (Melbourne, Victoria, Australia), March 3, 2011, Jason Steger, "Gifted Australian Biographer Dies in New York at 59."

*Australian,* March 3, 2011, Stephen Romei, "Hazel Rowley, 59, Dies in U.S."

*New York Times Book Review,* March 19, 2011, Margalit Fox, "Hazel Rowley, Who Wrote of Charismatic Lives, Dies at 59."

*Sydney Morning Herald,* March 10, 2011, Peter Craven, "An Irrepressible and Daring Storyteller."

*Washington Post Book World,* March 13, 2011, Emma Brown, "Hazel Rowley Dies: Acclaimed Biographer was 59."*

# Miri Rubin

## 1956-

## ■ Personal

Born 1956. *Education:* Hebrew University of Jerusalem, B.A., M.A., 1980; University of Cambridge, Ph.D., 1984.

## ■ Addresses

*Office*—Department of History, Queen Mary College, University of London, London E1 4NS, England. *E-mail*—m.e.rubin@qmul.ac.uk.

## ■ Career

Oxford University, Oxford, England, tutor, lecturer and reader in history, 1989-2000; University of London, Queen Mary College, London, England, professor, 2000—. Distinguished visiting professor at University of Connecticut, 1996, 1998, 2004, and University of Iowa, 2002.

## ■ Member

Royal Historical Society (councilor, 2004-07), Medieval Academy of America (corresponding fellow, 2007).

## ■ Awards, Honors

Cowinner in scholarship category, National Jewish Book Award, Jewish Book Council, for *Gentile Tales: The Narrative Assault on Late Medieval Jews;* AHRC Network Grant. Research fellowships from Cambridge University, Princeton University, and the University of London.

## ■ Writings

*Charity and Community in Medieval Cambridge,* Cambridge University Press (New York, NY), 1987.

*Corpus Christi: The Eucharist in Late Medieval Cambridge,* Cambridge University Press (New York, NY), 1991.

*Gentile Tales: The Narrative Assault on Late Medieval Jews,* Yale University Press (New Haven, CT), 1999.

*The Hollow Crown: A History of Britain in the Late Middle Ages,* Penguin (New York, NY), 2005.

*Emotion and Devotion: The Meaning of Mary in Medieval Religious Cultures,* CEU Press (New York, NY), 2009.

*Mother of God: A History of the Virgin Mary,* Yale University Press (New Haven, CT), 2009.

*EDITOR*

(With David Afulafia and Michael Franklin; and contributor) *Church and City, 1000-1500: Essays in Honour of Christopher Brooke,* Cambridge University Press (New York, NY), 1992.

(With Sarah Kay) *Framing Medieval Bodies,* Manchester University Press (New York, NY), 1994.

*The Work of Jacques Le Goff and the Challenges of Medieval History,* Boydell Press (Rochester, NY), 1997.

*European Religious Cultures: Essays Offered to Christopher Brooke on the Occasion of His Eightieth Birthday,* Institute of Historical Research (London, England), 2008.

(With Walter Simons) *Christianity in Western Europe c. 1100-c. 1500,* Cambridge University Press (New York, NY), 2009.

*Medieval Christianity in Practice,* Princeton University Press (Princeton, NJ), 2009.

(With Katherine L. Jansen) *Charisma and Religious Authority: Jewish, Christian, and Muslim Preaching, 1200-1500*, Brepols (Turnhout, Belgium), 2010.

## ■ Sidelights

Scholar Miri Rubin writes widely about the religious cultures of Europe between the twelfth and sixteenth centuries. Rubin is the author and editor of such works as *Framing Medieval Bodies* and *Gentile Tales: The Narrative Assault on Late Medieval Jews.*

### *Corpus Christi* and *Church and City, 1000-1500*

*Corpus Christi: The Eucharist in Late Medieval Cambridge* is Rubin's study of the "attempt in the late thirteenth and early fourteenth century to make the Eucharist the central symbol of a new culture through the creation of the feast of Corpus Christi," observed Roger E. Reynolds in the *Journal of Theological Studies.* In the work, Rubin examines the growth of the Corpus Christi celebration, including its sermons, processions, and liturgical practices, as well as its "new vocabulary of Christological spirituality emphasizing aspects of Christ's passion and its relation to the bread and wine used in the Eucharist," noted Reynolds. Robert W. Gaston, writing in the *Journal of Ecclesiastical History,* stated that *Corpus Christi* "is an admirable work of scholarship, replete with balanced, informative and incisively written chapters useful for a range of disciplines." Reynolds called the book "a fascinating and multifaceted examination of the cult that was the central symbol of late medieval culture, the Eucharist."

Rubin served as coeditor of *Church and City, 1000-1500: Essays in Honour of Christopher Brooke,* a collection of articles that explores the relationship between urban history and ecclesiastical practice in the Middle Ages. Dedicated to a noted medieval scholar, the festschrift contains fourteen essays, including Rubin's, a comparison of the differences in religious attitudes between cities and rural areas. According to Colin Morris in the *Journal of Theological Studies,* "all of these essays are of high quality, and most of them are models of specialist studies which contain wider implications for our understanding of medieval urban churches."

### *Framing Medieval Bodies* and *Gentile Tales*

In *Framing Medieval Bodies,* Rubin and coeditor Sarah Kay present twelve essays "that 'frame'—that is, conceptualize, represent, exhibit, or confine—the medieval body," observed Susan Groag Bell in *Signs.* The contributors approach the topic from a variety of scholarly disciplines, including theology, archaeology, art history, and psychology. "These essays are fascinating: ecstatics, hermaphrodites, Chaucer's Pardoner, anchoresses, medieval lepers, and psychotics crowd the pages of this book with a kaleidoscopic rigour that is almost vertiginous," Alexandra Barratt remarked in *Notes and Queries.* In *History Today,* Pauline Stafford remarked that "for most of the authors of *Framing Medieval Bodies,* the body has no universal, natural meaning. The body is conceptualized, 'framed' in many different ways. The resulting variety is fruitfully explored in a collection which will be a necessary addition to the growing literature on the medieval body."

In *Gentile Tales* Rubin examines "a particularly virulent form of narrative, the host desecration accusation, which developed from the increasing importance of the eucharist as sacrament and symbol around the end of the thirteenth century," noted Elisa Narin van Court in *Criticism.* In the host desecration narrative, a Jew acquires the eucharistic wafer and subjects it to various types of abuse, thereby striking at the Christian faith and even Christ himself. The desecration tales often led to violence by medieval European Christians against the Jews. Anna Sapir Abulafia, writing in *History Today,* stated that Rubin's work "does not deal primarily with the separate episodes of host desecration accusations. It aims to rise above the peculiarities of particular episodes in order to study the narrative aspect of this kind of anti-Judaism. The author asks what the basic components of the narrative are. She wonders what its role was and how it was disseminated." According to Michael Clanchy in the *Times Literary Supplement, Gentile Tales* "raises—as it is intended to do—deep and disturbing questions about the nature of persecution and mass hysteria, and not least about the ways in which Christian beliefs have caused the deaths of Jews." *Library Journal* contributor Hayim Y. Sheynin called the work "a welcome addition to the literature on public thought in medieval society and the history of Christianity and anti-Semitism."

### *Mother of God*

Rubin has since authored *The Hollow Crown: A History of Britain in the Late Middle Ages, Emotion and Devotion: The Meaning of Mary in Medieval Religious Cultures,* and *Mother of God: A History of the Virgin Mary.* The latter volume attempts to explore the integral role and influence of Mary in the foundations of Christianity (particularly Catholicism), as well as her changing meanings over time. Rubin writes that Mary is a symbol for forgiveness, motherhood, and faith. Furthermore, Mary inserts a feminine balance to Christianity, one that is perfectly juxtaposed to the masculine overtones of the holy trinity.

"Rubin combines sweeping historical vistas with lively anecdotes and stories of personal piety and economic largesse," Tina Beattie advised in her *Commonweal* review. However, she concluded her review with mild ambivalence: "All in all, this is a book to dip into and enjoy for its lavish and exuberant portrayal of the woman who emerged from the shadows of the New Testament text to play a formative role in the shaping of Western art, culture, and religion. Those seeking a deeper engagement with the subject will also have to look to other books and hope that one day Rubin might use her considerable scholarly skills to develop in greater detail some of the themes she touches on here." Sally Cunneen, writing in *America*, was far more laudatory, announcing: "In some 500 pages she unrolls the diversity as well as the continuity of meanings that different ethnic, national and religious groups have continued to find in the Jewish mother of Jesus." She added: "Rubin is strongest in her lengthy treatment of the European Middle Ages. Paying careful attention to the theology and liturgy of this period, when monasteries dominated the Christian world, she nevertheless concentrates on the human aspects of the widespread devotion to Mary that seemed to unite medieval Europe." In his *History Today* review, Simon Yarrow called *Mother of God* "a remarkable and original achievement. No one before has attempted a study of this scale and scope on Mary." Yarrow went on to state: "Rubin has followed and surveyed the course of Mary as might an explorer charting one of the world's great rivers from its rather unpromising trickle in the Gospels through its early alluvial accretions, its rapids, forks, and tributaries . . . before guiding us through changes in the mainstream, currents and countercurrents into an unexpected . . . but wonderfully warm and generous meditation by the author . . . on what Mary might mean today. I recommend that you read the book to find out."

## ■ Biographical And Critical Sources

### PERIODICALS

*America,* October 12, 2009, Sally Cunneen, "The Making of a Global Icon," p. 24.

*American Historical Review,* April, 1989, Ellen Wedemeyer, review of *Charity and Community in Medieval Cambridge,* p. 426; April, 1993, Pamela Shein-gorn, review of *Corpus Christi: The Eucharist in Late Medieval Cambridge,* p. 482; April, 1996, Karma Lochrie, review of *Framing Medieval Bodies,* p. 461.

*Catholic Historical Review,* July, 1993, David Burr, review of *Corpus Christi,* p. 522; April, 1994, Robert Brentano, review of *Church and City, 1000-1500: Essays in Honour of Christopher Brooke,* p. 336.

*Commonweal,* November 20, 2009, Tina Beattie, "BVM from A to Z," p. 26.

*Comparative Literature Studies,* spring, 1997, Celeste A. Patton, review of *Framing Medieval Bodies,* p. 184.

*Criticism,* spring, 2000, Elisa Narin van Court, review of *Gentile Tales: The Narrative Assault on Late Medieval Jews,* p. 269.

*English Historical Review,* April, 1990, Nicholas Orme, review of *Charity and Community in Medieval Cambridge,* p. 443; April, 1992, Nicholas Orme, review of *Corpus Christi,* p. 386; February, 1997, Peregrine Horden, review of *Framing Medieval Bodies,* p. 176.

*History,* June, 1988, J.R. Maddicott, review of *Charity and Community in Medieval Cambridge,* p. 289; June, 1992, R.N. Swanson, review of *Corpus Christi,* p. 287; October, 1994, Gary Dickson, review of *Church and City, 1000-1500,* p. 475.

*History Today,* December, 1995, Pauline Stafford, review of *Framing Medieval Bodies,* p. 58; December, 1999, Anna Sapir Abulafia, review of *Gentile Tales,* p. 56; May 1, 2005, Nigel Saul, review of *The Hollow Crown: A History of Britain in the Late Middle Ages,* p. 67; May 1, 2009, Simon Yarrow, review of *Mother of God: A History of the Virgin Mary,* p. 62; January 1, 2010, "A History of Christianity: The First Three Thousand Years," p. 58.

*Journal of Ecclesiastical History,* April, 1993, Susan Reynolds, review of *Church and City, 1000-1500,* p. 302; January, 1996, Robert W. Gaston, review of *Corpus Christi,* p. 157.

*Journal of Interdisciplinary Studies,* autumn, 1988, review of *Charity and Community in Medieval Cambridge,* p. 314; spring, 1994, Richard W. Pfaff, review of *Church and City, 1000-1500,* p. 690.

*Journal of Theological Studies,* October, 1993, Colin Morris, review of *Church and City, 1000-1500,* p. 750; April, 1994, Roger E. Reynolds, review of *Corpus Christi,* p. 386.

*Library Journal,* June 15, 1999, Hayim Y. Sheynin, review of *Gentile Tales,* p. 84.

*Medium Aevum,* fall, 1995, Derrick Pitard, review of *Framing Medieval Bodies,* p. 298; fall, 1998, review of *The Work of Jacques Le Goff and the Challenges of Medieval History,* p. 373; fall, 2000, John C. Hirsch, review of *Gentile Tales,* p. 338.

*New Statesman*, June 28, 1999, Lisa Jardine, review of *Gentile Tales*, p. 45.

*Notes and Queries*, June, 1996, Alexandra Barratt, review of *Framing Medieval Bodies*, p. 205; March, 2001, Ian P. Wei, review of *Gentile Tales*, p. 47.

*Signs*, spring, 1997, Susan Groag Bell, review of *Framing Medieval Bodies*, p. 765.

*Social History*, October, 1997, Catherine Peyroux, review of *Framing Medieval Bodies*, p. 339.

*Spectator*, March 26, 2005, "A Monumental Mediaeval Muddle," p. 44.

*Speculum*, April, 1989, Susanne F. Roberts, review of *Charity and Community in Medieval Cambridge*, p. 498; April, 1993, Gary Macy, review of *Corpus Christi*, p. 557; April, 1997, Helen Solterer, review of *Framing Medieval Bodies*, p. 504; April, 2001, Gavin I. Langmuir, review of *Gentile Tales*, p. 512.

*Theological Studies*, September, 1992, John F. Baldovin, review of *Corpus Christi*, p. 566.

*Times Literary Supplement*, November 1, 1991, Peter Heath, review of *Corpus Christi*, p. 26; June 18, 1999, Michael Clanchy, review of *Gentile Tales*, p. 34.

ONLINE

*Queen Mary, University of London, School of History Web site*, http://www.history.qmul.ac.uk/ (August 30, 2011), author profile.*

# Kirk Russell

## 1954-

■ **Personal**

Born December 28, 1954, in CA; married Judy Rodgers (a chef and restaurant owner); children: Kate, Olivia. *Education:* University of California at Berkeley, B.A., 1978. *Hobbies and other interests:* Hang gliding, mountain biking, skiing, cycling, backpacking.

■ **Addresses**

*Home*—Berkeley, CA. *Agent*—Philip G. Spitzer Literary Agency, 50 Talmage Farm Ln., East Hampton, NY 11937. *E-mail*—kirk@kirkrussellbooks.com.

■ **Career**

Novel and entrepreneur. Founder of construction company, until c. 1995. Continues to consult in green building.

■ **Writings**

*"JOHN MARQUEZ" SERIES; NOVELS*

*Shell Games,* Chronicle Books (San Francisco, CA), 2003.
*Night Game,* Chronicle Books (San Francisco, CA), 2004.
*Dead Game,* Chronicle Books (San Francisco, CA), 2005.
*Redback,* Severn House (London, England), 2011.

*"HOMICIDE INSPECTOR BEN RAVENEAU" SERIES; NOVELS*

*A Killing in China Basin,* Severn House (London, England), 2011.

■ **Sidelights**

Kirk Russell earned a living as a builder and owner of a construction company in his native California until the mid-1990s, when he began to devote himself to fiction writing. His breakthrough as a crime novelist came when he learned of an undercover unit of state agents who work in the wilderness finding game poachers and other criminals who exploit natural resources. The protagonist in Russell's first three novels is the fictitious John Marquez, a former Drug Enforcement Agency detective who has joined the California Department of Fish and Game's elite Special Operations Unit. In an online interview with Tracy Farnsworth for *Roundtable Reviews,* Russell said that, while he does not want to preach conservation in his thrillers, "We've got some very dedicated, very genuine good people out there fighting a quiet war for wildlife."

### *Shell Games* and *Night Game*

In Russell's debut work, *Shell Games,* Marquez and his unit search for poachers who illegally harvest abalones off the shores of California. Prized for its meat, abalone has been driven to the brink of extinction by over-harvesting. As Marquez tries to find the poachers, he discovers that a former drug dealer seeking revenge is tracking him. In *Booklist* Connie Fletcher described Marquez as "far and away the most inventive new detective hero," based on his worthy but unusual occupation. A *Kirkus Reviews* critic noted that the book does not follow the usual patterns of debut thrillers. "This is not a cliché fest," the critic noted. "The story is loaded with atmosphere."

Marquez continues fighting for wildlife in *Night Game.* In this outing the detective must find and stop a ruthless gang that kills bears for bile and paws—both prized on the alternative-medicine market. A *Kirkus Reviews* contributor styled the novel a "splendid second outing in a procedural series" and concluded that the thriller demonstrates "superb suspense, culminating in an exhausting but satisfying series of chases." Fletcher, writing again for *Booklist,* emphasized that Russell reveals the California wilderness with an insight that makes his work "achingly credible." In her *All Readers* online piece, Harriet Klausner suggested that the wild California mountains "come across as sinister and dangerous as any urban noir scene."

### *Dead Game* and *Redback*

The third Marquez procedural, *Dead Game,* finds Marquez tracking sturgeon poachers who value the endangered fish for its caviar. Russell told Jenna Glatzer on *AbsoluteWrite.com* that his books would not have been as plausible had the real California Fish and Game detectives not allowed him to accompany them on busts. "When I met the Fish and Game team something happened inside," he said. "I knew immediately this was a character I could truly care about, write, and believe in. I wanted to make a kind of modern-day hero and I saw the possibility in what this team was doing and the way they did it."

Russell published the fourth novel in the series, *Redback,* in 2011. Two decades earlier, Marquez and informant Billy Takado meet up with Mexican drug cartel leaders Luis and Miguel Salazar at a Baja California bull ring. Their undercover drug operation goes horribly wrong, however, when Takado is killed, resulting in Marquez's dismissal from the DEA. After settling with the California Department of Fish and Game, Marquez finds out that the poacher Emrahain Stoval was responsible for Takado's murder. With the FBI looking to apprehend Stoval, Marquez finds this chase too irresistible to sit out. He temporarily joins the FBI in order to help them catch the man who derailed his career so many years ago. Marquez is startled to find out, however, that someone he trusts is leaking personal information to Stoval about him and his family.

*Booklist* reviewer Emily Melton called the novel "outstanding" and "a superbly crafted, cleverly plotted, highly suspenseful thriller with a larger-than-life hero." A *Kirkus Reviews* critic observed: "Russell's narrative is so drastically compressed that you can barely take in the many action sequences, betrayals, and violent deaths in this breathless survey." Describing the prose as "smoothly understated," a contributor to *Publishers Weekly* remarked that "the tension rises as the unpredictable plot skitters and jitters along."

### ■ Biographical And Critical Sources

*PERIODICALS*

*Booklist,* July 1, 2003, Connie Fletcher, review of *Shell Games,* p. 1871; September 15, 2004, Connie Fletcher, review of *Night Game,* p. 214; August 1, 2005, Connie Fletcher, review of *Dead Game,* p. 2002; December 1, 2010, Emily Melton, review of *Redback,* p. 31.

*Kirkus Reviews,* July 15, 2003, review of *Shell Games,* p. 933; August 15, 2004, review of *Night Game,* p. 773; July 1, 2005, review of *Dead Game,* p. 711; December 15, 2010, review of *Redback.*

*Library Journal,* October 1, 2004, Teresa L. Jacobson, review of *Night Game,* p. 65.

*Midwest Book Review,* March 1, 2005, Harriet Klausner, review of *Night Game.*

*Publishers Weekly,* December 6, 2010, review of *Redback,* p. 32.

*ONLINE*

*AbsoluteWrite.com,* http://www.absolutewrite.com/ (October 17, 2005), Jenna Glatzer, "Interview with Kirk Russell."

*All Readers,* http://www.allreaders.com/ (October 17, 2005), Harriet Klausner, review of *Night Game.*

*Kirk Russell Home Page,* http://www.kirk-russell.com (August 16, 2011).

*Roundtable Reviews Online,* http://www.roundtablereviews.com/ (October 17, 2005), Tracy Farnsworth, "A Roundtable Interview with Kirk Russell."

# C.J. Sansom

## 1952-

### ■ Also Known As

Christopher John Sansom
The Medieval Murderers, a joint pseudonym

### ■ Personal

Born 1952, in Edinburgh, Scotland. *Education:* Birmingham University, B.A., Ph.D.; earned J.D.

### ■ Addresses

*Home*—Sussex, England.

### ■ Career

Writer. Former attorney in Sussex, England.

### ■ Member

Crime Writers' Association.

### ■ Awards, Honors

Ellis Peters Historical Dagger, Crime Writers' Association, 2005, for *Dark Fire.*

### ■ Writings

*Winter in Madrid,* Macmillan (London, England), 2006, Viking (New York, NY), 2008.

*"SHARDLAKE" SERIES*

*Dissolution,* Viking (New York, NY), 2003.
*Dark Fire,* Viking (New York, NY), 2005.
*Sovereign,* Macmillan (London, England), 2006, Viking (New York, NY), 2007.
*Revelation,* Macmillan (London, England), 2008.
*Heartstone,* Viking (New York, NY), 2011.

*UNDER JOINT PSEUDONYM THE MEDIEVAL MURDERERS*

*The Lost Prophecies,* Simon & Schuster (New York, NY), 2008.
*King Arthur's Bones,* Simon & Schuster (London, England), 2009.
*The Sacred Stone,* Simon & Schuster (London, England), 2010.
*Hill of Bones,* Simon & Schuster (London, England), 2011.

*COLLECTIONS; UNDER JOINT PSEUDONYM THE MEDIEVAL MURDERERS*

*The Tainted Relic,* Simon & Schuster (New York, NY), 2005.
*Sword of Shame,* Simon & Schuster (New York, NY), 2006.
*House of Shadows,* Simon & Schuster (New York, NY), 2007.

### ■ Sidelights

C.J. Sansom is a British writer. Born in Edinburgh, Scotland, in 1952, he earned a Ph.D. from Birmingham University. Sansom worked as a lawyer prior to becoming a full-time writer.

## "Shardlake" Series

Sansom's debut novel, *Dissolution*, "provides readers with a vivid Tudor historical mystery," according to Harriet Klausner in *Books 'n' Bytes*. *Dissolution* takes place in England in 1537 as Thomas Cromwell, vicar-general to King Henry VIII, is aiding the king in his efforts to undermine the authority of the Roman Catholic Church within England. Cromwell eagerly accepts the challenge, although he is concerned about a possible uprising from those opposed to the Crown as well as by demoralized Catholics. When an agent of the King turns up dead while on the King's business at the remote Monastery of St. Donatus the Ascendant in Scarnsea, Cromwell fears his worries have come to pass. He enlists the help of the hunchback lawyer Matthew Shardlake and Shardlake's young, handsome assistant, Mark Poer, in investigating the death and finding the agent's killer. Shardlake gladly accepts the case; he has been an enemy of the Catholic Church since being refused the priesthood due to his deformity. The task proves to be anything but easy, however, as Shardlake and Poer find themselves outnumbered and despised for being outsiders at the remote monastery, where they are surrounded by corruption, uncooperative monks, and sexual depravity. When Shardlake discovers the remains of another victim in the monastery pond, he realizes that all is not what it seems.

Michael Spinella, reviewing *Dissolution* in *Booklist*, stated that Sansom's debut novel "will not disappoint fans of historical fiction," while Toronto *Globe and Mail* contributor Margaret Cannon noted that the author's "great talent" brings to life the intrigue of pre-Elizabethan England "in all its squalor and fright." Laurel Bliss, writing in *Library Journal*, criticized the author's storyline, noting that although "Sansom clearly harbors a deep affection for and knowledge of this historical period . . . his novel is unrelentingly grim in tone." In contrast, a reviewer in *Publishers Weekly* complimented the novel, stating that "Sansom paints a vivid picture of the corruption that plagued England during the reign of Henry VIII, and the wry, rueful Shardlake is a memorable protagonist." Praising *Dissolution* as "cunningly plotted and darkly atmospheric," the contributor added that "Sansom proves himself to be a promising newcomer" in the historical fiction genre.

In *Dark Fire*, the award-winning second work in Sansom's "Shardlake" series, the hunchback attorney has just two weeks to uncover the truth behind an unusual murder and retrieve the secret formula for a terrible new weapon. After Shardlake fails in his defense of a young woman accused of murdering her cousin, Cromwell grants her a stay of execution when the attorney agrees to a dangerous mission. Accompanied by a tough-minded clerk, Jack Barak, Shardlake scours London for the source of Greek Fire, which Cromwell has promised to deliver to Henry VIII. "The seemingly ill-matched investigators start picking through all levels of London society, arriving ever just too late after pertinent murders and arson, dogged everywhere by a pair of singularly repulsive assassins," noted a critic in *Kirkus Reviews*. In *Dark Fire*, wrote *Guardian* reviewer Stella Duffy, Sansom offers "a broad view of politics—Tudor housing to rival Rachman, Dickensian prisons, a sewage-glutted Thames, beggars in gutters, conspiracies at court and a political system predicated on birth not merit, intrigue not intelligence." Duffy concluded: "Sansom gives Shardlake plenty of opportunities to debate the morality of his world and, by implication, our own."

Shardlake appears once again in *Sovereign*, set in 1541. At the request of Cardinal Cranmer, the barrister travels to the city of York to protect an imprisoned conspirator who possesses valuable information about the Tudor monarchy. Shardlake finds his own life in danger, however, after he stumbles upon a grisly murder. According to a *Kirkus Reviews* contributor, Sansom "fleshes out the detection with rich historic details presented at a stately pace."

Sansom published the fourth installment of the "Shardlake" series in 2008 with *Revelation*. The novel finds Shardlake's friend, Roger Elliard, drugged and murdered in a fountain, leaving him to figure out the identity of the murderer, despite the king's own personal interest in the case. Christina Hardyment, writing in the London *Times*, remarked: "Sansom's deft sense of dramatic timing takes us effortlessly through this fat, juicy book. For a while we jog along, building up connections, clues, suspense, and then wham, bang we're off at a skimble-scamble gallop. His skill lies not only in plotting and the creation of rounded and memorable characters, but in magicking up a richly textured backdrop." She added that this is "the best Shardlake yet." Writing in the London *Observer*, Stephanie Merritt pointed out that the "great appeal of these books, apart from the cast of regular characters, is the richness of Sansom's historical research." A contributor to *Material Witness* commented that "this is an involved and complex web but Sansom does not shy away from difficult territory and the result is extraordinarily rewarding," concluding that the novel "is crime-writing at its finest and historical fiction at its most sumptuous and Sansom is a lord and master of both arts." Jane Jakeman, reviewing the book in the London *Independent*, commented that the novel "is the apocalyptic nightmare of the Four Last Things;

Hell on earth—and this is a masterly evocation." Andrew Taylor, reviewing the book in *Spectator,* wrote that the novel "is head and shoulders above most historical crime novels. It's a tribute to Sansom's ability to plot that he not only controls his long and complex narrative but keeps the reader galloping through it, desperate to reach the climax (which does not disappoint). His knowledge of the period is another of the book's pleasures."

*Heartstone* marked the fifth novel in the "Shardlake" series. Shardlake is ordered by the English queen to look into the death of the son of one of her elderly servants. He is immediately threatened by group of thugs as he starts to investigate. Determined, he pushes forward with this case and also that of an institutionalized woman who suffers from agoraphobia.

A contributor to the *New Yorker* observed that despite some repetition, "Sansom has an unerring sense of pace and a deft historical touch." *Booklist* reviewer Michele Leber lauded that "the novel vividly captures the Tudor scene," calling it "historical mystery at its finest." Reviewing the novel in *Spectator,* Alan Judd commented that *Heartstone* may "be exceptional as a crime novel in that we don't actually see a body until p. 384, but it doesn't matter. The reason it doesn't is that Sansom's story develops naturally. And naturalness is perhaps the key to these books." Judd concluded: "This is good writing and it should be read."

### Other

In 2006 Samson published the novel *Winter in Madrid,* which was released in the United States in 2008. The novel follows three British men and their uneasy relationships in the early years of Franco's post-civil war rule in Spain. A contributor to the London *Telegraph* commented that "this is above all a novel about systems of authority and ideology: always, in the end, corrupting and corruptible, both beyond and beneath the scope of individual heroism," adding that the author "offers an intriguing and equivocal vision of a country in ideological turmoil." Writing in the *Philadelphia Inquirer,* Katherine Bailey observed: "Sansom's splendid novel is not only similar in backdrop to *For Whom the Bell Tolls;* it is also written in much the same plain and direct style (though Sansom's descriptive powers, particularly when introducing a change in setting or when portraying winter weather conditions, are quite remarkable)." A critic writing in *Kirkus Reviews* described the novel as "wise and melancholy and, eventually, very tense." *Booklist*

contributor Brad Hooper found that "this evocation of a dangerous diplomatic environment . . . will have widespread appeal."

In 2008 Sansom coauthored the novel *The Lost Prophecies,* under the joint pseudonym The Medieval Murderers with Bernard Knight, Ian Morson, Michael Jecks, Philip Gooden, and Susanna Gregory. The story centers on the prophetic Black Book of Bran, a book of prophecies that washed ashore in Ireland with an infant widely considered to be demonic. The authors chart the course of this book throughout Medieval European history, as it brings death and destruction in its way.

In a review in *Euro Crime,* Amanda C.M. Gillies stated: "If you like medieval mysteries then this book is definitely for you. If you aren't into medieval mysteries then I recommend it anyway." A contributor to *Tangled Web UK Review* called the novel "a refreshing change from the norm, as well as a brave attempt to buck the current decline of the short story in crime fiction, as fewer and fewer mainstream publishers consider anthologies."

## ■ Biographical And Critical Sources

### PERIODICALS

*Booklist,* April 1, 2003, Michael Spinella, review of *Dissolution,* p. 1382; November 15, 2004, Allison Block, review of *Dark Fire,* p. 566; March 15, 2007, Brad Hooper, review of *Sovereign,* p. 30; December 1, 2007, Brad Hooper, review of *Winter in Madrid,* p. 24; February 15, 2009, Brad Hooper, review of *Revelation,* p. 39; January 1, 2011, Michele Leber, review of *Heartstone,* p. 49; May 1, 2011, David Pitt, review of *Heartstone,* p. 52.

*Globe and Mail* (Toronto, Ontario, Canada), August 30, 2003, Margaret Cannon, review of *Dissolution.*

*Guardian* (London, England), November 6, 2004, Stella Duffy, review of *Dark Fire;* November 13, 2010, Sarah Crown, "A Life in Books: C.J. Sansom."

*Independent* (London, England), April 18, 2008, Jane Jakeman, review of *Revelation.*

*Kirkus Reviews,* March 1, 2003, review of *Dissolution,* p. 342; October 15, 2004, review of *Dark Fire,* p. 982; January 15, 2007, review of *Sovereign,* p. 47; October 15, 2007, review of *Winter in Madrid;* November 1, 2008, review of *Revelation;* December 15, 2010, review of *Heartstone.*

*Library Journal,* April 1, 2003, Laurel Bliss, review of *Dissolution,* p. 130; October 15, 2008, David Wright, review of *Winter in Madrid,* p. 104.

*New Yorker,* March 7, 2011, review of *Heartstone,* p. 85.

*Observer* (London, England), April 27, 2008, Stephanie Merritt, review of *Revelation.*

*Philadelphia Inquirer,* May 16, 2007, Desmond Ryan, review of *Sovereign;* January 20, 2008, Katherine Bailey, review of *Winter in Madrid.*

*Publishers Weekly,* March 17, 2003, review of *Dissolution,* p. 51; November 15, 2004, review of *Dark Fire,* p. 40; January 29, 2007, review of *Sovereign,* p. 45; September 24, 2007, review of *Winter in Madrid,* p. 42; November 24, 2008, review of *Revelation,* p. 40; December 15, 2008, review of *The Lost Prophecies,* p. 38; November 1, 2010, review of *Heartstone,* p. 30.

*Spectator,* April 1, 2006, Raymond Carr, review of *Winter in Madrid,* p. 52; May 10, 2008, review of *Revelation;* October 2, 2010, Alan Judd, review of *Heartstone,* p. 37.

*Telegraph* (London, England), February 26, 2006, review of *Winter in Madrid.*

*Times* (London, England), March 28, 2008, Christina Hardyment, review of *Revelation.*

ONLINE

*Blog Critics,* http://blogcritics.org/ (December 10, 2006), Natalie Bennett, review of *Sovereign.*

*Books 'n' Bytes,* http://www.booksnbytes.com/ (October 12, 2003), Harriet Klausner, review of *Dissolution.*

*Crime Time,* http://www.crimetime.co.uk/ (October 12, 2003), Ingrid Yornstrand, review of *Dissolution.*

*Euro Crime,* http://www.eurocrime.co.uk/ (September 1, 2009), Amanda C.M. Gillies, review of *The Lost Prophecies.*

*Material Witness,* http://materialwitness.typepad.com/ (March 14, 2008), review of *Revelation.*

*On the Tudor Trail,* http://onthetudortrail.com/ (March 15, 2011), author interview.

*PanMacmillan Web site,* http://www.panmacmillan.com/ (August 14, 2008), author interview.

*Tangled Web UK Review,* http://www.twbooks.co.uk/ (July 1, 2008), review of *The Lost Prophecies.**

# Harold Schechter

## 1948-

### ■ Personal

Born June 28, 1948, in New York, NY; son of Abraham Mark (a garment worker) and Celia (a statistician and homemaker) Schechter; married Avra Shapiro, January, 1970 (divorced, August, 1976); married Jonna Gormely Semeiks (a writer and teacher), July 15, 1979 (divorced, 2001); married Kimiko Hahn (a poet), August 29, 2002; children: (second marriage) Elizabeth Sara, Laura Suzanne. *Ethnicity:* "White." *Education:* City College of New York (now City College of the City University of New York), B.A., 1969; Purdue University, M.A., 1971; State University of New York at Buffalo, Ph.D., 1975. *Politics:* Democrat. *Religion:* Jewish.

### ■ Addresses

*Home*—New York, NY. *Office*—Department of English, Queens College of the City University of New York, Flushing, NY 11367. *Agent*—Loretta Barrett, 101 5th Ave., New York, NY 10003. *E-mail*—harold. schechter@qc.cuny.edu.

### ■ Career

Queens College of the City University of New York, Flushing, NY, assistant professor, 1975-80, associate professor, beginning 1981, became professor of English. Has appeared in documentaries, including *H.H. Holmes: America's First Serial Killer*, 2004, *Gorilla Trap*, 2007, and *Romeo Must Hang*, 2010.

### ■ Writings

*NONFICTION*

(With David Everitt) *Film Tricks: Special Effects in the Movies*, H. Quist (New York, NY), 1980.

*The New Gods: Psyche and Symbol in Popular Art*, Bowling Green University Popular Press (Bowling Green, OH), 1980.

(With Jonna Gormely Semeiks) *Patterns in Popular Culture: A Sourcebook for Writers*, Harper & Row (New York, NY), 1980.

(With David Everitt) *The Manly Handbook*, Berkley Books (New York, NY), 1982.

(With Jonna Gormely Semeiks) *Discoveries: Fifty Stories of the Quest*, Bobbs-Merrill Educational Publishing (Indianapolis, IN), 1982, 2nd edition, Oxford University Press (New York, NY), 1992.

(With David Everitt) *Not-the-A-Team Beauty Book*, photographs by James Prince, Pocket Books (New York, NY), 1984.

(Editor) *The City University of New York: CUNY English Forum*, AMS Press (New York, NY), 1985.

*Kidvid: A Parents' Guide to Children's Videos*, Pocket Books (New York, NY), 1986.

(Editor, with Warren Rosenberg and Jonna Gormely Semeiks) *American Voices: A Thematic/Rhetorical Reader*, Harper & Row (New York, NY), 1988.

*The Bosom Serpent: Folklore and Popular Art*, University of Iowa Press (Iowa City, IA), 1988, 2nd edition, Peter Lang Publishing (New York, NY), 2001.

(With David Everitt) *The Manly Movie Guide*, Boulevard Books (New York, NY), 1997.

(With David Everitt) *For Reel: The Real-life Stories That Inspired Some of the Most Popular Movies of All Time*, Berkley Boulevard (New York, NY), 2000.

*Savage Pastimes: A Cultural History of Violent Entertainment*, St. Martin's Press (New York, NY), 2005.

*The Whole Death Catalog: A Lively Guide to the Bitter End*, Ballantine Books (New York, NY), 2009.

*NOVELS*

*Outcry*, Pocket Books (New York, NY), 1997.
*Nevermore*, Pocket Books (New York, NY), 1999.

*The Hum Bug,* Pocket Books (New York, NY), 2001.

*The Mask of Red Death: An Edgar Allan Poe Mystery,* Ballantine Books (New York, NY), 2004.

*The Tell-Tale Corpse: An Edgar Allan Poe Mystery,* Ballantine Books (New York, NY), 2006.

### TRUE CRIME BOOKS

*Deranged: The Shocking True Story of America's Most Fiendish Killer,* Pocket Books (New York, NY), 1990.

*Depraved: The Shocking True Story of America's First Serial Killer,* Pocket Books (New York, NY), 1994.

(With David Everitt) *The A-Z Encyclopedia of Serial Killers,* Pocket Books (New York, NY), 1996.

*Deviant: The Shocking True Story of the Original "Psycho,"* Pocket Books (New York, NY), 1998.

*Bestial: The Savage Trail of a True American Monster,* Pocket Books (New York, NY), 1999, revised and updated edition (with David Everitt), 2006.

*Fiend: The Shocking True Story of America's Youngest Serial Killer,* Pocket Books (New York, NY), 2000.

*Fatal: The Poisonous Life of a Female Serial Killer,* Pocket Star Books (New York, NY), 2003.

*The Serial Killer Files: The Who, What, Where, How, and Why of the World's Most Terrifying Murderers,* Ballantine Books (New York, NY), 2004.

*The Devil's Gentleman: Privilege, Poison, and the Trial That Ushered in the Twentieth Century,* Ballantine Books (New York, NY), 2007.

(Editor and author of introduction) *True Crime: An American Anthology,* Library of America (New York, NY), 2008.

*Killer Colt: Murder, Disgrace, and the Making of an American Legend,* Ballantine Books (New York, NY), 2010.

### OTHER

(Selector, with Kurt Brown) *Conversation Pieces: Poems That Talk to Other Poems,* Alfred A. Knopf (New York, NY), 2007.

(Selector, with Kurt Brown) *Killer Verse: Poems of Murder and Mayhem,* Alfred A. Knopf (New York, NY), 2011.

Author of television scripts, including "Mirror, Mirror," an episode of *The Cosby Mysteries,* National Broadcasting Company, 1994; and "Castoff," an episode of *Law & Order,* National Broadcasting Company, 1998. Contributor to books, including *Original Sin: The Visionary Art of Joe Coleman,* HECK Editions (New York, NY), 1997. Contributor to journals, including *Studies in Short Fiction.*

### ■ Sidelights

Harold Schechter's specialty is the history of serial killers in the United States. Using newspaper clippings, court transcripts, and other sources, Schechter has documented the crimes and punishments of several of the most notorious American torture-killers. The subjects of his true crime tales include Herman Mudgett, a Chicago murderer; Albert Fish, who killed and ate at least fifteen children in the 1920s; and Ed Gein, whose Wisconsin crime spree inspired the movies *Psycho* and *The Texas Chain Saw Massacre.* These portraits of society's most dangerous denizens comprise just one aspect of Schecter's pursuit as a historian of popular culture in the nineteenth and twentieth centuries. He has also authored a series of mysteries featuring Edgar Allan Poe.

**True Crime**

In addition to biographies, such as *Deviant: The Shocking True Story of the Original "Psycho"* and *Depraved: The Shocking True Story of America's First Serial Killer,* Schechter coauthored an encyclopedia on serial killers. He is, as a *Publishers Weekly* reviewer put it, a "serial killer expert." The reviewer described Schechter as a "deft writer" whose strengths include "recreating from documentation the thoughts and perspectives of long-dead figures." *Booklist* correspondent Ray Olson found *Depraved* to be "first-rate true crime, first-rate popular history," and a *Publishers Weekly* contributor felt that in *Depraved,* Schechter does "a masterful job of reconstructing [the murderer's] killing spree."

*The Devil's Gentleman: Privilege, Poison, and the Trial That Ushered in the Twentieth Century* is the story of the trial and acquittal of Richard Molineux, son of a famous Civil War general, a prominent chemist, amateur athlete, and suspected poisoner. Henry Barnet, a rival for the affections of Molineux's intended, Blanche Chesebrough, and Harry Cornish, the manager of the Knickerbocker Athletic Club, were both poisoned by taking doses of patent medicines that had been adulterated with a toxic substance. Barnet died; Cornish survived, but the woman with whom he boarded (and to whom he had given a dose of the medicine) did not. Clues began to point to Molineux: he had tried to expel Cornish from his management position, and Barnet had been intimate with Blanche (she, in fact, wrote in her memoirs that she preferred Barnet's muscular attentions to those of the less powerful Molineux). Schechter "describes such new crime-solving techniques as fingerprinting and forensics," a *Kirkus Reviews* contributor declared, "and he takes a harrowing look inside Sing Sing's Death House. Though he rehashes the evidence rather repetitively, crime buffs will relish the extra details." The author "does little with his material other than keep events moving along, which is enough," stated William Grimes in the *New York Times Book Review.* "The book is like a fin-de-siècle version of Court TV, a riveting sequence of appalling events, weird testimony, courtroom theatrics and bungled justice." "The result," concluded a *Publishers Weekly* contributor, "is a riveting tale of murder, seduction and tabloid journalism run rampant in a New York not so different from today's."

For his next true crime effort, Schechter edited and wrote the introduction to *True Crime: An American Anthology.* The volume is a collection of crime writing in the United States from colonial times to today. Presented in chronological order, selections are from renowned writers and historical figures, including Benjamin Franklin, Mark Twain, Truman Capote, Ann Rule, and James Ellroy. Entries range in genre from ballads and magazine articles to Puritan sermons. Schechter's "introduction is a brilliant overview of styles of American crime writing," Connie Fletcher observed in her *Booklist* review. Karen Sandlin Silverman, writing in *Library Journal,* called the book a "delightful treasury encompassing some of the best crime writing from colonial times to today." Discussing the appeal of true crime writing in the *Weekly Standard,* Jon L. Breen wondered: "Is it a voyeuristic interest in the details of someone else's misfortune? Do we enjoy a reminder that our own lives, mundane and uneventful by comparison, could be much worse? Or perhaps our interest represents something more ennobling: a desire to understand the elements of the criminal justice system (police, courts, prisons), the conditions of society that breed crime, and the psychology of criminal behavior in the hope of making it all better. Most likely we just appreciate nonfiction writing with the high literary value that an excellent new anthology from the Library of America provides." Breen added: "Editor Harold Schechter was wise to arrange the selections in True Crime chronologically by date of publication, allowing the reader to trace the development of attitudes toward crime and styles of true crime writing."

In *Killer Colt: Murder, Disgrace, and the Making of an American Legend,* Schechter explores the Colt brothers, John and Samuel. Samuel invented the revolver and gained international success, but John murdered Samuel Adams in 1841. At the close of the nationally publicized trial, John was sentenced to death by hanging. He was murdered in his cell before his sentence could be carried out. According to Claire Franek in *Library Journal,* the volume is "recom-

mended for American history buffs with an interest in true crime stories." A *Kirkus Reviews* critic called the book an "energetic Wild West tale about two enterprising brothers" that is told with "lively, plentiful detail." The critic then stated that *Killer Colt* "possesses all the elements of lurid true crime and dark early American history." Allen Barra, writing in *American History,* was also impressed, finding that Schechter takes readers "through Colt's trial with such precision that you can smell the cigar smoke in the courtroom." Barra also observed that the author "succeeds in making us care about this story now by showing why it mattered to so many people then."

### Nonfiction

*Film Tricks: Special Effects in the Movies,* which Schechter wrote with David Everitt, details the evolution of special effects since the advent of motion pictures. Among the effects documented in *Film Tricks* are actress Fay Wray's capture by the giant ape in *King Kong,* actor/dancer Fred Astaire's gravity-defying dance in *Royal Wedding,* and the flying sequences in *Superman.* A reviewer in the *New York Times Book Review* described *Film Tricks* as a "carefully researched, pioneering study." Paul Stuewe, writing in *Quill and Quire,* deemed the book "an informative and liberally illustrated guide to the manufacture of illusion." Citing the gruesome effects of *Jaws* and *The Omen,* Stuewe added that *Film Tricks* "provides all the graphic examples necessary to relive such cinematic thrills and chills."

In *Savage Pastimes: A Cultural History of Violent Entertainment,* Schechter makes the case that not only is violent entertainment less prevalent and less gruesome today than in past generations and centuries, but most of the people who witnessed it throughout history, even at its worst, were decent people who never turned observation into action. Schechter compares violence in contemporary media (film, television, comics, video games) to historical equivalents (Roman amphitheaters, public tortures and executions, Puritan pillories, even the brutality in novels of classic masters such as Herman Melville). He claims that vicarious portrayals of violence occur (and always did) because people want to watch; furthermore, in the past people openly enjoyed the show. Today, at least, he suggests, most people seem satisfied by artificial reenactments. A *Kirkus Reviews* contributor described *Savage Pastimes* as "a bloody fine riposte to those who would censor with clouded hindsight and muddy reasoning." A reviewer in *Publishers Weekly* predicted: "This entertaining, provocative, not entirely convincing work will be a treat for literate readers."

## Novels

*Nevermore* is a historical mystery narrated by Edgar Allan Poe. The year is 1834, and young Poe, his great works still ahead of him, is working as a journalist. After Poe savages Davy Crockett's autobiography in print, the notorious frontier statesman seeks Poe out for a duel. Instead of fighting, the two men team up to solve a series of murders that give Poe grist for the macabre stories he will write. A *Publishers Weekly* reviewer noted that, while the prose is a bit "overwrought to contemporary eyes," the novel "has plenty of suspense and nicely integrated background detail." In the *New York Times Book Review*, James Polk found Schechter's "entertaining premise" to be "supported by rich period atmospherics."

Schechter continues to write novels featuring Poe as detective, and the critics who most appreciate them seem to be those who can read the tales for the fun of it: for the believable characterizations of Poe and his cohorts, the unlikely juxtapositions of historical figures who lived very different lives at the same time in history, and the preposterous backgrounds from which the stories emerge. *The Hum Bug* reveals that Poe has moved to New York City, where he is contacted by entrepreneur P.T. Barnum to solve a murder mystery that the media reporters of his day have linked to a grisly exhibit in Barnum's wax museum. Not only is the murder gruesome, but the sideshow characters are odd enough to demonstrate Schechter's confidence, based on his scholarly research in popular culture, that readers will gravitate toward the spectacle. Some reviewers noted that the plot pales in comparison to the people, while simultaneously recommending the book as an enjoyable entertainment. "A riveting experience," commented Fletcher in *Booklist*, while a *Kirkus Reviews* contributor called it "high fun." Positive reader response prompted Schechter to pair the Victorian sleuth with mountain man Kit Carson in *The Mask of Red Death: An Edgar Allan Poe Mystery*. In this adventure, one of Barnum's living exhibits, Chief Wolf Bear, is falsely suspected of a series of killings-by-scalping, and it is up to the detectives Poe and Carson to track down the real perpetrator, a monster out of the mountain country. A *Publishers Weekly* critic noted that Schechter's successive forays into Victorian-style fiction reflect improvements in "plotting and pacing" that result in a "competent" novel.

## Schechter Told *CA*:

"I'm less interested in the way pop culture affects us than in the way it reflects or symbolizes the hidden fears, fantasies, and desires that exist in our collective undermind. Pop art is a kind of communal dream—which is to say myth—and in much of my writing I examine the archetypal themes that are embodied in movies, comic books, television shows, and so on. That's one of the reasons I'm interested in Ed Gein. As the power and cult status of both *Psycho* and *The Texas Chainsaw Massacre* attest, Gein's story exerts a strange fascination. It's intriguing to me how closely certain elements of it parallel such fairy tales as 'Bluebeard' and 'Fitcher's Feathered Bird,' and my plan is to do a book that uses the Gein case as a way of getting at some basic questions about horror: why the human imagination craves these stories and why they are particularly popular in America right now. My interest in myth is also related to *Discoveries: Fifty Stories of the Quest*, a short story anthology whose contents are arranged according to the different stages of the archetypal hero's quest.

"The most interesting thing about my work—at least to me—is my ongoing effort to maintain two entirely separate writing careers, one as an academic producing scholarly pieces on Hawthorne, Melville, and Charles Brockden Brown; the other as a 'commercial' writer in the competitive world of trade paperbacks (a type of book I find strangely congenial to my talents). Which type of writing do I prefer? I find that, while each presents its own special problems, they both, in the end, produce an identical sense of satisfaction—one so deep that it more than compensates for the many frustrations and disappointments that seem to be an inescapable fact of life for anyone trying to make it as a professional writer."

Schechter later added: "*The Hum Bug* is the second in what was not intended as—but has turned out to be—a series of historical mysteries with Edgar Allan Poe as the detective. In each book, Poe teams up with a famous figure from his historical period—a person the actual Poe never met in real life but *could* have.

"I originally planned to do only a single novel—a kind of historical version of an action-adventure 'buddy movie' in which two totally contrasting personalities are thrown together and end up becoming the best of friends. My idea was to team up the pompous, intellectual Poe with the plain-talking, rough-and-tumble frontiersman Davy Crockett. That idea became my novel *Nevermore*.

"The book found enough readers to encourage me to a sequel, *The Hum Bug*, in which the celebrated showman P.T. Barnum hires Poe to help solve a murder. That book was followed by *The Mask of Red Death*, which pairs Poe with the legendary scout Kit

Carson. Another entry in the series is *The Tell-Tale Corpse: An Edgar Allan Poe Mystery*, in which Poe and his wife travel to Concord, Massachusetts, and meet the young Louisa May Alcott, future author of *Little Women*.

"Since I write the books from Poe's point of view, I have to read some of his fiction every day to get the sound of his voice going inside my head. It is hard work but fun. Unfortunately I'm starting to run out of famous people from his era to pair him up with."

## ■ Biographical And Critical Sources

PERIODICALS

*American Book Review Annual*, 1987, review of *Kidvid: A Parents' Guide to Children's Videos*, p. 352.

*American History*, June 1, 2011, Allen Barra, review of *Killer Colt: Murder, Disgrace, and the Making of an American Legend*, p. 80.

*Armchair Detective*, spring, 1990, review of *Deviant: The Shocking True Story of the Original "Psycho,"* p. 239.

*Biography*, January 1, 2008, review of *The Devil's Gentleman: Privilege, Poison, and the Trial That Ushered in the Twentieth Century*, p. 192.

*Booklist*, September 15, 1981, review of *Film Tricks: Special Effects in the Movies*, p. 84; June 15, 1986, review of *Kidvid*, p. 1491; May 15, 1989, review of *Deviant*, p. 1589; October 1, 1990, review of *Deranged: The Shocking True Story of America's Most Fiendish Killer*, p. 234; August, 1994, Ray Olson, review of *Depraved: The Shocking True Story of America's First Serial Killer*, p. 2002; January 1, 1999, Budd Arthur, review of *Nevermore*, p. 840; October 1, 2000, Ray Olson, review of *Fiend: The Shocking True Story of America's Youngest Serial Killer*, p. 295; October 1, 2001, Connie Fletcher, review of *The Hum Bug*, p. 303; September 15, 2008, Connie Fletcher, review of *True Crime: An American Anthology*, p. 9; May 1, 2009, Mike Tribby, review of *The Whole Death Catalog: A Lively Guide to the Bitter End*, p. 52.

*Choice*, July, 1988, review of *The Bosom Serpent: Folklore and Popular Art*, p. 1703.

*Come-All-Ye*, summer, 1989, review of *The Bosom Serpent*, p. 9.

*Cresset*, September, 1981, review of *The New Gods: Psyche and Symbol in Popular Art*, p. 30.

*Entertainment Weekly*, September 28, 2007, Chris Nashawaty, review of *The Devil's Gentleman*, p. 109.

*Film Quarterly*, summer, 1982, review of *Film Tricks*, p. 63; summer, 1989, Bruce Kawin, review of *Deviant*, p. 62; winter, 1989, Carol J. Clover, review of *The Bosom Serpent*, p. 46.

*Films in Review*, October, 1986, review of *Kidvid*, p. 498.

*Folklore*, August, 2004, Gillian Bennett, review of *The Bosom Serpent*, p. 241.

*Georgia Review*, fall, 1988, review of *The Bosom Serpent*, p. 657.

*Hollywood Reporter*, March 16, 2005, Gregory McNamee, review of *Savage Pastimes: A Cultural History of Violent Entertainment*, p. 30.

*Journal of American Culture*, September, 2005, Marshall W. Fishwick, review of *Savage Pastimes*, p. 337.

*Journal of Popular Culture*, fall, 1989, Ray B. Browne, review of *The Bosom Serpent*, p. 177.

*Kirkus Reviews*, July 1, 1994, review of *Depraved*, p. 917; December 15, 1998, review of *Nevermore*, p. 1756; September 1, 2000, review of *Fiend*, p. 1268; September 15, 2001, review of *The Hum Bug*, p. 1319; June 15, 2004, review of *The Mask of Red Death: An Edgar Allan Poe Mystery*, p. 556; December 15, 2004, review of *Savage Pastimes*, p. 1191; August 15, 2007, review of *The Devil's Gentleman*; August 1, 2010, review of *Killer Colt*.

*Kliatt*, May, 2000, review of *Nevermore*, p. 20, and review of *For Reel: The Real-life Stories That Inspired Some of the Most Popular Movies of All Time*, p. 38.

*Library Journal*, August, 1981, review of *Film Tricks*, p. 1563; June 1, 1986, John Smothers, review of *Kidvid*, p. 116; August, 1994, Gregor A. Preston, review of *Depraved*, p. 102; January, 2000, Kim R. Holston, review of *For Reel*, p. 114; September 15, 2001, Laurel Bliss, review of *The Hum Bug*, p. 117; July, 2004, Rex E. Klett, review of *The Mask of Red Death*, p. 63; September 15, 2008, Karen Sandlin Silverman, review of *True Crime*, p. 74; April 15, 2009, Lynne F. Maxwell, review of *The Whole Death Catalog*, p. 103; September 15, 2010, Claire Franek, review of *Killer Colt*, p. 87.

*Los Angeles Times*, June 1, 1986, review of *Kidvid*, p. 4.

*New York Times*, May 3, 1981, review of *Film Tricks*, p. 7.

*New York Times Book Review*, May 3, 1981, review of *Film Tricks*, p. 47; November 27, 1994, Thomas Maeder, review of *Depraved*, p. 25; January 31, 1999, James Polk, review of *Nevermore*, p. 16; October 24, 2007, William Grimes, "Murder by Mail in Gilded Age New York."

*Publishers Weekly*, July 18, 1994, review of *Depraved*, p. 232; December 21, 1998, review of *Nevermore*, p. 56; October 2, 2000, review of *Fiend*, p. 75; October 15, 2001, review of *The Hum Bug*, p. 49; May 31, 2004, review of *The Mask of Red Death*, p. 54; December 20, 2004, review of *Savage Pastimes*, p. 45; August 20, 2007, review of *The Devil's Gentleman*, p. 61; August 2, 2010, review of *Killer Colt*, p. 40.

*Quill and Quire,* May, 1981, review of *Film Tricks,* p. 35.

*Reference and Research Book News,* August, 2005, review of *Savage Pastimes,* p. 238.

*School Library Journal,* August, 1986, review of *Kidvid,* p. 40.

*South Carolina Review,* fall, 2001, review of *The Bosom Serpent,* p. 229.

*Virginia Quarterly Review,* summer, 1993, review of *Discoveries: Fifty Stories of the Quest,* p. 107.

*Washington Post Book World,* May 15, 2005, Juliet B. Schor, review of *Savage Pastimes,* p. 4.

*Weekly Standard,* January 3, 2005, Jon L. Breen, review of *The Mask of Red Death,* p. 31; November 24, 2008, Jon L. Breen, "Murder, They Wrote; the Art of Literary Mayhem."

*ONLINE*

*Harold Schechter Home Page,* http://haroldschechter. com (August 11, 2011).

*Queens College, City University of New York Web site,* http://www.qc.cuny.edu/ (August 11, 2011), author profile.

# Robert John Schneller, Jr.

## 1957-

### ■ Personal

Born November 29, 1957, in Allentown, PA; son of Robert J. (a teacher) and Joanne Schneller; married Rebecca Crutchley, April 19, 1986; children: Zachary Jacob, Noah Robert. *Ethnicity:* "WASP." *Education:* University of Pittsburgh, B.A., 1980; East Carolina University, M.A., 1986; Duke University, Ph.D., 1991. *Hobbies and other interests:* Bicycling.

### ■ Addresses

*Home*—Lake Ridge, VA. *Office*—Naval Historical Center, Washington Navy Yard, 901 M St. SE, Washington, DC 20374.

### ■ Career

U.S. Naval Historical Center, Washington, DC, historian, 1991—.

### ■ Awards, Honors

John Lyman Book Award for Biography, North American Society for Oceanic History, 1996.

### ■ Writings

*A Quest for Glory: A Biography of Rear Admiral John A. Dahlgreen,* U.S. Naval Institute Press (Annapolis, MD), 1996.

(With Edward J. Marolda) *Shield and Sword: The United States Navy and the Persian Gulf War,* Naval Historical Center (Washington, DC), 1998.

(Editor) *Under the Blue Pennant; or, Notes of a Naval Officer,* John Wiley (New York, NY), 1999.

*Farragut: America's First Admiral,* Brassey's (Washington, DC), 2002.

*Cushing: Civil War SEAL,* Brassey's (Washington, DC), 2004.

*Breaking the Color Barrier: The U.S. Naval Academy's First Black Midshipmen and the Struggle for Racial Equality,* New York University Press (New York, NY), 2005.

*Anchor of Resolve: A History of U.S. Naval Forces Central Command/Fifth Fleet,* Naval Historical Center (Washington, DC), 2007.

*Blue & Gold and Black: Racial Integration of the U.S. Naval Academy,* Texas A&M University Press (College Station, TX), 2008.

Contributor to periodicals, including *Naval War College Review.*

### ■ Sidelights

Naval historian Robert John Schneller, Jr., is the author of such biographies as *A Quest for Glory: A Biography of Rear Admiral John A. Dahlgreen, Farragut: America's First Admiral,* and *Cushing: Civil War SEAL.* Schneller has also addressed race relations in the navy in his books *Breaking the Color Barrier: The U.S. Naval Academy's First Black Midshipmen and the Struggle for Racial Equality* and *Blue & Gold and Black: Racial Integration of the U.S. Naval Academy.* The latter volume, based on detailed archival research, explores the long process of integration in the navy. According to Scheller, enlisted African Americans initially met with open hostility, both in naval policies and from their white counterparts. However, in 1965, a ten-year process toward full integration was put in place. Institutionally sanctioned discrimination gave way to a policy that favored equality.

Enlisted African American women faced doubly harsh discrimination, and Schneller explores their place in the navy as well. Aside from addressing the institutional changes that occurred between 1965 and 1976, Scheller examines more personal racial divides, and the actions and perceptions of white and black midshipmen at Annapolis.

For the most part, critics commended *Blue & Gold and Black* as a well-researched, informative, and insightful exploration of the progress of racial equality in the navy. Indeed, Brian G. Shellum, writing in *H-Net: Humanities and Social Sciences Online,* declared that the volume is "exceedingly well researched and written. It proves an excellent follow-up to . . . *Breaking the Color Barrier."* Shellum went on to call the volume "an absorbing account of how the U.S. Naval Academy struggled to deal with its racially intolerant past and ultimately succeeded in integrating the institution." Lauding the book further in his *Military Review* assessment, Bradford A. Wineman remarked: "Schneller's analysis does leave readers with overwhelming hope by reinforcing the progress of both the individual midshipmen and the institution to advance an environment of achievement, harmony, and understanding." *Journal of Southern History* contributor Michael Gelfand proffered praise as well, stating that the author "has provided such detailed coverage that this book will certainly inspire historians to address how the experiences of Latino/a, American Indian, and Asian American midshipmen differ from or resemble those of African Americans and women." Gelfand then called the book "a fascinating look at how the U.S. Navy, the Naval Academy, and the midshipmen themselves have worked to overcome the legacy of racism."

Schneller once told *CA:* "I write because it's fun."

## ■ Biographical And Critical Sources

### PERIODICALS

*Air Power History,* March 22, 2003, James R. FitzSimonds, review of *Shield and Sword: The United States Navy and the Persian Gulf War,* p. 52.

*Civil War History,* June 1, 1997, Joseph G. Damson, review of *A Quest for Glory: A Biography of Rear Admiral John A. Dahlgreen,* p. 180.

*Journal of Southern History,* February 1, 2010, H. Michael Gelfand, review of *Blue & Gold and Black: Racial Integration of the U.S. Naval Academy,* p. 201.

*Military Review,* May 1, 2009, Bradford A. Wineman, review of *Blue & Gold and Black.*

### ONLINE

*H-Net: Humanities and Social Sciences Online,* http://www.h-net.org/ (August 11, 2011), Brian G. Shellum, review of *Blue & Gold and Black.**

# Duane P. Schultz

## 1934-

### ■ Also Known As

Duane Philip Schultz

### ■ Personal

Born February 15, 1934, in Baltimore, MD; son of George Philip (an engineer) and Virginia Schultz; married Sydney Ellen Olman, June 17, 1962. *Education:* Johns Hopkins University, A.B., 1955; Syracuse University, M.A., 1957; American University, Ph.D., 1962.

### ■ Addresses

*Home*—Clearwater, FL; Washington, DC.

### ■ Career

Martin Co., Baltimore, MD, human factors engineer, 1958-60; American University, Washington, DC, instructor in psychology, 1960-61; Westinghouse Corp., Air Armaments Division, Baltimore, senior human factors engineer, 1961; Institute for Defense Analyses, Washington, DC, scientist, 1962; University of Virginia, Mary Washington College, Fredericksburg, assistant professor of psychology, 1963-66; University of North Carolina at Charlotte, associate professor, 1966-69, professor of psychology, beginning 1969. Visiting professor, University of Groningen, the Netherlands, 1970. *Military service:* U.S. Army, 1957.

### ■ Member

American Psychological Association, American Association of University Professors, Eastern Psychological Association, Southeastern Psychological Association.

### ■ Awards, Honors

Research grants from National Institute of Mental Health, 1962, and from Office of Naval Research, 1963-71.

### ■ Writings

*PSYCHOLOGY*

*Panic Behavior,* Random House (New York, NY), 1964.

*Sensory Restriction: Effects on Behavior,* Academic Press (New York, NY), 1965.

*A History of Modern Psychology,* Academic Press (New York, NY), 1969, 10th edition (with wife, Sydney Ellen Schultz), Cengage Learning (Belmont, CA), 2011.

(Compiler) *Psychology and Industry,* Macmillan (New York, NY), 1970.

(Editor) *The Science of Psychology: Critical Reflections,* Appleton (New York, NY), 1970.

*Psychology and Industry Today,* Macmillan (New York, NY), 1973, 10th edition (with wife, Sydney Ellen Schultz), published as *Psychology and Work Today: An Introduction to Industrial and Organizational Psychology,* Pearson Prentice Hall (Upper Saddle River, NJ), 2010.

*Theories of Personality,* Brooks/Cole (Pacific Grove, CA), 1976, 9th edition (with wife, Sydney Ellen Schultz), Wadsworth Cengage Learning (Belmont, CA), 2009.

*Growth Personality: Models of the Healthy Personality,* Van Nostrand (New York, NY), 1977.

*Psychology in Use: An Introduction to Applied Psychology,* Macmillan (New York, NY), 1979.

*Intimate Friends, Dangerous Rivals: The Turbulent Relationship between Freud and Jung,* J.P. Tarcher (Los Angeles, CA), 1990.

## HISTORY

*Wake Island,* Playboy Enterprises (Chicago, IL), 1978.

*Hero of Bataan: The Story of General Wainwright,* St. Martin's Press (New York, NY), 1981.

*The Last Battle Station: The Story of the USS Houston,* St. Martin's Press (New York, NY), 1985.

*The Maverick War: Chennault and the Flying Tigers,* St. Martin's Press (New York, NY), 1987.

*The Doolittle Raid,* St. Martin's Press (New York, NY), 1988.

*Month of the Freezing Moon: The Sand Creek Massacre, November, 1864,* St. Martin's Press (New York, NY), 1990.

*Over the Earth I Come: The Great Sioux Uprising of 1862,* St. Martin's Press (New York, NY), 1992.

*Glory Enough for All: The Battle of the Crater,* St. Martin's Press (New York, NY), 1993.

*Quantrill's War: The Life and Times of William Clarke Quantrill, 1837-1865,* St. Martin's Press (New York, NY), 1996.

*The Dahlgren Affair: Terror and Conspiracy in the Civil War,* W.W. Norton (New York, NY), 1998.

*The Most Glorious Fourth: Vicksburg and Gettysburg, July 4, 1863,* W.W. Norton (New York, NY), 2002.

*Custer: Lessons in Leadership,* Palgrave Macmillan (New York, NY), 2010.

Contributor of numerous articles to psychology journals.

## ■ Sidelights

Duane P. Schultz has written several major textbooks on psychology, as well as a comparative study of the lives and work of Sigmund Freud and Carl Jung. Retired from a long teaching career, he has focused more recently on writing about U.S. history, specializing in particular on subjects relating to the Civil War and the U.S. Indian Wars.

### Intimate Friends, Dangerous Rivals and Quantrill's War

In *Intimate Friends, Dangerous Rivals: The Turbulent Relationship between Freud and Jung* Schultz examines the intense and complex feelings between the two seminal figures in modern psychology. In Schultz's view, the men were bound together by mutual though different needs. For Freud, Jung was a submissive son figure; for Jung, Freud was an intellectual and spiritual mentor. Their relationship included jealousies and professional rivalries as well. Though a *Publishers Weekly* contributor found Schultz's argument oversimplified at times, the critic deemed the book "devastatingly intimate" and "rewarding."

Among Schultz's popular histories of the Civil War is *Quantrill's War: The Life and Times of William Clarke Quantrill, 1837-1865.* Quantrill was a guerilla fighter on the Confederate side who, in Schultz's view, was a career criminal who exploited the war to further his interests in theft and murder. During the war, he set himself up as the head of a raiding group that included Frank and Jesse James and other notorious outlaws. By the end of the war, though, Quantrill was no longer able to control these men. He then headed to Kentucky, where he was mortally wounded by Union forces. Schultz "retells Quantrill's life with dramatic flourish," observed a reviewer for *Publishers Weekly.*

### The Dahlgren Affair and The Most Glorious Fourth

*The Dahlgren Affair: Terror and Conspiracy in the Civil War* recounts the failed 1864 Yankee cavalry raid against Richmond, Virginia, and the controversy that erupted when it was discovered that this action, ostensibly mounted to free thousands of Union prisoners of war, had a covert mission: to assassinate Confederate president Jefferson Davis and his cabinet, and then to raze the city. Schultz narrates the events of the raid and the death in battle of Yankee colonel Ulric Dahlgren, on whose body the Confederate side claimed to have found the papers detailing the covert mission—papers the Confederates then published. Schultz explains that historians have not reached consensus on whether these documents were authentic or were fabricated in order to rouse the Confederate side to mount terrorist campaigns in the north. In Schultz's view, the papers were forged. Writing in *Contemporary Review,* Richard Mullen considered *The Dahlgren Affair* an "exciting and well told account," albeit with "a strong Northern bias."

In *The Most Glorious Fourth: Vicksburg and Gettysburg, July 4, 1863,* Schultz focuses on the momentous day on which the city of Vicksburg, Mississippi, surrendered to Union forces. The previous day, the Union Army had defeated Robert E. Lee's forces at Gettysburg, Pennsylvania. *Journal of Southern History* critic Anne Sarah Rubin observed that the dual focus provides the book with "unexpected resonance," and that Schultz's evocative use of detail allows him to tell his story "in vivid and moving terms." Acknowledging that the book is written for popular rather than academic audiences, Rubin concluded that it "succeeds admirably at this limited task."

### Custer

Schultz published *Custer: Lessons in Leadership,* in 2010. The book serves as a biography of nineteenth-century American General George Armstrong Custer, nicknamed the "boy general" for his relative youth. Despite graduating last in his class at West Point and with the most demerits, he quickly rose to the rank of general and was popular with the media. Custer became infamous for leading his 220-man army to near annihilation at the battle of Little Big Horn in 1876 and was subsequently blamed for the failure in historical records. Schultz aims to offer alternate perspectives on the situation, furthering the debate on Custer's role in the embarrassing military defeat.

Writing in *Civil War News,* Jonathan A. Noyalas lamented that "while portions of *Custer* have value, Custer enthusiasts, particularly those interested in Custer's Civil War service, will find this book frustrating and of little use." Noyalas suggested, though, that "perhaps the book's strongest element is its epilogue, which describes the reactions to Custer's death and examines how people attempted to understand" the tragic disaster that ended his life. A contributor to *Wild West* said that the book "is swiftly paced and well written. Certainly it does more than skim the surface of Custer's career" despite its "compact" size. A *Kirkus Reviews* critic remarked that *Custer* is "a competent overview, but readers in search of a rich character study or thoughtful analysis of military leadership should look elsewhere."

## ■ Biographical And Critical Sources

*PERIODICALS*

*American History,* October 1, 2010, Gene Santoro, review of *Custer: Lessons in Leadership,* p. 70.

*American Journal of Psychology,* December 1, 1981, review of *A History of Modern Psychology,* p. 667.

*American Legion,* January 1, 1982, review of *Hero of Bataan: The Story of General Wainwright,* p. 26.

*Best Sellers,* January 1, 1979, review of *Wake Island,* p. 325; January 1, 1982, review of *Hero of Bataan,* p. 381; May 1, 1985, review of *The Last Battle Station: The Story of the USS Houston,* p. 70.

*Booklist,* December 1, 1981, review of *Hero of Bataan,* p. 481; February 1, 1985, review of *The Last Battle Station,* p. 744; June 15, 1987, review of *The Maverick War: Chennault and the Flying Tigers,* p. 1560; October 1, 1988, review of *The Doolittle Raid,* p. 216; April 1, 1990, review of *Intimate Friends, Dangerous Rivals: The Turbulent Relationship between Freud and Jung,* p. 1510; April 1, 1992, Fred Egloff, review of *Over the Earth I Come: The Great Sioux Uprising of 1862,* p. 1426; September 1, 1993, Margaret Flanagan, review of *Glory Enough for All: The Battle of the Crater,* p. 38; September 15, 1996, Roland Green, review of *Quantrill's War: The Life and Times of William Clarke Quantrill, 1837-1865,* p. 216; September 15, 2001, Margaret Flanagan, review of *The Most Glorious Fourth: Vicksburg and Gettysburg, July 4, 1863,* p. 184.

*Chicago Tribune Books,* January 19, 2003, review of *The Most Glorious Fourth,* p. 6.

*Choice: Current Reviews for Academic Libraries,* March 1, 1982, review of *Hero of Bataan,* p. 986; December 1, 1987, review of *The Maverick War,* p. 680; October 1, 1992, W.E. Unrau, review of *Over the Earth I Come,* p. 371.

*Contemporary Psychology,* January 1, 1976, review of *A History of Modern Psychology,* p. 7; September 1, 1976, review of *Theories of Personality,* p. 660; August 1, 1978, "Growth Psychology," p. 593; November 1, 1978, review of *Psychology and Industry Today,* p. 957; November 1, 1979, review of *Psychology in Use: An Introduction to Applied Psychology,* p. 942; November 1, 1986, review of *Theories of Personality,* p. 909.

*Contemporary Review,* September 1, 1999, Richard Mullen, review of *The Dahlgren Affair: Terror and Conspiracy in the Civil War,* p. 163.

*Guardian* (London, England), December 13, 1981, review of *Hero of Bataan,* p. 18.

*Journal of Military History,* October 1, 1989, George M. Watson, Jr., review of *The Doolittle Raid,* p. 449.

*Journal of Southern History,* November 1, 2003, Anne Sarah Rubin, review of *The Most Glorious Fourth,* p. 929.

*Kirkus Reviews,* June 1, 1978, review of *Wake Island,* p. 629; October 1, 1981, review of *Hero of Bataan,* p. 1281; June 1, 1987, review of *The Maverick War,* p. 844; August 1, 1988, review of *The Doolittle Raid,* p. 1135; January 1, 1990, review of *Intimate Friends, Dangerous Rivals,* p. 35; May 1, 1990, review of *Month of the Freezing Moon: The Sand Creek Massacre,* p. 637; January 15, 1992, review of *Over the Earth I Come,* p. 103; August 15, 2001, review of *The Most Glorious Fourth,* p. 1199; July 15, 2010, review of *Custer.*

*Kliatt,* December 22, 1980, review of *Wake Island,* p. 50; September 22, 1986, review of *The Last Battle Station,* p. 64; May 1, 2003, Raymond L. Puffer, review of *The Most Glorious Fourth,* p. 38.

*Library Journal,* September 1, 1978, review of *Wake Island,* p. 1653; October 15, 1981, Mel D. Lane, review of *Hero of Bataan,* p. 2026; February 1, 1985, George E. Scheck, review of *The Last Battle Station,* p. 96; June 1, 1987, Mel D. Lane, review of *The Maverick War,* p. 112; October 15, 1988, Raymond L. Puffer, review of *The Doolittle Raid,* p. 88; March 1, 1990, Lucy Patrick, review of *Intimate Friends, Dangerous Rivals,* p. 107; June 1, 1990, Robert Stenzel, review of *Month of the Freezing Moon,* p. 146; February 15, 1992, Lisa A. Mitten, review of *Over the Earth I Come,* p. 182; May 15, 1997, Barbara Mann, review of *Quantrill's War,* p. 120; September 15, 1998, Ralph M. Miller, review of *The Dahlgren Affair,* p. 96; September 15, 2001, Brooks D. Simpson, review of *The Most Glorious Fourth,* p. 95.

*Los Angeles Times,* April 14, 1985, Paul Dean, review of *The Last Battle Station,* p. 6.

*New York Times Book Review,* January 24, 1982, D.J.R. J.R. Bruckner, review of *Hero of Bataan,* p. 14; March 22, 1992, Caleb Carr, review of *Over the Earth I Come,* p. 10; September 26, 1993, David Murray, review of *Glory Enough for All,* p. 20.

*Personnel Journal,* June 1, 1973, review of *Psychology and Industry Today,* p. 488.

*Publishers Weekly,* June 12, 1978, review of *Wake Island,* p. 78; October 9, 1981, Genevieve Stuttaford, review of *Hero of Bataan,* p. 58; January 11, 1985, review of *The Last Battle Station,* p. 62; June 5, 1987, Genevieve Stuttaford, review of *The Maverick War,* p. 66; October 21, 1988, Genevieve Stuttaford, review of *The Doolittle Raid,* p. 44; January 19, 1990, review of *Intimate Friends, Dangerous Rivals,* p. 89; May 11, 1990, Genevieve Stuttaford, review of *Month of the Freezing Moon,* p. 244; January 13, 1992, review of *Over the Earth I Come,* p. 40; July 19, 1993, review of *Glory Enough for All,* p. 237; September 9, 1996, review of *Quantrill's War,* p. 74; August 10, 1998, review of *The Dahlgren Affair,* p. 381; September 24, 2001, review of *The Most Glorious Fourth,* p. 79.

*Reference & Research Book News,* August 1, 1992, review of *Over the Earth I Come,* p. 9.

*School Library Journal,* April 1, 1982, review of *Hero of Bataan,* p. 92; November 1, 1992, Judy McAloon, review of *Over the Earth I Come,* p. 146; August 1, 1993, Beth Ann Mills, review of *Glory Enough for All,* p. 156; September 15, 1996, Robert A. Curtis, review of *Quantrill's War,* p. 76.

*Washington Post Book World,* November 22, 1981, review of *Hero of Bataan,* p. 1; December 20, 1987, review of *The Maverick War,* p. 10; July 15, 1990, review of *The Maverick War,* p. 13; January 6, 2002, review of *The Most Glorious Fourth,* p. 10.

*West Coast Review of Books,* February 1, 1982, review of *Hero of Bataan,* p. 40.

*Wild West,* June 1, 2011, review of *Custer,* p. 76.

ONLINE

*Civil War News,* http://www.civilwarnews.com/ (January 1, 2011), Jonathan A. Noyalas, review of *Custer.*

*Duane P. Schultz Home Page,* http://www.duaneschultz.com (August 25, 2008).*

# Michael Schumacher

## 1950-

■ **Personal**

Born May 22, 1950.

■ **Addresses**

*Home*—WI.

■ **Career**

Freelance journalist and writer.

■ **Writings**

*Reasons to Believe: New Voices in American Fiction* (criticism), St. Martin's Press (New York, NY), 1988.

*Creative Conversations: The Writer's Guide to Conducting Interviews,* Writer's Digest Books (Cincinnati, OH), 1990.

*Dharma Lion: A Critical Biography of Allen Ginsberg,* St. Martin's Press (New York, NY), 1992.

*Crossroads: The Life and Music of Eric Clapton,* Hyperion (New York, NY), 1995.

*There but for Fortune: The Life of Phil Ochs,* Hyperion (New York, NY), 1996.

*Francis Ford Coppola: A Filmmaker's Life,* Crown (New York, NY), 1999.

(Editor) Allen Ginsberg and Louis Ginsberg, *Family Business: Selected Letters between a Father and Son,* Bloomsbury (New York, NY), 2001.

*Mighty Fitz: The Sinking of the Edmund Fitzgerald,* Bloomsbury USA (New York, NY), 2005.

*Mr. Basketball: George Mikan, the Minneapolis Lakers, and the Birth of the NBA,* Bloomsbury USA (New York, NY), 2007.

*Wreck of the Carl D.: A True Story of Loss, Survival, and Rescue at Sea,* Bloomsbury USA (New York, NY), 2008.

(Editor, with Heikki Helin and Heiko Schuldt) *CASCOM: Intelligent Service Coordination in the Semantic Web,* Birkhaìuser (Basel, Switzerland), 2008.

*Will Eisner: A Dreamer's Life in Comics,* Bloomsbury (New York, NY), 2010.

■ **Sidelights**

Michael Schumacher, a freelance journalist, is the author of a number of nonfiction books and biographies that came about as a result of his work as an interviewer and chronicler of popular culture.

### Reasons to Believe

His first title, *Reasons to Believe: New Voices in American Fiction,* appeared in 1988, at a time when a fresh crop of novelists was being heralded as harbingers of a new American literary scene. The work was composed from a series of eighteen conversations Schumacher conducted with several of these rising young writers. Interweaving an overview of their life, analysis of their prose, and critical appraisals into his profiles, Schumacher discusses artistic motivations and publishing issues in dialogues with Tama Janowitz, Jay McInerney, Jayne Anne Phillips, and Bret Easton Ellis, among others.

*Reasons to Believe* also contains the transcripts of Schumacher's talk with short-story writer Raymond Carver, whom many of the new writers considered their literary mentor. Tragically, it was Carver's final interview given before his death in 1988. Some editors and other publishing professionals who were crucial to the emergence of the *New Voices* writers were also interviewed for the book. In *Publishers Weekly,* Penny Kaganoff granted that, though hopeful writers may find Schumacher's interviews insightful, "they are generally cursory, superficial, and too infrequently original."

### *Creative Conversations* and *Dharma Lion*

Schumacher utilized what he learned from his first book, as well as what he learned as a working journalist, and organized his insights in *Creative Conversations: The Writer's Guide to Conducting Interviews.* Published in 1990, the work offers a start-to-finish guide for the neophyte interviewer. Schumacher provides an overview of strategies for conducting research as well as various interview techniques commonly used by journalists and biographers. He also discusses interview etiquette and offers anecdotes from memorable interviews he conducted, including the Carver profile. In her *Booklist* review of *Creative Conversations,* Deanna Larson-Whiterod praised the work as containing a wealth of "dependable advice on the entire interview process."

Based on extensive interviews, Schumacher's *Dharma Lion: A Critical Biography of Allen Ginsberg* chronicles the life of Allen Ginsberg, an American poet associated with the iconoclastic Beat literary scene of the 1950s. Ginsberg, who died of liver cancer five years after this 1992 biography was published, enjoyed tremendous success during his career and became an important influence on writers and styles that followed him. Known for the subversive verve in his verse as well as for his frank, rebellious public persona, Ginsberg was one of the few American poets who was able to draw huge crowds to hear him read his work.

Schumacher's biography chronicles the difficult early life that inadvertently fostered such talent. Born in 1926 in New Jersey, Ginsberg endured a childhood devastated by his mother's schizophrenia and subsequent hospitalization. Growing up Jewish during the time of the Holocaust also fueled his loneliness and alienation, and as he entered adulthood the realization that he was gay only added to his despair. As Schumacher recounts, it was a move to San Francisco, a healthy love relationship, and a wise therapist that provided him with the impetus to lead the life he wished. Schumacher interviews those who knew Ginsberg from his early days as friend to Jack Kerouac, William Burroughs, and several other fellow iconoclasts in the Beat

movement. He also recounts some of the more memorable moments of Ginsberg's career, including an obscenity trial that attempted to censor his most famous poem, *Howl,* and his leadership of a crowd of protesters chanting the meditative "Om," en masse, outside the 1968 Democratic National Convention in Chicago.

Ginsberg's conversion to Buddhism inspired the biography's title, for the poet's spiritual mentor referred to him as the Lion of "Dharma," or ideal truth. Noting that while Schumacher "explores Ginsberg's activism and polemics at great length, and criticizes his work with fine, telling detail, his style tends toward the academic," explained *Los Angeles Times* contributor Gerald Nicosia, who dubbed *Dharma Lion* a "comprehensive biography." Rhoda Koenig, reviewing the work for *New York,* asserted that "Schumacher is at times too smooth and uncritical, but he provides a feast of anecdote and an engaging portrait of the protester-poet." Schumacher also served as editor of the letters exchanged between Ginsberg and his father, published in 2001 as *Family Business: Selected Letters between a Father and Son.*

### *Crossroads* and *There but for Fortune*

For Schumacher's next two projects, he explored the life and careers of two vastly different musical legends. *Crossroads: The Life and Music of Eric Clapton* is an in-depth look at the life and song of this blues and rock guitarist considered by many to be among the greatest living virtuosos. Clapton was born in England in 1945 and raised by his grandparents after his teenage mother abandoned him. He taught himself to play guitar, and by the mid-1960s he began a stellar trajectory that included stints with the Yardbirds, Cream, and Blind Faith. Clapton then went on to a Grammy-winning solo career. A friend of such musical luminaries as Bob Dylan, the guitarist also earned notoriety for his well-publicized personal life. He became involved with the wife of Beatle George Harrison, whom he later was married to briefly, he was plagued by alcohol and drug addiction, and his toddler son died from a fall out of a high-rise window in 1991. Clapton, as Schumacher relates, often used such difficulties as artistic inspiration, infusing his work with emotional resonance. A *Kirkus Reviews* contributor praised *Crossroads* as "an evenhanded biography that humanizes the guitar hero," while *Booklist* contributor Mike Tribby deemed the biography "a necessary addition to the pop-music library."

*There but for Fortune: The Life of Phil Ochs* tracks the career path of a far different musical artist: folk singer Phil Ochs. Schumacher was compelled to rely heavily on interviews with friends, family, and associates for this work because Ochs committed suicide twenty years before the book's 1996 publication. As the profile recounts, Ochs rose to prominence during the folk music boom of the early 1960s, but he never achieved the commercial success of many of his contemporaries, including Joan Baez and Peter, Paul & Mary. Schumacher's interviews reveal the extent of the bipolar illness that ultimately ended Ochs's career, as well as the musician's support of the civil rights crusade and the antiwar movement. Allowed access to Ochs's journals, Schumacher also quotes from the surveillance file on Ochs compiled by Federal Bureau of Investigation agents. As a *Publishers Weekly* contributor observed of the biography, "it seems odd, if not ludicrous, that the FBI once considered him a potential threat to American society; as Schumacher shows, he was, in fact, more of a threat to himself." Robin Lippincott, writing in the *New York Times Book Review*, called *There but for Fortune* "a heartfelt portrait of Ochs's life and times."

### Francis Ford Coppola

Schumacher chronicles another iconoclast whose personal life has not been without its difficulties in *Francis Ford Coppola: A Filmmaker's Life*. Although not authorizing Schumacher's biography, Coppola does contribute extensive recollections for the book, which Schumacher added after his main text was completed. Hailed as one of the greatest names in contemporary American filmmaking, but condemned by some as a self-aggrandizing shark, Coppola was the mastermind behind such classics as *The Godfather* and *Apocalypse Now*. Known for his contempt of the Hollywood studio status quo, Coppola, as Schumacher relates, struggled over the course of his career to break new ground, and at times met with astonishing failure.

*Francis Ford Coppola* relates many of the hardships in Coppola's personal life, including a bout with polio during his youth, the financial difficulties he caused his family because of his artistic vision, and the death of his son Gian-Carlo in a 1986 boating accident. "However unwise it was for Schumacher to invite his subject's collaboration, which turns the book into another exercise in Coppola self-promotion, the resulting quotations from Coppola and his close friends and family members prove to be the liveliest material" in the volume, asserted *New York Times Book Review* writer Joseph McBride, who added that Schumacher "gives ample evidence that Coppola's finest attribute as an artist is his penchant for taking risks." A *Publishers Weekly* reviewer offered a similarly positive appraisal, not-

ing that the biography's "real strength lies in its flavorful behind-the-scenes re-creation of the making of all of Coppola's movies."

### Mighty Fitz and Mr. Basketball

Shifting away from biography, Schumacher chronicles the tale of a famed Great Lakes shipwreck in *Mighty Fitz: The Sinking of the Edmund Fitzgerald*. The book was written to commemorate the thirtieth anniversary of the wreck, the subject of Gordon Lightfoot's popular song, "The Wreck of the Edmund Fitzgerald." The ship, the largest freighter on the Great Lakes at its launch in 1958, went down in a severe storm in 1975, taking with it all twenty-nine of its crew members. The event was a great shock; the ship had been deemed seaworthy and unsinkable. Schumacher, who has produced several documentary films about shipwrecks on the Great Lakes, recounts what is known of the tragedy and discusses various controversies about what made the ship sink. In addition, the book examines the rescue efforts and how the disposition of the ship's remains was handled. According to a contributor to *Kirkus Reviews*, *Mighty Fitz* is a "fastidious history of loss at sea, for casual reader and maritime maven alike."

In *Mr. Basketball: George Mikan, the Minneapolis Lakers, and the Birth of the NBA*, Schumacher writes about the first truly big man of basketball. Mikan, almost seven feet tall, began his career at DePaul University and then joined the Lakers as a center. He became an archetypal athlete, dominating his sport through the 1940s and 1950s. Indeed, Mikan's extreme height prompted the National Basketball Association (NBA) to change several rules in order to compensate for his advantage in shot-blocking and rebounding: the free-throw lane, for example, was widened from six feet to twelve feet, and the goaltending rule was created. Off the court, Mikan was an unprepossessing family man who was well liked. As many reviewers noted, Schumacher's book brings welcome attention to a sports star who had hitherto received comparatively little biographical notice.

Schumacher interviewed Mikan's teammates, family, coaches, and friends to shed light on the athlete as a player and a person. He also researched the annals of NBA history, interweaving Mikan's story with that of the rise of the NBA. A writer for *Atlantic Monthly* admired *Mr. Basketball* as "a detailed, atmospherically true tale of tallness." *Booklist* reviewer Wes Lukowsky also praised the book, observing that it provides not only an excellent overview of Mikan's life and career but also a valuable chronicle of the early years of the NBA. *Library Journal* contributor Douglas King, however, deemed *Mr. Basketball* unsuccessful because of its emphasis on "breezy recounts" of Mikan's major games, with long passages of statistics. A contributor to *Publishers Weekly* made a similar point, commenting that Schumacher does not succeed in bringing his subject to life off the court. A *Kirkus Reviews* critic, on the other hand, hailed *Mr. Basketball* as a "compelling portrait of a dynamic and influential man."

### Wreck of the Carl D.

In *Wreck of the Carl D.: A True Story of Loss, Survival, and Rescue at Sea,* Schumacher looks into the most expensive wreck in the history of maritime tragedies in the Great Lakes. Schumacher chronicles the demise of the "Queen of the Stone-Carrying Fleet" and also highlights the human losses incurred.

*Booklist* reviewer David Pitt found the book to be "a solid and sometimes heartbreaking addition to the maritime-tragedy genre." A contributor to *Kirkus Reviews* claimed that *Wreck of the Carl D.* is "a signal contribution to nautical Americana." A contributor to *Publishers Weekly* remarked that the author infuses "the book with dramatic substance to match the riveting narrative."

### Will Eisner

In *Will Eisner: A Dreamer's Life in Comics,* Schumacher looks at the professional success and personal life of one of the comic book industry's most celebrated figures. Schumacher shows how Eisner was able to set up one of the first comic syndicates in the country and raise the bar for the industry throughout his career.

Writing in the *Cleveland Plain Dealer,* William Kist commented that "one of the advantages of Schumacher's book is that it's told without the air of fanaticism that can cling to books about comics. This biography introduces a genre pioneer who doesn't enjoy the wide name recognition he deserves." Reviewing the book in the *Los Angeles Times,* Charles Solomon lamented that "too often, Schumacher talks about material that the book should have illustrated," adding that "even the largest plates in the 16-page color insert are smaller than the original comic book covers, and most of the color artwork is undated." A *Kirkus Reviews* critic opined that *Will Eisner* is "engaging for both the curious and the ardent fan."

## ■ Biographical And Critical Sources

### PERIODICALS

*Atlantic Monthly,* December 1, 2007, review of *Mr. Basketball: George Mikan, the Minneapolis Lakers, and the Birth of the NBA,* p. 115.

*Biography,* September 22, 2001, review of *Family Business: Selected Letters between a Father and Son,* p. 993.

*Bloomsbury Review,* March 1, 1993, review of *Dharma Lion: A Critical Biography of Allen Ginsberg,* p. 5.

*Booklist,* October 15, 1988, Brad Hooper, review of *Reasons to Believe: New Voices in American Fiction,* p. 359; May 15, 1990, Deanna Larson-Whiterod, review of *Creative Conversations: The Writer's Guide to Conducting Interviews,* p. 1773; October 15, 1992, Ray Olson, review of *Dharma Lion,* p. 393; April 1, 1995, Mike Tribby, review of *Crossroads: The Life and Music of Eric Clapton,* p. 1371; September 15, 1999, Bonnie Smothers, review of *Francis Ford Coppola: A Filmmaker's Life,* p. 213; October 1, 2005, Roland Green, review of *Mighty Fitz: The Sinking of the Edmund Fitzgerald,* p. 18; September 1, 2007, Wes Lukowsky, review of *Mr. Basketball,* p. 46; October 15, 2008, David Pitt, review of *Wreck of the Carl D.: A True Story of Loss, Survival, and Rescue at Sea,* p. 14; November 1, 2010, Donna Seaman, review of *Will Eisner: A Dreamer's Life in Comics,* p. 21.

*Bookwatch,* June 1, 1990, review of *Creative Conversations,* p. 2.

*California,* January 1, 1989, Greil Marcus, review of *Reasons to Believe,* p. 95.

*Chicago Tribune Books,* November 29, 1992, review of *Dharma Lion,* p. 1.

*Choice: Current Reviews for Academic Libraries,* February 1, 1997, review of *There but for Fortune: The Life of Phil Ochs,* p. 975; March 1, 2002, W. Britton, review of *Family Business,* p. 1237.

*Cleveland Plain Dealer,* November 30, 2010, William Kist, review of *Will Eisner.*

*English Studies,* October 1, 2005, Franca Bellarsi, review of *Family Business,* p. 469.

*Globe & Mail* (Toronto, Ontario, Canada), December 18, 1999, review of *Francis Ford Coppola,* p. D10; November 26, 2005, Orland French, review of *Mighty Fitz,* p. D31.

*Kirkus Reviews,* August 1, 1992, review of *Dharma Lion,* p. 977; March 1, 1995, review of *Crossroads,* p. 309; September 15, 1999, review of *Francis Ford Coppola,* p. 1487; October 1, 2005, review of *Mighty Fitz,* p. 1069; August 15, 2007, review of *Mr. Basketball;* September 15, 2008, review of *Wreck of the Carl D.;* August 1, 2010, review of *Will Eisner.*

*Kliatt,* January 1, 1989, review of *Reasons to Believe,* p. 24.

*Lambda Book Report,* January 1, 1993, Michael Bronski, review of *Dharma Lion,* p. 28.

*Library Journal,* September 1, 1992, William Gargan, review of *Dharma Lion,* p. 176; September 15, 1996, Lloyd Jansen, review of *There but for Fortune,* p. 71; August 1, 1999, Stephen Rees, review of *Francis Ford Coppola,* p. 93; September 1, 2001, William Gargan, review of *Family Business,* p. 178; October 15, 2005, Robert C. Jones, review of *Mighty Fitz,* p. 69; October 1, 2007, Douglas King, review of *Mr. Basketball,* p. 78.

*Los Angeles Times,* November 29, 1992, Gerald Nicosia, review of *Dharma Lion,* pp. 4, 13; November 21, 1999, review of *Francis Ford Coppola,* p. 6; November 30, 2010, Charles Solomon, review of *Will Eisner.*

*Newsweek,* October 12, 1992, David Gates, review of *Dharma Lion,* p. 80.

*New York,* October 26, 1992, Rhoda Koenig, review of *Dharma Lion,* pp. 95-96.

*New York Times Book Review,* September 15, 1996, Robin Lippincott, review of *There but for Fortune,* p. 31; December 12, 1999, Joseph McBride, review of *Francis Ford Coppola,* p. 42.

*Progressive,* March 1, 1993, review of *Dharma Lion,* p. 42.

*Publishers Weekly,* October 21, 1988, Penny Kaganoff, review of *Reasons to Believe,* p. 52; August 24, 1992, review of *Dharma Lion,* p. 68; March 13, 1995, review of *Crossroads,* p. 57; July 29, 1996, review of *There but for Fortune,* p. 79; November 1, 1999, review of *Francis Ford Coppola,* p. 61; August 6, 2001, review of *Family Business,* p. 73; September 12, 2005, review of *Mighty Fitz,* p. 59; July 23, 2007, review of *Mr. Basketball,* p. 51; September 15, 2008, review of *Wreck of the Carl D.,* p. 58; October 18, 2010, review of *Will Eisner,* p. 35.

*Reference & Research Book News,* September 1, 1993, review of *Dharma Lion,* p. 46; February 1, 2006, review of *Mighty Fitz.*

*School Library Journal,* July 1, 1990, John Lawson, review of *Creative Conversations,* p. 98.

*Times Higher Education Supplement,* June 30, 2000, Sandy Lieberson, review of *Francis Ford Coppola,* p. 29.

*Times Literary Supplement* (London, England), March 17, 2000, Chris Tayler, review of *Francis Ford Coppola,* p. 19.

*Washington Post Book World,* September 2, 2001, review of *Francis Ford Coppola,* p. 12.*

# Robert B. Shoemaker

## 1956-

■ **Also Known As**

Robert Brink Shoemaker

■ **Personal**

Born September 12, 1956, in Boston, MA; son of David (a chemistry professor) and Clara (a chemistry professor) Shoemaker; married; wife's name Catherine Wendy; children: one son. *Education:* Reed College, B.A. (with honors), 1978; Stanford University, A.M., 1980, Ph.D., 1986.

■ **Addresses**

*Office*—University of Sheffield, Department of History, Sheffield S10 2TN, England. *E-mail*—r. shoemaker@sheffield.ac.uk.

■ **Career**

Stanford University, Stanford, CA, lecturer in modern European history, 1984-86; Institute of European Studies, London, England, part-time lecturer in history, 1986-90; Lawrence University, London Programme, London, part-time lecturer in history, 1990; University of Sheffield, Sheffield, England, lecturer in history, beginning 1991, became professor, head of the history department, 2004-08, director of research and innovation, deputy director of the Centre for Criminological Research. Codirector, Old Bailey Proceedings Online Project, Open University. Visiting lecturer at Richmond College, 1986, Stanford University, 1988, Lansdowne College, 1989-90, and James Madison University, London Programme, 1989-90.

■ **Member**

Arts and Humanities Research Council, Economic and Social Research Council, Royal Historical Society (elected fellow), Phi Beta Kappa.

■ **Awards, Honors**

Cowinner, Longman-History Today Trustees Award, for the Old Bailey Proceedings Online Project.

■ **Writings**

*Prosecution and Punishment: Petty Crime and the Law in London and Rural Middlesex, c. 1660-1725,* Cambridge University Press (New York, NY), 1991.

(Editor, with Lee Davison, Tim Hitchcock, and Tim Keirn; and contributor) *Stilling the Grumbling Hive: The Response to Social and Economic Problems in England, 1689-1750,* Alan Sutton, 1992.

*Gender in English Society, 1650-1850: The Emergence of Separate Spheres?,* Longman (London, England), 1998.

(Editor, with Mary Vincent) *Gender and History in Western Europe,* Arnold (New York, NY), 1998.

(Project director, with Tim Hitchcock) *The Proceedings of the Old Bailey, London 1674 to 1834* (electronic resource), Old Bailey Proceedings Online (Sheffield, England), 2003.

*The London Mob: Violence and Disorder in Eighteenth-Century England,* Hambledon and London (New York, NY), 2004.

(With Tim Hitchcock) *Tales from the Hanging Court,* Hodder Arnold (London, England), 2006.

Contributor to *The Eighteenth Century Town, 1688-1820,* edited by Peter Borsay, 1990. Contributor of articles and reviews to history and British studies journals.

■ **Sidelights**

A longtime lecturer and professor of history at the University of Sheffield, Robert B. Shoemaker is an expert on England society in the seventeenth and eighteenth centuries. His first book, *Prosecution and Punishment: Petty Crime and the Law in London and Rural Middlesex, c. 1660-1725*, was published in 1991. For his next effort, Shoemaker edited *Stilling the Grumbling Hive: The Response to Social and Economic Problems in England, 1689-1750*, with Lee Davison, Tim Hitchcock, and Tim Keirn.

### Gender and History in Western Europe

He focuses on gender in his third and fourth volumes, *Gender in English Society, 1650-1850: The Emergence of Separate Spheres?* and *Gender and History in Western Europe*. The latter, which Shoemaker edited with Mary Vincent, explores women's history through the lens of gender studies. Essays are divided by theme, including religion, politics, and work, as well as sexuality and theory and method. Contributors include notable scholars, such as Phyllis Mack, Seth Koven, Thomas Laquer, and Catherine Hall.

Assessing *Gender and History in Western Europe* in the *Canadian Journal of History*, Henriette T. Donner remarked: "We may conclude from this survey that 'gender analysis' cannot and should not be defined. It is to its credit, that there are unlimited methods and interpretations." Donner went on to note that the book "illustrates the historical territory mapped by gender analysis. Not that gender analysis has already come of age. However, it has a large number of practitioners, and a wide audience. These are good reasons for gender analysis to begin working out the historical issues raised by its discoveries." According to Patricia Crawford in the *Journal of World History*, "Shoemaker and Vincent's collection and commentary reflect some British historiographical preoccupations with class and gender rather than race and feminism. But then, as the editors point out, in different languages and cultures gender itself can have different meanings." The critic added that "the impact of feminist scholarship on our understanding of the past can usually be guaranteed to lead to lively discussion in classes, for women's history has raised new questions and challenges for teachers and students alike. *Gender and History* will serve a useful purpose for those teaching European and American history from 1500."

### Tales from the Hanging Court

Turning from gender studies to criminal studies, Shoemaker wrote *The London Mob: Violence and Disorder in Eighteenth-Century England* in 2004. Two years later, he authored *Tales from the Hanging Court* with Tim Hitchcock. The historic true crime stories therein are taken from transcripts and reports of the Old Bailey trials (held between 1674 and 1834). By examining the thefts, murders, and rape trials during this period, Shoemaker and Hitchcock shed light on the justice system of early modern England. For instance, criminals were often arrested by common citizens, and prosecutions were conducted by the victims.

Nicholas Rogers, writing in *Labour/Le Travail*, was unimpressed, finding: "The problem with *Tales from the Hanging Court* is that it lets the Old Bailey Proceedings do too much of the talking; it makes the digital imperial; it doesn't follow all the possible leads in the stories that could make them interesting." On the other hand, *Journal of Social History* contributor Dana Rabin praised the "dramatic stories, well written analysis, and economical descriptions." She also noted: "As a teaching tool, this book would be extremely useful and effective. It animates the past, teaches many of the details of legal process, and draws attention to many other questions and approaches. For lay readers who are neither students nor scholars, this book has much to offer. The case studies featuring ordinary people and true crime make the eighteenth century accessible to many who consider the early modem to be 'ancient history.'"

## ■ Biographical And Critical Sources

### PERIODICALS

*Canadian Journal of History*, December 1, 1992, Louis A. Knafla, review of *Prosecution and Punishment: Petty Crime and the Law in London and Rural Middlesex, c. 1660-1725*, p. 548; August 1, 1999, Henriette T. Donner, review of *Gender and History in Western Europe*, p. 284.

*Historian*, June 22, 1993, Michael J. Galgano, review of *Prosecution and Punishment*, p. 762.

*History Today*, November 1, 2004, Patrick Dillon, review of *The London Mob: Violence and Disorder in Eighteenth-Century England*, p. 67.

*Journal of Social History*, March 22, 2010, Dana Rabin, review of *Tales from the Hanging Court*, p. 791.

*Journal of Women's History*, January 1, 2000, Allyson Lowe, review of *Gender and History in Western Europe*, p. 230.

*Journal of World History*, March 22, 2000, Patricia Crawford, review of *Gender and History in Western Europe*, p. 124.

*Labour/Le Travail*, September 22, 2007, Nicholas Rogers, "London's Marginal Histories," p. 217.

### ONLINE

*University of Sheffield Web site*, http://www.sheffield. ac.uk/ (August 16, 2011), author profile.*

# Mona Simpson

## 1957-

### ■ Also Known As

Mona Elizabeth Simpson

### ■ Personal

Born June 14, 1957, in Green Bay, WI; daughter of Abdulfata Jandali and Joanne Carol Schieble (later Joanne Simpson); married Richard Appel (a television comedy writer), 1995 (divorced); children: Gabriel Jandali-Appel, Grace Jandali-Appel. *Education:* University of California, Berkeley, B.A., 1979; Columbia University, M.F.A., 1983.

### ■ Addresses

*Home*—Santa Monica, CA. *Office*—University of California, Los Angeles, Dept. of English, 149 Humanities Bldg., Box 951530, Los Angeles, CA 90095-1530. *Agent*—Amanda Urban, International Creative Management, 40 W. 57th St., New York, NY 10019. *E-mail*—mona.s@ix.netcom.com.

### ■ Career

Writer and academic. Bard College, Annandale-on-Hudson, NY, Sadie Samuelson Levy Professor in Languages and Literature; University of California, Los Angeles, CA, professor of English.

### ■ Awards, Honors

Whiting Writers' Award and National Endowment for the Arts grant, both 1986; Hodder fellowship, Princeton University, 1987; fellowship, John Simon Guggenheim Memorial Foundation, 1988; Lila Wallace—Reader's Digest Award, 1995; Pen Faulkner Finalist, 2001; Chicago Tribune Heartland Prize, 2001, for *Off Keck Road*; Helen Foundation Award; Henfield Prize; literature award, American Academy of Arts and Letters, 2008.

### ■ Writings

*NOVELS*

*Anywhere but Here*, Knopf (New York, NY), 1986.
*The Lost Father*, Knopf (New York, NY), 1991.
*A Regular Guy*, Knopf (New York, NY), 1996.
*Off Keck Road* (novella), Knopf (New York, NY), 2000.
*Bea Maxwell*, Flammarion (New York, NY), 2002.
*My Hollywood*, Alfred A. Knopf (New York, NY), 2010.

Work represented in anthologies, including *Twenty under Thirty*, Scribner, 1985; *Louder than Words*, 1990; *The Pushcart Prize: Best of the Small Presses XI*; and *Best American Short Stories of 1986*. Contributor to periodicals, including *Harper's, Iowa Review, North American Review, Paris Review,* and *Ploughshares.*

### ■ Adaptations

*Anywhere but Here* was adapted by Alvin Sargent into a film directed by Wayne Wang, starring Susan Sarandon and Natalie Portman, released by Twentieth Century-Fox in 1999.

### ■ Sidelights

Mona Simpson is a novelist from the generation of writers that emerged in the 1980s. Her novels explore the complex ties in families torn apart by divorce or abandonment, usually focusing on daughters, their wayward mothers, and absent fathers. Born in Green Bay, Wisconsin, she grew up in California and earned a master of fine arts degree from Columbia University in 1983.

### Anywhere but Here

*Anywhere but Here*, Simpson's critically acclaimed first novel, set the framework for her fiction. In this book, Adele August is a twice-married woman who longs for her daughter, Ann, to become a child star in Hollywood. When Ann is twelve, Adele drives her from Wisconsin to luxurious Beverly Hills, California, hoping to make important connections with the film world's upper echelon there. Once in Beverly Hills, however, mother and daughter find life less than promising. Adele deludes herself with imagined love affairs while working mundane jobs, and Ann enjoys only limited success as a television performer. By novel's end, the emotionally trying—and occasionally violent—mother-daughter relationship is altered by Ann's growing need for independence.

Upon publication in 1986, *Anywhere but Here* was recognized as an important new work. Richard Eder, writing in the *Los Angeles Times*, described Simpson's debut as a "remarkably gifted novel," and Laurie Stone, in her *Village Voice* appraisal, called *Anywhere but Here* a "brilliant, true first novel." Further accolades came from *Newsweek* contributor Laura Shapiro, who called *Anywhere but Here* a "big, complex and masterfully written . . . achievement" that readily establishes Simpson as one of America's "best younger novelists."

As the accolades continued for *Anywhere but Here*, Simpson revealed in various interviews that producing her first novel was a demanding task. The book underwent several drafts—with some episodes revised as many as ten times—and was the subject of often severe criticism from friends and peers. Even after the novel was finally published and the acclaim came, Simpson expressed some dissatisfaction. "You really want to be proud of your work," she told *Washington Post Book World* contributor Paula Span. "You want the work to be as good as the vision you started with. For me, it never has been, so far."

### The Lost Father

Simpson continued to pursue her vision in *The Lost Father*, the sequel to *Anywhere but Here*. Ann, now grown, has left the West Coast—and the dream of

being a Hollywood star—for the East Coast and medical school in New York City. She is a gifted student with high expectations, but under the pressures of medical school, her long-suppressed questions about her absent father bubble to the surface and then consume her life. She knows that her lost father, John Atassi, was an Egyptian immigrant who came to study in the United States and then started a career as an academic. Along the way, he started and then abandoned a family. As her search takes on a life of its own, Ann Stevenson becomes Mayan Atassi, the name given to her by her father. She searches the United States and even takes a trip to Egypt to query her undiscovered family there. In the end, she finds him, a restauranteur in California with a new wife. When she at last finishes her quest, Ann/Mayan finds no answers and no satisfaction.

Ann/Mayan's quest for her father is long and all-consuming, characteristics that, according to a number of reviewers, create significant challenges for readers of Simpson's book. "There are problems in dramatizing such single-mindedness," noted Jim Shepard in the *New York Times Book Review*, "and the novel doesn't escape all of them." As Richard Eder pointed out in the *Los Angeles Times*, "Mayan is alive, believable, and real; and as with any live, real and engaging person who talks endlessly about herself and doesn't look up or out, you wish she would."

Even with such qualifications, Shepard deemed *The Lost Father* "a superb book." "The author's language can be breathtaking in the simple beauty of its imagery," he commented. "And," he wrote, "the portrait of Mayan that emerges is marvelous in its acuity and richness." Eder commended Simpson for treating the familiar theme of parental abandonment in a way that makes it come alive by keeping it personal. "What Simpson does," he observed, "is to work out in enormous, sensitive and highly imaginative detail the pattern this abandonment describes in one individual." *London Review of Books* contributor Jonathan Coe thought Mayan's deeply personal quest seemed to plod along at times, but he found that "eventually the narrative is allowed to get up a good head of steam, and the excitement of the final stages of the search—involving the inevitable trip to Egypt—is topped only by the exhilarating rightness of the novel's anti-climax, when Mayan does find her father and realises that she is no closer to solving the mystery which has been dogging her all her life."

### A Regular Guy

*A Regular Guy*, Simpson's third novel, is another story of a daughter, her unconventional mother, and her absent father. In this case, Jane and her mother,

Mary, are long forgotten by Tom Owens, Mary's high school sweetheart and Jane's father. Owens never finished college, but he did not need to. A biotechnology whiz kid, he has built his own company (named Genesis) from a home project into an extremely lucrative concern. (Reviewers have noted a parallel with real-life whiz kids such as Bill Gates and Simpson's brother, Steve Jobs.) The novel begins as Jane, not yet a teenager, learns to drive from her wayward mother and then sets out in a rickety truck in a journey from the California mountains to the California valleys to force her father to accept her. The resulting tale is "a luminous family saga," according to Sybil S. Steinberg in *Publishers Weekly*. Steinberg added: "Echoes of the Book of Genesis resonate throughout the novel, lending it an enchanting, allegorical air without overwhelming the uneasy, acutely observed family chemistry that is its focal point."

Because of the similarity of its theme to that of Simpson's earlier novels, reviewers were quick to compare *A Regular Guy* to *Anywhere but Here* and *The Lost Father*. In the opinion of *New York Times* reviewer Michiko Kakutani, *A Regular Guy* is "a novel that lacks the emotional immediacy of her earlier books, a stilted and strangely detached novel that feels as if it had been forcibly willed into creation." This detachment affects Simpson's characterization, according to Roxana Robinson in the *Washington Post Book World*. She wrote: "The characters—who are hard to like—never take on the psychological mass necessary to command our attention and sympathy. Never clearly defined, they cannot develop relationships or change through experience." *Library Journal* contributor Adam Mazmanian saw differences between this and earlier novels, but he still found much to praise in it. "Though this beautifully written novel lacks some of the humor of Simpson's earlier work," he observed, "the fully realized characters and the well-cast mood of ambivalence make this her best novel yet."

Martha Duffy, writing in *Time*, deemed *A Regular Guy* inferior to Simpson's previous treatments of the same themes. She remarked: "*A Regular Guy* has the same theme as much of her earlier work—a child searching for a lost father—and it lacks the energy and rude gusto of *Anywhere but Here*." Laura Shapiro, though, while seeing these novels as having similar origins, drew a different conclusion about the final products. "Simpson shows no sign of being tempted to write the same novel over and over," she maintained in a *Newsweek* review. "Her books may be inspired by similar emotional preoccupations, but her imagination works strictly from

scratch. For *A Regular Guy*, she has created a voice, a perspective and a style that are entirely fresh and that give her prodigious talents a challenging new playing field." She believed that "Simpson has never written a novel so teeming, nor one so technically daring." Steinberg concluded: "It is Simpson's delicate grasp of family planning and misplanning, of legitimate versus illegitimate parenting and the machinations of creativity and selling-out that make this rich and winding story so mesmerizing."

### *Off Keck Road*

*Off Keck Road* represents in some ways a departure for Simpson. Rather than following women on long, adventurous journeys, this short novel focuses on women who have spent most of their lives in their hometown, Green Bay, Wisconsin, which is also Simpson's home town. There are three primary characters. Bea, who comes from a wealthy family, leaves Green Bay for a time to work in advertising in Chicago, then returns to take care of her invalid mother and eventually goes into the real estate business. She develops an infatuation with her boss, but is unsuccessful at making emotional connections. June, a college friend of Bea's, is from the poorer side of town, the area that gives the book its title. She, too, leaves town briefly, marries and divorces, and returns to raise her daughter; she is free-spirited but a devoted mother. Shelley, also from Keck Road, is a survivor of polio, which left her with a bad leg. She works as a nurse; when Bea's boss becomes disabled, it is Shelley who takes care of him. The book chronicles the three women's lives from the 1950s to the end of the century.

Some reviewers described *Off Keck Road* as a sensitive, reflective portrait of its protagonists; although their lives are what one might call unremarkable, Simpson avoids condescending to them. Bea, June, and Shelley "mostly stand offstage as the dramas of passion, death and birth unfold around them," related Stacey D'Erasmo in the *New York Times Book Review*. "They tend parents, have or do not have affairs, but mostly they abide, living the sorts of lives that seem almost subliminal because they are so without event. . . . In its very slenderness, the novel embodies the unwrittenness of lives such as these. They can be implied, touched on, but not contained." *New York Times* daily reviewer Kakutani wrote that "*Off Keck Road* showcases the gifts of emotional sympathy and psychological observation that Ms. Simpson used to such enormous effect in *Anywhere but Here* and *The Lost Father*," with the author examining once again "the pull between rootlessness and freedom, domesticity and independence." Kakutani continued: "If the plot of *Off Keck Road* verges on the predictable, Ms. Simpson nonetheless manages to invest it with an unusual measure of felt emotion, delineating the myriad small choices, random events and missed opportunities than can determine the contours of a life." The novel also offers, Kakutani noted, an excellent sense of place, detailing the everybody-knows-everybody quality of small-town life along with the way many small towns lost their distinctive character in the late twentieth century, with their rural outskirts taken up by new construction and their locally owned businesses replaced by chain stores and franchised restaurants. *Booklist* reviewer Donna Seaman also remarked on this aspect of the novel, saying that Simpson "pauses often to contemplate the beauty of the land as it disappears beneath the hard edges of subdivisions and malls, an interment emblematic of how love is buried deep in the hearts of her modest but strong characters."

To certain reviewers, though, *Off Keck Road*'s modest characters and their understated story added up to boredom. "The narrative hovers more than it grips," commented a *Publishers Weekly* critic, while an *Economist* contributor found "this quiet tale of missed opportunities" to be "exceptionally dull." The *Economist* reviewer also termed Simpson's writing style "cruelly inert." The *Publishers Weekly* critic had no such complaint, saying: "Simpson's signature fine writing renders subtle quirks of character gently and realistically, and she again finds fresh ways of capturing the familiar." D'Erasmo allowed that some readers might find *Off Keck Road* disappointing compared with Simpson's other books and their intense portrayals of family relationships, but advised that for the patient, there is much of value in this "delicate and open-ended" study of women who live largely outside the traditional family structure. Kakutani concluded: "The novella isn't nearly as ambitious or compelling as *Anywhere but Here*, but in laying out a five-decade-long portrait of a small town and its residents, *Off Keck Road* leaves us with a melancholy sense of time and flux and loss."

Taken together, Simpson's novels offer her unique vision of American family life and its particular effect on young women. As Devoney Looser commented in *Contemporary Novelists*, "Simpson's novels are remarkable for their unsentimental versions of contemporary womanhood. Her female narrators are strong characters but not invincible heroines; they are victimized but not merely victims." The

books appeal directly to readers, suggested Looser, because they "read much more like memoir, providing readers with intricate and painful windows into her characters' psyches."

### *My Hollywood*

Simpson spent nearly a decade working on her 2010 novel *My Hollywood*. In an article in *UCLA Today*, Simpson shared: "I wanted to give people literary pleasure and to open doors onto new kinds of relationships, new kinds of unchronicled opportunities for love and generosity." Simpson added: "I thought a lot about the question, 'Can you buy love?' We all want children raised with love. Can you get that by hiring it? It's an interesting question."

In the novel, New York composer Claire moves to Hollywood when her husband gets a job opportunity there. She hires Lola, a fifty-something Filipina nanny, to help care for their baby son William. Lola has lived a remarkable life in the United States, supporting her children through university and a family in the Philippines. She serves as the leader of a group of Filipina nannies who are looking for a better understanding from their employers. Claire, unable to appreciate Lola for what she does for her family, takes her for granted and makes reckless decisions.

*Booklist* reviewer Seaman observed that throughout the novel, "Simpson subtly but powerfully traces the persistence of sexism and prejudice . . . and the complexity and essentiality of all domestic relationships." A *Kirkus Reviews* critic noted that "Simpson trades chapters between Claire and Lola's viewpoints, but Claire never becomes Lola's equal, as a character or as a human being." In a review in *Library Journal*, Evelyn Beck "recommended" *My Hollywood* to "readers intrigued by the rich but unseen lives of the domestic class a la Gosford Park," as well as fans of the author's other novels. A contributor to *Publishers Weekly* concluded: "Funny, smart, and filled with razor sharp observations about life and parenthood," *My Hollywood* "is well worth the wait."

### ■ Biographical And Critical Sources

*BOOKS*

*Contemporary Literary Criticism*, Volume 44, Gale (Detroit, MI), 1987.

*Contemporary Novelists,* 6th edition, St. James Press (Detroit, MI), 1996.

*PERIODICALS*

*Book,* November 1, 2000, Ann Collette, review of *Off Keck Road,* p. 84.

*Booklist,* August 1, 1996, Donna Seaman, review of *A Regular Guy,* p. 1856; November 1, 1999, Donna Seaman, review of *Anywhere but Here,* p. 511; September 1, 2000, Donna Seaman, review of *Off Keck Road,* p. 8; July 1, 2010, Donna Seaman, review of *My Hollywood,* p. 8; October 1, 2010, Kaite Mediatore Stover, review of *My Hollywood,* p. 40.

*Cosmopolitan,* February 1, 1992, Louise Bernikow, review of *The Lost Father,* p. 18.

*Economist* (U.S.), September 16, 2000, "New Fiction—Slenderly," p. 94.

*Entertainment Weekly,* February 14, 1992, L.S. Klepp, review of *The Lost Father,* p. 46; February 14, 1992, review of *Anywhere but Here,* p. 50; August 6, 2010, Missy Schwartz, review of *My Hollywood,* p. 75.

*Hollins Critic,* April 1, 1987, Meghan Gehman, review of *Anywhere but Here,* p. 17.

*Kirkus Reviews,* August 1, 2010, review of *My Hollywood.*

*Library Journal,* August 1, 1996, Adam Mazmanian, review of *A Regular Guy,* p. 114; October 15, 2000, Barbara Hoffert, review of *Off Keck Road,* p. 104; August 1, 2010, Evelyn Beck, review of *My Hollywood,* p. 74; November 1, 2010, Joyce Kessel, review of *My Hollywood,* p. 37.

*London Review of Books,* July 23, 1992, Jonathan Coe, review of *The Lost Father,* p. 22.

*Los Angeles Times,* January 4, 1987, Richard Eder, review of *Anywhere but Here,* p. 3; February 9, 1992, Richard Eder, review of *The Lost Father,* p. 3.

*Maclean's,* March 16, 1992, Judith Timson, review of *The Lost Father,* p. 54.

*Nation,* April 13, 1992, Carolyn Cooke, review of *The Lost Father,* p. 494.

*Newsweek,* February 2, 1987, Michiko Kakutani, review of *Anywhere but Here,* p. 69; October 7, 1996, Laura Shapiro, review of *A Regular Guy,* p. 78.

*New Yorker,* September 13, 2010, review of *My Hollywood,* p. 72.

*New York Times,* October 15, 1996, Michiko Kakutani, review of *A Regular Guy,* p. C15; October 20, 2000, Michiko Kakutani, "Dreams Chained in Place Restrain a Pair of Lives."

*New York Times Book Review,* February 9, 1992, Jim Shepard, review of *The Lost Father,* p. 10; November 12, 2000, Stacey D'Erasmo, "Life Is What Happens to Other People"; September 9, 2001, Scott Veale, review of *Off Keck Road,* p. 32; July 28, 2010, Celia McGee, "Mona Simpson Writes for Crowds, and Avoids Them."

*People,* February 16, 1987, Campbell Geeslin, review of *Anywhere but Here,* p. 15; March 9, 1992, Lorenzo Carcaterra, review of *The Lost Father,* p. 29; December 2, 1996, Joanne Kaufman, review of *A Regular Guy,* p. 36.

*Publishers Weekly,* November 22, 1991, review of *The Lost Father,* p. 39; August 19, 1996, review of *A Regular Guy,* p. 52; September 25, 2000, review of *Off Keck Road,* p. 89; June 28, 2010, review of *My Hollywood,* p. 101.

*Time,* April 13, 1987, review of *Anywhere but Here,* p. 76; November 4, 1996, Martha Duffy, review of *A Regular Guy,* p. 95.

*UCLA Today,* August 5, 2010, Wendy Soderburg, "UCLA Author's Latest Novel."

*Village Voice,* February 3, 1987, Laurie Stone, review of *Anywhere but Here,* p. 47; October 15, 1996, p. 45.

*Washington Post Book World,* January 27, 1987, Paula Span, review of *Anywhere but Here;* October 6, 1996, Roxana Robinson, review of *A Regular Guy,* p. 4.

*ONLINE*

*Mona Simpson Home Page,* http://www.monasimpson.com (August 2, 2011).*

# Christian Smith

## 1960-

### ■ Personal

Born October 23, 1960. *Education:* Gordon College, B.A., 1983; Harvard University, M.A., 1987, Ph.D., 1990.

### ■ Addresses

*Office*—University of Notre Dame, Department of Sociology and Center for the Study of Religion and Society, 816 Flanner Hall, Notre Dame, IN 46556. *E-mail*—chris.smith@nd.edu.

### ■ Career

Gordon College, Wenham, MA, instructor, 1987-89, assistant professor of sociology, 1989-94; University of North Carolina, Chapel Hill, assistant professor, 1994-99, professor, 1994-2003, Stuart Chapin Distinguished Professor of Sociology, 2003-05, associate chair of department, 2000-05; University of Exeter, Exeter, England, Leverhulme Fellow, visiting professor, and lecturer, 2006; University of Notre Dame, Notre Dame, IN, William R. Kennan, Jr., professor of sociology and director of the Center for the Study of Religion and Society, 2006—.

### ■ Awards, Honors

Award for Excellence in Teaching and Mentoring, University of North Carolina, Chapel Hill, Department of Sociology Graduate Student Association, 1995; Outstanding Article Award, American Sociological Association, 1999, for *Social Forces* article; Excellence in Mentoring Award, University of North Carolina, Chapel Hill, Department of Sociology Graduate Student Association, 2001; Outstanding Book Award, Society for the Scientific Study of Religion, 2001, for *Divided by Faith: Evangelical Religion and the Problem of Race in America*; Distinguished Book Award, *Christianity Today*, 2005, for *Soul Searching: The Religious and Spiritual Lives of American Teenagers,* and 2010, for *Souls in Transition: the Religious and Spiritual Lives of Emerging Adults*; Gordon College Alumnus of the Year, 2007. Grants from the Pew Charitable Trusts, Lilly Endowment Inc., and John Templeton Foundation.

### ■ Writings

*The Emergence of Liberation Theology: Radical Religion and Social Movement Theory,* University of Chicago Press (Chicago, IL), 1991.

*Resisting Reagan: The U.S.-Central American Peace Movement,* University of Chicago Press (Chicago, IL), 1996.

(With Michael Emerson and others) *American Evangelicalism: Embattled and Thriving,* University of Chicago Press (Chicago, IL), 1998.

*Christian America? What Evangelicals Really Want,* University of California Press (Berkeley, CA), 2000.

(With Michael O. Emerson) *Divided by Faith: Evangelical Religion and the Problem of Race in America,* Oxford University Press (New York, NY), 2000.

(With Robert Faris) *Religion and the Life Attitudes and Self-Images of American Adolescents,* University of North Carolina, National Study of Youth and Religion (Chapel Hill, NC), 2002.

(With Robert Faris) *Religion, American Adolescent Delinquency, Risk Behaviors, and Constructive Social Activities,* University of North Carolina, National Study of Youth and Religion (Chapel Hill, NC), 2002.

*Moral, Believing Animals: Human Personhood and Culture,* Oxford University Press (New York, NY), 2003.

(With Mark Regnerus and Melissa Fritsch) *Religion in the Lives of American Adolescents: A Review of the Literature,* University of North Carolina, National Study of Youth and Religion (Chapel Hill, NC), 2003.

(With Philip Kim) *Family Religious Involvement and the Quality of Family Relationships for Early Adolescents,* University of North Carolina, National Study of Youth and Religion (Chapel Hill, NC), 2003.

(With Melinda Lundquist Denton) *Soul Searching: The Religious and Spiritual Lives of American Teenagers,* Oxford University Press (New York, NY), 2005.

(With Michael Emerson and Patricia Snell) *Passing the Plate: Why American Christians Don't Give Away More Money,* Oxford University Press (New York, NY), 2008.

*The Religious and Spiritual Lives of America's Emerging Adults: Soul-Searching Five Years Later,* Oxford University Press (New York, NY), 2009.

(With Patricia Snell) *Souls in Transition: The Religious and Spiritual Lives of Emerging Adults,* Oxford University Press (New York, NY), 2009.

*What Is a Person? Rethinking Humanity, Social Life, and the Moral Good from the Person Up,* University of Chicago Press (Chicago, IL), 2010.

*The Bible Made Impossible: Why Biblicism Is Not a Truly Evangelical Reading of Scripture,* Brazos (Grand Rapids, MI), 2011.

(With Kari Christoffersen, Hilary Davidson, and Patricia Snell Herzog) *Lost in Transition: The Dark Side of Emerging Adulthood,* Oxford University Press (New York, NY), 2011.

*EDITOR*

*Disruptive Religion: The Force of Faith in Social-Movement Activism,* Routledge (New York, NY), 1996.

(With Joshua Prokopy) *Latin American Religion in Motion,* Routledge (New York, NY), 1999.

*The Secular Revolution: Power, Interests, and Conflict in the Secularization of American Public Life,* University of California Press (Berkeley, CA), 2003.

Contributor of essays to collections, including *Latin America: A Panorama,* edited by Gladys Varona-Lacey and Julio Lopez-Arias, Peter Lang (New York, NY), 1998; *Religion and Democracy in Latin America,* edited by William Swatos, Transaction Publishers (New Brunswick, NJ), 1995; *The Culture Wars Debate,* edited by Rhys Williams, Aldine (New York, NY), 1997; *God at the Grassroots: 1996,* edited by Mark Rosell and Clyde Wilcox, Rowman and Littlefield (New York, NY), 1997; *The Encyclopedia of Politics and Religion,* edited by Robert Wuthnow, CQ Books (Washington, DC), 1998; *The Blackwell Companion to Sociology,* edited by Judith Blau, Blackwell (Cambridge, England), 2001; *Passionate Politics: Emotions and Social Movements,* edited by Jeff Goodwin, James M. Jasper, and Francesca Polletta, University of Chicago Press (Chicago, IL), 2001; *Oxford Handbook of Religious Diversity,* edited by Chad Meister, Oxford University Press (New York, NY), 2009; and *The Believing Primate: Scientific, Philosophical, and Theological Perspectives on the Evolution of Religion,* Oxford University Press (New York, NY), 2009. Contributor to journals, including *Social Forces, Review of Religious Research, Sociology of Religion, Journal for the Scientific Study of Religion, Applied Developmental Science, Sociological Forum, Social Problems,* and *Gender and Society.*

■ **Sidelights**

Christian Smith, a professor of sociology at the University of North Carolina at Chapel Hill, has developed significant expertise in the study of movements for social change and American religion. He has written or edited several texts that explore key elements of this subject across a wide political spectrum, and has concentrated in particular on religious movements.

### *The Emergence of Liberation Theology* and *Resisting Reagan*

Smith's first book, *The Emergence of Liberation Theology: Radical Religion and Social Movement Theory,* is a revision of his Ph.D. thesis that examines the development of religious movements that advocated for social justice in Latin America. Using Doug McAdam's model of social change, Smith argues that liberation theology arose because three necessary conditions were present: favorable opportunities for change existed; facilitating organizations—in this case, the Catholic Church—were strong; and an "insurgent consciousness" had emerged. Smith provides extensive historical context for his analysis, which some critics admired both for its rigor and for its unbiased approach. In *Social Science Quarterly,* James E. Beckford welcomed Smith's "dispassionate and finely focused analysis" of a subject often mired in polemical arguments, and ventured that the book would attract the interest of scholars in several fields. Marie Augusta Neal commended the book in *American Journal of Sociology* as being "carefully researched and methodologically integrated." She recommended the title for both pastoral ministers and sociologists, noting that "the former will discover how pragmatically a sociologist approaches the holy and may be disenchanted; the latter will be challenged to try to add a variable that measures faith commitment and will probably conclude that it cannot be operationalized."

Smith again deals with Latin America in *Resisting Reagan: The U.S.-Central American Peace Movement*, a book critics welcomed for bringing scholarly attention to a relatively neglected subject. Hailing the book as a "major accomplishment," *Contemporary Sociology* writer James Hannon praised Smith's thorough research and skill at integrating a wide array of sources, including interview excerpts, into a coherent and readable analysis. Hannon also noted that, though Smith honestly acknowledges his own sympathy for the peace movement, he "successfully subordinates his own perspective" and considers the movement's failures as well as its successes. Though Hannon wished that the book had provided more answers to questions that the movement raised, he concluded that "Smith has written a definitive history of the Central American peace movement and provided a foundation for activists and students of the movement to build upon."

### *American Evangelicalism* and *Soul Searching*

In *American Evangelicalism: Embattled and Thriving*, Smith presents an analysis of contemporary evangelical movements in America. As with *Resisting Reagan*, Smith uses interview material to construct a text reviewers found lucid and engaging. Arguing that "evangelicalism flourishes on difference, engagement, tension, conflict and threat," Smith shows that religions can flourish in the pluralistic conditions of modern societies. "Evangelicals will find the book helpful in understanding themselves," wrote George Westerlund in *Library Journal*, while "academicians, politicians, and others will find that it unravels confusing ideas current in the field."

In *Soul Searching: The Religious and Spiritual Lives of American Teenagers*, Smith published the results of a survey he performed for the Lilly Endowment between 2001 and 2005. Based on hundreds of telephone surveys and interviews, *Soul Searching* shows that Americans between the ages of thirteen and seventeen—contrary to trends reported by many media outlets—actually are quite traditionally religious, and the majority of them describe themselves as Christian. In the opinion of many thinkers, Smith told Tony Jones in an interview posted on the *Youth Specialties* Web site, "the U.S. is more religiously pluralistic than it actually is. Some of my college students, for example, think that 25% of Americans are Jewish, and are shocked to find out that the actual number is 2%. Some advocate-scholars who evidently wish not only to describe but also to promote religious pluralism push the religious diversity story, which isn't really accurate." "Minority religions do have a cultural importance and influence disproportionate to their numbers," Smith continued, "but when it comes to actual numbers, the vast majority of Americans, including teenagers, are either Christian—practicing or nominal—or simply not religious at all."

Smith further reported that those teens who described themselves as highly believing Christians were doing particularly well, engaging in fewer risk behaviors and having better relations with their parents. However, the majority of teens who claimed to be Christian actually had little background in their religion and instead practiced something that Smith called "Moralistic Therapeutic Deism"—a belief system in which, Smith told Jones, "God functions as a combination divine butler and cosmic therapist." Popular opinion to the contrary, Smith told Michael Cromartie in *Books & Culture*, "youth actually want to be taught something, even if they eventually reject it. They at least want to have something to reject, rather than an attitude of anything goes. Teens need an opportunity to articulate, to think and to make arguments in environments that will be challenging to their faith. And I don't think they are getting that. In general, religious traditions that expect more and demand more of their youth get more," Smith concluded in his *Books & Culture* interview. "And those that are more compromising, more accommodating, more anything-goes, end up not getting much." In *Soul Searching*, declared Karen Gabriel on the *Higher Things* Web site, Smith and his coauthor Melinda Lundquist Denton "admonish the church to 'better attend to their faith particularities,' as well as observing the trend 'that many youth, and no doubt adults, are getting the wrong messages that historical faith traditions do not matter, that all religious beliefs are basically alike, that no faith tradition possesses anything that anybody particularly needs.'" "Scholars will surely agree," a *Publishers*

*Weekly* reviewer concluded, "that this study advances the conversation about contemporary adolescent spirituality."

### Passing the Plate

Smith teamed with Michael Emerson and Patricia Snell for *Passing the Plate: Why American Christians Don't Give Away More Money*, which explores Christian philanthropy. Based largely on surveys, the book reports that, on average, American Christian organizations donate 1.5 to 2 percent of their income. The authors point out that these findings are reported by the organizations themselves, so the reality is probably less. Smith, Emerson, and Snell break down giving percentages by Christian denomination, finding that Mormons donate most, followed by Protestants, with Catholics in the bottom rank. These relatively low charitable donations are explained by Americans' consumer culture and by churches' failure to set firm donating guidelines.

According to Cassie J. Moore in the *Chronicle of Philanthropy*, "the authors write that the goal of their book is not to condemn stingy Christians, but to understand and explain this lack of generosity." Critics found that Smith, Emerson, and Snell have reached this goal, and *Sojourners* magazine reviewer J. Dana Trent remarked: "The authors trust theologians and ethicists to evaluate the moral gravity of ungenerous giving. They allow the numbers to speak for themselves—awakening us to our tight-fisted ways, the needs of others, and reminding us to bring our 'first fruits' to God, even in the midst of economic struggle." Thus, Trent, concluded: "This book is a must-read for anyone who 'passes the plate.'" Joel A. Carpenter, writing in *Church History*, was also impressed, asserting "This book is a stunner. It dispels some myths about religious giving, such as who gives more, proportionately, well-off or low-income? Answer: low-income. Does 'talking about money too much' turn off givers? No, it is more a matter of how you talk about money. . . . If you give people news about the amazing things that their generosity helped to make happen, they want to hear—and give—more." Lauding the book further in *Books & Culture*, Ron Sider called it "a careful, scholarly analysis" and "a powerful study." He added: "I am convinced that *Passing the Plate* is urgently important for the American church. Every pastor should read it and beg God for the courage to insist that his or her congregation deal directly and systematically with this topic in an ongoing way. Every seminary professor and church leader should read it and take its lessons to heart. And every informed Christian layperson should pray over this book, asking God for a biblical understanding of stewardship and the strength to act accordingly."

## ■ Biographical And Critical Sources

### PERIODICALS

*American Journal of Sociology*, January, 1993, Marie Augusta Neal, review of *The Emergence of Liberation Theology: Radical Religion and Social Movement Theory*, pp. 965-967.

*Books & Culture*, January 1, 2005, "What American Teenagers Believe: A Conversation with Christian Smith," p. 10; November 1, 2008, Ron Sider, "A Lot of Lattes; Stingy Christians in an Age of Opulence."

*Choice: Current Reviews for Academic Libraries*, March 1, 2011, A.W. Klink, review of *What Is a Person? Rethinking Humanity, Social Life, and the Moral Good from the Person Up*, p. 1302.

*Christian Education Journal*, September 22, 2010, Steve Huerd, review of *Souls in Transition: The Religious and Spiritual Lives of Emerging Adults*, p. 466.

*Christianity Today*, April 1, 2005, "Compliant but Confused: Unpacking Some Myths about Today's Teens," p. 98.

*Chronicle of Philanthropy*, January 29, 2009, Cassie J. Moore, "Explaining the Relative Ungenerosity of Christians."

*Church History*, September 1, 2009, Joel A. Carpenter, review of *Passing the Plate: Why American Christians Don't Give Away More Money*, p. 709.

*Contemporary Sociology*, September, 1997, James Hannon, review of *Resisting Reagan: The U.S.-Central American Peace Movement*, pp. 600-601.

*Library Journal*, October 1, 1998, George Westerlund, review of *American Evangelicalism: Embattled and Thriving*, p. 98.

*Publishers Weekly*, March 27, 2000, review of *Christian America? What Evangelicals Really Want*, p. 76; May 29, 2000, review of *Divided by Faith: Evangelical Religion and the Problem of Race in America*, p. 76; January 24, 2005, review of *Soul Searching: The Religious and Spiritual Lives of American Teenagers*, p. 238.

*Social Science Quarterly*, December, 1992, James E. Beckford, review of *The Emergence of Liberation Theology*, p. 954; September 15, 2008, review of *Passing the Plate*, p. 63; September 14, 2009, review of *Souls in Transition*, p. 45; June 13, 2011, review of *The Bible Made Impossible: Why Biblicism Is Not a Truly Evangelical Reading of Scripture*, p. 43.

*Sociology of Religion*, March 22, 2001, Nancy T. Ammerman, review of *Latin American Religion in Motion*, p. 145.

*Sojourners*, March 1, 2009, J. Dana Trent, "Stingy Givers," p. 44.

ONLINE

*Catholic Books Review*, http://catholicbooksreview. org/ (May 10, 2008), Kafkazli Seyyed Javad, review of *The Secular Revolution: Power, Interests, and Conflict in the Secularization of American Public Life.*

*Christian Ethics Today*, http://www.christianethics today.com/ (May 10, 2008), Darold H. Morgan, review of *Divided by Faith.*

*Christian Odyssey*, http://www.christianodyssey. com/ (May 10, 2008), review of *Divided by Faith.*

*Higher Things*, http://higherthings.org/ (May 10, 2008), Karen Gabriel, review of *Soul Searching.*

*Human Nature*, http://human-nature.com/ (May 10, 2008), Mark Daims, review of *Moral, Believing Animals: Human Personhood and Culture.*

*Orthodox Presbyterian Church Web site*, http://www. opc.org/ (May 10, 2008), James W. Scott, review of *Moral, Believing Animals.*

*University of Notre Dame Web site*, http://www.nd. edu/ (August 11, 2011), author profile.

*Youth Specialties*, http://www.youthspecialties.com/ (May 10, 2008), Tony Jones, "Youth and Religion: An Interview with Christian Smith."*

# Timothy Snyder

## 1969-

■ **Also Known As**

Timothy David Snyder

■ **Personal**

Born August 18, 1969, in Kettering, OH; son of Estel Eugene and Christine Hadley Snyder; married June 10, 2005. *Education:* Brown University, B.A., 1991; University of Oxford, D.Phil., 1995.

■ **Addresses**

*Office*—Yale University, Dept. of History, Box 208324, 60 Canner St., New Haven, CT 06520-8324. *E-mail*—timothy.snyder@yale.edu.

■ **Career**

Writer, editor, historian, administrator, and educator. Yale University, assistant professor, 2001-04, associate professor, 2004-06, professor of history, 2006—, director of graduate studies, Department of History, 2006-08. Harvard Academy for International and Area Studies, former executive secretary.

■ **Awards, Honors**

Marshall Scholarship, government of the United Kingdom, 1991-94; IREX fellowship, Instytut Historii, Polska Akademia Nauk, Warsaw, Poland, 1992-95; fellowship, Centre Nationale des Recherches Scientifiques, Paris, France, 1994-95; fellowship, Institut fur die Wissenschaften vom Menschen, Vienna, Austria, 1996, 2004-05; Academy Scholar, Center for International Affairs, 1998-2001, and fellow, Olin Institute for Strategic Studies, Harvard University, 1997; Oskar Halecki Prize, Polish Institute of Arts and Sciences, 1998, for *Nationalism, Marxism, and Modern Central Europe;* Academy Scholar, Center for International Affairs, Harvard University, 1998-2001; George Louis Beer Prize, American Historical Association, 2003, and awards from the American Historical Association, American Association for Ukrainian Studies, Przeglad Wschodni, and Marie Curie-Sklodowska University, all for *The Reconstruction of Nations: Poland, Ukraine, Lithuania, Belarus, 1569-1999;* Pro Historia Polonorum Award, 2005, for *Sketches from a Secret War;* postdoctoral fellowship, American Council of Learned Societies; named among Top Young Historians, George Mason University, *History News Network,* 2005; Institut für die Wissenschaften vom Menschen, multiple winner.

■ **Writings**

*Nationalism, Marxism, and Modern Central Europe: A Biography of Kazimierz Kelles-Krauz, 1872-1905,* Ukrainian Research Institute, Harvard University (Cambridge, MA), 1997.

(Editor, with Peter Andreas) *The Wall around the West: State Borders and Immigration Controls in North America and Europe,* Rowman & Littlefield (Lanham, MD), 2000.

*The Reconstruction of Nations: Poland, Ukraine, Lithuania, Belarus, 1569-1999,* Yale University Press (New Haven, CT), 2003.

*Sketches from a Secret War: A Polish Artist's Mission to Liberate Soviet Ukraine,* Yale University Press (New Haven, CT), 2005.

*The Red Prince: The Secret Lives of a Habsburg Archduke,* Basic Books (New York, NY), 2008.

*Bloodlands: Europe between Hitler and Stalin,* Basic Books (New York, NY), 2010.

Contributor to books, including *Economic Consequences of Soviet Disintegration,* edited by John Williamson, Institute for International Economics (Washington, DC), 1993; *Nations Abroad: Diasporas and National Identity in the Former Soviet Union,* edited by Charles King and Neil Melvin, Westview (Boulder, CO), 1998; and *Memory and Power in Postwar Europe,* edited by Jan-Werner Muller, Cambridge University Press (Cambridge, England), 2002.

Contributor to periodicals and journals, including *Past and Present, Journal of Cold War Studies, Osteuropa, Polin: Studies in Polish Jewry, Times Literary Supplement, Truthdig, Nation, Prospect, New York Review of Books, Christian Science Monitor, Boston Globe, Chicago Tribune, Tygodnik Powszechny,* and *Yad Vashem Studies.*

Speaks and writes English, French, German, Polish, and Ukranian.

## ■ Sidelights

Writer and editor Timothy Snyder is a historian, professor of history, and administrator at Yale University. At Yale, Snyder has also served as the director of graduate studies in the university's Department of History. He holds a D.Phil. from the University of Oxford, where he was a Marshall Scholar. He specializes in modern nationalism and East European politics and political history, writing widely on the subjects and teaching a variety of related graduate and undergraduate courses. In 2005, Snyder was named one of *History News Network*'s Top Young Historians.

### The Wall around the West

Snyder is the editor, with Peter Andreas, of *The Wall around the West: State Borders and Immigration Controls in North America and Europe.* In this book, the editors assembled works that explore the concept of globalization and how it is affected by borders, real and imagined, that exist in the United States and Europe. John W. Critzer, writing in the *Journal of Ethnic and Migration Studies,* commented that "one of the most important aspects of this edited collection is to show that although territorial borders and the nation-state are being reshaped they continue to play a critical role in the age of globalisation." The book concentrates on borders in North America, between the United States and Mexico, and in Europe, between the European Union and Eastern European countries. The contributors focus on these borders and how they separate economically strong countries from their less wealthy neighbors. Whereas the United States wishes to restrict its borders with Mexico, the European Union seeks to add to its borders by welcoming new member countries.

Contributor Malcolm Anderson discusses the ineffectiveness of border controls, while David Spener attempts to reconcile the desire for border control with the need for a large pool of cheap labor represented by illegal immigrants. Milada Anna Vachudova looks at the requirements placed on new European Union members and how they are expected to be guardians of the EU's expanding borders. As in the United States, tighter European border controls have not managed to stem the flow of unauthorized immigrants, notes Rey Koslowski. Snyder himself contributes an essay that explores the book's title concept of the wall around the West, a border system that allows immigrants entry for factors that enhance U.S. and European economic standing. Critzer concluded the book would be "useful for students to begin thinking about such questions [as the effects of globalization]" and he considered it "highly recommended for courses focusing on immigration, globalisation, and international relations."

### Sketches from a Secret War

*Sketches from a Secret War: A Polish Artist's Mission to Liberate Soviet Ukraine* is Snyder's biography of Polish cubist painter Henryk Jozewski. An artist and theatrical scene-maker, Jozewski also served as governor of the Polish province of Volhynia in the days before World War II. "As Jozewski saw it, if modernity, artistic or otherwise, was ever to come to Volhynia, it would have to be brought there by the new Polish state, with the full cooperation and agreement of the majority Jewish and Ukrainian populations," commented Anne Applebaum in *Spectator.*

Jozewski hoped that reforms would occur and would be powered by the ethnic tolerance he had experienced and observed in the Polish-Lithuanian Commonwealth. Outside of his career as a painter, administrator, and hopeful reformer, Jozewski played another surprising role during the inter-war years of Poland and Eastern Europe: that of a successful, wide-ranging spy. He managed to place numerous agents throughout Ukraine in an attempt to spark a Ukrainian uprising against Soviet Communism. He was an active member of the anti-Nazi underground, and later resisted the Communists as a member of the anti-Communist underground. Jozewski conducted operations under the guise of a gardener until a relative informed on him in 1953. He spent his last days painting still lifes. Despite his efforts, Jozewski was unable to bring about the reforms he hoped for: he was unable to liberate Ukraine from the Soviets; he could not prevent ethnic conflict in Volhynia; and, perhaps most shattering of all, "he was also forced to witness the destruction of his own country, first by the Nazis, then by the Communists," Applebaum stated.

### The Red Prince

In *The Red Prince: The Secret Lives of a Habsburg Archduke,* Snyder tells the story of Wilhelm von Habsburg, a Ukrainian aristocrat who continued to seek independence for Ukraine even after the dissolution of the Austrian and Russian empires after World War I. Snyder finds that the idealistic Wilhelm possessed many favorable qualities, including a facility for language, skill at sword combat, and an unshakable aristocratic bearing and sense of entitlement. The multifaceted archduke also possessed proclivities, including dressing in women's clothing and a sexual appetite for both men and women. Yet he was a dedicated Ukrainian nationalist, who lived through many dangerous events as he fought against the Nazis, resisted the Soviets, and struggled in vain to win Ukraine's independence.

In Snyder's telling, von Habsburg emerges "as a restless spirit with dreams of grandeur who was attractive, even charismatic, without being particularly admirable," remarked Jay Freeman, writing in *Booklist.* "Snyder is probably the most intelligent and sensitive historian working on East Central Europe today, and he is eminently fitted for the task of telling this tale," commented Adam Zamoyski in *Spectator.* "Not often does scholarly history soar and entrap like a fine historical novel, but here it does," observed reviewer Robert Legvold in a *Foreign Affairs* assessment. Even though the "truth of Wilhelm's life seems stranger than fiction, Snyder does an excellent job of documenting this story," commented *Library Journal* contributor Antonio S. Thompson. Zamoyski concluded that *The Red Prince* is "a wonderful book, a gripping read full of surprises and memorable vignettes, which fills a gap in our knowledge and provides an accessible introduction to a badly neglected area of European history."

### Bloodlands

In 2010 Snyder published *Bloodlands: Europe between Hitler and Stalin.* Snyder looks at the period from 1933 until 1945 where the consolidation of power by Hitler and Stalin resulted in the deaths of fourteen million people. Focusing on the lands between Germany and Russia, the book shows the systematic murdering of millions, not only through concentration and work camps, but largely through intentional starvation.

*Booklist* reviewer Gilbert Taylor opined that the book's "solid and judicious scholarship . . . would engage those exposed to the period's chronology and major interpretive issues." *Tablet* contributor Adam Kirsch mentioned that "the relationship between Jews and Communism is probably the most explosive of all the subjects Snyder addresses, and here he benefits most from the strengths he shows throughout the bookdeep learning, wide compassion, and clear, careful moral judgment." Kirsch concluded that "anyone who wants to fully comprehend the Holocaust at least, as far as it can be comprehended should read *Bloodlands,* which shows how much evil had to be done in order to make the ultimate evil possible." A *Kirkus Reviews* critic called *Bloodlands* "a significant work of staggering figures and scholarship." Reviewing the book in *Maclean's,* Michael Petrou found the account to be "masterful." *Policy Review* contributor James Kirchick stated: "Surveying a time and subject that has been studied, dramatized, and argued about perhaps more thoroughly than any other in history, *Bloodlands* is an incredibly original work. It seeks to redirect our understanding of the Holocaust as primarily an eastern phenomenon, and one which took place among a spate of mass killing policies." Petrou concluded that "with this magisterial book, he has rendered the Holocaust, and the horrors that preceded and accompanied it, their rightful place."

## ■ Biographical And Critical Sources

*PERIODICALS*

*American Historical Review,* February 1, 2004, John-Paul Himka, review of *The Reconstruction of Nations: Poland, Ukraine, Lithuania, Belarus, 1569-1999,* p. 280; December 1, 2006, Kate Brown, review of *Sketches from a Secret War: A Polish Artist's Mission to Liberate Soviet Ukraine,* p. 1629.

*Atlantic,* July 1, 2008, review of *The Red Prince: The Secret Lives of a Habsburg Archduke,* p. 141.

*Austrian History Yearbook,* 2010, Steven Beller, review of *The Red Prince,* p. 261.

*Booklist,* May 15, 2008, Jay Freeman, review of *The Red Prince,* p. 19; September 15, 2010, Gilbert Taylor, review of *Bloodlands: Europe between Hitler and Stalin,* p. 18.

*Choice*, September 1, 2003, P.W. Knoll, review of *The Reconstruction of Nations*, p. 213.

*Economist*, June 3, 2011, "Hitler and Stalin."

*English Historical Review*, June 1, 1999, Raymond Pearson, review of *Nationalism, Marxism, and Modern Central Europe: A Biography of Kazimierz Kelles-Krauz, 1872-1905*, p. 1762.

*Ethics & International Affairs*, December 22, 2010, review of *Bloodlands*, p. 437.

*Foreign Affairs*, May 1, 2003, review of *The Reconstruction of Nations*, p. 160; November 1, 2008, Robert Legvold, review of *The Red Prince*, p. 172.

*Historian*, September 22, 2010, Paula Sitter Fichtner, review of *The Red Prince*, p. 708.

*History Today*, August 1, 2008, Graham Grandall Norton, review of *The Red Prince*, p. 62.

*International Affairs*, April 1, 2002, Ulla Holm, review of *The Wall around the West: State Borders and Immigration Controls in North America and Europe*, p. 383.

*International History Review*, June 1, 2006, David Goldfrank, review of *The Reconstruction of Nations*, p. 385.

*Journal of Ethnic and Migration Studies*, January 1, 2003, John W. Critzer, review of *The Wall around the West*, p. 176.

*Journal of Modern History*, June 1, 2008, Katherine R. Jolluck, review of *Sketches from a Secret War*, p. 459.

*Journal of the West*, December 22, 2005, Donald C. Cutter, review of *The Wall around the West*, p. 90.

*Kirkus Reviews*, April 15, 2008, review of *The Red Prince*; August 1, 2010, review of *Bloodlands*.

*Kritika*, March 22, 2006, Mark Mazower, review of *Sketches from a Secret War*, p. 379.

*Library Journal*, June 15, 2008, Antonio S. Thompson, review of *The Red Prince*, p. 75.

*London Review of Books*, August 14, 2008, Dan Jacobson, review of *The Red Prince*, p. 28.

*Maclean's*, January 31, 2011, Michael Petrou, review of *Bloodlands*, p. 61.

*Policy Review*, June 1, 2011, James Kirchick, review of *Bloodlands*.

*Publishers Weekly*, April 14, 2008, review of *The Red Prince*, p. 47.

*Reference & Research Book News*, February 1, 2006, review of *Sketches from a Secret War*.

*Sarmatian Review*, April 1, 2006, review of *The Reconstruction of Nations*, p. 1208.

*Slavic Review*, March 22, 2005, Brian Porter, review of *The Reconstruction of Nations*, p. 166; March 22, 2007, review of *Sketches from a Secret War*, p. 123.

*Spectator*, July 15, 2006, Anne Applebaum, review of *Sketches from a Secret War*; June 21, 2008, Adam Zamoyski, review of *The Red Prince*, p. 38.

*Tablet*, November 30, 2010, Adam Kirsch, review of *Bloodlands*.

*Times Higher Education*, August 14, 2008, Dan Jacobson, review of *The Red Prince*, p. 45.

*Times Literary Supplement*, December 19, 2003, Charles King, review of *The Reconstruction of Nations*, p. 34; December 22, 2006, Omer Bartov, review of *Sketches from a Secret War*, p. 30.

ONLINE

*History News Network*, http://hnn.us/ (February 10, 2009), "Top Young Historians."

*Nationmaster.com*, http://www.nationmaster.com/ (February 10, 2009), author profile.

*Yale University, Department of History Web site*, http://www.yale.edu/history/ (August 2, 2011), curriculum vitae of Timothy Snyder.

# Danielle Steel

## 1947-

■ **Also Known As**

Danielle Schuelein-Steel
Danielle Fernande Schuelein-Steel
Danielle Fernande Steel

■ **Personal**

Born August 14, 1947, in New York, NY; daughter of John and Norma Schuelein-Steel; married Claude-Eric Lazard (a banker), 1965 (marriage ended); married Danny Zugelder (marriage ended); married William Toth (marriage ended); married John Traina (a vintner), 1981 (marriage ended); married Thomas Perkins, 1998 (marriage ended, 2002); children: Nick (deceased); (first marriage) Beatrix; (third marriage) two stepsons, Samantha, Victoria, Vanessa, Maxx, Zara. *Education:* Graduated from Lycée Français de New York, 1963; attended Parsons School of Design, 1963, and New York University, 1963-67. *Religion:* Catholic.

■ **Addresses**

*Home*—Paris, France; San Francisco, CA. *Agent*—Janklow & Nesbit Associates, Inc., 445 Park Ave., New York, NY 10022.

■ **Career**

Writer and novelist. Supergirls, Ltd. (public relations firm), New York, NY, vice president of public relations, 1968-71; Grey Advertising, San Francisco, CA, copywriter, 1973-74. Has worked at other positions in public relations and advertising; and taught creative writing, 1975-76. American Library Associa-tion, national chair; Nick Traina Foundation to benefit mental health, founder; Steel Gallery of Contemporary Art, founder, 2003-07. National Committee for the Prevention of Child Abuse, spokesperson; American Human Association, national spokesperson.

■ **Awards, Honors**

Outstanding Achievement Award in Mental Health, California Psychiatric Association; Distinguished Service Award, American Psychiatric Association; Service to Youth Award for improving the lives of mentally ill adolescents and children, University of San Francisco Catholic Youth Organization and St. Mary's Medical Center, 1999; Chevalier of the Distinguished Order of Arts and Letters, Government of France, 2002; Outstanding Achievement Award for work with adolescents, Larkin Street Youth Services, 2003; inducted into the California Hall of Fame, 2009; Distinguished Service in Mental Health Award, New York Presbyterian Hospital, Columbia University Medical School, and Cornell Medical College, 2009.

■ **Writings**

*NOVELS*

*Going Home*, Pocket Books (New York, NY), 1973.
*Passion's Promise*, Dell (New York, NY), 1977.
*The Promise* (based on a screenplay by Garry Michael White), Dell (New York, NY), 1978.
*Now and Forever*, Dell (New York, NY), 1978.
*Season of Passion*, Dell (New York, NY), 1979.
*Summer's End*, Dell (New York, NY), 1979.
*The Ring*, Delacorte (New York, NY), 1980.

*Loving*, Dell (New York, NY), 1980.

*Remembrance*, Delacorte (New York, NY), 1981.

*Palomino*, Dell (New York, NY), 1981.

*To Love Again*, Dell (New York, NY), 1981.

*Crossings*, Delacorte (New York, NY), 1982.

*Once in a Lifetime*, Dell (New York, NY), 1982.

*A Perfect Stranger*, Dell (New York, NY), 1982.

*Changes*, Delacorte (New York, NY), 1983.

*Thurston House*, Dell (New York, NY), 1983.

*Full Circle*, Delacorte (New York, NY), 1984.

*Secrets*, Delacorte (New York, NY), 1985.

*Family Album*, Delacorte (New York, NY), 1985.

*Wanderlust*, Delacorte (New York, NY), 1986.

*Fine Things*, Delacorte (New York, NY), 1987, reprinted, Dell (New York, NY), 2007.

*Kaleidoscope*, Delacorte (New York, NY), 1987, reprinted, Dell (New York, NY), 2007.

*Zoya*, Delacorte (New York, NY), 1988.

*Star*, Delacorte (New York, NY), 1989.

*Daddy*, Delacorte (New York, NY), 1989.

*Message from 'Nam*, Delacorte (New York, NY), 1990.

*Heartbeat*, Delacorte (New York, NY), 1991, reprinted, Dell (New York, NY), 2007.

*No Greater Love*, Delacorte (New York, NY), 1991.

*Mixed Blessings*, Delacorte (New York, NY), 1992.

*Jewels*, Delacorte (New York, NY), 1992, reprinted, Dell (New York, NY), 2007.

*Vanished*, Delacorte (New York, NY), 1993.

*The Gift*, Delacorte (New York, NY), 1994, Spanish-language version with Maria Jose Rodellar published as *El Regalo*, 1994.

*Accident*, Delacorte (New York, NY), 1994.

*Wings*, Delacorte (New York, NY), 1994.

*Five Days in Paris*, Delacorte (New York, NY), 1995.

*Lightning*, Delacorte (New York, NY), 1995.

*Malice*, Delacorte (New York, NY), 1996.

*Silent Honor*, Delacorte (New York, NY), 1996.

*The Ranch*, Delacorte (New York, NY), 1997.

*Special Delivery*, Delacorte (New York, NY), 1997.

*The Ghost*, Delacorte (New York, NY), 1997.

*The Long Road Home*, Delacorte (New York, NY), 1998.

*The Klone and I: A High-Tech Love Story*, Delacorte (New York, NY), 1998.

*Mirror Image*, Delacorte (New York, NY), 1998.

*Now and Forever*, Delacorte (New York, NY), 1998.

*Bittersweet*, Delacorte (New York, NY), 1999.

*Granny Dan*, Delacorte (New York, NY), 1999.

*Irresistible Forces*, Delacorte (New York, NY), 1999.

*The House on Hope Street*, Delacorte (New York, NY), 2000.

*The Wedding*, Delacorte (New York, NY), 2000.

*Journey*, Delacorte (New York, NY), 2000.

*Leap of Faith*, Delacorte (New York, NY), 2001.

*Lone Eagle*, Delacorte (New York, NY), 2001.

*The Kiss*, Delacorte (New York, NY), 2001.

*The Cottage*, Dell (New York, NY), 2002.

*Answered Prayers*, Delacorte (New York, NY), 2002.

*Sunset in St. Tropez*, Delacorte (New York, NY), 2002.

*Dating Game*, Delacorte (New York, NY), 2003.

*Johnny Angel*, Delacorte (New York, NY), 2003.

*Safe Harbour*, Delacorte (New York, NY), 2003.

*Echoes*, Delacorte (New York, NY), 2004.

*Second Chance*, Delacorte (New York, NY), 2004.

*Miracle*, Delacorte (New York, NY), 2004.

*Ransom*, Dell (New York, NY), 2004.

*Impossible*, Delacorte (New York, NY), 2005.

*Toxic Bachelors*, Delacorte (New York, NY), 2005.

*The House*, Dell (New York, NY), 2006.

*Coming Out*, Dell (New York, NY), 2006.

*H.R.H.*, Delacorte (New York, NY), 2006.

*First Sight*, Delacorte (New York, NY), 2006.

*Sisters*, Delacorte (New York, NY), 2007.

*Bungalow 2*, Delacorte (New York, NY), 2007.

*Amazing Grace*, Delacorte (New York, NY), 2007.

*Honor Thyself*, Delacorte Press (New York, NY), 2008.

*Rogue*, Delacorte Press (New York, NY), 2008.

*A Good Woman*, Delacorte Press (New York, NY), 2008.

*Matters of the Heart*, Delacorte Press (New York, NY), 2009.

*One Day at a Time*, Delacorte Press (New York, NY), 2009.

*Southern Lights*, Delacorte Press (New York, NY), 2009.

*Family Ties*, Delacorte Press (New York, NY), 2010.

*Big Girl*, Delacorte Press (New York, NY), 2010.

*Legacy*, Delacorte Press (New York, NY), 2010.

*44 Charles Street*, Delacorte Press (New York, NY), 2011.

*Happy Birthday*, Delacorte Press (New York, NY), 2011.

*Hotel Vendome*, Delacorte Press (New York, NY), 2011.

*Betrayal*, Delacorte Press (New York, NY), 2012.

*The Sins of the Mother*, Delacorte Press (New York, NY), 2012.

*"MAX AND MARTHA" SERIES: FOR CHILDREN*

*Martha's Best Friend*, Delacorte (New York, NY), 1989.

*Martha's New Daddy*, Delacorte (New York, NY), 1989.

*Martha's New School*, Delacorte (New York, NY), 1989.

*Max and the Baby-sitter*, Delacorte (New York, NY), 1989.

*Max's Daddy Goes to the Hospital,* Delacorte (New York, NY), 1989.

*Max's New Baby,* Delacorte (New York, NY), 1989.

*Martha's New Puppy,* Delacorte (New York, NY), 1990.

*Max Runs Away,* Delacorte (New York, NY), 1990.

*Max and Grandma and Grandpa Winky,* Delacorte (New York, NY), 1991.

*Martha and Hilary and the Stranger,* Delacorte (New York, NY), 1991.

### "FREDDIE" SERIES: FOR CHILDREN

*Freddie's Trip,* Dell (New York, NY), 1992.

*Freddie's First Night Away,* Dell (New York, NY), 1992.

*Freddie's Accident,* Dell (New York, NY), 1992.

*Freddie and the Doctor,* Dell (New York, NY), 1992.

### OTHER

*Love Poems: Danielle Steel* (poetry), Dell (New York, NY), 1981, abridged edition, Delacorte (New York, NY), 1984.

(Coauthor) *Having a Baby* (nonfiction), Dell (New York, NY), 1984.

*Amando,* Lectorum Publications, 1985.

*His Bright Light: The Story of Nick Traina* (biography/memoir), Delacorte (New York, NY), 1998.

*The Happiest Hippo in the World* (children's book), illustrated by Margaret Spengler, HarperCollins (New York, NY), 2009.

*A Gift of Hope,* Delacorte Press (New York, NY), 2012.

Author maintains a blog at http://daniellesteel.net. Contributor to *The Fabergé Case: From the Private Collection of Traina,* by John Traina. Contributor of articles and poetry to numerous periodicals, including *Good Housekeeping, McCall's, Ladies' Home Journal,* and *Cosmopolitan.*

Author's works have been translated into twenty-eight languages.

## ■ Adaptations

Numerous works have been adapted for film or television: *Now and Forever,* adapted into a movie and released by Inter Planetary Pictures, 1983; *Crossings,* made into an ABC-TV miniseries, 1986; *Kaleidoscope* and *Fine Things,* made into NBC television movies, 1990; *Changes, Daddy,* and *Palomino,* aired by NBC, 1991; *Jewels,* adapted as a four-hour miniseries, 1992; *Secrets,* 1992; *Heartbeat, Star,* and *Message from 'Nam,* 1993; *Once in a Lifetime, A Perfect Stranger,* and *Family Album,* 1994; *Mixed Blessings,* 1995; the miniseries *Danielle Steel's "Zoya,"* 1996; *No Greater Love, The Ring, Full Circle,* and *Remembrance,* 1996; and *Safe Harbour,* 2007. Several of Steel's other novels, including *Wanderlust* and *Thurston House,* have also been optioned for television films and miniseries.

Audio adaptations include *The Ranch,* Bantam Books Audio, 1997; *Echoes, Five Days in Paris, The Ranch, Second Chance,* and *The Gift,* all Random House Audio, 2004; *The Ghost, The Long Road Home, Malice,* and *Silent Honor,* all Random House Audio, 2005.

## ■ Sidelights

Having produced a score of best-selling novels, Danielle Steel has been nothing less than a publishing phenomenon. Since the publication of her first hardcover in 1980, Steel has consistently hit both hardback and paperback best-seller lists; there are reportedly over 590 million of her books in print in twenty-eight languages in forty-seven countries. Her popularity has also spilled over into television, where several film versions of her books have been produced and garnered good ratings.

### Novels Published from 1980 to 1989

Steel's fiction is peopled by women in powerful or glamorous positions; often they are forced to choose the priorities in their lives. Thus, in *Changes* a New York anchorwoman who weds a Beverly Hills surgeon must decide whether her career means more to her than her long-distance marriage does. *Jewels* tells of the struggles of an American-born noblewoman, the Duchess of Whitfield, to find peace and raise her children in pre-World War II Europe. And while reviewers seldom express admiration for the style of romantic novelists in general—*Chicago Tribune Book World* contributor L.J. Davis claimed that *Changes* is written in "the sort of basilisk prose that makes it impossible to tear your eyes from the page even as your brain is slowly [turning] to stone"—some reviewers, such as a *Detroit News* writer, found that the author's "flair for spinning colorful and textured plots out of raw material . . . is fun reading. The topic [of *Changes*] is timely and socially relevant." Toronto *Globe & Mail* contributor Peggy Hill similarly concluded about 1988's *Zoya:* "Steel has the ability to give such formula writing enough strength to not collapse into an exhausted state of cliche. *Zoya* is a fine example of that achievement."

## Novels Published from 1990 to 1999

Steel sometimes confronts serious issues in her books. *Mixed Blessings* looks at issues of infertility in a work that a *Rapport* reviewer called "not only well written but extremely well researched." "On the whole," the reviewer concluded, "*Mixed Blessings* is definitely one of Steel's all-time best books." *Vanished* confronts the problem of kidnapped children in a story "set mainly in 1930's Manhattan," explained a *Kirkus Reviews* contributor. "The questions Steel raises about the tug-of-wars between guilt and responsibility . . . are anything but simple," stated Stuart Whitwell in *Booklist*. "The author of *Mixed Blessings* keeps her secrets well," stated a *Publishers Weekly* reviewer, "and . . . presents a strong portrait of a tormented young woman moving toward stability."

In *Accident*, Steel offers a story about the stresses placed on a family after a serious car accident puts a couple's teenaged daughter in the hospital from a brain injury. Romance reenters protagonist Page Clark's life when she falls for the Norwegian divorced father of her daughter's friend—this after having learned that her husband has been having an affair with another woman. "The ending is predictable but pleasant," declared a *Publishers Weekly* contributor, "bound to delight Steel's fans."

*Malice* is the story of Grace Adams's attempts to deal with her self-defense murder of her abusive father, while *The Gift* tells how a 1950s family slowly comes to accept the death of their youngest daughter and welcomes an unmarried expectant mother into their fold. "The narrative," stated a critic in a *Publishers Weekly* review of *The Gift*, has "well-meaning characters, uplifting sentiments and a few moments that could make a stone weep." A *Rapport* reviewer asserted that the most significant part of the story is "the affirmation of the grand design of tragedy and its transcendent message of purpose."

In 1998 Steel produced *The Klone and I: A High-Tech Love Story*. "While sticking to the typical Steel plot . . . this time around, she throws a bit of humor and weird sexual fantasy into the mix," commented Kathleen Hughes in *Booklist*. The story revolves around Stephanie, who, having been left by her husband, meets a new man, Peter, on a trip to Paris. Stephanie soon learns that Peter has cloned himself, and Stephanie must decide between the two of them. Critics were largely positive in their assessment of *The Klone and I*. "Give Steel points for turning from her usual tearjerkers . . . and trying her hand at a playful romantic comedy with a twist," wrote a contributor to *Kirkus Reviews*. A *Publishers Weekly* critic argued that although "the SF element

is minimal (approximately one part Ray Bradbury to thirty-five parts Steel), Steel's speculative whimsy spices her romantic concoction to produce a light but charming read."

## Novels Published from 2000 to 2009

In 2000, the prolific Steel published three new novels, *The House on Hope Street*, *The Wedding*, and *Journey*. Critics generally felt these novels gave Steel's fans exactly what they were looking for. In a *Booklist* review of *The Wedding*, for example, Patty Engelmann wrote: "All the key elements are here: a glamorous Hollywood setting along with the beautiful people and all their insecurities." Engelmann called the work "a good old-fashioned love story," claiming Steel is in "peak form." Engelmann felt similarly about *The House on Hope Street*: "Standard Steel fare and an excellent beach book, this will definitely please her readers." *Journey* received a similar reaction from critics. "Steel has her formula down pat, and she executes her story with her usual smooth pacing," concluded a critic in *Publishers Weekly*.

In *Second Chance*, Steel features a high-roller fashion editor who falls for a conservative businessman. Hughes remarked in *Booklist*: "Steel's fans will enjoy the detailed descriptions of privileged lifestyles and the ultimate happy resolution." A *Publishers Weekly* reviewer noted that although some readers will dislike the fact that the heroine gives up her career, "others will enjoy the usual Steel frills: plenty of gorgeous outfits, fine dining and exquisite real estate."

*Ransom*, like *Second Chance*, was released in 2004, amidst promises that it would be different from most of Steel's prior fiction. The story involves a kidnapping, and its characters include an ex-drug dealer, a widow, a shady businessman, and a police officer. In *Brandweek*, Ginger Danto suggested that the edgier flavor of the novel was a sign of the times. Danto wrote: "*Ransom* deals with crime, and apparently more violence than either writer or devoted reader are accustomed. As such, it is a deft reflection of the times, as movies and TV shore up more violence in the name of entertainment than ever before, perhaps to remain relevant alongside searing coverage of current events." A *Publishers Weekly* reviewer found the book disappointing: "The novel begins slowly . . . and never picks up speed, with Steel narrating as if from a distance, glossing over critical scenes and skimping on dialogue." Engelmann, writing again in *Booklist*, reached a similar conclusion: "This lackluster suspense novel and its plastic characters will have automatic appeal for Steel fans, but other readers may find it wanting."

Three hard-partying, serial-dating bachelors find their confirmed singles lifestyle endangered by love in *Toxic Bachelors*. Wealthy philanthropist Charlie Harrington, attorney Adam Weiss, and artist Gray Hawk are a trio of best friends, all in their forties, who have dedicated themselves to living lives free of romantic commitment. Instead, they party hard on Harrington's yacht and engage in a stream of never-ending serial dating with gorgeous but superficial women. All three bear the painful scars of a well-concealed past relationship that launched them on their freewheeling path. However, each man in turn finds his attitude changing when falling in love with a woman that defies their usual dating type and style: Gray with Sylvia, an art gallery owner, Charlie with Carole, a social worker, and Adam with Maggie, a waitress. A *Kirkus Reviews* critic named the novel a "by-the-numbers romance, with pop psychology overtones." The book displays one of the "happy endings that will keep her fans reading and waiting for more," commented *Booklist* contributor Hughes.

Veronica and Virginia, the twin-sister protagonists of *Coming Out,* are eighteen years old and decidedly different in attitude and temperament. Virginia is crazy over boys and shopping and being a girl, while Veronica is much more serious and politically and socially aware. When the two young women receive an invitation to a debutante ball, their mother, Olympia, who was a debutante herself, encourages them to attend. Virginia enthusiastically supports the idea, while Veronica finds the whole concept distasteful, elitist, and anti-Semitic, and refuses to participate. The situation worsens when their status-conscious father demands they both attend and threatens to cut off both girls' college fund if either refuses to go to the ball. As Veronica and Virginia spar with each other, older brother Charlie, a college senior, struggles with his own emerging identity as a gay man. A *Kirkus Reviews* critic called the book "a slight confection that spares no heartwarming family cliche, but one that acknowledges the unique challenges of today's mixed families."

Tanya Harris is a dedicated mother, loving wife, and up-and-coming writer in *Bungalow 2.* Her career as an author of stories and soap-opera scripts is flourishing, and her family life and marriage to husband, Peter, remain happy and stable. Tanya faces a difficult decision, however, when her agent presents her with an enticing offer: movie producer Douglas Wayne wants her and her alone to work on a new film screenplay, but it will require moving to Los Angeles for almost a year. Tanya is hesitant to leave her husband and children for an extended time, fearing repercussions as her daughters enter their senior year of high school. However, Peter realizes it's a once-in-a-lifetime opportunity and

encourages her to accept the offer. Eventually, she agrees to go, and finds the process of movie making both repulsive and deeply fascinating at the same time. She resists romantic overtures from Wayne, remaining faithful to her husband, but is devastated when Peter asks her for a divorce. Soon, Tanya finds herself single and adrift in Hollywood, where fantasies have a tendency to become unexpected reality. A *Kirkus Reviews* contributor called the book a "wholesome Cinderella story for the over-forty set."

Steel considers the effects of a natural disaster on both landscape and lives in *Amazing Grace.* When a powerful earthquake strikes Los Angeles, three women abruptly find their personal worlds shattered in the aftermath. The quake comes during a charity dinner organized by Sarah Sloane, a rich socialite. Soon after, Sarah discovers that her husband, Seth, a hedge-fund manager, is involved in illegal financial activity and cannot conceal his involvement because of the power outage caused by the quake. Melanie Free, a popular nineteen-year-old singer performing at the dinner, sheds her pop-star image and immediately dives into helping people, in the process revealing that she'd rather be a nurse than a performer. Both Sarah and Melanie are supported by Sister Maggie Kent, a nun who organizes and runs the camp for those displaced by the earthquake. Maggie finds herself in turmoil as she realizes she's falling in love with a photographer covering the aftermath of the disaster. "Typical Steel fare, this is a fast, uncomplicated read," commented *Booklist* reviewer Hughes. "Steel delivers a sparkly story with an uplifting spiritual twist," observed a *Publishers Weekly* reviewer.

Carole Barber, the fifty-year-old protagonist of *Honor Thyself,* is an award-winning actor who puts her career on hold after the death of her second husband. Reflecting on her past, she writes a semi-autobiographical novel but still struggles to make sense of where she's been and what she wants to accomplish. Hoping to recapture some of the happiness and excitement of her earlier days, she travels to Paris. There, however, she is severely injured in a terrorist bomb attack and lies brain-damaged and comatose for weeks. When she regains consciousness, she cannot remember any aspect of her life before her injury. Her adult children, ex-husband, and assistant try to help her recover her identity, with varied success. It is only when she encounters Matthieu, a lover from fifteen years prior, that she finds a renewed interest in life and the courage to embrace a renewed love and revitalized identity. "Faithful readers will be catapulted by Steel's staccato pacing and straightforward prose to a predictable yet satisfying conclusion," remarked Carol Haggas, writing in *Booklist.* A *Publishers Weekly* critic concluded that Steel "delivers a sympathetic heroine and a scene or two that makes the heartstrings quiver."

With *Rogue,* Steel "doctors up a familiar formula with fresh results," according to a *Publishers Weekly* reviewer. Maxine Williams is a forty-two-year-old psychologist specializing in childhood trauma and teen suicide. She is the single mother of three, having divorced her successful but immature dot-com husband Blake five years earlier. They are still friends, but he seems content enough to travel widely and bed as many young women as he can. Maxine finally finds another man who fits her model for a husband. Charles West is a doctor who seems serious and steady. Blake, in the face of a traumatic incident, however, suddenly takes another look at his life, and now wants to reconcile with Maxine, who now must make a hard decision. The *Publishers Weekly* reviewer felt that Steel, while never probing too deeply into her characters' inner lives, still "keeps the pages turning and offers a satisfying twist." *Fresh Fiction* Web site contributor Sandi Shilhanek termed *Rogue* a "story that gives readers character we love to hate, and that we truly love, and perhaps even envy just a bit." Likewise, *Genre Go Round Reviews* Web site reviewer Harriet Klausner found *Rogue* "an entertaining romantic triangle with a terrific final twist."

Steel delves into history for her novel *A Good Woman.* Annabelle Worthington loses her father and brother when they go down on the Titanic in 1912. Her mother survives but is badly shaken by the tragedy. Annabelle remained home because of the flu; now, to occupy herself she becomes a medical volunteer at Ellis Island where she meets much older Josiah Millbank, falls in love and gets married. However, after a couple of years of unconsummated marriage, Millbank admits that he has syphilis, and that he wants to leave her for his male lover. Annabelle refuses to give Millbank a divorce, so he puts it about that she is an adulterer, and society makes her the villain. Again she escapes into work, this time traveling to France where she works at a hospital during the fighting in World War I. And once more Annabelle finds a new and surprising turn in her life. Reviewing *A Good Woman* in the *Europe Intelligence Wire,* Sue McNab noted that Steel "takes us on another unforgettable journey and introduces us to a woman with unbreakable spirit." Similarly, *Booklist* reviewer Shelley Mosley felt Steel "has combined triumph and tragedy to create the story of a woman who . . . manages to survive on her own terms." A *Kirkus Reviews* contributor was less enthusiastic about the novel, commenting: "After a slow-moving start, the action accelerates during the war sections, but Steel's tin ear and simplistic prose, even more than the predictable

plot, make for a leaden tale." Higher praise came from a *Publishers Weekly* contributor who concluded: "Steel's fans will eat this up—Annabelle is one of the better protagonists Steel's conjured recently."

In *Matters of the Heart* Steel tells the story of photographer Hope Dunne, who is hired by award-winning author Finn O'Neill to take his photo for his next book. Traveling to London for the shoot, Hope is seduced by the charming Finn, who sweeps her off to his family home in Ireland. There Hope discovers that Finn is not quite right. He is in fact a sociopathic liar who has become obsessed with her. *Booklist* contributor Mosley felt that "Steel's fans will be delighted by this story of a woman seduced by a man who is too good to be true." A *Femail. com.au* contributor also had a positive assessment of *Matters of the Heart,* calling it "an unforgettable tale of danger and obsessive love."

*One Day at a Time* features wealthy young Coco Barrington, who gives up her fancy life in Los Angeles, drops out of law school, and moves to Northern California. There she lives a bohemian life style, finding romance with a young man who subsequently dies while hang gliding. In bereavement and house-sitting for her sister, Coco then meets British actor Leslie Baxter, a man on the run from a former lover with little control over her emotions. Coco and Leslie hit it off, face some initial difficulties, but then solidify their love, even as Coco begins to renew her relationship with her domineering mother. "Fairly brief and lighthearted; nonetheless, Steel's fans will enjoy," wrote *Booklist* contributor Hughes. *Associated Content* Web site reviewer Betty Alexander had similar praise for *One Day at a Time,* noting: "This latest novel from Danielle Steel has us mesmerized from beginning to end, as usual." And *Genre Go Round Reviews* contributor Klausner termed the novel "an engaging contemporary fiction tale."

## Novels Published in 2010 and Beyond

The plot in the 2010 novel *Family Ties* revolves around Annie Ferguson, an up-and-coming architect who is grieving for her sister and brother-in-law. Annie's loved ones die in a plane crash, leaving her to care for their three young children. Annie sacrifices dating in order to raise them while furthering her career. The children grow into successful adults, but Annie struggles to let them go. She distracts herself by reviving her romantic life, and she begins seeing a television news anchor. While the story is uplifting, critics were ambivalent, and a *Kirkus Reviews* contributor stated that it features "a listless narrative not helped by Steel's plodding prose." Despite this, the contributor acknowledged that Steel's "legion of fans aren't in it for the surprise." A *Publishers Weekly* reviewer was somewhat more evenhanded, remarking that Steel is "not known as a prose stylist, although there's a glimmer of a good plot." Seconding this neutral opinion in her *Xpress Reviews* article, Samantha J. Gust found that reading *Family Ties* is "not an unpleasant way to spend a few hours, thanks to the various characters and story lines." Engelmann, writing once more in *Booklist,* was far more impressed, announcing that the novel contains "all the trademark elements of Steel's novels . . . making her latest another sure hit with her loyal fans."

Additional novels that Steel released in 2010 are *Big Girl* and *Legacy.* In the latter, Brigitte Nicholson has just broken up with her boyfriend, an archaeologist. Less than forty-eight hours later she loses her job working for a university admissions office. Brigitte distracts herself from her woes by helping her mother with some family research. As she delves into her ancestry, Brigitte learns that a Dakota Sioux was buried in Brittany beside a long-lost relative. The Sioux was buried as Marquise de Margerac, but was once named Wachiwi. As Brigitte attempts to find out more about Wachiwi, she travels from Salt Lake City, Utah, to Sioux Falls, South Dakota, and then on to Paris, following in Wachiwi's footsteps. In Paris, she encounters a literature professor at the Sorbonne named Marc Henri. Brigitte and Marc inevitably fall for one another, and the narrative cuts back and forth between their love story and the progression of Wachiwi's adventures.

Like *Family Ties, Legacy* received mixed reviews. For instance, a *Kirkus Reviews* critic complained that "the two women's stories are compelling—if only they weren't weighted down by cliches and artless exposition." On the other hand, a contributor to the *Night Owl Reviews* Web site felt that the novel is "a good quick read, almost all the characters were positive while the rest of the characters' negativity was due to societal belief systems." Mosley, writing again in *Booklist,* was even more laudatory, finding Steel's work to be an "engrossing, exciting chronicle." Mosley went on to note that *Legacy* is "a novel that is sure to be a hit with a broad array of readers." Proffering further praise in *Publishers Weekly,* a critic called the book an "inspiring story" that portrays "a doubly absorbing romantic adventure."

In her next book, *44 Charles Street,* Steel presents another woman who has recently been dumped. Francesca Thayer, an art dealer based out of Manhat-

tan, is left financially destitute when her boyfriend (who is also her business partner) breaks up with her. In a desperate attempt to avoid foreclosure, Francesca rents her home's spare rooms to a teacher named Eileen, a good-looking father named Chris, and a well-known chef named Marya. The foursome bonds immediately and they support one another as Marya attempts to avoid a married man who wants to date her and as Eileen struggles with her attraction to quintessential bad boys. Chris, meanwhile, is in a nasty custody battle with his unstable ex-wife. Francesca's roommates' troubles allow her to forget her own, and she is finally able to let go of the life she planned in order to live the life she has been given.

While *44 Charles Street* received a warmer critical reception than its recent predecessors, it was still not without its detractors. For instance, Virginia Blackburn, writing in the online *London Express,* quipped: "Steel churned out a couple of bestselling page-turners and has continued the churning process ever since. They are still bestsellers but are they page-turners? One doesn't wish to be unkind." Gust, writing this time in *Library Journal,* however, commended the book for its thoughtful content. Indeed, she pointed out that *44 Charles Street* "touches on difficult social issues, such as abusive relationships and drug abuse." Yet, a *Kirkus Reviews* contributor called the novel "classic Steel, phoned in." According to the contributor, there is "much repetitious ruminating and a stultifying, unmusical prose style too often obstruct the intended edgy escapism." *Booklist* reviewer Mosley also called the book "classic Steel," but she qualified this statement by commenting that there is "lots of emotion, friendship, romance, heartbreak, tragedy, and danger." Mosley concluded that Steel's "countless fans are guaranteed to find it impossible to put down." A *Publishers Weekly* critic lauded the novel as well, announcing: "Steel keeps the tone gentle and soothing in this warm, cozy tale."

### Children's Books and Nonfiction

Steel has also written a number of books for younger readers, including the "Max and Martha" series and the "Freddie" series. The "Freddie" books feature a five-year-old boy as he first encounters significant, sometimes frightening events and learns to understand them. The books starring the young and earnest Freddie "deal realistically" with "milestone experiences of early childhood," commented a *Publishers Weekly* reviewer. *Freddie's First Night Away* concerns the young boy's anxieties at the prospect of spending a night at a friend's house, the first time he has ever been away from his family for an entire night. *Freddie's Trip* describes the youngster's reactions to his first lengthy car trip and how he learns to deal with the boredom of long stretches in the car. The *Publishers Weekly* contributor remarked that children will "enjoy spending time with the sprightly Freddie and his family."

Steel produces a stand-alone children's title with the 2009 *The Happiest Hippo in the World,* a cautionary tale about differences. The hippo in question is bright green, but born to a family of gray circus hippopotamuses. Too green for the circus, Greenie takes off for New York where he hopes to find a group to fit in with. While most children at a playground laugh at him, young Charlie thinks Greenie is just fine. "There's nothing subtle about Steel's . . . belabored narrative," noted a reviewer in *Publishers Weekly.*

In addition to her novels, children's fiction, and poetry, Steel ventured into biographical memoir in 1998 with *His Bright Light: The Story of Nick Traina.* The intensely personal memoir recounts the nineteen turbulent years of Steel's son's life—a life of manic depression, drugs, and ultimately suicide. Susan McCaffrey wrote in *Library Journal* that while Steel "is at times melodramatic and the pace is sometimes hampered by the inclusion of lengthy letters and poems, this is a compelling and surprisingly objective portrait of the devastating effects of mental illness." Steel founded the Nick Traina Foundation after her son's death to benefit mental health and other children's causes. Proceeds from *His Bright Light* went directly to the foundation.

Steel once told *CA:* "I want to give [readers] entertainment and something to think about."

## ■ Biographical And Critical Sources

### BOOKS

*Almanac of Famous People,* 6th edition, Gale (Detroit, MI), 1998.

Bane, Vickie L., with Lorenzo Benet, *The Lives of Danielle Steel: The Unauthorized Biography of America's Number One Best-selling Author,* St. Martin's Press (New York, NY), 1994.

*Bestsellers 89,* Issue 1, Gale (Detroit, MI), 1989.

*Bestsellers 90,* Issue 4, Gale (Detroit, MI), 1991.

*Contemporary Popular Writers,* St. James Press (Detroit, MI), 1997.

*Encyclopedia of World Biography,* 2nd edition, seventeen volumes, Gale (Detroit, MI), 1998.

*Newsmakers,* no. 2, Gale (Detroit, MI), 1999.

Steel, Danielle, *His Bright Light: The Story of Nick Traina,* Delacorte (New York, NY), 1998.

*Twentieth-Century Romance and Historical Writers,* 3rd edition, St. James Press (Detroit, MI), 1994.

### PERIODICALS

*Booklist,* April 1, 1992, Denise Perry Donavin, review of *Jewels,* p. 1413; October 15, 1992, review of *Mixed Blessings,* p. 380; October 15, 1994, Stuart Whitwell, review of *Vanished,* p. 372; April 15, 1995, Kathleen Hughes, review of *Lightning,* p. 1453; October 15, 1995, Kathleen Hughes, review of *Five Days in Paris,* p. 364; March 1, 1996, Kathleen Hughes, review of *Malice,* p. 1077; October 15, 1996, Kathleen Hughes, review of *Silent Honor,* p. 379; March 15, 1997, Mary Carroll, review of *The Ranch,* p. 1205; June 1, 1997, Melanie Duncan, review of *Special Delivery,* p. 1620; September 15, 1997, Kathleen Hughes, review of *The Ghost,* p. 181; February 1, 1998, Kathleen Hughes, review of *The Long Road Home,* p. 877; April, 1998, Kathleen Hughes, review of *The Klone and I: A High-Tech Love Story,* p. 1278; September 15, 1998, Sally Estes, review of *Silent Honor,* p. 220; October 15, 1998, Kathleen Hughes, review of *Mirror Image,* p. 371; March 1, 1999, Melanie Duncan, review of *Bittersweet,* p. 1104; May 1, 1999, Melanie Duncan, review of *Granny Dan,* p. 1559; February 1, 2000, Patty Engelmann, review of *The Wedding,* p. 997; March 15, 2000, Patty Engelmann, review of *The House on Hope Street,* p. 1294; August, 2000, Whitney Scott, review of *Journey,* p. 2076; February 1, 2001, Patty Engelmann, review of *Lone Eagle,* p. 1020; March 15, 2001, Diana Tixier Herald, review of *Leap of Faith,* p. 1333; August, 2001, Kathleen Hughes, review of *The Kiss,* p. 2053; September 15, 2001, Whitney Scott, review of *Lone Eagle,* p. 243; May 1, 2003, Kathleen Hughes, review of *Johnny Angel,* p. 1507; September 15, 2003, Kathleen Hughes, review of *Safe Harbour,* p. 181; January 1, 2004, Patty Engelmann, review of *Ransom,* p. 790; June 1, 2004, Kathleen Hughes, review of *Second Chance,* p. 1671; October 1, 2004, Kathleen Hughes, review of *Echoes,* p. 283; February 1, 2005, Kathleen Hughes, review of *Impossible,* p. 918; September 1, 2005, Kathleen Hughes, review of *Toxic Bachelors,* p. 7; March 15, 2006, Kathleen Hughes, review of *The House,* p. 6; April 15, 2007, Kathleen Hughes, review of *Bungalow 2,* p. 5; September 15, 2007, Kathleen Hughes, review of *Amazing Grace,* p. 4; December 1, 2007, Carol Haggas, review of *Honor Thyself,* p. 4; September 1, 2008, Shelly Mosley, review of *A Good Woman,* p. 5; December 1, 2008, Kathleen Hughes, review of *One Day at a Time,* p. 4; March 15, 2009, Shelley Mosley, review of *Matters of the Heart,* p. 5; September 1, 2009, Kathleen Hughes, review of

*Southern Lights*, p. 5; February 1, 2010, Kathleen Hughes, review of *Big Girl*, p. 5; April 1, 2010, Patty Engelmann, review of *Family Ties*, p. 4; July 1, 2010, Shelley Mosley, review of *Legacy*, p. 8; February 1, 2011, Shelley Mosley, review of *44 Charles Street*, p. 27.

*Books*, July, 1992, review of *Jewels*, p. 18.

*Bookseller*, March 21, 2003, Jason Ritchie, "Steel and Cox Are the Top Choices for Mother's Day," p. 15; October 28, 2005, review of *Toxic Bachelors*, p. 14; February 24, 2006, review of *The House*, p. 10.

*Brandweek*, March 15, 2004, Ginger Danto, "A Literary Bandwagon," p. 25.

*Chicago Tribune Book World*, August 28, 1983, L.J. Davis, review of *Changes*.

*Detroit News*, September 11, 1983, review of *Changes*.

*Duty-Free News International*, January 15, 2007, "Danielle by Danielle Steel," p. 43.

*Europe Intelligence Wire*, March 20, 2009, review of *A Good Woman*.

*Globe & Mail* (Toronto, Ontario, Canada), July 9, 1988, Peggy Hill, review of *Zoya*.

*Kirkus Reviews*, October 1, 1992, review of *Mixed Blessings*, p. 1212; June 1, 1993, review of *Vanished*, p. 685; January 1, 1994, review of *Accident*, p. 16; April 15, 1994, review of *The Gift*, p. 504; September 15, 1994, review of *Wings*, p. 1225; April 1, 1995, review of *Lightning*, p. 422; October 1, 1995, review of *Five Days in Paris*, p. 1377; March 1, 1996, review of *Malice*, p. 328; April 1, 1998, review of *The Klone and I*; August 15, 2000, review of *Journey*, p. 1141; August 15, 2001, review of *The Kiss*, p. 1160; August 15, 2002, review of *Answered Prayers*, p. 1170; April 15, 2003, review of *Johnny Angel*, p. 566; August 15, 2003, review of *Safe Harbour*, p. 1042; October 1, 2004, review of *Echoes*, p. 936; January 15, 2005, review of *Impossible*, p. 81; September 1, 2005, review of *Toxic Bachelors*, p. 941; May 1, 2006, review of *Coming Out*, p. 436; January 15, 2007, review of *Sisters*, p. 48; May 1, 2007, review of *Bungalow 2*; September 15, 2008, review of *A Good Woman*; April 1, 2010, review of *Family Ties*; August 1, 2010, review of *Family Ties*; August 15, 2010, review of *Legacy*; February 15, 2011, review of *Charles Street*.

*Library Bookwatch*, January, 2005, review of *Echoes*; February, 2005, review of *Echoes*.

*Library Journal*, October 15, 1993, review of *Vanished*, p. 110; October 15, 1994, review of *Wings*, p. 89; April 15, 1997, Kathy Ingels Helmond, review of *The Ranch*, p. 121; June 1, 1998, Kathy Ingels Helmond, review of *The Klone and I*, p. 161; December, 1998, Susan McCaffrey, review of *His Bright Light: The Story of Nick Traina*, p. 172; November 1, 2003, Carol J. Bissett, review of *Safe Harbour*, p. 126; March 1, 2005, Carol J. Bissett, review of *Impos-sible*, p. 80; October 1, 2005, Samantha J. Gust, review of *Toxic Bachelors*, p. 69; February 15, 2011, Samantha J. Gust, review of *44 Charles Street*, p. 102.

*M2 Best Books*, July 29, 2002, "Danielle Steel Becomes a Member of France's Order of Arts and Letters."

*New York Times Book Review*, August 19, 1984, review of *Full Circle*, p. 18; March 3, 1985, review of *Family Album*, p. 22; July 9, 1995, review of *Lightning*, p. 21.

*New York Times Magazine*, October 19, 2003, Deborah Solomon, "Rewriting Her Life," interview with Danielle Steel, p. 19.

*People*, November 7, 1983, review of *Now and Forever*, p. 10; June 18, 1984, Margot Dougherty, review of *Full Circle*, p. 21; April 29, 1985, Margot Dougherty, review of *Family Album*, p. 22; April 17, 1989, Joanne Kaufman, review of *Star*, p. 35; August 20, 1990, Ralph Novak, review of *Message from 'Nam*, p. 30; July 15, 1991, Ralph Novak, review of *Martha's New Puppy*, p. 29; December 16, 1991, Joanne Kaufman, review of *No Greater Love*, p. 39; September 29, 1997, Cynthia Sanz, review of *Special Delivery*, p. 40; December 22, 1997, Cynthia Sanz, review of *The Ghost*, p. 37; May 18, 1998, Cynthia Sanz, review of *The Long Road Home*, p. 45.

*PR Newswire*, October 18, 2006, "Danielle Steel and Elizabeth Arden Celebrate the Launch of the Fragrance, Danielle by Danielle Steel."

*Publishers Weekly*, June 18, 1984, Margot Dougherty, review of *Full Circle*, p. 21; April 13, 1990, Sybil Steinberg, review of *Message from 'Nam*, p. 56; October 18, 1991, review of *No Greater Love*, p. 49; March 30, 1992, review of *Jewels*, p. 88; June 15, 1992, review of *Freddie's First Night Away*, p. 103; June 15, 1992, review of *Freddie's Trip*, p. 103; October 26, 1992, review of *Mixed Blessings*, p. 55; June 7, 1993, review of *Vanished*, p. 52; January 10, 1994, review of *Accident*, p. 41; May 23, 1994, review of *The Gift*, p. 76; October 10, 1994, review of *Wings*, p. 60; May 1, 1995, review of *Lightning*, p. 41; October 16, 1995, review of *Five Days in Paris*, p. 44; March 25, 1996, review of *Malice*, p. 63; October 28, 1996, review of *Silent Honor*, p. 58; March 17, 1997, review of *The Ranch*, p. 74; June 16, 1997, review of *Special Delivery*, p. 46; October 27, 1997, review of *The Ghost*, p. 54; February 2, 1998, review of *The Long Road Home*, p. 78; April 20, 1998, review of *The Klone and I*, p. 44; June 1, 1998, review of *The Klone and I*, p. 34; October 26, 1998, review of *Mirror Image*, p. 45; March 15, 1999, review of *Bittersweet*, p. 46; May 24, 1999, review of *Granny Dan*, p. 65; February 14, 2000, review of *The Wedding*, p. 171; April 17, 2000, review of *The House on Hope Street*, p. 46; August 28, 2000, review of *Journey*, p. 50; March 5, 2001, review of *Lone Eagle*, p. 61; May 21, 2001, review of *Leap of Faith*, p. 82; August 19, 2002, review of

*Answered Prayers,* p. 64; June 2, 2003, review of *Johnny Angel,* p. 32; October 6, 2003, review of *Safe Harbour,* p. 58; January 12, 2004, review of *Ransom,* p. 36; May 31, 2004, review of *Second Chance,* p. 53; October 4, 2004, review of *Echoes,* p. 68; January 24, 2005, review of *Impossible,* p. 220; May 2, 2005, review of *Miracle,* p. 175; August 22, 2005, review of *Toxic Bachelors,* p. 34; April 24, 2006, review of *Coming Out,* p. 34; August 28, 2006, review of *H.R.H.,* p. 27; December 11, 2006, review of *Sisters,* p. 46; April 16, 2007, review of *Bungalow 2,* p. 29; August 13, 2007, review of *Amazing Grace,* p. 40; December 24, 2007, review of *Honor Thyself,* p. 28; April 21, 2008, review of *Rogue,* p. 33; August 11, 2008, review of *A Good Woman,* p. 26; August 24, 2009, review of *The Happiest Hippo in the World,* p. 61; September 7, 2009, review of *Southern Lights,* p. 26; January 4, 2010, review of *Big Girl,* p. 28; May 17, 2010, review of *Family Ties,* p. 28; August 2, 2010, review of *Legacy,* p. 30; February 7, 2011, review of *44 Charles Street,* p. 42.

*Rapport,* Volume 17, number 3, 1993, review of *Mixed Blessings,* p. 23; Volume 18, number 1, 1994, review of *The Gift,* p. 26.

*Saturday Evening Post,* January, 1999, Patrick Perry, review of *His Bright Light,* p. 65.

*School Library Journal,* November, 2001, Claudia Moore, review of *Leap of Faith,* p. 192.

*Soap, Perfumery & Cosmetics Asia,* March, 2007, "Novelist Danielle Steel," p. 9.

*Time,* November 25, 1985, review of *Secrets,* p. S1; October 13, 1986, review of *Wanderlust,* p. 102; March 16, 1987, review of *Fine Things,* p. 81; January 11, 1988, review of *Kaleidoscope,* p. 76.

*Xpress Reviews,* June 18, 2010, Samantha J. Gust, review of *Family Ties.*

ONLINE

*Associated Content,* http://www.associatedcontent. com/ (April 6, 2009), Betty Alexander, review of *One Day at a Time.*

*Bookreporter.com,* http://www.bookreporter.com/ (February 19, 2008), biography of Danielle Steel.

*Danielle Steel Home Page,* http://www.daniellesteel. net (August 16, 2011).

*Femail.com.au,* http://www.femail.com.au/ (September 3, 2009), review of *A Good Woman* and *Matters of the Heart.*

*Fresh Fiction,* http://freshfiction.com/ (July 18, 2008), Sandi Shilhanek, review of *Rogue.*

*Genre Go Round Reviews,* http://genregoround reviews.blogspot.com/ (June 12, 2008), Harriet Klausner, review of *Rogue;* (October 6, 2008), Harriet Klausner, review of *A Good Woman;* (March 2, 2009), Harriet Klausner, review of *One Day at a Time.*

*Internet Movie Database,* http://www.imdb.com/ (September 3, 2009), filmography of Danielle Steel.

*Inthenews.co.uk,* http://www.inthenews.co.uk/ (March 12, 2007), Chine Mbubaegbu, review of *Sisters.*

*London Express,* http://www.express.co.uk/ (April 10, 2011), Virginia Blackburn, review of *44 Charles Street.*

*Night Owl Reviews,* http://www.nightowlreviews. com/ (August 16, 2011), review of *Legacy.*

*Random House Web site,* http://www.randomhouse. com/ (September 3, 2009), biography of Danielle Steel.

*Thisisnottingham.co.uk,* http://www.thisis nottingham.co.uk/ (March 20, 2009), Sue McNab, review of *A Good Woman.**

# Elizabeth Stuckey-French

## 1958-

### ■ Personal

Born September 2, 1958, in Little Rock, AR; married (divorced); married Ned French (a teacher); children: (second marriage) two daughters. *Education:* Purdue University, B.A., M.A.; Iowa Writers Workshop, M.F.A., 1992.

### ■ Addresses

*Home*—Tallahassee, FL. *Office*—Department of English, Florida State University, 325 Williams Bldg., Tallahassee, FL 32306-1580. *E-mail*—estuckey-french@fsu.edu; esf@elizabethstuckeyfrench.com.

### ■ Career

Writer and educator. Florida State University, Tallahassee, began as assistant professor of English, became associate professor. Worked as an elementary school teacher and a social worker.

### ■ Awards, Honors

James Michener fellowship; O. Henry Prize, 2005, for the short story "Mudlavia"; grants from the Indiana Arts Commission, Howard Foundation, and Florida Arts Foundation.

### ■ Writings

*The First Paper Girl in Red Oak, Iowa, and Other Stories,* Doubleday (New York, NY), 2000.
*Mermaids on the Moon* (novel), Doubleday (New York, NY), 2002.

(With husband, Ned French, and Janet Burroway) *Writing Fiction: A Guide to Narrative Craft,* 7th edition, Pearson Longman (New York, NY), 2007.
*The Revenge of the Radioactive Lady: A Novel,* Doubleday (New York, NY), 2011.

Founding editor, *Sycamore Review.* Work represented in anthologies, including *New Territory: Contemporary Indiana Fiction.* Contributor to periodicals and literary journals, including *Atlantic Monthly, Gettysburg Review, Southern Review,* and *Five Points.*

### ■ Sidelights

Elizabeth Stuckey-French's collection *The First Paper Girl in Red Oak, Iowa, and Other Stories* contains twelve stories featuring a number of quirky characters, most of them Midwesterners and people who make bad choices. Among them are a woman who pays a gas station attendant to keep her and her children company on a cross-country road trip, a psychic who finds missing pets, and a scuba-diving female police officer who searches for dead bodies in the murky waters of polluted rivers.

Reviewing the collection for the *Austin Chronicle Online,* Martin Wilson found "Electric Wizard" to be the "best story." A student commits suicide, and his parents come to his poetry teacher asking for his work as proof that he was driven by genius. The student never wrote any poems, however, and the teacher is torn between telling them the devastating truth or a lie that will preserve their vision of their son. A *Publishers Weekly* reviewer noted that fiction writers are now forced to compete with bizarre situations and characters that populate daytime talk shows and concluded by saying that Stuckey-French "bests those spectacles of the everyday absurd, and does so with style and verve."

### Mermaids on the Moon and
### The Revenge of the Radioactive Lady

*Mermaids on the Moon*, Stuckey-French's debut novel, was called "wonderfully quirky" by a *Publishers Weekly* contributor. The novel centers on the mysterious disappearance of Grendy, a minister's wife and former performer in a synchronized swimming exhibition that was a tourist attraction in Florida many years ago. *Library Journal* reviewer Molly Gorman compared *Mermaids on the Moon* with the writing of Fannie Flagg and wrote: "As refreshing, crisp, and tangy as a summer drink, this is a beguiling read."

*The Revenge of the Radioactive Lady: A Novel* features Marylou Ahearn, an elderly woman who plans to get revenge on the man responsible for her eight-year-old daughter's death fifty years earlier. Her target is Dr. Wilson Spriggs, the man who knowingly exposed Marylou to radiation while she was pregnant. Marylou believed she was taking part in a benign scientific experiment, but she discovers the truth when her daughter is born with myriad health problems. Dr. Spriggs has long since retired and is living with his daughter's family in Florida, and Marylou moves to the same neighborhood. She poses as someone else and begins to slowly wreak havoc on Dr. Spriggs's life. Once her plan is complete, she intends to kill him. However, Marylou may be incapable of fulfilling her ultimate desire.

Horrifically, *The Revenge of the Radioactive Lady* is based in fact. Throughout the 1950s, scientists in the United States willingly exposed unwitting experiment participants to radiation. Stuckey-French learned about these experiments in Eileen Welsome's book *The Plutonium Files: America's Secret Medical Experiments in the Cold War*. The author told *New Yorker* interviewer Eileen Reynolds that "even though Welsome won a Pulitzer Prize for her reporting, neither I nor most people I talked to had heard the story. I wanted people to know about it. Part of my motivation was personal. In my early twenties I developed thyroid cancer, which most medical experts think is caused by radiation exposure, perhaps from dental x-ray machines or radioactive fallout drifting east from Nevada. I felt I had something in common with the subjects in the experiments."

Assessing the novel in the *Washington Post Book World*, Adam Langer found that Stuckey-French's "writing can be detailed and precise." According to Langer, "the most convincing aspects of *The Revenge of the Radioactive Lady* are not its grand aspirations but its more intimate moments: astute observations of the neuroses of married couples and their children, wittily rendered critiques of contemporary suburban life. Yet these are hardly damning criticisms. In fact, the same might be said of many excellent contemporary American novels." Reynolds proffered more straightforward praise, declaring: "So much that happens in this book is wildly improbable—we encounter at various points a massive hurricane, a nuclear reactor built in a backyard, and a crafty pedophile—but un-fantastical, deadpan prose grounds even the zaniest plot elements in everyday realism. Even as we laugh, we're moved to wonder how our own uniquely dysfunctional families might react in such circumstances."

## ■ Biographical And Critical Sources

*PERIODICALS*

*Booklist*, January 1, 2011, Carol Haggas, review of *The Revenge of the Radioactive Lady: A Novel*, p. 42.

*Kirkus Reviews*, May 1, 2002, review of *Mermaids on the Moon*, p. 609; December 15, 2010, review of *The Revenge of the Radioactive Lady*.

*Library Journal*, June 15, 2002, Molly Gorman, review of *Mermaids on the Moon*, p. 96; February 1, 2011, Leigh Wright, review of *The Revenge of the Radioactive Lady*, p. 57.

*New Yorker*, March 2, 2011, Eileen Reynolds, author interview and review of *The Revenge of the Radioactive Lady*.

*Publishers Weekly*, April 24, 2000, review of *The First Paper Girl in Red Oak, Iowa, and Other Stories*, p. 64; June 3, 2002, review of *Mermaids on the Moon*, p. 61; December 13, 2010, review of *The Revenge of the Radioactive Lady*, p. 36.

*School Library Journal*, December, 2000, Susanne Bardelson, review of *The First Paper Girl in Red Oak, Iowa, and Other Stories*, p. 169.

*Washington Post Book World*, February 8, 2011, Adam Langer, review of *The Revenge of the Radioactive Lady*.

*ONLINE*

*Atlantic Unbound*, http://www.theatlantic.com/ (June 11, 1998), Katie Bolick, "Wise Kids, Childish Adults: A Conversation with Elizabeth Stuckey-French."

*Austin Chronicle Online*, http://www.austinchronicle.com/ (September 29, 2000), Martin Wilson, review of *The First Paper Girl in Red Oak, Iowa, and Other Stories*.

*Elizabeth Stuckey-French Home Page*, http://elizabethstuckeyfrench.com (August 25, 2011).

*Florida State University, English Department Web site*, http://www.english.fsu.edu/ (August 25, 2011), author profile.*

# Scarlett Thomas

## 1972-

## ■ Personal

Born July 5, 1972, in London, England; daughter of Gordian (a manager in the music industry and racehorse business owner) and Francesca (an actress, political activist, and teacher) Troeller; partner of Rod Edmond. *Education:* Graduated from University of East London (with first-class honors); attended University of Kent. *Politics:* Old Labour; Socialist. *Hobbies and other interests:* Homeopathy, malfunctioning 60s architecture, artistic manifestoes, recreational mathematics, cricket, playing guitar and flute, visiting museums.

## ■ Addresses

*Home*—Kent, England. *Office*—School of English, Rutherford College, University of Kent, Canterbury, Kent CT2 7NX, England. *Agent*—Simon Trewin, PFD, Drury House, 34-43 Russell St., London WC2B 5HA, England. *E-mail*—s.thomas@kent.ac.uk.

## ■ Career

Writer and academic. University of Kent, England, English literature and creative writing instructor, beginning 2004, then director, Centre for Creative Writing director. Has also lectured at Dartmouth Community College, South East Essex College, and University of East London; served as a Edinburgh International Film Festival jurist, 2008.

## ■ Awards, Honors

Book of the Year, *Independent on Sunday,* 1999, for *In Your Face;* named one of the twenty best young British writers by the *Independent on Sunday,* 2001; Elle Style Award, 2002, for *Going Out.*

## ■ Writings

*"LILY PASCALE" TRILOGY; MYSTERIES*

*Dead Clever,* Hodder and Stoughton (London, England), 1998, Justin, Charles (Boston, MA), 2003.

*In Your Face,* Hodder and Stoughton (London, England), 1999, Justin, Charles (Boston, MA), 2004.

*Seaside,* Hodder and Stoughton (London, England), 2000.

*NOVELS*

*Bright Young Things,* Flame (London, England), 2001.

*Going Out,* Fourth Estate (London, England), 2002, Anchor/Vintage (New York, NY), 2004.

*PopCo,* Fourth Estate (London, England), 2004.

*The End of Mr. Y,* Harcourt (Orlando, FL), 2006.

*Our Tragic Universe,* Canongate (New York, NY), 2010.

Contributor to anthologies, including *All Hail the New Puritans* and *Big Night Out.* Contributor to newspapers and magazines, including *Guardian, Butterfly, Black Book, Literary Review, Scotland on Sunday,* and *Independent on Sunday.* Writer of radio play *Why My Grandmother Learned to Play the Flute,* experimental story/soundscape broadcast on Radio 4 (London, England), 2003.

## ■ Adaptations

Trillion Entertainment has optioned feature film rights to *Bright Young Things;* Greenlit Productions has optioned feature film rights to *Going Out.*

## ■ Sidelights

Hailed as one of the twenty best young British writers by the *Independent on Sunday* in 2001, Scarlett Thomas writes fiction centering on unorthodox young people often leading rather bohemian lives in England. She has written mysteries featuring an independent young woman detective, Lily Pascale, as well as novels outside the genre, and she contributed a short story to the anthology *All Hail the New Puritans*. This anthology aroused controversy with its manifesto calling for simple, straightforward prose, eschewing such devices as flashbacks and poetic license. In an interview published on her Home page, Thomas characterized *All Hail the New Puritans* as something of "an experiment, to see what would happen if those particular writers were given those particular rules," but also endorsed other styles of storytelling, saying, "It's the skill of the writer that determines whether a piece of writing works, not rules." Numerous reviewers have praised Thomas's skill; for instance, *Independent on Sunday* contributor Murrough O'Brien, critiquing *Going Out,* described her writing as "deeply original and provocative."

### *Dead Clever*

*Dead Clever,* Thomas's debut novel, introduces Pascale, a "smart, hip, and brilliant" sleuth, in the words of *USA Today* commentator Carol Memmott. Twenty-five-year-old Pascale, tired of life in London, returns to her hometown of Devon, where she finds a job teaching literature at a university. She loves detective stories, and she becomes a real-life detective after a student is raped and murdered and a witness dies under mysterious circumstances. Pascale's investigation brings her into contact with drug dealers, cult leaders, and a variety of other bizarre characters.

"Solid narrative and engaging dialog hold it all together," reported Rex E. Klett in *Library Journal.* A *Kirkus Reviews* critic was unimpressed, however, finding Pascale "drab" and the tale "preposterous." Memmott, on the other hand, deemed the story "slightly far-fetched but very Mary Shelley-ish," adding: "It's sure to satisfy readers who prefer a more literary crime novel." A *Publishers Weekly* reviewer summed up *Dead Clever* as an "engaging mystery . . . full of attractive characters in a lovingly evoked setting."

### *In Your Face, Seaside,* **and** *Bright Young Things*

Thomas continued Pascale's adventures in two more mysteries: *In Your Face,* which finds her trying to solve the murders of three young women who had discussed their experiences with stalkers in a magazine article written by a friend of Lily's, and *Seaside,* in which a teenage woman apparently commits suicide—but her surviving twin sister claims to be the dead girl. *Scotland on Sunday* contributor Susie Maguire deemed the latter book Thomas's "best to date."

Thomas next published *Bright Young Things,* a novel about six youths, all highly intelligent but frustrated with their lives, who are brought together when they answer a newspaper advertisement seeking "bright young things" for a "big project." When they report for their interviews, they are drugged, abducted, and taken to a faraway island. Some reviewers compared the novel to the television series *Big Brother,* in which strangers were forced to share a house, and Alex Garland's novel *The Beach,* about young Europeans on a Thai island. "It is right on the zeitgeist," related Vicky Allan in *Scotland on Sunday,* while Steve Jelbert, writing in the London *Times,* thought the book "wickedly satirized" hip young people.

### *Going Out* **and** *PopCo*

*Going Out* deals with twenty-five-year-old Luke, who is allergic to the sun and therefore has never left the home he shares with his cloying mother. He gets his perceptions of the world from television, the Internet, and his friend Julie, who is brilliant at mathematics but nonetheless unambitious, satisfied with being a waitress. They must leave their respective routines behind, however, when Luke decides to travel to meet a man who offers him a cure. Julie and a collection of quirky companions accompany him. London *Daily Mail* reviewer Amber Pearson described the story as "a modern take on *The Wizard of Oz,*" while *Scotsman* critic Casron Howat found the book "heartwarming and definitely funny."

Thomas' next novel, *PopCo,* was described by the author to *CA* as "my longest book so far (it's twice as long as *Going Out*), and the most ambitious. It's mainly about a toy company, and the process of developing a new idea in a remote, corporate 'thought camp.' But it's also about seventeenth-century pirates, World War II, early computing, number theory, secret codes, and ways of resisting authority. It's this crazy mix of things and I really hope it works." In an interview with *Bookslut* Web site reviewer Colleen Mondor, Thomas mentioned that she looked at *PopCo* as "the third book in a trilogy (the first two being *Bright Young Things* and *Going Out*). All three are about the effects of pop culture on people, and each one comes at the problem in a slightly different way."

## The End of Mr. Y

Thomas followed up *PopCo* with what Mondor described as "the genre busting" *The End of Mr. Y.* The novel's heroine, graduate student Ariel Manto, gets her hands on a copy of a supposedly cursed book, *The End of Mr. Y,* by nineteenth-century scientist Thomas E. Lumas, who died soon after writing it—along with everyone else ever involved with the book. This, however, does not deter Ariel. Through the book, she learns how to access the Troposphere, a place where one can travel through time and space via the thoughts of others. Ariel soon finds herself embarking on an adventure that could end up costing her life.

Many critics applauded Thomas' efforts with *The End of Mr. Y,* including Mondor, who felt: "With Mr. Y, Thomas showed again her utter fearlessness when it comes to attacking the big subjects and her determination to bring philosophical discussions into the realm of highly readable and entertaining literature." Critic Charlene Martel, in her review of *The End of Mr. Y* for the *Literary Word* Web site, noted: "This book explores so many theories about science, faith, consciousness, death and more. It's a book that will excite the senses, inspire the imagination, and tease the intellect." Martel added that "the author has a way of drawing the reader into the book, even when just sharing details of Ariel's day to day life. The characters are vivid, realistic and very easy to connect with." *New York Times Book Review* contributor Gregory Cowles felt that "amid all the novel's engaging questions about the nature of reality, it's hard to get worked up about a subplot that has Ariel traveling through time to save laboratory mice. Still, she spins Derrida and subatomic theory into a wholly enchanting alternate universe that should appeal to a wide popular audience, and that's something no deconstructionist or physicist has managed to do."

## Our Tragic Universe

In 2010 Thomas published the novel *Our Tragic Universe.* Book reviewer Meg finds her perspective of the whole world rocked after reading a stimulating book. She starts to research the universe on a scientific and philosophical level, letting it take over her daily life. With her relationship strained, she begins to question the point of the novel she has always wanted to write. It consumes her as she tries to manipulate the lives of those around her.

A contributor to the *New Yorker* mentioned that Thomas "creates a compelling novel that ably dodges the conventions she's sending up." *Booklist*

contributor Heather Paulson suggested the novel to "readers who enjoy the ideological push and pull of philosophical fiction," calling it "definitely worth reading." A *Kirkus Reviews* critic stated: "For the omnivorous reader who, like Meg, can't get enough of the insights and passions and theories and inner lives of others, Thomas's fifth novel . . . should be an addictive delight." In a review in *Library Journal,* Laurel Bliss admitted that "few writers can mix science, philosophy, and humor as cleverly as Thomas." A contributor to *Publishers Weekly* observed that Thomas "provides a cast of characters who come across as credible owing to their recognizable foibles."

## Thomas once told *CA:*

"I find the world a rather confusing, often alienating place. I always wanted to explore this and to create imaginary utopias where the anxieties of contemporary life can be resolved. Narrative is a good place to find resolution, if that's what you are seeking. In my most recent books, *Bright Young Things, Going Out,* and *PopCo,* the characters tend to go on journeys of some sort. I think that's important.

"My work is influenced by a lot of reading. The more I write, the more I seem to read. I go to a public library every day with a flask of coffee. Paul Erdos once said that a mathematician is a machine for turning coffee into proofs. Perhaps an author is another kind of machine—it's the same fuel but you get a different result at the end. I like writing in public spaces. It keeps me connected with what I am writing about.

"When I read an exciting writer, that gives me more inspiration than anything. Jean Baudrillard, William Gibson, Douglas Coupland, Marge Piercy, Margaret Atwood, and Mary Shelley have all influenced me in some way. I read a lot of math and science books too, which send my imagination racing. Recently, I found Stanley Milgram's study, 'Obedience to Authority,' absolutely fascinating.

"I was quite unpleasantly surprised by the 'corporate' side of writing. I never realized how much of writing is driven by sales and marketing targets, and how your readership can be determined by bookshop policy. It is also much less glamorous than I thought it would be, which is probably a good thing.

"Occasionally I get e-mails from people who say that one of my books has made them look at the world in a slightly different way, or even better, that the book has made them feel that they are not the only person experiencing loneliness or confusion or alienation. Getting an e-mail like that beats even the most brilliant review. In my books, it's OK to be a dreamer, to walk out of your job, to become a vegetarian, to try to start a revolution. I want my books to make people realize that these things are all completely OK—that they are desirable and logical in the world in which we live. On another level, I want my books to make people think, 'Huh?,' to make the reader try to solve the puzzles (there are lots of puzzles in *PopCo*), and to feel happy, at least on some level, at the end."

■ **Biographical And Critical Sources**

*PERIODICALS*

*Booklist*, January 1, 2004, Emily Melton, review of *Dead Clever*, p. 835; April 1, 2004, Jennifer Mattson, review of *Going Out*, p. 1349; September 1, 2005, Allison Block, review of *PopCo*, p. 67; November 1, 2005, Jenny McLarin, review of *Seaside*, p. 29; August 1, 2006, Allison Block, review of *The End of Mr. Y*, p. 44; September 1, 2010, Heather Paulson, review of *Our Tragic Universe*, p. 45.

*Bookmarks*, January 1, 2011, review of *Our Tragic Universe*, p. 39.

*Bookseller*, June 8, 2007, Benedicte Page, review of *The End of Mr. Y*, p. 21.

*Daily Mail* (London, England), August 9, 2002, Amber Pearson, review of *Going Out*, p. 54.

*Detroit Free Press*, November 16, 2005, Ron Bernas, review of *Seaside*.

*Entertainment Weekly*, September 3, 2010, Keith Staskiewicz, review of *Our Tragic Universe*, p. 77.

*Independent on Sunday* (London, England), April 13, 2003, Murrough O'Brien, review of *Going Out*, p. 19; July 13, 2007, Roz Kaveney, review of *The End of Mr. Y*.

*Kirkus Reviews*, December 1, 2002, review of *Dead Clever*, p. 1740; December 15, 2003, review of *In Your Face*, p. 1429; April 1, 2004, review of *Going Out*, p. 297; August 1, 2005, review of *PopCo*, p. 813; October 1, 2005, review of *Seaside*, p. 1056; July 15, 2006, review of *The End of Mr. Y*, p. 698; August 1, 2010, review of *Our Tragic Universe*.

*Library Journal*, January 1, 2003, Rex E. Klett, review of *Dead Clever*, p. 162; January 1, 2004, Rex E. Klett, review of *In Your Face*, p. 164; April 1, 2004,

review of *Going Out*, p. 297; August 1, 2005, Lisa Rohrbaugh, review of *PopCo*, p. 73; November 1, 2005, Rex E. Klett, review of *Seaside*, p. 56; October 15, 2006, Andrea Kempf, review of *The End of Mr. Y*, p. 56; July 1, 2010, Laurel Bliss, review of *Our Tragic Universe*, p. 79; January 1, 2011, Donna Bachowski, review of *Our Tragic Universe*, p. 48.

*New Yorker*, October 4, 2010, review of *Our Tragic Universe*, p. 95.

*New York Times Book Review*, October 29, 2006, Gregory Cowles, "Reading Minds," p. 26.

*Publishers Weekly*, December 16, 2002, review of *Dead Clever*, p. 48; January 5, 2004, review of *In Your Face*, p. 43; August 1, 2005, review of *PopCo*, p. 42; September 26, 2005, review of *Seaside*, p. 65; June 26, 2006, review of *The End of Mr. Y*, p. 26; July 26, 2010, review of *Our Tragic Universe*, p. 42.

*Scotland on Sunday*, October 24, 1999, Susie Maguire, review of *Seaside*, p. 11; March 11, 2001, Vicky Allan, review of *Bright Young Things*, p. 12.

*Scotsman* (Edinburgh, Scotland), March 29, 2003, Casron Howat, review of *Going Out*, p. 6; May 16, 2010, Claire Black, "Interview: Scarlett Thomas, Writer."

*Telegraph* (London, England), May 14, 2010, Ed Cumming, "Scarlett Thomas: Profile."

*Times* (London, England), August 4, 2001, Steve Jelbert, review of *Bright Young Things*.

*Times Literary Supplement*, August 3, 2007, "Go to the Goose Fair," p. 19.

*USA Today*, April 17, 2003, Carol Memmott, "'Dead Clever' Unveils a Hip Literary Detective," p. 5D.

*ONLINE*

*Bookslut*, http://www.bookslut.com/ (December 4, 2007), Colleen Mondor, "An Interview with Scarlett Thomas."

*Literary Word*, http://www.theliteraryword.blogspot.com/ (July 19, 2007), Charlene Martel, review of *The End of Mr. Y*.

*PopMatters*, http://www.popmatters.com/ (November 1, 2006), Megan Milks, review of *The End of Mr. Y*.

*Scarlett Thomas Home Page*, http://www.scarlettthomas.co.uk (August 3, 2011).

*University of Kent, School of English Web site*, http://www.kent.ac.uk/english/ (August 3, 2011), author profile.

# Leonard Todd

## 1940-

### ■ Personal

Born February 10, 1940, in Greenville, SC; son of Leonard M. (a banker) and Lena-Miles (a poet) Todd; married Laurel Blossom (a poet). *Education:* Attended Sorbonne, University of Paris, 1959; Yale University, B.A. (cum laude), 1961, M.A., 1965.

### ■ Addresses

*Home*—Edgefield, SC. *Agent*—John Cushman Associates, 25 W. 43rd St., New York, NY 10036.

### ■ Career

Writer and graphic designer. Sea Pines Plantation, Hilton Head Island, SC, design director, 1967-71; one-man show of design work at American Museum of Natural History, 1975; freelance writer, 1971—. Production and design director, *Coda*, 1976—; former resident at the Virginia Center for the Creative Arts and the Paris Cité Internationale des Arts; guest speaker.

### ■ Awards, Honors

Fulbright scholar, 1965-67; finalist, South Carolina Center for the Book Award, for writing, for *Carolina Clay*; National Award for Arts Writing, 2008, for *Carolina Clay*.

### ■ Writings

*Trash Can Toys and Games,* Viking (New York, NY), 1974.

*The Best Kept Secret of the War,* Knopf (New York, NY), 1984.
*Squaring Off* (young-adult novel), Viking (New York, NY), 1990.
*Carolina Clay: The Life and Legend of the Slave Potter Dave,* W.W. Norton (New York, NY), 2008.

Contributor of articles to periodicals, including *Family Circle, Viva, Village Voice, Cosmopolitan, Americana,* and *Travel & Leisure,*

### ■ Sidelights

Leonard Todd is an American writer and graphic designer. Born in South Carolina, in 1940, he graduated with multiple degrees from Yale University in the 1960s and began working as a designer. Todd began freelance writing in the 1970s and published his first book, *Trash Can Toys and Games,* shortly thereafter.

#### *Squaring Off* and *Carolina Clay*

In 1990 Todd published the young-adult novel *Squaring Off.* Widower Trag and his teenage son Willy both fall for local stripper LuJane Jessup in this southern novel set in the 1950s. A contributor to *Publishers Weekly* found the narrative to be "graphically realistic," noting that LuJane and Trag "may be stereotypes, but they have personalities that are distinctly their own."

Todd published *Carolina Clay: The Life and Legend of the Slave Potter Dave* in 2008. Todd researched the story of a nineteenth-century slave named Dave who was once owned by his ancestors. Todd uncovered a talented and educated man who was not only versed at pottery but also poetry.

A *Kirkus Reviews* critic opined that the book is "well-informed, but colored by the legends that have grown up around his magnificent vessels," adding that it is "captivating, though necessarily speculative." In a review in *School Library Journal*, Joanne Ligamari claimed: "This book provides a real feel for a slave's life and experience." Reviewing the book in *American Scholar*, Scott Reynolds Nelson remarked that the book "is rich with telling quotations from contemporary sources that come from approximately the same time and place as events in Dave's life. It is a brilliant evocation of the skilled work of slaves in a South Carolina whose white citizens were growing increasingly bellicose and violent. The research on Dave himself is amazing, and the picture of the antebellum South Carolina backcountry is extremely rich." Nelson concluded that "*Carolina Clay* will likely stand as the most complete history of Dave." Writing in the *Journal of Southern History*, P. Sterling Stuckey commented that "if at times Leonard Todd, in his fascinating book . . . appears eager to get things 'right' between the slave potter Dave and Todd's relatives who owned him, Todd's basic humanity and scholarly integrity restore the reader's trust and admiration."

### Todd once told *CA:*

"Before becoming a writer, I studied and practiced architecture for more than a decade. The two disciplines couldn't be more different, yet I find they share a similar creative process. For me, designing a building and writing a novel both involve bringing order to disparate parts—establishing a form within which various needs and impulses can come together, find expression, take on life. The form I find most useful in my writing, for now at least, is the same that the early skyscraper architects employed; they always gave their buildings a beginning, a middle, and an end—like a column, they said. Within that simple framework wonders can happen."

### ■ Biographical And Critical Sources

*PERIODICALS*

*American Scholar*, September 22, 2008, Scott Reynolds Nelson, review of *Carolina Clay: The Life and Legend of the Slave Potter Dave*, p. 134.

*Journal of Southern History*, February 1, 2010, P. Sterling Stuckey, review of *Carolina Clay*, p. 145.

*Kirkus Reviews*, August 15, 2008, review of *Carolina Clay*.

*Publishers Weekly*, August 11, 2008, review of *Carolina Clay*, p. 39.

*School Library Journal*, March 1, 2009, Joanne Ligamari, review of *Carolina Clay*, p. 179.

*ONLINE*

*Leonard Todd Home Page*, http://leonardtodd.com (August 3, 2011).

*Renegade South*, http://renegadesouth.wordpress.com/ (December 21, 2009), David Woodbury, "David Woodbury's Q&A with Leonard Todd."*

# Nick Trout

## ■ Personal

Born in England; married; children: two daughters. *Education:* University of Cambridge, England, degree in veterinary medicine, 1989; M.A., 1990; earned D.V.M.

## ■ Addresses

*Home*—Boston, MA. *Office*—MSPCA-Angell Headquarters, 350 S. Huntington Ave., Boston, MA 02130.

## ■ Career

Veterinarian. Member of Royal College of Veterinary Surgeons, 1989; diplomate of American College of Veterinary Surgeons, and European College of Veterinary Surgeons, 1995. University of Liverpool, Liverpool, England, house officer, 1989-91; Tufts University School of Veterinary Medicine and Angell Animal Medical Center, Boston, MA, resident in small animal surgery, 1991-94, staff surgeon, 1994—.

## ■ Writings

*MEMOIRS*

*Tell Me Where It Hurts: A Day of Humor, Healing, and Hope in My Life as an Animal Surgeon,* Broadway Books (New York, NY), 2008.
*Love Is the Best Medicine: What Two Dogs Taught One Veterinarian about Hope, Humility, and Everyday Miracles,* Broadway Books (New York, NY), 2010.
*Ever by My Side: A Memoir in Eight [Acts] Pets,* Broadway Books (New York, NY), 2011.

Contributing columnist to the *Bark* and *Prevention.*

## ■ Sidelights

Nick Trout is a staff surgeon at the Angell Animal Medical Center in Boston, Massachusetts, a very large, internationally known humane society and veterinary hospital. Trout, who is board-certified in veterinary surgery, specializes in soft tissue surgery and orthopedic surgery. Hip replacements and arthroscopic surgeries are among his specialties. In an interview with Joan Brunwasser in *OpEdNews.com,* Trout admitted: "I started to think about writing some seven or eight years ago. Every veterinarian can tell you a funny, sad, shocking or emotional story about an animal or a pet owner they have worked with. This job provides a writer with wonderful material. I began writing them down. Then I began to think about how these interactions made me feel, what I could learn from them. Take this to the next level and you have the beginnings of a story."

### *Tell Me Where It Hurts*

In his first memoir, *Tell Me Where It Hurts: A Day of Humor, Healing, and Hope in My Life as an Animal Surgeon,* Trout offers "a thoroughly charming book on his experiences as a vet surgeon," according to a writer for the *Dolittler* Web site. The book reflects a twenty-four-hour cycle, although the stories are drawn from many different days over the course of twenty-five years of veterinary practice. Trout hoped that in this way, he would convey a sense of the rushed, intense pace of life at the Angell Animal Medical Center. The anecdotes he shares include that of a late-night emergency operation on a dog's twisted intestine, and a Boxer dog who, although he appeared to be male, actually had a uterus—and an infection in it. He reflects on the emotional and moral difficulties inherent in veterinary medicine, including the changing sense of ethics about euthanasia and the dilemma of the rising cost of good veterinary care. The result is an "addictively readable" account of modern veterinary medicine, said Nancy Bent in *Booklist*.

The *Dolittler* Web site reviewer commented that Trout describes events in "glorious detail. The stories are whisked together in a masterfully wandering course that simulates the process of developing clinical and emotional competence in the real world of veterinary medicine." As a final recommendation for *Tell Me Where It Hurts*, the *Doolittler* reviewer commented: "Even veterinarians will want to read it."

Bent compared *Tell Me Where It Hurts* to the famous series of memoirs by a rural veterinarian, James Herriot, which began with the book *All Creatures Great and Small*. Trout's book is "equally heartwarming, yet high-tech," stated Bent. She noted that Trout writes just as well about the clinical, technical aspects of life as an animal surgeon as he does about the emotional bond that people share with their pets. "This is the perfect gift for anyone considering becoming a veterinarian," wrote a *Publishers Weekly* reviewer, adding that it shows the sensitivity, intelligence, and writing talent of its author. Another reviewer, Miriam Tuliao, wrote in her *Library Journal* review: "Modern veterinary medicine is potently explored in this noteworthy debut."

### Love Is the Best Medicine

In 2010 Trout published *Love Is the Best Medicine: What Two Dogs Taught One Veterinarian about Hope, Humility, and Everyday Miracles*, his second memoir. The tale discusses two of Trout's canine clients and the unique stories that brought them into his life and vice versa. The fourteen-month-old miniature pinscher Cleo comes from top-class breeders, while the ten-year-old black cocker spaniel mix Helen has been a loner most of her life.

A contributor to *Two Little Cavaliers* "highly recommended" *Love Is the Best Medicine*, noting that "this is, ultimately, a feel-good story that will be appreciated and enjoyed by most who have shared their lives with a much-loved pet." Writing in *Fetchdog*, Tanya Turgeon remarked that "Trout can be wordy at times, but it's well worth the extra syllables for a peak into the mind, life, and lessons learned by a veterinarian who represents the profession so many of us depend on to keep our loved ones healthy." *Booklist* contributor Colleen Mondor suggested that "Trout's chronicle will appeal to readers from teens to grandparents."

### Ever by My Side

Trout published s third memoir, *Ever by My Side: A Memoir in Eight [Acts] Pets*, in 2011. This personal account relates the relationship Trout had with his animal-loving father and the pets they had as a family. Numerous visits to the veterinarian piqued the young man's interest in the field.

Writing in Missouri's *Webster-Kirkwood Times*, Linda Jarrett stated: "Written in a style similar to John Grogan who wrote *Marley and Me*, Trout tells hilarious tales." Reviewing the memoir in *Bookloons*, Rheta Van Winkle opined "that anyone who has had beloved pets themselves would enjoy reading this book. It's funny in places and sad in others, with lots of interesting information about the dogs and one fearless cat belonging to the Trout family." A *Kirkus Reviews* critic described the memoir as "a tender tribute to the author's father, sure to please fans of Trout's previous two pet-focused books."

## ■ Biographical And Critical Sources

*BOOKS*

Trout, Nick, *Tell Me Where It Hurts: A Day of Humor, Healing, and Hope in My Life as an Animal Surgeon*, Broadway Books (New York, NY), 2008.
Trout, Nick, *Love Is the Best Medicine: What Two Dogs Taught One Veterinarian about Hope, Humility, and Everyday Miracles*, Broadway Books (New York, NY), 2010.
Trout, Nick, *Ever by My Side: A Memoir in Eight [Acts] Pets*, Broadway Books (New York, NY), 2011.

*PERIODICALS*

*Bark*, August 24, 2011, Lee Harrington, "Talking Dogs with Nick Trout, DVM."
*Booklist*, February 1, 2008, Nancy Bent, review of *Tell Me Where It Hurts*, p. 12; September 1, 2008, Kaite Mediatore Stover, review of *Tell Me Where It Hurts*, p. 119; February 15, 2010, Colleen Mondoor, review of *Love Is the Best Medicine*, p. 17; July 1, 2010, Laurie Hartshorn, review of *Love Is the Best Medicine*, p. 72.
*Boston*, March 1, 2010, "Pets: Q&A with Dr. Nick Trout."
*Keizer Times* (Keizer, OR), June 20, 2011, Terri Schlichenmeyer, review of *Ever by My Side*.
*Kirkus Reviews*, February 1, 2008, review of *Tell Me Where It Hurts*; December 15, 2010, review of *Ever by My Side*.

*Kliatt,* July 1, 2008, Francine Levitov, review of *Tell Me Where It Hurts,* p. 56.

*Library Journal,* February 1, 2008, Miriam Tuliao, review of *Tell Me Where It Hurts,* p. 88; April 1, 2010, Judy Brink-Drescher, review of *Love Is the Best Medicine,* p. 91; October 15, 2010, review of *Love Is the Best Medicine,* p. S14.

*Publishers Weekly,* December 24, 2007, review of *Tell Me Where It Hurts,* p. 39.

*Webster-Kirkwood Times* (Webster Groves, MO), March 25, 2011, Linda Jarrett, review of *Ever by My Side.*

ONLINE

*Bookloons,* http://www.bookloons.com/ (August 24, 2011), Rheta Van Winkle, review of *Ever by My Side.*

*Colorado State University Libraries Web site,* http://lib.colostate.edu/ (April 6, 2011), "An Evening with Dr. Nick Trout."

*Doolittler,* http://www.dolittler.com/ (April 20, 2008), review of *Tell Me Where It Hurts.*

*Feathered Quill Book Reviews,* http://featheredquill.blogspot.com/ (February 28, 2011), "Author Interview with Nick Trout."

*Fetchdog,* http://www.fetchdog.com/ (August 24, 2011), Tanya Turgeon, review of *Love Is the Best Medicine.*

*MSPCA-Angell Web site,* http://www.mspca.org/ (October 21, 2008), biographical information on Nick Trout.

*Nick Trout Home Page,* http://www.drnicktrout.com (August 24, 2011).

*OpEdNews.com,* http://www.opednews.com/ (August 24, 2011), Joan Brunwasser, "Veterinarian Nicholas Trout on *Ever by My Side.*

*Philly Dog,* http://www.thephillydog.com/ (March 31, 2011), review of *Ever by My Side.*

*Random House Web site,* http://www.randomhouse.com/ (October 21, 2008), author profile.

*Read It Forward,* http://read-it-forward.crownpublishing.com/ (August 24, 2011), "Meet the Author."

*Seattle Kennel Club Web site,* http://www.seattlekennelclub.org/ (August 24, 2011), Ranny Green, review of *Love Is the Best Medicine.*

*Two Little Cavaliers,* http://twolittlecavaliers.com/ (June 22, 2011), review of *Love Is the Best Medicine.*\*

# Di Wang

## 1956-

## ■ Personal

Born June 20, 1956, in Chengdu, Sichuan, China; son of Guangyuan (a musician) and Yiaolin (an artist) Wang; married Wei Li (an office manager), December 31, 1983; children: Ye. *Ethnicity:* "Chinese." *Education:* Sichuan University, B.A., 1982, M.A. (history), 1985; Johns Hopkins University, M.A. (East Asian history), Ph.D., 1999.

## ■ Addresses

*Home*—College Station, TX. *Office*—Dept. of History, Texas A&M University, College Station, TX 77843-4236; fax: 979-862-4314. *E-mail*—di-wang@tamu.edu.

## ■ Career

Academic and historian. Sichuan University, Chengdu, China, lecturer, 1985-87, associate professor, 1987-92; Texas A&M University, College Station, assistant professor, 1998-2004, associate professor of history, 2004-09, professor of history, 2009—. Visiting research fellow, University of Michigan, 1991-92; visiting scholar, Michigan State University, 1992; visiting professor, Central China Normal University, 2003—; fellow, University of Tokyo, 2005; fellow, Hopkins-Nanjing Center, Nanjing University, 2005; visiting research fellow, Academy of Chinese Social Sciences, 2005—; fellow, National Humanities Center, 2006-07; visiting scholar, University of California at Berkeley, Center for Chinese Studies, 2009; visiting associate professor, University of California at Berkeley, Department of History, 2009; Zijiang Distinguished Visiting Professor, Normal University, 2009—; East Asian Institute research fellow, National University of Singapore, 2010.

## ■ Member

Chinese Historians in the United States (president), Association for Asian Studies, American Historical Association, Historical Society for Twentieth Century China.

## ■ Awards, Honors

Outstanding junior faculty award, Sichuan University, 1986; recipient of grants from American Council of Learned Societies/National Endowment for the Humanities, 2002, Institute for International Research, and Japan Society for the Promotion of Science, 2004; Bernadotte E. Schmitt Grant for Research in European, African and Asian History, American Historical Association, 2004; best book award, Urban History Association, 2006, for non-North American books, for *Street Culture in Chengdu.*

## ■ Writings

*Kuachu fengbi de shijie: Changjiang shangyu guyu she hui yanjiu, 1644-1911* (title means "Striding Out of a Closed World: Social Transformation of the Upper Yangzi Region, 1644-1911"), Zhonghua Book (Beijing, China), 1993.

*Street Culture in Chengdu: Public Space, Urban Commoners, and Local Politics, 1870-1930,* Stanford University Press (Stanford, CA), 2003.

*The Teahouse: Small Business, Everyday Culture, and Public Politics in Chengdu, 1900-1950,* Stanford University Press (Stanford, CA), 2008.

*Qing Mo Xian Dai Qi Ye Yu Guan Shang Guan Xi* (title means "Merchants, Mandarins, and Modern Enterprise in Late Qing China"), Zhongguo she hui ke xue chu ban she (Beijing, China), 2010.

Contributor of articles to academic journals, including *Modern China, Journal of Urban History, Late Imperial China, Twentieth-Century China, European Journal of East Asian Studies, Chinese Historical Review, Journal of Modern Chinese History,* and *Lishi yanjiu;* contributor of book reviews to academic journals, including *Chinese Historical Review, Qingshi yicong, International Journal of Asian Studies, Lishi renleixue xuekan, China Review International, Dushu,* and *American Historical Review;* contributor of chapters to academic books in English and Chinese.

Manuscript reviewer for publishing houses and academic journals, including *Journal of Asian Studies, Modern China, Late Imperial China, Chinese Historical Review, Journal of History and Anthropology, International Journal of Asian Studies, Modern China Studies, Lishi Yanjiu, Jindaishi yanjiu, Journal of Architecture, Urban and Rural Studies of National Taiwan University,* Stanford University Press, Oxford University Press, Houghton Mifflin, Bedford/Martin's, and Wadsworth; editorial board member of *Shehui kexue luntan, Xin shixue,* and *Frontiers of History in China,* as well as coeditor of the latter.

## ■ Sidelights

Di Wang is an academic and historian. Born in 1956 in Chengdu, China, he studied history at Sichuan University before earning a Ph.D. from Johns Hopkins University in 1999. Wang lectured at Sichuan University in the 1980s and early 1990s and became an assistant professor of history at Texas A&M University in 1998, becoming a full professor by 2009. Wang has contributed articles and reviews to a number of academic journals on his research interests, which cover the social and cultural history of China. He has also served as a manuscript reviewer for journals and publishing houses. Wang's

2003 book *Street Culture in Chengdu: Public Space, Urban Commoners, and Local Politics, 1870-1930* won the best non-North American book award from the Urban History Association.

Wang published *The Teahouse: Small Business, Everyday Culture, and Public Politics in Chengdu, 1900-1950* in 2008. The scholarly account looks at the teahouses of Chengdu in southwestern China. Wang first looks at the operations of the teahouses themselves and the role the Teahouse Guild has played. He then describes the social hierarchy and openness of teahouses, something comparatively unique to Chengdu. Wang also highlights how these teahouses serve as a forum for discussion on current affairs. Writing in *Pacific Affairs,* Michael Tsin observed that throughout the text, "the details are occasionally repetitive but always illuminating." Tsin concluded by calling the book "a judicious and informative piece of scholarship."

## ■ Biographical And Critical Sources

*PERIODICALS*

*Canadian Journal of History,* August 1, 2004, Bill Sewell, review of *Street Culture in Chengdu: Public Space, Urban Commoners, and Local Politics, 1870-1930,* p. 421.

*Pacific Affairs,* June 22, 2004, Michael Tsin, review of *Street Culture in Chengdu,* p. 325; March 1, 2010, Michael Tsin, review of *The Teahouse: Small Business, Everyday Culture, and Public Politics in Chengdu, 1900-1950,* p. 155.

*Reference & Research Book News,* November 1, 2008, review of *The Teahouse.*

*ONLINE*

*Department of History, Texas A&M University Web site,* http://history.tamu.edu/ (August 4, 2011), author profile.*

# John C. Waugh

## 1929-

---

### ■ Also Known As

John Clinton Waugh

### ■ Personal

Born October 12, 1929, in Biggs, CA; son of Arthur Fletcher (in highway maintenance) and Pauline (a homemaker) Waugh; married (marriage ended); married Kathleen Diane Lively (a social work administrator), June 11, 1982; children: Daniel Charles, Eliza Marie. *Education:* University of Arizona, B.A. (magna cum laude), 1951; graduate study at University of California—Los Angeles and St. Johns College. *Politics:* Democrat. *Religion:* Protestant.

### ■ Addresses

*Home and office*—Pantego, TX. *Agent*—Mitchell J. Hamilburg, 292 S. La Cienega Blvd., Ste. 312, Beverly Hills, CA 90211. *E-mail*—rivermule@gmail.com.

### ■ Career

Journalist, freelance writer, and editor. *Christian Science Monitor,* Western News Bureau, bureau secretary, 1956-57, staff correspondent, 1957-65, focus editor in Boston, MA, 1965-66, bureau chief in Los Angeles, CA, 1966-70, national series writer, 1970-73, Watergate scandal reporter in Washington, DC, 1973; Office of Vice President Nelson Rockefeller, media specialist, 1973-76; freelance writer and editor, 1976-83; Office of U.S. Senator Jeff Bingaman, press secretary, 1983-89. Has served as editorial consultant for West Virginia Public Radio, West Virginia Department of Natural Resources, New York State Energy Office, U.S. Department of Energy, Atlantic Richfield Company, Public Broadcasting Service (PBS), and the President's Council on Environmental Quality. *Military service:* U.S. Navy, 1951-55, commissioned officer, 1952-55.

### ■ Member

Phi Beta Kappa, Phi Kappa Phi.

### ■ Awards, Honors

Silver Gavel Award for best national reporting, American Bar Association, 1972, for a series of articles in *Christian Science Monitor;* Fletcher Pratt Award for best nonfiction book on the Civil War, History—New York Civil War Round Table, 1994, for *The Class of 1846: From West Point to Appomattox—Stonewall Jackson, George McClellan and Their Brothers;* History Award Medal, Daughters of American Revolution, 1998; Grady McWhiney Award of Merit, Dallas Civil War Round Table, 2000.

### ■ Writings

*NONFICTION*

*The Class of 1846: From West Point to Appomattox—Stonewall Jackson, George McClellan and Their Brothers,* Warner Books (New York, NY), 1994.
*Sam Bell Maxey and the Confederate Indians,* Ryan Place Publishers (Fort Worth, TX), 1995.
*Reelecting Lincoln: The Battle for the 1864 Presidency,* Crown (New York, NY), 1997.

*Last Stand at Mobile*, McWhiney Foundation Press (Abilene, TX), 2001.

*Surviving the Confederacy: Rebellion, Ruin, and Recovery—Roger and Sara Pryor during the Civil War*, Harcourt (New York, NY), 2002.

*Edwin Cole Bearss: History's Pied Piper*, Edwin C. Bearss Trust Fund (Washington, DC), 2003.

*On the Brink of Civil War: The Compromise of 1850 and How It Changed the Course of American History*, Scholarly Resources (Wilmington, DE), 2003.

*Twenty Good Reasons to Study the Civil War*, McWhiney Foundation Press (Abilene, TX), 2004.

*Kansai International Airport: Airport in the Sea*, Children's Press (New York, NY), 2004.

*One Man Great Enough: Abraham Lincoln's Road to Civil War*, Harcourt (Orlando, FL), 2007.

(Interviewer, with Drake Bush) *How Historians Work: Retelling the Past, from the Civil War to the Wider World*, edited by Judith Lee Hallock, State House Press (Buffalo Gap, TX), 2010.

*Lincoln and McClellan: The Troubled Partnership between a President and His General*, Palgrave Macmillan (New York, NY), 2010.

Contributor of articles to periodicals, including *American Heritage, Civil War Times Illustrated, USAir* magazine, *Country, New York Times, Sports Illustrated, Outside, New Republic, Nation, Los Angeles Times, Boston Herald-American, Boston Globe, West, Kiwanis* magazine, *Think, American Banker, American Education, Black Politician, Goldenseal,* and *National Observer.*

## ■ Sidelights

Journalist and author John C. Waugh once told *CA:* "I have never considered not writing. I started young aiming for a career in journalism, pointing myself in that direction from the day I started school. My goal was to grow up and be a correspondent for the *Christian Science Monitor*. Being easily fascinated by almost any subject, and prone to diversions, I flirted momentarily with careers in paleontology and history, but managed in the end to stay on the preordained track, graduating from the University of Arizona in 1951 with a degree in journalism.

"Following a five-year stint in the U.S. Navy, I joined the Western News Bureau of the *Christian Science Monitor* in 1956 as secretary to the bureau chief, more or less on my self-imposed schedule. Nine months later I was a staff correspondent. In my nearly twenty-year career on the *Monitor,* I was a general utility infielder, writing about every conceivable subject, but mainly politics, and finally

doing special series for the paper on a wide range of topics." Waugh spent a long and distinguished career with the *Christian Science Monitor* before he left that publication to concentrate on freelance work. He has also served on the staffs of both Vice President Nelson Rockefeller, a Republican, and the Democratic U.S. senator from New Mexico, John Bingaman.

### Early Nonfiction

Waugh's first book was the acclaimed history volume *The Class of 1846: From West Point to Appomattox—Stonewall Jackson, George McClellan and Their Brothers.* The volume explores the United States Military Academy at West Point's class of 1846. The class produced many famed generals, most of whom, after strengthening the bonds of school friendship in the Mexican American War and in battles against Native American tribes, had to fight one another in the U.S. Civil War. George McClellan, Jesse Reno, and George Stoneman fought for the Union, while the Confederates boasted Stonewall Jackson, George Pickett, and A.P. Hill. Commending the study's examination of "the four bloody years from Fort Sumter to Appomattox through the lives of the members of the West Point Class of 1846 who participated in the war," *Washington Post Book World* reviewer Jonathan Yardley praised the book's "penetrating analysis."

Other critics offered similar opinions. David Murray, writing in the *New York Times Book Review,* maintained that in *The Class of 1846,* Waugh "has done his homework well, and has deftly translated his findings into a complicated but compelling narrative." Guy Halverson, writing in the *Christian Science Monitor,* called the work a "first-rate and moving account," and *History Book Club Review* reviewer William C. Davis summed it up as "a moving, important book that goes beyond the story of these . . . young men to speak of the America from which they came and which, in one way or another, all of them risked themselves to help defend and define."

In *Reelecting Lincoln: The Battle for the 1864 Presidency,* Waugh turns his attention toward what has long been considered one of the most critical elections in American history. In the midst of the Civil War, the results of the 1864 election would determine the fate of a nation. *Booklist* contributor Brad Hooper noted in his review: "The candidates, the issues, and the consequence of the election are analyzed with perfect clarity." Using a variety of sources, including old newspaper articles, memoirs, and letters, Waugh relates the story of Lincoln's reelection to the presidency. Stephen B. Oates, reviewing the volume in the *New York Times Book Review,* thought that "Waugh . . . recounts the 1864 election with great narrative skill. The story sweeps along, with brilliant vignettes of all the players in the drama and one vivid scene after another: life in wartime Washington, the Democratic convention in Chicago, Lincoln in the War Department telegraph office, anxiously awaiting news from the battlefronts." While noting that Waugh "adds nothing new to the story" of the 1864 election, Oates nevertheless remarked: "As popular history, *Reelecting Lincoln* is highly entertaining."

### Mid-Career Nonfiction

Waugh continued his study of the Civil War in *Last Stand at Mobile,* which tells the story of the capture of Mobile, Alabama, one of the Confederacy's most important cities. He followed *Last Stand at Mobile* with *Surviving the Confederacy: Rebellion, Ruin, and Recovery—Roger and Sara Pryor during the Civil War,* in which he recounts the tale of a Confederate couple who manage to remain together before, during, and after the Civil War, even as their country is torn apart. Roger and Sara Pryor were well known in the South, and Waugh tells the story of the Civil War from their perspective. He traces Roger from his prewar position as an editor to his service in the Confederate army and his rise as a lawyer in New York after the war. Waugh follows Sara as she cares for her children while her husband is away at war. Using diaries and letters, Waugh captures not only the facts of the Civil War, but also the emotions.

Waugh received some negative criticism for over-dramatizing certain scenes and reconstructing the dialogue in *Surviving the Confederacy.* A *Publishers Weekly* contributor remarked: "Waugh describes vividly the society in which the Pryors moved and their struggles during the war, but the reconstructed dialogue and breathless descriptions . . . may deter the more historically minded." *Library Journal* reviewer Randall M. Miller echoed that sentiment, writing: "Waugh overdramatizes by including dialogue and imputing motives to actions that the sources do not wholly sustain." Despite these shortcomings, Paul Christopher Anderson, in his review in *Civil War History,* credited Waugh "with understanding what many academic historians often seem unwilling to explore or unable to confront: the Civil War was an emotional experience, an intensely human drama." Mary Seaton Dix, contributor to the *Journal of Southern History,* also found merit in *Surviving the Confederacy.* Dix wrote: "This dramatic account of Sara and Roger Pryor's marriage helps to explain why there are so few Civil War novels. Fact simply outstrips fiction, especially when historians turn to the letters, diaries, and memoirs that provide such rich descriptions of life before, during, and after the war."

*On the Brink of Civil War: The Compromise of 1850 and How It Changed the Course of American History* is Waugh's account of one of the major events that eventually led to the Civil War. Following the U.S.-Mexican War, North and South argued over the fate of the newly acquired land. Among the people populating the events in the book are several politicians, including Henry Clay, Daniel Webster, John C. Calhoun, Henry Seward, Stephen A. Douglas, Salmon P. Chase, and Jefferson Davis. On one side of the debate, the North wanted the new territories to be free. On the opposing side, the South wanted the new land to become slave-holding territories. The Compromise of 1850 established a system of popular sovereignty in the new territories, which vaguely determined that the settlers to each territory would determine whether that territory would eventually become a free or slave-holding state. This same compromise also ushered in the Fugitive Slave Law, a divisive piece of legislation that drew many Northerners off the sidelines and into the fight against slavery. In an effort to prevent a civil war, the Compromise of 1850 practically drew the battle lines.

### Later Nonfiction

In *One Man Great Enough: Abraham Lincoln's Road to Civil War,* Waugh addresses the early years of Lincoln's life that served as the foundation for his thoughts and behavior during his time as the president, and his actions relating to the Civil War. He begins with Lincoln's childhood and provides a thorough picture of the man as he grew up, studied, and eventually entered the law and then politics. Waugh addresses each phase of Lincoln's life by analyzing the actions that eventually led him to become leader of the country. The themes of the book focus heavily, as a result, on the maintenance of the Union, war, and attitudes toward slavery. He relies heavily upon the plethora of material available in Lincoln's own words, including journals and letters as well as speeches, and the writings of Lincoln's law partner before he took public office, William Herndon. A reviewer in *Publishers Weekly* noted that "Waugh is particularly adept at weaving details of Lincoln's family life into the narrative, which focuses on decidedly political matters." A contributor to *Kirkus Reviews* found the book less in-depth than some of the other biographies of Lincoln that are available but still worthwhile, concluding that the volume is "unlikely to impress jaded Lincoln devotees, but sure to charm newcomers."

Waugh followed *One Man Great Enough* with *How Historians Work: Retelling the Past, from the Civil War to the Wider World* and *Lincoln and McClellan: The Troubled Partnership between a President and His General.* In the latter, Waugh explores the working relationship between President Abraham Lincoln and General George McClellan. Their strategizing during the Civil War is addressed, and Waugh notes that Lincoln and McClellan were essentially at odds. Lincoln was raised in poverty; McClellan was well bred (and a snob). Lincoln provided the supplies and men that McClellan demanded during the war, but he was disappointed by the general's failure to capture Virginia. According to Michael J. Deeb in the online *Civil War Novels,* "this short study goes beyond just the Lincoln-McClellan relationship. In fact it is principally about how McClellan handled the great authority given him by President Lincoln in 1861. The author brings to the table a better understanding of how McClellan's rigid arrogance, mistrust and fear of failure impeded his ability to work with civilian authority and subordinates or lead his troops effectively. It is well worth the read." Jay Freeman, writing in *Booklist,* was also laudatory, noting that "general readers who wish to learn more . . . will find this work informative and easily digestible." In the words of *Library Journal* reviewer Gayla Koerting, *Lincoln and McClellan* is "highly recommended for history buffs and academic libraries and as a good supplemental text for an undergraduate Civil War course."

## Waugh Once Told *CA:*

"I fancy myself not so much a historian as a historical reporter, uniting my supposed skills as a journalist with my preoccupation with the past. I look on history as a series of dramatic scenes, and try to write it that way. Put yourself down anywhere in the past, anywhere at all, and something damned interesting and dramatic is going on. My goal is to bring what is going on back to life, so you can see it, smell it, feel it. There is basically no difference in telling a story from the past from covering a breaking news story in the present. The only difference is my sources are all dead, which is no handicap.

"When I am at work with a book, I spend the first few months researching—enough to prime the pipeline. Then, when I have enough to begin writing, I write mornings and continue researching afternoons and evenings, generally keeping one chapter ahead of myself, one jump ahead of the sheriff. Invariably after the writing is done, I continue to write, reshaping, refining, until some editor tears the manuscript out of my hands and says 'enough already.'

"My purpose in writing is first and foremost to tell a good story, to make the past come alive, to try to help readers enjoy reading about what happened so long ago. Winston Churchill once said, 'History with its flickering lamp stumbles along the trail of the past, trying to reconstruct its scenes, to revive its echoes, and kindle with pale gleams the passion of former days.' I consider my mission as a writer is to help history along its stumbling trail as best I can, to reconstruct its scenes, revive its echoes, and rekindle the passion of former days.

"Several writer-historians have shown me the way. Among them is Shelby Foote, whose three-volume work on the Civil War is literature. 'Literature' also describes the works of Bruce Catton, and Abraham Lincoln's biographer Carl Sandburg. There have been some fine historian-writers whom I admire as well: James M. McPherson, James Randall, David M. Potter, Benjamin Thomas, and Arthur Schlesinger, Jr. I have also admired some fine writers who were also major actors in history: Abraham Lincoln and John Hay come to mind.

"I think a lot of history written today is heavy going, lacking poetry. History is exciting, it is about people, and it is about drama. Whenever anybody tells me they hated history in school and are bored by it in adulthood, it is because it was not taught right and is not written right. Historians should also be writers. The research may be strong, but without a good, compelling writer, the history remains dead and meaningless. So I believe historians today generally need to give equal time not just to what they are saying, but to how they are saying it.

"My advice to young writers is to approach their writing as storytellers. Their job is to tell the reader a story. Their job, if they are writing history, which is what I am addressing here, is to tell what happened in the past and tell it in human terms, as dramatically and poetically as they can and still be true to their facts."

## ■ Biographical And Critical Sources

*PERIODICALS*

*American History,* April 1, 2003, Floyd B. Larcent, Jr., review of *Surviving the Confederacy: Rebellion, Ruin, and Recovery—Roger and Sara Pryor during the Civil War,* p. 67.

*Booklist,* November 1, 1997, Brad Hooper, review of *Reelecting Lincoln: The Battle for the 1864 Presidency,* p. 452; April 15, 2010, Jay Freeman, review of *Lincoln and McClellan: The Troubled Partnership between a President and His General,* p. 22.

*Book World*, February 8, 1998, review of *Reelecting Lincoln*, p. 3; July 4, 1999, review of *The Class of 1846: From West Point to Appomattox—Stonewall Jackson, George McClellan and Their Brothers*, p. 10.

*Christian Science Monitor*, April 5, 1994, Guy Halverson, review of *The Class of 1846*.

*Civil War History*, September, 2003, Paul Christopher Anderson, review of *Surviving the Confederacy*, p. 311.

*History Book Club Review*, March, 1994, William C. Davis, review of *The Class of 1846*, pp. 3-6.

*Journal of Southern History*, February, 2004, Mary Seaton Dix, review of *Surviving the Confederacy*, pp. 169-171; February 1, 2004, Mary Seaton Dix, review of *Surviving the Confederacy*, p. 169.

*Kirkus Reviews*, December 1, 1997, review of *Reelecting Lincoln*, p. 1764; August 15, 2007, review of *One Man Great Enough: Abraham Lincoln's Road to Civil War*; March 15, 2010, review of *Lincoln and McClellan*.

*Library Journal*, November 1, 1997, Patricia Ann Owens, review of *Reelecting Lincoln*, p. 92; October 1, 2002, Randall M. Miller, review of *Surviving the Confederacy*, p. 115; October 1, 2002, Randall M. Miller, review of *Surviving the Confederacy*, p. 115; April 1, 2010, Koerting Gayla, review of *Lincoln and McClellan*, p. 84.

*New York Times*, February 18, 1998, review of *Reelecting Lincoln*, p. E8.

*New York Times Book Review*, June 12, 1994, David Murray, review of *The Class of 1846*, p. 23; February 15, 1998, Stephen B. Oates, review of *Reelecting Lincoln*, p. 14.

*Publishers Weekly*, December 15, 1997, review of *Reelecting Lincoln*, p. 39; September 9, 2002, review of *Surviving the Confederacy*, p. 57; September 17, 2007, review of *One Man Great Enough*, p. 45; April 19, 2010, review of *Lincoln and McClellan*, p. 44.

*Wall Street Journal*, February 12, 1998, review of *Reelecting Lincoln*, p. A20.

*Washington Post Book World*, February 13, 1994, Jonathan Yardley, review of *The Class of 1846*.

ONLINE

*Civil War Novels*, http://www.civilwarnovels.com/ (August 11, 2011), Michael J. Deeb, review of *Lincoln and McClellan*.

*John C. Waugh Home Page*, http://www.johncwaugh.com (August 11, 2011).*

# Charles Webster

## 1936-

---

### ■ Personal

Born October 23, 1936, in Lowdham, England. *Education:* Earned D.Sc.

### ■ Addresses

*Office*—All Souls College, Oxford OX1 4AL, England.

### ■ Career

Writer, editor, and educator. Corpus Christi College, Oxford, fellow, 1972-88; Wellcome Unit for Medicine, Oxford, director, 1972-88; University of Oxford, reader in history of medicine, 1972-88; All Souls College, Oxford, senior research fellow, then emeritus fellow, 1988-2004.

### ■ Writings

(Editor) *Samuel Hartlib and the Advancement of Learning,* Cambridge University Press (London, England), 1970.

(Editor) *The Intellectual Revolution of the Seventeenth Century,* Routledge & Kegan Paul (Boston, MA), 1974.

*The Great Instauration: Science, Medicine, and Reform, 1626-1660,* Duckworth (London, England), 1975, Holmes & Meier (New York, NY), 1976.

(Editor, with Francis Maddison and Margaret Pelling) *Essays on the Life and Work of Thomas Linacre, c. 1460-1524,* Clarendon Press (Oxford, England), 1977.

*Utopian Planning and the Puritan Revolution: Gabriel Plattes, Samuel Hartlib, and "Macaria,"* Wellcome Unit for the History of Medicine (Oxford, England), 1979.

(Editor) *Health, Medicine, and Mortality in the Sixteenth Century,* Cambridge University Press (New York, NY), 1979.

(Editor) *Biology, Medicine, and Society, 1840-1940,* Cambridge University Press (New York, NY), 1981.

*From Paracelsus to Newton: Magic and the Making of Modern Science,* Cambridge University Press (New York, NY), 1982, Dover (Mineola, NY), 2005.

*Problems of Health Care: The National Health Service before 1957,* HMSO (London, England), 1988.

(Series editor, with Charles Rosenberg) William H. Schneider, *Quality and Quantity: The Quest for Biological Regeneration in Twentieth-Century France,* Cambridge University Press (New York, NY), 1990.

(Editor) *Caring for Health: History and Diversity,* Open University Press (Philadelphia, PA), 2nd edition, 1993, 3rd edition, 2001.

*Government and Health Care: The British National Health Service, 1958-1979,* Stationary Office (London, England), 1996.

(Editor, with Irvine Louden and John Horder) *General Practice under the National Health Service, 1948-1997,* Clarendon Press (New York, NY), 1998.

*The National Health Service: A Political History,* Oxford University Press (New York, NY), 1998, 2nd edition, 2002.

*The Practice of Reform in Health, Medicine, and Science, 1500-2000: Essays for Charles Webster,* edited by Margaret Pelling and Scott Mandelbrote, Ashgate (Burlington, VT), 2005.

(Editor, with Pamela Michael) *Health and Society in Twentieth-Century Wales,* University of Wales Press (Cardiff, Wales), 2006.

*Paracelsus: Medicine, Magic, and Mission at the End of Time,* Yale University Press (New Haven, CT), 2008.

## ■ Sidelights

Charles Webster is a respected author and editor of numerous volumes on the history of medicine and education, focusing on the advancements in England during the sixteenth and seventeenth centuries. Several of his books examine the work of reformers such as Samuel Hartlib and Gabriel Plattes, known for their efforts to democratize the educational system in England, while later works address health service policies in the modern era, in each case showing how early reform affected the development of public services, resulting in modern-day standards.

### Samuel Hartlib and the Advancement of Learning and The Intellectual Revolution of the Seventeenth Century

In *Samuel Hartlib and the Advancement of Learning,* Webster presents a collection of mid-seventeenth century tracts on educational reform that were the basis for the beliefs of Samuel Hartlib and John Dury. Hartlib and Dury strove for universal education, working under the principle that all children deserved to attend school, and not just those from wealthy homes. In addition, they were advocates of updated teaching methods and curricula. The timing of this proposal, at the heart of the English Civil War, ultimately proved its downfall, as the Restoration forced educational reform and focus on subjects such as science into the background. J.R. Ravetz, in a review for the *English Historical Review,* called Webster's introduction to the volume "penetrating and erudite," and a contributor to the *Times Literary Supplement* wrote: "This volume will enlighten students of education and give historians of the period a better understanding of an important aspect which has not had the attention it deserves."

*The Intellectual Revolution of the Seventeenth Century* collects a number of articles from the historical journal, *Past and Present.* Paul S. Seaver, reviewing for *Church History,* praised Webster's introduction, calling it "substantial." He continued, saying: "Webster is particularly illuminating in his discussion of that complex debate which concerns the transformation of natural philosophy which we have come to call the scientific revolution."

### The Great Instauration and From Paracelsus to Newton

Webster delves more deeply into the relationship between the scientific revolution of the seventeenth century and the changes to English society in his book, *The Great Instauration: Science, Medicine, and Reform, 1626-1660.* He focuses on Samuel Hartlib, using his papers as reference, then widens his range to include such reformers as Gabriel Plattes, Comenius, and Benjamin Worsley. These men attempted to improve the state of education, scientific exploration, economics, and foreign policy. *Times Literary Supplement* contributor Quentin Skinner referred to Webster's book as "a work of monumental scholarship, full of new information, beautifully organized, opening up new areas for discussion, culminating in a challenging new theory about the whole development of English science." Frances Yates, reviewing for the *New York Review of Books,* commented: "One feels a certain narrowness in Webster's approach, a restriction to the 'special field' of English Puritan science. Nevertheless, within his limits he has performed a valuable work in his exhaustive account of Puritan science, medicine, and reform between 1626 and 1660 . . . the specific task which he set himself."

*From Paracelsus to Newton: Magic and the Making of Modern Science* addresses the ways in which magic and prophecy overlapped with more conventional science as the latter developed as a discipline. Webster explains that even those known for the cutting-edge advances of the seventeenth century, such as Isaac Newton, were prone to consulting religious scripture when trying to determine God's will. Steven Shapin, in a piece for the *British Book News,* wrote that "according to Webster, late-seventeenth-century 'physico-theology' was designed not so much to 'explain away' miracles as to justify the correctness of biblical chronology." Shapin went on to refer to Webster's work as "the best introduction to current understanding of the relation between science and prophetic religion in this period."

### Problems of Health Care and The National Health Service

With *Problems of Health Care: The National Health Service before 1957,* Webster tackles the National Health Service (NHS), an institution that came into existence following World War II and provides free health care at point of consumption. He traces the system from its origins as part of the Poor Law, legislation for public health and national insurance, through wartime reconstruction, to its current incarnation. *London Review of Books* contributor Jose Harris pointed out that "though the story is told with almost exaggerated restraint and detachment, there are few signs here that this is an 'official,' government-inspired history in any pejorative sense." Robert Pinker, in a piece for the *Times Literary Supplement,* wrote that the book "strikes the right balance between detailed analysis and an interesting narrative," and went on to conclude: "Charles Webster has made a splendid, scholarly start to his history, strong in narrative and fair in its judgments." Kenneth O. Morgan, writing for the *English Historical Review,* referred to the book as "a marvelously exciting work, full of new information and new insights," and said of Webster that "his lucid, scholarly, and dispassionate account will provide the basis for all future research on public health policy in modern Britain."

Webster revisits the NHS in *The National Health Service: A Political History,* a volume that spans the history of the system from its origins to its modern incarnation and focuses on the changes made by successive governments, particularly on that of Margaret Thatcher who was known for her healthcare policies. Writing for the *London Review of Books,* Richard Horton noted: "Webster is at his most interesting in writing about Thatcher. He shows how she . . . exchanged the status quo for a revolutionary reappraisal of how to govern the Health Service. She and her ministers . . . replaced the consensus with confrontation. . . . Efficiency replaced effectiveness as Thatcher's goal." Webster addresses questions of rising population and concerns about care for the elderly, comparing Britain's policies to those of neighboring countries. *English Historical Review* contributor Arthur Marwick called *The National Health Service* a "gem of a book."

### Health and Society in Twentieth-Century Wales

Webster coedited *Health and Society in Twentieth-Century Wales* with Pamela Michael in 2006. The account derives from a conference at the University of Wales, Bangor, in 2000 that aimed to discuss the history of medicine in Wales and its academic literature. The first seven chapters cover the history, while the remainder of the book covers more contemporary issues. Reviewing the book in *Medical History,* Anne Borsay called the book "a welcome addition to the still relatively scant academic literature on the history of medicine in Wales."

### Paracelsus

In 2008 Webster published *Paracelsus: Medicine, Magic, and Mission at the End of Time.* The account examines the nonscientific writings of the sixteenth-century Swedish-born doctor Paracelsus. Webster shows how his unorthodox views based on his belief that the end of the world was drawing near

made him an outcast from his fellow doctors of his time. A contributor to *Times Higher Education* commented: "While this work will be especially interesting for historians of science, medicine and the Reformation, Webster's work will appeal to a wide audience, for it captures in lucid prose and fascinating stories the medicine, science, magic and apocalyptic angst of early modern Europe." A contributor to the *New Yorker* called the book "the first major consideration in fifty years of the Renaissance doctor, alchemist, and theologian." Reviewing the book in *Church History,* Eric Lund remarked that "a tribute on the cover of this book claims that it will undoubtedly replace Pagel's classic study. This is an overstatement because Pagel and others still provide a fuller analysis of Paracelsus's scientific theories. Aspects of this book may also be challenging for those who are looking for an entry point to the study of Paracelsus. Nevertheless, it will provide a valuable resource for contextualizing his thought and clarifying its scope and focus."

## ■ Biographical And Critical Sources

*PERIODICALS*

*American Historical Review,* April 1, 1984, Brian Easlea, review of *From Paracelsus to Newton: Magic and the Making of Modern Science,* p. 401.

*British Book News,* August 1, 1983, review of *From Paracelsus to Newton,* p. 496.

*British Medical Journal,* April 12, 1997, Gordon Macpherson, review of *Government and Health Care: The British National Health Service, 1958-1979,* p. 1136; April 11, 1998, J.P. Bunker, review of *The National Health Service: A Political History,* p. 1177.

*Choice,* June 1, 1980, review of *Health, Medicine, and Mortality in the Sixteenth Century,* p. 559; September 1, 1983, review of *From Paracelsus to Newton,* p. 124.

*Church History,* June 1, 1975, Paul S. Seaver, review of *The Intellectual Revolution of the Seventeenth Century,* p. 263; September 1, 2009, Eric Lund, review of *Paracelsus: Medicine, Magic, and Mission at the End of Time,* p. 685.

*Economic History Review,* February 1, 1999, Bernard Harris, review of *The National Health Service,* p. 167.

*Economist,* September 28, 1974, review of *The Intellectual Revolution of the Seventeenth Century,* p. 104.

*English Historical Review,* January 1, 1972, J.R. Ravetz, review of *Samuel Hartlib and the Advancement of Learning,* p. 188; April 1, 1981, C.S.L. Davies, review of *Health, Medicine, and Mortality in the Sixteenth Century,* pp. 393-394; April 1, 1982, Christopher Hill, review of *Utopian Planning and* the Puritan Revolution: Gabriel Plattes, Samuel Hartlib, and "Macaria," p. 426; April 1, 1983, K. Theodore Hoppen, review of Biology, Medicine, and Society, 1840-1940, pp. 388-390; July 1, 1991, Kenneth O. Morgan, review of Problems of Health Care: The National Health Service before 1957, pp. 681-682; September 1, 1999, Arthur Marwick, review of The National Health Service, p. 1034; June 1, 2000, Helen Jones, review of General Practice under the National Health Service, 1948-1997, p. 760.

London Review of Books, June 23, 1988, Jose Harris, "One Nation," p. 9; July 2, 1998, Richard Horton, "A Revision of Expectations," p. 22.

Medical History, October 1, 2007, Anne Borsay, review of Health and Society in Twentieth-Century Wales, pp. 572-573.

Mennonite Quarterly Review, July 1, 2010, Gary K. Waite, review of Paracelsus, p. 453.

New Statesman, November 14, 1975, Christopher Hill, "Scientists of the Republic," pp. 613-614; March 27, 1998, Polly Toynbee, review of The National Health Service, p. 48.

New Yorker, January 12, 2009, review of Paracelsus, p. 69.

New York Review of Books, May 27, 1976, Frances Yates, "Science, Salvation, and the Cabala," review of The Great Instauration: Science, Medicine, and Reform, 1626-1660, pp. 27-29; December 16, 1982, Lawrence Stone, "Madness," review of Health, Medicine, and Mortality in the Sixteenth Century, pp. 28-36.

Political Quarterly, July 1, 1997, Rudolf Klein, review of Government and Health Care, p. 301; January 1, 1999, Rudolf Klein, review of The National Health Service, p. 108.

Public Administration, March 22, 1999, Rodney Lowe, review of The National Health Service, p. 221.

Quarterly Review of Biology, September 1, 1992, Elof Axel Carlson, review of Quality and Quantity: The Quest for Biological Regeneration in Twentieth-Century France, pp. 337-341.

Reference and Research Book News, February 1, 1994, review of Caring for Health: History and Diversity, p. 56.

Renaissance Quarterly, September 22, 2009, Tara Nummedal, review of Paracelsus, p. 995.

Science and Society, December 22, 1976-1977, C.H. George, review of The Intellectual Revolution of the Seventeenth Century, pp. 479-486.

SciTech Book News, June 1, 2006, review of The Practice of Reform in Health, Medicine, and Science, 1500-2000: Essays for Charles Webster.

Times Higher Education, March 5, 2009, review of Paracelsus.

Times Literary Supplement, April 2, 1970, review of Samuel Hartlib and the Advancement of Learning, p. 365; July 2, 1976, Quentin Skinner, review of The Great Instauration, p. 810; March 19, 1982, Jane Lewis, review of Biology, Medicine, and Society, 1840-1940, p. 300; September 9-15, 1988, Robert Pinker, review of Problems of Health Care, p. 987.

ONLINE

All Souls College, Oxford University Web site, http://www.all-souls.ox.ac.uk/ (August 4, 2011), author profile.*

# Lauren Weisberger

## 1977-

■ **Personal**

Born March 28, 1977, in Scranton, PA; married Mike Cohen (a writer), April 5, 2008. *Education:* Cornell University, B.A., 1999.

■ **Addresses**

*Home*—New York, NY. *Agent*—Deborah Schneider, Gelfman & Schneider Literary Agents, 250 W. 57th St., Ste. 2515, New York, NY 10107. *E-mail*—lauren@laurenweisberger.com.

■ **Career**

Writer. *Vogue*, New York, NY, personal assistant, c. 2001; *Departures*, New York, staff writer, c. 2003. Actress, including appearance in the film *The Devil Wears Prada*; guest on television programs, including *Today*, 2003, and *Tout le monde en parle*, 2006.

■ **Awards, Honors**

Galaxy British Book Award, film book of the year, 2007, for *The Devil Wears Prada*.

■ **Writings**

(With Jennifer Weiner and Adriana Trigiani) *American Girls about Town* (short stories), Downtown Press (New York, NY), 2004.

*NOVELS*

*The Devil Wears Prada*, Doubleday (New York, NY), 2003.

*Everyone Worth Knowing*, Simon & Schuster (New York, NY), 2005.
*Chasing Harry Winston*, Simon & Schuster (New York, NY), 2008.
*Last Night at Chateau Marmont*, Atria (New York, NY), 2010.

Author of a blog.

■ **Adaptations**

*Everyone Worth Knowing* was adapted as an audiobook, released by Simon & Schuster in 2005; *The Devil Wears Prada* was adapted as a film, released by Fox 2000 Pictures in 2006.

■ **Sidelights**

Lauren Weisberger is an American writer. Born in 1977 in Scranton, Pennsylvania, she graduated from Cornell University and set off to work in New York City. Weisberger began working as the personal assistant to *Vogue* editor-in-chief Anna Wintour and writing reviews for *Departures* magazine while taking some creative writing classes.

### The Devil Wears Prada

In *The Devil Wears Prada*, Weisberger's first novel, recent Ivy League graduate Andrea Sachs lands the job of a lifetime as the personal assistant to Miranda Priestly, the tough-as-nails, Prada-wearing editor in chief of *Runway* magazine, the country's leading fashion publication. As Andrea simmers through the menial and demeaning tasks that comprise her days, she dreams of a more fulfilling career as a staff writer for the *New Yorker* and hopes that her current job will be a stepping stone to the next one. Even though she is constantly reminded that "millions of girls would kill for her job," she finds it hard to be grateful for the opportunity to be humiliated in public by her boss, even if she gets free designer shoes in the process. At the bottom of the publishing pecking order, Andrea's hours are long, recognition is nonexistent, and the boss keeps her on call twenty-four hours a day. Her exciting life in New York City leaves her no time for her friends and family and makes her suspect that her college education was a waste of time. The biggest names in the fashion world—Hilfiger, de la Renta, Versace, et al—serve as the backdrop for this novel.

When *The Devil Wears Prada* was published in the spring of 2003, it became a best seller as much for what it was about as for who it was about. Prior to writing the book, Weisberger worked as the personal assistant for Anna Wintour, the editor in chief of the American edition of *Vogue,* and the book was widely rumored to be a thinly veiled exposé of what it was like to work for the notoriously difficult fashion icon. Interest in the book even before it was finished led to a bidding war that gained Weisberger a lucrative deal for both the book and film rights.

Like her heroine, Weisberger graduated from an Ivy League school in 1999 and soon began her job at *Vogue,* where she was propelled into the fashion world with little preparation or experience. She resigned after a year, and when her next job left her with enough time to enroll in a writing seminar, she compiled a collection of vignettes based on her work experiences that her instructor urged her to submit to an agent. The agent, Deborah Schneider, generated lots of advance publicity about the book, and by the time it was published, expectations were high. As Kate Betts noted in the *New York Times:* "Does it even matter what's actually on the page when everybody is reading between the lines?"

In the story, the fashion-unconscious Andrea has only taken the *Runway* job because she hopes that Miranda will recommend her to the editor of the *New Yorker.* She arrives at the office wearing modest Nine West shoes, and soon enough a kind soul gives her a makeover, raiding the office's vaunted "closet" in the process, a raid that gives her a pair of thousand-dollar Gucci pants that no one else can wear because they are a hefty size six. Add a pair of Jimmy Choo stiletto-heeled shoes, and Andrea's fashion consciousness begins to improve. But Miranda makes her life so miserable that she is unable to enjoy playing dress-up. The boss is an overbearing, undersized "size zero" who eats bacon, steak, and ice cream and throws her clothes away after she wears them twice. She makes unreasonable demands: Andrea must not eat in her presence; Andrea must pack her travel clothes in velvet; Andrea must locate copies of the yet-to-be-published Harry Potter book to ship to Miranda's children in Paris.

The pressure prompts Andrea to indulge in revenge fantasies. "You don't want her to die," she thinks, "because if she does, you lose all hope of killing her yourself. And that would be a shame." Andrea relaxes over late-night drinks with her friends, but she regretfully finds herself losing touch with her childhood friend, whose drinking habit is escalating nearly out of control. Also neglected is Andrea's boyfriend, Alex, a fourth-grade teacher of disadvantaged kids, who is perennially disappointed over having to take a back seat to his girlfriend's career. Apart from the magazine, her career plan involves attracting the attention of Christian Collinsworth, a budding literary celebrity whose first book was hailed "as one of the most significant literary achievements of the 20th century." Bolstered by encouraging words from him, Andrea musters the nerve to confront Miranda at a Paris fashion show that becomes the scene of a showdown.

Critics reacted to the "tell-all" nature of the story with varying shades of amusement. Some of them compared the book to other recent muckraking novels considered to be of special interest to female readers, such as *The Nanny Diaries.* Stacy Alesi of the *Library Journal* called *The Devil Wears Prada* a "fast-paced black comedy [that] has enough dirt to please any fashionista." A reviewer for *Publishers Weekly* wrote that the book has "plenty of dead-on assessments of fashion's frivolity and realistic, funny portrayals of life as a peon." A *Kirkus Reviews* contributor dubbed the novel an "on-the-money kiss-and-tell debut."

In interviews, Weisberger attempted to place distance between the character of Miranda and any comparison to her former boss at *Vogue,* and she discouraged comparisons between the magazine and *Runway.* Miranda "is certainly not modeled after Anna," she told David D. Kirkpatrick for a *New York Times* article. On the contrary, she continued, "there was something amazing about getting to work for and see this incredibly bright, powerful woman." Furthermore, Weisberger believes the scope of the novel is broader than critics have described it. "I think it goes beyond the fashion industry," she told Lynn Andriani for *Publishers Weekly.* "It's a year in the life of this girl: her relationships, and what it's like to be right out of college and living in New York." The author continued: "You're in so far over your head, you have no idea of up from down." Furthermore, she stated that the narrative "is composed of stories from my friends," adding: "And a lot of it is my slightly overactive imagination." But not everyone was convinced. "*The Devil Wears Prada* is a roman a clef of the unsubtlest sort," wrote Diane Roberts in the *Atlanta Journal-Constitution,* "maybe more a roman a vengeance." Summarizing the wide-ranging opinions of many critics, Lisa Lockwood wrote in *Women's Wear Daily* that "the book is far from a literary masterpiece, but its in-depth knowledge of the inner workings and absurdities of the fashion magazine world should keep both outsiders and insiders chuckling through the breathless sentences."

### Everyone Worth Knowing and Chasing Harry Winston

In her next novel, *Everyone Worth Knowing,* Weisberger tells the story of Bettina "Bette" Robinson, who leaves the staid world of banking to work for an upscale public relations firm. Bette's new job requires her to socialize with the rich and famous, and her relationship with a high-profile bachelor leads to her name appearing in the gossip columns. Bette, however, finds herself attracted to "nobody," which, coupled with the growing negative gossip, leads her to introspection about what is really important in life. A *Kirkus Reviews* contributor noted that the author "again traces the misadventures of a hapless young thing sucked into a glamorous career that is psychologically and physically crushing." Misha Stone, writing in the *Library Journal,* called the book "a solid sophomore novel," adding that the author creates "a smart, complex character" in the form of Bette.

*Chasing Harry Winston* tells the story of three Manhattan "twenty-ish" women, friends since college, now looking for new experiences after failed relationships. Emmy's ongoing relationship has ended because her boyfriend left her for a younger girl who works as a personal trainer. Leigh is on the verge of becoming a senior editor at the publishing house where she works, but she is beginning to have concerns about the life she will need to lead in order to make her dreams come true. Brazilian-born Adriana is eyeing her rapidly approaching thirtieth birthday with misgivings; her mother (a former supermodel) is pressing her to marry before her looks begin to fade. Emmy and Adriana resolve to address their respective problems through a pact: in the next year, they agree that Emmy, who has been (serially) monogamous in her relationships, will go on a long tour in connection with her job, with the side goal of bedding as many men as possible. Adri-

ana, for her part, will forgo her sexual-predator reputation to enter a single committed relationship. Leigh makes no promises, but she is so obsessed with her new job—editing a new, but badly written, novel from one of the superstars under contract to her publishing house—that she is not even thinking about male-female relations. Once she meets the author whose book she has been assigned to rescue, the handsome and married Jesse Chapman, however, her emotions begin to churn in much the same way as those of her friends. "These girls have been best friends for years," explained Alexandra Perich, writing for the Web site *Celebrity Cafe.* "As they near thirty, they're looking toward their future, but they're not quite sure they like what they see."

Reviews for *Chasing Harry Winston* were mixed. Some critics found the novel disappointing, especially after the success of *The Devil Wears Prada.* "There's something to disappoint everyone in Lauren Weisberger's flashy new novel, *Chasing Harry Winston,*" *Entertainment Weekly* reviewer Jennifer Reese reported. "Anyone looking forward to a dishy beach read a la *The Devil Wears Prada*" will be disappointed, because "the fluffy fun bits are lost in a blobby mess of a narrative." "Weisberger's third effort . . . with the requisite girls' nights out and disappointing men," observed a *Kirkus Reviews* contributor, "has some well-observed passages—and Adriana is a hoot—but it's nothing we haven't seen before, many times."

Other critics found the novel an entertaining contribution to the contemporary romance genre, and the Harry Winston jewelry chain welcomed the book and the publicity it brought: according to Olivia Barker in *USA Today,* the U.S. stores all created window displays for Weisberger's work. In addition, the book jacket evoked the image of the hit movie made from *The Devil Wears Prada;* it featured, Barker wrote, "a stiletto heel that, instead of being crowned by a pitchfork, spears a trio of multi-carat diamond rings." Other critics drew comparisons between the novel and the popular television series *Sex and the City.* "In fact, the only difference between *Chasing Harry Winston* and *Sex and the City,*" observed *Cornell Daily Sun* contributor Suzanne Baumgarten, "is that the women are in their late-20s instead of mid-40s, and there are three instead of four of them." "*Chasing Harry Winston,*" wrote *Bookreporter.com* reviewer Jamie Layton, "is one of those warm weather reads good enough to take you out of yourself for a while and into the fabulous lives of pretty, young, up-and-coming Manhattanites." *Chasing Harry Winston,* commented Lisa Davis-Craig in *Library Journal,* should interest "the [large] number of readers who enjoy following characters willing to spend $8000 on a 'makeover' for a parrot." "For an afternoon of escape into a world of friendship, fun and success," Melissa Mack wrote in the Adelaide *Independent Weekly,* "this is your book." "Even though it won't be standard reading for a literary class," commented Jennifer Melville in her review of the novel for *Story Circle Book Reviews,* "*Chasing Harry Winston* makes for a pleasant beach read."

### Last Night at Chateau Marmont

In 2010 Weisberger published the novel *Last Night at Chateau Marmont.* Nutritionist Julian Alter works two jobs to support her aspiring musician husband Julian. When he signs a big recording contract, their marriage is put to the test. His constant touring and absence creates a void in their lives while the frequency of last-minute leaves from work to attend his events threatens her professional career.

A *Chick Lit Reviews* Web site reviewer remarked that the novel "is written really well by Weisberger, and I can't understand why everyone says she's a one-book-pony (if you will) and can't write for toffee." The contributor stated: "I found the book absorbing, and I could barely put the book down once I got into it," adding that "I'm definitely going to be reading Lauren's other novels as she clearly can write a good story." Writing in the London *Metro,* Andrew Williams found the novel to be "diverting in a predictable, overlong, made-for-TV-movie-type way," admitting that it is "probably best savoured by devotees of the genre." A *Kirkus Reviews* critic described the novel as "a sudsy insider's look at the celebrity machine-and the cruel world it creates." Reviewing the novel in *USA Today,* Olivia Barker claimed that "the tale may end on a disappointingly cheesy pop vs. rock 'n' roll note, but [*Last Night at Chateau Marmont*] nonetheless is as fervently flippable as a gossip magazine." A contributor to *Publishers Weekly* concluded that "Weisberger has insightful takes about the price of success in our celebrity-obsessed culture."

### ■ Biographical And Critical Sources

*BOOKS*

Weisberger, Lauren, *The Devil Wears Prada,* Doubleday (New York, NY), 2003.

*PERIODICALS*

*Atlanta Journal-Constitution,* April 25, 2003, Diane Roberts, "Devil Skewers Fashion Maven," p. E1.

*Atlantic,* July 1, 2003, Caitlin Flanagan, review of *The Devil Wears Prada,* p. 146.

*Book,* May 1, 2003, Kristin Kloberdanz, review of *The Devil Wears Prada,* p. 79.

*Booklist,* April 1, 2003, Kathleen Hughes, review of *The Devil Wears Prada,* p. 1355; July 1, 2005, Kathleen Hughes, review of *Everyone Worth Knowing,* p. 1878.

*Cornell Daily Sun* (Ithaca, NY), October 9, 2008, Suzanne Baumgarten, review of *Chasing Harry Winston.*

*Daily Mail* (London, England), August 20, 2010, Lina Das, "Think the Boss in *The Devil Wears Prada* Was a Total Monster?"

*Entertainment Weekly,* May 30, 2008, "Costume Jewelry," p. 90; August 20, 2010, Annie Barrett, review of *Last Night at Chateau Marmont,* p. 129.

*Globe and Mail* (Toronto, Ontario, Canada), May 31, 2008, Maggie Wrobel, review of *Chasing Harry Winston,* p. L6; August 2, 2008, Joanna Goodman, review of *Chasing Harry Winston,* p. D8.

*Independent Weekly* (Adelaide, South Australia, Australia), July 23, 2008, Melissa Mack, review of *Chasing Harry Winston.*

*Kirkus Reviews,* February 15, 2003, review of *The Devil Wears Prada,* p. 268; July 15, 2005, review of *Everyone Worth Knowing,* p. 764; April 15, 2008, review of *Chasing Harry Winston;* August 1, 2010, review of *Last Night at Chateau Marmont.*

*Library Journal,* April 1, 2003, Stacy Alesi, review of *The Devil Wears Prada,* p. 132; September 15, 2005, Misha Stone, review of *Everyone Worth Knowing,* p. 57; May 1, 2008, Lisa Davis-Craig, review of *Chasing Harry Winston,* p. 62.

*Metro* (London, England), September 8, 2010, Andrew Williams, review of *Last Night at Chateau Marmont.*

*Midwest Book Review,* November 1, 2004, Harriet Klausner, review of *American Girls about Town.*

*Newsweek,* April 28, 2003, Cathleen McGuigan, "Prada, Yada, Yada: A Wintour's Tale," p. 60.

*New York Observer,* March 31, 2003, Alexandra Jacobs, "The Underling's Revenge, by Conde Nast's Whistleblower," p. 11.

*New York Times,* May 27, 2002, David D. Kirkpatrick, "An Insider's View of Fashion Magazines," p. C6; April 14, 2003, Janet Maslin, "Elegant Magazine, Avalanche of Dirt," p. E1.

*New York Times Book Review,* April 13, 2003, Kate Betts, "Anna Dearest," p. 30.

*Philadelphia Inquirer,* January 11, 2006, Elizabeth Wellington, review of *Everyone Worth Knowing.*

*Publishers Weekly,* March 17, 2003, review of *The Devil Wears Prada,* and Lynn Andriani, author interview, p. 53; October 4, 2004, review of *American Girls about Town,* p. 70; August 22, 2005, review of *Everyone Worth Knowing*, p. 35; April 7, 2008, review of *Chasing Harry Winston*, p. 41; July 5, 2010, review of *Last Night at Chateau Marmont*, p. 28.

*Sunday Telegraph* (London, England), March 9, 2003, Jenny McCartney, "In the Fashion Business, It's Cool to Be Cruel."

*USA Today,* April 11, 2003, author interview; April 14, 2003, Donna Freydkin, "To Speak of the 'Devil' Is in Vogue"; May 28, 2008, "'Prada' Nips at Author's Heels," p. 1; August 26, 2010, Olivia Barker, review of *Last Night at Chateau Marmont,* p. 4D.

*Women's Wear Daily,* May 24, 2002, Lisa Lockwood, "What's in Vogue for 2003," p. 13.

## ONLINE

*BookBrowse,* http://www.bookbrowse.com/ (January 27, 2009), author interview.

*BookLoons,* http://www.bookloons.com/ (January 27, 2009), Kim Atchue-Cusella, review of *American Girls about Town.*

*Bookreporter.com,* http://www.bookreporter.com/ (January 27, 2009), Carlie Kraft, review of *The Devil Wears Prada;* Jamie Layton, review of *Chasing Harry Winston.*

*Celebrity Cafe,* http://thecelebritycafe.com/ (January 27, 2009), Alexandra Perich, review of *Chasing Harry Winston.*

*Chick Lit Reviews,* http://chicklitreviews.com/ (September 24, 2010), review of *Last Night at Chateau Marmont.*

*Conversations with Famous Writers,* http://conversationsfamouswriters.blogspot.com/ (October 11, 2005), Cindy Bokma, review of *Everyone Worth Knowing.*

*Curled Up with a Good Book,* http://www.curledup.com/ (January 27, 2009), Amanda Cuda, review of *American Girls about Town.*

*Lauren Weisberger Home Page,* http://www.laurenweisberger.com (August 5, 2011).

*Readers Read,* http://www.readersread.com/ (April 7, 2006), author interview.

*Something Jewish,* http://www.somethingjewish.co.uk/ (June 10, 2006), Caroline Westbrook, author interview.

*Story Circle Book Reviews,* http://www.storycirclebookreviews.org/ (July 15, 2008), Jennifer Melville, review of *Chasing Harry Winston.*\*

# Fay Weldon

## 1931-

### ■ Also Known As

Franklin Birkinshaw

### ■ Personal

Born September 22, 1931, in Alvechurch, Worcester-shire, England; daughter of Frank Thornton (a physician) and Margaret (a writer) Birkinshaw; married (divorced); married Ronald Weldon (an antiques dealer), 1962 (divorced, 1994); married Nick Fox (a poet); children: (first marriage) Nicholas; (second marriage) Daniel, Thomas, Samuel. *Education:* University of St. Andrews, M.A., 1954.

### ■ Addresses

*Home*—Dorset, England. *Office*—Brunel University, Department of English, Kingston Ln., Uxbridge UB8 3PH, England. *Agent*—Casarotto, Ltd., National House, 62/66 Wardour St., London W1V 3HP, England. *E-mail*—fay.weldon@brunel.ac.uk.

### ■ Career

Writer, novelist, playwright, television and radio scriptwriter. Brunel University, London, England, Department of English, Brunel chair and professor of creative writing, 2006—. Propaganda writer, British Foreign Office; market researcher, *Daily Mirror.* Former member, Art Council of Great Britain literary panel and GLA's film and video panel; chair, judges' panel for the Booker McConnell Prize, 1983; writer-in-residence, Savoy Hotel, 2002. Has also worked as an advertising copywriter.

### ■ Awards, Honors

Society of Film and Television Arts award for best series, 1971, for an episode of *Upstairs, Downstairs;* Writer's Guild award for best radio play, 1973, for *Spider;* Giles Cooper Award for best radio play, 1978, for *Polaris;* Society of Authors' traveling scholarship, 1981; PEN/Macmillan Silver Pen Award, c. 1995, for *Wicked Women;* Commander of the British Empire (CBE), 2001. D.Litt., University of St. Andrew's, 1990.

### ■ Writings

*NOVELS*

*The Fat Woman's Joke* (also see below), MacGibbon & Kee (London, England), 1967, published as . . . *And the Wife Ran Away,* McKay (New York, NY), 1968.

*Down among the Women,* Heinemann (London, England), 1971, St. Martin's Press (New York, NY), 1972.

*Female Friends,* St. Martin's Press (New York, NY), 1974.

*Remember Me,* Random House (New York, NY), 1976.

*Words of Advice,* Random House (New York, NY), 1977, published as *Little Sisters,* Hodder & Stoughton (London, England), 1978.

*Praxis,* Summit Books (New York, NY), 1978.

*Puffball,* Hodder & Stoughton (London, England), 1979, Summit Books (New York, NY), 1980.

*The President's Child,* Hodder & Stoughton (London, England), 1982, Doubleday (New York, NY), 1983.

*The Life and Loves of a She-Devil,* Hodder & Stoughton (London, England), 1983, Pantheon (New York, NY), 1984.

*The Shrapnel Academy,* Viking (New York, NY), 1986.

*The Hearts and Lives of Men,* Viking (New York, NY), 1987.

*The Rules of Life* (chapbook), HarperCollins (New York, NY), 1987.

*Leader of the Band,* Viking (New York, NY), 1988.

*The Heart of the Country,* Viking (New York, NY), 1988.

*The Cloning of Joanna May,* Viking (New York, NY), 1990.

*Darcy's Utopia,* Viking (New York, NY), 1991.

*Life Force,* Viking (New York, NY), 1992.

*Trouble,* Viking (New York, NY), published as *Affliction,* HarperCollins (London, England), 1993.

*Splitting,* Atlantic Monthly Press (New York, NY), 1995.

*Worst Fears,* Atlantic Monthly Press (New York, NY), 1996.

*Big Girls Don't Cry,* Atlantic Monthly Press (New York, NY), 1997.

*Growing Rich,* Penguin (New York, NY), 1998.

*Rhode Island Blues,* Atlantic Monthly Press (New York, NY), 2000.

*The Bulgari Connection,* Grove/Atlantic (New York, NY), 2001.

*Mantrapped,* Grove/Atlantic (New York, NY), 2005.

*She May Not Leave,* Atlantic Monthly Press (New York, NY), 2005.

*The Spa Decameron,* Quercus (London, England), 2007, also published as *The Spa,* Grove (New York, NY), 2009.

*The Stepmother's Diary,* Quercus (London, England), 2008.

*Chalcot Crescent,* Corvus (London, England), 2009.

*Kehua!,* Corvus (London, England), 2010.

## PLAYS

*Permanence* (produced in the West End at Comedy Theatre, 1969), published in *Mixed Blessings: An Entertainment on Marriage,* Methuen (New York, NY), 1970.

*Time Hurries On,* published in *Scene Scripts,* edited by Michael Marland, Longman (London, England), 1972.

*Words of Advice* (one-act; produced in Richmond, England, at Orange Tree Theatre, 1974), Samuel French (New York, NY), 1974.

*Friends,* produced in Richmond, England, at Orange Tree Theatre, 1975.

*Moving House,* produced in Farnham, England, at Redgrave Theatre, 1976.

*Mr. Director,* produced in Richmond, England, at Orange Tree Theatre, 1978.

*Action Replay* (produced in Birmingham, England, at Birmingham Repertory Studio Theatre, 1979; produced as *Love among the Women* in Vancouver, British Columbia, at City Stage, 1982), Samuel French, 1980.

*I Love My Love,* produced in Exeter, England, at Northcott Theatre, 1981.

*After the Prize,* produced off-Broadway at Phoenix Theatre, 1981, produced as *Woodworm,* in Melbourne, Australia, at Playbox Theatre, 1983.

## TELEVISION PLAYS

*The Fat Woman's Tale,* Granada Television, 1966.

*Wife in a Blond Wig,* British Broadcasting Corp. (BBC-TV), 1966.

*Office Party,* Thames Television, 1970.

*Hands,* BBC-TV, 1972.

*Poor Baby,* ATV Network, 1975.

*The Terrible Tale of Timothy Bagshott,* BBC-TV, 1975.

*Aunt Tatty* (dramatization based on an Elizabeth Bowen short story), BBC-TV, 1975.

*Pride and Prejudice* (five-part dramatization), BBC-TV, 1980.

*Life for Christine,* Granada Television, 1980.

*Little Miss Perkins,* London Weekend Television, 1982.

*Loving Women,* Granada Television, 1983.

*The Wife's Revenge,* BBC-TV, 1983.

## RADIO PLAYS

*Housebreaker,* BBC Radio 3, 1973.

*Mr. Fox and Mr. First,* BBC Radio 3, 1974.

*The Doctor's Wife,* BBC Radio 4, 1975.

*All the Bells of Paradise,* BBC Radio 4, 1979.

*Polaris,* American Broadcasting Company (ABC Radio), 1980, published in *Best Radio Plays of 1978: The Giles Cooper Award Winners,* Eyre Methuen (London, England), 1979.

*The Hearts and Lives of Men,* BBC Radio 4, 1996.

## OTHER

(Editor, with Elaine Feinstein) *New Stories 4: An Arts Council Anthology,* Hutchinson, 1979.

*Watching Me, Watching You* (short stories; also includes the novel *The Fat Woman's Joke*), Summit Books (New York, NY), 1981.

*Letters to Alice on First Reading Jane Austen* (nonfiction), Michael Joseph, 1984, 2nd edition, Carroll & Graf (New York, NY), 1999.

*Polaris and Other Stories,* Hodder & Stoughton (London, England), 1985.

*Moon over Minneapolis; or, Why She Couldn't Stay* (short stories), Viking (New York, NY), 1992.

*So Very English,* Serpent's Tail (London, England), 1992.

*Wicked Women: A Collection of Short Stories,* Flamingo (London, England), 1995, Atlantic Monthly Press (Boston, MA), 1997.

*Godless in Eden: A Book of Essays,* Flamingo (London, England), 1999.

*Auto da Fay* (memoir), Grove (New York, NY), 2003.

*What Makes Women Happy,* Fourth Estate (London, England), 2006.

Also author of children's books, including *Wolf the Mechanical Dog,* 1988, *Party Puddle,* 1989, and *Nobody Likes Me,* 1997. Author of the short story collections *Angel, All Innocence: And Other Stories,* 1995, *A Hard Time to Be a Father,* 1998, and *Nothing to Wear and Nowhere to Hide: A Collection of Short Stories,* 2002. Author of the chapbook *The Roots of Violence,* 1989. Author of the nonfiction books *Rebecca West,* 1985, and *Sacred Cows,* 1989.

Author of *Watching Me, Watching You,* a stage adaptation of four of her short stories; *Jane Eyre,* a stage adaptation of the novel by Charlotte Brontë, 1986; and the play *The Hole in the Top of the World,* 1987. Also author of the radio plays *Spider,* 1972, and *If Only I Could Find the Words,* BBC.

Author of *Big Women,* a four-part series, for Channel 4 television. Author of teleplays for television series, including *Upstairs, Downstairs,* London Weekend Television, 1971; *Six Women* BBC-TV, 1977; and *Leap in the Dark* BBC-TV, 1980. Author of radio plays to radio shows, including *Just before Midnight,* BBC Radio 4, 1979.

## ■ Adaptations

*The Life and Loves of a She-Devil* was adapted into the film *She-Devil* in 1989, written by Barry Strugatz and Mark R. Burns, directed by Susan Seidelman, starring Roseanne Barr and Meryl Streep; also adapted for film or television were *The Cloning of Joanna May,* 1991, and *The President's Child,* 1992.

## ■ Sidelights

After her parents divorced when she was only five, Fay Weldon grew up in New Zealand with her mother, sister, and grandmother. Returning to England to attend college, she studied psychology and economics at St. Andrews in Scotland. As a single mother in her twenties, Weldon supported herself and her son with a variety of odd jobs until she settled into a successful career as a copywriter. After marrying in the early sixties, Weldon had three more sons, underwent psychoanalysis as a result of depression, and subsequently abandoned her work in advertising for freelance creative writing. (She would later marry a third time.) Her first novel, *The Fat Woman's Joke,* appeared in 1967 when she was thirty-six years old. Since that time she has published many novels, short stories, and plays for the theater, television, and radio. Throughout her work, Weldon's "major subject is the experience of women," wrote Agate Nesaule Krouse in *Critique.* "Sexual initiation, marriage, infidelity, divorce, contraception, abortion, motherhood, housework, and thwarted careers . . . all receive attention." Products of a keen mind concerned with women's issues, Weldon's novels have been labeled "feminist" by many reviewers. Yet, Weldon's views are her own and are not easily classified. In fact, feminists have at times taken exception to her portrayal of women, accusing the author of perpetuating traditional stereotypes.

Weldon's fiction fosters disparate interpretations because its author sees the complexity of the woman's experience. Weldon accepts feminist ideology as a liberating force, but she also understands its limitations. Thus, what emerges from Weldon's writing is more than an understanding of women's issues; she appreciates the plight of the individual woman.

### Early Novels

Weldon's early novels, especially *Down among the Women, Female Friends,* and *Remember Me,* gained recognition for both their artistry and their social concerns. "Vivid imagery, a strong sense of time and place, memorable dialogue, complex events, and multiple characters that are neither confusing nor superficially observed" characterize these novels, according to Krouse, making them "a rich rendering of life with brevity and wit."

Although each of these books possesses elements typical of a Weldon novel, they focus on different aspects of the female experience and the forces that influence them. *Down among the Women* reflects how three generations of women, each the product of a different social climate, react to the same dilemma.

Krouse found that, in this book, Weldon creates "a work whose very structure is feminist." She added in her *Critique* review: "The whole novel could profitably be analyzed as a definition of womanhood: passages describing how one has to live 'down among the women' contrast with anecdotes of male behavior." The image of womanhood offered here is not ideal, but as Krouse commented, Weldon's ability to blend "the terrible and the ridiculous is one of the major reasons why a novel filled with the pain endured by women . . . is neither painfully depressing nor cheerfully sentimental."

As its title suggests, *Female Friends* examines relationships among women and how the companionship of other women can be comforting to a woman wearied by the battle of the sexes. "The most radical feminist could not possibly equal the picture of injustice [Weldon] paints with wry, cool, concise words," wrote L.E. Sissman in the *New Yorker*. Sissman found that "the real triumph of *Female Friends* is the gritty replication of the gross texture of everyday life, placed in perspective and made universal; the perfectly recorded dialogue, precisely differentiated for each character; the shocking progression of events that, however rude, seem real." Weldon does not overlook the injustices committed by women in this day-to-day struggle, however. Ultimately, her characters suggest, women are responsible for their own lives. As Arthur Cooper noted in *Newsweek*, Weldon "has penetrated the semidarkness of the semiliberated and shown that only truth and self-awareness can set them free."

*Remember Me* is the story of one man's impact on the lives of three women and how the resentment of one of those women becomes a disruptive force even after her death. This novel suggests that elements beyond the control of the individual often dictate her actions. "Scores of . . . coincidences . . . emphasize the theme that chance, misunderstanding, and necessarily limited knowledge play a significant part in human life," observed Krouse in *Critique*. Human frailties, Krouse added, body functions, pain, sickness "and death are recurrent images underscoring human mortality." Phyllis Birnbaum, writing in *Saturday Review*, commented: "Precise satire, impassioned monologue, and a sense of limited human possibility make this novel a daring examination of twentieth-century discontent."

By the time she had written her sixth novel, *Praxis* (the fifth, *Words of Advice*, appeared in 1977), Weldon had become a widely respected author. Kelley Cherry pointed out in the Chicago *Tribune Books* that *Praxis* is a novel about endurance. The central character, Praxis Duveen, must endure in a world filled with rampant chauvinism.

A novel in which so many misfortunes plague one character runs the risk of becoming unbelievable. Nonetheless, Cherry wrote: "The writing throughout is brisk and ever so slightly off the wall—sufficiently askew to convey the oddness of events, sufficiently no-nonsense to make that oddness credible."

In her next novel, *Puffball*, "Weldon mixes gynecology and witchcraft to concoct an unusual brew," Joan Reardon noted in the *Los Angeles Times Book Review*. Here, more than before, Weldon confronts the woman's condition on a physical level, focusing on pregnancy. "Weldon has the audacity to include technical information on fertility, conception, and fetal development as an integral part of the story," commented Lorallee MacPike in *Best Sellers*. "She makes the physical process preceding and during pregnancy not only interesting but essential to the development of both story and character."

In the eyes of some reviewers, however, the technical information weakens the novel. Reardon wrote that in *Puffball*, "perspicacity has given way to whimsy and 'the pain in my soul, my heart, and my mind' has become a detailed analysis of the pituitary system." Moreover, some feminists faulted this book for its old-fashioned images of women; Anita Brookner pointed out in the *Times Literary Supplement*: "Superficially, it is a great leap backwards for the stereotype feminist. It argues in favour of the old myths of earth and motherhood and universal harmony: a fantasy for the tired businesswoman." Yet a reviewer in the *Atlantic* found that "the assertion of the primacy of physical destiny that lies at the center of *Puffball* gives the book a surprising seriousness and an impressive optimism."

In *The President's Child*, Weldon breaks new ground, exploring the impact of political intrigue on individual lives. Her next novel, however, is reminiscent of *Praxis*. Like Praxis, the protagonist of Weldon's ninth novel, *The Life and Loves of a She-Devil*, is buffeted by the injustice of her world. But whereas Praxis endures, Ruth gets revenge. Losing her husband to a beautiful romance novelist, tall, unattractive Ruth turns against husband, novelist, and anyone else who gets in her way. Unleashing the vengeance of a she-devil, she ruins them all; the novelist dies and the husband becomes a broken man. In the end, having undergone extensive surgery to make her the very image of her former competitor, she begins a new life with her former husband. "What makes this a powerfully funny and oddly powerful book is the energy that vibrates off the pages," wrote Carol E. Rinzler in the *Washington Post Book World*.

Seeing Ruth's revenge as a positive response to the injustice of the male establishment, some reviewers were disappointed by her turnaround at the novel's end. As Michiko Kakutani pointed out in the *New York Times:* "Her final act—having extensive plastic surgery that makes her irresistible to men—actually seems like a capitulation to the male values she says she despises."

### Mid-Career Novels

Annette Horrocks, the pregnant protagonist of *Trouble* is the second wife of a chauvinistic businessman who becomes threatened when his wife publishes a novel. In a twist, the husband runs not into the arms of another woman, but into the clutches of a pair of pseudo-therapists, who convince him that Annette is his enemy.

Weldon's twentieth novel, *Splitting,* features seventeen-year-old former rock star Angelica White, who is determined to become the perfect female companion in order to endear herself to dissolute but wealthy Sir Edwin Rice and obtain a marriage commitment. She discards her image as the rock queen Kinky Virgin, doffs the nose rings and the spectacularly colored hair, and becomes overweight, drug-abusing Edwin's helpmate. "In effect, Angelica's troubles begin when she resolves that it's 'time to give up and grow up,'" according to Bertha Harris, writing in the *New York Times Book Review.* Soon the typical flock of avaricious females descend on Angelica, breaking up her home and causing her to fracture into four separate personalities. Ultimately banished from the Rice estate, her money having long since been usurped by her husband, Angelica ultimately avenges herself through the savvy, recklessness, and sense of fun created by her multiple selves. "The splitting device works shamelessly well," explained Kate Kellaway in the London *Observer.* "Weldon uses it as a way of exploring and rejoicing in the theatricality of women, their volatility, their love of disguise, of fancy dress, of playing different parts."

Weldon has since continued her pace, not only with novels such as 1996's *Worst Fears,* but also with a short story collection, appropriately titled *Wicked Women: A Collection of Short Stories,* which was published in 1995. In *Worst Fears,* a widowed woman suddenly realizes that her life has not in fact been the rosy picture she imagined it. Snubbed by her friends and lacking sympathy in favor of her husband's mistress, Alexandra soon finds that such deception by the living is nothing compared to the deceptions practiced on her by her now dead husband. Left with nothing, she plans her revenge in true Weldon fashion in a novel in which the author "has filed down a few sharp edges," according to *New York Times Book Review* contributor Karen Karbo, adding: "and that makes it one of her best

novels yet." Variations on this traditional Weldon theme are also played out in the sixteen short stories in *Wicked Women.*

Writing in the *Knight-Ridder/Tribune News Service,* Jean Blish Siers wrote: "Perhaps the funniest of all Fay Weldon's very funny novels, *Big Girls Don't Cry* tackles the feminist movement head-on with the wry, ironic comedy for which Weldon is famous." This 1997 volume is also typical of Weldon's work in that its story is presented episodically, with short paragraphs and scenes often delivered in a temporally fragmented fashion. "It is a tapestry Weldon weaves," observed a critic in the online *Complete Review,* "and the story does come together very well. Weldon's succinct style, with few wasted words, her dialogue brutally honest and straightforward, her explanations always cutting to the quick make for a powerful reading experience. Not everyone likes their fiction so direct, but we approve heartily and recommend the book highly." The plot of *Big Girls Don't Cry* moves from the early 1970s to the present and concerns five women who founded a feminist publishing house called Medusa. As the novel opens we meet Zoë, a young mother in a loveless marriage, the beautiful Stephanie, the sexy Layla, the intellectual Alice, and Nancy, who has just broken off an unsatisfying engagement. While the publishing house thrives over the next three decades, the women's lives evolve dramatically. Husbands and friends change; children are abandoned; internecine conflicts sometimes plague the five while at other times they must rally in support of one another. "In the end," noted Siers, "the five—older but not much wiser—must face the consequences of decisions made a quarter-century earlier." The *Complete Review* contributor commented: "The characters are all very human, and while they profess idealism Weldon ruthlessly shows how difficult it is to live up to it."

### Later Novels

In 2005, two of Weldon's books were published: *Mantrapped* and *She May Not Leave.* In *Mantrapped* the novel's female protagonist, Trisha, wakes up one morning to discover that she has switched bodies with a man named Peter. "Weldon is a master of cosmic and comical sexual shenanigans," wrote Eileen Zimmerman Nicol in a *Bookreporter.com* review of *Mantrapped.* "Despite the inherent difficulty in specifying which character is doing, thinking or saying what, she makes the most of the situation."

In *She May Not Leave,* Weldon tells the story of a couple who hire a Polish au pair to care for their young daughter. Although Martyn is initially against the idea, his unmarried partner Hattie is anxious to have someone help out around the house so she can go to work. They hire Agnieszka, who quickly proves indispensable. However, when Agnieszka is threatened with deportation, Martyn and Hattie decide that she must get married to Martyn so she can stay and work for them. "Weldon's trademark acid wit is very much in evidence here," wrote Tina Jordan in *Entertainment Weekly.* Joanne Wilkinson, writing in *Booklist*, noted that "Weldon aims some well-honed barbs at political correctness in this amusing send-up of modern relationships and child-rearing practices."

*Chalcot Crescent* is a dystopian novel set in London in 2013. The heroine, Frances, is based on Weldon's own stillborn sister. Thus, the story imagines an alternate reality in which Weldon's sibling survived. Frances struggles to get by after a deep economic recession toppled London's parliament and left an iron-fisted dictatorship in its place. The National Unity Government oversees food rationing and monitors the entire city via CCTV. Although she was once a successful novelist, Frances is now deeply in debt. She spends her days in her home hiding from creditors and reminiscing about her life. The resulting story is "a heavy subject made palatable, even engaging, because Fay Weldon does the telling," Carol Gladstein stated in *Booklist.* Barbara Love, writing in *Library Journal,* was equally impressed, calling the book "a rollicking story that may inspire readers to greener habits before the apocalypse." In *Kirkus Reviews,* a critic found that "what's memorable is the author's mischievous, sinister/comic tone and deft, multilayered levels of fictionalization." The critic then added that *Chalcot Crescent* is an "impressive work from a seasoned cynic." As a *Publishers Weekly* reviewer pointed out: "This marvelously sardonic work shows a future that is all too close to reality."

The long-standing struggle between stepdaughters and stepmothers takes center stage in *The Stepmother's Diary.* Sappho is overjoyed at her recent marriage to Gavin, but his daughter Isobel proves problematic. She is a good student who volunteers with the elderly, and she can do no wrong in Gavin's eyes. However, Isobel resents Sappho's presence in her life, and she rejects all of Sappho's efforts to befriend her. When Isobel learns about Sappho's unsavory past, she holds this knowledge over the head of her well-meaning stepparent. In addition, Isobel begins demanding, and receiving, the bulk of her father's love and attention, leaving Sappho as little more than a third wheel. This poignant spin on the evil stepmother paradigm

leaves readers questioning "whether any character is capable of having the best interests of anyone else at heart," Charlotte Moore asserted in the *Spectator.* Moore went on to remark: "Weldon's clever puppetry means that *The Stepmother's Diary* is never less than entertaining, but her refusal to engage the reader's sympathy means that it can't be very much more." David Horspool, writing in the London *Times,* was also ambivalent, commenting: "It is a shame that this intelligent if sometimes workmanlike novel has been packaged as the flimsiest sort of chick-lit. . . . In a way, it subverts much of what her fiction exemplifies: that what women do, and think, and write about, is serious stuff, which can't be prettified, pigeonholed, or tidied away."

More positive critiques of *The Stepmother's Diary* were given by Geraldine Bedell in the *Observer* and Sue Magee in the online *Bookbag.* For instance, Bedell observed: "Much of the novel's success is down to the prose, which is sardonic but confiding, acerbic but gossipy. Weldon holds these positions in tension and trips between them in a high-wire act." Bedell also wrote: "Lest this all sound too self-consciously literary, *The Stepmother's Diary* also feels very contemporary and is often extremely funny. Weldon's novels can read like fables . . . but this one is wholly convincing and involving." Magee praised the novel for different reasons, announcing: "It's not just down to the technical brilliance of the writing either—the ear for dialogue is faultless, whatever the age or sex and the characters come off the page so well-formed that you're surprised not to find them in the room with you."

### Essays and Nonfiction

In 1999 Weldon published *Godless in Eden: A Book of Essays.* Therein she covers a wide range of topics and examines a variety of controversial issues, including sex and society, the feminization of politics, the royal family, therapy, her own life and loves, and the changing roles of men and women in the contemporary world.

Weldon's understanding of the individual woman, living in a world somewhere between the nightmare of male chauvinism and the feminist ideal, has allowed her to achieve a balance in her writing. "She has succeeded in uniting the negative feminism, necessarily evident in novels portraying the problems of women, with a positive feminism, evident in the belief that change or equilibrium is possible," wrote Agate Nesaule Krouse in *Critique.* Having found an audience for her writing—insights into the condition of woman, shaped by her intelligence and humor—Fay Weldon has risen to prominence in literary circles.

Weldon's 2003 memoir, *Auto da Fay,* follows Weldon's life from her birth and young life in New Zealand through her first marriage as a young women to a much older man and her eventual successful career as a writer, which she began when she was in her thirties. "This delightful autobiography is imbued with the same audaciousness and perspicacity as is her other works," wrote *Book reporter.com* contributor Barbara Lipkien Gershenbaum. "As a woman of deep insights she highlights the key, transcendent events of her life."

In *What Makes Women Happy,* the author writes about the constant battles that women face between nature and nurture and, through morality-based parables, explores the issue of women's happiness. In a review of *What Makes Women Happy* in *Booklist,* Carol Haggas noted that the author provides "a multidisciplinary exploration of this endlessly fascinating conundrum." Haggas added that "Weldon's theory [on womens' happiness] is completely thought-provoking." *Library Journal* contributor Erica L. Foley referred to the book as "an engaging read that will delight women."

## ■ Biographical And Critical Sources

### BOOKS

Barreca, Regina, *Fay Weldon's Wicked Fictions,* University Press of New England (Lebanon, NH), 1994.

*Contemporary Literary Criticism,* Volume 122, Gale (Detroit, MI), 2000.

*Dictionary of Literary Biography,* Volume 194: *British Novelists since 1960, Second Series,* Gale (Detroit, MI), 1998.

Dowling, Finuala, *Fay Weldon's Fiction,* Fairleigh Dickinson University Press (Madison, NJ), 1998.

Faulks, Lana, *Fay Weldon,* Twayne (Boston, MA), 1998.

Weldon, Fay, *Auto da Fay,* Grove (New York, NY), 2003.

### PERIODICALS

*Best Sellers,* October, 1980, Lorallee MacPike, review of *Puffball.*

*Booklist,* February 1, 2006, Joanne Wilkinson, review of *She May Not Leave,* p. 6; February 1, 2007, Carol Haggas, review of *What Makes Women Happy,* p. 7; September 1, 2010, Carol Gladstein, review of *Chalcot Crescent,* p. 39.

*Bookseller,* April 7, 2006, "Weldon Takes Brunel Chair," p. 48.

*Critique,* December, 1978, Agate Nesaule Krouse, author profile.

*Entertainment Weekly,* Tina Jordan, review of *She May Not Leave,* p. 141.

*Kirkus Reviews,* February 1, 2006, review of *She May Not Leave,* p. 111; August 15, 2010, review of *Chalcot Crescent.*

*Knight-Ridder/Tribune New Service,* January 20, 1999, Jean Blish Siers, review of *Big Girls Don't Cry.*

*Library Journal,* February 15, 2006, Christine Perkins, review of *She May Not Leave,* p. 112; February 15, 2007, Erica L. Foley, review of *What Makes Women Happy,* p. 139; August 1, 2010, Barbara Love, review of *Chalcot Crescent,* p. 75.

*Los Angeles Times Book Review,* September 7, 1980, Joan Reardon, review of *Puffball.*

*Newsweek,* November, 1974, Arthur Cooper, review of *Female Friends.*

*New Yorker,* March 3, 1975, L.E. Sissman, review of *Female Friends.*

*New York Times,* August 21, 1984, Michiko Kakutani, review of *The Life and Loves of a She-Devil.*

*New York Times Book Review,* June 11, 1995, Bertha Harris, *Splitting,* p. 48; June 9, 1996, Karen Karbo, review of *Worst Fears,* p. 19.

*Observer* (London, England), May 7, 1995, Kate Kellaway, review of *Splitting;* September 14, 2008, Geraldine Bedell, review of *The Stepmother's Diary.*

*Publishers Weekly,* January 9, 2006, review of *She May Not Leave,* p. 29; January 22, 2007, review of *What Makes Women Happy,* p. 172; August 9, 2010, review of *Chalcot Crescent,* p. 29.

*Saturday Review,* December, 1976, Phyllis Birnbaum, review of *Remember Me.*

*Spectator,* September 15, 2007, "Not Much Good Clean Fun," p. 48; September 27, 2008, Charlotte Moore, "Meet the Disposable Family," p. 40; September 12, 2009, "Family Album," p. 37.

*Times* (London, England), October 19, 2008, David Horspool, review of *The Stepmother's Diary.*

*Times Literary Supplement,* February 22, 1980, Anita Brookner, review of *Puffball.*

*Tribune Books* (Chicago, IL), November 12, 1978, Kelley Cherry, review of *Praxis.*

*Washington Post Book World,* September 30, 1984, Carol E. Rinzler, review of *The Life and Loves of a She-Devil.*

ONLINE

*Bookbag,* http://www.thebookbag.co.uk/ (March 1, 2009), Sue Magee, review of *The Stepmother's Diary.*

*Bookreporter.com* http://www.bookreporter.com/ (December 27, 2000), interview with author; (June 16, 2007), Judith Handschuh, biography of author; (June 16, 2007), Marge Fletcher, review of *She May Not Leave;* (June 16, 2007), Eileen Zimmerman Nicol, review of *Mantrapped;* (June 16, 2007), Barbara Lipkien Gershenbaum, review of *Auto da Fay;* (June 16, 2007), Heather Grimshaw, review of *The Bulgari Connection;* (June 16, 2007), Jana Siciliano, review of *Rhode Island Blues;* (June 16, 2007), Judith Handschuh, reviews of *Big Girls Don't Cry, Wicked Women, Worst Fears,* and *Trouble.*

*British Council Contemporary Writers Web site,* http://www.contemporarywriters.com/ (June 16, 2007), biography of author.

*Brunel University Web site,* http://www.brunel.ac.uk/ (June 16, 2007), faculty profile of author.

*Complete Review,* http://www.complete-review.com/ (August 8, 2000), review of *Big Girls Don't Cry* and *Big Women.*

*HarperCollins Web site,* http://www.harpercollins.co.uk/ (June 16, 2007), biography of author.

*Internet Movie Database,* http://www.imdb.com/ (June 16, 2007), information on author film and television work.

*NNDB,* http://www.nndb.com/ (June 16, 2007), information on author and author's works.

*Redmood.com,* http://www.redmood.com/ (August 16, 2011), biography of author.*

# Lauren Willig

## 1977-

■ **Personal**

Born March 28, 1977, in Philadelphia, PA. *Education:* Yale University, B.A., 1999; Harvard University, M.A., 2001, J.D. (magna cum laude), and doctoral study.

■ **Addresses**

*Home*—New York, NY; Cambridge, MA. *E-mail*—willig@post.harvard.edu.

■ **Career**

Writer. Former lawyer. Cravath, Swaine & Moore, New York, NY, associate. Visiting faculty, Yale University, 2010.

■ **Member**

Beau Monde (Regency chapter of Romance Writers of America); New York Bar Association.

■ **Writings**

*"PINK CARNATION" HISTORICAL NOVEL SERIES*

*The Secret History of the Pink Carnation,* Dutton (New York, NY), 2005.

*The Masque of the Black Tulip,* Dutton (New York, NY), 2006.

*The Deception of the Emerald Ring,* Dutton (New York, NY), 2006.

*The Seduction of the Crimson Rose,* Dutton (New York, NY), 2008.

*The Temptation of the Night Jasmine,* Dutton (New York, NY), 2009.

*The Mischief of the Mistletoe: A Pink Carnation Christmas,* Dutton (New York, NY), 2010.

*The Betrayal of the Blood Lily,* Dutton (New York, NY), 2010.

*The Orchid Affair,* Dutton (New York, NY), 2011.

*The Garden Intrigue,* Dutton (New York, NY), 2012.

■ **Sidelights**

Lauren Willig's first novel was rejected the first time she sent it to a publishing house. Handwritten and spanning 300 pages, her Nancy Drew-inspired mystery was returned and her dreams of becoming a best-selling author were crushed. Fortunately, Willig did not let this rejection stop her (she was only nine years old, after all), and she has since gone on to pen several successful historical romance novels.

### The Secret History of the Pink Carnation

In *The Secret History of the Pink Carnation,* Eloise Kelly is a Harvard graduate student working on a dissertation about two English spies, the Scarlet Pimpernel and the Purple Gentian, who performed gallant, clandestine deeds for the British during the Napoleonic wars of the early nineteenth century. Hoping to learn as much as she can about the two spies, Eloise travels to London, where she meets Arabella Selwick-Aderly, a descendant of Lord Richard Selwick, who was the Purple Gentian. Arabella grants Eloise access to the family's papers. After a bit of research, Eloise stumbles upon the journal of a young woman named Amy Balcourt and learns of another, more elusive spy: the Pink Carnation. As Eloise peruses Amy's journal, readers are transported back to the nineteenth century to follow Amy and her cousin Jane as they travel to France in hopes of joining the Purple Gentian's league. In the meantime, Eloise delves further into her research, despite attempts by Arabella's nephew, Colin, to restrict her access to his family's hidden secrets. Not one to be deterred, Eloise perseveres and uncovers the Pink Carnation's true identity.

A critic in *Kirkus Reviews* termed Willig's debut novel "a sexy, smirking, determined-to-charm historical-romance." In a *Library Journal* critique, Anna M. Nelson observed that Willig "has an ear for quick wit and an eye for detail." A *Publishers Weekly* contributor commented that the identity of the Pink Carnation seems a bit obvious, but noted that Willig "does a good job painting a picture of the tumultuous era." *Booklist* contributor Kristine Huntley concluded her review by calling the novel "a decidedly delightful romp."

### The Masque of the Black Tulip

*The Masque of the Black Tulip* finds Eloise continuing her research on the Pink Carnation when she discovers correspondence between the mysterious spy and Lady Henrietta Selwick, Richard Selwick's sister, stating that a deadly French spy known only as the Black Tulip is planning a murder. Readers are once again transported back in time as Henrietta and her brother's friend, Miles, work to stop the Black Tulip before it is too late. Writing in *Library Journal*, Bette-Lee Fox commented that *The Masque of the Black Tulip* is "a bit more clichéd" than Willig's first novel, but noted that it is still "terribly clever and funny." Likewise, a *Publishers Weekly* contributor commented that "many . . . will delight in this easy-to-read romp and line up for the next installment." One *Kirkus Reviews* contributor remarked on Willig's appealing characters and plots.

In an interview posted on the Barnes and Noble Web site, Willig offered this advice to writers: "Write the story you want to tell, in a way that pleases you—you, after all, are the one living with this plot and these characters for months on end. . . . Reading—reading broadly, in a variety of genres and styles—is the best education for any author, and the only real training is to write, write, and write some more.

### The Deception of the Emerald Ring

In *The Deception of the Emerald Ring,* the third book in the "Pink Carnation" series, Eloise is still working on her Ph.D. in history. She uncovers another tale of nineteenth century spies in the archives. This time, the story focuses on Letty Alsworthy, a nineteen-year-old who marries Lord Geoffrey Pinchingdale-Snipe. When Geoffrey is nowhere to be found on their wedding night, Letty thinks she's been abandoned. However, in reality, Geoffrey is a spy and a member of the Purple Gentian. He has actually gone to Ireland to help prevent the Irish Rebellion. When Letty finally tracks down her husband, she finds herself involved in espionage.

"Willig's latest is riveting, providing a great diversion and lots of fun," wrote Patty Engelmann of *The Deception of the Emerald Ring* in *Booklist.* A *Publishers Weekly* contributor noted that "the historic action is taut and twisting."

### The Seduction of the Crimson Rose

*The Seduction of the Crimson Rose* marks the fourth installment in the "Pink Carnation" series. Readers continue to learn more about the Pink Carnation through Eloise's research efforts, as well as about Eloise herself and her blooming love affair with Colin. In this book, Mary Alsworthy, who was treated so scandalously by her now-former fiancé in the previous book, finds herself agreeing to be used as bait by Lord Vaughn in an attempt to lure the attentions of the mysterious and dangerous French spy known as the Black Tulip. Mary has the dark-haired looks that the Black Tulip seems to favor, and so she seems an ideal candidate to lure him into the open. However, when the Tulip does notice Mary, she learns that he has more interest in her than she previously imagined, and what he asks she may not be willing to give, no matter the greatness of the cause.

A reviewer in *Publishers Weekly* praised the book for its "witty repartee and arch conversations," and concluded that "the novel handily fulfills its promise of intrigue and romance." A contributor to *Kirkus Reviews* noted that "Willig's research grounds this adventure in solid detail, from the dresses to the deadly weaponry." Huntley, writing again in *Booklist,* found that Willig's books improve "with each addition, and her latest is filled with swashbuckling fun, romance, and intrigue."

### The Temptation of the Night Jasmine

In *The Temptation of the Night Jasmine,* Eloise spends a week at Colin's country estate, and it is there that she discovers a bundle of letters that reveals this novel's adventure story. Twenty-year-old Lady Charlotte Lansdowne—author of the letters—is a heroine in love with fantastical concepts, including the idea of a unicorn and of a man whom one can trust. She has a tendency toward reading and rereading her favorite romance novels, so it is unsurprising that she should envision herself as the heroine in one of her favorites, particularly when her distant cousin Robert Dovedale, a longtime officer serving in India, returns to England and sparks her imagination. Robert, of course, has other things on his mind besides romance. His mentor and superior officer, Colonel Arbuthnot, was murdered while he was still abroad, shot in the back by a fellow Englishman during a battle, and Robert is determined to discover which of the Colonel's men was responsible for so dastardly and cowardly an act. He merely knows that the traitorous individual has returned to England as well and is living a life of apparent leisure among the wealthy, even as he plots with the French.

Despite his mission, Robert is not immune to Charlotte's charms. In fact, he is drawn in by her innocence, especially attractive to him after so long at war, and in direct contrast to the ugliness he faces in his work. However, he cannot bring himself to abandon his search for the Colonel's killer, and when his investigation leads him in dangerous territory—namely, the Hellfire Club, a group whose membership is notorious for its mysterious activities and debauchery—he seeks to end his relationship with Charlotte for her own protection, writing her a quick note before following his latest lead. Charlotte, naturally, is devastated by his abrupt departure and his—in her eyes—cruel ending of their relationship. When she learns a piece of information that, ironically, would have proven useful to Robert's investigation, she does not take it to him. Instead, she and her friend Henrietta set out to save the king on their own, based on the information Charlotte has acquired, trading girlish dreams and fantasies for real-life espionage and dangerous dealings. Through these daring actions, Charlotte finds that is a strong, capable woman who need not rely on a man for every happiness, and of course finds that happiness often comes to those who seize the reins of their destiny.

Reviewers expressed primarily favorable opinions of this installment of the "Pink Carnation" series, with several noting that Willig seems to be improving with each book as her skills as a writer improve and she further develops the intricately woven world in which she sets her romantic intrigues. In

*Kirkus Reviews*, a writer opined that "smart characters of both genders, fast-paced plotting and a dash of self-conscious humor make this installment a winner." A reviewer on the *Readings and Ruminations* Web site commented of Charlotte and Robert: "I felt like their relationship was more real than any of the relationships in the previous novels. They talked about how things might or might not work, and I think their story ended with far more realistic expectations than other characters." A reviewer in *Publishers Weekly* remarked that the "conflation of historical fact, quirky observations and nicely rendered romances results in an elegant and grandly entertaining book." Laurel Ann, writing on the *Austen Prose* Web site, concluded of the book that "Willig's effervescent style is almost tongue-in-cheek in its playfulness. Her strength, however, lies in her rendering of her characters unique and endearing personalities. Like Austen, she chooses an array of foibles and follies in human nature illustrated in her secondary characters to frame her hero and heroine." Lori Lamothe, reviewing on the *Mostly Fiction* Web site, found the work "a clever, entertaining diversion for a rainy day."

### The Mischief of the Mistletoe

Turnip Fitzhugh, the nobleman who is wrongly believed to be the Pink Carnation, appears in *The Mischief of the Mistletoe: A Pink Carnation Christmas*. His path crosses with Arabella after she takes a teaching job against the advice of her friend, Jane Austen. Turnip and Arabella discover a strange note on the inside of a Christmas pudding wrapper. The note, which is written in French, draws the pair into a mystery that leads them to discover the identity of the English spies who have gone missing in France.

Applauding the story in *Kirkus Reviews*, a critic observed: "A shift of focus away from espionage and toward Jane Austen makes for a fun, fresh installment in a successful series." Huntley, writing once more in *Booklist*, was also impressed, asserting: "This delectable, exciting holiday tale will appeal to longtime fans of the series and newcomers alike." According to an online *Write Meg* contributor, "Turnip and Arabella's slow realization of their feelings for one another was wonderfully done. . . . Willig gave us just enough to whet our appetites but keep us wanting more, and I turned the pages hoping to get another taste of their blooming love affair. The story's mystery came as a surprise to me, too, and was one I didn't see coming."

### The Betrayal of the Blood Lily

Willig sets the action in India in *The Betrayal of the Blood Lily*, the sixth "Pink Carnation" installment. Lady Frederick Staines elopes and moves with her new husband to Hyderabad to avoid a scandal in London. But new intrigues await her in India, and Lady Frederick learns of a plot to remove the British from power. She teams up with Captain Alex Reid to disrupt the conspiracy, galloping throughout the country to avoid assassins. The spy known as Marigold is at the heart of the conspiracy, and Lady Frederick and Captain Alex hope to discover Marigold's identity before it is too late.

Critics applauded *The Betrayal of the Blood Lily*, calling it an entertaining and intriguing series addition. For instance, *Booklist* reviewer Huntley felt that the author "injects a new energy in her already thriving, thrilling series, and presents the best entry to date." Stacey Hayman, writing in *Library Journal*, proffered additional praise, dubbing the novel "a great choice for readers who like their mysteries with historical or romantic elements." A *Publishers Weekly* contributor stated that "Willig hasn't lost her touch," adding: "This outing has all the charm of the previous" series novels.

### ■ Biographical And Critical Sources

*PERIODICALS*

*Booklist*, November 15, 2004, Kristine Huntley, review of *The Secret History of the Pink Carnation*, p. 558; August 1, 2006, Patty Engelmann, review of *The Deception of the Emerald Ring*, p. 56; January 1, 2008, Kristine Huntley, review of *The Seduction of the Crimson Rose*, p. 46; December 1, 2009, Kristine Huntley, review of *The Betrayal of the Blood Lily*, p. 21; September 15, 2010, Kristine Huntley, review of *The Mischief of the Mistletoe: A Pink Carnation Christmas*, p. 50.

*Kirkus Reviews*, November 1, 2004, review of *The Secret History of the Pink Carnation*, p. 1028; October 15, 2005, review of *The Masque of the Black Tulip*, p. 1107; August 1, 2006, review of *The Deception of the Emerald Ring*, p. 752; November 15, 2007, review of *The Seduction of the Crimson Rose*; December 1, 2008, review of *The Temptation of the Night Jasmine*; August 15, 2010, review of *The Mischief of the Mistletoe*; December 15, 2010, review of *The Orchid Affair*.

*Library Journal*, November 15, 2004, Anna M. Nelson, review of *The Secret History of the Pink Carnation*, p. 53; November 15, 2004, Tania Barnes, "Q&A: Lauren Willig," p. 52; November 1, 2005, Bette-Lee Fox, review of *The Masque of the Black Tulip*, p. 70; September 1, 2006, Bette-Lee Fox, review of *The Deception of the Emerald Ring*, p. 140; November 15, 2008, Bette-Lee Fox, review of *The Temptation of the Night Jasmine*, p. 66; October 1, 2009, Barbara Hoffert, review of *The Betrayal of the Blood Lily*, p. 58; November 1, 2009, Stacey Hayman, review of *The Betrayal of the Blood Lily*, p. 60.

*Marie Claire*, December 1, 2006, review of *The Deception of the Emerald Ring*, p. 68.

*Publishers Weekly*, January 24, 2005, review of *The Secret History of the Pink Carnation*, p. 223; October 31, 2005, review of *The Masque of the Black Tulip*, p. 32; August 21, 2006, review of *The Deception of the Emerald Ring*, p. 47; November 26, 2007, review of *The Seduction of the Crimson Rose*, p. 27; November 10, 2008, review of *The Temptation of the Night Jasmine*, p. 30; October 5, 2009, review of *The Betrayal of the Blood Lily*, p. 32.

*Xpress Reviews*, November 12, 2010, Stacey Hayman, review of *The Orchid Affair*.

*ONLINE*

*All about Romance*, http://www.likesbooks.com/ (October 21, 2009), Linnie Gayl Kimmel, review of *The Temptation of the Night Jasmine*.

*Austen Prose*, http://austenprose.wordpress.com/ (October 21, 2009), Laurel Ann, review of *The Temptation of the Night Jasmine*.

*Barnes and Noble.com*, http://www.barnesandnoble.com/writers/ (October 21, 2009), "Meet the Writers: Lauren Willig," interview with author.

*Best Reviews*, http://thebestreviews.com/ (October 21, 2009), Harriet Klausner, review of *The Secret History of the Pink Carnation*; (January 14, 2005), Suan Wilson, review of *The Secret History of the Pink Carnation*; Harriet Klausner, review of *The Masque of the Black Tulip*.

*Genre Go Round Reviews*, http://genregoroundreviews.blogspot.com/ (October 21, 2009), Harriet Klausner, review of *The Temptation of the Night Jasmine*.

*Lauren Willig Home Page*, http://www.laurenwillig.com (August 12, 2011).

*Loaded Questions*, http://www.loaded-questions.com/ (October 21, 2009), Kelly Hewitt, author interview.

*Maya Rodale Blog*, http://mayarodale.com/ (October 21, 2009), Maya Rodale, "Lauren Willig Answers the Same Six Questions I Always Ask."

*Medieval Bookworm*, http://chikune.com/ (October 21, 2009), review of *The Temptation of the Night Jasmine*.

*Mostly Fiction*, http://www.mostlyfiction.com/ (October 21, 2009), Lori Lamothe, review of *The Temptation of the Night Jasmine*.

*MSNBC Web site,* http://www.msnbc.msn.com/ (October 21, 2009), "A Sultry Dose of Romance—from Harvard; Author Lauren Willig Gives a Historical Twist to Dating," profile of author.

*Reading and Ruminations,* http://readingand ruminations.wordpress.com/ (October 21, 2009), review of *The Temptation of the Night Jasmine.*

*Risky Regencies,* http://riskyregencies.blogspot. com/ (October 21, 2009), "The Not-So-Secret Interview with Lauren Willig."

*Romance Readers Connection,* http://www.the romancereadersconnection.com/ (October 21, 2009), Debora Hosey, review of *The Temptation of the Night Jasmine.*

*What Is Kim Reading?,* http://whatiskimreading.blog spot.com/ (October 21, 2009), review of *The Temptation of the Night Jasmine.*

*Write Meg,* http://writemeg.com/ (December 5, 2010), review of *The Mischief of the Mistletoe.*\*

# Mark Winne

## 1950-

---

## ■ Personal

Born March 7, 1950. *Education:* Bates College, B.A.; Southern New Hampshire University, M.S.

## ■ Addresses

*Home*—Santa Fe, NM. *Office*—Mark Winne Associate, 41 Arroyo Hondo Trail, Santa Fe, NM 87508. *E-mail*—win5m@aol.com.

## ■ Career

Writer. Hartford Food System, Hartford, CT, executive director, 1979-2003; Member of the Santa Fe Food Policy Council and the Southwest Grass-fed Livestock Alliance. Food and society policy fellow, W.K. Kellogg Foundation, 2002-04; visiting scholar, John Hopkins University School of Public Health, 2010-11; working Lands Alliance organizer and chair; founder of Connecticut Farmland Trust; cofounder of City of Hartford Food Policy Commission, Connecticut Food Policy Council, End Hunger Connecticut!, and Community Food Security Coalition.

## ■ Awards, Honors

Secretary's Plow Honor Award, U.S. Department of Agriculture, 2001; Leadership Award, Community Food Security Coalition, 2003.

## ■ Writings

*Closing the Food Gap: Resetting the Table in the Land of Plenty*, Beacon Press (Boston, MA), 2008.

*Food Rebels, Guerrilla Gardeners, and Smart-Cookin' Mamas: Fighting Back in an Age of Industrial Agriculture*, Beacon Press (Boston, MA), 2010.

Contributor of essays and articles to periodicals and Web sites, including *Hartford Courant, Boston Globe, Nation, In These Times, Sierra, Orion, Yes!, Food for Thought, Civil Eats*, and *Successful Farming;* author of a blog.

## ■ Sidelights

Mark Winne has more than thirty years of experience working for nonprofit agencies seeking to bring relief to underprivileged communities and individuals, especially those lacking basic needs such as food. Winne has served for Connecticut's Hartford Food System, the Connecticut Food Policy Council, and the W.K. Kellogg Foundation as a Food and Society Policy fellow, and he has participated in the U.S. delegation to the World Conference on Food Security in Rome, Italy.

### *Closing the Food Gap*

Winne's first book, *Closing the Food Gap: Resetting the Table in the Land of Plenty*, addresses food consumption and production issues as well as food politics and trends. According to Mark Knoblauch's review in *Booklist, Closing the Food Gap* explores the "relationships between consumers and producers" and promotes the supply of "better tasting, more nutritional food available to the poor." Winne illustrates the problems stemming from urbanization and government policies regarding agriculture and offers solutions, already successfully implemented, such as community farming, youth involvement, and local farmers' markets. Although Mindy Rhiger stated that *Closing the Food Gap* is "more suitable for academic readers than general audiences," in her article for *Library Journal*, she pointed out that the text offers diverse information, including "factual accounts of various food-systems projects" and "memoirlike accounts" that reflect Winne's involvement with these issues. Winne also addresses the irony of the presence of underfed and malnourished people living in the relatively wealthy United States, the limited availability of proper education regarding nutrition and healthy alternatives to commercially processed and mass-produced foods, and the degree to which food issues affect communities across the nation.

A contributor to *Kirkus Reviews* claimed that Winne "salts his personal history with pertinent reportage" without appearing as "a puritanical moralizer" due to his advocacy of "a unified federal program, less dependence on food banks, more slow food, and more investment in healthy viands." A reviewer for *Publishers Weekly* called *Closing the Food Gap* an "articulate and comprehensive book" containing "a calm, well-reasoned, and soft-spoken call to arms to fight for policy reform."

### Food Rebels, Guerrilla Gardeners, and Smart-Cookin' Mamas

In 2010 Winne published *Food Rebels, Guerrilla Gardeners, and Smart-Cookin' Mamas: Fighting Back in an Age of Industrial Agriculture*. The account criticizes industrial food practices across the United States, lamenting the lack of sustainable methods and poor regulation. In the book, Winne chronicles programs in various parts of the country that help people, particularly those in areas most in need, reclaim a healthier lifestyle through food, cooking, and local food-production industries.

A contributor to the *Seattle Post-Intelligencer* claimed that "Winne . . . packs a mean mouthful in the title of his new book." In the same article, Winne explained that the "smart-cookin' mamas" he refers to in his book are part of a community of mostly Mexican immigrants in Austin, Texas, who learned how to cook more healthily. Winne commented that "they were often living in food deserts, places where you just can't find affordable places to shop for healthy food." After having gone through the program, however, Winne pointed out that these women were living healthier lives and felt good about themselves, noting: "It was really heartening to see that kind of energy. They looked you in the eye and had a firm handshake. They could tell you their story with confidence." A contributor to *Reference & Research Book News* pointed out that the author "offers a harsh critique of industrial food practices in the U.S." A *Kirkus Reviews* critic observed that Winne's "examination challenges readers to galvanize and bolster reform efforts and, by example, continue the revolutionary concept of 'food sovereignty.'" The same contributor concluded by calling *Food Rebels, Guerrilla Gardeners, and Smart-Cookin' Mamas* "a good combination of solid research and affirmative testimonials."

## ■ Biographical And Critical Sources

*PERIODICALS*

*Booklist*, December 15, 2007, Mark Knoblauch, review of *Closing the Food Gap: Resetting the Table in the Land of Plenty*, p. 7.

*Kirkus Reviews*, October 15, 2007, review of *Closing the Food Gap*; July 15, 2010, review of *Food Rebels, Guerrilla Gardeners, and Smart-Cookin' Mamas: Fighting Back in an Age of Industrial Agriculture*.

*Library Journal*, November 1, 2007, Mindy Rhiger, review of *Closing the Food Gap*, p. 90.

*Publishers Weekly*, October 8, 2007, review of *Closing the Food Gap*, p. 44.

*Reference & Research Book News*, April 1, 2011, review of *Food Rebels, Guerilla Gardeners, and Smart-Cookin' Mamas*.

*Seattle Post-Intelligencer*, January 27, 2011, review of *Food Rebels, Guerilla Gardeners, and Smart-Cookin' Mamas*.

*ONLINE*

*Food and Society Policy Fellows Web site*, http://www.foodandsocietyfellows.org/ (August 14, 2008), author profile.

*Mark Winne Home Page*, http://www.markwinne.com (August 5, 2011).

# Rick Yancey

## ■ Also Known As

Richard Yancey

## ■ Personal

Born in FL; married; wife's name Sandy; children: Jonathan, Joshua (stepsons), Jacob. *Education:* Roosevelt University, B.A.

## ■ Addresses

*Home*—Gainesville, FL. *Agent*—Brian DeFiore, DeFiore & Company, 72 Spring St., Ste. 304, New York, NY 10012.

## ■ Career

Internal Revenue Service, former revenue officer; columnist and theater critic for the *Ledger*, Lakeland, FL. Also worked as a typesetter, drama teacher, actor, ranch hand, playwright, and telemarketer.

## ■ Member

Screenwriters Guild of America, Authors Guild.

## ■ Awards, Honors

Best Books for Children selection, *Publishers Weekly,* 2005, and Carnegie Medal nominee, Chartered Institute of Library and Information Professionals, 2006, both for *The Extraordinary Adventures of Alfred Kropp;* Michael L. Printz Award, 2010, for *The Monstrumologist.*

## ■ Writings

(As Richard Yancey) *A Burning in Homeland* (novel), Simon & Schuster (New York, NY), 2003.

(As Richard Yancey) *Confessions of a Tax Collector: One Man's Tour of Duty inside the IRS* (memoir), HarperCollins (New York, NY), 2004.

Also author of screenplays, under name Richard Yancey, including *The Orbit of Venus* and *The Cricket.*

*"MONSTRUMOLOGIST" SERIES*

*The Monstrumologist* (young adult novel), Simon & Schuster (New York, NY), 2009.

(Editor) William James Henry, *The Curse of the Wendigo,* Simon & Schuster Books for Young Readers (New York, NY), 2010.

(Editor) William James Henry, *The Isle of Blood,* Simon & Schuster Books for Young Readers (New York, NY), 2011.

*"ALFRED KROPP" SERIES; NOVELS FOR YOUNG ADULTS*

*The Extraordinary Adventures of Alfred Kropp,* Bloomsbury (New York, NY), 2005.

*The Seal of Solomon,* Bloomsbury (New York, NY), 2007.

*The Thirteenth Skull,* Bloomsbury (New York, NY), 2008.

*"TEDDY RUZAK" SERIES; MYSTERY NOVELS UNDER NAME RICHARD YANCEY*

*The Highly Effective Detective*, Thomas Dunne Books (New York, NY), 2006.

*The Highly Effective Detective Goes to the Dogs*, St. Martin's Minotaur (New York, NY), 2008.

*The Highly Effective Detective Plays the Fool*, St. Martin's Minotaur (New York, NY), 2010.

*The Highly Effective Detective Crosses the Line*, Minotaur Books (New York, NY), 2011.

## ■ Adaptations

*The Extraordinary Adventures of Alfred Kropp* was optioned for film by Warner Bros. Pictures, 2006.

## ■ Sidelights

Rick Yancey has a varied body of work. A former employee of the Internal Revenue Service, he mines his experiences working for this much-maligned government agency in his memoir, *Confessions of a Tax Collector: One Man's Tour of Duty inside the IRS.* He has also written several adult novels, including the "Teddy Ruzak" detective series, in addition to penning the "Alfred Kropp" books for a younger readership. "Yancey is an honest, uningratiating writer, whose characters are grittily convincing, though rarely charming," commented a *Publishers Weekly* critic in appraising the author's adult novel *A Burning in Homeland.*

### *A Burning Homeland*

*A Burning in Homeland,* a southern gothic, begins in 1960 and reaches back to the 1940s in its complex storyline. Set in Homeland, Florida, Yancey's story is narrated by three characters: Robert Lee "Shiny" Parker, a precocious seven-year-old; Mavis, a Baptist preacher's wife; and Mavis's strange daughter, Sharon-Rose, all of whom come to live with the Parkers after the preacher's house suspiciously burns to the ground and its owner is hospitalized. In another part of town, Halley Martin reflects on the last twenty years he spent pining for Mavis while he was in prison for the murder of Walter Hughes, who was accused of raping Mavis. Through the help of Ned Jeffries, a young Baptist preacher from Homeland who acts as prison chaplain, Halley writes to Mavis. Once again, however, Halley loses

his love: through her letters, Mavis reveals the reasons she has decided to marry Ned, even though she still loves Halley.

The novel received praise from several reviewers. A *Kirkus Reviews* contributor dubbed *A Burning in Homeland* "a beguiling, old-fashioned tale of desperate love and cruelty." In *Booklist,* Kaite Mediatore wrote of the novel: "Dripping with atmosphere and drama, it's a pleasure as guilty as a third helping of pecan pie." Valerie Sayers commented in the *New York Times Book Review* on the character of Shiny, writing that although his voice does not sound like that of a seven-year-old, "we suspend our disbelief because that voice is so appealing. Shiny wins us over because of his glorious anxiety, his crying fits and especially his terror of Mavis's daughter, Sharon-Rose, a great fictional misfit, a determined pursuer of boys and a good comic foil to her mother, that faded object of desire." Sayers noted that Yancey includes black characters as servants and that a black man named Elias first informs Halley of Mavis's rape, a reversal of the stereotypical scene, in which the black man is accused of rape and a white man takes the first steps toward revenge.

### *Confessions of a Tax Collector* and *The Extraordinary Adventures of Alfred Kropp*

*Confessions of a Tax Collector* recounts Yancey's twelve-year stint at the Internal Revenue Service working as a revenue officer. Discussing actual cases in which identities have been protected, he describes how he confiscated property to satisfy back taxes owed to the government and examines what he describes as "the 'cowboy' attitude of the old days," before the Revenue Restructuring Act of 1998 cut back on the extreme tactics and harassment that revenue officers employed. Yancey also recounts the dangers he encountered in facing delinquent taxpayers and of his isolation and obsession with his job. The story has a happy ending, however. Yancey married his supervisor and then quit the job at about the time his writing career began to take off. *Library Journal* contributor Richard Drezen described the memoir as "an engaging insider's account of life inside the dreaded IRS."

Yancey's writing career includes a couple of well-received series. Inaugurating a series geared for teen readers, *The Extraordinary Adventures of Alfred Kropp* is the story of a sixteen-year-old boy who is involved in a scheme to steal Excalibur, the sword of King Arthur. Yancey described his relationship with the character in an interview posted on the Bloomsbury Publishing Web site: "Growing up, I often felt like an outcast, kind of a loner like Alfred. I feel connected to Alfred's story, because it was written at a time when I was going through some professional challenges (becoming a full-time writer)."

*The Extraordinary Adventures of Alfred Kropp* begins as the orphaned Alfred is sent to live with his Uncle Farrell, a security guard who works the night shift. An extraordinarily large boy, Alfred frequently feels like a loser, performing poorly in school and in sports. Offered a million dollars to retrieve a sword, Uncle Farrell readily accepts the task and enlists the help of his reluctant nephew. Retrieving the sword turns out to be quite easy, and Alfred readily gives the object to the evil Mogart. Upon becoming aware that he has actually handed over Excalibur, the famed weapon of King Arthur, to an evil ex-knight looking to rule the world, Alfred undertakes to help Bennacio, an ancestor to a knight of the Round Table, in his efforts to recapture the powerful weapon.

Some critics found Yancey's hero to be an endearing character and predicted that adventure fans will find *The Extraordinary Adventures of Alfred Kropp* a good choice. "Alfred's naivete and basic good nature . . . make this pageturner stand out in the crowded fantasy adventure genre," remarked a *Publishers Weekly* commentator. *School Library Journal* contributor Hillias J. Martin similarly called the volume "lighthearted, entertaining, occasionally half-witted, but by and large fun," while *Booklist* reviewer Michael Cart described *The Extraordinary Adventures of Alfred Kropp* as "a white-knuckle, page-turning read."

### *The Seal of Solomon* and *The Highly Effective Detective*

Alfred returns in *The Seal of Solomon,* "a rip-roaring story that teens will love and won't be able to put down," according to June H. Keuhn in *School Library Journal.* When a fired member of the Office of Interdimensional Paradoxes and Extraordinary Phenomena (OIPEP) steals one of King Solomon's rings along with a vessel said to contain trapped demons, OIPEP Operative Nine seeks the help of Alfred to track down the thief. Noting that *The Seal of Solomon* also works as a stand-alone title, *Booklist* contributor Todd Morning wrote that Yancey combines "action-packed scenes with tongue-in-cheek humor and occasional heart-on-sleeve sincerity" in Alfred's second adventure.

In 2006, Yancey began a series of detective novels for adult readers. Left with a small inheritance, gumshoe Teddy Ruzak opens a private investigating agency in *The Highly Effective Detective,* despite having no training or experience in the field. Looking into a seemingly minor case of goslings killed by a speeding motorist, Ruzak stumbles upon a murder mystery involving a missing spouse. Some reviewers found much to like in the new series, with a *Kirkus Reviews* critic describing it as "an adorably quixotic adventure from mystery first-timer Yancey." A *Publishers Weekly* contributor observed that Yancey's "narrative takes unforeseen, utterly believable twists that wind to an extremely satisfying close."

### *The Highly Effective Detective Goes to the Dogs*

Yancey's follow-up novel featuring Ruzak, *The Highly Effective Detective Goes to the Dogs,* also earned praise from critics as the unlicensed private investigator searches for the killer of a homeless man. As the only one who believes Cadillac Joe was murdered, Ruzak looks for the culprit in a second installment that is "even funnier than the first," reported *Booklist* reviewer David Pitt. Also finding *The Highly Effective Detective Goes to the Dogs* enjoyable, a *Publishers Weekly* commentator predicted that the detective's "distinctive voice . . . will endear this surprisingly effective bumbler" to mystery fans.

### *The Highly Effective Detective Plays the Fool* and *The Highly Effective Detective Crosses the Line*

The third novel in the "Teddy Ruzak" series, *The Highly Effective Detective Plays the Fool,* was published in 2010. Ruzak is hired and subsequently fired by Katrina Bates after he discovers that her husband is having an extramarital affair. After he is approached by a representative looking for the case file, Bates goes missing. Knowing the connection to the cheating husband, Ruzak pursues the matter independently.

A contributor to *Kirkus Reviews* described Teddy as "the anti-Spenser—unmasculine, weak, klutzy, and hilariously garrulous." Writing in *Booklist,* Pitt said of the series that "reader response should be unanimous: keep 'em coming, please." A contributor to *Publishers Weekly* observed that "the appealing if bizarre narrative voice carries the action briskly along."

In 2011 Yancey continued the series with *The Highly Effective Detective Crosses the Line*. Ruzak is hired to protect the unwilling and unappreciative twenty-three-year-old Isabella Farrell from her deranged ex-boyfriend. She has even him arrested for breaking and entering her apartment. Ruzak is determined, however, and is able to link the ex with a neo-Nazi group.

Writing in the *Wall Street Journal*, Tom Nolan called the novel "charming." *Booklist* reviewer Pitt suggested that "readers new to the Ruzak novels will have a great time and be eager for more." A *Publishers Weekly* contributor commented that "despite the dip in quality, fans will want to see more of Ruzak." A contributor to *Kirkus Reviews* observed that "Teddy continues to grow and deepen as he charts a developmental path like no other in the genre."

### The Monstrumologist

*The Monstrumologist* is intended to launch a new series for young adults. Its narrator and protagonist is William Henry James, a New England orphan boy apprenticed to Dr. Pellinore Warthrop, a "monstrumologist," or scholar of monsters. The novel takes the form of Will's journal, and chronicles events occurring in 1888, when he is twelve years old. The story is set in motion when a grave robber delivers two bodies to the monstrumologist; one is that of a young girl, the other of a mysterious cannibalistic creature called an Anthropophagus, which originated in Africa but somehow made it to the United States. Will and the doctor discover a local Anthropophagi coven and find their own lives in danger while there are further grisly murders, including that of a minister's family. Enlisting the help of ruthless monster hunter John Kearns, Will and Warthrop set out to eliminate the Anthropophagi threat. Meanwhile, Will continues to grieve his deceased parents and seeks a father figure in the distant doctor, who is considered peculiar by most of the area residents.

Several reviewers thought *The Monstrumologist* a well-written, chilling tale that would find favor with teenage readers. "Gory perhaps over the edge to disgusting, this is horror at its worst, which means at its exciting entreating best," commented Harriet Klausner in *Genre Go Round Reviews*. Charlie Wendell, writing in *Open Letters Monthly*, described the book as "a lightning-fast read and highly entertaining, a ripping yarn." *School Library Journal* critic John Peters noted that while the novel features ample "gore and violence," it offers something more: "surprising depth and twists" in "plot and cast alike." Wendell explained the characters' appeal thus: "Yancey writes characters just broad enough to be compelling without being ridiculous, with just a hint of cartoonishness." Some reviewers also remarked on the relationship between Will and Warthrop. *St. Petersburg Times* contributor William Harvey observed that unlike some other horror novels aimed at young adults, *The Monstrumologist* does not trade in romance but instead "involves paternal love, which is a welcome change of pace." Not that the story lacks for thrills, Harvey added: "If you enjoy white-knuckle terror you will want to read this book faster than an Anthropophagi can shred a victim to bits." Benjamin Boche, a reviewer for the Web site *Teenreads.com*, predicted that readers would be "compelled to keep turning pages to see what happens next" and found the novel overall "a glorious start to what looks to be another promising horrific series."

### The Curse of the Wendigo

Yancey published the second novel in the "Monstrumologist" series, *The Curse of the Wendigo*, in 2010. Will and the doctor assist a woman who insists her husband went missing while looking for a flesh-eating, vampire-like monster called the Wendigo. They speak to a Canadian shaman who offers a supernatural version of what happened to the man. The doctor's inability to accept mythological monsters, however, puts them all in danger.

Writing in *School Library Journal*, Tim Wadham claimed that the novel "is certain to be popular with fans of *The Monstrumologist*." However, Wadham pondered that "the disturbing, cynical tone makes the most appropriate audience for this book uncertain." Reviewing the novel in the *Voice of Youth Advocates*, Donna Miller opined: "Once again, Yancey skillfully weaves a tale that touches readers at a visceral level and will linger long in the imagination." Noting that few literary horror books are "finer than *The Monstrumologist*," *Booklist* contributor Daniel Kraus lauded that "Yancey's second volume sustains that high bar with lush prose, devilish characterizations, and more honest emotion." A contributor to *Kirkus Reviews* noted that "the narrative, flecked with the same surgical illustrations as the first installment, flows evenly." A contributor to *Publishers Weekly* thought that the growing "relationship between hapless Will and the demanding monstrumologist is the most rewarding aspect of the story."

## ■ Biographical And Critical Sources

### BOOKS

Yancey, Richard, *Confessions of a Tax Collector: One Man's Tour of Duty inside the IRS*, HarperCollins (New York, NY), 2004.

### PERIODICALS

*Booklist*, January 1, 2003, Kaite Mediatore, review of *A Burning in Homeland*, p. 854; November 15, 2003, David Pitt, review of *Confessions of a Tax Collector: One Man's Tour of Duty inside the IRS*, p. 546; August, 2005, Michael Cart, review of *The Extraordinary Adventures of Alfred Kropp*, p. 2019; March 15, 2006, David Pitt, review of *The Highly Effective Detective*, p. 32; May 15, 2007, Todd Morning, review of *The Seal of Solomon*, p. 54; June 1, 2008, David Pitt, review of *The Highly Effective Detective Goes to the Dogs*, p. 50; September 1, 2009, Daniel Kraus, review of *The Monstrumologist*, p. 92; January 1, 2010, David Pitt, review of *The Highly Effective Detective Plays the Fool*, p. 52; September 1, 2010, Daniel Kraus, review of *The Curse of the Wendigo*, p. 96; December 1, 2010, David Pitt, review of *The Highly Effective Detective Crosses the Line*, p. 30.

*BookSmack! Reviews*, October 21, 2010, review of *The Curse of the Wendigo*.

*Entertainment Weekly*, July 21, 2006, Tina Jordan, review of *The Highly Effective Detective*, p. 74.

*Horn Book*, January 1, 2011, Jonathan Hunt, review of *The Curse of the Wendigo*, p. 103.

*Horn Book Guide*, March 22, 2010, T. Borregaard, review of *The Monstrumologist*, p. 112; March 22, 2011, Jonathan Hunt, review of *The Curse of the Wendigo*, p. 117.

*Houston Chronicle*, June 27, 2003, Melanie Danburg, review of *A Burning in Homeland*.

*Journal of the American Taxation Association*, March 22, 2005, Christine C. Bauman, review of *Confessions of a Tax Collector*, p. 110.

*Kirkus Reviews*, November 15, 2002, review of *A Burning in Homeland*, p. 1656; December 15, 2003, review of *Confessions of a Tax Collector*, p. 1444; September 15, 2005, review of *The Extraordinary Adventures of Alfred Kropp*, p. 1037; May 15, 2006, review of *The Highly Effective Detective*, p. 501; June 1, 2008, review of *The Thirteenth Skull*; July 1, 2008, review of *The Highly Effective Detective Goes to the Dogs*; September 1, 2009, review of *The Monstrumologist*; January 1, 2010, review of *The Highly Effective Detective Plays the Fool*; September 15,

2010, review of *The Curse of the Wendigo*; December 15, 2010, review of *The Highly Effective Detective Crosses the Line*.

*Legal Times*, June 7, 2004, Steve Weinberg, review of *Confessions of a Tax Collector*.

*Library Journal*, March 15, 2003, Rebecca Sturm Kelm, review of *A Burning in Homeland*, p. 118; December, 2003, Richard Drezen, review of *Confessions of a Tax Collector*, p. 134.

*New York Times Book Review*, March 2, 2003, Valerie Sayers, review of *A Burning in Homeland*, p. 30; April 5, 2004, Janet Maslin, review of *Confessions of a Tax Collector*, p. E8.

*Publishers Weekly*, December 2, 2002, review of *A Burning in Homeland*, p. 31; January 19, 2004, review of *Confessions of a Tax Collector*, p. 60; August 29, 2005, review of *The Extraordinary Adventures of Alfred Kropp*, p. 57; April 10, 2006, review of *The Highly Effective Detective*, p. 48; April 2, 2007, review of *The Seal of Solomon*, p. 57; June 23, 2008, review of *The Highly Effective Detective Goes to the Dogs*, p. 40; September 7, 2009, review of *The Monstrumologist*, p. 48; January 18, 2010, review of *The Highly Effective Detective Plays the Fool*, p. 33; October 4, 2010, review of *The Curse of the Wendigo*, p. 50; November 22, 2010, review of *The Highly Effective Detective Crosses the Line*, p. 44.

*St. Petersburg Times* (St. Petersburg, FL), November 1, 2009, William Harvey, "Rick Yancey's 'Monstrumologist' Is White-Knuckle Reading."

*School Library Journal*, October 1, 2005, Hillias J. Martin, review of *The Extraordinary Adventures of Alfred Kropp*, p. 178; June 1, 2006, Francisca Goldsmith, review of *The Highly Effective Detective*, p. 192; June 1, 2007, June H. Keuhn, review of *The Seal of Solomon*, p. 165; November 1, 2008, Samantha Larsen Hastings, review of *The Thirteenth Skull*, p. 139; November 1, 2009, John Peters, review of *The Monstrumologist*, p. 125; March 1, 2010, Amanda Raklovits, review of *The Monstrumologist*, p. 67; December 1, 2010, Tim Wadham, review of *The Curse of the Wendigo*, p. 132; March 1, 2011, Amanda Raklovits, review of *The Curse of the Wendigo*, p. 73.

*USA Today*, April 12, 2004, Carol Knopes, review of *Confessions of a Tax Collector*, p. B11.

*Voice of Youth Advocates*, December 1, 2010, Donna Miller, review of *The Curse of the Wendigo*, p. 478.

*Wall Street Journal*, February 12, 2011, Tom Nolan, review of *The Highly Effective Detective Crosses the Line*.

*Washington Post*, March 7, 2004, Nancy McKeon, "A Tax Dodger Meets the Man," interview, p. F1.

*ONLINE*

*Bloomsbury Publishing Web site,* http://www.bloomsbury.com/ (August 27, 2005), "A Conversation with Rick Yancey."

*BookPage,* http://www.bookpage.com/ (August 27, 2005), Harold Parker, review of *A Burning in Homeland.*

*Children's Bookshelf,* http://www.publishersweekly.com/ (April 5, 2007), Sue Corbett, "Children's Bookshelf Talks with Rick Yancey."

*Downright Creepy,* http://www.downrightcreepy.com/ (April 27, 2011), "The Monstrumologist Author Rick Yancey."

*Genre Go Round Reviews,* http://genregoroundreviews.blogspot.com/ (September 17, 2009), Harriet Klausner, review of *The Monstrumologist.*

*Open Letters Monthly,* http://www.openlettersmonthly.com/ (December 16, 2009), Charlie Wendell, review of *The Monstrumologist.*

*Rick Yancey Home Page,* http://www.rickyancey.com (August 25, 2011).

*Teenreads.com* http://www.teenreads.com/ (March 7, 2010) Benjamin Boche, review of *The Monstrumologist.**

# Ching-Hwang Yen

## 1937-

### ■ Personal

Born September 10, 1937, in Yung Ch'un, Fukien, China; son of Yen Chang-shu and Ong Kheong; married Yong Kwee-ying; children: Pei-fen (daughter), Kuo-liang (son), Kuo-wei (son), Kuo-kang (son). *Education:* Nanyang University, B.A. (with first-class honors), 1960; Australian National University, Ph.D., 1970.

### ■ Addresses

*Office*—Dept. of History, University of Adelaide, Adelaide, South Australia 5001, Australia; fax: 8-8303-3443. *E-mail*—chinghwang.yen@adelaide. edu.au.

### ■ Career

Academic and historian. Nanyang University, Singapore, tutor in history, 1963-65; University of Adelaide, Adelaide, Australia, lecturer in history, 1968-76, senior lecturer, 1977-86, reader, 1987-88, reader in history, beginning 1991, then adjunct associate professor; University of Hong Kong, professor and head of department of history, 1988-90; writer. Member of the police-ethnic liaison committee of the South Australian Police Department, 1980-86, and of the multicultural education coordinating committee of the South Australian Government, 1982-85; chair of the Multicultural and Dragon Boat Festival Committee of South Australia, 1986-87; member of the Australian government's immigration review panel, 1987-88, and of the Hong Kong selection committee for the Commonwealth Scholarship and Fellowship Plan, 1990.

### ■ Member

Chinese Association of South Australia (president, 1975-78 and 1981-87), Overseas Chinese Foundation of Hong Kong (founding member and member of executive committee, beginning 1989).

### ■ Writings

*The Overseas Chinese and the 1911 Revolution: With Special Reference to Singapore and Malaya,* Oxford University Press (New York, NY), 1976.

*Coolies and Mandarins: China's Protection of Overseas Chinese during the Late Ch'ing Period,* Ohio University Press (Athens, OH), 1985.

*A Social History of the Chinese in Singapore and Malaya, 1800-1911,* Oxford University Press (New York, NY), 1986.

(Editor and contributor) *Ethnic Chinese Abroad: A Special Issue of Asian Culture,* Singapore Society of Asian Studies, 1990.

*The Ethnic Chinese in East and Southeast Asia: Business, Culture, and Politics,* Times Academic Press (Singapore), 2002.

*Hai Wai Hua Ren De She Hui Bian Ge Yu Shang Ye Cheng Zhang,* Xiamen da xue chu (Xiamen, China), 2005.

*Cong Li Shi Jiao Du Kan Hai Wai Hua Ren She Hui Bian Ge,* Xinjiapo qing nian shu ju (Xinjiapo, China), 2007.

*The Chinese in Southeast Asia and Beyond: Socioeconomic and Political Dimensions,* World Scientific (Hackensack, NJ), 2008.

Yen's works have been translated into Chinese.

### ■ Sidelights

Ching-Hwang Yen is a Chinese academic and historian. Born in Yung Ch'un, Fukien, China, on September 10, 1937, he graduated from Nanyang

University in 1960 and served as a tutor in history there in the mid-1960s. Yen subsequently completed a Ph.D. from the Australian National University in 1970. He began lecturing in history at the University of Adelaide in 1968 and became a senior lecturer in 1977. In 1987 he became a reader at the university and later an adjunct associate professor. Yen also served for two years as a professor and head of department of history at the University of Hong Kong.

Yen published *The Chinese in Southeast Asia and Beyond: Socioeconomic and Political Dimensions* in 2008. The account compiles essays and lectures on the Chinese Diaspora in Southeast Asia, focusing largely on Singapore and Malaysia before they became independent states. Yen looks into a number of topics, including the economic history, kinship associations, the origins of Chinese capitalism, and Sun Yat Sen and his relationship to the Chinese in Malaysia and Singapore.

Writing in *Pacific Affairs*, Jemma Purdey commented: "To say that this book succeeds in presenting its readers with the totality of coverage of the region's ethnic Chinese would be going too far. However, the compilation serves as a good introduction for those students looking for a broad perspective on the subject." Purdey later admitted that "as an established and senior scholar Yen's comments and critique of the study of the history of Southeast Asia's ethnic Chinese . . . are extremely interesting."

## ■ Biographical And Critical Sources

*PERIODICALS*

*Pacific Affairs*, March 1, 2010, Jemma Purdey, review of *The Chinese in Southeast Asia and Beyond: Socioeconomic and Political Dimensions*, p. 195.
*Reference & Research Book News*, November 1, 2008, review of *The Chinese in Southeast Asia and Beyond.*

*ONLINE*

*Department of History, University of Adelaide Web site*, http://www.adelaide.edu.au/ (August 5, 2011), author profile.*

# Merla Zellerbach

## 1930-

### ■ Personal

Born August 27, 1930, in San Francisco, CA, daughter of Eliot M. and Lottie Burstein; married Stephen Anthony Zellerbach, 1950; children: Gary Allen. *Education:* Attended Stanford University, 1948-50.

### ■ Addresses

*Home*—San Francisco, CA.

### ■ Career

Writer. ABC Television, regular panelist for the program *Oh My World,* 1965-70; Enrichment Lecturer and cruise ship writing instructor, 1975-93; *Nob Hill Gazette,* San Francisco, CA, editor, 1996-2007, editor emerita, 2007—. Leukemia & Lymphoma Society trustee; Compassion & Choices board member.

### ■ Member

American Association for United Nations (organizer, president of San Francisco Sponsors, member board of directors), Psychiatric Day Center, St. Francis Yacht Club, International Hospitality Center.

### ■ Awards, Honors

Queen of Mardi Gras, City of San Francisco, 1956; Mayor Dianne Feinstein Proclamation of Merla Zellerbach Day, November 1, City of San Francisco, 1983; international achievement award, *Where,* 1994, for best article writing; Governor Pete Wilson commendation award, 1996; U.S. Senate Certificate of Commendation, 2000; California State Assembly Certificate of Recognition, 2000; Mayor Gavin Newsom Proclamation of Merla Zellerbach Day, October 1, City of San Francisco, 2007.

### ■ Writings

*Love in a Dark House,* Doubleday (New York, NY), 1961.

(With Alan S. Levin) *The Type One/Type Two Allergy Relief Program: Including Information on Testing Procedures,* research assistant Debra Lynn Dadd, Tarcher (Los Angeles, CA), 1983.

(With Phyllis Saifer) *Detox: A Successful and Supportive Program for Freeing Your Body from the Physical and Psychological Effects of Chemical Pollutants (at Home and at Work), Junk Food Additives, Sugar, Nicotine, Drugs, Alcohol, Caffeine, Prescription and Nonprescription Medications, and Other Environmental Toxins,* Tarcher (Los Angeles, CA), 1984.

*Wildes of Nob Hill,* Ballantine Books (New York, NY), 1986.

*Love the Giver,* Ballantine Books (New York, NY), 1987.

*Cavett Manor,* Ballantine Books (New York, NY), 1987.

*Rittenhouse Square,* Random House (New York, NY), 1989.

*Sugar,* Ballantine (New York, NY), 1989.

*The Allergy Sourcebook: Everything You Need to Know,* foreword by Vincent A. Marinkovich, Contemporary Books (Chicago, IL), 1995, 3rd edition, 2000.

*Secrets in Time,* Firefall Media (Canyon, CA), 2009.

*Mystery of the Mermaid,* Firefall Media (Canyon, CA), 2009.

*The Missing Mother,* Firefall Media (Canyon, CA), 2010.

Contributor to *Saturday Evening Post, Cosmopolitan, Travel & Leisure, Reader's Digest, Prevention, Women's World, This Week, SF Focus, Gentry, Nob Hill Gazette, Where, Town & Country,* and *Dining Out in San Francisco*; contributor to *The Stanford Century,* 1991; author of the *"My Fair City"* column in *San Francisco Chronicle,* 1962-85.

## ■ Sidelights

Merla Zellerbach is an American writer. Born in San Francisco, California, on August 27, 1930, she studied at Stanford University. Zellerbach served as the "My Fair City" columnist for the *San Francisco Chronicle* from 1962 until 1985. She also served as a regular panelist on the ABC television program *Oh My World* in the 1960s and as an Enrichment Lecturer and cruise ship writing instructor from 1975 until 1993. Starting in 1996, she became the editor of San Francisco's *Nob Hill Gazette.*

In 1989 Zellerbach published *Rittenhouse Square.* Developer Vittoria "Torie" Di Angelo has a lot to prove to herself as she makes a name for herself in this rags-to-riches story. Torie takes on historical preservationists in her attempt to make her mark on the city of Philadelphia and finds love along the way. A contributor to *Publishers Weekly* opined that in addition to creating a protagonist "who is brainy, tough, and simpatico, Zellerbach provides an impressively detailed view of the urban renewal scene."

Zellerbach created the "Hallie Marsh" mystery series in 2009 with the publication of *Mystery of the Mermaid.* While on a six-week-long cruise, public relations executive Hallie Marsh is hesitant to pursue a relationship with journalist Dan "Cas" Casserly after her double mastectomy. The pair get distracted, however, by working together to solve a disappearance-cum-murder case at sea. Speaking of Hallie and Cas's relationship, a *Publishers Weekly* critic noted that the author "manages to put a humorous spin on the couple's courtship."

In 2010 Zellerbach published the next book the "Hallie Marsh" series, *The Missing Mother.* Hallie and now-fiancé Cas look into two murders surrounding the disappearance of a journalist while Hallie's physical therapist roommate, Sara, becomes romantically involved with her wealthy client. A contributor to *Publishers Weekly* suggested that "smooth prose and careful plotting will remind readers of early Mary Higgins Clark."

## ■ Biographical And Critical Sources

*PERIODICALS*

*Consumer Health Information Source Book, Edition 5,* 1998, Alan M. Rees, review of *The Allergy Sourcebook: Everything You Need to Know,* p. 102.

*Publishers Weekly,* January 1, 1990, review of *Rittenhouse Square;* October 26, 2009, review of *Mystery of the Mermaid,* p. 37; November 15, 2010, review of *The Missing Mother,* p. 42.

*San Francisco Chronicle,* November 23, 2008, Carolyne Zinko, "Merla Zellerbach's Career in High Society."

*ONLINE*

*Firefall Media Web site,* http://www.firefallmedia.com/ (August 5, 2011), author profile.

*Merla Zellerbach Home Page,* http://www.merla zellerbach.com (August 5, 2011).*